THE OXFORD HANDBOOK OF
VIRGINIA WOOLF

THE OXFORD HANDBOOK OF

VIRGINIA WOOLF

Edited by
ANNE E. FERNALD

Great Clarendon Street, Oxford, OX2 6DP,
United Kingdom

Oxford University Press is a department of the University of Oxford.
It furthers the University's objective of excellence in research, scholarship,
and education by publishing worldwide. Oxford is a registered trade mark of
Oxford University Press in the UK and in certain other countries

© The several contributors 2021

The moral rights of the authors have been asserted

First Edition published in 2021

All rights reserved. No part of this publication may be reproduced, stored in
a retrieval system, or transmitted, in any form or by any means, without the
prior permission in writing of Oxford University Press, or as expressly permitted
by law, by licence or under terms agreed with the appropriate reprographics
rights organization. Enquiries concerning reproduction outside the scope of the
above should be sent to the Rights Department, Oxford University Press, at the
address above

You must not circulate this work in any other form
and you must impose this same condition on any acquirer

Published in the United States of America by Oxford University Press
198 Madison Avenue, New York, NY 10016, United States of America

British Library Cataloguing in Publication Data

Data available

Library of Congress Control Number: 2020952296

ISBN 978–0–19–881158–9

DOI: 10.1093/oxfordhb/9780198811589.001.0001

Printed and bound by
CPI Group (UK) Ltd, Croydon, CR0 4YY

Links to third party websites are provided by Oxford in good faith and
for information only. Oxford disclaims any responsibility for the materials
contained in any third party website referenced in this work.

Acknowledgements

An undertaking as massive as this must begin with gratitude for the generosity of the community of Woolf scholars, most especially the contributors to this volume. Many thanks, too, to my editors at Oxford University Press, Jacqueline Norton and Aimee Wright, who helped shepherd this volume to completion. Among those who helped me keep on track, I owe a tremendous debt to my graduate students at Fordham University. First among them is Ellis Light, who not only expertly helped with citation checking and final edits of most chapters, but helped mentor others to do the same. Ellis's work solved many editorial challenges. Freelance editor Miranda Dubner, and graduate students Amal Zaman and Lionel Spencer were of tremendous help in the final stages. I thank George Hong and my colleagues at the Office of Research at Fordham for ensuring that my graduate students and freelancer were compensated for their time. Thanks, too, to my beloved family and friends for their many kindnesses.

Contents

List of Figures — xi
List of Contributors — xiii
Works by Virginia Woolf — xix

Introduction — 1

PART I LIFE

1. Family and Place — 7
   URMILA SESHAGIRI

2. Friends and Lovers — 27
   KATHRYN SIMPSON

3. Traditions and Transformations — 44
   REGINA MARLER

PART II TEXTS

4. Private Writings — 63
   CAROLINE POLLENTIER

5. Early Novels and Stories (1915–1923) — 76
   JOCELYN RODAL

6. Mature Works I (1924–1927) — 89
   GABRIELLE McINTIRE

7. Mature Works II (1928–1932) — 102
   ELSA HÖGBERG

8. Late Works (1933–1941) — 117
   ALICE WOOD

PART III EXPERIMENTS IN FORM AND STYLE

9. Stream of Consciousness 133
   Dora Zhang

10. Character, Form, and Fiction 149
    Amy Bromley

11. Time 164
    Jesse Matz

12. Narrative Ethics 180
    Janine Utell

13. Allusion and Metaphor 197
    Jane de Gay

14. Biography and Autobiography 212
    Laura Marcus

PART IV PROFESSIONS OF WRITING

15. Literary London 227
    Helen Southworth

16. The Hogarth Press 246
    Alice Staveley

17. Woolf as Reviewer-Critic 262
    Eleanor McNees

18. The Essays 277
    Beth C. Rosenberg

19. The Lyrical Mode of Translating 291
    Claire Davison

PART V CONTEXTS

20. Woolf's Feminism 311
    Stephanie J. Brown

21. Queer Theory — 326
    CHRIS COFFMAN

22. Woolf and Education — 344
    ANNA SNAITH

23. Woolf and Suffrage — 362
    BARBARA GREEN

24. Impressionism and Post-Impressionism — 377
    TAMAR KATZ

25. Oceans and Empire — 392
    MAXWELL UPHAUS

26. Biopower — 408
    MADELYN DETLOFF

27. The Natural World and the Anthropocene — 422
    CLIFF MAK

28. War and Peace — 440
    BERYL PONG

29. Work — 456
    MARY WILSON

30. Consumer Culture — 472
    ELIZABETH M. SHEEHAN

PART VI AFTERLIVES

31. Feminist Theory — 489
    JEAN MILLS

32. Disability, Illness, and Pain — 504
    ELIZABETH OUTKA

33. The Academy and Publishing — 521
    VARA NEVEROW

34. Modern Woolfian Fiction — 536
    ROXANA ROBINSON

35. Magic Realism and Experimental Fiction 553
    LAURA Mª LOJO-RODRÍGUEZ

36. Virginia Woolf in the Canon of Women's Literature: Narrative
    Futures of the Feminist Novel 573
    TONYA KROUSE

37. Creative Non-fiction and Poetry 590
    STACEY D'ERASMO

38. Virginia Woolf, Filmmaker 605
    JACQUELINE SHIN

39. Woolfian Afterlives 622
    LAURA SMITH

Index 641

Figures

1.1	Talland House, Leslie Stephen Photograph Album, Mortimer Rare Book Collection (MRBC-MS-00005), Smith College Special Collections, Northampton, Massachusetts	12
1.2	Julia Duckworth Stephen and Leslie Stephen, with young Virginia, Leslie Stephen Photograph Album, Mortimer Rare Book Collection (MRBC-MS-00005), Smith College Special Collections, Northampton, Massachusetts	16
38.1	Mark Cousins, *What is This Film Called Love?*	612
38.2	David Lowery, *A Ghost Story*	616
38.3	Alex Garland, *Annihilation*	617
39.1	Vanessa Bell, *Studland Beach* © Estate of Vanessa Bell. All rights reserved, DACS 2020. Photo © Tate	625
39.2	Dora Carrington, Farm at Watendlath, Tate. Photo © Tate	626
39.3	Rebecca Horn, *Orlando,* © 2020 Artists Rights Society (ARS), New York / VG Bild-Kunst, Bonn. Photo © Tate	630
39.4	Aleana Eagan. *It is noon and one of them wanders off* (2012) Image courtesy of artist and Kerlin Gallery, Dublin	632
39.5	Aleana Eagan. *Room after room* (2012) Image courtesy of artist and Kerlin Gallery, Dublin	633
39.6	Wayne McGregor, *Woolf Works*. Premiere: The Royal Ballet, 2015. Image: Tristram Kenton	635

Contributors

Amy Bromley completed her Ph.D. on 'Virginia Woolf and the Work of the Literary Sketch' at the University of Glasgow. She is the co-editor, with Elsa Högberg, of *Sentencing Orlando: Virginia Woolf and the Morphology of the Modernist Sentence* (2018), shortlisted for the Modernist Studies Association Book Prize in 2019.

Stephanie J. Brown is Assistant Professor of English at the University of Arizona. She is the editor of Edith Ayrton *Zangwill's The Call: A New Scholarly Edition* (2019). Her current book project is on how women writers from the early twentieth century represented state surveillance of feminist activism in Britain.

Chris Coffman is Chair of the Department of English and Professor of English at the University of Alaska Fairbanks. The author of *Gertrude Stein's Transmasculinity* (2018) and *Insane Passions* (2006), she also has articles in print on modernism, queer film, and theory in *TSQ*; *GLQ*; *Postmodern Culture*; *Culture, Theory, and Critique*; *Angelaki*; *Texas Studies in Literature and Language*; and *Arizona Quarterly*. She is currently completing a book on psychoanalytic queer and transgender theory called *Queer Traversals*.

Claire Davison is Professor of Modernist Studies at the Université Sorbonne Nouvelle, Paris. She is currently preparing a monograph on modernist broadcasting and sonic modernity 1925–1945, and co-editing a critical edition of the Collected Letters of Katherine Mansfield. She is the author of *Translation as Collaboration—Virginia Woolf, Katherine Mansfield and S. S. Koteliansky* (2014), and co-editor of *Cross-Channel Modernisms* (2020).

Stacey D'Erasmo is Associate Professor of Writing and Publishing Practices at Fordham University. She is the author of the novels *Tea* (2000), *A Seahorse Year* (2004), *The Sky Below* (2009), *Wonderland* (2014), *The Complicities* (2022), and the non-fiction book *The Art of Intimacy* (2013). She is working on a book of essays, *The Long Run*.

Madelyn Detloff is Professor and Chair of English and Professor of Global and Intercultural Studies at Miami University. She is author of *The Value of Virginia Woolf* (2016) and *The Persistence of Modernism: Loss and Mourning in the 20th Century* (2009), and co-editor of *Queer Bloomsbury* (2016) and *Virginia Woolf: Art, Education, and Internationalism* (2008).

Anne E. Fernald is Professor of English and Women's, Gender, and Sexuality Studies at Fordham University. She is the author of *Virginia Woolf: Feminism and the Reader*

(2006) and the editor of the Cambridge University Press edition of *Mrs Dalloway* (2014). She co-edits the journal *Modernism/modernity*.

Jane de Gay is Professor of English Literature at Leeds Trinity University. She is the author of *Virginia Woolf's Novels and the Literary Past* (2006) and *Virginia Woolf and Christian Culture* (2018).

Barbara Green is Professor of English and Concurrent Professor in Gender Studies at the University of Notre Dame. She is the author of *Feminist Periodicals and Daily Life: Women and Modernity in British Culture* (2017), *Spectacular Confessions: Autobiography, Performative Activism, and the Sites of Suffrage, 1905–1938* (1997), and she is the co-editor of *Women's Periodicals and Print Culture in Britain, 1918–1939* (2018). She co-edits the *Journal of Modern Periodical Studies*.

Elsa Högberg is a research fellow in English Literature at Uppsala University. She is the author of *Virginia Woolf and the Ethics of Intimacy* (2020), editor of *Modernist Intimacies* (2021), and co-editor, with Amy Bromley, of *Sentencing* Orlando: *Virginia Woolf and the Morphology of the Modernist Sentence* (2018).

Tamar Katz is Associate Professor of English and Associate Professor of Urban Studies at Brown University. She is the author of *Impressionist Subjects: Gender, Interiority, and Modernist Fiction in England* (2000). She is working on *City Memories: Modernism and Urban Time in New York City*.

Tonya Krouse is Professor of English, Northern Kentucky University. She is the author of *The Opposite of Desire: Sex and Pleasure in the Modernist Novel* (2008) and co-author of *Introducing English Studies* (2020). She is working on *The Magnetism of D.H. Lawrence*.

Laura Mª Lojo-Rodríguez is Senior Lecturer in English, University of Santiago de Compostela, Spain. She is the author of '"Thought in American and for the Americans": Victoria Ocampo, Sur and European Modernism' (*Philosophy in the Condition of Modernism*, 2018) and '"England's Most Precious Gift": Virginia Woolf's Transformations into Spanish' (*A Companion to World Literature*, 2020), and has co-edited *Gender and Short Fiction: Women's Tales in Contemporary Britain* (2018) and *Borders and Border Crossing in the Contemporary English Short Story* (2019).

Gabrielle McIntire is Professor of English Literature at Queen's University, Canada. She is the author of *Modernism, Memory, and Desire: T.S. Eliot and Virginia Woolf* (2008), and the editor of *The Cambridge Companion to* The Waste Land (2015).

Eleanor McNees is a professor of English at the University of Denver. She edited the four-volume *Critical Assessments of Virginia Woolf* (1994), annotated and wrote the introduction for the Harcourt edition of *The Years* (2008), and has published essays on Woolf's literary affiliation with Victorian authors.

Cliff Mak is an Assistant Professor of English at Queens College, City University of New York. He is author of the essays 'On Falling Fastidiously: Marianne Moore's Slapstick Animals' in *English Literary History* (2016) and 'Joyce's Indifferent Animals: Boredom and the Subversion of Fables in Finnegans Wake' in *Modernist Cultures* (2016). He is completing a volume on modernist instinct and stylistic virtuosity.

Laura Marcus is Goldsmiths' Professor of English Literature at the University of Oxford. Her book publications include *The Tenth Muse: Writing about Cinema in the Modernist Period* (2007) (winner of the MLA's James Russell Lowell prize), *Dreams of Modernity: Psychoanalysis, Literature, Cinema* (2014) and *Autobiography: A Very Short Introduction* (2018).

Regina Marler is an independent scholar and critic based in the San Francisco Bay Area. She edited *Selected Letters of Vanessa Bell* (1993) and *Queer Beats: How the Beats Turned America On to Sex* (2004). She is the author of *Bloomsbury Pie: The Making of the Bloomsbury Boom* (1996) and contributes regularly to *The New York Review of Books* and elsewhere.

Jesse Matz is Professor of English at Kenyon College. He is the author of *Lasting Impressions: the Legacies of Impressionism in Contemporary Culture* (2016) and *Modernist Time Ecology* (2019).

Jean Mills is Associate Professor of English Literature at John Jay College/CUNY. She is the author of *Virginia Woolf, Jane Ellen Harrison, and the Spirit of Modernist Classicism* (2014) and is currently at work on her second book *Literary Approaches to Peace*. She recently edited and wrote the Introduction and Afterword for the late Jane Marcus's unfinished manuscript, *Nancy Cunard: Perfect Stranger* (2020).

Vara Neverow is a professor of English and Women's and Gender Studies at Southern Connecticut State University. She organized the second Annual Conference on Virginia Woolf and served as President of the International Virginia Woolf Society for two terms (2000–2005). She has been the editor of the *Virginia Woolf Miscellany* since 2003. She is co-editor of the four-volume set *Virginia Woolf: Critical and Primary* and *Virginia Woolf: Twenty-First-Century Approaches* (2014).

Elizabeth Outka is Professor of English, University of Richmond. She is the author of *Viral Modernism: The Influenza Pandemic and Interwar Literature* (2020) and *Consuming Traditions: Modernity, Modernism, and the Commodified Authentic* (2009). Her articles have appeared in *Modernism/modernity, NOVEL, Contemporary Literature*, and numerous edited collections.

Caroline Pollentier is Associate Professor of English, Sorbonne Nouvelle University. She founded the French Society for Modernist Studies in 2013 and co-edited, with Sarah Wilson, *Modernist Communities Across Cultures and Media* (2019).

Beryl Pong is a Vice-Chancellor's Fellow in English at the University of Sheffield and an Assistant Professor at the National University of Singapore. She is the author of *British*

Literature and Culture in Second World Wartime: For the Duration (2020). She is currently working on a study of semicolonialism and modernist short fiction, and an interdisciplinary project on drone aesthetics.

Roxana Robinson is Distinguished Writer in Residence at Hunter College, and former president of the Authors Guild. She is the author of the biography *Georgia O'Keeffe: A Life*, and nine works of fiction, including the novel *Cost*. She has received fellowships from the NEA and the Guggenheim Foundation; she has twice won the Maine Fiction Award from the MWPA; she has won the James Webb Award for Fiction and has twice been a finalist for the Nona Balakian Award for Criticism given by the NBCC.

Jocelyn Rodal is an Associate Research Scholar and Lecturer in English at Princeton University. She is currently at work on a book manuscript titled *Modernism's Mathematics: From Form to Formalism*. That project reads literary modernism alongside a contemporaneous modernist movement in mathematics, arguing that formalism has structural and historical roots in mathematics.

Beth C. Rosenberg is Professor of English at the University of Nevada, Las Vegas. She is the author of *Virginia Woolf and Samuel Johnson: Common Readers* (1995) and co-editor of *Virginia Woolf and the Essay* (1997). She is currently working on a comparative study of Virginia Woolf and Elena Ferrante.

Urmila Seshagiri is Associate Professor of English at the University of Tennessee. She is the author of *Race and the Modernist Imagination* (2010) and the editor of Virginia Woolf's *'Sketch of the Past' The First Scholarly Edition* (forthcoming). She is writing a book about the legacy of modernism in contemporary fiction. Her essay 'Orienting Virginia Woolf' (2004) won the Margaret Church Prize for best publication in *Modern Fiction Studies*.

Elizabeth M. Sheehan is Associate Professor of English and Women, Gender, and Sexuality Studies at Oregon State University. She is the co-editor of *Cultures of Femininity in Modern Fashion* (2011) and author of *Modernism à la Mode: Fashion and the Ends of Literature* (2018). She is editing a book of essays on fashion and literature.

Jacqueline Shin is Associate Professor of English at Towson University. She is the author of articles on Elizabeth Bowen, Graham Greene, Sylvia Townsend Warner, and Virginia Woolf, published in *Modernism/modernity* and elsewhere. She is writing a book on detached perspectives in works of twentieth-century fiction and contemporary film.

Kathryn Simpson is former Senior Lecturer in English Literature at the University of Birmingham (UK). She is author of *Gifts, Markets and Economies of Desire in Virginia Woolf* (2008) and *Virginia Woolf: A Guide for the Perplexed* (2016). She is co-editor of *Virginia Woolf: Twenty-First-Century Approaches* (2014) and of *Virginia Woolf: Critical and Primary Sources* (2020).

Laura Smith is Curator at Whitechapel Gallery, London. In her previous role as Curator at Tate St. Ives she was responsible for the exhibition: 'Virginia Woolf: an exhibition inspired by her writings' (2018). Throughout her career to date she has presented numerous exhibitions of the work of women artists and on the subject of feminism. She is currently writing a monograph on the work of Eileen Agar.

Anna Snaith is Professor of Twentieth-Century Literature at King's College London. She is the author of *Virginia Woolf: Public and Private Negotiations* (2000) and *Modernist Voyages: Colonial Women Writers in London 1890–1945* (2014), and editor of Woolf's *The Years* (The Cambridge Edition of Virginia Woolf, 2012), *A Room of One's Own* and *Three Guineas* (Oxford Worlds Classics, 2015), and *Sound and Literature* (2020). She is currently working on a monograph on interwar British literature and noise.

Helen Southworth is Professor of English at the University of Oregon. She works in the fields of modernism, book and publishing history, life writing, archives and digital humanities. She is the author of *Fresca: A Life in the Making* and *The Intersecting Realities and Fictions of Virginia Woolf and Colette* and co-author of *Scholarly Adventures in Digital Humanities*. She edited *Leonard and Virginia Woolf, the Hogarth Press and the Networks of Modernism* and is a founding member of the Modernist Archives Publishing Project team (modernistarchives.com).

Alice Staveley is Senior Lecturer in English at Stanford University. She is co-founder of the Modernist Archives Publishing Project (modernistarchives.com) and co-author of *Scholarly Adventures in Digital Humanities* (2017). She has published broadly on Woolf's publishing practices, including the history of her 'lost' press manager, Norah Nicholls. With Stanford undergraduates, she heads a DH project quantifying book sales data for the Hogarth Press. In 2017, she won the Dean's Award for Distinguished Teaching.

Maxwell Uphaus was an English literature faculty member for two years at Montana State University and three years at the University of Toronto, during which time his research focused on the role of the sea in the historical imagination of British modernism. He is the author of articles that have appeared or are forthcoming in *Modern Fiction Studies*, *Modernist Cultures*, *Soundings: An Interdisciplinary Journal*, *English Language Notes*, and *Comparative Literature*. He is currently a developmental editor and staff writer for Broadview Press.

Janine Utell is Homer C. Nearing, Jr Distinguished Professor in English at Widener University. She is the author of *James Joyce and the Revolt of Love* (2010), *Engagements with Narrative* (2015), and *Literary Couples and 20th-Century Life Writing* (2019), and the editor of *The Comics of Alison Bechdel* (2020) and *Teaching Modernist Women's Writing in English* (forthcoming). She is working on a monograph about modernist women's writing and anger and a biography of Howard Cruse.

Mary Wilson is Associate Professor of English at the University of Massachusetts Dartmouth. She is the author of *The Labors of Modernism: Domesticity, Servants, and Authorship in Modernist Fiction* (2014) and co-editor of *Rhys Matters: New Critical Perspectives* (2014). She is currently working on a new book project on imagining queer domesticities.

Alice Wood is Senior Lecturer in English Literature at De Montfort University. She is the author of *Virginia Woolf's Late Cultural Criticism* (2013) and *Modernism and Modernity in British Women's Magazines* (2020).

Dora Zhang is Associate Professor of English and Comparative Literature at University of California, Berkeley. She is author of *Strange Likeness: Description and the Modernist Novel* (2020).

Works by Virginia Woolf

ARO	*A Room of One's Own*, in *A Room of One's Own and Three Guineas*, ed. Anna Snaith (Oxford: Oxford University Press, 2015), 1–86.
BA	*Between the Acts*, ed. Mark Hussey (Cambridge: Cambridge University Press, 2011).
CSF	*The Complete Shorter Fiction of Virginia Woolf*, ed. Susan Dick, 2nd ed. (Orlando: Harcourt, 1989).
D1–5	*The Diary of Virginia Woolf*, ed. Anne Olivier Bell and Andrew McNeillie, 5 vols (London: Penguin, 1979–1985).
F	*Flush*, ed. Kate Flint (Oxford: Oxford University Press, 2009).
E1–6	*The Essays of Virginia Woolf*, 6 vols, vols 1–4 ed. Andrew McNeillie; vols 5–6 ed. Stuart N. Clarke (London: Hogarth, 1986–2011).
HPGN	*Hyde Park Gate News: The Stephen Family Newspaper* [by Virginia Woolf, Vanessa Bell, and Thoby Stephen], ed. Gill Lowe (London: Hesperus, 2005).
JR	*Jacob's Room*, ed. Kate Flint (Oxford: Oxford University Press, 2008).
L1–6	*The Letters of Virginia Woolf*, ed. Nigel Nicolson and Joanne Trautmann, 6 vols (London: Hogarth, 1975–1980).
MB	*Moments of Being*, ed. Jeanne Schulkind, 2nd edn, London: Hogarth, 1985
MD	*Mrs Dalloway*, ed. Anne E. Fernald (Cambridge: Cambridge University Press, 2015).
ND	*Night and Day*, ed. Michael H. Whitworth (Cambridge: Cambridge University Press, 2018).
O	*Orlando*, ed. Suzanne Raitt and Ian Blyth (Cambridge: Cambridge University Press, 2018).
P	*The Pargiters, the Novel-Essay Portion of The Years*, ed. Mitchell A. Leaska (New York: Harcourt, 1977).
PA	*A Passionate Apprentice: The Early Journals 1897-1909*, ed. Mitchell A. Leaska (London: Hogarth, 1990).
RF	*Roger Fry*, (London: Hogarth, 1940).
TG	*Three Guineas*, in *A Room of One's Own and Three Guineas*, ed. Anna Snaith (Oxford: Oxford University Press, 2015), 87–253.

TL   *To the Lighthouse*, ed. Margaret Drabble (Oxford: Oxford University Press, 2000).

TR   *Translations from the Russian*, trans. S. S. Koteliansky, ed. Stuart N. Clarke (Southport: Virginia Woolf Society of Great Britain, 2006).

VO   *The Voyage Out*, ed. Lorna Sage (Oxford: Oxford University Press, 2009).

W   *The Waves*, ed. Michael Herbert and Susan Sellers (Cambridge: Cambridge University Press, 2011).

Y   *The Years*, ed. Anna Snaith (Cambridge: Cambridge University Press, 2015).

INTRODUCTION

VIRGINIA Woolf (1882–1941) wrote prolifically and experimentally. In all she wrote and did, she strove for the rights of women artists: she was a feminist. This volume's six parts take her feminism and her experiments in language as foundational to her legacy: Part I has a biographical focus; then the chapters in Part II examine her career, holistically and chronologically; Part III offers more detail on the extent of her experimental practices, taking aspects of her innovation and examining each along the span of her career; Parts IV and V situate Woolf in her historical moment; and the final part explores the many ways Woolf's ideas and words continue to show their influence.

Throughout Virginia Woolf's career, she turned from writing essays and reviews to writing novels and stories, often on the same day. Recognizing this, chronological chapters look at her writing across genres, considering a phase of Woolf's career as it unfolds, with life events and all of her writing—fiction, nonfiction, and the private writing of diaries and letters—side by side. Woolf's deep engagement with prior literature and her restless commitment to experimentation is represented here by a cluster of chapters devoted to a range of ways in which she broke new ground with language. Woolf's writing was also profoundly engaged with the larger world, and an ample section on contexts explores those connections, from her connections to the literary field to her writings on war, empire, and consumer culture. This volume concludes with chapters tracing Woolf's ongoing influences in a range of theoretical and creative discourses, including across multiple subgenres of fiction, as well as within creative nonfiction, and the nonverbal arts.

For all of Woolf's rebellion against Victorian verbosity, her collected work spans many volumes. Her work in fiction and nonfiction stretches the limits of the genre so thoroughly that it is difficult to enumerate how her books fit into discrete genre categories. The seldom-read *Roger Fry* (1940) is an experimental biography of the artist and critic who was also her friend (and, although unmentioned in the book, her sister's lover from 1911–1913); critics typically count *Orlando* (1928) among her novels despite the fact that its setting, Knole House, relies on many facts from the family history of her friend and lover Vita Sackville-West; but how do we count *Flush* (1933), a fictional biography of Elizabeth Barrett-Browning's dog that highlights what we might call canine stream of consciousness? Even books we can more confidently categorize challenge genre boundaries. Her first novel, *The Voyage Out* (1915), thwarts expectations of the bildungsroman not only by killing the heroine but by continuing on for several chapters beyond her death; her final novel, *Between the Acts* (1941), depicts scenes from English history through the frame of a village pageant that features a raucous juxtaposition of genres (music, dramatic monologues, newspaper clippings, and poetry) that defy easy categorization. She considered calling *To the Lighthouse* (1927) an elegy. The feminist polemic *A Room of One's Own* (1929) is adapted from a lecture and uses a fictionalized narrator; her second book-length feminist work, *Three Guineas* (1938), is composed as a series of letters to an imaginary gentleman but includes voluminous footnotes, extensive descriptions of photographs of war trauma alongside actual photographs of men in uniform that are not described at all. Her shorter works, too, often crossed boundaries. Her first and most daring experiments came in her short fiction: the stories 'Kew Gardens', 'The Mark on the Wall', and others playing with stream of consciousness techniques while she was composing the more realist *Night and Day* (1919).

Woolf's broad and deep reading extended from ancient Greek up through modern physics and tell-all memoir. She read English literature, poetry, drama, and prose, from Middle English to her day—including some American literature; devoured biography, letters, and memoirs; and read widely in Greek, French, and Russian literature, three languages she studied. This reading informed her writing. For all of this study, she never enrolled in school as a child at all and despite many classes at university, she was never a degree-seeking student. Her parents did not believe in women earning university degrees, and this injustice, among others, fuelled the feminism that informed her writing. Throughout her oeuvre, Woolf explored the ways that social structures, particularly patriarchy, cramp lives, especially the lives of women of her own class. She spoke out against subtle and explicit discrimination from passing slights up to and including sexual violence and abuse.

This volume looks broadly and holistically at Woolf's friendships and her relationships to her contemporaries, within and beyond London's Bloomsbury, to situate her writing in a more diverse, less familiar context. We know that Virginia Woolf moved in a network of London literary and social life, her intimates extending far beyond her most famous affiliation with the Bloomsbury Group, a loose affiliation of artists and intellectuals who gathered in that neighbourhood. Indeed, several of her most important relationships—with Violet Dickinson, Katherine Mansfield, and Ethel Smyth—were not, strictly speaking, with members of the group. Literary London of the early twentieth century had many circles that connected to Woolf's professional life, as a novelist, reviewer, feminist, and publisher. Beyond her abundantly documented and richly interesting personal history, Woolf lived through a tumultuous time in the history of England. As a child, she witnessed the procession of Queen Victoria through London's streets; at the time of her death, the blitzkrieg had bombed her London home and displaced her to the countryside.

Woolf's feminism was foundational to her thinking: every chapter assumes her deep interest in exploring questions of feminism and gender roles, even as many also interrogate limitations in her thinking. This volume includes essays on Woolf's relationship to the feminist concerns of her day, including not only her relationship to feminism itself but to issues such as education, where her feminist commitments were unwavering;

suffrage, where some of her dismissive comments have led critics to underestimate her engagement or to fully understand her work in the larger context of the struggle for the right to vote. It also presents essays on how this legacy continues to influence current conversations, in both feminist and queer theory. More equivocal, but still a topic of Woolf's direct attention, is her work on social class. Woolf was precise, often snobbish, in her class affiliations, but her scrutiny of her position shifted with changing circumstances in illuminating ways.

By contrast, Woolf's occasional participation in discourses of race are notable, but seldom innovative, and often racist. Rather than replicate the extant critiques of Woolf's thinking on race, contributors in many chapters consider race as part of their engagement with other issues, addressing the complex ways that her critiques of patriarchy, capitalism, and empire often failed to imagine her own complicity with structures of racism. Whatever Woolf's failings, this volume takes seriously our contemporary responsibility to engage with issues of race and takes heart in the fact that, as Woolf learned from writers who would have been sexist toward her, so her successors are far more diverse in racial and national background than she might have anticipated. Thus, in every chapter on Woolf's afterlives, you will find discussion of writers of colour who draw on Woolf as an influence, recognizing both her inspiration and her limitations. Part of this legacy continues in the diversity of contributors to this volume itself.

PART I
LIFE

CHAPTER 1

FAMILY AND PLACE

URMILA SESHAGIRI

WHERE did Virginia Woolf feel herself most at home? The historical record and a mass of biographical materials suggest many familiar answers. Over the course of her fifty-nine years, Woolf's residences included a seaside summer home in Cornwall, a gloomy, elegant Kensington house, a sequence of flats and houses in Bloomsbury, and the carefully tended grounds of Monk's House in Sussex.[1] And Woolf made herself at home in numerous other places, whether as a frequent weekend guest at Lady Ottoline Morrell's Oxfordshire estate Garsington Manor House, or as Vita Sackville-West's intimate companion at the latter's ancestral home Knole, or, perhaps most significantly, as a witness to the aesthetic energies coursing through her sister Vanessa Bell's farmhouse-turned-atelier in Charleston.[2] But let us set aside these storied places—bracketing, in true Woolfian spirit, what is preserved in history books—and consider the idea of home apart from mappable geographies and architecture. Woolf's literary worldmaking endeavoured to solve the elemental condition of belonging: and from her early fictions *The Voyage Out* (1915) and 'The Mark on the Wall' (1917) to her unfinished final works 'Sketch of the Past' (1939–1941) and *Between the Acts* (1941), Woolf reinvented the idea

---

[1] Illustrated histories of Woolf's residences include Marion Dell and Marion Whybrow, *Virginia Woolf & Vanessa Bell: Remembering St Ives* (Cornwall: Tabb House, 2003); Ruth Webb, *Virginia Woolf* (London: The British Library, 2000); Frances Spalding, *The Illustrated Letters of Virginia Woolf* (London: Collins & Brown, 1991; London: National Trust Books, 2017); Christopher Reed, *Bloomsbury Rooms: Modernism, Subculture, and Domesticity* (New York: Bard Center, 2004); Nuala Hancock, *Charleston and Monk's House: The Intimate House Museums of Virginia Woolf and Vanessa Bell* (Edinburgh: Edinburgh University Press, 2012) and *Virginia Woolf at Monk's House: A National Trust Guidebook* (Sussex: The History Press, 2018).

[2] See Ottoline Morrell, *Ottoline at Garsington: Memoirs of Lady Ottoline Morrell, 1915–1918* (New York: Knopf, 1975) and Miranda Seymour, *Ottoline Morrell: Life on the Grand Scale* (New York: Farrar, Straus and Giroux, 1993); Vita Sackville-West, *Knole and the Sackvilles* (1922) and Robert Sackville-West, *Knole (Kent)* (London: Tempus, 1996); Quentin Bell and Virginia Nicholson, *Charleston: A Bloomsbury House and Garden* (London: White Lion, 2018); and Sarah Milroy and Ian A. C. Dejardin, *Vanessa Bell* (London: Dulwich Picture Gallery, 2017).

of home to express the tension between alienation and intimacy. We may know all of her addresses, but her theories of home unsettle the stability that such knowledge promises.

Two moments from Woolf's last writings illustrate this destabilizing work and set the stage for understanding her conceptions of home. The first hails from Woolf's memoir 'Sketch of the Past' and paints a portrait of St Ives, the small Cornish village where Woolf and her family spent their summers from 1882 to 1894:[3]

> The town was then much as it must have been in the sixteenth century, unknown, uninvited, unvisited, a scramble of granite houses crusting the slope in the hollow under the Island. It must have been built for shelter; for a few fishermen, when Cornwall was more remote from England than Spain or Africa is now.... The eighteenth century had left no mark upon St Ives, as it has so definitely upon every southern village. It might have been built yesterday; or in the time of the Conqueror. It had no architecture; no arrangement. The market place was a jagged cobbled open place; the Church was on one side; built of granite, ageless, like the houses; the fish market stood beside it. (*MB* 128)

Woolf's evocation of St Ives—a town changed and yet unchanged by the centuries, a town at one time 'more remote from England than Spain or Africa is now'—accommodates Cornwall's enduring Englishness alongside a sense of its foreignness. The *here and now* of Woolf's Victorian childhood summer home, the passage suggests, are not more powerful than their geohistorical counterpoints or antecedents. In a different tenor, a passage from Woolf's final novel *Between the Acts* imagines how people's connections to their homes can both offer and obscure meaning. *Between the Acts*, the story of a pageant play staged for the members of an English village, takes as its main setting a large country house whose aspect conveys simultaneous solidity and unsteadiness:

> Pointz Hall was seen in the light on an early summer morning to be a middle-sized house. It did not rank among the houses that are mentioned in Guide Books. It was homely. But this whitish house with the grey roof, and the wing thrown out at right angles [...] was a desirable house to live in. Driving past, people said to each other: 'I wonder if that'll ever come into the market?' And to the chauffeur: 'Who lives there?'
> The chauffeur didn't know. The Olivers, who had bought the place something over a century ago, had no connection with the Warings, the Elveys, the Mannerings or the Burnets; the old families who had all intermarried, and lay in their deaths intertwisted like the ivy roots beneath the churchyard wall. (*BA* 5)

---

[3] On the interleaved histories and memories that went into Woolf's composition of 'Sketch of the Past', see Julia Briggs, *Virginia Woolf: An Inner Life* (New York: Harcourt, 2005); Alex Zwerdling, *The Rise of the Memoir* (Oxford: Oxford University Press, 2017); and Hannah Sullivan, *The Work of Revision* (Cambridge, MA: Harvard University Press, 2013).

As the site of the Oliver family's varied experiences of history, Pointz Hall embodies the uncertain condition of community in interwar England.[4] Purchased rather than inherited, architecturally insignificant, and now inhabited by a family unknown to local residents, Pointz Hall represents the broken promises of the once constitutive mutuality between genealogy and property. Home and family, in other words, signal discontinuity and unknowability rather than the stable forward-moving flow of 'intertwisted' lives. Yet a yearning for that flow generates as much narrative momentum as the act of acknowledging its absence.

These passages from 'Sketch of the Past' and *Between the Acts* illuminate a strategy that Woolf deploys throughout her oeuvre: the use of 'home' to locate an elusive equilibrium between past and present. And Woolf's pursuit of that temporal equilibrium opens up two interrelated lines of argument about the vital conceptual role of home in her life and work. On one hand, such a pursuit shaped the author's experience of diverse private and public milieux between her childhood and her move to Bloomsbury in 1904, where her identity as an Englishwoman was both anchored and displaced by each place she called home. At the same time, Woolf's curiosity about balancing the past and the present pervades her best-known novels, an array of modernist works in which feminist literary inventiveness produces a sense of home that is—as the two passages above demonstrate—simultaneously definitive and unstable. Through the act of reimagining home, Woolf's literary and non-literary writings seek answers to no smaller a query than, in Clarissa Dalloway's words, 'What did it mean to her, this thing she called life?' (*MD* 105). The form and substance of Clarissa's query, which falls at a key moment in Woolf's 1925 novel *Mrs Dalloway*, open the avenues through which the modernist arts were forged. Against the conventional phrasing *what is the meaning of life?* and its implicitly static, singular answer, Clarissa's query names 'life' as 'this thing' that lacks another name and carries multiple meanings for different questioners. And life's 'supreme mystery', for Clarissa Dalloway, expresses itself in the language of domestic architecture: 'Here was one room, there another' (*MD* 114). Or, in the words of Lily Briscoe, the artist-protagonist of Woolf's *To the Lighthouse* (1927) who longs to access the 'chambers of the mind and heart' of her beloved friend Mrs Ramsay, 'What art was there, known to love or cunning, by which one pressed through into those secret chambers?' (*TL* 70). Rooms, chambers, houses: what connects and divides them from one another? The question yields aesthetic form as well as philosophical grounding in Woolf's writings, where the work of home and the work of art are inseparable. Home is the place where literary genres bend and break; it is the site where Woolf remakes historical masternarratives and national subjects.

To tell the story of Virginia Woolf's life is to tell the story of many families in many English houses. Quentin Bell's compendious 1972 *Virginia Woolf: A Biography*,

---

[4] See Jed Esty, *A Shrinking Island* (Princeton: Princeton University Press, 2003); Melba Cuddy-Keane, 'The Politics of Comic Modes in Virginia Woolf's *Between the Acts*', *PMLA* 105, no. 2 (1990), 273–85; Mark Hussey, 'Introduction', in Virginia Woolf, *Between the Acts* (Cambridge: Cambridge University Press, 2011).

which declares that 'The purpose of the present volume is purely historical', begins chapter 1 with the words 'Virginia Woolf was a Miss Stephen. The Stephens emerged from obscurity in the eighteenth century' and chapter 2 with 'Virginia was born on 25 January 1882, at 22 Hyde Park Gate.'[5] Bell grounds his story in biography's traditional generic foundations, the lineage and location of the subject's family. And unsurprisingly, most writers who have told the story of Virginia Woolf's life, whether before or after Bell, invoke the same reliable building blocks of biography: genealogy, cultural context, precise dates, and geographical coordinates.[6] But Hermione Lee counters the accumulated weight of such biographies, dispensing with Quentin Bell's 'purely historical' optic in order to train her gaze on the subversive life-writing techniques that Woolf pioneered. Lee's authoritative 1996 *Virginia Woolf* (which has replaced Bell's more anecdotal, intimate biography of his aunt as the standard-bearer for Woolf's life history) points out: 'What no longer seems possible is to start: "Adeline Virginia Stephen was born on 25 January 1882, the daughter of Sir Leslie Stephen, editor of the *Dictionary of National Biography*, and of Julia Stephen, née Jackson." '[7] Thus, any life of Woolf seems best produced in a space between the factual and the experiential, a space where Woolf's own narratives came into being. We start, then, in the manner of most of Woolf's biographers, on what appears to be stable ground.

In 1881, Sir Leslie Stephen signed a lease for Talland House, a large villa in the seaside town of St Ives, in Cornwall. Newly appointed as the first editor of *Dictionary of National Biography*, that sixty-three-volume 'monument to the Victorian age',[8] Stephen wrote a happy letter from St Ives to the publisher, George Smith: 'We are having lovely weather here, and the place is perfectly charming. I think that we have made a great hit in taking the house, which is perfect for our requirements. I shall, I hope, come back ready to write and edit biographies by the dozen.'[9] The 'we' Stephen refers to included the large, complicated family he had created with his second wife, Julia Prinsep Duckworth Stephen. By the time he acquired Talland House, Sir Leslie Stephen was recognized as one of the intellectual titans of late nineteenth-century England. His father, Sir James Stephen, had been a Clapham Sect abolitionist who educated his son at Eton, King's College, London, and Trinity College, Cambridge.[10] Leslie inherited his father's abolitionist convictions; he studied Divinity at Cambridge and was ordained as a deacon in 1855. Soon after, however, influenced by the variously secular theories of Charles

---

[5] Quentin Bell, *Virginia Woolf: A Biography* (London: Hogarth Press, 1972), xv, 1, 22.

[6] For example: David Daiches, *Virginia Woolf* (New York: New Directions, 1942); Monique Nathan, *Virginia Woolf* (New York: Grove Press, 1961); Panthea Reid, *Art and Affection: A Life of Virginia Woolf* (Oxford: Oxford University Press, 1996); James King, *Virginia Woolf* (New York: W. W. Norton & Co., 1995); Lyndall Gordon, *Virginia Woolf: A Writer's Life* (New York: W. W. Norton & Co., 2001); and Christine Froula, *Virginia Woolf and the Bloomsbury Avant-Garde: War, Civilization, Modernity* (New York: Columbia University Press, 2004).

[7] Hermione Lee, *Virginia Woolf* (New York: Vintage, 1996), 3.

[8] Noel Annan, *Leslie Stephen: The Godless Victorian* (New York: Random House, 1984), 87.

[9] Frederic Maitland, *The Life and Letters of Leslie Stephen* (London: Duckworth & Co., 1910), 349.

[10] See S. P. Rosenbaum, *Victorian Bloomsbury, Volume 1: The Early History of the Bloomsbury Group* (New York: Palgrave Macmillan, 1987).

Darwin, John Stuart Mill, Thomas Henry Huxley, and other Victorian intellectuals, he rejected the Stephen family's religiosity and resigned from his post as a tutor at Cambridge, no longer able to deliver weekly chapel talks with conviction. His agnosticism would subsequently inform a prolific authorial and editorial career that spanned philosophy, politics, criticism, and biography.[11] In 1867, Leslie Stephen married Minny Thackeray, the daughter of the novelist William Makepeace Thackeray. They spent nine happy years living amidst literary circles in London and travelling through Europe (Leslie was an accomplished alpinist); their only child, Laura Stephen, was born in 1870 and afflicted by a still-unspecified mental or intellectual condition.[12] But Minny died in premature labour during her second pregnancy in 1875, and Leslie, grieving and now alone in caring for Laura, moved to a new home in Hyde Park Gate, Kensington, next door to Julia Duckworth.[13] Julia, the Calcutta-born daughter of an English father and French mother raised among poets, painters, and writers and renowned for her Pre-Raphaelite beauty, was also widowed and was caring for children (George, Stella, and Gerald) following the sudden death of her barrister husband Herbert Duckworth.[14] She and Leslie married in 1878 and moved into 22 Hyde Park Gate, and together had four children: Vanessa, Thoby, Virginia, and Adrian. It was this large clan that Leslie had in mind when he leased Talland House in Cornwall, and the Stephens would spend every summer there between 1882 and 1894 (Fig. 1.1).

Talland House was the source of a childhood sensory intensity that flooded Virginia Woolf's adult writings.[15] Here, released from the conventions of their London life, she and her siblings would take long walks, capture moths and butterflies, watch sailboats, play cricket, converse with townspeople, and gaze at Godrevy Lighthouse, the inspiration for *To the Lighthouse*.[16] Talland House is the first place, as she tells us in this famed passage from 'Sketch of the Past', that she remembers:

> If life has a base that it stands upon, if it is a bowl that one fills and fills and fills—then my bowl without a doubt stands upon this memory. It is of lying half asleep, half

---

[11] See Leslie Stephen, 'An Agnostic's Apology: Poisonous Opinions', in Leslie Stephen, *Selected Writings in British Intellectual History*, ed. Noel Annan (Chicago: University of Chicago Press, 1979); Annan, *Leslie Stephen*; Maitland, *The Life And Letters*, 130–54; and John Bicknell, ed., *Selected Letters of Leslie Stephen: Volume I (1864-1882)* (Columbus: Ohio State University Press, 1996), 6–19.

[12] Leslie Stephen, *Mausoleum Book* [1895] (Oxford: Oxford University Press, 2001), 7–23; Lee, *Virginia Woolf*, 99–103; and Gillian Gill, *Virginia Woolf and the Women Who Shaped Her World* (Boston: Harcourt, 2019), 104–24. On disability and Woolf, see Janet Lyon, 'On the Asylum Road with Mew and Woolf', *Modernism/modernity* 18, no. 3 (2012), 551–74; and Maren Tova Linett, *Bodies of Modernism: Physical Disability in Transatlantic Modernist Literature* (Ann Arbor: University of Michigan Press, 2017).

[13] Stephen, *Mausoleum Book*, 22.

[14] Diane Gillespie and Julia Steele, eds, *Julia Duckworth Stephen: Stories for Children, Essays for Adults* (Syracuse, NY: Syracuse University Press, 1987); Vanessa Curtis, *Virginia Woolf's Women* (Madison: University of Wisconsin Press, 2003), 31–56; and Gill, *Virginia Woolf and the Women*, 127–60.

[15] See Lee, *Virginia Woolf*, 21–34 for detailed connections between Woolf's experiences at Talland House and her evocation of childhood in *Jacob's Room*, *To the Lighthouse*, and *The Waves*.

[16] See Marion Whybrow, *Virginia Woolf & Vanessa Bell: A Childhood in St Ives* (Wellington: Halstar, 2014).

FIGURE 1.1 Talland House, Leslie Stephen Photograph Album, Mortimer Rare Book Collection (MRBC-MS-00005), Smith College Special Collections, Northampton, Massachusetts

> awake, in bed in the nursery at St Ives. It is of hearing the waves breaking one, two, one, two, and sending a splash of water over the beach; and then breaking one, two, one, two, behind a yellow blind. It is of hearing the blind draw its little acorn across the floor as the wind blew the blind out. It is of lying and hearing the splash and seeing this light, and feeling, it is almost impossible that I should be here; of feeling the purest ecstasy I can conceive. (*MB* 64–5)

Endowing her memory of Talland House with the status of a 'base' or 'bowl' that supports and receives life's subsequent experiences, Woolf rhapsodizes about formative childhood summers spent with her family in this home, 'the best beginning to life conceivable ... perennial, invaluable' (*MB* 128). And yet, reflecting on this childhood at the age of fifty-eight, she questions whether her first memory owes anything to the family history we have just outlined:

> Who was I then? Adeline Virginia Stephen, the second daughter of Leslie and Julia Prinsep Stephen, born on 25 January 1882, descended from a great many people, some famous, others obscure; born into a large connection, born not of rich parents, but of well-to-do parents, born into a very communicative, literate world; so that I could if I liked to take the trouble, write a great deal here not only about my mother

and father but about uncles and aunts, cousins and friends. *But I do not know how much of this, or what part of this, made me feel what I felt in the nursery at St Ives.* (MB 65, my emphasis)

The factual destabilized by the ephemeral: here is the gesture that Woolf had perfected over decades of writing, the creation of self-conscious aesthetic tension between modes of the real. Indeed, an early typed draft of 'Sketch' originally employed the word 'stem'— 'If life has a stem that it stands on'—which Woolf struck out and replaced with the handwritten word 'base'.[17] In choosing the metaphor of a base over the organic foundation of a stem, Woolf's compositional process itself foregrounds a tension between genetic and cultural influence, asking whether we inherit our foundational selves from our families or from other sources: 'But I do not know how much of this, or what part of this, made me feel what I felt in the nursery at St Ives.'

Woolf's admission that 'I do not know' speaks to an intriguing distance between what Talland House *was* and the multiple meanings that accrued to it over the years. This distance often manifests itself in Woolf's experimental fictions as an oscillation between embracing and refusing the idea of home as a fixed point of origin. For example, the unifying motif of her anti-bildungsroman *Jacob's Room* (1922) is of furnished but empty domestic spaces that thwart our understanding of the titular protagonist:

> Jacob's room had a round table and two low chairs. There were yellow flags in a jar on the mantelpiece; a photograph of his mother; cards from societies with little raised crescents, coats of arms, and initials.... Listless is the air in an empty room, just swelling the curtain; the flowers in the jar shift. One fibre in the wicker armchair creaks, though no one sits there. (*JR* 48)

Jacob Flanders's possessions in his Cambridge room (native flowers, a maternal photograph, cards bearing ancestral insignias) evoke longstanding networks of English masculine social belonging. But the 'listless' room's uninhabited armchair – a passage repeated verbatim on the novel's final page – foretells Jacob's premature death during the Great War. As violence tears the world apart, domesticity itself furnishes the language of mortality rather than comforting continuity: fatal gunfire sounds to Jacob's bereft mother 'as if nocturnal women were beating great carpets' (*JR* 246). In this novel—Woolf's third, and the work where, as she wrote in her diary 'I have found out how to begin (at 40) to say something in my own voice' (*D2* 186)—the alienated protagonist's empty room signifies the monstrous homelessness of an entire generation of men.[18] But Woolf's most radical novel, *The Waves* (1930), finds freedom in the absence

---

[17] University of Sussex, Monk's House Papers, MH/5/A.e.
[18] Alex Zwerdling, '*Jacob's Room*: Woolf's Satiric Elegy', *ELH* 48, no. 4 (1981), 894–913; Kathleen Dobie, 'This is the Room that Class Built: the Structures of Race and Class in *Jacob's Room*', in Jane Marcus, ed., *Virginia Woolf and Bloomsbury: A Centenary Celebration* (London: Macmillan, 1987), 195–207.

of conventions associated with home. Here is the voice of Louis, one of the novel's six narrating children, calibrating the social distances between himself and his English peers: 'My father is a banker in Brisbane and I speak with an Australian accent.... I could know everything in the world if I wished. But I do not wish to come to the top and say my lesson. My roots are threaded, like fibres in a flower-pot, round and round about the world' (*W* 13–14). Refusing to be confined or displaced by colonial attitudes, the adult Louis plants his 'roots' successfully in the crosscurrents of international business: 'I am half in love with the typewriter and the telephone. With letters and cables and brief but courteous commands on the telephone to Paris, Berlin, New York, I have fused my many lives into one; I have helped by my assiduity and decision to score those lines on the map there by which the different parts of the world are laced together' (*W* 133–4). Fittingly, in a work that Woolf characterized as her 'abstract mystical eyeless book: a play-poem' (*D3* 203), Louis lays bold claim to a 'fused', polylinear life, casting aside British imperial centre/periphery conceptions of 'home' in favour of cosmopolitan belonging. And these currents of dispossession in *Jacob's Room* and of renunciation in *The Waves* combine in Woolf's polemic *Three Guineas* (1938), where the trope of home illuminates the massed historical weight of sexual and socioeconomic injustice. The narrator of *Three Guineas* speculates that an Englishwoman, a perpetual outsider in her own nation, would not summon patriotic energy during wartime but would instead avow, 'As a woman, I have no country. As a woman I want no country. As a woman, my country is the whole world' (*TG* 185). Whether as a call to an inclusive global feminism or a willed refusal of any domestic collectivity, this oft-cited line from *Three Guineas* exemplifies the form-giving elusiveness that Woolf consistently associates with home.[19]

That elusiveness reverberates throughout Woolf's writings, producing sometimes exhilarating, sometimes frightening aesthetic modes that challenge the impact of birthplace and family on selfhood: again, 'I do not know how much of this, or what part of this, made me feel what I felt.' The memoir 'Sketch of the Past' attributes the condition of not-knowing—ontological as well as epistemological—to the difficulty of retrieving childhood remembrances accurately: 'As an account of my life [these first memories] are misleading.... If I could remember one whole day I should be able to describe, superficially at least, what life was like as a child. Unfortunately, one only remembers what is exceptional' (*MB* 69). But if that difficulty derives from the uneven workings of memory, it also comes from the dialectical quality of Woolf's formative domestic experiences. The first thirteen years of her life were divided between 22 Hyde Park Gate and Talland House, and her earliest associations with home are therefore doubled. The very journey between London and Cornwall furnished the other memory she names as her 'first' in her memoir: 'This was of red and black flowers on a black ground—my mother's dress; and she was sitting either on a train or in an omnibus, and I was on her

---

[19] On the question of Woolf's feminism in relation to her global politics, see Susan Stanford Friedman, 'Wartime Cosmopolitanism: Cosmofeminism in Virginia Woolf's *Three Guineas* and Marjane Satrapi's *Persepolis*', *Tulsa Studies in Women's Literature* 32, no. 1 (2013), 23–52; and Naomi Black, *Virginia Woolf as Feminist* (Ithaca, NY: Cornell University Press, 2004).

lap' (*MB* 64). Thus, two memories compete for primacy in Woolf's consciousness: one of lying alone in a nursery and yet feeling kinaesthetic unity with the elements, the other of being securely cradled by her mother and yet moving between two residences. These 'equiprimordial memories', as Laura Marcus describes them,[20] furnish an entry point into Woolf's ambivalence about the Stephen family's late Victorian world. Summers in Talland House may have seemed to Woolf and her siblings 'an unforgettable Paradise',[21] but the months spent in 22 Hyde Park Gate harboured complexities borne of the age and the distinct temperaments of Leslie and Julia Stephen.[22] (Fig. 1.2)

Much has been written—a great deal of it by Woolf herself—about life in Hyde Park Gate.[23] Woolf lived there from her birth until 1904, when she, Vanessa, and Adrian moved to a house in Bloomsbury following the death of Leslie Stephen. One of a 'series of architecturally undistinguished row houses designed as single-family homes for upper middle-class families',[24] 22 Hyde Park Gate was a locus of ur-Victorian mores in the heart of Kensington, a household wedded to protocol and propriety in all class- and sex-based relations.[25] In a short 1922 piece written for the Bloomsbury Memoir Club,[26] Woolf would recall the "muffled silence" (*MB* 184) of childhood in Hyde Park Gate where "everybody knew everybody, and everything about everybody" (*MB* 121):

> There were chests of heavy family plate. There were hoards of china and glass. Eleven people aged between eight and sixty lived there, and were waited upon by seven

---

[20] Laura Marcus, 'Experiments in Form: Modernism and Autobiography in Woolf, Eliot, Mansfield, Lawrence, Joyce, and Richardson', in Adam Smyth, ed., *A History of English Autobiography* (Cambridge: Cambridge University Press, 2016), 298–312, at 310.

[21] Bell, *Virginia Woolf*, 30.

[22] Roger Poole, *The Unknown Virginia Woolf* (Cambridge: Cambridge University Press, 1978); Steve Ellis, *Woolf and the Victorians* (Cambridge University Press, 2007); Mary Jean Corbett, *Family Likeness: Sex, Marriage, and Incest From Jane Austen to Virginia Woolf* (Ithaca, NY: Cornell University Press, 2008), 174–200.

[23] All five of Woolf's pieces in *Moments of Being: Unpublished Autobiographical Writings* ('Old Bloomsbury', '22 Hyde Park Gate', 'Reminiscences', 'Sketch of the Past', and 'Am I a Snob?') have contributed to our understanding of her Kensington childhood. See also Woolf's anonymous contribution to F. W. Maitland's *The Life and Letters of Leslie Stephen* (New York: G. P. Putnam & Sons, 1906), a chapter titled 'The Sunset' (474–6) that recalls Leslie Stephen in 22 Hyde Park Gate; and Woolf, *Letters Volume 1* and her early journals, *A Passionate Apprentice*. Writings by other family members include Gill Lowe, ed., *Hyde Park Gate News: The Stephen Family Newspaper, by Virginia Woolf, Vanessa Bell, and Thoby Stephen* (London: Hesperus, 2005); Vanessa Bell, *Sketches in Pen and Ink* (London: Chatto & Windus, 1997); Q. Bell, *Virginia Woolf*, 22–39. Andrew McNeillie offers an intellectual history of the Stephen family's circle in 'Bloomsbury', in Sue Roe and Susan Sellers, eds, *The Cambridge Companion to Virginia Woolf* (Cambridge: Cambridge University Press, 2000), 1–28.

[24] Victoria Rosner, *Modernism and the Architecture of Private Life* (New York: Columbia University Press, 2005), 69.

[25] Alison Light, *Mrs Woolf and the Servants: An Intimate History of Domestic Life in Bloomsbury* (London: Bloomsbury, 2009), 1–78.

[26] The Memoir Club was founded by the Woolfs' friend Molly McCarthy in 1920. Members included Leonard and Virginia Woolf, E. M. Forster, John Maynard Keynes, Vanessa Bell, Clive Bell, Desmond MacCarthy, Lytton Strachey, Roger Fry, and others. See S. P. Rosenbaum, *The Bloomsbury Group Memoir Club* (New York: Palgrave Macmillan, 2014).

FIGURE 1.2 Julia Duckworth Stephen and Leslie Stephen, with young Virginia, Leslie Stephen Photograph Album, Mortimer Rare Book Collection (MRBC-MS-00005), Smith College Special Collections, Northampton, Massachusetts

> servants, while various old women and lame men did odd jobs with rakes and pails by day.
> The house was dark because the street was so narrow that one could see Mrs Redgrave washing her neck in her bedroom across the way; also because my mother who had been brought up in the Watts-Venetian-Little Holland House tradition had covered the furniture in red velvet and painted the woodwork black with thin gold lines on it. The house was also completely quiet. Save for an occasional hansom or butcher's cart nothing ever passed the door. One heard footsteps tapping down the street before we saw a top hat or a bonnet; one almost always knew who it was that passed. (*MB* 182–3)

As they grew up in this steady, tradition-heavy atmosphere, the Stephen children played in Kensington Gardens and visited the Natural History Museum; they attended Queen Victoria's Diamond Jubilee in 1897; sons were educated in exclusive public schools and universities while daughters were taught at home. But although they observed the ritual practices of dressing for dinner and of taking part in Mrs Stephen's Sunday Afternoons, the members of the Stephen family inhabited a rarefied, occasionally eccentric intellectual sphere populated by the day's leading writers and thinkers. The American writer James Russell Lowell was Woolf's godfather; Henry James, Thomas Hardy, and George Meredith counted among the family's intimate circle, as did the social reformer and industrialist Charles Booth and painters such as Edward Burne-Jones and G. F. Watts, whose portraits of Woolf's family members and ancestors hung on the walls of the six-story house.[27] Family discourse was as literary and liberal as it was repressive. Anne Olivier Bell, the editor of Woolf's diaries, tells us, 'The coarsest passages of Swift and Sterne would have been perfectly familiar to Leslie Stephen, but he could no more have quoted them than he could have alluded to a visit to the lavatory. He was a man who was ready to lead a revolution against God, who would not have been afraid of political innovations, but who so completely accepted the conventions and prohibitions of his age and class that he was ready to regard them almost as laws of nature' (*D*1 vi–vii). To be a child in the Stephen household, thus, required balancing rigid social habits with an intellectual elasticity that fostered critique of such rigidity.

Perhaps the most telling—and charming—evidence of the culture of letters in Woolf's childhood is *The Hyde Park Gate News*, a newspaper created by the Stephen children whose witty reports about familial activity reflect, in Gill Lowe's words, 'a precocious mastery of diverse techniques: pastiche, slapstick, comedy, satire, euphemism, hyperbole, whimsy and suspense' (*HPGN* xi–xvii).[28] Produced from 1891 to 1895 and modelled on Victorian papers (perhaps most closely resembling the children's beloved penny periodical *Tit-Bits*), this newspaper records daily domesticity in its predictability as well as its variety. Formatted in neat columns and illustrated with sketches by the budding artist Vanessa, *The Hyde Park Gate News* documents the trivial (weather, haircuts, dance classes) and the momentous (Christmas Day, the joyful adoption of a dog named Shag, periodic visits home from Thoby Stephen and Gerald Duckworth). Comical tensions among the siblings arise in a report about Adrian Stephen's fruitless plan to start a rival publication called 'The Talland Gazette'; Woolf's earliest literary talents appear in short fictions such as 'A Midnight Ride' (1892) and 'A Cockney's Farming Experiences' (1892). Referring to themselves as 'the juveniles', the Stephen children style their domestic reportage as a gleeful tug-of-war between propriety and impropriety: 'There is a vulgar little song coming into fashion who's [sic] chorus is "Ta ra ra bomteay." We are sure that the proper mind of Mrs Jackson [Julia Stephen's mother] would be properly shocked to know that this vulgar little ditty has actualy [sic] been sung under the same house as the one she is in' (*HPGN* 47).

The Hyde Park Gate News offers a miniature cartography of late nineteenth-century English middle-class life, inspired by the household explorations of inquisitive children. The young Virginia Stephen captured 'the grown-up world into which I would dash for a moment and pick off some joke or little scene and dash back again upstairs

---

[27] Steve Ellis, *Woolf and the Victorians*.
[28] See also Quentin Bell, *Virginia Woolf*, 28–32; Katherine Dalsimer, *Virginia Woolf: Becoming a Writer* (New Haven, CT: Yale University Press, 2001), 25–38.

to the nursery' (*MB* 94), a domestic adventuring that rendered permeable the social divisions between adults and children and laid a feminist foundation for her later writing. (Fittingly, Woolf's earliest published pieces—unsigned review-essays in *The Guardian* and the *Times Literary Supplement*—were meditations on the relationships between Victorian writers and their homes.)[29] Further, her entries for the family newspaper reveal an understanding of how the present moment, emerging from the past, moved, easily or uneasily, towards a future governed by different social rules. Consider this satirical mini-biography of a fictional social reformer named 'Miss Smith', written for *The Hyde Park Gate News* just before Woolf's thirteenth birthday and wonderfully predictive of later writings:

> From her infancy upwards Miss Smith had known that she was remarkable. She had been once upon a time the most remarkable baby ever known, and as she became older her intellect surprised her more and more.... When she appeared in society, as she did at the age of 20, her curiosity to see the world having overcome her contempt of it, she protested that society must be entirely reorganised. The position of men and women towards each other was altogether disgraceful. She wrote the most remarkable essays upon Woman's Rights, and declared herself to be a temperance lecturer.... At 30 she had deserted Woman's Rights and Temperance was settling down into a mild hobby. She thought bitterly of her former self and prepared to live her life alone. It was just about this time, when she had with many pangs allowed herself to be only a woman, that a gallant gentleman appeared, and so lonely had Miss Smith become, and so much did she feel the need of someone stronger and wiser than herself that she consented to become his wife. So they two married like ordinary human beings, and she proved to be an excellent wife, and later on a devoted mother. (*HPGN* 164–6)

Despite her efforts to escape a marriage plot, the 'remarkable' Miss Smith finds herself in the roles of wife and mother, consigned to the world of 'ordinary human beings'. The character's fate reveals that at thirteen, Virginia Stephen could critique but not yet break free of what Susan Stanford Friedman calls the 'identification, interdependence, and community'[30] that conventionally give form to women's life stories. Woolf's later works, of course, successfully reshape the arc of women's lives, aligning rather than opposing the 'remarkable' and the 'ordinary'. Her influential 1924 manifesto 'Modern Fiction' calls attention to 'an ordinary mind on an ordinary day', declaring that if writers reconsidered the established hierarchies of value that shape literature, 'there would be no plot, no comedy, no tragedy, no love interest or catastrophe in the accepted style'.

---

[29] 'Haworth, November, 1904' (originally published in *The Guardian*) and 'Literary Geography' (Woolf's first contribution to the *TLS*, published in 1905) discuss the merits and risks of visiting the houses of the Brontës, the Carlyles, and Dickens. See also *E*1 5–9, 32–5.

[30] Susan Stanford Friedman, "Autobiographical Selves: Theory and Practice," in Shari Benstock, ed., *The Private Self: Theory and Practice of Women's Autobiographical Writings* (London: Routledge, 1988), 34-62.

And to justify this new aesthetics of the real, 'Modern Fiction' delivers a statement as relevant to readers of *The Hyde Park Gate News* as to readers of *To the Lighthouse*: 'Let us not take it for granted that life exists more fully in what is commonly thought big than in what is commonly thought small' (*E4* 160). Remarkable and ordinary, big and small: these changing terms of what matters in fiction acquire a powerful feminist edge in Woolf's 1929 treatise *A Room of One's Own*, which upbraids a literary culture in which 'this is an important book, the critic assumes, because it deals with war. This is an insignificant book because it deals with the feelings of women in a drawing-room' (*ARO* 96). What prevents Miss Smith from revolutionizing 'the position of men and women towards one another', as Virginia Stephen intuited as a child and articulated as an adult in *A Room of One's Own*, is the Englishwoman's experience of 'a sudden splitting off of consciousness, say in walking down Whitehall, when from being the natural inheritor of that civilization, she becomes, on the contrary, outside of it, alien and critical' (*ARO* 73). And indeed, the final entry for *The Hyde Park Gate News* describes a young female 'Author' alone in her room and alienated by such a 'splitting off', her literary creations forced to remain unpublished because she is unable to express her views persuasively to her 'Editor'. That inarticulate frustration would consistently be linked in Woolf's mind with 'the rules of the game of Victorian society' and with a domesticity that muzzled her earliest published writings: 'When I read my old *Literary Supplement* articles, I lay the blame for their suavity, their politeness, their sidelong approach, to my tea-table training' (*MB* 150). The child writer and editor of *The Hyde Park Gate News*, bound by late Victorian mores, exulted in early flashes of the literary freedom that would, in later years, characterize novels where barriers once posed by culture, history, and sex would waver and vanish.[31]

The Hyde Park Gate News ceased publication in 1895, a year that ushered in a sequence of traumatic events in Woolf's girlhood. The next decade would be splintered by the deaths of several family members, the onset of mental health difficulties, and, consequently, the diminishing of early certainties about the idea of home. In 1895, Julia Stephen, Virginia's beloved mother and 'the very centre of that great Cathedral space which was childhood' (*MB* 81), died unexpectedly of rheumatic fever at the age of forty-eight.[32] Virginia's older half-sister Stella Duckworth served briefly as a surrogate maternal figure for the younger Stephen children, but married soon after Julia's death and left 22 Hyde Park Gate. Stella, too, died suddenly, due to complications from an infection contracted during her honeymoon in 1897. The deaths of mother and sister within a span of two years left fifteen-year-old Virginia and eighteen-year-old Vanessa to assume the duties of caring for Leslie Stephen. These duties became frequently intolerable as their isolated father's self-pity degenerated into verbal and psychological abuse; and the

---

[31] See Jane Goldman, *The Feminist Aesthetics of Virginia Woolf: Modernism, Post-Impressionism and the Politics of the Visual* (Cambridge: Cambridge University Press, 1998) and Frances Spalding, *Virginia Woolf: Art, Life and Vision* (London: National Portrait Gallery, 2014).

[32] Viviane Forrester, *Virginia Woolf: A Portrait* (New York: Columbia University Press, 2015), 69–108.

sisters experienced relief alongside their sorrow when their father succumbed to cancer in 1904. Two decades later, Woolf reflected, 'His life would have entirely ended mine.... No writing, no books;—inconceivable' (*D3* 208). They had barely recovered a sense of centre when, in 1906, their brother Thoby Stephen died of typhoid after a vacation in Greece.

Scholars and biographers have observed that the devastating losses of this period haunted Woolf's psyche and her fiction for decades, perhaps resonating most profoundly through *To the Lighthouse*, the 1927 'Elegy' (*D3* 34) for Victorian domesticity where Woolf memorialized her parents in the characters of Mr and Mrs Ramsay.[33] *To the Lighthouse* describes in exquisite detail a summer day in the world of a family with eight children, its opening section the epitome of locating the 'remarkable' in the 'ordinary', but the novel's centre shatters that very world with a single, pitiless sentence enclosed in square brackets:

> [Mr Ramsay, stumbling along a passage one dark morning, stretched his arms out, but Mrs Ramsay having died rather suddenly the night before, his arms, though stretched out, remained empty.] (*TL* 128)

This rupture—the inexplicable, incomprehensible death of a matriarch, the unknowable future ahead—speaks as much to the loss of Julia Stephen as it does to the violence of the Great War: both occurrences were fatal to the integrity of domestic fabric.[34] *To the Lighthouse* evokes the premature deaths of Stella Duckworth and Thoby Stephen through the stark, parenthetical deaths of Prue and Andrew Ramsay; the impersonal narrative voice of the novel's middle section, 'Time Passes', announces that '(Prue Ramsay died that summer in some illness connected with childbirth)' (*TL* 180) and that '(Twenty or thirty young men were blown up in France, among them Andrew Ramsay)' (*TL* 181). The Ramsays' house itself, an architectural signifier for late Victorian customs and mores, decays in emptiness until housekeepers revive it:

> The house was left; the house was deserted. It was left like a shell on a sand-hill to fill with dry salt grains now that life had left it. The long night seemed to have set in the trifling airs, nibbling, the clammy breaths, fumbling, seemed to have triumphed. The saucepan had rusted and the mat decayed. Toads had nosed their way in.... Slowly and painfully, with broom and pail, mopping, scouring, Mrs McNab, Mrs Bast stayed the corruption and the rot rescued from the pool of Time that was fast closing over them now a basin, now a cupboard[.] (*TL* 187–9)

---

[33] See Anne E. Fernald, '*To the Lighthouse* in the Context of Virginia Woolf's Diaries and Life', in Allison Pease, ed., *The Cambridge Companion to* To the Lighthouse (Cambridge: Cambridge University Press, 2015), 6–18; Louise DeSalvo, *Virginia Woolf: The Impact of Childhood Sexual Abuse on Her Life and Work* (New York: Ballantine Books, 1990), 99–206; and Briggs, *Virginia Woolf: An Inner Life*.

[34] See Mark Hussey, ed., *Virginia Woolf and War: Fiction, Reality, and Myth*. (Syracuse, NY: Syracuse University Press, 1991).

'Rescued from the pool of Time', the house takes on fresh meaning after the war, opening up the novel's celebration of memory's unreliable meshes, and of the past's overflow into the present as a phenomenon that renews lives and homes. As the reader follows Lily Briscoe's wandering consciousness in the novel's final section, the absent Mrs Ramsay comes into focus anew, a character with hitherto unknown dimensions and contradictions. Woolf's literary works thus resist the very biographical readings they encourage: the deaths that plunged Virginia Stephen into such darkness are reinvented by the adult Woolf as an unexpected source of vitality in her most formally daring fictions. Death, neither a fixed end point nor a harbinger of paralysis, often serves as a phenomenon that forces Woolf's characters to reconcile their ambivalence about home and belonging.[35]

Consider the climax of *Mrs Dalloway*. What makes the novel's 'caves connect', in Woolf's celebrated metaphor, is not Clarissa's entrance into her party with the Prime Minister (a visible affirmation of her success as 'the perfect hostess' (*MD* 7)), but instead the more rarefied moment when Clarissa learns of the shell-shocked veteran Septimus Warren Smith's suicide: 'Oh! thought Clarissa, in the middle of my party, here's death, she thought' (*MD* 104):

> Death was defiance. Death was an attempt to communicate, people feeling the impossibility of reaching the centre which, mystically, evaded them.... She felt somehow very like him— the young man who had killed himself. She felt glad that he had done it; thrown it away while they went on living. The clock was striking. The leaden circles dissolved in the air. But she must go back. She must assemble. She must find Sally and Peter. And she came in from the little room. (*MD* 166–7)

Here, Woolf condenses the novel's metropolitan panoramas and its enormous arc of historical time into the innermost spaces of Clarissa's home, a collision of the remarkable and the ordinary that releases Clarissa from her fears. The party occasions the work of moving in and out of rooms to 'assemble'; it also allows Clarissa the apparently impossible experience of living and dying in a single moment.

If the relationship between domesticity and mortality takes on a sacred quality in *Mrs. Dalloway,* Woolf lightens it with a teasing, irreverent sensibility in her comic biographies *Orlando* (1928) and *Flush* (1931). That title spaniel, abducted from Elizabeth Barrett's Westminster home and imprisoned in Whitechapel, experiences displacement as vividly as any human character: 'This was now the truth—this room, these ruffians, these whining, snapping, tightly tethered dogs, this murk, this dampness. Could it be true that he had been in a shop, with ladies, among ribbons, only yesterday? Was there such a place as Wimpole Street? ... The whole of that life and its emotions floated away, dissolved, became unreal' (*F* 57).

---

[35] On the Woolfian pivot between living and not-living, see Bill Brown, 'The Secret Life of Things: Virginia Woolf and the Matter of Modernity', *Modernism/modernity* 6, no. 2 (1999), 1–28.

A desire to dissolve and render unreal the world of 22 Hyde Park Gate, perhaps, compelled Woolf's first steps as an independent adult in Bloomsbury, the unstylish London neighbourhood where she, Vanessa, and Adrian moved after Leslie Stephen's death. The decision to leave Kensington to 'start life afresh' (*MB* 184) in a succession of flats in Bloomsbury (46 Gordon Square, 29 Fitzroy Square, and 38 Brunswick Square) stands as the most storied domestic shift of Woolf's life. No longer encumbered by her father and half-brothers' patriarchal expectations, twenty-two-year-old Woolf regarded 46 Gordon Square as 'the most beautiful, the most exciting, the most romantic place in the world' (*MB* 184):

> We were going to do without table napkins, we were to have [large supplies of] Bromo instead; we were going to paint; to write; to have coffee after dinner instead of tea at nine o'clock. Everything was going to be new; everything was going to be different. (*MB* 185)

Embarking on a daringly modern life that rebuked their Kensington years, the Stephen sisters formed a social, intellectual, artistic, and sexual network that came to be known as the Bloomsbury Group. They befriended young men from Cambridge University, including the economist John Maynard Keynes, the biographer Lytton Strachey, the artist and historian Roger Fry, and the art-critic Clive Bell (who married Vanessa in 1907); they kept company with rising modernist talents such as T. S. Eliot, E. M. Forster, Katherine Mansfield, and Dora Carrington; and their increasingly international social and professional circles included the Argentine writer and publisher Victoria Ocampo, the Indian novelist Mulk Raj Anand, and the French photographer Gisèle Freund. 'Bloomsbury', mythologized and demythologized by its original members (as well as by every successive generation of scholars and critics), made the idea of home synonymous with artistic rule-breaking, sexual liberation, and feminist-pacifist idealism.[36] In this radical new environment, Woolf began publishing the reviews that inaugurated her four-decade career as a professional writer; in Andrew McNeillie's words, 'she made of the personal essay, the review, the biographical study, the commemorative article, an art of her own' (*E1* ix). She intuited that she would contribute to literary fiction by revolutionizing it: 'I think a great deal of my future, and settle what books I am to write', she told her brother-in-law Clive Bell in 1908, 'how I shall re-form the novel and capture multitudes of things at present fugitive, enclose the whole, and shape infinite strange shapes' (*L1* 356).[37] And this sense of social and aesthetic possibility flourished, in her

---

[36] On the history and culture of the Bloomsbury group, see Jane Marcus, ed., *Virginia Woolf and Bloomsbury: A Centenary Celebration* (London: Palgrave Macmillan, 1987); Gloria Naylor, *Bloomsbury: Its Authors, Artists, and Designers* (London: Bullfinch Press, 1990); Jesse Wolfe, *Bloomsbury, Modernism, and the Reinvention of Intimacy* (Cambridge: Cambridge University Press, 2011), Victoria Rosner, ed., *The Cambridge Companion to the Bloomsbury Group* (Cambridge: Cambridge University Press, 2014); Sara Blair, 'Local Modernity, Global Modernism: Bloomsbury and the Places of the Literary', *ELH* 71, no. 3 (Fall 2004), 813–38.

[37] See Barbara Lounsberry, *Becoming Virginia Woolf: Her Early Diaries and the Diaries She Read* (Gainesville: University Press of Florida, 2014).

view, because 'the gulf which we crossed between Kensington & Bloomsbury was the gulf between respectable mum[m]ified humbug & life crude & impertinent perhaps, but living' (*D1* 206).

In 1912, Virginia married Leonard Woolf, a Cambridge graduate and aspiring writer returned from seven years' civil service in Ceylon.[38] They lived at first in rented properties in London and Richmond, and then leased Hogarth House in Richmond from 1915 to 1924. Hogarth House gave its name to the influential publishing enterprise the Woolfs ran together for more than three decades. From its humble beginnings in 1917 as a hand-press in Richmond to a thriving institution in London, the Woolfs' Hogarth Press shaped the arc of twentieth-century literature, publishing diverse modern writing by figures such as Eliot, Mansfield, Hope Mirlees, W. H. Auden, Sigmund Freud, Gertrude Stein, Rebecca West, C. L. R. James, and Maxim Gorky.[39] And although her first two novels, *The Voyage Out* and *Night and Day*, were published by Duckworth & Co., Woolf published all of her subsequent works at the Press from 1917 until her death in 1941. The Hogarth Press supplied a powerful answer to the question that opens *A Room of One's Own*: 'But, you may say, we asked you to speak about women and fiction—what has that got to do with a room of one's own?' (*ARO* 3). Sex, literature, and autonomy, historically and aesthetically inseparable for Woolf, found a happy conjunction in her identity as a publisher. A well-known passage from her 1925 diary revels in the doubling of her creative authority: 'I'm the only woman in England free to write what I like' (*D3* 43). If the world of Bloomsbury offered Woolf a new family, the Hogarth Press offered her a new home.

Leonard and Virginia divided the three decades of their marriage between residences in London and Sussex. In 1919, they purchased Monk's House, a sunlit eighteenth-century cottage in the village of Rodmell where Virginia felt at home immediately.[40] Even before moving in, she wrote, 'That will be our address for ever and ever; Indeed I've already marked our graves in the yard which joins our meadow' (*L2* 382). They spent weekends and holidays in Monk's House, as well as summers, and the pace of village life—gardening, cooking, walking the six miles to Vanessa Bell's farmhouse, Charleston—provided Woolf with the solitude she needed for her art. Monk's House was the measured, simpler counterpoint to the social and professional bustle of 52 Tavistock Square in London, which the Woolfs acquired in 1924 and where they lived until 1939, when they moved to 37 Mecklenburgh Square.[41] Both of the Woolfs' London properties served as business headquarters for the increasingly successful Hogarth Press, and both houses were destroyed in 1940 during the

---

[38] See Victoria Glendinning, *Leonard Woolf: A Biography* (New York: Free Press, 2006).

[39] See Helen Southworth, *Leonard and Virginia Woolf, The Hogarth Press and the Networks of Modernism* (Edinburgh: Edinburgh University Press, 2010); J. H. Willis, *Virginia and Leonard Woolf as Publishers: The Hogarth Press, 1917–41* (Charlottesville: University of Virginia Press, 1992); John Lehmann, *Virginia Woolf and Her World* (New York: Harcourt, 1977); Lee, *Virginia Woolf*, 357–71.

[40] Peter Fullager, *Virginia Woolf at Richmond* (Twickenham: Aurora Metro Press, 2018) supplies a detailed account of Woolf's life in Monk's House.

[41] Both houses were destroyed by German bombs in 1940. See Lee, *Virginia Woolf*, 706–32.

Blitz. After German bombs fell on Mecklenburgh Square in September and on Tavistock Square in October, Woolf recorded the physical and psychic devastations of war:

> So by Tube to the Temple; & there wandered in the desolate ruins of my old squares: gashed; dismantled; the old red bricks all white powder, something like a builders yard. Grey dirt & broken windows; sightseers; all that completeness ravished & demolished. (D5 353)

Exiled from the city of her birth, she and Leonard subsequently made Monks House their permanent residence.

Monk's House had been where Woolf wrote the literary masterpieces that brought international fame and considerable prosperity. Rich with fruit trees and flowering plants and decorated lavishly by Vanessa Bell, Monks House welcomed Virginia and Leonard's friends, relatives, artists, and literary collaborators. It was where Woolf felt the absurdity as well as the comfort of domestic routine amidst the terror of war. ('It wd [sic] have been a very peaceful matter of fact death to be popped off on the terrace playing bowls this very fine cool sunny August evening', she penned acidly in her 1940 diary (D5 313)). She and Leonard made a suicide pact as they lived through dozens of German air-raids that killed friends and fellow villagers, and Woolf's evolving theories of home and nation expressed themselves in two influential meditations on art, patriotism, and belonging, 'Thoughts on Peace During an Air-Raid' and 'The Leaning Tower'.[42] These late essays, along with *Roger Fry* (1940), *Between the Acts*, and "Sketch of the Past," were largely composed at Monks House in the custom-built writing-lodge that was Woolf's most generative room of her own.

It was, of course, from Monk's House that Woolf set out to the River Ouse on 28 March 1941, after composing loving epistles to Leonard and to her sister, Vanessa, describing the voices in her head that she could no longer ignore. What might her final journey—a walk through familiar terrain to an unknowable endpoint—have contained? The possibility of an answer shimmers, unexpectedly, through 'Kew Gardens' (1917), one of Woolf's earliest experiments with short fiction, written at the age of thirty-five and hand-printed at the then-new Hogarth Press. 'Kew Gardens' describes a snail, a creature for whom self and home are literally inseparable. The snail embarks on an odyssey that, despite its smallness, traverses entire worlds:

> In the oval flower bed the snail, whose shell had been stained red, blue, and yellow for the space of two minutes or so, now appeared to be moving very slightly in its shell, and next began to labour over the crumbs of loose earth which broke away and rolled down as it passed over them. It appeared to have a definite goal in front of it, differing in this respect from the singular high stepping angular green insect who attempted to cross in front of it, and waited for a second with its antennae trembling

---

[42] Clara Jones traces the evolution of Woolf's complex sense of national belonging in *Virginia Woolf: Ambivalent Activist* (Edinburgh: Edinburgh University Press, 2006), 154–206.

as if in deliberation, and then stepped off as rapidly and strangely in the opposite direction. Brown cliffs with deep green lakes in the hollows, flat, bladelike trees that waved from root to tip, round boulders of grey stone, vast crumpled surfaces of a thin crackling texture— all these objects lay across the snail's progress between one stalk and another to his goal. (*CSF* 91–2)

The snail's 'labour' as he moves 'between one stalk and another' is not less rich or nuanced than the labours of the story's human characters. And the transposition of the remarkable and the ordinary in this exquisite early piece, refracted through the eyes of the snail, anticipates the domains that Woolf created for beloved characters in lengthier fictions that bind the socially complex and the aesthetically liberating: Septimus Warren Smith, displaced in London but at home in a mysterious chorus of voices, Orlando, the androgynous time-traveller captivated by an ancestral estate, Miss LaTrobe, the outcast artist weaving history into the present moment. 'Kew Gardens' reconceives the short story in order to balance the realities and unrealities of home, a fugitive balance that eluded the fifty-nine year-old Woolf mourning a war-darkened world's "completeness ravished & demolished". As the little snail ends its journey through the flower bed, the story catapults us out to immense London "like a vast next of Chinese boxes all of wrought steel turning ceaselessly one within another" (95). It is a dramatic scalar shift that enacts the range and the significance of "home" in Woolf's life and her oeuvre, where diverse architectures – lived, remembered, forbidden, obliterated, imagined – always accompanied literary metamorphosis.

Selected Bibliography

Briggs, Julia, *Virginia Woolf: An Inner Life* (New York: Harcourt, 2005).
Brown, Bill, 'The Secret Life of Things: Virginia Woolf and the Matter of Modernity,' *Modernism/modernity* 6, no. 2 (1999), 1–28.
Fernald, Anne E., '*To the Lighthouse* in the Context of Virginia Woolf's Diaries and Life', in Allison Pease, ed., *The Cambridge Companion to* To the Lighthouse (Cambridge: Cambridge University Press, 2015), 6–18.
Goldman, Jane, *The Feminist Aesthetics of Virginia Woolf: Modernism, Post-Impressionism and the Politics of the Visual* (Cambridge: Cambridge University Press, 1998).
Hancock, Nuala, *Charleston and Monk's House: The Intimate House Museums of Virginia Woolf and Vanessa Bell* (Edinburgh: Edinburgh University Press, 2012).
Jones, Clara, *Virginia Woolf: Ambivalent Activist* (Edinburgh: Edinburgh University Press, 2006).
Lounsberry, Barbara, *Becoming Virginia Woolf: Her Early Diaries and the Diaries She Read* (Gainesville: University Press of Florida, 2014).
Lowe, Gill, ed., *Hyde Park Gate News: The Stephen Family Newspaper, by Virginia Woolf, Vanessa Bell, and Thoby Stephen* (London: Hesperus, 2005).
Reed, Christopher, *Bloomsbury Rooms: Modernism, Subculture, and Domesticity* (New York: Bard Center, 2004).
Rosner, Victoria, ed., *The Cambridge Companion to the Bloomsbury Group* (Cambridge: Cambridge University Press, 2014).

Southworth, Helen, *Leonard and Virginia Woolf, The Hogarth Press and the Networks of Modernism* (Edinburgh: Edinburgh University Press, 2010).

Spalding, Frances, *Virginia Woolf: Art, Life and Vision* (London: National Portrait Gallery, 2014).

CHAPTER 2

FRIENDS AND LOVERS

KATHRYN SIMPSON*

'THE TRUTH IS ONE HAS ROOM FOR A GOOD MANY RELATIONSHIPS.' (*D3* 117)

For Woolf, friendship was the centre of life and pleasure; it was a vital source of love, desire, support, and inspiration as well as of challenge, jealousy, conflict, and loss. Her wide and eclectic social circle included family and family friends, aristocrats and wealthy socialites, artists, critics, musicians, political activists, scholars, literary professionals, and the Bloomsbury Group. These friendships waxed and waned over time and Woolf often reflected on her friendships, assessing the number, place, and importance of each in her life: 'How many friends have I got?' she asks (*D1* 234). Many of her friendships were richly complex and, as she explained to her close friend of her later life, Ethel Smyth, 'Where people mistake … is in perpetually narrowing and naming these immensely composite and wide-flung passions—driving stakes through them, herding them between screens' (*L4* 200). What is also very apparent is that Woolf depended on her friends and used them to satisfy her complicated, unconventional, and sometimes contradictory needs and desires. Importantly, 'the maternal protection' which she 'always most wished from everyone' (*D3* 52) further intensified and complicated her friendships. As she continues to Smyth, 'But how do you define "Perversity"? What is the line between friendship and perversion?' (*L4* 200). Woolf's claim that she is 'diverse enough to want Vita and Ethel and Leonard and Vanessa' confirms this complexity (*L4* 199). Fluctuating in intensity and intimacy, many of her closest bonds blurred lines so that mixed feelings of desire, love, and jealousy for some rendered 'friends' and 'lovers' synonymous.

Woolf's heightened feelings of vulnerability and sensitivity could lead her to be superior and snide in her scrutiny, and duplicitous and malicious when she felt hurt or

---

* I'm indebted to my friend, Gill Lowe, for her insightful advice on this chapter.

betrayed. In her role as literary mentor to a number of younger writers and employees at the Hogarth Press (such as Elizabeth Bowen, John Lehmann, and Marjorie Thomson Joad) she could also be kind and generous as well as critical. Although in many ways introspective and protective of her time alone, Woolf loved to embody 'party consciousness' and could be gregarious, playful, witty, clever, and highly entertaining. She took great pleasure in social interaction and Hermione Lee's sense that 'her dazzling, unstoppable conversational displays' had 'a dangerous, reckless, perhaps also a sexual element'[1] is confirmed by Woolf's own reflection on the sensual pleasure she derived from being the centre of attention:

> Yet this showing off, which is not copulating, necessarily, nor altogether being in love, is one of the great delights, one of the chief necessities of life. Only then does all effort cease; one ceases to be honest, one ceases to be clever. One fizzes up to some absurd delightful effervescence of soda water or champagne through which one sees the world tinged with all the colours of the rainbow. (*MB* 211)

What is telling is that this performance with and for her friends is not '*necessarily*' synonymous with 'copulating' or 'being in love' (emphasis added), but it seems it certainly could be. What she sought and gained from her friendships was varied and complex, sometimes platonic, sometimes erotic or sexual, and sometimes a precarious mixture of both. The menagerie of creature companions and pet names Woolf used to describe and imagine her relationships indicates how she positioned herself in relation to others. They were companions, sparring partners, and love(r)s providing affirmation, admiration, inspiration, and intellectual stimulation; the erotic quality of this animal discourse adds further to the ambiguity that characterizes many of Woolf's more intimate friendships.

Woolf had a number of suitors and marriage proposals; what Vanessa referred to as her 'harem' included Saxon Sydney-Turner, Walter Headlam, Edward Hilton Young, Walter Lamb, and Sydney Waterlow. All were 'Cambridge men' and all were refused. Lytton Strachey's proposal and acceptance in 1909 was perhaps the most bizarre given the circumstances: he was still reeling from the shock of discovering that his love, Duncan Grant, was in love with Maynard Keynes, and was simultaneously encouraging Leonard to propose to Virginia. It was during this period, following the birth of Julian Bell (in February 1908), that Virginia and Clive Bell began a dangerously playful affair, 'a game of intimacy and intrigue which lasted for perhaps two years'. Motivated as it was by a shared sense of jealousy about Vanessa's maternal preoccupation and Woolf's sense of grateful pleasure for Clive's attentiveness to her writing and support as she worked on her first novel, this was also perhaps one of the more complex and messier blurrings of the friend/lover boundaries. As Lee explains, this relationship 'shifted into the more satirical and distrustful friendship which continued all their lives'.[2]

---

[1] Hermione Lee, *Virginia Woolf* (London: Chatto and Windus, 1996), 110.
[2] Lee, *Virginia Woolf*, 249.

Throughout her life Woolf's friendships were instrumental to her sense of herself as a writer, and writers were among her closest and most important friends and lovers. Woolf demanded a great deal from her friendships and this chapter focuses on six friends that, in different ways, sustained her as she developed her modernist techniques and competitively sought to distinguish herself in the literary world: Violet Dickinson, E. M. Forster, Lytton Strachey, Katherine Mansfield, Vita Sackville-West, and Ethel Smyth.

'WOMEN ALONE STIR MY IMAGINATION.' (*L4* 203)

In 1925, Woolf wrote to her friend Jacques Raverat, 'Much preferring my own sex as I do, ... [I] intend to cultivate women's society entirely in future' (*L3* 164), suggesting a new intention. In fact, her devotion to women's society and all it had to offer began much earlier. It was Violet Dickinson with whom she shared the most intimate, intense, and ambiguous relationship of her early adult life but many other women friends were powerful 'mentor/mother[s]' for her and helped shape her thinking, writing, and politics.[3] Her tutors in Latin and Greek, Clara Pater (from 1898) and Janet Case (from 1902), and her friendship with Jane Ellen Harrison, informed her feminist and pacifist thinking and, crucially, provided Woolf with 'the intellectual and emotional protection to rebel, challenge, and question nearly everything.'[4] Kitty Maxse, Madge Symonds Vaughan, and Nelly Cecil (Lady Eleanor Cecil) provided maternal care, particularly following the deaths of her parents and as she recovered from her subsequent breakdowns. These early friendships nurtured her emotional and erotic life, and the sharing of manuscripts and mutual encouragement formed a powerful kernel of intellectual and creative support for her literary endeavours. Even once Woolf had begun her new life in Gordon Square with a very different circle of friends, her old friends continued to inspire characters and fictional scenes, indicating Woolf's lasting emotional attachment to them.

The architect of her own home—Burnham Wood in Hertfordshire—and of her own life, Violet Dickinson was a woman of independent wealth, socially well-connected, a Quaker, and a philanthropist; she was also widely adored. During an emotionally fraught period of Woolf's life from 1902 until around 1907, Dickinson was Woolf's single most important friend and confidante, and her affectionate and sympathetic letters were received 'like balm on the heart' (*L1* 75). She was patient with Woolf's wildly varying moods and responded generously to her often petulant and melodramatic demands

---

[3] Mills, *Virginia Woolf, Jane Ellen Harrison, and the Spirit of Modernist Classicism* (Columbus: Ohio State University, 2014), 42.

[4] Mills, *Virginia Woolf*, 42. On Woolf's formal education, see Christine Kenyon and Anna Snaith's '"Tilting at universities": Woolf at King's College London', *Woolf Studies Annual* 16 (2010), 1–44.

for love, attention, and approval. For Woolf this was a 'romantic friendship', a phrase encapsulating the devotion and erotically charged desire Woolf felt for Dickinson, whom she claims stirred in her 'hot volcano depths... hitherto entirely quiescent' (L1 75, 85). Her letters to Dickinson tease with erotic suggestion: Dickinson's letters are 'like the scent of profane Violets on my plate at breakfast, such as grow in the unhallowed part of a churchyard' where Woolf declares she 'shall be buried one day' and she asserts that Dickinson can write 'nice hot letters' though she feels she 'oughtn't to' (L1 95, 76). Critics debate whether this suggestively seductive correspondence (which Woolf wanted to keep private) was testimony to a sexual relationship, or whether it was in part at least a literary performance, Woolf showing off her capacity to excel in 'cram[ming] in the amount of pure hot affection' into half a sheet of writing (L1 84). What is clear is that whether physically consummated or not, 'Violet was the first true emotional and physical love of Virginia's early adult life.'[5]

Dickinson's friendship remained important to Woolf. She likened a surprise visit from her and her praise of *Night and Day* to 'the breath of life in my nostrils' and recalled that it was because of Violet that she 'ever survived to write at all' (L2 402). Glossed in the *Collected Letters* as referring to Dickinson's nursing of Virginia in 1904, this statement seems also to acknowledge the pivotal role Dickinson played in initiating and continuing to encourage Woolf's professional life as a writer—not least in enabling her to make contact with Margaret Lyttelton, editor of the Women's Supplement of the *Guardian*, resulting in Woolf's first paid publications in 1904. Dickinson marked this turning point with a birthday gift of 'a huge china inkpot' (PA 227). Woolf considers it 'rather too large to be practicable', but her decision to 'cultivate a bold hand & a quill pen' (PA 227)—'a delightful pun on authorial and sexual explorations'[6]—seems a fitting acknowledgement of Dickinson's belief in Woolf's literary talents and of their affectionate and erotic bond. The confidence Dickinson imbued and the careful criticism she gave on Woolf's early pieces, as well the playfulness of their relationship, inspired Woolf's earliest experimental fiction—'Friendships Gallery'—which Woolf typed in purple ink and bound in violet leather to give as a gift to Dickinson in August 1907.[7] This comic and fantastical life of her friend, with its self-conscious narrative voice and satirical refusal of the generic conventions of biography, has been seen as a vital first step in Woolf's emergence as a feminist writer who creatively and adeptly mocks established male-dominated literary conventions and radically revises narrative techniques to more fully represent women's experience. It

---

[5] Vanessa Curtis, *Virginia Woolf's Women* (Stroud: Sutton Publishing Limited, 2003), 88. On the debate around their correspondence and possible sexual intimacy, see, for example, Jane Lilienfield, '"The Gift of a China Ink Pot": Violet Dickinson, Virginia Woolf, Elizabeth Gaskell, Charlotte Bronte, and the Love of Women in Writing', in Eileen Barrett and Patricia Cramer, eds, *Virginia Woolf: Lesbian Readings* (New York and London: New York University Press, 1997), 37–56.

[6] Lilienfield, '"The Gift"', 45.

[7] This was published for the first time in 1979. See Virginia Woolf, '"Friendships Gallery"', Ellen Hawkes, ed., *Twentieth-Century Literature* 25 (1979), 270–302.

anticipates, as many have noted, Woolf's more elaborate and 'revolutionary' revision of a woman's biography in *Orlando*.[8]

'THE SOCIETY OF BUGGERS HAS MANY ADVANTAGES—IF YOU ARE A WOMAN [WRITER].' (*MB* 211)

Woolf's friendships within the Bloomsbury Group could also 'stir [her] imagination' and give impetus to her creative ambitions, though for different reasons. In her memoir, 'Old Bloomsbury', Woolf makes clear what she gained from these friendships—the pleasure of intellectual stimulation and challenge, the inspiration to contribute and debate, and, as the friendships matured, the freedom to gossip. However, the critical edge that marks her friendships with these privileged men and the sexist world of Cambridge that shaped them stemmed from her anger and resentment at the many injustices women suffer, and she wrote in opposition to their views and defied what she sometimes felt was a patronizing attitude.[9] As a number of critics have also argued, however, 'queer filiation'[10] was important to Woolf and many critics celebrate the sexual subversiveness of Bloomsbury as productive and affirming.[11] While Woolf maintained a number of long-standing relationships with other men (and women) in the group, her complex friendships with two of its literary 'buggers'—E. M. Forster and Lytton Strachey—spurred her creative and critical writing and thinking in particular ways.

Beginning in 1910 until her death in 1941, Woolf's 'complex literary friendship' with Forster was her longest relationship with a fellow writer outside her family circle and one 'that goaded and nourished' them both.[12] Through publications and in private they

[8] For example, see Karin E. Westman, 'The First "Orlando": The Laugh of the Comic Spirit in Virginia Woolf's "Friendships Gallery"', *Twentieth Century Literature* 47, no. 1 (2001), 39–71.

[9] Lee, *Virginia Woolf*, 213–14. For example, Phyllis Rose, Jane Marcus, and Julie Taddeo offer fierce feminist criticism of this male-dominated group. See Jane Marcus, 'Liberty, Sorority, Misogyny', in Caroline G. Heilbrun and Margaret Higonnet, eds, *Representations of Women in Fiction: Selected Papers from the English Institute, 1981* (Baltimore: Johns Hopkins University Press, 1983), 60–96; Phyllis Rose, *Woman of Letters: A Life of Virginia Woolf* (New York: Oxford University Press, 1978); Julie Taddeo, 'A Modernist Romance? Lytton Strachey and the Women of Bloomsbury', in Elizabeth Jane Harrison and Shirley Peterson, eds, *Unmanning Modernism: Gendered Re-readings* (Knoxville: University of Tennessee Press, 1997), 132–52.

[10] Stephen Barber, 'Lip-Reading: Woolf's Secret Encounters', in Eve Kosofsky Sedgwick, ed., *Novel Gazing: Queer Readings in Fiction* (Durham, NC: Duke University Press, 1997), 401–43, at 414.

[11] Carolyn G. Heilbrun was one of the first to put forward this perspective, 'The Bloomsbury Group', *Midway: A Magazine of Discovery in the Arts and Sciences* 9, no. 2 (1968), 71–85. See Brenda S. Helt and Madelyn Detloff, *Queer Bloomsbury* (Edinburgh: Edinburgh University Press, 2016).

[12] Michael J. Hoffman and Ann Ter Haar, '"Whose Books Once Influenced Mine": The Relationship between E. M. Forster's *Howards End* and Virginia Woolf's *The Waves*', *Twentieth Century Literature* 45, no. 1 (Spring 1999), 46–64, at 46.

carried out a twenty-five-year-long argument about the development of the modern novel, each vying for position in the literary sphere and sparring with one another as they tried 'to establish the narrative aesthetics of their time'.[13] This provided a stimulus for Woolf to develop and assert her own daring experimental modernist form, an approach in sharp contrast to the 'conventional paraphernalia' she saw in Forster's novels.[14]

However, Woolf needed Forster's approbation and took care to distinguish their private debate from her more forceful public views. This is evident, for example, in her letter to Forster following the publication of her critical review of *Aspects of the Novel* (1927) where the 'official and impersonal' typewritten part of her letter continues their sparring, but which includes a handwritten apology for any hurt or annoyance caused (*L3* 437). Woolf valued Forster's critical assessments of her style and technique, and these boosted her self-esteem: 'with each successive novel it is Forster's judgment she awaits and his critique that—other than Leonard's—she values most highly'.[15] In fact, as she explains to Gerald Brenan following the publication of *Mrs Dalloway*, 'I always feel that nobody, except perhaps Morgan Forster, lays hold of the thing I have done' (*L3* 189). Five years later, her reputation assured, she describes Forster's books (and implicitly 'the novelist' himself) to Ethel Smyth as 'impeded, shrivelled and immature', but nonetheless her desire for his 'critical approbation was ardent and undiminished' (*L4* 218), even to the final work she published in her lifetime, *Roger Fry* (1940).[16] Each saw the other as cool and aloof, but they both had an acute sensitivity to criticism and praise. Their shared belief in artistic freedom, particularly in relation to sexuality, was also key in their joint defence of Radclyffe Hall's *The Well of Loneliness* when it was put on trial for obscenity in 1928.

As her final two entries in her diary reveal, however, for Woolf there was a persistent tension at the heart of their friendship, which had its source in her feminist anger directed at the male privilege and sexism of Forster and other Bloomsbury men. She may have eagerly awaited Forster's critical and personal response to *Roger Fry* in July 1940, but in November she took great pleasure in refusing his offer of being proposed as a committee member for the London Library given his prejudice against women five years earlier: 'He sniffed about women on Cttee. One of these days I'll refuse I said silently. And now I have' (*D5* 337).

Woolf's friendship with Forster pivoted around the very different 'critical axioms' they each held 'sacred'[17] and was marred by a difference in personality (Forster experienced Woolf's rivalry as supercilious and malicious, for example). Her intimacy

---

[13] Hoffman and Haar, '"Whose Books"', 47.
[14] Ann Henley, '"But We Argued About Novel-Writing": Virginia Woolf, E. M. Forster and the Art of Fiction', *Ariel* 20, no. 3 (1989), 73–83, at 80.
[15] Hoffman and Haar, '"Whose Books"', 48.
[16] Henley, '"But We Argued"', 74.
[17] David Dowling, *Bloomsbury Aesthetics and the Novels of Forster and Woolf* (Basingstoke: Palgrave Macmillan, 1985), 87.

with Lytton Strachey, on the other hand, was sparked by their similar 'tenacious ... [and] treacherous' traits,[18] as well as their inability to trust the other. Woolf admired 'his wit & infinite intelligence' (*D1* 89) and his taste in literature. She relished his dazzling, clever (sometimes malicious) conversation and excessive social performance, as others relished the same in her, and found that 'his great gift of expression ... ma[de] him in some respects the most sympathetic & understanding friend to talk to' (*D1* 89). With their 'tastes in common' and her understanding of his feelings 'even in their more capricious developments', she experienced a rare intimacy: 'he is a figure not to be replaced by any other combination' (*D1* 89). She is, nonetheless, critical in her delineation of Strachey's qualities as a friend: her 'chronicle of Lytton' considers him 'slightly stingy' with emotion, lacking in generosity in a number of ways—he is 'infinitely cautious, elusive & unadventurous' (*D1* 236). While Strachey's biographer, Michael Holroyd, sympathetically reads in St. John Hirst (*The Voyage Out*) a sensitive recognition of Strachey's deep-seated loneliness and distance from others,[19] this 'version' of Strachey (amongst others in Woolf's fiction) was also intended to undermine male privilege and ambition and to parody what she found most unappealing in her friend.

Nonetheless, Strachey has been seen as inspiration for Woolf's most playful and sexually daring work, *Orlando*, influencing the 'exaggerated, theatricalized version of Sackville-West's biography' that produced the 'campy artifice' enabling the novel to dodge the censors and so become 'Woolf's first best seller'.[20] As Woolf's diary records, 'Vita should be Orlando, a young nobleman. There should be Lytton. & it should be truthful; but fantastic' (*D3* 157). It seems fitting that Woolf's aim to 'revolutionise biography in a night' via her fantastically queer character and plot (*L3* 429) should be 'animate[d]' by the 'queer style' of her old friend,[21] a writer known for his own revolutionizing of biography in *Eminent Victorians* (1918), *Queen Victoria* (1921), and *Elizabeth and Essex* (1928).

Strachey was also instrumental in encouraging another of the most important literary friendships in Woolf's life—that with Katherine Mansfield. Indeed, the quality of the emotional connection Woolf felt for both Strachey and Mansfield seems similar. Although their social interaction was less frequent in later years, Woolf felt a lifelong connection to Strachey: 'He was one of the people whose death she would most mind and could least bear to imagine.'[22] In the autumn of 1931, before Woolf knew that he was seriously ill, she had a dream 'more vivid than real life' in which they were young and laughing (*L4* 412). Lee refers to this as 'an extraordinary moment of telepathic sympathy'.[23] It prompted Woolf to contact 'the bearded serpent' and this was her final

---

[18] Lee, *Virginia Woolf*, 255.
[19] Michael Holroyd, *Lytton Strachey: A Biography* (London: Book Club Associates, 1973), 408.
[20] Christopher Reed, 'Bloomsbury as Queer Subculture', in Victoria Rosner, ed., *The Cambridge Companion to The Bloomsbury Group* (New York and Cambridge: Cambridge University Press, 2014), 71–89, at 76.
[21] Reed, 'Bloomsbury', 74, 76.
[22] Lee, *Virginia Woolf*, 627.
[23] Lee, *Virginia Woolf*, 627.

communication with him (*L4* 412). Woolf's words to Carrington following Strachey's death also echo her feelings following news of Mansfield's death: 'I find I cant [sic] write without suddenly thinking Oh but Lytton wont [sic] read this, and it takes all the point out of it' (*L5* 11).

'THE QUEEREST SENSE OF ECHO' (*D2* 61)

Shortly after Mansfield's death Woolf records her mixed emotions, which coalesce into the sense that 'When I began to write, it seemed to me there was no point in writing. Katherine wont [sic] read it. Katherine's my rival no longer' (*D2* 226). This friendship was one of the most intense and complex of bonds being at once profoundly intimate and mutually supportive but also personally vituperative, professionally rivalrous, and at times deliberately distant: an 'uneasy sisterhood',[24] as many critics agree. This friendship, however, most dramatically accelerated Woolf's development as an experimental writer and the volatile power dynamic between the two, which hinged on class and colonialism as well as literary rivalry, contributed to this.[25] At times they felt a close professional bond and mutual personal fascination; their shared literary goal to revitalize and reshape modern writing as women created a heightened sense of affinity between them, 'a queer sense of being "like"' (*D2* 45). However, at times Mansfield felt herself to be an outsider and powerless—'I am the little colonial walking in the London garden patch—allowed to look, perhaps, but not to linger.'[26] Her early effusive and flirtatious letters to Woolf are a kind of courtship and play up Woolf's power and influence, but she also mocks Woolf's elitism and superiority and was unafraid to publish a critical review of *Night and Day* (in the *Athenaeum*, 1919). Mansfield, though younger, already had publications in modernist journals and newspapers, and from the beginning Woolf perceived her as a threat. Mansfield's assertion that they are 'after so very nearly the same thing'[27] was affirming but also signalled a challenge and put Woolf on her guard. A few months after receiving Mansfield's letter, Woolf's diary records that Mansfield is 'so intelligent & inscrutable that she repays friendship', but also criticizes her 'commonness' and 'cheap[ness]' (*D1* 58). What is most shocking and revealing is the animal image Woolf employs to describe her initial impression of Mansfield: 'she stinks like a—well civet cat that had taken to street walking' (*D1* 58). Anna Snaith notes that

---

[24] Ann L. McLaughlin, 'An Uneasy Sisterhood: Virginia Woolf and Katherine Mansfield', in Jane Marcus, ed., *Virginia Woolf: A Feminist Slant* (Lincoln: University of Nebraska Press, 1983), 152–61.

[25] See Anna Snaith, '"Curious slides and arrests": Class and Colonialism in the Relationship Between Katherine Mansfield and Virginia Woolf', in Stéphanie Amar-Flood and Sara Thornton, eds, *Lectures d'une oeuvre: Selected Stories de Katherine Mansfield* (Paris: Editions du Temps, 1997), 143–58.

[26] Katherine Mansfield, Notebook 16, in Margaret Scott, ed., *Katherine Mansfield Notebooks Volume 2*, (New Zealand: Lincoln University Press, 1997), 166.

[27] Katherine Mansfield, *The Collected Letters of Katherine Mansfield*, 4 vols. ed. Vincent O'Sullivan and Margaret Scott (Oxford: Clarendon Press, 1984), 327.

this 'mammal native to Africa and Asia ... emit[s] a greasy, highly scented secretion for the purposes of marking territory'.[28] This image denigrates Mansfield as foreigner, but also belies Woolf's sense of Mansfield's trespass on her territory: on both the geographical space of London, which she loved, and the cultural territory of literary London in which Woolf was beginning to make her name.

In many ways Woolf found their friendship to be precarious and unpredictable, 'almost entirely founded on quicksands', with periods of 'intimate, intense ... intercourse' (D1 243) followed by what were to Woolf inexplicable hurtful silences—usually due to a decline in Mansfield's health. However, Woolf found their intense discussions of writing in a 'disembodied way' to be profound and 'priceless', creating for her 'the queerest sense of echo coming back to me from her mind the second after I've spoken' (D2 45, 61). Their friendship evolved through 'mutual mentorship'.[29] Mansfield was instrumental in the genesis and development of Woolf's 'Kew Gardens' (1919), a publication that truly launched Woolf's career as an experimental modernist writer and bolstered the success of the Hogarth Press. In transforming her story 'The Aloe' into *Prelude* (1918) for publication as the second Hogarth Press title, Mansfield honed her distinctive narrative technique and fixed her authorial identity as Katherine Mansfield (one of several of her pen names).

Mansfield continued to function as both accomplice and rival, even after her death. Woolf asserted her own superiority as a writer but also acknowledged that 'she [Mansfield] ... could do what I can't!' (D2 226). She also recalled her last meeting with her friend: 'For our friendship was a real thing we said, looking at each other quite straight. It would always go on whatever happened.... that friendship persists' (D2 227). Woolf's sense of connection with Mansfield did persist for the rest of Woolf's life as Woolf dreamt of her, recalled her haunting presence in certain places, and still weighed the value of her own work in relation to Mansfield's. Her inspiration and influence can be perceived in Woolf's writing from the first story Woolf wrote once they had become friends, to her last posthumously published novel, *Between the Acts*. With her origins in Tasmania (in an earlier draft, New Zealand), Mrs Manresa is perceived as a foreign intruder on this English scene, 'common' with her makeup and fashionable clothes, and sexually adventurous. However, she is the only audience member courageous enough to face herself and the present moment with composure and candour, as Miss La Trobe's experimental technique seems to require. The ambiguity of this character seems a fitting final tribute to a friend with whom Woolf had such a complex relationship. Mansfield's sense of identity as merely a mask and performance of the moment also finds the 'queerest sense of echo' in Woolf's comment on her own sense of identity at this late

---

[28] Snaith, '"Curious Slides"', 149.

[29] Janet Winston, 'Reading Influences: Homoeroticism and Mentoring in Katherine Mansfield's "Carnation" and Virginia Woolf's "Moments of Being": "Slater's Pins Have No Points"', Eileen Barrett and Patricia Cramer, eds, *Virginia Woolf: Lesbian Readings* (New York: New York University Press, 1997), 57–77, at 58.

stage of her career: 'Each [book] accumulates a little of the fictitious V.W. whom I carry like a mask about the world' (*D5* 307).

'ONE OF THE VERY FEW CONSTANT PRESENCES' (*L6* 355)

While Woolf's friendship with Mansfield had been at times seemingly erotic in its intensity ('queer' is how Woolf repeatedly describes the uniqueness and reciprocity of their bond), it is 'the new apparition Vita' (*D2* 225) who, with her bounty of literary and other gifts, would seduce Woolf's mind *and* body. They met for the first time at a dinner party hosted by Clive Bell in December 1922 and, as Lee argues, Sackville-West seems to have replaced Mansfield in Woolf's life.[30] The juxtaposition of two diary entries recording Woolf's need to 'write to ... Vita' and that 'Katherine has been dead a week' seems to confirm this (*D2* 225).

Although Sackville-West was already a successful writer, 'donkey West', as Woolf teasingly called her, she was not a writer with whom she felt the same creative affinity, nor the sharp sting of rivalry as with Mansfield. Nonetheless, their intimacy was shaped by the power dynamic of their relationship as writers as well as by the positive effect that Sackville-West's emotional acceptance and erotic intensity had on Woolf and her writing.[31] Again, Woolf's love and friendship for another woman writer was entwined with her role as publisher: Sackville-West was flattered to be invited to publish with the Hogarth Press and the Press benefitted significantly from the bestselling success of her novels and travel writing. The entanglements of their professional, personally intimate, and creative lives were richly productive, and writing played a pivotal role in intensifying their bond. In letters they flirted, teased, and exchanged 'verbal caress[es]'[32] in ways not always possible when face to face. During Sackville-West's two long visits to Persia in early 1926 and 1927, for instance, distance fuelled not only their desire for one another but also their creativity in the articulation of their desire. Their communications across the miles 'created an *epistolarium* of love that was large, complicated and obsessive'.[33]

In many ways, the production of Sackville-West's *Seducers in Ecuador* (1924) encapsulates the complex dynamic of their relationship, revealing what tantalized and seduced the other. Sackville-West was captivated by Woolf's charm, poise, and intellect

---

[30] Lee, *Virginia Woolf*, 493.
[31] On their power dynamic, see Suzanne Raitt, *Vita and Virginia: The Work and Friendship of V. Sackville-West and Virginia Woolf* (Oxford: Clarendon Press, 1993), 3. On Sackville-West's positive effects on Woolf's writing, see Karyn Z. Sproles, *Desiring Women: The Partnership of Virginia Woolf and Vita Sackville-West* (Toronto, Buffalo, and London: University of Toronto Press, 2006).
[32] Mitchell A. Leaska, Introduction, *The Letters of Vita Sackville-West to Virginia Woolf*, ed. Louise DeSalvo and Mitchell A. Leaska (London: Virago Press, 1992), 9–46, at 9.
[33] Leaska, Introduction, 26.

and responded with generosity and compassion to her vulnerability. In Woolf's eyes Sackville-West was the assured aristocrat, competent woman, and confident writer who accepted the flattering (and challenging) invitation to produce a novel for the Hogarth Press within six months, even while she would be walking in the Dolomite mountains in Italy. Her success confirmed Woolf's initial impression of her as 'ha[ving] her hand on all the ropes' (*D2* 217) and she 'marvel[s] at [Sackville-West's] skill, & sensibility; for is she not mother, wife, great lady, hostess, as well as scribbling?' (*D2* 313). Sackville-West's willingness to offer the maternal affection and protection Woolf craved led Woolf to feel 'virgin, shy, & schoolgirlish' (*D2* 217) and to declare her 'childlike dazzled affection' for her (*L3* 131). Woolf recognized and was willing to respond to her own fascination for Sackville-West as 'a pronounced Sapphist' who was also attracted to Woolf (*D2* 235).

Sackville-West's dedication of her aptly titled novel to Woolf produced the desired effect. Seeking to impress Woolf and to appeal to her tastes, she wrote, uncharacteristically, in a style of ironic detachment to produce what is 'perhaps [her] most imaginatively conceived novel'.[34] In writing 'the sort of thing [Woolf] should like to write [herself]' (*L3* 131), she flattered and reassured by imitation—something Woolf recognized, and she praised 'the beauty and fantasticallity of the details' (*L3* 131). Sackville-West's role as seducer frames the production of this novel. Her letter promising to write the novel speaks also of 'entic[ing]' Woolf to 'play truant to Bloomsbury and culture' by travelling alone with Sackville-West so they could know one another more fully and intimately. Her description of her novel as 'our joint progeny' compounds her literary seduction in its suggestion of a greater intimacy than is usual between writer and publisher.[35]

Woolf's 'severer taste' initially led her to judge Sackville-West harshly, describing her as 'florid, moustached, parakeet coloured, with all the supple ease of the aristocracy, but not the wit of the artist' (*D2* 216–17). However, what she self-mockingly describes as her penchant for titles (in 'Am I a Snob?') finds satisfaction in Sackville-West's strength and voluptuous sensuality inherited through her family line: 'All these ancestors & centuries, & silver & gold, have bred a perfect body' (*D2* 306). Woolf's relationship with Sackville-West as friend and lover fulfilled Woolf physically and emotionally in a way not experienced before. If Dickinson had first stirred 'hot volcano depths', Sackville-West brought this heat to the surface with her 'candle lit radiance' and her magnificent legs, 'like beech trees' (*D3* 52). The intensity of their physical relationship reached a peak in December 1925 when they spent time alone at Long Barn. Diary entries and letters imply physical lovemaking and a sense of mutual seduction. Although Woolf records her response as 'very mixed', she was clearly carried away by Sackville-West's 'maturity & full breastedness: her being so much in full sail on the high tides' and 'her being in short (what I have never been) a real woman' (*D3* 52). 'These Sapphists *love* women; friendship is never untinged with amorosity' (*D3* 51), Woolf asserts, and, caught up in this amorosity herself, she records an erotically charged impression of Sackville-West

---

[34] Leaska, Introduction, 23.
[35] Louise DeSalvo and Mitchell A. Leaska, eds, *The Letters of Vita Sackville-West to Virginia Woolf*, 54, 61.

as 'pink glowing, grape clustered, pearl hung' (*D3* 52) as she shops in the grocers in Sevenoaks.

Following Sackville-West's return from Persia in 1926 they met often, went to the theatre and ballet, and spent nights alone, but both express uncertainty about the nature of their relationship. Writing to her husband, Harold Nicolson, Sackville-West describes her 'love for Virginia [as] a very different thing: a mental thing, a spiritual thing if you like, an intellectual thing ... She makes me feel protective.'[36] Woolf reflects that she is 'amused' at their relationship, 'I like her presence & her beauty. Am I in love with her? But what is love? Her being "in love" (it must be comma'd thus) with me, excites & flatters; & interests. What is this "love"?' (*D3* 86–7).

Unsurprisingly, Woolf traces the root of this uncertainty about Sackville-West to her writing; both she and her work lack a 'central transparency': 'There's something that doesn't vibrate in you: ... something reserved, muted' (*L3* 244, 302). By the following year, despite Woolf's enticement to 'throw over your man' and join Woolf for 'moonlight', 'wine', and the revelation of Woolf's imagination, the 'millions, myriads' of things Woolf had in her head (*L3* 393), Sackville-West was embarking on other affairs, notably with Mary Campbell, which she had confessed to Woolf by the end of the year. Lee suggests that Woolf's decision to write *Orlando* was a means of 't[aking] control of the relationship in a new form'.[37] Woolf explained to Sackville-West that 'its [sic] all about the lusts of your flesh and the lure of your mind' (*L3* 429) and Woolf's novel makes full use of both Sackville-West's life, personality, and personal and family history as well as the products of her mind in drawing on Sackville-West's literary, historical, and biographical writing.[38]

Sackville-West was 'dazzled' by this novel so excessively dedicated to her, but also overwhelmed and alarmed, and gradually their friendship became less intense. For all of Sackville-West's deviance from sex, gender, and marital norms, she was a traditionalist in values and views, her life and work expressing her 'social and aesthetic conservatism'.[39] Although she accompanied Woolf when she lectured at Cambridge and reviewed *A Room of One's Own*, what she praised about Woolf's 'little book' reveals a significant gap between their political perspectives: 'Mrs Woolf is too sensible to be a thoroughgoing feminist', she asserts.[40] Nonetheless, Sackville-West and Woolf remained important to one another until the end of Woolf's life, writing to each other with great affection, taking pleasure in meeting and discussing Sackville-West's old loves by way of confirming their continuing close friendship (*L6* 461–2). In 1929 Woolf explains that

---

[36] Nigel Nicolson, ed., *Vita and Harold, The Letters of Sackville-West and Harold Nicolson, 1910–1962* (London: Phoenix, 1994), 158.

[37] Lee, *Virginia Woolf*, 511.

[38] See Sproles, *Desiring Women*, and Nicki Hallett, 'Anne Clifford as Orlando: Virginia Woolf's Feminist Historiology and Women's Biography', *Women's History Review* 4, no. 4 (2006), 505–24.

[39] Raitt, *Vita and Virginia*, 11.

[40] 'Sackville-West, from a review, *Listener*' (6 November 1929), in Robin Majumdar and Allen McLaurin, eds, *Virginia Woolf: The Critical Heritage* (Boston: Routledge and Kegan Paul, 1975), 257–8, at 257, 258.

Sackville-West is 'one of the very few constant presences' (*L6* 355) and in 1940 Woolf is 'glad that [their] love has weathered so well' (*D5* 328). Sackville-West went to speak about Persia to the Rodmell Women's Institute on 18 February 1941. It was one of the last times they saw one another and Woolf's 'look[ing] forward [to it] as a drowning sailor to a Spice Island' (*L6* 470) perhaps reflects how the earlier period of emotional and erotic intensity—heightened by Sackville-West's trips to Persia—functioned as an emotional centre in their long-lasting friendship.

'MY OLD STRIPED TIGER CAT, WITH HER GROWL AND HER CLAWS AND HER SOFT FUR' (*L6* 301)

Dame Ethel Mary Smyth was the last great friend of Woolf's life. She was a feminist activist, composer, writer, and would-be lover. Woolf admired her sharp wit, intellect, creativity, and her honest and fearless approach to life and to the expression of emotions and opinions. She was 'not merely ... a musician and a writer, but also ... a blaster of rocks and the maker of bridges'.[41] Although different from one another in age and artistic focus, 'the two women had much in common', both seeking professional success in male-dominated cultural fields and writing polemical texts that challenged the deep-seated sexism inimical in those fields.[42] The feminist political impetus underlying Woolf's literary experiments found a correlation in Smyth's more strident memoirs and other publications, and they also shared pacifist goals. Smyth encouraged Woolf to be more open, candid, self-reflective, and self-revealing; her impact on Woolf and Woolf's later, less subjectively focused, writing can be seen to be substantial. As Herbert Marder argues, '[h]er friendship with Ethel coincided with Virginia's growing desire to address social problems, the crisis of European civilization, in a language that would appeal to the ordinary educated reader'.[43] After reading Smyth's early memoirs, Woolf's diary records her interest in Smyth's 'friendships with women' (*D1* 315) and the fact that, for both, long-lasting intimate and homoerotic relationships with women were central to their lives was powerful in the deepening of their friendship. Like others of Woolf's women friends, Smyth provided a degree of protection and maternal care and praised her writing effusively; from Smyth she could demand love and command attention.

---

[41] In Mitchell A. Leaska, Introduction, *The Pargiters* (London: Hogarth Press, 1977), xxviii.

[42] Christopher Wiley, '"When a Woman Speaks the Truth About Her Body": Ethel Smyth, Virginia Woolf, and the Challenges of Lesbian Auto/biography', *Music and Letters* 85, no. 3 (August 2004), 388–414, at 2.

[43] Herbert Marder, *The Measure of Life: Virginia Woolf's Last Years* (Ithaca, NY: Cornell University Press, 2001), 27.

In her diary Woolf records a summary of their first three-and-a-half-hour conversation in terse phrases that convey the sense of Smyth's energy, enthusiasm, and forthright manner—'a bluff, military old woman ... bounced into the room'—but Woolf also perceives 'something fine & tried & experienced about her besides the rant & the riot & the egotism' (*D3* 290, 292). It is this combination of qualities that led Woolf to seek her company, to crave her attention, praise, and love, but which could also irritate and enrage her, leading Woolf to ridicule and mock her to others. Woolf also presented challenges for Smyth and was not always easy company, as Smyth records in her diary: 'How far V. is human I don't know. She is very incalculable, and has never been known to admit that she can be in the wrong. And yet you love her, love her.'[44] The profusion of letters they exchanged is an indication of the importance of their friendship: Woolf sent over four hundred letters to Smyth in the eleven years of their friendship,[45] which was 'substantially more than to any of her other correspondents during this period'.[46] Although 'Ethel took Woolf into her confidence, and Woolf reciprocated willingly',[47] Smyth's egotism, intensity, and her being in love with Woolf was also experienced as overwhelming: 'It is like being caught by a giant crab', Woolf explained (*L4* 171). It is not clear whether Woolf reciprocated Smyth's passion, but in response to Smyth's sense that Woolf's letters 'intoxicate' (*L6*, 439, n1), Woolf reflects on their 'intercommunicativeness' as a 'queer collocation' which exists (she teasingly suggests) regardless of their difference: they are 'two people who have nothing alike—, except—well, I cant [sic] go into that' (*L6* 439).

Before their first meeting Smyth had 'delighted' Woolf with a letter conveying her great admiration for *A Room of One's Own*. However, in a sense their relationship began before this meeting, with a number of close connections between their Anglo-Indian families and shared family stories,[48] mutual friends, and through their familiarity with each other's work. Woolf had attended the première of Smyth's opera, 'The Wreckers', in 1909 and began to know and admire her through reading her memoirs (*Impressions that Remained*) in 1919, positively reviewing her *Streaks of Life* in *The New Statesman* in 1921 ('Ethel Smyth') where she praised Smyth's 'vivid pen' and her 'extreme courage and extreme candour' (*E3* 299, 298). What Woolf initially admired in Smyth's writing—her outspokenness and honesty—were the qualities she admired in Smyth as a friend. Although she was seventy-one and Woolf forty-eight when they first met, Smyth's 'astonishing vitality' (*E3* 298) continued to energize and sustain their friendship.

As their friendship deepened, so Woolf's criticism of Smyth's literary techniques and her egotism was given more freely. However, in her speech to a meeting of the London [and] National Society for Women's Service on 21 January 1931, on a shared platform with Smyth, Woolf praised Smyth's books as 'masterpieces' and in letters privately

---

[44] Cited in Marder, *The Measure*, 32.
[45] Stephen Barkway, '"This sheet is a glass": Virginia Woolf, Woman of Letters', *Nineteenth Annual Virginia Woolf Birthday Lecture* (Southport: Virginia Woolf Society of Great Britain, 2018), 19.
[46] Wiley, '"When a Woman Speaks"', 6–7.
[47] Barkway, '"This sheet"', 17.
[48] Lee, *Virginia Woolf*, 585–6.

encouraged Smyth to continue to write her memoirs. This was not only because she recognized the importance of recording her friend's great achievements 'for posterity' but also because Woolf also took genuine pleasure in Smyth's writing and her seemingly effortless ability to bring people and scenes to life (*L6* 39).

Although by the 1930s Smyth, due to increasing deafness, was no longer composing, both were attuned to the synergies between their different creative spheres. Following their first meeting, Woolf records Smyth's view that 'writing music is like writing novels. One thinks of the sea—naturally one gets a phrase for it' (*D3* 291–2). This description corresponds with Woolf's earlier explanation to Sackville-West of her own creative experience: 'Style is a very simple matter; it is all rhythm.... A sight, an emotion, creates this wave in the mind, long before it makes words to fit it' (*L3* 247). Such preoccupations with rhythm and the musical qualities of her writing were particularly heightened for Woolf during the first years of her friendship with Smyth as she worked, with profound concentration, on *The Waves*, a process of creativity she explains to Smyth as 'writing to a rhythm and not to a plot' (*L4* 204). While Woolf appreciated Smyth's performance as a conductor in rehearsal, she was unsure about her compositions: 'I suspect the music is too literary—too stressed—too didactic for my taste' (*D4* 9–10). However, more recent critical appreciation has analysed the subversive qualities of Smyth's compositions, identifying elements that resonate with Woolf's own politically and sexually subversive literary techniques.[49] In *Between the Acts* (1941), the creative woman and orchestrator of the village pageant at the novel's heart seems to draw inspiration in part from Smyth. Like Smyth, Miss La Trobe is a passionate fighter and outsider whose egotism and bellicose approach can be a source of irritation and friction. That she is also a source of energetic and subversive creativity beyond the pages of this final novel—hearing 'Words without meaning—wonderful words' rising up from the rhythmical 'plodding' of the 'dumb oxen' (*BA* 152)—reaffirms the synergy of words and music that was so central to Woolf's relationship with Smyth and to Woolf's belief in friendships that sustain the creative act.

'MAKING A LIVING, AS I DO BY THE PEN, IT IS INDECENT TO USE IT FOR THE PURPOSE OF FRIENDSHIP.' (*L1* 189)

For Woolf life *was* writing and, although she resisted being pinned down as a specific type of author, her friends and lovers were central to her success. Her message to Dickinson concerning the indecency of using her pen *merely* for the purpose of

---

[49] See Elizabeth Wood, 'Performing Rights: A Sonography of Women's Suffrage', *Musical Quarterly* 79, no. 4 (Winter 1995), 606–43.

friendship is part of Woolf's teasing complaint about the paucity of news in letters received from her friend. Woolf thrived on letters and communications of all kinds from her friends so that 'living', 'pen', and 'friendship' are synonymous. From her friends Woolf derived new perspectives, ideas, and inspiration; she looked to them to stimulate her intellect and imagination and to bring things to life. As she explained to Smyth, 'But what I want of you is illusion—to make the world dance' (*L4* 200). But she also demanded a great deal from her friends—love and attention, maternal care and admiration, challenge and competition. Smyth's reference to Woolf as '4d. for 9d'[50] sums up her sense that Woolf took more than she gave and Woolf repeatedly weighs the value of her friendships realizing that, although she may feel that her 'map of the world lacks rotundity', it is her friends who will fill it out (*D3* 316). Her recognition of her reliance on her friends and lovers to satisfy her need for experience and an ever-expanded vision seems encapsulated in her assertion that 'I use my friends rather as giglamps; Theres [sic] another field I see: by your light. Over there's a hill. I widen my landscape' (*D3* 316). While, as she asserts in 'Modern Fiction', our life experiences are not ordered into a neat series of discrete events—'gig lamps, symmetrically arranged'—but are rather 'a luminous halo; a semi-transparent envelope' (*E4* 160), so her gig lamps of friendship create an expansive network of interconnections that support her as a writer, respond to her complex and contradictory needs, and sustain her as a woman.

Selected Bibliography

DeSalvo, Louise, and Mitchell A. Leaska, eds, *The Letters of Vita Sackville-West to Virginia Woolf* (London: Penguin, 1992).

Barber, Stephen, 'Lip-Reading: Woolf's Secret Encounters', in Eve Kosofsky Sedgwick, ed., *Novel Gazing: Queer Readings in Fiction* (Durham, NC: Duke University Press, 1997), 401–43.

Barkway, Stephen, '"This sheet is a glass": Virginia Woolf, Woman of Letters', *Nineteenth Annual Virginia Woolf Birthday Lecture* (Southport: Virginia Woolf Society of Great Britain, 2018).

Helt, Brenda S. and Madelyn Detloff, *Queer Bloomsbury* (Edinburgh: Edinburgh University Press, 2016).

Henley, Ann, '"But We Argued About Novel-Writing": Virginia Woolf, E. M. Forster and the Art of Fiction', *Ariel* 20, no. 3 (1989), 73–83.

Hoffman, Michael J., and Ann Ter Haar, '"Whose Books Once Influenced Mine": The Relationship between E. M. Forster's *Howards End* and Virginia Woolf's *The Waves*', *Twentieth Century Literature* 45, no. 1 (Spring 1999), 46–64.

Lee, Hermione, *Virginia Woolf* (London: Chatto and Windus, 1996).

Lilienfield, Jane, '"The Gift of a China Ink Pot": Violet Dickinson, Virginia Woolf, Elizabeth Gaskell, Charlotte Bronte, and the Love of Women in Writing', in Eileen Barrett and Patricia

---

[50] Cited in Wiley, '"When a Woman Speaks"', 8 n28.

Cramer, eds, *Virginia Woolf: Lesbian Readings* (New York and London: New York University Press, 1997), 37–56.

McLaughlin, Ann L., 'An Uneasy Sisterhood: Virginia Woolf and Katherine Mansfield', in Jane Marcus, ed., *Virginia Woolf: A Feminist Slant* (Lincoln: University of Nebraska Press, 1983), 152–61.

Mills, Jean, *Virginia Woolf, Jane Ellen Harrison, and the Spirit of Modernist Classicism* (Columbus: Ohio State University, 2014).

Raitt, Suzanne, *Vita and Virginia: The Work and Friendship of V. Sackville-West and Virginia Woolf* (Oxford: Clarendon Press, 1993).

Reed, Christopher, 'Bloomsbury as Queer Subculture', in Victoria Rosner, ed., *The Cambridge Companion to The Bloomsbury Group* (New York and Cambridge: Cambridge University Press, 2014), 71–89.

Snaith, Anna, ' "Curious slides and arrests": Class and Colonialism in the Relationship Between Katherine Mansfield and Virginia Woolf', in Stéphanie Amar-Flood and Sara Thornton, eds, *Lectures d'une oeuvre: Selected Stories de Katherine Mansfield* (Paris: Editions du Temps, 1997), 143–58.

Sproles, Karyn Z., *Desiring Women: The Partnership of Virginia Woolf and Vita Sackville-West* (Toronto: University of Toronto Press, 2006).

Westman, Karin E., 'The First "Orlando": The Laugh of the Comic Spirit in Virginia Woolf's "Friendships Gallery" ', *Twentieth Century Literature* 47, no. 1 (2001), 39–71.

Wiley, Christopher, ' "When a Woman Speaks the Truth About Her Body": Ethel Smyth, Virginia Woolf, and the Challenges of Lesbian Auto/biography', *Music and Letters* 85, no. 3 (August 2004), 388–414.

Winston, Janet, 'Reading Influences: Homoeroticism and Mentoring in Katherine Mansfield's "Carnation" and Virginia Woolf's "Moments of Being": "Slater's Pins Have No Points" ', Eileen Barrett and Patricia Cramer, eds, *Virginia Woolf: Lesbian Readings* (London and New York: New York University Press, 1997), 57–77.

Wood, Elizabeth, 'Performing Rights: A Sonography of Women's Suffrage', *Musical Quarterly* 79, no. 4 (Winter 1995), 606–43.

CHAPTER 3

TRADITIONS AND TRANSFORMATIONS

REGINA MARLER

MODERNIST, feminist, experimental: the terms we now most associate with Virginia Woolf all presuppose a break with conventions (social, domestic, artistic) and a rejection of the status quo in art and power relations. We can even find—as Woolf herself enjoying finding—moments that symbolize that break: 'On or about December, 1910, human character changed', as she famously hazarded in 'Mr Bennett and Mrs Brown' in 1924 (*E2* 421). With her friends in the Memoir Club, she played up the spring evening early in Vanessa Bell's marriage, when Lytton Strachey pointed at a stain on Vanessa's dress and asked, 'Semen?' 'With that one word', Woolf declared, 'all barriers of reticence and reserve went down' (*MB* 195). Yet all her life, Virginia Woolf kept returning in memory to her childhood home, to the Victorian family in which she was raised—eleven family members and seven long-suffering servants—where boys went to the best schools that Sir Leslie Stephen could afford, and girls, however clever or gifted, were shaped for charitable work, for motherhood, for marriage to prominent men.

This obsessive turning back is a kind of pained nostalgia: a lament, a grievance, a comfort—and the engine of even her most avant-garde work. The traditions and assumptions of that potent childhood world pull against (but also significantly underpin) the changes Woolf observed and tried to enact in her own life as she trailblazed new ways of writing, made a modern marriage, and witnessed the rise of the working class.

A wicker perambulator advances up Hyde Park Gate toward Kensington Garden in, say, September 1882, on a rare clear day. Gripping the pram handle are a nursemaid and a three-year-old girl of serious demeanour wearing a pinafore over her frock. Her toddler brother dawdles behind. Add a second nursemaid, holding the little boy's hand. A well-heeled matron steps out her front door with another maid, her paid companion. They say good morning. Stop here, at this fictional but plausible moment, with the infant Ginia Stephen's legs wheeling amid the folds of her yard-long cambric gown, and her cap-string bow tight under her chin.

We can interpret this scene—or, indeed, similar real-life scenes captured in the Stephen and Duckworth families' photograph albums—in several ways, focusing, for example, on class, money, family dynamics, empire, London, fashion, or the status(es) of women. All preoccupied the adult Virginia Woolf. In fact, the Stephen children's newspaper, *Hyde Park Gate News* (c. 1891–1895), demonstrates such a comfortable grasp of British class structure and its comic potential that it is clear Virginia's dawning awareness of such issues dates from the nursery. The children's pleasure reading included the conservative satire in *Punch Magazine*, the digest *Tit-Bits*, with its sensational human-interest stories, and the Grossmith brother's comic masterpiece on social climbing, *The Diary of a Nobody*, serialized in *Punch* from 1888 to 1889. Along with Victorian children's classics like Lewis Carroll's Alice books, they also had their mother Julia Stephen's light, didactic stories for children.

Before Virginia and her sister Vanessa launched into their adolescent readings of the English classics—'I can still hear much of George Eliot and Thackeray in her voice', Vanessa Bell recalled in her memoir, 'Notes on Virginia's Childhood'—they pored over the works of the prolific Charlotte M. Yonge. Virginia even brought Yonge's enormously popular romance, *The Heir of Redclyffe* (1853), on her honeymoon to Spain, France, and Italy—an odd choice given its message of moral uprightness, not to mention the hero's death on his Italian honeymoon. A mention of the crucifixion could make Vanessa and Virginia dissolve into giggles as children, but neither of them seems to have objected to Yonge's religiosity. These stories, then, along with the dark interiors at 22 Hyde Park Gate formed part of the 'granite' of Virginia's childhood—the material and socio-political realities of her late Victorian world. They would have appeared immutable to her as a young girl.

When the Stephen children fled Kensington for Bloomsbury in the wake of their father's death in 1904, they left many dreaded social obligations behind. But to the end of her life, Woolf was evoking the numinous objects and interiors of St. Ives and Hyde Park Gate, and grappling with more complicated legacies from Julia Stephen, including the conservative women reformers and philanthropists whom she had held up as models for her daughters. In Woolf's complex relationship to servants—a source of frustration and painful insight—we see another way in which the past continued to pull on and inform her work.

Totemic objects associated with Virginia Woolf include her favourite kind of umbrella (green with a white lining), her oak standing desk (given to Quentin Bell and now at Duke University),[1] the black pen that had been her mother's and became hers—'*the* pen, as I used to think it, along with other objects, as a child, because mother used it' (*D1* 214)—and the crook handle faux bamboo walking stick left on the banks of the Ouse at her death, with its faint, associative echo of Uncle Thoby Prinsep's walking stick,

---

[1] See Leslie Kathleen Hankins' 'Heritage Hoarding: Artifacts, Archives, and Ambiguity, or, The Saga of Virginia Woolf's Standing Desk', in Jane de Gay, Tom Brekin, and Anne Reus, eds, *Virginia Woolf and Heritage: Selected Papers from the Twenty-Sixth Annual International Conference on Virginia Woolf* (Clemson, SC: Clemson University Press, 2017), 73–9.

near Julia's bed when she died. Woolf's cane was given to Louie Mayer, cook-general at Monks House, and is now at the Berg Collection.[2]

Who cherishes a beloved parent's dipping pen now, let alone writes with it, as did Virginia Woolf? One can alight on almost any surviving (or described) object from her youth and gain a similar vertiginous sense of the past—as close as we get to time travel—and a somatic empathy with the young Virginia. Woolf does the same in 'A Sketch of the Past' when she walks her reader through the entrance hall of 22 Hyde Park Gate, with its maxims for gentlemen pinned above the mantelpiece. Naturally, however, much fell away—the 'cotton wool' of daily life, as she wrote: yet 'the things one does not remember are as important; perhaps they are more important' (*MB* 69).

Despite Woolf's interest in clothes, for example, she does not think to recall the shape of women on the street in her childhood—cloth bells, many-layered—now so striking to us in period photographs. Perhaps there is a hint in the 'triangular purple shape' of the mother and child in Lily Briscoe's painting in *To the Lighthouse* (*TL* 72). In Leslie Stephen's photograph album, Julia Stephen can be seen outside Talland House wearing a voluminous black cloak, dress, and apron combination that almost entirely obscures her body: she puts the 'mater' in 'material'.[3] Perhaps this was the black cloak recalled by a St. Ives woman in a 1964 letter to Leonard: 'a black cloak which [Mrs Stephen] wore to the water's edge and cast off when bathing'.[4]

Her sister Vanessa also produced adept memoirs of life at Hyde Park Gate. Though capable of comic exaggeration, Vanessa's wry humour resembles her mother's tone in *Notes from Sick Rooms* more than Virginia's aerobatics. Vanessa delved into fascinated detail about their grandmother's elaborate mid-Victorian toilette, assisted by 'her strict German maid, Minna': the unusual 'delicious soap' with which Maria Jackson perfected her already-clean hands, and the eventual placing of a shawl of 'softest Cashmir over her shoulders and I think another of most delicate Shetland':

> Then tiny shawls of finest wool—but that seems almost too coarse a word—were folded on her head and fastened with an old-fashioned (even then) brooch. One layer over another—at last she was ready—and on good days she would be carried down to the drawing room and there receive her guests.[5]

The late Victorian world of her shared childhood with Virginia was of course vastly, intentionally different from the less supervised, somewhat chaotic, and clothes-optional Edwardian childhood that Vanessa created for her sons, Julian and Quentin, and for her daughter, Angelica. In Virginia's memoirs, we glimpse Sir Leslie Stephen's yellow tin hip bath, a vessel in which he had bathed all his life, to be filled by servants from brass hot water cans (*MB* 118). From Quentin Bell's *Charleston Bulletin*, we have the bathtub at

---

[2] See antiquestradegazette.com/news/2002/making-waves/.
[3] c. 1894, Plate 38b, Leslie Stephen's Photograph Album, Smith College.
[4] Quoted in Hermione Lee, *Virginia Woolf* (London: Chatto & Windus, 1996), 26.
[5] Vanessa Bell, 'Memoir Relating to Mrs Jackson', in Lia Giachero, *Sketches in Pen and Ink*, 50.

Charleston Farmhouse, its chipped basin touched up with white paint and improperly dried before the next unlucky bather. A tale of two tubs: the traditional and the (spottily) transformative.

Alex Zwerdling, in his *Virginia Woolf and the Real World* (1986), was among the first to recognize that Woolf has been wrongly regarded as the poster girl for dreamy abstraction. Despite her formulation of the 'granite and rainbow' needed in fiction, the material culture of her Kensington upbringing and later life only sparked serious inquiry after the 1976 publication of Virginia Woolf's memoirs (replete with material details of life at Hyde Park Gate) and after Monk's House and Charleston Farmhouse were restored and opened to the public in the 1980s. These homes and their 'emotionally textured interiors'[6] offer profound experiences for those who study their former inhabitants. Even the 1980 Sotheby's auction to benefit the Charleston Trust made it possible for the Woolfian to imagine the Stephen children eating from the tiny eggcups used at Hyde Park Gate, sized for Victorian chicken eggs—not only a touching survival of Stephen family life but also an evocation of class, culture, markets, and the Indian investments from which the residents of Hyde Park Gate derived much of their income. In short: the British Empire in an eggcup.

It may seem greedy to ask such relics for insights beyond those in the various Bloomsbury Group memoirs and letters. But contemporary documentation of Woolf's early childhood is somewhat scrappy—her fault in arriving seventh of eight children. Only as she learns to write can we gradually trace in *Hyde Park Gate News*, then in her letters and early journals, and a few of her father's letters, the growing girl's awareness of social structures, of the power dynamics operating between servants and children, between parents and children, between servants and their employers, between husband and wife, between subjects and society, and subjects and the state. There is a world of difference between Virginia Stephen at fifteen, who pressed through crowds to catch sight of Her Majesty's bonnet as Queen Victoria passed in procession in 1897 (*PA* 42), and the mature Virginia Woolf, who declared, 'As a woman, I have no country' (*TG* 185).

The Stephen sisters were so relieved to have torn free from Kensington society after Sir Leslie's death—so self-congratulatory, frankly—that it took time for them to view their rebellion in context, as part of the immense societal shifts in early twentieth-century Britain. Feminism per se and suffrage are covered in detail elsewhere in this volume, so the aim here is more contextual—a sketch of an era, with attention to some interesting crosscurrents and divergences. For example, the Married Women's Property Act passed in 1882, the year of Woolf's birth. Woolf herself noted it—literally—when jotting down points of interest on women's evolving legal status from Albert Venn Dicey's *Law and Opinion* at the bottom of her reading list for 1904-5.[7] On a timeline of women's history,

---

[6] Nuala Hancock, *Charleston and Monk's House: The Intimate House Museums of Virginia Woolf and Vanessa Bell* (Edinburgh: Edinburgh University Press, 2012).

[7] Albert Venn Dicey, *Lectures on the Relation between Law and Public Opinion in England During the Nineteenth Century* (London: Palgrave Macmillan, first ed. 1905).

the concurrence of Woolf's birth and the Married Women's Property Act would merit a small red star. But it was no breakthrough for the female denizens of 22 Hyde Park Gate.

When Julia Prinsep Duckworth married Leslie Stephen in 1877, her male relations apparently arranged for a settlement that permitted her to retain inheritances from her first husband and (later) her parents. Julia Stephen had money of her own to bequeath, not only the handful of personal mementos she bequeathed on her deathbed. (Her list of bequests—and that of her mother, Maria Jackson—is among the Stephen family papers at the British Library.) Probate from Herbert Duckworth's 1870 death was to Julia. Without a settlement, Julia's chief legal protection would have been an earlier, much more restrictive Married Women's Property Act of 1870, inspired by the terrible divorce of Caroline Norton in the 1830s and the legal kidnapping of her children. The 1870 act granted wives the ability to earn and control their own money, and to inherit small sums under their own names during marriage, but stipulated that everything they owned before marriage would be yielded to their new husband. Until the Inheritance Act of 1938, a man had complete testatory freedom (as Woolf addressed in *Three Guineas*). On his death, his house and estate could pass entirely away from his wife and children with no consideration for their maintenance.

Julia Stephen left the substantial sum of £5,483 (the equivalent now of roughly £629,582) to Leslie Stephen, and was free to do so because the children of her first marriage—including her daughter Stella—already had money in trust from the Duckworth cotton fortune. Stella's branch of the Duckworths descended from George Duckworth (1749–1815), Lord of the Manor at Over Darwen near Blackburn, once at the heart of the Lancashire textile industry. Her inheritance brought wealth to her husband, the solicitor Jack Waller Hills, a second son of modest means. Such arrangements had become common among the wealthy or professional classes. Money held in trust was exempt from the coverture laws. As soon as families had accrued enough money and status to afford legal help, they could arrange some financial protection of their daughters. Further generosity depended on the individual. After Stella Duckworth died intestate, her widower made allowances from his income from Stella's marriage settlement to her surviving half-siblings until his remarriage in the 1920s. (Probate to Hills was £25,896.) Stella's wealth, in part, enabled him to pursue his later political career.

Yet considerable financial uncertainty remained for women, even those of 'the lower division of the upper middle class', as Quentin Bell placed the Hyde Park Gate ménage.[8] Julia Stephen did not control the family finances. The well-worn stories of Sir Leslie raging at the weekly bills presented to him by Julia, then, after her death, by Stella, and finally by Vanessa are based both on Victorian ideals of womanhood and the fact that these women had no legal standing to sign checks. Their names were not on the household bank account. (At his death, Sir Leslie Stephen's estate of £15,715—the rough equivalent of £1,822,940 today—was divided among his children.)

---

[8] Quentin Bell, *Virginia Woolf: A Biography* (New York: Harcourt Brace Jovanovich, 1972), 21.

Although the details of Vanessa and Clive Bell's early financial discussions are unclear, she did write her own checks and control—or fail to control—household expenses. Vanessa had also been 'supposed to be in control of the [Stephen] family finances' at Gordon Square, a source of some uneasiness, offset by her joy that 'at last we were free'.[9] At Hyde Park Gate, she and Virginia had struggled to clothe themselves and buy books and art supplies on the £50 a year allowance Sir Leslie had been persuaded to give them. Two days after Sir Leslie's funeral in 1904, Adeline Virginia Stephen lavished £40 on a life membership to the London Library ('age: 22 ... Occupation: Spinster').[10] For a ravenous reader, this must have felt like buying a fiefdom. The purchase also memorialized her father, President of the London Library from 1892 until his death. Yet the almost complete exclusion of women as trustees on the Library committee was to remain a lasting source of irritation—dry twigs that would fuel the fire of *Three Guineas*.

Virginia brought £9,000 to her union with Leonard Woolf in 1912—far exceeding his assets.[11] This collection of inheritances from her father, her half-sister Stella, her aunt Caroline Emilia Stephen, and her brother Thoby might not have provided enough for the couple to live on, given Virginia's medical expenses. Leonard took charge of their investments—by custom, one assumes, and perhaps also because Virginia fell ill so quickly after their marriage. Scholars have found no evidence that Virginia ever participated in investment decisions. She was not granted a bank account and chequebook until 1927, after tearful arguments: 'a great advance in dignity' (*D*3 175).

These financial arrangements were among the lived conditions that complicated, ameliorated, and reinforced the legal and social restrictions into which Virginia Stephen and her female relations were born. Woolf explored implications of women's exclusion from the world of finance that went far beyond a demand for inclusion or the imagined pleasures of wealth: when the professions and the Stock Exchange open to both sexes, Woolf argued in *Three Guineas*, women might simply become 'champions of the capitalist system', leading the same benighted, money-obsessed lives as the men at the heart of those institutions (*TG* 150).[12]

Woolf's attitude to capital wavered between pragmatism and distaste. In her essay 'Professions for Women' (1932), she describes her battles, as a young writer, with 'the Angel in the House'—that tenacious mid-Victorian ideal of sympathetic and self-sacrificing womanhood: 'In those days—the last of Queen Victoria—every house had its Angel. And when I came to write I encountered her with the very first words. The

---

[9] Quoted in Frances Spalding, *Vanessa Bell* (London, Ticknor & Fields, 1983), 49.

[10] See www.londonlibrary.co.uk/newblog/entry/archive-advent-calendar-13-december-2013. See a photograph of her handwritten membership application here: blog.londonlibrary.co.uk/wp-content/uploads/2013/12/VWoolf.jpg.

[11] See Paul Delaney's 'A Little Capital: The Financial Affairs of Leonard and Virginia Woolf' in *The Charleston Magazine* 7 (Summer/Autumn 1993), 5–8, and Hermione Lee's chapter 'Money and Fame' in her biography of Virginia Woolf.

[12] See Diane F. Gillespie, 'Adventures in Common: Investing with Woolfs and "Securitas"', in Helen Wussow and Mary Ann Gillies, eds, *Virginia Woolf and the Common(wealth) Reader* (Clemson, SC: Clemson State University, 2014), 205–11.

shadow of her wings fell on my page; I heard the rustling of her skirts in the room'. Killing the Angel was 'the one act for which I take some credit to myself', Woolf asserted. Less often quoted is her quick concession that 'the credit rightly belongs to some excellent ancestors of mine who left me a certain sum of money—shall we say five hundred pounds a year?—so that it was not necessary for me to depend solely on charm for my living'.[13]

One of Woolf's goals for 1931 was not to think about making money. Yet, as Hermione Lee shrewdly observes, 'Like her father, she thought a great deal, probably every day, anxiously and greedily, about how much money she had and how much she could spend.'[14] She did not want to hoard her extra money but to spend it on beautiful objects, travel, and gifts. She had been controlled too long not to relish her hard-won liberties. *A Room of One's Own* (1929) 'could be read as her own disguised economic autobiography', Hermione Lee posits, for Woolf was completing revisions to the essay (drawn from lectures delivered at Cambridge in 1928) at the point when financial success finally arrived for her as a writer.[15] That year she earned £3,050, 'the salary of a civil servant: a surprise to me, who was content with £200 for so many years' (*D*3 285).

About 'The Woman Question' in Victorian England we have abundant scholarship. Vanessa Bell's and Virginia Woolf's memoirs are part of that record, as are Julia Stephen's one book, *Notes from Sick Rooms (1883)*, and her three unpublished essays, but only a mile away at 44 Phillimore Gardens in the mid-1860s, Charlotte Manning had hosted meetings of the Kensington Society, an important precursor to the London National Society for Women's Suffrage, and the great suffrage leader Millicent Fawcett (also a Kensington lady) had married one of Leslie Stephen's oldest friends, Henry Fawcett. Julia Stephen wrote only indirectly about marriage in her essay on women agnostics, but reveals her old-fashioned views on gender roles and women's capacities.

Julia Stephen's convictions can also be surmised through the surviving half (his) of her correspondence with Leslie Stephen, and can be wrung from the treacle of his memoir, the *Mausoleum Book*. These records show Julia's efforts to placate her second husband, to jolly him out of his dark moods, while nevertheless resisting his demand that she do less for others—less nursing, specifically. We can also glimpse a ghostly reverse image of the Stephens' marriage in the very different marriages made by Virginia and Vanessa, whose husbands supported their art and allowed them both time and privacy.

The steely side of Julia Stephen has left historical traces, as well. Her doctrine of personal duty would brook no challenge, nor would she curtail her seemingly endless work. She had warned Leslie Stephen before marriage that she would often be away nursing, and in fact spent much of their engagement nursing her uncle Thoby Prinsep through his final illness. 'My darling was always making her rounds', he recalled, 'more alas!

---

[13] Virginia Woolf, 'Professions for Women', in *Virginia Woolf: Women and Writing*, ed. Michele Barrett (Orlando, FL: Harvest Press, 1980), 59.
[14] Lee, *Virginia Woolf*, 558.
[15] Lee, *Virginia Woolf*, 556.

than her strength justified—among people whom she could help'.[16] Stella had wanted her mother's tombstone to record that she 'went about doing good' (*MB* 96). Like the role models she proposed for her daughters, Julia enjoyed exercising her skill and independence in what both she and Leslie considered the womanly spheres of nursing, teaching, and philanthropy. She may have 'fully endorsed the Victorian models for female behavior', but she was no martyr to her husband's desire to keep her home.[17] If, as Woolf wrote in 'A Sketch of the Past', Hyde Park Gate in 1900 was 'a complete model of Victorian society', then Julia Stephen's self-determination cannot be glossed over.

This self-determination was supported by the labour of other women. 'Seven people waited on eleven', as Alison Light writes in her superb study *Mrs Woolf and the Servants*, 'they slept and ate there, in the attics and the basement, living a parallel life'.[18] Live-in servants were one of the great givens of Virginia Stephen's childhood. Period memoirs are full of casual references to this necessity, even in modest middle-class homes of the professional classes. Sophia Farrell had entered Julia Duckworth's service at twenty-six, rose to the esteemed position of cook, and remained with various members of the family for her whole working life. She was 'one of the abiding mother-figures in Virginia's life', as Alison Light notes, and the Stephens' version of the old family retainer, with all the awkward obligations and emotions this entailed.[19] The quasi-familial position of domestic servants—never patriarchs but often surrogate mothers, uncles, aunts, children—complicates the analysis. (Winston Churchill, for example, died with one photo on his bedside: that of Elizabeth Everest, his beloved nanny.)

The lives of female domestic servants and their middle-class 'mistresses' can be usefully examined together because employer and employee lived together and were so often intertwined. But domestic service also provided a daily, imperfect model for that larger, Evangelical ideal of service that Julia Stephen took for granted, which partook also of Thomas Carlyle's stirring call to work in *Past and Present* (1843) and elsewhere. The ideals of work and service were driving forces for the three women she held up as role models for her daughters: Octavia Hill (1838–1912), Florence Nightingale (1820–1910), and Mary Augusta Ward (1851–1920).[20]

Here were three conservative philanthropists burning with moral purpose whose views on women's suffrage seem not unlike Julia Stephen's. Florence Nightingale strongly supported married women's property rights and reluctantly signed the early petition for women's suffrage that her friend John Stuart Mill presented in Parliament in 1866. But women's rights in the abstract bored her. Even opening the professions to women left her cold. Why push to become doctors when the nation desperately needed nurses? The housing reformer Octavia Hill distrusted legislative solutions to the poverty she saw

---

[16] Leslie Stephen, *The Mausoleum Book* (Oxford: Oxford University Press, 1977), 81.
[17] Lee, *Virginia Woolf*, 85.
[18] Alison Light, *Mrs Woolf and the Servants* (New York: Bloomsbury Press, 2008), 9.
[19] Light, *Mrs Woolf and the Servants*, 71.
[20] Jane Garnett, 'Julia Stephen', entry in the *Dictionary of National Biography* (Oxford: Oxford University Press, 2004).

all around her and the degradations of poor women's lives. Like Julia, she endorsed the doctrine of separate spheres; both were among the hundred or so women who signed Mrs Humphry Ward's appeal against female suffrage published in *Nineteenth Century* in 1889. Anti-suffragism has been described as 'the obvious destination for a well-to-do late Victorian literary woman',[21] but Mary Augusta Ward threw herself at the cause, risking her popularity as a novelist. 'None of the great Victorian reputations has sunk lower than that of Mrs Humphry Ward', remarked Virginia Woolf in reviewing Ward's biography in 1924.

As Julia Stephen's exemplars of Victorian womanhood, however, these three complicated, ambitious figures reward a second glance.[22] Their energy alone is worth noting, in light of Anne Thackeray Ritchie's memory of the 'superabundant vitality' of the Pattle sisters—Julia's maternal relations—and Woolf's remarks that Julia Stephen exhausted herself doing good and managing her husband's emotions.[23]

To some extent, female achievement in the public realm—even if directed toward charitable ends—flew in the face of prescriptive notions of femininity and the mid-century doctrine of separate spheres, as articulated by many writers, including John Ruskin in his 1864 lecture, 'Of Queen's Gardens', according to which man is the doer and the creator: 'His intellect is for speculation and invention ... But the woman's power is for rule, not for battle,—and her intellect is not for invention or creation, but for sweet ordering, arrangement, and decision ... Her great function is Praise.'[24]

Naturally, the home is 'woman's true place and power' in this formulation. The doctrine of separate spheres enforces male supremacy by granting women the 'equal but different' roles that have remained a hallmark of conservative thought. Women like Octavia Hill and Julia Stephen felt empowered by this ideology, which seemed to acknowledge their talents, even as it circumscribed their application: 'Women do not stand on the same ground as men with regard to work', Julia Stephen wrote in her essay on agnostic women, 'though we are far from allowing that our work is lower or less important than theirs, but we ought and do claim the same equality of morals.'[25]

Ruskin had abandoned his Evangelical faith by the time he wrote 'Of Queen's Gardens', but he might as well be describing Eve, the biblical helpmeet. Thus, a girl's education should 'enable her to understand, and even to aid, the work of men'. She should learn language and science 'only so far as may enable her to sympathize in her husband's pleasures, and in those of his best friends'. Biological determinism seemed

---

[21] Brian Harrison, *Separate Spheres: the Opposition to Women's Suffrage* (London: Croom Helm, 1978), 22.

[22] See Gertrude Himmelfarb's *Victorian Minds* (London: Weidenfield & Nicolson, 1968) and her essay collection, *Marriage and Morals Among the Victorians* (London: Faber, 1986). See also Elaine Showalter's essay, 'Florence Nightingale's Feminist Complaint: Women, Religion, and *Suggestions for Thought*' in *Signs* 6, no. 3 (Spring 1981), 395–412.

[23] Quoted in Caroline Dakers, *The Holland Park Circle: Artists and Victorian Society* (New Haven, CT: Yale University Press, 1999), 28.

[24] John Ruskin, *Of Queens' Gardens* (London: George Allan, 1902), 20–1.

[25] Quoted in Gillespie and Steele, 246–7.

only common sense to most Victorians, including the Stephens. When Leslie Stephen mentioned educating their daughters, Julia adopted a wounded, defensive posture: what must he think of her, with her gentlewoman's smattering of home learning, if he valued female education so highly? Her essay on agnostic women was written to refute an article in *Nineteenth Century*, in which it was argued that agnosticism would encourage men to open the professions to women, since they were 'cut off from all their natural occupations' as caregivers and housewives. 'Such dreams are vain', Julia Stephen replies:

> Will competitive examinations cease? Will women surmount all these obstacles of their sex which have hitherto happily restrained them? And, should Agnosticism place women in the Cabinet and in the houses of the stock exchange, what will it mean for men? Will their chivalry have no reward?[26]

This passage quietly burns behind much of Woolf's writings, like a gas jet in an inner room—not, decisively, a room of one's own. She could not reasonably quote her own mother in *Three Guineas*, but she does quote an ermine-draped judge who declared that women's interest in fashion was 'one of nature's solaces for a constant and insuperable physical handicap' (*TG* 221–2). If only we could see how or if Julia responded to Philippa Fawcett becoming the first woman to top the Mathematical Tripos at Cambridge in 1890, ranking above the Senior Wrangler. Prizes and university honours mattered to the Stephens, and Fawcett's achievement made news worldwide. She would go on to a distinguished career in educational reform—being paid the same salaries as men for her work. In his 1886 biography of Henry Fawcett, Leslie Stephen mentions his daughter only in passing. He also remarks that in Fawcett's last years, Philippa was reaching 'an age in which she could frequently be her father's companion, and the development of her talent was a source of constant and growing interest to him'.[27]

'Man must be pleased, but him to please is woman's pleasure', wrote Coventry Patmore in his popular narrative poem of wedded bliss, *The Angel in the House* (published in four parts from 1854 to 1863). Were any of these three role models Angels in the house? Angels, perhaps, but Ward and Hill were rarely in the house: they were women of action. Although considered a minor poet now—'the laureate of the tea table', as Edmund Gosse called him—Patmore was at the centre of Victorian literary life, and a close friend of both Maria Jackson and her sister, Julia Margaret Cameron, who titled one of her photographs *The Angel in the House* (1873). Woolf kept a surprising number of books by him, including the copy of *The Angel in the House* inscribed to her mother in her youth.

As it happens, Patmore's 'Angel' had its uses for Florence Nightingale, whose departure for the Crimean in October 1854 sparked debate and outrage about the impropriety and dangers of sending gentlewomen into battle. A public relations campaign followed, in which two anonymous letters attesting to Miss Nightingale's femininity, religious feeling, and filial devotion circulated in the national press. She longed to stay at

---

[26] Quoted in Gillespie and Steele, 246.
[27] Leslie Stephen, *Life of Henry Fawcett* (London, 1885), 453.

home, the writers argued, but felt called to render '"the holiest of woman's charities"' to the wounded and dying soldiers. As Mark Bostridge, a recent biographer, writes: 'What is being offered here is an acceptable public counterpart to "The Angel in the House", Coventry Patmore's portrayal of the perfect wife and mother, published for the first time that autumn: an "Angel of Mercy" to validate a woman's sudden appearance at the scene of war.'[28] It worked, and helped establish Nightingale's 'secular sainthood'.

Nightingale had, in fact, felt called by God to nursing. After years of oppression from her affluent family, she seized an opportunity to study at a nursing convent in Germany. Her friend Sidney Herbert, who headed the War Office during the Crimean War, suggested she go to Scutari in 1854 and organize nursing efforts at the crowded and filthy military hospital. Until Herbert's death in 1861, she would use him as her agent in revolutionizing military medical services; she also exploited her own myth as 'The Lady of the Lamp' in marshalling the work of others, enjoying her position of command. Due to her gender, as well as chronic illness contracted in Scutari, she was obliged to work indirectly through men. Soon after the return from Scutari, when she began superintending a Harley Street 'Establishment for Gentlewomen during Illness', she wrote her father:

> I do all my business by intrigue. I propose in private to A. B. and C. the resolutions I think A B. and C. most capable of carrying in committee, and then leave it to them, and I always win. I am now in the hey-day of my power.[29]

Nightingale founded modern nursing, introduced statistics to the medical and social sciences, wrote two volumes on health and sanitation in colonized India, and on sleepless nights penned long religious works—all from her invalid's bedroom in Mayfair. In *Cassandra* (written in 1852, but only circulated among friends) she offers a radical revisionist theology and lashes out at the Victorian family and the forced idleness of girls. Woolf read and admired *Cassandra* on its first publication in Ray Strachey's *The Cause* (1928), but recoiled at Nightingale's unrestrained account of personal suffering.

In *Notes on Nursing* (1859) and elsewhere, Nightingale's tone is voluble, emphatic, and opinionated. (The only stylistic similarity between Julia Stephen's *Notes From Sick Rooms* and the volume that inspired it is an arresting attention to detail: Nightingale points out the annoyance caused by spilled tea in a patient's saucer, for example, and Julia Stephen insists that nurses use a cupped palm rather than two fingers to support the patient's head.) One can poke fun at Nightingale's fervour, as did Lytton Strachey in *Eminent Victorians*—'A Demon possessed her!'—but it is difficult, even for him, not to admire this Victorian dynamo: 'In the real Miss Nightingale there was more that was interesting than in the legendary one; there was also less that was agreeable.'[30]

---

[28] Mark Bostridge, *Florence Nightingale: The Making of an Icon* (Farrar, Straus and Giroux, 2008).
[29] Quoted in Boyd, 181.
[30] Lytton Strachey, *Eminent Victorians* (London: Chatto, 1918), 1.

Some letters from Octavia Hill to Stella Duckworth addressing their joint building project in Lisson Grove, a notorious slum in Marylebone, recently sold at auction.[31] Two of these cottages survive on Ranston Street, showing the 'windows here' that Hill, a lover of light and open space, emphasized in a sketch for her young follower. Hill's work in Lisson Grove followed her usual pattern: she bought and demolished dilapidated tenement houses in the worst parts of London, and, with the help of donors and her team of middle-class 'Fellow Workers', constructed small, airy dwellings for workers and artisans. These were let at reasonable rents—so reasonable that landlords (like Eleanor in *The Years*, the character inspired by Stella) had difficulty putting aside enough cash for repairs. Hill typically collected the rent herself, convinced that the personal connection between a concerned landlord and a responsible tenant ennobled both parties. She rented only to the 'deserving poor'.

Hill knew hardship at first hand. Her father had lost his fortune—in part through ambitious social schemes—and from the age of fourteen, she helped support her family, mostly as a teacher in the Notting Hill school she ran with her sisters. Her mother had also kept school and then managed a co-operative enterprise to help foster economic independence for poor women. In fact, Hill was steeped in the Christian social reform movement from early childhood, in the way that Virginia Stephen was steeped in the literary world. Even Hill's grandfather, Dr Thomas Southwood Smith, had been a pioneer in the model dwelling movement. From her management of a toy-making workshop for child workers, Hill moved on to manage affordable houses (the first three leases bought in 1865 by her friend John Ruskin), then a Southwark complex of dwellings, where Stella volunteered. Hill trained many such 'lady volunteers to oversee the properties', wrote Martha Vicinus in her important study of Victorian women's communities, *Independent Women*, 'each week collecting the rent and using the occasion to assist—or interfere—in the affairs of her tenants'.[32]

The young Virginia resented having to chaperone Stella on workhouse and slum visits, from at least one of which they fled in fear. Virginia also spent the morning of her fifteenth birthday running errands with Stella and accompanying her to a meeting with Octavia Hill. Jo Fisher had brought the plans for Stella's cottages: 'All three learnedly argued over them for half an hour, I sitting on a stool by the fire and surveying Miss Hills [sic] legs' (*PA* 21). One can view these visits as a failed apprenticeship. While Stella gladly followed her mother into good works, her younger Stephen sisters balked. The extent to which Woolf may have later associated ladies' philanthropic endeavours with her grief and breakdown after her mother's death—for Stella was assigned to guard Virginia and supervise her continued recovery—warrants further exploration. Illness and constraint dogged Virginia in the two years between her mother's death and Stella's, and, as her

---

[31] The letters date from 1893 to January 1897, shortly before Stella's wedding, and were written at Grace Dieu Manor, Leicestershire, the home of Charles Booth.

[32] Martha Vicinus, *Independent Women: Work & Community for Single Women 1850–1920* (Chicago: Chicago University Press, 1985), 217.

biographers have noted, she was sometimes restricted from reading and study in favour of these more ladylike pursuits.

Octavia Hill also fought to maintain open spaces for public use and co-founded the National Trust. She flogged her ideas relentlessly in the press. She has been described as the founder of modern social work, but, like Florence Nightingale, she did not want to lose social workers and helpful moneyed ladies to the vote. In a 1910 letter to the *Times*, she argued that political power for Englishwomen would 'militate against their usefulness in the large field of public service. This service is, to my mind, far more valuable now than any voting power could possibly be'.[33] Yet she was the first woman invited to sit on a Royal Commission. Statesmen wrote and called on her daily. Her organization survives as Octavia Housing, and provides thousands of affordable housing units in England, including some acquired by Octavia Hill herself.

Like Florence Nightingale, Hill remained unmarried. Flouting the conventional view that marriage was woman's highest goal and destiny—and, of course, almost the only career aside from 'governess' available to most middle-class women—they not only blazed their own paths but opened the way for other women, creating the new careers of trained nurse and social worker. In her diary, after rejecting one of her suitors, Nightingale confided: 'I have a moral, an active nature which requires satisfaction and that I would not find in his life'.[34] In choosing not to marry, her money, time, and priorities would remain her own.

Even for less prodigiously gifted women, like Julia Stephen or her daughter Stella, 'the potential fulfilment of a life of self-sacrifice was obvious', Vicinus points out, 'when compared with endless hours whiled away with flower arranging, visiting, and tea parties'.[35] Of course, the charitable work expected of middle-class and wealthy women could (and did) expand by degrees, from the bun handed out the kitchen door to a beggar to the church bazaar to the founding and administration of settlements in London—conducting business, essentially, under the mantle of womanly goodness. Julia Stephen visited the poor and sick and donated money to Octavia Hill, but Stella organized her week around her charitable duties, like a part-time job: collecting rents and arranging repairs for the Southwark tenants on Tuesday mornings, and on Thursday afternoons reading to workhouse inmates.

Mary Augusta Ward was a family friend of the Stephens, yet she is perhaps the most surprising of Julia Stephen's role models for her daughters. Ward's passion for universal education exceeded even her anti-suffrage zeal. Formidably intelligent and exceptionally well-educated for the period, Ward was also as religious as Octavia Hill and Florence Nightingale. Her family connections rivalled those of Virginia Woolf: her grandfather Thomas Arnold was the revered mid-Victorian head of Rugby (later mocked by Lytton

---

[33] Quoted in Nancy Boyd, *Josephine Butler, Octavia Hill, Florence Nightingale: Three Victorian Women Who Changed their World* (London: Macmillan, 1982), 141.

[34] Quoted in *Ever Yours, Florence Nightingale: Selected Letters*, ed. Martha Vicinus (Cambridge, MA: Harvard University Press, 1990), 40.

[35] Vicinus, *Independent Women*, 51.

Strachey in *Eminent Victorians*), her uncle was Matthew Arnold, and her father Tom Arnold was a literary scholar. Her nephews were Julian and Aldous Huxley. After studying at girls' schools, she acquired the major European languages while her family lived at Oxford, and then married a fellow writer and had three children. She published over thirty novels under her married name, Mrs Humphry Ward, and never shied from social or religious controversy. While Virginia Woolf was coming of age as a reader (1890–1905), Mrs Humphry Ward was the bestselling novelist in the English language. She channelled her ample royalties toward good works and reform, and entertained on a grand scale.

One critical study of Mary Augusta Ward is aptly titled *Behind Her Times*. Certainly, in Woolf studies, Ward remains a byword for reactionary late Victorianism. She believed that suffrage beyond the level of local government would diminish women's moral influence, yet she strongly supported women's education and was a co-founder of Somerville Hall (later Somerville College), Oxford. She became involved with the settlement movement—in which middle-class volunteers moved into slums to bring knowledge and 'culture' to the residents—and was among the first to provide education for disabled children, as well as a flexible School for Mothers. Her legacy is the Mary Ward Centre in Queen Square, an adult education centre. Virginia and Leonard Woolf would have walked daily past the original 1898 building on Tavistock Place, the Passmore Edwards Settlement (named for a major donor), now the Mary Ward House Conference and Exhibition Centre, which includes a Virginia Woolf Conference Room.

In her journal for 10 January 1905, Virginia jotted: 'Mrs. H. Ward, curiously, wrote to suggest Passmore Edwards work to N[essa] & me, but I have a valid excuse!' Although not spelled out, her excuse becomes clear in context. Her journal entry began, 'Found this morning on my plate my first instalment of wages—£2.7.6. for Guardian articles, which gave me great pleasure' (*PA* 219–20). By remarkable coincidence, the cheque for Virginia Stephen's first paid writing arrived on the same day as Mrs Humphry Ward's solicitation: the old world beckoned just as she had reached new shores.

As Hermione Lee observes, Woolf 'partly admired' these slum-travellers and social activists, especially her friend Margaret Llewellen Davies, head of the Women's Co-operative Guild: 'But the ethos of public service ... also filled Virginia Woolf with sceptical reservations. Her private opinion of the women involved in such activities was in sharp contrast to her public appreciation of them in a work such as *Three Guineas*'.[36] And she would never forgive the measly education she was accorded at a time when girls' schooling was no longer a rare or radical prospect: the £100 or so (compared to perhaps £2,000 each for her brothers) that her father doled out for her tutors in the classics and her classes in the Ladies' Department at King's College, London (where there is now a Virginia Woolf building).

Woolf and her sister shrugged off Julia Stephen's role models as hopelessly outdated, not fully appreciating how ground-breaking, semi-autonomous, and politically

---

[36] Lee, *Virginia Woolf*, 124.

powerful these women were, regardless of their anti-suffrage stance—and how much they accomplished toward the advancement of women. Modernism demanded a break from the past, and it was hard to disentangle the oppressive aspects of their Victorian upbringings from the progressive. Mary Ward in particular became a figure of fun in Bloomsbury. She was among the Kensington socialites whom the Stephen girls made a point of dropping when they started their new, unchaperoned lives in Gordon Square. (Earlier, after Stella's death, the well-meaning but clueless Sir Leslie had specifically asked Mrs Ward to help guide his daughters.)[37] Vanessa roared with laughter over Mrs Ward's autobiography, *A Writer's Recollections* (1918), reading it at least twice, as late as the 1930s. She and Duncan Grant memorized parts of it. 'What is the peculiar mixture of commonplace banality, snobbishness, arrivism and boastfulness', she asked Virginia, 'which makes her hit the bull's eye of British middle-class taste with such amazing skill each time?'[38] During Mrs Ward's life, Virginia wrote respectfully (though critically) about her novels; afterwards, she trounced them. 'While her imagination always attempts to soar', she concluded, 'it always agrees to perch' (*E3* 383).

But viewed from a greater distance these role models represent—as Woolf wrote of Lady Strachey—'the type of the Victorian woman at her finest—many-sided, vigorous, adventurous, advanced'.[39] Yes, even advanced: for they crossed barriers that stopped many other women, and invited others to follow. Did Julia Stephen intend these examples to inspire in her daughters only an attitude of selflessness and a kindly disposition toward the poor and sick? Why point out the eagle if you want only sparrows?

Selected Bibliography

Bell, Quentin, *Virginia Woolf: A Biography* (New York: Harcourt Brace Jovanovich, 1972).
Bell, Vanessa, 'Memoir Relating to Mrs Jackson', in Lia Giachero, ed., *Vanessa Bell: Sketches in Pen and Ink* (London: Pimlico, 1998), 50.
Boyd, Nancy, *Josephine Butler, Octavia Hill, Florence Nightingale: Three Victorian Women Who Changed their World* (London: Macmillan, 1982).
Delany, Paul, 'A Little Capital: The Financial Affairs of Leonard and Virginia Woolf', *The Charleston Magazine* 7 (Summer/Autumn 1993), 5–8.
Gillespie, Diane F., 'Adventures in Common: Investing with Woolfs and "Securitas"', in Helen Wussow and Mary Ann Gillies, eds, *Virginia Woolf and the Common(wealth) Reader* (Clemson, SC: Clemson State University, 2014), 205–11.
Harrison, Brian, *Separate Spheres: The Opposition to Women's Suffrage* (London: Croom Helm, 1978).

---

[37] Leslie Stephen, *Selected Letters of Leslie Stephen*, ed. John Bicknell (London: Palgrave, Macmillan, 1996), 482.
[38] Quoted in Frances Spalding, 166. See also Regina Marler, *Selected Letters of Vanessa Bell* (New York: Pantheon), 386–7.
[39] Virginia Woolf, 'Lady Strachey: Obituary', in *The Platform of Time*, ed. S. P. Rosenbaum (United Kingdom: Hesperus Press, 2007), 110.

Hancock, Nuala, *Charleston and Monk's House: The Intimate House Museums of Virginia Woolf and Vanessa Bell* (Edinburgh: Edinburgh University Press, 2012).

Hankins, Leslie Kathleen, 'Heritage Hoarding: Artifacts, Archives, and Ambiguity, or, The Saga of Virginia Woolf's Standing Desk', in Jane de Gay, Tom Brekin, and Anne Reus, eds, *Virginia Woolf and Heritage* (Clemson, SC: Clemson University Press, 2017), 73–9.

Lee, Hermione, *Virginia Woolf* (London: Chatto & Windus, 1996).

Light, Alison, *Mrs Woolf and the Servants* (NY: Bloomsbury Press, 2008).

Ross, Ellen, ed. *Slum Travelers: Ladies and London Poverty, 1860–1920* (Berkeley and Los Angeles: University of California Press, 2007).

Spalding, Frances, *Vanessa Bell* (London, Ticknor & Fields, 1983).

Stephen, Leslie, *The Mausoleum Book* (Oxford: Oxford University Press, 1977).

Stephen, Julia Duckworth, *Notes from Sick Rooms*, in Diane F. Gillespie and Elizabeth Steele, eds, *Julia Duckworth Stephen: Stories for Children, Essays for Adults* (Syracuse, NY: Syracuse University Press, 1993), 216–40.

Vicinus, Martha, *Independent Women: Work & Community for Single Women 1850–1920* (Chicago, IL: Chicago University Press, 1985).

Woolf, Virginia and Quentin Bell, *The Charleston Bulletin Supplements*, ed. Claudia Olk (London: British Library, 2013).

PART II
TEXTS

CHAPTER 4

PRIVATE WRITINGS

CAROLINE POLLENTIER

'Back from Garsington, & too unsettled to write—I meant to say read; but then this does not count as writing. It is to me like scratching; or, if it goes well, like having a bath' (*L2* 179). Virginia Woolf's self-reflexive comment in this diary entry dated 17 July 1917 playfully suggests the artlessness of private writing, thus relegated to domestic, bodily matters. Similar to how Clive Bell and Roger Fry established a Kantian divide between art and ordinary life—the sphere of aesthetic ends and that of practical uses—Woolf here mockingly looks back on her journal along formalist lines. The trope of 'scratching', however, implicitly complicates such dualism between art and life. Unlike contemporary theorists of everyday life aesthetics, Woolf by no means suggests that 'scratching an itch'[1] could produce an aesthetic experience, but insofar as 'scratching' evokes a somatic phenomenon as well as the technique of writing by hand, it also blurs the divide between art and non-art, at least on a figural level. Despite their moot literariness, these private 'scraps and scratches' (*D3* 67) encode an organic continuum between art and life.

Woolf kept a diary consistently throughout her life and wrote several thousands of letters; she also kept reading notebooks, of which sixty-seven volumes remain.[2] Her private archives of 'scribbling', as she often alluded to these everyday forms of writing, have patently defied critical consensus, being read either as less than art or artworks per se. They can be approached as the proto-artistic epitexts of her published artworks, providing metatextual insights on her published works.[3] Alternatively, they have been revalued as self-conscious artforms, reinscribed within distinctive generic traditions[4]

---

[1] Sherri Irvin, 'Scratching an Itch', *Journal of Aesthetics and Art Criticism* 66 (Summer 2008), 25–35.
[2] See Brenda R. Silver, *Virginia Woolf's Reading Notebooks* (Princeton, NJ: Princeton University Press, 1983).
[3] See, for instance, Anne E. Fernald, '*To the Lighthouse* in the Context of Virginia Woolf's Diaries and Life', in Allison Pease, ed., *The Cambridge Companion to To the Lighthouse* (Cambridge: Cambridge University Press, 2015), 6–18.
[4] On Woolf's relation to the diaristic tradition, see Barbara Lounsberry's *Becoming Virginia Woolf* (Gainesville: University Press of Florida, 2014) and *Virginia Woolf's Modernist Path* (Gainesville: University Press of Florida, 2016).

or aligned with the fragmentary patterns of modernist subjectivities.[5] To revise further this critical divide between life and art—and not just reclaim the artistic value of Woolf's daily writings—entails analysis of more extensive crossings between texts and lives. Private writings testify to what Michel Foucault theorized in his later work as an 'aesthetics of existence'.[6] Foucault extended art to existential techniques of craft by raising a radically democratic question: 'couldn't everyone's life become a work of art?'[7] Binding aesthetics to ethics, Foucault identified ancient correspondences and *hupomnêmata* (commonplace books) as various 'practice[s] of self-examination'[8] constitutive of the aesthetic crafting of *bios*. The subject shapes her life through daily acts of self-care—'regular and deliberate practice[s] of the disparate',[9] which, as Judith Butler argued after Foucault, 'maintain a critical relation to existing norms'.[10]

In the light of Foucault's ethics of self-writing, I propose to read Woolf's notebooks, letters, and diaries as ethical and political technologies of privacy. Woolf's private writings can be apprehended as various 'techniques of living' [11] rehearsing an elusive tension between immediacy and self-consciousness. The archival impulse of her notebooks, the pragmatics of intimacy at work in her letters, and the aesthetics of daily life outlined in her diaries configure various acts of self-making, ranging from social critique to psychological immunity. Woolf's notebooks, letters, and diaries can, moreover, only be fully understood within their own technological era in which, as Friedrich Kittler stated, 'writing ceased to be synonymous with the serious storage of data'.[12] Woolf was keenly aware of the extent to which her daily 'scribbling' or 'scratching' was becoming increasingly entangled with and replaced by new technologies of recording (the cinema and photography), new communicational technologies (the telegraph, the telephone, radio, and television in its prototypical state) as well as mass-produced journalism—her diaries, letters, and notebooks testify to such intermedial entanglement. While relating these archaic media to the social rise of 'the very private' in modernity (*E6* 226), Woolf mobilized her private 'notes' as untimely techniques of resistance, generating founding, if vulnerable, forms of micro-power.

As interrelated quotidian disciplines of writing, the vast corpus of Woolf's private texts can first be considered within the frame of an ordinary day. While she usually wrote fiction in the morning and took notes for her essays in the afternoon—what she

---

[5] See Susan Sellers, 'Virginia Woolf's Diaries and Letters', in Sue Roe and Susan Sellers, eds, *The Cambridge Companion to Virginia Woolf* (Cambridge: Cambridge University Press), 109–26.

[6] Michel Foucault, 'Self Writing', in *Essential Works of Foucault 1954–1984*, vol. 1, ed. Paul Rabinow, trans. Robert Hurley et al (New York: New Press, 1997), 207.

[7] Foucault, 'On the Genealogy of Ethics: Overview of Work in Progress', in *Essential Works of Foucault*, vol. 1, 261.

[8] Foucault, 'Self Writing', 219.

[9] Foucault, 'Self Writing', 212.

[10] Judith Butler, *Giving an Account of Oneself* (New York: Fordham University Press, 2005), 17.

[11] Butler, *Giving an Account*, 221.

[12] Friedrich A. Kittler, *Discourse Networks 1800/1900*, trans. Michael Metteer (Stanford: Stanford University Press, 1992), 229.

called 'read[ing] with a pen & notebook, seriously' (*D5* 145), Woolf turned to her journal during intervals of time (her 'usual 5 minutes for notes' (*D5* 144)), most often just after teatime when she was left 'in tatters' (*D2* 198) by her visitors—but also just before lunch or dinner (she notes she has just '25 minutes to lunch' or '30 minutes to fill' (*D4* 25; *D4* 30)). Embedded in daily life, diary writing repeats each day 'so as to make each day last longer' or to 'revive' a 'skeleton day' (*D4* 17; *D3* 248) but also helped Woolf structure her day, when she turned it into a calendar or a schedule for writing and reading. She recurringly mentions gaps or blank leaves, apologizing for 'the anaemic state' of her journal (*D3* 76). Missing sequences of time, pictured as 'a tap left running' (*D1* 239) might be recorded in her letters, especially letters devoted to daily facts—'diary letters' as opposed to 'dumb letters […] leaving immense tracts unnamed' (*D5* 452; *D3* 242). Woolf sometimes wrote several letters a day and usually made sure, before going on trips abroad, to give her correspondents a list of addresses to keep receiving mail around Europe. Referring indiscriminately to her diary and letters as 'notes', Woolf considered both media, together with the notebooks, as daily archives, defined by the mundane but fundamental mnemonic technique of writing by hand.[13]

This archival function underpins Woolf's reading notebooks, which constitute highly composite texts.[14] When revising old essays or preparing new ones, Woolf compiled various sets of notes originally written on loose pages, sometimes torn from spiral notepads, so that she mixed multiple periods of time into single bound notebooks. She did not annotate her books, using instead this mnemonic technique of notation, with lists of quotations facing a column of page numbers. Quotations occasionally alternated with first-hand reading impressions and fragments of drafts, sometimes blurring the line between life and writing—volume XIX, for instance, features a quote from Catullus evoking her dead brother and a map of London sketched while devising *Mrs Dalloway*. Within such heterogeneity, one can retrace a technical evolution in the way Woolf adapted the act of collecting textual fragments over the course of her career. From 1905 onwards, her notebooks testify to a vast enterprise of literary criticism, which, from 1931 up to the publication of *Three Guineas*, partly transformed into an archaeology of the social.

The preface of *The Common Reader*, based on a sentence by Samuel Johnson first registered in volume XXXVIII, self-reflexively picked up on the intertextual process of notetaking at work in the six notebooks from which the volume itself resulted seven years later[15]—Woolf's Montaignian common reader, like the matter of his book, collects 'whatever odds and ends he can come by' (*E4* 19). More than mere systems of notation,

---

[13] Apart from some reading notes for *Three Guineas*, some professional correspondence, and typewritten letters addressed to correspondents who could not read her handwriting, Woolf's private writings were mostly written by hand, in a variety of inks and pens, and very rarely rewritten (the 1940 letter to Ben Nicolson is a notable exception (*L6* 421–2)).

[14] The holographs have been classified by Brenda R. Silver but remain unpublished. Michèle Barrett and Brenda R. Silver are currently working on the digitization of the notebooks. Silver's numbering of the notebooks will be used below.

[15] See volumes XIX, XXV, XXX, XXXVIII, XLVII, and LXIX.

reading records were for Woolf testcases for a reader-oriented, democratic criticism. She patently included herself in this critical shift of authority—insofar as 'all criticism is done when the book is read', as she states in volume XVIII, her notebooks often record her own immediate reception. In her notes on *The Faery Queen*, for instance, she writes in the first person: 'I have decided to stop reading Faery Queen at the end of the 4th book because I am completely out of the mood.'[16] This first-hand reading experience then turns into the mockingly authoritative, but deeply anti-authoritarian, starting point of her essay: 'The first essential is of course not to read "*The Faery Queen*"' (E6 487). In her last critical projects, Woolf suggested that 'the truest account of reading Shakespeare would be not to write a book with beginning middle and end; but to collect notes, without trying to make them consistent.'[17] As anti-totalizing, lacunary forms of criticism, reading notes suggest a concrete resistance to institutional discourse, affording subversive tactics of daily life as later theorized by Michel De Certeau.[18]

In the eleven notebooks she wrote in preparation for *Three Guineas*, Woolf retooled the private process of commonplacing—the '*captur[ing] [of]* the already-said', to quote Foucault[19]—into a radical project of documentation, at the intersection of sexual and international politics. The thousands of references she identified between 1931 and 1937 in literature, history, philosophy, and modern journalism constituted the groundwork for her pamphlet's extensive footnotes. Woolf's method of quotation became significantly intermedial, as she started collecting journalistic material from which she later selected various clippings.[20] Her three scrapbooks of press cuttings form a series of archival assemblages, in which multiple fragments from various dates and sources are often juxtaposed critically. A single page from volume XL, for instance, features an ironic collage rebutting the totalizing discourse of patriarchy: a typed quote taken from an article on 'Womens Love of Economic Dependence', a second one on 'The Fellows attitude to Oxford and women', a quote in French by George Sand on community, and a typed note on 'Deaths in childbirths'. Woolf recast citations as techniques of counter-interpellation, allowing her to dismantle from within the discursive formation of women. In 1937, the social research project of Mass Observation carried out a comparable work of documentation involving, before the Day Surveys of 12 May, the compilation of a 'library of press-cuttings'.[21] Contrary to the intended objectivity of Mass

---

[16] Woolf, Monk's House Papers, B2m.

[17] Woolf, quoted in Brenda R. Silver, '"Anon" and "The Reader": Virginia Woolf's Last Essays', *Twenty Century Literature* 25 (Fall/Winter 1979), 431–2.

[18] Michel De Certeau, *The Practice of Everyday Life*, trans. Steven Randall (Berkeley: University of California Press, 1988).

[19] Foucault, 'Self Writing', 210.

[20] See Silver, volumes LVIII, LIX, and LX. On Woolf's scrapbooks, see Alice Wood, *Virginia Woolf's Late Cultural Criticism* (London: Bloomsbury, 2013), 74–82.

[21] Mass Observation, *May the Twefth*, eds Humphrey Jennings and Charles Madge (London: Faber and Faber, 2009), 3. Fully engaged in the writing of *Three Guineas*, Woolf declined to review *May the Twelfth* when asked by Kingsley Martin (L6 172).

Observation,[22] Woolf's documentary project rested, however, on a feminist politics of subversion. Woolf harnessed her own genealogy of the present to the interpretive operation of critique, which, as a matter of fact, underpins her juxtaposition of a clipping on the Coronation ('Clothes at Coronation. What Some Peers Must Wear. New Coiffures for Peeresses', 17 February 1937, volume LIX) with anti-pacifist statements made by Church officials.

Woolf's feminism also inflected her committed defence of the epistolary form. As early as 1914, she voiced her support for Margaret Llewelyn Davies's publication of *Maternity: Letters from Working-Women Collected by the Women's Co-Operative Guild* (L2 54) and was, through her own reading of the letter tradition, acutely aware of how the genre participated in the public articulation of female experience. As a relational and yet intimate medium, letters extend the sphere of privacy to 'a public of one' (E5 384) in an alternative, in-between space between private and public. In her essay on Dorothy Osborne's letters—written in October 1928 before giving her Cambridge lectures and revised in March 1932 when she had just conceived the project of *Three Guineas*[23]— Woolf sketched a feminist aesthetics of epistolary privacy, promoting the genre as 'a form of literature' per se and positing it as the prehistory of women's published writing. Picturing the letter as an outsider's artform, Woolf used the ecological and sonic metaphor of 'the undergrowth' to launch a revisionist critique of female silence that finally hinted at Osborne's missing archive—'the letters that Dorothy did not write' (E5 388).

While Woolf reclaimed women's letters as artforms in their own right, the epistolary metaphors she used in her own letters often connoted the immediacy of the domestic sphere. Letter writing comes 'out of the spout of the teapot', it 'is a mere tossing of omelettes' (L5 98; L3 80). Woolf often opposed the dailiness of her letters to art but also valued the loose, unintentional randomness of the epistolary form—she preferred, indeed, the fluency of pen writing over typewriting. She also pondered on the letter writer's interiorization of aesthetic value and public appreciation: 'Do you think people […] do write letters to be published? I'm vain as a cockatoo myself; but I don't think I do that. Because when one is writing a letter, the whole point is to rush ahead' (L5 98). The moot question of artistic intentionality appears earlier as an unresolved contradiction: 'I'm breaking myself of the habit of profuse and indiscriminate letter writing. I can only write, letters that is, if I don't read: once I think I destroy' (L3 63). Woolf's letters are pervaded by such ambivalence between self-consciousness and immediacy, which explains to some extent not just her mixed feelings about letters—her 'appetite for letters' being often overshadowed by the 'misery' and sometimes 'hate' of letter writing

---

[22] See Humphrey Jennings and Charles Madge, 'Poetic Description and Mass-Observation', *New Verse* 24 (February–March 1937): 'the process of observing raises [the observer] from subjectivity to objectivity', 3.

[23] Between the first two versions, published in the *New Republic* and the *Times Literary Supplement* in October 1928 (E4 553–9, 605–9) and the 1932 second *Common Reader* version (E5 382–90), Woolf expanded her feminist reading of Osborne's letters, mainly through counterfactual thinking ('Had she been born in 1527 she would never have written at all') and a final emphasis on Osborne's silence.

(*L*4 153; *L*1 298; *L*4 166)—but also her intermittent consideration of letters as archives. Even though on several occasions Woolf asked her correspondents not to share her letters with posterity, she was very conscious of her own letters as posthumous, public archives of herself; as a matter of fact, she read the correspondence of her parents, of Roger Fry, and Julian Bell, using their letters as biographical material. Deciding nonetheless not to publish her correspondence with Ethel Smyth in particular, she defined epistolary relations as a disparate archive in becoming: 'Lets leave the letters till we're both dead. Thats my plan. I dont keep or destroy but collect miscellaneous bundles of odds and ends, and let posterity, if there is one, burn or not' (*L*4 272).

Alongside this archival self-consciousness, Woolf envisioned letter writing through the technological mutations of communication: 'The wireless and the telephone have intervened. The letter writer has nothing now to build with except what is most private' (*E*6 226). As an archaic medium, contemporary letters have become, she argued, unique if perishable repositories of the 'very private' (*E*6 226). Reflecting on the technological constitution of privacy, Woolf foregrounded a reciprocal relation between the technological emergence of new media—telephony, telegraphy, and mass journalism—and the emergence of new forms of intimacy through the obsolete medium of letter writing. Unlike the metanarrative of decline she sketches in 'The Humane Art', she formulated various vivid defences of modern letters, repeatedly rebutting conservative timelines of the genre such as voiced by literary critic John Bailey, author of the 1899 *Studies in Some Famous Letters*.[24] In 'Modern Letters' and 'Letter to a Young Poet', for instance, she rejected the critical commonplace that 'the art of letter writing is dead' (*E*6 456)—'the art of letter writing has now reached a stage, thanks to the penny post and telephone, where it is not dead […] but so much alive as to be quite unprintable' (*E*6 459). Diagnosing a shift of private communication from voice and news to pen, which she partly explained by the letter's destructibility as a cheap medium (allowing for the burning of secrets), Woolf paradoxically reclaimed letters as new ethical affordances. Instead of turning nostalgically to the belletrist tradition—with which she sometimes mockingly associated her own 'well-known eighteenth-century style' (*L*3 307)—she perceived the very obsolescence of the epistolary medium as a way of remediating intersubjectivity.

Technological matters also surface in her own letters. In a letter from March 1928, Woolf depicts a Transatlantic telephone conversation in optical terms: 'That sort of instant communication between two rooms fascinates me' (*L*3 474). This visual representation of international telephony closely followed the first Transatlantic television signal carried out one month earlier. The fact that letters could actually transform into remote vision is explicitly addressed in a 1935 letter to Julian Bell, then based in China: 'I wish television were now installed and I could switch on and see you, instead of tap tapping' (*L*5 432)—Woolf typed her letters to Julian, who could not read her handwriting. By extending letter writing to a utopian form of television (then known as the Emitron),

---

[24] In her letters, Woolf often took John Bailey as a rhetorical counter-model by referring to his authority in an ironic way. See *L*1 79, 98, 109, 167.

Woolf anchored the archaic artefact within a future-oriented, global network of communication. As a matter of fact, her letters did not just regularly mention other communicational media—mainly phone calls and telegrams—but occasionally incorporated them through an experimental intermedial poetics, when she recorded telephone conversations (*L4* 49, 60; *L6* 322) or compared her letters to wireless telepathy (*L1* 98). By speculating on the place of letter writing in the first media age and enmeshing her own letters with new media, Woolf transformed letters into hybrid technologies of contact.

In an October 1929 letter to her writer friend Gerald Brenan, Woolf pondered on the ways of 'seeing' people (*L4* 95), distinguishing not just the familiar sense of the phrase in everyday language but actual verbal interactions from more authentic relations such as achieved through epistolary distance: 'one tries to imagine oneself in contact, in sympathy' (*L4* 96). Woolf configured epistolary relationality as an ethics of contact producing, rather than replacing, the intimacy of friendship. As Jessica Berman argued more broadly, Woolf negotiates 'a model of ethics that is built upon intimacy rather than radical alterity',[25] a model in which 'intimate relations'[26] are nonetheless predicated on difference rather than similarity. Halfway between closeness and distance, letter writing records the material construction of intimacy. Defining friendship as 'letter writing of some sort', Woolf places the reader—'the other's influence'—as the premise of her letters, every letter being but a way of 'giv[ing] back a reflection of the other person' (*L1* 79; *L5* 317; *L4* 98).[27] In aligning Woolf's 'epistolary performances'[28] with theatre, Catharine R. Stimpson did much to uncover the reader-oriented pragmatics of her letters. Woolf created multiple postures and 'masks' (*L3* 136) for each of her correspondents, but also brought together many voices and fragments of conversation, creating a similar polyglossia to the ones she identified in Madame de Sévigné's or Dorothy Osborne's letters—'the voices mingle' (*E6* 501). Through these multiple selves, epistolary contact developed as a self-reflexive tension between 'sympathy' and 'egotism'—which does not so much imply, indeed, a duality nor similarity between self and other, but rather distributes care within 'entwined' relations (*L4* 108), as Woolf phrased it when describing her somatic entanglement with Vita's pain. In a recurring critique of her epistolary ego, she often depreciated her 'egotistical sheet' or 'invalidish egotism' (*L1* 332; *L4* 23), but simultaneously expressed care for her friends—for instance, she apologizes for 'an egotistical letter which says nothing about [her] really complete sympathy for [Ethel Smyth]' (*L4* 223). The embodied 'entwining' of self and other within both proximity and distance constantly remodels the affective ethics of letter writing, thus giving rise

---

[25] Jessica Berman, 'Woolf and the Private Sphere', in Bryony Randall and Jane Goldman, eds, *Virginia Woolf in Context* (Cambridge: Cambridge University Press, 2012) 467.

[26] Berman, 'Woolf and the Private Sphere', 467.

[27] See also Ian Blyth's analysis of the epistolary gift in 'Woolf, Letter writing, and Diary Keeping', in *Virginia Woolf in Context*, ed. Bryony Randall and Jane Goldman (Cambridge: Cambridge University Press, 2012), 353–61.

[28] Catharine R. Stimpson, 'The Female Sociograph: The Theater of Virginia Woolf's Letters', in D. C. Stanton, ed., *The Female Sociograph: Theory and Practice from the Tenth to the Twentieth Century* (Chicago: University of Chicago Press, 1987), 169.

to experiences of co-being—Woolf uses, for instance, the somatic figure of the membrane to describe herself without her friends (*L4* 203)—as well as experiences of dissensus. Indeed, various forms of misunderstanding and disagreement also come to light through the epistolary exchanges—with Ethel Smyth in particular[29]—leading Woolf to contemplate 'the general impossibility [...] of *any* understanding between two people' (*L4* 328).

Woolf often gave her 'egotistic diary' an epistolary turn by addressing it as a 'confidante', acknowledging it as 'a face of its own' (*D4* 47; *D2* 106; *D1* 317), or even addressing herself as 'Old Virginia' ('greetings, my dear ghost' (*D2* 24)). Although the ethical reflexivity underpinning Woolf's diary is based on the care of the self rather than on the care of others as in the letters, Woolf distanced herself from solipsism in both forms. Woolf's private writings shape a relational subjectivity, situating the self in a polyphonic, communal network of voices, textual fragments, and media. In her diary, Woolf more specifically negotiated the possibility of self-immunity, which one should not associate too readily with introspective isolation. Even as a therapeutic means of 'uncramp[ing]' and 'steady[ing] the fidgets' (*D5* 80; *D4* 318), the recording of daily life constitutes for Woolf the basis for an aesthetics of living as well as a concrete politics of resilience.

Woolf's diaries, first published between 1977 and 1984, originally consisted in thirty notebooks written from her thirties onwards, from 1915 and 1941. The subsequent publication of *The Passionate Apprentice* disclosed a further seven notebooks previously written between 1897 and 1909, including a reference to a diary kept in 1896. From 1891 to 1895, the Stephen children collaborated on a weekly family journal, *Hyde Park Gate News*, first published in 2005. Taking into account the whole of Woolf diaristic oeuvre helps one retrace a life-long engagement with dailiness. As a parody of popular penny papers such as *Tit-Bits*, Woolf's very first diaristic literary undertaking as a child reappropriated the popular journalism of the time. This entertaining, often satirical record of daily life in the Stephen household can be read as Victorian juvenilia, but the fictional personae of the paper (in the 'Extracts from the Diary of Miss Sarah Morgan' of the fifth volume, for instance (*HPGN* 167–70)) anticipated Woolf's later use of diaristic personae, such as the character of Miss Jan in the 1897 diary. In keeping with this early experiment, Woolf's diary later intersected with a plurality of media, as a recording technique of daily life rooted in technological modernity as much as in the diaristic tradition. In 1930, for instance, Woolf tried to regularly incorporate newspaper headlines into a series of entries 'to give this book continuity' (*D3* 332). She also compared her diary to cinema in January 1922: 'I feel time racing like a film at the Cinema. I try to stop it. I prod it with my pen. I try to pin it' (*D2* 158). The diary is also often pictured as telegraphy, associated with urgency (*D2* 14; *D4* 19). Alongside these technological metaphors, Woolf reflected on the diaristic forms she devised to document the everyday. She tried, for instance, to 'record conversations verbatim' by devising theatrical '[s]cenes' (*D2* 251–2), thus turning real persons into a cast of characters (*D2* 252–7); she also used emotional

---

[29] See, for instance, *L4* 352–4.

graphs (*D6* 64), entitled notes as in a commonplace book (*D3* 102–5), and commented on her use of parentheses (allowing one to 'read two things at the same time' (*D3* 106)) as well as present participles—she often condemned the present participle as sloppy diary writing (*D2* 262) but noticed the device helped her in writing the end of *Mrs Dalloway* (*D2* 312).

As a 'technique of living', Woolf's diary documents ways of turning one's life into a work of art, to take up Foucault's words. This is not to say that Woolf's diary aestheticizes everyday life—the diary does not defamiliarize, but rather records the familiar. In the 'stylistics of existence'[30] outlined by Foucault, and more recently developed by literary critics Caroline Levine and Marielle Macé in their distinct rethinkings of formalism,[31] forms shape lives as well as artefacts so that texts map forms of life, and lives can be given significant forms. Though Woolf's meta-aesthetic thinking was influenced by early twentieth-century formalism, her diaries ultimately question dualistic separations between artistic and daily forms, creating instead a self-reflexive continuum between art and the everyday. Instead of considering them as the 'running ground' for her novels (*D5* 90), or conversely, as 'distinct works of art',[32] one could thus rethink them as shared existential forms. As ordinary writings, Woolf's diaries delineate an aesthetics of the everyday extending beyond artworks themselves. In that respect, Foucault's interrogation ('couldn't everyone's life become a work of art?'[33]) becomes an incentive for modernist scholars to explore jointly Woolf's diaries and the diaries of ordinary men and women, such as the five hundred or so diarists of *Mass Observation*—the most important modernist collection of diaries that ran intermittently from 1939 to 1967 in the wake of the 1937 Day Surveys.

If the diaries of Mass Observers, such as that of Lillian Rogers for example, also involved a 'reflexive modern selfhood',[34] what distinguishes Woolf's diaries is arguably their prominent aesthetic reflexivity—Woolf constantly reflected on literature as well as on the diary's potential to become literature. Through frequent meta-aesthetic comments looking back on her journal, she alternatively downplayed and promoted the aesthetic value of her diarizing. She often undermined her 'scribbling', noting that she had 'not thought of a form for this book' (*D4* 89), but very early on, she also saw her diaries as an aesthetic form in becoming: 'I should like to come back and find that the collection has sorted itself & refined itself & coalesced […] into a mould, transparent

---

[30] Michel Foucault, *The History of Sexuality, Volume 3: The Care of the Self*, trans. Robert Hurley (New York: Vintage, 1988), 71.

[31] Caroline Levine, *Forms: Whole, Rhythm, Hierarchy, Network* (Princeton: Princeton University Press, 2015) and Marielle Macé, *Styles. Critique de nos formes de vie* (Paris: Gallimard, 2016). See Macé's rephrasing of Foucault in 'Ways of Reading, Modes of Being', *New Literary History* 44, no. 2 (2013), 213: 'What does it mean to give style to our existence? It is not something reserved for artists, esthetes, or heroic lives, but the distinctive trait of human life[.]'

[32] Sellers, 'Virginia Woolf's Diaries and Letters', 114.

[33] Foucault, 'On the Genealogy of Ethics', 261.

[34] James Hinton, *Nine Wartime Lives: Mass Observation and the Making of the Modern Self* (Oxford: Oxford University Press, 2010), 134.

enough to reflect the light of our life, & yet steady, tranquil, composed with the aloofness of a work of art' (*D1* 266). Woolf subsequently hypothesized that the disjointed, heterogenous form of the diary could become an aesthetic paradigm in itself ('suppose one can keep the quality of a sketch in a finished & composed work?' (*D2* 312)) and even suggested that this non-artistic effect might derive from an intrinsic self-consciousness ('a false anti-literariness' (*D4* 95)). Against formalist theories of the time and outside any systematic thinking, the diary form led Woolf to apprehend how the external finalities of prosaic life might grow into, overlap with, or even originate from internal aesthetic finalities.

Woolf's meta-aesthetic reflection on diarizing could equally be read as a meta-ethical reflection on life, defining '*bios* as material for an aesthetic piece of art'.[35] This continuum between aesthetics and ethics becomes salient in her consistent engagement with Michel de Montaigne throughout the diaries. Woolf did not simply quote the *Essays*, she sketched, like Montaigne, a heterogeneous 'art of life' out of the recording of 'every fact of existence' (*E4* 73, 77). As Nicola Luckhurst has shown, Woolf kept misquoting Montaigne in her diaries, turning his thought into an ethical leitmotiv and a psychological spur—'But enough of death, it is life that matters' (*D2* 301).[36] The ethics of Woolf's diaries, like that of Montaigne's *Essays*, is discontinuous: she quotes Wordsworth on happiness (*D6* 78), Seneca on unhappiness (*D5* 282), supports a philosophy of the free soul (*D5* 68), notes the importance of 'hug[ging] the present moment' (*D5* 262), and insists above all on the value of change, presenting it as an artistic value that might extend to life—'Never settle, is my principle in life'; 'to upset everything every 3 or 4 years is my notion of a happy life' (*D2* 259; *D3* 70). She uses in particular the Montaignian metaphor of the weathercock, after devoting a whole diary entry to the extreme feeling of unhappiness caused by a humiliating remark made to her about her hat. Reflecting back on her unhappiness in the next entry, she writes: 'These reflections about the hat read rather amusingly I think. What a weathercock of sensibility I am!' (*D3* 91).[37] The image of the weathercock has elsewhere been analysed in parallel with neurology,[38] but the fact that Woolf derives it from Montaigne's 'Of Constancy' should not go unnoticed. Montaigne applies this empiricist image to ordinary men: 'all the vulgar, and we are all of the vulgar, would have their belief as turnable as a weathercock; for the soul […] would be forced incessantly to receive other and other impressions'.[39] By appropriating the figure of the

---

[35] Foucault, 'On the Genealogy of Ethics', 260.

[36] See Nicola Luckhurst, '"To Quote my Quotation from Montaigne"', in Sally Greene, ed., *Virginia Woolf: Reading the Renaissance*, (Athens: Ohio University Press, 1999), 41–64.

[37] See also *D4* 44.

[38] Susie Christensen, '"What a weathercock of sensibility I am!": Sensory Self-observation in the Diaries of Virginia Woolf and "A Human Experiment in Nerve Division" by Henry Head and W. H. R. Rivers', *Textual Practice* 29, no. 6 (2015), 1117–42.

[39] Michel de Montaigne, 'Apology for Raimond de Sebonde', *Essays of Michel de Montaigne*, vol. 2, trans. Charles Cotton (London: G. Bell and sons, 1913), 280.

weathercock, Woolf reworks it as a cathartic cognitive affordance—a 'metaphor we live by', as understood by Lakoff and Johnson.[40]

Metaphors, as they are used in the diary form, are cognitively embedded in everyday life. 'Why do I write such metaphors?' Woolf asks (D3 199). She sees herself as a weathercock, pictures the reader's mind as an aeroplane propeller (D5 151), life as a strip of pavement (D2 72), her friendships as a game of marbles (D2 157), days as pebbles on a beach (D2 234), diary writing as dancing on hot bricks (D5 55), humanity as a vast wave (D3 22); she also famously sees 'a fin passing far out', an image first employed to 'make a note of a curious state of mind' (D3 113) before being reincorporated in her fiction. These numerous conceptual crossings cannot be understood as preliterary or proto-artistic; they amount instead to mundane acts of creativity performing self-reflexive acts of 'reviewing', according to Foucault's analogy between criticism and the technique of self-examination—'reviewing one's day'.[41] The critical act of reviewing that pervades the diaries—Woolf includes reading notes in her entries, shows how her reading superimposes itself on her day, and even envisions a critical book written in 'the diary form' (D5 210)—extends into ethical forms of self-care, as in this entry dated 5 September 1927 in which Woolf soothes her 'agitated mind' with therapeutic metaphors, after an upsetting day trip to Peacehaven, a seaside town of mass tourism: 'The mind is like a dog going round & round to make itself a bed. So give me new & detestable ideas, I will somehow trample a bed out of them' (D3 155–6). As Woolf refigures the unaesthetic 'turning & tumbling energy' of Peacehaven into a soothing kinetic simile, her diary entry finally affords a satisfying object of craft, an imaginary bed.

The cathartic effect Woolf ascribes to diary writing alerts us to the politics of self-immunity she binds to this private technology in wartime. 'Immunity is an exalted desirable state', Woolf writes in July 1932 (D4 117). This hyperbolical feeling is then recorded as an existential state of ataraxia—'its a holy, calm, satisfactory flawless feeling—To be immune, means to exist apart from rubs, shocks, suffering' (D4 117). 'Private peace', however, is precisely that which is 'invaded'[42] in wartime (D5 213, 131), when, as Hermione Lee puts it, Woolf's diary notes start morphing into 'telegrams from a disaster zone'.[43] On 1 September 1939, the imminence of the war is strikingly cast in the deixis of a present tense: 'War is on us this morning' (D5 232). Now imbricated with the national timescale of the radio broadcast, the diary gives way to an hour-by-hour schedule of the country's entry into war two days later: 'This is I suppose certainly the last hour of peace. The time limit is out at 11. PM to broadcast at 11. 15' (D5 233). Substituting itself with collective listening, the journal entry first implicitly quotes the BBC's urging listeners

---

[40] George Lakoff and Mark Johnson, *Metaphors We Live By* (Chicago: University of Chicago Press, 1980).

[41] Foucault, 'Self Writing', 219.

[42] Woolf used this war metaphor shortly after Hitler's invasion of Austria and her acquiring a new radio.

[43] Hermione Lee, *Virginia Woolf* (New York: Vintage, 1999), 704. On the presence of war in Woolf's diaries, see Barbara Lounsberry, *Virginia Woolf, the War Without, the War Within* (Gainesville: University Press of Florida, 2018).

to 'stand by' for Chamberlain's declaration of war ('L. & I "stood by" 10 minutes ago') but finally desynchronizes itself from the public announcement, left unrecorded. Very quickly, Woolf identified her diary as an alternative practice of resistance in the world conflict: 'the only contribution one can make—This little pitter-patter of ideas is my whiff of shot in the cause of freedom' (*D5* 235). A couple of months later, she extended this pacifist reclamation of private thinking in the essay 'Thoughts on Peace in an Air Raid', but the diary, in which she initially recorded her intuition about thinking as fighting[44] as well as the accident of the German plane later staged in the essay,[45] remains singular in its form and function—'this book will serve to accumulate notes' (*D5* 235). The wartime logic of parataxis—featuring increasing juxtapositions and short, elliptical nominal sentences—exemplifies a stylistic and existential bareness that suggests at once the immediacy of vulnerability and a strategy of resilience. Woolf explicitly privileges 'little exact notes' over 'reflections', explaining that 'she could read notes only' during the war (*D5* 233, 304). Even as they reveal the subject's precarious state—her 'generalized capacity to be killed',[46] to quote Roberto Esposito—bare notes function as a communal and yet idiosyncratic medium of immunitarian resistance. Outside the national endeavour publicly broadcast by the radio and newspapers, the journal turns into an archaic biopolitical technology, documenting the endurance of *bios* in wartime. While in her ever-shifting meditation on 'the drifting material of life' Woolf often suggested that 'most of life escapes' (*D1* 266; *D2* 298)—in Foucault's words, 'discourse is not life'[47]—her private notes bear witness, in their very precariousness, to the political persistence of daily living through writing.

Selected Bibliography

Berman, Jessica, 'Woolf and the Private Sphere', in Bryony Randall and Jane Goldman, eds, *Virginia Woolf in Context* (Cambridge: Cambridge University Press, 2012) 461–74.
Blyth, Ian, 'Woolf, Letter writing, and Diary Keeping', in *Virginia Woolf in Context*, ed. Bryony Randall and Jane Goldman (Cambridge: Cambridge University Press, 2012), 353–61.
Butler, Judith, *Giving an Account of Oneself* (New York: Fordham University Press, 2005).
deCerteau, Michel, *The Practice of Everyday Life*, trans. Steven Randall (Berkeley: University of California Press, 1988).
Esposito, Roberto, *Communitas: The Origin and Destiny of Community*, trans. Timothy Campbell (Stanford: Stanford University Press, 2017).
Fernald, Anne E., '*To the Lighthouse* in the Context of Virginia Woolf's Diaries and Life', in Allison Pease, ed., *The Cambridge Companion to To the Lighthouse* (Cambridge: Cambridge University Press, 2015), 6–18.

---

[44] 'This idea struck me: the army is the body: I am the brain. Thinking is my fighting' (*D5* 285).
[45] See *D5* 313 and *E6* 245.
[46] Roberto Esposito, *Communitas: The Origin and Destiny of Community*, trans. Timothy Campbell (Stanford: Stanford University Press, 2017), 13.
[47] Foucault, quoted in Butler, 36.

Foucault, Michel, 'On the Genealogy of Ethics: Overview of Work in Progress', in *Essential Works of Foucault 1954-1984, volume 1*, ed. Paul Rabinow, trans. Robert Hurley et al (New York: New Press, 1997), 253–80.

Foucault, Michel, 'Self Writing', in *Essential Works of Foucault 1954-1984, volume 1*, ed. Paul Rabinow, trans. Robert Hurley et al (New York: New Press, 1997), 207–22.

Irvin, Sherri, 'Scratching an Itch', *Journal of Aesthetics and Art Criticism* 66 (Summer 2008). 25–35.

Kittler, Friedrich A., *Discourse Networks 1800/1900*, trans. Michael Metteer (Stanford: Stanford University Press, 1992).

Lakoff, George and Mark Johnson, *Metaphors We Live By* (Chicago: University of Chicago Press, 1980).

Levine, Caroline, *Forms: Whole, Rhythm, Hierarchy, Network* (Princeton: Princeton University Press, 2015) and

Macé, Marielle, *Styles. Critique de nos formes de vie* (Paris: Gallimard, 2016).

Sellers, Susan, 'Virginia Woolf's Diaries and Letters', in Sue Roe and Susan Sellers, eds, *The Cambridge Companion to Virginia Woolf* (Cambridge: Cambridge University Press), 109–26.

Silver, Brenda R., *Virginia Woolf's Reading Notebooks* (Princeton, NJ: Princeton University Press, 1983).

Stimpson, Catharine R., 'The Female Sociograph: The Theater of Virginia Woolf's Letters', in D. C. Stanton, ed., *The Female Sociograph: Theory and Practice from the Tenth to the Twentieth Century* (Chicago: University of Chicago Press, 1987), 168–79.

CHAPTER 5

EARLY NOVELS AND STORIES (1915–1923)

JOCELYN RODAL

THE period from 1915 to 1923 saw Virginia Woolf searching for new forms of fiction. She sought out 'new shapes' for writing, 'a completely new form', because, amid 'the respectful hostility which is the only healthy relation between old and young', she felt acutely the inadequacy of the traditions that had been handed down to her (*L2* 167; *E3* 384). In 'Modern Novels' (1919), Woolf declared that 'All that fiction asks of us is that we should break her and bully her, honour and love her, till she yields to our bidding, for so her youth is perpetually renewed and her sovereignty assured' (*E3* 36). Between 1915 and 1923, Woolf continually broke and reinvented her own writing, perpetually renewing herself. Her commitment to finding a new method, a new vessel, for fiction was unyielding. That commitment continued throughout Woolf's life: as late as 1931, she wondered if *The Waves* might be 'my first work in my own style' (*D4* 53). Woolf reinvented herself throughout her career. Yet that trend is especially striking in her early writing, when Woolf was still inventing as well as reinventing herself as an author.

Forging something new took time and struggle. Virginia Woolf's early writing is diverse, by turns experimental and careful, brazen and circumspect. In terms of style, her first three novels, *The Voyage Out* (1915), *Night and Day* (1919), and *Jacob's Room* (1922), could hardly be more different from each other. The unifying factor can be found in the determined but often stumbling efforts of a new generation: these three novels are all, haltingly, about young people striving to move forward into a new era. They each centre on protagonists who are coming of age. That can tempt comparisons to the *Bildungsroman*, wherein a young character learns the way of the world, growing from childhood to maturity, but Woolf defies the *Bildungsroman* genre as well, because here the young person herself cannot quite carry us forward: two out of three of these novels end with the deaths of their protagonists, so that we are left with the new era absent the new person, as if it is the reader, and not the character, who is ultimately forced to mature.

Throughout these first novels writing tends to be a shaky ambition, as if indicating ambivalence about the great difficulties of moving literature forward. Writers in these novels struggle to follow through, while those around them often doubt the value of their efforts. In *The Voyage Out* Terence wants 'to write a novel about Silence', but by his own admission he is 'very lazy', and it seems doubtful that he ever will (*VO* 249, 327). In *Night and Day*, Mrs Hilbery spends more than a decade writing a biography that she is unlikely to ever finish. In *Jacob's Room*, Jacob sometimes fancies himself a writer, but he isn't particularly dedicated to it. In fact, in Woolf's early books the one character who does complete significant quantities of writing is William Rodney, but his dramatic verse is not very good, producing 'a sense of chill stupor in the audience' (*ND* 143). William tells us, 'Of course, I've failed, as all the moderns fail' (*ND* 365). Comments such as this, directed against modern literature, spring up again and again in Woolf's first three novels, frequently from the mouths of dubious characters, and yet left uncorrected. In *The Voyage Out*, Mrs Elliott proclaims, '"I don't think people *do* write good novels now—not as good as they used to, anyhow." No one took the trouble to agree with her or to disagree with her' (*VO* 433). In *Jacob's Room*, Jacob remarks that 'the moderns were futile', and explains that 'he never read modern novels' (*JR* 167–8). A good deal of anxiety about the literary future lingers throughout these three novels, as does the occasionally smothering weight of the past, from which younger characters struggle to escape. In that sense Woolf's early work is generally about modernism, in advance of modernism. This writing struggles to imagine a new kind of novel while acknowledging that that new kind of novel does not exist: not quite yet. This essay will examine how Woolf's early work persistently ponders and imagines what a new era of novels will offer, even as Woolf refuses to specify and delimit what has yet to come to pass.

The Voyage Out, Woolf's first book, was published in 1915 after years of torturous rewriting. Christine Froula describes it as a 'protomodernist novel of manners',[1] but it is more accurate to say that it oscillates jarringly between a conventional novel of manners and something utterly strange and new. It settles into Jane Austen-infused parlour conversations for long stretches and then, in the next moment, offers up impressionist wonderments. At its centre is Rachel Vinrace, a young woman who travels to South America, meets an assortment of people, becomes engaged, and then abruptly falls ill and dies. Rachel's naïveté is glaring, and nearly everyone around her tries to remediate it by recommending books. The conservative politician prescribes Burke. A scholarly young man admonishes her to read Gibbon. From her uncle, 'You should read Balzac' (*VO* 192). Rachel's aunt, Helen Ambrose,

> desired that Rachel should think, and for this reason offered books... But when Mrs Ambrose would have suggested Defoe, Maupassant, or some spacious chronicle of family life, Rachel chose modern books, books in shiny yellow covers, books with a great deal of gilding on the back, which were tokens in her aunt's eyes of harsh

---

[1] Christine Froula, *Virginia Woolf and the Bloomsbury Avant-garde* (New York: Columbia University Press, 2005), 39.

wrangling and disputes about facts which had no such importance as the moderns claimed for them. But she did not interfere. Rachel read what she chose, reading with the curious literalness of one to whom written sentences are unfamiliar, and handling words as though they were made of wood, separately of great importance, and possessed of shapes like tables or chairs. (*VO* 137–8)

Everyone around Rachel tells her to read older books, works of tradition, but Rachel insistently chooses whatever she can find that is new. She doesn't explain her preference for modern literature, which seems almost instinctual. Helen perceives Rachel's way of reading as evidence of her ignorance, but it is a beautiful thing to imagine words possessed of the physicality that Rachel imparts to them. After all words *should* be examined as 'separately of great importance', and what a poetry it would be with words that were 'made of wood ... possessed of shapes like tables or chairs'. Woolf employs some strategic vagueness here. We know that Rachel has been reading a good deal of Ibsen ('a brightly-covered red volume') as well as *Diana of the Crossways*, but we never learn what these 'modern books ... in shiny yellow covers' contain. If Rachel physicalizes words, Woolf, for her part, emphasizes the physicality of these modern books as if to avoid describing their contents, perhaps because these particular modern books do not yet exist. Instead, they are hopefully undetermined, a wonder that will come to pass.

The Voyage Out becomes experimental particularly as it draws to a close, first with the chaotic engagement scene, and then further so with Rachel's final illness, as Woolf plunges us into the confusion of her growing delirium, flooding us with overwhelming sensory impressions. Then, with Rachel's death, the novel abruptly resumes the gently satirical parlour conversations that we had been accustomed to before, but something has changed: the strangeness of Rachel's death has shaken our trust in the pattern on which those dialogues rested, rendering them weird and new. E. M. Forster declared that these closing chapters 'have an atmosphere unknown in English literature'.[2] By ending *The Voyage Out* with her most strikingly experimental passages and her most avant-garde narrative decisions, Woolf renders the book itself an odd kind of literary history, one that seems to chart the passage from nineteenth-century forms toward something surprising and hitherto unseen. As the story comes to a close it is newly tempting to imagine *The Voyage Out* itself as one of the 'modern books ... in shiny yellow covers' that Rachel reads but never invites us inside.

Night and Day was often accused of being a step backwards, seeming to resemble the books Helen might recommend rather than one of Rachel's modern yellow volumes. In an early review Katherine Mansfield described it as 'a novel in the tradition of the English novel. In the midst of our admiration it makes us feel old and chill: we had never thought to look upon its like again!'[3] Mansfield was not alone in this view. Forster

---

[2] E. M. Forster, 'A New Novelist' [1915], in Robin Majumdar and Allen McLaurin, eds, *Virginia Woolf: The Critical Heritage* (London: Routledge, 1975), 52–5, at 54.

[3] Katherine Mansfield, 'A Ship Comes into Harbor' [1919], in Majumdar and McLaurin, eds, *Virginia Woolf: The Critical Heritage* (1975), 79–82, at 82.

described *Night and Day* as 'a deliberate exercise in classicism'.[4] Woolf herself seemed to submit to this opinion when she told a friend, years later, that in writing it she had made herself 'copy from plaster casts, partly to tranquillise, partly to learn anatomy. Bad as the book is, it composed my mind, and I think taught me certain elements of composition' (*L4* 231). However, there is reason to be careful about how we read this admission from Woolf. As Suzanne Raitt has pointed out, Woolf often made comments that might 'appear to authorise developmental readings of her *œuvre*'.[5] The trouble with developmental readings is that they both undervalue Woolf's early work and risk imposing a false inevitability, understanding her future writing as if it were, *ex post facto*, predetermined. *Night and Day* deserves to be examined on its own terms. Yet that novel is also about the past and future of literary production, rendering it difficult to think about without reference to all that came before and after.

Although the style of *Night and Day* is generally traditional,[6] it revolves around a yearning to express modernity. Its early working title was *The Third Generation* (later *Dreams and Realities*) and indeed it depicts a younger generation who look back at the accomplishments of their Victorian forebears and dream of what they will achieve in their own day. Four young people are at the centre of *Night and Day*: William Rodney and Ralph Denham each dream of writing books; Mary Datchet works for women's suffrage and later for a socialist society; Katharine Hilbery, the protagonist, longs to study mathematics. To work in mathematics as a woman in 1919 was itself a brave break with expectations, but Katharine's family heritage further pulls against her ambitions. Katharine's grandfather was a renowned poet, and she chafes at the burden of that heritage, and against the weight of literary tradition that it imposes. Katharine knows she must somehow break free from the past, even as she acknowledges not knowing how:

> Perhaps it is a little depressing to inherit not lands but an example of intellectual and spiritual virtue; perhaps the conclusiveness of a great ancestor is a little discouraging to those who run the risk of comparison with him ... The glorious past, in which men and women grew to unexampled size, intruded too much upon the present, and dwarfed it too consistently, to be altogether encouraging to one forced to make her experiment in living when the great age was dead. (*ND* 33)

Katharine chooses mathematics, and not literature, as her vocation directly because of her own family's storied literary past. 'Isn't it difficult to live up to your ancestors?' Ralph asks Katharine. 'I dare say I shouldn't try to write poetry', Katharine replies (*ND* 10). Yet Katharine's mathematics quickly begins to evoke a new kind of writing, because

---

[4] E. M. Forster, 'The Novels of Virginia Woolf' [1926], in Majumdar and McLaurin, eds, *Virginia Woolf: The Critical Heritage* (1975), 171–8, at 173.

[5] Suzanne Raitt, 'Finding a Voice: Virginia Woolf's Early Novels', in Sue Roe and Susan Sellers, eds, *The Cambridge Companion to Virginia Woolf* (Cambridge: Cambridge University Press, 2000), 29–49, at 29.

[6] There has been some debate on this point. See Elizabeth Outka, 'The Transitory Space of *Night and Day*', in Jessica Berman, ed., *A Companion to Virginia Woolf* (Chichester: Wiley, 2016), 55–66.

Woolf repeatedly and reliably describes it in terms of written marks on paper, very much like the physicalized modern books that Rachel attends to. Katharine's mathematics are 'sacred pages of symbols and figures' (*ND* 480). She 'cast her mind alternately towards forest paths and starry blossoms, and towards pages of neatly written mathematical signs' (*ND* 226). Woolf describes the written form of mathematics rather than its intellectual content, and Katharine treasures and romanticizes the material manifestations of her study. While Katharine insists that 'in her mind mathematics were directly opposed to literature' (*ND* 40), that opposition is complicated by Woolf's choice to describe mathematics consistently in terms of the written form it shares with literature. In fact, although Katharine claims to dislike literature, her dislike is particular to traditional writing such as William's, and to the writing of previous generations, by which she feels cowed. She nurtures a quiet interest in newer writing:

> Katharine did her best to interest her parents in the works of living and highly respectable authors; but Mrs Hilbery was perturbed by the very look of the light, gold-wreathed volumes, and would make little faces as if she tasted something bitter as the reading went on; while Mr Hilbery would treat the moderns with a curious elaborate banter such as one might apply to the antics of a promising child. (*ND* 103–4)

As Katharine struggles to attain independence from the past, these 'light, gold-wreathed' modern novels push back against an older generation that regards them as 'the antics of a promising child'. Modern novels, like Katharine, are doing battle to make their adulthood recognized. And Katharine's ardent desire to strike out on her own, to do the opposite of her storied literary ancestors, poses a tempting analogy with Woolf, who in 1919 was determined to write something very different from the writing of her own celebrated Victorian family (from her father Leslie Stephen to her relation by marriage William Makepeace Thackeray).[7] In this way, *Night and Day* is about the struggle toward modernism: Woolf's struggle toward modernism.

Night and Day follows a marriage plot, ending in two engagements, part of what led Mansfield to declare that 'It is impossible to refrain from comparing *Night and Day* with the novels of Miss Austen.'[8] However, as Jane Marcus has pointed out, for the heroines of *Night and Day* 'both marriage and the rejection of marriage are the means to an end, domestic peace and freedom to work ... We expect these marriages to produce not babies, but books.'[9] Katharine in particular hopes that by marrying she will at last become able to work, envisioning with marriage 'a pile of books in her hand, scientific books, and books about mathematics and astronomy which she had mastered' (*ND* 141). In the novel's closing pages, she and her fiancé Ralph imagine their future:

---

[7] Early in her career Woolf sometimes bristled at intimations that in writing she was simply following familial tradition. See, for example, *L*1 306.

[8] Katherine Mansfield, 'A Ship Comes into Harbor', in Majumdar and McLaurin, eds, *Virginia Woolf: The Critical Heritage* (1975), 79–82, at 82.

[9] Jane Marcus, *Virginia Woolf and the Languages of Patriarchy* (Bloomington: Indiana University Press, 1987), 27.

> Together they groped in this difficult region, where the unfinished, the unfulfilled, the unwritten, the unreturned, came together in their ghostly way and wore the semblance of the complete and the satisfactory. The future emerged more splendid than ever from this construction of the present. Books were to be written, and since books must be written in rooms ... they sketched a habitation for themselves upon the outline of great offices in the Strand and continued to make an account of the future. (*ND* 537)

Night and Day ends imagining the books that are yet to be written. It works to envision 'the unwritten' with 'the semblance of the complete and the satisfactory'. In the process, it directly prefigures one of Woolf's later works, because this passage, with its insistence that 'books must be written in rooms', is a definite precursor to Woolf's declaration in *A Room of One's Own* (1929) that a woman must have 'a room of her own and five hundred a year' in order to write (*ARO* 71). If Katharine reimagines marriage, Mary Datchet remains ardently single at the end of *Night and Day*, thus retaining a room of her own.[10] With both characters, *Night and Day* contemplates what it will take for women to gain the space in which to write something new.

'The Mark on the Wall' (1917), which Woolf wrote and published while she was at work on *Night and Day*, presents a very different method. Here, for the first time, we see something resembling Woolf's later use of stream of consciousness, the rhapsodic and eclectic musings about thought that themselves compose thought. 'The Mark on the Wall' begins with a physical book—'the steady film of yellow light upon the page of my book'—but the narrator isn't reading it (*CSF* 83). Instead she thinks her own thoughts. And here, finally, we get contemplation of what modern writing will contain, when it does come to pass:

> As we face each other in omnibuses and underground railways we are looking into the mirror; that accounts for the vagueness, the gleam of glassiness, in our eyes. And the novelists in future will realise more and more the importance of these reflections, for of course there is not one reflection but an almost infinite number; those are the depths they will explore, those the phantoms they will pursue, leaving the description of reality more and more out of their stories. (*CSF* 85–6)

Here Woolf specifies some of what she expects modern writing will comprise. Yet even here that content is emphatically multifarious, for 'there is not one reflection but almost an infinite number', and Woolf hopes novelists will pursue a multiplicity of 'depths' and 'phantoms'; her critique of 'reality', perhaps, is that it is menacingly singular, and as such does not make space for the variability of human experiences. In 'The Mark on the Wall' Woolf rebukes the traditions of her childhood, but she objects particularly to the traditions that impose one and only one way of looking, acting, and being: 'There was a

---

[10] When Katharine visits Mary's flat she contemplates how 'in such a room one could work—one could have a life of one's own' (*ND* 286).

rule for everything. The rule for tablecloths at that particular period was that they should be made of tapestry with little yellow compartments marked upon them ... Tablecloths of a different kind were not real tablecloths' (*CSF* 86). The absurdity of this anecdote belies its seriousness, because the stakes of the memory lie in writing and in personhood itself: if tablecloths without little yellow compartments were not real tablecloths, then books of the wrong sort might not be real books; people behaving the wrong way might not be recognized as people. Woolf celebrates the memory of 'How shocking, and yet how wonderful it was to discover' that these rules could be discarded, remembering the 'intoxicating sense of illegitimate freedom' that came from setting them aside, turning instead toward the undetermined future (*CSF* 86). Here the future becomes the opportunity for freedom itself.

This beckons toward why modernity was so important to Woolf. She insisted on change because she was determined to throw out the corsets and cages that the past handed down to the present: she was determined to articulate life as she saw it and not as she was expected to see it, and as such she insisted on breaking the groundless rules that writers too often took for granted. Her protest was not against history or tradition in itself but against the blindness toward the variability of individual human life that history risked imposing. In the opening lines of 'Modern Novels', Woolf declares that 'In making any survey ... of modern fiction it is difficult not to take it for granted that the modern practice of the art is somehow an improvement upon the old'; fighting this impulse to treat modernity as an intrinsic good, Woolf insists instead that over the centuries 'we do not come to write better; all that we can be said to do is to keep moving' (*E3* 31). Modernity is no better than history, but 'the problem before the novelist at present, as we suppose it to have been in the past, is to contrive a means of being free to set down what he chooses' (*E3* 34–5). That is, the problem of *now*-ness is ultimately a problem of freedom.

This essay has, up to this point, used 'modern', 'modernity', and even 'modernism' in a slightly naïve way, to refer simply to that which was insistently different from whatever had come before: avowing change, but leaving that change notably unspecified. That non-specific usage follows from Woolf herself, who pondered and returned to the modern throughout her early writing in a way that was insistent and yet carefully undetermined: because if the modern was to be free, then it must not be pinned down. The word itself comes up again and again in her work, and Woolf repeatedly used it to head her essays (e.g. 'Modern Novels' (1919), 'Modern Essays' (1922)), but in those essays and elsewhere she generally defends the modern while labouring to avoid defining it. Occasionally she did hazard a guess as to what had changed: in 'How it Strikes a Contemporary' (1923) she puts the Great War at the origin of the shift (*E3* 357), and in a draft of 'Character in Fiction' (1924) she posits that it might stem from Freud—although she notably removes that specification from the published essay (*E3* 504, 421). More often she simply insists that there has been a great change, and refuses to specify the nature of the change, not wanting to delimit or contain it in any way. She would do this most famously in 'Character in Fiction', with her assertion that 'on or about December 1910 human character changed', specifying the date (maddeningly) but not the nature of the change itself (*E3* 421). As Jesse Matz has pointed out, this kind of strategic non-specification was a pattern throughout Woolf's essays on modern fiction:

> [S]he winningly advises modern writers to trade material detail for 'life itself', but she does not say what 'life itself' is, or how modern fiction will treat it. In fact she ends her essays on modern fiction admitting failure—failure to come up with any alternative, and failure to replace Edwardian Materialism with credible new conventions. Failure, if anything, is her answer to Arnold Bennett, since failure is a sure sign of the effort to make it new. But of new terms for modern fiction Woolf offers none.
>
> She offers no positive alternative to 'Materialism' in part because she wants to keep the field open. Her adversary is less Bennett's writing than his rules... Had she simply switched modernist rules for Edwardian ones, Woolf would have traded one trap for another.[11]

A growing body of work has investigated how Woolf used various kinds of semantic non-specification to afford authorial freedom. Megan Quigley has argued that Woolf characteristically leaned on vagueness as a positive good in her writing.[12] Dora Zhang has attended to Woolf's use of demonstratives to circumvent limited descriptions.[13] An essay of my own examines how Woolf placed deliberately undetermined figures at the centre of her novels.[14] Matz lays out how she used non-specification to particularly impressive ends in her essays on modern fiction. In this vein, Woolf often used the word 'modern' as a kind of placeholder for her hopes for how writing might break free from the limitations of the past. To define exactly how it would do so risked imposing a new set of limitations, and so she found roundabout ways to express the thing without delimiting it.

Jacob's Room does battle at every turn to keep its subject undetermined in this way. The narrator frequently professes uncertainty regarding the character of her protagonist. Toward the end of the novel she wonders, 'how far was he a mere bumpkin? How far was Jacob Flanders at the age of twenty-six a stupid fellow?' and her questions go unanswered (*JR* 214). In 1922 an early review declared that 'We do not know Jacob as an individual, though we promptly seize his type',[15] and contemporary scholars have generally agreed. Julia Briggs describes Jacob as 'both unknown and unknowable'.[16] Christine

---

[11] Jesse Matz, *Literary Impressionism and Modernist Aesthetics* (New York: Cambridge University Press, 2001), 174.
[12] Megan Quigley, *Modernist Fiction and Vagueness: Philosophy, Form, and Language* (New York: Cambridge University Press, 2015).
[13] Dora Zhang, 'Naming the Indescribable: Woolf, Russell, James, and the Limits of Description', *New Literary History* 45, no. 1 (Winter 2014), 51–70.
[14] Jocelyn Rodal, 'Patterned Ambiguities: Virginia Woolf, Mathematical Variables, and Form', *Configurations* 26, no. 1 (Winter 2018), 73–101.
[15] Unsigned review, *Times Literary Supplement* [1922], in Majumdar and McLaurin, eds, *Virginia Woolf: The Critical Heritage* (1975), 95–8, at 97.
[16] Julia Briggs, *Virginia Woolf: An Inner Life* (Orlando, FL: Harcourt, 2005), 93.

Froula writes that 'he is at once an elusive being no net of words can capture and ... a puppet moved hither and thither by fate'.[17]

Jacob's Room is littered with descriptions of characters reading, and, especially, of characters writing. It begins with Jacob's mother writing a letter, 'pale blue ink' 'slowly welling from the point of her gold nib', and it ends with her gazing in shock at Jacob's 'letters strewn about for anyone to read' after he has died (*JR* 3, 246). In between characters are forever taking pen to paper. The focus here is most often on letter writing, which *Jacob's Room* contemplates as 'the sheet that perishes'—unlike literature, 'the sheet that endures' (*JR* 126). Yet the most striking thing about letters in *Jacob's Room* is how very often they *don't* perish, as with the personal letters that linger in Jacob's room after he is gone. In fact, in *Jacob's Room* contemplations of letters very often seem to become contemplations of books,[18] but these are not the undetermined books of the future. Instead these are books already written, with all the accompanying discomforts of completion: 'for to see one's own envelope on another's table is to realize how soon deeds sever and become alien. Then at last the power of the mind to quit the body is manifest, and perhaps we fear or hate or wish annihilated this phantom of ourselves, lying on the table' (*JR* 125). This passage echoes the shame that Woolf sometimes felt when she looked back at her own completed writing, as when she described *Night and Day* as 'bad' some ten years after its publication, or when, checking the proofs of *Jacob's Room*, she declared that 'I could depress myself adequately if I went into that. The thing now reads thin and pointless' (*L4* 231; *D2* 199). It can be mortifying to read one's own words after the fact, particularly when we can no longer revoke them.

The future offers the comfort of having not yet arrived, and having thus not yet disappointed us. When the future becomes the present so many of its possibilities must naturally shrivel. *Jacob's Room* occupies a futurity that Jacob himself can never enjoy, insofar as it was published in 1922, four years after the Great War—which ended his life—had in turn ended. Thus this strange little novel exists in a future that can never quite be reached even as it is also forced, like Jacob himself, to turn always toward the past. Unlike Rachel and Katharine, Jacob's literary tastes turn to the past. He prefers the Elizabethans and the Greeks, 'and Fielding if you must read novels' (122). But he sees this preference as forward-looking, and he is filled with brash ambitions for the future:

> But what brought Jacob Flanders to read Marlowe in the British Museum?
> Youth, youth—something savage—something pedantic. For example, there is Mr Masefield, there is Mr Bennett. Stuff them into the flame of Marlowe and burn them to cinders. Let not a shred remain. Don't palter with the second rate. Detest your own age. Build a better one. And to set that on foot read incredibly dull essays upon

---

[17] Froula, *Virginia Woolf and the Bloomsbury Avant-Garde*, 63.
[18] John Lurz argues that, when *Jacob's Room* exhorts 'Let us consider letters' (*JR* 125), 'The pun is obvious: let us think about the correspondence we write to each other as well as the alphabetic building blocks of written signification.' John Lurz, *The Death of the Book: Modernist Novels and the Time of Reading* (New York: Fordham University Press, 2016), 120. See also Rachel Hollander, 'Novel Ethics: Alterity and Form in *Jacob's Room*', *Twentieth Century Literature* 53, no. 1 (Spring 2007), 40–66.

Marlowe to your friends. For which purpose one must collate editions in the British Museum. One must do the thing oneself. Useless to trust the Victorians, who disembowel, or to the living, who are mere publicists. The flesh and blood of the future depends entirely upon six young men. And as Jacob was one of them, no doubt he looked a little regal and pompous as he turned his page. (*JR* 145–6)

Marlowe is Jacob's response to his 'own age', and he is comfortably convinced that he will 'build a better one', because although for readers his death in the war often feels inevitable, Jacob never sees it coming. Yet Woolf's ricocheting use of free indirect discourse in this passage lays bare the fact that although she has built this book around Jacob, she will not be entrusting her future to him. Her jabbing satirical critiques of Jacob ('something savage—something pedantic', 'incredibly dull essays upon Marlowe', 'he looked a little regal and pompous') alternate sharply with lines that are distinctively in Jacob's own voice ('Stuff them into the flame of Marlowe and burn them to cinders'; 'The flesh and blood of the future depends entirely upon six young men'). Discomfortingly, as Woolf mocks Jacob, here she also agrees with him: about the Edwardian generation of authors, such as John Masefield, whom Woolf criticized as, unlike Geoffrey Chaucer, a 'self-conscious story-teller', which in her diary became simply 'Why isn't Masefield as good as Chaucer' (*E*4 27; *D*3 71); and Arnold Bennett, who had argued in 1920 that 'intellectually and creatively man is the superior of woman'.[19] Bennett would provoke some of Woolf's angriest—and best—polemics on modern fiction. When Woolf describes Jacob contemplating the future that he intends to make happen, she uses his mind as the vehicle for a peculiar kind of agreement. Because, definitively, Woolf agreed with Jacob that Bennett was 'second rate'. But Jacob is unaware that she is lampooning him, too, for all the same reasons.

One of the oddest things about *Jacob's Room* is how its hopes unpeel from its protagonist. Had Jacob lived, he still could not have been a bearer of the future Woolf hopes to bring about, because he is complicit in the cultural systems that will ultimately kill him.[20] Instead the hopes of *Jacob's Room* can be found in its daring new form, what it offers in the way of a new vision of the novel. These hopes fall particularly onto the shoulders of the novel's diffident and self-referential female narrator, who announces herself repeatedly, doubting her own narrative decisions and openly questioning her own trustworthiness. Her self-doubts contrast strikingly with Jacob's overconfidence, and they promise a self-awareness that he could never muster. In this vein, *Jacob's Room* repeatedly refers to itself by name: 'in the middle of Jacob's room'—'What do we seek through millions of pages? Still hopefully turning the pages—oh, here is Jacob's room' (*JR* 246, 132). This self-referral provides another version of Rachel's 'books in shiny yellow covers', the book within the book, less undetermined and yet even more insistently new.

---

[19] Arnold Bennett, *Our Women: Chapters on the Sex-discord* (New York: George H. Doran, 1920), 112.
[20] See Briggs, *Virginia Woolf: An Inner Life*, 93; Froula, *Virginia Woolf and the Bloomsbury Avant-Garde*, 69–73; and Alex Zwerdling, '*Jacob's Room*: Woolf's Satiric Elegy', *ELH* 48, no. 4 (Winter 1981), 894–913, at 904.

In *Jacob's Room*, with its irresolvable uncertainties and its innovative narrative methods, Woolf did a range of things that had never been done before.

That experimentation, in turn, is exactly what would incite the ire of Bennett (though Jacob's threat to 'burn [him] to cinders' can't have helped). In 1923 Bennett dismissed *Jacob's Room* for 'attach[ing] too much weight to cleverness, which is perhaps the lowest of all artistic qualities'. He concluded that 'the characters do not vitally survive in the mind because the author has been obsessed by details of originality and cleverness'.[21] It bears saying that in one sense Bennett was right: Jacob is not what survives *Jacob's Room*. But what Bennett terms mere 'cleverness' is in fact remarkably light-handed storytelling. It is free indirect discourse jumping lithely from one mind to the next. It is 'myriad impressions—trivial, fantastic, evanescent, or engraved with the sharpness of steel. From all sides they come, an incessant shower of innumerable atoms, composing in their sum what we might venture to call life itself' (*E3* 33). What Bennett derides as mere 'cleverness' could be termed the seeds of modernism. In fact, the great irony of Bennett's brutal review of *Jacob's Room* lies in the blindness that is particular to its temporality. After dismissing *Jacob's Room* Bennett pivots to declare that 'nevertheless ... I am fairly sure that big novelists are sprouting up. Only we do not know where to look for them. Or we cannot recognize them when we see them.'[22] Bennett had found an early novel by a writer whose reputation would, in time, dramatically outstrip his own. But not only did he fail to 'recognize ... the spring of greatness' in her early work, he used it to exemplify the absence of greatness.[23] Bennett accurately described how the expectations of the present can impart blindness toward the future: the irony is that the future emerged from exactly the corner he had most forcefully dismissed.

'Character in Fiction' (1924), in which Woolf responded to Bennett, is by turns brazen and diffident, characterized by 'some very sweeping ... assertions' ('on or about December 1910 human character changed') but also moments of striking humility ('if I speak to you in the first person, with intolerable egotism, I will ask you to excuse me. I do not want to attribute to the world at large the opinions of one solitary, ill-informed, and misguided individual' (*E3* 421)). In this way, it reads a little like the oscillating free indirect discourse of *Jacob's Room*, except that here the daring and circumspect are not two colliding male and female voices, but instead the complex single voice of one brave but self-aware author, challenging the misogyny of literary tradition with all the tools at her disposal. In 'Character in Fiction' Woolf recounts sitting in a train car opposite a Mrs Brown, a stranger who transfixed her imagination, proffering the seeds of a novel: 'The impression she made was overwhelming. It came pouring out like a draught, like a smell of burning ... I believe that all novels begin with an old lady in the corner opposite' (*E3* 425). Woolf's argument hinges on how the literary future emerges from the literary past, because Mrs Brown's train car 'is travelling, not from Richmond to Waterloo, but from

---

[21] Arnold Bennett, 'Is the Novel Decaying?' [1923], in Majumdar and McLaurin, eds, *Virginia Woolf: The Critical Heritage* (1975), 112–14, at 113.

[22] Bennett, 'Is the Novel Decaying?', 114.

[23] Bennett, 'Is the Novel Decaying?', 114.

one age of English literature to the next' (*E3* 430). Woolf declares that great invention has become newly indispensable in the writing of her era. But then, in some ways, her ending to 'Character in Fiction' is sombre. She predicts that 'we are trembling on one of the great ages of English literature', yet she also declares that 'We must reconcile ourselves to a season of failures and fragments.' She closes with an injunction to writers 'never to desert Mrs Brown' (*E3* 436).

Up against that famous essay, Woolf's earlier version, 'Mr Bennett and Mrs Brown'[24] (1923), is remarkable for its hope. The earlier essay is not nearly so bold. Here the famous assertion about December 1910 is nowhere to be found. Here Mrs Brown is a mere possibility, invoked but, like Rachel's yellow books, her story never told. And yet here Woolf's convictions that the literary future is bright are if anything even more stunning than are the sweeping assertions of 'Character in Fiction'. In place of the later version's solemn closing injunction, the earlier essay closes instead with an emphatic and celebratory prediction:

> Let us prophesy: Mrs Brown will not always escape. One of these days Mrs Brown will be caught. The capture of Mrs Brown is the title of the next chapter in the history of literature; and, let us prophesy again, that chapter will be one of the most important, the most illustrious, the most epoch-making of them all. (*E3* 388)

Woolf's insistence—put forward insistently and without justification—that her own era would be 'one of ... the most epoch-making of them all' is remarkable. Here we see all of Woolf's bravery without her evidence. Here she does not characterize Mrs Brown, does not tell us her story: she simply declares that someday someone will. As it happens, Woolf someday would. But it cannot be called prophecy if the prophet is the one who makes the future happen. That isn't future-telling, it's simple determination.

The attempt to read Woolf's early work in and of itself is the effort to view modernism proleptically, to envision what it might have looked like to those determined to make it happen, before it had happened. Woolf's early writing persistently contemplates future novels, and yet describes those novels in a way that is insistently undetermined: because how do you represent something of which the very concept is that it will change the terms of representation? This is the central problem in Woolf's early work, which aspires to bring modernism into being. It is often a struggle to understand an author's early work on its own terms, to avoid seeing it only through the lens of what would follow. Indubitably, Woolf's early writing is no mere preface. But the struggle particular to understanding Woolf's early writing on its own terms is how it itself insists on beckoning toward her later work, especially to *Mrs Dalloway*, which was so much in conversation with *The Voyage Out*, *Night and Day*, and *Jacob's Room* as to recycle characters from all

---

[24] Woolf later republished 'Character in Fiction' under the original title, and so both versions sometimes get referred to as 'Mr Bennett and Mrs Brown'. To avoid confusion, this essay preserves the unique titles for the earlier and later versions.

three.[25] Those first three novels, in turn, are adamantly prescient, at every turn imagining what will come next, even constituted by their vision of what would come next.

Selected Bibliography

Bennett, Arnold, *Our Women: Chapters on the Sex-discord* (New York: George H. Doran, 1920).
Briggs, Julia, *Virginia Woolf: An Inner Life* (Orlando, FL: Harcourt, 2005).
Froula, Christine, *Virginia Woolf and the Bloomsbury Avant-garde* (New York: Columbia University Press, 2005).
Hollander, Rachel, 'Novel Ethics: Alterity and Form in *Jacob's Room*', *Twentieth Century Literature* 53, no. 1 (Spring 2007), 40–66.
Lurz, John, *The Death of the Book: Modernist Novels and the Time of Reading* (New York: Fordham University Press, 2016).
Majumdar, Robin, and Allen McLaurin, eds, *Virginia Woolf: The Critical Heritage* (London: Routledge, 1975).
Marcus, Jane, *Virginia Woolf and the Languages of Patriarchy* (Bloomington: Indiana University Press, 1987).
Matz, Jesse, *Literary Impressionism and Modernist Aesthetics* (New York: Cambridge University Press, 2001).
Outka, Elizabeth, 'The Transitory Space of *Night and Day*', in Jessica Berman, ed., *A Companion to Virginia Woolf* (Chichester: Wiley, 2016), 55–66.
Quigley, Megan, *Modernist Fiction and Vagueness: Philosophy, Form, and Language* (New York: Cambridge University Press, 2015).
Raitt, Suzanne, 'Finding a Voice: Virginia Woolf's Early Novels', in Sue Roe and Susan Sellers, eds, *The Cambridge Companion to Virginia Woolf* (Cambridge: Cambridge University Press, 2000), 29–49.
Rodal, Jocelyn, 'Patterned Ambiguities: Virginia Woolf, Mathematical Variables, and Form', *Configurations* 26, no. 1 (Winter 2018), 73–101.
Zhang, Dora, 'Naming the Indescribable: Woolf, Russell, James, and the Limits of Description', *New Literary History* 45, no. 1 (Winter 2014), 51–70.
Zwerdling, Alex, '*Jacob's Room*: Woolf's Satiric Elegy', *ELH* 48, no. 4 (Winter 1981), 894–913.

---

[25] See Paul Saint-Amour, 'Mrs Dalloway: of Clocks and Clouds', in Jessica Berman, ed., *A Companion to Virginia Woolf* (2016), 79–94, at 92 n1.

CHAPTER 6

MATURE WORKS I (1924–1927)

GABRIELLE MCINTIRE

During the years 1924 to 1927 Virginia Woolf was in the early stages of her mature and most prolific phase of writing, and fully in command of her powers after the critical success of *Jacob's Room* (1922). She worked in multiple genres and for both popular and more strictly literary audiences, producing two of her most important novels, *Mrs Dalloway* (1925) and *To the Lighthouse* (1927), a collection of her own essays, *The Common Reader* (1925), extensive journalism,[1] hundreds of letters and diary entries, and more than a dozen short stories. She also worked as a publisher at her own Hogarth Press. For Woolf, every genre was integral to the whole of her vision, with lessons and inflections pouring across the boundaries of her work. In her diary of October 1924 she stresses the value of her journaling for her creative process: 'in this book I *practise* writing; do my scales; yes & work at certain effects. I daresay I practised Jacob here,—& Mrs D. & shall invent my next book here' (*D2* 319).[2] In each mode she consciously sought to experiment, strove to reinvigorate exhausted literary forms, and emphasized the unique power of poetic language for conveying elusive truths about the ungraspability of identity, self, otherness, and human being-ness. She also consistently problematized what truth is and how it signifies. Truth, for Woolf, is at once crucial, ineffable, and various in its hermeneutics and expressions while it demands stringent efforts at discovery, elucidation, and representation. Indeed, across all of her disparate genres during these years we find a remarkably persistent return to an animating ethical problem: how

---

[1] Julia Briggs points out that Woolf's 'earliest and steadiest earnings derived from reviewing rather than from fiction': *Reading Virginia Woolf* (Edinburgh: Edinburgh University Press, 2006), 63.

[2] Following Rachel Bowlby, Elena Gualtieri 'stresses the fluidity of generic boundaries between Woolf's early journals, her essays and her short stories': *Virginia Woolf's Essays: Sketching the Past* (New York: Palgrave Macmillan, 2000), 18. Christine Reynier also reminds us that most of Woolf's novels are 'surrounded by short stories, leading to them and sprouting from them', and she directs us to Beth R. Daugherty's argument that '"novels grow out of short stories and short stories grow out of novels"': *Virginia Woolf's Ethics of the Short Story* (New York: Palgrave Macmillan, 2009), 8, 150.

best to render, within the confines of language and textuality, what is most true and real about how we exist and relate to both ourselves and the world.³ Her ethics of the page sought to designate, illuminate, and even parse ontologies of truth (and the truths of ontologies), relations, aesthetics, and literary representation, and these preoccupations led her to infuse her novels, stories, essays, and even her journalism with poetry as she sought to do justice to the complexities of what she persistently called the soul.

Woolf believed that literature should not only engage us, but change us. If we allow ourselves to respond to the invitation that the best works offer us (and Woolf does believe there are literary successes and failures) we will be improved; we will be more ethical. But reading well is difficult labour. She confesses, 'It is very rare—the right mood for reading—in its way as intense a delight as any; but for the most part pain' (*D3* 32). As we read Woolf we are absorbing some of what Benjamin Hagen calls her 'sensuous pedagogy', where she 'enjoins [her] readers to hold revelation and reason in concert,'⁴ and one of the best places to turn for a meta-critical addendum to her fiction is her own *The Common Reader*, which can help guide us through her project, like an elaborate manual. In one of the essays, 'On Not Knowing Greek', Woolf proposes that 'novelists are always devising some substitute' for the chorus's 'undifferentiated voices who sing like birds in the pauses of the wind; who can comment, or sum up, or allow the poet to speak himself or supply, by contrast, another side to his conception' (*E4* 43). *The Common Reader* gathers and garners a critical 'chorus' that publicly accompanies and supplements her fiction, singing in its lyrical and deliberately poetic voice that counters and challenges restrictive, established prose-essay forms. The collection offers a playground for her developing ideas about how best to write, passionately inviting readers to consider essential 'truths' about subjects ranging from Greek literature to gender, from the state of 'Modern Fiction' (1921) to biographical and critical sketches of an incredible range of writers including Plato, Chaucer, Montaigne, Shakespeare, Defoe, Addison, George Eliot, Charlotte Brontë, Joseph Conrad, Jane Austen, Tolstoy, Chekov, Dostoevsky, and others, some more obscure. Central to the project of *The Common Reader* is instruction in the ethics of reading, and through the essays Woolf insists that the very act of reading is a core value. Reading, for Woolf, always involves intense encounters with the intimacy of others and otherness: an attempt to bridge the estrangement between the complicated alterities among fictional characters, the author, and the reader. Woolf argues, after Montaigne, that 'to communicate is our chief business' in life (*E4* 76), and she affirms that writing is an effort to communicate, while reading attempts to draw near and invite listening. Communication is almost always troubled, though, in Woolf's fiction, where she renders alienation as an inescapable aspect of human existence and

---

[3] Jessica Berman asserts that 'so much of her writing takes up the question of ethical reality', and points us to the work of Mark Hussey, Ann Banfield, and Martha Nussbaum on the centrality of the ethical domain in Woolf's work: *Modernist Commitments: Ethics, Politics, and Transnational Modernism* (New York: Columbia University Press, 2011), 159.

[4] Benjamin Hagen, 'Feeling Shadows: Virginia Woolf's Sensuous Pedagogy', *PMLA* 132, no. 2 (March 2017), 266–80, at 270

repeatedly stages the radical difficulty of grasping the meaning or intentions of others, frequently suggesting that we are always-already doomed to misreading ourselves and others. Nevertheless, Woolf never abandons desires to find the ground we might have *in common* with other people, across what Jessica Berman describes as a Deleuzeian ethical 'fold in the text that brings subjects into relationship with other subjects across this gap without conflating them, assuming their commensurability, or eliminating their distance'.[5] Woolf titled her collection *The Common Reader*, after all, and this gesture affirms a perpetually reinvented commonality (a being-in-common and a being-in-community) between and among her readers and herself. This feminist, democratizing interpolation wants to include and reach out to everyone who reads it, minimizing disparateness while honouring difference.

The Common Reader also participates in what Lee Oser calls, more broadly, 'the modernist moral project', with Woolf delineating the exercise and activity of truth-seeking as both an ethical call and a supreme pleasure.[6] In reading Plato, Woolf invites us to celebrate with her 'the indomitable honesty, the courage, the love of truth which draw Socrates and us in his wake to the summit where, if we too may stand for a moment, it is to enjoy the greatest felicity of which we are capable' (*E4* 32). The argument is inflected by Woolf's wide reading in Aristotle, who proposes that happiness is possible only through acting justly and bettering the world: happiness is not a stasis point that one achieves and settles into, but 'an activity of the soul in accordance with virtue'.[7] This active ethics-as-foundation for the good life—this love for truth-*seeking*—remains a necessity, for Woolf, for living, reading, and writing. Woolf contends that Austen's continued relevance comes, in part, from her 'exquisite discrimination of human values' (*E4* 150), while it is Chaucer who helps Woolf delineate, ahistorically, 'the morality of ordinary intercourse, the morality of the novel' (*E4* 32). Literature teaches us, and not only intellectually. It facilitates a visceral didacticism that seeps into our bodies: 'as we read [Chaucer], we are absorbing morality at every pore' (*E4* 31), while Plato's dialogues affirm that 'Truth is to be pursued with all our faculties.... we are made to seek truth with every part of us' (*E4* 33). Woolf's quest for truth's meaning thus tries to translate into language-art the palimpsestic nature of values and ideas, the plasticity and permeability of identity, and the elusive dynamism of dialogic exchange. Ethics layer into us, penetrating and shaping us.

But Woolf knows that seeking (or finding) truth is radically un-simple, and that truth is always multifarious, polyvalent, and polydimensional, with singular yet shifting meanings for each of us. In 'On Not Knowing Greek', Woolf emphasizes—steeped, as she was, in the modernist philosophies of T. E. Hulme and G. E. Moore—that 'truth is various; truth comes to us in different disguises; it is not with the intellect alone that we perceive it' (*E4* 46). Both perceiving and representing truth require patient attention

---

[5] Berman, *Modernist Commitments*, 41.

[6] Lee Oser, *The Ethics of Modernism: Moral Ideas in Yeats, Eliot, Joyce, Woolf and Beckett* (Cambridge: Cambridge University Press, 2007), 1.

[7] Aristotle, *Nicomachean Ethics* (Cambridge: Cambridge University Press, 2000), 16.

to overlapping axes of ethics, insight, and aesthetics as well as some degree of uncertainty and epistemological incompleteness; the hermeneutics of truth will always be jostled, unsettled, and troubled, both by the difficulty of discovering any definite truth and, crucially, by the limitations of translating that truth into communicable language or art. To find a just and adequate recognition by others, for instance, means that truth's troubled iterability is also always in contest with the mutability of what Woolf calls the 'soul', which she understands to be in flux, 'restive ... the strangest creature in the world' (*E4* 73).

In 'Modern Fiction', a slightly earlier statement about her writing goals, Woolf maligns realist contemporaries such as 'Mr Wells, Mr Bennett, and Mr Galsworthy' (*E4* 158) as 'materialists' because they fail to capture what really matters: they 'write of unimportant things ... they spend immense skill and immense industry making the trivial and the transitory appear the true and enduring', but, 'Whether we call it life or spirit, truth or reality, this, the essential thing, has moved off, or on, and refuses to be contained any longer in such ill-fitting vestments as we provide' (*E4* 159–60). For Woolf, one of art's most fundamental duties is to represent elusive, quasi-transcendent elements of experience—fragments of *quidditas*, or *whatness*, to borrow from Aquinas. James Joyce stands as her best contemporary example of a writer who does justice to these ineffable elements of our selves that are bound up with neuropsychology, physiology, and even transcendence: his work is 'spiritual; he is concerned at all costs to reveal the flickerings of that innermost flame which flashes its messages through the brain' (*E4* 161).

In 'Character in Fiction' (1924) Woolf outright asks, with some frustration, 'what is reality? And who are the judges of reality'? (*E3* 426), and she declares with a sense of the 'sanguine' that her age is one of 'smashing' and 'crashing': 'we hear all round us, in poems and novels and biographies, even in newspaper articles and essays, the sound of breaking and falling, crashing and destruction' (*E3* 433–4). The 'crashing' and 'smashing' signify the demolition of conventional forms in the face of present realities of rapidly shifting social, cultural, political, and existential landscapes of post-war 1920s British life. Truth itself was changing, and form had to adapt to accommodate its new horizons. Still, she recognized that this renovation of literary textuality inevitably involved frustrations, false starts, and distortions: 'we must reconcile ourselves to a season of failures and fragments', she complains. 'We must reflect that where so much strength is spent on finding a way of telling the truth the truth itself is bound to reach us in rather an exhausted and chaotic condition' (*E3* 435). Modernist innovation did not necessarily mean that 'truth' was suddenly more apparent, only that there were new tools to help expose and grasp it.

Woolf was writing *The Common Reader* during the same period that she was drafting *Mrs Dalloway*, and within this span of intense productivity she composed roughly nine stories about Mrs Dalloway's party, though she only published one of them, 'Mrs Dalloway in Bond Street', in *The Dial* in 1923. The stories offer another sketchbook that clarifies her emerging conviction that writing is ethical only insofar as it strives to render something truthful. In her story, 'The Introduction', the narrator has a sudden insight—one of Woolf's early 'moments of being'—that individual realities are composed of both facts and fictional fantasies, both of which we hold dear:

> One divided life (she felt sure of it) into fact, this essay, and into fiction, this going out, into rock and into wave, she thought, driving along and seeing things with such intensity that for ever she would see the truth and herself, a white reflection in the driver's dark back inextricably mixed: the moment of vision. (*CSF* 184)

Her momentary sense of the permanence of this hazy, dream-like insight of herself as a 'white reflection' on someone else's 'dark back' (whether this means a dark piece of clothing or signifies a veiled comment on race) renders self-knowledge as occurring through an impossible non-'reflection' on something that would, at best, show herself as a shadow. The 'vision' dissipates quickly—it 'wobbled, began melting' (*CSF* 184)—as soon as she encounters the anxiety-provoking strangeness of others (and otherness) in 'the world' (*CSF* 184) of Mrs Dalloway's party where the insincerity of the socius undoes the brief certainty of her personal vision. Similarly, in 'The New Dress', Mrs Dalloway's guest, Mabel, struggles to reconcile her public and private selves in the flux of what she perceives to be a thoroughly disingenuous social milieu: ' "Lies, lies, lies!" ' she exclaims, 'For a party makes things either much more real, or much less real, she thought; she saw in a flash to the bottom of Robert Haydon's heart; she saw through everything. She saw the truth. *This* was true, this drawing room, this self, the other false' (*CSF* 172). In another story, the sarcastically titled 'The Man Who Loved His Kind' (1925), Woolf laments and exposes 'the evil, the corruption, the heartlessness of society' (*CSF* 196), while in *Mrs Dalloway*, Septimus Smith—Mrs Dalloway's double and foil—suffers ontological distress as he echoes Matthew Arnold's desolate statement at the end of 'Dover Beach' (c. 1851) that our world 'Hath really neither joy, nor love, nor light, / Nor certitude, nor peace, nor help for pain':[8] 'For the truth is (let [Rezia] ignore it) that human beings have neither kindness, nor faith, nor charity beyond what serves to increase the pleasure of the moment' (*MD* 80). Woolf's critiques about the 'heartless' qualities of personal attachments continues in *To the Lighthouse*, where Mrs Ramsay reflects on 'human relations,' 'how flawed they are, how despicable, how self-seeking, at their best' (*TL* 58); she later genders this critique to claim that 'human relations' between men and women were the 'worst' since 'Inevitably these were extremely insincere' (*TL* 125). These bleak portraits of 'human relations' continue in Woolf's diary, too, where she worries about 'the slipperiness of the soul', the duplicity of people, and their 'insane instinct for life', which she regards as innately selfish, making a Hobbesian-like judgement about the nature of human connection: 'The truth is people scarcely care for each other' (*D2* 244).

Despite Woolf's pessimism about the human capacity either to face the truth or to tell the truth (even to oneself), she creates two male protagonists in *Mrs Dalloway* who weave through the heart of Clarissa's story driven by a search for meaningful truth: Peter

---

[8] Matthew Arnold, 'Dover Beach', in *Matthew Arnold: Poems* (London: British Library, 2011), 33–4.

Walsh and Septimus Smith. Peter Walsh pleads with Clarissa as a young man at their life-altering break-up scene, '"Tell me the truth, tell me the truth," he kept on saying. He felt as if his forehead would burst. She seemed contracted, petrified. She did not move. "Tell me the truth," he repeated.... "Tell me the truth," he repeated' (*MD* 58). His yearning for direct, unriddled knowledge about what they have meant to each other and what (and whom) Clarissa really wants is excruciating, and underscored by Woolf's *dedoublement* of showing *and* telling, repeatedly, that he is repeating. Clarissa, though, leaves him through silence, refusing to answer his pleas, foreclosing communication or 'truth', and causing trauma. Decades later, while Peter is contemplating whether he should attend Clarissa's party, he ruminates that 'the truth about our soul' is that, 'fish-like [it] inhabits deep seas and plies among obscurities' (*MD* 144). At the party itself Peter confesses to Sally that his romantic relationship with Clarissa 'had spoilt his life', while Sally has carried an entirely disparate version of their love story, believing that 'Clarissa had cared for him more than she had ever cared for Richard' (*MD* 171–2). Septimus Smith—a double for Peter as well as for Clarissa—yearns to discover a single, 'whole', unbroken truth that might break the spell of his shell-shocked depressive terror. He fantasizes that his salvation might come when 'he, Septimus, was alone, called forth in advance of the mass of men to hear the truth, to learn the meaning, which now at last, after all the toils of civilisation—Greeks, Romans, Shakespeare, Darwin, and now himself—was to be given whole to' (*MD* 61). Elsewhere, during one of Septimus's quasi-ecstatic moments, he paraphrases Keats: 'all of this, calm and reasonable as it was, made out of ordinary things as it was, was the truth now; beauty, that was the truth now. Beauty was everywhere' (*MD* 62–3). Keats had chiasmatically posited in 1819, '"Beauty is truth, truth beauty,"—that is all / Ye know on earth, and all ye need to know',[9] and the Romantics remain a super-saturation for Woolf. We begin to see that Woolf constructs a post-Aristotelian and post-Romantic modernist logic that still wants to connect fraught instabilities of truth and self-insight with fragmentary, broken beauty as a mode of fragile, aesthetic awakening. Her philosophical posture infinitely demands that we self-scrutinize, surrender to the ephemerality of insight, and be willing to re-calibrate self-narrativizations with the jarring truths (or lies) of others.

Woolf makes the impulse to find and to know truth a vital concern for almost every major character in *To the Lighthouse*. Central to Lily Briscoe's quest is a persistent longing to get 'at the truth of things' (*TL* 199), which she approaches principally via the maternal in her abstract expressionist avant-garde painting of Mrs Ramsay and James, a secularized version of the Madonna and child. Lily, too, must withdraw from the social sphere in order to confront truth and create: the effort of painting draws Lily 'out of gossip, out of living, out of community with people into the presence of this formidable ancient enemy of hers—this other thing, this truth, this reality' (*TL* 214). Lily's creative method, like Woolf's, borrows from Cubism, which aimed to draw reality on varying

---

[9] John Keats, 'Ode on a Grecian Urn', in *The Complete Poems*, 3rd edition, ed. John Barnard (London: Penguin, 1988).

planes, sometimes asynchronically, offering different angles of vision, prompting the viewer to register the ever-shifting and always plural nature of how we think, perceive, and experience, even as we ourselves change: 'One wanted fifty pairs of eyes to see with, she reflected. Fifty pairs of eyes were not enough to get round that one woman' (*TL* 255). Again Woolf suggests that seeking to render any adequate truth about even a single person, beloved figure, or mother is an impossible task; even if we dare try we must adopt a multiplicity of perspectives.

Mrs Ramsay herself has an 'instinct for truth', even as she finds it 'painful to be reminded of the inadequacy of human relationships, that the most perfect was flawed', and 'could not bear' too much close 'examination' (*TL* 56). Her son, James, remembers her, a decade after her death, as beloved especially because of her singular capacity both to articulate her own truth and to invite truth and welcome it from others; he recollects her as both the mouthpiece of truth and as the ultimate receptacle of *his* truth: 'She alone spoke the truth; to her alone could he speak it' (*TL* 252). Mr Ramsay, too, is preoccupied with truth, though not so much with finding truth as with making others comply with his version of it: 'What he said was true. It was always true. He was incapable of untruth; never tampered with a fact' (*TL* 8). This rigidity that Woolf frames as endemic to both patriarchy and tyranny—a problem she revisits in *Three Guineas* (1938)—compels Mr Ramsay to teach his children that 'life is difficult; facts uncompromising ... one needs, above all, courage, truth, and the power to endure' (*TL* 8–9). Indeed, the Oedipal conflict between Mr Ramsay and James is aggravated precisely because of divergent notions of what is true and what is real or realizable. Mr Ramsay's insistence on possible inclement weather that would forbid a voyage is in near total opposition to Mrs Ramsay's supportive valorisation of James's six-year-old passion-driven imaginative idealism and his desire to travel to the numinous lighthouse—a place and destination across an expanse of sea that corresponds, as symbol, she understands, with the dream-language of children and their truth. Further, it is the tension between Mr and Mrs Ramsay's starkly contrasting ways of seeing what is real or true—and what one might dare to *make* real—that seriously strains their marriage. Years later, in 'A Sketch of the Past', Woolf would describe her own father, Sir Leslie Stephen, as a model for Mr Ramsay: 'tyrannical', oppressive, and 'entrenched away from all truth' (*MB* 106–7).

Part of what is at stake in *To the Lighthouse*, then, are contestations between kinds of truths and versions of realities, with each character existing within a quasi-existentialist isolation, set brilliantly on the remote, already isolated Isles of Skye. Here, within a microcosm of family and friends, the characters exist within what I want to call *permeable solitudes*, where it is a challenge (and not the norm) to discover sustaining and meaningful connections with otherness. The isolation of each person corresponds with that underlying alienation that Woolf addresses in her short stories. In 'A Simple Melody' (1925), Woolf posits our soul's 'extreme unlikeness to anyone else's' (*CSF* 205) while contending that untangling the knotty dialectical estrangement between our sameness and difference from others is one of the great riddles of human being-ness. We are both 'the same' and 'by [our] very nature opposed, different, at war', and her narrator wonders whether a desire to discover our commonalities is authentic, fair, and 'true': 'which is the more profound?'—'similarity' or 'dissimilarity' (*CSF* 206). But, crucially, Woolf insists in *To the Lighthouse* that incongruous interpretations of truth and reality can actually be constitutive of intimacy. Through her mobile, free, indirect discourse that acknowledges truth's complexities via frequently shifting points of view and varying sites of iterability, she insists that we both know and fail to know even our closest friends and family members in large part because of ongoing misprisions that nevertheless draw us near to one another in our dedicated efforts at reading and re-reading beloved alterities.

While Woolf remains unsure whether our 'similarity' or 'dissimilarity' is the more profound, I argue that her work is animated by an ethics of redemption that resists generating or perpetuating artificial alienations. In both *Mrs Dalloway* and *To the Lighthouse* moments of happiness occur through sudden, unexpected experiences of both aesthetic and communal unity. During the climactic dinner-party scene of *To the Lighthouse*, when the 'light' of 'eight candles' 'brought them into sympathy momentarily' (*TL* 131), Woolf creates a Last Supper tableau around Mrs Ramsay's final meal with family and friends where alterity is briefly diminished, and it is precisely through being and seeing together that the guests feel the presence of 'eternity'. Similarly, at the close of the book, Woolf pairs Lily Briscoe's painterly and quasi-ecstatic momentous 'vision' with the long-anticipated voyage and arrival of Mr Ramsay, James, and Cam at the aptly named *light*house. Mrs Dalloway, too, has visions and revelations that bear the burden of redeeming ordinary time: in certain moments she felt 'a sudden revelation, a tinge like a blush ... with some pressure of rapture', and she draws near to an otherwise untouchable truth without quite being able to grasp it: 'she had seen an illumination; a match burning in a crocus; an inner meaning almost expressed' (*MD* 29). As in so many of Woolf's exemplary moments the insight comes with a stunning flare of new perspective and then dies away. Both novels convey an economics of scarcity and brevity about these potent, redemptive instances that are ordinary, yet extraordinary, even while they are tasked with nothing less than renewing and sustaining us: 'Moments like this are buds on the tree of life', thinks Mrs Dalloway (*MD* 26).

During the years 1924 to 1927 Woolf also wondered explicitly, in ethical terms, about the nature of and the motivation behind her own impulse for writing. She asks herself meta-critically what kind of writer she will be, how she *ought* to *be* as a writer, and what creative writing can and should attempt to realize. As Panthea Reid writes in her biography of Woolf, 'Whether thinking of love or art or public responsibility, Virginia always debated which was truer, more valuable', and she was often torn between the 'artistic and the ethical'.[10] In Woolf's diary of June 1923, while she was drafting 'The Hours', which would become *Mrs Dalloway*, her admiration for Dostoevsky prompts her to wonder: 'Am I writing The Hours from deep emotion? ... Have I the power of conveying the true reality? Or do I write essays about myself? Answer these questions as I may, in the uncomplimentary sense, & still there remains this excitement. To get to the bones'

---

[10] Panthea Reid, *Art and Affection: A Life of Virginia Woolf* (Oxford: Oxford University Press, 1996), 318.

(*D2* 248). Like Chaucer's ability to infuse morality transdermally, through our pores, and Plato's encouragement to pursue truth with 'every part of us' (the flesh, soul, and intellect), Woolf wanted her writing to enter, affect, and change us in our inmost corporeality and frame. She concurs with Arnold Bennett that 'I haven't that "reality" gift' (*D2* 248) of her less experimental contemporaries, but she wanted to invent a new kind of realism that would creatively and convincingly render a post-Freudian and post-Bergsonian phenomenology in which the unconscious has at least as large a role as the conscious mind. Again positing a hierarchy among writers, she argues that only the best 'attain that unconsciousness which means that the consciousness is stimulated to the highest extent' (*E4* 50). Following Joyce's *Ulysses*, Woolf was seeking to 'trace the pattern, however disconnected and incoherent in appearance, which each sight or incident scores upon the consciousness' in an 'attempt to come closer to life' (*E4* 161).

But Woolf regrets the descriptive rather than illuminative qualities of even the best prose fiction because, unlike poetry, novels possess inadequate literary tools for 'extremes of passion' and are limited in what they can convey about the complexities of character. Even of Tolstoy's *Anna Karenina* she wonders, 'How then can we compare this lumbering and lagging art with poetry?' (*E4* 66). In 1923 she writes in her diary that 'It is a general sense of the poetry of existence that overcomes me' (*D2* 246), while 'The Narrow Bridge of Art'[11] (1927) finds her wondering—poetically, rhythmically— whether prose can 'chant the elegy, or hymn the love, or shriek in terror, or praise the rose, the nightingale, or the beauty of the night? Can it leap at one spring at the heart of its subject as the poet does? I think not. That is the penalty it pays for having dispensed with the incantation and the mystery, the rhyme and metre' (*E4* 436). Woolf's language-driven poetic prose sought to minimize this penalty, and to discover a way 'to liberate us of the enormous burden of the unexpressed' (*E4* 67) by throwing off genre-bound restrictions to allow for freer passionate expressivity and the felicities of poetic *jouissance*. Her fiction does take us to 'that higher air which is generally reached only by the more extreme measures of poetry—it is this art which plays upon us in so many ways at once and brings us to an exultation of mind which can only be reached when all the powers are called upon to contribute their energy to the whole' (*E4* 47). It has become well recognized that Woolf was uneasy with the generic designation of 'novel' for her books, and while writing both *To the Lighthouse* and *The Waves* (1931) she proposes adopting a new term—'elegy'—acknowledging the elegiac testimony of her novels in working through some of the astonishing early losses of her mother, half-sister, father, and brother; all before she was twenty-five. She was chafing at the restrictions of genre, language, communication, and form all at once, hoping to discover a new freedom of expression for the ineffability of modern experience. Genre, form, and content had to change to accommodate an expanding horizon of the sayable; these had to change because truth itself was changing.

---

[11] Originally entitled 'Poetry, Fiction and the Future' (*E4* 428–40).

We come to understand that Woolf wants us to read her fiction as if we were reading poetry—that she was trying to poeticize fiction, and that her novels should be read with the diligence of poetic scansion. Consider a passage near the opening of 'Time Passes' in *To the Lighthouse*:

> The autumn trees, ravaged as they are, take on the flash of tattered flags kindling in the gloom of cool cathedral caves where gold letters on marble pages describe death in battle and how bones bleach and burn far away in Indian sands. The autumn trees gleam in the yellow moonlight, in the light of harvest moons, the light which mellows the energy of labour, and smooths the stubble, and brings the wave lapping blue to the shore. (174)

With its alliteration, internal and half rhymes, rhythmic beats (including a striking fifty-seven monosyllabic words here of the total seventy-eight, which create multiple spondees that are softened and brushed by embedded anapaests), additive accretions (four 'ands', with a further echo in 'sands'), personification, assonance, sibilance, repetition, layers of metaphor, and highly suggestive, fantastical imagery, Woolf takes us to the poetic territory of the 'chant', 'hymn', 'shriek', and 'praise', that she misses from traditional prose fiction.

We also see poetry in her characters—many of whom have a powerful sense of proximity to poetry and poetic language, and who live fabled and poetic lives that they self-interpret as poeticized narrative and story. Septimus writes poetry, reads Shakespeare's *Antony and Cleopatra* in Regent's Park on the day he is to die, and his wife asks, 'Was he not like Keats?' (*MD* 76). When Woolf sketches an early version of *Mrs Dalloway* in her story, 'Mrs Dalloway in Bond Street' (which she sent to T. S. Eliot in 1923), Mrs Dalloway murmurs, almost chants, poetry on her walks through the streets of London, dwelling on Shelley's elegy for Keats, 'Adonais'—as she does in *The Voyage Out* (1915). This early Mrs Dalloway is highly literate, knows Shakespeare's sonnets 'by heart', has opinions about Shakespeare's Dark Lady, repeats a line from Shakespeare's *Cymbeline* that will become a refrain in *Mrs Dalloway*—'Fear no more the heat o' the sun'—quotes Edward Fitzgerald, jokes about Keats and fashion, and considers giving Elizabeth Gaskell's *Cranford* as a gift to her servant. In the present tense of the novel Mrs Dalloway is less of a reader than she used to be—'she scarcely read a book now, except memoirs in bed' (*MD* 8)—but she acknowledges the absorbing role reading had in her personal formation. When she dwells on memories of being in love with Sally Seton at Bourton, for instance, she recalls her own excitement about devouring literature—she read 'Plato in bed before breakfast... Morris... Shelley by the hour'—as if sexual awakening and desire were continuous with the thrilling pleasure of reading philosophy and poetry (*MD* 30).

In *To the Lighthouse* Woolf's characters similarly contemplate, repeat, give voice to, and inhabit poetry. Mr Ramsay murmurs fragments from Tennyson's 'The Charge of the Light Brigade' through the whole first section as he wanders through the gardens of the family home; he quotes Shelley (*TL* 96); and he recites from Charles Elton's 'Luriana Lurilee' at the group's supper together. Indeed, Mrs Ramsay worries that his 'habit' of 'saying poetry aloud, was growing on him' (*TL* 96). Mr Carmichael becomes a successful poet and reads Virgil in bed (*TL* 171); Paul, Andrew, Prue, and Nancy all 'sing' and 'shout out together' lyrics from Minta's song, 'Damn your eyes, damn your eyes' (*TL* 101); and Mrs Ramsay reads aloud to James, but, like Mrs Dalloway, feels that she 'never had time to read' books for herself (*TL* 38). Woolf nevertheless renders Mrs Ramsay as a creative presence who is traversed and stirred by poetry. In the last glimpse we have of her before her death, Mrs Ramsay reads from a collection of poems, 'swinging herself, zigzagging this way and that' (*TL* 160), inspired to turn to textuality by Mr Ramsay's partial recitation of 'Luriana, Lurilee' at dinner. Mrs Ramsay then echoes and extends Mr Ramsay's recitation by saying inwardly three additional lines from 'Luriana, Lurilee', slightly altering the words. Her longing for 'something I have come to get' whose exact meaning escapes her, prompts her to feel with her hands for a book, leading her to read 'at random' among Renaissance literature, pausing on William Browne of Tavistock's 'The Sirens Song'—'Steer, hither steer your winged pines, all beaten Mariners'—and on Shakespeare's Sonnet 98—'As with your shadow I with these did play' (*TL* 160). Despite the narrator's claim that it is the rhythm of the words rather than their semantic meaning that initially affects her ('She did not know at first what the words meant at all' (*TL* 160)), Mrs Ramsay knows enough to designate the sonnet form, and to feel physically, emotionally, and intellectually moved as she reads, finding in the poem a tangible compression of meaning that she can hold in both her mind and her hand: 'the essence sucked out of life and held rounded here' (*TL* 163). These words of Shakespeare's also 'shadow' and echo the time remaining to Mrs Ramsay, with the sonnet's language, poetry, and otherness bleeding through the diegetic narrative access to Mrs Ramsay's mind as she feels 'the shadow' of her intimacy with Mr Ramsay alongside a shadow of intellectual and emotional violence 'folding them in', making her feel she needed to 'beg[] ... as if for help' (*TL* 165). Her husband's 'mind,' she feels, is 'like a raised hand shadowing her mind' bringing her 'involuntarily' into proximity with him; we are unsure if his 'raised hand' is one that might strike, that might offer protection, or that casts shadow (*TL* 165). Once again, uncertainty and undecidability are intrinsic to intimacy, while the co-extensive connection both of Mrs Ramsay's self with literary textuality and of herself with her husband's needs, desires, and demands propel and sustain intimacy's intense bonds as Woolf describes an indefinite ground of hiatus, hesitation, merging, and ambivalence that is never either here or there, but perpetually, and provokingly, in between.

Woolf infuses her novels, essays, and even her journalism with poetry because she is seeking to do justice to the complexities of that shadowy, half-known part of ourselves that she consistently calls the soul. Many of her contemporaries 'have disappointed us', she argues in 'Modern Fiction', 'because they are concerned not with the spirit but with the body ... they have left us with the feeling that the sooner English fiction turns its back upon them, as politely as may be, and marches, if only into the desert, the better for its soul' (*E4* 158). 'Soul' is, nevertheless, a strong word for Woolf to use in the 1920s as a self-professed atheist, but she uses it often, and she regularly connects it with the ethical responsibility she felt in creating literary text-events. In an essay on Montaigne published in the *Times Literary Supplement* while Woolf was composing *Mrs Dalloway*,

Woolf admires Montaigne's essays for taking on the supremely important 'attempt to communicate a soul' (*E*4 76). She agrees with Montaigne that 'To tell the truth about oneself, to discover oneself near at hand, is not easy'; in fact, no one since 'the ancients' have managed to '"follow a pace so rambling and uncertain, as that of the soul"' (*E*4 71). Woolf wants to be the modern writer who most succeeds in the arduous task of rendering 'our enthralling confusion, our hotch-potch of impulses, our perpetual miracle—for the soul throws up wonders every second' (*E*4 75). Again, she connects the soul with the body and the compass of our passions and neurobiologies, affirming that 'the soul is all laced about with nerves and sympathies which affect her every action' (*E*4 78). Similarly, in one of Woolf's many reviews of Chekhov, she notes Chekhov's edifying, ethico-spiritual effect on us: 'as we read these little stories about nothing at all, the horizon widens; the soul gains an astonishing sense of freedom' (*E*4 185).

Woolf's diaries, too, reflect ongoing, if ambivalent, desires to 'speak of the soul' (*D*2 234). In February 1924 she notes with pride that E.M. Forster had 'said I had got further into the soul in Jacob's Room [sic] than any other novelist' (*D*2 292). A few months later she links growing desires—and a decreasing resistance—to 'write about the soul' with her sense of her burgeoning poeticism: 'I think its [sic] time to cancel that vow against soul description. What was I going to say? Something about the violent moods of my soul. How describe them [sic], even with a waking mind? I think I grow more & more poetic' (*D*2 304). And she affirms that she has been doing soul-work in writing *Mrs Dalloway*: 'But oh the delicacy and complexity of the soul—for, haven't I begun to tap her & listen to her breathing after all?' (*D*2 308).

When writing about the poetics rather than the hermeneutics of Greek writers—on *how* they wrote and achieved their effects, rather than on *what* they wrote—Woolf deductively concludes that their poetry depended on a sustaining ambiguity together with a musical, percussive way of touching the body: in Aeschylus 'The meaning is just on the far side of language' while 'Every sentence had to explode on striking the ear' (*E*4 45). This is what Woolf wanted to achieve in the musicality of her fiction: a fusion of aesthetic intensity with the enigma of meaning expressed in such a way that its form, purpose, and moment in 'striking the ear' would cause simultaneous ontological, epistemological, psychological, and aesthetic arousal, and awakening, and recognition. Part of her contribution to modernist literature, then, is in fusing, blurring, and blending the capabilities of poetry, fiction, and non-fictional prose as if to generate a new palette that would allow her reader to recognize poetry as *both* superimposed and continuous with prose—in the same spaces, within the same constructions and words, as doubles that sustain and stimulate each other.

Woolf believed that she and her contemporaries were 'trembling on the verge of one of the great ages of English literature' (*E*3 436), and to grasp her project, to do justice to it today, we would do well to heed Woolf's affirmation that reading changes us and causes small miracles:

> For we are apt to forget, reading, as we tend to do, only the masterpieces of a bygone age, how great a power the body of a literature possesses to impose itself: how

it will not suffer itself to be read passively, but takes us and reads us; flouts our preconceptions; questions principles which we had got into the habit of taking for granted, and, in fact, splits us in two parts as we read. (*E4* 62)

Roland Barthes would write decades later that 'the subject of history' is always 'a split subject, who simultaneously enjoys, through the text, the consistency of his selfhood and its collapse, its fall'.[12] Reading, according to Woolf, breaks us apart; reading splits the self. But it is only in this splitting that we are able to *become*; that we, as her future (common) readers, are made, and re-made as we confront the experiments with culture, self, identity, language, form, narrative, and consciousness that span Woolf's unremitting attempts to write what matters.

Selected Bibliography

Aristotle, *Nicomachean Ethics* (Cambridge: Cambridge University Press, 2000).
Arnold, Matthew, 'Dover Beach', in *Matthew Arnold: Poems* (London: British Library, 2011).
Barthes, Roland, *The Pleasure of the Text*, trans. R. Miller (New York: Hill and Wang, 1975).
Benzel, Kathryn N., and Ruth Hoberman, eds, *Trespassing Boundaries: Virginia Woolf's Short Fiction* (New York: Palgrave Macmillan, 2004).
Berman, Jessica, *Modernist Commitments: Ethics, Politics, and Transnational Modernism* (New York: Columbia University Press, 2011).
Briggs, Julia, *Reading Virginia Woolf* (Edinburgh: Edinburgh University Press, 2006).
Gualtieri, Elena, *Virginia Woolf's Essays: Sketching the Past* (New York: Palgrave Macmillan, 2000).
Hagen, Benjamin, 'Feeling Shadows: Virginia Woolf's Sensuous Pedagogy', *PMLA* 132, no. 2 (March 2017), 266–80.
Keats, John, 'Ode on a Grecian Urn', in *The Complete Poems*, 3rd edition, ed. John Barnard (London: Penguin, 1988).
Oser, Lee, *The Ethics of Modernism: Moral Ideas in Yeats, Eliot, Joyce, Woolf and Beckett* (Cambridge: Cambridge University Press, 2007).
Reid, Panthea, *Art and Affection: A Life of Virginia Woolf* (Oxford: Oxford University Press, 1996).
Reynier, Christine, *Virginia Woolf's Ethics of the Short Story* (New York: Palgrave Macmillan, 2009).

---

[12] Roland Barthes, *The Pleasure of the Text*, trans. R. Miller (New York: Hill and Wang, 1975), 21.

CHAPTER 7

MATURE WORKS II (1928–1932)

ELSA HÖGBERG

Woolf's writing during the prolific period 1928–1932 evinces a persistent concern with the poetic and prosaic impulses of fiction. While her literary journalism in these years frequently privileges the poetic, aesthetic detachment from prosaic, socio-political causes that informs her ideal of androgynous art as outlined in *A Room of One's Own* (1929), for the past decades Woolf scholars have revealed how her aesthetic experiments undermine such distinctions between poetic and committed writing. We have been made to see that the playfully poetic style of *A Room of One's Own* composes the fabric of its feminist critique; that *Orlando: A Biography* (1928), with its rewriting of history and intricate rhapsodic narrative, is far more than a mere *jeu d'esprit*; and that the abstract, lyrical *The Waves* (1931) is fervently anti-imperialist and anti-fascist. However, we have yet to fully appreciate how the lyrical features and formal-generic hybridity of these texts (*Orlando* is at once novel, mock biography, and 'love letter' to its dedicatee, Woolf's friend and lover Vita Sackville-West;[1] *A Room of One's Own* political essay and poetic reverie; *The Waves* 'prose yet poetry; a novel & a play' (*D3* 128)) become the very site for Woolf's socio-political commitments. Such deep integration of the poetic/aesthetic and the prosaic/political was richly theorized by Woolf herself, notably in her 1927 manifesto 'Poetry, Fiction and the Future', and formal-generic hybridity as conceptualized in that little-known essay lies, I propose, at the heart of Woolf's work in this extraordinarily creative period. Taking this premise as its starting point, the present chapter illuminates connections between *Orlando*, *A Room of One's Own*, and *The Common Reader: Second Series* (1932), and between *The Waves* and the pacifism of the Women's Co-operative Guild, to name a few.

---

[1] Sackville-West's son Nigel Nicolson famously called *Orlando* 'the longest and most charming love-letter in literature' (*Portrait of a Marriage* (London: Futura Publications, 1974), 209).

The years 1928–1932 form the peak of the increasingly successful period that saw the publication of Woolf's idiosyncratic, modernist experiments in poetic prose from *Jacob's Room* (1922) to *The Waves*. Anne Olivier Bell thus perceives a 'unity' marking a 'distinct period' in Woolf's life and work (1925–1930), 'in which she attained full maturity as an artist and at the same time achieved a secure and respected position in the world of letters' (*D3* vii); as Bell notes, *The Waves* was 'the zenith of that happy exploration' (*D4* vii). The years framing this chapter arguably constitute the climax of this trajectory: *Orlando* sold far better than any of Woolf's novels to date, bringing about her widespread recognition as a novelist, and the early reception of *The Second Common Reader* was 'almost universally favourable' (*E5* xii). This progressive 'unity' was also aesthetic insofar as each of her novels explored further dimensions of the lyrical prose she theorized in her contemporaneous essays, including *A Room of One's Own*—itself a hybrid text overflowing the boundaries separating political essay and modernist fiction, argumentative prose and poetic lyricism. And yet, *Orlando* and *The Waves* still tend to be conceived as opposite poles of the poetic prose spectrum, as the two extremes of Woolf's fictional development in the years 1922–1931. An initial idea for her long essay 'Phases of Fiction' (1929) might serve as a description of these two 'ends' of her own course as a novelist: 'I don't think it's a matter of "development" but something to do with prose & poetry, in novels. For instance Defoe at one end: E. Brontë at the other. Reality something they put at different distances' (*D3* 50).

Until recently, critics have largely accepted Woolf's own idea of *Orlando* a delightful 'escapade' written in 'clear & plain' narrative prose—'it is all a joke, & yet gay & quick reading [...] a writers holiday' (*D3* 131, 162, 177)—a pleasurable relief from 'these serious poetic experimental books whose form is always so closely considered' (*D3* 162). *The Waves* has similarly been read as the culmination of the 'serious poetic' experiments that Woolf saw as her primary vocation as a writer, and from which *Orlando* provided release. Consequently, *Orlando* has been taken less seriously than *The Waves*, which has been elevated, reverentially or unfavourably, as Woolf's most abstract novel, beautifully poetic and therefore detached from socio-political concerns. Even if this picture has been challenged in recent years, it lingers as a residue of the long obsolete notion of Woolf's fiction as the exquisite 'tea-room modernism' of a socially privileged writer who could afford to indulge in 'pleasant trifles' like *Orlando*, or in poetic reveries like *The Waves*,[2] as if such texts could not quite be accommodated into the now prevalent conception of Woolf's aesthetic modernism as furthering progressive political stances from feminism and socialism to anti-fascism, anti-imperialism, as well as an ethically compelling pacifism. The one novel, it would seem, is not poetic enough, and the

---

[2] In his review 'Prose-de-Société', J.C. Squire called *Orlando* 'a very pleasant trifle' (in Robin Majumdar and Allen McLaurin, eds, *Virginia Woolf: The Critical Heritage* (London and Boston: Routledge and Kegan Paul, 1975), 229). Gerald Sykes's notion of *The Waves* as 'tea-room modernism' ('Modernism', in Eleanor McNees, ed., *Virginia Woolf: Critical Assessments*, vol. IV (Mountfield: Helm Information, 1994), 11) resonates with that of detractors such as F.R. and Q.D. Leavis.

other—too poetic. In this, these two texts appear to occupy a somewhat awkward place in her oeuvre.

A more holistic picture of this particular period in Woolf's career, and of the many intersections between *Orlando*, *The Waves*, and political writings such as *A Room of One's Own*, begins to emerge if we consider these texts through the lens of her contemporaneous essay 'Poetry, Fiction and the Future'. Among Woolf's works, *Orlando* and *The Waves* achieve the perhaps most experimental realization of her vision for the hybrid, poetic novel of the future as outlined in this essay—a vision that also came to permeate the political argument as much as the lyrical prose style of *A Room of One's Own*. The latter text, in turn, is compositionally intertwined with *Orlando*, with which it shares many themes and stylistic features: *Orlando* was published in the United Kingdom on 11 October 1928, a couple of weeks before Woolf presented the talks at Newnham and Girton colleges, Cambridge, which eventually became *A Room of One's Own*. And, as we shall see, central political as well as aesthetic dimensions of Woolf's feminist essay were channelled, although perhaps more obliquely, into *The Waves*, so that *A Room of One's Own* forms a bridge between the two novels.

'Poetry, Fiction and the Future' was first published on 14 and 21 August 1927 in the *New York Herald Tribune*, and Andrew McNeillie calls it 'the most direct manifesto Woolf ever produced, being effectively a programme for writing *The Waves*' (*E4* xix). He also, however, points to links between this essay and *Orlando* (*E4* xviii), and the editors of the recently published Cambridge University Press edition of Woolf's novel-biography stress that her description of the poetic prose novel of the future 'anticipates *Orlando* almost exactly' (*O* xl). The novel Woolf imagines

> will be written in prose, but in prose which has many of the characteristics of poetry [...] it will have little kinship with the sociological novel or the novel of the environment [...] it will give the relation of the mind to general ideas and its soliloquy in solitude. For under the dominion of the novel [...] we long sometimes to escape from the incessant, the remorseless analysis of falling into love and falling out of love [...] We long for some more impersonal relationship. We long for ideas, for dreams, for imaginations, for poetry. (*E4* 435–6)

This sketch of an impersonal, modernist novel lyricism dissolves a poetry-prose dichotomy that Woolf frequently upholds in her critical essays—'poetry has always been overwhelmingly on the side of beauty [...] She has never been used for the common purpose of life. Prose has taken all the dirty work on her shoulders' (*E4* 434):

> [the future novel] will clasp to its breast the precious prerogatives of the democratic art of prose; its freedom, its fearlessness, its flexibility. For prose is so humble that it can go anywhere; no place is too low [...] this unnamed variety of the novel will be written standing back from life, because in that way a larger view is to be obtained of some important features of it; will be written in prose because prose, if you free it from the beast of burden work which so many novelists necessarily lay upon it of carrying loads of details, bushels of fact—prose thus treated will show itself capable

of rising high from the ground, not in one dart, but in sweeps and circles, and of keeping at the same time in touch with the amusements and idiosyncrasies of [...] daily life. (*E4* 436, 438)

If we trace the transposition of Woolf's vision into the aesthetic-political vision of *A Room of One's Own*, this 'larger view' of life proves capable of revealing much more than its 'amusements and idiosyncrasies'. Read alongside each other, these essays suggest a break with the widespread notion that a novel's democratic work—in the triple sense of socially egalitarian, 'consistent with the principles of democracy' and 'relating to the common or ordinary people in a state or polity'[3] —is most effectively carried out in prose at its most prosaic. And these visions of a democratic, socio-politically grounded, yet poetic, modernist novel form materialized in the vastly different shapes of *Orlando* and *The Waves*. In their singular formal and generic hybridity, these two novel experiments arguably form Woolf's most radical rupture of the novelistic mould, as advocated in her brief essay 'What is a Novel?' (1927):

> It is high time that this imaginary but still highly potent bogey was destroyed [...]
> When they write a novel let [the novelists themselves] define it. Let them say that they have written a chronicle, a document, a rhapsody, a fantasy, an argument, a narrative or a dream.
> For there is no such thing as 'a novel'. (*E4* 415)

Woolf's insistence, in this period, on the need to rethink, and perhaps even do away with, the novel as genre is central, I believe, if we are to do justice to *Orlando* and *The Waves* as two of her most aesthetically as well as socio-politically compelling books from the years 1922–1931.

In *A Room of One's Own*, the narrator's preference for the 'contemplative' or poetic novelist[4] is deeply embedded in Woolf's feminist argument. Like the novelist in 'Poetry, Fiction and the Future', the imagined woman writer of Woolf's projected future will 'knoc[k] [the novel form] into shape [...] providing some new vehicle, not necessarily in verse, for the poetry in her' (*ARO* 58). Unlike Shakespeare's gifted sister or the nineteenth-century female novelist, 'whose original impulse [...] to poetry' (*ARO* 50) was thwarted because of the systematic patriarchal oppression excluding women from public life, historiography, and literary tradition, the female writer of the early twentieth century can begin the monumental task of recording, through the aesthetic means of a necessarily impersonal novel lyricism, women's increasing presence in the public world of the professions, politics, and letters. As in 'Women and Fiction' (1929), which aligns a poetic orientation towards 'wider questions [...] of our destiny and the

---

[3] On Woolf's democratic intellectual ethos, see Melba Cuddy-Keane, *Virginia Woolf, the Intellectual, and the Public Sphere* (Cambridge: Cambridge University Press, 2003), chapter 1.

[4] Virginia Woolf, *A Room of One's Own and Three Guineas* (Oxford: Oxford University Press, 2015), 66.

meaning of life' with 'the greater impersonality of women's [public] lives' (*E5* 34), Woolf foresees, in *A Room of One's Own*, an expanding turn in women's writing from the personal and emotional (as necessitated by the patriarchal system of separate spheres) to the impersonal, the poetic, and professional, in which women's future fiction will be enriched by women's research and scholarship on literature, but also in other fields (*ARO* 60). Thus, the fictional Mary Carmichael's novel *Life's Adventure*, a pioneering literary illumination of female same-sex desire and women's professional relations, conjures the chemist's laboratory where 'Chloe liked Olivia', a scene that begins to 'catch those unrecorded gestures, those unsaid or half-said words […] when women are alone, unlit by the capricious and coloured light of the other sex' (*ARO* 64).[5] Woolf's narrator urges Mary Carmichael to use her art as a novelist to bring into public light this 'accumulation of unrecorded life': 'All that you will have to explore […] holding your torch firm in your hand. Above all, you must illuminate your own soul' (*ARO* 67–8). This advocacy of contemplative, poetic, 'incandescent' prose as a 'tool' and 'weapon' (*ARO* 58) by which to claim women's rightful place as scientists, lovers of other women, and inheritors of a literary tradition yet to be appropriated from a virtually all-male lineage indicates just how entangled the poetic and the political are in *A Room of One's Own*. And while decades of Woolf criticism have done much to elucidate this entanglement, its full extent has yet to be explored.

Overall, as Laura Marcus observes about the trajectories of feminist scholarship on Woolf, there has been a tendency to endorse either her polemical outrage, or her ideal of pleasurable, creative androgyny. As Marcus notes, these predispositions have alternated, with 'anger' and the prosaic *Three Guineas* being the focal points of predominantly historical-materialist traditions, and 'androgyny' and the poetic *A Room of One's Own* those of more theorized, especially psychoanalytically oriented, scholarship.[6] We could add that the various lineages of politically informed Woolf criticism have tended to sustain deep-seated binaries such as poetic/prosaic, stylized/authentic, and aesthetic/historically grounded. At the present juncture of historicist and new aestheticist approaches to Woolf and modernism, one challenge, particularly for critical explorations of the texts covered by this chapter, will be to stay close to Woolf's vision in 'Poetry, Fiction and the Future' to appreciate more fully how she integrates the poetic and the prosaic in *Orlando*, *A Room of One's Own*, and *The Waves*.

There is still a great deal to discover in how the poetic dimensions of these texts further their socio-political, democratic work: *Orlando*'s subversive treatment of sex, gender, censorship, and inheritance; the anti-fascism and anti-imperialism of *The Waves*; and the convergence of all these in the feminism of *A Room of One's Own*. Contemporary scholarship on the public and political dimensions of affect, lyric, and in particular voice (as a physical-acoustic as well as discursive phenomenon) can do much to illuminate the

---

[5] See Jane Goldman, 'Burning Feminism: Virginia Woolf's Laboratory of Intimacy', in Elsa Högberg, ed., *Modernist Intimacies* (Edinburgh: Edinburgh University Press, 2021); *ARO* 132.

[6] Laura Marcus, 'Woolf's Feminism and Feminism's Woolf', in Susan Sellers, ed., *The Cambridge Companion to Virginia Woolf* (Cambridge University Press, 2010), 162–8.

commitments specific to these hybrid texts. Thus, the poetic-political articulations of the multiple ballad voices composing *A Room of One's Own* (a residue and development of Woolf's original, vocal address to her audiences at Newnham and Girton) amount to much more than the dismantling of subject positions once heralded by poststructuralist critics.[7] Can the polyvocal lyricism of this essay perhaps be understood as the very material of its feminist, socialist politics?[8] *Orlando* and *The Waves* are similarly multivocal, and just as the democratic valences of *Orlando*'s 'plain' narrative prose can only be fully understood through close study of this text's unrivalled, artful ventriloquism— its playful yet aesthetically intricate voicing of other writers, literary traditions, and discourses (of law, sexology, religion, history, and biography)—so the lyrical soliloquies of *The Waves* have all too often been read as an expression of solipsistic interiority and disembodied thought (taken as signs of the author's socio-political alienation), rather than as physical, vocal enunciation: the poetic-theatrical performance of speech to an audience, with its vital political possibilities, as suggested by Woolf's own conception of this book as 'prose yet poetry; a novel & a play' (*D3* 128).

Orlando, described by Woolf herself as 'too freakish & unequal [...] Not, I think "important" among my works' (*D3* 177), has been widely recognized as one of her most dynamic modernist experiments since the rise of LGBTQ studies in the 1990s, which brought substantial focus on this hybrid novel's transgressive configurations of biography,[9] sexuality, and same-sex desire. Published in the same year that Radclyffe Hall's realist novel *The Well of Loneliness* was convicted for obscenity because of its lesbian subject matter, the overtly erotic *Orlando* famously escaped censorship by virtue of its poetic and stylistic playfulness. The composition of the text, which intensified the sensual relationship between Woolf and Vita Sackville-West (the model for Orlando), may well have channelled what Sackville-West once called Woolf's 'suppressed randiness'.[10] Even so, Woolf's erotically charged novel also remains politically compelling from a

---

[7] In her Introduction to the Oxford University Press edition of *A Room of One's Own*, Anna Snaith notes that its 'complex polyvocality' blurs spoken and written expression, thereby 'relat[ing] social critique to the politics of voice, genre, and tone' (*ARO* xxiii, xii–xiii). In this, Snaith is preceded by earlier scholars such as Jane Marcus, who brilliantly analysed the feminist, socialist, critical, and female erotic valences of the essay's multivocal address (see chapters 7 and 8 of *Virginia Woolf and the Languages of Patriarchy* (Bloomington: Indiana University Press, 1987), and 'Still Practice, A/Wrested Alphabet: Toward a Feminist Aesthetic', in *Art and Anger: Reading like a Woman* (Columbus: Ohio State University Press, 1988).

[8] Is it a coincidence that the perhaps most lyrical passage of *A Room of One's Own*, an ecstatic depiction of the wild gardens of the fictional women's college Fernham, culminates in a tribute to classical scholar Jane Ellen Harrison, whose feminist pacifism inspired Woolf's own?

[9] On Woolf's reforming of the biographical genre in *Orlando*, away from the Victorian conventions of the *Dictionary of National Biography* towards the artful 'new biography' developed by, amongst others, Harold Nicolson and Lytton Strachey, see Suzanne Raitt, *Vita and Virginia: The Work and Friendship of V. Sackville-West and Virginia Woolf* (Oxford: Clarendon Press, 1993), chapter 1, and Suzanne Raitt and Ian Blyth, 'Introduction' in Raitt and Blyth, eds, *Orlando: A Biography* (Cambridge: Cambridge University Press, 2018), xlvi–xlviii. See also Woolf's 'The New Biography' (1927).

[10] Adam Parkes, 'Lesbianism, History and Censorship: *The Well of Loneliness* and the Suppressed Randiness of Virginia Woolf's *Orlando*', *Twentieth Century Literature* 40, no. 4 (Winter 1994).

queer theory and gender studies perspective,[11] and scholarship now abounds on her lyrical engagement with 'prosaic' topics including historiography, colonialism, the gift (as a material and aesthetic phenomenon), intertextuality, and the literary past.[12] Suzanne Raitt and Ian Blyth write:

> The day after she wrote the last word of *Orlando*, Virginia Woolf noted in her diary that it was 'all a joke' (*D3* 177). But in fact, *Orlando* is one of her most ambitious and complex texts. In it, Virginia experiments with a new form for the novel; [...] she rewrites the history of the Sackville family; she re-imagines the genre of biography; she offers a detailed social history of England; she recreates some of the golden moments of British literature [...] The novel was a gift in more ways than one. (*O* xxxvii)

With its massive textual apparatus and notes as well as detailed explanatory notes unpacking the novel's myriad historical and literary references and allusions, their volume is an unparalleled scholarly effort to demonstrate that *Orlando* is so much more than a *jeu d'esprit* or 'love letter' to Sackville-West. The book is both of these things, but such terms have tended to obscure its jointly aesthetic and socio-political achievements. If Raitt and Blyth's edition follows the now predominant historicist and archival approaches to Woolf, the discreet notations at the bottom of each page also enable a double reading mode: an immersion in the novel's rhapsodic, fluid narrative prose, as well as concentrated attention to the many voices, echoes, and allusions composing its unique modernist style.

Such a double reading mode, pleasurable and playful as well as acutely perceptive to contextual and aesthetic detail, is also cultivated in *Sentencing* Orlando: *Virginia Woolf and the Morphology of the Modernist Sentence* (2018), the first scholarly collection dedicated specifically to Woolf's novel-biography. Each chapter focuses on a single sentence from *Orlando*, examining its aesthetic and historical resonances. This simultaneously immersive and rigorous method uncovers *Orlando's* extraordinary rendering, through satire and parodic mimicry, of literary and historical voices, a modernist polyphony that is as aesthetically complex as it is transformative. As the contributors reveal,

---

[11] On lesbian and queer approaches to Woolf and Bloomsbury, see Patricia Morgne Cramer, 'Woolf and Theories of Sexuality', and Madelyn Detloff, 'Woolf and Lesbian Culture: Queering Woolf Queering', both in Bryony Randall and Jane Goldman, eds, *Virginia Woolf in Context* (Cambridge: Cambridge University Press, 2012). Landmark works include Eileen Barrett and Patricia Cramer, eds, *Virginia Woolf: Lesbian Readings* (New York: New York University Press, 1997), and Brenda S. Helt and Madelyn Detloff, eds, *Queer Bloomsbury* (Edinburgh: Edinburgh University Press, 2016).

[12] See Angeliki Spiropoulou, *Virginia Woolf, Modernity and History: Constellations with Walter Benjamin* (Basingstoke: Palgrave Macmillan, 2010), chapter 4; Randi Koppen, 'The Negress and the Bishop: On Marriage, Colonialism and the Problem of Knowledge', in Elsa Högberg and Amy Bromley, eds, *Sentencing* Orlando: *Virginia Woolf and the Morphology of the Modernist Sentence* (Edinburgh: Edinburgh University Press, 2018); Kathryn Simpson, *Gifts, Markets and Economies of Desire in Virginia Woolf* (Basingstoke: Palgrave Macmillan, 2009), chapter 3; Anne E. Fernald, *Virginia Woolf: Feminism and the Reader* (Basingstoke: Palgrave Macmillan, 2006); and Jane de Gay, *Virginia Woolf's Novels and the Literary Past* (Edinburgh: Edinburgh University Press, 2006), chapter 5.

Orlando puts into play Woolf's theory of the sentence in *A Room of One's Own*, in which a subversive gender and genre politics operates on the level of aesthetics: the literary sentence emerges there as aesthetic property to be handed down an exclusionary male line of descent, and the poetic prose sentence becomes the woman writer's 'weapon' with which to transform the novel genre (*ARO* 57–8). Woolf herself advocated a democratic reading practice in which the common, or unprofessional, reader's pleasurable savouring of a good sentence becomes the precondition for literary study at its most rewarding,[13] and the epigraph to *The Second Common Reader* recalls her ambivalent treatment of male writers in *Orlando*: Samuel Johnson's voice—'I rejoice to concur with the common reader [...] uncorrupted by [...] the dogmatism of learning'—enriched her own original definition of the common reader as someone who reads primarily 'for his own pleasure' (*E4* 19), even as the same voice resonates in *A Room of One's Own* as a striking example of men's centuries-long suppression of women's intellectual and creative work (*ARO* 42). A formally attuned reading of *Orlando's* ventriloquism reveals that her *Common Reader* ethos inspired her writing of the novel as something like an act of piracy: we could say that through her immense erudition and stylistic mastery, Woolf pirates aesthetic property—the male sentences of writers such as those acknowledged in her spoof Preface—and transforms it into a symbolic gift for her female lover of material property (the Knole estate) that she could not inherit because of the laws of primogeniture.[14] The densely allusive yet democratically accessible narrative of *Orlando*, with its polyvocality and appeal to the common reader, ultimately enacts a key tenet of *A Room of One's Own*: 'masterpieces are not single and solitary births; they are the outcome of many years of thinking in common, of thinking by the body of the people, so that the experience of the mass is behind the single voice' (*ARO* 49).[15]

One of the closest inspirational 'friends' listed in *Orlando's* Preface was Thomas De Quincey, who also occupies a central place in *The Second Common Reader*. In 'De Quincey's Autobiography', an essay written for that volume, Woolf describes his poetic, 'impassioned prose' in terms strongly reminiscent of 'Poetry, Fiction and the Future', and her own writing in *Orlando* achieves a De Quinceyan combination of 'the rapid passage of events and actions' and 'the slow opening up of single and solemn moments of concentrated emotion' (*E5* 457). The result is a dream-like, impersonal lyricism;[16] Woolf's passion for Sackville-West saturates *Orlando*, but if we begin to appreciate

---

[13] See, for instance, 'On Re-reading Novels' (1922, *E3* 340) and *A Room of One's Own* (60–1).

[14] In its manipulation of canonical writers' sentences, *Orlando* arguably pirates exclusionary intellectual and aesthetic property in Caren Irr's feminist sense of the term (*Pink Pirates: Contemporary American Writers and Copyright* (University of Iowa Press, 2010)).

[15] Jane Marcus reads this tenet as 'a Marxist-feminist theory of literary criticism' (*Woolf and the Languages of Patriarchy*, 75). See Cuddy-Keane's account of Woolf's democratic commitment to a classless literary education in relation to contemporaneous debates around 'the common reader' (*Virginia Woolf, the Intellectual*).

[16] Cf. '[De Quincey's] most perfect passages [...] are not cries of anguish [...] they are descriptions of states of mind' (Woolf, '"Impassioned Prose"', *E4* 367), and her dissatisfaction, in 'Poetry, Fiction and the Future', with the novel's 'remorseless analysis of falling into love and falling out of love' (*E4* 435).

this exuberant 'writer's holiday' (*D3* 177) as integral to her poetic prose experiments of the period 1922–1931, we can detect a carefully crafted lyricism that made possible the writing of this novel as a form of piracy and gift, whereby her appropriation of his style becomes an aesthetically as well as politically charged act of mimicry disrupting a predominantly male lineage of material and aesthetic inheritance.[17] Central to this act is *Orlando*'s generic hybridity as novel-biography, with its alluring mix of fact and fiction, which counters the role of biographical and novelistic conventions in sustaining this lineage.[18] In this, the text develops De Quincey's own hybrid style, poised between fact-bound life writing and a lyrical prose in which 'hard fact' becomes 'cloud-like and supple' (*E4* 365).

Woolf's De Quinceyan concern with hybrid and poetic writing also pervades her essay 'How Should One Read a Book?', which promotes the common reader's vital role, distinct from that of professional critics, in setting aesthetic standards to ensure a democratic, co-creative dialogue between writers and 'people reading for the love of reading' (*E5* 582). Originally published in 1926, this text was substantially revised as the closing essay of *The Second Common Reader*, even if the reworked version retains a forceful articulation of Woolf's co-creative reading ethos. A comparison of the two versions illuminates her transition from the mindset generating *Orlando* to her preoccupations when composing *The Waves*: the first version celebrates the pleasurable cross-fertilization of 'hybrid books' such as biographies with poetry and fiction—'Books [...] are always overflowing their [generic] boundaries' (*E4* 393, 395, 390)—whereas the second favours 'the greater abstractness, the purer truth of fiction', stressing the poetic and formal qualities of fiction as an art form (*E5* 577–9). In 1928, while conceiving *The Waves*, Woolf noted her desire

> to give the moment whole; whatever it includes. Say that the moment is a combination of thought; sensation; the voice of the sea [...] this appalling narrative business of the realist: getting on from lunch to dinner: it is false, unreal [...] Why admit anything to literature that is not poetry—by which I mean saturated? (*D3* 209–10)

An echo of this thought found its way into 'De Quincey's Autobiography': 'then suddenly the smooth narrative parts asunder, arch opens beyond arch [...] and time stands still' (*E5* 458). These visions materialized in *The Waves*, itself a realization of the novel envisioned in 'Poetry, Fiction and the Future', giving 'as poetry does, the outline rather than the detail [...] [the mind's] soliloquy in solitude [...] mould[ing] blocks' (*E4* 435, 439).[19] Early reviewers stressed the novel's lyricism, complex formal design, and

---

[17] See Elsa Högberg, 'Woolf, De Quincey and the Legacy of "Impassioned Prose"', in Högberg and Bromley, *Sentencing Orlando*.

[18] See Karyn Z. Sproles, *Desiring Women: The Partnership of Virginia Woolf and Vita Sackville-West* (Toronto: University of Toronto Press, 2006), chapter 5, on *Orlando* as a generically unstable, feminist biography.

[19] In *A Room of One's Own*, the novel is similarly figured as an art form with 'a certain looking-glass likeness to life, though of course with [...] distortions innumerable [...] a structure leaving a shape on the mind's eye' (*ARO* 54).

radical break with novelistic conventions. In its dream-like visual 'scenes' and musical aesthetic virtuosity, the text displays a De Quinceyan 'gift of composition' already manifest in *Orlando*,[20] but like the earlier novel, it also playfully crafts the generic hybridity characterizing Woolf's novel of the future: 'It will have something of the exultation of poetry, but much of the ordinariness of prose. It will be dramatic, and yet not a play. It will be read, not acted' (*E4* 435). However, unlike the hybrid and poetic qualities of *Orlando*, the innovative soliloquy form of *The Waves* (which combines prose, poetry, and drama) was read, for decades, as an indication of its author's retreat from sociopolitical concerns into the poetic realm of interiority.[21] Until relatively recently, *The Waves* was generally thought to have little to say about the political climate in the years of its composition, and, as Jane Marcus noted in her ground-breaking 1991 essay 'Britannia Rules *The Waves*', its long-standing 'status as "difficult" or only available to an elite' brought about its 'relegation to the unread, except in formalist or philosophical terms'.[22]

Marcus's essay opened up an entirely new way of reading Woolf's 'antinovel' in claiming it to be 'a cultural icon of the 1930s' '[c]onsistent with the socialist politics and antifascist ethics of *The Years* and *Three Guineas*'.[23] Exposing the patriarchal bias informing assessments of *The Waves* as difficult and inaccessible, Marcus shows the novel's formal experimentalism to be the very vehicle for an anti-imperialist politics addressed to an audience of common readers. Following Marcus's transformative account, a feminist, democratic, and non-conformist political stance has been ascribed to the novel's aesthetic strategies by scholars attuned to its critique of nationalism, imperialism, and the fascist movements spreading in Europe at the time of its composition.[24] Jessica Berman has insightfully explored the text's poetic resistance to the political rhetoric of Oswald Mosley's New Party (a part of the British Union of Fascists from 1931).[25] As these field-defining studies reveal, the lyricism of *The Waves* erupts like the 'fountain of creative energy' defended in *A Room of One's Own* as the anti-fascist novelist's counter-force against the arid, hyper-masculine 'I' of the (proto-)fascist writer at home and abroad, whose protests against women's increasing gains in the public

---

[20] On these features of De Quincey's prose, see Woolf's 'De Quincey's Autobiography' (*E5* 453–5), and '"Impassioned Prose"' (*E4* 363–6).

[21] In a representative early review titled 'Virginia Woolf Soliloquises', Gerald Bullet speaks of an unworldly, introspective lyricism (in McNees, *Critical Assessments*). Even Alex Zwerdling's *Virginia Woolf and the Real World* (Berkeley: University of California Press, 1986) considered *The Waves* to lack the historical and political engagement of Woolf's later 1930s works (9, 12).

[22] Jane Marcus, 'Britannia Rules *The Waves*', in McNees, *Critical Assessments*, 77.

[23] Marcus, 'Britannia', 76–7, 81.

[24] See in particular Cathy J. Phillips, *Virginia Woolf against Empire* (Knoxville: University of Tennessee Press, 1994); Jessica Berman, *Modernist Fiction, Cosmopolitanism and the Politics of Community* (Cambridge: Cambridge University Press, 2001), chapter 4; and Christine Froula, *Virginia Woolf and the Bloomsbury Avant-Garde: War, Civilization, Modernity* (New York: Columbia University Press, 2004), chapter 6.

[25] Berman, *Modernist Fiction*, chapter 4.

sphere had already, in Italy, played a major role in bringing about 'an age to come of pure, of self-assertive virility' (*ARO* 75–8).²⁶ These reflections anticipate Woolf's much debated claim, in *Three Guineas*, that nationalism, imperialism, and fascism all originate in patriarchal family structures, and that combatting such structures at home is essential to the international battle against fascism.²⁷ It is remarkable that *The Waves* is still so rarely read together with this the most prosaic of Woolf's books, especially given their entangled composition histories. In 1931, Woolf gave her speech 'Professions for Women', which she thought might open a sequel to *A Room of One's Own*, and the previous year she composed her Introductory Letter for Margaret Llewelyn Davies's collection *Life as We have Known It*, outlining her impressions from her work for the Women's Co-operative Guild, whose pacifist struggle 'for peace and disarmament and the sisterhood of nations' (*E5* 188) she found particularly compelling.²⁸

While such reassessment of Woolf's lyricism as a primary channel for the politics of *The Waves* would not have been possible without the pioneering scholarship represented by Marcus and Berman, this critical trajectory also exhibits a difficulty accommodating Woolf's poetic soliloquies into its politicized interpretations. Thus, Marcus speaks of Woolf's 'exhaustion' of the soliloquy form through her intertextual parody of the Romantic poet's introspection and its sustainment of British imperialism.²⁹ More recent criticism on *The Waves* points towards potential ways of discerning the novel's challenge to (poststructuralist) notions of an inevitable affinity between poetic introspection and a Western fantasy of self-possessed individualism culminating in the fascist's aggressive 'I'. This century's ethical direction in literary studies has produced compelling readings of *The Waves* notably through Emmanuel Levinas's philosophy, which focus on the text's poetic dislocation of the autonomous subject with its violent political, philosophical, and linguistic legacy. Tamlyn Monson thus reads the soliloquies' rhythmic, wave-like 'shattering and piecing together' of the self (*W* 216)³⁰ in Levinasian and Kristevan terms as the cyclical rise and fall of the eloquent, autonomous 'I', a process whereby subject formation entails an ethical exposure to the other and outside.³¹ Such scholarship

---

²⁶ This passage of *A Room of One's Own* offers a compelling aesthetic solution to the Benjaminian problem outlined elsewhere in the essay (*ARO* 13–14, 16–17) and in 'Poetry, Fiction and the Future': that the years following World War I saw the exhaustion of lyricism, conceived in terms of affective continuity and effusion. See Walter Benjamin, 'On Some Motifs in Baudelaire' (1939; trans. 1969) on the impossibility of lyric in the age of modernity.

²⁷ On Woolf's anti-fascism and critique of the fascists' reactionary gender politics, see Merry M. Pawlowski, ed., *Virginia Woolf and Fascism: Resisting the Dictators' Seduction* (Basingstoke: Palgrave, 2001).

²⁸ 'Professions for Women' was both the first working title for *Three Guineas* and the title of the posthumously published version of the talk Woolf gave to the London/National Society for Women's Service on January 21, 1931.

²⁹ Marcus, 'Britannia', 83–4.

³⁰ Cf. 'I am writing [*The Waves*] to a rhythm and not to a plot [...] the rhythmical is more natural to me than the narrative' (*L4* 204).

³¹ Tamlyn Monson, '"A Trick of the Mind": Alterity, Ontology, and Representation in Virginia Woolf's *The Waves*', *Modern Fiction Studies* 50, no. 1 (Spring 2004).

continues to illuminate an ethically as well as aesthetically charged question resonating across Woolf's work, and *The Waves* in particular: 'what's between us?', a question 'of what holds us together or apart—nation, empire, class, gender, city, body, house, self'.[32] Indeed, philosophical, ethical, and socio-political approaches to Woolf have tended for some time to be closely intertwined. And while philosophical readings of *The Waves* have proliferated since at least the 1960s,[33] the relatively recent philosophical turn in Woolf studies has brought a vital focus on the novel's ethico-politically resonant exploration of aesthetics and the materiality of a world that exceeds human life.[34]

The novel's points of contact between embodied perception and the vibrancy of matter have been analysed by scholars alert to its aesthetic engagement with the new physics. Derek Ryan's post-humanist reading situates *The Waves* at a fruitful intersection between physics and philosophy, building on scholarship such as that of Gillian Beer.[35] Considering the novel's rhythmic, poetic incorporation of the language of wave-particle theory in relation to the anti-militarism of Arthur Eddington and Gerald Heard (whose scientific work Woolf read), Beer points to a 'common danger for artists and physicists' as fascism was gaining ground: 'a withdrawal from [...] the political fray, in the light of an emphasis on emptiness, porousness, atomism, undecidability'.[36] This observation captures a problem surfacing in the most perceptive critical assessments of *The Waves*: if its fervently anti-fascist aesthetic floods the boundaries that violently separate self and other, subject and object, mind and matter in the history of Western art, philosophy, and politics, what progressive, democratic force (if any) might such a poetics hold in a world where the wave of militaristic nationalism rises again and again? And if the novel's aesthetic is one of excess (manifest in the breaking wave, the rhythmic undoing of the sovereign subject), how account for the co-opting of 'oceanic feeling', primal rhythms, and effaced individual boundaries by the aesthetic and political rhetoric of fascism? These are some of the most challenging questions about aesthetics and politics that the novel itself prompts us to ask through its oceanic rhythm, its pulsating soliloquies following one another like the rising and falling of waves.[37]

---

[32] Laura Doyle, 'Introduction: What's Between Us?', *Modern Fiction Studies* 50, no. 1 (Spring 2004 [special issue on Woolf]), 6.

[33] Mid-twentieth-century philosophical approaches to *The Waves* often 'reinforced earlier stereotypes of Woolf as an [...] otherworldly writer' (Jane Goldman, ed., *Virginia Woolf, To the Lighthouse, The Waves* (New York: Columbia University Press, 1998), 69; see 53–85).

[34] A notable precursor of this century's philosophical turn is Ann Banfield's *The Phantom Table: Woolf, Fry, Russell and the Epistemology of Modernism* (Cambridge: Cambridge University Press, 2000), which unravels Woolf's depictions of a world existing independently of human consciousness.

[35] Derek Ryan, *Virginia Woolf and the Materiality of Theory: Sex, Animal, Life* (Edinburgh: Edinburgh University Press, 2013).

[36] Gillian Beer, *Virginia Woolf: The Common Ground. Essays by Gillian Beer* (Edinburgh: Edinburgh University Press, 1996), 122.

[37] Jessica Berman begins to consider this problematic (*Modernist Fiction*, 139–56), and Lyndsey Stonebridge argues that *Between the Acts* explores rhythm's potential to cultivate fascist ideology (*The Destructive Element: British Psychoanalysis and Modernism* (Basingstoke: Palgrave, 1998), 82, 94). I would argue that Woolf explored the politically regressive implications of rhythm already in *The Waves*.

And yet, Woolf insisted on the humanizing potential of literary works written 'for more than one voice', to cite the title of an unparalleled book by feminist philosopher Adriana Cavarero, works whose poly-vocal transformation of the novel genre in the direction of poetry might revive 'the democratic art of prose; its freedom, its fearlessness, its flexibility' (E4 436). 'Soliloquy' was Woolf's own term (D3 312) for what has been almost exclusively read as a form of silent interior monologue, rather than the voiced performance suggested by her playful combination of prose narrative, poetic introspection, and dramatic address. What would it mean to read Woolf's lyrical-dramatic soliloquies precisely as speech to be delivered by six voices?[38] Cavarero's *For More than One Voice: Toward a Philosophy of Vocal Expression* takes us in one compelling direction, arguing that the relational uniqueness of the voice, which signals the speaker's singularity, has been (violently) supressed, throughout the history of Western philosophy, by the solipsistic construct of the self-possessed individual. Considered as a dramatic-poetic staging of vocalized introspection, Woolf's soliloquies offer philosophical as well as political resistance to both 'the soliloquy of an *I* whose disembodied ear concentrates on its own mute voice'[39] and the chanting of a clamorous 'chorus', a term used repeatedly in the novel to figure the conformist thinking and silencing of the singular voice characterizing group psychology at its most regressive.[40]

Thus conceived, Woolf's lyrical dramatization of multiple speaking voices becomes the very locus of an anti-totalitarian, democratic, and non-violent textual politics, one that arguably inspired the generic hybridity and poly-vocality specific also to *Orlando* and *A Room of One's Own*. Gillian Beer, one of few critics to appreciate the deep resonances between these radically different works, writes:

> Each of the books Woolf wrote around the time strained across genre, attempted to break through—or disturb—the limits of the essay, the novel, the biography, to touch realities denied by accepted forms. In all her work there was an astute awareness that apparently literary questions—of genre, language, plot—are questions that touch the pith of how society constitutes and contains itself.[41]

And if these hybrid texts realize Woolf's vision, in *A Room of One's Own* and contemporaneous essays such as 'Poetry, Fiction and the Future' and 'Women and Fiction', of

---

[38] The proliferation of inter-art approaches to Woolf has shed new light on *The Waves* and other hybrid texts. See especially Maggie Humm, ed., *The Edinburgh Companion to Virginia Woolf and the Arts* (Edinburgh: Edinburgh University Press, 2010).

[39] Adriana Cavarero, *For More than One Voice: Toward a Philosophy of Vocal Expression* (Stanford: Stanford University Press, 2005), 46.

[40] See Elsa Högberg, *Virginia Woolf and the Ethics of Intimacy* (London: Bloomsbury Academic, 2020), 181–6. The political connotations of the dramatic chorus in *The Waves* have yet to be fully explored. In this novel, the chorus lacks the democratic and inter-artistic function it holds in later works such as *Between the Acts* and 'Anon'; rather, it anticipates Woolf's Freudian analysis, in *Three Guineas*, of societies as essentially prone to aggression.

[41] Beer, *Virginia Woolf*, 77.

an impersonal prose lyricism 'stand[ing] further back from life' than fiction, essays and biographies tend to do (*E4* 435), their poetic detachment enables 'not withdrawal but a means of observing patterns other than those formerly recorded'.[42] Steeped in Woolf's democratic aesthetic and political ethos, *Orlando*, *A Room of One's Own*, and *The Waves* all enkindle 'the desire to create' uniting the writer and the common reader in her account, a desire frequently lost in the 'historian and critic['s]' prosaic emphasis on the external conditions shaping a novel (*E5* 41). We would do well to take this as an admonishment to critics today: a pleasurable attentiveness to the politically transformative potential of Woolf's own novel lyricism has much to offer the vigorous, historicist scholarship of recent years, particularly in extending its archive beyond *Three Guineas* and her post-*Waves* fiction. Woolf knew, and her work from the years 1928–1932 brilliantly demonstrates, that if 'We long for ideas, for dreams, for imaginations, for poetry' in times of patriarchal, nationalist, and fascist aggression, a lyrical revival of 'the democratic art of prose' can become a vital means of resistance.

Selected Bibliography

Beer, Gillian, *Virginia Woolf: The Common Ground. Essays by Gillian Beer* (Edinburgh: Edinburgh University Press, 1996).
Berman, Jessica, *Modernist Fiction, Cosmopolitanism and the Politics of Community* (Cambridge: Cambridge University Press, 2001).
Cavarero, Adriana, *For More than One Voice: Toward a Philosophy of Vocal Expression* (Stanford: Stanford University Press, 2005).
Cuddy-Keane, Melba, *Virginia Woolf, the Intellectual, and the Public Sphere* (Cambridge: Cambridge University Press, 2003).
Froula, Christine, *Virginia Woolf and the Bloomsbury Avant-Garde: War, Civilization, Modernity* (New York: Columbia University Press, 2004).
Goldman, Jane, 'Burning Feminism: Virginia Woolf's Laboratory of Intimacy', in Elsa Högberg, ed., '*Modernist Intimacies* (Edinburgh: Edinburgh University Press, 2021), 52–73.'
Helt, Brenda S., and Madelyn Detloff, eds., *Queer Bloomsbury* (Edinburgh: Edinburgh University Press, 2016).
Humm, Maggie, ed., *The Edinburgh Companion to Virginia Woolf and the Arts* (Edinburgh: Edinburgh University Press, 2010).
Högberg, Elsa, and Amy Bromley, eds., *Sentencing* Orlando: *Virginia Woolf and the Morphology of the Modernist Sentence* (Edinburgh: Edinburgh University Press, 2018).
Marcus, Jane, 'Britannia Rules *The Waves*', in Eleanor McNees, ed., *Virginia Woolf: Critical Assessments*, vol. IV (Mountfield: Helm Information, 1994), 75–96.
Marcus, Jane, *Virginia Woolf and the Languages of Patriarchy* (Bloomington: Indiana University Press, 1987).
Monson, Tamlyn, '"A Trick of the Mind": Alterity, Ontology, and Representation in Virginia Woolf's *The Waves*', *Modern Fiction Studies* 50, no. 1 (Spring 2004), 173–96.

---

[42] Beer, *Virginia Woolf*, 49.

Pawlowski, Merry M., ed., *Virginia Woolf and Fascism: Resisting the Dictators' Seduction* (Basingstoke: Palgrave Macmillan, 2001).

Raitt, Suzanne, *Vita and Virginia: The Work and Friendship of V. Sackville-West and Virginia Woolf* (Oxford: Clarendon Press, 1993).

Simpson, Kathryn, *Gifts, Markets and Economies of Desire in Virginia Woolf* (Basingstoke: Palgrave Macmillan, 2009).

CHAPTER 8

LATE WORKS (1933–1941)

ALICE WOOD

On 25 April 1933, Virginia Woolf wrote excitedly of her present project, 'The Pargiters': 'I think this will be a terrific affair. I must be bold & adventurous. I want to give the whole of the present society—nothing less: facts, as well as the vision. And to combine them both. I mean, The Waves going on simultaneously with Night & Day. Is this possible?' (*D4* 151–2). This ambitious work had its origins in Woolf's conception of 'an entire new book—a sequel to a Room of Ones [sic.] Own—about the sexual life of women' on 20 January 1931, a day before giving her speech on 'Professions for Women' to the Junior Council of the London & National Society for Women's Service (*D4* 6). Begun in late 1932 as 'an Essay-Novel' (*D4* 129), *The Pargiters* evolved into two works: Woolf's penultimate novel *The Years* (1937) and her anti-war pamphlet *Three Guineas* (1938). By February 1933 Woolf had abandoned the hybrid format, but her plans for the text remained innovative. Facts would be compacted into the fiction, combined with 'the vision', and she hoped to include 'satire, comedy, poetry, narrative' too, asking herself 'what form is to hold them all together?' (*D4* 151–2). The political aims of the project notably drove its radical formal intentions. This book was to hold 'millions of ideas but no preaching—history, politics, feminism, art, literature' (*D4* 152). Feminism and literary experimentalism were closely intertwined throughout Woolf's career. In her late works, including *The Years*, *Three Guineas*, and her final novel *Between the Acts* (1941), politics became central to guiding her creative practice. During 1933–1941, in the context of the Great Depression, fascism, and war, Woolf's urge to document and analyse the society around her—to express 'all I know, feel, laugh at, despise, like, admire hate & so on'— energized and directed her writing in new ways (*D4* 152).

During her lifetime, however, Woolf's late turn to socio-political analysis and its impact on her literary experiments went largely unnoticed. This chapter's use of 'late' to identify a distinct and final phase in Woolf's oeuvre is shaped of course by a retrospective viewpoint and knowledge of her death on 28 March 1941. In the turbulent economic and political climate of the 1930s and early 1940s, in contrast, during which explicitly political and socially engaged literature thrived in Britain, Woolf was routinely caricatured as a remote, outmoded, and declining aesthete. Following her high modernist fiction of the 1920s and *The Waves* (1931), her published works of 1933–1941 seemed to retreat from stylistic innovation. *Flush* (1933), her playful biography of Elizabeth Barrett Browning's dog, presented a clear narrative that appealed to a broad audience, selling 'over 18,000 copies in its first six months in the UK alone'.[1] Reviewing the book in *Harper's Bazaar* (UK), Sylvia Lynd praised its 'straightforward pleasing quality'.[2] *The Years* was read on publication as a similarly straightforward family chronicle despite Woolf's radical aspirations for the text. The novel topped the *New York Herald Tribune*'s bestselling fiction list from 9 May to 18 July 1937[3] and was reviewed in *Time* on 12 April 1937 with a photograph of Woolf by Man Ray on the cover, carrying with it, as Brenda R. Silver notes, 'connotations of celebrity, of stardom'.[4] Meanwhile, Edwin Muir in the *Listener* concluded that 'after *The Waves* this is a disappointing book'.[5] The popular success of *Flush* and *The Years* compounded the critical perception of a highbrow writer past her peak; at the same time, the social criticism of both works was overlooked. When Woolf did address politics directly in *Three Guineas*, many critics resisted her feminist analysis and pacifist position by presenting her thinking as outdated or ill-informed. Though Theodora Bosanquet in the feminist weekly *Time and Tide* celebrated Woolf's anti-war polemic as 'a revolutionary bomb of a book', Graham Greene in the *Spectator* rather misogynistically dismissed it as 'a little old-fashioned', 'a little shrill', and the product of 'a too sheltered life'.[6] Attacking *Three Guineas* in *Scrutiny*, Q.D. Leavis declared: 'Mrs Woolf is not living in the contemporary world ... [and] is quite insulated by class'.[7] The publication of *Roger Fry* (1940), Woolf's biography of her friend the Bloomsbury art critic, perpetuated the impression of her privileged isolation. Herbert Read admired the book's 'directness' while characterizing the Bloomsbury set as an antiquated '*élite*' who 'turned with a shudder from ... "the herd" '.[8] Published posthumously in July 1941, *Between the Acts* marked a return to overt experimentalism but the novel's apparently nostalgic setting—an English country house prior to World War II—supported the view that her art and politics were backward and obsolete. Woolf's suicide, erroneously reported in the press as being a result of her inability to face the anxiety of wartime, overshadowed early readings of the novel.[9] The *Times Literary Supplement* ruled that '*Between the Acts* is not among Virginia Woolf's best work'.[10]

---

[1] Julia Briggs, *Virginia Woolf: An Inner Life* (London: Penguin, 2006), 300.
[2] Sylvia Lynd, 'Literary News', *Harper's Bazaar* (UK), October 1933, 68.
[3] See Anna Snaith, 'Introduction' to Virginia Woolf, *The Years*, ed. Anna Snaith (Cambridge: Cambridge University Press, 2012), lxxxvii.
[4] Brenda R. Silver, *Virginia Woolf: Icon* (Chicago and London: University of Chicago Press, 1999), 79.
[5] Quoted in Robin Majumdar and Allen McLaurin, eds, *Virginia Woolf: The Critical Heritage* (London: Routledge, 1975), 388.
[6] Quoted in Majumdar and McLaurin, *Virginia Woolf*, 402, 407–8.
[7] Quoted in Majumdar and McLaurin, *Virginia Woolf*, 409.
[8] Quoted in Majumdar and McLaurin, *Virginia Woolf*, 420–1.
[9] See Mark Hussey on the novel's early critical reception in his 'Introduction' to Virginia Woolf, *Between the Acts*, ed. Mark Hussey (Cambridge: Cambridge University Press, 2011), lvi–lix.
[10] Quoted in Majumdar and McLaurin, *Virginia Woolf*, 439.

Subsequent critical accounts of Woolf's late works have rewritten these first impressions. Feminist critics of the 1970s and 1980s began this process by reinstating *Three Guineas* as a key text in Woolf's oeuvre and highlighting interrogations of patriarchy, nationalism, imperialism, fascism, and war across her late writing.[11] A turn to the archive yielded copious private and pre-publication documents—including the unabridged diary, letters, notebooks, and drafts—revealing Woolf's attention to contemporary society and politics throughout her life and especially in the years approaching and following the outbreak of World War II. Between 1931 and 1937, Woolf kept scrapbooks of newspaper cuttings and extracts from books and articles relating to the oppression of women and national and international politics.[12] Study of her eight-volume *Pargiters* manuscript has shown this research informed the composition of *The Years* and *Three Guineas* and uncovered explicit socio-political commentary in the novel at draft stage.[13] Woolf submerged and dramatized her feminist analysis in *The Years*, which expands and elucidates her lifelong criticism of Britain's patriarchal values, social structures, and public institutions by depicting their influence on three generations of the upper-middle-class Pargiter family from 1880 to the present day. In *Three Guineas*, envisaged as a separate political pamphlet from 1935, Woolf carefully set out her complex feminist-pacifist argument that the dictator abroad extended from the patriarch at home, and that women of her own class—the daughters of educated men—must reject and oppose the acquisitive and patriotic ideals of patriarchal society to help prevent war. *Between the Acts* further examined English culture and society in the face of international conflict, satirizing patriarchy, patriotism, and imperialism while exploring collective fears for England's survival through portraying the residents of Pointz Hall, their insular community, and Miss La Trobe's subversive village pageant on one day in June 1939. Scholarly interpretations from a range of theoretical perspectives have analysed the breadth as well as the limitations of Woolf's political thinking in these texts.[14] In

---

[11] See, for example, the *Bulletin of the New York Public Library* 80, no. 2 (Winter 1977), a special issue on *The Years* and *Three Guineas*; Jane Marcus, ed., *New Feminist Essays on Virginia Woolf* (London: Macmillan, 1981); Jane Marcus, ed., *Virginia Woolf: A Feminist Slant* (Lincoln: University of Nebraska Press, 1983).

[12] Virginia Woolf, *The Three Guineas Scrapbooks*, 3 vols, Monks House Papers Archive, University of Sussex, B.16f.

[13] See Grace Radin, *Virginia Woolf's* The Years: *The Evolution of a Novel* (Knoxville: University of Tennessee Press, 1981); Susan M. Squier m, 'The Politics of City Space in *The Years*: Street Love, Pillar Boxes and Bridges', in Jane Marcus, ed., *New Feminist Essays on Virginia Woolf* (London: Macmillan, 1981), 216–37; Susan Squier, 'A Track of our Own: Typescript Drafts of *The Years*,' in Jane Marcus, ed., *Virginia Woolf: A Feminist Slant*, 198–211; Alice Wood, *Virginia Woolf's Late Cultural Criticism: The Genesis of* The Years, Three Guineas *and* Between the Acts (London: Bloomsbury Academic, 2013).

[14] For a sample of this work, see Alex Zwerdling, *Virginia Woolf and the Real World* (Berkeley: University of California Press 1986); Rachel Bowlby, *Virginia Woolf: Feminist Destinations* (Oxford: Blackwell, 1988); Mark Hussey, ed., *Virginia Woolf and War: Fiction, Reality, and Myth* (Syracuse, NY: Syracuse University Press, 1991); Pamela L. Caughie, *Virginia Woolf and Postmodernism: Literature in Quest & Question of Itself* (Urbana: University of Illinois Press, 1991); Katherine J. Phillips, *Virginia Woolf Against Empire* (Knoxville: University of Tennessee Press, 1994); Gillian Beer, *Virginia Woolf: The Common Ground* (Edinburgh: Edinburgh University Press,

the twenty-first century, her late works continue to attract sustained interest in Woolf studies[15] and from scholars of 'late modernism', a critical category used to identify a more politically alert and participatory model of literary modernism from the later interwar period and after.[16] This chapter approaches Woolf's late writing thematically, reading across *The Years*, *Three Guineas*, *Between the Acts*, and beyond, with a focus on her responses to mixing literature and politics, to patriarchy and fascism, and to nationalism and war. It stresses the close relationship between these works and between political engagement and literary experimentalism through her late career. Far from precipitating a creative decline, Woolf's late political turn drove the desire to 'be bold & adventurous' in her art (*D4* 151).

MIXING ART AND POLITICS

The relationship between art and politics was a recurrent concern for Woolf during 1933–1941. Writing in an age of propaganda, she was deeply distrustful of literature produced as part of a political programme, yet also maintained that writers and their works are indelibly connected to, and the product of, their society and historical moment. In 'Why Art To-Day Follows Politics' (1936), an article written in support of the Artists' International Association and published by the Communist Party of Great Britain's *Daily Worker*, she argued that 'the practice of art, far from making the artist out of touch with his kind, rather increases his sensibility' (*E6* 77). In the past, Woolf contends, it was held that 'to mix art with politics ... was to adulterate it', but in the present moment (this essay was printed five months into the Spanish Civil War) she claims the artist is 'affected as powerfully as other citizens when society is in chaos' and 'is forced to take part in politics' (*E6* 76–7). Woolf's reflections on this topic speak to wider debates in the period, during which overtly political writing flourished in Britain against a backdrop of national and international unrest.

1996); Merry M. Pawlowski, ed., *Virginia Woolf and Fascism: Resisting the Dictators' Seduction* (Basingstoke: Palgrave, 2001).

[15] See Anna Snaith, *Virginia Woolf: Public and Private Negotiations* (Basingstoke: Palgrave, 2000); Naomi Black, *Virginia Woolf as Feminist* (Ithaca, NY: Cornell University Press, 2004); Anne E. Fernald, *Virginia Woolf: Feminism and the Reader* (New York: Palgrave, 2006); Judith Allen, *Virginia Woolf and the Politics of Language* (Edinburgh: Edinburgh University Press, 2010); John Whittier-Ferguson, 'Repetition, Remembering, Repetition: Virginia Woolf's Late Fiction and the Return of War', *Modern Fiction Studies* 57, no. 2 (2011), 230–53; Evelyn Tsz Yan Chan, *Virginia Woolf and the Professions* (Cambridge: Cambridge University Press, 2014); and Wood, *Woolf's Late Cultural Criticism*.

[16] See Jed Esty, *A Shrinking Island: Modernism and National Culture in England* (Princeton, NJ: Princeton University Press, 2004); Marina MacKay, *Modernism and World War II* (Cambridge: Cambridge University Press, 2007); Thomas S. Davis, *The Extinct Scene: Late Modernism and Everyday Life* (New York: Columbia University Press, 2015).

'The thirties was the decade in which young writers became involved in politics', Stephen Spender recalled in 1978, and '[t]he politics of this generation were almost exclusively those of the left'.[17] Woolf's uneasy dialogue with these younger writers—dubbed 'the Auden generation' by Samuel Hynes's classic study—was informed by their antagonism towards her own generation and her difference from them in literary method and outlook.[18] In 'The Leaning Tower' (1940), an essay derived from her lecture on modern literature for the Brighton branch of the Workers' Education Association on 27 April 1940, Woolf addressed the work of 'Day Lewis, Auden, Spender, Isherwood, Louis MacNeice and so on' and lamented 'the pedagogic, the didactic, the loud speaker strain that dominates their poetry' (*E6* 267, 272). Here, as in her *Letter to a Young Poet* (1932), Woolf characterizes the work of the male, public-school-educated, leftist writers of the 1930s as marred by 'rage' and a tendency to 'preach' (*E5* 310; *E6* 272). These objections recall her claim in *A Room of One's Own* (1929) that Charlotte Brontë's works are 'deformed and twisted' because she writes 'in a rage where she should write calmly', and writes 'of herself where she should write of her characters' (*ARO* 90). For Woolf, personal anger damages the artistic integrity of a literary work. Antagonism and didacticism impair the poetry of the Auden generation in her view, though she acknowledges the political direction of literature is inevitable in the current climate.

As Jane Marcus has influentially argued, 'Woolf used her own art for propagandistic purposes'.[19] While resisting didacticism, Woolf consistently expressed her politics through her art and nowhere more so than in her late works. Woolf's major literary undertaking of the 1930s, the hybrid project that became *The Years* and *Three Guineas*, was shaped by the wish to expand and vocalize her feminist cultural analysis and to evidence this analysis with thorough research. In the early stages of composition, she applied to friends for information—including Ethel Smyth in December 1932 for 'a few facts' on 'Mrs Pankhurst and the suffrage' (*L5* 141)—and sifted historical and cultural sources through her practice of collating newspaper articles in scrapbooks. These three volumes are usually termed the '*Three Guineas* scrapbooks' by critics, but their research first informed *The Pargiters*. The five fictional chapters of her 'novel-essay' were written as extracts from a voluminous 'novel of fact' in which 'scarcely a statement ... cannot be ... verified' (*P* 9). By January 1933 Woolf was becoming 'afraid of the didactic' and the essays were soon omitted, but she continued to weave her feminist commentary and research through the fiction of *The Years* (*D4* 145). Thus, the campaign for women's suffrage remains present through oblique references to Rose Pargiter's suffragette activity, such as in '1911' when Eleanor Pargiter confirms Rose has 'been had up in a police-court' because she 'threw a brick' (*Y* 184).

---

[17] Stephen Spender, *The Thirties and After: Poetry, Politics, People (1933–75)*, (Basingstoke: Palgrave, 1978), 13.

[18] Samuel Hynes, *The Auden Generation: Literature and Politics in England in the 1930s* (London: Bodley Head, 1976).

[19] Jane Marcus, *Art & Anger: Reading Like a Woman* (Columbus: Ohio State University Press, 1988), 103.

Ultimately, *The Years* conveys Woolf's feminism covertly, but the desire to fuse politics and aesthetics nevertheless directed its literary method. The parallel composition of *Three Guineas* as an overtly polemical work of 1930s peace propaganda further demonstrates her conviction in 'Why Art To-Day Follows Politics' and 'The Leaning Tower' that writers must address politics with war approaching. Written as three interlinking letters replying to requests for money from three campaigning societies, this propagandistic text fuses fiction with argument; 'its narrator is not Woolf herself', Naomi Black observes, and 'the addressees of the letters are imagined instead of actual identifiable individuals'.[20] Its challenging structure, supported by a set of explanatory notes, is Woolf's creative answer to the problem of responding directly but not didactically to totalitarianism and war. An intensively self-reflexive text, *Between the Acts* also asks how art can address and influence a society threatened by violence through the figure of Miss La Trobe and her precarious pageant. The novel's explicit references to pre-war contexts—the French Prime Minister, 'M. Daladier … pegging down the franc', for example, and 'Europe, bristling with guns'—insist that neither life nor art are immune from politics in the face of international conflict, paradoxically evoking the moment before Britain's entry into World War II for readers living through that event (*BA* 10, 39). Woolf's late works blend fact with fiction and art with argument in an experimental response to the pressing political contexts of her time.

Patriarchy and Fascism

When Woolf began drafting *The Pargiters* in October 1932, her innovative 'novel-essay' focused on the restrictions placed on women's private and public lives. The second *Pargiters* essay cites an article drawn from Woolf's first research scrapbook on 'The Chaperonage Age' by Countess Lovelace, for example, in which Lovelace describes 'the social taboo' that made it unthinkable 'for my sisters and me to go out alone into the streets' in the nineteenth century (*P* 37).[21] When the essays were dropped, the fiction continued to depict the impact of chaperonage on unmarried middle-class women and the wider implications of women's historical exclusion from public space. In the '1880' chapter of *The Years*, Eleanor wonders which of her sisters will accompany her father to a dinner party, while Delia and Milly look longingly into the street as a young man visits their neighbour. Turning back into the room, Delia exclaims 'Oh my God!' and considers her situation 'hopeless' (*Y* 17–18). Fifty years later in the 'Present Day' chapter, when asked by her niece Peggy, a doctor, whether she was 'suppressed when [she] was young', Eleanor suddenly remembers: 'Delia standing in the middle of the room; Oh my

---

[20] Black, *Woolf as Feminist*, 73.
[21] Mary Caroline Wortley, Countess of Lovelace, 'Fifty Years, Society and the Season, The Chaperoned Age', *The Times*, 9 March 1932, 13–14. This article can be found in Woolf, *Three Guineas Scrapbooks*, Monks House Papers Archive B.16f, vol. 1, 29.

God! Oh my God! she was saying; a hansom cab had stopped at the house next door; and she herself was watching Morris—was it Morris?—going down the street to post a letter' (*Y* 302-3). Woolf's novel shows how the Pargiter sisters' inability to move freely outside the home in their youth restricted their opportunities for intellectual growth, financial independence, emotional fulfilment, and a sexual life—denying Eleanor a formal education and profession like her niece. The image of Morris stepping out to post a letter signifies their brothers' easy freedoms in comparison and may recall for the reader Rose's childhood encounter with a predatory man by the local 'pillar-box', symbolizing male domination over public space and its physical as well as psychological and economic threat to women (*Y* 25).

In *Flush*, drafted during 1931–1932, Woolf had already depicted the constraints of chaperonage and the confines of the nineteenth-century upper-middle-class home. Her spoof biography explores British hierarchies of gender, class, and race through a dog's-eye view. Living at Wimpole Street with Elizabeth Barrett, Flush discovers 'the dogs of London ... are strictly divided into different classes' and that he is 'a dog of birth and breeding' (*F* 23). He consequently 'accept[s] the protection of the chain' around his neck and curbs his instinct to 'run wild' like the 'unkempt and uncollared' (*F* 22-3). Trapped in 'a cushioned and firelit cave' due to his owner's poor health and domineering father, Flush learns, as Barrett Browning has, '[t]o resign, to control, to suppress the most violent instincts of his nature' (*F* 24-5). The taming of Flush parallels the subjugation of nineteenth-century middle-class women, like his writer owner, who must similarly accept restrictions on their independence in return for a comfortable home and the preservation of their social status. As Pamela Caughie has noted, however, Flush is also Barrett Browning's personal property—a commodity bought, stolen, and ransomed— and as such 'resembles less the woman writer than the writer's servant'.[22] Woolf's canine subject invites multiple interpretations. Anna Snaith observes that 'Flush's value in London relies on ideas of purity, the exclusive, unadulterated pure-bred' and shows how his responses to the Whitechapel dog-snatchers evoke nineteenth-century stereotypes of the working classes and contemporary anti-Semitic discourse towards Jews in the East End.[23] 'By attributing the "bestial" view of Whitechapel to an aristocratic *dog*', she argues, 'Woolf exposes the ridiculousness of the hierarchies'.[24] '*Flush* is,' Snaith compellingly suggests, 'part of Woolf's anti-fascist writing of the 1930s', which mocks 'the language of eugenics and racial superiority' and the ideology it supports.[25]

For Woolf, fascism was fundamentally an extension of patriarchy. When invited to join the committee of an anti-Fascist exhibition by Elizabeth Bibesco in late 1934, she insisted on the relevance of 'the woman question' to the project (*D4* 273). Bibesco

---

[22] Pamela L. Caughie, '*Flush* and the Literary Canon: Oh Where Oh Where Has That Little Dog Gone?', *Tulsa Studies in Women's Literature* 10, no. 1 (1991), 60.

[23] Anna Snaith, 'Of Fanciers, Footnotes, and Fascism: Virginia Woolf's *Flush*', *Modern Fiction Studies* 48, no. 3 (2002), 622.

[24] Snaith, 'Of Fanciers, Footnotes, and Fascism', 624 (original emphasis).

[25] Snaith, 'Of Fanciers, Footnotes, and Fascism', 631.

objected: 'I am afraid that it had not occurred to me that in matters of ultimate importance even feminists c[oul]d wish to segregate & label the sexes' (*D4* 273). 'What about Hitler?' Woolf replied (*D4* 273). In *Three Guineas*, her narrator contends that the British patriarch is 'the egg of the very same worm that we know under other names in other countries.... Dictator as we call him when he is Italian or German, who believes that he has the right ... to dictate to other human beings how they shall live' (*TG* 228–9). She argues that the patriarchal system and its institutions—from public schools and universities to the professions and the church—not only oppress women, but breed in men 'unreal loyalties', 'possessiveness', 'jealousy', 'pugnacity', and 'greed', which together create the conditions for tyranny and war to thrive (*TG* 271, 275).

Photographs of continental dictatorial figures from newspaper cuttings in Woolf's second research scrapbook—Austria's former vice chancellor, Major Emil Fey, for example, and Count Galeazzo Ciano, Mussolini's son-in-law and chief propagandist—reveal a familiarity with European politics rarely explicit in her writing, but which crucially informed her feminism and the symbolic use of newspapers and photographs in her late works.[26] Fascist tyranny looms through a photograph in the 'Present Day' chapter of *The Years* as Eleanor stutters 'Damned ... bully!' in response to a 'blurred picture of a fat man gesticulating' (presumably Mussolini) in the evening newspaper (*Y* 298). *Three Guineas* includes five photographs of British patriarchal figures rather than fascist leaders, reflecting Woolf's insistence on the need to recognize the dictator at home, which resonate portentously with the text's repeated description of 'photographs of dead bodies' and 'ruined houses' from the Spanish Civil War (*TG* 164–5).[27] In *Between the Acts*, newspaper reports of violence and persecution disrupt the pre-war holiday atmosphere of Pointz Hall, to which Giles Oliver arrives having read of 'sixteen men ... shot, others prisoned, just over there, across the gulf in the flat land which divided them from the continent' (*BA* 34). Through the character of Giles, Woolf illustrates her *Three Guineas* argument that patriarchy creates domestic dictators. Unhappy in his life and profession as a stockbroker—'[g]iven his choice, he would have chosen to farm'—Giles tyrannically turns his resentment towards others (*BA* 34). His aunt Lucy Swithin, perceived as 'foolish' and 'free', provides one target for his misogynist anger; William Dodge, the Olivers' unobtrusive homosexual lunch guest, supplies 'another peg on which to hang his rage' (*BA* 34, 44). Only violent action 'relieve[s] him' as he stamps dead a snake choking on a toad (*BA* 72). Giles displays 'the desire for aggression; the desire to dominate and enslave' that Woolf identified in her 1940 essay 'Thoughts on Peace in an Air Raid', citing Lady Astor in *The Times*, as 'a subconscious

---

[26] Woolf, *Three Guineas Scrapbooks*, Monks House Papers Archive B.16f, vol. 2, 5, 20.

[27] On the use of photographs in *Three Guineas*, see Alice Staveley, 'Name That Face', *Virginia Woolf Miscellany*, 51 (1998), 4–5; Maggie Humm, 'Memory, Photography, and Modernism: The "dead bodies and ruined houses" of Virginia Woolf's *Three Guineas*', *Signs* 28, no. 2 (2003), 645–63; Emily Dalgarno, *Virginia Woolf and the Visible World* (Cambridge: Cambridge University Press, 2001); and, Rebecca Wisor, 'About Face: The *Three Guineas* Photographs in Cultural Context', *Woolf Studies Annual* 21, (2015), 1–49.

Hitlerism in the hearts of men' (*E6* 243). His silent attack on William as '[a] toady; a lickspittle; not a downright plain man of his senses' evokes the persecution of homosexuals alongside Jews and other minorities under fascism (*BA* 44). Driving through Germany in May 1935, Woolf had witnessed first-hand '[b]anners stretched across the street' declaring 'The Jew is our enemy' as she and her Jewish husband Leonard inadvertently encountered a rally for Göring in Bonn (*D4* 311).

'The whole iniquity of dictatorship', Woolf argues in *Three Guineas*, 'whether in Oxford or Cambridge, in Whitehall or Downing Street, against Jews or against women, in England, or in Germany, in Italy or in Spain is now apparent' (*TG* 304). Her narrator identifies nineteenth-century feminists as 'the advance guard' of the contemporary anti-fascist movement and, by burning the divisive word 'feminist', hopes to see the sons and daughters of educated men 'working together for the same cause' (*TG* 303). Yet Woolf insists in *Three Guineas* that as women enter higher education, the professions, and public life, they must reject the acquisitive and patriotic values of patriarchal institutions, maintain indifference to militarism, and absent themselves from 'all such ceremonies as encourage the desire to impose "our" civilization or "our" dominion upon other people' (*TG* 314). Her narrator will not join her male correspondent's society campaigning for peace and the protection of culture and intellectual liberty, but proposes to form an alternative 'Outsiders' Society', through which the daughters of educated men can work apart 'but in co-operation' with their brothers against patriarchy, fascism, and war (*TG* 309).

Nationalism and War

In the final chapter of *Three Guineas*, the narrator tells her male correspondent that she 'has no wish to be "English" on the same terms that you yourself are "English"' (*TG* 301). She gives her guinea to his cause, but 'does not claim in return ... admission to any profession; any honour, title, or medal; ... any seat upon any society, committee or board' (*TG* 301). This argument had been rehearsed in the '1910' chapter of *The Pargiters*, in which Elvira (Sara in *The Years*) determines to reject the vote after attending a suffrage meeting with her cousin Rose and deciding she 'do[es]n't want to be an Englishwoman'.[28] Discussing the matter with her sister Maggie, Elvira sets out their position in a letter that anticipates the epistolary form and polite but combative tone of *Three Guineas*: 'In our opinion the acceptance of a vote makes us liable to honours we deplore, & to services which we abominate—meaning by that titles, degrees & shooting savages with muskets'.[29] Elvira's letter was omitted from *The Years* and this debate was

---

[28] Virginia Woolf, *The Pargiters* MS, 8 vols, Henry W. and Albert A. Berg Collection of English and American Literature, New York Public Library, M.42, vol. 4, 57.

[29] *The Pargiters* MS, Berg Collection M.42, vol. 4, 64.

deferred until *Three Guineas*, where it was reframed as feminist resistance to war.[30] In that text, speaking in the voice of the female outsider, Woolf asserts:

> 'Our country' ... throughout the greater part of its history has treated me as a slave; it has denied me education or any share in its possessions.... Therefore if you insist upon fighting to protect me, or 'our' country, let it be understood, soberly and rationally between us, that you are fighting to gratify a sex instinct which I cannot share.... [A]s a woman, I have no country. As a woman I want no country. As a woman my country is the whole world. (*TG* 313)

Woolf's anti-patriotism and internationalist stance were closely bound to her feminist rejection of patriarchal values and traditions, but they also represent a broader political position aligned with the peace movement in the interwar period. The notion of international citizenship was advocated by numerous women's organizations in the 1920s and 1930s, including the Women's Co-operative Guild with which Woolf was associated, and its aspirations were epitomized by the League of Nations, of which Leonard Woolf was an influential proponent.[31] Internationalist politics accorded with Woolf's lifelong pacifism and infused much of her late writing, which is acutely alert to connections between patriotism, militarism, and war.

At the same time, however, Woolf's late works are preoccupied with exploring the past, present, and future of her society and national culture. During 1933–1941, she interrogated the patriarchal and imperialist legacies she viewed as corrosive in Britain and Europe, while responding nostalgically to everyday English life now threatened by fascism and war. In the '1911' chapter of *The Years*, Eleanor Pargiter contemplates England with mixed feelings as she visits Morris and Celia in rural Dorset following a trip to Southern Europe. This chapter prefigures *Between the Acts* in setting—a country house on the day of a village play and bazaar raising funds for the local church—and through its ambivalent probing of Englishness. 'England was disappointing,' Eleanor reflects as she looks out on 'the burnt, dry lawn' before dinner; 'it was small; it was pretty; she felt no affection for her native land' (*Y* 179). Yet, after dinner on the terrace, she concedes that the landscape 'ha[s] its beauty' and cries out '"How lovely it is!" ... as if she were making amends to England after Spain' (*Y* 185). Eleanor's patriotic impulse parallels that of the female outsider in *Three Guineas*, who, after declaring herself a citizen of the world, finds that 'still some obstinate emotion remains, some love of England' (*TG* 313). This patriotic emotion is evident, too, in Eleanor's delight in

---

[30] For further discussion of this revision process see Squier, 'A Track of Our Own', and Wood, *Woolf's Late Cultural Criticism*.

[31] On Woolf's association with the Women's Co-operative Guild, see Alice Wood, 'Facing *Life as We Have Known It*: Virginia Woolf and the Women's Co-operative Guild', *Literature & History*, 23, no. 2 (2014), 18–34; and chapter 3 in Clara Jones's *Virginia Woolf: Ambivalent Activist* (Edinburgh: Edinburgh University Press, 2016). Leonard Woolf's *International Government* (Westminster: Fabian Society, 1916) encouraged the British government to promote the establishment of a League of Nations after World War I, in which Leonard was involved until its collapse in the mid-1930s.

'commonplace words, spoken by Celia quite simply', which strike her as 'pure English' (*Y* 186). While Eleanor romanticizes England's landscape and Celia's speech, the narrative gently mocks Celia's provincialism as she talks of Eleanor's cousin Maggie, now married to René, and the prospect of their baby's birth abroad. '"I do wish it could have been born in England"', Celia muses: '"Her children will be French, I suppose?"' (*Y* 186). The thought that Maggie's children will not be English unsettles Celia by exposing the arbitrariness of nationality, especially for women, which Woolf addressed explicitly in *Three Guineas* with a reminder that '[a woman] becomes a foreigner if she marries a foreigner' according to British law at this time (*TG* 312). Anticipating *Three Guineas* and *Between the Acts*, *The Years* evokes the contingency of nationality alongside depicting Eleanor's examination of her national feeling.

Between the Acts expands this exploration of English national identity with increased urgency and intensity in response to wartime contexts: from Nazi Germany's invasion of Austria on 12 March 1938, three weeks before the text was begun, to nightly air raids during the Battle of Britain, which hit the Woolfs' London home in September 1940. Echoing '1911' in *The Years*, the Pointz Hall residents idealize the English countryside and their view of 'flat, field-parcelled land' that seems impervious to change, though Giles portentously imagines '[a]t any moment guns would rake that land into furrows' (*BA* 38–9). Jed Esty interprets the novel as part of an 'anthropological turn' by late modernist writers as 'the political crises of the time compelled intellectuals to think nationally, but also shifted the real terms of national identity away from aggressive Britishness, toward humane Englishness'.[32] The book's action centres on Miss La Trobe's anti-nationalistic pageant, which deviates from popular Empire Day pageants of the day by surveying English history through its literature—Middle English poetry, Restoration comedy, Victorian music hall, Edwardian drama—rather than national or military events. By omitting patriotic elements, Miss La Trobe, and Woolf, explore communal English identity without inciting the 'national self-praise' that *Three Guineas* identified as fuelling militarism and war (*TG* 314). Instead, the satirical scenes of the Pointz Hall pageant invite a critical response. Mr Budge, the local publican, dressed as 'a Victorian Constable', delivers a monologue exposing nineteenth-century patriarchy and imperialism to ridicule; wielding his truncheon, he commands 'the traffic of 'Er Majesty's Empire' and the morals of 'Her Majesty's minions', asserting his dominion '[o]ver thought and religion; drink; dress; manners; marriage too' and pompously declaring that 'to direct the traffic … at 'Yde Park Corner … is a whole-time, white man's job' (*BA* 116–8). 'Tut-tut-tut … There were grand men among them', one pageant spectator retorts defensively to this portrayal of Victorian authority, feeling 'a sneer had been aimed at her father; therefore at herself' (*BA* 118). Another spectator tuts too, but then reflects: 'children did draw trucks in mines … and divorced ladies were not received at Court. How difficult to come to any conclusion!' (*BA* 118).

---

[32] Esty, *A Shrinking Island*, 2, 17.

Alongside examining England's past, *Between the Acts* evokes the present and urges readers to consider their country's future. The pageant's expected patriotic finale, with a 'Grand Ensemble, round the Union Jack', is replaced with Miss La Trobe's final speech calling her cast and audience 'Liars most of us. Thieves too' (*BA* 114, 134). 'Look at ourselves, ladies and gentlemen!' Miss La Trobe begs the pageant-goers; 'ask how's this wall, the great wall, which we call, perhaps miscall, civilisation, to be built by ... orts, scraps and fragments like ourselves?' (*BA* 135). The ominous sound of droning in the novel—from the 'drone of the trees' in the garden to the 'drone' of the '[t]welve aeroplanes in perfect formation' that interrupt Reverend Streatfield's speech—suggests the intrusive drone of aircraft during the Battle of Britain and emphasizes that English culture and society cannot remain '[i]solated on a green island' (*BA* 11, 138–9). References to Pointz Hall's close proximity to the Channel—'Thirty-five [miles] only'—combine with the novel's allusions to international events to undercut the notion of England as a sheltered island nation (*BA* 21). *Between the Acts* explores English communal life alongside critiquing patriotism, militarism, and imperialism, and, in accord with Woolf's pacifist internationalism, insists that England must recognize and refashion itself as an active and co-operative member of a wider European community.

Conclusions

'Thinking is my fighting', Woolf wrote in her diary on 15 May 1940 (*D5* 285). The desire to expand and express her feminist thinking in response to the political crises of her time dominated Woolf's late writing. Always wary of didacticism, she sought new ways to fuse aesthetics and politics in her late works. The wish to include 'millions of ideas but no preaching' in her creative output propelled her experimentalism and re-energized her literary practice during 1933–1941 (*D4* 152). Woolf's major late works are particularly tightly entwined within her oeuvre due to their mutual concern with blending fact with fiction, narrative with argument, and their overlapping analyses of patriarchy, fascism, nationalism, and war. This chapter has demonstrated close correspondences between *The Years*, *Three Guineas*, and *Between the Acts* as well as Woolf's wider late writings, through which she articulated her evolving feminist-pacifist response to European fascism and war as she endeavoured to negotiate a new relationship between her politics and her art.

Selected Bibliography

Beer, Gillian, *Virginia Woolf: The Common Ground* (Edinburgh: Edinburgh University Press, 1996).
Black, Naomi, *Virginia Woolf as Feminist* (New York: Cornell University Press, 2004).
Briggs, Julia, *Virginia Woolf: An Inner Life* (London: Penguin, 2006).

Caughie, Pamela L., '*Flush* and the Literary Canon: Oh Where Oh Where Has That Little Dog Gone?', *Tulsa Studies in Women's Literature* 10, no. 1 (1991), 47–66.

Esty, Jed, *A Shrinking Island: Modernism and National Culture in England* (Princeton, NJ: Princeton University Press, 2004).

Humm, Maggie, 'Memory, Photography, and Modernism: The "dead bodies and ruined houses" of Virginia Woolf's *Three Guineas*', *Signs* 28, no. 2 (2003), 645–63.

Marcus, Jane, *Art & Anger: Reading Like a Woman* (Columbus, OH: Ohio State University Press, 1988).

Radin, Grace, *Virginia Woolf's The Years: The Evolution of a Novel* (Knoxville: University of Tennessee Press, 1981).

Snaith, Anna, 'Of Fanciers, Footnotes, and Fascism: Virginia Woolf's *Flush*', *Modern Fiction Studies* 48, no. 3 (2002), 614–636.

Squier, Susan M., 'The politics of city space in *The Years*: Street love, pillar boxes and bridges', in Jane Marcus, ed., *New Feminist Essays on Virginia Woolf* (London: Macmillan, 1981), 216–37.

Squier, Susan M., 'A track of our own: typescript drafts of *The Years*,' in Jane Marcus, ed., *Virginia Woolf: A Feminist Slant* (Lincoln: University of Nebraska Press: 1983), 198–211.

Wisor, Rebecca, 'About Face: The *Three Guineas* Photographs in Cultural Context', *Woolf Studies Annual* 21 (2015), 1–49.

Wood, Alice, *Virginia Woolf's Late Cultural Criticism: The Genesis of* The Years, Three Guineas *and* Between the Acts (London: Bloomsbury Academic, 2013).

Wood, Alice, 'Facing *Life as We Have Known It*: Virginia Woolf and the Women's Co-operative Guild', *Literature & History* 23, no. 2 (2014), 18–34.

PART III
EXPERIMENTS IN FORM AND STYLE

CHAPTER 9

STREAM OF CONSCIOUSNESS

DORA ZHANG

FEW terms are as associated with the formal innovations of the modernist novel as *stream of consciousness*, a mode of writing that records the flickering parade of impressions across a character's mind from a subjective point of view. Pioneered in the English tradition by Dorothy Richardson and James Joyce, Virginia Woolf is acknowledged to be one of its most skilled practitioners. But despite the ubiquitous familiarity of the term in general, and its association with Woolf in particular, her innovations in this arena have not been clearly recognized. This stems first of all from a confusion over whether the term refers to a particular stylistic technique, or whether it refers to something like a genre, constituted by shared themes.[1] 'Stream of consciousness' is often used interchangeably with one particular technique: interior monologue. However, this conflation is misleading, and I will use the term to refer to a genre that employs many aesthetic strategies, among which interior monologue is just one.[2] By expanding its definition, we are better equipped to appreciate the range of techniques that make up stream-of-consciousness texts, and Woolf's contributions in particular. For while it is famously associated with irregular or absent punctuation, fragmented or incomplete sentences, ellipses, and discontinuous syntax, as in Molly Bloom's soliloquy at the end of *Ulysses*, Woolf's innovations in stream of consciousness writing announce themselves more quietly. Moreover, a gendered association of the genre with the personal, the private, the small, and the detail has led writing by women to be more often considered 'formless', obscuring the precise nature of their formal contributions.

---

[1] This confusion is noted in the entry title in at least one encyclopaedia. See Alan Palmer, 'Stream of Consciousness or Interior Monologue', in David Herman, Manfred Jahn, and Marie-Laure Ryan, eds, *Routledge Encyclopedia of Narrative Theory* (London: Routledge, 2010), 570–1.

[2] Robert Humphrey makes a similar point in *Stream of Consciousness in the Modern Novel* (Berkeley: University of California Press, 1954), 5. For more recent discussions see Hoyt Long and Richard Jean So, 'Turbulent Flow: A Computational Model of World Literature', *Modern Language Quarterly* 77, no. 3 (2016), 345–67; Vicki Mahaffey, 'Streams Beyond Consciousness', in Jean-Michel Rabaté, ed., *A Handbook of Modernist Studies* (Hoboken: John Wiley & Sons, 2013), 35–54.

Woolf's contributions to stream of consciousness include at least three features, which form my focus here. First, I will look at her virtuosic use of free indirect discourse, which enables her to shift perspectives with unparalleled fluidity, and which in turn allows her to overcome what she herself felt was the great drawback of the novel of subjective experience: the egotism of the first person. Second, I examine Woolf's experiments with evoking a collective stream of consciousness in her late novel *Between the Acts*. While there are dangers to collective thinking, as Woolf, a vocal critic of fascism, was well aware, she was also drawn to moments of shared perception as a way of overcoming individual isolation. Third, I make the case that her use of analogies, something not ordinarily associated with stream of consciousness, constitutes an important technique of this genre. These analogies, which are directed above all at conveying the feeling of being conscious, also illuminate unappreciated links between Woolf and William James, the psychologist who popularized the term. Taken together, Woolf's stream-of-consciousness strategies refute a major critique of this genre: its intense individualism and liability to lapse into solipsism.

Early Tributaries

But first, let us return to the head of the stream. The term is usually credited to William James, specifically the famous 'Stream of Thought' chapter of his 1890 *Principles of Psychology*.[3] Insisting on the continuous rather than successive nature of thought, James writes:

> Consciousness ... does not appear to itself chopped up in bits. Such words as 'chain' or 'train' do not describe it fitly as it presents itself in the first instance. It is nothing jointed; it flows. A 'river' or a 'stream' are the metaphors by which it is most naturally described. In talking of it hereafter, let us call it the stream of thought, of consciousness, or of subjective life.[4]

Literary commentators have rarely paid close attention to the meaning of this term and its significance in James, and I will return to his affiliations with Woolf towards the end of the chapter. Suffice it for now to note that James was deploying the metaphor in order to refute Associationism, the prevailing theory of mind at the time in which substantive thoughts occurred in consciousness discretely and discontinuously. For James, the problem with Associationism was that it tended to both emphasize and atomize the terms being associated (i.e. ideas) at the expense of the actual association (i.e. the

---

[3] James himself came to it by way of the now largely forgotten British philosopher, Shadworth Hodgson, who first used the term in *Time and Space: A Metaphysical Essay* (London: Longman Green, 1865).

[4] William James, *Principles of Psychology*, 2 vols (New York: Dover Books, 1950), 1: 239.

relations) between them. As we will see, it was precisely these relations that Woolf, too, sought to capture.

The literary usage of 'stream of consciousness' was first introduced by May Sinclair in a 1918 review of Dorothy Richardson's novels in *The Egoist*. 'Nothing happens', Sinclair wrote, 'It is just life going on and on. It is Miriam Henderson's stream of consciousness going on and on.'[5] From the first, this mode was understood as an attempt to obtain direct contact with its object—called variously consciousness, experience, reality, or life—without mediation or intervention, and freed from the falsification of plot and story. Joyce and Richardson were cited as pioneers of the method, but Woolf's name was rarely absent from any discussion, usually evoked as one of its most prominent practitioners. So in a 1926 article in *The Atlantic* defending stream-of-consciousness fiction from those who called it 'an eccentric fad', Ethel Wallace Hawkins wrote, 'the evolution—or, more accurately, the gradual intensification—of this method may best be traced in the three novels of Virginia Woolf—*The Voyage Out*, *Jacob's Room*, and *Mrs Dalloway*.[6] By the end of the 1920s, after the publication of *Mrs Dalloway* and *To the Lighthouse*, as well as nine volumes of Richardson's *Pilgrimage* sequence, *Ulysses*, and *The Sound and the Fury*, stream of consciousness had become the hallmark of the modern novelist.[7] Joseph Warren Beach and Percy Lubbock both used the term in their influential treatises on the craft of fiction, and by 1927, the phrase was familiar enough that the American writer and critic Katherine Fullerton Gerould could write in *The Saturday Review*, 'I do not know whence the phrase came, nor does it matter, since it has become familiar to us all within the last decade.'[8]

Genre and Gender

While stream of consciousness quickly spread across the literary landscape in the early twentieth century, it was not universally praised. Common criticisms charged it with tedium, self-absorption, and triviality. Lamenting the absence of drama and action in the style, Gerould concluded, 'the dullness of books like "Dark Laughter" and "Mrs Dalloway" almost makes the comic strips seem amusing'; and D.H. Lawrence famously remarked caustically, '"Did I feel a twinge in my little toe or didn't I", asks every character of Mr Joyce, Miss Richardson or M. Proust.'[9] Although these criticisms extended to

---

[5] May Sinclair, 'The Novels of Dorothy Richardson', *The Egoist* 5, no. 4 (1918), 58.
[6] Ethel Hawkins, 'The Stream of Consciousness Novel', *The Atlantic Monthly*, September 1926, 356–60, esp. 358.
[7] The characteristic modern novelist, the influential critic J. Middleton Murry wrote, attempted 'to record immediately the growth of a consciousness. Immediately, without any effort at mediation by means of an interposed plot or story.' See Murry, *Discoveries* (London: W.W. Collins & Sons, 1924), 98.
[8] Katharine Fullerton Gerould, 'Stream of Consciousness', *The Saturday Review*, 22 October 1927, 233–5, 223.
[9] Gerould, 'Stream of Consciousness', 234; D. H. Lawrence, *Selected Literary Criticism*, ed. Anthony Beal (New York: Viking Books, 1956), 114.

male as well as female writers, it is important to note that stream of consciousness was, from the first, discussed in gendered terms. The idea that the genre was formless, that it was concerned only with trivialities, and that it was self-involved were all cast in terms of gendered binaries: soft versus hard, small versus big, internal versus external, and individual versus social. It also fell on one side of a gendered divide within the tropology of modernist poetics: the very metaphor of the stream, with its associations of vague, misty, amorphous flow, contrasts with the valorizations of the hard, rigid, precise, and granite in the poetics of Ezra Pound, Wyndham Lewis, and T.E. Hulme, among others.[10] The charges of formlessness, or absent or failed design, were also levelled much more at female writers like Woolf, Richardson, and Katherine Mansfield. In contrast, a male stream-of-consciousness writer like Joyce was more often credited with being guided by intellect rather than 'intuition' or 'impression', and what might be called the absence of form in one context became innovative and revolutionary in another.[11] Stream-of-consciousness writing was and, in many ways, remains associated with the delicate, the miniature, the precious, and disorganized detail over the cohesive pattern—all decidedly feminized traits.[12]

At the same time, the supposedly feminine nature of this style was sometimes a rallying cry for its practitioners. In a 1938 foreword to *Pilgrimage* Richardson characterized her project as forging a new literary form in an attempt 'to produce a feminine equivalent of the current masculine realism'.[13] Feminine prose, she wrote, 'should properly be unpunctuated, moving from point to point without formal obstructions'.[14] In reviewing volumes of *Pilgrimage*, Woolf too aligned Richardson's linguistic innovation with her womanhood. 'She has invented ... a sentence which we might call the psychological sentence of the feminine gender. It is of a more elastic fibre than the old, capable of stretching to the extreme, of suspending the frailest particles, of enveloping the vaguest shapes' (*E3* 367). We cannot fail to be reminded here of Woolf's own formulation of the aim of the novel in manifestos such as 'Modern Fiction'. While conceding that Richardson is working on 'an infinitely smaller scale', Woolf does not hesitate to rank her achievement with that of Chaucer, Donne, and Dickens, each of whom has also

---

[10] On this hard/soft divide as one of the oppositions of modernism see Sanford Schwartz, *The Matrix of Modernism: Pound, Eliot and Twentieth Century Thought* (Princeton: Princeton University Press, 1985).

[11] So where Robert Humphrey sees Richardson as having moments of brilliance but finally becoming 'lost in the overflow—a formless, unending deluge of realistic details' (9), he writes of Joyce: 'What the ends of *Ulysses* finally are, I do not expect to determine', suggesting that the failing of incomprehension lies with the critic, not the author. See Jesse Matz, *Literary Impressionism and Modernist Aesthetics* (New York: Cambridge University Press, 2001), 83–4 for a discussion of the different critical treatments of male and female modernist writers.

[12] On the gendered history of the devaluation of the detail, see Naomi Schor, *Reading in Detail* (New York: Routledge, 2007).

[13] Dorothy M. Richardson, 'Foreword', *Pilgrimage*, 4 vols (London: Virago, 1979), 1: 9–10. In her *Atlantic* article, Hawkins also singles out 'three brilliant women writers' (Richardson, Katherine Mansfield, and Woolf) as key practitioners of the method, 'interesting for their individuality in likeness' ('Stream of Consciousness', 356).

[14] Richardson, 'Foreword', 1: 12.

shown that the heart 'is a body which moves perpetually, and is thus always standing in a new relation to the emotions which are its sun' (*E3* 367).

In alluding to the smallness of the scale on which Richardson is working, Woolf is highlighting a criticism that she herself often encountered. The charge of triviality levelled at stream-of-consciousness texts depends on assumptions about whose interiority is worthy of representation, and whose experience can stand for broader conditions or reach out toward larger social, historical threads, instead of remaining confined to the personal. Woolf herself resisted the usual hierarchies of size and value, insisting, 'let us not take it for granted that life exists more fully in what is commonly thought big than in what is commonly thought small' (*E4* 161). We may certainly take her to task for not expanding the purview of her own representations of consciousness beyond a relatively narrow segment of the upper middle class, but this does not thereby negate the importance of her assertion that 'everything is the proper stuff of fiction' (*E4* 164).[15]

Woolf's point can also be read in light of a Marxist critique of stream of consciousness within a wider critique of modernism as representative of a bourgeois individualism.[16] In this view, where modernist works are said to retreat into fragmented, private, subjective perspectives and abandon any attempt to represent an objective social totality, stream of consciousness would appear to be the very embodiment of an alienated, reified form. But whatever the merits of such a critique as a demystification of modernist ideology, we should also not overlook the gendered assumptions it contains. In many ways it extends an old association of the feminine with interiority and the private and domestic spheres, in contrast to the outward-looking masculine domains of political and economic history. But of course, the doctrine of the separate spheres is something that feminist critics have long refuted, not least Woolf herself. In 'Mr Bennett and Mrs Brown', she grounds her critique of the Edwardians in the fact that while the nature of social relationships has changed, the forms of the novel have not kept up. 'When human relations change there is at the same time a change in religion, conduct, politics, and literature' (*E3* 422). As Nancy Armstrong observes, for Woolf, history does not take place in the world outside the house: 'Rather, history makes its mark on human experience in such small personal ways as when "Mrs Brown took out her little white handkerchief and began to dab her eyes." Here, at the centers of little networks of human relations, occur those changes that will eventually show in "religion, conduct, politics, and literature."'[17] The idea that stream of consciousness is simply expressive of a bourgeois individualist ideology has

---

[15] For a recent argument about the politics of Woolf's overturning of aesthetic hierarchies, see Jacques Rancière, *The Lost Thread: The Democracy of Modern Fiction*, trans. Steve Corcoran (London: Bloomsbury, 2016).

[16] For the earliest formulation of this idea, see Georg Lukács, 'The Ideology of Modernism', in *Realism in Our Time: Literature and the Class Struggle*, trans. John and Necke Mander (New York: Harper & Row, 1971), 17–46. For responses to Lukács and a robust debate on the politics of modernism and expressionism, see Ernst Bloch et al, eds, *Aesthetics and Politics* (New York: Verso Books, 2007).

[17] Nancy Armstrong, *Desire and Domestic Fiction* (New York: Oxford University Press, 1987), 247.

caused it to be regarded with a certain embarrassment among leftist critics. But I argue here that Woolf's contributions to the genre—by experimenting with collective streams, and by attempting to capture the nuances of 'networks of human relations' within the form of the novel—allow us to re-evaluate the association of stream of consciousness with solipsistic interiority.

Interior Monologue and Free Indirect Discourse

We have seen some criticisms of stream of consciousness, but even sympathizers noted the formal challenges posed by the attempt to represent consciousness in a new way. These challenges centred especially on the limitations of interior monologue and its first-person perspective. In a 1921 interview entitled 'The Future of the Novel', May Sinclair observes that while stream of consciousness was the developmental endpoint of the psychological novel, it is really only suited to novels that centre on a single character and a single point of view. 'It certainly remains to be seen whether it will be successful in dealing with groups of characters all equally important.'[18] Moreover, by inhabiting characters' perspectives so thoroughly, readers are prevented from knowing more than the characters do. According to Sinclair, the challenge for authors, then, is to 'present things so that they appear both as they really are and as they appear to the consciousness of his one subject'.[19]

These reservations were shared by Woolf herself. In her diaries she criticized the 'egotistic' tendency in Joyce (*D2* 189), writing a little later, 'if one lets the mind run loose it becomes egotistic; personal, which I detest' (*D2* 321). While this passage has sometimes been read as evidence of Woolf's competitive anxieties about her achievements in light of Joyce's, we should take it seriously as an expression of her aesthetic priorities, whatever its merits (or lack thereof) as an assessment of Joyce's work. For Woolf, the problem of egotism is exemplified by the dominance of a single perspective, as in interior monologue. These limitations are especially clear in the novel that Joyce credited with inaugurating the method of interior monologue, Édouard Dujardin's *Les lauriers sont coupés* (1888). In this passage, the narrator, Daniel Prince, is preparing to leave a restaurant. 'I get up; I put my coat back on; the waiter's pretending to help me; thank you; my hat; my gloves; here in my pocket; I'm going ... a waiter opens the door for me; good night; it's cold; let's button up my coat.'[20] The exposition in the first person here is not only awkward but also creates a sense of claustrophobia when sustained over the course

---

[18] Sinclair, 'Future of the Novel', *Pall Mall Gazette*, 10 January 1921.
[19] Sinclair, 'Future of the Novel'. Also cited in Mahaffey, 45.
[20] Édouard Dujardin, *The Bays are Sere*, 16; *Les lauriers sont coupés* (Paris: Librarie de la Revue Indépendante, 1888), 30.

of the novel. We never get access to the thoughts of any other character, including Léa, the actress who is the object of Daniel's affection.

Joyce circumvents the limitations of the single perspective in *Ulysses* by gathering a chorus of voices, and by eliminating the narration of exposition he mitigates the clumsiness of Dujardin. But to do so Joyce has to mix interior monologue with other narrative modes, including free indirect discourse, supplementing the first person with the third. And while different points of view are represented in *Ulysses*, as in other prominent stream of consciousness works such as Faulkner's *The Sound and the Fury*, narrative perspective is organized by chapter and remains discretely divided. That is, the gathering of multiple voices remains separated, with transitions from one perspective to another clearly marked. Woolf's innovation lies in the fluidity, subtlety, and frequency with which she shifts between points of view without imposing boundaries between them. Moreover, by playing perspectives against one another, her use of the 'dual voice' of free indirect discourse also answers Sinclair's second challenge to stream of consciousness, enabling her to present things both as they are *and* as they appear to a perceiving subject.[21]

To be sure, Woolf is by no means the first writer to employ free indirect discourse, which has been used in the English novel since at least Jane Austen. Gustave Flaubert brought it to prominence in the European novel in the mid-nineteenth century, and by the modernist period this technique was ubiquitous. Free indirect discourse is a particularly novelistic grammatical form that combines elements of both direct and indirect speech, eliminating the first-person pronoun and replacing it with a third-person 'he' or 'she' rendered subjective. Suppressing the quotation marks that are characteristic of direct speech, it nevertheless represents the thoughts, speech, and perceptions of a character directly, without the intervention of a narrator who reports or comments on them.[22] When early on in *Mrs Dalloway* we read, 'But how strange, on entering the Park, the silence; the mist; the hum ... and who should be coming along with his back against the Government buildings, most appropriately, carrying a dispatch box stamped with the Royal Arms, who but Hugh Whitbread; her old friend Hugh—the admirable Hugh!' (*MD* 5) we understand that even though this passage is written in the third person, we're witnessing Clarissa thinking these thoughts, rather than receiving a report of her thoughts from a narrator. Instead of being told what a character is perceiving, saying, or thinking, free indirect discourse grants direct access to a character's mind. In her diaries Woolf acknowledges her preference for 'oratio obliqua' (*D3* 106), as she called it, contrasting it with her 'few direct sentences', and indeed most of her mature fiction is written in this style, with the notable exception of *The Waves*.

---

[21] See Roy Pascal, *The Dual Voice: Free Indirect Speech and Its Function in the Nineteenth Century European Novel* (Manchester: Manchester University Press, 1977).

[22] Ann Banfield gives a thorough linguistic account of free indirect discourse in *Unspeakable Sentences: Narration and Representation in the Language of Fiction* (Boston: Routledge, 1982). For an accessible explanation aimed at the general reader, see James Wood, *How Fiction Works* (New York: Farrar, Straus, and Giroux, 2008). For an argument about its ideological functions, see D. A. Miller, *The Novel and the Police* (Berkeley: University of California Press, 1988).

In addition to allowing us to inhabit a character's perspective with great intimacy, free indirect discourse also enables the narrative to move easily between different minds, all looking out onto the same external world. Sometimes, the shift occurs within a single sentence, as in this example from the climactic dinner scene in the first section of *To the Lighthouse*: 'What damned rot they talk, thought Charles Tansley, laying down his spoon precisely in the middle of his plate, which he had swept clean, as if, Lily thought (he sat opposite to her with his back to the window precisely in the middle of view), he were determined to make sure of his meals' (*TL* 115). In one economical sentence Woolf reveals a number of things: Charles Tansley's resentment (born of shame about his poverty coupled with his sense of intellectual superiority), Lily Briscoe's perceptiveness, underscoring her role as the novel's chief observer, and her dislike of Tansley (spurred by his misogyny), which is tinged here with a certain class prejudice of her own—she sees him as determined to make sure of his meals because she finds him smug and self-serving, but there's also an implicit sneer at his eagerness for food. In this passage the pivot in the perspective shift is the spoon, which Charles Tansley lays down in the middle of his plate—and the sentence—as if for Lily to pick up as we move into her point of view. This move is typical of Woolf, who tends to use a publicly observable fact, in this case the plate and the spoon, as a hinge to shift between different characters' perspectives and their private thoughts. In scenes such as these, free indirect discourse allows for layered and refracted descriptions that tell us something about both the observer and the observed, revealing not only insights of individual psychology but also of social analysis.

Woolf is especially interested in the epistemological affordances of the play of perspectives that opens up once narration is liberated from the tyranny of the first person. Her novelistic universe is woven through piecing together fragments—sometimes very brief, sometimes quite extended—from a tapestry of perspectives.[23] Accordingly, Woolf's use of free indirect discourse is especially effective in scenes that bring together a variety of people, whether during a family dinner, on a busy London street, or at a glittering party, as we see in this passage below from *Mrs Dalloway* involving Ellie Henderson, Clarissa's poorer, shabbier cousin, and Richard Dalloway.

> 'Well, Ellie, and how's the world treating *you*?' [Richard Dalloway] said in his genial way, and Ellie Henderson, getting nervous and flushing and feeling that it was extraordinarily nice of him to come and talk to her, said that many people really felt the heat more than the cold.
>
> 'Yes they do,' said Richard Dalloway. 'Yes.'
>
> But what more did one say?
>
> 'Hullo, Richard,' said somebody, taking him by the elbow, and, good Lord, there was old Peter, old Peter Walsh. He was delighted to see him—ever so pleased to see him!... And off they went together walking right across the room, giving each other little pats, as if they hadn't met for a long time, Ellie Henderson thought, watching

---

[23] For more on this point, see Ann Banfield, *The Phantom Table: Woolf, Fry, Russell, and the Epistemology of Modernism* (New York: Cambridge University Press, 2000).

them go, certainly she knew that man's face. A tall man, middle aged, rather fine eyes, dark, wearing spectacles, with a look of John Burrows. (*MD* 169–70)

In the space of a few lines, we see the interaction from both Ellie and Richard's perspectives—his sense of obligation to talk to her, her nervousness in front of her grander relatives—in what is roughly the literary equivalent of a split screen with subtitles of thoughts. Note that the perspective in the line 'But what more did one say?' is ambiguous; it could belong to either Ellie or Richard, or in fact both, briefly uniting them in a moment of shared social unease. When the pause is broken by the appearance of Peter Walsh, Ellie's observation of him gives us the only external description of Peter that we get in the book. Coming so close to the end, it is defamiliarizing to see a character whom we have known so intimately be described as 'a tall man, middle aged ... dark, wearing spectacles', but it shows us a view of him that accords with the knowledge of the describer, in this case Ellie, situating both perceiver and perceived within layered psychological and sociological matrices.

'One wanted fifty pairs of eyes to see with', Lily Briscoe thinks in *To the Lighthouse*, 'Fifty pairs of eyes were not enough to get round that one woman [Mrs Ramsay] with' (*TL* 198). With free indirect discourse, Woolf finds the linguistic resources to represent the perspectives of fifty pairs of eyes, as well as some eyeless ones representing 'the world seen without a self' (*W* 287). The world is pieced together from what is seen through these individual points of view, and through them the reader is granted from moment to moment the intimate knowledge of another that Lily Briscoe seeks. One of Woolf's great themes is the limits of what we can know of other people, and the gap between the public and the private self is at once a philosophical problem stemming from the fact that we never have access to other people's minds, and also a social problem about how we fashion ourselves according to certain conventions, as well as how we read each other according to such predetermined categories. She thus uses free indirect discourse to enact on the level of form something her novels are preoccupied with on the level of theme. For Sinclair, the challenge of the stream-of-consciousness writer was to 'present things so that they appear both as they really are and as they appear to the consciousness of his one subject'. Woolf does not posit any simple objective/subjective divide between things as they are and things as they appear, but by stitching together multiple perspectives with unprecedented fluidity, she creates a common reality while allowing her readers glimpses of how this reality is differently experienced by different subjects.

'I REJECTED, WE SUBSTITUTED': COLLECTIVE STREAMS

Even as it remains true that, for Woolf, the supreme mystery remains, 'here was one room, there another' (*MD* 127), in her works the acute awareness of the breach between two minds is balanced by brief moments of communal feeling. Stream-of-consciousness writing is usually taken to be concerned exclusively with individual minds; an idea exacerbated by its conflation with interior monologue. But in the late fiction, we see Woolf's experiments with free indirect discourse take on yet another, less recognized dimension: the rendering of collective consciousness. The best-known novel that experiments with a group is, of course, *The Waves*, which is sometimes described as six voices raised in a single soliloquy. But the characters of Bernard, Susan, Neville, Rhoda, Ginny, and Louis retain distinct perceptions, even as they also seem to have an uncanny access to each other's thoughts. I will return to *The Waves* momentarily in order to consider the dangers of communal feeling, but first, I want to look at several moments in a lesser-known novel, *Between the Acts* (1941), when a group of characters seem to be thinking and perceiving as one. The idea that stream-of-consciousness writing is solely individualistic has obscured Woolf's interest in rendering collective streams, while the failure to recognize her experiments in this regard has exacerbated a narrow view of the genre.

Woolf's interest in group consciousness was not isolated among her contemporaries. There was a flurry of interest in ideas of 'group mind', crowd theory, and group psychology in the early decades of the twentieth century, especially after the outbreak of World War I, and again in the 1930s as the prospect of World War II loomed. As Allen McLaurin has documented, Woolf and her Bloomsbury associates were aware of and fascinated by these developments.[24] In 1913 Woolf reviewed a novel by the French writer Jules Romains, leader of the Unanimism movement, which propounded the doctrine of a communal psychic life among groups, and McLaurin proposes that Romains had an unacknowledged influence on Woolf.[25] Fascinating as this intellectual history is, what I am concerned with here are the ways in which shared perceptions find *formal* expression in free indirect discourse.

It should not be surprising that we find it in *Between the Acts*, a novel that takes community—that of a family, a village, and a nation—as its theme. The story is set in a bucolic English village, where Miss La Trobe, a misfit outcast, directs the annual village pageant, which tells of the history of the England. In the novel, which begins and ends with the Olivers, a family of landed gentry, there are several noteworthy interludes of anonymous, collective speech among the villagers who form the audience for the pageant. '... Dressing up. That's the great thing, dressing up. And it's pleasant now, the

---

[24] See Allen McLaurin, 'Virginia Woolf and Unanimism', *Journal of Modern Literature* 9, no. 1 (1981–2), 115–22; and 'Consciousness and Group Consciousness in Virginia Woolf', in Eric Warner, ed., *Virginia Woolf: a Centenary Perspective* (New York: Palgrave Macmillan, 1984), 28–40. In the latter piece McLaurin also notes that the association of stream of consciousness with individual minds has obscured Woolf's interest in a group mind ('Group Consciousness', 29–30). For more on this movement, see Felix J. Walter, 'Unanimism and the Novels of Jules Romains', *PMLA* 51, no. 3 (1936), 863–71.

[25] The novel, *Les Copains*, was translated into English by Sydney Waterlow and Desmond MacCarthy, the latter of whom was the model for Bernard in *The Waves* (McLaurin, 'Group Consciousness', 34).

sun's not so hot ... That's one good the war brought us—longer days ... Where did we leave off? D'you remember? The Elizabethans ... Perhaps she'll reach the present, if she skips ... D'you think people change? Their clothes, of course ... But I mean ourselves ...' (*BA* 121, original ellipses). These overheard snatches of conversation are so many elliptical 'scraps, orts, and fragments' (*BA* 188); they form momentary lines of continuity and response, but the voices remain distinct, even if anonymously grouped together.

Subtler and more merged are the moments when characters seem to perceive together as one, as in this early scene when a group of young people are preparing the barn for the pageant:

> Young men and women—Jim, Iris, David, Jessica—were even now busy with garlands of red and white paper roses left over from the Coronation. The seeds and the dust from the sacks made them sneeze. Iris had a handkerchief bound round her forehead; Jessica wore breeches. The young men worked in shirt sleeves ...
>
> 'Old flimsy' (Mrs Swithin's nickname) had been nailing another placard on the Barn ... The workers were laughing too, as if old Swithin had left a wake of laughter behind her. The old girl with a wisp of white hair flying, knobbed shoes as if she had claws corned like a canary's, and black stockings wrinkled over the ankles, naturally made David cock his eye and Jessica wink back, as she handed him a length of paper roses ... So they laughed; but respected. If she wore pearls, pearls they were. (*BA* 26-7).

The present tense indexicals and past tense, 'were even now', along with colloquial language like 'the old girl', alert us to the fact that this is free indirect discourse. But whose point of view is being represented? Jim, Iris, David, and Jessica, reminiscent of the sextet of *The Waves*, are minor characters who are only briefly mentioned here. The affectionately teasing perception of Mrs Swithin, 'the old girl with a wisp of white hair flying, knobbed shoes as if she had claws corned like a canary's, and black stockings wrinkled over the ankles', seems to be a shared one, or at the very least shared between David and Jessica, who are explicitly named in the sentence. Whereas in *Mrs Dalloway* and *To the Lighthouse* free indirect discourse is used primarily to highlight the differences in people's perceptions, both of each other and themselves, here it is used to render the easy camaraderie between this high-spirited gang. This is notably a very ordinary kind of intimacy—an everyday experience of shared perception and understanding that stands in contrast to the more visionary moments of communion in *The Waves*. This passage holds no great significance for the story of *Between the Acts*, but we see in this almost throwaway moment the possibility of a collective stream of consciousness reflecting ordinary moments of shared feeling and perceiving, which stand in counterbalance to the emphasis on isolation and dispersion elsewhere in the novel.

Of course, group feeling has its dangers, as Woolf was well aware. The Unanimists were optimistic about the possibility of a communal spirit animating a group, portraying it in ecstatic terms. But Woolf was also aware of works that painted a more pessimistic view, such as Wilfred Trotter's *Instincts of the Herd in Peace and War* (1916), which she discussed with Leonard and with Roger Fry.[26] Trotter's book, influenced by the work of the crowd psychologist, Gustave Le Bon, emphasized the irrationality of the masses and their susceptibility to influence and control. Woolf was pulled in two directions: at once drawn to the idea of communal feeling and perceiving as a way of bridging the divide between individual minds, and also wary of the violence that can result from the manipulation of the 'herd instinct'.[27] We find evidence of this tension throughout her works, especially in *The Waves*, the novel concerned most overtly with group consciousness. In an influential essay, Jane Marcus reads the ending of the novel, with Bernard telling the story of the other characters' lives, as a cautionary tale of a fascist and imperialist instinct, the domination of a single voice over a heteroglossic chorus.[28] And Jessica Berman has persuasively argued that *The Waves* is intricately bound up with the fantasies of community offered by the proto-fascist movement gathering in Britain in the early 1930s, whose power Woolf recognizes even as she also sees and critiques its limitations.[29] For my purposes here, it is significant that what is at stake in the conclusion of *The Waves* is not so much a group mind or a communal feeling so much as Bernard's own feeling of being indistinct from his friends, manifest in his narration of their stories. Unlike *The Waves*, which cedes the last word to Bernard, in *Between the Acts*, the pendulum remains swinging between individual isolation and a sense of community, summed up in the repeated refrain of the gramophone, 'dispersed are we; who have come together' but also 'let us retain whatever made that harmony' (*BA* 95). It is crucial that the moments of collective consciousness like the group perception of Mrs Swithin and the anonymous fragmented speech of the villagers concerns brief, intermittent flashes of fellow-feeling rather than the sustained resolution of multiple voices into a single one, as at the end of *The Waves*. Such flashes are arguably less prone to devolving from fellow-feeling into groupthink, even if Woolf, especially in her writing of the 1930s, never forgot this danger.

---

[26] See McLaurin, 'Group Consciousness', 36–7.

[27] In her diary she writes: 'Old Roger [Fry] takes a gloomy view, not of our life, but of the world's future; but I think I detected the influence of Trotter & the herd, & so I distrusted him. Still, stepping out into Charlotte Street, where the Bloomsbury murder took place a week or two ago, & seeing a crowd swarming in the road & hearing women abuse each other & at the noise others come running with delight—all this sordidity made me think him rather likely to be right' (*D1* 80, cited in McLaurin, 'Group Consciousness', 37).

[28] See Jane Marcus, 'Britannia Rules the Waves,' in Karen Lawrence, ed., *Decolonizing Tradition: New Views of Twentieth-Century 'British' Literary Canons* (Urbana: University of Illinois Press, 1992), 136–62; and Gabrielle McIntire, 'Heteroglossia, Monologism, and Fascism: Bernard Reads *The Waves*', *Narrative* 13, no. 1 (2005), 29–45.

[29] Jessica Berman, 'Of Waves and Opposition: *The Waves*, Oswald Mosley, and the New Party', in Merry M. Pawlowski, ed., *Virginia Woolf and Fascism* (Basingstoke: Palgrave, 2001), 105–21.

Psycho-analogies and the Feeling of Relations

We have just seen Woolf's experiments in rendering collective perception, and in the final part of this chapter I want to turn to a still lesser-known technique that I propose belongs to the stylistic repertoire of stream-of-consciousness writing: the use of analogies, often extended, to represent thought and feeling. These analogies, which Woolf uses with particular frequency and agility, bring her together with William James, and it will show us another way of understanding the deep concern with relationality that underlies her stream-of-consciousness writing.

Although Dorrit Cohn identified what she called 'psycho-analogies' as a narrative mode of representing consciousness in *Transparent Minds* (1978), critics have not subsequently recognized the use of comparative strategies as a feature of stream of consciousness writing.[30] And yet psycho-analogies are prevalent in modernist works. Citing examples from Proust, Nathalie Sarraute, and Robert Musil (of whom one scholarly count found an astonishing 337 similes in thirty-eight pages), Cohn calls Woolf 'the stream-of-consciousness novelist who employs psycho-analogies most copiously'.[31] These often extended similes distend narrative time and underscore the contradictory nature of thoughts and feelings while bypassing 'not only self-articulation, but also self-understanding', since they are not part of the character's own inner discourse.[32] Although they can be attributed either to a narrator or 'infused more directly into the thought-stream of the character', psycho-analogies are not accounts of what a character is thinking, and so serve a different purpose than the narration of inner speech that comprises interior monologue.[33] Their primary aim, we could say, is not so much to convey the content of a character's thoughts, but rather the process of thinking. More precisely, psycho-analogies are used to describe in highly specific and evocative ways the *feeling* of thinking.

Woolf is an extremely adept practitioner of such analogies. Take these examples, from *Mrs Dalloway* and *To the Lighthouse*:

> But—but—why did she suddenly feel, for no reason that she could discover, desperately unhappy? As a person who has dropped some grain of pearl or diamond into

---

[30] For instance, Humphrey cites as the basic stream of consciousness techniques only 'direct interior monologue, indirect interior monologue, omniscient description, and soliloquy' (23). It is also missing from the long list of techniques given by Hoyt Long and Richard Jean So in their recent computational study of stream of consciousness ('Turbulent Flow', 346).

[31] Dorrit Cohn, *Transparent Minds* (Princeton: Princeton University Press, 1978), 44. In fact Cohn finds a 'hypertrophy of analogies' in modernist fiction (43).

[32] Cohn, *Transparent Minds*, 42.

[33] Cohn, *Transparent Minds*, 42.

the grass and parts the tall blades very carefully, this way and that, and searches here and there vainly, and at last spies it there at the roots, so she went through one thing and another ... (*MD* 120–1)

What then was this terror, this hatred? Turning back among the many leaves which the past had folded in him, peering into the heart of that forest where light and shade so chequer each other that all shape is distorted, and one blunders, now with the sun in one's eyes, now with a dark shadow, he sought an image to cool and detach and round off his feeling in a concrete shape. (*TL* 185)[34]

In the first example, Clarissa Dalloway rummages in her mind for the cause of an emotion, and in the second, James Ramsay attempts to identify a feeling by combing through his past. Incidentally, James's search for 'an image to cool and detach and round off his feeling in a concrete shape' is an apt description of Woolf's own process. Both analogies concern states of confusion, a sense of not quite knowing and then seeking to discover what one is thinking or feeling by turning over various memories and ideas. The ensuing images in the analogies—of someone searching for a dropped pearl in the grass, and of a person blundering in a forest blinded by chequered rays of light—aim to give a sense of how this state of mind feels. It is also characteristic of Woolf that these comparisons are dynamic—in both cases, the analogous image is not a static tableau but involves some active process. More than *what* is thought, felt, or sensed, these descriptions are concerned with conveying what it is *like* to think, which, for Woolf, is never separate from feeling and sensing.

The deployment of psycho-analogies brings Woolf, a preeminent writer of stream of consciousness, close to William James, a pioneer of this term in psychology. Recall that for James, the stream metaphor was intended to reorient us toward relations and to see these as being no less important as the terms they connected. Rather than a train with discrete albeit connected cars, James argues that our mind is closer to a continuously flowing stream. Every substantive thought is ineluctably inflected by myriad relations to what has preceded it and what will follow. 'Every definite image in the mind is steeped and dyed in the free water that flows round it. With it goes the sense of its relations, near and remote, the dying echo of whence it came to us, the dawning sense of whither it is to lead.'[35] For James, this free water with its dying echoes and dawning senses is crucially constitutive of the way consciousness feels, which we neglect in our blinkered view of thoughts as '"about" this object or "about" that, the stolid word *about* engulfing all their delicate idiosyncrasies in its monotonous sound.'[36] If a thunderclap breaks into silence, for instance, 'the awareness of the previous silence creeps and continues; for what we hear when the thunder crashes is not thunder *pure*, but thunder-breaking-upon-silence-and-contrasting-with-it ... The thunder itself we believe to

---

[34] These examples are also cited by Cohn in *Transparent Minds*, 44.
[35] James, *Principles of Psychology*, 1: 255.
[36] James, *Principles of Psychology*, 1: 246.

abolish and exclude the silence; but the *feeling* of the thunder is also a feeling of the silence as just gone.'[37]

It is this deeply relational aspect of consciousness, hazy and impossible to isolate though these relations may be, that Woolf's writing is also particularly interested in conveying. Thus, her works tend to be highly associative, darting back and forth across time and space as one impression recalls another. In our focus on the 'aboutness' of thoughts, James observes, we have been misled by our use of language. 'We ought to say a feeling of *and*, a feeling of *if*, a feeling of *but*, and a feeling of *by*, quite as readily as we say a feeling of *blue* or a feeling of *cold*. Yet we do not: so inveterate has our habit become of recognizing the existence of the substantive parts alone, that language almost refuses to lend itself to any other use.'[38] Gertrude Stein's radical experiments with prepositions is one inheritance of this Jamesian insight in literature, but we can also see it importantly, if less directly, in the work of Woolf. Her psycho-analogies are keyed especially to the relations between substantive thoughts, not only conveying particular thoughts about particular things but also evoking the ways in which one thought or memory is ineluctably inflected by other experiences and associations. This is reflected in the very form of the analogy itself, in which the 'like' or 'just as' or 'as if' reaches toward other terms and experiences, weaving an intricate web of relations.

We find a beautiful image for the feeling of relating in *Mrs Dalloway*, just after Peter Walsh leaves Clarissa after their first reunion. As he walks down Victoria Street, Peter hears the bell of St Margaret's toll and experiences 'an extraordinarily clear, yet puzzling, recollection of her, as if this bell had come into the room years ago, where they sat at some moment of great intimacy, and had gone from one to the other and had left, like a bee with honey, laden with the moment' (*MD* 49–50). The feeling at issue here is an uncanny sense of déjà vu, but unlike the Proustian involuntary memory, which collapses past and present time, the distance travelled between the two moments is here delicately preserved in the flight of the bee. If William James reminds us that when we hear a crash of thunder it is not the thunder alone but 'thunder-breaking-upon-silence-and-contrasting-with-it', the flight of the bee is an analogy for all the variegated shades of relations that colour any experience.

Including such analogies in our account of stream of consciousness offers us a new view onto the genre. Of course, the juxtapositional energies of analogy can be put to any number of uses, including to shock, ironize, and play, all of which Woolf deploys at different moments. But one important use, evident in her analogies to describe the feeling of being conscious, is to highlight and to evoke the cognitive habit of relating itself. What Woolf conveys in these analogical descriptions of thinking, remembering, and searching through the mind is the feeling of 'if' and the feeling of 'and', the feeling of 'like' and the feeling of 'as'. She highlights the propensity to make connections, and in this sense reading analogies solely for their content would be to take them only in their 'aboutness'. What they equally illustrate in each case is the feeling of relationality itself.

---

[37] James, *Principles of Psychology*, 1: 240–1.
[38] James, *Principles of Psychology*, 1: 245–6.

Although Woolf, along with many of her modernist contemporaries, has often been accused of being overly preoccupied with individual minds, sometimes to the point of solipsism, we can in fact discern in the very textures of her stream of consciousness writing a deeply relational worldview that reaches out to other domains of experience, social, historical, and natural. 'All human relations have shifted—those between masters and servants, husbands and wives, parents and children' (*E3* 422). We can look to thematic representations in her novels for an account of these shifting relations—perhaps best depicted in *The Years*, which follows several generations of the Pargiter family—but we can also look to the level of form itself. In her deft use of free indirect discourse to braid a common reality out of different perspectives, in her experiments with rendering collective perception, and in her analogical descriptions of the feeling of consciousness, Woolf shows us in different ways the ineluctably relational nature of consciousness.

SELECTED BIBLIOGRAPHY

Banfield, Ann, *The Phantom Table: Woolf, Fry, Russell, and the Epistemology of Modernism* (New York: Cambridge University Press, 2000), 307–11.

Berman, Jessica, 'Of Waves and Opposition: *The Waves*, Oswald Mosley, and the New Party', in Merry M. Pawlowski, ed., *Virginia Woolf and Fascism* (Basingstoke: Palgrave, 2001), 105–21.

Cohn, Dorrit, *Transparent Minds* (Princeton: Princeton University Press, 1978).

Gerould, Katharine Fullerton, 'Stream of Consciousness', *The Saturday Review*, 22 October 1927, 233–5, 223.

Hawkins, Ethel, 'The Stream of Consciousness Novel', *The Atlantic Monthly*, September 1926, 356–60.

James, William, *Principles of Psychology*, 2 vols (New York: Dover Books, 1950).

Long, Hoyt and Richard Jean So, 'Turbulent Flow: A Computational Model of World Literature', *Modern Language Quarterly* 77, no. 3 (2016), 345–67.

Lukács, Georg, 'The Ideology of Modernism', in *Realism in Our Time: Literature and the Class Struggle*, trans. John and Necke Mander (New York: Harper & Row, 1971), 17–46.

Mahaffey, Vicki, 'Streams Beyond Consciousness', in Jean-Michel Rabaté, ed., *A Handbook of Modernism Studies* (Hoboken: John Wiley & Sons, 2013), 35–54.

Marcus, Jane, 'Britannia Rules *The Waves*', in Karen Lawrence, ed., *Decolonizing Tradition: New Views of Twentieth-Century 'British' Literary Canons* (Urbana: University of Illinois Press, 1992), 136–62.

McIntire, Gabrielle, 'Heteroglossia, Monologism, and Fascism: Bernard Reads *The Waves*', *Narrative* 13, no. 1 (2005), 29–45.

McLaurin, Allen, 'Virginia Woolf and Unanimism', *Journal of Modern Literature* 9, no. 1 (1981–1982), 115–22.

Palmer, Alan, 'Stream of Consciousness or Interior Monologue', in David Herman, Manfred Jahn, and Marie-Laure Ryan, eds, *Routledge Encyclopedia of Narrative Theory* (London: Routledge, 2010), 570–1.

Pascal, Roy, *The Dual Voice: Free Indirect Speech and Its Function in the Nineteenth Century European Novel* (Manchester: Manchester University Press, 1977).

Schwartz, Sanford, *The Matrix of Modernism: Pound, Eliot and Twentieth Century Thought* (Princeton: Princeton University Press, 1985).

CHAPTER 10

CHARACTER, FORM, AND FICTION

AMY BROMLEY

In 'Character in Fiction' (1924) Virginia Woolf sets the stage for her discussion of novelistic style with some rhetorical declarations on the concept of character:

> My first assertion is one that I think you will grant—that every one in this room is a judge of character. Indeed it would be impossible to live for a year without disaster unless one practiced character-reading and had some skill in the art. Our marriages, our friendships depend on it; our business largely depends on it; every day questions arise which can only be solved by its help. And now I will hazard a second assertion, which is more disputable perhaps, to the effect that on or about December 1910 human character changed. (*E3* 421)

While the 'disputable' nature of Woolf's second claim has been taken up in modernist studies, and has often been appropriated as a defining maxim for modernism,[1] the preceding assertions—that 'every one in this room is a judge of character' and it is a skilled art upon which many practical matters hang—are just as crucial to Woolf's suggestive discussion and deployment of character in this essay. By pointing out that it is something we have everyday experiences of, she encourages us to dwell on the word 'character' and foregrounds the sense in which it is a site of inscription, representation, and interpretation. Her rhetoric invites us to decipher the complex work to which the concept of character is put throughout the essay. Although they ostensibly function as a springboard from which to land the more contentious and provocative claim, her

---

[1] Makiko Minow-Pinkney's collection of essays, *Virginia Woolf and December 1910: Studies in Rhetoric and Context* (Grosmont: Illuminati Books, 2014), testifies to the enduring resonances of Woolf's provocative phrase. In particular, Brenda Silver's contribution, 'On or about 1910: The Iconic Life of a Familiar Quotation', discusses its uses and misuses in recent decades (167–73).

proposals about interpreting character as an everyday activity and a critical survival skill also establish the high stakes of that coy exaggeration, 'on or about December 1910 human character changed'. Setting the tone for such a statement, at once glib and weighted with contextual significance, Woolf's preliminaries indicate the serious importance of being able to read, write, and understand the typification of seismic shifts that she is about to perform in this essay. Structuring her argument as a series of character sketches, Woolf uses the concept of fictional character to synecdochally typify certain novelistic styles, making the element of character stand for and describe a 'type' of novel in its entirety. Playing, as Laura Marcus notes, 'with the complexities and multiple definitions of "character",[2] Woolf also casts differences in novelistic style as characteristic of, and characterized by, certain broadly sketched historical, national, and gendered ways of seeing.

Throughout her writing, as in the punning, metaphoric mode of 'Character in Fiction', Woolf conceptualizes character as 'figure' and as 'type': as a material, printed textual entity, but also as a representation of what she calls, in 'Modern Fiction' (1925), 'the essential thing', 'life itself' (E4 160-1). As Eric Sandberg points out in his study of Woolf's *Experiments in Character* (2014), her 'interest in human subjectivity was filtered through and shaped by a fascination with the process of *writing* character'.[3] For Woolf, characters are textual entities and constructs of literary language, and the sense in which a character is a typographical symbol is key to its manifestation on the page—in words, building sentences, building stories. This aspect of Woolf's writing on character—of character as a structuring formal principal and a complex linguistic figure—highlights its inherent tensions between surface and depth. By interpreting the significations that mark the surface, we come to create a representative idea of 'the essential thing'. In *To the Lighthouse* (1927), Lily Briscoe thinks: 'Our apparitions, the things you know us by, are simply childish. Beneath it is all dark, it is all spreading, it is unfathomably deep; but now and again we rise to the surface and that is what you see us by' (*TL* 53). As an 'apparition' in the sense of something that *appears*, but that is also elusive and ghostly, 'character' is a stand-in for something that would otherwise be unnameable. This is a narrative and textual predicament that often haunts Woolf's characterizations. Her work consistently asks how to make the surface of the page and the words printed there manifest the life, or 'being', of a person: how to inscribe the surface in such a way as to suggest depths, and how to imbed character in the formal composition of the novel. Here, the importance of caricature for Woolf is a helpful idea. As an aesthetic of bold, exaggerated outlines

---

[2] Laura Marcus, *Dreams of Modernity: Psychoanalysis, Literature, Cinema* (Cambridge: Cambridge University Press, 2017), 134. For example, Marcus notes Woolf's 'linking the term at one point to "the character of one's cook", so that "character" shades off into "character-reference", the implication being that the Edwardians [...] depict their fictional characters in ways that look more like references or testimonials than they do depictions of complex modern subjectivities'.

[3] Eric Sandberg, *Virginia Woolf: Experiments in Character* (New York: Cambria Press, 2014), 6 (emphasis mine).

invoking visual art, satire, and comedy, caricature might appear antithetical to the complexity and depth of Woolf's novelistic structures: yet her narrative strategies and perspectives often display the hand of the writer at work, pointing to the essential provisionality of the signs by which we read character, to the changeability of these signs and, often, to their misleading inadequacy in capturing the 'essential thing' they supposedly represent. Instead, Woolf's fiction performs suggestive, often exaggerated, outlines of character, highlighting its inseparability from the form in which it is iterated and its mutual constitution of the narrative in which it appears.

These ideas of materiality, form, and figuration are central to this chapter on character in Woolf's fiction. After examining Woolf's rhetoric around 'character' in her essays in more detail, it traces the inscription of character across different genres and modes of writing. Rather than proceeding in chronological order through Woolf's writing, it begins by foregrounding the character sketch as an important form for Woolf's technique in her longer works, focusing through 'An Unwritten Novel' (1920) as an important pre-text for her developments in the novel. This sketch iterates a self-aware, performative mode of writing, which draws attention to the hand of the writer at work, and dwells on surface impressions as they may or may not relate to a deeper essence. My close reading of this sketch, where Woolf demonstrates the interdependence of form and character, establishes a basis for examining characterizations in her longer works. Since it is not possible here to fully discuss all ten novels, focus is turned on three key examples in which the character's name appears in the title: *Jacob's Room* (1922), *Mrs Dalloway* (1925), and *Orlando: A Biography* (1928). These texts act as nodes from which to connect the ideas of character, form, and the material act of writing as they resonate throughout Woolf's oeuvre. Their narrative strategies demonstrate the ways in which her experiments with character in fiction are simultaneously a theoretical engagement with fiction writing in general, and with novelistic form in particular. Throughout, the chapter acknowledges that Woolf's private writing often serves as a sketchbook for character. Attending to her writing of character across these genres brings to light the importance of caricature in widely different types of narrative, from memoir, to free indirect discourse, to auto/biographical sketches. This focus on caricature can, in turn, help us to make sense of the tension between permanence and mutability inherent in Woolf's materialist conception of character. With regard to form, the aesthetic presence of caricature in her novels enables her, as she wanted to do in writing *Mrs Dalloway*, to keep 'the quality of the sketch in the finished and composed work' (*D2* 312).

In her essays, Woolf continually foregrounds the inextricability of character and form. 'Character in Fiction' itself represents a complex oratory as well as literary and textual performance: in making her proposals, Woolf has her eye not only on an audience of readers, but also on those physically present when she delivered a version of this paper to the Cambridge Heretics Society in May 1924 (*E3* 436 n1). Her talk developed an earlier essay, 'Mr Bennett and Mrs Brown', which had been published in the *New York Evening Post* and *Nation & Athenaeum* in 1923. There, it had entered into debate with Arnold Bennett's ideas of modern character in his review of *Jacob's Room*. In 'Is the

Novel Decaying?', published in *Cassell's Weekly*, Bennett had complained that Woolf's 'characters do not vitally survive in the mind'.[4] Bracketing momentarily the question of Woolf's character-sketching in *Jacob's Room*, and the related discussion of elusive character in modernist writing that Bennett's criticism raises, it is important to note the significant changes between versions of Woolf's response, which themselves engage a dialogue between permanence and mutability. The revised version of 'Mr Bennett and Mrs Brown', via the paper read to the Heretics, appeared as 'Character in Fiction' in *Criterion* (1924) where, as Makiko Minow-Pinkney points out, Woolf's 'assertion "on or about December 1910 human character changed" appears for the first time'.[5] The *Essays of Virginia Woolf* reprints the *Criterion* version, representing as fixed a text that had been and was to continue to be a site of continual rewriting, reframing, and refining. The representative value of this version has, as Minow-Pinkney notes, 'been the preferred text' from which scholars have discussed the December 1910 passage,[6] and is the main one I have referred to for my examination of Woolf's rhetoric in this chapter. Although the text itself is historically unstable, rhetorically it performs exactly the kind of broad-stroke, lasting impression of which Bennett thought Woolf incapable.

Woolf creates for her purpose the figure of Mrs Brown—a 'will-o'-the-wisp, a dancing light, an illumination gliding up the wall and out of the window', who 'changes the shape, shifts the accent, of every scene in which she plays her part' (*E3* 387–8). Mrs Brown is an allegory of character itself, a phantom to be caught, a vessel to be filled; she is mutably characteristic. She has the power not only of transformation, but of satire and caricature in her potential for 'freakish malice', with the agency to turn 'the most solemn sights […] to ridicule' (*E3* 387). Using Mrs Brown as an exaggerating mirror on which to reflect modes of literary characterization, Woolf sketches 'three different versions' of a writer's attempt to capture Mrs Brown:

> The English writer would make the old lady into a 'character'; he would bring out her oddities and mannerisms; her buttons and wrinkles; her ribbons and warts. Her personality would dominate the book. A French writer would rub out all that; he would sacrifice the individual Mrs Brown to give a more general view of human nature; to make a more abstract, proportioned, and harmonious whole. The Russian would pierce through the flesh; would reveal the soul—the soul alone, wandering out into the Waterloo Road, asking of life some tremendous question which would sound on and on in our ears after the book was finished. (*E3* 426)

In each of their ways, Woolf's characterizations of these writers show them in the act of sketching: the English exaggerating details, the French drawing broad-stroke

---

[4] Arnold Bennett, 'Is the Novel Decaying?', *Cassell's Weekly* 47, 28 March 1923, reprinted in Robin Majumdar and Allen McLaurin, eds, *Virginia Woolf: The Critical Heritage* (London: Routledge, 1975), 112–13. See Minow-Pinkney, 'Appendix' in *Virginia Woolf and December 1910*, 190. For the revised typescript of 'Character in Fiction' and notes on the revision and publication history of these two essays, see also *E3* 501–17.

[5] Minow-Pinkney, 'Appendix', in *Virginia Woolf and December 1910*, 190–1.

[6] Minow-Pinkney, 'Appendix', in *Virginia Woolf and December 1910*, 190–1.

generalizations, and the Russian aiming to express an essence by stripping away all superfluity.⁷ Woolf's characterization of Edwardian fiction in contradistinction to Victorian and Georgian is, she acknowledges, a caricature created in the same way 'as painters do when they wish to reduce the innumerable details of a crowded landscape to simplicity—step back, half shut the eyes, gesticulate a little vaguely with the fingers, and reduce Edwardian fiction to a view' (*E3* 385). Reducing something to a metaphorical 'view' results in a generalization that is nevertheless useful for argument and criticism. Through the allegorical figure of Mrs Brown, Woolf's argument also inflects a critical point about form, style, and gender politics: in their approach to writing novels, none of these men really see, nor do they allow the reader to see, Mrs Brown. Of course, part of the point is that she is not really there to be seen: she is a fiction, and any attempt to write of Mrs Brown's character will necessarily be a creative projection of the writer. Furthermore, as Woolf writes in her diary, her main point is that 'character is dissipated into shreds now: the old post-Dostoevsky argument' (*D2* 248).

Woolf's understanding of writing character as a contextually specific act—entwined with literary form and changing with the times—entails a set of conventions that the character sketch carries as a classical literary genre. The character sketch has a lineage, as Jacques Bos has shown, from Theophrastus's *Characters* to seventeenth-century satirical caricature.⁸ As a form used 'for what may have been ethical, rhetorical or entertainment purposes,'⁹ Bos traces the Ancient Greek etymology of the word 'character' to two distinct words: ἦθος (ethos, 'dwelling-place'), and χαράσσειν (charassein, 'to sharpen' and 'to inscribe onto a surface').¹⁰ The dichotomy between essence and appearance suggested by the etymology of 'character' informs the use of the sketch as a technique in classical rhetoric, by which a speaker would outline their opponent's appearance or actions to typify and attack their essential being. In his discussion of 'The Vissicitudes of Character' in Woolf's work, Terry Eagleton fleshes out this etymology:

> In the English language, the word 'character' does not originally denote a person at all. It means a sign, trait or mark which identifies an individual, as in the surviving use of the word to mean written letters. One could speak of a man's character, meaning those traits and marks which, like a signature, lent his existence some continuity. The word thus served as a metonym of an individual; but, as often happens, the part came after a while to merge with the whole, and 'character' began to signify an individual as such.¹¹

---

⁷ The influence of Russian fiction on Woolf is a vast topic, particularly in terms of character. See, for example, Roberta Rubenstein, *Virginia Woolf and the Russian Point of View* (New York: Palgrave Macmillan, 2009).
⁸ Jacques Bos, 'Individuality and Inwardness in the Literary Character Sketches of the Seventeenth Century', *Journal of the Warburg and Courtauld Institutes* 61 (1998), 142–57.
⁹ Bos, 'Individuality and Inwardness', 144.
¹⁰ Bos, 'Individuality and Inwardness', 144.
¹¹ Terry Eagleton, 'The Vissicitudes of Character', in Minow-Pinkney, ed., *Virginia Woolf and December 1910*, 86.

Mirroring this move from metonymy to synecdoche, and retaining the idea of 'continuity' in tension with historical specificity, in 'Character in Fiction', Woolf draws from the form of the character sketch in the Theophrastean rhetorical tradition, describing typical behaviours which suggest and come to stand for a deeper ἦθος. She engraves representative marks, which, though they be reductive caricatures, enable her to differentiate the aesthetic projects in the novel undertaken by her generation and its predecessors. She also makes character sketches of the novelist (*E3* 422), the reader (*E3* 421), the English public (*E3* 436), and James Joyce (*E3* 434). With this kind of broad-stroke typification in mind, Sandberg contends that Woolf would 'have been familiar with the tradition of Theophrastean character types' through her father's library collection, and he sees them at work in Woolf's first novel, *The Voyage Out* (1915).[12] Satirical caricature as a demonstration of rhetorical skill is also present in Woolf's juvenilia: as Hermione Lee notes in prefacing *Hyde Park Gate News*, we see Woolf there 'trying out' character sketches 'like "the tall stout lively person with a fatal habit of talking to herself"' (*HPGN* ix). Woolf has a stock cast of such characters in most of her novels (e.g. the scholar, the spinster, the poet, the politician), wherein it is possible, as Vassiliki Kolocotroni suggests, to identify a 'recognizable Woolfian type'.[13]

It is also important to note that the rhetorical history of the character sketch as a literary form complements its context in visual portraiture, where Woolf finds familial influences in the work of Vanessa Bell and Julia Margaret Cameron; but her sketch of the novelist in 'Character in Fiction' is a particularly interesting example of a specifically literary type: 'The study of character becomes to them an absorbing pursuit; to impart character an obsession.'[14] Casting the narrator in this role of the typical Woolfian novelist, in 'An Unwritten Novel', the compulsion of the narrator to make a 'character' of a woman on a train drives the whole plot. As a character sketch of, by, and for a novelist, this sketch presents a scene of simultaneous reading and composition that, for the narrator, remains unfulfilled, and for Woolf was generative of new experiments in the novel.

For Woolf, thinking about the novel necessarily entails thinking about character. How, then, does her conception of modern character as 'dissipated into shreds' marry with her experiments in novelistic form, and with the novelist's compulsion to 'impart character'? With character and the novel as its subject, 'An Unwritten Novel' displays in miniature some of the techniques that Woolf later develops in her novels; but it also provokes theoretical engagement with the material processes of writing and interpreting character. Published in *London Mercury* (July 1920), and later included in Woolf's collection of short fiction, *Monday or Tuesday* (1921), the process of writing 'An

---

[12] Sandberg, *Experiments in Character*, 53.
[13] Vassiliki Kolocotroni, 'Strange Cries and Ancient Songs: Woolf's Greek and the Politics of Intelligibility', in Bryony Randall and Jane Goldman, eds, *Virginia Woolf in Context* (Cambridge: Cambridge University Press, 2013), 424–5.
[14] Kolocotroni, 'Strange Cries and Ancient Songs', 422.

Unwritten Novel' suggested to Woolf 'immense possibilities' in novelistic form. In her diary, while planning what was to become *Jacob's Room*, she writes:

> conceive mark on the wall, K[ew]. G[ardens]. & unwritten novel taking hands & dancing in unity. What the unity shall be I have yet to discover: the theme is a blank to me […] I must still grope & experiment but this afternoon I had a gleam of light. Indeed I think from the ease with which I'm developing the unwritten novel there must be a path for me there. (*D2* 13–14)

Combined with the essayistic meditation of 'The Mark on the Wall' and the cinematic scene-making of 'Kew Gardens', the narrative strategies of 'An Unwritten Novel' set the tone for Woolf's later experiments in unwriting the novel. While it is, like 'The Mark on the Wall', effectively an interior monologue that sketches the narrator as the main character, 'An Unwritten Novel' also foregrounds the processes of reading and writing, interpretation, and inscription, as they relate to 'life'. The novel that this sketch sets up is as yet unwritten, but it is also actively unwritten in that it is simultaneously constructed and dismantled as the narrative progresses (which arguably also applies to *Jacob's Room*, *Mrs Dalloway*, and *Orlando* in their own ways). As Julia Briggs argues, however, '[t]he unwriting of the title is never entirely effected, since the most memorable part of the story is the imagined narrative of a life; its status as speculation had, in any case, been established at the outset'.[15] This speculative mode of character-sketching creates a complex, layered text that, while seeking to undermine the possibility of neutral or truthful representation, 'stands as a testament to the power of imaginative acts'.[16] This is not therefore simply a character sketch in the sense of being a caricature or portrait of a person, but it also makes a performance of characterization by drawing attention to suggestion, gesture, and process, making character itself the subject of the sketch.

The ability to read character as a supposed ontological certainty is interrupted, distorted, and fractured throughout this sketch. The grammatical strategies of deferral begin in the line 'Life's what you see in people's eyes; life's what they learn, and, having learnt it, never, though they seek to hide it, cease to be aware of—what? That life's like that, it seems' (*CSF* 112). The deferral of 'life', as a concept that appears as semblance ('it seems'), is embodied in the physical strategies that people hide behind. These strategies, like the grammatical interruption of the dash and the question, 'what?', figure as 'marks' to be read:

> Marks of reticence are on all those faces: lips shut, eyes shaded, each one of the five doing something to hide or stultify his knowledge. One smokes, another reads; a third checks entries in a pocket book; a fourth stares at the map of the line framed opposite; and the fifth—the terrible thing about the fifth is that she does nothing at

---

[15] Julia Briggs, *Reading Virginia Woolf* (Edinburgh: Edinburgh University Press, 2006), 35.
[16] Briggs, *Reading Virginia Woolf*, 69.

all. She looks at life. Ah, but my poor, unfortunate woman, do play the game—do, for all our sakes, conceal it! (*CSF* 112)

Through the marks that these people display, their characters are sketched lithographically: the men deflect 'life' and attention (one even does so by reading) whereas the woman absorbs them, and appears as a surface on which the narrator's ink will stick. The narrator can project a psychological identification with the woman who looks back, leading to a process of embodied mimicry when she involuntarily imitates the woman's twitch: 'She saw me. A smile of infinite irony, infinite sorrow, flitted and faded from her face. But she had communicated, shared her secret, passed her poison; she would speak no more' (*CSF* 114). The 'infinite irony' in the woman's smile here suggests that she is satirically aware of the process she has set in motion. Like Mrs Brown, the figure is one whose gestures inspire fear and despair, at the same time as she challenges the writer to attempt to account for her. There is also arguably a certain violence in the narrator's projections and manipulations of this woman into the position of silent muse. In at least one layer of the text, this woman is, as Briggs points out, an allegorical figure: 'Woolf's first archetypal anonymous middle-aged woman in a railway carriage' such as later became Mrs Brown.[17] Through this 'type', Woolf is ultimately concerned with the literary impulses and gestures of the writer.

Pointing to the writing process itself, Woolf highlights the mechanisms of scene-making and invention in square brackets: '[But this we'll skip; ornaments, curtains, trefoil china plate, yellow oblongs of cheese, white squares of biscuit—skip—oh, but wait! Half-way through luncheon one of those shivers; Bob stares at her, spoon in mouth...]' (*CSF* 114). In a technique that later has sustained importance in *Jacob's Room* and *Orlando*, the narrator thus sets a scene in the third-person present tense, and begins an address to the character in second person outside the brackets:

> Now, Minnie, the door's shut; Hilda heavily descends; you unstrap the straps of your basket, lay on the bed a meagre nightgown, stand side by side furred felt slippers. The looking-glass—no, you avoid the looking-glass. Some methodical disposition of hat-pins. Perhaps the shell box has something in it? You shake it; it's the pearl stud there was last year—that's all. (*CSF* 114)

The introduction of the pronoun 'you' has the simultaneous effect of stage-directing the character and placing the reader in her position. The present tense direct address gives the sense that this is a hypothetical situation unfolding as we watch it, suggesting the autonomy of characters even as it also highlights the narrative mechanisms that control them: 'A moment's blankness—then, what are you thinking?' (*CSF* 115). While the

---

[17] Briggs, 35. See also Jean Guiguet, *Virginia Woolf and her Works*, trans. Jean Stewart (London: Hogarth Press, 1965), 332: 'Minnie Marsh in "An Unwritten Novel" is elder sister to Mrs Brown, and Virginia Woolf undoubtedly bore in mind the sketch—written in 1919-1920, when elaborating the typical figure on whom she based her theory.'

narrator asks rhetorical questions of their own imagined character, that character itself is also reduced to a set of signifying marks to be interpreted: 'Have I read you right?' (*CSF* 117).

With each development in the story undoing the previous work, we are encouraged to think that the ending provides the 'true' story about this woman's life, as she leaves the train to be met by her son. Yet, this information is, again, inferred by the narrator, whose perspective we never escape. There is an almost involuntary temptation, on the reader's part, to extrapolate a whole picture as the narrator has just done: the narrator 'pass[es] her poison' to the reader. The character sketch, whose mechanisms have just been laid bare by Woolf as a *mis-en-abyme* of signs and gestures, crucially depends on the reader's participation in constructing the whole image from a few parts—it relies on a scene-making impulse on the part of the reader, stimulated by the outlines which inevitably bear the imprint of the writer.

The light-touch provisionality of the sketch is therefore in dialectical tension with ideas of permanence and inscription in the form of a printed book, speaking to the contradictions of reading and/or constructing the essence of a person from the marks on the surface. As well as in the newspaper/character reading that happens on public transport in 'An Unwritten Novel', in Woolf's work more generally, as Marcus notes, 'there is a recurrent play on "character" as a printing term, and on the relationship between "character" and "type" to subvert received definitions of "character" as psychological "type" and to explore the concept of reading character as one would read a map or navigate a city'.[18] Woolf's punning exploitation of etymology in this way highlights the material and discursive nature of the literary construction of character, as a phenomenon of language and text. As Marcus suggests in her metaphor of mapping and navigation, Woolf uses character as a means of orientating the reader in the text. This is particularly evident in *Mrs Dalloway*, where the metaphorical city is also the recognizable interwar London scene, and where the characters provide the kind of 'tunnel' vision that Woolf used to describe her way of writing the past 'in instalments' (*D2* 272). This 'tunnelling process' maps onto her 'discovery', while drafting *Mrs Dalloway*, that she 'dig[s] out beautiful caves behind [her] characters': 'I think that gives exactly what I want; humanity, humour, depth. The idea is that the caves shall connect and each comes to daylight at the present moment' (*D2* 263). Again, she invokes the tensions between surface and depth, essence and historicity, in the concept of character. These play out in the suggestive, accumulated outlines of the novel—*Mrs Dalloway*—as a sketchbook of characters, in which she developed the stripped-back, architectural simplicity of the sketch that were first at work, via 'An Unwritten Novel', in *Jacob's Room*.

In her review of *Jacob's Room*, Rebecca West highlights the affinities between Woolf's fiction and visual art, suggesting that the book be read 'not as a novel but as a portfolio'.[19] Indeed, Jacob seems to be a hypothetical character in a book constructed as a series of

---

[18] Marcus, *Dreams of Modernity*, 136.
[19] Rebecca West, 'Review of *Jacob's Room*', in Majumdar and McLaurin, *The Critical Heritage*, 101.

character sketches, including many named but incidental characters. Some of these have no interaction with Jacob, while others directly touch and divert his life in certain directions. Introducing temporal leaps and changes of scene, the following passage about Mr Floyd, who tutored Jacob and his brothers, is an intriguing example:

> Then Mr Floyd spoke about the King's Navy (to which Archer was going); and about Rugby (to which Jacob was going); and next day he received a silver salver and went—first to Sheffield, where he met Miss Wimbush, who was on a visit to her uncle, then to Hackney—then to Maresfield House, of which he became the principal, and finally, becoming editor of a well-known series of Ecclesiastical Biographies, he retired to Hampstead with his wife and daughter, and is often to be seen feeding the ducks on Leg of Mutton Pond. [...] Meeting Jacob in Piccadilly lately, he recognized him after three seconds. But Jacob had grown such a fine young man that Mr Floyd did not like to stop him in the street. (*JR* 24)

This cursory biographical account of Mr Floyd—who becomes a biographer himself—gives a set of coordinates for Jacob's life. After slipping into free indirect discourse where we witness Mr Floyd's thoughts, the narrative then shifts back in time, using the points plotted by this paragraph to return to Jacob's story and hint forwards to his eventual death: 'They were all alive, that is to say, while poor Mr Floyd was becoming Principal of Maresfield House' (*JR* 25). With Mr Floyd's biography imbedding a spoiler for Jacob's fate, the implication here is that, at a later point, they would not be 'all alive'. Rooted in a moment of 'becoming', the sentence begs the question of what happened to Jacob and his family by the time Mr Floyd *was* Principal; though he had seen Jacob 'lately', it suggests that they are not 'all alive' now, when Mr Floyd '*is often* to be seen feeding the ducks'. Such complexities of temporality and perspective are perhaps what elude Arnold Bennett: on the simplest level, as Mark Hussey points out, 'Jacob is *dead*; it is the experience of his *absence* that Woolf evokes in her novel. Character as Cenotaph'.[20] Character as *always* an empty yet symbolic signifier is arguably one of the ways in which Woolf develops a new form out of 'An Unwritten Novel'. As Randi Koppen suggests, however, this unravelling and 'unwriting' had already been at work in Woolf's first novel, *The Voyage Out*. There, 'it is the dissolution rather than formation of character that marks the beginnings of Woolf's modernist aesthetic'.[21] This 'dissolution' continues through 'An Unwritten Novel', to the central absence of Jacob, and is figured again in the laconic presence of Percival in *The Waves* (1931).

In all these novels, the permanent textual nature of character stands in for the impossibility of capturing or constructing a fully fleshed-out vision. The narrator of *Jacob's Room* often reflects on the processes of reading character, at one point materially

---

[20] Mark Hussey, 'Woolf: After Lives', in Randall and Goldman, eds, *Virginia Woolf in Context*, 17. See Bennett, 'Is the Novel Decaying?', 47.

[21] Randi Koppen, 'The Negress and the Bishop: On Marriage, Colonialism, and the Problem of Knowledge', in Elsa Högberg and Amy Bromley, eds, *Sentencing Orlando: Virginia Woolf and the Morphology of the Modernist Sentence* (Edinburgh: Edinburgh University Press, 2018), 192.

comparing people to books: 'Each had his past shut in him like the leaves of a book known to him by heart; and his friends could only read the title' (*JR* 85). This metaphor invoking the dimensions of the book encapsulates the difficulties of interpreting what is displayed on the surface, and points to the split between private and public lives with which Woolf is concerned throughout her fiction.[22] This tension highlights a difficulty in constructing literary characters:

> It is no use trying to sum people up. One must follow hints, not exactly what is said, nor yet entirely what is done. Some, it is true, take ineffaceable impressions of character at once. Others dally and loiter, and get blown this way and that. [...] There is also the highly respectable opinion that character-mongering is much overdone nowadays. (*JR* 214)

The impossibility of brevity and the pitfalls of loquaciousness in trying to take a characteristic 'impression' echoes into Woolf's 1929 essay, 'Phases of Fiction'. There, Woolf takes a meandering, anachronistic path through literary history, guided by the whims of 'interest and pleasure' (*E5* 40), and the phrase 'character-mongers' is fleshed out in another typification of novelistic style comprising 'Truth-Tellers', 'Romantics', 'Character-Mongers and Comedians', and 'Psychologists'. 'The Character-Mongers and Comedians' section begins with Dickens, who encourages the reader to 'enter into the spirit of exaggeration' (*E5* 55), and whose boldly drawn characters are solidified through repetition to become points of orientation for the reader: they 'serve as stationary points in the flow and confusion of the narrative' (*E5* 56). From Dickens's landmark 'unmitigated and extreme' characters (*E5* 57), Woolf moves to Jane Austen, where 'the sentence has taken on a different character': it 'runs like a knife, in and out, cutting a shape clear. It is done in a drawing-room. It is done by the use of dialogue' (*E5* 58). Highlighting the intertwining of character and form, Woolf foregrounds the relationality of Austen's characters who are brought into being through interaction with each other: like in Tolstoy, 'the pressure of character upon character is never relaxed. The tension is perpetual, every nerve in the character is alive' (*E5* 58). Such contrastive juxtaposition, mirrored in the structure of Woolf's essay itself, informs her own use of dialogue as a structuring principle of the novel: *The Voyage Out* and *Night and Day* are largely composed of dialogues that counterpoint different types of characters; *Mrs Dalloway*, *To the Lighthouse*, and *The Years* juxtapose shifting perspectives in free indirect discourse; *The Waves* intersperses the monologues of six main characters with poetic interludes that separate the chapters; and *Orlando* and *Between the Acts* are Bakhtinian carnivals of multivocal dialogic discourses.

'But', Woolf cautions, 'personal relations have limits, as Jane Austen seems to realise by stressing their comedy. Everything, she seems to say, has, if we could discover it, a reasonable summing up' (*E5* 61). This 'summing up' would have to come from a point of

---

[22] See Anna Snaith, *Virginia Woolf: Public and Private Negotiations* (Basingstoke: Palgrave Macmillan, 2000).

view external to the characters themselves, perhaps with the comedic distance of dramatic irony. In her discussion of the final author in this section, Woolf attends to George Eliot's use of first-person framing narratives, which, much as they iterate the 'I' as a character in its own right, distance us from the main characters: 'we are not going to get the relations of people together, but the spectacle of life so far as "I" can show it to us' (*E5* 61–2). Where 'Austen went in and out of her people's minds like the blood in their veins' (*E5* 63), Eliot stands detached enough to philosophize about their situations. The effect is not so much comedy as it is characterization by analysis, moving us into the 'far more dubious region' of 'The Psychologists' (*E5* 63). The narrators of *Jacob's Room* and *Orlando* perform similar functions in telling the life of someone else, with varying degrees of distance and exteriority: it is the 'dubious' effect of supposed neutrality in such frameworks—mocked in 'An Unwritten Novel'—which informs Woolf's use of irony, satire, and parody in these texts.

The ambivalence of 'summing people up' in frame narratives is important to *Mrs Dalloway*, where Clarissa vows in the opening pages 'she would not say of anyone in the world now that they were this or were that' (*MD* 7). In a novel predominantly narrated through her interior discourse, Clarissa is also seen through the eyes of other characters: often, sparse and incisive characterization is shown as a mode of social criticism, but also of memory, if not exactly of elegiac memorialization. The passing of time and the workings of memory are shown to have the potential of both deepening an impression and heightening loss: for Septimus Smith, the experience of war trauma dissolves character itself into a flow of fleeting sensations and impressions, superimposed memories, and hallucinations. While Peter Walsh finds that 'it was a mere sketch, he often felt, that even he, after all these years, could make of Clarissa' (*MD* 70), the novel nevertheless ends with the ultimate summary: 'For there she was' (*MD* 174). These performative final words are structurally important markers of *Mrs Dalloway*'s experimental form and characterization, jettisoning exhaustive description but nevertheless attempting to get to the heart of something. In her diary while writing the conclusion of *Mrs Dalloway*, Woolf planned to have an 'ending on three notes, at different stages of the staircase, each saying something to sum up Clarissa' (*D2* 312). The four words that replace these summaries take us a step further. Summary is something that happens on the surface, in retrospect, with recourse to key characteristics: in *Mrs Dalloway*, Clarissa shows us that there can be no truthful, retrospective 'summing up' of character—but it is important to make the attempt; to say that she was there.

In its accumulation and juxtaposition of perspectives, *Mrs Dalloway* is as much a portfolio as is *Jacob's Room*. Developing the latter's passages of memoiristic interior discourse, *Mrs Dalloway* also takes up and extends character sketches of people who had previously appeared in earlier novels: the Dalloways figured prominently in *The Voyage Out*; on the streets of London we encounter Moll Pratt from *Jacob's Room* (*MD* 17); and Clara and Mrs Durrant appear at Clarissa's party, along with Mrs Hilbery of *Night and Day* (*MD* 156–7). *Mrs Dalloway* itself is part of a set of character sketches and scenes that Woolf wrote around the novel (one of which is, tellingly, entitled 'A Summing Up'), collected posthumously in Stella McNichol's *Mrs Dalloway's Party: A Short Story*

Sequence (1973). The central characters, then, have a life outside of this novel; they permeate the world of Woolf's fiction, moving in multiple places and changing the scenes in which they appear. They create continuities, as characteristic Woolfian types, and a sense of character as something that endures between the pages of these texts; but they are also altered by the perspectives and contexts in which they appear, imprinted anew in each novelistic setting.

In all of Woolf's novels, Orlando might be the character who most fully allegorizes this idea of character as historically specific. A collage of different literary styles, *Orlando* grew out of Woolf's character-sketching in her diaries, where she recorded portraits of her family, friends, and visitors, often creating exaggerated types and practising technique without fleshing out the whole description. Woolf explicitly ponders the formal possibilities of the sketchbook in an entry that describes the beginnings of her idea for *Orlando*: 'One of these days, I shall sketch here, like a grand historical picture, the outlines of all my friends. [...] It might be a way of writing the memoirs of one's own times during people's lifetimes. It might be a most amusing book. The question is how to do it' (*D3* 156–7). Combining caricature and memoir, as Diane Gillespie points out, Woolf's 'diary entries [are] her equivalent of the visual artist's sketches, [and] serve in part as exercises for fictional characterizations'.[23] H. Porter Abbot also notes that Woolf 'engraves [character portraits in her diaries] with the sharp instrument of her wit'.[24] Her understanding of the diary as a collection of caricatures, with possibility of working up to a 'grand' visual artwork, not only informs *Orlando*, but is a crucial aspect of Woolf's investment in the character sketch as a form of life-writing.

In the scenes of her own early life recounted in her unfinished memoir, 'A Sketch of the Past', Woolf finds that attempting to write people through the lenses of memory and childhood vision figures them as caricatures: '[T]hese people were very like characters in Dickens. They were caricatures; they were very simple; they were immensely alive. They could be made with three strokes of the pen, if I could do it' (*MB* 86). The accumulation of such outlines has the potential to proliferate, but it also requires some skill to compose a text that affords kaleidoscopic and comical insight, such as Woolf performs in *Orlando*. Retrospectively writing about this mock-biography in her diary, with a contortion of tense, Woolf sees that: 'I want (and this was serious) to give things their caricature value' (*D3* 136). John Graham, citing this sentence in epigraph to his essay on the subject, notes that caricature views people 'with momentary detachment, and [...] may go beyond recognition to the discovery of something new about his face and character': 'Caricature can explore because it ignores the complexity of the total object and isolates only its relevant features, thereby allowing a sharper focus of attention than is possible in a full treatment'.[25] This definition foregrounds the instantaneous,

---

[23] Diane F. Gillespie, *The Sisters' Arts: Writing and Painting of Virginia Woolf and Vanessa Bell* (Syracuse, NY: Syracuse University Press, 1991), 171.

[24] H. Porter Abbot, 'Character and Modernism: Reading Woolf Writing Woolf', *New Literary History* 24, no. 2 (Spring 1993), 395.

[25] John Graham, 'The "Caricature Value" of Parody and Fantasy in Orlando', *University of Toronto Quarterly* 30, no. 4 (July 1961), 345 (italics in original).

preliminary, and experimental aspect of caricature, positioning it as both of the moment and as an exercise in technique: it is a way of testing various possibilities through suggestion and impression rather than prolonged analysis, and cuts to the essential by selection, 'simplification[,] and exaggeration'.[26] Thus, caricature both inscribes a bold, lasting image and acknowledges its own reductive provisionality.

As a series of signifying marks and gestures, which must be read correctly, the changeability of character in different contexts is important to *Orlando*. As well as invoking 'real-life' historical and literary figures in its satire of English biographical tradition, the novel casts Woolf's aristocratic lover, Vita Sackville-West, as the title character. *Orlando* presents character as full-bodied caricature, imbedding character sketches within parodies of certain literary forms and novelistic styles, typifying eras of literary history from the Elizabethan to 'the present moment' (1928) (*O* 272). Orlando alters with the times, and spontaneously changes sex midway through the novel. This supposedly fundamental change, integral to the novel's structure, is a change of signifiers that, we are told, leaves the 'essence' of Orlando fundamentally unchanged: 'Orlando had become a woman—there is no denying it. But in every other respect, Orlando remained precisely as he had been. The change of sex, though it altered their future, did nothing whatever to alter their identity. Their faces remained, as their portraits prove, practically the same' (*O* 128). With the shifting pronouns of these sentences, the character changes even as the biographer is asserting an essentialist, static conception of who Orlando is, was, and would be. With their contradictory recourse to Orlando's surface appearance as proof that, on the face of things, deep down, the character is unchanged, the targets of Woolf's satire here are the conventions of traditional life-writing and the illusory positivism of the realist novel.

In 'The Art of Biography' (1939), Woolf invokes 'the creative fact; the fertile fact; the fact that suggests and engenders' as an index of successful literary form (*E6* 187). Her language is suggestive in its advocacy of 'shaping the whole so that we perceive the outline': unlike monumental works, such sketches are a spur to memory, a form in which the character outlasts the moment of writing and of reading, but through which they also have the ability to change. Rather than 'capturing' character, the sketch in its open-ended provisionality is arguably a form that enables the capricious mutability of character that Woolf had begun to theorize through Mrs Brown. As well as its sense of accentuation, brevity, and distillation of the essential, the caricature crystallizes character in a 'fertile' biographic mode, which asks the reader to help fill out the picture. The brevity of the character sketch provides an opportunity to isolate surface impressions, to read them in detail, but also to take these signs as a starting point for further creative recontextualization. Woolf's novelistic character-sketching acknowledges that, ultimately, perhaps only an outline is after all possible; that caricature is inevitable—and that it is, in both senses of the word, vital.

---

[26] Graham, 'The "Caricature Value"', 345.

Selected Bibliography

Abbot, H. Porter, 'Character and Modernism: Reading Woolf Writing Woolf', *New Literary History* 24, no. 2 (Spring 1993), 393–405.

Bos, Jacques, 'Individuality and Inwardness in the Literary Character Sketches of the Seventeenth Century', *Journal of the Warburg and Courtauld Institutes*, 61 (1998), 142–57.

Briggs, Julia, *Reading Virginia Woolf* (Edinburgh: Edinburgh University Press, 2006).

Graham, John, 'The "Caricature Value" of Parody and Fantasy in *Orlando*', *University of Toronto Quarterly* 30, no. 4 (1961), 345–66.

Hussey, Mark, 'Woolf: After Lives', in Bryony Randall and Jane Goldman, eds, *Virginia Woolf in Context* (Cambridge: Cambridge University Press, 2013), 13–27.

Majumdar, Robin, and Allen McLaurin, eds, *Virginia Woolf: The Critical Heritage* (London: Routledge, 1975).

Minow-Pinkney, Makiko, *Virginia Woolf and December 1910: Studies in Rhetoric and Context* (Grosmont: Illuminati Books, 2014).

Sandberg, Eric, *Virginia Woolf: Experiments in Character* (New York: Cambria Press, 2014).

Woolf, Virginia, *Mrs Dalloway's Party: A Short Story Sequence*. Edited by Stella McNichol (London: Hogarth Press, 1973).

CHAPTER 11

TIME

JESSE MATZ

> But Time, unfortunately, though it makes animals and vegetables bloom and fade with amazing punctuality, has no such simple effect upon the mind of man. The mind of man, moreover, works with equal strangeness upon the body of time. An hour, once it lodges in the queer element of the human spirit, may be stretched to fifty or a hundred times its clock length; on the other hand, an hour may be accurately represented on the timepiece of the mind by one second. This extraordinary discrepancy between time on the clock and time in the mind is less known than it should be and deserves fuller investigation. (*O* 90)

Subjective time was a constant fascination for Virginia Woolf. The 'timepiece of the mind' freely measures all her fiction, and its extraordinary discrepancies are always under investigation in fiction obsessed with the experience of time at every level. Subjective time works with surpassing strangeness upon Woolf's narrative forms, and that queer element is also her thematic concern in fiction that is so variously rendered tragic or comic, Romantic or ironic by the power—or the failure—of the mind's own kind of time. Moments of epiphany in which time stops or, inversely, flashing impressions of flux are the two main alternatives within which Woolf patterns out myriad temporalities. Thematically, the effect ranges from a blissful sense of plenitude to a tragic sense of life wasting away, and here too Woolf patterns out every possibility, so aware of all the implications of this shift from the limits of time on the clock to the freedoms, opportunities, and terrors of time in the mind.

Of course, Woolf's interest in subjective time was part of a larger modernist trend. By the time Woolf published *Orlando* in 1928, 'time in the mind' had become a common site of resistance to time's growing standardization. Modernity had asserted the time-schemes of factories and railway schedules, of global time-zones, and other public standards. These standards seemed to rule out more human rhythms and practices, and in response, many modernist writers and artists sought subjective discrepancies.

The well-known history of this response often singles out the establishment of the Greenwich Meridian as a critical moment. In 1884, the International Meridian

Conference established the basis for the time-zone system that joins the world into a total order; objective time became a global force, transforming what had been a diversity of time-cultures into a singular regime, not only at the level of time-zones but of all the clocks, schedules, and regulations they entailed.[1] Once established, this total system could only provoke dissent: its regularity could only seem out of sync with the real human experience of time, and that real human temporality became the focus for a host of cultural productions.

One example often singled out in this history of the reaction against time's standardization is Joseph Conrad's 1905 novel *The Secret Agent*. The novel's central event is an attempt to destroy the Greenwich Observatory—symbolically, to reject objective time. The subjective alternative is embodied in the novel itself, which turns upon a central time-shift that is a kind of formal equivalent to the attack on the Greenwich Meridian. Another such symbolic event occurs in William Faulkner's 1929 novel *The Sound and the Fury*, in which Quentin Compson smashes his watch—a family heirloom explicitly described as an oppressive measure of inhumane uniformity. Faulkner's novel also represents the subjective alternative in its forms of narration, which correspond entirely to 'time in the mind', departing all external measures for total immersion in what Woolf calls the 'queer element of the human spirit'. Woolf's own interest in such a departure was similar, and part of the larger culture of temporal subjectivism represented by Conrad, Faulkner, and the many others who reacted against objective time by representing what they took to be the truer human experience of it.

But although Woolf recognized the 'extraordinary discrepancy between time on the clock and time in the mind', that did not mean she wholly abandoned the former in favour of the latter. Much to the contrary, the discrepancy only made her more keenly aware of the validity of all the different temporalities at work in the world. Objective time was also a decisive force for her—most notably in *To the Lighthouse* (1927). Famously centred on 'Time Passes', a harrowing evocation of time passing without any significant reference to human subjectivity, *To the Lighthouse* very much recognizes the reality of the temporality that has nothing to do with the human spirit. Similarly, many of Woolf's fictions engage with history and natural patterns of time, all with a view toward achievements that go beyond the kind of subjective time characteristic of modernist culture.[2]

---

[1] For the full history of this shift and its effect on the literature and the arts, see Stephen Kern, *The Culture of Time and Space 1880-1918* (Cambridge, MA: Harvard University Press, 2003), 10–20; and Adam Barrows, *The Cosmic Time of Empire: Modern Britain and World Literature* (Berkeley: University of California Press, 2011), 22–52. More specifically, see Kern's account of the reasons Woolf felt it necessary to 'go beyond "the formal railway line of a sentence"' (31), and Barrows' account of 'Woolf's interest in the dangers of temporal standardization' (120).

[2] Woolf's diverse engagements with time have recently been recognized in an array of critical interventions explaining her relevance to ideas of periodization (Susan Stanford Friedman, 'Alternatives to Periodization: Literary History, Modernism, and the "New" Temporalities', *Modern Language Quarterly* 80, no. 4 (December 2019), 379–402), futurity (Paul K. Saint-Amour, *Tense Future: Modernism, Total War, Encyclopedic Form* (Oxford University Press, 2015), 90–132), everydayness and daily life (Bryony Randall, *Modernism, Daily Time, and Everyday Life* (Cambridge: Cambridge University

In some cases, Woolf's project is to reconcile these diverse patterns, and to attribute such reconciliation to aesthetic engagement. To the extent that Woolf contributes to a certain modernist effort at aesthetic redress, her visions of discrepant temporalities harmonize them in reparative aesthetic forms. As we will see, *To the Lighthouse* might be such a vision, succeeding 'Time Passes' with an optimistic realization of human projects that synthesize personal moments of being with objective time. But Woolf's interest in all kinds of time is more importantly an expression of her lifelong intellectual and artistic restlessness—itself a function of time, and perhaps her most characteristic response to it.

For Woolf's temporality was above all a dialectical one. Any idea of time in Woolf seems to provoke its opposite. For every commitment to a subjective form, there is recognition of time's objective reality; for any joy Woolf seems to take in time's true freedom, there is despair over it, and Woolf finds cause for celebration and dejection in clock-time as well. This dialectic obtains right from the start, in Woolf's earliest modernist writings—the essays and short stories through which she began to work out her fundamental principles. In her essays on modern fiction and the short fictions that correspond to them, Woolf rejects the static material forms of the Edwardian writers in favour of the flux of impressions. In these writings, flux is 'life itself', and subjective temporal disorder is at once the very life of the mind and the truth of human existence (*E3* 33). But as soon as she says so, Woolf is compelled to recognize the problem with flux as a measure of existence and a format for fiction. Her dialectical habit of mind asserts itself, and Woolf admits that the flux of impressions may never stabilize into anything like the conventional format necessary for public discourse. In 'Character in Fiction' (the later version of her better-known essay 'Mr Bennett and Mrs Brown'), Woolf regrets the 'season of failures and fragments' produced by the modernist effort at representational liberty (*E3* 420–38). In 'an Unwritten Novel', she has the liberatory flux of impressions run up against a contradictory factual reality, and despair is the result. If the narrator of 'An Unwritten Novel' then resumes her pursuit of subjective impressions and recommits to the flux of subjective time—'And yet the last look of them ... floods me anew'; 'I hasten, I follow'—it is with a sense that no single representational format will suffice to capture this 'adorable world' (*CSF* 121). Dialectically for Woolf, the flux that is a force for freedom—'life itself'—easily becomes that which undoes everything and wastes life away. The alternative may seem sustaining for a time, but it becomes a lifeless objectivity, provoking in turn its opposite—and a new phase in the dialectic. This pattern not only gives Woolf's work a unique relationship to time, but also gives a certain shape to her

---

Press, 2007), 155–184), transcendence (Robert Baker, 'What Do We Mean When We Talk about Transcendence?': Plato and Virginia Woolf', *Philosophy and Literature* 43, no. 2 (October 2019), 312–35), trauma (Martin Hägglund, *Dying for Time: Proust, Woolf, Nabokov* (Cambridge, MA: Harvard University Press, 2012), and memory (Gabrielle McIntire, *Modernism, Memory, and Desire: T. S. Eliot and Virginia Woolf* (Cambridge: Cambridge University Press, 2008) just to name a few of the topics and studies that continue to make the question of time a central focus in Woolf studies.

whole career as a writer, which is uniquely patterned according to the problem of time itself.

Woolf's career-long engagement with the problem of time begins in earnest with *Jacob's Room*. Although time is not explicitly at issue in this novel (as it is in the subsequent major time novels of the 1920s), *Jacob's Room* (1922) does take subjective time as its pattern, because it is essentially impressionistic. The effort to see its protagonist from many different points of view fragments the novel; its different perspectives on Jacob disallow any continuously linear progress, producing instead a dispersed multiplicity of incommensurate impressions. Flux dissolves narration from the outset, as Jacob's mother Betty Flanders sees her son's childhood landscapes (and her own writing) through her tears. As Jacob then ages from boyhood to young manhood, radically episodic observations of him dissolve chronological progression in favour of thematic and characterological priorities, as when an early view of Jacob's tutor Mr Floyd launches the narration far into the future—from the present moment of Jacob's childhood to just 'the other day', when Mr Floyd discovers that 'Jacob had grown … a fine young man' (*JR* 24). Although the tutor is a minor character important only in Jacob's early boyhood, recognizing his view of Jacob requires the narrator to depart the narrative present into the future moment in which he sees Jacob grown up. Departing so decisively from linear sequence, *Jacob's Room* indicates its greater interest in human truths apart from their order in time. That is, what matters to the novel is the truth about human character, and it ranges everywhere necessary to discover and deliver that essential reality.

As *Jacob's Room* 'proceeds', it continues to reach around for all possible insights into Jacob's life, wherever and whenever they might obtain—often pausing for the kind of timeless truths that justify this nonlinear procedure. For example, observing Jacob amid the multitudes at the theatre makes Woolf's narrator reflect upon the problem of choosing narratorial subjects: once linear progression has been abandoned, Woolf's narrator implies, possibilities come flooding in, threatening total flux unless narration can develop alternative methods. And *Jacob's Room* does develop them, even to the point of doing without the kind of climactic moments that ordinarily structure chronological narration. Notoriously, the novel never presents the critical moment of Jacob's death. We only learn about it afterwards, indirectly, from the impressions of his empty room registered by his mother and his best friend: 'Listless is the air in an empty room', Woolf's narrator tells us, without any more vivid account of the death that has left it so (*JR* 247). Those impressions are what matter to a novel dedicated to 'life itself', the experience of it, regardless of the way such experience must undo narrative's more conventionally progressive chronology.

This experience of time becomes the explicit concern of *Mrs Dalloway* (1925), in which the flux of life and thought not only unstructures narration implicitly but becomes a thematic problem. Here too time is immediately a factor, as Clarissa Dalloway's first venture into the busy life of London provokes memories, reviving her past. As she plunges into the fresh morning air, she remembers doing so elsewhere years ago, and it is difficult to distinguish the memory from Clarissa's present experience. That ambiguity becomes a main preoccupation for a novel aware of the way memory determines the present—the way the past endures, conditioning present awareness.

Two contexts typically explain this tendency in Woolf's fiction. One is her own account of what she called her method of 'tunnelling' or submerging backward as necessary into the past to discover the experiential backing of life in process.[3] The other is the work of the time-philosopher most often cited as a counterpart for Woolf: Henri Bergson. Bergson famously theorized 'duration', arguing that time does not pass but *endures*, and this distinction was key to a foundational and highly influential account of time as flux, as evolutionary change, and an intensive property utterly different from the kind of spatial manifold that tends to define it. Bergson noted that our dominant ideas of time are actually all borrowed from space; such things as clocks and calendars distort our sense of time by subjecting it to extensive criteria. 'When we speak of *time*', Bergson explains, 'we generally think of a homogeneous medium in which our conscious states are ranged alongside one another as in space', and we therefore get time exactly wrong.[4] That tendency is not only misleading but ruinous, in Bergson's account, because pure duration—time itself—is also the medium of human freedom. Subjecting it to false external measures, we also limit ourselves, and if we could only enter into the fuller freedom of duration, change would become more fully possible and active in our actual lives: 'by invading the series of our psychic states, by introducing space into our perception of duration, [spatial representation] corrupts at its very source our feeling of outer and inner change, of movement, and of freedom', and it is essential to try to rediscover duration in spite of this corruption.[5] Woolf seems to have shared this idea of duration and *Mrs Dalloway* appears to pursue it: as Clarissa's present consciousness loses focus upon the moving present and resorts to living memory for its sense of direction, she seems to get back to what Bergson calls pure duration, and as Woolf develops patterns that reflect this possibility, she appears to join the Bergsonian effort to discover the larger benefits that accrue to this truer sense of time. Bergson offers this definition of duration:

> Pure duration is the form which the succession of our conscious states assumes when our ego lets itself *live*, when it refrains from separating its present state from its former states.... In a word, pure duration might well be nothing but a succession of qualitative changes, which melt into and permeate one another, without precise outlines, without any tendency to externalize themselves in relation to one another. Without any affiliation with number: it would be pure heterogeneity.[6] (*MD* 100)

Woolf too tried for this heterogeneity, these melting changes that permeate one another, and the vitality they entailed.[7]

---

[3] 'It took me a year's groping to discover what I call my tunnelling process, by which I tell the past by instalments, as I have need of it' (*D2* 272).

[4] Henri Bergson, *Time and Free Will: An Essay on the Immediate Data of Consciousness* [1889], trans. F. L. Pogson (London: George Allen Unwin, Ltd., 1910), 90.

[5] Bergson, 74.

[6] Bergson, 100.

[7] For a more thorough account of the many ways Woolf's work (as well as that of like-minded modernists) aligns with Bergson's theories see Mary Ann Gillies, *Henri Bergson and British Modernism* (Montreal: McGill-Queen's University Press, 1996), 109, which argues, for example, that 'far from being moments out of time, Woolf's moments of being are instances of pure duration, moments during which

But there are limits to Woolf's Bergsonism, and reasons to question this familiar association. Even if there were evidence that Bergson influenced Woolf directly, there are practical differences that should encourage us to explain the temporality of *Mrs Dalloway* in contrast to Bergson as well. Bergson questioned the possibility that any literary language might actually be adequate to time itself, stressing the essential spatiality of language and its consequent incompatibility with duration as such. This idealism tended to commit Bergson to the kind of Romantic ideals Woolf tended to question. Committed to literary language, Woolf believed more fully in its suggestive power, earnestly pursuing the possibility of inhabiting time's truer freedom. Simultaneously, however, she knew the limits of such freedom, especially for people who were, like Clarissa Dalloway, subject to very real social and political limits. This is to say that a focus on women's lives could only qualify the Romanticism implicit in duration as Bergson theorized it, and that other points of critical reference might be necessary to place Woolf in relation to this aspect of temporal engagement.

For example, the work of the much lesser-known psychologist and fiction writer Mary Sturt. Sturt published *The Psychology of Time* in 1925, and it has much in common with *Mrs Dalloway*, published that same year.[8] Generally, Sturt's work is very much of its moment—the modernist moment shaped by Bergsonian ideas and their cultural corollaries. Like Bergson, Sturt concerns herself with the difference between the concept of time and the experience of it as well as the problem of defining duration in relation to (and apart from) the concepts and experiences that effectively constitute time. Unlike Bergson, however, Sturt recognizes the value and the necessity of the practical view of time, aiming not for a Romantic ideal of some escape into pure duration but a kind of compromise between that ideal and practical reality. It is this compromise that makes Sturt perhaps a better counterpart for Woolf—a more apt theoretical context for Woolf's way of navigating through the complexities that make time at once a matter of conceptual speculation, experiential psychology, and narrative action.

In the last paragraph of *The Psychology of Time*, Sturt observers that although 'time ... is part of our adaptation to our environment', 'most men crave to be free of it'.[9] The necessity of adaptation and the wish for freedom have both been important to Sturt's discussion of time, and in this last paragraph she draws conclusions about their relative claims upon us. She recognizes that 'it is indeed possible to gain this freedom,

---

past and present time not only literally coexist, but during which one is aware of their coexistence. In a Bergsonian sense, these are moments of pure *durée*'.

[8] Sturt (1896–1994) was also author (with E.C. Oakden) of the textbook *Modern Psychology and Education* (1926), and her focus upon the intersection of these two fields characterized her work as well as what made her approach to the question of time unique. She sought ways to make the psychology of time more relevant to practical interests—in education but also in anthropological and cultural studies (A. C. Grayling et al., eds, *The Continuum Encyclopedia of British Philosophy*, vol. 4 (London: Bloomsbury, 2006), 3084–5). Sturt's range of interests extended to fiction writing as well. She wrote three novels: *Swallows in Springtime* (1934), *Be Gentle to the Young* (1937), and *The Hours of the Night* (1938).

[9] Mary Sturt, *The Psychology of Time* [1925] (London: Routledge, 2001), 149.

but at the price of cutting one's self off from external objects, and thus from much of the society of mankind and its advantages'.[10] This ambivalent view matches Woolf's own ambivalence, especially because Sturt admits that there is the problem of 'the person who practices such detachment being thought mad'.[11] Woolf, too, was aware that any radical transcendence of time—or, rather, of time understood as a 'force'—could be delusional or worse. She therefore sought the kind of compromise Sturt imagines here:

> A compromise is, however, possible; a certain limited freedom from time can be achieved without a complete severance of our connexion with external objects. A mind supplied with stories of the past and dreams of the future has a certain freedom. Supposing the affairs of everyday do not press too heavily on it, it can slip away for many hours and walk with poets long dead in the green dusk of a twilight wood, or pass to the calm unchanging regions of speculation where the roar of the passing centuries dies as a whisper on the air.[12]

Reminiscent of Woolf's own temporal lyricism, this passage identifies a time-sense similar to the one operative in Mrs Dalloway. It involves a Bergsonian 'severance of connexion' and a freedom at once timeless and more true to temporal duration. But it is a 'certain freedom' rather than an absolute one, a mixed relationship to 'the affairs of everyday', and it involves a literary form of imagination. Woolf similarly seeks this balance between subjective freedom and objective affairs, between timeless epiphany and routine existence, at least so that the two might enhance each other. And Woolf shows us minds supplied with stories of the past and dreams of the future, herself dedicated to the further creation of stories and dreams made upon this heterodox pattern of time.

Thus, in Mrs Dalloway we see not only Clarissa freely searching her way forward in time motivated by yet-present stories of her past, escaping time while subject to it, but also Septimus Smith beset by an inverse sort of compromise. The subjective time-sense available to him is a traumatic one; past violence overwhelms the present, leaving Septimus without any futurity at all. When in a manic state of dissociation he dreams up an 'ode to Time', it is terribly real—a bad combination of freedom to 'slip away' from the affairs of everyday and the roar of time's passing (MD 63). Woolf's representations of subjective time explore these complex implications of duration, recognizing not only the idea of a temporality that might depart from objective, linear, chronological measures— not only *pure* duration—but also and more significantly the effects of the many possible and ultimately necessary compromises with time's objectivity.[13] At certain moments,

---

[10] Sturt, *Psychology of Time*, 150.

[11] Sturt, *Psychology of Time*, 150

[12] Sturt, *Psychology of Time*, 150.

[13] Recent discussions of the actual complexity of temporal engagement in Mrs Dalloway include Paul Tolliver Brown, 'The Spatiotemporal Topography of Virginia Woolf's *Mrs Dalloway*: Capturing Britain's Transition to a Relative Modernity', *Journal of Modern Literature* 38, no. 4 (2015), 20–38; and Bryony Randall, 'A Day's Time: The One-Day Novel and the Temporality of the Everyday', *New Literary History* 47, no 4 (2016), 581–610.

Mrs Dalloway affirms the possibility of epiphanic forms of transcendence: when Clarissa who had 'feared time itself' and 'the dwindling of life' finds in the past a sustaining sense of herself as an abiding central force in the world, when she 'plunged into the very heart of the moment, transfixed it', she achieves the kind of moment of being through which subjective power overcomes time's passing (*MD* 27, 33). But such moments regularly give way to an opposite dynamic, as time reasserts itself and demands its due beyond any possibility of compromise or reconciliation.[14]

This interest in possible compromises, this dualism or view toward reconciliations, made *Mrs Dalloway* one of the three exemplary 'tales about time' discussed by Paul Ricoeur in his landmark *Time and Narrative*.[15] Ricoeur's approach to the question of time in narrative is that of phenomenological hermeneutics—appropriate for Woolf, who does focus so much on the *poiesis* of time, the making of time itself, in human consciousness. Ricoeur's phenomenological hermeneutics focuses more specifically on the way narrative engagement constructs human temporality.[16] His central argument is circular: 'time becomes human time to the extent that it is organized after a narrative; narrative, in turn, is meaningful to the extent that it portrays the features of temporal experience'.[17] Narrative is how we give time—otherwise so elusive and fraught with *aporias* or gaps between its diverse forms—a meaningful shape; in turn, the effort to make sense of our lives in time motivates narrative forms of engagement. Time shapes narrative and narrative shapes time; a reciprocal relationship keeps driving this dialectical process, so that a time-narrative reciprocity perpetually generates new narrative forms and new temporal possibilities.

Narrative fiction specifically plays a vital role because what Ricoeur calls the 'fictive experience of time' produced by narrative dynamics best captures time's 'discordant concordance'.[18] All narrative fictions have this special potential to make time meaningful, but Ricoeur identifies certain texts as particularly telling 'tales about time'. Three *Zeitromane* (time novels) make time meaningful with special thematic attention to it: Marcel Proust's *In Search of Lost Time*, Thomas Mann's *The Magic Mountain*, and Woolf's *Mrs Dalloway*. Woolf's novel achieves this distinction by engaging with time at different levels of experience and understanding and finding ways to navigate the differences among them. Set on a single day, patterned according to the flux of consciousness, regularly punctuated by the public measures of time embodied by London's

---

[14] For a revisionist discussion of the pedagogical power of Woolfian 'moments of being' see Benjamin D. Hagen, 'Feeling Shadows: Virginia Woolf's Sensuous Pedagogy', *PMLA* 132, no. 2 (March 2017), 266–80.

[15] Paul Ricoeur, *Time and Narrative*, vol. 2, trans. Kathleen McLaughlin and David Pellauer (Chicago: University of Chicago Press, 1985), 100.

[16] For an explanation of the process of creation of new realities that links Ricoeur's theory to Woolf's work, see Teresa Prudente, *A Specially Tender Piece of Eternity: Virginia Woolf and the Experience of Time* (Plymouth: Lexington Books, 2009), 161–2.

[17] Ricoeur, *Time and Narrative*, vol. 1, 3.

[18] 'By fictive experience I mean a virtual manner of living in the world projected by the literary work as a result of its capacity for self-transcendence'. Paul Ricoeur, *Time and Narrative*, vol. 2, trans. Kathleen McLaughlin and David Pellauer (Chicago: University of Chicago Press, 1985), 159.

different church-bells, *Mrs Dalloway* explores the varieties of time that might keep life from taking a meaningful shape. Aware of the perils of temporal confusion represented so bleakly by traumatic experience and the social disjunctions of urban life in modernity, *Mrs Dalloway* enacts in its narrative forms the patterns that would humanize time.[19] That tendency takes the novel far from what might otherwise seem to be its temporal focus upon the personal, private time experience of a single day. It accords Woolf's fiction a more monumental status in relation to phenomenological hermeneutics. *Mrs Dalloway* performs the reciprocity of time and narrative with rare thematic virtuosity. Indeed, Ricoeur argues, its way of thematizing this reciprocity gives it exceptional power over the fictive experience of time.[20]

This power increases in *To the Lighthouse*. As we shift now to the time-project at work in Woolf's next *Zeitroman*, the larger temporal shape of her fictive engagements with time starts to emerge. We can begin to see the pattern that structures Woolf's development as a writer—a temporality that suggests just how much Woolf herself was open to time and its transformations. *Jacob's Room* developed her awareness of the subjectivity of time, as we have seen, and its narrative forms deformed in response to that awareness. But *Mrs Dalloway* does not then continue in the same mode. Rather, it asks subsequent questions about the relation of this subjective temporality to the demands of everyday life and the more public, objective structures of life at large. Weaving together different minds and their social environments, *Mrs Dalloway* pursues the reconciliations and reciprocities celebrated by Paul Ricoeur. Next, *To the Lighthouse* makes that pursuit more explicit—a self-aware objective of literary form. And this pattern continues—in *Orlando*, where history becomes a part of the puzzle; in *The Waves* (1931), a novel that radicalizes both subjectivity and the objective forms of time separate from human experience; and later texts in which Woolf continues to follow the dialectical relationship between time and narrative toward new discoveries.

If *Mrs Dalloway* looks for ways to reconcile disparate temporalities, performing the fictive experience of time toward that end, *To the Lighthouse* explicitly suggests that such a reconciliation is the effect of aesthetic form. The first part of the novel ('The Window') explores the subjectivity of time, much like *Mrs Dalloway*, courting those moments of being or epiphanies that might seem to give subjective consciousness power over the passing of time. The climactic moment of 'The Window' comes when a dinner party, at first inauspiciously pointless and fractious, comes together into a luminous vision of human solidarity and timeless happiness:

> [It all] seemed now for no special reason to stay there like a smoke, like a fume rising upwards, holding them safe together. Nothing need be said; nothing could be said.

---

[19] For Ricoeur's account of *Mrs Dalloway* as a 'tale about time' see *Time and Narrative*, vol. 2, 101–12.

[20] This possibility has been a main focus for readings of this text at least since Erich Auerbach's landmark discussion of the way 'the exterior objective reality of the momentary present ... is nothing but an occasion' for the extensive subjective reflections that go well beyond its timeframe (Erich Auerbach, *Mimesis: The Representation of Reality in Western Literature*, trans. Willard R. Trask (Princeton: Princeton University Press, 1946), 541).

> There it was, all round them. It partook, she felt, carefully helping Mr Bankes to a specially tender piece, of eternity; as she had already felt about something different once before that afternoon; there is a coherence in things, a stability; something, she meant, is immune from change, and shines out (she glanced at the window with its ripple of reflected lights) in the face of the flowing, the fleeting, the spectral, like a ruby; so that again tonight she had the feeling she had had once today already, of peace, of rest. Of such moments, she thought, the thing is made that remains for ever after. This would remain. (*TL* 141–2)

But it would not remain, and 'The Window' suggests that such moments on their own cannot really stay—that something more must be 'made' for them do so. Even as they occur, 'vanishing even as she looked', they are 'already the past', as Mrs Ramsay recognizes as she gives one last look at the scene in which her epiphanic moment has occurred (*TL* 150). And if *Mrs Dalloway* had already demonstrated that subjective time alone could not give adequate meaning to human life, *To the Lighthouse* increases the challenge to it: in 'Time Passes', the section that follows the epiphanies of 'The Window', objective time asserts itself with a force—and a narrative correlate—unprecedented in the literature of time. 'Time Passes' notoriously demonstrates the wasting power of a temporality not subject to any humanization—or the truth about time apart from our humanizing fantasies about it. And in accordance, the narrative mode of this section shifts to a radical omniscience, a distant authorial mode as inhuman as 'The Window' was subjectively engaged.[21]

But 'Time Passes' is not the last word on time in *To the Lighthouse*. The novel's alternatives (the blighting power of time, the relatively inconsequential and therefore tragic human moment of being) set the stage for something that might put them into positive relation to each other. That thing is the work of art, and, by implication, the novel itself. Lily Briscoe has been making a painting, trying all these years to capture Mrs Ramsay in a manner not unlike the way Mrs Ramsay herself seemed to be able to make a moment matter. But Lily's approach is aesthetic, not sentimental, and as she comes to realize, better able to capture timeless truth. When she finally adds the decisive stroke to her picture and completes it, she knows that she has had her timeless vision, even if the picture itself will be 'hung in the attics' and forgotten (*TL* 242). Simultaneously, Mr Ramsay and his children finally reach the lighthouse—the structure that has been an aspirational chronotope for time itself throughout the novel, a symbol of something at once timeless (ceaselessly abiding) and persistent (with its intermittent beam a constant pattern across the landscape). Featuring these twin achievements, *To the Lighthouse* calls attention to itself as a phenomenological form. That is, the novel's three parts presented dialectically with thematic stress upon their dialectical process construct what we might

---

[21] For a fuller account see Ann Banfield, 'Time Passes: Virginia Woolf, Post-Impressionism, and Cambridge Time', *Poetics Today* 24, no. 3 (2003), 471–516. See also Charles Tung, 'Baddest Modernism: The Scales and Lines of Inhuman Time', *Modernism/Modernity* 23, no. 3 (September 2016), 515–38.

call (modifying Ricoeur's phrase) a 'tale *for* time', a narrative explicitly poised for time's remediation. It shows Woolf suggesting that her form of narrative fiction might itself make a difference to time.

As a kind of overarching chronotope for time itself, Woolf's lighthouse aligns her with the theorist of the chronotope, Mikhail Bakhtin. And this association also provides us with another way to understand how Woolf goes well beyond the interest in the classic modernist interest in subjective time. Bakhtin defines the chronotope as time's spatial configuration, 'the intrinsic connectedness of temporal and spatial relationships that are artistically expressed in literature'.[22] In the chronotope, 'spatial and temporal indicators are fused into one carefully thought-out, concrete whole. Time, as it were, thickens, takes on flesh, becomes artistically visible; likewise, space becomes charged and responsive to the movements of time, plot and history'.[23] Chronotopes obtain as figures within a text but also as a narrative pattern and, beyond that, a historical form specific to a historical moment. In *To the Lighthouse*, Woolf similarly embodies her idea of time in a figure that also corresponds to the shaping force of her narrative form and to a historical formation. The form is that of a timeless landmark and a regular rhythm—the permanent abstract horizontal in the landscape and the source of the 'steady stroke' so reassuring to Mrs Ramsay (*TL* 86). This form is Woolf's narrative form, too, because of the way *To the Lighthouse* seeks to reconcile timeless moments with time's passing. And the lighthouse chronotope corresponds to a historical formation by serving as a kind of pastoral guide to safe passage within modernity. If *To the Lighthouse* is riven by war as well as time's passing—if indeed the war has lent new violence to the effect of time's passing, and so radically undermined any chance of meaning in spite of it—the lighthouse figures an abiding safety, an idea of something that might enable survival of radical historical rupture. As a spatial object so fully charged with time, as a figure that is also a reflexive narrative form and a historical property, Woolf's chronotope is an example of what Bakhtin calls the 'creative chronotope', the point of interchange between a literary text and its world: Bakhtin speaks of 'a special *creative* chronotope inside which this exchange between work and life occurs, which constitutes the distinctive life of the work', and this category might well apply to the way Woolf's lighthouse signifies beyond its text.[24] *To the Lighthouse* suggests that Woolf shared Bakhtin's idea of the way narrative forms could embody time, and, more than that, his larger sense of the worldly reasons to assert that capacity.

To survey Woolf's engagements with time from *Jacob's Room* to *the Lighthouse* is to discover the development of a project that subsequently ramifies in different directions. If *To the Lighthouse* brings temporal *poiesis* to a high point of metafictional surety,

---

[22] Mikhail Bakhtin, 'Forms of Time and of the Chronotope in the Novel: Notes Toward a Historical Poetics', in *The Dialogic Imagination: Four Essays by M. M. Bakhtin*, ed. Michael Holquist, trans. Caryl Emerson and Michael Holquist (Austin: University of Texas Press, 1981), 84.
[23] Bakhtin, Forms of Time and of the Chronotope, 84
[24] Bakhtin, 254

stressing how its own forms might enact that reciprocity of time and narrative identified by Paul Ricoeur, subsequent texts explore the diverse ramifications of this idea about shaping power of the fictive experience of time. *Orlando*, the text in which Woolf's narrator reflects upon the 'extraordinary discrepancy between time on the clock and time in the mind' (*O* 90), actually has objectives that go well beyond the identification of this discrepancy. For *Orlando* takes a subjective approach to history, structuring the history of English culture in accordance with the perspective of a single strong personality.[25] As Orlando develops from a young Elizabethan gentleman to a modern woman, the periods through which they pass are registered as such by Orlando's changing body, mind, and prospects. And because this subjectivity is that of literary form—because *Orlando* is a history of genres, or a matter of history as genre—this novel suggests that the purchase upon time developed in *To the Lighthouse* has become a transformative historical sense. In other words, the aesthetic performance that reconciles moments of being and time's passing in Lily's picture (and, by extension, Woolf's novel) becomes a structure for periodization. Of course, the result is satirical. Woolf's biographer-narrator is a parody of historicist fiat, characterizing each age and Orlando's relation to it with absurd licence. Woolf thereby takes a wry view of what Ricoeur and other narrative theorists tend to celebrate: the questionable way the fictive experience of time cycles back into the narrative sense of history, the potential distortions enabled by the power of our fictions to refigure history itself.

A diurnal chronotope structures *The Waves*, but not in the manner of the classic pastoral, for which such natural rhythms could foster a conservative or nostalgic mode of literary cultivation. In *The Waves*, this chronotope provides a fixed but free structure for subjective consciousness, serving as the ideal foil to time's human subjectivity. The structure of *The Waves* is the lighthouse writ large, Woolf's most aesthetically utopian enactment of the reciprocal relationship between human time and narrative form. Form and flux complement each other; natural time correlates to the stages of human life, not to naturalize it in a pastoral mode but rather to reduce the artificiality of narrative. That is, the bare and simple form of a day's natural progress enables Woolf to see life apart from conventional narrative expectations—and to transform narrative itself in the process. This reduction becomes the occasion for a new approach to interior monologue. What could have been impossible—a novel composed entirely of interior monologue, or 'autonomous monologue', to use Dorrit Cohn's term for Woolf's technique in *The Waves*—does take narrative form, through the complementary relationship between purely lyrical acts of consciousness and the kind of objectively natural time Woolf had explored in 'Time Passes'.[26] In other words, Woolf puts narrative fiction on an entirely

---

[25] The queerness of the temporality that results is the subject of Melanie Micir's 'The Queer Timing of *Orlando: A Biography*', *Virginia Woolf Miscellany* 82 (Fall 2012), 11–13.

[26] Dorrit Cohn, *Transparent Minds: Modes for Presenting Consciousness in Fiction* (Princeton University Press, 1978), 263–5. Autonomous monologue occurs in those very rare instances in which interior monologue is not framed by an authorial narrator, and Cohn claims that *The Waves* involves a uniquely 'timeless' version of it (264). Cohn therefore gives Woolf the last word in her study of modes for

new temporal foundation by wholly splitting but then newly reintegrating what she calls 'time in the mind' and 'time on the clock'.

In *Aspects of the Novel*, E.M. Forster argued that the latter must dominate the former—that fiction only works if an objective timeline (or 'life in time') organizes the flux of human existence (the 'life by values').[27] Writers who wish to resist the forward drive of narrative form must make essential sacrifices to it. But in *The Waves*, Woolf manages to have it both ways, at once taking her narrator-characters out of time and actually giving the 'life in time' even greater narrative primacy. Forster may have regretted the need to capitulate to chronology, but Woolf manages to make chronology itself a new form for *human* time. She embraces its artifice by exaggerating its aesthetic potential. Rigidifying chronological measures to the point of aesthetic abstraction, she develops an open form of representation: the 'life in time' gets transformed into a symbolic pattern for the 'life by values', as a kind of neutral design scheme, an open form for registering the flux of human existence.

This combination of aesthetic form and free consciousness, this most fully developed way of reconciling subjective and objective temporalities, shows Woolf reaching an experimental breaking point in the relationship between time and narrative. If Ricoeur is right to suggest that narrative forms give human meaning to time and, inversely, that the result cycles back into new narrative forms, *The Waves* would seem to represent a limit case, a mannerist performance of temporal *poiesis*. It makes sense then that Woolf's next move—her next dialectical turn in the time-narrative reciprocity—would involve a highly practical version of the rarefied aesthetic form she achieves in *The Waves*.

In the early 1930s, Woolf embarked upon what she called an 'essay-novel', a combination of narrative fiction and factual commentary based around the story of an exemplary English family across the decades: 'Its to be an Essay-Novel', she wrote, 'called the Pargiters—& its to take in everything, sex, education, life, &c; & come, with the most powerful & agile leaps, like a chamois across precipices from 1880 to hear & now' (*D*4 129). Very different from *The Waves*, this next project nevertheless had something essential in common with the time-scheme of Woolf's most experimental novel. In both cases, Woolf separated out the temporalities normally integrated by narrative engagement. Just as *The Waves* developed a powerfully complementary polarization of subjective flux and natural time, the essay-novel project tried for a complementarity of life in process (and all the wayward heterogeneity it entails) and the gnomic timelessness of narratorial commentary. Here too Woolf attempted a limit-case arrangement for narrative temporality, albeit an inverse one, and one she could not sustain in finished form. What *The Waves* held together through the *poiesis* available to aesthetic forms fell apart when it became a matter of a more pragmatic arrangement—probably because Woolf was actually attempting to pre-empt reception. The essay portions of the

---

presenting consciousness in fiction, noting that *The Waves* 'could be accommodated in this study only *in extremis*' (265).

[27] E. M. Forster, *Aspects of the Novel* [1927] (New York: Harcourt, 1955), 28.

essay-novel did the work of interpretation, work typically done not just by narrators but also by readers. Woolf's major *Zeitromane* prepare for a fictive experience that implicitly occurs in readerly reception, and though these novels do make that intended effect fairly explicit, they do not themselves perform it. Woolf's essay-novel seems to have verged too far into a next stage of the time-narrative process—the stage of reception—to work as Woolf wished or to have the kind of unity she preferred.

When Woolf chose to separate the essay and novel portions of this essay-novel into two separate texts—*Three Guineas* (1938) and *The Years* (1937), respectively—she recognized that she had taken temporal experimentation beyond the breaking point, subjecting narrative temporality to a range it could not itself run.[28] The fact that these two texts are outliers in Woolf's canon is telling, since the polemics of *Three Guineas* and the relative best-seller conventionality of *The Years* are tendencies that were originally meant to develop together the kind of dialectical complexity typical of Woolf's major works. Woolf herself knew it and struggled with the implications of this inadvertent duality. The 1930s were a particularly bad time for it, given the need, explained so well by Woolf herself in 'The Leaning Tower' and other non-fictional works, to sustain the sort of aesthetic synthesis to which she had always been so strongly committed. This is to say that the question of narrative temporality—in Woolf's terms, how to reconcile 'time in the mind' with 'time on the clock' ('moments of being' with 'time passes') and how to make narrative fiction the proving ground for this dialectic—became by this point in Woolf's career not only a principle question about literary structure but a political question as well, since she had attempted to make the kind of synthesis available to narrative a way also to do art and politics at the same time. Failing at that in the 1930s was for Woolf a problem of historic proportions.

All this is context for the visionary return to history that was *Between the Acts* (1941). If *Orlando* had been a playful approach to the possibility that fictive experience transforms historical time, *Between the Acts* takes that possibility more seriously. If *The Waves* had attempted to make objective time structure 'time in the mind' with an enabling narrative form, *Between the Acts* looks to dramatic performance for a more critical version of this relationship. What had begun for Woolf as an interest in the subjective experience of time developed through dialectical engagements with the alternatives to end in this highly self-conscious enactment of what time and narration do for each other. As Miss La Trobe tries and fails and tries again to produce her vision of English history, history constantly intervenes at other levels, asserting the more idiosyncratic contingencies of unpredictable events. As individual life stories and communal activities do and don't harmonize with the larger performance of history, *Between the Acts* wonders about the representational force of narrative temporality.[29] Sometimes its sequences and other

---

[28] For an account of the contradictions involved see Anna Snaith, '*The Years* and Contradictory Time', in Jessica Berman, ed., *A Companion to Virginia Woolf* (Oxford: Wiley Blackwell, 2016), 137–49.

[29] That the implications might be feminist or another form of ideology critique is a possibility explored in different ways in Karin E. Westman, 'History as Drama: Towards a Feminist Materialist Historiography', in Diane F. Gillespie and Leslie K. Hankins, eds, *Virginia Woolf and the Arts: Selected Papers from the Sixth Annual International Conference on Virginia Woolf* (New York: Pace University

attributions of human meaning to larger events fall absurdly flat; sometimes they come off, even creating the kind of public solidarity that makes cultural history most practically meaningful. When Miss La Trobe's pageant ends finally with its vision of the present moment, reflecting the audience in a fragmentary array of mirrors—'Our selves! Our selves!', 'as we are, here and now'—*Between the Acts* offers a last figure for the kind of temporal intervention Woolf has long pursued in such various ways (*BA* 132, 133). But whereas a theorist of narrative temporality like Paul Ricoeur asserts an optimistic view of the power of the fictive experience of time to address the *aporias* disabling to human temporality, Woolf finally takes a more uncertain view, showing us how our most ambitious narrative representations might mirror back to us something that is finally—even despite Woolf's lifelong explorations of possible alternatives, even in the face of world catastrophe—a matter of tragic subjectivity.

This account of Woolf's career as a writer would be a very questionable biographical progress-narrative if it were not for the justification of phenomenology. This view of Woolf's dialectical progress through versions of narrative temporality takes its cue from the possibility, developed in such powerful and influential terms by Ricoeur, that time and narrative shape each other not only reciprocally, and not only dialectically, but on through history, urging each other toward new refigurations. This dynamic is an apt theoretical framework for the fiction of Virginia Woolf because she seems to have shared Ricoeur's view of it, to the point of putting it into a more active and purposive practice. That is, Woolf seems to have begun each new project with a sense of the temporal possibilities the prior one had created, eager to pursue the next stage in the dialectic, to discover how narrative form ought to respond to the version of time her own prior narrative form had invented. No writer has pursued this project of temporal *poiesis* so actively or so completely. Indeed it may be the most extraordinary achievement of a writer whose many achievements might be understood as functions of this restless dialectic driven by narrative temporality itself.

Selected Bibliography

Auerbach, Erich, *Mimesis: The Representation of Reality in Western Literature*, trans. Willard R. Trask (Princeton University Press, 1946).
Bakhtin, Mikhail, 'Forms of Time and of the Chronotope in the Novel: Notes Toward a Historical Poetics', in Mikhail Bakhtin, *The Dialogic Imagination: Four Essays*, ed. Michael Holquist, trans. Caryl Emerson and Michael Holquist (Austin: University of Texas Press, 1981).
Banfield, Ann, 'Time Passes: Virginia Woolf, Post-Impressionism, and Cambridge Time', *Poetics Today* 24, no. 3 (2003), 471–516.
Barrows, Adam, *The Cosmic Time of Empire: Modern Britain and World Literature* (Berkeley: University of California Press, 2011).

Press, 1977), 335–43; and Jed Esty, *A Shrinking Island: Modernism and National Culture in England* (Princeton University Press, 2003), 85–107.

Bergson, Henri, *Time and Free Will: An Essay on the Immediate Data of Consciousness* [1889], trans. F. L. Pogson (London: George Allen Unwin, Ltd., 1910).
Hagen, Benjamin D., 'Feeling Shadows: Virginia Woolf's Sensuous Pedagogy', *PMLA* 132, no. 2 (March 2017), 266–80.
Hägglund, Martin, *Dying for Time: Proust, Woolf, Nabokov* (Harvard University Press, 2012).
Kern, Stephen, *The Culture of Time and Space 1880-1918* [1983] (Cambridge, MA: Harvard University Press, 2003).
Prudente, Teresa, *A Specially Tender Piece of Eternity: Virginia Woolf and the Experience of Time* (Plymouth: Lexington Books, 2009).
Randall, Bryony Randall, *Modernism, Daily Time, and Everyday Life* (Cambridge University Press, 2007).
Ricoeur, Paul, *Time and Narrative*, vol. 2, trans. Kathleen McLaughlin and David Pellauer (Chicago: University of Chicago Press, 1985).
Sturt, Mary, *The Psychology of Time* [1925] (London: Routledge, 2006).
Tung, Charles, 'Baddest Modernism: The Scales and Lines of Inhuman Time', *Modernism/Modernity* 23, no. 3 (September 2016), 515–38.

CHAPTER 12

....

NARRATIVE ETHICS

....

JANINE UTELL

VIRGINIA *Woolf is a profoundly ethical writer.* Depending on one's position as a reader in the world, this might seem to be an intuitively true statement, a controversial statement, a statement that conjures scenes such as Clarissa Dalloway's party—or that hearkens back to the polemic of *Three Guineas* (1938). Readers might understand Woolfian narrative ethics as drawing upon a Boothian form of judgement, or perhaps a commitment to a more pointedly political stance, one calling for the reimagination of the individual's relationship to the world. One might recall Woolf's reading of G.E. Moore or Aristotle, or Martha Nussbaum's claims for narrative fiction as essential for an understanding of the 'good life'. As Nussbaum writes in *Love's Knowledge*, literature is 'deeper and more central' to us because, in its particularity, 'it speaks *about us*, about our lives and choices and emotions, about our social existence and the totality of our connections'.[1] Woolf's novels would seem to exemplify this point: the human network that comprises the experience of the Pargiters in *The Years* (1937), the mosaic of voices that makes up *The Waves* (1931). A pre-eminent preoccupation of Woolf as a novelist is the exploration of who we are in our relationality, in our sociality, and what the forging and sustaining of connections means for how we are in the world and the choices we make in making a meaningful life with others. Moreover, the ways in which her work evinces multiplicity and ambiguity, and how these shape her characters, their choices and actions, situates her texts in the realm of a specifically modernist ethics, as defined by Melba Cuddy-Keane.[2] Across her career, Woolf's radical innovations in the representation of character and everyday experience have profound implications for ethical thinking and reading.

At the same time, to suggest that Woolf is an ethical writer might seem to suggest that moral lessons are to be had, or that some universal system of values, a systematizing of thought, might be found. As a modernist, as a woman, as a thinker approaching the world from a stance of multiple ambiguities and a rejection of the systematic, Woolf

---

[1] Martha Nussbaum, *Love's Knowledge* (New York: Oxford University Press, 1990), 171.
[2] Melba Cuddy-Keane, 'Ethics', in Stephen Ross, ed., *Modernism and Theory: A Critical Debate* (New York: Routledge, 2009), 208–18.

resists attempts to impose the norms and rules one might associate with ethics and moral philosophy. How can the author of *To the Lighthouse*—'Nothing is just one thing'—give us 'rules' for living? Yet to consider whether Woolf is an ethical writer, to examine Woolf's narrative ethics, is to acknowledge that these forms of judgement, emerging from narrative form, are idiosyncratic and contingent. If Woolf's narrative ethics teaches us anything, it might be that. It depends on the particular relationship and recognition, on a near constant interrogation of what it means to live meaningfully with others. Furthermore, based on this characterization of her narrative practice and the philosophical concerns manifested therefrom, we might say not only that Woolf is a profoundly ethical writer; we might also say that her work is embedded within a particularly feminist ethics. We find in Woolf a dismantling of the 'logic of binary oppositions' that 'is also a logic of subordination and domination' as well as a 'revalu[ing of] such goods as connectedness, emotional responsiveness, and care', which have served as a feminist critique of masculinist arguments for ethics predicated on autonomy and rationality and have been used to make powerful claims for justice and flourishing.[3]

It was not so long ago that Nussbaum held literary critics to account for a lack of attention to ethics and moral philosophy in their work on narrative. In *Love's Knowledge*, Nussbaum argued that literary criticism turned away from ethical theory not only due to a preoccupation with poststructuralism and 'textuality' but also because of a sense that 'ethical writing must *do violence* to the literary work'.[4] An understanding of ethical reading grounded in duty or utility, for Nussbaum, has the potential to do violence because it refuses to recognize the radical openness of the literary text, an openness engendered and met by the perceptive reader's attempts to work through the infinite possibilities of what it means to live a good life suggested by the expression of narrative form and our own embodied experience.[5] Narrative fiction, by providing a site for the judgement of character and the exercise of practical wisdom (or *phronesis*), can offer readers a space to do the experiential work of discerning virtue and right action. For Nussbaum, perception, not rules, is key.

Nussbaum's writing about literature and ethics was on the cusp, however, of what has come to be known as the 'ethical turn' in literary studies, a move described by both David Parker and Liesbeth Korthals Altes. In the years shortly after Nussbaum's words were first published, numerous critics turned toward ethical theory, not to find the kind of universalizing vision for moral conduct advocated by the arguments of Wayne Booth in such writings as *The Company We Keep: An Ethics of Fiction* (which Adam Zachary Newton has characterized as 'the self-adequating ethos of the critic, who ... matches form to content, and content to conduct'[6]), but to theorize reading through the kind

---

[3] Seyla Benhabib, *Situating the Self: Gender, Community, and Postmodernism in Contemporary Ethics* (New York: Routledge, 1992), 15; qtd in David Parker, 'Introduction: The Turn to Ethics in the 1990s', in Jane Adamson, Richard Freadman, and David Parker, eds, *Renegotiating Ethics in Literature, Philosophy, and Theory* (Cambridge: Cambridge University Press, 1998), 1–17, at 3.
[4] Nussbaum, 172. Emphasis added.
[5] Nussbaum, 173–4.
[6] Adam Zachary Newton, *Narrative Ethics* (Cambridge, MA: Harvard University Press, 1995), 9.

of openness suggested by Nussbaum. Reading after the ethical turn is not necessarily preoccupied with answering the question, *what does it mean to live a good life?*, and it is certainly not in the service of suggesting that there is a universal response. Rather, it seeks relationship with the text through an understanding of alterity, and it attends to narrative form as a means of recognizing singularity and difference.

Such work, informed by the philosophy of Emmanuel Levinas, envisions the text making demands on the reader, and the reader as responsible to the text for accepting its embodied phenomenon, its singularity, in all its difference and radical unknowability. To be otherwise, to attempt to fully know, and likewise to attempt to represent, to impose a totalizing universality, is to perform a kind of violence. Derek Attridge, in an argument for Levinasian reading, writes, 'A reading that glides over the work's challenges, or converts otherness to sameness by imposing a common meaning on an uncommon one, or that disregards the context within which the work is being read, is refusing to accept the responsibility being demanded.'[7] Attridge here describes the kind of interpretive violence Nussbaum also calls upon us to resist.[8] For Levinas, as put forth in *Totality and Infinity* and *Time and the Other*, this is precisely the relationship, the obligation, we have to others.[9] We are each confronted by the other, unknowable in their alterity and impossible to fully represent. Nevertheless, essential to human relationship is the recognition of such alterity and the obligation to enter into ethical relationship despite difference. Levinasian ethics rejects universalizing norms, privileging instead the singularity of the other, and claiming alterity as the fundament upon which relationality, and care, must be generated and sustained. As we shall see, this has implications for form—the relationship created between the reader and the text—and substance—the representation of ethical relationality, sociality, intimacy, care.

We might then discern three major areas of narrative ethics: the question of the 'good life', and the ways in which an engagement with narrative fiction informed by fine perception and practical wisdom gives readers the opportunity to work through the question via a praxis-oriented and experiential form of reading; the necessity of recognizing alterity, unknowability, and responsibility, and the demands placed upon us thereby; and finally, a third, emerging from the tensions between the first two. This third way we find to be a suspicion of the ethical project, a resistance to the totalizing impulse of humanism, and a focus on oppression and intersectionality.[10] The first two

---

[7] Derek Attridge, *The Work of Literature* (New York: Oxford University Press, 2015), 121.

[8] For additional takes on Levinasian reading, see Jill Robbins, *Altered Reading: Levinas and Literature* (Chicago: University of Chicago Press, 1999); Andrew Gibson, *Postmodernity, Ethics, and the Novel: From Leavis to Levinas* (New York: Routledge, 1999). Melba Cuddy-Keane's formulation of Woolf's 'dialogic reading' has echoes of 'ethical reading', with its 'both/and' stance and commitment to 'empathy and changing viewpoint': see Melba Cuddy-Keane, *Virginia Woolf, the Intellectual, and the Public Sphere* (New York: Cambridge University Press, 2003), 118.

[9] Emmanuel Levinas, *Time and the Other*, trans. Richard Cohen (Pittsburgh: Duquesne University Press, 1990); Emmanuel Levinas, *Totality and Infinity*, trans. Alphonso Lingis (Pittsburgh: Duquesne University Press, 1969).

[10] Liesbeth Korthals Altes, 'Ethical Turn', in David Herman, Manfred Jahn, and Marie-Laure Ryan, eds, *The Routledge Encyclopedia of Narrative Theory* (New York: Routledge, 2005), 142–6, at 142–3.

in particular have deeply informed readings of Woolf's narratives. After a consideration of these important strands in Woolf scholarship, we will turn our attention to what the third area of narrative ethics means for reading Woolf's fiction.

While the attention to Woolf's form and substance around the questions of *what does it mean to live a good life?* and *how do I meaningfully engage with the other in a relationship of care, responsibility, and recognition?* is essential, and her novels do indeed provide a generative space for working through these questions (as many critics have noted), I will spend the rest of this chapter putting forth a *resistant* reading of Woolf's narrative ethics. Much of Woolf's fiction offers in substance a vision of connection and community, or at least it has been perceived as doing so by many astute readers; her form, as exemplified by the polyvocal symphony of *The Waves* or the reimagining of biography in *Orlando* (1928) or *Flush* (1933), provides a 'model' of 'narrative practices that would allow for representation that is ethical'.[11] Her novels, deeply concerned with the epistemological and ethical nature of subjectivity, call upon us indeed to process our understanding of the subjectivity of others and the significance of choices and actions for meaningful life and relationship. However, in what follows, I will focus on figures of resistance in *Mrs Dalloway* and *The Years* in order to propose that we should read Woolf's narrative ethics more ambivalently, in the tension between connection being the highest good and a desire to 'opt out', in Mari Ruti's phrase.[12] These novels, often taken up for their representations of community, family, and connection, bear within them ethically (if not narratively) significant figures of failed sociality—outsiders—and thereby prompt us to re-envision Woolfian ethics from a position of scepticism. We can move beyond even Jil Larson's conceptualization of a feminist narrative ethics, one that seeks out the idiosyncratic, the particular, the socially situated, the emotional; one that pushes against a normative or universalist approach; one that interrogates whether the 'dismantling of philosophical tradition will lead to positive change for women'.[13] A resistant reading, taking into account Woolf's rejection of normativity, her feminism, and her ambivalence around queer sexuality, might find that the novelist is concerned with attempting to define the 'good life' while also feeling that flourishing is elusive, even impossible, for those on the margins.

Many accounts of Woolf's narrative ethics begin with her 1908 reading of G.E. Moore's *Principia Ethica*, published in 1903. Moore's critique of Aristotle's *Nicomachean Ethics* had a significant influence on the Bloomsbury group, of which Moore was a member by 1910, but it has also had a possibly even greater—possibly overdetermining—effect on our understanding of Bloomsbury's ethics and aesthetics. For instance, the legal

---

[11] Rebecca Nicholson-Weir, ' "There Are Things That Can't Be Said": Levinas and the Ethics of Representation in Virginia Woolf's *Jacob's Room*', in Donald R. Wehrs, ed., *Levinas and Twentieth-Century Literature: Ethics and the Reconstitution of Subjectivity* (Newark: University of Delaware Press, 2013), 49–66, at 50.

[12] Mari Ruti, *The Ethics of Opting Out: Queer Theory's Defiant Subjects* (New York: Columbia University Press, 2017).

[13] Jil Larson, *Ethics and Narrative in the English Novel, 1880–1914* (New York: Cambridge University Press, 2001), 5.

scholar David A.J. Richards has gone so far as to argue that Moore's ethics and the Bloomsbury group's embracing thereof contributed to the resistance to patriarchy and rise of gay rights, which ultimately led to the decline and end of the British empire.[14] It is true that Moore's conceptualization of the beautiful and the good appear in Roger Fry's writings on art and Leonard Woolf's writings on politics, and that the emphasis on personal relationships in the self-conscious construction of a meaningful life we find in the novels of E.M. Forster as well as Virginia Woolf may be traced back to Moore. On the other hand, Madelyn Detloff points out that while the Woolfs owned three copies of the *Nicomachean Ethics*, there is no evidence that Woolf read it, though she would have encountered it via her reading of Moore.[15]

Nevertheless, it might be worth considering the possibility that as often (and as uncritically) as scholars of Bloomsbury return to the *Principia Ethica* as an originary moment in Woolf's ethics, there may be potential to read her novels as critiques of Moore's work emerging from a feminist stance and a deep ambivalence about the capacity of human beings to truly flourish, as well as to sustain flourishing in others. As I will show, a resistant reading of Woolf's narrative ethics suggests something other than an uncritical embrace of Moore's early influence; it suggests instead an ambivalence towards a model predicated on the unmixed good of personal affection that may not be able to account for the marginalized, excluded, or oppressed.

What Moore calls 'the pleasures of human intercourse or of personal affection' is an unmixed good, as is the perception of the beautiful and the pleasure derived from aesthetic experience.[16] In what was seen to be a radical departure from Aristotle's formulation of ethics, Moore claims these are simply inherently good, in and of themselves. They cannot be categorized, and they cannot be analysed through the assignation of properties.[17] (In a famous formulation, Moore writes that the apprehension of personal affection and aesthetic pleasure as 'good' occurs in the way we understand yellow as 'yellow'.) Furthermore, the good is what we desire to desire, and to contemplate the good is of high ethical value. Therefore, if one desires to desire human intercourse and affection, as well as the good for another for whom one feels affection, then 1) that relationship and the ethical obligation to enrich it is of the highest good; and 2) contemplating it as part of desiring to desire is also good.

---

[14] David A. J. Richards, *The Rise of Gay Rights and the Fall of the British Empire* (New York: Cambridge University Press, 2013). For additional accounts, see Michael Holroyd, 'Bloomsbury and the Fabians', in Jane Marcus, ed., *Virginia Woolf and Bloomsbury: A Centenary Celebration* (New York: Macmillan, 1987), 39–51; Ann Banfield, 'Cambridge Bloomsbury', in Victoria Rosner, ed., *The Cambridge Companion to Bloomsbury* (New York: Cambridge University Press), 33–53; Lorraine Sim, *Virginia Woolf: The Patterns of Ordinary Experience* (Burlington, VT: Ashgate, 2010); Christine Reynier, 'Virginia Woolf's Ethics and Victorian Moral Philosophy', *Philosophy and Literature* 38, no. 1 (2014), 128–41; Derek Ryan, 'Following Snakes and Moths: Modernist Ethics and Posthumanism', *Twentieth Century Literature* 61, no. 3 (2015), 287–304.

[15] Madelyn Detloff, *The Value of Virginia Woolf* (New York: Cambridge University Press, 2016), 15.

[16] G. E. Moore, *Principia Ethica* (New York: Cambridge University Press, 1971), 188.

[17] Nicholson-Weir, 51.

Readers of Woolf who have made the ethical turn have discerned numerous instances where Moore's ethics do not hold. While scholars such as Jesse Wolfe have noted, not wrongly, that for Bloomsbury writers and thinkers 'friendship and art are among life's highest goods',[18] in fact, many instances occur throughout Woolf's narratives of characters seeking ethical relationship and performing ethical judgements and actions despite a lack of human affection. In attending to the ways in which members of the Bloomsbury group privilege intimacy, as Wolfe does, one might miss the encounters characterized by failures of friendship and connection, and the ways in which those encounters allow us to read against the ethical grain. In addition to *Mrs Dalloway* and *The Years* (as discussed later), we might also look to: *The Waves*, where instances of failed or incomplete sociality proliferate alongside moments of connection, especially involving Rhoda and Louis ('We differ, it may be too profoundly ... for explanation' (*W* 100)); *To the Lighthouse*, were we to examine not the famous *boeuf en daube* scene but perhaps rather instances with Lily and Charles Tansley, or Mr Ramsay's relationship with his children; and moments where ideas of community are complicated and thwarted in more explicitly political ways in *Between the Acts* (1941).

In her Aristotelian reading of *Mrs Dalloway*, Patricia Curd focuses particularly on character: the importance of emotional states to moral discernment at various stages for each of the characters, and the significance of virtue theory to reading Woolf's characters. (It might be worth pausing for a moment to note that as affect theory has taken an important place in critical conversations about ethics, particularly those evincing more of a resistant strain, we will return to the issue of emotions.) Curd notes that flaws in Woolf's characters are the result of improper or incorrect deployment of particular virtues, and those who do not discern the value of emotion, and seek to facilitate the flourishing of others, are less virtuous.[19] Her case in point is Miss Kilman, 'whose resentment at the goods and virtues of others ... motivates her actions and shapes her attitudes'.[20] For Curd, Woolf is performing a feminist re-envisioning of Aristotle that places the emotional life of fictional characters at the centre of our comprehension of character. Thus, here, the failure of human connection is essential to grappling with the nature of virtue, which depends upon the extent to which we do or do not facilitate the flourishing of others, and correctly perceive our own capacity for flourishing. Miss Kilman does not further the flourishing of others, true, but she also does not recognize in herself the potential for flourishing and self-realization.[21]

A neo-Aristotelian reading of Woolf within the context of modernist fiction, such as that put forth by Lee Oser, shows that while the concept of character as delineated

---

[18] Jesse Wolfe, *Bloomsbury, Modernism, and the Reinvention of Intimacy* (New York: Cambridge, 2011), 31.

[19] Patricia Curd, 'Aristotelian Visions of Moral Character in Virginia Woolf's *Mrs Dalloway*', in Julie K. Ward, ed., *Feminism and Ancient Philosophy* (New York: Routledge, 1996), 141–54, at 144–5.

[20] Curd, 146.

[21] See Eileen Barrett, 'Unmasking Lesbian Passion: The Inverted World of *Mrs Dalloway*', in Eileen Barrett and Patricia Cramer, eds, *Virginia Woolf: Lesbian Readings* (New York: New York University Press, 1997), 146–64.

by Curd is complicated by a modernist rejection both of Aristotelian ethical notions of 'character'—excellence, strength, weakness, badness—and of the notion that a literary character might be a coherent, unified self moving through the world as a rational actor, a theorizing of 'ethical narrativity' is still a worthwhile endeavour.[22] The value comes from the question of the ways in which modernist fiction, with the deployment of the aesthetic, performative self, raises questions about 'the ethics of authenticity'.[23] Oser writes, 'Moore's influence on Woolf, though profound, is not the last word on her ethics. It fits into a larger ethics of authenticity, outlined in "Modern Fiction" with the terms "spirit", "utmost sincerity", "free will", and "saintliness". The ethics of authenticity connects Woolf's literature to her feminist politics and the church of Judith Shakespeare.'[24] The ethics of authenticity requires the individual to pursue the intuition of goodness in the 'common world',[25] while not imposing one's own apprehension of the nature of goodness on others; this attentiveness to subjectivity and perception serves as a form of dissent.

'Authenticity' as found in Oser's examination of the modernist self and the Woolfian subjectivity bears a family resemblance to the openness to alterity at the core of Levinasian ethics. Those who have undertaken Levinasian readings of Woolf's narrative have done compelling work.[26] Both Rebecca Nicholson-Weir and Rachel Hollander have considered *Jacob's Room* (1922) from the perspective of the responsibility of the self to the other and the imperative of the ethical encounter, Hollander in particular illuminating narrative ethics further by framing it within the Derridean concept of hospitality (an important moment in postmodern ethics emerging from Derrida's ongoing conversations with Levinas). For Hollander, Woolf's ethics of the encounter 'cal[l] into question the legitimacy of existing systems of thought'.[27] I see here an echo of Attridge's claim for the 'alterity' of a text: its 'challenge to existing frameworks of knowledge, feeling, and behavior'.[28] Likewise, Jessica Berman sees an accounting of Woolf's ethics drawing on Deleuze's idea of the 'fold', as well as the epistemological knot at the core of Levinasian ethics, as essential for reckoning with 'the incommensurable experiences of separate beings'.[29] Moments of seeming gaps that are transformed into moments of connection—'gaps, interruptions, and moments of narrative incoherence'[30]—for Berman demonstrate that Woolf's 'powerful, nonnormative, feminist ethics can arise

---

[22] Lee Oser, *The Ethics of Modernism* (New York: Cambridge University Press, 2007), 9.
[23] Oser, 91.
[24] Oser, 91
[25] Oser, 86.
[26] See also David Sherman, 'A Plot Unraveling into Ethics: Woolf, Levinas, and "Time Passes"', *Woolf Studies Annual* 13 (2007), 159–79.
[27] Rachel Hollander, *Narrative Hospitality in Late Victorian Fiction: Novel Ethics* (New York: Routledge, 2013), 11.
[28] Attridge, 219.
[29] Jessica Berman, *Modernist Commitments: Ethics, Politics, and Transnational Modernism* (New York: Columbia University Press, 2011), 40.
[30] Berman, 41.

not only from the difficult leap toward the life of a stranger but also from the possibilities and limits of intimacy, eros, and care, which supplement but do not erase the challenge of alterity'.[31] Berman's theorizing of Woolf's ethics is also a critique of Levinasian ethics and its insistence on radical unknowability, which, she points out, renders impossible the intimacy Woolf values. A Woolfian narrative ethics can be informed by the epistemological problems of unknowability and alterity—but there must be a way to imagine a coming together in intimacy across the gap.

The concept of the 'fold' and its application to Woolf's narratives to more fully uncover and enact the author's ethical vision—even in moments of interruption and seemingly disrupted connectedness—moves us closer, in my mind, to a fuller accounting of Woolf's narrative ethics. Bringing together 'the substance of content' and the 'form of content', in Leona Toker's words, enables us to see the gaps, the aesthetic of the interrupted encounter, where Woolf's ethics are manifest. [32] What I intend to do now, though, is read against the grain (somewhat) of those who find those gaps to be fillable moments of connection, rich with the potential for intimacy; what if the folds are unfolded, left hanging, in moments of unfulfilled encounter and refused responsibility? We turn, now, to the third ethical turn, one that demands visibility for bad affect instead of affection, shame instead of sympathy. Where do characters resist the attempts of others—and ourselves—to generate moments of intimacy and shared feeling? If we persist in erasing or evading Woolf's attempts to problematize ethical relationships and the sociality, the intimacy, at the foundation of those relationships, are we performing the kind of unethical reading Attridge cautions against: the 'gliding' over a work's 'challenges', an 'imposition' of 'common meaning'? If connection has become the ethical norm in reading Woolf, what would a non-normative reading of Woolf's narrative ethics and ethical form look like?

Mrs Dalloway: 'For surely a girl has a right to some kind of happiness?' (*MD* 110)

In some ways, *Mrs Dalloway* is the ur-text of Woolf's narrative ethics, the novel that has taught us how to read Woolf ethically. The form of the novel—including the parallel storylines of Clarissa Dalloway and Septimus Smith; the permeable and covert third-person narrative consciousness and the use of free indirect discourse; and the catastrophe/resolution of the death of Septimus and the party held by Clarissa—has led numerous readers to make entirely sound claims for *Mrs Dalloway* as exemplifying

---

[31] Berman, 40.
[32] Leona Toker, *Towards the Ethics of Form in Fiction: Narratives of Cultural Remission*. (Columbus: Ohio State University Press, 2010), 2–3.

ethical engagement with narrative as well as the power of narrative to facilitate ethical thinking and recognition. Mark Hussey has identified 'the desire to combine with others' as the essential feeling driving the novel, while Makiko Minow-Pinkney has argued that the floating narrative consciousness, having 'no single identity or position', disallows the conventional work of a narrator involving 'judging, interpreting, explaining'.[33] At the same time, as we have seen in Curd's reading, the novel does put forth a judgement of characters who *lack* judgement, who fail to discern the proper feelings needed for ethical relationships with others.[34] Yet again, Molly Hite's study of tonal cues and affect in *Mrs Dalloway* shows that Woolf's experimental third-person narrator makes ethical judgement difficult. Tonal cues from the narrator that might facilitate our judgement of a character are seemingly absent, leading to a kind of 'affective indeterminacy'.[35] Crucial for the discussion here is Hite's entirely valid point that without the affective certainty generated by a narrator's clear stance towards a character, discerned through tone, the ethical understanding generated by readers suspended in such a state of indeterminacy must be incomplete. More pointedly, Hite asks, can we really read Clarissa as the model of empathy she becomes on the point of Septimus's death, over the course of the novel's conclusion?[36] Does doing so instrumentalize Septimus within the narrative in an unethical way?

Lorraine Sim in her reading of 'the ethics of the ordinary' finds 'the ordinary'—ordinary moments, events, and encounters that form the narrative fabric of *Mrs Dalloway*—to be the locus for 'ethical significance in Woolf's writing ... it *invariably* serves as the basis for moments of sympathy, intimacy, and understanding between people ... To recognize or *create*—even *imaginatively*—a common ground through an awareness of our mutual share in the ordinary, while not denying or simplifying difference, is the space within which an ethics of care for, and intimacy with, the other arises.'[37] Sim thus reads Clarissa Dalloway's 'reverence for the everyday' as 'connected to her ethics'.[38] In Sim's claim for our ability to imagine shared experience, and thus shared feeling, we might recall Attridge's formulation of ethical reading from earlier: in ethical reading, we invent ways of being with the other that embrace the encounter with difference and the obligation therein. Woolf's narratives, in readings such as Sim's, privilege those moments of inventiveness among characters, which then serve as models for our own inventiveness in encountering the alterity of the text. Yet, we might push back on the claim being made by using the word 'invariably'. Do the kinds of cues we do or do

---

[33] See Mark Hussey, *The Singing of the Real World: The Philosophy of Virginia Woolf's Fiction* (Columbus: Ohio State University Press, 1986), 49; Makiko Minow-Pinkney, *Virginia Woolf and the Problem of the Subject* (New Brunswick, NJ: Rutgers University Press, 1987), 58.

[34] Oser, 88; see also Molly Hite, 'Tonal Cues and Uncertain Values: Affect and Ethics in *Mrs Dalloway*', *Narrative* 18, no. 3 (2010), 249–75, at 255–9.

[35] Hite, 249.

[36] Hite, 252–4.

[37] Sim, 177. Emphasis added.

[38] Sim, 192.

not receive, as in Hite's thinking, really lead to us *invariably* seeing Woolf's characters clearly in ethical terms?

In Woolf's novels, we do in fact find moments of what Sara Ahmed calls 'bad feeling', negativity generated by the figures she terms 'affect aliens', and connections are formed among people not through care or intimacy but the 'stickiness' of resistance, rejection, isolation, and inhospitality.[39] Attridge is useful to recall here again: to fully engage with a work's alterity, we must recognize the challenge it presents to existing frameworks of thought. Reading against the grain of Woolf's narrative ethics demands we enter into that challenge—the challenge here to the existing frameworks of thought readers have created through an insistence on *invariably*. Ahmed reads Clarissa Dalloway as a figure of sadness and suffering, one who was promised a social norm (marriage, children) as the highest good, and who finds instead that the possibility for flourishing has been foreclosed.[40] This is in marked contrast to Jesse Wolfe's reading of Woolf and intimacy, wherein he sees Clarissa's choice to marry as ultimately contributing to her flourishing.[41] It is thus their shared suffering that creates the 'odd intimacy' with Septimus,[42] as bad feelings, negative feelings, circulate throughout the book. In Ahmed's reading of the novel, negative feelings become a form of resistance to normative conceptualizations of flourishing and community. Furthermore, this is an explicitly feminist resistance, one that accounts for Woolf's ambivalence regarding forms of sociality as pure good.

We might turn again to Miss Kilman, clad in her mackintosh. Miss Kilman exemplifies what Ahmed has described as the ways in which some bodies encounter resistance in the world; they are not 'housed' as hospitably as others.[43] Even that mackintosh, which Celia Marshik has noted gestures towards Miss Kilman's 'abject body', rather than providing protection for that body from the elements, is an object around which negative feeling circulates.[44] As Miss Kilman emerges from Elizabeth Dalloway's bedroom—a space of queer intimacy that is in fact disavowed by Clarissa, and, through her perspective, elided from the novel, thereby remaining unknown and invisible—her mackintosh is rendered into a signifier for her unwantedness, for the failure of sociality: 'Miss Kilman in her mackintosh listening to whatever they said.... Yes, Miss Kilman stood on the landing, and wore a mackintosh' (*MD* 110). The mackintosh is made affective, 'sticky' with bad feeling.[45] That 'yes' is the portal through which we access Miss Kilman's consciousness, and through which her bad feelings are made visible. She has her reasons for wearing the mackintosh—age, poverty—but as we shall see, Clarissa's affective response to the coat alters our relationship to both women. The repetition of 'in a mackintosh'

---

[39] Sara Ahmed, *The Promise of Happiness* (Durham, NC: Duke University Press, 2010), 43, 49.
[40] Ahmed, 71.
[41] Jesse Wolfe, *Bloomsbury, Modernism, and the Reinvention of Intimacy* (New York: Cambridge, 2011), 163.
[42] Ahmed, 72.
[43] Ahmed, 12.
[44] Celia Marshik, *At the Mercy of Their Clothes: Modernism, the Middlebrow, and British Garment Culture* (New York: Columbia University Press, 2017), 97.
[45] Ahmed, 44.

has constellated around it a spectrum of negative affect: 'She had been cheated' (*MD* 110). The thought 'she had been cheated' elicits an expression of the feeling of what Miss Kilman believes herself entitled to: 'She considered she had a perfect right to anything that the Dalloways did for her. She had been cheated. Yes, the word was no exaggeration, for surely a girl has a right to some kind of happiness?' (*MD* 110). What follows in the scenes of the novel devoted to Miss Kilman's outing with Elizabeth, to the shop and to tea, reveals that according to the novel, Miss Kilman in fact does *not* have the right to happiness, to flourishing. If we follow Ahmed's line of thinking, that happiness is a social norm disguised as a social good, then what Miss Kilman imagines herself entitled to is a kind of normativity of which the novel insists on depriving her.

Yet her own feeling of desiring happiness, and imagining she has a right to flourishing, is ambivalent. She rejects the impulse to normativity, insisting on her outsiderness, even as she asserts her 'right'. She is characterized by an ambivalence to others, and to herself, a lack of awareness of her own feelings that renders human connection impossible. She thinks, 'Now she did not envy women like Clarissa Dalloway; she pitied them,' and just a sentence later, 'She pitied and despised them' (*MD* 111). Moments later the narrator reports, 'But Miss Kilman did not hate Mrs Dalloway' (*MD* 112). Further on, recalling the perception that Clarissa sees her as ugly, she thinks, 'But why wish to resemble her? Why? She despised Mrs Dalloway from the bottom of her heart' (*MD* 115). In her thinking, Miss Kilman rejects the (hetero)normative impulse to resemble Clarissa, to value what she values. Both pity and hatred make the kind of empathic and ethical relationship the novel would seem to value impossible. I would argue that here, and further on, Miss Kilman is electing to opt out of the potential for social, and therefore ethical, relationship.

The mackintosh is an object that reveals how bad feeling is 'contagious'; its presence on Miss Kilman alters Clarissa's affect, which is unambiguously negative.[46] The narrator reports:

> For now the body of Miss Kilman was not before her, it overwhelmed her—the idea. The cruellest things in the world, she thought, seeing them clumsy, hot, domineering, hypocritical, eavesdropping, jealous, infinitely cruel and unscrupulous, dressed in a mackintosh coat, on the landing. (*MD* 113)

This response of Clarissa's, wherein the mackintosh becomes all of the negativity associated with Miss Kilman, puts the lie to at least some critics' assertions that she holds a reverence for ordinary moments of connection and the seeking out of union. Clarissa's rejection of connection with Miss Kilman is indeed engendered by the woman's queer body, which Clarissa can barely account for in its embodied reality; the very 'idea' is 'overwhelming'. In 'clumsy' and 'hot', we hear resonances with Marshik's reading of Miss Kilman's body as abject, and we might even discern Clarissa's referring to it as a 'thing',

---

[46] Ahmed, 20.

among the 'cruellest things'. Her vision of Miss Kilman as nonhuman precludes any ethical relationship at all.

Once Elizabeth and Miss Kilman sit down to tea, the affective dynamic shifts. Elizabeth in her own way resists connection with Miss Kilman, even as she is drawn to a relationship with her. She regards Miss Kilman, and the narrator reports, 'Elizabeth rather wondered ... what Miss Kilman was thinking.... Elizabeth rather wondered whether Miss Kilman could be hungry' (*MD* 116). It is the use of 'rather' I would like to attend to; the qualifier on Elizabeth's wondering marks a distinct lack of curiosity. As the scene in the teashop progresses, we see that the narrator only reports Elizabeth's words and thoughts indirectly, and, relative to Miss Kilman's words and thoughts, Elizabeth's are few: 'But perhaps it was a little flat somehow, Elizabeth felt'; 'Elizabeth supposed she was going; her mother wanted her to go'; 'She did not much like parties, Elizabeth said' (*MD* 118). That final instance is noteworthy in the absence of quotation marks, denoting indirect speech. Rarely do we have direct access to Elizabeth's thoughts and words, and only in the most superficial sense. In this way, it seems, she is withholding connection from Miss Kilman, even from the reader. She is affectless, hiding her own emotional responses and desires from Miss Kilman's need.

Miss Kilman's need, her desire, her affect, cluster around different objects in the teashop: that is, cakes and pastries. As Miss Kilman and Elizabeth sit down, Elizabeth notices Miss Kilman minding a child taking a pink cake, and then, midway through the paragraph reporting the scene, the consciousness shifts from Elizabeth's 'rather wondering' to Miss Kilman's really 'minding': 'She had wanted that cake—the pink one. The pleasure of eating was almost the only pure pleasure left her, and then to be baffled even in that!' (*MD* 116). From that moment, she informs Elizabeth that she has no reserves of happiness on which to draw, and is 'jolted by every pebble' (*MD* 116). The desire to possess, the desire for pleasure, and the thwarting of those desires, reveals to Miss Kilman her own lack of happiness; she attempts to share this lack with Elizabeth, using her own lack of *eudemonia* to create connection, yet even that too is thwarted (Elizabeth thinks later that 'it was always talking about her own sufferings that made Miss Kilman so *difficult*'(*MD* 122; emphasis added)). Shortly thereafter, her desire to possess manifests in connection with a chocolate éclair, which she eats with such hedonistic gusto she winds up getting pastry on her fingers once she has 'swallowed [it] down' (*MD* 118). After finishing the pastry she thinks, 'She was about to split asunder, she felt. The agony was so terrific. If she could grasp her, if she could clasp her, if she could make her hers absolutely and for ever and then die; that was all she wanted' (*MD* 118). The eroticization of the encounter—splitting, grasping, clasping, dying—makes manifest Miss Kilman's queer desire, her need to possess, in language that might strike one as ethically problematic were it to be read in purely Levinasian terms. However, a resistant reading of this scene might suggest that the failure of others to engage with Miss Kilman, the ethical failure on the part of the characters of Clarissa and then her daughter to recognize Miss Kilman, results in the imperative to make Miss Kilman's affective position visible. Her shame, her negative experience of her own queerness, are rendered visible in order for us to truly begin to account for it.

The episode with Miss Kilman ends as she decides to go to Westminster Abbey after Elizabeth has left her in the teashop. She is described as blundering, lurching doggedly, 'very red in the face' (*MD* 119). The world is inhospitable to her body in this moment, and she seeks to 'rid herself both of hatred and of love', to be 'not a woman, a soul' (*MD* 120). In the final moments of the scene, she desires to reject all affect, which to her mind is part of being a woman. She attempts to opt out of feeling, and to opt out of what it means to be a gendered being in the world, to have a gendered sociality. Her queer desire for Elizabeth, and what she perceives as the world's failure to truly recognize her in its insistence she be more like Clarissa, make her own non-normativity, and the negative feelings that engenders, visible to her; thus, she rejects all relations that refuse her happiness, that call forth her 'difficulty'. The narrative does not necessarily endorse this act, but it does suggest that a meaningful ethical judgement is at work in resisting the failure of meaningful human interaction.

THE YEARS: 'THAT THRILL SHE KNEW MEANT BITTERNESS' (*Y* 295)

Readers of *The Years* have emphasized its status as Woolf's most realist novel, as well as her most political. Katherine Saunders Nash, in her reading of the text's feminist narrative ethics, points out that despite the political concerns of the novel, attention to its ethics has not followed. Nash reads *The Years* as intervening in specific 'ethical questions about power and control' distinct from Woolf's earlier novels, which, as Hite has noted, engage with the indeterminacy of ethical positions more broadly.[47] Reading the holograph novel-essay *The Pargiters* (1977), the early draft of *The Years*, and building on Melba Cuddy-Keane's reading of dialogic technique as integral to Woolf's rejection of didacticism around political and ethical issues, Nash arrives at an argument for the narrative ethics in the published novel as grounded in non-coercive rhetorical strategies.[48] Woolf's narratives deliberately and artfully reject the impulse to coerce; in Nash's formulation of tacit persuasion, non-coercive rhetorical strategies in *The Years* are deployed by an implied author to lead the reader to participate in a feminist argument against power.

However, a consideration of outsiders in *The Years* might reveal that the novel also interrogates subtle forms of social coercion as unethical, calling upon readers to take up the position of outsider even as they participate in a realist mode that, on the surface, seems to endorse normative forms of sociality. The ways in which coercion, and the rejection thereof as an ethical act, is made manifest in the storyworld of *The Years* might

---

[47] Hite, 91.
[48] Katherine Saunders Nash, *Feminist Narrative Ethics: Tacit Persuasion in Modernist Form* (Columbus: Ohio State University Press, 2014), 93.

be examined productively in a character who insists on outsiderness: Eleanor Pargiter's niece Peggy, an unmarried doctor in her thirties in the last section of the novel, 'Present Day'. The events of 'Present Day' are leading up to a party being given by Delia Pargiter, a party that fits uncomfortably within the universe of such social events in Woolf (the party at the conclusion of *Mrs Dalloway*, the *boeuf en daube* scene in *To The Lighthouse*). Delia's party is characterized by interrupted connections, enforced sociability, the imperative to enjoy oneself. One might even read Nicholas's ineffectual speech as a failure (as Clare Hanson does, indicative of his taboo sexuality[49]), and Eleanor's falling asleep as a version of opting out. Woolf deploys these incomplete or failed scenes of sociability—Miss Kilman's tea with Elizabeth Dalloway, Delia's party, even the occasionally prickly gatherings in *The Waves*, to offer another example—in order to resist our insistence on (if not our experience of) sociality as a site of normative ethics.

As Peggy and Eleanor are preparing to go to the party, finishing dinner together, Peggy thinks of Sara and her relationship with Nicholas:

> What a fool, she thought bitterly, and a thrill ran down her thigh. Why was she bitter? For she prided herself on being honest—she was a doctor—and that thrill she knew meant bitterness. Did she envy her because she was happy, or was it the croak of some ancestral prudery—did she disapprove of these friendships with men who did not love women? (*Y* 295).

Peggy's 'bitterness', her affective response to thinking of the relationship between Sara and Nicholas, is embodied, almost sexualized; she might be read here as deriving pleasure from regarding human connection with negative feeling. In critical responses to *The Years*, Sara is often read as an outsider, along with Nicholas and often via their unusual relationship. Madelyn Detloff, for instance, in her consideration of Woolf's 'queer outsiders', not only regards the pair as disrupting heteronormative cultural imperatives but also attempts to render queer bodies 'culturally intelligible'.[50] Here, Peggy at once rejects the positive feeling that comes with encountering intimacy in others and situates herself as an outsider opting out of intimate relationships. If the novel valorizes the kind of queer outsiderness evinced by Sara and Nicholas, Peggy refuses to play along.

Furthermore, Peggy establishes her own outsiderness by holding up her status as a professional woman, a doctor. Such a social position would have been unusual in 1930s England, and, interestingly, while doctors are figures central to the social tapestry of the realist mode (think Lydgate in George Eliot's *Middlemarch*, for example), Peggy's position as a doctor in Woolf's one realist novel marks her as a woman outside the norm, something she embraces and deploys to unfold connection with others. As she and

---

[49] Clare Hanson, 'Virginia Woolf in the House of Love: Compulsory Heterosexuality in *The Years*', *Journal of Gender Studies* 6, no. 1 (1997), 55–62, at 58.

[50] Madelyn Detloff, 'Woolf and Lesbian Culture: Queering Woolf Queering', in Bryony Randall and Jane Goldman, eds, *Virginia Woolf in Context* (New York: Cambridge University Press, 2012), 342–52, at 351.

Eleanor arrive at the party, her identity as 'affect alien', to return to Sara Ahmed's term, is made clear: 'She went in; but she felt plated, coated over with some cold skin' (*Y* 316). Again, her refusal to be open to encounter is manifested in bodily terms, much like Miss Kilman's red face. She observes the performance of human intimacy with a kind of cynicism: 'Making believe, Peggy thought to herself as she shook hands with Delia and passed on, that something pleasant is about to happen' (*Y* 316). The appositive gestures towards the social performance expected of her, but Peggy's internal thought reporting exposes social performance for what it is: an imperative to participate in normative social encounters.

For Peggy, to opt out of encounter is to resist the falsity of intimacy. She regards intimacy as a form of coercion, and refuses responsibility to the other. Every time she seeks to find herself alone, she is trapped in conversation; she participates perfunctorily, as all the while the narrator reports her racing thoughts to the reader. In this way, Peggy as a character is able to form a kind of intimacy with the reader that serves as a critique of enforced sociality. As she looks out the window at the stars—'She felt nothing'—she is interrupted once again by a young man ('Was his name Leacock or Laycock?') (*Y* 325). Peggy's moments with others are characterized by half-listening and wandering attention, and here the young man himself is interrupted by the reporting of her thoughts: 'She had heard it all before. I, I, I—he went on. It was like a vulture's beak pecking, or a vacuum-cleaner sucking, or a telephone bell ringing.... He had to expose, had to exhibit. But why let him? she thought, as he went on talking. For what do I care about his "I, I, I"?' (*Y* 326). Peggy recognizes the otherness of the young man, and yet she persists in rejecting responsibility to him; she holds him out at a distance in his difference. The 'aridity' of the 'I', as Woolf writes in *A Room of One's Own*, makes the self—the ego, if you like—an 'obstacle' and 'impediment' to fulfilling the obligations of relationality (*ARO* 76). The assertion of the 'I' forecloses the possibility of connection in its insistence on its 'dominance' (*ARO* 76). Peggy here denies the young man his insistence not only on her attention but on her attending to his alterity because she cannot bear his assertion of self.

For Peggy to act thusly is to violate a gender norm as well as a normative ethics of difference, a move we see throughout Woolf's work, as in, for instance, Lily Briscoe as she grapples with a (perhaps misplaced) sense of obligation to male characters like Charles Tansley and Mr Ramsay. The climactic moment of Peggy's refusal is her outburst at her cousin North, who has just returned from Africa. The moment occurs shortly after Eleanor has insisted to Peggy that she is enjoying herself. Not that she *should* enjoy herself, but that she *is*: 'But we're enjoying ourselves.... Come and enjoy yourself too' (*Y* 346). To have one's affect dictated to one, especially in the realm of enjoyment is, it seems, a form of tyranny, what Slavoj Žižek has defined as a form of aggression. Sara Ahmed has designated women who identify and resist this form of aggression as 'feminist killjoys', a helpful and sort of glorious turn of phrase that allows us to read Peggy's ethical moves in this moment and throughout as feminist. Peggy resists internally the imposition of affect by thinking about the suffering of others: 'But how can one be "happy"?' (*Y* 350). Once again, we see an 'affect alien', one of Woolf's characters interrogating the ethical implications of norms of sociality. Peggy's internal response to her aunt's imperative serves as an answer to those who might read uncritically Woolf's endorsement of 'authenticity', to return to Oser's term. Happiness as an unquestioned good is up for critique in scenes where one is supposed to be experiencing pleasure; in fact, it is the imperative to enjoy oneself in the company of others that leads precisely to these moments of critique.

Peggy's moment here leads to her feeling called upon to resist what she sees as the scriptedness of her cousin North's life: 'A feeling of animosity possessed her.... "What's the use?" she said, facing him. "You'll marry. You'll have children. What'll you do then? Make money. Write little books to make money...." She had got it wrong. She had meant to say something impersonal, but she was being personal' (*Y* 352). First, we see the culmination of Peggy's negative affect—'a feeling of animosity possessed her'—and it sets her at odds with the rest of the Pargiters, who have taken North's return (from his work as an instrument of conquest, colonial imperialism, and oppression in Africa) as a cause for celebration. Next, Peggy enacts a moment of recognition: she faces him. In Levinasian terms, the encounter with 'the face' is the paramount instance of recognition, the moment where one recognizes the alterity of the other and is called upon to recognize the ethical obligation to be responsible that is inherent in human relationships. Here, Woolf subverts that call to responsibility. Peggy faces North, but it is to reject him and his complicity in socio-political norms. Finally, Peggy is forced to acknowledge that her move must be personal. Her resistance and refusal have implications for personal relationships, for intimacy; such resistance and refusal can never be entirely impersonal.

North and Peggy come together briefly after this outburst: 'The touch of his flesh, bringing back to her the nearness of human beings and their distance.... But I mustn't make a fool of myself again' (*Y* 358). The third-person omniscient heterodiegetic narrator shares with us Peggy's insight into the intractable problem of intimacy, the failure of the 'fold'. Yet Peggy's consciousness then takes over, asserting resistance: 'I mustn't make a fool of myself again.' Earlier, she thinks of Sara as a fool for her intimacy with Nicholas; to seek and attempt to sustain connection is 'foolish'. As the party draws to a close, Peggy is nowhere to be found. The 'affect alien' has been quietly removed from the scene, and all that remain are the fools who greet the dawn. The novel does not entirely endorse Peggy's judgement, but neither does it silence her moments of resistance.

Virginia Woolf may be a profoundly ethical novelist, but to read Woolf's narrative ethics as monolithic would be to read Woolf's work unethically. We are required to be open to characters who put forth a form of feminist resistance to normativity, even as a kind of ambivalence is evinced towards non-normative characters. Their positions may be narratively tenuous, their bad feelings requiring their time in the world of the story to be brief. Nevertheless, they offer essential critiques of the ethical demands of sociality and the problem of intimacy.

Selected Bibliography

Altes, Liesbeth Korthals, 'Ethical Turn', in David Herman, Manfred Jahn, and Marie-Laure Ryan, eds, *The Routledge Encyclopedia of Narrative Theory*, (New York: Routledge, 2005), 142–6.

Banfield, Ann, 'Cambridge Bloomsbury', in Victoria Rosner, ed., *The Cambridge Companion to Bloomsbury* (New York: Cambridge University Press, 2014), 33–53.

Cuddy-Keane, Melba, 'Ethics', in Stephen Ross, ed., *Modernism and Theory: A Critical Debate* (New York: Routledge, 2009), 208–18.

Curd, Patricia, 'Aristotelian Visions of Moral Character in Virginia Woolf's *Mrs Dalloway*', in Julie K. Ward, ed., *Feminism and Ancient Philosophy* (New York: Routledge, 1996), 141–54.

Detloff, Madelyn, *The Value of Virginia Woolf* (New York: Cambridge University Press, 2016).

Gibson, Andrew, *Postmodernity, Ethics, and the Novel: From Leavis to Levinas* (New York: Routledge, 1999).

Hite, Molly, 'Tonal Cues and Uncertain Values: Affect and Ethics in *Mrs Dalloway*', *Narrative* 18, no. 3 (2010), 249–75.

Larson, Jil, *Ethics and Narrative in the English Novel, 1880–1914* (New York: Cambridge University Press), 2001.

Nicholson-Weir, Rebecca, '"There Are Things That Can't Be Said": Levinas and the Ethics of Representation in Virginia Woolf's *Jacob's Room*', in Donald R. Wehrs, ed., *Levinas and Twentieth-Century Literature: Ethics and the Reconstitution of Subjectivity* (Newark: University of Delaware Press, 2013), 49–66.

Oser, Lee, *The Ethics of Modernism* (New York: Cambridge University Press, 2007).

Robbins, Jill, *Altered Reading: Levinas and Literature* (Chicago: University of Chicago Press, 1999).

Ryan, Derek, 'Following Snakes and Moths: Modernist Ethics and Posthumanism', *Twentieth Century Literature* 61, no. 3 (2015), 287–304.

Sherman, David, 'A Plot Unraveling into Ethics: Woolf, Levinas, and "Time Passes"', *Woolf Studies Annual* 13 (2007), 159–79.

Sim, Lorraine, *Virginia Woolf: The Patterns of Ordinary Experience* (Burlington, VT: Ashgate, 2010).

Wolfe, Jesse, *Bloomsbury, Modernism, and the Reinvention of Intimacy* (New York: Cambridge, 2011).

CHAPTER 13

ALLUSION AND METAPHOR

JANE DE GAY

Virginia Woolf, in *Night and Day* (1919), provides a witty insight to her own allusive process in a comic sketch of the attempts of Mrs Hilbery, lover of literature and would-be biographer, to make progress with her book:

> She was haunted by the ghosts of phrases. She gave herself up to a sensual delight in the combinations of words. She sought them in the pages of her favourite authors. She made them for herself on scraps of paper, and rolled them on her tongue when there seemed no occasion for such eloquence. (*ND* 321)

In four sentences that subtly elide reading and writing, Woolf demonstrates the intrinsic connection between the two, suggesting that, in order to be a writer, you need first to be a reader. In the first sentence, Mrs Hilbery hears echoes of past writings coming as though from without: a feeling of being 'haunted' by other writers' words. In the second, she responds viscerally as she experiences 'sensual delight': it is indeterminate whether the combinations are her own or those of other writers. In the third, she turns to literary works for inspiration, seeking both direct quotations and the 'ghosts of phrases' or literary echoes within them. Finally, using nothing more refined than 'scraps of paper' she tries out her own phrases, albeit ones that are too elaborate for their purpose, and experiences them physically by rolling them on her tongue.

The passage is also an example of how Woolf uses metaphor to examine the nature of text and of intertextual relationships. Metaphor is a figure of speech by which something is described in terms more appropriate to something else, resulting in properties being transferred between the two. Metaphor, now seen as an essential component of language (not just the decorative feature that Aristotle had suggested), draws attention to the fundamental inadequacy of language. Woolf addresses this problem, which exercised many modernist writers, by giving words presence and substance. Past literature is given a spectral presence in 'ghosts of phrases', while the expression 'rolled them on her tongue' both reminds us of the physiological processes involved in the speech act and lends words physical substance. As this chapter will show, Woolf's allusions are often supported by metaphors that draw attention to the longevity of past literature that is essential to the act of allusion.

Woolf's allusive practices were shaped by her habits as an attentive and empathetic reader with extensive knowledge of literary, cultural, classical, philosophical, and biblical texts. Woolf spent her formative years reading in her father's library (which she subsequently inherited); she read at the British Museum and London Library; she studied with Janet Case and Clara Pater, and at King's College London;[1] but most importantly, as her reading notes and diaries attest, she conducted a lifelong practice of systematic reading in tandem with writing fiction and non-fiction.[2] Therefore, as my research into Woolf's novels and the literary past has shown, her reading and writing practices were closely interfused: she read for intellectual stimulation, to release her creativity, and to make sense of the world and its problems.[3] To give two examples: she began drafting her first novel, *The Voyage Out* (1915), after a six-year period of extensive reading, and her composition of *The Waves* (1931) went alongside an intensive reading of the Romantic poets and Dante: a year after her first vision for *The Waves*, she described the experience as being 'visited by the "spirit of delight"', a phrase from Shelley that she recalls 'singing this time last year ... so poignantly that I have not forgotten it' (*D3* 153). Shelley is seen as a companion in her creativity, and she uses his words to express her own emotions.

As a result of this intimate engagement with literature, Woolf's allusions are both transformative and dialogic. Her essay 'How Should One Read a Book?' (1932), throws light on this. She notes that reading should firstly be attentive, immersive, and empathetic: she urges us to 'banish all ... preconceptions when we read', not to 'dictate' to an author but to become a 'fellow-worker and accomplice' (*E5* 573). However, she notes that we should then review our 'multitudinous impressions' of a book, for 'we must make of these fleeting shapes one that is hard and lasting' (*E5* 579). The 'transition' between the two stages is enabled by 'Nature', not by our own volition: an organic metaphor to which we will return shortly. Through this process, a book becomes part of us, for we review both it and our impressions of it. In the process, books can be transformed through misremembering and misquotation, as words are re-contextualized and adapted to serve new purposes. However, Woolf's transformative use of allusion goes alongside dialogism in the Bahktinian sense of 'turning persuasive discourse into speaking persons', as a way of 'experimentally objectifying another's discourse'.[4] Woolf often envisaged an authorial presence (even to the extent of representing an author as a character, as we will see) in order to create a foil for argument and debate.

---

[1] Hermione Lee, *Virginia Woolf* (London: Chatto and Windus, 1996), 143–4; Christine Kenyon Jones and Anna Snaith, '"Tilting at Universities": Virginia Woolf at King's College London', *Woolf Studies Annual* 16 (2010), 1–44.

[2] Brenda R. Silver, ed., *Virginia Woolf's Reading Notebooks* (Princeton, NJ: Princeton University Press, 1983).

[3] Jane de Gay, *Virginia Woolf's Novels and the Literary Past* (Edinburgh: Edinburgh University Press, 2006), 212.

[4] Mikhail Bakhtin, *The Dialogic Imagination: Four Essays*, ed. Michael Holquist, trans. Caryl Emerson and Michael Holquist (Austin: University of Texas Press, 1994), 348.

The dialogic approach was necessary because Woolf's relationship to literature and its traditions was vexed as well as inspired. As she noted in *A Room of One's Own* (1929), 'It is useless to go to the great men writers for help, however much one may go to them for pleasure' (*ARO* 57). Woolf was exercised by the difficulties female writers faced both in finding conducive reading material and in gaining acceptance for their work when canonical writers were predominantly male. This makes Woolf's allusiveness distinctly feminist: not only because she drew on past women writers, but because she explored what it meant to read male writers as a woman. Unlike Mrs Hilbery, who is inhibited by her father, a famous poet, and lives in his shadow and those of her illustrious ancestors, Woolf embraces male alongside female antecedents to engage with the literary past holistically: the problematic 'pleasure' that Woolf took in reading past male writers was an important dynamic within her work. However, as we will see, Woolf also thought beyond the figure of the author: she had a love of simple, anonymous verses, inculcated from childhood onwards by 'English voices murmuring nursery rhymes' (*TG* 185), and she often imagined literature to originate from the land itself rather than from individual writers. As she wrote in her essay 'Reading' (1919): 'Instead of being a book it seemed that what I read was laid upon the landscape not printed, bound, or sewn up, but somehow the product of trees and fields and the hot summer sky' (*E3* 142).

Although literary allusion has often been recognized as a characteristic of modernism, Woolf's allusiveness should not be seen as a response to the male modernists but as a parallel development that took its own distinct course. Modernist allusion is often regarded as a device for preserving links with the past while pioneering new forms of literature. David Lodge, for example, has suggested that allusions were used to provide structure to counterbalance experimental approaches to form and narrative:[5] James Joyce's appropriation of the *Odyssey* for *Ulysses* and T.S. Eliot's adoption of mythological structures for *The Waste Land* are particularly prominent examples of this. Woolf's use of allusion is less structured than those of Eliot or Joyce for, apart from her use of lines from *Cymbeline* as a refrain in *Mrs Dalloway* (1925), she tends to hint at rather than telegraph her sources. As a result, Woolf's allusions offer the reader 'secret founts of pleasure', as Anne Fernald has shown.[6]

Allusions were also used by modernist writers to gain credibility for new writing by invoking a pedigree: for example, Eliot's footnotes to *The Waste Land* seek to tie it to a body of literature through identifying quotations, a counterpoint to his argument in 'Tradition and the Individual Talent' that 'not only the best, but the most individual parts' of a modern poet's work 'may be those in which the dead poets, his ancestors, assert their immortality most vigorously', because '[n]o poet, no artist of any art, has his complete meaning alone.... You cannot value him alone; you must set him, for contrast and comparison, among the dead.'[7] Woolf was sceptical of this view. Unlike Eliot

---

[5] David Lodge, *The Modes of Modern Writing: Metaphor, Metonymy, and the Typology of Modern Literature* (London: Bloomsbury, 1977), 46.

[6] Anne E. Fernald, 'Woolf and Intertextuality', in Bryony Randall and Jane Goldman, eds, *Woolf in Context* (Cambridge: Cambridge University Press, 2012), 52–64, at 55.

[7] T. S. Eliot, *Selected Essays* (London: Faber, 1932), 14, 15.

and Joyce, who approached literature from the perspective of university-educated men, Woolf asserted her intellectual independence by refusing to 'admit authorities, however heavily furred and gowned, into our libraries and let them tell us how to read, what to read, what value to place upon what we read' (*E5* 573). Allusions for Woolf were not about invoking the authority of earlier texts or of their scholarly interpretations, but about transforming and interrogating texts.

Woolf therefore differed from Eliot's view that tradition 'cannot be inherited, and if you want it you must obtain it by great labour' and 'sweat for it'.[8] As an Englishwoman, Woolf regarded its literature as a birth right, an inheritance from her father (*L3* 344), and an organic product of the land, in contrast to Eliot and Joyce, who as an American and Irishman saw English literature as something that needed to be attained with effort. Woolf's approach was therefore distinctly different from Eliot's emphasis on conformity and the 'extinction of personality' when studying literature.[9] Eliot used an architectural metaphor to describe the literary tradition as a collection of 'existing monuments' whose appearance could be changed by the construction of a new edifice among them; by contrast, Woolf adopted more organic metaphors including the natural growth of seeds, plants, and flowers; familial metaphors of conception, birth, and reproduction, and the more ethereal metaphor of haunting.[10] All these emphasize a process whereby the literary past continues into the present but constantly takes on new forms. Literary history was evolving, not fixed, for Woolf; the literary canon was not a site of authority; indeed, as we will see, Woolf's writing demonstrates a growing desire to question the canon, and an increasing interest in reinvigorating old literature as an ongoing presence and common inheritance. This chapter will demonstrate these dynamics of Woolf's allusive practice as we examine how she uses allusions to articulate relationships with the literary past first in *A Room of One's Own*, and then in three examples of her treatment of female writers in her novels: Mrs Hilbery, Orlando and her poem 'The Oak Tree', and Miss La Trobe's pageant in *Between the Acts* (1941).

A Room of One's Own is Woolf's most developed statement on the relation of the woman writer to the literary tradition, for here she speculates that 'we think back through our mothers if we are women' (*ARO* 57) and sketches out a history of women writers as an alternative to the male canon. However, the essay's allusive pattern demonstrates intricate relationships with male as well as female writers. Expounding her frustrations with the male writer, Woolf notes that although a woman writer cannot 'lift anything substantial from him successfully', because the man's sentence is different from the woman's, she can nonetheless 'adapt' a 'few tricks' (*ARO* 57). This adaptation

---

[8] Eliot, *Selected Essays*, 14, 17.
[9] Eliot, *Selected Essays*, 17.
[10] Bonnie Kime Scott notes that male modernist writers tend to use architectural metaphors, while female ones more shifting ones, such as webs and weaving. Bonnie Kime Scott, *Refiguring Modernism*, 2 vols (Bloomington: Indiana University Press, 1995).

merits further scrutiny, for *A Room of One's Own* encompasses dialogism, as Woolf cites and quotes from past writers, and transformation, as she melds echoes from their works to generate fresh meanings.

Woolf uses allusion to establish a relationship with past writings from the first pages of the essay, where she inscribes into her own prose the work of one of 'the great men writers' (*ARO* 57), the eighteenth-century essayist Charles Lamb. The allusion starts obliquely, as Lamb comes 'to mind' through 'some stray memory of revisiting Oxbridge in the long vacation': Woolf almost names his essay 'Oxford in the Vacation' here, while ambivalently claiming that 'the name escapes me'. Woolf progresses from remembering Lamb to revivifying him, first recalling how Thackeray regarded him as a 'saint', and then projecting him as a Bakhtinian dialogic partner:

> Indeed, among all the dead (I give you my thoughts as they came to me), Lamb is one of the most congenial; one to whom one would have liked to say, Tell me then how you wrote your essays? (*ARO* 5–6)

Woolf's phrasing here initially recalls Eliot's statement that 'you must set [the contemporary writer] for contrast and comparison, among the dead', but she proceeds to do the opposite, for Lamb is not dead but an animate, 'congenial' presence with whom she desires personal interaction. As Woolf expresses a wish to know how Lamb wrote, she also signals her affinities with him: her description of Lamb's essays having a 'wild flash of imagination ... starred with poetry' (*ARO* 6) would also be a good description of *A Room of One's Own* itself.

This seemingly localized mention of Lamb hints at a wider context, for echoes of his Oxford essay ripple out into the opening passage of *A Room of One's Own*, as Woolf writes herself into a tradition of essayists. Both essays begin by anticipating that readers will be puzzled: Lamb draws attention to his pseudonym ('Casting a preparatory glance at the bottom of this article ... methinks I hear you exclaim, Reader, *Who is Elia?*'), and Woolf to her title ('But, you may say, we asked you to speak about women and fiction—what has that got to do with a room of one's own?' (*ARO* 3)).[11] They both tease readers as to what they might be expecting based on earlier writings: for Lamb, this would be tales of office-workers; for Woolf it would be conventional remarks on women writers, including the 'sketch of Haworth Parsonage under snow', her homage to Elizabeth Gaskell from one of her earliest published pieces.

Both essays proceed to assert the creative potential of distraction, demonstrating the point by launching into extended digressions linked with physical *flâneries*. In both cases, they venture to Oxbridge as outsiders: although Woolf casts Lamb as a graduate

---

[11] Charles Lamb, 'Oxford in the Vacation', in Charles Lamb, *The Essays of Elia*, 2nd ed. (Boston: Crosby, Nichols, Lee, 1860), 19.

'revisiting' Oxford, he was not university-educated, having been 'defrauded in his young years of the sweet food of academic institution'. However, whereas Woolf highlights her outsider status, symbolized by her female narrator being chased from a college lawn by the Beadle, Lamb being a man can successfully masquerade as an insider, imagining himself a scholar, a Master of Arts, and a doctor winning acceptance and welcome: 'I have seen your dim-eyed vergers, and bed-makers in spectacles, drop a bow or a curtsy, as I pass, wisely mistaking me for something of the sort.' Nonetheless, both Lamb and Woolf are concerned to claim space: Lamb can occupy Oxford colleges that are emptied of students for the vacation, as 'the walks at these times are so much one's own';[12] Woolf, echoing Lamb's phrase in her title, appeals for a room in which to write.

Lamb becomes a half-buried marker of Woolf's sceptical engagement with literary scholarship when she raises the question of manuscripts. Woolf misremembers Lamb's essay because, although she claims that it is 'about' the manuscript of Milton's *Lycidas* and Lamb's shock at finding that it existed in different versions, in fact Lamb only mentions this in a footnote to his original article in the *London Magazine* (1820): 'I had thought of the Lycidas as of a full-grown beauty—as springing up with all its parts absolute—till, in an evil hour, I was shown the original written copy of it … How it staggered me to see the fine things in their ore! interlined, corrected! as if their words were mortal, alterable, displaceable at pleasure!'[13] In the version collected in his *Essays of Elia* (1823), he merely states that he dislikes manuscript research, finding that those '*variae lectiones*, so tempting to the more erudite palates, do but disturb and unsettle my faith'.[14] What Woolf does, then, is destabilize Lamb's text by taking his provisional material to be central to his essay. Woolf's narrator plans to go and see *Lycidas* for herself to see how Milton's text, which Lamb wants to preserve as a perfect, immortal work of art, was actually the result of change and process.

Woolf therefore unsettles the status of canonical male writers in general, leaving their work open to revision, misremembering, and creative misquotation: as Amanda Golden has noted, Woolf's reference to Milton's manuscript draws attention to the alternative version of history with which her essay is concerned.[15] Woolf significantly ignores Lamb's most famous work—the retellings of Shakespeare in *Tales of Shakespeare*—and as a result, occludes his collaborator, his sister Mary. Instead, Woolf makes her own creative response to Shakespeare by giving him a sister, Judith, as the epitome of a lost tradition of women writers traceable back to the figure of 'Anon', writer of ballads and folksongs, who Woolf speculates, was 'often a woman'.

---

[12] Lamb, 'Oxford in the Vacation', in *Essays of Elia*, 22.
[13] Charles Lamb, 'Oxford in the Vacation', *London Magazine* 10 (October 1820), 365–69, at 367), at https://babel.hathitrust.org, last accessed 24 January 2019.
[14] Lamb, 'Oxford in the Vacation', in *Essays of Elia*, 24.
[15] Amanda Golden, 'On Manuscripts: Virginia Woolf and Archives', in Nicola Wilson and Claire Battershill, eds, *Virginia Woolf and the World of Books* (Clemson, SC: Clemson University Press, 2018), 26–30, at 27.

Woolf sees Shakespeare as congenial and adaptable, but she frequently castigates Milton for epitomizing all that is wrong with canonical writers. Woolf frequently plays them off against one another: Shakespeare's work reflects a mind that is 'incandescent', free of impediments, egotism, and opinions, unlike Milton who, along with Donne and Ben Jonson, displays 'his grudges and spites and antipathies' (*ARO* 43). Shakespeare, she concludes later, was 'androgynous', like Lamb and Coleridge (from whom she drew the concept), again in contrast to Milton who, along with Ben Jonson, 'had a dash too much of the male in them' (*ARO* 78). If Shakespeare's sister is to be 'born again' through the efforts of women writers, one of the necessary conditions is that we should 'look past Milton's bogey, for no human being should shut out the view' (*ARO* 86).

Woolf pushes Milton aside to make way for female writers. The narrator says that she is freed to write by a legacy from her aunt that 'unveiled the sky to me, and substituted for the large and imposing figure of a gentleman, which Milton recommended for my perpetual adoration, a view of the open sky' (*ARO* 30). Here, Woolf rejects not only Milton, but the male-centred universe of *Paradise Lost*: 'he for God only, she for God in him', which in turn alludes to Saint Paul's statement from 1 Corinthians 11:3 that 'the head of every man is Christ; and the head of the woman is the man'. Woolf hereby rejects social and religious strictures that had suppressed women, and the literary canon that had enforced such values. She later supplants Milton when she celebrates the hidden literary tradition of women, imagining 'a lost novelist, a suppressed poet … some mute and inglorious Jane Austen' (*ARO* 37), incorporating a transformative allusion to Thomas Gray's 'Elegy Written in a Country Churchyard', by replacing the name of Milton with that of Jane Austen as a figure worthy of recall.

Although Milton is her rhetorical opponent on matters of the canon, his writing returns to support her argument that a woman needs the intellectual freedom afforded by personal space and an independent income. She therefore alludes to a line from *Comus*, where the Lady refuses temptation: 'Thou canst not touch the freedom of my mind', to challenge the prohibitive Beadle and champion a woman's right to read: 'Lock up your libraries if you like; but there is no gate, no lock, no bolt that you can set upon the freedom of my mind' (*ARO* 57). The narrator also alludes to Milton to articulate the crippling effect that society's demands can have on a woman's writing. The narrator comments that 'the thought of that one gift which it was death to hide—a small one but dear to the possessor—perishing and with it my self, my soul,—all this became like a rust eating away the bloom of the spring, destroying the tree at its heart' (*ARO* 29). This alludes to Milton's Sonnet 19, 'On His Blindness': 'that one talent which is death to hide / Lodg'd with me useless, though my soul more bent / To serve therewith my Maker'. However, Woolf replaces the 'talent' (which in Milton's biblical source was a coin) with the organic metaphor of literary creativity as a living gift: impediments to writing are like disease in trees, preventing the flowering of poetry. In order to live, a literary work needs to have organic roots in a tradition.

Woolf develops these organic metaphors when, as a counterpart to her argument from Milton, she quotes from 'The Spleen' by Anne Finch, Lady Winchilsea. 'The Spleen' contends that anger and domestic strife cloud a woman's ability to express herself and although this is the very point that Woolf makes in her essay, she stresses that such argumentative discourse has no place in poetry. Instead, she rescues Finch by extracting fragments of 'pure poetry' from 'The Spleen':

> Nor will in fading silks compose,
> Faintly the inimitable rose.
> Now the jonquille o'ercomes the feeble brain;
> We faint beneath the aromatic pain.[16]

Significantly, these phrases accentuate the organic: in moments when Finch writes about nature, her poetry comes to life. But Woolf's overall point is that this element of Finch's work did not survive: '[h]er gift is all grown about with weeds and bound with briars. It had no chance of showing itself for the fine distinguished gift it was' (ARO 46). Like the 'rust' destroying the tree in Woolf's earlier metaphor, Finch's anger has choked the growth of her poetry. Finch's problem, in Woolf's view, is that where Milton was too masculine, Finch's work is marred by its anger towards men.

In parallel with her vegetal metaphors, Woolf employs an extended metaphor of literature as the product of a lengthy process of collaboration and breeding: 'masterpieces are not single and solitary births; they are the outcome of many years of thinking in common, of thinking by the body of the people, so that the experience of the mass is behind the single voice' (ARO 49). Woolf alludes to the classical metaphor of the Muse, one that implies a sexualized view of poetry as the product of intercourse, for she envisages English poetry as arising from the exchange of love songs between male and female poets, setting Tennyson's 'There has fallen a splendid tear' in dialogue with Christina Rossetti's 'My heart is like a singing bird' as a refrain throughout the essay. Although this image is, as Madelyn Detloff has noted, 'fanciful, almost pathetically heteronormative',[17] Woolf develops and queers it when she notes that such fertilization can occur when male and female qualities are found in the same mind, such as Coleridge's: 'when one takes a sentence of Coleridge into the mind, it explodes and gives birth to all kinds of other ideas, and that is the only sort of writing of which one can say that it has the secret of perpetual life' (ARO 76–7). This metaphor melds the sexual and the organic, for 'perpetual' is a horticultural term for plants that flower or fruit recurrently or continuously, showing the continual process of renewal and development that Woolf sees in literature.[18] The truly creative mind is one that preserves past literature, fusing echoes together to generate fresh writings. This profoundly dialogic, transformative allusive process is, precisely, Woolf's technique in the essay itself.

With *A Room of One's Own* in mind, we can now look back and see Woolf's allusive and metaphorical practice in embryonic form in her description of Mrs Hilbery. Woolf

---

[16] Anne Finch, Lady Winchilsea, 'The Spleen', in Sandra M. Gilbert and Susan Gubar, eds, *The Norton Anthology of Literature by Women,* 2nd ed. (New York: W. W. Norton, 1985), 170–3.
[17] Madelyn Detloff, *The Value of Virginia Woolf* (Cambridge: Cambridge University Press, 2016), 20.
[18] *Oxford English Dictionary* 2c.

uses organic metaphors for Mrs Hilbery's inspiration when spring enlivens her 'emotional powers':

> The first signs of spring, even such as make themselves felt towards the middle of February, not only produce little white and violet flowers in the more sheltered corners of woods and gardens, but bring to birth thoughts and desires comparable to those faintly coloured and sweetly scented petals in the minds of men and women. (*ND* 319)

This inspiration comes from the natural world, demonstrating the organic nature of literature, but it also comes from the past, for the image of spring producing spiritual and emotional reinvigoration along with the flowers is found in the earliest English poetry: the early lyrics at the start of the *Oxford Book of English Verse*, such as 'Springtide' (c. 1300), which tells how 'Lenten ys come with love to toune, / With blosmen and with bridles roune', and bringing 'Dayes-eyes in this dales'.[19] Here, Woolf is already drawing on the anonymous ballads that she suggested in *A Room of One's Own* might be the earliest output from a woman writer. Mrs Hilbery's emotional awakening, similarly stimulated by the spring, stirs her awareness of the 'shapes and colours of the past', and leads her to consume literature.

The image also recalls in the opening lines of Chaucer's *The Canterbury Tales*, where April showers bathe 'every veyne in swich licour, / Of which vertu engendred is the flour' and inspire people to go on pilgrimages. Woolf makes a playful allusion at Mrs Hilbery's expense in her desire to visit Shakespeare's tomb in Stratford-upon-Avon: a quasi-religious quest to find inspiration in relics, for she is enthused by 'the certainty that there was existing in England a spot of ground where Shakespeare had undoubtedly stood, where his very bones lay directly beneath one's feet' (*ND* 322). Here, Woolf envisages Shakespeare as quite literally melded into the soil, making him part of the land. The discussion of Shakespeare is also transformative, for Mrs Hilbery expresses the whimsical idea that Shakespeare's sonnets were written by Anne Hathaway: a joke that can be taken more seriously as an attempt to insert women writers into literary history that foreshadows Woolf's creation of a female Shakespeare in his hypothetical sister Judith.

Woolf continues to use allusion to write herself and other women writers into literary history in *Orlando* (1928), but she broadens her scope even further by drawing on her vast knowledge of literary history. In contrast to Mrs Hilbery, whose book never progresses beyond fragments (*ND* 36–7), the protagonist becomes a successful female writer when her poem 'The Oak Tree' is published in the twentieth century to critical acclaim, financial gain, fame, and the awarding of a literary prize (*O* 284). Orlando represents Vita Sackville-West, the bestselling writer who had won the Hawthornden Prize for her poem *The Land*, but she also has parallels with Woolf herself, not least because Orlando's composition of 'The Oak Tree' takes place over the duration of the novel and thus evolves in tandem with Woolf's own composition. In taking the narrative over

---

[19] Arthur Quiller-Couch, ed., *The Oxford Book of English Verse* [1900] (Oxford: Clarendon Press, 1966), 3.

three centuries and a half, depicting Orlando writing 'The Oak Tree' as boy and woman from 1586 to 1928, Woolf demonstrates how it is not just the result of a lifetime's effort, but has emerged organically from the English countryside (as its title suggests) *and* from the body of English literature, for Woolf's allusive layers throughout the novel demonstrate an accretion of literary styles and echoes across the centuries. Woolf's incorporation of past writings into Orlando's writing and her own is therefore an outworking of the concept that 'masterpieces are not single and solitary births' (*ARO* 49).

On the other hand, Woolf uses allusions to pinpoint Orlando's struggles with the weight of the literary past and the canon, for she suggests that Orlando's prodigious reading is a disease: as a young nobleman he is 'afflicted with a love of literature' leaving him, in an unhealthy organic metaphor, 'infected by a germ said to be bred of the pollen of the asphodel' (*O* 68–9). He eagerly picks up the inflections of other writers, appropriately beginning his poetic career in an age that prioritized imitation over originality: one of his earliest attempts is 'Æthelbert: A Tragedy in Five Acts'. In counterpoint to her protagonist's struggles, on the other hand, Woolf seamlessly blends allusions into her own prose to show how Orlando's thoughts reflect the concerns of the age: 'poets sang beautifully how roses fade and petals fall. The moment is brief they sang, the moment is over; one long night is therefore to be slept by all' (*O* 26). Woolf invokes a literary cliché of the time but also calls specific writings to mind, melding the words of Vita's ancestor, Thomas Sackville, 'The fields so fade, that flourish'd so beforn',[20] with Shakespeare's conception of death as a sleep, as in 'our little life / Is rounded with a sleep', or Hamlet's 'sleep of death'.

Woolf also invokes allusions to show how Orlando, like Mrs Hilbery, is haunted by literature, for reading leads him to 'substitute a phantom for reality' (*O* 69) and neglect his aristocratic duties (Orlando later describes herself as being 'haunted' by Shakespeare from childhood (*O* 285)). Woolf evokes Sir Thomas Browne (a writer who, alongside Lamb, 'never helped a woman yet' (*ARO* 57)), as Orlando reads to distract himself from love, fame, and the trials of writing:

> Like an incantation rising from all parts of the room, from the night wind and the moonlight, rolled the divine melody of those words which, lest they should outstare this page, we will leave where they lie entombed, not dead, embalmed rather, so fresh is their colour, so sound their breathing. (*O* 75)

Browne's words, arising like an 'incantation', seem to come from outside his book and outside of Orlando's mind, to disarming effect. Browne's work exists between life and death, both 'embalmed' and 'breathing'. This idea evokes Browne's 'Urn Burial' in which he marvels on the vibrancy of grave goods: 'incinerable substances were found so fresh, that they could feel no singe from fire.... In their hardness and yellow colour they most resembled box, which, in old expressions, found the epithet of eternal, and perhaps in such conservatories might have passed uncorrupted.'[21] Woolf therefore circumvents

---

[20] Thomas Sackville, 'Mirror for Magistrates', *Thomas Sackville: Poetical Works* (London: Chappell, 1820), 119.

[21] *Hydriotaphia: Urn Burial* [1658] (London: Charles Whittingham, 1893), 40.

Orlando's problems to allow herself and the reader to enjoy the pleasure of unearthing Browne's words which, like the grave goods, exist in a zombie-like state to haunt Orlando.

Remaining one step ahead of her character, Woolf challenges conventional scholarly accounts of literary periodization and, along with these, a sense of the inevitable pressures of tradition, for although Orlando's career progresses chronologically and although Woolf sometimes gives Orlando's writing a period flavour, she does not mimic changing styles as Joyce does in the 'Oxen of the Sun' episode of *Ulysses*, as I have demonstrated elsewhere,[22] but plays fast and loose with time frames. Romantic ideas are pervasive: Woolf presents them anachronistically in the Elizabethan era, when Orlando's attempts to write break down when he tries to address the Romantic theme of nature: 'Green in nature is one thing, green in literature another' (*O* 16). This challenges the reader to consider the possibility that Elizabethan writers experienced the love of nature, often seen as a Romantic phenomenon. In particular anachronistic buried allusions to Keats's statement that '"Beauty is truth, truth beauty"', from 'Ode on a Grecian Urn', appear in the sixteenth century as Orlando considers 'the problem of what poetry is and what truth is'; in the seventeenth, she writes a 'long, blank version poem' from a train of thought that engages Romantic debates over how the mind interacts with the natural world: 'She began to think, was Nature beautiful or cruel; and then she asked herself what this beauty was; whether it was in things themselves, or only in herself; so she went on to the nature of reality, which led her to truth' (*O* 134).

By creating a fantastic character who can cross the boundaries of age and gender, Woolf envisages that writers may be able to disentangle themselves from time-bound and gender-specific approaches. The rejection of periodization reaches a zenith in the Victorian age, which is inimical to Orlando's creativity. Ironically invoking Hazlitt's concept of the spirit of the age, Woolf points out that social forces can hamper creativity: 'One might see the spirit of the age blowing, now hot, now cold, upon her cheeks. And if the spirit of the age blew a little unequally, the crinoline being blushed for before the husband, her ambiguous position must excuse her' (*O* 215). Like the 'Angel in the House' (Coventry Patmore's epitome of domestic virtue that Woolf castigates in 'Professions for Women'), the spirit of the age criticizes Orlando's writings, didactically pointing at 'The Oak Tree' with a 'ruler such as governesses use', questioning her expressions, not least the erotically charged reference to 'girls' (*O* 242). Woolf rescues Orlando by making her trans-historical and resistant of her time: 'it is probable that the human spirit has its place in time assigned to it; some are born of this age, some of that; and now that Orlando was grown a woman ... the lines of her character were fixed, and to bend them the wrong way was intolerable' (*O* 222).

Just as Woolf shows that certain literary fashions and trends can cramp women's creativity, so she satirizes the literary canon as an unhelpful ideology. The canon is both an inhibition and an inspiration for Orlando, even as a young man, for the 'great

---

[22] de Gay, *Virginia Woolf's Novels and the Literary Past*, 47–8.

names' make him eager for fame but aware that such fame is elusive. Having praised Shakespeare in *A Room of One's Own* for his androgyny, Woolf mocks those who make him a yardstick for judging other writers, making him an anonymous, unassuming 'rather fat, rather shabby man, whose ruff was a thought dirty, and whose clothes were of hodden brown' (*O* 20). In the seventeenth-century sequence, Woolf comically merges Shakespeare's head with the newly built dome of St. Paul's Cathedral to mock those who appropriate Shakespeare to support British supremacy. She even suggests that male greatness is a product of Orlando's gullibility: 'the glory of poetry, and the great lines of Marlowe, Shakespeare, Ben Jonson, Milton began booming and reverberating, as if a golden clapper beat against a golden bell in the cathedral tower which was her mind' (*O* 152). Woolf satirizes the critic Nick Greene's adulation of famous male writers to undermine contemporary ones: 'The great days of literature are over. Marlowe, Shakespeare, Ben Jonson—those were the giants. Dryden, Pope, Addison—those were the heroes. All, all are dead now. And whom have they left us? Tennyson, Browning, Carlyle!' (*O* 254).

Woolf is ironical about Orlando attaining canonical status by winning a prize, mocking 'old Greene getting upon a platform the other day comparing her with Milton (save for his blindness) and handing her a cheque for two hundred guineas' (*O* 296–7). However, Woolf also suggests that the literary past has been inspiring because Greene admires Orlando's mature poem precisely because it has a literary tradition behind it: 'It reminded him, he said as he turned over the pages, of Addison's *Cato*. It compared favourably with Thomson's *Seasons*' (*O* 256). And indeed, Woolf, through her own allusive practice that demonstrates her virtuoso knowledge of canonical literature, has likewise anchored her own writing into a much wider literary tradition.

Woolf continues to challenge literary historians, and firmly rejects the canon, in Miss La Trobe's literary-historical pageant in *Between the Acts*. At the same time, Woolf reinvigorates past literature as an ongoing presence and common inheritance in this novel, even more prominently than the others. La Trobe is heir to Mrs Hilbery as a frustrated female writer, as she stands fuming in the wings when the audience fails to see her point, but she is also heir to Orlando and all she represents, for the pageant does not originate from her own creativity but from centuries of English literature. Lucy Swithin indicates this heritage when she speculates that La Trobe has 'the whole of English literature to choose from' (*BA* 43), anticipating that La Trobe is going to reject the conventional form of the nationalistic and militaristic historical pageant. As Jed Esty notes, the pageant in this novel 'gives form to communal values rather than to individual impressions or divisive ideologies'.[23]

Woolf's interest in critiquing the assumptions of literary historiography, seen in both *A Room of One's Own* and *Orlando*, surfaces even more ironically and playfully in *Between the Acts*. The pageant subjects conventional literary history to review/revue with parodic chronological episodes alluding to Chaucer's pilgrims, Elizabethan

---

[23] Jed Esty, *A Shrinking Island: Modernism and National Culture in England* (Princeton, NJ: Princeton University Press, 2004), 87.

comedy, Restoration comedy, and Victorian melodrama (*BA* 59, 64–8, 91–100, 118–24). Significantly, Woolf's playful approach in *Between the Acts* emerged in tandem with her planning of a non-fictional reappraisal of literary history, a project that was to involve extensive re-reading of work including Shakespeare, Ben Jonson, Milton, Donne, '& all the rest'.[24] As Brenda R. Silver notes, this project was entwined with the novel, for Woolf's diary from October 1940 to March 1941 'records side by side with the progress of *Pointz Hall*, the original title of *Between the Acts*, a steady stream of reading for the book she now described as threading a necklace through English life and literature'.[25] Woolf started drafting two essays, 'Anon' and 'The Reader', immediately after finishing the first typescript and wrote the essays as she revised the novel.

Woolf delivers a final riposte to the concept of canonicity in 'Anon' and *Between the Acts*, for both works point to the origins of literature in anonymous sources rather than named authors. In 'Anon', Woolf revises her earlier idea that the writer of ballads and folksongs was 'often a woman' to envisage an androgynous figure: 'Anon is sometimes man; sometimes woman'; no longer an individual but 'the common voice singing out of doors' (*E6* 582). Woolf develops her organic metaphor into an argument that literature began in the natural world as birdsong, which the huntsmen mimicked, initiating an oral tradition of songs and stories preserved in folklore and popular memory (*E6* 582). Echoing a phrase from *Orlando* 'that flowers fade; that death is the end', Woolf now categorically attributes this to 'Anon the lyric poet' (*E6* 598). Woolf suggests that the arrival of the concept of literary personality, with the invention of the printing press, was not progress but a detrimental moment: the death of 'Anon'. And yet, even as names became enshrined, even as Malory's name became attached to the 'Morte D'Arthur', for example, the voice of 'Anon' was encapsulated within it, and the characters represented were 'ourselves' (*E6* 583–4).

Woolf presents Miss La Trobe as an embodiment of 'Anon', often called 'Miss Whatsername', as Silver has noted.[26] La Trobe is less defined as a character than either Mrs Hilbery or Orlando: the villagers can only speculate on her life story, she hides in the bushes during the play and refuses to come out to accept thanks. As a masculine woman, she reflects the androgyny embodied in *Orlando* and championed in *A Room of One's Own* and 'Anon'. La Trobe's play bears many of the hallmarks of the literature of 'Anon' as Woolf described it: it is performed outdoors, it incorporates birdsong, and it ends with a performance piece in which the players hold up '[a]nything that's bright enough to reflect, presumably, ourselves?' (*BA* 132). This drama in which a community represents itself, in which members act and the audience participates, is a communal production rather than an individual endeavour.

Woolf unsettles the supremacy of the 'great names' of literature in *Between the Acts* by emphasizing that literature is an organic process. On the rare occasions when authors

---

[24] Brenda R. Silver, ed., '"Anon" and "The Reader": Virginia Woolf's Last Essays', *Twentieth-Century Literature* 25 (1979), 356–441, at 359.

[25] Silver, ed., '"Anon" and "The Reader"', 357.

[26] Silver, ed., '"Anon" and "The Reader"', 380.

are named, their work is decontextualized: when Bart Oliver recalls Byron and quotes 'She walks in beauty, like the night' and 'So we'll go no more a-roving / By the light of the moon', his daughter-in-law Isa turns the words into natural objects: 'the words made two rings, perfect rings, that floated them, herself and Haines, like two swans down stream' (*BA* 4). Literary quotations are transformatively blended into everyday speech, such as when Giles expresses himself by distractedly quoting *King Lear*'s 'I fear I am not in my perfect mind' and misquoting Gray's 'Elegy', as 'from yonder ivy-mantled tower / The moping owl does to the moon complain' becomes 'the owl hoots and the ivy mocks tap-tap-tapping on the pane' (*BA* 62). Anonymous works and nursery rhymes provide the soundscape for the novel when Bart hears someone practising on the piano, playing 'Hark, hark, the dogs do bark', and 'Lady I love till I die', a generic sentiment, attributed by Mark Hussey to another anonymous lyric from *The Oxford Book of English Verse*, 'There is a lady sweet and kind' (*BA* 85, 215).

This process reaches its climax in the closing scene of the play, in which radically decontextualized quotations appear as fragments (*BA* 132–3). Although Woolf introduces the collage by saying that each actor 'declaimed some phrase or fragment from their parts', very few of these lines come from the play as it has appeared in the novel: Reason is a person in the pageant, but does not declaim the quoted words 'Reason am I'; a top hat is a piece of costume, and it does not say 'I'm the old top hat'; Papa reads, but no one invites him to 'take your book and read aloud'. The only phrase taken from the pageant is from a popular stage ballad by a minor writer of the Romantic era: 'I'd be a butterfly' by Thomas Haynes Bayly.

Other phrases in the collage echo the frame narrative of the novel: life between the acts, rather than the pageant. The snatches of music heard by Bart are echoed, as are Giles' quotations from *King Lear* and Gray's 'Elegy'. Most of the literary fragments have not appeared in the novel at all: 'Home is ... the hunter, home from the hill', from R.L. Stevenson's 'Requiem'; 'maiden faith is rudely strumpeted', from Shakespeare's Sonnet 66; 'Sweet and low; sweet and low, wind of the western sea' from Tennyson's 'The Princess', 'Is this a dagger which I see before me?' from *Macbeth*; and 'In thy will is our peace', from Dante's *Divine Comedy*. The words of famous poets, none of whom is named, are placed alongside those of anonymous others and interspersed with ellipses denoting silence. The collage suggests that it is difficult for anyone to claim ownership of literature. With *Between the Acts*, the novel Gillian Beer describes as being 'combed through' with quotations,[27] Woolf takes her art of allusion to its logical conclusion: echoes are fully 'hidden founts of pleasure'; canonicity and the order of great names are overthrown; literature is fully interwoven into language itself. In doing so, Woolf gives past literature vibrancy in the present.

Woolf's art of allusion is subtle, complex, and deeply informed by her reflections on literature and its origins. In the four works explored here, Woolf invokes a wide range of

---

[27] Gillian Beer, *Virginia Woolf: The Common Ground* (Edinburgh: Edinburgh University Press, 1996), 134.

literature as she meditates on the writer's relationship to the past, while using allusion to root her own writing in a vast network of literary works. As we have seen, these two approaches work in counterpoint: while showing real and fictional writers such as Anne Finch, Mrs Hilbery, and Orlando struggling with past literature, Woolf adroitly harnesses it herself. Woolf's metaphors all speak of a quest for origins: from elusive ghosts, to progeny, to family relationships, but most powerfully the sense of literature evolving from the natural world: an image suggested by Orlando's poem 'The Oak Tree', that comes into focus in 'Anon', and is engaged creatively in *Between the Acts*. By the time she wrote her final novel, Woolf was embedding her intertexts very deeply, not to conceal her sources but to enfold a chorus of literary voices in her own work.

Selected Bibliography

Bakhtin, Mikhail, *The Dialogic Imagination: Four Essays*, ed. Michael Holquist, trans. Caryl Emerson and Michael Holquist (Austin: University of Texas Press, 1994).

Beer, Gillian, *Virginia Woolf: The Common Ground* (Edinburgh: Edinburgh University Press, 1996).

de Gay, Jane, *Virginia Woolf's Novels and the Literary Past* (Edinburgh: Edinburgh University Press, 2006).

Detloff, Madelyn, *The Value of Virginia Woolf* (Cambridge: Cambridge University Press, 2016).

Eliot, T. S., *Selected Essays* (London: Faber, 1932).

Esty, Jed, *A Shrinking Island: Modernism and National Culture in England* (Princeton, NJ: Princeton University Press, 2004).

Fernald, Anne E., 'Woolf and Intertextuality', in Bryony Randall and Jane Goldman, eds, *Woolf in Context* (Cambridge: Cambridge University Press, 2012), 52–64.

Golden, Amanda, 'On Manuscripts: Virginia Woolf and Archives', in Nicola Wilson and Claire Battershill, eds, *Virginia Woolf and the World of Books* (Clemson, SC: Clemson University Press, 2018), 26–30.

Jones, Christine Kenyon, and Anna Snaith, '"Tilting at Universities": Virginia Woolf at King's College London', *Woolf Studies Annual* 16 (2010), 1–44.

Lamb, Charles, *The Essays of Elia*, 2nd ed. (Boston: Crosby, Nichols, Lee, 1860).

Lee, Hermione, *Virginia Woolf* (London: Chatto and Windus, 1996).

Lodge, David, *The Modes of Modern Writing: Metaphor, Metonymy, and the Typology of Modern Literature* (London: Bloomsbury, 1977).

Scott, Bonnie Kime, *Refiguring Modernism*, 2 vols (Bloomington: Indiana University Press, 1995).

Silver, Brenda R., ed., '"Anon" and "The Reader": Virginia Woolf's Last Essays', *Twentieth-Century Literature* 25 (1979), 356–441.

Silver, Brenda R., ed., *Virginia Woolf's Reading Notebooks* (Princeton, NJ: Princeton University Press, 1983).

CHAPTER 14

BIOGRAPHY AND AUTOBIOGRAPHY

LAURA MARCUS

BIOGRAPHY and autobiography—as literary genres and as ways of representing the lives and identities of others and of the self—were at the heart of Virginia Woolf's cultural world and of her writing life. Her Bloomsbury circle was fuelled by the arts of conversation, gossip, and memoir. The 'Memoir Club', founded in 1920 and lasting for many decades, was a forum in which Bloomsbury members—the Club's original members included Leonard and Virginia Woolf, E.M. Forster, Molly and Desmond MacCarthy, Lytton Strachey, John Maynard Keynes, Duncan Grant, Vanessa and Clive Bell, and Roger Fry—read autobiographical sketches to each other, sustaining their collective identity through their personal, and group, stories and anecdotes. 'I doubt that anyone will *say* the interesting things but they can't prevent their coming out', Woolf commented of the Club's first meeting (*D2* 22).

Throughout her life, Woolf read extensively and absorbedly in biographies, autobiographies, journals, memoirs, and collections of letters, and reviewed many such works for the literary journals. A prolific diarist and correspondent, her personal writings were forums for perceptions, observations, and descriptions which also became shaping forces in her fiction and essays. Woolf's novels are deeply intertwined with life-writing forms, from the bildungsroman of *The Voyage Out* (1915) to the play with conventional biographical forms of *Jacob's Room* (1922), *Orlando* (1928), *The Waves* (1931), and *Flush* (1933) and the autobiographical foundations of *To the Lighthouse* (1927). Her earliest short stories, including 'Memoirs of a Novelist' (1909) and 'The Journal of Mistress Joan Martyn' (1906), were experiments in the writing of historical and fictional biography, which also, in taking a distance from the conventions of the Victorian 'lives and letters' form, began the process by which Woolf, over the course of her writing life, would (as she put it in describing her plans for *Orlando*) help to 'revolutionize' biography (*L3* 429). One of her final works, the incomplete and, in her lifetime, unpublished memoir 'A Sketch of the Past', has become one of the most significant texts of modern autobiography, opening out to questions of identity ('Who was I then?'), the nature of memory and recall, and the relationship between past and present time and selves ('I now, I then') in ways that have come to define the key aspects of twentieth-century autobiographical acts.

The milieu in which Virginia Woolf—then Virginia Stephen—grew up was also one to which biography was central. Her paternal and maternal lineages were eminent: her ancestors and relations were part of the network of intellectual and professional families who shaped Victorian society and knowledge production in its literary, philosophical, religious, cultural, scientific, and political dimensions, and whose members' lives were deemed entirely worthy of record. Many of their number, both male and female, were also prolific essayists, biographers, autobiographers, and authors of memoirs and reminiscences. The 'lives of great men', from which Woolf would come to take a critical and parodic distance, was the substance of the work that occupied her father, the philosopher and essayist Sir Leslie Stephen, for many years of his life and for much of her childhood: the monumental *Dictionary of National Biography* (*DNB*). The *DNB* undoubtedly changed the nature of Victorian biographical writing, substituting brevity for the voluminous 'lives and letters' form and dismissing undue piety towards the departed with its unwritten motto of 'no flowers by request'. Nonetheless, its near exclusively masculine focus and its hierarchy of value in relation to lives and careers were aspects that Woolf would repeatedly counter in her chosen focus on women's lives, 'the lives of the obscure', and the importance of 'Anon'. Of her numerous essays, reviews, and character-sketches, a very substantial proportion are concerned with women and women's writing, including many works of biography and autobiography, memoir, and reminiscence. A late essay, 'The Art of Biography' (1939), returned to the questioning of biography's commitment to 'the lives of great men':

> Is not anyone who has lived a life, and left a record of that life, worthy of biography—the failures as well as the successes, the humble as well as the illustrious? And what is greatness? And what smallness? He [the biographer] must revise our standards of merit and set up new heroes for our admiration. (*E6* 186)

Into the new century, 'the moderns' would mark their distance and difference from the Victorian past both by their irreverent attitudes to the conventions of life-writing and by the complex understandings of identity and selfhood that the new psychologies, including an emergent psychoanalysis, were bringing into being. If Leslie Stephen and his co-editor on the *DNB*, Sidney Lee (whose writings on biography continued into the 1910s), were among the shaping figures of late Victorian biographical writing, it was in the cultural milieu surrounding Woolf in the first decades of the twentieth century that new modes of life-writing flourished, their popularity intimately connected to the perception that biography had been reinvented for the modern age. Woolf's close friend Lytton Strachey's *Eminent Victorians* (1918) was a key text of 'the new biography', in its destruction through satire of the reputations of the 'great men' (and, in Florence Nightingale, 'great women') of Victorian Britain. 'I have attempted', Strachey wrote in the Preface to the work, 'through the medium of biography to present some Victorian visions to the modern eye',[1] 'visions' becoming a synonym for 'illusions' and 'delusions', not least those of the blind subservience to God and Country that had led to the mass destruction of a world war (which was still, at the time of the book's publication, running its course).

Strachey followed *Eminent Victorians* with numerous biographical 'portraits' and with his *Queen Victoria* (1921) and *Elizabeth and Essex* (1928), the latter published in the same year as *Orlando*, which has its own representation of the great queen. Other members of Woolf's intimate and broader circles also produced a significant number of works of biography and biographical criticism. Vita Sackville-West's biographical works included studies of *Aphra Behn* (1927) and *Joan of Arc* (1936); Sackville-West's husband Harold Nicolson published an experiment in biography, *Some People* (1927)—the subject of Woolf's essay 'The New Biography'—and a study entitled *The Development of English Biography* (1927), published by the Woolfs' Hogarth Press, which was in production as Woolf worked on *Orlando*. The French critic André Maurois, who became linked to the Bloomsbury circle in the 1920s, gave a series of lectures that were published as *Aspects of Biography* in 1929.[2] Maurois debates closely with Nicolson's critical study in this text, defending his own romanticized biographies of Shelley and Disraeli in his argument that the writing of history and biography belonged to the domains of creativity and imagination and that 'poetic truth' should be as central to biography as to any literary genre.

Maurois also addresses the ways in which Woolf had taken up similar questions in 'The New Biography' (1927), inventing the term that would come to define modern biographical writing. The essay explores the vexed question of biographical 'truth', in relation to (in Sidney Lee's phrase) 'the truthful transmission of personality'.[3] Woolf suggests that, whereas Lee failed to perceive the conflict between these two aims, their conjunction in fact constitutes 'the whole problem of biography as it presents itself to us today' (*E4* 473). Combining a brief history of biography with a review of Nicolson's *Some People*, Woolf suggests that the biographical genre achieved its highest point in the eighteenth century (with Boswell's *Life of Johnson* (1791) as a work in which 'truth of fact' and the revelation of 'personality' were seamlessly brought together) and its lowest in the Victorian age, when, while 'truth of fact' was scrupulously observed, 'the personality which Boswell's genius set free was hampered and distorted', primarily 'by the idea of goodness' (*E4* 474). In Victorian biography, Woolf suggested, 'the living man' became 'a fossil' (*E4* 475), and the writing of life (*bios*) became a death-dealing form. This is the paradox that she played with throughout her mock-biography *Orlando*, satirizing the 'cradle to grave' form of the conventional biography: 'without looking to right or left, in the indelible footprints of truth; unenticed by flowers; regardless of shade; on and on

---

[1] Lytton Strachey, *Eminent Victorians: Cardinal Manning, Florence Nightingale, Dr Arnold, General Gordon* (London: Chatto & Windus, 1918), vii.
[2] André Maurois, *Aspects of Biography* (Cambridge: Cambridge University Press, 1929).
[3] Qtd. in André Maurois, *Aspects of Biography*, trans. S. C. Roberts (Cambridge: Cambridge University Press, 2014), 33.

methodically till we fall plump into the grave and write *finis* on the tombstone above our head' (*O* 61).

'The Art of Biography', in which Woolf discussed Lytton Strachey's biographical writings, pursued this theme: 'the majority of Victorian biographies are like the wax figures now preserved in Westminster Abbey that were carried in funeral processions through the streets—effigies that have only a smooth superficial likeness to the body in the coffin' (*E6* 182). The representation of the living body, and of bodily experience, was for Woolf one of the most important challenges for biographers, failed by most of its practitioners. 'One might read the lives of all the Cabinet Ministers since the accession of Queen Victoria without realizing that they had a body between them', Woolf wrote in a review-essay (of the US writer William Roscoe Thayer's 1919 biography of Theodore Roosevelt) entitled 'Body and Brain' (*E4* 224).

The change that came over biography in the twentieth century, Woolf argues, was most visible in its compression and, more fundamentally, in a radical alteration in its point of view. The biographer was now an equal to their subject, no longer obliged to document every element of a life but, as Strachey observed in his Preface, permitted to select. In Woolf's words: 'He chooses; he synthesizes; in short, he has ceased to be the chronicler; he has become an artist' (*E4* 475). *Some People*, she writes, is a prime illustration of 'the new attitude to biography', in that Nicolson 'has devised a method or writing about people and about himself as if they were at once real and imaginary' (*E4* 475). The text alternates biographical and autobiographical sketches with the portrayal of invented characters, deploying 'truth' and 'fiction' in both types of portrait. Laudatory as her account is, Woolf nonetheless takes a critical distance from Nicolson's experiment, suggesting that 'the truth of real life' and 'the truth of fiction' (*E4* 477), 'granite and rainbow', are ultimately incompatible, and expresses reservations about the collapsing of distinctions between biography and fiction in the modern age: 'if [the biographer] carries the use of fiction too far, so that he disregards the truth, or can only introduce it with incongruity, he loses both worlds; he has neither the freedom of fiction nor the substance of fact' (*E4* 478).

Despite her doubts about this mixed genre (which, while identified as a new form of writing, in fact developed out of the 'imaginary portraits' of the nineteenth century) Woolf herself wrote a number of short fictional portraits or, in S.P. Rosenbaum's phrase, 'fantasy memoirs' (*E6* 515–49), primarily of friends and relatives, including Violet Dickinson and Nelly Cecil (in an early piece entitled 'Friendship's Gallery'), Sydney Saxon-Turner, and John Maynard Keynes. The last two works were outlines for sketches, and in the piece on 'JMK' Woolf produced a radical, and fantastical, compression of a life. This sketch, unpublished in her lifetime, bears on Woolf's declared intention for her novels to eliminate 'waste, deadness, superfluity' (*D3* 209–10) (as in the 'prodigious waste' (*E4* 475) she identified in Victorian biographies in 'The New Biography'), while pointing up the ways in which lives can contain the most incompatible of elements whose strange and fascinating coexistence is falsified when smoothed out and regulated by chronological narrative form. In 'JMK' Woolf placed in parenthesis the assertion that 'The art of biography is in its infancy. It has not yet learnt to walk without leading strings' (*The Platform of Time*, 223), an argument she developed in 'The Art of Biography': 'Biography thus is only at the beginning of its career; it has a full and active life before it, we may be sure—a life full of difficulty, danger and hard work' (*E6* 186).

Orlando was Woolf's most complete creation in the realm of fictional biography, and one in which the 'fantasy' element is central. The narrator of *Orlando* (like that of *Jacob's Room*) is a biographer, or would-be biographer, in pursuit of an elusive subject; one who lives, in the case of Orlando, as man and then woman, through four hundred years of history. Woolf was reading Strachey's *Queen Victoria* as she worked on *Jacob's Room* and commented in her diary that Strachey's biography was 'a remarkably composed & homogenous book' but that 'I doubt whether these portraits are true—whether that's not too much the conventional way of making history' (*D2* 65). Her 'experimental mood' in the construction of *Jacob's Room* led to the observation of her central character in 'glimpses': repeated throughout the novel is the assertion that 'It is no use trying to sum people up' (*JR* 37).

In September 1925, Woolf wrote to Vita Sackville-West: 'I try to invent you for myself, but find I really have only 2 twigs and 3 straws to do it with. [...] This proves what I could write reams about—how little we know anyone, only movements and gestures, nothing connected, continuous, profound' (*L3* 204–5). 'Inventing' Vita was precisely what Woolf would go on to do in *Orlando*, the plan for which was made by October 1927: 'a biography beginning in the year 1500 & continuing to the present day, called Orlando; Vita; only with a change about from one sex to another' (*D3* 161). In a letter to Sackville-West on the book's completion, Woolf asked: 'will my feelings for you be changed? I've lived in you all these months—coming out, what are you really like? Do you exist? Have I made you up?' (*L3* 474). Questions of identity become particularly complex and uncertain in *Orlando*'s final section, set in the present day, as Woolf indicates the ways in which modern psychology posits the existence of the multiple selves that compose a single individual: 'For [Orlando] had a great many selves to call upon, far more than we have been able to find room for, since a biography is considered complete if it merely accounts for six or seven selves, whereas a person may well have many thousand' (*O* 282). Katherine Mansfield expressed a similar thought in her journals: 'True to oneself! which self! Which of my many—well really, hundreds of selves ... there are moments when I feel I am nothing but the small clerk of some hotel without a proprietor, who has all his work cut out to enter the names and hand the keys to the wilful guests.'[4]

Yet Mansfield also indicated her simultaneous belief in 'a self which is continuous and permanent', and Woolf, too, in the closing pages of *Orlando*, refers to a 'Captain self, the Key self, which amalgamates and controls' all the others, and also to 'what is called, rightly or wrongly, a single self, a real self' (*O* 286). Both Mansfield and Woolf were addressing a question central to both classical and modern thought, as in Henri

---

[4] Margaret Scott, ed., *The Katherine Mansfield Notebooks*, vol. 2 (Canterbury, NZ: Lincoln University Press, 1997), 204.

Bergson's exploration of the issue of the unity and the multiplicity of selfhood in the philosophy of Plotinus, whose central question was, in Bergson's words: 'How can our person be on the one hand one or single, on the other hand multiple'. Plotinus's answer was, Bergson wrote, that 'each of us was multiple "in our lower nature" and single "in our higher nature"',[5] a hierarchy that Bergson did not embrace, though he acknowledged its force. For Woolf, as for Mansfield, the concept of a single and continuous self was to some extent connected to a model of unconscious life. Orlando, despite his sex change and the radical reshaping of his/her outward appearance and manners by the 'spirit of the age[s]' (O 215) through which he/she lives, remains fundamentally the same.

The concept of the 'Captain self, the Key self' also bears on a fundamental tenet of 'the new biography': that there is a 'key to character' in each life, which provides a structure and a pattern to the life both as lived and as represented by the biographer. For Maurois: 'A human life is always made up of a number of such motifs: when you study one of them, it will soon begin to impress itself upon you with a remarkable force.'[6] For some of Maurois's biographer contemporaries, including the German Emil Ludwig and the American Gamaliel Bradford, the narrative of development and the chronological depiction of a life were resisted in favour of a focus on an essential self, transcending time. Biography becomes closely connected to portraiture, an aspect of the genre with which Woolf played in her inclusion in *Orlando* of portraits (including those of Vita's Sackville ancestors) and of photographs of Vita at different stages of life. *Orlando* is written in full awareness of the biographical theories of the time, and both entertains and parodies these.

The text also repeatedly poses the question of sexual identity: 'she seemed to vacillate; she was man; she was woman; she shared the secrets, shared the weakness of each' (O 147). A fascination with sexuality fuelled much of the concern with 'character' in the early twentieth century. Nicolson, in *The Development of English Biography*, postulated a future for 'scientific biography': 'there will be biographies examining the influence of heredity—biographies founded on Galton, on Lombroso, on Havelock Ellis, on Freud; there will be medical biographies—studies of the influence of character on the endocrine glands, studies of internal secretions.'[7] The sexologist Havelock Ellis had, in his account of 'scientific biography', explored homosexuality and the part played by heredity and embryology in the 'making' of the homosexual.

Woolf undermined such scientific certainties in her account of Orlando's sex change—'Let biologists and psychologists determine. It is enough for us to state the simple fact; Orlando was a man till the age of thirty, when he became a woman and has remained so ever since' (O 128)—while interweaving, both seriously and satirically, the narratives of sexual and gender identity of her times. Her assertion that 'Different though the sexes are, they intermix' (O 173), for example, seems to echo Freud's claims that 'both in male and female individuals masculine as well as feminine instinctual

---

[5] Henri Bergson, *Mélanges*, ed. André Robinet (Paris: Presses Universitaires de France, 1972), 1055.
[6] Maurois, *Aspects of Biography*, 71–2.
[7] Harold Nicolson, *The Development of English Biography* (London: Hogarth Press, 1927), 154–5.

impulses are found, and ... each can equally well undergo repression and so become unconscious'.[8] In her posthumously published journals, Sackville-West repeatedly referred to her 'dual' nature—'I advance, therefore, the perfectly accepted theory that cases of dual personality do exist, in which the feminine and the masculine elements alternately preponderate'[9]—and one of the 'gifts' that Woolf made to her in the writing of *Orlando* was the narrative embodiment of this theme. Sackville-West alludes in the journals to her own adventures in cross-dressing (in Paris with her lover Violet Trefusis), in which she writes of masquerading as a boy: 'I never appreciated anything so much as living like that with my tongue perpetually in my cheek, and in defiance of every policeman I passed'.[10]

In the final section of the novel/biography, Orlando wins a prize for the poem, 'The Oak Tree', which he/she has been writing over the course of the centuries 'and we must snatch space to remark how discomposing it is for her biographer that this culmination to which the whole book moved, this peroration with which the book was to end, should be dashed from us on a laugh casually like this; but the truth is that when we write of a woman, everything is out of place—culminations and perorations; the accent never falls where it does with a man' (*O* 284–5). *Orlando* transgresses the absoluteness of the division between the sexes, putting into question what it might be to write 'of a woman', or indeed 'of a man', but the passage is nonetheless at one with Woolf's broader commitment to the expression of the 'difference' of women's lives, central to the arguments of *A Room of One's Own*, and to exploration of the ways in which the writing of those lives would necessitate a different understanding of the 'life-course' to that of conventional biography. 'To try the accepted forms', Woolf wrote in a review-essay titled 'Men and Women', 'to discard the unfit, to create others which are more fitting, is a task that must be accomplished before there is freedom or achievement' (*E3* 195).

Orlando was followed by *The Waves* and *Flush*. *The Waves* developed as a form of group biography, at a time when Woolf was closely considering questions of ageing and changing and the shape of lives. The novel (whose first working title was *The Moths*) was also to be a form of 'impersonal' autobiography: 'This shall be Childhood; but it must not be my childhood', she wrote in her diary (*D3* 236). Biography—the charting of the lives and thoughts of the novel's six characters—was intertwined with autobiography, a dimension of 'the new biography' to which Woolf had pointed with her enjoinder to 'Consider one's own life'; that is, to impart to the biographical subject the felt complexities of one's own selfhood. Of *The Waves* Woolf wrote that 'the six characters are supposed to be one' adding: 'I come to feel more and more how difficult it is to collect oneself into one Virginia; even though the special Virginia in whose body I live for the moment is violently susceptible to all sorts of separate feelings' (*L4* 397). The experience of identity and the question of 'the one and the many', of unity and multiplicity

---

[8] Freud, 'A Child is Being Beaten', *The Complete Works of the Standard Edition*, vol. 17 (London: Hogarth Press), 202.

[9] Harold Nicolson, *Portrait of a Marriage* (London: Futura, 1974), 118.

[10] Nicolson, *Portrait of a Marriage*, 127.

(discussed earlier in relation to Plotinus and Bergson), are thus pursued throughout *The Waves*, as Woolf traces the six lives from childhood to adulthood. Bernard, who recounts their stories in the final part of the text to an unnamed auditor, is both a biographer and a biographical subject, though he questions the very notion of 'stories' and the adequacy of biographical narration to the intricacies of lives.

On completing *The Waves* and beginning *Flush*, her 'biography' of Elizabeth Barrett Browning's spaniel, Woolf wrote in her diary: 'It is a good idea I think to write biographies; to make them use my powers of representation reality accuracy; & to use my novels simply to express the general, the poetic. Flush is serving this purpose' (*D4* 40). *Flush* was inspired by Woolf's reading of the Browning love letters: 'the figure of their dog made me laugh so I couldn't resist making him a Life' (*L5* 161–2). As in the case of *Orlando*, *Flush* is closely connected to the debates about biographical writing of the period, including the question of 'the ethics of biography', recently raised in response to Rudolf Besier's stage-play *The Barretts of Wimpole Street* (1934), in which Besier had hinted at Elizabeth Barrett's father's incestuous desires for his daughter as the underlying reason for his tyrannical possessiveness towards her. *Flush* was also in dialogue with Strachey's biographical methods. As Woolf wrote to David Garnett: 'Yes, the last paragraph as originally written was simply Queen Victoria dying all over again—but I cut it out, when he was not there to see the joke' (*L5* 232). (Strachey died in 1932, as Woolf worked on the book.)

Woolf's perception of biography (for all the fantastical and experimental forms it took in her writing) as a 'solid world' (*D5* 141), in contrast to her fictional works, was most fully realized in her one 'straight' biography, the life of the art critic and artist Roger Fry, which his family asked her to write after Fry's death in September 1934. Woolf frequently referred, in her diaries and letters, to the difficulties of its writing, calling it 'drudgery' and a 'grind'. As she wrote in a letter to Ethel Smyth: 'Odd what a grind biography is. This is my favourite reading: what hard writing' (*L6* 262). Increasingly concerned as she was throughout the 1930s, as the political situation became ever more exigent, with the nature (and the complexities) of 'facts'—she first conceived *The Years* (1937) as a 'Novel-Essay', 'a novel of fact', and the question of 'fact' is central to *Three Guineas* (1938)—the marshalling of biographical evidence, and in particular the mass of Fry letters that were made available to her, proved a daunting (though ultimately rewarding) task.

Woolf's comments in her private writings on the choices she made in the biography's composition open up, in revealing ways, approaches to 'the art of biography' (the topic on which she wrote her 1939 essay), and her own doubts about her abilities as a biographer. She followed her own prescriptions, as laid out in her essay 'The New Biography', for the biographer's commitment to 'the truth of fact', describing her alternations between the Roger Fry biography and her early work on the novel that would become *Between the Acts* (1941) as 'switching from assiduous truth to wild ideas' (*D5* 159). At moments Woolf considered adopting the more novelistic approach taken by many of the biographers of her generation—'I think I will go on doggedly till I meet him myself—1909—& then attempt something more fictitious' (*D5* 155)—but this was ultimately not the line she followed, and she introduces her personal relationship to him in oblique and glimpsing ways: 'And another impression floated over the first glimpse of Roger Fry in the flesh—a glimpse caught a year or two before on a lawn at Cambridge' (*RF* 149). In the final version of the biography, the early chapters draw heavily on Fry's autobiographical writings; the biography opens with a fragment that formed part of a paper Fry had given to the Memoir Club, in which he described his early passion for the colour of a cluster of red poppies in his childhood garden (*RF* 15–16), so that autobiography enters strongly into the biographical text. In a later section, Woolf offers 'a skipping summary' of the pages of his letters (*RF* 66), thus refusing the comprehensive, and often numbing, duplication of letters characteristic of the Victorian 'lives and letters' mode.

While, then, Woolf did not produce anything like a 'fictitious' biography, there are traces of Strachey's model in the combining of documentation with the biographical subject's thoughts and feelings and faint echoes of the mock-biographical modes of *Jacob's Room* and *Orlando*. She returned, both in describing her ideas for the biography in her diaries and in the biography itself, to an image of 'a humming-bird hawk-moth hanging over a flower, quivering yet still' (*RF* 152). In *Roger Fry* (1940) this description refers to Fry's relationship to works of art, but it also looks back to the subversions of the biographer's task in *Jacob's Room*: 'But something is always impelling one to hum vibrating, like the hawk moth, at the mouth of the cavern of mystery, endowing Jacob Flanders with all sorts of qualities he had not at all ... Yet over him we hang vibrating' (*RF* 61). The 'skipping summary' of the letters in *Roger Fry* recalls a line in *Orlando* in which we are told of one 'episode' that Orlando 'skipped it, to get on with the text', and there are yet stronger echoes of *Orlando* in Woolf's account of Fry's early travels in Italy, in which she draws on his letters home: 'On he walked. He stayed with peasants in a farmhouse and had "a delightful feeling of being perfectly at home with them". Adventures befell him. He was taken for a brigand in his great straw hat; for some mysterious reason a man picked a quarrel with him' (*RF* 72). In the writing of *Roger Fry*, then, Woolf brought into the text elements of earlier works that had been highly subversive of the biographical act, even as she reiterated her commitment to 'assiduous truth'.

While *Roger Fry* is ostensibly structured along the lines of the familiar life-course of a man of privilege of his period—early childhood in an eminent family, public school days, Cambridge, European travel, marriage and family, career, and writings—Woolf shows throughout the biography that her subject was never at peace, or at one, with this conventional trajectory: 'he had a tradition, a background, behind him ... But another result of the profound peace was also obvious—it seemed necessary to revolt against it, to break it up' (*RF* 82–3). Fry was, she wrote, 'a man who lived many lives, the active, the contemplative, the public and the private' (*RF* 200). Woolf also alludes to the homosexual milieu of his early years, as in his friendships with G. Lowes Dickinson at Cambridge and John Addington Symonds and Horatio Brown in Venice. In 'The Art of Biography' (1939), written during the composition of *Roger Fry*, Woolf argued, in the context of a discussion of the centrality of 'facts', and their alteration by changes of culture and opinion: 'What was thought a sin is now known, by the light of facts won for us by the psychologists, to be perhaps a misfortune; perhaps a curiosity, perhaps neither one nor the other, but a trifling foible of no great importance one way or the other.

The accent on sex has changed within living memory' (*E6* 186). More difficult for Woolf were the personal elements of Fry's life in which she was closely involved, and in particular his love affair with her sister Vanessa Bell, which had begun in 1911: as Woolf wrote to her: 'I'm flummoxed entirely how to deal with your own letters. [...] What am I to say about you. [...] Do give me some views; how to deal with love so that we're not all blushing' (*L5* 285). Her decision (additionally affected by the fact that the Fry family would be asked to approve the biography) was to omit any reference to the relationship, though it was a shaping force in Fry's life.

Roger Fry was very well received, both by Woolf's circle (with the exceptions of Leonard Woolf, who was critical of the methods she had adopted, and Maynard Keynes, who suggested she write 'the real life', as opposed to 'The official life', for the Memoir Club (*D5* 314)) and by the broader reading public. 'Of course the great difficulty', Woolf wrote to Clive Bell, 'was not to intervene oneself, and yet not to be colourless. I've never done anything so devilishly difficult' (*L5* 411). To her friend the composer Ethel Smyth, Woolf wrote: 'It was an experiment in self-suppression; a gamble in R's power to transmit himself. And so rich and to me alive and various and masterly was he that I was certain he would shine by his own light better than through any painted shade of mine' (*L5* 417).

In December 1940, Woolf wrote to Smyth of the planned next volume of her voluminous autobiography: 'I'm awfully proud ... that you've started again on the autobiography, partly owing to me. I was thinking the other night that there's never been a womans [sic] autobiography. Nothing to compare with Rousseau. Chastity and modesty I suppose have been the reason' (*L5* 453). As Woolf was working on *Roger Fry*, she had begun to compose the autobiographical work that would be published posthumously as 'Sketch of the Past'. On 25 April 1939, she wrote in her diary: 'My mother, I was thinking, had 2 characters. I was thinking of my memoirs. The platform of time. How I see father from the 2 angles. As a child condemning; as a woman of 58 understanding—I shd say tolerating. Both views true?' (*D5* 281).

'The platform of time' became the structuring principle of the memoir, which includes memories and episodes Woolf had explored in her early journals. In her 1905 Cornwall diary, she had recorded her return with her siblings to the landscapes of her childhood, and their desire that 'we should find our past preserved, as though through all this time it had been guarded & treasured for us to come back to one day—it mattered not how far distant' (*PA* 281). The questions of time and distance and of loss and reparation lie at the heart of her most autobiographical novel, *To the Lighthouse*: 'So much depends then, thought Lily Briscoe [...] upon distance' (*TL* 258). In 'Sketch of the Past', 'the present' becomes a 'platform to stand on. It would be interesting to make the two people, I now, I then, come out in contrast. And further, this past is much affected by the present moment. What I write today I should not write in a year's time' (*MB* 75).

As she wrote these lines, war was being threatened, and the writing of the memoir (which is substantially structured in diary form) continued after war had been declared: 'I continue (22nd September 1940) on this wet day—we think of weather now as it affects invasions, as it affects raids, not as weather that we like or dislike privately' (*MB* 126). The question of how, or if, any semblance of 'private' life or of individuality could be sustained in the inevitable shift from the individual to the mass in a society at war—'"I" rejected: "We" substituted'—became the key image of her final, posthumously published novel *Between the Acts*—was a matter of grave concern to Woolf at this time. The writing of Roger Fry's biography and of her memoir seems to have provided her with some solace and refuge from public events, which she nonetheless assiduously recorded in her diaries.

Woolf's mother, Julia Stephen, and the impact of her death is at the heart of the memoir. The opening passages recall 'the first memory' (two memories in fact vie for primordiality) 'of red and purple flowers on a black ground—my mother's dress' and then 'of lying half-asleep, half-awake, in bed at the nursery at St Ives ... It is of lying and hearing this splash [of the waves] and seeing this light [behind a yellow blind], and feeling, it is almost impossible that I should be here, of feeling the purest ecstasy I can conceive' (*MB* 64). The first memory is of closeness to the mother, who fills the child's vision and who is, like the pattern on her dress, both foreground and background. 'There she was', Woolf writes later in the memoir, 'in the very centre of that great Cathedral space which was childhood; there she was from the very first' (*MB* 81). The second ('first') memory seems to mark the emergence of self-consciousness, of a sense of separate identity that is also a sense of oneness with the surrounding world. The sensory recall of these first memories is pursued throughout the memoir, as Woolf seeks not only to capture the moment's immediacy but also to recreate the quickness and vitality of her mother, whose image had become fixed by portraits and photographs and by the grieving Leslie Stephen's 1895 memoir of his dead wife, known by his children as 'The Mausoleum Book'.[11]

In the late 1939s, Woolf was reading Freud, perhaps for the first time in any depth: the concept that most struck her was that of 'ambivalence', the mixture of love and hate, which she applied to her feelings towards her father. Writing of her adolescent years, she notes: 'it was the tyrant father—the exacting, the violent, the histrionic, the demonstrative, the self-centred, the alternately loved and hated father—that dominated me then' (*MB* 116). 'Two different ages', she observed, 'confronted each other in the drawing room at Hyde Park Gate [her childhood home]. The Victorian age and the Edwardian age ... We looked at him with eyes that were looking into the future' (*MB* 147). This division becomes the material of the last part of the memoir, as Woolf describes the life she and Vanessa endured with her grieving and increasingly 'tyrannical' father and her conventional (but sexually rapacious) half-brothers in the years after her mother's death.

Early in the text Woolf describes an episode of sexual abuse that she endured, as a very young child, at the hands of her half-brother Gerald Duckworth, then a young man: 'I remember resenting disliking it—what is the word for so dumb and mixed a feeling? It must have been strong, since I still recall it' (*MB* 69). The incident and the feelings associated with it are linked to the memory of the guilt she experienced in looking at herself in a hall-mirror at Talland House in St. Ives: 'the looking-glass shame has lasted all

---

[11] Alan Bell, ed., *Sir Leslie Stephen's Mausoleum Book* (Oxford: Clarendon Press, 1977).

my life' (*MB* 68). Woolf offers several reasons—none of them definitive—for the 'shame' associated with both memories, which she suggests might be the product of 'some ancestral dread': 'It proves that Virginia Stephen was not born on the 25th January 1882, but was born many thousands of years ago; and had from the very first to encounter instincts already acquired by thousands of ancestresses in the past' (*MB* 69). Critics have tended to read this assertion as a way of displacing the 'trauma' of the childhood sexual experience, but it might also be suggested that Woolf was in fact particularly concerned with the emotion of 'shame', not only as an 'inherited characteristic'[12] but also as a powerful element in autobiographical writing, including that of Rousseau, who recounts 'shaming' memories as formative in his life. Woolf described the episode with Gerald Duckworth to Ethel Smyth in a letter of January 1941, connecting it closely to the question of reticence and candour about sexual matters in autobiographical writings:

> [A]s so much of life is sexual—or so they say—it rather limits autobiography if this is blacked out. It must be, I suspect, for many generations, for some; for its like breaking the hymen—if that's the membrane's name—a painful operation, and I suppose connected with all sorts of subterranean instincts. I still shiver with shame at the memory of my half brother, standing me on a ledge, aged about 6, and so exploring my private parts. Why should I have felt shame then? (*L6* 459–60)

Truth-telling—which might entail a woman's writing herself out of shame—thus becomes closely connected to the shaming memory. The relationship between the 'I now, I then', which, for Woolf, is both the structure and the problematic of autobiography, is at one with the question of the shaming memory in relation to the shame experienced at the time: 'Why should I have felt shame then?' In the letter, and in 'A Sketch of the Past', Woolf points towards the complexities of instincts, experiences, sensations, and feelings in ways that certainly suggest an engagement with Freud's thought, though the broader issue is that of the profound difficulties entailed in answering the question 'Who was I then?'

For all its immediacy—and Woolf was concerned to recapture 'the child's vision' of what had become the past—the memoir is deeply reflective about the act of memoir-writing, just as *Roger Fry* encodes in its composition the choices available to biographers. Woolf comments on the question of memory and the act of recall throughout *Sketch of the Past*—'I feel that strong emotion must leave its trace; and it is only a question of discovering how we can get ourselves attached to it, so that we shall be able to live our lives through from the start' (*MB* 67)—and on the difficulties confronting the memoir writer. The reason why 'so many are failures', she suggests, is because 'they leave out the person to whom things happened. The reason is that it is so difficult to describe any human being. So they say: "This is what happened"; but they do not say what the person

---

[12] See Laura Marcus, '"Some Ancestral Dread": Woolf, Autobiography, and the Question of "Shame"', in Jane de Gay, Anne Reus, and Tom Brecking, eds, *Virginia Woolf and Heritage* (Clemson, SC: Clemson University Press, 2017), 264–79.

was like to whom it happened' (*MB* 65). 'A Sketch of the Past' intertwines what Woolf had described in an essay on Thomas de Quincey as 'the two levels of existence' that the autobiographer 'must devise some means' to record: 'the rapid passage of events and actions; the slow opening up of single and solemn moments of concentrated emotion' (*E5* 457).

Woolf had already written about many of the events and experiences described in 'A Sketch of the Past': the piece now known as 'Reminiscences'[13] was written as an account of Julia Stephen and Vanessa Bell and addressed to Vanessa's oldest son Julian; '22 Hyde Park Gate' (*E5* 31–42) (delivered in November 1920) was a Memoir Club contribution, in which Woolf offered a comic and unsparing account of the characters of, and life with, her Duckworth half-brothers, Gerald and George, before the Stephen children made their escape to Bloomsbury. These materials, however, take on a different light in 'A Sketch of the Past', in which Woolf seeks not only to remember and represent the world of her childhood but also to explore, as I have suggested, fundamental questions of identity and, more specifically, of 'what makes me a writer' (*MB* 72). The memoir is where Woolf came closest to describing a 'philosophy' of life: 'that behind the cotton wool there is a pattern; that we—I mean all human beings—are connected with this; that the whole world is a work of art; that we are parts of the work of art' (*MB* 72). For Woolf, to live and to write were one and the same.

Selected Bibliography

Bell, Alan, ed., *Sir Leslie Stephen's Mausoleum Book* (Oxford: Clarendon Press, 1977).
Marcus, Laura, '"Some Ancestral Dread": Woolf, Autobiography, and the Question of "Shame"', in Jane de Gay, Anne Reus, and Tom Brecking, eds, *Virginia Woolf and Heritage* (Clemson, SC: Clemson University Press, 2017), 264–79.
Maurois, André, *Aspects of Biography* (Cambridge: Cambridge University Press, 1929).
Nicolson, Harold, *The Development of English Biography* (London: Hogarth Press, 1927).
Nicolson, Harold, *Portrait of a Marriage* (London: Futura, 1974).
Strachey, Lytton, *Eminent Victorians: Cardinal Manning, Florence Nightingale, Dr Arnold, General Gordon* (London: Chatto & Windus, 1918).

---

[13] Woolf began this memoir in 1907, and it was posthumously published in *Moments of Being*.

PART IV
PROFESSIONS OF WRITING

CHAPTER 15

LITERARY LONDON

HELEN SOUTHWORTH

On 9 January 1924, when Virginia Woolf purchased the ten-year lease that would seal her move to Tavistock Square in Bloomsbury, after an eleven-year absence from central London, nine of which she lived in Richmond at Hogarth House, she waxed poetic in her diary.[1] Paraphrasing poet William Dunbar, Woolf celebrated the social, artistic, and literary importance of London: 'London thou art a jewel of jewels, & jasper of jocunditie—music, talk, friendship, city views, books, publishing, something central & inexplicable, all this is now within my reach' (*D2* 283). In the middle of writing *Mrs Dalloway*, one of many, but perhaps her best-known London novel, finished at the end of 1924 and published in the spring of 1925, and seven years into her work with husband Leonard Woolf at their Hogarth Press (1917–1946), which would find its most permanent home at Tavistock Square in Bloomsbury, Woolf was ready to be back at the heart of the culturally, socially, and professionally rich capital.

Woolf's 1924 paean encapsulates her attachment to literary London, as it celebrates, in the wake of Modernism's *annus mirabilis*, the intertwined networks of books and publishing, talk and friendship, and music and city views that epitomized the capital. Although often downplayed as a 'modernist city', as Malcolm Bradbury argues, 'London saw extraordinary artistic turbulence over the crucial years of 1880 to 1920'. At this period, London was a 'cultural frontier'; a place where 'clusterings of migrant artists', 'willing and unwilling [expatriates] and exiles' drove the production of 'interfusing movements and tendencies.'[2] London was also 'a "world city" with a world hinterland, an entrepôt for culture, publishing, finance and shipping, a magnet for internal migration, from other parts of England, and for external migration from the rest of the world.'[3] But,

---

[1] The actual move took place on 13 and 14 March, with the first night in the house 15 March (*D2* 297).

[2] Malcolm Bradbury, 'London 1890–1920', in Malcolm Bradbury and James McFarlane, eds, *Modernism: A Guide to European Literature* (London: Penguin, 1976), 79, 13. Bradbury identifies the generation in London before the war as Pound, H.D., Frost, Eliot, Mansfield, and Lewis 'looking for new art of twentieth-century *Risorgimento*'. Before them came Conrad, Harland, Crane, Moore, Wilde, Yeats, and Shaw (177).

[3] Asa Briggs, qtd in Bradbury and MacFarlane, *Modernism*, 180.

as Bradbury goes on to argue, a view supported by the recent work of Alexandra Harris among others, London was also a place with a strong local culture, and the local meshed with these external influences in very complicated and productive ways.[4] Bradbury notes, for example, that while 'Bloomsbury was famously Francophile', it also had strong native ties to Ruskin, Pater, and G.E. Moore.[5]

How did the work of Woolf, in many ways the homegrown, quintessentially English writer, contribute to or grow out of this turbulent metropolitan mix of the local and global? What does it mean to consider Woolf as a London writer? Does such a designation limit her or is it conversely to acknowledge the rich cosmopolitanism of her imagination? What did London mean to Woolf? Did it imply a sense of being at 'the centre of things' or was it about access to culture?[6] And what was culture for Woolf? Was it the theatre and the museum or the weight of patriarchy and empire in Whitehall, or was it the Hogarth Press and the agency her own publishing house afforded her?

Place matters, as Sara Blair argues in her 'Local Modernity, Global Modernism: Bloomsbury and the Places of the Literary'. Borrowing from new cultural geographers such as David Harvey, Saskia Sassen, and Anthony Giddens, Blair suggests that it means something for 'culture and subjects to be located'.[7] Thus, Blair reads Bloomsbury not as an aura, but as a 'local world', a 'geocultural landscape' in which '[the work and works of modernism] unfold': and she defines modernism as 'among other things a determined response to the specific spaces in which it takes shape, advertises its cultural value, and contests for social power'.[8] In this sense, for Blair, Bloomsbury is both a 'project', 'a cultural phenomenon constituted through networks of conversation, contact and exchange', and a 'place'. It is only by disentangling these two, she suggests, that one can, perhaps counterintuitively, better understand its global dimensions.[9] Following Blair here, this chapter interrogates London as both project and place, as professional and social milieu, as well as an inspiration for Woolf's imagination. Expanding

---

[4] Alexandra Harris, *Romantic Moderns: English Writers and Artists and the Imagination from Virginia Woolf to John Piper* (London: Thames and Hudson, 2010).

[5] Bradbury, 'London 1890–1920', 176.

[6] In *Night and Day*, Mary Datchet thinks about her life in 'the wonderful maze of London, which still seemed to her, in spite of her constitutional level-headedness, like a vast electric light, casting radiance upon the myriads of men and women who crowded round it. And here she was at the *very centre of it*, that centre which was constantly in the minds of people in remote Canadian forests and on the plains of India, when their thoughts turned to England' (44; emphasis added). In her diary, Woolf wrote: 'My theory is that for some reason the human mind is always seeking what it conceives to be the centre of things: sometimes one may call it reality, again truth, again life' (D1 205).

[7] Sara Blair, 'Local Modernity, Global Modernity: Bloomsbury and the Places of the Literary', *English Literary History* 71, no. 3 (Fall 2004), 813.

[8] Blair, 'Local Modernity', 814.

[9] Blair, 'Local Modernity', 815. Using guidebooks from the period (1900–1915), Blair productively interrogates the tension between built space and social practice in terms of defining 'Bloomsbury', real place, and social phenomenon; she 'embeds' 'Bloomsbury' in Bloomsbury (830).

on Blair, this chapter moves outside Bloomsbury and explores a larger London scene.[10] Focusing on the period up to 1924, it follows Woolf from Kensington to Bloomsbury, from Bloomsbury to Richmond, and then back.

From Kensington to Bloomsbury

The Stephen family was well connected in literary and artistic coterie London well before Virginia Stephen's birth. Leslie Stephen's first marriage connects Virginia Woolf to the Thackerays and to the evangelical Christian social reformer Clapham sect, considered a Bloomsbury precursor; her mother's aunt was photographer Julia Margaret Cameron and her uncle was Thoby Prinsep, whose Little Holland House artistic salon in Kensington, with painter George Frederic Watts, would provide Woolf's mother, Julia Jackson (later Duckworth, then Stephen) an education in Pre-Raphaelite painting.[11] When they lived at Hyde Park Gate, in Kensington, where Leslie Stephen was born, the Stephen-Duckworth's neighbours included *Times Literary Supplement* editor Bruce Lyttleton Richmond (from its founding in 1902 until 1937). Richmond was, early on, according to Anne Olivier Bell and Andrew McNeillie, 'VW's staunchest patron' (*D2* 11). Richmond's wife Elena (Rathbone) had been part of the Duckworth-Stephen social circle, known as the 'Hyde Park Gaters', in Kensington in Virginia Stephen's youth.

Following Leslie Stephen's death (1904), when Virginia was twenty-two years old, Vanessa Stephen moved the Stephen siblings in 1905 to Gordon Square in the then unfashionable Bloomsbury. In 'Old Bloomsbury', Woolf suggests that one motivating factor for Vanessa's choice of Bloomsbury was precisely its spiritual distance from upper-middle-class Kensington; in her diary, Woolf describes 'the gulf which we crossed between Kensington & Bloomsbury [as] the gulf between respectable mum[m]ified humbug & life crude & impertinent perhaps, but living' (*D1* 206). It was here in 1905 that Virginia, Vanessa, and Thoby established first an Apostles-like insular 'club' in London with Thoby's Thursday nights. Vanessa Bell's more capacious art exhibition and discussion Friday Club was established at the same time (1904–1922), involving many artists from outside Bloomsbury, including John Nash, Derwent Lees, C.R.W. Nevinson, and Edward Wadsworth, as well as a good number of women artists such as Sylvia Milman and Gwen Raverat.[12] Both of these clubs were seeds from which the Bloomsbury Group would grow. When Vanessa married Clive Bell, Virginia ceded the Gordon Square house to the newlyweds and moved with brother Adrian to Fitzroy Square in 1907, described by Duncan Grant as 'a derelict square', 'houses [...] decayed', 'taken as offices, lodgings,

---

[10] Dorothy Brewster, *Virginia Woolf's London* (New York: New York University Press, 1960), 7. Brewster argues that Woolf's London is 'more like an insubstantial pageant than a city that can be mapped in a guide-book. Yet her London is abundantly, though not always precisely, identifiable.'
[11] Hermione Lee, *Virginia Woolf* (London: Vintage, 1997), 51–2, 90.
[12] See Richard Shone, 'The Friday Club', *The Burlington Magazine* 117, no. 866 (May 1975), 278–84.

nursing homes, artisans' workshops'.[13] And in 1911, Virginia Stephen and Adrian moved to their third Bloomsbury square, Brunswick, where they set up home with John Maynard Keynes, Grant, and Leonard Woolf.[14]

The Bloomsbury Group was never 'official'. As Hermione Lee reminds us, there was neither a Bloomsbury manifesto nor a subscription, nor was there a single address or headquarters.[15] However, as S.P. Rosenbaum's work, and, more recently, work in Victoria Rosner's *Cambridge Companion to the Bloomsbury Group* and Derek Ryan's and Stephen Ross's *Handbook to the Bloomsbury Group* demonstrates, there was a certain orthodoxy.[16] 'Old' or original Bloomsbury was, at its core and to start, the indigenous and the connected, more provincial than metropolitan, more Cambridge than London, more male than female. Woolf describes Cambridge somewhat derisively in *Jacob's Room* (1922) as 'a suburb where you go to see a view and eat a special cake' (*JR* 50); Oxbridge is a place Woolf's narrator turns her back on in favour of London in *A Room of One's Own* (1929), a book Lee describes as 'as much [...] about London as about the history, education and writing of women in England'.[17] Examples of connected Bloomsbury include Desmond and Molly MacCarthy and Lytton Strachey. Both men were at Cambridge and both were Apostles, and all three had family ties to the Stephens.[18] However, despite this tight knit core, the individuals who made up the Bloomsbury Group were not exclusive nor were they always tied to the London neighbourhood called Bloomsbury. Complicating the locational implications of the moniker, while Bloomsbury was where the group met to start, many of those considered core Bloomsbury Group members did not live in Bloomsbury or limit themselves to Bloomsbury, including the Woolfs who lived in Richmond between 1914 and 1924 and the MacCarthys who lived in Chelsea. As Regina Marler suggests, 'a collective name', although useful, 'was slightly absurd'. And Marler cites Virginia Woolf's playful habit in the 1930s of '[calling] her younger friends "Maida Vale" or "Hampstead."'[19]

Around 1908–1910, as the Bloomsbury Group quickly transitioned away from the more exclusive Cambridge Apostle model, new groups shaped and contributed to it. Among these groups were the Cambridge Neo-Pagans, including painters

---

[13] Qtd. in Morag Shiach, 'Domestic Bloomsbury', in Victoria Rosner, ed., *The Cambridge Companion to the Bloomsbury Group* (Cambridge: Cambridge University Press, 2014), 61.

[14] Harris, *Romantic Moderns*, 47. Lee argues that while 'Bloomsbury' (the term, used as a joke to start, dates to 1910) represented a reaction against Victorian life, it did, 'in fact developed ... the social habits, mannerisms and ways of thinking of *an excluding network*' (55). Virginia Woolf compared Bloomsbury at this period to 'the lion's cage at the Zoo. One goes from cage to cage. All the animals are dangerous, rather suspicious of each other, and full of fascination and mystery' (*L2* 451).

[15] Lee, *Virginia Woolf*, 263.

[16] For example, S. P. Rosenbaum, ed., *Edwardian Bloomsbury* and *Victorian Bloomsbury. A Collection of Memoirs and Commentary* (Toronto: University of Toronto Press, 1995).

[17] Lee, *Virginia Woolf*, 553. Woolf's narrator visits Cambridge (mixed with Oxford), but remains an outsider there, in *A Room of One's Own* (1929).

[18] Lee, *Virginia Woolf*, 209. Molly MacCarthy was related to the Stephens via Anne Ritchie.

[19] Regina Marler, 'Bloomsbury's Afterlife', in Rosner, ed., *The Cambridge Companion to the Bloomsbury Group*, 217.

Augustus John, Jacques Raverat and friends, and Ottoline Morrell's Oxfordshire satellite Garsington Manor set.[20] In London, the Slade art school cohorts, which included Percy Wyndham Lewis and John, and in a next generation, Dora Carrington, Mark Gertler, Paul Nash, and Stanley Spencer, had an important influence on the Bloomsbury Group, as did those who congregated at Wyndham Lewis's short-lived Rebel Art Centre (1914) and Roger Fry's longer standing Omega Workshops (1913–1920), all of these in Bloomsbury. Other addresses significant in terms of the broader London art and literature scene in the late 1910s and the early 1920s included the Eiffel Tower restaurant in the then somewhat lugubrious Soho, haunt of American Imagists Hilda Doolittle (H.D.) and Ezra Pound. H.D. had moved to London in 1911 and had lived with D.H. Lawrence (1885–1930) for a time in Mecklenburgh Square.[21] Mecklenburgh Square would be briefly the home of the Woolfs' Hogarth Press between 1939 and 1940. London's equivalent to Parisian cafes were its nightclubs, such as the Cave of the Golden Calf at 9 Heddon Street, just off Regent Street (1912–1914), also frequented by Pound, Katherine Mansfield, Ford Madox Ford, John, and Wyndham Lewis. Clive Bell and Mary Hutchinson, in 1918, favoured the Café Royale at 68 Regent Street in Piccadilly (*D*1 151).

That Virginia and Leonard Woolf's friend network always extended beyond Bloomsbury is illustrated by a 1919 entry from Woolf's diary. The meandering quality of Woolf's description beautifully exemplifies the organic way in which her social circles changed over time. It also suggests the degree to which Woolf identified people with places. Anticipating a return to her own diary in search of memoir material, perhaps, she thinks, at age fifty, Woolf, then almost thirty-seven years old, plans 'an account of my friendships & their present condition, with some account of my friends [sic] characters.' She begins: 'How many friends have I got?' and continues:

> There's Lytton, Desmond, Saxon; they belong to the Cambridge stage of life; very intellectual; cut free from Hyde Park Gate; connected with Thoby; but I can't put them in order, for there are too many. Ka & Rupert & Duncan, for example, all come rather later; they belong to Fitzroy days; the Oliviers & all that set are stamped as the time of Brunswick Sqre; Clive I put a little aside; later still there are the cropheads, Alix, Carrington, Barbara, Nick, Bunny. I must insert too the set that runs parallel but does not mix, distinguished by their social & political character, headed perhaps by Margaret & including people like Goldie, Mrs Hamilton & intermittent figures such as Matthaei, Hobson, and Webbs—no, I can't include either the darkies, or Dr Leys, though they stand for the occasional visitor who lunches & retires to L.'s room to talk seriously. I have not placed Ottoline or Roger, & again there are Katherine & Murry & the latest of all, Hope Mirrlees, who recalls Pernel & Pippa & outlying

---

[20] Lee, *Virginia Woolf*, 239. Interestingly, in terms of the layering of the local and the cosmopolitan, Woolf would send the manuscript of her London novel *Mrs Dalloway* to Raverat as he lay dying in France.

[21] See Robert Crunden, 'London, Where Ezra Pound Appropriated the Salons of Yeats and Hueffer', in *American Salons* (Oxford: Oxford University Press, 1993), on connections with George Orwell, Stevie Smith, Mulk Raj Anand, and Inez Holden.

figures such as Ray & Oliver. Gertler I must omit (& Mary Hutch. too.) for reasons which if my account gets written I might give; & Eliot I liked on the strength of one visit & shall probably see more of, owing to his poems which we began today to set up. (*D1* 234–5)

Woolf's catalogue takes in Cambridge, Bloomsbury, Leonard's political and journalistic sphere in London and beyond, and closes with the spaces of the Hogarth Press. As it does so, it highlights the degree to which the exclusivity and insularity of Cambridge and the values inherited from Hyde Park Gate, where Bloomsbury had its roots, were impossible in a broader modern(ist) London. Woolf's use of the term 'darkies' is racist and is, unfortunately, not isolated to this instance.[22] It is likely a reference to, among others, Parmenas Githendu Mockerie, Kenyan colleague of Scottish Doctor and anti-imperialist Norman Leys, and like Leys, a Hogarth Press author (Githendu Mockerie published *An African Speaks for his People* in 1934 and Leys *Kenya* in 1924, *A Last Chance in Kenya* in 1931, and *The Colour Bar in East Africa* in 1941). Although Leonard's political activities and Woolf's own work at the press clearly broadened her scope, these opportunities did not erase her own biases. This passage shows how cosmopolitan Woolf's life was even in 1919, when American T.S. Eliot, in London since 1914, makes a first appearance. In London, Woolf's social circles inevitably expanded and proliferated. Bloomsbury's borders were 'loose and fluid': parallel sets emerged; some groups mixed, others did not.[23]

In her biography of Roger Fry (1866–1934), Woolf captures this new openness when she describes Fry's vision of Bloomsbury as a 'society of moderate means, a society based upon the old Cambridge ideal of truth and free speaking, but alive, as Cambridge never had been, to the importance of the arts' (*RF* 184). Fry was just one of several key figures in terms of opening Bloomsbury up to the outside. Along with Duncan Grant and Carrington and their Slade art school friends, Fry turned everyone's attention from philosophy to art at the same time as Clive Bell introduced French art and socializing to Bloomsbury.[24] Fry was very close to the Woolfs, spending time working at the Hogarth Press in its earliest days in Richmond, Fry 'scraping at his woodcuts while [Woolf] sewed [books]'. When he started collaborating with the Woolfs, Fry brought 'people [to Hogarth House] in shoals' (*D2* 108). As a result of his work at the Grafton Galleries, located first on Grafton Street in Mayfair and then in Bond Street, where he curated the first of two Post-Impressionist art shows in 1910, *Manet and the Postimpressionists*, including work of Seurat, Van Gogh, Gauguin, and Cézanne, Fry brought Paris to London. His editorship of the London-based *The Burlington Magazine* from 1909 to 1919, produced first in New Burlington Street and later in Fitzrovia's Berners Street, as well as his creation of The Omega Workshops in Fitzroy Square beginning in 1913, put

---

[22] See Gretchen Holbrook Gerzina's 'Bloomsbury and Empire' in Rosner ed. *The Cambridge Companion to the Bloomsbury Group*, 112–27.

[23] Rosner, *The Cambridge Companion to the Bloomsbury Group*, 2.

[24] Lee, *Virginia Woolf*, 239.

Fry at the heart of the London art scene.[25] As he distanced himself from older garde British artists, encouraged by new, although mixed, experiences in the United States working for J.P. Morgan, Fry's hosting of the second, 1912 Post-Impressionist art show, this time featuring French, Russian, and British artists, with Leonard Woolf as secretary, brought him closer to a younger generation of English artists. Among these younger artists was Woolf's sister Vanessa Bell, Fry's lover for a time.

E.M. Forster (1879–1970), like Fry, had one foot in Bloomsbury and the other outside. Forster had been at King's College, Cambridge from 1897 to 1901, becoming an Apostle in 1901, and had forged friendships with Leonard Woolf, Strachey, and Keynes there. But, as David Garnett contended, 'Morgan Forster was on the periphery rather than at the heart of [the Bloomsbury] circle'.[26] Woolf knew Forster by reputation first; they became friends after he presented at the Friday Club in 1910. Forster did not move to London until 1925, and he chose Brunswick Square and later Chiswick. While Woolf appears to have found Forster misogynistic, he was clearly a close friend and very influential in terms of her writing.[27] In 1924 when the Woolfs moved to Tavistock Square, Forster published his last novel *A Passage to India* following *Pharos and Pharillon* in 1923 and thereafter just biography. His *Anonymity: An Enquiry* was published as a pamphlet by the Hogarth Press in 1925.

Forster would bring into Bloomsbury internal and external migrants like gay Birmingham Group writer John Hampson and Indian writer Mulk Raj Anand, whom Forster had met when Anand was working for Eliot at the *Criterion*. The Hogarth Press published Hampson's work in the late 1920s and Anand's in John Lehmann's journal *New Writing* in 1938. Anand recorded his time in London as *Conversations in Bloomsbury*, published in 1981, as did West-Indian writer C.L.R. James, another Hogarth Press author, in his *Letters from London*, a column originally written in 1932 for readers of Trinidad's *Port of Spain Gazette* and collected in a volume in 2003.[28] As Blair points out, many South Asian writers, including Anand, who studied philosophy in 1929, were in Bloomsbury for University College in Gower Street. University College had come into existence precisely for non-Anglicans, barred from Oxbridge until 1871.[29] Embedded

---

[25] 'Editorial: Fifty Years of the Burlington Magazine', *Burlington Magazine* 95, no. 600 (March 1953), 63–5.

[26] Qtd. in David Medalie, 'Bloomsbury and Other Values', in David Bradshaw, ed., *The Cambridge Companion to E.M. Forster* (Cambridge: Cambridge University Press, 2007), 36. Medalie argues that '[Forster's] fiction in particular, is much more profitably read as an exploration, even a critique, of Bloomsbury values than as an exposition of them'.

[27] Jane Goldman, 'Forster and Women', in David Bradshaw, ed., *The Cambridge Companion to Forster* (Cambridge: Cambridge University Press, 2007), 128. Bill Goldstein has a more positive take on the relationship shared by Woolf and Forster: *The World Broke in Two* (New York: Henry Holt, 2017), 24–26. Woolf says she 'likes [Forster] very much, though I find him whimsical & vagulous to an extent that frightens me with my own clumsiness & definiteness' (D1 291).

[28] C. L. R. James, *Letters from London*, ed. Nicholas Laughlin, Introduction by Kenneth Ramchand (London: Signal Books, 2003). James's *The Case for West-Indian Self Government* was published by the Hogarth Press in 1933.

[29] Blair, 'Local Modernity', 821.

in London's emergent culture industries, Anand apprenticed with the Woolfs at the Hogarth Press, as he had with Eliot. During World War II, he worked, along with Forster, George Orwell, and Tamil poet, critic, and publisher M.J. Tambimuttu, at the BBC. These collaborations demonstrate the social and cultural richness of interwar London life in the context of which Bloomsbury emerges as a cross section of something much more alive, sprawling, ambitious and ambiguous than Bloomsbury has sometimes been understood to be.

From Bloomsbury to Richmond

Virginia Woolf's move to suburban Richmond in 1913 represented an exile of sorts. However, it also enabled a revaluation of London from the periphery. Woolf wrote her first novel, *The Voyage Out* (1915), in the early years of her marriage while living with Leonard in Bloomsbury's Cliffords Inn (Chancery Lane), an address that ties her biographically and literarily to one of the greatest London writers, Charles Dickens. However, she wrote and published *Night and Day* (1919) and *Jacob's Room*, and wrote most of *Mrs Dalloway* (1925), while living in then suburban Richmond. Woolf also launched the Hogarth Press from Richmond; famously announcing in her diary of 25 January 1913, on her thirty-third birthday, her intention to buy Hogarth House, a printing press, and a bulldog named John, at the same time.

Susan Squier sees Woolf's 'retreat' from the city as 'the primary solution to the conflict between social and intellectual duties in a woman's life'; Squier characterizes Woolf's move back to Bloomsbury in 1924 and in *Mrs Dalloway* as a return to the maternal and the social she had previously avoided.[30] Woolf's relationship with London changed when she was in Richmond and the distance from and subsequent return to the centre translated itself into a new kind of vision. Certainly, there is a sense of celebratory rediscovery in *Jacob's Room* where Jacob comes of age in London between chapters 5 and 10 of fourteen, a perspective revisited again in *Mrs Dalloway*, where Elizabeth Dalloway's coming of age in the capital echoes Jacob's. A change in style and form, a move from the greater realism of *The Voyage Out* and *Night and Day* to the stream of consciousness of *Jacob's Room* and *Mrs Dalloway*, also accompanies Woolf's move back into the city.

Woolf knew London and its neighbourhoods well and her careful representation of real locations affirms her connection to the city and its history. However, as Jean Moorcroft Wilson argues, 'London is rarely used simply as a convenient setting'. For Dorothy Brewster, Woolf's representations of London are at the centre of her artistic dilemma about how to square the internal and the external, and, as Catherine Lanone suggests, London was Woolf's palimpsest, 'a cityscape' she constantly 'shap[ed] into

---

[30] Susan M. Squier, *Virginia Woolf and London: The Sexual Politics of the City* (Chapel Hill: University of North Carolina Press, 1985), 91–2.

textual experience'.[31] David Bradshaw notes that '*The Voyage Out* begins with Helen and Ridley Ambrose walking down from the Strand to the freighted milieu of the Victoria Embankment', for Bradshaw a 'majestic-cum-iniquitous location' symbolic in terms of 'Woolf's thematic priorities'.[32] In *Night and Day*, Ralph Denham's middle-class family live in suburban Highgate, while Katharine Hilbery's more well-to-do and connected people live in Knightsbridge. In the opening pages of the novel, Denham enters the Hilbery's home 'with the omnibuses and cabs still running in his head, and his body still tingling with his quick walk along the streets and in and out of traffic and foot-passengers' (*ND* 2). The first conversations of the gathering pertain to a Hilbery relative who has been exiled from London to Manchester (a reference to Woolf's exile in Richmond). When Denham escapes the Hilbery's stifling drawing-room he's 'glad' for the 'raw fog' and the 'the unpolished people who only wanted their share of the pavement allowed them' and we get a sense of Woolf's own love of walking in the city as the young man relishes the 'beat of his foot upon the pavement, and the glimpse which half-drawn curtains offered him of kitchens, dining-rooms, and drawing-rooms, illustrating with mute power different scenes from different lives' (*ND* 16). Denham's disappointment at his return to suburban Highgate, where he finds 'damp shrubs growing in front gardens and the absurd names painted in white upon the gates of those gardens', was surely somewhat Woolf's on returning to Richmond (*ND* 18).

When Woolf embarked on *Jacob's Room* in 1920, she envisioned 'a new novel' with 'a new form' where 'one thing should open out of another [giving] the looseness & lightness I want ... no scaffolding; scarcely a brick to be seen; all crepuscular, but the heart, the passion, humour, everything as bright as fire in the mist' (*D2* 13–14). Moorcroft Wilson argues that London precisely 'help[ed] [Woolf] shape her material, [helped her] give form to her novel'.[33] Indeed, in chapter 5 of *Jacob's Room*, the pace of the work changes as we find Jacob, formerly in Scarborough and Cambridge, newly lodged in the vicinity of Bloomsbury's Lamb's Conduit Street. In our first glimpses of Jacob in London he is in traffic at the colourful and bustling Mudie's corner in Oxford Street, where 'all the red and blue beads had run together on the string', from where he escapes into the half-lit silence of St. Paul's Cathedral (*JR* 85). Thereafter, Jacob, with London's 'multitudes' always at his shoulder, criss-crosses London (*JR* 87): among his haunts, the less reputable Soho and Hampstead-adjacent Haverstock Hill by night, and Holborn/Bloomsbury and the British Museum by day.

A sense of a London divided, similar to that found in *Jacob's Room*, organizes *Mrs Dalloway*, where Clarissa Dalloway's Westminster sits in opposition to Septimus's Bloomsbury. Clarissa's London consists of St. James's Park, Bond Street, Piccadilly, and Hatchard's bookshop. Septimus lodges first off the Euston Road and then with Italian

---

[31] Catherine Lanone, 'The Non-Linear Dynamics of Virginia Woolf's London: from Elation to Street Haunting', *Caliban: French Journal of English Studies* 25 (2009), 315–22.

[32] David Bradshaw, 'Woolf's London', in Bryony Randall and Jane Goldman, eds, *Virginia Woolf in Context* (Cambridge: Cambridge University Press, 2013), 231.

[33] Jean Moorcroft Wilson, *Virginia Woolf: Life and London* (London: Tauris Parke, 2000), 130.

wife Rezia on the Tottenham Court Road. Reminding us of the rich racial and social diversity of London, immigrant Rezia has heard of the shops in London from an aunt who lives in Soho and Septimus studies Shakespeare with Isabel Pole in Waterloo Road, a reference to Morley Memorial College for Working Men and Women, which was housed at the Old Vic. Balancing Clarissa's high society country life at Bourton is Septimus's provincial past and suburban future: he's from Stroud, Gloucestershire; he might have ended up in Purley, an allusion to Leonard Woolf's family's suburban Putney home (*MD* 76).

The tolling of Westminster's Big Ben, and of a second clock, St. Margaret's, functions as an essential structuring and linking device in *Mrs Dalloway*, as do other London sights and sounds. A passing unidentified dignitary, a backfiring car, a plane soaring overhead in the sky advertising toffee, all draw the eyes and ears of multiple characters. Clarissa and Septimus come together in Bond Street outside Mulberry's florist and flâneur Peter Walsh traverses the city from Clarissa's house to a bench in Regent's Park where he crosses paths with Rezia and Septimus (*MD* 19). Regent's Park and London's other parks, like Kew Gardens, were rich spaces for Woolf's imagination.

In his autobiography, Leonard Woolf remarks how the move to Tavistock Square in 1924 alerted him to London's contradictions, at once 'its huge, anonymous, metropolitan size' and, at the same time, 'its pockets of provincial, almost village life'. Leonard averred that 'if you scratch the surface of [the lives of Londoners] in 1924 you find yourself straight back in 1850 or even 1750 and 1650', adding that '[i]n the 15 years I lived in Tavistock Square I got to know a gallery of London characters who themselves lived in a kind of timeless London and in a society as different from that of Fleet Street, Westminster, Kensington, or Putney—all of which I have known—as Sir Thomas Bertram's in Mansfield Park must have been from Agamemnon's behind the Lion Gate in Mycenae'.[34] Virginia Woolf too cherished London's gallery of characters, from the 'seedy-looking nondescript man carrying a leather bag stood on the steps of St. Paul's Cathedral' (*MD* 25) to perhaps one of Woolf's best-remembered 'Anons', the beggar woman singing outside Regent's Park tube station:

> the voice of an ancient spring spouting from the earth; which issued, just opposite Regent's Park Tube station from a tall quivering shape, like a funnel, like a rusty pump, like a wind-beaten tree for ever barren of leaves which lets the wind run up and down its branches singing
> *ee um fah um so*
> *foo swee too eem oo*
> and rocks and creaks and moans in the eternal breeze. (*MD* 72–3)

During her partial suburban exile in Richmond, Woolf voyaged into central London regularly. Trains and buses figure prominently on Woolf's cityscapes: among the most

---

[34] Leonard Woolf, *Downhill All the Way: An Autobiography of the Years 1919–1939* (London: Harvest, 1967), 120.

famous examples 'the journey from Richmond to Waterloo [station]' in her 1924 essay 'Mr Bennett and Mrs Brown'. Other examples include Elizabeth Dalloway's bus ride up Whitehall and the Strand in *Mrs Dalloway*, 'a pirate', 'reckless, unscrupulous, bearing down ruthlessly, circumventing dangerously' (*MD* 121), and Jacob's joyous journey atop a Holborn bus in *Jacob's Room*: 'Oh yes, human life is very tolerable on the top of an omnibus in Holborn, when the policeman holds up his arm and the sun beats on your back, and if there is such a thing as a shell secreted by man to fit man himself here we find it, on the banks of the Thames, where the great streets join and St Paul's Cathedral, like the volute on the top of the snail shell, finishes it off' (*JR* 86).

One reason for Woolf's central London trips was the city's independent bookshops, which flourished in the Charing Cross Road. Woolf's many descriptions of her visits to this part of London on book-buying missions demonstrate what a source of inspiration it was for her. A favourite circuit for Woolf, according to Moorcroft Wilson, took in 'Partridge and Cooper's stationery shop in Fleet Street, Gordon Square, Mudie's Lending Library in New Oxford Street, and the 17 Club in Soho'.[35] Foyles Bookshop, founded in 1903, opened its first store in 1904 and moved in 1906 to 135 Charing Cross Road. Zwemmer's (est. c. 1922), specializing in art and modern literature, and F.B. Neumayer were also both in the Charing Cross Road. Simpkin and Marshall (1814–1955), wholesale bookseller and distributor, was based in Paternoster Row, long a hub for the book trade. In 1921, Charles Lahr took over the Progressive Bookshop in Holborn, from where he would publish the *New Coterie* magazine between 1925 and 1927 and in 1931 launch the Blue Moon Press. Friends and clients included D.H. Lawrence, C.L.R. James, and, later, Olive Moore.

The British Museum's Reading Room was also an important destination for Woolf, as it was for many women writers, and it figures in both *Jacob's Room* and *A Room of One's Own*. Not only did Katherine Mansfield write there, but Pound and H.D. are said to have created Imagism in the museum tea room in 1912. Both Virginia and Leonard Woolf also frequented the London Library at 14 St. James's Square, although Virginia found it too stuffy (*D3* 80). The London Library was a private institution of which Leslie Stephen had been president, following Tennyson in this role. It features in Woolf's short story 'A Society' as Poll's domain; her father has left her his fortune on the condition she read all the books contained therein.

Another important city meeting place for Woolf during this period of exile was the Bloomsbury adjacent 1917 Club. The 1917 was a club for socialists established by Leonard Woolf and Ramsay MacDonald in October 1917, in the same year as the Hogarth Press, and funded by Maynard Keynes and others. It was located at 4, then 5, Gerrard Street, Soho. Leonard identifies Gerrard Street as 'in those days the rather melancholy haunt of prostitutes daily from 2.30 pm onwards', a location appropriate to the ethos of the 1917 Club in its capacity as 'the zenith of disreputability'; for Leonard, the

---

[35] Moorcroft Wilson, *Virginia Woolf: Life and London*, 140.

1917 Club was the antithesis of the Athenaeum Gentlemen's Club, long a Pall Mall fixture.[36] In *Jacob's Room*, we find Slade art school student Fanny Elmer in Gerrard Street 'wish[ing] that she had read books' (*JR* 167). Glendinning describes the membership of the 1917 Club as 'primarily political', including J.A. Hobson, H.N. Brailsford (both names associated with the Hogarth Press), and Molly Hamilton. While the mornings at the 1917 Club were political, in the afternoons 'art and culture' took over.[37] Members in this second category included Aldous Huxley, H.G. Wells, Rose Macaulay, E.M. Forster, actress Elsa Lanchester, and composer Cyril Scott. The 1917 Club was a place where, according to P.N. Furbank, Bloomsbury met during the war with 'every kind of progressive: labour politicians, pacifists, communists, vegetarians, free lovers and theosophists'.[38] Reminding us of the diversity of the capital, Jamaican poet Claude McKay, in London between 1919 and 1921, frequented the 1917 Club with Charles Kay Ogden; McKay would have had a loose tie to the Woolfs through Sydney Olivier and Olivier's daughters. According to Gemma Romain and Caroline Bressey, McKay 'found in Soho an engaging and multi-cultural, though complex and at times alienating, social life where he met activists, writers, artists, sailors and boxers'.[39] A reflection of this complexity and alienation, when McKay tried to organize, in 1917, an exhibition of the work of artist Henry Bernard at the 1917 Club, a negative interaction marred his experience.[40]

The Gerrard Street 1917 Club was a location essential to Virginia Woolf in the years when she was still in Richmond. She mentions the club over and over in her diary of this period characterizing it as a home away from home in London's centre where she was able to hold court. In a January 1918 letter to Vanessa Bell, Woolf exclaims: 'The centre of life I should say; is now undoubtedly the 1917 club' (*L2* 210) and again, in 1920, in her diary she writes: 'The 1917 club has the merit of gathering my particular set to a bunch about 4:30 on a week day' (*D2* 6). In 1922, Woolf would find Marjorie Joad there, one of a number of early partners and employees at the Hogarth Press. It is interesting to consider this unconventional club as in some ways akin to Gertrude Stein's 27 rue de Fleurus salon in Paris in operation between 1903 and 1938, and to explore it as a location that was, for Woolf, in its capacity as a precursor to Tavistock Square and the Hogarth Press, more inclusive than Gordon Square. Like 27 rue de Fleurus, the 1917 Club functioned as what Blair calls 'a social form' or 'a genuinely new kind of space of cultural exchange', that can be 'link[ed] to other spaces of avant-garde cultural production' in, in this case, interwar London.[41]

---

[36] Leonard Woolf, *Beginning Again: An Autobiography of the Years 1911–1918* (London: Harvest, 1989), 216.

[37] Victoria Glendinning, *Leonard Woolf: A Biography* (New York: Free Press, 2006), 192.

[38] Furbank, qtd. in Lee, *Virginia Woolf*, 263.

[39] Gemma Romain and Caroline Bressey, 'Claude McKay: Queer Interwar London and Spaces of Black Radicalism', in Katherine M. Graham and Simon Avery, eds, *Sex, Time and Place: Queer Histories of London, c.1850 to the Present* (London: Bloomsbury Academic, 2016), 116–7.

[40] See Jane Marcus, *Hearts of Darkness: White Women Write Race* (New York: Rutgers, 2004), 54–5.

[41] Sara Blair, 'Home Truths: Gertrude Stein, 27 Rue de Fleurus, and the Place of the Avant-Garde', *American Literary History* 12, no. 3, (Fall 2000), 419, 424. In her article on Gertrude Stein and her Paris salon at 27 rue de Fleurus, Blair has us attend 'more closely, more materially, to the places of

At the same time that Woolf presided over afternoons at the 1917 Club, there were several other groups forming in adjacent London neighbourhoods with which Woolf found herself caught up. Two such coteries were based in Hampstead and Chelsea, the former shorter lived than the latter. Woolf's reactions to and observations of these sets and coteries suggest the degree to which London life at once stimulated and unsettled her. They also remind us how important such geographical groupings together were during this period of literary and artistic ferment.

Hampstead had long attracted writers and artists, in part due to its proximity to 'the wild beauty of [Hampstead] Heath', but also through 1920 due to relatively low rents for London (especially in Hampstead town, the Vale of Health, or North End). Poet John Keats lived in Hampstead from 1819 to 1820, as did his contemporary Romantic poet Leigh Hunt and later D.H. Lawrence, fixing the association of the neighbourhood with poets and novelists. In her 'Great Men's Houses', Woolf writes: 'Even in the twentieth century this serenity still pervades the suburb of Hampstead. Its bow windows still look upon vales and trees and ponds and barking dogs and couple sauntering arm in arm and pausing, here on the hill top, to look at the distant domes and pinnacles of London, as they sauntered and paused and looked when Keats lived there' (*E6* 296). Other Hampstead residents include John Galsworthy (*Forsyte Saga*) and Lytton Strachey, as well as artists Henry Lamb, Mark Gertler, Barbara Hepworth, and Ben Nicholson. Freud lived in Hampstead briefly at the very end of his life, and Woolf visited him there in January 1939.

Between 1915 and 1920, the Woolfs spent a lot of time in Hampstead. Adrian Stephen and his wife Karin Costelloe lived there, as did Janet Case and Margaret Llewelyn Davies. Leonard Woolf was frequently there on political business, lecturing, for example, to the Hampstead group of the Union of Democratic Control (*D1* 162, 213). In this context, Woolf portrays Hampstead as serious, populated by 'clean, decorous, uncompromising & high minded old ladies & old gentlemen; & the young wearing brown clothes, & thinking seriously, the women dowdy, the men narrow shouldered; bright fire & lights & books surrounding us, & everyone of course agreeing beforehand to what was said' (*D1* 83). On their 'Hampstead afternoons', Virginia would go to Janet and Leonard to Margaret (*D1* 213).

Hampstead took on particular significance for Woolf in the late 1910s in its capacity as home to her rival Katherine Mansfield, an immigrant who left an important mark on literary London and Bloomsbury. Like Woolf, Mansfield both wrote and engaged in the culture industries in her capacity as editor, alongside editor husband John Middleton Murry. Mansfield had come to London from her native New Zealand first to study in 1903 before returning permanently in 1908. Before meeting the Woolfs in

---

the literary: the sites of its formation, the circuits of its dissemination and the literal and symbolic boundaries it breaches and creates' (418). Blair asks how home is linked to other sites of literary 'production, marketing and display'. She looks at the relationship between 27 rue de Fleurus and 'expatriate Paris [and] the world of the Lost Generation' and she asks us to considers the '[r]elations of literary production [...] to the imaginative and social spaces in which it takes place' (419).

1916/1917, Mansfield came to the Woolfs' attention through A.R. Orage (*New Age*), Murry, and Ottoline Morrell. In November 1918, when preparing Mansfield's *Prelude* as one of the earliest publications at the Hogarth Press, Woolf visited Mansfield and Murry in Hampstead in the 'tall ugly villa looking over the valley', known as 'the Elephant' (*D1* 216). At this point, Mansfield was already ill with the tuberculosis that would kill her in 1923. The Murrys had taken the house, in East Heath Road, in the summer of 1918; they were neighbours of Janet Case at Windmill Hill, Hampstead (*D1* 151).

In 1921, Woolf makes a reference to a group in Hampstead hosted by Slade-trained painter Dorothy Brett, daughter of the Second Viscount Esher. Woolf knew Brett through Ottoline Morrell at whose Garsington Manor Brett had stayed during World War I. Brett had also studied at the Slade art school between 1910 and 1916 with Bloomsbury intimate Dora Carrington. Woolf identifies 'Brett's salon' as made up of Ukrainian S.S. Koteliansky or 'Kot'[42] with whom the Woolfs would collaborate on Russian translations for the Hogarth Press, and Sydney Waterlow, translator, editor, and author of *Shelley* (1912); painter Mark Gertler; classical scholar Herbert J.M. Milne; journalist, editor, and writer John William Navin Sullivan, as well as Murry and Mansfield (*D2* 149–50).

Giving a sense of Woolf's ambivalence about London neighbourhood cliques, in December 1921, Woolf appears unafraid of 'Brett's salon', deciding it 'need give no one the gooseflesh [since] it is a group without teeth or claws'. In fact, she announces fearlessly, if they were to denounce her, she would sleep the sounder. 'For one thing they have no faith in each other. In my day groups were formidable because they coalesced' (*D2* 149–50). However, Woolf's later trepidation on being invited into Hampstead speaks volumes about her love–hate relationship with London literary society. She realizes she needs the stimulation of others than her familiars, even though, at the same time, she fears such contact:

> And if I can only protect this for the present, I shall be able to write. So the question for me is, how far to withdraw from unsympathetic society in the future? Is this cowardly, or merely good sense? For instance, here is Brett already inviting us into the heart of the enemies camp—Hampstead Thursday evenings. If I go I shall be rasped all over, or at any rate dulled & blunted, by the presence of [JWN] Sullivan, Kot and Sydney. *If I don't go shall I soften & rot in the too mild atmosphere of my own familiars?* Perhaps the best plan would be to live in a neutral territory—neither friend nor foe, & by this means sink the exacting claims of egoism. *Is there such a society possible though?* (*D2* 192; emphasis added)

Although not mentioned by Woolf here, D.H. Lawrence, who had lived in the Vale of Health in Hampstead in 1915 and then variously elsewhere in Hampstead with wife

---

[42] Lee suggests that Mansfield's 'colonialism and her itinerant uprootedness were the opposite of Virginia's ancestral network': 'Katherine had met Kot through Lawrence, and in the summer of 1916 she infiltrated Garsington, where Ottoline lent her *The Voyage Out*. Lytton met her, and—as he had with Leonard—it was he who whetted Virginia's interest' (Lee, *Virginia Woolf*, 387–8).

Frieda, was also part of Brett's set. Despite collaborations with the Woolfs at the Hogarth Press, Lawrence remained distant from and hostile to Bloomsbury.

Concurrent to Hampstead, Woolf contended with another overlapping social set in Chelsea. Andrea P. Zemgulys suggests that Woolf felt threatened by Chelsea because of its resemblance to Bloomsbury. Both groups were 'an admixture of innovation and tradition, fashion and stability, bohemianism and social establishment'.[43] David Pryce-Jones agrees that 'much united Chelsea and Bloomsbury', but sees more distinction than does Zemgulys in terms of 'definitions of the purposes of literature and art':

> To Chelsea, self-expression was a means, the chief means perhaps, to enjoyment of a fuller life; to Bloomsbury, it was more strictly an end requiring no further justification. The Pearsall Smith set looked at Bloomsbury and deplored people who for all their gifts and privileges were stuck in class-consciousness and money-conscious attitudes, self-denying people, in short parochial and priggish. The Woolf set looked at Chelsea and envied people who had travelled too widely, who were at ease in foreign languages and settings, treated money and status loosely, self-indulgent people who were, in short, suspiciously worldly.[44]

As Zemgulys argues, 'Chelsea provoked Virginia Woolf' in its capacity as a former enclave to Victorian predecessors, and because it was later home to 'Woolf's so-called "bohemian" contemporaries'.[45] Chelsea past was painters D.G. Rossetti, J.M.W. Turner, John Singer Sargent, and Holman Hunt and writers George Meredith, Algernon Swinburne, Leigh Hunt, and Thomas Carlyle.[46] Contemporary Chelsea included painter Ethel Sands, who resided at 15 The Vale, Chelsea, with partner Nan Hudson. Sands's salon accommodated Walter Sickert, George Moore, Henry and William James, Ottoline Morrell, Logan Pearsall Smith, and Woolf herself. Another important Chelsea figure was socialite Sibyl Colefax whose Argyll House was situated 'at the rural end of the King's Road'.[47] Lady Colefax first invited Virginia Woolf in late 1919. Other Chelsea residents were literary gatekeepers Bloomsbury's Desmond MacCarthy, Affable Hawk in the *New Statesman*, and J.C. Squires, *London Mercury* editor from 1919 to 1934 and *Observer* book critic from 1921 to 1931. Also in Chelsea were Mary Hutchinson, Maurice Baring, Bob and Hilda Trevelyan, and Bloomsbury antagonist Cyril Connolly.

---

[43] Andrea P. Zemgulys, '"*Night and Day* is Dead": Virginia Woolf in London "Literary and Historic"', *Twentieth Century Literature* 46, no. 1 (Spring 2000), 56.

[44] David Pryce Jones, *Cyril Connolly: Journal and Memoir* (London: Ticknor & Fields, 1984), 93.

[45] Zemgulys, '"*Night and Day* is Dead"', 56. Zemgulys argues that by situating *Night and Day* in Chelsea, and by portraying it as a place where 'innovation and imitation' vied for prominence, the former winning out when the heroine moves away from Chelsea, Woolf symbolically broke free from standard form and embarked on the experimentalism that marked her novels beginning with *Jacob's Room*. Zemgulys continues: 'In her subsequent novels *Jacob's Room* and *Orlando*, Woolf will rework literary and historic London to render it as fiction rather than fact and reduce it to an effect rather than a condition of modernity' (74).

[46] Zemgulys, '"*Night and Day* is Dead"', 69.

[47] Lee, *Virginia Woolf*, 468.

Woolf bore the provocation from Chelsea with more maturity and amusement than she did Hampstead. Confirming that intimacy predominated in London literary society despite perceived division, on discovering the Sitwell siblings, Osbert, Sacheverell, and Edith, in Chelsea in 1918, having just published a review of Edith's poetry in the *Times*, Woolf accepted an invitation only to find she knew almost everyone there:

> It's strange how whole groups of people suddenly swim complete into one's life. This group to which Gertler & Mary H. [Hutchinson] are attached was unknown to me a year ago. I surveyed them with considerable, almost disquieting calm. What is there to be excited about, or to quarrel over, in a party like this, I asked myself; & found myself saying the most maternal things to Gertler [...] Edith Sitwell is a very tall young woman, wearing a permanently startled expression ... Otherwise, I was familiar with everyone, I think. Nina Hamnet[t], Mary H., Jack H., Ottoline, Sheppard, Norton & so forth. (*D1*, 202)

In her 1965 autobiography, *Taken Care Of*, Edith Sitwell provides the Chelsea perspective on Bloomsbury, whose company she believed too 'serried' to accommodate her own idiosyncracies: 'silence was much prized, sometimes to the embarrassment of people outside the inner circle of Bloomsbury ... nothing was more unconventionally conventional than the company of Bloomsbury'.[48]

BACK TO BLOOMSBURY: FROM HOGARTH HOUSE TO TAVISTOCK SQUARE

One reason for the move back to Bloomsbury, from Hogarth House to 52, Tavistock Square, in March 1924 was Leonard Woolf's assumption of the literary editorship of the *Nation and Athenaeum* (*N&A*) in 1923, his first salaried role in the field of journalism and a position he would fill for the next seven years.[49] This was a move that would put Leonard, and by extension Virginia and the Hogarth Press, at the heart of literary London. *N&A*'s offices were in Great James Street in Bloomsbury, under a mile away from Tavistock Square. In his autobiography, Leonard Woolf confirms that a motivation for the move to Tavistock Square was how taxing it had become for Virginia to keep up with social events at a distance. But it was clearly about more than these practicalities for Virginia. In 1922, Virginia had told Leonard: 'If she lived in London [...] 'I might go & hear a tune, or have a look at a picture, or find out something at the British Museum, or go adventuring among human beings. Sometimes I should merely walk down

---

[48] Edith Sitwell, *Taken Care Of: The Autobiography of Edith Sitwell* (London: Atheneum, 1965), 93–4.
[49] J. H. Willis, *Leonard and Virginia Woolf as Publishers: The Hogarth Press 1917-1941* (Charlottesville: University of Virginia Press, 1992), 78.

Cheapside. But now I'm tied, imprisoned, inhibited [...] surely we could get more life than we do [...]' and she continues:

> this social side is very genuine in me. Nor do I think it reprehensible. It is a piece of jewellery I inherit from my mother—a joy in laughter, something that is stimulated, not selfishly wholly or vainly, by contact with my friends. And then ideas leap in me. Moreover, for my work now, I want free intercourse, wider intercourse—& now, at 41, having done a little work, I get wages partly in invitations. I might know people. In Richmond this is impossible. Either we have arduous parties at long intervals, or I make my frenzied dashes up to London, & leave, guiltily, as the clock strikes 11. (*D2* 250–1)

By 1924, although she was grateful for the calm and stability Hogarth House, and the eponymous press that had taken shape there 'on this very green carpet' (*D2* 283), had provided, Virginia Woolf felt, according to Leonard, 'cabined and confined' in Richmond. Among her greatest fear was 'for ever to be suburban'.[50]

With the move back to Bloomsbury and into Tavistock Square in 1924, with their thriving press in tow, the Woolfs settled into a neighbourhood abuzz with creative industry. On its way out, but having left a mark on the neighbourhood, was Fry's Omega Workshops (1913–1920), which had recently ceased operations at 33 Fitzroy Square. Harold Monro's Poetry Bookshop (1913–1932), publishing house, bookshop, and performance space, although already struggling in 1924, moved from its Devonshire Street location (now Boswell Street) in 1926 to Great Russell Street, and remained open until 1935. New additions to the neighbourhood included publishing house Jonathan Cape, which began operations at 11 Gower Street in 1921 with Edward Garnett as chief literary adviser. Faber & Gwyer would open offices at 24 Russell Square in 1925 with T.S. Eliot, freshly quit of his Lloyds Bank job, as poetry editor, and American publishing house, Alfred A. Knopf, Inc. would follow in 1926 with a London office, in Bloomsbury, manned by author and agent Storm Jameson and Guy Chapman, her soon to be husband.[51] Francis Birrell and David Garnett's Bloomsbury Bookshop (1919–1924), also a very small publishing operation, was at 19 Taviton Street, and later in Gerrard Street, its personnel tightly linked to that of the Hogarth Press. Francis Meynell's, Vera Mendel's, and David Garnett's Nonesuch Press would emerge from the basement of Birrell and Garnett's shop in 1922. And Mudie's Circulating Library was at 509, 510, and 511 New Oxford Street, right next to the British Museum.

Already established in neighbourhoods adjacent to Bloomsbury, in Covent Garden, Charing Cross Road, Adelphi, and Paternoster Row, were publishers Edward Arnold (est. 1890), E.M. Forster's major publisher and publisher of Leonard's fiction (in 1913 and 1914), Allen & Unwin/T Fisher Unwin (est. 1882), publishers of Leonard's nonfiction,

---

[50] Leonard Woolf, *Downhill All the Way*, 118; *D2* 250.
[51] Laura Claridge, *The Lady with the Borzoi: Blanche Knopf, Literary Tastemaker Extraordinaire* (New York: Farrar Straus and Giroux, 2016), 118.

and William Heinemann, established in Covent Garden in 1890 before moving in 1908 to Bedford Street, Strand, WC. Virginia Woolf's half-brother's publishing house, Gerald Duckworth & Co. (est. 1898), which published both Woolf's *The Voyage Out* (1915) and *Night and Day* (1919), was at 3 Henrietta Street, Covent Garden. These were operations alongside which the Hogarth Press located itself and from which the Woolf's publishing industry drew energy.

The Little Magazine revolution was also underway not far off: Dora Marsden's, Harriet Weaver's, and Pound's *The Egoist* magazine began life at Oakley House, Bloomsbury Street, but by 1919, when the cessation of magazine production and a move into book publishing was announced, The Egoist Ltd. was at 23 Adelphi Terrace House, 2 Robert Street, Adelphi, London WC2 (The Egoist Press published Lewis's *Tarr* in July 1918). *The Little Review* was at the same address. Murry's *Rhythm*, 1911–1913, was published by the Catherine Press in Norfolk Street to start, then Stephen Swift and Company Ltd., 16 King Street in Covent Garden, and last by Martin Secker, 5 John Street, Adelphi, London WC. The *Times* (and the *Times Literary Supplement*) was at Printing House Square in Queen Victoria Street in EC1.

Coincident with the move from Richmond back to Bloomsbury, the Hogarth Press entered what J.H. Willis calls its 'mature' phase (1924–1930), which saw considerable expansion of its list. In 1922, the Woolfs published six titles and in 1923, eleven titles. In 1924, sixteen titles appeared and in 1925, twenty-eight. To its strong fiction offerings, the Woolfs added pamphlets on 'political, social and economic issues', their first *International Psychoanalytical Library* publications, which included Freud's first appearances in England in 1919, and the *Hogarth Essays* series, the first of a number of series the press would produce. With increased space and a more central location, the Hogarth Press staff also grew, as did their pool of contributors. Press staff members, Marjorie Joad and Dadie Rylands, were brought onboard in 1923 and 1924 respectively, and Sackville-West first published with the press in 1924.

With this expansion of press operations came the need for further socializing and networking, both in and beyond Bloomsbury, at once a boon and a burden for both Woolfs. This responsibility to a whole new constituency in the capital represented an especially ambiguous honour for Virginia Woolf whose love–hate relationship with company and society is mirrored in her ambivalent relationship with London. As Anna Snaith suggests, Woolf 'dreamed of extreme privacy, of being immune to society ... but she needed society for its own sake as well as for inspiration, hence her love of walking through the busy streets of London.' The city was 'a public world of professional men, but also a place where, in contrast to her social engagements, she could walk and be private and anonymous'.[52] Similarly, the comings and goings of the press at once inspired her and devoured her time.

Despite, or in fact as a consequence of, the challenges the urban and newly professional environment brought to Woolf's comfort threshold, London, in all of its

---

[52] Anna Snaith, *Virginia Woolf: Private and Public Negotiations* (Basingstoke: Palgrave, 2000), 40.

diversity, represents a key element in almost all of her works subsequent to her 1924 return to Bloomsbury, from *A Room of One's Own*, *Orlando*, and *Flush* to *The Waves* and *The Years*. London's reality, its geography, would never cease to 'attract' and 'stimulate' Woolf: to '[give her] a play & a story & a poem, without any trouble, save that of moving [her] legs through the streets' (*D3* 186). At the same time, the dynamism and elusiveness of London society, playfully parodied here in *Orlando*, would never cease to nourish her rich imagination:

> To give a truthful account of London society at that or indeed at any other time, is beyond the powers of the biographer or the historian. Only those who have little need of the truth, and no respect for it—the poets and the novelists—can be trusted to do it, for this is one of the cases where the truth does not exist. Nothing exists. The whole thing is a miasma—a mirage. (*O* 113)

SELECTED BIBLIOGRAPHY

Blair, Sara, 'Local Modernity, Global Modernity: Bloomsbury and the Places of the Literary', *English Literary History* 71, no. 3 (Fall 2004), 813–38.

Bradbury, Malcolm, 'London 1890–1920', in Malcolm Bradbury and James McFarlane, eds, *Modernism: A Guide to European Literature* (London: Penguin, 1976).

Bradshaw, David, 'Woolf's London', in Bryony Randall and Jane Goldman, eds, *Virginia Woolf in Context* (Cambridge: Cambridge University Press, 2013).

Brewster, Dorothy, *Virginia Woolf's London* (New York: New York University Press, 1960).

Evans, Elizabeth, *Thresholds Modernism* (Cambridge: Cambridge University Press, 2018).

Moorcroft Wilson, Jean, *Virginia Woolf: Life and London* (London: Tauris Parke, 2000)

Snaith, Anna, *Virginia Woolf: Private and Public Negotiations* (Basingstoke: Palgrave Macmillan, 2000).

Squier, Susan M, *Virginia Woolf and London: The Sexual Politics of the City* (Chapel Hill: University of North Carolina Press, 1985).

Zemgulys, Andrea P, *Modernism and the Locations of Literary Heritage* (Cambridge: Cambridge University Press, 2008).

CHAPTER 16

THE HOGARTH PRESS

ALICE STAVELEY

ALL families have origin stories. So do most businesses. For Virginia Woolf and the Hogarth Press, the stories are twinned. During the course of a celebratory outing to Buzzard's Tea Rooms on Oxford Street in honour of her thirty-third birthday, 25 January 1915, Woolf records the indelible moment she and Leonard determined to buy their own printing press: 'Sitting at tea we decided three things: in the first place to take Hogarth, if we can get it; in the second, to buy a Printing press; in the third to buy a Bull dog, probably called John. I am very much excited at the idea of all three—particularly the press' (*D1* 28). The Trinitarian overtones of this memory—in what was, moreover, the third year of her marriage—are light-hearted but not misplaced. In terms of the artistic, domestic, and economic transformations the Hogarth Press would exert on Woolf's life and career, her anecdote reads like a prophecy. While they didn't end up with the bulldog, they did secure a home, Hogarth House in suburban Richmond, which lent its name to the small handpress they purchased two years later during a walk in London along the South Bank, close to Clifford's Inn, where they had lived when they were first married. This decision to name the press after their home signalled a domestic patrimony, a marital and entrepreneurial joint venture. Somewhat auspiciously, it also evoked manifold enlightenment promises and perils, including the cultural criticism and social satire of William Hogarth, and the public sphere of the eighteenth-century coffee-house, not to mention the much maligned 'bluestockings' whose private lives and scribbling aspirations were, as Woolf would come to depict them in *A Room of One's Own* (1929), open targets for prominent male critics like Alexander Pope and John Gay. Having a 'press of her own' would go a long way to creating the material, intellectual, emotional, and institutional spaces necessary for cultivation of Woolf's feminist modernism, undergirding her bravura claim, just eight years after the Hogarth Press's founding, 'Yet I'm the only woman in England free to write what I like' (*D3* 43).

The Woolfs' handpress, purchased on 23 March 1917 from the Excelsior Supply Company on Farringdon Street—a shop described by Leonard as 'not a large firm, but it sold every kind of printing machine and material, from a handpress to a composing stick'[1]—reset the course of the Woolfs' marriage, intensifying its habitus as a professional and creative working partnership. With greater velocity than either of them had anticipated, it turned them into owners of a rapidly growing, upstart publishing house. 'MSS pour in; & this press becomes a serious business' writes Virginia in 1924 (D2 307). During their married life, the Hogarth Press published over five hundred books and pamphlets, including all Virginia's book-length publications after 1922. It boasted a list of over three hundred individual authors. It published, on average, twenty-six titles a year.[2] This significant contribution to twentieth-century print culture was all the more impressive considering neither Virginia nor Leonard were solely publishing proprietors: they both had extensive and time-consuming responsibilities as writers and reviewers, public speakers, and public intellectuals. They might have been forgiven for not lending their hands (and minds) to cultivating a new generation of writers under their own imprint. Instead, they chose to curate, by soliciting, reviewing, editing, and marketing a wide array of authors, in a diverse set of genres, whose manuscripts, as they poured into the Woolfs' home, had palpable presence: 'I am weighed down by innumerable manuscripts', Woolf writes to Vita Sackville-West, 'Edith Sitwell; 20 dozen poets; one man on birth control; another on religion in Leeds; and the whole of Gertrude Stein, which I flutter with the tips of my little fingers, but dont open. I think her dodge is to repeat the same word 100 times over in different connections, until at last you feel the force of it' (L3 198).

To fulfil similar bibliophilic ambitions, the Woolfs might have engaged a more modest or antiquarian enterprise in the tradition of fine arts printing, like the Kelmscott Press, producing beautifully illuminated and typeset editions of the classics (forsaking the dodge of Stein, or other modernists, altogether). They chose instead to publish and promote mainly living writers—a crucial testament of their modernity, in the sense of their investment in contemporaneous cultural production—rather than the works of the late and great. Their decision, as Ursula McTaggart rightly notes, 'generated a literary and political conversation instead of beautifying personal libraries'.[3] Privileging living writers to envelop in Hogarth Press covers, not dead writers gilded in letterpress and gold-leaf, the Woolfs aspired to the mandate they set forth on the fifth anniversary of the press in 1922, promising not 'to embellish our books beyond what is necessary for ease of reading and decency of appearance', and that 'cheapness and adequacy' trumped 'high prices and typographical splendor'.[4] Nonetheless, they did experiment with a variety of material formats, from handprinted art paper-covered pamphlets typeset, printed, and bound in their own home, to hardbacked novels edited in-house sporting dust jackets illustrated by leading graphic designers and outsourced to largescale commercial

---

[1] Leonard Woolf, *Beginning Again* (New York: Harcourt Brace Jovanovich, 1963), 234.
[2] J. H. Willis, Jr., *Leonard and Virginia Woolf as Publishers: The Hogarth Press 1917–1941* (Charlottesville and London: University Press of Virginia, 1992), 369.
[3] Ursula McTaggart, '"Opening the Door": The Hogarth Press as Virginia Woolf's Outsiders' Society', *Tulsa Studies in Women's Literature* 29, no. 1 (Spring 2010), 63–81, at 63.
[4] Qtd in S. P. Rosenbaum, *Aspects of Bloomsbury* (London: Palgrave Macmillan, 1998), 152.

printers and binders. Their generic range was equally hybrid, various, and diverse. Poems, novels, translations, political tracts, literary essays, histories, biographies, art historical books, children's literature, popular fiction, and even etiquette and medical manuals all merited their attention as acquisition editors and press directors. As Claire Battershill has recently described the broad and idiosyncratic press backlist, '[w]hat the Woolfs liked and what interested them mattered enormously to the Hogarth Press: it was really the main factor [...] that determined their selections. Nearly any kind of book, and any style of writing, if it were "modern" in the sense of seeming relevant to the contemporary moment, might be published by the press.'[5]

This additive ethos cultivated by the Hogarth Press—including its constitutive identity as a privately owned, in-house publisher, even when its actual footprint became much larger—was emblematized on the black and gold lettered business shingle mounted at the entry to Hogarth House: Mr & Mrs L. Woolf and The Hogarth Press.[6] A marriage united by an ampersand iterated as a conjunction forged a publishing business that toggled between any number of distinctive but compound identities, '[...] an operation at once domestic and commercial; English and international; homegrown and ambitious'.[7] The press was never backward looking but constantly moving forward, diversifying its outputs, and innovating its production practices. It was always in the business of soliciting new writers. Woolf herself often joked about asking everyone she met to write for the press. The Hogarth Press machinery overtook the rooms of their home in Richmond, and when they moved to central London in 1924, it occupied the entire ground floor of 52 Tavistock Square.[8] Anticipating this move, Woolf pays homage to the press, anthropomorphizing its vital force, its insistent and unstoppable progress, against the mordancy of a house packed up, ready for departure. Yet, her elegiac impulses are undermined by a press refusing inscription in the past: '[...] nowhere else could we have started the Hogarth Press, whose very awkward beginning had rise in this very room, on this very green carpet. Here that strange offspring grew & throve; it ousted us from the dining room, which is now a dusty coffin; & crept all over the house' (*D2* 283).

Critical reception of the Hogarth Press has not always reflected this narrative of expansion, hybridity, and disruptive progress. Although J.H. Willis, Jr published a landmark history in 1992, *Leonard and Virginia Woolf as Publishers*, and J. Howard Woolmer

---

[5] Claire Battershill, *Modernist Lives: Biography and Autobiography at Leonard and Virginia Woolf's Hogarth Press* (London: Bloomsbury Academic, 2018), 6.

[6] This door sign is in the Hogarth Press archives at the E. J. Pratt Library, Victoria College, University of Toronto; you can see an image of it on the landing page of the *Modernist Archives Publishing Project* (MAPP): www.modernistarchives.com.

[7] Battershill, *Modernist Lives*, 7.

[8] For a whimsical but architecturally well remembered floor plan of 52 Tavistock Square with a pull-out diagram of the basement press rooms, see Richard Kennedy, *A Boy at the Hogarth Press* (London: Whittington Press, 1972). This house was destroyed in the bombings of World War II, but Hogarth House, Richmond survives today, the birthplace of the Woolfs' press commemorated by an iconic blue plaque.

contributed a bibliography in 1986 chronicling every Hogarth Press publication alongside print runs, the dominant narrative, until quite recently, has been of a small-scale, coterie press given to handprinted publications and cultivation of avant-garde taste. It is a compelling storyline rooted partly in fact—the press did start out small and its first publications were handprinted pamphlets—but one that trades on the cultural capital associated with a New Critical view of modernism itself as highbrow, insular, private, and non-commercial. Some iterations of this narrative have a long shelf-life, often acting to mediate parochial or implicitly anti-Bloomsbury sentiments. Faye Hammill and Mark Hussey note that as late as 2010, Iain Stevenson, in a book devoted to a history of twentieth-century British publishing, could argue that the Hogarth Press was 'still a cottage industry in the 1930s, "amateur dabbling" that would not have survived without the Woolfs' "personal wealth and the patronage of their friends"'.[9]

This view of the Hogarth Press as a cliquish enterprise, a hobby, informs what we might associate, to adapt a term popularized in Woolf studies by Hermione Lee, with the 'biomythographies' of the Hogarth Press: its influence on the Woolfs' creative lives, and its contributions, not just to interwar print culture, but also, given its recent revival as a Penguin Random House imprint, to its stature as a legacy brand promoting new writers.[10] Even in the 1960s when he was publishing his autobiography, Leonard felt compelled to rebut misperceptions about the press's origins: 'I have often been told and I have seen it stated more than once in print that Virginia and I started the Hogarth Press on the money which I had won in the sweepstake. The statement is ludicrously untrue.'[11] He proceeds to detail the capital they both put into the purchase of the Excelsior Press, the costs of the first production—a pamphlet *Two Stories* (1917) containing his short story 'Three Jews' and Virginia's 'The Mark on the Wall'—which recouped expenses and made a small profit that was returned to the press. This initial success established an important precedent: 'the business financed itself out of profits and we never had to "find capital" for it'.[12] Leonard's defensive tone might have been responding to anti-elitist accusations about the press as a dilettantish and privileged pursuit, but his words arguably implicate other implicit (sexist) antagonisms amongst his class and generation about Virginia's private capital; a sense she too brought 'unearned' wealth into the marriage—capital akin to a sweepstakes perhaps—adding to suspicions, at a time when her literary reputation was at a post-Leavisite nadir, that any creative sustenance afforded by her own press was negligible or irrelevant, another iteration of the 'coterie' or cottage press formulary.

---

[9] Faye Hammill and Mark Hussey, *Modernism's Print Cultures* (London: Bloomsbury, 2016), 102.

[10] The Hogarth Press was sold in 1946 to Chatto & Windus who were later bought by Random House (since 2013, Penguin Random House). In 2011, Random House reactivated the Hogarth imprint as 'a home for a fresh generation of literary talent: an adventurous fiction imprint with an accent on the pleasures of storytelling and a broad awareness of the world'. See https://www.penguin.co.uk/company/publishers/vintage/hogarth.html.

[11] Leonard Woolf, *Beginning Again*, 54.

[12] Leonard Woolf, *Beginning Again*, 54.

Most striking, however, in Leonard's depiction of the Hogarth Press's founding is his emphasis on its self-supporting identity, independent of external collateral. This narrative stresses its independence and autonomy within the landscape of literary publishing, suggesting a crucial prerequisite for its survival that both Virginia and Leonard appear to have shared ('*we* never had to find capital for it'). Indeed, in the mid-1920s when the Woolfs briefly flirted with a buy-out offer from the larger commercial firm Heinemanns—'we sniff patronage' (*D2* 215) writes a wary Woolf—she expressed her delight at rejecting the offer by alliterating liberation with defiant plural possession, 'We [...] have decided for freedom & a fight with great private glee' (*D2* 215). With financial autonomy, however precarious, comes creative and editorial freedom, both freedom *as* an editor to select one's own lists, and to be spared, in Woolf's case, from the interventions *of* editors. This executive liberation undergirds one of her most frequently cited feminist aphorisms: 'Yet I'm the only woman in England free to write what I like. The others must be thinking of series' & editors' (*D3* 43).

Woolf makes clear that small scale success for her life as a publisher or writer was *not* an option, yet the intimate congruence between Woolf's creative ambitions and the fortunes of the Hogarth Press are rarely underscored in critical discussion. Here she is again on the eve of the move to Tavistock Square, prescient of risk, but candid, and pointed, about her aspirations as a publisher: 'The next ten years must see the press into fame or bankruptcy; to loiter on here is a handicap' (*D2* 285). '[F]ame or bankruptcy' is an uncompromising antithesis, rooted in unabashed ambition. It gives the lie to etherealized portraits of Woolf as disinterested in the real world of print manufacture, a cultural fiction rooted in an antifeminist press biomythography that has had rather more staying power in both popular and academic portraits of Woolf than in almost any other critical arena. One of the solecisms committed by the 2002 Academy-award winning movie version of Michael Cunningham's novel, *The Hours*, a deft reimagining of *Mrs Dalloway* (1925), is, despite rich and detailed cinematic depictions of the Hogarth Press and its outputs, Woolf's portrayal by Nicole Kidman as living proximate to her own press but terrified of touching its machinery. In one telling scene, Kidman as Woolf escapes the printing room to get some air, leaving a disgruntled Leonard labouring over typesetting while giving irritated voice to the wish that he too might take walks. Actually, while Leonard and Virginia shared typesetting in the early days of the press, Leonard's hand tremor made the activity difficult and latterly, with the help of hired women assistants, Virginia spent countless hours at the typecase.[13]

The stakes within the academy of the resistance to reading the cultural and historical implications of Woolf as a woman printer and publisher—herself acutely aware of how that identity was catalytic of her break into modernism—reflect larger tensions within narrative theory, book history, and modernist studies, particularly as the field

---

[13] Hermione Lee takes issue with a film that 'evacuates [Woolf's] life of political intelligence or social acumen, returning her to the position of doomed, fey, mad victim', wishing '[Woolf] could have been seen setting type at the Press alongside Leonard, as she so often did'. Lee, *Virginia Woolf's Nose: Essays on Biography* (Princeton, NJ: Princeton University Press, 2005), 55.

has undergone the cultural materialist turn, ambiguously problematic for feminist inquiry, within the past two decades.[14] For Woolf, however, the press was not intended to sequester or cut off her creative life as a woman writer from her printer's life, her editorial life, her social life, or her business life. It was instead to be a thriving hub, an intergenerational, mutually energizing makerspace recirculating and reintegrating intellectual and somatic currents across generations, sprung from and spun out of the marital reciprocity of the first person plural: '[W]e shall be benefactors of our age; & have a shop, & enjoy the society of the young, & rummage & splash in the great bran pie, & so never, never stop working with brains or fingers or toes till our limbs fly asunder & the heart sprays off into dust' (D2 271). These whirligig energies suturing mind and body, self and society, generated networks of social, economic, and affective capital that Woolf understood to be highly interconnected, interdependent, and, as her analogy to the 'great bran pie' suggests, generative of secret or hidden gifts almost limitlessness in their sought-after acquisition.[15] It is why she writes so often about the Hogarth Press in terms of adulation and indebtedness, terms that often imply a preferential trade-off between the hand that composes the (unpublished) holograph, and the typesetter's hand that composes the text for public consumption: 'How my handwriting goes downhill! Another sacrifice to the Hogarth Press. Yet what I owe the Hogarth Press is barely paid by the whole of my handwriting' (D3 42).

In the last decade, criticism on Woolf as a publisher, influenced by the broader cultural-historical turn within modernist studies, has begun to tap into this rich, contextual, and crucially networked understanding of the Hogarth Press and its role in the publishing history of modernism. Helen Southworth's important edited collection, *Leonard and Virginia Woolf: The Hogarth Press and the Networks of Modernism*, published in 2010, represented the first book-length intervention in revising the dominant view of the Hogarth Press as coterie, non-commercial, and a singular conduit for Woolf's writings. Compelled to add archival and literary critical heft to incisive commentary of Laura Marcus's in the mid-1990s about the 'heterogeneity' of the press,[16] Southworth's collection 'shift[s] the emphasis onto the networks generated and

---

[14] For recent critiques the 'everywhere and nowhere' place of feminism within the new modernist studies, see Seshagiri, 'Mind the Gap! Modernism and Feminist Praxis', *Modernism/Modernity Print Plus* 2, no. 2 (August 2017); and Anne Fernald, 'Women's Fiction, New Modernist Studies, and Feminism', *Modern Fiction Studies* 59, no. 2 (Summer 2013), 229–40. Within book history, there is a more severe disciplinary split, which Trysh Travis, citing Leslie Howsam, suggests relates to the fact that '[l]audable attention to the presence of women [in book history] ha[s] not translated into a feminist book history'. Travis, 'The Women in Print Movement: History and Implications', *Book History* 11, no. 1 (2008), 275–300, at 275.

[15] Wiktionary defines this colloquial phrase as 'A tub filled with bran in which small gifts are buried as a lucky dip.' In *The Waves* (1931), Woolf ascribes it to the artist-figure Bernard's inner life, his undergraduate sense of surprised multiplicity contrasted with agentive self-invention: 'Every hour something new is unburied in the great bran pie. What am I? I ask. This? No, I am that' (*W* 59).

[16] Laura Marcus, 'Virginia Woolf and the Hogarth Press', in Ian Willison, Warwick Gould, and Warren Chernaik, eds, *Modernist Writers and the Marketplace* (London: Palgrave Macmillan, 1996), 124–50, at 128.

intersected by the Hogarth Press [...] broader than the Bloomsbury Group, [...] to evaluate the Woolfs' contributions to the making of modernism'.[17] Contributors contextualize key outputs of the Hogarth Press author list, including their middlebrow (Melissa Sullivan) and working-class (Helen Southworth) fictions, their global and anti-colonial publications (John Young and Anna Snaith), their cultivation of an avant-garde female child poet, Joan Adeney Easdale (Mark Hussey) and surveys on contemporary religion (Diane Gillespie), the 'radical politics' of their Russian translations (Jean Mills), and the larger institutional, economic, and business apparatus the Woolfs knew intimately as actors in a wider industry where books were commodities needing marketing, promotion, and packaging (Elizabeth Willson Gordon and Stephen Barkway).

Complementing the essays in Southworth's collection, much recent scholarship on the Hogarth Press interrogates how, as an 'institution of modernism', to borrow Lawrence Rainey's influential phrase, it navigated the often competing imperatives of commercial success (or at least prosperous solvency) and cultural capital.[18] Elizabeth Willson Gordon, for instance, examines the sometimes contradictory ways the press managed coterie and commercial market demands to build a private press at once 'elitist and democratic'[19]; she recounts a delightful irony (and alternative origin story) of how the press began, not with the Woolfs learning to print by typesetting a piece of fiction but rather with an advertisement—uneven, poorly inked, but aspirational—notifying prospective buyers of their forthcoming inaugural booklet, *Two Stories* (1917).[20] This episode recalls the Woolfs' youthful optimism at the outset of their adventures in publishing, two novices excitedly setting up shop. Yet it also captures the intermingling of consumptive pleasures—material, economic, somatic—that Leonard himself recounts when he and Virginia stood outside the Excelsior Supply Company, salivating over the tools of the trade for sale through the plate glass windows: 'Nearly all the implements of printing are materially attractive and we stared through the window at them rather like two hungry children gazing at buns and cakes in a baker shop window'.[21]

How the Hogarth Press managed Woolf's distribution and marketing to maintain her cultural prestige while she became a bestseller has generated significant critical attention, which, in Claire Battershill's terms, helps to 'reconsider the Woolfs as not just literary figures but specifically as business people'.[22] John Young and Lise Jaillant have both separately examined the Hogarth Press's decision to publish a Uniform Edition of Woolf's works in the late 1920s, including the competing imperatives of what Young

---

[17] Helen Southworth, ed., *Leonard and Virginia Woolf, The Hogarth Press, and the Networks of Modernism* (Edinburgh: Edinburgh University Press, 2010), 2.

[18] Lawrence Rainey, *Institutions of Modernism* (New Haven, CT: Yale University Press, 1998).

[19] Elizabeth Willson Gordon, 'How Should One Sell a Book? Production Methods, Material Objects and Marketing at the Hogarth Press', in Lisa Shahriari and Gina Potts, eds, *Virginia Woolf's Bloomsbury, Volume 2* (London: Palgrave Macmillan, 2010), 107–23, at 112.

[20] Willson Gordon, 'How Should One Sell a Book?', 119.

[21] Leonard Woolf, *Beginning Again*, 234.

[22] Claire Battershill, 'The Hogarth Press', in Lise Jaillant, ed., *Publishing Modernist Fiction and Poetry* (Edinburgh: Edinburgh University Press, 2019), 70–87, at 72.

terms 'canonicity and commerciality' in Woolf's representation and distribution.[23] Elsewhere, John Young discusses more broadly Woolf's investment in the business of making and producing books from her vantage point 'as an author not isolated from textual production but as one immersed [in it]'.[24] Edward Bishop, Benjamin Harvey, and Catherine Hollis variously explore how Vanessa Bell's dust jackets filter Woolf's reception and navigate currents related to fame and iconicity, including Woolf's desire for female colloquy in her working relationship with Bell in ways that complement, and complicate, what Hollis characterizes as Woolf's lifelong fascination with 'anonymity and collectivity'.[25] Mining extensive publishers' archives to prove just how much Woolf's wide readership was cultivated by strategic business and hiring practices in-house, Alice Staveley and Nicola Wilson have shown, respectively, how the Hogarth Press target-marketed women professionals as readers in the late 1930s, thanks to the hiring of a female press Manager, Norah Nicholls, and actively solicited one of the premier competitive book clubs to have Woolf win coveted billing and promotion as a Book Society author.[26] Diane Gillespie's body of work on the Hogarth Press similarly excavates unknown histories of the writers and readers cultivated by the Woolfs.[27]

The impact that printing and the mechanical forms of typesetting had on Woolf's narrative aesthetics has also been the focus of a variety of recent inventive analyses, including Leslie Hankins's study of Woolf's typesetting of Katherine Mansfield's 'Prelude' as a 'unique form of reading (and un-reading)'; Edward Bishop's and Julia Briggs's examinations of typesetting's formalist effects on Woolf's sense of page design

---

[23] John Young, 'Canonicity and Commercialization in Woolf's Uniform Edition', in Bonnie Kime Scott and Ann Ardis, eds, *Virginia Woolf Turning the Centuries* (New York: Pace University Press, 2000), 236–43. Lise Jaillant, *Cheap Modernism: Expanding Markets, Publishers' Series and the Avant-garde* (Edinburgh: Edinburgh University Press, 2017), 120–39.

[24] John Young, '"Murdering an Aunt or Two": Textual Practice and Narrative Form in Virginia Woolf's Metropolitan Market', in Jeanne Dubino, ed., *Virginia Woolf and the Literary Marketplace* (Palgrave, 2010), 183.

[25] Edward L. Bishop, 'From Typography to Time: Producing Virginia Woolf", in Beth Daugherty, ed., *Virginia Woolf: Texts and Contexts* (New York: Pace University Press, 1996), 50–63; Benjamin Harvey, 'The Twentieth Part: Virginia Woolf in the British Museum Reading Room', *Literature Compass* 4, no.1 (January 2007), 218–34; Benjamin Harvey, 'Lightness Visible: An Appreciation of Bloomsbury's Books and Blocks', in Nancy E. Green and Christopher Reed, eds, *A Room of Their Own* (Ithaca, NY: Herbert F. Johnson Museum of Art, Cornell University, 2008), 88–117; Catherine Hollis, 'Virginia Woolf's Double Signature', in Karen Kukil, ed., *Virginia Woolf in the Real World* (Clemson, SC: Clemson University Digital Press, 2005), 19–24.

[26] Alice Staveley, 'Marketing Virginia Woolf: Women, War, and Public Relations in *Three Guineas*', *Book History* 12 (2009), 295–339; Nicola Wilson, 'Virginia Woolf, Hugh Walpole, the Hogarth Press, and the Book Society', *English Literary History* 79, no. 1 (Spring 2012), 237–60.

[27] Diane F. Gillespie, '"Can I Help You?": Virginia Woolf, Viola Tree, and the Hogarth Press', in Jeanne Dubino, Gill Lowe, Vara Neverow, and Kathryn Simpson, eds, *Virginia Woolf: Twenty-First-Century Approaches* (Edinburgh: Edinburgh University Press, 2015), 51–71; Diane F. Gillespie, 'Publishing on the Brink of World War II: The Woolfs, The Hogarth Press, and The Refugees', *South Carolina Review* 48, no. 2 (Spring 2016), 14–30; Diane F. Gillespie, 'Advise and Reject: Virginia Woolf, The Hogarth Press, and a Forgotten Woman's Voice', in Julie Vandivere and Megan Hicks, eds, *Virginia Woolf and Her Female Contemporaries* (Clemson, SC: Clemson University Press, 2016), 191–7.

and white space; Drew Shannon's exploration of the Benjaminian 'aura' of originality surrounding Woolf's handprinted booklets; Anna Fewster's doctoral work on Woolf's handprinting, informed by her work as a letterpress artist; and Emily Kopley's forthcoming investigations of the intimate 'reciprocal encouragement between conscientious printing and fine writing' made possible by the Woolfs' prioritizing of poetry selections in their early lists.[28] One particular poem, 'Paris', by Hope Mirrlees, has drawn special attention, editorially and critically, since it forced Woolf very early in her role as publisher to confront, palpably, modernist poetics as a form of typographic radicalism.[29] More recently, graphic designer Ane Thon Knutsen has taken inspiration from Woolf's typesetting experiments to complete a doctorate in graphic design on Woolf's works as well as creating her own installation art exhibitions based on Woolf's radical typographic experimentalism.[30]

Several recent books and one digital humanities initiative have attended broadly to materiality and publishing contexts at the Hogarth Press: Jennifer Sorensen's *Modernist Experimentations in Genre, Media, and Transatlantic Print Culture*[31] interpolates Woolf's early handprinted publications, notably her best-selling mock biography, *Flush* (1933), for 'their hypermediated mixed media material forms [...] centrally focused on human and object relations'; Claire Battershill's *Modernist Lives*[32] investigates in broad terms not just Woolf's iterative engagements in life writing but the Hogarth Press's role as a cultural institution in experimenting with and promoting autobiography and biography as genres. *The Modernist Archives Publishing Project* (MAPP) leverages technology to build a 'critical digital archive' of modernist presses, beginning with the thousands of pieces of paperwork generated by the Hogarth Press. It aims to open modernist publishers' archives to wider interest and scrutiny, aggregating documents across geographically dispersed brick-and-mortar archives, to reveal the often hidden or underrecognized

---

[28] Leslie Hankins, 'Printing "Prelude": Virginia Woolf's Typesetting Apprenticeship and Katherine Mansfield on "Other People's Presses"', in Helen Wussow and Mary Ann Gillies, eds, *Virginia Woolf and the Common(wealth) Reader* (Clemson, SC: Clemson University Digital Press, 2014), 212–22, at 219; Edward Bishop, 'Mind the Gap: The Spaces in *Jacob's Room*', *Woolf Studies Annual* 10 (2004), 31–48; Julia Briggs, 'Search for Form (i)', in Julia Briggs, *Reading Virginia Woolf* (Edinburgh: Edinburgh University Press, 2006), 96–112; Drew Shannon, '"The Book is Still Warm": The Hogarth Press in the Age of Mechanical Reproduction', in Lisa Shahriari and Gina Potts, eds, *Virginia Woolf's Bloomsbury, Volume 2* (London: Palgrave Macmillan, 2010), 124–37; Anna Fewster, *Bloomsbury Books: Materiality, Domesticity, and the Politics of the Marked Page* (PhD diss., University of Sussex, 2009); Emily Kopley, *Virginia Woolf and Poetry* (Oxford: Oxford University Press, forthcoming).

[29] Julia Briggs, 'Modernism's Lost Hope', in Julia Briggs, *Reading Virginia Woolf* (Edinburgh: Edinburgh University Press, 2006), 80–95, at 80–1; Megan Beech, '"Obscure, Indecent and Brilliant" Female Sexuality, the Hogarth Press, and Hope Mirrlees', in Claire Battershill and Nicola Wilson, eds, *Virginia Woolf and the World of Books* (Clemson, SC: Clemson University Press, 2019), 70–5; Sandeep Parmar, ed., *The Collected Poems of Hope Mirrlees* (Manchester: Carcanet Press, 2011).

[30] For Knutsen's installations, see https://cargocollective.com/anethonknutsen and for her thesis see https://www.researchcatalogue.net/view/598364/602024.

[31] Jennifer Sorensen, *Modernist Experimentations in Genre, Media, and Transatlantic Print Culture* (London: Routledge, 2017), 189.

[32] Claire Battershill, *Modernist Lives* (London: Bloomsbury, 2018).

stories behind the production, distribution, and reception of modernist books.[33] The site was launched at the 2017 International Virginia Woolf conference at the University of Reading in celebration of the Hogarth Press's centenary. The conference generated many papers focused on the material textuality of Woolf's oeuvre, selections from which appear in Claire Battershill and Nicola Wilson's edited collection, *Virginia Woolf & the World of Books*.[34]

Notwithstanding this recent renaissance of scholarship on textual materiality in Woolf studies, one crucial question remains undertheorized: how *did* Woolf's modernist aesthetic emerge from a feminist materialist confrontation with the hands-on practices of printing, publishing, and editing at her own press? She may well have been the self-declared 'freest' woman in England, but how did that freedom gain traction—literally—because she learned to typeset and to oversee the operations, industrial and managerial, of a publishing business? How, to paraphrase William Morris, did she conceptualize and enact a modernist artistic practice rooted in the 'resistance in the materials' catalysed by making her own books?[35] A commonplace of Woolf criticism has been that with the arrival of the Hogarth Press in 1917, Woolf's modernism emerged spontaneously, Woolf herself a quasi-modernist Athena sprouting unbidden from the head of Zeus. Her first two novels, *The Voyage Out* (1915) and *Night and Day* (1919) were realist novels, depicting the experiences of modernity, especially between the sexes, but they were not formally experimental. Their generic conventionality was mirrored if not compromised by their entrée into the public sphere as outputs of Duckworth and Co., a successful mainstream press founded in 1898 by Woolf's sexually abusive half-brother, Gerald Duckworth.[36] With the arrival of the Excelsior Press, however, and the accompanying sixteen-page guide book to setting up and operating a home press, Woolf began writing highly experimental short fictions, beginning with 'The Mark on the Wall' (1917), in order to have small, compact units of text to handset and print. Form followed function within the practical exigencies of tabletop printing.

---

[33] A companion print volume, *Scholarly Adventures in Digital Humanities: Making the Modernist Archives Publishing Project* (New York: Palgrave Macmillan, 2017) written by the site's founders, Claire Battershill, Elizabeth Willson Gordon, Michael Widner, Nicola Wilson, Helen Southworth, and Alice Staveley puts their digital work into dialogue with theories and practices long established in book history.

[34] Claire Battershill and Nicola Wilson, eds, *Virginia Woolf & the World of Books* (Liverpool: Liverpool University Press, 2018).

[35] For a brilliant study of the origins of this phrase in Morris's writing, especially its meaning for digital humanists, see Bethany Nowviskie's article 'resistance in the materials', http://nowviskie.org/2013/resistance-in-the-materials. See also Anna Fewster's chapter 'Black Shapes on a White Page: The Influence of Hand Printing on Virginia Woolf's Fiction', especially her inspired reading of the feminist materialism encoded in Woolf's dots and dashes, in Fewster, *Bloomsbury Books*.

[36] Edward L. Bishop reminds us that Woolf's comments about Duckworth 'pawing over' her books implicated his objectification and abuse. See Bishop, 'From Typography to *Time*', 50. Duckworth's is still active today as Duckworth Overlook. Its landing page invokes Woolf's name, not Gerald's, a strategic if still exploitative revisionary history, in describing its origins as 'founded by the family of Virginia Woolf'. https://www.duckworthbooks.co.uk

But why did modernist form follow in the inaugural text Woolf wrote for her own press, the interiorized, consciousness-saturated short fiction, 'The Mark on the Wall'? It wasn't that Woolf was new to short fiction, since she had several unpublished stories in her portfolio going back at least a decade, many of which depict the experiences of women whose narratives or perceptual desires find inadequate generic forms or, in practical terms, publication venues not associated with male familial gatekeepers. For instance, 'Memoirs of a Novelist'—a metafictional mock biography of a fictional female novelist that critiques moribund conventions of biography—was rejected in 1909 by *The Cornhill Gazette*, a periodical formerly edited by Woolf's father, Leslie Stephen, and the story remained unpublished during Woolf's lifetime. Notably, Woolf doesn't resurrect any of her pre-1910 short pieces to practice her typesetting skills. Instead, under pressure to come up with something new, she conjures 'The Mark on the Wall', a reverie about a stationary narrator whose mind, focused on the obscurity of the titular mark, has been liberated to follow its own neural contours, the loops and curves and nonlinear movements of a perambulating, self-searching, associational imagination.

Yet this heightened, even hyperbolic interiority, in the history of the story's conceptualization, is deeply imbricated with Woolf's new print cultural environment. A narrative allegedly about intense inwardness is actually about embodied creative outwardness. Grounded by her press, Woolf's critical lyricism takes flight. The brand of handpress the Woolfs purchased, the Excelsior Press, conjures in its Latinate name—'ever upward'— the intermingling of fixity and flight, rootedness and ascension of a story that revels, metacritically, in the transgressive aspirations of a woman printer composing and compositing her own fictions. At first, the 'mark' that catalyses the mental esprit appears insignificant, even exiguous, 'a small round mark, black upon the white wall, about six or seven inches above the mantelpiece' (*CSF* 83). To an aspirant printer or compositor, this description suggests a diacritical mark like a period, a full stop, on a white page. In intradiegetic terms, however, the narrator *strategically* sets up the mark as worthy of her perceptual attention: aesthetically, in compositional terms in that it is imagined, pointedly, as 'interrupt[ing] [...] an old fancy, an automatic fancy'; practically, when Woolf begins typesetting the story and has to select the punctuational typeface from a casebox (*CSF* 83). The visual mark elides a haptic signifier at once there and not there, the Schrödinger's cat of the printer's case. This controlled dualism between what exists and what does not yet exist but is coming into being—a journey from conception of an idea to holographic text to published booklet guided by the typesetter's hand as she chooses when, where, and how to place that mark on the forbidding wall of the white page—undergirds the speculative start-and-stop perambulations of narratorial cogitation: 'And if I were to get up at this moment and ascertain that the mark on the wall is really—[...] what should I gain?' (*CSF* 87). In short, in making her own books out of her own stories, Woolf self-consciously narrates the material and cognitive processes— and the stakes—of taking back, reclaiming, or limiting the full stop that an overweening patriarchal society has iteratively borne upon women's lives: the ways they can narrate those lives; and the venues available to publish them. This reclamation is not just a thematic thread woven deeply into the story; it is the story of the making of 'The Mark on the Wall' itself. To read its materiality as constitutive of its feminist modernism is to understand the epistemological and political costs of evacuating textual criticism of material history. As Leslie Howsam puts it more generally:

> The book is a material object. From the literary and historical perspectives, the materiality of books is often overlooked, so powerful are their texts and the impacts of those texts upon their times. But bibliographical scholarship demonstrates that the *book-as-object holds the evidence of its own making*; it carries not only the obvious text on its pages but a further 'text' in its format, materials, design and impression.[37]

As a story about cognition that demarcates a shift in Woolf's own consciousness for how to remake narrative form, 'The Mark on the Wall' inaugurates a feminist modernist aesthetic combining an imaginative with a haptic, or hands-on, apprehension for material textuality. Woolf's contemporaneous reflections on her writing process reveal the aspirational but precarious promise of a book's 'lifecycle' from conception, to composition, to printing and publication when administered by a woman's hands.[38] Indeed, Woolf had a habit of eliding the rhetoric of composition (in terms of writing) and that of production (in terms of printing and publication) in her excitement about the arrival of her press. A casual conflation between writing and production—between composition as an author's private writing practice and compositing as a typesetter's practice, which sets up, quite literally, a text for public readership—informs the conceptualization of 'The Mark on the Wall' before Woolf even puts pen to paper. In a letter to Vanessa Bell, Woolf confesses, 'We have just started printing Leonards story ["Three Jews"]; I haven't produced mine yet, but there's nothing in writing compared with printing' (*L2* 155–6). 'It [printing] is tremendous fun, and it makes all the difference writing anything one likes, and not for an Editor' (*L2* 169).

Woolf continually fastens upon the somatically empowering experience of compositing, describing it in gilded language: 'exciting, soothing, ennobling, and satisfying' (*L2* 151). Daily experience she often refracts through the prism of the Hogarth Press. During the long months it took to handset Katherine Mansfield's story, *Prelude*, Woolf channels her inner materialist flâneuse: 'I keep thinking of different ways to manage my scenes; conceiving endless possibilities; seeing life, as I walk about the streets, an immense opaque block of material to be conveyed by me into its equivalent of language' (*D1* 214). These diarized thoughts, her innermost self-reflections, start to become concretized in a hybridized language merging metal and paper, a mind-meld where an ingot awaiting disseveration into tiny pieces of type (or 'sorts')

---

[37] Leslie Howsam, 'The Study of Book History', in Leslie Howsam, ed., *Cambridge Companion to the History of the Book* (Cambridge: Cambridge University Press, 2015), 1–14, at 4. Italics added.

[38] See Robert Darnton's famous 'communications circuit' in 'What is the History of Books (Revisited)?', *Modern Intellectual History* 4, no. 3 (November 2007), 495–508. Revisions of Darnton's original model appear in Nicolas Barker, ed., *A Potencie of Life: Books in Society: The Clarke Lectures* (London: British Library, 1993), 5–43. For a feminist critique of the circuit, see Michelle Levy, 'Do Women Have a Book History', *Studies in Romanticism* 53, no. 3 (Fall 2014), 297–317.

commingles with the suggestive separability of paper: 'Suppose I buy a block, with detachable leaves, I think I shall snare a greater number of loose thoughts' (*D1* 228). These idiomizations of the printer's workshop are not limited to those early years when Woolf is most involved in typesetting her own and others' texts. Here she is again, conceptualizing that most abstract and 'ethereal' of novels, *The Waves* (1931), in uncannily familiar terms, this time less narratorial than characterological:

> There is a square; there is an oblong. The players take the square and place it upon the oblong. They place it very accurately; they make a perfect dwelling-place. Very little is left outside. The structure is now visible; what is inchoate is here stated; we are not so various or so mean; we have made oblongs and stood them upon squares. This is our triumph; this is our consolation. (*W* 128–9)

To understand the embodied, affective experience for Woolf in handling typeface, it is crucial to interrogate how that sense of liberation came twinned with prohibition—a formative triumphal consolation or consolatory triumph perhaps—at the outset of her experiments in printing given the longstanding cultural bias against women compositors. Women had been struggling since at least the mid-nineteenth century to be accepted into the printing trades. The site of the most ferocious resistance was in the compositing rooms of printing houses where, as Michelle Tusan argues, 'male printers had long considered themselves part of a "labor aristocracy," receiving high wages for producing culturally valued products'.[39] Women were often barred from these rooms and passed off with lighter, less remunerative, and more 'feminized' jobs like sewing quires and binding books. The technologized, materialized, and spatialized sex binaries characteristic of a putatively civilized world are what Woolf takes as her target in 'The Mark on the Wall'. Early in the narrator's musings, this thought emerges: 'To show how very little control of our possessions we have—what an accidental affair this living is after all our civilization—let me just count over a few of the things lost in our lifetime, beginning, for that seems always the most mysterious of losses—what cat would gnaw, what rat would nibble—three pale blue canisters of book-binding tools?' (*CSF* 84). Woolf here casts off with playful, sharped-edged irony not only the segregation of book work along a sex/gender axis; she also implicates the powerful symbolism arising from and a priori to it: a privileged metonymy between the materiality of print and the morphology of the male body that produces—or gets to 'handle'—cultural capital in the form of books, newsprint, playbills, money, and so on where letters that 'line up' in the compositor's stick make meaning far beyond the mere 'words on the page'. Woolf was herself an avid bookbinder before becoming a compositor, a sign of the cultural privilege of her youth, but also of its circumscriptions.[40] Recognizing the loss of those tools in 'The Mark on

---

[39] Michelle Tusan, *Women Making News: Gender and Journalism in Modern Britain* (Urbana and Chicago: University of Illinois Press, 2005), 40.

[40] Alan Isaac, *Virginia Woolf, The Uncommon Bookbinder* (London: Cecil Woolf, 2000). See also Anna Fewster's chapter 'Covering and Binding: Virginia Woolf and the Subversive Stitch', in *Bloomsbury Books*.

the Wall' is whimsical but tactical; she now has other less stereotypically feminine tools to play with. When she and Leonard approached St. Bride's Institute after purchasing their press in order to learn the ropes, they were turned away, an exclusion Leonard explains in terms of age and class, but which was most obviously compounded by the profound sexism within the trade unions.[41] So what critics, academic and popular alike, tend to emphasize as the hobbyist cult of the small press, and its amateurish appeal, obscures deeper material historical factors about the costs of women's exclusion from these worlds that lands its mark in 'The Mark on the Wall'.

That Woolf was especially attuned to the rarity of women compositors informs the circumstances surrounding the hiring of the Hogarth Press's first full-time employee, Marjorie Thomson Joad. Woolf was drawn to Joad during a meeting at the 1917 Club when she overhears Joad expatiating on the omission of women compositors to a luckless man sitting having his tea: 'They say there's never been a woman printer; but I mean to be one' (*D2* 213). Woolf, a woman printer of five years standing, puts her eavesdropping into action, following Joad to the writing room to solicit her interest in joining the Hogarth Press. Woolf identifies with Joad, then allies with her. As Nicola Wilson writes, Woolf's outreach coincides with the moment the Woolfs are struggling with the press's workload, and the temptation to sell out to a bigger firm.[42] The 'fight for freedom' Woolf triumphs in when they reject outside offers references Joad: 'we incline to Miss Tomson & freedom' (*D2* 215). Pay parity is not, however, (yet) a goal: Joad is paid £100 a year and 50 per cent of net profits, though this is the same amount for full-time employment earned by the previous (male) incumbent of the job, Ralph Partridge, working only part time.[43]

Woolf enjoys the many hours she spends at the typesetter's case with Joad. She describes them in terms that conflate—even more pronouncedly than when she's writing 'The Mark on the Wall'—shared female compositing work with the cultural capital of a poem that will come in time to epitomize high (male) modernism, T.S. Eliot's *The Waste Land*: 'As for the press, we have finished Tom, much to our relief. He will be published this August by Marjorie; & altogether we have worked at full speed since May' (*D2* 259). Of course, Marjorie can only be seen as the publisher of *The Waste Land* if Woolf conflates printer/compositor with publisher (which technically only she has standing to claim) and if she considers Joad's labour, administrative as well as technical, not only as equal to her own, but also as bearing, in a kind of metonymic metamorphosis, the sacral importance of a woman's laying on (of) hands in making products of cultural value. Far from Eliot's 'typist home at teatime' in *The Waste Land*, these are women setting type, not tea, taking a stand together composing and distributing (or

---

[41] Leonard Woolf, *Beginning Again*, 233. For sexism in the printing trades, see Siân Reynolds, *Brittanica's Typesetters* (Edinburgh: Edinburgh University Press, 1989).

[42] Nicola Wilson, paper presented at Centre for Printing History and Culture, Birmingham, September 2018 and forthcoming in Nicola Wilson and Helen Southworth, 'Early Women Workers at the Hogarth Press (c.1917–25)', in Helen Williams, ed., *Women in Print* (Oxford: Peter Lang, forthcoming).

[43] This translates into about £6,000/year in today's currency.

'dissing' as Woolf liked to say, casting unwitting but proleptic shade on the old orders) letters from an in-home typecase.

Where does this leave future scholarship on Woolf and the Hogarth Press? The short answer: everywhere. The longer answer: with a recognition of how difficult it can be to write Woolf into histories of women and the book precisely because books are an often-overlooked form of technology and technology is an always already gendered enterprise. Woolf's critique of patriarchal norms and practices didn't begin with the Hogarth Press, but it was radically altered by it. 'Seeing the book as a technology means understanding it', writes the book historian Leah Price, 'not just as a statement about the world outside its pages, but as a set of instructions about how those pages themselves should be handled and read'.[44] Woolf was ever conscious of the private coercions, industrial hierarchies, monied interests, and private/public divides lurking behind that subjective imperative, 'should'. Owning a press heightened those interests and gave her a stake in attempting to redress them. When she argues in *A Room of One's Own* (1929) that there is 'no mark on the wall to measure the precise height of women' (*ARO* 64), her allusion to her own feminist modernist practice is redolent of 'biobibliographic' resistance: a bookish retort to manifold attempts to circumscribe what women might achieve; to not placing a limit on their prospects by forcing them to conform to a number or prescribed category.[45]

Underlying much of the essayistic experimentation in *A Room of One's Own*, unheralded and unheard, is Woolf's life as a printer, publisher, and editor. In the narrator's frustrated but perseverative attempts to read *Life's Adventure*, the 'failed' novel of Mary Carmichael's, is the spirit of a generous editor, making quick marginalia notes, wanting to encourage and promote, even if Mary's attempt to break first the sentence, and then the sequence has not yet achieved full narrative transformation (*ARO* 60). For all the interruptions that Woolf argues plague women's attempts to write, the essay itself is full of gestural interruptions to women readers to become the writers who might fill in the missing histories of women that have left capacious gaps on the libraries' shelves. At the Hogarth Press, those writers would, Woolf implies, receive welcome. This textual trace was undoubtedly rooted in oratorical strategy; there are few recorded accounts from the all-female audiences who heard the original lectures on which *A Room of One's Own* was based, but one young woman, E.E. Phare, recounts Woolf's admonition that they should 'all write novels and send them to be considered by the Hogarth Press'.[46]

Reimaging Woolf's transformative contributions to the history of the novel, and to feminist theory and criticism, requires envisioning her inhabiting the multivalent and manifold roles she undertook during her twenty years as owner, editor, reviewer,

---

[44] Leah Price, *What We Talk About When We Talk About Books* (New York: Basic Books, 2019), 31.

[45] David Greetham, *Textual Transgressions: Essays Towards the Construction of a Biobibliography* (New York: Garland, 1998).

[46] Quoted in Woolf, *Women & Fiction: The Manuscript Versions of* A Room of One's Own, ed. S. P. Rosenbaum (Oxford: Blackwell, 1992), xv.

printer, publisher, and writer at the Hogarth Press; roles that were as generative, fluid, integrated, social, and material as she knew them to be:

> I am back again in the thick of my novel [*To the Lighthouse*], and things are crowding into my head: millions of things I might put in—all sorts of incongruities, which I make up walking the streets, gazing into the gas fire. Then I struggle with them, from 10–1: then lie on the sofa, and watch the sun behind the chimneys: and think of more things: then set up a page of poetry in the basement, and so up to tea and Morgan Foster. (*L*3 238)

Selected Bibliography

Battershill, Claire, 'The Hogarth Press', in Lise Jaillant, ed., *Publishing Modernist Fiction and Poetry* (Edinburgh: Edinburgh University Press, 2019), 70–87.

Battershill, Claire, *Modernist Lives: Biography and Autobiography at Leonard and Virginia Woolf's Hogarth Press* (London: Bloomsbury Academic, 2018).

Darnton, Robert, 'What is the History of Books (Revisited)?', *Modern Intellectual History* 4, no. 3 (November 2007), 495–508.

Gordon, Elizabeth Willson, 'How Should One Sell a Book? Production Methods, Material Objects and Marketing at the Hogarth Press', in Lisa Shahriari and Gina Potts, eds, *Virginia Woolf's Bloomsbury*, vol. 2, (London: Palgrave Macmillan, 2010), 107–23.

Hammill, Faye and Mark Hussey, *Modernism's Print Cultures* (London: Bloomsbury, 2016).

Isaac, Alan, *Virginia Woolf, The Uncommon Bookbinder* (London: Cecil Woolf, 2000).

Marcus, Laura, 'Virginia Woolf and the Hogarth Press', in Ian Willison, Warwick Gould, and Warren Chernaik, eds, *Modernist Writers and the Marketplace* (London: Palgrave Macmillan, 1996), 124–50.

McTaggart, Ursula, '"Opening the Door": The Hogarth Press as Virginia Woolf's Outsiders' Society', *Tulsa Studies in Women's Literature* 29, no. 1 (Spring 2010), 63–81.

Southworth, Helen, ed., *Leonard and Virginia Woolf, the Hogarth Press, and the Networks of Modernism* (Edinburgh: Edinburgh University Press, 2010).

Staveley, Alice, 'Marketing Virginia Woolf: Women, War, and Public Relations in *Three Guineas*', *Book History* 12, no. 1 (2009), 295–339.

Tusan, Michelle, *Women Making News: Gender and Journalism in Modern Britain* (Urbana: University of Illinois Press, 2005).

Willis, J. H., Jr, *Leonard and Virginia Woolf as Publishers: The Hogarth Press 1917–1941* (Charlottesville: University Press of Virginia, 1992).

Wilson, Nicola, 'Virginia Woolf, Hugh Walpole, the Hogarth Press, and the Book Society', *English Literary History* 79, no. 1 (Spring 2012), 237–60.

Woolf, Leonard, *Beginning Again* (New York: Harcourt Brace Jovanovich, 1963).

Young, John, '"Murdering an Aunt or Two": Textual Practice and Narrative Form in Virginia Woolf's Metropolitan Market', in Jeanne Dubino, ed., *Virginia Woolf and the Literary Marketplace* (New York: Palgrave, 2010), 181–195.

CHAPTER 17

WOOLF AS REVIEWER-CRITIC

ELEANOR MCNEES

Serious attention to Woolf's essays and reviews was sparse and sporadic until publication of Mark Goldman's 1965 *PMLA* essay, 'Virginia Woolf and the Critic as Reader', and his subsequent 1976 book, *The Reader's Art: Virginia Woolf as Literary Critic*. Goldman was one of the first to investigate Woolf's dual role as critic and reader in her essays and reviews and to dispel the tendency to view her as an undisciplined impressionist critic, victim of the 'subjective taint of the Pater-Wilde inheritance'.[1] Goldman pinpointed the movement from reader to critic most prominently enunciated in Woolf's insistence on two kinds of reading in her 1926 essay 'How Should One Read a Book'. Throughout her career and well before the publication of that essay, Woolf's reviews already evoked the tension between impressionistic reader and evaluative critic. Gradually, and especially in the 1920s, Woolf's reviews (as instanced by her assessments of Conrad and Hemingway) begin to negotiate this tension more fluidly as they shift between perspectives, between inner recorder of perceptions and external analysis. This move in the reviews and essays parallels her increasing facility with free indirect discourse in the great novels of the 1920s as well—her discovery of the 'tunnelling process' in *Mrs Dalloway* (1925) and her movement from interior consciousnesses to impersonal interlude and back to interior consciousness in *To the Lighthouse* (1927). Assuming confidence as both a reviewer and a novelist whose own works were subject to multiple reviews, Woolf grew from a reviewer into a critic, subsequently criticizing other reviewers who failed to demonstrate a similar growth.[2] Her April 1931 assessment of Keats's harshest reviewer, John Lockhart,

---

[1] Mark Goldman, 'Virginia Woolf and the Critic as Reader', *PMLA* 80, no. 3 (June 1965), 275–84, at 276.

[2] Since Goldman's study, scholars have conflated Woolf's essays and reviews to focus specifically on Woolf's dialogic partnership with the reader. See especially Edward L. Bishop, 'Metaphor and the Subversive Process of Virginia Woolf's Essays', *Style* 21, no. 4 (1987), 573–88; Leila Brosnan, *Reading Virginia Woolf's Essays and Journalism* (Edinburgh: Edinburgh University Press, 1997); Elena Gualtieri, *Virginia Woolf's Essays* (New York: St. Martin's Press, 2000); Katerina Koutsantoni, *Virginia Woolf's Common Reader* (London: Ashgate, 2009); and Randi Saloman, *Virginia Woolf's Essayism* (Edinburgh: Edinburgh University Press, 2012). On dialogic method borrowed from Bakhtin's discourse

faults Lockhart less for his famously savage attack on Keats and more for his failure to move from the reviewer 'who skims the surface' to the critic who must 'push on into those calm and austere regions where the mind settles down to think things out and has its dwelling in a mood of gentle and universal contemplation'.[3]

En route from reviewer to critic, Woolf followed in her father Leslie Stephen's footsteps though, unlike Stephen, she never wholly abandoned reviewing. Both Leslie Stephen and Virginia Woolf entered the profession of reviewing through family connections. Leslie's older brother, James Fitzjames (a barrister who wrote reviews and 'middles' for the *Saturday Review* and *The Pall Mall Gazette*), secured Leslie's introduction to the editor of the *Saturday Review*. Similarly, family friend Violet Dickinson introduced Woolf (Virginia Stephen until 1912) in 1904 to Kathleen (Margaret) Lyttelton, editor of the *Women's Supplement* of the Anglo-Catholic *Guardian*. From the late 1850s, both Stephen brothers reviewed a wide range of literature for the *Saturday Review*, and both frequently commented on the quasi-respectability of journalism as a profession.[4] In one incisive discussion, 'The Two Sides of Criticism', Fitzjames Stephen, conflating reviewer and critic, sums up the biased role of the reviewer-critic when he notes that 'The critic either approaches his subject moved to sympathy with it, or disposed to attack it; and the exigencies of his calling preclude his perfect impartiality'.[5] The reviewer-critic (arguably the dual role Virginia Woolf would assume), he continues, need not worry about their own harshness or leniency as another will likely balance out opinion, a view that, as Woolf asserts in her late essay 'Reviewing' (1939) invalidates the criticism. In suggesting, however, a critical method for the reviewer, J.F. Stephen anticipates Woolf's own process of reviewing, particularly her emphasis on capturing a dominant impression that reflects the work's merits or deficits. Stephen states that the reviewer 'has to ask himself what is the predominating impression which he wishes to produce'.[6] He also indicates

---

model and often aligned with reader-response theory in Woolf's essays, see Beth Carole Rosenberg, *Virginia Woolf and Samuel Johnson: Common Readers* (New York: St. Martin's Press, 1995); Hermione Lee, 'Virginia Woolf's Essays', in Sue Roe and Susan Sellers, eds, *The Cambridge Companion to Virginia Woolf* (Cambridge: Cambridge University Press, 2000), 91–108; Jim Stewart, ' "Poetics ... will fit me for a reviewer!": Aristotle and Woolf's Journalism', in Bryony Randall and Jane Goldman, eds, *Virginia Woolf in Context* (Cambridge: Cambridge University Press, 2012), 322–31; Jeanne Dubino, 'Virginia Woolf: From Book Reviewer to Literary Critic, 1904-1918', in Beth Carole Rosenberg and Jeanne Dubino, eds, *Virginia Woolf and the Essay* (New York: St. Martin's Press 1997), 25–40; and Beth Daugherty, 'Virginia Stephen, Book Reviewer: or The Apprentice and her Editors', in Eleanor McNees and Sara Veglahn, eds, *Woolf Editing / Editing Woolf* (Clemson, SC: Clemson University Press 2009), 63–9; Beth Daugherty, 'Reading, Taking Notes, and Writing: Virginia Stephen's Reviewing Practice', in Jeanne Dubino, ed., *Virginia Woolf and the Literary Marketplace* (New York: Palgrave Macmillan 2010), 27–41.

[3] Virginia Woolf, 'Lockhart's Criticism', in Stuart N. Clarke, ed., *The Essays of Virginia Woolf: Vol. 5* (London: Hogarth Press, 2009), 241–7, at 244, 245.

[4] See James Fitzjames Stephen, 'The Profession of Journalism', *Saturday Review* 1 (January 1859), 9–10; and Leslie Stephen's grudging respect for the *Saturday Review*'s elevation of journalistic standards: Leslie Stephen, 'Journalism', *Atlantic Monthly* 92 (November 1903), 611–22.

[5] James Fitzjames Stephen, 'The Two Sides of Criticism', *Saturday Review* 6 (18 December 1858), 611–12, at 611.

[6] J. F. Stephen, 'Two Sides', 611.

the structure Woolf elaborates in many of her early reviews. For Stephen, a mixed review consists of a 'qualification' followed by 'the substance', a move Woolf's reviews notice in her persistent use of 'but'.[7]

Virginia Woolf's debt to Leslie Stephen's journalistic career and specifically to his reviews was more obvious than her unacknowledged debt to her uncle. Frequently, their methods were strikingly similar as in Leslie Stephen's 'Thoughts on Criticism by a Critic' (1876) and Woolf's 'How It Strikes a Contemporary' (1923): the ironic tone, the use of analogy and metaphor, and their assessment of the role of the reviewer-critic work to highlight an author's merits or failings.[8] Both found themselves in their early journalistic years reviewing what Leslie Stephen termed 'ephemeral' literature. Stephen frequently disparaged his own role as reviewer, calling himself a 'penny-a-liner' who 'read[s] some of the greatest rubbish that appears in the English language in order to criticize it in the paper'.[9] Woolf's essay, 'How It Strikes a Contemporary' (1923), reaches a similar conclusion: the contemporary critic, if such a figure even exists, should try to 'see the present in relation to the future' (*E3* 359). Too often the reviewer lacks perspective in a rush to offer an immediate verdict. Though, like Leslie Stephen, Woolf tended to elevate the critic over the reviewer, she increasingly merged them into the reviewer-critic as her own reviews of the 1920s began both to expound and enact her own critical standards.

Aware of her paternal literary heritage and of her privileged entrance into the world of reviewing by means of family connections, Woolf remained in dialogue with her father's essays and reviews and used that dialogue to legitimize her own role as a female reviewer-critic. Her apprenticeship to Leslie Stephen and to her first editors, Kathleen Lyttelton and Bruce Richmond, and to a lesser extent, *Cornhill's* Reginald Smith, was provisional but formative. Woolf's first published review (of some seventy reviews and notices for the *Women's Supplement* to the *Guardian*) was a short evaluation of American novelist William Dean Howells's *The Son of Royal Langbrith* in the 14 December 1904 issue—less than a year after her father's death.[10] Even in this early piece, Woolf exhibits a trait that characterizes many of her later reviews: she begins with a definitive declarative sentence that places the work or the author in one of two opposite literary camps: 'Mr Howells is the exponent of the novel of thought as distinct from the novel of action' (*E1* 3). Throughout her reviewing career Woolf praised writers (novelists, poets, memoirists, biographers) who prized thought as evidence of their sincerity. The rest of the review

---

[7] J. F. Stephen, 'Two Sides', 611.

[8] Andrew McNeillie acknowledges Leslie Stephen's considerable influence on Woolf's reading and writing practices, ones akin to Stephen's own. See *The Essays of Virginia Woolf*, vol. 4, ed. Andrew McNeille (London: Hogarth Press, 1994), xi–xii.

[9] Leslie Stephen to Oliver Wendell Holmes, Jr, 8 November 1866, in *Selected Letters of Leslie Stephen*, vol. 1, ed. John W. Bicknell (Columbus: Ohio State University Press, 1996), 32.

[10] Kathleen Lyttelton was an advocate of female suffrage and author of a book, *Women and their Work* (1901), though she held a religious and conservative view about separate spheres for men and women (Serena Kelly, *Oxford Dictionary of National Biography*, https://doi-org.du.idm.oclc.org/10.1093/ref:odnb/50712).

summarizes the plot (an 'obligatory' exercise she would almost entirely abandon by the 1920s) with a final sentence that sounds naively stilted as she dons the mask of formal reviewer: 'It is needless to say that the whole is beautifully proportioned, and told in the reserved and expressive language of a man who has much skill in writing' (E1 5).

In February 1905, Woolf published her first review of a book by a major author—Henry James's *The Golden Bowl*—in the *Guardian*. She was initially excited to receive a work by a writer whom her father had serialized in *Cornhill Magazine* and who by 1905 was a respected novelist. (Woolf would write six more articles and/or reviews of James's works both for the *Guardian* and the *Times Literary Supplement* (*TLS*).) However, as she read the '550 pages of James's novel', she noted 'the long drawn out Henry James' adding, 'I shall have earned the shillings I make by this review at any rate' (*PA* 235). After she submitted the review, she was irritated to hear from the editor that it had to be cut by a third. She fumed in her journal, 'So I must cut it down, spoil it, & waste I dont know how many hours work, all because the worthy Patronesses want to read about midwives' (*PA* 235).[11] Still, the review is striking for its persistently critical tone couched in an extended simile. Doubtless, the guise of anonymity allowed Woolf more freedom to be honest, even though her conclusion, like that of the Howells review, reverses course to offer self-consciously stilted praise. As she would complain in later reviews, James's novel, though 'exquisite [in its] felicity of word or thought which alone would illumine a whole chapter of an ordinary novel', finally fails to capture living characters (*E1* 22, 24). In a simile she reprises in her response to James's editor Percy Lubbock's *Craft of Fiction* six years later, she asserts that 'Mr James is like an artist who, with a sure knowledge of anatomy, paints every bone and muscle in the human frame; the portrait would be greater as a work of art if he were content to say less and suggest more' (*E1* 23). The review announces two critical yardsticks by which Woolf would measure other fiction in subsequent reviews: the crucial importance of creating living characters, and the power of suggestion over statement, best embodied in works by the Russian novelists Tolstoy and Dostoevsky, and also by Conrad.

Woolf's shift in late 1905 to reviewing for the *TLS* was to establish her as the foremost female reviewer amongst a small clique of male contributors to the periodical.[12] Her diaries relate the history of her professional relationship with the *TLS* over nearly four decades of Bruce Richmond's editorship. After an arranged invitation to a dinner in February 1905 where she was introduced to Richmond, she received a request to review new works for the *TLS*: 'So I said yes', she reports, '& thus my work gets established, & I suppose I shall soon have as much as I can do—which is certainly satisfactory' (*PA* 234). Aside from having Richmond solicit and then reject one review (on Catherine de Medici in April 1905, because Woolf was not 'a professed historian'),

---

[11] For Woolf's careful attention to detail in the process of reading and responding to a text slated for review, see her ten pages of notes in the Monks House Collection (SxMs-18/2/B/1/A).

[12] For an assessment of Woolf's key role amidst a radical group of young male reviewers for the *TLS*, see Derwent May, *Critical Times: The History of the* Times Literary Supplement (New York: Harper Collins, 2001), 52, 70.

Woolf was to receive from him a steady stream of books of all literary genres—novel, memoir, biography, letters, essays—for the next three decades. As she comments ironically in her diary on 14 March 1905: 'Another book from the Times!—a fat novel, I'm sorry to say. They pelt me now' (*PA* 252). And in a 10 November 1905 letter to her friend Nelly (Lady Robert) Cecil (with whom she would subsequently collaborate on a 'Books on the Table' series of reviews for *Cornhill Magazine*), she playfully states, 'The Times sends me one novel every week; which has to be read on Sunday, written on Monday, and printed on Friday. In America, you know, they make sausages like that' (*L1* 211–12). Her professional relationship with Richmond was mutually valuable, especially as Woolf's reputation as a novelist rose, though in December 1921 she expressed frustration at Richmond's insistence that she delete the 'vulgar' adjective 'lewd' from an essay about James's Ghost Stories (*D2* 151), later vowing, 'No more reviewing for me, now that Richmond re-writes my sentences to suit the mealy mouths of Belgravia' (*D2* 155). By July 1927, when she had begun to review works for a wider range of journals, she was confident enough to ask Richmond for a raise as she 'can't always refuse £60 in America for the *Times*' £10' (*D3* 149). In 1938, wistfully recalling her long connection with Richmond and the *TLS*, she admitted, 'I learnt a lot of my craft writing for him: how to compress; how to enliven; & also was made to read with a pen & notebook, seriously' (*D5* 145).

Woolf's first brief departure from anonymous reviewing occurred in 1908 when she shared the *Cornhill Magazine* series 'Books on the Table' with Nelly Cecil. Under the editorship of Reginald Smith, she signed her six reviews as her father had signed his contributions to the 'Hours in a Library' series in *Cornhill* in the 1870s. Of Woolf's *Cornhill* reviews, the first, 'The Memoirs of Sarah Bernhardt' (February 1908), and the fourth, 'A Week in the White House with Theodore Roosevelt' (August 1908), reveal two distinct aspects of her reviewing persona. They also emphasize Woolf's preoccupation with character, her attempt, as she would famously enunciate in 'Mr Bennett and Mrs Brown' (1922), to capture the essence of personality—the spirit of life.[13] In her review of Bernhardt's memoirs, and throughout her reviewing career, Woolf tries, according to Hermione Lee, 'to connect reading and writing. She gets inside the writer, feels her way to the essence, saturates herself, and then tries to communicate that saturation.'[14] In this early review, Woolf 'saturates herself' with Bernhardt's written voice to extract and enact specific scenes from the actress's account. Attempting to demonstrate how Bernhardt inhabits a character on stage, Woolf reverts to pictorial analogies, to the 'precision and vitality of colored and animated photographs' Bernhardt's words conjure (*E1* 166). Woolf offers Bernhardt's receptivity to impressions as an analogy for a similar receptivity in the

---

[13] Leila Brosnan regards Woolf's *Cornhill* reviews as marking a turning point with the discovery of her 'method of arguing by analogy and association'. Brosnan, *Reading Virginia Woolf's Essays and Journalism*, 63.

[14] Hermione Lee, '"Crimes of Criticism": Virginia Woolf and Literary Journalism', in Jeremy Treglown and Bridget Bennett, eds, *Grub Street and the Ivory Tower: Literary Journalism and Literary Scholarship from Fielding to the Internet* (Oxford: Clarendon Press, 1998), 132.

reader: 'It is her business to be able to concentrate all that she feels into some gesture perceptible to the eye, and to receive her impressions of what is going on in the minds of others from the same tokens also' (E1 166). The review concludes by raising a dilemma that troubles Woolf from her early to her late reviews (and one she seeks to solve in 'How Should One Read a Book'): the reviewing persona acknowledges the difficulty of shifting from reader to reviewer after the reader has been 'under the obsession of a book' (E1 169). In trying to capture the fleeting qualities of Bernhardt, Woolf (echoing Walter Pater's Conclusion to *The Renaissance*) embodies her theory of personality in a metaphorical question: 'Are we not', she asks, trying to grasp the peculiarly elusive quality of Bernhardt's personality, 'each in truth the center of innumerable rays which so strike upon one figure only, and is it not our business to flash them straight and completely back again, and never suffer a single shaft to blunt itself on the far side of us?' (E1 170).[15] Woolf's method here (along with her frustration)—the oxymoronic attempt to 'grasp' and elucidate the ephemeral personality—persists throughout her reviewing career, culminating in her final published essay on another actress, Ellen Terry in 1941. She resorts to free indirect discourse making it difficult to distinguish the reviewer's voice from that of the subject in the work under review.[16] Especially in memoirs and letters where the audience is private—either oneself or one other person—this ventriloquist technique allows Woolf to connect reader and memoirist or letter-writer by obscuring the reviewer's middle-voiced position.

Woolf's *Cornhill* review of Hale's 'A Week in the White House' adopts an alternative reviewing persona to convey character. Instead of submerging her voice beneath that of the character via free indirect discourse, she devises what Hermione Lee terms her 'scene-making' technique to place the reader of the review in the character's room, in this case Roosevelt's study in the White House. She quotes Hale's detailed commonplace description to set the keynote of Roosevelt's 'rough and ready' peculiarly American quality, one that is radically democratic in its general interest in humanity and the common man but oblivious to subtlety. Roosevelt, like his study, she surmises, prefers 'the simplest form of life' to the '"worlds of poetry and romance"' (E1 208). The pronominal shift to 'you' in the final paragraph unites the reviewer and the British audience against Roosevelt and the American people. The American people (like Roosevelt), she asserts, 'forced as they are to do without the luxuries of tradition, must find in themselves a raw material and exalt it above the finished form' (E1 209). In her subsequent reviews of American writers, Woolf invokes this raw democratic impulse that elevates vitality above subtlety and sophistication. These early *Cornhill* reviews illustrate two different methods Woolf would pursue in her later reviews: a ventriloquistic

---

[15] 'Experience, already reduced to a group of impressions, is ringed round for each one of us by that thick wall of personality through which no real voice has ever pierced on its way to us, or from us to that which we can only conjecture to be without.' See Walter Pater, *The Renaissance: Studies in Art and Poetry* [1873] (New York: Oxford University Press, 1986), 151.

[16] For a useful description of Woolf's subtle manipulation of free indirect discourse see Anna Snaith, *Virginia Woolf: Public and Private Negotiations* (New York: St. Martin's Press, 2000), 63–64.

presentation of character or a telescopic focus on a single trait to imprint the character on the reader's mind.

The lead article 'Modern Fiction' in the *TLS* in 1919 signals the end of Woolf's early period of reviewing and the beginning of a middle period in the 1920s when her reviews staged the growth of reviewer into critic. Between 1907 and 1919 she had written primarily for the *TLS* with the exception of her signed ventures in *Cornhill Magazine*. However, when Desmond MacCarthy assumed editorship of the *New Statesman* in 1920, she began to branch beyond anonymous reviews to signed pieces in other periodicals. When Leonard Woolf accepted the position of literary editor of the newly merged *Nation and Athenaeum* in 1923, she published reviews and essays frequently there as well. By 1925, she had begun to penetrate the American market with essays and reviews (mostly signed) in *Vogue*, the *New York Herald Tribune*, and the *Yale Review*. Still, her production in *TLS* contained some of her most trenchant theoretical and methodological principles from 'Modern Fiction' to her critical essays 'On Re-Reading Novels' (*TLS* 20 July 1922) and 'How it Strikes a Contemporary' (*TLS* 5 April 1923). 'On Re-reading Novels' mounts an internal debate on the merits and limitations of Percy Lubbock's *The Craft of Fiction*, the first book, as she admits, to devote itself to form in fiction. Woolf's response to and continuing preoccupation with Lubbock's work mark a new self-conscious awareness of stylistic elements in her later reviews. At first, she rails against Lubbock's suggestion that the author's intended form—and not the emotion—is the central ingredient in a novel: 'We must receive impressions, but we must relate them to each other as the author intended; and we can only do his bidding by making ourselves acquainted with his method. When we have form itself ... it is this which endures, however mood or fashion may change' (*E3* 339). Woolf continued to wrestle with Lubbock's emphasis on form in her reviews as well as in her essays and novels, and she returned to it when she was writing her biography of Roger Fry.[17] Yet, ultimately, she disagreed that form governs impression or emotion. As in the double readings of 'How Should One Read a Book', she argues emotion must precede any formal reading: 'The novelist's method is simply his device for expressing his emotion', though she concedes, 'if we discover how that effect is produced we shall undoubtedly deepen the impression' (*E3* 342).

In the 1920s, Woolf began to embed her critical theories of reading and reviewing in reviews in *New York Herald Tribune*—'Life and the Novelist' (7 November 1926)—and in 'An Essay in Criticism' (9 October 1927). Her unpublished typescript, 'Byron and Mr Briggs', however, most explicitly dramatizes these theories. Intended as the introductory chapter to an unfinished book, tentatively titled 'Reading', Woolf enacts the dilemma of the reviewer about to assess a novel by a first-time novelist: 'what could be easier [she asks] than to run through the four hundred pages of sufficiently large print? (type between tea & dinner)' (*E3* 474). Her reply evinces the ironic humour typical of

---

[17] Telling Fry in 1924 that she has been writing about Lubbock's *The Craft of Fiction*, she distinguishes it from Fry's idea of form in painting: 'I say it is emotion put into the right relations; and has nothing to do with form as used of painting. But this you must tidy up for me when we meet' (*L3* 133).

her reviews: 'And next morning, perhaps with labor, perhaps without, the impression would be floated onto paper and would be found to measure not less than two, but certainly not more than five, of what printers call Long Primer' (E3 474). The ensuing thirty-eight typescript pages between this facile solution and the final sentence of the piece produce a lengthy series of procrastinations and digressions at the end of which the review remains unwritten. The typescript concludes with the narrator's admonition to herself: 'It is high time to begin the review' (E3 499).

This interval between the opening intention and the unfulfilled action contains some of Woolf's most astute remarks on the relationships among readers, reviewers, critics, and writers.[18] She introduces her 'common reader' who stands in deliberate contrast to both reviewer and critic. Hinting at the two kinds of reading (impressionistic and judicial) elaborated in 'How Should One Read a Book', the narrator/reviewer persona of 'Byron and Mr Briggs' begins by aligning herself with the subhuman reviewer: 'Any parrot can repeat their blunders', and 'Any pig can sort the critics into schools. There is the biographic; the psychological; the socio-political; the historical; the aesthetic, the impressionist; (the scientific) analytic' (E3 476). The porcine reviewer, she suggests, performs the mindless task of sorting and categorizing, while increasingly specialized critics have cut themselves off from common readers. Neither critic nor reviewer, consequently, offer satisfactory evaluations of the work: whereas the critic approaches a literary work with a particular bias, the reviewer 'never penetrated(s) deep enough to lay hold upon a principle' (E3 477). The contemporary reviewer, forced to read a book or two a week and then compress her impressions into a column or two, becomes a predator: 'Like a man in a shooting gallery...he sees...books move steadily past in front of (past) him. Bang! He lets fly. The rabbit is missed...but he has only just time to reload before taking aim at the pheasant' (E3 477). Consequently, both critic and reviewer are inferior to the 'common reader' who, lacking the bias of the critic and having more leisure time than the reviewer, is free to approach the literary work directly. This triangular conversation between reviewer, critic, and common reader persists particularly in the performative reviews of the 1920s. 'Byron and Mr Briggs' illustrates the complex triadic relationship that pervades Woolf's reviews as she alternately dons the persona of common reader and then doffs it for that of the reviewer-critic. It also reinforces the two types of reading—the receptive absorption of impressions followed by active analytical reflection. The common reader (and sometimes the too hasty reviewer) often halts at the first reading whereas the critic proceeds to the second reading. In her early reviews Woolf tries to perform both readings simultaneously, but as she gained stature as a reviewer, essayist, and novelist she moved more confidently between receptive and analytic modes.

---

[18] Andrew McNeillie notes the significance of 'Byron and Mr Briggs' to Woolf's emerging theory of criticism and the common reader: 'For it is here that she begins to explore, in the person of Mr Briggs...the nature of the relationship between Dr. Johnson's "common reader" and "literature"' (E3 xvi).

Woolf's development from reviewer to reviewer-critic is most evident in her series of reviews of Conrad's works as well as those of Russian authors from Dostoevsky to Turgenev. As she surveys their productions, she steeps herself in a broader historical and aesthetic context, and her reviews assume a critical authority that extends beyond her earlier common reader persona. In 1923 in the last—and most experimental—of her six reviews of Conrad's writings, Woolf dramatizes a fictitious debate between a reviewer-critic and his common reader interlocutor. The only Conrad review to be published in *Nation and Athenaeum* (all others appeared anonymously in *TLS*), this radical departure from her previous more conventionally structured reviews forces the (common) reader to oscillate from one perspective to another and so to form a more independent view of Conrad's merits. The gendered debate hinges on the critical question as to whether Conrad is a 'classic' author (*E3* 376). The *male* reviewer-critic Lowe (echoing Woolf's previous critical assessments of Conrad's limitations) argues that Conrad fails to rise to classic status because he has a 'mind of one facet' (*E3* 376). But the *female* common reader Otway disagrees; she avers that a great novelist can 'reconcile ... opposites'. Conrad's books, she concludes, 'are full of moments of vision'. 'They light up a whole character in a flash' (*E3* 378). Yet the male critic Lowe has the last word in the debate when he characterizes Conrad as a foreigner who is 'too formal, too courteous, too scrupulous in the use of a language which is not his own' (*E3* 379). Though Woolf's earlier reviews evinced the same ambivalence enacted in this staged conversation between critic and common reader, this new overtly dialogic and performative method challenges the reader/audience to participate in a debate about critical standards. If, in this final review, Woolf manipulates the debate to favour the critic, her earlier reviews of Conrad's works praise a technique she strove throughout her own novels to adopt—the tension between surface and depth. From her 1917 review of *Lord Jim* with its 'silent surfaces and their immense reserves of strength' (*E2* 143) to her review of *Notes on Life and Letters* (1921) where 'The waves heave ever so slightly on the surface, but the waters beneath are unfathomably deep' (*E3* 290), she reveals her dual roles as novelist and reviewer-critic. The 'great' writers whom she both admires and faults challenge her to refine her critical approach, to move beyond the superficiality of a hasty review.

Woolf's reviews of the Russian novelists Tolstoy and Dostoevsky similarly engage both her critical and novelistic personae in their agile movement between surface and depth. Tolstoy, with his ability to make each detail an index of internal character and his 'continuous vein of thought', perhaps outpaces Conrad, but both writers possess 'that extraordinary union of extreme simplicity combined with the utmost subtlety' (*E2* 77–9). Likewise, Dostoevsky, though inferior to Tolstoy, forces the reader to enter a 'labyrinth of soul' English writers do not mine (*E2* 85). Woolf admires Dostoevsky's ability to follow thought beneath the surface, 'to suggest the dim and populous underworld of the mind's consciousness where desires and impulses are moving blindly beneath the sod' (*E2* 85).

Woolf writes another experimental review on 9 October 1927 for the American *New York Herald Tribune* of Ernest Hemingway's *Men Without Women* where she engages Hemingway's method as an excuse to announce her shift from reviewer to critic. Purposely conflating review with critical essay in its title, 'An Essay in Criticism', it enacts (as did her final Conrad review) Woolf's debate between reviewer-critic and common reader. Here, however, the reviewer-critic bullies the common reader into distrusting one's personal impressions.[19] Woolf devotes two-thirds of the review to a discussion of the critic's problematic relation to the common reader. The now conflated reviewer-critic makes the reader so self-conscious and timid that 'He [the reader] begins to doubt and conceal his own sensitive, hesitating apprehensions when they conflict with the critics' decrees' (E4 450). Yet this reviewer-critic occupies a difficult position: he 'has to give us his opinion of a book that has been published two days, perhaps, with the shell still sticking to its head' (E4 450). A critical opinion that doesn't allow for a second evaluative reading is necessarily flawed.

Deploying a method increasingly typical of her longer reviews (and dramatized in the Conrad debate)—slipping back and forth between common reader and reviewer-critic—Woolf self-deprecatingly aligns herself with the 'humble' common reader as opposed to the strident reviewer-critic: 'So the crude trumpet blasts of critical opinion blow loud and shrill, and we, humble readers that we are, bow our submissive heads' (E4 450). The dialogic model that critics identify in Woolf's essays is on full display here as Woolf jumps from critic to common reader and back to critic. This review of Hemingway, an American author with whom she cannot empathize, marks, like the final Conrad review, Woolf's merging of reviewer and critic in dialogue with the 'common' reader.[20] It also illustrates the various narrative methods and the more assured tone she began to employ in the 1920s within her longer reviews, especially in those published in American periodicals. This enhanced freedom to stage critical debates within a review coincided with Woolf's burgeoning fame as a novelist. Her signed reviews during the 'middle' period of the 1920s allowed her to announce her own critical methodology, whereas the anonymous TLS reviews (though increasingly longer and more prominently placed) still followed a more traditional review format. Woolf's Hemingway review demonstrates another characteristic of her more sophisticated reviews—manipulation of metaphor (here the bullfighting scene)—to display what for her is a central flaw in Hemingway's writing—its falsity: 'Mr Hemingway's writing ... gives us now and then a real emotion, because he keeps absolute purity of line in his movements and lets the horns (which are truth, fact, reality) pass him close each time. But there is something faked, too, which turns bad and gives an unpleasant feeling—that also we must face in course of time' (E4 452). As in her earlier reviews, she reverts to the 'pivotal' conjunction

---

[19] See Melba Cuddy-Keane, *Virginia Woolf: The Intellectual and the Public Sphere* (New York: Cambridge University Press, 2003). Cuddy-Keane discusses the complicated reading process Woolf performs in this review; she argues that Woolf creates a 'self-reflexive evaluative critic' and uses Hemingway as a 'test case' to 'write a metacritical commentary on the evaluative process itself' (187).

[20] Ironically, as McNeillie recounts in his notes to the review, Hemingway read Woolf's review in Paris's Shakespeare and Company bookshop and became 'so furious that he punched a lamp and broke it' (E4 456n1).

'but' to turn praise to blame.[21] Stepping into the role of critic, she reminds the reader of her comparative method: the critic 'has to decide which are the most salient points of the book he has just read; to distinguish accurately to what kind they belong, and then, holding them against whatever model is chosen for comparison, to bring out their deficiency or their adequacy' (E4 452). At the close of the review, Woolf reprises the bullfighting metaphor to condemn a lack of truth in Hemingway's story, characters, and style: 'For in truth story writing has much in common with bullfighting' (E4 455). In the final sentence Woolf returns to the self-conscious persona of the reviewer-critic: 'So we sum him up. So we reveal some of the prejudices, the instincts and the fallacies out of which what it pleases us to call criticism is made' (E4 455). Yet the irony of the critic's biased position undermines his/her authority and makes one question the validity of the judgement. Are 'prejudices ... instincts ... fallacies' valid standards of criticism, or are they, in fact, the tools of the reviewer? Scrutinizing the method and content of the Hemingway review midway through Woolf's reviewing career offers readers a keener awareness of her multiple reviewing personae and the devices these personae employ to engage readers.

Woolf's review of Harold Nicolson's *Some People* (30 October 1927), like her review-manifesto of Hemingway, shows her working to codify the processes of writing and to erect new standards for evaluating works. In this review she first coins her terms of 'granite-like solidity' and 'rainbow-like intangibility' to describe the biographer's difficulty in reconciling two seemingly opposing qualities. The formal skeleton Lubbock stressed must mesh somehow with the kaleidoscopic rainbow of impressions from which a biographer has to select in writing a life.

Woolf's reviews of the late 1920s anticipate her own projected critical book, 'Phases of Fiction'. Originally advertised as a pamphlet in the Hogarth Press series, the work ultimately resulted in three sequential essays in the American publication, *The Bookman*, in the spring of 1929. 'Phases of Fiction', like her two *Common Readers*, builds on her extensive practice in reviewing a wide range of novels, and especially on new editions of 'classic' works. Woolf revisited her review of a new edition of Defoe's *Robinson Crusoe* for the *Nation and Athenaeum* in February 1926 to journey over several centuries of novelists and to contrast Defoe's complete sense of reality where 'no shadow mitigates the solidity of any object', with the atmospheric density of Hardy and Proust (E3 334). Fifteen years of reviewing editions of most of the novels she discusses underpin Woolf's deceptively casual method of *Phases of Fiction* where she nudges the reader from one kind of novel to another. This process foreshadows her late unfinished book on reading with its chapter, 'Reading at Random', again deceptively simple but reinforced by extensive notes on literature and history. The note-taking that Woolf learned in preparing her earliest reviews here in her final project provides the foundation for her recuperative presentation of the history of reading.

---

[21] Woolf's reviews, as Edward Bishop comments, 'pivot ... on a disclaimer; her most common one, "But", works to shift the reader from one view to its opposite as metaphor frequently jerks one from one mental image to a completely unfamiliar one'. See Bishop, 'Metaphor and the Subversive Process', 574.

A decade after 'Phases of Fiction', Woolf published her mordantly satirical 1939 pamphlet 'Reviewing', a savage indictment of reviewers who failed to become critics. By then Woolf herself had been the target of both laudatory and hostile reviews for three decades.[22] Consequently, she understood her own ambivalent position as reviewer and author, as she confessed in a letter to the *New Statesman and Nation* in response to a highly critical review of 'Reviewing'. Personifying the reviewer as a parasitic insect, Woolf admitted, 'I am a louse myself, and well aware of it; but if ... the rest of my colleagues are gay little crickets chirruping about the house to their own content ... I withdraw every word and keep both contempt and pity for myself' (*L6* 370). In his review of Woolf's pamphlet, 'Y. Y.' (Robert Lynd) had called Woolf's cynical assessment of reviewers 'surely the most contemptuous yet uttered'.[23] He defended the role of the reviewer as useful to a society hungry for books but in need of 'advice'. For 'Y. Y.' the reviewer should be 'at once a reporter and a guide', sometimes even a critic if 'he is lucky enough to come on a work of genius'.[24] The reviewer's duty to the public is 'to discover and announce excellence, whatever its kind ... to say whether a new book is or is not excellent for its intended purpose'.[25] Siding with Leonard Woolf's postscript to Woolf's pamphlet, 'Y. Y.' agrees that a reviewer is ultimately 'the go-between between the public and literature, even if most of this is only temporary literature'.[26] The review goaded Virginia Woolf into offering her sarcastic response the following week.

At the heart of Woolf's tirade against early twentieth-century reviewing practices is the proliferation of both books and reviewers, so many, in fact, that (echoing J.F. Stephen's 'Two Sides of Criticism') reviews appear to cancel each other out: 'Now that he has sixty reviews where in the nineteenth century he had perhaps six, he finds that there is no such thing as "an opinion" of his work. Praise cancels blame; and blame praise. There are as many different opinions of his work as there are different reviewers' (*E6* 198). The only justification then for a review is its ability to influence sales; it has ceased to be of value to the writer or to persuade the prospective reader to read the work. If so, Woolf quips, 'Why bother to write reviews or to read them or to quote them if in the end the reader must decide the question for himself?' (*E6* 198). She offers two solutions to this dilemma—one for the prospective reader: a Gutter and Stamp system whereby the reviewer could quickly dispense with a work by indicating its merit or demerit with an asterisk or a dagger; and one for the writer—a private colloquy between reviewer and writer—in which the writer, too often operating in isolation, might benefit from a critical conversation with the reviewer. Throughout the pamphlet Woolf deploys the metaphor of a tailor or dressmaker behind a shop window into which the reviewers peer,

---

[22] For a discussion of how negative reviewers, especially F.R. and Q.D. Leavis, may have contributed to the rancorous tone of 'Reviewing', see Eleanor McNees, 'Colonizing Virginia Woolf: *Scrutiny* and Contemporary Cultural Views', in Jeanne Dubino and Beth Carole Rosenberg, eds, *Virginia Woolf and the Essay* (New York: St. Martin's Press, 1997), 41–58.

[23] Y. Y. [Robert Lynd], 'Last of the Reviewers?' *New Statesman and Nation* 18 (4 November 1939), 640.

[24] Lynd, 'Last of the Reviewers?', 640.

[25] Lynd, 'Last of the Reviewers?', 641.

[26] Lynd, 'Last of the Reviewers?', 641.

scrutinizing the work. In the private colloquy between reviewer and writer, the writer instead 'would withdraw into the darkness of the workshop; he would no longer carry on his difficult and delicate task like a trouser mender in Oxford Street, with a horde of reviewers pressing their noses to the glass and commenting to a curious crowd upon each stitch' (*E6* 204).

In his addendum to Virginia Woolf's denigration of the reviewer and the reviewing process, Leonard Woolf claims the role of the reviewer 'is to give to readers a description of the book and an estimate of its quality in order that he may know whether or not it is the kind of book which he may want to read' (*E6* 206). For Leonard Woolf (as for 'Y. Y.') the reviewer speaks only to the prospective reader in a one-to-one conversation; for Virginia Woolf, the dialogic model becomes triadic to incorporate reader, *author*, and reviewer. A worthy reviewer is a mediator (or a hostess) who first seasons a dish before serving it to her guests.[27] Responding to a letter from W.J.H. Sprott the following year about her biography of Roger Fry, Woolf again alludes to the distinction between critic and reviewer, but here, in a telling metaphor, she qualifies that distinction: 'I never meant to be severe on critics, as you say I've been: only on the reviewers *who ought to grow into critics* instead of remaining sprats and minnows' (*L6* 416, emphasis added). This statement, recalling her criticism of Lockhart as a reviewer who failed to grow into a critic, exemplifies Woolf's own trajectory as reviewer-grown-into-critic, a gradual though not necessarily linear process.

The year after her indictment of reviewers, Woolf published three final reviews, all in *The New Statesman and Nation*. These late reviews of Coleridge and Coleridge's daughter (Fall 1940) and her last review of 'Mrs Thrale' (March 1941) return to two of Woolf's persistent preoccupations as reviewer-critic: how to enact a conversation between reviewer-critic and common reader and how to capture elusive lives of women obscured by their more famous male companions. Throughout her essays and reviews from the early *TLS* review, 'Coleridge as Critic' (7 February 1918) to her final 'The Man at the Gate', Woolf included Coleridge in her list of the great English critics against whom she implicitly measured contemporary critics and reviewers. In the 1918 review, she suggests her ideal of the unmediated conversation between a speaking critic and his reader and interlocutors, a conversation towards which she was striving in her final versions of 'Anon'. Listening to Coleridge's talk, one comes face to face with 'the individual mind', a mind she first quotes Coleridge as saying must be 'androgynous' (*E2* 222). Coleridge's conversational criticism reveals but does not impose, and thus he becomes Woolf's ideal example of the impersonal, anti-authoritarian critic. Over thirty years later, with a heightened focus on the shapes and sounds of spoken words, she considers his words as reverberating, 'so that as we enter his radius he seems not a man, but a

---

[27] Although Anna Snaith argues that Leonard Woolf has the 'final word' in the pamphlet—'Rather than holding a private consultation, Leonard is the reviewer here, gazing into the shop window', it seems more likely that the Woolfs chose to make this debate public to underscore the two sides and to encourage readers to engage in the dialogue for themselves. See Snaith, *Virginia Woolf*, 51.

swarm, a cloud, a buzz of words, darting this way and that, clustering, quivering and hanging suspended' (*E6* 235).

Woolf's review of a biography of Coleridge's daughter Sara (26 October 1940) hints at the difficulty 'children of great men' (Woolf's similar predicament) face in trying to express their own particular identity against their more powerful and famous fathers, especially in an age when women were not expected to assert their professional independence. Sara Coleridge, Woolf explains, never succeeded in breaking away from her father; instead, she was a 'continuation … of his mind, his temperament' (*E6* 249). Editing his works, as Woolf was *not* to do with her father's, Sara 'found her father in those blurred pages, as she had not found him in the flesh; and she found that he was herself. She did not copy him, she insisted; she was him. Often she continued his thoughts as if they had been her own' (*E6* 251). Woolf wields this late review both to capture the spirit of 'Mrs Brown', here embodied as Sara Coleridge, and to imply her own independence from her father whose critical writings loomed behind so many of hers.

Woolf's final review sidesteps a major male figure, Samuel Johnson, to focus instead on Johnson's female friend, Hester Lynch Thrale Piozzi, who after marrying an 'Italian music master & harpsichordist', would end her friendship with Johnson. Puzzling over the break with Johnson that coincided with the death of Hester's first husband, Woolf suggests, as she had in the Sarah Bernhardt review of 1908, that no biographer or reviewer of a biography can capture the spirit of a person: 'The more we know of people the less we can sum them up.' 'Just as we think to hold the bird in our hands, the bird flits off' (*E6* 292). Throughout her reviews Woolf doggedly pursues this impossibly elusive task as she tries to penetrate and impersonate the subject under review. Consequently, her reviews possess an insistent immediacy; they stage a virtual encounter between the reader and the book under review. It is not surprising then, that Woolf's final published piece, neither strictly review nor critical essay, returns us to her preoccupation with the impossible task of capturing and conveying personality. 'Ellen Terry', published in the *New Statesman* (and rejected by *Harper's Bazaar*) in 1941 just before Woolf's death, harkens back to Woolf's 1908 review of Sarah Bernhardt. Both actresses, Woolf stresses, abandoned their own personalities in order to inhabit their characters—a process that suggests Woolf's own ventriloquist method of reviewing memoirs, letters, and biographies. Regardless of the disparaging comments about reviewing and reviewers scattered throughout her diaries and letters and articulated most sardonically in 'Reviewing', Woolf realized the cumulative value of her journey over the course of more than three decades as a reviewer. Her early *Guardian* and *TLS* reviews laid the foundation for her later critical essays; they also formed her professional identity as a reviewer-grown-into-critic, merging the two into a formidable 'reviewing persona'.[28] Woolf conceded that the 'sidelong approach' of her early 'tea-table training'—the acquired 'surface manner'—allowed her 'to slip in things that would be inaudible if one marched straight up and spoke out loud' (*MB* 150). While the surface manner required 'discipline

---

[28] Daugherty, 'Reading', 36.

and restraint', it also helped her develop a style that feminist critics, in particular, labelled an 'ironic twist ... typical of her critical *persona*'; an 'ironic distance' ensured by the anonymity of the early reviews; and a 'language of disguise' as a 'textual tactics of resistance' in response to her (mostly male) editors' stipulations.[29] Woolf's attempt in her final project 'Anon' to recall the voices of Anon to a readership no longer familiar with oral culture implicitly challenges the judicial voices of the editor and the reviewer-critic. In this last unfinished work, the divisions among author, common reader, and reviewer-critic collapse in Woolf's effort to render a pre-literate world in which song and dramatic performance require participation instead of critical comment.

Selected Bibliography

Bishop, Edward L., 'Metaphor and the Subversive Process of Virginia Woolf's Essays', *Style* 21, no. 4 (Winter 1987), 573–88.

Brosnan, Leila, *Reading Virginia Woolf's Essays and Journalism: Breaking the Surface of Silence* (Edinburgh: Edinburgh University Press, 1997).

Cuddy-Keane, Melba, *Virginia Woolf: The Intellectual and the Public Sphere* (Cambridge: Cambridge University Press, 2003).

Dubino, Jeanne, and Beth Carole Rosenberg, eds, *Virginia Woolf and the Essay*. (New York: St. Martin's Press, 1997).

Dubino, Jeanne, *Virginia Woolf and the Literary Marketplace* (New York: Palgrave Macmillan, 2010).

Goldman, Mark, 'Virginia Woolf and the Critic as Reader', *PMLA* 80, no. 3 (June 1965), 275–84.

Gualtieri, Eleana, *Virginia Woolf's Essays: Sketching the Past* (New York: St. Martin's Press, 2000).

Koutsantoni, Katerina, *Virginia Woolf's Common Reader* (Burlington, VT: Ashgate, 2009).

Lee, Hermione, 'Virginia Woolf's Essays', in Sue Roe and Susan Sellers, eds, *The Cambridge Companion to Virginia Woolf* (Cambridge: Cambridge University Press, 2000), 91–108.

May, Derwent, *Critical Times: The History of the Times Literary Supplement* (London: HarperCollins, 2001).

McNees, Eleanor, and Sara Veglahn, eds, *Woolf Editing / Editing Woolf* (Clemson, SC: Clemson University Digital Press, 2009).

Saloman, Randi, *Virginia Woolf's Essayism* (Edinburgh: Edinburgh University Press, 2012).

Snaith, Anna, *Virginia Woolf: Public and Private Negotiations* (New York: St. Martin's Press, 2000).

Stewart, Jim, '"Poetics ... will fit me for a reviewer!": Aristotle and Woolf's Journalism', in Bryony Randall and Jane Goldman, eds, *Virginia Woolf in Context* (New York: Cambridge University Press, 2012), 322–31.

---

[29] Gualtieri, *Virginia Woolf's Essays*, 26: Snaith, *Virginia Woolf*, 89; Brosnan, *Reading Virginia Woolf's Essays and Journalism*, 65–6. See also Hermione Lee, '"Crimes of Criticism"', 121 on Woolf's dual censors: 'Like the Angel in the House, the invisible censors seem to be both external and internalized. And the debate between authorial desire and the pressures which make the modern author self-conscious is one of the main stories of Virginia Woolf's writing life.'

CHAPTER 18

THE ESSAYS

BETH C. ROSENBERG

Virginia Woolf's essays fall into many genres, including book reviews, literary criticism, biography, memoir, and occasional pieces. Her topics range from the home of Thomas Carlyle in 'Great Men's Houses' (1932) to aerial battles in 'Thoughts on Peace in an Air Raid' (1940) to the nature of sickness in 'On Being Ill' (1926). She documents seemingly trivial events, like a moth's struggle to escape a window frame in 'The Death of the Moth' (1942) or a walk to a stationer's store in 'Street Haunting' (1927). Her memoirs 'A Sketch of the Past' (1939) and 'Am I a Snob?' (1936) are highly personal narrative essays. She theorizes the nature of fiction in 'Mr Bennett and Mrs Brown' (1923) and 'Modern Fiction' (1925). She writes the biographical essays in 'Lives of the Obscure' and essays on women writers who were unstudied in Woolf's time, such as 'Mary Wollstonecraft' and 'Dorothy Wordsworth', as well as women writers she revered like 'Jane Austen' and 'George Eliot'. Woolf's deep understanding of the essay's form and history, her drive to construct a female literary history and female narrative form, culminate in *A Room of One's Own* (1929), where she employs a feminist rhetoric of affect and emotion. Woolf's particular contribution to the essay includes a new kind of literary history that focuses on women, gender, and politics. Hers is a uniquely feminine and feminist voice that is created through a visceral and sensual rhetoric that addresses the body's response to experience and exploits emotions in order to persuade her readers.

As a student of the essay and its history, Woolf studied the form from the only models available to her, and these were almost exclusively male. Montaigne, Hazlitt, Pater, and Beerbohm are among her greatest models—and through their work she learns to make the essay her own, turning from the masculine tradition that she was trained in and reinventing the genre to argue for a uniquely female and feminist perspective. Woolf's theory of the essay, what it should say and do, includes an emphasis on voice and personality, a conversational tone, and a style that is clear yet visual and aesthetic. Ultimately, she breaks from her predecessors by expanding nineteenth-century aestheticism to include tropes of emotion—anger, love, and enthusiasm, among others—that are commonly associated with women. Rather than weaken her rhetoric, the use of emotion empowers it, making her prose appeal to a visceral and bodily knowledge in the reader.

Woolf's essays do not deploy the detached critical tone or a sense of absolute authority that her friend T.S. Eliot affected. Compared to her contemporaries, Woolf's essays were considered impressionistic and antiquarian. Her casual conversational tone, where the reader is her peer, and her subjective responses to art and life were misunderstood and dismissed. She strove for a personal voice that the common reader understands. She refers to the soul, the inner self, but it is really the psychological and aesthetic self that she describes; Woolf's inner self is defined by her gender and, through style and voice, she presents a female experience. She also uses fictional techniques, creating story out of her subject, to engage the reader and stimulate both the imagination and emotions. Her form of argumentation is based on an intuitive logic, where she emphasizes affective responses to cultural and economic conditions. This mode of writing, for Woolf, is the antidote to the masculine essay of reason, logic, and ego, flaws she found even in the male essayists she adored.

Woolf's earliest exposure to the essay was through her father, Leslie Stephen. Stephen, an influential essayist and biographer in his own right, introduced the idea of the essay as an integral part of literary history. Not only did he write full-length biographies of figures such as Samuel Johnson and George Eliot, but he published essays on literature, history, biography, and agnosticism. Woolf was intimately familiar with his *Hours in a Library* (1874–1879), *An Agnostic's Apology and Other Essays* (1893), *Studies of a Biographer* (1898–1902), and his contributions as editor to *The Dictionary of National Biography* (1882–1891). Through Stephen, Woolf was introduced to the notion of literary history, which is not only a guiding principle of many of her essays but essential to her use and critique of the essay form.

Woolf began her essay-writing career as a book reviewer.[1] While she published reviews as early as 1904, and while, from the start, she strove to do more than simply assess a book but to put it in a larger context and develop her point of view as a critic, she always had the essay and its form in mind. Some of her early works, such as 'Haworth, November, 1904' (1904), 'Journeys in Spain' (1904), and 'A Walk by Night' (1905), take the tone of her later more personal and occasional essays. The style of the book reviews is more conventional, limited to space, topic, and an editor's hand. The essays, on the other hand, have a clear and definitive voice, point of view, and personality, and they engage with the reader in a more affective and sensory way. Her apprenticeship in essay writing taught Woolf to use greater aesthetic and visual language to make abstract ideas and experiences concrete; she also develops and refines the novelist's sense of story and character in her non-fiction. It is in the essays too that she follows her attraction to nineteenth-century aestheticism, which she learns from Pater and Hazlitt, and where she vividly articulates the rhetoric of emotional response to and in non-fiction.

---

[1] For more on Woolf as a reviewer, see Chapter 17 'Woolf as Reviewer-Critic' in this volume, where Eleanor McNees describes in detail Woolf's history as a book reviewer. See also Jeanne Dubino, 'Virginia Woolf from Book Reviewer to Literary Critic, 1904-1918' in Beth Carole Rosenberg and Jeanne Dubino, eds, *Virginia Woolf and the Essay* (New York: St. Martin's Press, 1997), 25–40.

Woolf revised and collected some of her reviews and published them as collections of essays, *The Common Readers*, first series (1925) and second series (1932). Anne Fernald notes the 'difficulty in comprehending this impressive collection as a whole', arguing that the essays are organized according to a voice and point of view that belong to 'a kind of every person, a blank common reader' and yet Woolf 'slips in' women writers and unknown female histories.[2] Future work on Woolf's self-edited collections will help us to understand her as an essay writer with agency and purpose, one who makes her own aesthetic and structural choices, not the passive, imitative subject of a male-dominated literary history.

Early critics such as Winifred Holtby and Ruth Gruber recognized the significance of Woolf's essays.[3] Leonard Woolf would later collect the essays in four volumes and publish them between 1966 and 1967.[4] Leonard's *Collected Essays*, as Andrew McNeillie points out, was a kind of extended *Common Reader*,[5] without annotations or even notes on date and place of first publication. However, in 1989 McNeillie began to edit a six-volume series of collected essays, including footnotes and appendixes. It took over twenty years for the collection to be completed, with Stuart N. Clarke editing the last two volumes.[6]

The 1970s and 1980s focused more on Woolf's feminism, politics, and novels.[7] None address Woolf's use of the essay to create literary history, let alone a specifically female history. Woolf began to articulate her theories of the essay long before she wrote her own. Her focus, throughout her essay-writing career, was on voice and the speaking

---

[2] Anne Fernald, '"Writing for everybody, for nobody, for our age, for her own": *The Common Reader* as Writer's Manual', in Eleonora Basso, Lindsey Cordery, Emilio Irigoyen, Claudia Pérez, and Matías Núñez, eds, *Virginia Woolf en América Latina: Reflexiones desde Montevideo* (Montevideo: Librería Linardi y Risso, 2013), 219–43.

[3] Ruth Gruber, *Virginia Woolf: The Will to Create as a Woman* (New York: Avalon Publishers, 1935); Winifred Holtby, *Virginia Woolf: A Critical Memoir* (London: Bloomsbury, 2007).

[4] Virginia Woolf, *Collected Essays*, ed. Leonard Woolf, 4 vols (London: Hogarth Press, 1967).

[5] Andrew McNeillie, Introduction to *The Essays of Virginia Woolf 1904-1912*, vol. 1 (New York: Harcourt, 1989) explains the need for republishing Woolf's essays. Since the publication of Leonard's 1967 collection, Woolf's journals, diaries, and shorter fiction, as well as her reading notebooks and a bibliography and guide to her literary sources and allusions have been published. McNeillie's and Stuart N. Clarke's editions of the essays are complete with annotations and references.

[6] For a survey of earlier criticism of Woolf's essays, see Mark Goldman, *The Reader's Art: Virginia Woolf as a Literary Critic* (Paris: Mouton & Co., 1976), 1–6. See also Eleanor McNees, ed., *Virginia Woolf Critical Assessments*, 4 vols (Mountfield, East Sussex: Helm Information, 1994).

[7] A series of studies began to emerge in the mid-1990s that re-evaluated the importance of the essays, including Beth Rosenberg and Jeanne Dubino, *Virginia Woolf and the Essay* (London: Palgrave Macmillan, 1997) and Leila Brosnan, *Reading Virginia Woolf's Essays and Journalism* (Edinburgh: Edinburgh University Press, 1999); Elena Gualtieri, *Virginia Woolf's Essays* (London: Palgrave Macmillan, 2000); and Randi Saloman's *Virginia Woolf's Essayism* (Edinburgh: Edinburgh University Press, 2014). These works situate Woolf within the traditions of the essay and non-fiction prose and illustrate Woolf's deep understanding of the genre. They focus primarily on the aesthetic nature of her essays, her feminism, her journalistic impulses, and the influence of European 'essayism'.

'I'. She rejected what she calls the 'egotistical' I of her contemporaries to argue for a more authentic personality that could communicate her experience to her audience, whether that experience was aesthetic, personal, or in the world. Woolf believed that essays should deal with truth, not fact, reflect the movement and change of our being, be passionate and emotional, have a 'fierce attachment to an idea' (E4 224), and, ultimately, give pleasure to their readers. In the 1920s, she not only refined her first-person voice but brought a more self-consciously gendered perspective, first by writing about women and their unknown histories, and then by finding the means to create a uniquely feminine subjective voice and rhetorical style.

The female voices and styles she creates in 'Street Haunting' and 'The Death of the Moth', for example, illustrate her innovative approach to the essay. Both essays are ostensibly about small, trivial subjects and use first person to suggest an intimacy with the narrator's thoughts and feelings. Though the underlying themes about death and the nature of the self are abstract, the language she uses in both essays is concrete and specific. The power of a moth that struggles against death is compared to the human struggle: 'One could watch the extraordinary efforts made by those tiny legs against an oncoming doom which could, had it chosen, have submerged an entire city, not merely a city, but masses of human beings; nothing, I knew, had any chance against death' (E6 444). Woolf is concerned with the metaphysical, and her use of first person brings a personal tone often associated with the feminine. A walk to buy a pencil can allow us to 'leave the straight lines of personality and deviate into those footpaths that lead beneath brambles and thick tree trunks into the heart of the forest where live those wild beasts, our fellow men' (E4 490–1). Here the narrator talks of empathy for 'those wild beasts, our fellow men', also a traditionally female emotion. Metaphor and connotation, diction, the appeal to the reader's senses to see, hear, and feel what she is describing, allow her style to become highly aesthetic as it persuades on intuitive and emotional levels through the colour of her prose.

To write her own feminine and feminized version of the essay, Woolf culled from her male predecessors techniques that they themselves did not identify as 'feminine'. From Pater, Beerbohm, Montaigne, and Hazlitt, she learns techniques that bring a confidential trust between the author and her reader: a voice that reflects the personality of the author, the desire to create pleasure for the reader with a conversational and accessible tone, movement of thought, artful, sensuous, and emotional language, and the use of a painter's visual imagery. Though she gives the most detailed attention to male essayists, she is aware of her own historical position. Woolf applies the lessons she learns to many essays about individual woman writers and the obscure women who made writing possible for men, including 'Lives of the Obscure', 'The Duchess of Newcastle', and 'Outlines' in *The Common Reader*, but it is not until *A Room of One's Own* that she confronts the problems of writing as a woman about women through a distinctly female rhetoric where emotion and affect become modes of persuasion.

Woolf's more detailed thoughts on the essay's power to move its readers are sketched out in 'The Modern Essay', written in 1922 for the *Times Literary Supplement* (*TLS*), which covers fifty years of essay writing, is historical and chronological in structure, and theoretically frames Woolf's ideas about how 'certain principles appear to control the chaos' (E4 216) of the essay's form. In this essay she writes of two Victorian essayists, Pater and Beerbohm, whom she greatly admires. She spends a considerable amount of space defining the history and nature of the essayist's audience. According to Woolf, the most significant change in audience came at the turn of the nineteenth century, when the Victorian reader changed to a modern one. The change 'came from a small audience of cultivated people to a larger audience of people who were not quite so cultivated' (E4 220). The modern 'public needs essays as much as ever ... The demand for the light middle not exceeding fifteen hundred words, or in special cases seventeen hundred and fifty, much exceeds the supply' (E4 222). The 'light middle' brow reader wants to read but hasn't the time to wade through a beautifully wrought essay of more than fifteen hundred words. Woolf states that to 'write weekly, to write daily, to write shortly, to write for busy people catching trains in the morning or for tired people coming home in the evening, is a heart-breaking task for men who know good writing from bad' (E4 223). The challenge for the modern essayist is how to bring pleasure to a reader preoccupied by modern life while revealing the true personality of the writer.

The guiding principle of the essay is that it should 'give pleasure', and everything in the essay 'must be subdued to that end'. A good essay will 'lay us under a spell with its first word' and in 'the interval we may pass through the most various experiences'. It must 'lap us about and draw its curtain across the world'. This is seldom accomplished by the essayist, Woolf claims, though the reader is partially to blame: 'Habit and lethargy have dulled his palate'. To produce pleasure in the reader, the essayist must know 'how to write'. This is not just a matter of reproducing knowledge on a page, but an essay 'must be so fused by the magic of writing that not a fact juts out, not a dogma tears the surface of the texture' (E4 216). Though the essay's purpose is to reproduce knowledge, pleasure is derived from the writer's ability to communicate knowledge while nothing blatant, explicit, or jarring appears on the writing's surface.

The knowledge communicated is 'some fierce attachment to an idea. It is on the back of an idea, something believed in with conviction or seen with precision and thus compelling words to shape it'. The good essay 'must have this permanent quality about it; it must draw its curtain round us, but it must be a curtain that shuts us in, not out' (E4 224). The way the essay does this is to let the personality of the writer come through and embrace the reader, an act seemingly so easy but difficult to achieve. How does an essay achieve its 'permanent quality'? It is through concrete and visual language, according to Woolf, that the essayist can provoke an affective response from her reader. No phrase is wasted, no word is lost. Her study of the essay's history, and her attention to her male precursors, taught her how to use language to move her reader's emotions.

The first writer who taught Woolf how to appeal to affect is Walter Pater, and her response to him defines a style she tries to achieve in her own essays. Perry Meisel's study on Woolf and Pater establishes Pater's influence on Woolf by way of Pater's aestheticism. He traces Pater's figurative language, particularly the image of the 'hard gemlike flame' of aesthetic experience, in Woolf's novels.[8] Her notion of the 'moment', Meisel argues, is Pater's influence.[9] Woolf also learned from Pater the power of nineteenth-century aestheticism, its use of colourful rhetoric as well as its focus on the reader's visceral and bodily experience of language. Woolf borrowed from Pater techniques that make her prose appeal to our senses—taste, sight, sound, touch—to give something other than a concrete fact. It is through our bodies' senses that Woolf communicates to us. If our senses help to define our experience, then the emphasis of emotions, too, are expressions of our physical bodies and part of the vocabulary of aestheticism.

Woolf describes Pater's aestheticism and how he uses it in his essay on Leonardo da Vinci:

> [H]e has somehow contrived to get his material fused. He is a learned man, but it is not knowledge of Leonardo that remains with us, but a vision.... Only here, in the essay, where the bounds are so strict and facts have to be used in their nakedness, the true writer like Walter Pater makes the limitations yield their own quality. Truth will give it authority; from its narrow limits he will get shape and intensity. (E4 218)

Even within the conventions of the essay, which limits Pater to 'facts', he is able to give these facts their own quality that Woolf names 'vision' and 'truth'. These abstract qualities—not objective facts—are what the essay writer must strive for. Even as Woolf moves through the history of the essay into the twentieth century, she demands these qualities and ultimately passes harsh judgement on the essay writer who can't achieve them.

Woolf goes on to quote images from Pater's work, like ' "the smiling women and the motion of the great waters" ', as examples of how Pater's concrete language appeals to our senses and emotions; his writing reminds us 'that we have ears and we have eyes'. Pater's style is one where 'every atom of its surface shines' (E4 218), a style Woolf finds grounded in the physical world and is also found in her own intensely visual style, her use of metaphor and connotation, and her desire to give the reader a visceral, bodily experience of language. If Pater has flaws for Woolf, it is his insistence on detachment and objectivity in his tone and his inability to write as himself, to use the human, individual voice to speak to his audience.

Unlike Pater, Woolf's essays distinguish themselves by their constant intimate tone, loaning itself to a more feminine point of view. Her use of first person, singular and plural, is deliberate. It is a rhetoric that appeals to affect and emotion, the visceral response that moves the reader along a train of thought. She learns this from Beerbohm who, unlike Pater, is an essayist who cultivates a speaking voice in his essays. Woolf writes that in Beerbohm's essays readers of the 1890s found themselves 'addressed by

---

[8] Walter Pater, Conclusion to *The Renaissance*, in Harold Bloom, ed., *Selected Writings of Walter Pater* (New York: Columbia University Press, 1974), 60.

[9] See Perry Meisel, *The Absent Father: Virginia Woolf and Walter Pater* (New Haven, CT: Yale University Press, 1980).

a voice which seemed to belong to a man no larger than themselves'. Beerbohm uses the 'essayist's most proper but most dangerous delicate tool' by bringing 'personality into literature'. He does so 'consciously and purely' (*E4* 220). We know that the 'spirit of personality permeates every word he writes'. It is only 'by knowing how to write that [Beerbohm] can make use in literature of [the] self; the self which, while it is essential to literature, is also its most dangerous opponent'. There are many essayists who show 'trivial personalities decomposing in the eternity of print', though Beerbohm 'possessed to perfection' the art necessary to bring personality to the essay (*E4* 221). Although the use of first person, especially to write about experience, is typically understood as the feminine mode of writing, Woolf learns from Beerbohm how to bring personality and voice to her writing. Her use of a personal voice is most obvious, for example, in 'Mr Bennett and Mrs Brown' (1924), where she speaks in first person to pull her reader into her experience of observation on the train. In this essay she also brings to our attention the imaginative impulse that goes into creating a personality, as she does with the character of Mrs Brown, whose personality is so clearly defined that it resonates in the mind long after we have finished reading.

Woolf continued to develop her narrative voice and personality studying other essayists. Two years after publishing 'The Modern Essay' Woolf published 'Montaigne', which was first a review of *Essays of Montaigne* for the *TLS* in 1924 and later published in *The Common Reader*. She explains the vitality of voice in Montaigne's essays. We 'never doubt for an instant that his book was himself' (*E4* 72). He brings art to 'this talking of oneself, following one's own vagaries, giving the whole map, weight, colour, and circumference of the soul in its confusion, its variety, its imperfections' (*E4* 71). The revelation of the self, to 'tell the truth about oneself, to discover oneself near at hand' through language is 'not easy' (*E4* 71). Montaigne teaches Woolf that the essayist does not condescend or tell others how to live their lives, but rather traces the flexibility of identity and its ability to reflect self-consciousness in the narrative.

When Woolf writes of Montaigne's determination to represent his 'soul', she is referring to his subjective self, his personality, his voice. This inner self is 'the strangest of creatures ... so complex, so indefinite' that a man might spend his life trying to discover her (*E4* 74). Yet there is the 'pleasure of pursuit' of the self. Montaigne can say nothing of 'other people's souls' since he can 'say nothing ... about his own' (*E4* 74). Woolf learns from Montaigne how to focus on her personality, her own truth and perception of the world and experience; it is the art of presenting a unique self through the writer's voice that Woolf practices throughout her essay-writing career.

Montaigne's essays are then an 'attempt to communicate a soul' for 'Communication is health; communication is truth; communication is happiness' (*E4* 76). A version of this assertion will reappear in *Mrs Dalloway* (1925), when Septimus contemplates suicide and his message for the world in Regents Park (*MD* 75). The ability to communicate the self is healthy, truthful, and brings contentment. But real communication is difficult. The successful essayist can share her thoughts, 'to go down boldly' into the self and 'bring to light those hidden thoughts which are most diseased; to conceal nothing; to pretend nothing', to tell her own truth and therefore connect with others (*E4* 76). The essayist's most authentic communications reveal what is most difficult for the reader to acknowledge—dark thoughts that potentially tell us things about ourselves we don't want to be aware of. We are all 'ordinary men and women' in Montaigne's essays (*E4* 77). Montaigne shows Woolf how to look deeply into her own responses and feelings, to communicate those to her readers without demanding that they follow her.

For Woolf, William Hazlitt brings together voice and style, and he models for her how to make her language visual and engaging. His essays are written with the language of a visual artist and stylist. It is Hazlitt's self-consciousness as he writes that Woolf feels is his greatest contribution to the essay form. In her essay 'William Hazlitt', a revised *TLS* review that was republished in *The Common Reader: Second Series*, she introduces Hazlitt's essays favourably: 'His essays are emphatically himself. He has not reticence and he has no shame. He tells us exactly what he thinks' (*E5* 494). He also tells us 'exactly what he feels' (*E5* 494) and has 'the most intense consciousness of his own experience' (*E5* 494).

In addition to Hazlitt the thinker there is 'Hazlitt the artist'. This man is 'sensuous and emotional, with his feeling for colour and touch ... with his sensibility to all those emotions which disturb the reason' (*E5* 498). As she did with Pater, Woolf comments on the aesthetic qualities of Hazlitt's essays. She calls attention to the sensuality and emotionality of his language, his 'feeling for the colour' of language, and how his 'sensibility' is open to all 'emotions' that overcome reason (*E5* 499). Hazlitt's inner conflict is reflected in his style as he vacillates between thinker and artist. In his essays, we sense the movement of his thought: '[H]ow violently we are switched from reason to rhapsody—how embarrassingly our austere thinker falls upon our shoulders and demands our sympathy' (*E5* 499). It is this movement of tone and mood, from logic to emotion, which Woolf admires.

It is Hazlitt's visual language that Woolf attempts to imitate. Hazlitt has the 'great gift of picturesque phrasing' that allows him to "float ... over a stretch of shallow thought' (*E5* 500). He has the 'freest use of imagery and colour' and the 'painter's imagery' that keeps his reader engaged. And though there are weaknesses in his essays—they can be 'dry, garish ... monotonous'—each essay has 'its stress of thought, its thrust of insight, its moment of penetration'. His aim is to 'communicate his own fervour', and according to Woolf he succeeds (*E5* 501). Hazlitt's ability to articulate his ideas through his visual language, to pursue his ideas in the finest detail, allow 'the parts of his complex and tortured spirit [to] come together in a truce of amity and concord' (*E5* 502). In the end, there 'is then no division, no discord, no bitterness'. Hazlitt's 'faculties work in harmony and unity'. His sentences are constructed with determination and energy: 'Sentence follows sentence with the healthy ring and chime of a blacksmith's hammer on the anvil'. His 'words glow and the sparks fly; gently they fade and the essay is over' (*E5* 503). Hazlitt is a craftsman who cobbles his words together with such expertise that they explode with energy. He brings passion to his essays through his imagery, figurative language, and consistency of style. The tension between the thinker and artist is refined and unified with his prose. These qualities become useful for Woolf's essays and her feminist rhetoric.

Woolf adapts the essay form to express a woman's experience, sometimes her own, sometimes others', in literature, education, marriage, and the domestic sphere. From her male precursors and teachers she borrows their more 'feminine' and unconventional techniques of style and rhetoric. The freedom to use an individual voice and personality, to show thoughts moving and changing, to communicate a truth that is not a fact, to use language visually and sensually to appeal to our visceral senses are the lessons she learned. These things are used most forcefully in A Room of One's Own, which on the one hand is a personal essay that utilizes first person, and other hand is a treatise, a call for a collective history of women in culture, meant to appeal to a woman's sensibility and experience. She not only lists a range of writers who might be considered part of her great tradition of women's writing—Jane Austen, George Eliot, the Brontës, among others—but she analyses the historic and socioeconomic conditions of women in society. Woolf introduces specific themes, such as female friendship and love, women's education, the desire to write, and the inability to do so, financial, social, and economic barriers the female artist must confront. These themes have been well discussed by feminist and modernist literary scholars from the time of its publication to the present. In addition to the critical issues that confront women writers, Woolf addresses other innovative and provocative qualities in this long and experimental essay. It is Woolf's reinvention of the essay form that really reflects her genius and ingenuity. Unlike male essayists before her, she brings gender to her understanding of form, and she goes beyond their influences by adding to and amplifying the rhetoric of affect and emotions.

Written in 1929, *A Room of One's Own* challenges our understanding of the personal essay with its mixture of non-fiction and fiction.[10] From the first paragraphs, Woolf undermines our assumptions about the narrator in her essay. Based on a series of lectures Woolf gave in 1928 at Newnham and Girton, the essay immediately calls into question the authority of the speaker: ' "I" is only a convenient term for somebody who has not real being' (ARO 4). It contains a full-voiced narrative persona whose thought represents the movement of an active and lively mind in direct conversation with her audience.

The accessibility of the speaker is found in her playful tone: 'But, you may say, we asked you to speak about women and fiction—what has that got to do with a room of one's own?' (ARO 3). The first sentence is an equivocation, an uncertainty, a small rebellion. We know from the start that Woolf does not plan to make us secure in her meaning. Her narrative wanders like the river she sits by to contemplate her subject. The narrator alludes to Montaigne's tenet that truth and fact are not the same things. She will not be able to tell her audience the 'truth' about women and fiction; nor will she be able to hand them 'after an hour's discourse a nugget of pure truth to wrap up between the pages of

---

[10] Anne Fernald, 'A Room of One's Own, Personal Criticism, and the Essay', *Twentieth Century Literature* 40, no. 2 (Summer, 1994), 165–89. Fernald outlines the qualities of personal prose, which she distinguishes from personal criticism and autobiography. Woolf wrote about 'thinking as a deeply personal act in her criticism' (168). Fernald's discussion 'of the personal in Virginia Woolf emphasizes thought' and why 'various readers come to take Woolf so personally' (172).

[their] notebooks' (ARO 3). This is because 'fiction here is likely to contain more truth than fact', and she proposes 'making use of all the liberties and licences of a novelist' to tell the 'story' of the two days that preceded her lecture (ARO 4).

She tells us that hers is an 'opinion upon one minor point', an idea she is fiercely attached and loyal to throughout the essay, 'that a woman must have money and a room of her own if she is to write fiction' (ARO 3). Like Hazlitt, she will develop in our presence (if we as readers should consider ourselves part of her audience) 'as fully and freely' as she can 'the train of thought that led [her] to think this' (ARO 4). At this point she undermines any confidence the reader might have that Woolf is the narrator or that the speaking 'I' is identified with the author. The 'I' in *A Room of One's Own* becomes a fictional construct, one meant to engage and entertain the reader. In fact, 'lies will flow' from her lips, though 'there may be some truth mixed up with them' (ARO 4). It is her audience's responsibility to 'seek out this truth and to decide whether any part of it is worth keeping' (ARO 4). Here the influence of her predecessors is clear—the essay is meant to address truth, reflect a mind in process, and contain a clear speaking voice (even if the 'I' of the narrative is fictional).

She begins to narrate the extended argument *A Room of One's Own* will make about the importance of a female literary tradition for women writers. It is not only what she says, but the way she presents her case by appropriating the techniques of essayists like Montaigne and Hazlitt; she never dwells too long on any subject, and her thoughts move along to Oxbridge, an invented university modelled on Oxford and Cambridge. Also invented is Fernham, the women's college she compares with Oxbridge. Her aesthetic and sensory language to make a socioeconomic argument provokes readers into a visceral and instinctual realm, the realm of connotative and fictive language, where we can see, taste, and feel the differences in social class. The narrator walks by the library at Oxbridge and admires the grand spires and buildings of this awe-inspiring institution. She contemplates how much gold and silver it has taken to build it and eventually describes the sumptuous meal she eats. These images are tangible, vivid, and appeal to a range of senses. In comparison, the language used to describe the women's college is stark, empty, and has no aesthetic attraction. Colourful, concrete, sensory language is associated with the power and authority of one institution while the lack of aesthetic description reflects the powerlessness of the other. This is done to make an argument, using a more feminine, concrete language to point to inequities of experience.

The use of aesthetic language in her essays, encouraged by Pater and Hazlitt, resembles what we find in Woolf's great novels from the 1920s, *Mrs Dalloway* and *To the Lighthouse* (1927), where she also tries to convey some abstract truth for her readers. What we do not find in those novels, or in many of her earlier essays, is a tone of disaffection with the *status quo*. What begins in *A Room of One's Own* as a kind of restlessness, like the narrator who unconsciously walks off the path, quickly grows into discontent and frustration, dissension, hostility, and anger, and then back. In this essay, Woolf alludes to and describes a range of emotions and uses them as rhetorical tropes to persuade her readers of a female logic, one that is visceral, sensual, and bodily. For Woolf, emotions are the body's response to experience, and aestheticism's attachment to the senses is a way Woolf exploits emotions to her purpose.

A Room of One's Own appeals to the reader's emotions, names and discusses emotions, and employs tropes of emotion and affect to move the reader to a female and feminist point of view. There is the appeal to enthusiasm, for example, found at the end of the essay when Woolf calls on her readers to work in 'poverty and obscurity' (*ARO* 86) to help Judith Shakespeare come into being. The most powerful and disturbing affect that Woolf invokes is anger. It is the affect of anger, an emotion that is most provocative, aggressive, inappropriate, and unreasonable that she uses most successfully. Woolf names anger, both in women and men, when she visits the British Museum to research the history of women.

Woolf's representation of anger has been discussed by feminist critics Jane Marcus and Brenda Silver, among others, who argue that Woolf's anger (emotion) is repressed, sublimated, or destructive.[11] These readings view anger as a psychological construct rather than a rhetorical figure. They see these passages as Woolf's expression of her personal anger instead of a rhetorical trope functioning within the tradition of the essay. Rhetorician and feminist Barbara Tomlinson argues for a 'socioforensic discursive analysis'.[12] Discursive analysis, by focusing on how emotions function rhetorically, allows us to reveal underlying ideologies and authority in social discourse. It demands that we analyse 'textual emotion in the light of larger discourses about social power'.[13] Narratives move through a 'modulation' of emotion, some moments stronger than others, and textual markers of anger in Woolf's essay reveal what Tomlinson calls its 'textual vehemence', a critique of the institutional forces that undermines traditional modes of writing and argument.[14]

Sara Ahmed's work on emotion and affect also helps us to look at what she calls the 'emotionality of texts'.[15] Her method calls on us to investigate how 'texts name or perform different emotions'.[16] Most important to understanding Woolf's use of emotion is Ahmed's ideas that emotions are 'performative' and that they 'involve speech acts'. She argues that emotion is not 'in' texts, but rather 'effects of the very naming of emotions'.[17] Woolf's essay names anger, her own and others', and by doing so reveals and exposes what is hidden under the rhetoric she critiques. In what ways does she 'perform' anger in her essay and how does it affect the reader?

In *A Room of One's Own*, Woolf hypothesizes that emotions, while expressed through the body's physical responses and grounded in an aesthetic ethos, are tools of persuasion.

---

[11] Jane Marcus, *Art and Anger: Reading Like a Woman* (Columbus: Ohio State University Press, 1988). Brenda Silver, *Virginia Woolf Icon* (Chicago: University of Chicago Press, 1999).
[12] Barbara Tomlinson, *Feminism and Affect at the Scene of Argument: Beyond the Trope of the Angry Feminist* (Philadelphia: Temple University Press, 2010), 19.
[13] Tomlinson, *Feminism and Affect*, 19.
[14] Tomlinson, *Feminism and Affect*, 57.
[15] Sarah Ahmed, *The Cultural Politics of Emotion* (New York: Routledge, 2004), 13.
[16] Ahmed, *The Cultural Politics of Emotion*, 13.
[17] Ahmed, *The Cultural Politics of Emotion*, 13.

In acknowledging the rhetorical power of emotion, Woolf reverses a Victorian taboo against emotional prose, tempts her critics to dismiss her, and, at the same time, evokes an older history of the essay as a genre open to recording a range of responses. The contribution Woolf's *A Room of One's Own* makes to the history of the essay is an increased awareness that we cannot separate gender from personality, voice, and point of view, since these things are a function of the body. Building on Pater's aestheticism and Hazlitt's painterly language, Woolf writes a careful, sensual, sensory, detailed prose; in addition to the reader's aesthetic response, Woolf hopes for an emotional one, where emotion resides in the interaction between the naming of emotion and emotion itself. Woolf's representation of emotions reveals the ways she makes her own theory of personality in non-fiction; not only does her essay contain a distinct voice and strong sense of audience but she also uses affect to communicate the power of her experience.

The first time we see the representation of anger is in the second chapter of *A Room of One's Own*. We find the narrator at the British Museum researching her talk on women and fiction. Woolf takes us through her argument that institutions of great literature, like the British Museum, contain nothing to help the female writer develop as an artist and individual—there is no tradition for her to follow. Her frustration is revealed in her unconscious sketching of Professor X, and the sketch itself reflects her own, as yet unacknowledged, anger. She describes her sketch of the Professor: 'His expression suggested that he was labouring under some emotion that made him jab his pen on the paper as if he were killing some noxious insect as he wrote.... Whatever the reason, the professor was made to look very angry and very ugly' (*ARO* 24). In the physical expression of his body, we see his anger as he jabs his pen, a phallic allusion, to kill the 'noxious insect' he condescends to write about. Not only is he angry, but his anger makes him 'ugly', much in the same way women's anger has historically been represented.

Woolf consciously uses the trope, if not of the 'angry feminist', then of the 'angry woman'. She subverts this highly charged metaphor to argue against the ideological power of the male intellectual institutions by making the Professor angry too, with all the traditional associations of irrationality and inappropriateness. Not only does the narrator become aware of men's anger toward women, but with a conscious reflection on the sketch, she becomes aware of her own. The narrator knows that what she has done is transfer her anger onto her drawing. The sketch is a manifestation of an emotion, a symptom communicated through her body with her pen to her page. When she reads about the inferiority of women the first thing she notices is her bodily response: her 'heart leapt', her 'cheeks had burnt', and she was 'flushed'. Not only are her emotions felt through her body but she understands how it is an anger that 'mixed itself with all kinds of emotions' (*ARO* 25). The narrator's anger is expressed through her body and senses and is inextricably linked to the aesthetic response Woolf wants to inspire in her reader. Her sketching begins the act of naming emotion.

Where Professor X is angry at women, and the narrator becomes aware of her anger toward him, the story of Judith Shakespeare escalates anger to violence and rage. Through this visual anecdote Woolf comments on the psycho-manipulation of anger toward women by men. Judith Shakespeare endures her father's anger through his violence: 'She cried out that marriage was hateful to her, and for that she was severely beaten by her father. Then he ceased to scold her. He begged her instead not to hurt him, not to shame him in this matter of her marriage' (*ARO* 36). Judith's 'hate' is manifested through her cries, and her body becomes the site of emotion and severe punishment. Knowing that his anger will not change Judith's mind, her father turns her pain into his 'hurt' and 'shame', emotions he uses to persuade her. These appeals do not stir pathos in Judith, but rebellion. Judith seeks freedom, circumstances lead to suicide, and the narrator asks: '[W]ho shall measure the heat and violence of the poet's heart when caught and tangled in a woman's body?' (*ARO* 37). Anger is trapped in the body, which literally feels the sensation of 'heat', of passion and fury, but finds no expression. However, Woolf has expressed it for us, by naming the emotion and connecting it to female experience and allowing the reader to feel Judith's rage through a language that is sensory, visceral, and undoubtedly female.

Woolf writes in *A Room of One's Own* that it is 'useless to go to the great men writers for help, however much one may go to them for pleasure', just as she goes to the male essayists Montaigne, Pater, Beerbohm, and Hazlitt for pleasure. She too 'may have learnt a few tricks from them and adapted them to her use' (*ARO* 57). From the history of male essayists Woolf inherited—and reinvented for her own use—the sensual, visceral, and painterly language of aestheticism. Hers is a rhetoric of affect and emotion, and she makes a literary space for herself and the women essayists who follow through a decidedly female strategy—the employment of emotions that in the past were considered weak and unconvincing. The narrator's anger at the Professor and Judith's anger with her father reverses conventional readings of the trope of the angry woman by showing how anger moves the subject to action. By making anger explicit, Woolf gives it new power. It is an anger of one's own and is used both as resistance and a vehicle for change.

Not only does she use anger and rage to illustrate the socioeconomic inequities women suffer but Woolf's notion of a female literary history also hinges on the emotion of anger. In chapter 4 of *A Room of One's Own*, Woolf begins to piece together her literary history. Intense emotions, like anger and fear are flaws in the fiction of women who precede Woolf. She begins with the seventeenth-century poet Lady Winchilsea. Woolf finds her poetry 'bursting out in indignation' (*ARO* 44). Had she 'freed her mind from hate and fear and not heaped it with bitterness and resentment' (*ARO* 45) her poetry would have been much better. By the nineteenth century women writers had 'training in the observation of character, in the analysis of emotion' (*ARO* 51). She praises Jane Austen for writing 'without hate, without bitterness, without fear' (*ARO* 71), while she finds Charlotte Brontë unable to transcend her emotions in writing. Describing Brontë's anger, Woolf cites a long passage from *Jane Eyre* that explains how 'women feel just as men feel ... they suffer from too rigid a restraint, too absolute a stagnation, precisely as men would suffer' (*ARO* 52). The entrance of Grace Poole at this point in the novel is an 'awkward break' that represents the 'marks and jerks' of the novel, and by noticing these 'one sees that [Brontë] will never get her genius whole and entire'. Woolf finds that Brontë writes 'in a rage where she should write calmly' (*ARO* 52). But Woolf also acknowledges that 'she puts her finger exactly not only upon her own defects but upon those of her sex at that time' (*ARO* 53). For Woolf, anger is a deformity in women's fiction—it scars and stains it.

Woolf was conflicted about the purpose and role of emotions in women's writing, but she knew that it is through affect that the woman writer writes. Naming emotion engages the reader and influences her to see the world differently. Like the 'dead poet who was Shakespeare's sister', the contemporary woman essayist must draw 'her life from the lives of the unknown who were her forerunners' (*ARO* 86). Woolf sees herself as part of a cultural family, where the physical body expresses the emotions of experience. Using the techniques of clear prose, the speaking voice, the portrayal of a mind in the process of thought, and concrete and aesthetic imagery to help express the passionate intensity of her subject, she creates *A Room of One's Own*, an essay that has profoundly influenced female essayists of the twentieth and twenty-first centuries.

Woolf's late nineteenth-century education in biography, history, and literary criticism creates a foundation for her interest in genealogy, lineage, and canon formation. Her own essays helped her to understand the tradition and development of the genre. She disregarded gender in her evaluations of male essay writers because, beyond techniques and formal qualities she found helpful to her own writing, there were no allusions to gender in their work. She uses her inheritance from Montaigne, Pater, Beerbohm, Hazlitt, and others to create in her own essays, including *A Room of One's Own*, what she herself lacked, a defined tradition of women's essay writing that allows further possibilities in content and form.

Selected Bibliography

Brosnan, Leila, *Reading Virginia Woolf's Essays and Journalism* (Edinburgh: Edinburgh University Press, 1999).

Dubino, Jeanne, 'Virginia Woolf from Book Reviewer to Literary Critic, 1904–1918', in Beth Carole Rosenberg and Jeanne Dubino, eds, *Virginia Woolf and the Essay* (New York: St. Martin's Press, 1997).

Fernald, Anne, '*A Room of One's Own*, Personal Criticism, and the Essay', *Twentieth Century Literature* 40, no. 2 (Summer 1994), 165–89.

Goldman, Mark, *The Reader's Art: Virginia Woolf as a Literary Critic* (Paris: Mouton & Co., 1976).

Gualtieri, Elena, *Virginia Woolf's Essays* (London: Palgrave Macmillan, 2000).

McNees, Eleanor, ed., *Virginia Woolf: Critical Assessments*, 4 vols. (Mountfield: Helm Information, 1994).

Rosenberg, Beth, and Jeanne Dubino, eds, *Virginia Woolf and the Essay* (New York: St. Martin's Press, 1997).

Saloman, Randi, *Virginia Woolf's Essayism* (Edinburgh: Edinburgh University Press, 2014).

CHAPTER 19

THE LYRICAL MODE OF TRANSLATING

CLAIRE DAVISON

'I would venture to guess', writes Virginia Woolf in one of the most-quoted passages of *A Room Of One's Own* (1929), 'that Anon, who wrote so many poems without signing them, was often a woman' (*ARO* 38). In 'Anon'—a panoramic book-project she was planning in the 1930s—Anon is likewise 'sometimes man; sometimes woman'; they are also 'a simple singer, lifting a song or story from other people's lips' and finding the words 'to give voice to the old stories' (*E6* 582). Pursuing the same vein, this chapter 'ventures to guess' that Anon, the gender-crossing, unnamed, itinerant minstrel, not signing but singing their words in the 'uncouth jargon of their native tongue' (*E6* 582), is also a translator, in both the most intimately literal and radically metaphorical senses of the term. Anon's part in cultural transmission is very much that of the translator in their rambling, Babel-defying missions to up-anchor historically and culturally grounded source texts, and set them off on an odyssey of sorts during which they will be tested and refashioned. Historically, like Woolf's Anon, translators and translation play the ancillary role, quite literally that of the *ancilla* or handmaiden, holding up a mirror that reflects a face other than their own; like Anon, translators' works mostly went unsigned before the late nineteenth century. And as historians of translation have shown, the anonymous translator was often a woman, venturing into the world of print by the back door, beneath a cloak of invisibility (and economic precariousness), and via other people's words.

Translators have only a cameo role in Woolf's fiction, but their realm is her entire oeuvre. Their voice can be heard from *The Voyage Out* (1915), where Ambrose Ridley restores Pindar to the world, and interpretative pianist Rachel guffaws when she reads a mawkishly adapted Wagner libretto, to *Between the Acts* (1941) when William Dodge spontaneously renders lines from *Phèdre* into English. Woolf's nonfiction, while rarely centred on translation, frequently explores the literal and conceptual dynamics of language-crossing, border-crossing transactions. This is especially true of her earliest essays. 'An Andalusian Inn' (1905) recounts with evident relish how the everyday runs amok for travellers in foreign lands when languages misconnect. Conversely

'The Stranger in London' (1908) revisits London as a trans-European, trans-linguistic marketplace drawing in foreign travellers.[1] Nor is translation merely an encompassing metaphor within the poetics of rambling and dislocating.[2] Woolf was familiar with the minutiae of translating as praxis; as a publisher, she helped define the Hogarth Press's energetic commitment to commissioning, editing, and circulating foreign translations. Varying degrees of proficiency in Russian, French, and Greek combined with a vivid curiosity about literatures and cultural identities prompted her to undertake translations of her own. What all these ventures share are 'brief, intimate, colloquial' moments when translation—as if aspiring to the condition of song—rings dazzlingly true (*E6* 588).[3] This is the 'lyrical mode' of the translator, and it traverses Woolf's fictional and non-fictional writings like the minstrels and storytellers of the Middle Ages.[4]

The year 1917, however grimly resonant today in terms of the ruthlessness of war, civil wars, and revolution, proved richly productive in terms of Woolf's translational thinking, especially, as will be seen later, when observed 'under the Russian magnifying glass'.[5] As passing reflections in letters, diary notes, and essays attest, and in keeping with established pedagogical practices, prior to this date, translation had played a practical part in a literary and linguistic apprenticeship: rendering passages of French, German, and Greek into English and vice versa was considered a reliable gauge of comprehension and grammatical precision.[6] With the publication of 'The Perfect Language' Woolf problematizes translation for the first time, homing in on that undefined no-man's land between languages where translation supposedly happens.[7] She does this via the figure

---

[1] See Jessica Berman's essential conceptualization of translation within Modernist cosmopolitan thinking: '[t]ranslation functions as a metaphor for the liminal zone between the punctual and the fragmented self, between the self and its communities of affiliation, both past and present, as well as between the loyalties and allegiances demanded by those communities, both large and small' in *Modernist Fiction, Cosmopolitanism and the Politics of Community* (Cambridge: Cambridge University Press, 2001), 17.

[2] Writing as critic and translator of Woolf, Bernard offers an astute exploration of figures of translation within Woolf's ethics of cultural displacement in Claire Davison and Anne-Marie Smith-Di Biasio, eds, *Trans-Woolf* (Perugia: Morlacchi, 2017), 23–39.

[3] See also Elsa Högburg, 'The Melancholic Translations of Anon' in Claire Davison and Anne-Marie Smith-Di Biasio, eds, *Trans-Woolf* (Perugia: Morlacchi, 2017), 45–52.

[4] Many critics have linked Woolf's translational thinking to Benjamin's in 'The Task of the Translator'. For most recent examples, see in particular Goldman, Di Biasio, and Högberg in *Trans-Woolf*. Thinking through translation to the voices of a wandering 'Anon', however, illuminates closer links with Benjamin's 'The Storyteller' in Walter Benjamin, *Illuminations*, trans. Harry Zohn (London: Fontana, 1992), 83–107.

[5] See the unfinished essay 'Tchekhov on Pope' (*E6* 550). This incomplete essay, which thinks through translations, and through French, English, and Russian literatures, makes extensive metaphorical use of the dissolving boundaries and fluid horizons Woolf evokes whenever assessing translational encounters.

[6] For Woolf's apprenticeship in these languages, see Emily Dalgarno's *Virginia Woolf and the Visible World* (Cambridge: Cambridge University Press, 2007), 40–2 and *Virginia Woolf and the Migrations of Language* (Cambridge: Cambridge University Press, 2012), 1–6.

[7] See Raterman's incisive exploration of Woolf's subversive approach to translational transactions, and her deconstruction of translational transparency and its ideological underpinnings in 'Reading from the outside: The uses of translation for Virginia Woolf's "common reader"', *Translation Studies* 3, no. 1 (January 2010), 78–93.

of what we might call a 'common translator'—the enraptured amateur who, with a literal translation placed side-by-side with a text in its original language, could venture into foreign worlds 'with his feet on the fender', while also experiencing the thrill of language as a dislocation of native sure-footedness (*E2* 114).[8] There were rewards for such diligence: 'those moments of instant understanding which are the flower of reading. In them we seem not so much as to read as to recollect what we have heard in some other life' (*E2* 115).

The year 1917 also marked the publication of Woolf's first essay on Russian literature, a review of Tolstoy's *The Cossacks*, which likewise bears the imprint of translation's estranging, dislocative powers that by deflecting the path of the senses can reveal the world slantwise. And it was the year she and Leonard met S.S. Koteliansky, a Ukraine-born professional translator and literary intermediary, and an émigré eking out survival by finding new markets for newly published Russian works. His pro-active political militancy and multilingualism would help define the mission of the Hogarth Press: it was Russian translations that marked the shift from a hand-press to a respected, financially viable company.[9]

This gateway to professional success was also a byway into the exceptional bonds of intimacy that translation weaves, between an author's printed voice, and the translator or co-translators by whose intermediary they will speak anew. Woolf soon began taking lessons with Koteliansky, learning to pronounce the complex clusters of Russian consonants, exploring the subtleties of time recollected in verbal declensions, and gauging textual valency by reciting the translation aloud. This was Koteliansky's preferred method[10]—a clear indication that voice mattered. That Russian, like Greek, also involved deciphering an unknown alphabet, and turning strange print into partly familiar sounds, could only enhance 'the requisite remoteness, the associative eeriness of the validated original'.[11] Nor was this mere fetishized exoticism: there is a distinctly ethical edge to each encounter with foreignness, when, with a 'start of surprise', 'we constantly realise [...] that we have met it before in ourselves' (*E2* 86). This is the barrier-raising power of translation, opening up new dimensions between lands, languages,

---

[8] For the dislocative, outlandish experience of foreign languages in translation, see Claire Davison, 'Bilinguals and Bioptics: Virginia Woolf and the Outlandishness of Translation', in Jeanne Dubino, Gill Lowe, Vara Neverow, and Kathryn Simpson, eds, *Virginia Woolf: Twenty-First Century Approaches* (Edinburgh: Edinburgh University Press, 2015), 73–8.

[9] See Laura Marcus, 'The European Dimension of the Hogarth Press' in Mary Ann Caws and Nicola Luckhurst, eds, *The Reception of Virginia Woolf in Europe* (London: Continuum, 2002), 328–34.

[10] This collaborative praxis is attested by nearly all Koteliansky's co-translators, including Katherine Mansfield, Leonard and Virginia Woolf, and John Middleton Murry. See Claire Davison, *Translation as Collaboration: Virginia Woolf, Katherine Mansfield and S. S. Koteliansky* (Edinburgh: Edinburgh University Press, 2014), 51–6.

[11] Vassiliki Kolocotroni, 'Strange Cries and Ancient Songs: Woolf's Greek and the Politics of Intelligibility' in Bryony Randall and Jane Goldman, eds, *Virginia Woolf in Context* (Cambridge: Cambridge University Press, 2012), 423–38, at 427. Kolocotroni's exploration of the tensions between strange codes, archaic sounds, cultural unknowability, and familiar soundtracks opens up a previously unsuspected vibrancy in Woolf's thinking between languages and eras.

and dimensions of the self; it untethers texts from the here-and-now, and harnesses the 'nameless wandering voice' of Anon, who roams in 'the world beneath our consciousness; the anonymous world to which we can still return' (*E6* 589, 584).

An overview of the Hogarth Press translations shows the lyrical, performative dimension of translation in practice. Step one is acknowledging translation's transformative, performative powers on the reader, the most telling illustration being Woolf's review of Hogarth's unexpected bestseller: Gorky's *Reminscences of Tolstoy* (1920), translated by Leonard Woolf and Koteliansky. The essayist's eye is caught by the startling aesthetics of Gorky's portrait. Tolstoy's physical characteristics are captured in synecdoche, devoid of monumental grandeur; the fragments are assembled pell-mell, in collage-form: 'his legs were short', 'he showed a curious lack of taste in his neck-ties', 'the hands clutching the stick were thick and clumsy' (*E3* 253). The greatness of Tolstoy's mind is glimpsed only in shards: 'accidentally throwing off profound, coarse, wise sayings, as if they were sparks struck out by his mind in collision with some reality which existed only for him' (*E3* 253). Meanwhile, intimations of the private man's brooding psychological complexity undercut any claim to 'truth', while allegorically capturing what it means to live *in* translation: 'silent, vast and lonely, like someone who has never got caught up in the ordinary round of existence, [...] a person "just arrived from some distant country, where people think and feel differently and their relations and language are different" '.[12]

Dislocated, tangential, reawakening the senses: thus likened in effect to 'an untouched amateur photograph', Gorky's essay seemingly topples the conventions of nineteenth-century biographizing in one fell swoop (*E3* 252). It offers new models for mediating between life as it is lived, and figures of life observed; it also reads as a blueprint for Woolf's poetics of translation, metaphorically catching the sound of an author's lost voice, heard 'at the back door', thereby assuring them the 'afterlife' for which, as Benjamin demonstrated, all works yearn.[13] It also sounds the keynote of the Hogarth Press's translations to come. Each volume revisits the supposed megaliths of the literary world tangentially, via extracts from various self-fashioning modes of writing—letters, diaries, snapshots, and self-portraiture—which recreate the materiality and rhythms of a self that is caught in trifling acts of unobtrusive everydayness. And by translating previously unknown, self-representing writings, and miscellany, rather than the writers' classic oeuvre, the translators' first step is to lend their voice to the author's 'I', in a form of recreative ventriloquism that lets selves and others, male voices and female voices, change places.

---

[12] Leonard Woolf and S. S. Koteliansky, eds and trans., *Reminiscences of Leo Nicolayevitch Tolstoi* (London: Hogarth Press, 1920), 32.

[13] Jean Mills likewise correlates Woolf's experience as a translator and her reading of *Avvakum* and Harrison. See 'The Writer, The Prince and the Scholar: Virginia Woolf, D. S. Mirsky and Jane Harrison's Translation from Russian of *The Life of the Archpriest Avvakum by Himself*, in Helen Southworth, ed., *Leonard & Virginia Woolf, the Hogarth Press and the Networks of Modernism* (Edinburgh: Edinburgh University Press, 2010), 154–9.

Take *Tolstoi's Love Letters* (1923), co-translated by Koteliansky and Virginia Woolf. It comprises a preface, and a substantial postface on Tolstoy's indirectly auto-fictional poetics written by Paul Biryukov, one of Tolstoy's closest friends; in-between are the 'love' letters whose publication Sophia Tolstoy had forbidden until after her death. Despite the romantic lure of the title (another addition by the translators/publisher), these are mostly letters 'not about love', as Shklovsky memorably put it.[14] Even the would-be admirer's opening epistle is haughtily ironic, sneering at his beloved's previous description of a red-currant-printed dress worn at an official outing: 'How glad I am that your currant pattern dress was crumpled at the parade, and how stupid the unknown baron who saved you. If I had been in his place, I would have joined the crowd and smeared the currants on the white dress' (*TR* 118). Despite such cantankerous beginnings, a romance of sort takes shape *in absentia*, once the letter writer has deliberately estranged himself from his beloved to gauge the depth of his emotions. The letters therefore read as a hypothesis on love, reflecting less on the sincerity or integrity of 'real' emotion than on the fictionalizing craft of the novelist. Tolstoy gives his two potential lovers fictional masks—Khrapovitsky and Mrs Dembitsky—and draws pictures of a married life that might be theirs: 'Lovely Mrs Dembitsky has not yet felt anything of the sort; for her happiness consists in balls, bare shoulders, a carriage, diamonds, acquaintances with chamberlains, lieutenant-generals, etc. but it so happened that Khrap. and Demb. seemed to love each other (perhaps I am lying to myself, but at this instant I love you terribly)' (*TR* 127). Tolstoy falls in love with the fictional creation, but out of love with his 'lovely lady', however, recommending that she 'go abroad, enter a nunnery, bury yourself in the country' (*TR* 138). Having reasoned that 'we became entangled, but let us try to remain friends', he ends 'the love story' with a portrait of himself as insouciant author, happily settled in Paris, inspired by new passions: 'The French play Beethoven, to my great surprise, like Gods, and you can imagine how I enjoy hearing this musique d'ensemble, executed by the best artists in the world' (*TR* 69, 144).

Woolf's translational incursions into Russian lives and works are even more veiled, if not entirely invisible, in another publication by the Hogarth Press, *The Autobiography of Countess Sophie Tolstoi*, translated by Koteliansky and Leonard Woolf; this too is a volume whose rich paratexts include letters, extensive explanatory notes, and source documents on Tolstoy's well-publicized 'Going away' in 1910. Sophie Tolstoi's commissioned testimony reconstructs domestic life married to an overbearing, yet inspirational and gifted writer, and the concomitant stifling of her own creativity—as a writer and a musician. The influence that such alternative, proto-feminist historiography and biographizing had on Woolf as a reader can only be surmised—although Sophia surely provides a prototype for the women's lives later lifted from obscurity by *A*

---

[14] See Shklovsky's *Zoo, or Letters not about Love* (1923), one of the founding modernist studies of estrangement and not belonging, encapsulated by epistolary form and decentred, dehumanized masks of the self.

Room of One's Own. One letter reads: 'Tomorrow I shall be sixty-nine years old, a long life; well, *what* out of that life would be interesting to people? I have been trying to find some woman's autobiography for a model, but have not found one anywhere.'[15] More important in terms of Anon and the translator's craft is that fact that it was Virginia Woolf who copy-edited first drafts of Leonard and Koteliansky's translation, sometimes 'quite substantially'.[16] By weaving her annotations into the manuscript, she therefore joins the chorus of voices in translation as an uncredited, anonymous 'singer'.[17] Surviving drafts also reveal that among the source texts Koteliansky initially provided were more damning accounts of Sophie's behaviour and mental state, which incited readers to side firmly with the great man bullied by an increasingly deranged wife. It is therefore eloquent indeed that in the Hogarth Press montage, such texts are not included; in this way, as the translators underline, 'Countess Sophie Andreevna Tolstoi herself states her own case in full'.[18]

Lost voices in the byways of translation provide a fitting bridge from 'Not Knowing Russian' to 'On Not Knowing Greek'.[19] In both essays, translation is initially posited as a species without pedigree, doomed to fall short of its pure, authoritative 'source'. They soon open up, however, to reveal the serendipitous moments evoked earlier, when translation works wonders. These are the reserve of the 'unknowing' translator, who blithely transgresses divine authority and Babelian censure. Paradoxically empowered by 'the outsider's privilege', they venture feelingly into the mellow, alluring cadences of words spoken 'foreignly', or heard from afar across temporal, geographical, or atmospheric boundaries (*E6* 582). Recited, chanted, or sung, these unexpected, sensuous encounters with 'little' words in all their materiality bridge the gap between the unspoken and the unsayable, between spontaneously expressed emotion and subjective experience reiterated by proxy. This is where translation is found aspiring to the condition of lyric,[20]

---

[15] Sophie Tolstoi, *The Autobiography of Countess Sophie Tolstoi*, trans. S. S. Koteliansky and Leonard Woolf (London: Hogarth Press, 1922), 12. Although Woolf could not have known about it, Sophie Tolstoi also composed a transposition of Tolstoy's *Kreutzer Sonata* from a very Judith Shakespeare-angled, female-centred perspective, called *So Who's to Blame?*

[16] See Rebecca Beasley, 'On Not Knowing Russian: The Translations of Virginia Woolf and S. S. Kotelianskii', *Modern Language Review* 108, no. 1 (January 2013), 1–29, at 19.

[17] 'Chorus' is not used metaphorically. Koteliansky's first drafts are wide spaced on the page, allowing his co-translators to add their versions or suggestions above or below. The montage effect, in terms of coloured inks, writing styles, and juxtaposed translations reads very much like a musical score. I would like to express my warmest thanks to Rebecca Beasley for so generously sharing her copies and impressions of the drafts.

[18] Sophie Tolstoi, *Autobiography of Sophie Tolstoi*, 6.

[19] As Roberta Rubenstein suggests, 'The Russian Point of View' essentially tells of 'Not Knowing Russian'. See *Virginia Woolf and the Russian Point of View* (New York: Palgrave, 2009), 10.

[20] The musical component of translational 'lyric' is essential. As musicologists have underlined, unlike poetry, musical lyric has always been construed as a second-hand or public mode of intimacy. The singer's 'I' is a self-evident performance mask, shared in part with the 'I' of the lyricist, the composer and the listener. In Woolf's words, 'Everybody shared in the emotion of Anon's song' (*E6* 581).

prompting a sensual renewal that recalls Keats, who *looks* into Chapman's Homer, but *hears* Chapman's Homeric voice:

> Oft of one wide expanse had I been told
> That deep-brow'd Homer ruled as his demesne;
> Yet did I never *breathe* its pure serene
> Till I *heard* Chapman *speak out* loud and bold.[21] (italics added)

Three major works show this working in practice, as words are released from the tethers of print, and the path of the senses is displaced. In *The Voyage Out*, Ridley Ambrose represents the decentred figure of the translator. He plays a complicating, disruptive role, always out of time and place, and, in terms of the novel's surface linearity, entirely out of sync. A cloaked, perplexing figure, he roams restlessly on the periphery of the action intoning other people's verses, from the opening prologue scene until the deathbed climax. It is his point of view as a classicist, nonetheless, that transposes Helen's unaccounted sobbing—the first figuration in Woolf's work of a woman who 'must weep'[22]—into a choric commentary on maternal grief (*VO* 5). Similarly, the indecent intimacy of Rachel's feverish delirium is translated by Ridley into the agitated pacing and intonations of a requiem's 'Libere Me' [Deliver Me] performed outside—uncomfortable, distressing, and yet as ineluctable as labour in childbirth: 'the sounds of Ridley's song and the beat of his pacing worked into the minds of Terence and St John'; 'The sound of these words were strangely discomforting to both the young men, but they had to be borne' (*VO* 409). Ridley's repertoire of songs, performed 'at the back door' of the unfolding plot, is essentially classical. This is not solely because he is a classics scholar devoted to annotating Greek fragments. Ridley's 'home' is in translation: '"This *is* nice," said Hewet. "But where is Mr Ambrose?" "Pindar," said Helen' (*VO* 170).

The transgressive, dislocative essence of translating Greek recurs unexpectedly in the church service. While 'baaing inexpressive human voices' intone empty versicles (*VO* 265), an alternative 'prayer' book discreetly provided by Hirst quite literally resurrects another body, from a subversively female world, and time immemorial:

> Hirst politely laid the book before [Mrs Flushing], pointing to the first line of a Greek poem and then to the translation opposite. [...] She gulped down the Ode to Aphrodite during the Litany, keeping herself with difficulty from asking when Sappho lived, and what else she wrote worth reading, and contriving to come in punctually at the end with 'the forgiveness of sins, the Resurrection of the body, and the life everlastin'. Amen.' (*VO* 266-7)

---

[21] John Keats, 'On first looking into Chapman's Homer', in Edward Hirsch, ed., *The Complete Poems of John Keats* (New York: Modern Library, 2001), 43.
[22] 'Women Must Weep—or Unite Against War' was the title Woolf gave her abridged version of *Three Guineas* published in *Atlantic Monthly* in 1938.

As odes, the illicit verses gesture to the condition of the lyric. They also illustrate Woolf's subtle understanding of translation's subversive powers—mischievously blasphemous, slippery in gender, yet artfully indirect.[23]

The Years offers a host of similar shifts from a scholar's exhaustive annotations to sensuous, interstitial, barrier-dissolving feats. The novel features two slightly disconnected, dislocated translators. First, there is an 'Anon': 'the man Peggy called Brown; the others called Nicholas; whose real name he did not know' (*Y* 373). Like Ridley, Brown lives in translation. His thoughts and statements are frequently interrupted mid-sentence; even his name reflects a veiled, inaccessible origin, suggesting either a Hobson-Jobson approximation of an unpronounceable, unintelligible patronym, or a mundane, semantic universal—the sort that slips most effortlessly through languages and across temporalities. Brown's counterpart is the scholar Edward, who is ultimately even more out of place in the novel's temporal, generational plot than either his forebear Ridley or the exile/refugee Brown. Edward is just an undergraduate when first encountered in the role of translator, teetering on the boundary between authorized, printed words and an illicit Siren's song. As in the church scene in *The Voyage Out*, translation's subversive counterpoint looms up from a complex sonic backcloth of intermingling cultures, objects, music, and voices:

> All sounds were blotted out. He saw nothing but the Greek in front of him. But as he read, his brain gradually warmed; he was conscious of something quickening and tightening in his forehead. He caught phrase after phrase exactly, firmly, more exactly, he noted, making a brief note in the margin, than the night before. Little negligible words now revealed shade of meaning which altered the meaning. He made another note; *that* was the meaning. (*Y* 44)

Unable to keep a scholar's grip on the misbehaving words, Edward sips a little wine. At this point, with his senses alert and the words resonating from the page, time, and space are disrupted. Like Keats rediscovering Homer via Chapman and Cortez, 'a new planet swims into [Edward's] ken' and he looks on 'with a wild surmise'. Two worlds—the personal, intimate, and libidinal, and the ancestral, impersonal, and political—intertwine:

> And whether it was the wine or the words or both, a luminous shell formed, a purple fume, from which out stepped a Greek girl; yet she was English. There she stood among the marble and the asphodel, yet there she was among the Morris wall-papers and the cabinets—his cousin Kitty. [...] She was both of them—Antigone and Kitty; here in the book; there in the room. (*Y* 46)

Here is translation working on the translator unknowingly, releasing impossible, inadmissible connections. The scholar in Edward curbs these temptations; his official,

---

[23] See also Kolocotroni, '"This Curious Silent Unrepresented Life": Greek Lessons in Early Virginia Woolf', *Modern Language Review* 100, no. 2 (April 2005), 313–22.

finished version earns him his place in the academy. Despite being bound and sealed, however, the translation retains its magic as a potentially unruly, world-transforming recitative. This includes the power to weave a subtle thread that connects one character to another. When Sara randomly takes up Edward's volume and begins reading 'broken words', a similar shift from one world and one soundscape to another recurs. Translation casts its spell, and she *becomes* Antigone:[24]

> She came whirling out of the dust-cloud to where the vultures were reeling and flung white sand over the blackened foot. She stood there letting fall white dust over the blackened foot. Then behold! there were more clouds; dark clouds; the horsemen leapt down; she was seized; her wrists were bound with withies; and they bore her, thus bound—where?
> There was a roar of laughter from the garden. (*Y* 121)

The irrevocable, performative powers of a translation that ring true are revealed in this impossible merging of two worlds and two mind- and soundscapes within Sara's consciousness: the partying outside sounds alongside the scandal of violent arrest that shattered Antigone's private rituals of mourning. Once caught by Edward, and released anew by Sara, this intuitively re-embodied voice-in-translation then passes on, across the generations of the Pargiters, assuring the posterity of an original as surely as it does in Walter Benjamin's now classic essay 'The Task of the Translator', but without the theological aura. Years later, when Eleanor, Edward, and North converse at the party that brings the novel's 'Present Day' to a close, Antigone's voice rings out quite unexpectedly again. The first person to hear her is Eleanor:

> 'Yes! The Antigone!' she exclaimed. 'And I thought to myself, just what you say, Edward—how true—how beautiful...'
> She broke off, as if afraid to continue.
> Edward nodded. He paused. Then suddenly he jerked his head back and said some words in Greek: 'οὔτοι συνέχθειν, ἀλλὰ συμφιλεῖν ἔφυν.'
> North looked up.
> 'Translate it,' he said.
> Edward shook his head. 'It's the language,' he said. (*Y* 372)

What might this untranslated foreignness left in mid-air signify? What prompts Edward, irrespective of his authority as translator, to leave the words on the borderline of audibility and intelligibility? Is he still wary of the heady effects translating the *Antigone* once had? Is this the 'bondage' in which language has us, 'the desire for that which perpetually lures us back'? (*E4* 48).[25] Would Antigone's defiant credo be out of place at the

---

[24] For an extended exploration of the interwoven textual/musical soundscape, see Elicia Clements, 'The Efficacy of Musical Performance in *The Years*', in Adriana Varga ed., *Virginia Woolf and Music* (Bloomington: Indiana University Press, 2014), 180–203.

[25] See also Kolocotroni's analysis of this 'uncomfortable dramatization of unintelligibility', in 'Strange Cries', 432.

warmly hospitable party? Or does her sonorous appeal perform a new political parable by remaining untranslated, thereby keeping foreignness safe in an era when national and racial barriers were closing in again? The riddle is left for the reader to ponder. By breaking the flow of homely English print on the page, in any case, the text continues to bear witness to translation's subversive valency.

Antigone's defiant words also resonate between *The Years* and the deftly layered textual montage of *Three Guineas*—a contemporary drama in epistolary form, whose generic instability is in part the result of translatable and untranslated foreignness joining forces with the lost voices of 'Anon'.[26] The classical reference is first introduced to illustrate 'the public psychometer', Woolf's neologistic and therefore transparency-defying figure for the collective pulse. Both the referenced text and the translator, however, will be presented as something of a riddle:

> To take one example, since we are pressed for time. The *Antigone* of Sophocles has been done into English prose or verse by a man whose name is immaterial. [...] Lame as the English rendering is, Antigone's five words are worth all the sermons of all the archbishops (*TG* 162)

Like the photos of Spanish atrocities, the words are withheld, however, making their radical potency hover as 'cultural "background noise"' on the page.[27] Readers must turn to the footnotes, as they might to a dictionary, to look up meaning. Even here, the foreign lure, the encoded script, and the disruptive sonorities of Antigone's words do not surface easily. They are disseminated between two footnotes, with a series of translational obstacles hampering the way. These include practical questions of scholarship; a digression on the inadequacies of linguistic equivalence; an admission that literature, even translated, will escape the propagandist's designs; and a transposition of the classical plot into modern times: 'Antigone herself could be transformed either into Mrs Pankhurst, who broke a window and was imprisoned in Holloway; or into Frau Pommer' (*TG* 238). When the five Greek words finally cry out from the silent page, the eleven-word crib performs its role as a translation even as it admits its inability to do so. In other words, the resonant words and Woolf's quoted source text—'"Tis not my nature to join in hating, but in loving (*Antigone*, line 523, Jebb)' (*TG* 239)—buried beneath layers of other meanings, and segregated from the main body of the text, seemingly dramatize, metaphorize, and translate the drama of Antigone herself, condemned for speaking out against tyranny, and sentenced to being buried alive. Once released from the marginal spatiality of footnotes, however, translation *and* the residue of untranslatability serve to defy Creon's order that his law-defying niece be immured in silence. Here, surely, is a new incarnation of Anon's boundary-crossing song, 'rising, bursting

---

[26] My reading of soundscapes resonating with the taking place of translation is indebted to Dimock's theory of resonance as read by Anne Fernald in 'Woolfian Resonances', *Literature Compass* 4, no. 1 (January 2007), 271–83.

[27] See Fernald, 'Woolfian Resonances', 276.

up, from beneath' in a 'voice that stumbles [...] the voice of reason, of humanity, of common sense' (*E6* 590, 586–7).[28]

The stumbling voice of the vernacular, as spoken by the common people, in 'Anon' is gradually contrasted, in Woolf's essay, by an elevated, elegant language imposed by the patriarchal authorities of Church and State: 'Upstairs they spoke French' (*E6* 582). This is no passing jibe. As the essay title 'On Not Knowing French' announces, there remains a third, more unexpected port of call on Woolf's odyssey of languages-in-translation, which binds French, Greek, and Russian and their cultural 'demesnes' together.[29] The cross-Channel challenge of 'not knowing French' dislocates what is supposedly close to home, however, disrupting any too-easily opposed binaries. For this reason, the paradox of French familiarity is perhaps where the most radical edge of her forays into unhinged subjectivities and performed 'foreignness' can be found:

> Let us start from a letter written in 1934, quoted here in full:
>
> Voilà, chère Janie, le brouillon que vous avez commandé. Après l'avoir lu je pense que peutêtre il sera mieux de ne pas l'envoyer. Cette image de l'elepant [sic] et la sylphe n'est pas tout à fait réussie: c'est un peu—peut on dire 'rosse'?
>
> J'avais l'intention de vous aborder au Square hier soir, mais le sommeil m'a vaincu, et j'ai eu le plaisir en dormant de vous revoir, et de vous entendre dire que vous m'aimez, et que je sais très bien la différence entre les imparfaits et les parfaits—ce qui m'a tellement ravie que je me suis éveillée et hélas—c'était un reve. (*L5* 316)

The note encapsulates the paradoxical essence of Woolf's poetics of translation. It is a covering letter sent to Jane Bussy—who was giving her French lessons—enclosing a draft text in French that Woolf admits might be better *not* sent. Embedded in this playful breach of etiquette is an incongruous image of 'an elephant and a sylph', which is 'might we say rather uncouth' ['peut on dire rosse']. The adjective 'rosse' is a little-used, pejorative, or ironic term, whose mongrelized etymology bespeaks a trans-European odyssey: it harks back to base Norman, old Germanic, and (via Don Quixote's Rocinante) Spanish, and can signify both an old nag and a waspish or shrewish commentator.[30] The animalesque fantasy, in other words, ranging from elephants to carthorses via sylphs to portray one's own (self) composition, is part of an incongruous, language-crossing parable. Lacking Woolf's enclosed composition or translation into French, we can only surmise the referent. Given Woolf's fondness for animal nicknames and for creative lines of escape from stable, single identities, it might allude to a playful

---

[28] Woolf's focus here is on Latimer's discovery of the appalling plight of the common people, rather than on Anon the singer. However, the essayist suggests that the scandals of what he witnessed incited Latimer to abandon his role as preacher, appointed to transmit the voice of the Church, and to take up the more subversive song of Anon, 'tearing down' the dogmas of the law.

[29] Woolf's intertwining experience of the languages included reading the classics and the Russians at times via the French. I explore her three-way thinking through languages in 'Bilinguals and Bioptics'.

[30] 'Rosse', Alain Rey, dir., in *Dictionnaire historique de la langue française*, vol. 2 (Paris: Robert, 1992), 1834.

musical 'translation' of Saint-Saens's 'Carnival of the Animals', in which 'The Elephant' is 'a humorous distortion for double-bass and piano of Berlioz's 'Danse des Sylphes'.³¹

Irrespective of what the elephant and sylph may signify, the embedded tale of language's border-crossing exploits continues in the second paragraph. Woolf evokes a dream, in French, in which she hears Jane Bussy saying that she 'loves' her (or 'likes'—the French word hovers artfully between the two), before praising her pupil for distinguishing between imperfectives and perfectives. So delightful is the news that the dreamer awakes, to discover, 'alas—it was a dream'. The short letter, in other words, contains a host of tantalizing hints, concealed and revealed by veils of French. These affirm that Woolf could not only read and write in French, she was even dreaming in it, which is a gauge of finer linguistic prowess if 'On Not Knowing French' is to be trusted: 'There are a few who claim—and who shall deny them?—that it is the language of their dreams' (*E5* 5). So what are we to make of an essay that, like Mansfield's short story, 'Je ne parle pas français', dismantles its own linguistic and logical base in the act of constructing it?

Setting aside the self-deprecating modesty and the lip-service paid to native French wisdom and wit, it is the text's status as pre-translational and post-translational reflection that interests me here.³² Where is the source, and where the mirror-image? Who speaks this text, and to whom is it addressed? As Stuart N. Clarke indicates, it was a 'signed review in the *New Republic*' of André Maurois's novel *Climats*, to be 'printed in England France and America, simultaneously' (*E5* 7). It was the first of nine commissioned essays, published on the front page of *Le Figaro*, and the only one to address French literature rather than English. It was therefore conceived as a language-and-culture-crossing riddle, worded with its own translation-to-come in mind, and speaking of matters French to the French. To choose to review a French novel, and to question along the way both what chances a native Anglophone has of truly, un(self)-consciously knowing French, and contrariwise what a native Francophone might hear and mishear when ostensibly understanding English, is in itself something of a provocation in jest. Beyond its own performative paradox, however, and even as it meanders through the landscapes of Maurois's supposedly quintessential French novel, the review articulates a rich reflection on the effects of being translated, or 'in translation', oneself.

Maurois and his novel were operative choices in this linguistic odyssey. Widely acknowledged as France's most anglophile novelist, he was also an acclaimed biographer and theorist of biography, whose 1928 Clark lectures (later translated 'back' into French) reflect an on-going conversation with his Bloomsbury fellows. His first biographies (translated almost immediately into English) likewise recount the lives of

---

³¹ Posthumously published in 1922, the suite was regular concert and radio repertoire in the early 1930s.
³² See Edwin Gentzler, *Translation and Rewriting in the Age of Post-Translation Studies* (London: Routledge, 2017). In Gentzler's incisive conceptualisation, 'post-translation' deliberately 'erase[s] the border' between pre-translation and post-translation, thereby underlying translation's centrality 'as an always on-going process of *every* communication' (5).

eminent British romantics—Shelley and Disraeli.[33] Whether read in Maurois's 'original' French or in English translation, these works, like Woolf's essay, occupy a strange world that both precedes and proceeds from translation. The same is true of *Climats*, which in French is not exactly a 'roman' (novel) but a 'récit'—an untranslatable term denoting either a fictional or self-fictionalising chronicle, or a lyric recitative. Diptych in form, and loosely epistolary, it transposes the myth of Orpheus and Eurydice into a post-war domestic tragedy set in provincial France. Quintessentially 'French' as it may be, Maurois's novel proves, as Proust claimed all works of literature should, to be written in 'a sort of foreign language'.[34] Its theme meanwhile—unrequited or belated love, always missing its mark—is as old as literature itself, more at home in 'troubadour lyric' than in a single nation's literature, finding expression not just in Anon's tales but in performances—operas, ballets, song cycles, poems, and most recently, Maurois's 'récit'.

These linguistic reflections ricochet throughout Woolf's reading of *Climats* (in French) in 'On Not Knowing French'. The essayist reads through Englishness and England to grasp Frenchness and France; she writes English in the knowledge that it is imminently to become French—and even, as agreed with the *Figaro* editor, to be published in French first (*E5* 662). It is an essay, in other words, with no 'original', written to be written differently; either version 'mak[es]' visible a "significant form" residing somehow beyond and within both the English and the French versions of the text'.[35] Nor would Woolf lose all sight of her text in translation: she would be able to read it once it had been translated, even if she no longer 'knew' it. Bearing in mind these iridescent inter-reflecting mirrors, which dissolve all boundaries between originals, sources, selves, and others, what becomes of Woolf's voice in *Le Figaro*?

As the English version puts it only too well, the change in language gives words 'a body rather different from their faces' (*E5* 3). The first differences are grammatical. In the (unsigned) *Figaro* version, the 'language that is not one's own' gains inflections and variants that English 'words' don't have, because the French language brings gender into play. In French, both 'word' *and* 'language' can be masculine *and* feminine: 'le mot' and 'la parole'; 'la langue' and 'le langage'. Likewise, in keeping with the requisite French style, the specific (grammatical) subject will at times gain a gendered echo:

'C'est le langage de leurs rêves. Mais pour bien posséder une langue, il faut l'avoir oubliée.'

'Un étranger, avec une parfaite maîtrise d'une langue, pourra écrire dans un style correct et musical.'

---

[33] Maurois's commitment to disseminating British literary and culture in France was lifelong. His biographies went on to include Bryon, Edward VII, and Fleming; he also wrote a cultural history of the nineteenth century and a study of British romanticism.

[34] In an article later included in Marcel Proust's *Contre Saint-Beuve* [1895] (Paris: Gallimard, 1997), Proust affirms that 'Beautiful works are written in a sort of foreign language' (297), a notion that later formed the bedrock of Gilles Deleuze's *Critique et clinique*.

[35] Jane Goldman, 'Translation, Secondary Rendering and Textual Genesis', in Claire Davison and Anne-Marie Smith-Di Biasio, eds, *Trans-Woolf* (Perugia: Morlacchi, 2017), 97–120, at 102.

'Cet anglais inconscient où on sent le passé de chaque parole, avec ses souvenirs et ses points d'attache.'[36]

Beyond grammatical wavering between 'his' and 'her', between masculines and feminines, perceptual differences occur as one language's metaphors are reshaped into another's. Take the dislocation of the senses as they are first defamiliarized and reawakened within Woolf's 'On Not Knowing French', and then heard anew in 'Quand on ne sait pas le français'. Registered by the French body, sensual impressions are not quite the same:

> 'the words come together somehow incongruously'
>
> '[les mots] ont quelque peu l'air de ne pas s'entendre entre eux' [*The words look as if they aren't quite understanding / hearing each other*]
>
> 'the novelty with which he endowed them'
>
> 'il a jeté un regard neuf sur de vieux sujets [*he has looked anew at old subjects*]
>
> And this novelty was the more striking because there was perhaps a grain of truth that custom had overlaid.'
>
> Et il a réussi à remettre en lumière [*shed light*] un grain de vérité que la coutume et la routine avaient fini par voiler.' [*veiled over*]
>
> 'It is a delight, after mumbling over the old stories of our old memoirs in the familiar English atmosphere...'
>
> 'Quel délice! [*How delightful*] Avoir longtemps remâché [*chewed over*] les vieilles rengaines [*the old tunes*] de nos vieux mémoires, respiré l'antique atmosphère [*breathing in the old English air*] anglaise avec son décor familier...' (E5 4)[37]

Like the senses, bodies, beasts, and even landscapes behave differently as they are transposed from one language to the other:

> 'what takes the French taste in contemporary English literature'
>
> 'ce qui séduit [*seduces*] particulièrement les Français'
>
> 'The very foxes are different.'
>
> 'Les renards même ne ressemblent pas aux nôtres.' [*Even their foxes don't look like ours.*]
>
> 'Our ramblings lead us into *châteaux* that have much more than the formality of our country houses.'
>
> 'Ces promenades [*These strolls*] nous conduisent aussi dans des châteaux qui évoquent quelque chose de plus que nos manoirs à l'air un peu apprêté.' [*our rather starchy-looking manor-houses*]

---

[36] Virginia Woolf, 'Quand on ne sait pas le français', *Le Figaro* 41, (February 1929), 1–2, at 1. Underlinings and bracketed translations are my own.

[37] Woolf, 'Quand on ne sait pas le français', 1.

'We race through half a dozen chapters at top speed.'

'Pendant une demi-douzaine de pages, nous restons haletants.' [*We remain breathless.*] (E5 4–5)[38]

Inevitably, as two languages constantly readjust to say almost the same thing, Woolf's *Figaro* 'original' creates oddly different impressions of the place from which it started. 'Home' is not where it once was, but nor are the 'strange' and the 'familiar', in fact:

'There is an oddity in every page.'
'On éprouve une impression de bizarrerie.' [*One senses bizarreness*]

'Some queer, a little lopsided version'
'des jugements d'un équilibre imparfait' [*judgements with an imperfect sense of balance*]

'Novelty, and the strangeness'
'ce charme complexe' [*this complex charm*]

'Strange swift streams'
'leurs rivières rapides et pittoresques' [*picturesque*]

'A formidable civilisation, more articulate, less homely than our own'
'cette civilisation française est impressionnante, plus souple, moins bourgeoise que la nôtre' [*awesome, more flexible, less bourgeois*]

'Earlier and more elegant than our homely violets and primroses'
'plus précoces et plus gracieuses que les modestes violettes et primevères de chez nous' [*the modest violets and primroses where we live*] (E5 5–6)[39]

Shifts like these invite more attenuated, less qualitative readings of Woolf's responses to translation. As they accumulate, they show precisely how 'the ear collects a thousand hints and suggestions from one's own tongue', or why, as she notes in her diary 'One *feels* the immeasurable difference between the text & the translation' (E5 6; D1 184; italics added).

Thinking back through Maurois's 'récit' thus provides essential insights into Woolf's reflections on and reflections in translation, and why, 'If one wants to see what style is, it is best to read a translation'.[40] It points exactly to how she read French 'unknowingly', through the diffracting mirror images of lives expressed in contemporary re-enactments of classical tragedy, of lyrical laments exchanged by lovers loving belatedly across the grave, of deflected selves of biography, and of her own voice, spoken to echo back in another key. To return to the figure of the wandering minstrel, Maurois's strangely English-haunted Frenchness read by Woolf points to ways in which thinking through translation

[38] Woolf, 'Quand on ne sait pas le français', 1–2.
[39] Woolf, 'Quand on ne sait pas le français', 2.
[40] This is what Dalgarno refers to as Woolf's 'tantalizing' note on Proust's *Germantes*. See Dalgarno, *Migrations*, 37.

via speaking selves and once-lived lives plays an essential cameo part in Woolf's alternative literary panorama, as it reads at random, restoring 'less visible connections' and clearing the tracks that had been grown over. Anon the translator thus spans the gulf between the civic unrest of times immemorial, and the urgent political realities of the late 1930s, alighting along the way upon Tolstoy, heard in translation, and still resounding 'loud and bold':

> I read Tolstoy at breakfast—Goldenweiser, that I translated with Kot in 1923 & have almost forgotten. Always the same reality—like touching an exposed electric wire […] Thus more disturbing, more 'shocking' more of a thunderclap, even on art, even on lit.re that any other writer (D5 273)

Freed from 'the tethers of a single mind',[41] Anon the translator merits his and her place alongside Woolf's extensive cast of minor, mostly female, characters. These overlooked and yet essential intermediaries, working 'with nameless vitality' (E6 598) in the sidelines rather than the limelight, are busy ensuring that there will be afterlives for the languages and literatures that desire nothing more than to continue roaming anonymous and forgetful across histories, geographies *and* genders:

> English words marry French words, German words, Indian words, Negro words, if they have a fancy. Indeed, the less we enquire into the past of our dear Mother English the better it will be for that lady's reputation. For she has gone a roving, a-roving fair maid. (E6 96)

In 'Craftsmanship', the song serves to recount a life of the English language, but it is referenced in song books as 'The Maid of Amsterdam'.

Selected Bibliography

Beasley, Rebecca, 'On Not Knowing Russian: The Translations of Virginia Woolf and S. S. Kotelianskii', *Modern Language Review* 108, no. 1 (January 2013), 1–29.
Bernard, Catherine, 'Translation/Transport in *Flush* and Other Hybrids: Virginia Woolf's Ethics of Cultural Displacement', in Claire Davison and Anne-Marie Smith-Di Biasio, eds, *Trans-Woolf* (Perugia: Morlacchi, 2017), 23–44.
Davison, Claire, *Translation as Collaboration: Virginia Woolf, Katherine Mansfield and S. S. Koteliansky* (Edinburgh: Edinburgh University Press, 2014).
Davison, Claire, 'Bilinguals and Bioptics: Virginia Woolf and the Outlandishness of Translation', in Jeanne Dubino, Gill Lowe, Vara Neverow, and Kathryn Simpson, eds, *Virginia Woolf: Twenty-First Century Approaches* (Edinburgh: Edinburgh University Press, 2015), 72–92.

---

[41] Although 'Street Haunting' is not specifically about translating, or language, Woolf uses the essay to explore a 'self-translational' experiment in which 'one is not tethered to a single mind but can put on briefly for a few minutes the bodies and minds of others' (E4 490).

Gentzler, Edwin, *Translation and Rewriting in the Age of Post-Translation Studies* (London: Routledge, 2017).

Goldman, Jane, 'Translation, Secondary Rendering and Textual Genesis', in Claire Davison and Anne-Marie Smith-Di Biasio, eds, *Trans-Woolf* (Perugia: Morlacchi, 2017), 97–120.

Högberg, Elsa, 'The Melancholic Translations of Anon', in Claire Davison and Anne-Marie Smith-Di Biasio, eds, *Trans-Woolf* (Perugia: Morlacchi, 2017), 45–66.

Kolocotroni, Vassiliki, '"This Curious Silent Unrepresented Life": Greek Lessons in Early Virginia Woolf', *Modern Language Review* 100, no. 2 (April 2005), 313–22.

Mills, Jean, 'The Writer, The Prince and the Scholar: Virginia Woolf, D. S. Mirsky and Jane Harrison's Translation from Russian of *The Life of the Archpriest Avvakum by Himself*, in Helen Southworth, ed., *Leonard & Virginia Woolf, the Hogarth Press and the Networks of Modernism* (Edinburgh: Edinburgh University Press, 2010), 150–75.

Raterman, Jennifer, 'Reading from the outside: The uses of translation for Virginia Woolf's "common reader"', *Translation Studies* 3, no. 1 (January 2010), 78–93.

Rubenstein, Roberta, *Virginia Woolf and the Russian Point of View* (New York: Palgrave Macmillan, 2009).

Tolstoi, Sophia, *The Autobiography of Countess Sophie Tolstoi*, trans. S. S. Koteliansky and Leonard Woolf (London: Hogarth Press, 1922).

Woolf, Leonard and S. S. Koteliansky, eds and trans., *Reminiscences of Leo Nicolayevitch Tolstoi* (London: Hogarth Press, 1920).

PART V
CONTEXTS

CHAPTER 20

WOOLF'S FEMINISM

STEPHANIE J. BROWN

Two questions immediately confront anyone tasked with evaluating Virginia Woolf's feminism: 'which Woolf?' and 'which feminism?' Just as feminism itself passed through various and sometimes competing iterations over the course of Woolf's lifetime, so Woolf herself shifts according to the light: different Virginia Woolfs (and Stephens) come into view depending on whether we go looking for Woolf the novelist, Woolf the essayist and diarist, or the Woolf who circulated in the world, cycling around London during the General Strike of May 1926 to drum up signatures of prominent writers in support of the strikers[1] or 'passing out [suffrage] handbills in the street' with her sister Vanessa.[2] These Woolfs are not entirely distinct, of course, but focusing on any one of them will reveal different inflections of feminist engagement, and these differences are at times difficult to reconcile.[3]

Two specific concerns have long motivated readers of Woolf's feminism. Quentin Bell's biography of his aunt appeared in 1972, a watershed moment that resulted in the now widely held view that 'Woolf's life and work ... have a densness and complexity that were not evident earlier'.[4] Offering an account of her feminism has entailed attempting to unravel the relationship between aesthetics, politics, and the conduct of everyday life in Woolf's work ever since, and a pair of common lines of inquiry were laid out early in this debate. The first foregrounded the public, intellectual, and often extra-textual elements of Woolf's politics (although this strain of Woolf's feminism was usually understood to include *A Room of One's Own* (1929)) as her major contribution

---

[1] Hermione Lee, *Virginia Woolf* (London: Chatto & Windus, 1996), 533.
[2] Barbara Strachey Halpern, 'Ray Strachey—A Memoir', in Wayne K. Chapman and Janet M. Manson, eds, *Women in the Milieu of Leonard and Virginia Woolf: Peace, Politics, and Education* (New York: Pace University Press, 1998), 76–86, at 78.
[3] This observation is not novel. Different critical ways of solving the issue, including implicitly or explicitly focusing on one element of Woolf's work or life to the exclusion of others, or separating considerations formally, occupy space in the introductions to many critical studies of Woolf.
[4] Alex Zwerdling, *Virginia Woolf and the Real World* (Berkeley: University of California Press, 1986), 2–3.

to feminism. The second explored Woolf's aesthetics, including her resistance to overtly polemical literature, as a canny, reasoned response to the inevitable limitations of what fiction—especially fiction that implicitly endorsed authoritarian or patriarchal modes of thought by replicating them in its narratives strategies—could accomplish for women in the world outside the text.[5] This chapter takes up both of these threads, which remain central to considerations of Woolf's career, in its holistic consideration of central questions that remained consistent for her feminism, and the ways in which their inflections varied, over the course of her life.

Woolf's career spans a period of radical change in women's status in Britain. These changes included major milestones in first-wave feminism, during which women made significant legal and social gains. Legislatively, these gains were enshrined in the terms of the Married Women's Property Act of 1882, which ended coverture for married women and allowed them to own property in their own name, the Representation of the People Acts of 1918 and 1928, the latter of which enfranchised women on the same terms as men, the seating of the first female members of parliament in 1919,[6] the Sex Disqualification Removal Act 1919, which ended sex-based discrimination in the professions and civil service,[7] and greater parity in how women and men were treated under the divorce laws by the Matrimonial Causes Act of 1923. In the later 1910s and early 1920s, Marie Stopes worked to establish that birth control advice could legally 'be given by organisations under the control of the government'.[8] (She also opened the first birth control clinic in England in 1921, and in 1925 opened 'what appeared to be the first provincial birth-control clinic' in an attempt to ensure access to women outside the metropolis.[9]) Institutionally, the founding of Girton and Newnham Colleges at Cambridge in 1866 and 1872 established women's access to university education, although it would be 1920 before women were granted Oxford degrees on the same terms as men; Cambridge didn't follow suit until 1936. Socially, these victories represented progress in bringing

---

[5] These distinct approaches were formalized by two of the earliest scholarly monographs on Woolf's politics, both of which appeared in 1986. Alex Zwerdling's *Virginia Woolf and the Real World* notes that the persistent if ambivalent interest in feminism in Woolf's work was accompanied by a the lack of 'a historical sense of her place in and particular contribution to the women's movement' (211). Zwerdling argues that Woolf's contribution 'was to restore a sense of the complexity of the issues after the radical simplification of that had seemed necessary for political action' (217) during the women's suffrage movement. Pamela J. Transue's *Virginia Woolf and the Politics of Style* (New York: State University of New York Press, 1986), in contrast, locates the efficacy of Woolf's feminist works in their 'strategies for transforming her feminist vision into an art unfettered by the tone of grievance... Woolf offers a rare opportunity for the study of the processes by which ideology can be transformed into successful art' (15).

[6] Nancy Astor was the first female MP to take her seat; Constance Markievicz was the first woman to be elected to the House of Commons in 1918, but like all members of Ireland's Sinn Féin, left her seat vacant.

[7] Sex-based but not marital-status-based: a marriage bar remained in place in the civil service, for example, until 1946: Cheryl Law, *Suffrage and Power: The Women's Movement 1918–1928*, (London: I. B. Taurus Publishers, 1997), 93.

[8] Johanna Alberti, *Beyond Suffrage: Feminists in War and Peace, 1914–1928* (London: Macmillan, 1989), 121–4.

[9] Alberti, *Beyond Suffrage*, 123.

the public around to a positive view of women's education, sexual and financial autonomy, and involvement in public life. Although some of these gains were neutralized after World War I, when women faced renewed hostility in the civil services and the professions, campaigns for international solidarity and pacifism in the post-war years were two areas where women could be seen as unthreatening contributors, and women developed a common rhetoric of the helpful feminist working with international bodies on issues where female experts were considered appropriate, such as the trafficking of women and children.

At the same time, emergent discourses around women's sexuality, including women's decisions to acknowledge and act on same-sex desire, drove acute changes in public perceptions of feminism. Woolf's life coincides with what David Trotter has taxonomized as three waves of feminist activity, each tied to different ways of conceptualizing lesbian identity, between the 1870s and the 1930s; these waves are, in a parlance he borrows from the New Woman debates of the 1890s, the 'New' (1870s–1890s), 'Newer' (1900s–1910s), and 'Newest' (late 1910s–early 1930s) women.[10] The first of these waves took up the problems depicted in the New Woman novel, namely women's education and emancipation; the second was 'concern[ed] with the economic and political destinies of women who had chosen not to marry[, which] found a focus in campaigns to improve living and working conditions, and to secure the vote'. The third, women who came of age in the post-war years, benefited by the gains of the first two waves, and 'found a focus in androgynous modernity and in the emergence of a lesbian subculture'.[11] While women in the first of these two waves 'sometimes came under the suspicion of lesbianism ... but did not think of themselves as lesbians and were not necessarily thought of as lesbians', this was not the case for the third wave.[12] Woolf's own lesbian relationships, her representation of her lover Vita Sackville-West as the inspiration for *Orlando* (1928), and her reactions to the increasing public awareness of

---

[10] David Trotter, 'Lesbians before Lesbianism: Sexual Identity in Early Twentieth-Century British Fiction', in Billie Melman, ed., *Borderlines: Genders and Identities in War and Peace, 1870-1930* (London: Routledge, 1998), 193–211, at 193–4.

[11] Trotter, 'Lesbians before Lesbianism', 194.

[12] Trotter, 'Lesbians before Lesbianism', 194. See also Laura Doan's chapter on the question of how women understood sex acts between women during the war, '"We Cannot Use That Word": On the Habits of Naming, Name Calling, and Self-Naming', in Laura Doan, *Disturbing Practices: History, Sexuality, and Women's Experience of Modern War* (Chicago: University of Chicago Press, 2013), 133–63. Doan offers a close reading of the practices surrounding naming lesbian identity in the post-war years. Looking at whether and how women named lesbian identity at two moments, 1918 and 1931, Doan finds that 'there is scant evidence ... that, concerning sexuality, these women felt themselves to be anything, least of all a name ... some women had little sense of sexual selfhood or subjectivity'; as a result, she argues 'we need to pause—as historians and historicists—and consider the habit of naming the sexual being as historically contingent' (140). Doan troubles the practice of 'assuming as naturalized the attaching of a name to a practice or an identity' (136) in documenting the slippage between reported acts, ascribing categories of sexual identity on the basis of those acts, and the very different terms in which the (here alleged) participants might have articulated, or been entirely uninterested in articulating, a sense of self that connected to sexual identity, whether lesbian or not.

lesbianism as a phenomenon necessarily intersect with her feminism and the depiction of women in her work.

These three historical period's understandings of women's sexuality corresponded roughly with three phases of feminism, each with a different rhetorical and political orientation. Her youth coincided with the end of Queen Victoria's reign, and the canon of literary luminaries in her family's Victorian intellectual milieu function as the dominant points of reference for her non-fiction until surprisingly late in her career.[13] This was a period in which the implications of the women's rights reform legislation of the mid- and late 1800s were being worked through in the courts.[14] This included the court of public opinion, where crusading journalists like W.T. Stead drew attention to issues that were coded as women's concerns, and where the 'woman question' and the 'New Woman' were objects of sustained debate. This period also saw the rise of groups like the National Vigilance Association, which promoted temperance and attempted the 'rescue' of fallen women. Judging by the public's voracious appetite for press coverage of scandal trials, and the increasingly explicit media coverage of these trials, it was also a moment of increasingly public discourse around sexual scandal and (initially male) queerness.[15] In the women's suffrage movement, the period of the late 1800s was a moment of relative calm that preceded the militancy of the early 1900s.[16]

There were also cultural movements that crossed these chronological divisions: women's access to formal education and the professions, as well as information about reproductive health, were among those that Woolf engaged with throughout her life. Feminists became increasingly curious about everyday intersections of gender and class as socialist thought (and the Independent Labour Party) gained traction within the British mainstream. Toward the end of Woolf's life, advocates of internationalism

---

[13] For the intellectual influence of Victorian writers and thinkers on Woolf's work, see Steve Ellis, *Virginia Woolf and the Victorians* (Cambridge: Cambridge University Press, 2007).

[14] This was neither a simple process nor a quick one: for example, it was not until 1935 the courts determined that women could be held personally liable for financial contracts undertaken in their own names: see Carole Pateman, *The Sexual Contract* (Stanford, CA: Stanford University Press, 1988), 165. Until this determination was made, banks and creditors lacked legal assurance that women could be compelled to repay their debts, and so were unlikely to enter into financial contracts with them.

[15] While the Oscar Wilde trial is the best-documented of these late nineteenth-century trials, Gretchen Soderlund's *Sex Trafficking, Scandal, and the Transformation of Journalism, 1885 to 1917* (Chicago: University of Chicago Press, 2013) discusses the media's role in sustaining the sexual scandal trial as a phenomenon. Jodie Medd's *Lesbian Scandal and the Culture of Modernism* (Cambridge: Cambridge University Press, 2012) and Lucy Bland's *Modern Women on Trial: Sexual Transgression in the Age of the Flapper* (Manchester: Manchester University Press, 2013) both document the permutations of the sexual scandal trial throughout the modernist period.

[16] Although suffrage scholars like Maureen Wright have worked in recent years to demonstrate that the late Victorian era was not a fallow period for the women's suffrage movement, but rather an important period in which traditional arguments were re-evaluated, new societies and networks formed, and increasing recruitment of young people to the cause, it remains the case that this is a perspective from inside the movement, and that this progress was not necessarily a part of the general public's view of the movement. See Maureen Wright, *Elizabeth Wolstenholme Elmy and the Victorian Feminist Movement: The Biography of an Insurgent Woman* (Manchester: Manchester University Press, 2011).

and pacifism became increasingly visible in these conversations, as did arguments that critiqued imperial expansion and the suppression of national independence movements in British colonies, especially those colonies that had mobilized troops in large numbers to the British cause during World War I.[17] British women of the early twentieth century had increasing access to the critiques of empire, and were increasingly aware of the ways in which the British economy relied on transnational exchange for its everyday domestic operations. These factors prompted the tenuous beginnings of what we might follow Kimberlé Crenshaw in calling an intersectional feminism that included the voices of colonized women and women of colour in ways that had not been possible in the nineteenth century—even if that work did not always travel under the *name* of feminism.[18]

Woolf wrote short stories, reviews, and her earliest novels, *The Voyage Out* (1915) and *Night and Day* (1919), during the period of around 1903 to 1918 when women's suffrage and, after 1914, women's relationships to the war effort functioned as the framework through which the public most commonly engaged with feminist questions.[19] The emphasis on equality under the law and equal access to resources, women's positions in the workplace (and, for working class women, in the trades unions) as well as an emphasis on women's ability to contribute to a wartime economy, entailed arguments that framed feminism as a question of equal (or at least equivalent) contributions and rights.

Woolf's mature novels and non-fiction appeared in the post-war years. After the war, a form of difference feminism emerged in Britain to displace the egalitarian model of the pre-war and war years. High levels of post-war unemployment among men, and in particular demobilized soldiers, made feminist arguments in favour of equal access to jobs, and equal work for equal pay, deeply unpopular. Public opinion, which had celebrated women's efforts on the home front during the war, came to view women's desire, and in many cases their economic need, to remain in the workforce as a whim that could only be indulged at the expense of the working man in the post-war years—a situation that was not much ameliorated during the global depression of the late 1920s and early 1930s. In response to the allegations that such women wilfully took jobs that properly belonged to returning men and a public backlash to women in the workplace, feminist rhetoric shifted to arguments that emphasized difference: these arguments relied on women's unique abilities as mothers, wives, and workers in ways that were often calculated to appear unthreatening to a patriarchal status quo.[20] Stopes's work meant that the 1920s

---

[17] On the role of colonial soldiers in the War, see Santanu Das, *Race, Empire, and First World War Writing* (Cambridge: Cambridge University Press, 2014).

[18] Kimberlé Crenshaw defines and elaborates the implications of intersectionality in her groundbreaking essay 'Demarginalizing the Intersection of Race and Sex: A Black Feminist Critique of Antidiscrimination Doctrine, Feminist Theory and Antiracist Politics', *The University of Chicago Legal Forum* 1989, no. 139 (1989), 139–67.

[19] Barbara Green's chapter in this volume offers an extended consideration of Woolf's engagement with the suffrage movement and its politics.

[20] For a detailed consideration of these arguments, see Dierdre Beddoe, *Back to Home and Duty: Women between the Wars, 1918-1939* (London: Pandora Press, 1989) and Martha Vicinus, 'Revolt against Redundancy', in Martha Vicinus, *Independent Women: Work and Community for Single Women, 1850–1920* (Chicago: The University of Chicago Press, 1985), 10–45.

and 1930s saw a shift in the terrain of arguments that had supported women's reproductive autonomy and sexual education to concerns of public hygiene and responsible motherhood and citizenship. In the post-war years, women were figured in many feminist arguments as supplementing men's abilities rather than supplanting them; the task of mainstream feminism often revolved around finding an outlet for women's abilities that did not appear to threaten a precarious economic order that already faced challenges from the socialist left, anti-colonial resistance movements, and the depression. In addition, 'feminism' itself had come to be such an unpopular label that some activist women intentionally eschewed it in favour of other frameworks for discussing women's rights and issues: as Caitriona Beaumont has shown, 'Using the terminology of citizenship to enhance women's status in society, instead of feminism, mainstream women's groups succeeded in avoiding any association with what was then perceived as an extreme, unpopular, and controversial ideology.'[21] Although Woolf famously, if figuratively (and perhaps sarcastically), burned the word 'feminist' in *Three Guineas* (1938) as 'a vicious and corrupt word that has done much harm in this day and is now obsolete' (*TG* 179), this is nonetheless the period in which her work is most at odds with mainstream women's activism, as she increasingly advocated abolishing not only patriarchal social and economic structures but also the masculinist rhetoric that validated and upheld them.

Constant across the decades is Woolf's engagement with feminism from outside the mainstream. Even in the late 1920s and 1930s, years marked, according to Catherine Clay, by 'the emergence of a public association of women writers at an historic moment of professional opportunity for a new generation of middle-class women' in the periodical press as well as in literary work, Woolf's feminism can hardly ever be situated neatly within the terms of the debate as the social reformers and other feminist thinkers of her time framed them.[22]

Woolf's historical moment necessarily shaped her feminism, even as she attempted to shape it in return. The same is true of her immediate social circles, which changed dramatically over the course of her life as the death of her parents, her work, her marriage to Leonard Woolf, and later her literary fame all allowed her increasing freedom to determine the contours of her social world. The feminism of Woolf's work is inevitably shaped by her sense of audience, the occasion of a given piece of writing, and her cultural positioning, and all these factors changed radically over the course of her career. The need for feminist arguments to be consistently situated in multiple, at times contradictory, discourses that exceeded them must be recognized if we are to make sense of her

---

[21] Caitriona Beaumont, 'Citizens not Feminists: the Boundary Negotiated between Citizenship and Feminism by Mainstream Women's Organizations, 1928–39', *Women's History Review* 9, no. 2 (December 2000), 411–29, at 415.

[22] Catherine Clay's *British Women Writers, 1914–1945: Professional Work and Friendship* (Burlington, VT: Ashgate, 2006) uses the periodical *Time and Tide* as one case study that develops this claim quite persuasively.

work's engagement with feminism and the increasingly broad audiences she pursued for her ideas as her career progressed.

In the years before her parents' deaths in 1895 (Julia Stephen) and 1904 (Leslie Stephen), a division obtained between the general tendency of the Stephens' social circles and the policy positions within Virginia's immediate family:

> Woolf grew up in an environment that nurtured beliefs in the value of education, professional opportunity, political equality, and organized political effort for and by women.... Yet no one in Woolf's immediate family was directly involved in feminist activism, and her mother was unusual in her opposition to change in the situation of women; Julia Stephen even signed the notorious [1889] 'Appeal against Female Suffrage'... and disapproved of formal education for women.[23]

Virginia Stephen became acquainted with the women of this wider milieu in the years immediately before Julia Stephen's death. In the decade that followed, Virginia would become close to several women closer to Julia's age who hailed from her parents' social circle. Unlike her mother, many of these women campaigned for women's education, emancipation, or suffrage. Notable among these were Violet Dickinson, who was an early, key supporter for Virginia Stephen's writing in the 1890s, her tutor Janet Case, Kitty Maxse, Nelly Cecil, Madge and Emma Vaughan, and, a few years later, Mary Sheepshanks, the vice president of Morley College, under whom Woolf taught from 1905 to 1907.[24] In the early 1900s, however, Woolf's emergent friendships with the Cambridge men who would later be identified with Bloomsbury—Duncan Grant, Clive Bell, Lytton Strachey, Leonard Woolf, Maynard Keynes, and, later, E.M. Forster and Roger Fry—led to the attenuation of these relationships. In this period, Woolf put 'these earlier friendships with older women ... behind her, sometimes ruthlessly'.[25] It is clear that this turn from a circle of politically active women entailed judgements and ultimately a profound ambivalence about the efficacy of the feminist social and political reforms they pursued.

The intellectual milieu of Woolf's early family life and her later association with Bloomsbury accustomed her to being in proximity to sites of elite intellectual endeavour and coded that endeavour as masculine. Woolf had consistent access to elite male social and intellectual spaces that many of her female contemporaries lacked, but these spaces were not uniformly hospitable to women (or feminism). As one of a very small number of female Bloomsberries after the Stephen siblings moved to Gordon Square in 1904, Woolf's work was consistently submitted to rigorous aesthetic and intellectual

---

[23] Naomi Black, *Virginia Woolf as Feminist* (Ithaca, NY: Ithaca University Press, 2004), 35–6.

[24] Lee, *Virginia Woolf*, 144, 160–1, 166, 222. Woolf's relationship with Margaret Llewellyn Davies, who developed a friendship with both Woolfs in 1913 that would lead to their life-long entanglement with the Women's Co-operative Guild, would be subject to similar ambivalence in the decades that followed. Chapter 2 by Katheryne Simpson in this volume considers Woolf's move away from this network of female supporters, in particular Violet Dickinson, Nelly Cecil, and Madge Vaughan, in greater depth.

[25] Lee, *Virginia Woolf*, 161.

critique by men whose university training she freely acknowledged was more systematic than her own, but that did not make them particularly well-equipped (and, in fact, as *Three Guineas* (1938) and *A Room of One's Own* suggest, may have rendered them singularly *ill*-equipped) to respond judiciously to the feminist elements in her work.[26] It is nonetheless clear that the critiques of these interlocutors, and the fact that the discursive community in which she tested the written expression of her ideas before publishing them was overwhelmingly male, did shape her presentation of feminist ideas, especially in her early career.[27] It is nearly impossible to imagine Woolf writing polemic in the style of Cicely Hamilton's *Marriage as a Trade* (1909) or Christabel Pankhurst's *The Great Scourge* (1913), both of which deal with social problems that animate Woolf's early novels and later essays, and this may be partly due to Woolf's recognition that the men of Bloomsbury would have condemned attempts to work within a feminist argumentative style that could be denigrated as aesthetically unsophisticated.[28] As Woolf was beginning her career, she doubtless recognized, and may have internalized, the standards of taste that would have led her Bloomsbury readers to wince or snicker at the earnest exhortation, unsubtle satire, and middle- or lowbrow conventions common to much feminist polemic and creative work.

Woolf's engagement with Bloomsbury was concomitant with an apparent lack of engagement with contemporary women writers. The distance Woolf maintained from her contemporaries in her writing creates some unease for readers who would celebrate her feminist politics. This disengagement is especially relevant to an assessment of Woolf's feminism, because it raises the suspicion that she may have embraced the sexist exceptionalism or tokenism through which a women's satisfaction at successfully making herself heard or seen is heightened by being the *sole* woman afforded an entry to an otherwise exclusively male conversation. To embrace the role of exception creates

---

[26] This is not least the case because the men who were most often the targets of Woolf's animus and satire were precisely the men of (roughly) her own class. 'Woolf's loyalties were... complicated by her strong feeling that the men of her own class were not worth imitating. The whole arena of men's work seemed to be dominated by a competitive ethic that Woolf found repugnant' (Zwerdling, *Virginia Woolf and the Real World*, 235).

[27] In 1908, for example, Clive Bell was the first, very attentive, reader of the *Melymbrosia* drafts that would be revised and published as Woolf's first novel, *The Voyage Out*, in 1915 (Lee, *Virginia Woolf*, 254–5).

[28] Hamilton and Pankhurst each work in an explicitly political and economic vein of feminism, but with very different tones and points of inflection to Woolf and to one another. Cicely Hamilton, *Marriage as a Trade* [1909] (Detroit: Singing Tree Press, 1971) makes economic arguments for women's emancipation that Woolf would echo in *A Room of One's Own* and *Three Guineas*, but it does so with an explicitness about questions of women's sexuality and the structural proximity of marriage to prostitution that Woolf never allowed herself in her published works, and with the free expression of female anger that would be carefully tempered and revised out of drafts of Woolf's fiction and essays before publication. Likewise, Christabel Pankhurst's *The Great Scourge and How to End It* (London: E. Pankhurst, 1913), in its frenzied rhetoric of men's inherent viciousness as the cause of venereal disease, engages questions of sexuality and sexual health with a resolute lack of subtlety that would have horrified Woolf on aesthetic grounds.

obstacles to championing other women's work.[29] When it does not lead to outright antagonism (as it sometimes did in her relationship with Katherine Mansfield), it may replace meaningful female solidarity with condescension toward other women, who are presumed to be less capable.[30]

The Hogarth Press is an instructive enterprise to consider in this light: while the Hogarth catalogue included a number of female authors and translators, with the exception of Mansfield, none of these women were in danger of stepping on the toes of Woolf's literary fiction. As the press's co-owner, Woolf entered these relationships in a position of patronage—a position she may have found more congenial than equality. Though Woolf as an editor was 'not an especially generous champion of her woman contemporaries … [she] shows a taste for an idiosyncratic, humorous fiction by women like F. M. Mayor … and Julia Strachey'—a sensibility at a distance from that of her own fiction.[31] In the late 1910s and 1920s, the press also brought her into contact, with a younger generation of women like Alix Strachey, who worked briefly at Hogarth Press and collaborated with both Woolfs on the research for Leonard's book *Empire and Commerce in Africa* (1919).[32] For Woolf, Alix emblematized a cultural divide between herself and younger women who 'provoked her into "me and them" comparisons' in which they were 'doing all the things she had not done'.[33] The tensions in Woolf's relationships with her female near-contemporaries, and their implications for her feminism, do not allow easy resolution, but rather need to be seen as part of her ongoing negotiation of her identity as a writer and public figure.

Woolf's work 'in public'—speeches and occasionally essays—form the most legibly feminist domain within her larger body of work. The belief that Woolf wrote exclusively for coterie audiences is untenable considering the publication venues and the settings of her political speech. While her best-known feminist work, *A Room of One's Own*, grew out of talks commissioned for the highly educated women of Newnham and Girton

---

[29] Mary Jean Corbett argues that this dynamic is especially pronounced if one filters out Woolf's work on women writing prior to the twentieth century: this reveals a refusal to engage with, or even name, her immediate contemporaries in essays and reviews ('Considering Contemporaneity: Woolf and the "Maternal Generation"', in Julie Vandivere and Megan Hicks, *Virginia Woolf and Her Female Contemporaries: Selected Papers from the Twenty-Fifth Annual International Conference on Virginia Woolf* (Clemson, SC: Clemson University Press, 2016), 2–7, at 3–4).

[30] Woolf's relationship with Mansfield is notoriously complicated. A diary entry from December 1920 gives some indication of the nature of those complications: 'I was happy to hear K[atherine Mansfield] abused the other night. Now why? Partly some obscure feeling that she advertises herself … & then how bad the Athenaeum stories are; *yet in my heart I must think her good, since I'm glad to hear her abused*' (D2 78–9, my emphasis).

[31] Lee, *Virginia Woolf*, 374.

[32] For a detailed history of this collaboration, see Wayne K. Chapman, '"L's Dame Secretaire": Alix Strachey, the Hogarth Press, and Bloomsbury Pacifism, 1917-1960', in Wayne K. Chapman and Janet M. Mason, eds, *Women in the Milieu of Leonard and Virginia Woolf: Peace, Politics, and Education* (New York: Pace University Press, 1998), 33–57.

[33] Lee, *Virginia Woolf*, 384.

Colleges (*ARO* 3), Woolf wrote for a variety of audiences, many of them predominantly working or middle class, across a number of popular genres.[34]

Importantly, this diversity among the audiences she chose grew over the course of her career, signalling an increasing awareness of the need to address these particular groups. Woolf gained rhetorical flexibility in addressing audiences of working-class women later in life. Clara Jones uses Woolf's talk to the Rodmell Women's Institute (WI) in 1940 as an example that not only communicates *Three Guineas*' political content, framed humorously for this particular audience, but also enacts its polemic thrust:

> The fact that Woolf was speaking to a more diverse audience than the rather rigid one she formulated in *Three Guineas* suggests that this WI talk was *an instance in which her social practice was more ambitious than her written theory*. By camouflaging her didacticism with raucous, for the most part inclusive, humour, Woolf secures the WI women's collusion in their critique through their laughter.[35]

From Jones' work, it is clear that Woolf's WI work involved an element of signal boosting: in arranging and promoting talks for the WI, Woolf was not averse to promoting female voices other than her own, or to seeking out friends and family to participate in these projects, she 'took responsibility for the format', and was 'involved in what is always the less glamorous, more technical side of organizing events'.[36] Jones notes that the willingness to get others involved in causes, even as she was ambivalent about their efficacy herself, was 'one of the few lines of continuity we can trace throughout her activism'.[37] If the willingness to importune one's friends and family about something is a sign of one's commitment, then this continuity is an important one.

While work like Jones' has undermined or at least complicated critical arguments that Woolf did not engage with her female contemporaries, a reasonable concern over the degree to which she was thinking and speaking with rather than to women, especially other feminist writers and women writing about political issues, lingers.[38]

---

[34] A comprehensive list of publication venues for Woolf's explicitly feminist articles and essays can be found in chapter 5 of Black, *Virginia Woolf as Feminist*, 99–123; these include the suffrage periodical *The Woman's Leader*, the highbrow *TLS* and feminist *Time and Tide*, as well as popular monthlies like *Vogue*. Black omits *Good Housekeeping*, where the essays later collected as *The London Scene* were first published (presumably because those essays were not primarily feminist in focus); this was another forum aimed at an inclusive audience of women.

[35] Clara Jones, *Virginia Woolf, Ambivalent Activist* (Edinburgh: Edinburgh University Press, 2016), 172–4, my emphasis.

[36] Jones, *Ambivalent Activist*, 167.

[37] Jones, *Ambivalent Activist*, 167.

[38] Christine Kenyon Jones and Anna Snaith have demonstrated that Woolf's ideas about the cultural function of women's education emerged from her relationship with Clara Pater and her coursework at King's College ('"Tilting at Universities": Woolf at King's College London', *Woolf Studies Annual* 16 (2010), 1–43), and Anne Fernald notes the influence of Janet Case and Jane Harrison on the feminist form taken by her engagement with the study of Greek (*Feminism and the Reader* (New York: Palgrave Macmillan, 2006), 25–7).

Sowon S. Park describes Woolf's feminism as 'specified to the highest degree'[39]; this description highlights how the constellation of concerns shaping Woolf's engagement with feminism are not simply different than the concerns of many of her feminist contemporaries. Woolf is not unique in the issues she considers or the causes she champions. What, then, were the specific determinants of Virginia Woolf's own feminism? Her relationship to Bloomsbury is one. Two others bear consideration: her insistence on mediating her feminism through a system of aesthetic value; and her growing conviction that existing institutions are structured by an ineradicably patriarchal logic, and therefore inadequate to the needs of women and to the requirements of a just society. These determinants explicitly proceed from Woolf's disposition as an artist. Equally, they stem from the deeply seated conviction that the problems women faced could not be resolved without radical, structural change in the forms of life and governance available to women— a conviction articulated with increasing clarity and force over the course of her career.

The importance that Woolf places on aesthetic judgement, when considered in light of the fact that she repeatedly ascribed a lack of aesthetic capacity to people whose class status was unequal to her own, indicates a limitation of her imagination, feminist and otherwise. This concern arises most clearly in connection with two common observations about Woolf's feminism. First, that Woolf is a snob, deprecating the merit of works by women that do not meet her standards of taste and intellectual complexity. Second, that Woolf's awareness of her aesthetic commitments as a (highbrow) woman writer mediates her relationship to feminism, foregrounding questions of form to the point of occluding other considerations. These observations are, of course, not unrelated to one another. Anne Fernald diagnoses Woolf's snobbery unequivocally: 'Bloomsbury encouraged the intense individualism that she made central to her feminism. Woolf, who once wrote an essay entitled, "Am I a Snob?" was indeed a snob, and her snobbery persisted until the end of her life: she nourished this quality even as she acknowledged more communitarian ways of knowing and connecting.'[40] Fernald emphasizes Woolf's snobbery as one that is intentionally cultivated ('nourished') by means of an individualist rhetoric and a scale of values that places a premium on aesthetic discernment rather than the more traditional grounds of class: 'part of her unforgiving judgments of others emerges ... from her effort to distinguish good writing from bad and, more importantly good from great'.[41] This argument exemplifies an elision between Woolf's constructed image of herself as a writer and the terms of her snobbery—an elision that Woolf embraced.[42]

---

[39] Sowon S. Park, 'Suffrage and Virginia Woolf: "The Mass Behind the Single Voice"', *The Review of English Studies*, n.s., 56, no. 223 (February 2005), 119–134, at 134.
[40] Fernald, *Feminism and the Reader*, 2.
[41] Fernald, *Feminism and the Reader*, 2.
[42] The tendency of some recent critics to dismiss the role that 'snobbery' played in Woolf's work seems reactive at best: Jean Mills, to take one example, deploys specious ad hominem logic to sidestep the issue of class entirely in 'Virginia Woolf and Class', in Jessica Berman, ed., *A Companion to Virginia Woolf* (London: John Wiley & Sons, 2016), 219–34, at 219. More productive is Melba Cuddy-Keane's warning in *Virginia Woolf, the Intellectual, and the Public Sphere* (Cambridge: Cambridge University Press, 2003)

Some of the most uncomfortable moments in Woolf's critical writings are those in which she acknowledges that she stands at a remove from the immediate concerns of less privileged women. This discomfort is generated by the simultaneity with which Woolf acknowledges the disadvantages and difficulties that make other women's lives different from her own while disavowing the possibility of a transformative empathy with them. The best known of these moments occur in Woolf's introduction to Margaret Llewelyn Davies' *Life as We Have Known It* (1931), the book of life-writing by members of the working-class Women's Co-operative Guild compiled by Davies and published by the Hogarth Press. In her introductory letter, addressed to Davies but intended to open the published collection, Woolf recalls her experiences at a Women's Co-operative Guild conference in 1913.

In this letter, Woolf famously questions the efficacy of the reforms the women's speeches propose, claiming that 'If every reform they demand was granted this very instant it would not touch one hair of my comfortable capitalist head' (*E5* 178).[43] Yet the certainty she expresses here is undermined by the real threat that cross-class solidarity seems to pose: the threat that such solidarity may lead, not to progress in the terms desired by the Guildswomen, but instead to an atavistic collapse of middle- and upper-class women into the historical conditions of women in the Victorian era. She claims that 'To expect us, whose minds, such as they are, to fly free at the end of a short length of capital to tie ourselves down again to that narrow plot of acquisitiveness and desire is impossible' (*E5* 182). Once noticed, it is equally impossible to discount the intense anxiety attendant on the simple 'again' in this passage.

Woolf goes on to suggest that the division between the working classes and the rest of society leaves everyone 'equally deprived. For we have as much to give them as they to give us—wit and detachment, learning and poetry, and all those good gifts which those who have never answered bells or minded machines enjoy by right. But the barrier is impassible' (*E5* 232). Woolf's contribution to *Life as We Have Known It* makes it all too easy to cherry-pick sentiments that, in isolation, make Woolf sound entirely reprehensible. She erects 'impassible barriers', which consistently foreground aesthetic experience as the crux of her difference from working class women. Specifically, she denies the working classes aesthetic judgement and the desire for aesthetic fulfilment. This would matter less were it not for the fact that throughout her work, sound aesthetic judgement, and not political perspicuity or efficacy, guarantees a person recognition as possessing the full range of human capacities. She refuses to imagine that the working

---

against allowing class analytics to stand in for analysis of Woolf's politics tout court. Cuddy-Keane argues against both the reduction of Woolf's aesthetics to snobbery and 'recent accusations that she was an aesthetic capitalist bent on acquiring cultural and economic power through self-commodification' (2) and posits that Woolf was unique in her ability to 'envision possibilities for moving beyond [oppositions between high- and lowbrow in politics and art] in a way that most others involved in the cultural debates could not' (18).

[43] See also Margaret Llewyn Davies, ed., *Life as We Have Known It, by Cooperative Working Women* (New York: W.W. Norton & Company, 1975), xv–xxxix.

women's demands for reform policies could be connected to an aesthetic sensibility that already exists in the working classes. In 'The Docks of London', her narrator observes that 'The aptness of everything to its purpose, the forethought and readiness which have provided for every process, come, as if by the back door, to provide that element of beauty which nobody in the Docks has ever given half a second of thought to.... Hence beauty begins to steal in' (*E5* 278–9). The appreciation of beauty, which is forced to 'steal in' to a scene from which it would otherwise be excluded, is denied the inhabitants of the docklands, who are insultingly described as incapable of considering or perceiving it, let along creating it intentionally. Similarly, Woolf renders the community of prostitutes in *Orlando* as 'full subjects, and by extension, potential writers': one inevitably entails the other.[44] Whatever we may think of this criterion, her refusal to recognize working-class people's capacities to meet it leads to a severely limited feminist solidarity, at least in those terms that Woolf herself identified as meaningful.

Recognizing the shortcomings in Woolf's thinking about class does not require that we dismiss the truly radical elements in her thoroughgoing critique of patriarchy. Early in her career, Woolf's proximity to emergent modernism leads her to posit that the work women will do in the world holds the potential of the radically new and the heretofore unknown: in 'The Feminine Note in Fiction' (1905) she asks: 'Is it not too soon after all to criticize the "feminine note" in anything? And will not the adequate critic of women be a woman?' (*E1* 15). It is revolutionary to assert, as Woolf does here, that the only 'adequate critic' may be woman, and that the novelty of new forms of women's life and work might provide a standard by which to correct the misprisions that have enabled patriarchal power to make a hash of it.

The many points in Woolf's life when women, like men, appeared to have failed at the task, equally render this a frightening responsibility for women's art or feminist politics to bear. Yet in at least one respect, Woolf's feminism was inherently more radical in its aspirations than nearly all her contemporaries: her consistent dismissal of a liberal politics that aimed at ameliorating rather than abolishing the structures that upheld women's oppression.

One biographical difference that separates Woolf from many other feminists of her day is her freedom to sustain a holistic inquiry into the underlying structures that enabled women's oppression and marginalization. In her adult life, Woolf's intellectual, cultural, and economic resources, and the choice of a husband and other partners who valued her intellectual and artistic work, made her increasingly free of the more forceful forms of oppression that circumscribed the lives of so many of her female contemporaries, and that drew them into unavoidable entanglements with immediate political problems or legislative issues.[45] The result is a relative detachment that allowed

---

[44] Fernald, *Feminism and the Reader*, 108.

[45] It is not that Woolf didn't experience gendered forms of oppression or discrimination—sexual abuse at the hands of her stepbrother, her interactions with the medical profession, and the difficulties in being taken seriously as a female artist would all render such an argument nonsensical. Rather, her sense of increasing financial stability and artistic successes through the early twentieth century enabled her to

her to think synoptically rather than reactively, and to pursue a consistent intellectual project over the course of several decades. It is important, as readers, not to overestimate the intellectual value of this detachment on the grounds that it may give rise to an apparently 'universal' or dispassionate feminist critique in a way that the more obviously historically contingent feminism of (for example) the suffragists or female trades-unionists does not.

For many of her readers, Woolf's feminism could (and did) appear innocuous or mystifying, or even remain imperceptible, inasmuch as it seldom entails concrete policy proposals. Such a reading mistakes the scope of her critique, which consistently calls her fellow Englishmen and women to remake the social order via different forms of lived relations between men and women, and among women. Her ambivalence around suffrage activism, for example, entailed a deep suspicion of the vote as an effective tool of reform, not least because having the vote was no guarantee that women would be able to use it effectively to disrupt the patriarchal capitalist forms of power that impoverished women's lives. In light of this suspicion, the fact that Woolf's writing calls for a renegotiation of the existing forms and language of intimacy becomes an index of its ambition, not its toothlessness. Woolf's work calls for a radical overhaul of the existing social structures and ways of thinking, speaking, and moving through public and private spaces as requisite for substantive change in women's positions.

Ultimately, a capacious horizon of expectations may have guided Woolf's feminist targets and aspirations: to advocate for a revolution in language and lived experience may require uncoupling from the details of quotidian experience (even as the disappointments those experiences repeatedly entail are rendered in intimate detail in many of Woolf's novels, essays, and short stories). Such a rarefied perspective enables grand ambitions for feminism that are liberating in the face of an exhausting present precisely because of their transformative sweep. But this perspective also risks diminishing without addressing the distinctions within quotidian feminism that matter most to how many twenty-first century feminists situate our own work: those of race, colonial positioning, class, and sexual and gender identity, as well as our understanding of intersectional forms of oppression. Woolf's implicit shuttling between the two scales can result in a divided temporality, a divide that threatens to be irreconcilable: pessimism about the present and the immediate future, and something like optimism on a scale likely longer than that of a single human life.

Select Bibliography

Alberti, Johanna, *Beyond Suffrage: Feminists in War and Peace, 1914–1928* (London: Macmillan, 1989).
Black, Naomi, *Virginia Woolf as Feminist* (Ithaca, NY: Ithaca University Press, 2004).

---

develop her feminism without many of the immediate domestic and economic constraints faced by other feminists.

Chapman, Wayne K., '"L's Dame Secretaire": Alix Strachey, the Hogarth Press, and Bloomsbury Pacifism, 1917-1960', in Wayne K. Chapman and Janet M. Mason, eds, *Women in the Milieu of Leonard and Virginia Woolf: Peace, Politics, and Education* (New York: Pace University Press, 1998), 33-57.

Clay, Catherine, 'Citizens not Feminists: the Boundary Negotiated between Citizenship and Feminism by Mainstream Women's Organizations, 1928-39', *Women's History Review* 9, no. 2 (December 2000), 411-29.

Clay, Catherine, *British Women Writers, 1914-1945: Professional Work and Friendship* (Burlington, VT: Ashgate, 2006).

Crenshaw, Kimberlé, 'Demarginalizing the Intersection of Race and Sex: A Black Feminist Critique of Antidiscrimination Doctrine, Feminist Theory and Antiracist Politics', *The University of Chicago Legal Forum* 1989, no. 1 (1989), 139-67.

Doan, Laura, *Disturbing Practices: History, Sexuality, and Women's Experience of Modern War* (Chicago: University of Chicago Press, 2013).

Fernald, Anne E., *Virginia Woolf: Feminism and the Reader* (New York: Palgrave, 2006).

Halpern, Barbara Strachey, 'Ray Strachey—A Memoir', in Wayne K. Chapman and Janet M. Manson, eds, *Women in the Milieu of Leonard and Virginia Woolf: Peace, Politics, and Education* (New York: Pace University Press, 1998), 76-86.

Jones, Christine Kenyon, and Anna Snaith, '"Tilting at Universities": Woolf at King's College London', *Woolf Studies Annual* 16 (2010), 1-43.

Jones, Clara, *Virginia Woolf, Ambivalent Activist* (Edinburgh: Edinburgh University Press, 2016).

Lee, Hermione, *Virginia Woolf* (London: Chatto & Windus, 1996).

Pateman, Carole, *The Sexual Contract* (Stanford, CA: Stanford University Press, 1988).

Sowon S., Park, 'Suffrage and Virginia Woolf: "The Mass behind the Single Voice"', *The Review of English Studies*, n.s., 56, no. 223 (February 2005), 119-34.

Trotter, David, 'Lesbians before Lesbianism: Sexual Identity in Early Twentieth-Century British Fiction', in Billie Melman, ed., *Borderlines: Genders and Identities in War and Peace, 1870-1930* (London: Routledge, 1998), 193-211.

Zwerdling, Alex, *Virginia Woolf and the Real World* (Berkeley: University of California Press, 1986).

CHAPTER 21

QUEER THEORY

CHRIS COFFMAN

Many of Virginia Woolf's books from the 1920s and early 1930s feature characters whose queer longings emerge in otherwise heterosexual contexts. In *Mrs Dalloway* (1925), an orgasmic description of 'some pressure of rapture' that 'split its thin skin and gushed and poured' precedes middle-aged housewife Clarissa Dalloway's memory of having fallen 'in love' with Sally Seton in young adulthood (*MD* 29); in *To the Lighthouse* (1927), blocked painter Lily Briscoe throbs with aesthetic and erotic desire for Mrs Ramsay, the angel in the patriarchal house; in *The Waves* (1931), Neville's 'heart rises' while admiring Percival, foreshadowing the adult poet's male lover (*W* 96). By the late 1930s, Woolf positions queer characters as alternatives to heteronormativity. As London is bombed in *The Years* (1937), Eleanor Pargiter sees in a Polish gay man, Nicholas, a 'new world' in which people are 'free' to 'live adventurously, wholly' (*Y* 268); in *Between the Acts* (1941), William Dodge lusts after the 'hirsute, handsome, virile' Giles Oliver while lesbian Miss La Trobe directs a pageant countering fascism (*BA* 77).

The latter two texts position queers as members of the intersectional 'Society of Outsiders' that *Three Guineas* (1938) identifies as resistant to patriarchy (*TG* 186). Woolf's other writings also anticipate Sara Ahmed's analysis of queer spatiality and Elizabeth Freeman's examination of queer temporality.[1] As Ahmed notes, *A Room of One's Own* (1929) foregrounds '[h]ow important it is, especially for women, to claim ... space' for solitary writing: women writers who 'take up space' defy heteronormative expectations and 'their bodies in turn acquire new shapes'.[2] The potential queerness of these shapes is made clear when *A Room of One's Own*'s narrator envisions the challenge to patriarchy that could ensue if 'Chloe liked Olivia' and 'they shared a laboratory' amenable to homosocial and homosexual bonds (*ARO* 62–3). Similarly, Woolf's mock biography *Orlando*

---

[1] Sara Ahmed, *Queer Phenomenology: Orientations, Objects, Others* (Durham: Duke University Press, 2006); Elizabeth Freeman, 'Introduction', *GLQ: A Journal of Lesbian and Gay Studies* 13, no. 2–3 (2007), 159–76; Elizabeth Freeman, *Time Binds: Queer Temporalities, Queer Histories* (Durham: Duke University Press, 2010).

[2] Ahmed, *Queer Phenomenology*, 11, 61.

(1928) crosses space and time to find queer potential in eighteenth-century prostitutes' 'society of their own', within which Orlando experiences 'the love of both sexes equally' by cross-dressing as a man (*O* 200, 202).

Orlando's protagonist—a figure for Woolf's lover, Vita Sackville-West—begins male yet wakes up one morning female. Literalizing Monique Wittig's assertion that '[l]esbians are not women', this plotline shakes up fixed ontologies of gender identity and sexual orientation, demonstrating Woolf's potential for feminist, lesbian, and queer scholarship.[3] As Melanie Micir observes, because of the '[h]elpful critical capaciousness of the term "queer,"' one need not 'choose between a lesbian and queer Woolf'; her texts sustain both readings.[4] Nor need one choose between these Woolfs and a trans Woolf.[5] Of her books, *Orlando* has been especially productive: it anticipates all of these formations while hinting at their transnational implications by registering the desires and gendered embodiments its protagonist experiences in different cultural and historical contexts. This invites comparisons to the challenges to patriarchal genders advanced by twentieth-century Islamic novelists: Indian Iqbalunnisa Hussain, Egyptian Nawal El Saadawi, and Moroccan Tahar Ben Jelloun. Contemporary English writer Jeanette Winterson further stretches Woolf's critique of patriarchy as well as her expansion of possibilities for sexuality and embodiment. Read together, these authors reveal Woolf's far-ranging implications for queer scholarship.

A love letter to Sackville-West, *Orlando* features a protagonist who lives through several centuries of English history in both male and female embodiments. Orlando's story does not exactly match those of contemporary transgender people, whose transitions are often—but not always—preceded by unease about their bodies.[6] Although Orlando's gender identity is not explicitly questioned until after transition, from the novel's opening line—'there could be no doubt of his sex'—Woolf interrogates desire and gender across multiple eras of British history (*O* 13).[7] As Pamela Caughie observes, *Orlando* emphasizes that '[g]ender ... is a historically specific cultural process', negotiated through the 'literary forms and legal institutions, psychology and medicine, fashion and social customs' Orlando encounters at different times.[8] Because the

---

[3] Monique Wittig, *The Straight Mind and Other Essays* (Boston: Beacon Press, 1992), 32.

[4] Melanie Micir, 'Queer Woolf', in Jessica Berman, ed., *A Companion to Virginia Woolf* (Hoboken: John Wiley, 2016), 347–58, at 349, 352.

[5] See Micir, 'Queer Woolf', for an overview of queer Woolf scholarship. See Jessica Berman, 'Is the Trans in Transnational the Trans in Transgender?', *Modernism/modernity* 24, no. 2 (April 2017), 217–44; Pamela Caughie, 'The Temporality of Modernist Life Writing in the Era of Transsexualism: Virginia Woolf's *Orlando* and Einar Wegener's *Man Into Woman*', *Modern Fiction Studies* 59, no. 3 (Autumn 2013), 501–25; and Chris Coffman, 'Woolf's *Orlando* and the Resonances of Trans Studies', *Genders* 51 (2010), 1–18, for discussion of trans Woolf scholarship.

[6] See Coffman, 'Woolf's *Orlando*', for analysis of *Orlando* in light of contemporary transgender identities as well as discussion of passages not reproduced here.

[7] See Berman, 'Is the Trans in Transnational the Trans in Transgender?'; Caughie, 'The Temporality of Modernist Life Writing'; and Coffman, 'Woolf's *Orlando*', for different arguments about *Orlando* and transgender issues. In the spirit of Berman's argument that Orlando is transgender, I refer to Orlando as 'they'.

[8] Caughie, 'The Temporality of Modernist Life Writing', 518.

narrative crosses centuries and cultures, each with its own 'institutions and discourses', Orlando's gender and sexuality are 'orientated' and 'reoriented' in response to varied demands.[9] As Ahmed argues, 'life gets "directed"' through means that are 'often hidden from view' until one refuses them.[10] People then undergo a process of resettlement after departing from normative 'lines' guiding dominant ways of being 'gendered, sexualized, and raced'.[11] *Orlando* illustrates this process. Its protagonist's adjustments after transition trace a 'desire line' of 'unofficial paths' that Woolf, Sackville-West, and others traversed at a 'queer slant' to institutionally sanctioned forms of relationship.[12]

Orlando's use of the fantastic allows readers to imagine queer desires and trans embodiments as futures 'that might be lived, and livable' in another time.[13] Using 'both analepsis and prolepsis', Woolf explores what Elizabeth Freeman calls queer time's 'wrinkles and folds'.[14] Written when British genders and sexualities were changing significantly, Woolf's novel tracks the possibilities created by Orlando's varied experiences of history and embodiment.[15] In the late twentieth and early twenty-first centuries, *Orlando*'s 'paths' have solidified into 'alternative lines' that continue to gain official sanction.[16]

Anticipating early twenty-first-century trans activists' challenges to grammatical conventions, *Orlando* initially describes its transitioned protagonist using 'they', 'them', and 'their' pronouns. Reporting that 'there is no denying' that 'Orlando had become a woman', the narrator insists that 'in every other respect, Orlando remained precisely as he had been. The change of sex, though it altered their future, did nothing whatever to alter their identity. Their faces remained, as their portraits prove, practically the same' (*O* 128). Although the narrator eventually capitulates, conceding that 'in future we must, for convention's sake, say "her" for "his," and "she" for "he"' even though Orlando's 'memory ... went back though all the events of her past life without encountering any obstacle', proleptic redoubling of the protagonist's 'faces' raises unresolved questions about gender and sexuality (*O* 128). *Orlando* thereby asks readers to consider the queer sexualities that emerge from what Jason Cromwell calls 'transsituated identities and bodies' as well as the ways the book's queerings of gender and sexuality cross time and space.[17] If 'the manipulation of time' can 'produce' queer 'bodies and relationalities', *Orlando* creates novel forms of desire and gendered embodiment by placing its protagonist in varied historical and cultural situations.[18]

---

[9] Caughie, 'The Temporality of Modernist Life Writing', 518; Ahmed, *Queer Phenomenology*, 4–5.
[10] Ahmed, *Queer Phenomenology*, 20.
[11] Ahmed, *Queer Phenomenology*, 14, 5.
[12] Ahmed, *Queer Phenomenology*, 19, 19, 72.
[13] Caughie, 'The Temporality of Modernist Life Writing', 518.
[14] Caughie, 'The Temporality of Modernist Life Writing', 517; Freeman, 'Introduction', 163.
[15] Caughie, 'The Temporality of Modernist Life Writing', 517.
[16] Ahmed, *Queer Phenomenology*, 19–20.
[17] Jason Cromwell, *Transmen & FTMs: Identities, Bodies, Genders & Sexualities* (Urbana: University of Illinois Press, 1999), 132.
[18] Freeman, 'Introduction', 159.

Orlando's marriage to Shelmerdine is one such relation. Marked as 'she' and 'he', respectively, Orlando and Shel participate in heterosexual marriage by inverting dominant genders: the realization that ' "You're a woman, Shel!" ' and ' "You're a man, Orlando!" ' confirms their bond (*O* 230). Becoming 'engaged' mere 'minutes' after meeting, they defy Victorian scripts for courtship, and their married life is anything but temporally normative (*O* 228). Shel's sailings around Cape Horn counter domesticity's rhythms; Orlando wanders each 'autumn … into the heart of the woods in solitude', floating 'as a spirit might through the spectre-pale beech trees' (*O* 236). By embracing 'nonsequential forms of time' enabling extreme connection and detachment, Orlando and Shel subsist 'aslant from dominant forms of object-choice, coupledom, family, marriage, sociability, and self-presentation and thus out of synch with state-sponsored narratives of belonging and becoming'.[19]

Orlando also interrogates its protagonist's geographical reorientations. Desiring change after a failed love affair, Orlando accepts a 'lifeline': an ambassadorial position furthering Britain's impulse 'to possess, and to occupy' other lands.[20] As Ahmed explains, the word 'lifeline' has a double meaning, referring both to 'lines' such as 'inheritance' and 'reproduction', which 'we are given as our point of arrival into familial and social space'—that is, to 'lines' we feel 'pressure' to follow—and to a new direction that 'saves us' from 'an impossible world or an unlivable life'.[21] The move to Turkey is a 'lifeline' implicating Orlando in colonialist practices driven by orientalist '[l]ines of desire', yet it simultaneously holds queer potential: according to one 'legend', Orlando 'became the adored of many women and some men' while abroad (*O* 116).[22] These 'lines of desire' propel the gender transition and stay with gypsies that allow Orlando temporary relief from Englishness.[23]

The novel's orientalism is legible from the opening scene showing Woolf's sixteen-year-old protagonist re-enacting colonialist violence, 'slicing at the head of a Moor which swung from the rafters' of 'the attic rooms of the gigantic house of the lord who had slain him' (*O* 13). Introducing 'doubt about' Orlando's gender, this episode foreshadows the way Woolf queers gender, sexuality, and time by orientalizing English concerns (*O* 13). Because the concept of 'the nation "coheres" as an effect' of orientalist 'repetition', this 'direction' forms the protagonist's national identity, whose differences from the gypsies' gender-bending 'alternative line' ultimately propel Woolf's protagonist back to England once Orlando's susceptibility to the 'English disease, a love of Nature', is revealed (*O* 132).[24]

Orlando's transnational movements are problematic but generative. Jessica Berman observes that 'Woolf reaches for Orientalist tropes in *Orlando* … because she rightly

---

[19] Freeman, *Time Binds*, xi–xv.
[20] Ahmed, *Queer Phenomenology*, 17, 115.
[21] Ahmed, *Queer Phenomenology*, 17–18.
[22] Ahmed, *Queer Phenomenology*, 114.
[23] Ahmed, *Queer Phenomenology*, 114.
[24] Ahmed, *Queer Phenomenology*, 118, 118, 20.

recognized that English civic discourses about gender and nationality allowed no room for narratives of transgression or change on her home turf. For the British subject, both transnational and transgender positions are much harder to put on and take off than Orlando's Turkish trousers, which 'can be worn indifferently by either sex' (*O* 129).[25] Because Orlando is '[i]nhabiting a body that is not extended by the skin of the social', the trousers resignify gender beyond early twentieth-century English constructs, revealing 'the mediated quality of embodiment as well as the multiple ways our bodies and their situations challenge normate regimes of civic identity and power'.[26] For example, after Orlando's transition, conflicting lawsuits threaten their property, one presuming 'that she was dead', another 'that she was a woman', and another 'that she was an English Duke' (*O* 155). These contradictions expose English law's limitations, proliferating queer genders and desires.

Orlando extends contemporary queer and trans theories by examining ways patriarchy's implication with binary gender crosses borders. Eve Kosofsky Sedgwick describes queerness as 'multiply transitive', moving 'across genders, across sexualities, across genres, across "perversions" ';[27] Susan Stryker, Paisley Currah, and Lisa Jean Moore show that words such as 'straight, bent, deviate', and 'perverse' work to 'describe patterns of bodily movements through, and occupations of, space' and time.[28] 'Queer' and 'trans' are free-floating modifiers that range across seemingly different categories, couple with words such as 'gender' or 'national', and reveal embodiment's shiftiness.[29] *Orlando* and other Woolfian texts are similarly multiple, moving across space and time to challenge dominant genders and sexualities.

Whereas *Orlando* queers English genders and sexualities through border-crossing, Woolf's other works struggle with patriarchy in ways similar to a mid-century Indian novel and two late twentieth-century North African books: Hussain's *Purdah and Polygamy* (1944); El Saadawi's *Woman at Point Zero* (1975); and Ben Jelloun's *The Sand Child* (1985).[30] These texts reorient Woolf's questioning of gender and sexual inequities to illuminate contemporary feminist, queer, and transgender concerns in different parts of the world. Set in 1970s Egypt and 1940s India, respectively, *Woman* and *Purdah and Polygamy* share *A Room*'s and *Three Guineas*'s searches for space for feminist resistance within patriarchy. *A Room* contends that women need regular income and space of their own to write; *Three Guineas* adds that they deserve 'intellectual liberty' without 'unreal loyalties' to patriarchal institutions (*TG* 168, 159). Like Woolf's writings, El Saadawi's

---

[25] Berman, 'Is the Trans in Transnational the Trans in Transgender?', 235.

[26] Ahmed, *Queer Phenomenology*, 20; Berman, 'Is the Trans in Transnational the Trans in Transgender?', 235.

[27] Eve Kosofsky Sedgwick, *Tendencies* (Durham, NC: Duke University Press, 1993), xii.

[28] Susan Stryker, Paisley Currah, and Lisa Jean Moore, 'Introduction: Trans-, Trans, or Transgender?', *WSQ* 36, no. 3–4 (2008), 11–22, at 13.

[29] Stryker, Currah, and Moore, 'Introduction', 12.

[30] Iqbalunnisa Hussain, *Purdah and Polygamy: Life in an Indian Muslim Household* (Bangalore: Hosali Press, 1944); Nawal El Saadawi, *Woman at Point Zero* (London: Zed Books, 1983); Tahar Ben Jelloun, *The Sand Child*, 1985 (New York: Harcourt, 1987).

and Hussain's novels associate queerness with feminist resistance. *The Sand Child*, by contrast, uses a trans scenario—the story of Ahmed, a female at birth but publicly socialized as a boy—to critique patriarchy. By detailing struggles that *Orlando*'s orientalist fantasies obscure, these three texts reveal Woolf's misunderstandings about the parts of the world to which she turns to critique English genders and sexualities.

El Saadawi's *Woman at Point Zero* tracks the systemic sexual violence its protagonist, Firdaus, endures. Born to a 'poor peasant farmer' who dies during her childhood, Firdaus is left with an uncle who educates but molests her.[31] While a boarding student at a girls' secondary school, she discovers that she can share 'secrets' with her classmates.[32] Her love of learning and leadership also helps her realize that she 'was not like other women, nor like the other girls around me who kept talking about love, or about men'.[33] When a teacher, Iqbal, discovers Firdaus alone on the playground at night, Firdaus begins to cry. When Iqbal takes 'her hand' to console her, Firdaus notes that '[t]he feeling of our hands touching was strange, sudden'; she feels her 'body tremble with a deep distant pleasure, more distant than the age of my remembered life'.[34] Recalling the 'Sapphic primitivism' Robin Hackett finds in Woolf, this language hints at Firdaus's suppressed potentialities.[35] She senses 'a part of my being which had been born with me when I was born, but had not grown with me when I had grown'; '[a] cloudy awareness of something that could have been, and yet was never lived'.[36]

This revelation of Firdaus's sexual and intellectual orientation recalls Sally and Clarissa's kiss in *Mrs Dalloway*, which takes place in a similarly liminal space: Bourton's terrace. Both moments echo Woolf's account of the new relationships possible if 'Chloe liked Olivia' because 'they shared a laboratory together' (*ARO* 62–3). Queer scholars have long noted the erotic potential *A Room* locates in feminist solidarity, rendered vaginally as 'a vast chamber where nobody has yet been' (*ARO* 63). Yet *Mrs Dalloway*'s third-person narrator remarks that some 'scruple picked up Heaven knows where' blocks Clarissa from acknowledging same- and opposite-sex eroticism she can only 'dimly perceive' (*MD* 28). When 'yielding to the charm of a woman', Clarissa 'did undoubtedly then feel what men felt': a momentary

> tinge, like a blush which one tried to check and then, as it spread, one yielded to its expansion, and rushed to the farthest verge and there quivered and felt the world come closer, swollen with some astonishing significance, some pressure of rapture, which split its thin skin and gushed and poured with an extraordinary alleviation over the cracks and sores. (*MD* 28–9)

---

[31] El Saadawi, *Woman at Point Zero*, 12.
[32] El Saadawi, *Woman at Point Zero*, 24–5.
[33] El Saadawi, *Woman at Point Zero*, 25.
[34] El Saadawi, *Woman at Point Zero*, 29–30.
[35] Robin Hackett, *Sapphic Primitivism: Productions of Race, Class, and Sexuality in Key Works of Modern Fiction* (New Brunswick, NJ: Rutgers University Press, 2004), 3.
[36] El Saadawi, *Woman at Point Zero*, 30.

This passage's orgasmic language reveals Woolf's and the narrator's sexual awareness, yet Clarissa feels only 'an illumination; ... an inner meaning almost expressed' (*MD* 29). Firdaus, too, cannot admit her desire. Clutching Iqbal's hand, 'memory' reveals the life Firdaus 'never lived'; though her 'lips opened to speak', her 'voice failed to come through' and her 'heart faltered, stifled by a frightened, frenzied beating over something precious I was on the point of losing, or had just lost, for ever'.[37]

Unlike Clarissa, who kisses Sally in young adulthood and explicitly looks back from middle age upon the 'question of love, ... this falling in love with women', Firdaus denies her feelings (*MD* 29). When asked by a classmate whether she is 'in love with Miss Iqbal', Firdaus rejects the idea even though her 'heart beat' and she 'wanted to reach out, and take' Iqbal's 'hand'.[38] Asking 'How could I be in love with a woman?' Firdaus cannot put emotions or bodily sensations into language.[39] When Firdaus places 'second in the school and seventh countrywide' on her examinations, Iqbal leads her through her graduation ceremony, the teacher's 'two jet black eyes encircled by two rings of dazzling white' that are her charge's only 'glimmer of light'.[40] Taking Iqbal's hand, Firdaus shivers 'with a pain so deep that it was almost like pleasure, or a pleasure so deep it bordered on pain, ... a remote pleasure, buried in such far away depths that it seemed to have arisen a very long time ago'.[41] Although she nearly reveals her feelings, Iqbal says, '"Don't say anything Firdaus"'.[42] In the courtyard the night before returning to Cairo, Firdaus breaks into a sweat: as she believes Iqbal is 'moving towards' her, she feels that '[m]y heart beat wildly and the blood rushed to my head'.[43] After crying out for Miss Iqbal, she is 'awakened' by her 'own voice' from 'what appeared to be a dream', and recognizes that she had mistaken a 'low ... wall' for her teacher.[44]

Like Woolf and *Mrs Dalloway*'s narrator, El Saadawi infuses Firdaus's first-person narration with erotic language revealing her repressed desire for Iqbal. *Woman* also shares *Mrs Dalloway*'s emphasis on women's sexual suppression within patriarchy. Although Firdaus's uncle's wife suggests sending her to the women's dormitory at the university, he instead marries her to Sheikh Mahmoud, an abuser. Clarissa's retreat to the chaste whiteness of the ever '[n]arrower and narrower bed' of the 'attic room' representing the 'emptiness about the heart of life' with her husband suggests that she, too, is sexually unsatisfied within heterosexual marriage (*MD* 28). Sheikh Mahmoud's violence toward Firdaus is far harsher than Richard's distanced affection for Clarissa, though.

Fleeing after a bloody beating, Firdaus is taken in by Bayoumi, who repeatedly rapes her. After being recruited into prostitution through a female pimp's homosocial

---

[37] El Saadawi, *Woman at Point Zero*, 30.
[38] El Saadawi, *Woman at Point Zero*, 30–1.
[39] El Saadawi, *Woman at Point Zero*, 31.
[40] El Saadawi, *Woman at Point Zero*, 32–3.
[41] El Saadawi, *Woman at Point Zero*, 33.
[42] El Saadawi, *Woman at Point Zero*, 33.
[43] El Saadawi, *Woman at Point Zero*, 34.
[44] El Saadawi, *Woman at Point Zero*, 34.

attentions, Firdaus regains respectability through office work, but comes to understand wifehood as a profession after a failed romance with a man who marries another woman to secure his professional advancement. Seeking autonomy, she self-employs as a prostitute, the 'least deluded' of options, enabling her to control her circumstances and gain respect for her donations.[45] Firdaus's desire for women remains unfulfilled, but she has her own flat and supports herself. Her gains are temporary, however: after a pimp strong-arms a substantial cut of her earnings, she knifes him and is executed for murder. Despite Firdaus's suppressed queerness, refusal to remarry, and room of her own, the space she finds within patriarchy proves unviable.

Hussain's *Purdah and Polygamy* focuses on the third of its four wives, Maghbool, whose relative privilege allows her to establish a viable private space within patriarchy and—unlike Clarissa—ultimately escape her husband's home. Maghbool displays several characteristics Woolf identifies as queer challenges to patriarchy. Marked 'a sinner' by 'her old lady relations' for having 'wasted her age, energy, and beauty' on masculine pursuits such as fiscal management and the arts, she is pressured into marrying Kabeer.[46] Swayed by 'romance' music describing an 'ideal … life' with 'a man who would be all love and would care for her desires, comfort and even whims and fancies', Maghbool imagines that marriage would leave her 'freer to make use of her talents'.[47] Her life with Kabeer debunks these fantasies by placing her in situations that complicate idealizations of female bonding.

Although Maghbool is lured into marriage through feminization within a romance narrative, her masculine traits re-emerge within the zenana, motivating feminist solidarities like Chloe's. Whereas Kabeer's wealthy first wife, Nazni, exacerbates polygamy's rivalries, Maghbool is kind to his second wife, Munira, a poor and devoutly religious woman whom he treats 'worse than a servant'.[48] When Munira gives birth as Kabeer seduces Nazni, Maghbool attends to the newborn and its mother, who calls her 'an angel on earth' for defying cultural norms that enable the rich to mistreat 'the poor and ugly'.[49] Although Munira initially doubts Maghbool's intentions and declares that 'I have to live according to my destiny', without assistance from a wealthier 'rival', the new mother eventually gains 'confidence' in Maghbool and cares for her when she is burnt in the kitchen.[50] When Kabeer takes a fourth wife, Noorjahn, Maghbool's solidarities extend even to Nazni: '[s]ince all the three creatures had the same grievance they were united' as 'friends against the formidable enemy'.[51]

Unlike Woolf's characters and El Saadawi's Firdaus, Maghbool does not show sexual interest in women. However, her care for them is masculinized. Unswayed by her

---

[45] El Saadawi, *Woman at Point Zero*, 86.
[46] Hussain, *Purdah and Polygamy*, 140.
[47] Hussain, *Purdah and Polygamy*, 141.
[48] Hussain, *Purdah and Polygamy*, 183.
[49] Hussain, *Purdah and Polygamy*, 182.
[50] Hussain, *Purdah and Polygamy*, 183.
[51] Hussain, *Purdah and Polygamy*, 280.

father, who claims she is unhappy because she 'think[s] for herself' and lacks 'implicit faith' in Kabeer, Maghbool refuses to gain her husband's respect 'by disrespecting herself' through submission.[52] Moreover, by allowing her cousin Azeem to visit her room, Maghbool defies the rule that '[n]o two members of opposite sexes are expected to be in any place without a third person', especially with the woman 'laughing'.[53] These actions move Maghbool beyond given gender categories.[54]

Maghbool is also educated and 'economically independent'.[55] Because her father ensures that she owns rent-generating property, she embodies Woolf's argument that for a woman writer to succeed, she must have an independent income and her own room. Architecturally enforced gender segregation enables Maghbool to write in her private chamber, but her public emergence as an author and possession of an income 'better than most men' infuriate Kabeer.[56] Declaring that 'to give money to a woman is to give a dagger to her', he abuses her for inattention to household tasks.[57] Although the 'rebel' Maghbool pays a high price for her integrity, her ability to support herself confirms Woolf's insight that giving women space and economic power helps them defy traditional gender roles.[58] This ultimately allows Maghbool to leave after her husband's death.

As Berman observes, even though she does not transition, 'Maghbool is in many ways a trans figure, one who not only crosses over the gender binary, but also challenges the assumptions that this household (and by extension, the institutions of purdah and polygamy) make about women.'[59] If Berman is right that Hussain thereby 'mobilizes what we might call a trans critique on several levels' by challenging 'gender, religious, and national/social standards', I would add that she anticipates contemporary transfeminism.[60] As Finn Enke observes, trans theory shares with '[f]eminist, women's and gender studies' the view that '*every*one's gender is made: Gender, and also sex, are made through complex social and technical manipulations that naturalize some while abjecting others'.[61] Maghbool's incursions into masculine domains are trans moves that highlight gender's constructedness. Moreover, her solidarity with Kabeer's other wives is based on their shared suffering under patriarchy, regardless of whether they accept cultural definitions of 'woman'. However, the alliances Maghbool forms with Munira and Nazni differ from those Woolf addresses in *Orlando*. By implying that gender is constructed, Woolf emphasizes the homophobia Orlando internalized while male and

---

[52] Hussain, *Purdah and Polygamy*, 188–9.
[53] Hussain, *Purdah and Polygamy*, 200.
[54] Hussain, *Purdah and Polygamy*, 32.
[55] Hussain, *Purdah and Polygamy*, 171.
[56] Hussain, *Purdah and Polygamy*, 242.
[57] Hussain, *Purdah and Polygamy*, 242.
[58] Hussain, *Purdah and Polygamy*, 257.
[59] Berman, 'Is the Trans in Transnational the Trans in Transgender?', 237.
[60] Berman, 'Is the Trans in Transnational the Trans in Transgender?', 236, 238.
[61] A. Finn Enke, ed., *Transfeminist Perspectives in and beyond Transgender and Gender Studies* (Philadelphia: Temple University Press, 2012), 1.

the sexism they endured while female.⁶² Hussain, by contrast, stresses the oppression those assigned as 'women' experience within polygamous households.

Instead of exploring feminist and queer oppression and resistance within private space, Ben Jelloun's *The Sand Child* uses the lonely Ahmed's story to stress the injustice of barring women from public life. Like *Orlando*, *The Sand Child* is not premised on the protagonist's struggle against a gender based on birth sex. Instead, Ahmed's difficulties come from having his gender publicly reassigned as 'male' to create an heir and thereby circumvent cultural and legal constructs favouring men. Although *Orlando*, too, calls attention to the sexism and threat of dispossession its protagonist experiences once reassigned as female, Orlando's newfound embodiment is not tortuous.

The Sand Child gives readers access to Ahmed's journals and allows them to spy on him when he 'thinks he is alone', twisting Woolf's strategies in *A Room* and *Orlando*.⁶³ Invoking the magistrate at the obscenity trial of Radclyffe Hall's *The Well of Loneliness*, *A Room* taunts readers by prefacing the passage on Chloe and Olivia by ascertaining that 'behind that red curtain over there the figure of Sir Chartres Biron is not concealed' (*ARO* 62).⁶⁴ *Orlando*'s narrator correspondingly publicizes private spaces' feminist and queer potential by constructing a sense of secrecy about the solidarity Orlando enjoys with prostitutes, joking, 'hist … is that not a man's step on the stair?' (*O* 200). Ben Jelloun places *The Sand Child*'s readers in a similarly voyeuristic position—but does so to challenge the injustices that led to Ahmed's situation.

Like *The Well*—on whose behalf Woolf testified—*The Sand Child* attaches shame and stigma to Ahmed's situation even as multiple voices provide different interpretations of it, leaving not only his adolescent motivations but also the very fact of his existence open for speculation. First, an unnamed 'reader' imagines that Ahmed experienced 'crisis' because he was 'torn between the development of his body and his father's determination to make him wholly and fully a man'; a second states that Ahmed 'had no doubts' and 'willingly took up the challenge'; a third highlights forms of socialization through which 'In due course, he became a man'; and finally, a fourth asserts the 'truth' that 'If Ahmed had really existed, he would have ended up in a madhouse.'⁶⁵ These divergences prepare readers for excerpts from Ahmed's journal that ask who is responsible for his predicament, in which '[t]he truth goes into exile.'⁶⁶ This articulation of 'the unbearable intimacy of a truth that can't be spoken' recalls *The Well*.⁶⁷ Although *Orlando* similarly engages essentialist and social constructionist views of gender through open questions, contradictions, and aporias, Woolf's novel contrasts to *The Sand Child* by taking a playful rather than mournful approach to the binary gender system's injustices.

---

⁶² See Coffman, 'Woolf's *Orlando*'.
⁶³ Ben Jelloun, *The Sand Child*, 82.
⁶⁴ Radclyffe Hall, *The Well of Loneliness* (New York: Random House, 1990).
⁶⁵ Ben Jelloun, *The Sand Child*, 28–9.
⁶⁶ Ben Jelloun, *The Sand Child*, 29–30.
⁶⁷ Ben Jelloun, *The Sand Child*, 29.

Orlando's initially male protagonist does not begin life as a feminist, but is forced to confront legal and social gender inequities after transitioning. As female, Orlando is threatened with loss of their estate and subjected to Alexander Pope's misogyny. These experiences cause a change in consciousness prompting Orlando to seek 'great enjoyment in the society of her own sex' and to 'change frequently from one set of clothes to another', dressing as a man to circumvent restrictions on women's public movement (*O* 201). Orlando 'reaped a twofold harvest' by cross-dressing: 'the pleasures of life were increased and its experiences multiplied' the novel's feminist and queer trajectories (*O* 202).

The Sand Child similarly offers a feminist critique of gender inequities. Ahmed is initially an anti-feminist who embraces male privilege without using it for feminist purposes. He differs from Maghbool in *Purdah and Polygamy* by rejecting solidarity with women: he devalues their community in the hammam, becomes 'a petty tyrant' who makes 'his sisters wait on him at lunch and dinner', and refuses 'any show of tenderness toward his mother'.[68] These anti-feminist gestures conform to masculine scripts maintaining 'appearances'.[69] Having decided that being a man is both 'his father's will' and his own, he says that he 'likes' the condition he initially questioned and will 'endure it' because '[i]t gives me privileges'.[70] Claiming that he is thereby 'choosing life', he implies that womanhood amounts to social death.[71] To conform to the prevailing gender system, he marries a 'sacrificial woman' whose physical disability he dehumanizes.[72] After his father's death, he also claims 'the duty and right' to watch over his mother and sisters.[73] Insisting that they 'owe' him 'obedience and respect', he asserts that 'if in our house women are inferior to men it's not because God wishes it or because the prophets decided it thus, but because the women accept this fate'.[74] He then orders them to 'submit and live in silence!'[75] Insisting that gender is cultural rather than imposed through divine will, Ahmed highlights women's agency in consenting to patriarchy. However, he overlooks the difficulties they have in resisting legally codified gender inequality: challenges El Saadawi exposes.

Although Ahmed is a patriarchal tyrant, the book's narrator also challenges misperceptions that he is monstrous for falling outside the binary gender system. Objecting to his anti-feminism while emphasizing his incongruous status as a 'monster who writes poems', the narrator reflects on Ahmed's loneliness.[76] Writing that 'I am trying not to die', he identifies with the 'wind ... inside my head'.[77] Sounding like Rhoda

[68] Ben Jelloun, *The Sand Child*, 35.
[69] Ben Jelloun, *The Sand Child*, 32.
[70] Ben Jelloun, *The Sand Child*, 32–4.
[71] Ben Jelloun, *The Sand Child*, 34.
[72] Ben Jelloun, *The Sand Child*, 37.
[73] Ben Jelloun, *The Sand Child*, 46.
[74] Ben Jelloun, *The Sand Child*, 46.
[75] Ben Jelloun, *The Sand Child*, 46.
[76] Ben Jelloun, *The Sand Child*, 38.
[77] Ben Jelloun, *The Sand Child*, 38.

in Woolf's *The Waves*, whose identification with the sea and claim to 'have no face' dislocate and split her identity, Ahmed invents and affirms 'other faces', asking whether the wind will 'fall where I rest my head to welcome other lives, to stroke other faces'.[78] He notes, too, that '[s]ometimes the winter of those faces chills my blood'.[79] Although he seeks 'other faces', they reject him with 'grimaces', so he 'set[s] them aside' and '[t]hey suffer'.[80]

In a passage recalling the dream of life as a caveman concluding Hall's 'Miss Ogilvy Finds Herself', Ahmed's interrogation of identity sparks a fantasy in which his 'body dances to some African rhythm ... I'm in the bush and mingle with the naked men'.[81] Primitive masculinist sociality allows him to imagine supportive 'faces and hands'.[82] He declares that '[m]y reclusion is willed, chosen, loved. Moreover, I shall get faces and hands from it, journeys and poems'.[83] Dismissing '[t]he others' who 'understand nothing', he deems them 'unworthy of my madness', stating that 'I am building a palace in which death will have no place'.[84] Going within to combat loneliness, Ahmed does what Woolf's suicidal Rhoda ultimately cannot: he uses creativity to survive.

However, *The Sand Child* also mobilizes essentialist assumptions about gendered embodiment to register Ahmed's struggle. Ben Jelloun includes a story of another Moroccan leader who lived as a man but was ultimately exposed as female. This 'isolated leader', '[f]eared and respected', was eventually 'venerated' as a 'saint' by 'wanderers' who 'run away' from their circumstances, 'seeking the inner face of truth'.[85] Ahmed, too, flees after his wife's death. As his struggle with 'solitude' intensifies, he writes of 'desire' that he is 'tired of carrying its insinuations in my body'; 'I shall remain profoundly unconsoled, with a face that is not mine and a desire that I cannot name.'[86] Shortly thereafter, he declares that he wants to return to his body's 'origins', for 'nature' to reclaim 'her rights'.[87] After heterosexual dreams, he states that 'I have lost my body's language; indeed, I never possessed it.'[88] His subsequent questioning of whether he is 'a woman' or 'a man' is followed by masturbation, fantasies of sex with agender bodies, and bodily 'desires' for men.[89] Although some of Ahmed's yearnings reflect Cromwell's observation that

---

[78] Woolf, *The Waves*, 102; Ben Jelloun, *The Sand Child*, 38.
[79] Ben Jelloun, *The Sand Child*, 38.
[80] Ben Jelloun, *The Sand Child*, 38.
[81] Radclyffe Hall, 'Miss Ogilvy Finds Herself' [1926], in Terry Castle, ed., *The Literature of Lesbianism: A Historical Anthology from Ariosto to Stonewall* (New York: Columbia University Press, 2003), 635–48; Ben Jelloun, *The Sand Child*, 39.
[82] Ben Jelloun, *The Sand Child*, 39.
[83] Ben Jelloun, *The Sand Child*, 39.
[84] Ben Jelloun, *The Sand Child*, 39.
[85] Ben Jelloun, *The Sand Child*, 60–1.
[86] Ben Jelloun, *The Sand Child*, 64–5.
[87] Ben Jelloun, *The Sand Child*, 67.
[88] Ben Jelloun, *The Sand Child*, 71.
[89] Ben Jelloun, *The Sand Child*, 72, 79.

'transsituated' sexualities defy 'the binary of heterosexual and homosexual', his fantasies build to the desire to conceive a child through heterosexual intercourse.[90]

After Ahmed declares that he is 'ready to be a woman', he acknowledges the necessary process of becoming, that 'I must go back to childhood, become a little girl, an adolescent girl, a girl in love, a woman.'[91] However, *The Sand Child*'s essentialism returns once he leaves home, removes his 'chest bandages', and masturbates.[92] After a witchlike vagabond kisses his body, Ahmed goes to a hotel and touches his 'vagina'.[93] After being felt up and digitally penetrated in a corner alley, he witnesses a drag performance. Differing from the book's earlier tales of transmasculine leaders, Ahmed agrees to replace the performer and enjoys his role in the freak show as Lalla Zahra.

Different storytellers then offer divergent endings to his story: a violent death while defending himself against rape by his employer; a death in 'ecstatic beatitude' while writing 'before the sky, before the sea' after giving his money to his sisters;[94] a freeing 'pilgrimage' to 'Mecca' that leads him to join impoverished children in 'confronting' an oppressive 'army'.[95] The third variation opposes war and oppression through violent resistance rather than Woolfian pacifism. Told by the elderly Fatuma, this is 'an old' version, 'from before Islam',[96] much like Firdaus's encounter with Iqbal feels 'more distant than the age of' her 'remembered life'.[97] Fatuma's story does not conclude the novel, however. In a fourth ending, a blind man who confesses that 'I have spent my life falsifying or altering other people's stories' recalls a series of encounters with an agender person reminiscent of a character from the *Thousand and One Nights*, a text whose frame narrative *The Sand Child* echoes.[98] This man's labyrinthine narration moves from North Africa to Andalucía to Buenos Aires and back, only to 'admit failure' and leave readers seeking a conclusion from 'the moon when it is full'.[99]

The sequel, *The Sacred Night* (1987), reduces these ambiguities, showing the protagonist's subsequent life as a woman 'to establish the facts'.[100] Although at one point *Sacred Night* observes that Lalla Zahra has 'to become a woman', it emphasizes that she played with 'dolls' and women's clothes as a child.[101] As an adult, she undoes the effects of an 'adolescence rejecting desire' by following the ways it 'direct[s]' her 'body by instinct' toward heterosexual satisfaction.[102] In a variation on Firdaus's execution, she is

---

[90] Cromwell, *Transmen & FTMs*, 130.
[91] Ben Jelloun, *The Sand Child*, 73.
[92] Ben Jelloun, *The Sand Child*, 84.
[93] Ben Jelloun, *The Sand Child*, 87.
[94] Ben Jelloun, *The Sand Child*, 118–19.
[95] Ben Jelloun, *The Sand Child*, 128–32.
[96] Ben Jelloun, *The Sand Child*, 132.
[97] El Saadawi, *Woman at Point Zero*, 30.
[98] Ben Jelloun, *The Sand Child*, 134.
[99] Ben Jelloun, *The Sand Child*, 165.
[100] Tahar Ben Jelloun, *The Sacred Night* (New York: Harcourt, 1989), 3.
[101] Ben Jelloun, *The Sacred Night*, 23, 74.
[102] Ben Jelloun, *The Sacred Night*, 128, 118.

jailed after shooting Fatima's father, who sought her out in a 'rage' for 'revenge'.[103] And in a plotline echoing El Saadawi's and Hussain's critiques of idealizations of sisterhood, Lalla Zahra's sisters—having joined a 'brutal and fanatical' sect—find her in prison and avenge themselves through female 'circumcision' despite its being unsanctioned by 'Islam' or 'any other religion'.[104] Her 'body' then returns to feeling like the 'sandbag' that characterized her life as a man.[105] This suggests that despite the feminism of these books, they assume that binary gender and heterosexuality are essential rather than constructed.[106]

Thus, although *The Sand Child*'s insistence that Ahmed's life raises unanswered questions recalls *Orlando*'s undecidabilities, Woolf and Ben Jelloun treat gender and sexuality quite differently. Whereas Ben Jelloun's account of Ahmed's pain and loneliness is grounded in essentialist assumptions about the biological basis of the femininity supposedly denied by masculine gender socialization, *Orlando* mobilizes—yet refuses to resolve—the 'debate between essentialist and social constructionist accounts of sex, gender and sexuality'.[107] Although both books interrogate patriarchy's mutual implication with binary gender, their critiques serve different ends. While *The Sand Child* suggests that Ahmed suffers from sacrificing femaleness to access legal privileges, *Orlando* is not founded on such assumptions. As Berman argues, Orlando's right to property is questioned not because they have become female but 'because English law cannot grant civic status to a non-normate body and must mark Orlando as irrevocably female, and therefore unable to inherit': 'the potentially transgressive power of' Orlando's transition 'is diminished by the operation of jurisprudence, its "trans" status erased by the state's insistence on a binary logic of identity within an asymmetrical sex/gender system'.[108] This makes *Orlando*'s feminist critique of injustices toward women equally a queer and trans critique of the binary system constraining gender and desire.

Woolf's challenges to binary genders and sexualities directly inform those of contemporary English novelist Jeanette Winterson, whose texts—like El Saadawi's, Hussain's, and Ben Jelloun's—critique patriarchy and idealizations of sisterhood. A writer whose *Art Objects* openly acknowledges her debt to Woolf, Winterson rearticulates Woolf's queer and trans themes by expanding their spatial and temporal scope.[109] *Written on the Body* (1992) employs a narrator whose gender is unmarked; *Sexing the Cherry* (1981), *The Passion* (1987), *The Daylight Gate* (2012), and *The Gap of Time* (2015) reinflect *Orlando*'s plastic treatment of time, queering gender, sexuality, size, spatiality, and temporality by deploying 'historiography as a mode of fantasy' rather than to verify facts.[110] Expanding

---

[103] Ben Jelloun, *The Sacred Night*, 132.
[104] Ben Jelloun, *The Sacred Night*, 149–50, 155.
[105] Ben Jelloun, *The Sacred Night*, 160.
[106] Ben Jelloun, *The Sacred Night*, 160.
[107] Coffman, 'Woolf's *Orlando*'.
[108] Berman, 'Is the Trans in Transnational the Trans in Transgender?', 234.
[109] Jeanette Winterson, *Art Objects: Essays on Ecstasy and Effrontery* (New York: Vintage, 1995).
[110] Jeanette Winterson, *Written on the Body* (New York: Vintage, 1992); Jeanette Winterson, *Sexing the Cherry* (New York: Grove, 1989); Jeanette Winterson, *The Passion* (New York: Grove, 1987);

upon *Orlando*'s themes in new contexts, Winterson's novels create 'points of resistance to' dominant conceptions of futurity, creating 'other possibilities for living in relation to indeterminately past, present, and future others' while also exploring queer subversion's limits.[111]

Like *Orlando* and the other novels I have discussed, Winterson's work advances queer and trans challenges to unjust patriarchal norms. Orlando is threatened with loss of the family estate upon being designated female; two of Winterson's characters are treated as property. In *The Passion*, which queers the Napoleonic era, young military cook Henri falls in love with Villanelle, a Venetian who takes 'pleasure with both men and women' and is sold to the army as a sexual slave by the man she marries after the Queen of Spades breaks her heart.[112] Like the female Orlando, Villanelle cross-dresses; she marries because her husband likes her 'to dress as a boy' and she enjoys it.[113] Her birdlike webbed feet, typical of Venetian boatmen, also mark her as intersex, simultaneously queering her gender and blurring the distinction between animal and human. *Sexing* features Dog-Woman, whose size, scale, and personality are similarly subversive. Strong enough to catapult an elephant 'into the sky', so large that male lovers cannot feel her vagina, Dog-Woman defies norms.[114] After her 'father tried to steal' and 'sell' her, she murders him; at another point her son, Jordan, cross-dresses as a woman.[115]

Jordan also falls in love with a princess, Fortunata. Revising 'The Twelve Dancing Princesses', Winterson introduces Fortunata as the one sibling who 'never came to live' in the home her sisters own and inhabit after escaping marriage.[116] Their stories re-envision Orlando's marriage through tales of unhappy heterosexual unions and thwarted queer relationships. Although the princess, whose tale begins their stories, leaves her husband to live 'in perfect salty bliss' with a 'mermaid' before rejoining her sisters, other narratives recount homophobia and transphobia.[117] One princess, married to a man who loves 'a boy', murders them both 'with a single arrow'.[118] Another lives 'in a tower' with her beloved 'Rapunzel' until a man 'who had always liked to borrow his mother's frocks' masquerades 'as Rapunzel's lover' to capture her and blind the 'witch', who is eventually 'found by her sisters' and lives with them after her husband becomes 'a frog'.[119] A tale of a sister whose collection of relics includes 'the still-born foetus of the infamous Pope Joan who had so successfully posed as a Man of God until giving birth

---

Jeanette Winterson, *The Daylight Gate* (New York: Grove, 2012); Jeanette Winterson, *The Gap of Time* (London: Hogarth, 2015); Ellis Hanson, 'Kink in Time', *b20*, 6 October 2016, http://www.boundary2.org/2016/10/ellis-hanson-kink-in-time.

[111] Freeman, 'Introduction', 163; Freeman, *Time Binds*, xxii.
[112] Winterson, *The Passion*, 59–60.
[113] Winterson, *The Passion*, 96.
[114] Winterson, *Sexing the Cherry*, 21.
[115] Winterson, *Sexing the Cherry*, 122.
[116] Winterson, *Sexing the Cherry*, 61.
[117] Winterson, *Sexing the Cherry*, 48.
[118] Winterson, *Sexing the Cherry*, 50.
[119] Winterson, *Sexing the Cherry*, 52.

in the Easter parade' foreshadows the erotically resplendent story of a princess who lives with her butch lover 'alone in a windy castle' until 'someone' finds them, realizes the prince 'she had married was a woman', and comes 'to burn her': a spectacle thwarted when the princess pre-emptively murders her lover.[120] Winterson's emphasis on the lovers' bliss contrasts to Ahmed's painful marriage in *The Sand Child* and distinguishes *Sexing* from *Orlando*, whose protagonist experiences sexism without homophobic and transphobic violence.

Fortunata's refusal to live with her sisters undercuts the feminist sisterhood whose homoerotic potential Woolf highlights. This challenge also appears in *Daylight*, a rewriting of the Pendle witch trials that echoes the ancient Mesopotamian tale 'The Descent of Inanna'. 'Descent' takes its protagonist to the underworld to mourn the husband of her sister, queen Ereshkigal. After Inanna is stripped, condemned, and killed at Ereshkigal's behest, their father sends two creatures 'neither male or female' to rescue Inanna.[121] After the 'judges of the underworld' demand a substitute to secure her release, Inanna assigns her husband and his sister to that role so she can ascend from the underworld and rule over heaven and earth.[122]

Daylight's protagonist—Alice Nutter—avoids becoming a sacrificial 'substitute' for her former lover, Elizabeth Southern, who seeks to reverse the physical decline that resulted from selling her soul.[123] Whereas Elizabeth dies an imprisoned pauper, the wealthy Alice is convicted of witchcraft after unsuccessfully protecting Elizabeth's family, the Demdikes. The grim situation of the Demdike youngster who supports their execution—Jennet Device, 'neglected' by her mother and 'sold' to a rapist by her 'brother'—exposes the limitations of sisterhoods that do not alter patriarchal structures.[124] Alice's love for Jesuit priest Christopher Southworth is also queer, entailing shared defiance of the norms embodied in the crusade against '[w]itchery popery popery witchery' and persisting despite his castration by anti-Catholic torturers.[125]

In *Sexing*, Fortunata's fate is far happier than Alice's. Such a passionate dancer that 'any other life would have been a lie', she 'didn't burn in secret with a passion she could not express; she shone' on stage after giving up 'hope of being rescued' and learning 'to dance alone'.[126] This suggests that by surpassing eroticism, art avoids patriarchal marriage's and communal sisterhood's traps. Like *Orlando*, *Sexing* inflects aestheticism through temporal 'wrinkles and folds' interrogating gender, sexuality, and love, concluding a disquisition on the 'experience of time' by observing that '[p]assion, delirium, meditation, even out-of-body, are words we use to describe the heightened condition of

---

[120] Winterson, *Sexing the Cherry*, 49, 54.
[121] Diane Wolkstein and Samuel Noah Kramer, 'The Descent of Inanna', in *Inanna, Queen of Heaven and Earth: Her Stories and Hymns from Sumer* (New York: Harper & Row, 1983), 64.
[122] Wolkstein and Kramer, 'The Descent of Inanna', 68.
[123] Winterson, *The Daylight Gate*, 127.
[124] Winterson, *The Daylight Gate*, 215.
[125] Winterson, *The Daylight Gate*, 22.
[126] Winterson, *Sexing the Cherry*, 61, 112.

superconductivity' characterizing 'true art'.[127] Art 'take[s] us where the artist has been, to' a 'different place where we are free' and 'drawn out of ourselves'.[128]

Rearticulating these themes in the context of the 2008 global financial crisis, *Gap* rewrites William Shakespeare's *The Winter's Tale. Gap*'s protagonist, Leo, loved his gay best friend, Xeno, in childhood; in adulthood, Leo initiates a fatal chain of aggression and broken relationships after imagining that Xeno is sleeping with his wife, Mimi. By depicting Leo as irrationally violent and prone to devouring seafood as aggressively as *Mrs Dalloway*'s Doris Kilman consumes cakes, Winterson suggests that queer desire can remain as repressed in the twenty-first century as in previous eras.

Moreover, *Gap* critiques capitalism through butch Roni Horn and trans woman Lorraine La Trobe. Like her namesake—the pageant director in *Between the Acts* who uses an authoritarian style to produce a play undermining fascism—Winterson's La Trobe mixes progressive and regressive traits. Whereas Horn is a politically pure anti-capitalist who protests one of Leo's housing developments, La Trobe defends him and moonlights at a fetish club; her dual roles suggest queerness's potential complicities with capitalism.

Through this critique of queer subversion's limits, Winterson builds on El Saadawi's, Hussain's, and Ben Jelloun's challenges to Woolf's idealization of feminist sisterhood. Refusing to simplify ideological contradictions, *Gap* rearticulates Winterson's themes in contemporary contexts by queering time's 'wrinkles and folds'.[129] In so doing, *Gap* joins the other texts I have analysed in examining the cultural and historical conditions informing their protagonists' trajectories. Sharing *Orlando*'s invention of new embodiments and Fortunata's search for a 'place where we are free', these novels—like all of the texts I have discussed—reveal one of Woolf's most important legacies for queer and trans scholarship: a critique of patriarchy that invents new possibilities for desire and gendered embodiment.[130]

Selected Bibliography

Ben Jelloun, Tahar, *The Sacred Night* (New York: Harcourt, 1989).
Ben Jelloun, Tahar, *The Sand Child* [1985] (New York: Harcourt, 1987).
El Saadawi, Nawal, *Woman at Point Zero* (London: Zed Books, 1983).
Hall, Radclyffe, 'Miss Ogilvy Finds Herself' [1926], in Terry Castle, ed., *The Literature of Lesbianism: A Historical Anthology from Ariosto to Stonewall* (New York: Columbia University Press, 2003), 635–48.
Hall, Radclyffe, *The Well of Loneliness* (New York: Random House, 1990).
Hussain, Iqbalunnisa, *Purdah and Polygamy: Life in an Indian Muslim Household* (Bangalore: Hosali Press, 1944).

---

[127] Freeman, 'Introduction', 163; Winterson, *Sexing the Cherry*, 98–101.
[128] Winterson, *Sexing the Cherry*, 101.
[129] Freeman, 'Introduction', 163.
[130] Winterson, *Sexing the Cherry*, 101.

Winterson, Jeanette, *Art Objects: Essays on Ecstasy and Effrontery* (New York: Vintage, 1995).
Winterson, Jeanette, *The Daylight Gate* (New York: Grove, 2012).
Winterson, Jeanette, *The Gap of Time* (London: Hogarth, 2015).
Winterson, Jeanette, *The Passion* (New York: Grove, 1987).
Winterson, Jeanette, *Sexing the Cherry* (New York: Grove, 1989).
Winterson, Jeanette, *Written on the Body* (New York: Vintage, 1992).
Wolkstein, Diane, and Samuel Noah Kramer, *Inanna, Queen of Heaven and Earth: Her Stories and Hymns from Sumer* (New York: Harper & Row, 1983).

CHAPTER 22

WOOLF AND EDUCATION

ANNA SNAITH

'To Maidens who Desire the Higher Education' (*Ladies' Department Magazine*, King's College London 1898, 12–13).

> 'Hail, cultivated maidens who design
> To wrest your learning from a lecturer's lips,
> And take your dose of intellectual wine
> In sips.
> See what we offer you, choose what you please,
> Professors (gowned) are ready at your call
> To set your feet in wisdom's path. The fees
> Are small. [...]
> Come, then, aspiring maids, and let us show,
> In Art, in Letters, Science, Game, and Song,
> That they who rate our sex's standard low
> Are wrong!'
>   A. Hood

THE spring of 2018 saw sustained industrial action in many UK universities over significant changes to academic pensions. The dispute became about so much more: the marketization of higher education, soaring tuition fees, vice-chancellors' salaries, increasingly precarious contracts for early career academics. Placards bearing slogans such as 'we are the university' and 'students not consumers' seemed to resonate with Woolf's insistence not only on equal access to education but also on the transformation of the university (its syllabi, pedagogy, and rationale). The hiatus created a moment of utopian possibility when the university community (staff and students) meditated upon what an inclusive higher education might look like; manifestos were written and demands were made. This moment, too, reverberated with Woolf's own vision for the university in *Three Guineas* (1938):

> The aim of the new college, the cheap college, should be not to segregate and specialise, but to combine [...] there would be none of the barriers of wealth and

ceremony, of advertisements and competition which now make the old and rich universities such uneasy dwelling places [...] what could be of greater help to a writer than to discuss the art of writing with people who were thinking not of examinations or degrees or of what honour or profit they could make literature give them but of the art itself? (*TG* 119)

In the late 1930s, and interrogating questions about the university's role in militarized and nationalistic cultures, Woolf envisages an even more radical response to the university in *Three Guineas*: 'Set fire to the old hypocrisies [...] And let the daughters of educated men dance round the fire [...] "Let it blaze! Let it blaze! For we have done with this 'education'!"' (*TG* 120).

Virginia Woolf was a complex and progressive thinker on education. Our attention, in the twenty-first century, has increasingly turned to those parts of the globe where girls and women still do not have access to education. Woolf's attention was on the gender disparity in access to education in early twentieth-century Britain, as well as the limitations and constraints of educational institutions for the girls and women who managed to enter them. Her thinking on education is intertwined with her feminism, pacifism, and anti-authoritarianism. Her two major essays—*A Room Of One's Own* (1929) and *Three Guineas*—revolve around institutions of higher education and the manifestations of gendered inequality: from prohibitions around entry, to the syllabi, the built environment, to the lasting impact of higher education on men and women. The young male characters in Woolf's novels are often to be found in their study or university quadrangles while female characters are either at a remove or awkward in their habitation of the university. Woolf, like the narrator of *A Room of One's Own*, had associations with Cambridge—giving lectures and visiting family members and friends who were studying or teaching there—but she remained outside such institutional structures for most of her life, famously refusing honorary degrees from Manchester and Liverpool (1933 and 1939). But despite her outsider status, she devoted much thought to considering how institutions of higher education might be reformed from without and within. She conducted extensive research into pioneering female educators and read memoirs and biographies about the experience of education in Victorian and early twentieth-century Britain.

Furthermore, her engagement operates across genres and in a range of modes from the pragmatic to the utopian. When understood in relation to contemporary thinking on the nature and purpose of the education of women and girls, debates about working-class education, and the study of English as a university discipline, her explosion of the term 'education' (and related categories such as specialization and professionalization) appears all the more prescient. Her thinking chimes with progressive educational thinkers of her day (such as Friedrich Froebel) as well as with concepts such as child-centred or life-long learners in our current moment. Her oeuvre might be said to enable a reconceptualization of the terms 'knowledge' and 'education' themselves, partly through her numerous essays on practices of reading (including reviewing and criticism). These are central to her endorsement of a predominantly non-institutional understanding of education. Her commitment to the idea of the common reader, and her support for public libraries, are part of her alternative pedagogy. Critical attention to Woolf's representation of education has been a fairly recent development, galvanized, in part, by archival discoveries relating to her own education, her work as an educator, and her research into and knowledge of educational battles. This chapter will lay out these debates and discoveries in order to emphasize the multifarious nature of her interest, whether institutional, resistant, theoretical, or pragmatic. When viewed in relation to wider debates in Britain in the early twentieth century, Woolf is shown to be not only *au fait* with the key issues (remarkably so, given how little time she spent within educational institutions) but to offer a particular intervention around the university teaching of English literature. Her essays train and conceptualize their readers so as to emphasize active, pluralistic, and rigorous self-education.

WOOLF IN EDUCATION

In the manuscript version of what would become Woolf's 1937 novel, *The Years*, she deliberates at length on the consequences of educational disparity between male and female siblings. She notes the financial disparity in education costs with £300 a year spent on school and college fees for the sons versus £50 on violin and sketching lessons for the Pargiter daughters: Eleanor, Milly, Delia, and Rose (*P* 31). The issue is ideology rather than availability: 'there were colleges for women in existence—Girton was opened in 1873—and Eleanor, Milly and Delia might therefore have gone either to Girton or to Newnham or to Somerville. But there was a certain prejudice against women's colleges' (*P* 33–4). Milly wants to study at the Slade, already open to women, but 'painting at the Slade meant painting from the nude [...] Captain Pargiter did not like the idea' (*P* 29–30). Woolf traces this educational inequality and the long-lasting rift it causes within families and between siblings. In the Victorian household, spaces of learning are clearly demarcated as male. Rose is shunned and made to feel ignorant when she tries to enter her brother's domain—the 'school room'—and the published novel tracks the psychological imprint of this memory decades later (*Y* 40).

In *Three Guineas*, Woolf's female narrator turns immediately to the question of educational opportunities to describe the difference in point of view from her interlocutor: an educated barrister. She takes the trope of Arthur's Education Fund, from William Thackeray's *The History of Pendennis*, to symbolize the 'voracious receptacle' into which 'all educated families from the thirteenth century to the present moment have paid money' (*TG* 90). The fund provides young men with not only 'book-learning' but the games, travel, and friendships that broaden the mind and body. Women, looking through the 'shadow' of the Fund, see 'a schoolroom table; an omnibus going to a class; a little woman with a red nose who is not well educated herself but has an invalid mother to support' (*TG* 91). The 'noble courts and quadrangles of Oxford and Cambridge' become 'petticoats with holes in them, cold legs of mutton' (*TG* 91). When Woolf addresses *Three*

Guineas to the 'daughters of educated men', she questions the meaning of 'educated': how enlightened are those fathers who refuse to allow their daughters the same experiences they themselves enjoyed, and what are the merits of an education system that trains elite men in the preservation of their own privilege to the exclusion of women?

Woolf watched the men around her—brothers and friends—make the expected journey from public school to Cambridge. Her father, Leslie Stephen, studied first at Eton, then between the ages of sixteen and eighteen at King's College London as preparation for his entrance to Cambridge University. Her brothers, Thoby and Adrian, attended Clifton College and Westminster respectively before both going on to Trinity College, Cambridge. Woolf's husband to be, Leonard, also studied at Trinity Cambridge where he met other key members of the Bloomsbury group including E.M. Forster, John Maynard Keynes, Lytton Strachey, and Clive Bell.

For many years the narrative about Woolf's own education was that she did the occasional course in Greek at King's College London, had private tutors including Janet Case, but was essentially an autodidact, helped by her free-ranging access to her father's library. The appended chronology in Quentin Bell's biography of Woolf lists studies at King's in Greek and History but in the body of the biography only her private tuition with Clara Pater features.[1] Subsequent biographers follow this lead, noting some study in Greek but placing the emphasis on lonely study in the home. The *Oxford Dictionary of National Biography* entry by Lyndall Gordon states that she was 'largely self-educated, and continued with a programme of reading throughout her life. Her only sustained formal study was in Greek. At fifteen she attended a few Greek classes at King's College in London'.[2] Hermione Lee notes briefly that during the 'years of lonely self-education' in the autumn of 1897 Virginia 'started classes in Greek and Latin with Dr George Warr [...] one of the founders of the Ladies Department of King's College, in Kensington. She didn't take the exams'.[3]

Woolf's own comments seem to corroborate these accounts. In 1932, in response to a request for biographical information from Harmon Goldstone, who wanted to write a book on her, she replied: 'Partly from reasons of health I was never at any school or college. My father allowed me to read any book in his library when I was a girl; and it was a large library' (*L5* 91). In that same year when she was invited to deliver the Clark Lectures at Cambridge University (given by her father in 1883) she felt that the invitation was an affirmation of her years of self-study:

> This, I suppose, is the first time a woman has been asked; & so it is a great honour—think of me, the uneducated child reading books in my room at 22 H. P. G.—now advanced to this glory. (*D4*, 79)

---

[1] Quentin Bell, *Virginia Woolf: A Biography* (London: Grafton Books, 1978), 191–2.
[2] *Oxford Dictionary of National Biography*; ODNB online, entry for 'Virginia Woolf', www.oxforddnb.com/view/article/37018, accessed 3 July 2018.
[3] Hermione Lee, *Virginia Woolf: A Biography* (London: Vintage, 1996), 143.

So important to her, however, was her outsider position, and so abhorrent to her the lecture form, that she refused the invitation.

In 2009, extensive material was discovered relating to Woolf's studies at King's College London's Ladies' Department between 1897 and 1901. These archival records indicate much more sustained studies across a range of subjects including Greek (Intermediate and Advanced), Latin (with her sister Vanessa), History (English and Continental), and German (in which she took exams).[4] At that point, the Ladies' Department was located at 13 Kensington Square near to the Stephen family home. Woolf's mother, Julia, had died in 1895 and her father was clearly worried about the impact of the studies on his 'fragile' daughter. He writes to her Greek tutor, his friend, George Warr, Professor of Classical Literature and one of the founders of the Ladies' Department:

> My daughter is attending your Greek class. I hope you will allow me to give you one hint. She has been in a very nervous state, wh[ich], though [...] explicable, has given me some anxiety. I have allowed her to go to the class, for wh[ich] she was very anxious; because I think that it does her some good to have the occupation. [...] I should be grateful if you would just remember this & let her off with light work.[5]

Woolf's own comments on her studies indicate that she was neither anxious nor let off with easy work: 'I am, however, feeling a little triumph over the Latin language as though I had stolen a march on it—great rough beast that it is! As for Greek, it is my daily bread, and a keen delight to me' (*L1* 35).

King's College London was founded in 1829. Its 'Lectures for Ladies' were launched in 1871 in Richmond, and this enterprise then moved to Kensington and grew into the Ladies' Department of King's College, constituted formally in 1885. In 1878 King's became the first institution in England to allow women to take degrees although female students would not join their male counterparts on the Strand until 1915. By 1897, when Virginia was a student there, the King's Ladies' Department had over five hundred students and was offering a wide variety of courses at a range of educational levels, requiring varying amounts of commitment, and including preparation for London and Oxford university degree exams. The then Principal, Lilian Faithfull, describes the varied student body:

> [w]omen and girls of all ages from seventeen to seventy came to the lectures, some only to do one course, once a week, and some to several. Old ladies followed a

---

[4] See Christine Kenyon Jones and Anna Snaith, '"Tilting at Universities": Virginia Woolf at King's', *Woolf Studies Annual* 16 (2010), 1–44 for more details of Woolf's studies as well as reproductions of archival materials including syllabi and registrations. Sections of this article have been reproduced here with the permission of my co-author, Christine Kenyon Jones, and Pace University Press.

[5] Quoted in Emily Dalgarno, *Virginia Woolf and the Visible World* (Cambridge: Cambridge University Press, 2001), 41. The original letter is now in the Archives of American Art at the Smithsonian Institution, Washington DC, catalogue identifier AAA 3480.

favourite Professor and came year after year. [...] Married women arrived gasping for a 10 o'clock lecture, having snatched an hour with difficulty from their household duties at that time in the morning. And there were innumerable girls who had just left school and were anxious to continue their education, and others who were in the hands of governesses unable to teach them this or that subject, and glad to supplement their lessons by lectures.[6]

Archival records include registrations, syllabi, lists of tutors, and a magazine. This has afforded a full picture of what, when, and how Woolf (or Virginia Stephen as she was then) studied as well as the possible impact of her studies on her later reading and writing. Between 1897 and 1899, for example, she was taught 'English and Continental History 1660–1789' by naval historian John Knox Laughton, Professor of Modern History at King's from 1885. Laughton was known to Leslie Stephen as a prolific contributor (926 entries) to the *Dictionary of National Biography*. A specialist on Nelson, Laughton inaugurated the sub-discipline of naval history, advancing the thesis that 'the key to the growth of the British Empire lay in maritime power'.[7] Not only that, Laughton contributed to the professionalization of history as a 'scientific' and 'rigorous' discipline, so no wonder the young Virginia Stephen was anxious about his feedback: 'I have to write essays upon historical subjects for my history class, and on Tuesday I will have my first essay given back to me with the masters corrections' (*L1* 11). Two years in, Woolf decided not to continue with her studies in History but the setting of her first novel, *The Voyage Out* (1915), with its emphasis on British naval power and the trade routes of empire may be a critical response to Laughton's imperialism.

Woolf started studying Greek in 1897 under the tutelage of George Warr, one of the foremost Greek scholars of his day and one of the prime movers behind the founding of the Ladies' Department. By 1897 she had progressed to Warr's 'Advanced Grammar and Reading Class' and was working at degree level on Sophocles' *Oedipus* amongst other texts. In 1898 she began Latin (along with her sister Vanessa) with Clara Pater, working through a syllabus that included Virgil's *Aeneid*, and the following academic year Virginia was studying both Greek and Latin with Pater covering texts such as Plato's *Ion* and later Sophocles' *Antigone*.[8] This was a play that caught her imagination and remained a life-long influence given its depiction of a woman's subversion of state and patriarchal power. The play appears in both *The Years* and *Three Guineas*, in the latter as an 'instructive analysis of tyranny' in the context of the late 1930s (*TG* 162). In 1934, Woolf wrote: 'Reading Antigone. How powerful that spell is still—Greek. Thank heaven I learnt it young' (*D4* 257). Woolf described Pater as 'perfectly delightful' (*L1* 26), clearly

---

[6] Lilian M. Faithfull, *In the House of My Pilgrimage* (London: Chatto and Windus, 1924), 105.
[7] See Andrew Lambert, *The Foundations of Naval History: John Knox Laughton, the Royal Navy and the Historical Profession* (London: Chatham, 1998), 196.
[8] Kenyon Jones and Snaith, 'Tilting', 34.

as enamoured of her tutor as the subject itself. Pater had been active in the Association for Promoting the Higher Education for Women in Oxford and would go on to become the Vice President of Somerville College, Oxford. The portrait of the queer relationship between a student and her female tutor, Julia Craye, in 'Moments of Being: Slater's Pins Have No Points' emerges out of Woolf's study with Pater, again suggesting the legacy of her studies at King's. It is intriguing that Woolf chose not to study English literature at King's, particularly given the prevalence of women tutors during her years of attendance. Staff there at the time included the Principal Lilian Faithfull and Edith Morley, who as Professor of English Language at University College, Reading, became the first woman appointed to a chair at an English university.

The Ladies' Department also offered amenities and extra-curricular activities that Woolf may have enjoyed. The *Department Magazine* offers insight into the Library, consisting of around eight hundred volumes during Woolf's time, but growing rapidly due to donations (including from Jane Harrison). Many clubs, activities, and lectures were on offer to the female students, such as the Browning Society run by Edith Morley, boating, tennis, bicycling, hockey, a Ladies' Orchestra, and a drama club. In one of her editorials in the magazine, Lilian Faithfull praises the value of residential attendance following the opening of King's Hall for Ladies' Department students in 1897. In the 'resident colleges', Faithfull describes how:

> [t]he greater part of each day is spent by the student in her own room. Sometimes girls prefer to work together, but as a rule they seem to find that solitude conduces to concentration, and that a self-imposed isolation is advisable. This solitude in a corporate life is surely most valuable, and the necessity for it is too often forgotten in home life. [...] The possession of a castle of one's own is, perhaps, the first keen joy of College life.[9]

Faithfull here prefigures the emphasis on autonomous space in *A Room of One's Own*, but other of her contributions to the Magazine indicate the dire financial situation of the Ladies' Department: 'we were desperately poor [...] We had no endowment, no scholarships, and a debt on our buildings'.[10] This anticipates Woolf's interrogation of the poverty of women's colleges in *A Room of One's Own*: without the ability to 'amass great wealth', or to 'possess what money they earned' or to decide where their husband's money should best be donated, 'to raise bare walls out of earth was the utmost they could do' (*ARO* 18).

Woolf's early experience as a student must surely have impacted on her work, only a few years later in 1905, as a tutor at Morley College, an adult co-educational establishment in south London. Morley College was founded by Emma Cons, who had

---

[9] *King's College Magazine, Ladies' Department*, number XI, Michaelmas term 1900, 5–6. King's College Archives (K/SER1/170).

[10] Faithfull, *Pilgrimage*, 110.

worked with social reformer Octavia Hill, as had Woolf's half-sister Stella Duckworth.[11] Woolf's brother, Adrian, also taught at Morley, as well as at the Working Men's College established in 1848 by F.D. Maurice.[12] At the request of Mary Sheepshanks, the college's Vice-Principal, Woolf taught weekly classes in literature, composition, and history from January 1905 until 1907. Her letters and diary entries from this period are full of references to her teaching and her regular commitment as an educator certainly occupied her alongside her early work as a journalist. We see her taking her students— 'nice, enthusiastic working women who say they love books' (PA 218)—on trips, lending them books and meditating on how to make her syllabus come alive.

Clara Jones emphasizes the impact of her studies with Laughton on her own teaching of history. In Woolf's 'Morley Sketch', an account of her teaching written in July 1905, she describes the 'four working women' in her class and her attempts to 'make the {?} real interest of history—as it appears to me—visible to them'.[13] She preserves a chronological approach and works through texts by E.A. Freeman and J.R. Green: 'So we {tramped through} made our way through Early British, & Roman, & Angles Saxons & Danes, & Normans, till we {had} were on the more substantial ground of the Plantagenet Kings'.[14] Jones notes that Woolf demonstrates 'a certain attachment to a progressivist story of England, which is rarely addressed in accounts of her theory of history' and is undermined in her own writings from *The Voyage Out* onwards.[15] Her studies with Laughton influenced her early desire to offer her own students a chronological understanding of English history, but against her own tutor's emphasis on a scientific and archival based historiography we see her insistence on the 'flesh & blood' of history, her desire to make things come alive through narrative.[16]

Given Morley's position as an institution devoted to working-class education, critics have focused on Woolf's cross-class encounters while in the classroom. Beth Rigel Daugherty notes, for example, that 'the first and most important lesson Virginia Stephen learns at Morley: to transcend class difference and identify with her students'.[17] Daugherty traces Woolf's experience as a teacher to her essayistic style, more specifically the content and structure of her *Common Reader* volumes. The essays become classrooms, and the techniques Woolf developed at Morley, given the diverse group of students she faced, fed into her own non-fiction writing. Among the strategies

---

[11] Clara Jones, *Virginia Woolf: Ambivalent Activist* (Edinburgh: Edinburgh University Press, 2015), 18.
[12] Melba Cuddy-Keane, *Virginia Woolf, the Intellectual and the Public Sphere* (Cambridge: Cambridge University Press, 2003), 82.
[13] Virginia Woolf, 'Morley Sketch' reproduced in Jones, *Woolf*, 210–15, 212.
[14] Jones, *Ambivalent*, 212.
[15] Jones, *Ambivalent*, 30.
[16] Jones, *Ambivalent*, 212. Jones also reads this early teaching of history in relation to the historiography of Woolf's early short stories, especially 'The Journal of Mistress Joan Martyn'.
[17] Beth Rigel Daugherty, 'Virginia Woolf Teaching/Virginia Woolf Learning: Morley College and the Common Reader', in Helen Wussow, ed., *New Essays on Virginia Woolf* (Dallas: Contemporary Research Press, 1995), 61–77, at 63. See also Beth Rigel Daugherty, 'Teaching Woolf/Woolf Teaching', *Woolf Studies Annual* 10 (2004), 275–308.

Daugherty identifies are identification with audience or reader and the inclusion of context and vivid detail. As Daugherty argues: 'her strategies lower the barriers between teacher and student, writer and reader, reader and reader, and by implication, class and class'.[18] This emphasis on conversation and an abhorrence of lecturing runs throughout Woolf's oeuvre but can be seen to derive from her direct experience as an educator. Jones, however, complicates Rigel Daugherty's emphasis on class solidarity, noting Woolf's 'mixture of hostility, curiosity and fellowship' in relation to one of her students in particular, a Miss Williams who was working as a journalist.[19] Woolf seems intrigued, perhaps threatened, by this student, noting dismissively that 'she could turn out a review as with the precision of a machine'.[20] For Jones, class difference was not so easily transcended or set aside.

Melba Cuddy-Keane reads Woolf's response to Morley in terms of contemporary debates about the methods and purposes of working-class education. We see Woolf concerned that Morley's curriculum privileged more popular courses and therefore lacked the depth and rigour required to develop the potential of its students. As Cuddy-Keane writes, 'Woolf's difficulties reflect one of the basic problems in adult education of the time: despite the fine ideals of fellowship, the education was situated in the discourse of the educated upper middle class, reinforcing inequalities between teacher and student'.[21] These debates led to the formation in 1903 of the Workers' Educational Association (WEA), for which Woolf would later write and lecture, in an attempt to bring together University Extension programmes with working class organizations such as the Co-operative and the Trade Union Movements. The WEA 'endorsed generalist, non-specialised education—education that was neither vocational in orientation nor designed for material advancement or class mobility' and brought debates about the 'nature, goals, and methods of adult education' into the public realm.[22] These debates and differences would lead to the founding, in 1908 at Ruskin College, Oxford, of the Plebs' League focusing on Marxist education. For Cuddy-Keane, Woolf's involvement with Morley College must be viewed in the context of her focus on broad reading which is neither vocational nor about entry into a '"high" cultural tradition'.[23] Her comments about non-professionalized, non-specialized education in *Three Guineas* can, in part, be traced back to this early experience. And although her teaching at Morley ended in 1907, she would continue giving lectures—in the university, in girls' schools, for the WEA, the Women's Institute, and the London and National Society for Women's Service—throughout her life.

---

[18] Daugherty, 'Virginia Woolf Teaching', 62.
[19] Jones, *Ambivalent*, 45.
[20] Jones, *Ambivalent*, 211.
[21] Cuddy-Keane, *Intellectual*, 83.
[22] Cuddy-Keane, *Intellectual*, 87, 86.
[23] Cuddy-Keane, *Intellectual*, 88.

Woolf on Education

Much of Woolf's fictional writing on education treats the effects of the exclusion of girls and women from the education system: inequalities within the family and the circumscription of their physical, intellectual, and social environments. The narrator of her first novel, *The Voyage Out*, describes the protagonist Rachel Vinrace's sporadic and inconsistent education at some length: 'she had been educated as the majority of well-to-do girls in the last part of the nineteenth century were educated. Kindly doctors and gentle old professors had taught her the rudiments of about ten different branches of knowledge [...] But there was no subject in the world which she knew accurately' (*VO* 31). More broadly, the novel questions the parameters, purpose, and locations of 'education' by contrasting the book learning of male characters such as Rachel's uncle, scholar Ridley Ambrose, with the educational possibilities of travel and cultural encounters. Rachel is continually given canonical tomes to read, including by her uncle: 'You should read Balzac. Then we come to Wordsworth and Coleridge. Pope, Johnson, Addison, Wordsworth, Shelley, Keats. One thing leads to another' (*VO* 192). She instead prefers 'modern books, books in shiny yellow covers' and can be found devouring Ibsen alongside developing her own musical education (*VO* 136–7). With the rise in literacy rates that followed the Education Acts of 1870 and 1880, and the beginnings of a commitment to national, non-denominational primary education, came anxiety about the 'right' kind of reading, particularly for women and working-class people. It was Woolf's cousin, H.A.L. Fisher, who drew up the 1918 Education Act, which raised the school leaving age to fourteen. In the concerns of those around Rachel with what she should and should not be reading (as well as playing), Woolf engages with topical debates around the potential of education through reading.

Woolf was as interested in the deleterious effects of educational institutions on those within as she was concerned with those forced to remain outside. Her oeuvre contains recurrent images of 'the procession of the sons of educated men [...] who have been educated at public schools and universities' into the professions (*TG* 142). In *Jacob's Room* (1922), the eponymous protagonist's linear path from Rugby, to Trinity College Cambridge and into professional life is disrupted and undone by World War I. As Nicholas Midgley has argued, not only did the war destroy the 'narrative of Bildung' on which the university was based but also the 'novel of education', which reinforced such a grand narrative.[24] All sense of a progressive and homogeneous development of 'character' disappears as the female narrator struggles to 'know' Jacob. So too, the purpose and effects of his formal education seem hard to discern apart from its bestowing of a sense of entitlement and privilege, of 'magisterial authority' (*JR* 59). Jacob, like the young male scholars in *The Years*, confidently occupies an

---

[24] Nicholas Midgley, 'Virginia Woolf and the University', *Woolf Studies Annual* 2 (1996), 147–59, at 151.

intellectual tradition as well as the spaces that embody it. His study not only contains Spinoza, Spenser, 'all the Elizabethans', and Dickens, but his own work confirms and reifies the white, male tradition in his essay "'Does History consist of the biographies of Great Men?"' (*JR* 48). Not only that, Woolf depicts an education system training its students in competition, patriotism, imperialism, and belligerence—leading them to and preparing them for war. In a key scene we see undergraduates processing into King's College Chapel: 'Look as they pass into service, how airily the gowns blow out, as though nothing dense and corporeal were within. What sculptured faces, what certainty, authority controlled by piety, although great boots march under the gowns. In what orderly procession they advance' (*JR* 38). The military language indicates men already conscripted (as Jacob is already absent in the opening of the novel), subsumed into the military machine where church, state, and university coalesce. This nexus of power operates around the exclusion of women. Spying a woman in the congregation, he thinks: 'No one would think of bringing a dog into church [...] a dog destroys the service completely. So do these women' (*JR* 40). Through this allusion to Samuel Johnson, Woolf depicts Jacob's adoption of misogynist views about the 'unnaturalness' of women's habitation of spaces of scholarship and worship. It is not only institutional inequality that requires reform but the pervasive ideological barriers. This is the 'odour' or 'atmosphere' that she identifies in *Three Guineas*: the 'impalpable' yet powerful enemy that affects 'solid bodies, like salaries, which might have been thought impervious to atmosphere' (*TG* 134–5).

In *Jacob's Room*, as later in *The Years*, Woolf depicts a constellation of male scholarship, privilege, and homosocial interaction that revolves around the study of Greek. We see Jacob reading and translating Greek, he eventually travels to modern Greece, and his friendship with Durrant is crystallized around this sanctified access to knowledge: 'It seemed to both that they had read every book in the world [...] Civilisations stood round them like flowers ready for picking [...] we're the only people in the world who know what the Greeks meant' (*JR* 101–2). Yet as the novel unfolds, Woolf gradually unravels the assumed benefits and results of such an education. Jacob seems ignorant of the past—he 'knew no more Greek that served him to stumble through a play. Of ancient history he knew nothing'—and ill-equipped to deal with or form independent opinions on political issues (*JR* 102). Education is here depicted as rote learning and passive absorption rather than critical engagement (*JR* 144).

In her essay 'On Not Knowing Greek' (1925), written for the first *Common Reader* volume, Woolf 'plunges right to the heart of the power structure that placed different readers in hierarchically ordered locations'.[25] She immediately evokes issues of gender and privilege: 'our ignorance' places us 'at the bottom of any class of schoolboys' (*E4* 38). But as the essay unfolds Woolf not only exhibits her ability to read and translate Greek (as a result, in part, of her studies at King's), but also unpacks the verb 'to know' by suggesting that no contemporary readers 'know' Greek given the issues

---

[25] Cuddy-Keane, *Intellectual*, 138.

of temporal, geographical, and cultural difference. 'We do not know how the words sounded, or where precisely we ought to laugh, or how the actors acted' (*E4* 38). We move from literal to cultural translation and access to the past. Furthermore, our post-war context determines a particular vantage point on the classical past, which is about nostalgia for the uninjured male body. The essay in this way becomes a meditation on the limits of education and the contingency of knowledge at the same time as it rehearses and undercuts the associations between class privilege and Greek education.

But a classical education, Greek in particular, also signified subversively for Woolf in relation to Jane Harrison's work and position within the university. In *A Room of One's Own*, the ghostly depiction of Fernham, the women's college, is frequented by the 'famous scholar [...] J---- H-----' (*ARO* 13). A young Virginia Stephen was introduced to Harrison by her Greek tutor, Janet Case, in 1904 at Newnham College. Harrison had gone up to Cambridge in 1874, making her 'one of the first generation of English women to earn a college education'.[26] In her work at Newnham (where she was known for her unorthodox teaching methods) as well as her scholarship on the matrifocal aspects of Greek culture, Harrison was a feminist pioneer and a role model for Woolf as a female career academic and public intellectual.[27] More specific lines of influence can be found, too, as in Harrison's essay, 'Scientiae Sacra Fames', originally given as a lecture entitled 'Women and Knowledge' in 1913, which prefigures many of the central arguments about women's creativity and autonomous space in *A Room of One's Own*.[28]

Woolf took a particular interest in the position of women within the university and knew many of the pioneers who fought for equal access.[29] The night before she gave the 1928 lecture at Newnham that became *A Room of One's Own*, Woolf stayed with the College's Principal, Pernel Strachey, sister to Lytton, and Woolf's own cousin, Katherine Stephen, had been Principal of Newnham between 1911 and 1920. Cambridge University was notoriously intransigent on the question of female students and staff and the narrator of *A Room of One's Own*, trespassing on the grass and asking to see Milton's manuscripts in the library, is a transgressive presence that demands to be seen in the context of these battles. Indeed, the respective histories of Girton and Newnham represent the varying approaches to the higher education of women: the former's founder, Emily Davies, insisting that women sit the Tripos examinations, whereas Newnham favoured a separate suite of subjects for women and eschewed competition with male students. It was a long road to full equality at Cambridge. Women could not hold degree

---

[26] Jean Mills, *Virginia Woolf, Jane Harrison and the Spirit of Modernist Classicism* (Columbus: Ohio State University Press, 2014), 14.
[27] Mills, *Harrison*, 6.
[28] See Harrison, *Alpha and Omega* (London: Sidgwick and Jackson, 1915).
[29] For a contemporary, Woolf-related exploration of the position of women in academia see Isabelle Stengers and Vinciane Despret, *Women Who Make A Fuss: The Unfaithful Daughters of Virginia Woolf*, trans. April Knutson (Minnesota: University of Minnesota Press, 2014).

titles or attend lectures by right until 1923, were not allowed to hold university posts until 1926 or to become full members of the university until 1948 (compared with the University of London in 1900 and Oxford in 1920).[30] Woolf was well aware of the history of resistance to these restrictions, in 1897 and then the renewed campaigns after World War I that led to a vote for full membership for women, which was defeated in 1920. This was followed in 1921 by another vote to grant women titular degrees. When this passed, a riot broke out and the Newnham College Clough Memorial Gates were demolished.[31] Woolf records this event in *Three Guineas*, noting that, rather than teaching generosity, education makes the educated 'anxious to keep their possessions' (*TG* 114–5).

Suzana Zink reads the composition of *Jacob's Room* in relation to these high profile campaigns and establishment fears around the impact on both genders of this 'intrusion' of women into the sanctified spaces of male scholarship. In the published novel, women are present in the university via 'old Miss Umphelby' whose 'lectures [...] are not half so well attended as those of Cowan, and the thing she might have said in elucidation of the text for ever left out' (*JR* 53). But in manuscript, Woolf included a scene depicting a female student, Angela Williams, in her Newnham room (later published as 'A Woman's College from Outside' in 1926).[32] As Zink argues, the excision 'may be read not only as an indication of women's exclusion but also as a means of preserving their "outsiderness," in the same way in which the protagonist's empty room ultimately fails to "capture" Jacob'.[33] *A Room of One's Own* takes up this image of the female trespasser when the narrator—keen to examine the manuscript of Milton's *Lycidas* as well as the details of Thackeray's eighteenth-century style in *Esmond*—is barred from entering Trinity College Library. The woman intellectual is an aberration, a monstrosity. Derived from two lectures Woolf gave at Newnham and Girton in 1928, the text acknowledges the marginalized position of those women students who have managed to enter the gates of the university. The impoverished position of 'Fernham' (as reflected in the catering on offer) is also a benefit, a freedom from the stultifying effects of wealth and tradition. And the text itself becomes an alternative site of education in its delineation of a tradition of women writers: an education that the narrator continually invites the female audience to play a role in shaping (see, for example, *ARO* 42).

Woolf continues her focus on education into the 1930s with the 'Oxford' scenes of her novel, *The Years*, which treat the marginalization of women and working-class men within the university. Woolf read voraciously in preparation for writing, including biographies of Dorothea Beale (Principal of Cheltenham Ladies' College), Anne Jemima Clough (Principal of Newnham), and Emily Davies (founder of Girton).[34]

---

[30] Rita McWilliams Tullberg, *Women at Cambridge*, rev. ed. (Cambridge: Cambridge University Press, 1998), 1.

[31] For full details of the campaigns see McWilliams Tullberg, *Cambridge*, 121–50.

[32] In *Virginia Woolf: The Complete Shorter Fiction*, ed. Susan Dick (New York: Harcourt Brace Evanovich, 1985).

[33] Suzana Zink, *Virginia Woolf's Rooms and the Spaces of Modernity* (Basingstoke: Palgrave Macmillan, 2018), 121.

[34] Her reading included Cecily F. Steadman's *In the Days of Miss Beale* (London: J. Burrow, 1931), Elizabeth Raikes, *Dorothea Beale of Cheltenham* (London: Constable, 1908), Blanche Athena Clough,

The scrapbooks she kept while writing *The Years* and *Three Guineas* contain newspaper articles entitled, 'Does University Education Fit Modern Women for Life' (which linked women's education to the breakdown of domestic life) and 'The Position of the Woman Student' (a piece arguing against the regulations restricting women within the university) (see *Y* liii). This research fed into the 1880 section of the novel and the character of Kitty Malone, whose father is master of the fictional Katharine's College. In *The Pargiters*, Woolf describes Kitty's dreams 'of becoming a learned woman, an historian herself' but her father's insistence that she shares 'the inability of your sex to grasp historical truth' (*P* 103). Kitty is well aware of the wider response to campaigns for women's education: 'the contempt which these efforts roused in the ordinary don and undergraduate, the opposition [with] which all requests for money to build, or for the right to attend lectures or share in the educational advantages of men were received could scarcely fail to impress the mind of an intelligent girl of twenty-one' (*P* 125). Even her mother was 'not at all in favour of the women's colleges that were just coming into existence' (*P* 103). Kitty studies history with medieval historian Miss Lucy Craddock. In the manuscript we learn that Miss Craddock, 'had gone to classes at Queens College London—& then Miss Beale had asked her to teach at Cheltenham, & [*she had written*] a little book on the Angevin Kings' (*P* 102). In the published novel, Kitty relishes her tutelage while being conscious that 'so many of the Dons sneered at her' and how this relates to her modest living conditions: 'Was this her only room, she wondered? Did she sleep on the lumpy-looking sofa with the shawl thrown over it?' (*Y* 62, 59).

While working on *The Years*, Woolf was reading a biography of Thomas Hardy and noting his anger about 'the treatment of working men at Oxford; hence Jude' (*D4* 118–19). *The Years* also engages with questions of class and education via the character of Sam Robson, described as an academic 'who had done it all off his own bat' (*Y* 59).[35] Robson offers not only a depiction of the class barriers in higher education in the Victorian period but also a new model of feminist masculinity.[36] In *The Pargiters*, Woolf makes clear that Robson is based on the philologist Joseph Wright (1855–1930) author of the six-volume *English Dialect Dictionary* (1898–1905). Wright was primarily an autodidact (born before compulsory elementary education) who completed a PhD in Heidelberg before moving to Oxford to teach for the Association for the Education of Women and eventually becoming Professor of Comparative Philology in 1901. Woolf had been reading Elizabeth Wright's 1932 biography of her husband and incorporating aspects into *The Pargiters*, particularly in relation to his working-class, Yorkshire roots and his feminism, linked explicitly in *The Pargiters* to his self-education and maternal influence (*P* 155–8). As Natasha Periyan discusses, Wright was not only the acknowledged model

---

A Memoir of Anne Jemima Clough (London: Edward Arnold, 1897), Barbara Stephen, *Emily Davies and Girton College* (London: Constable & Co. Ltd, 1927). She quotes from these sources in *The Pargiters* and *Three Guineas*.

[35] See also the reference to 'Runcorn's boy' in the Present Day section of *The Years*.

[36] For further reading on class and higher education see Jonathan Rose, *The Intellectual Life of the British Working Classes* (New Haven: Yale University Press, 2001).

for Robson and his dictionary the source of the word 'Pargiter', but the song sung by the working-class children (learnt at school) at the close of the novel bears close resemblance to dialect words from his *Dictionary*. Here, as Periyan argues, given the middle-class audience's inability to comprehend the song, Woolf enters into wider debates about the politics of working-class education and cultural division.[37]

Periyan argues more broadly that the ending of *The Years* and 'The Leaning Tower' (a paper delivered to the Brighton WEA in 1940) are 'informed by early manifestations of debates surrounding the role of education in the cultivation of social and cultural democracy', specifically multilateral or comprehensive secondary education.[38] The essay describes the waning influence of 'a particular brand of public-school masculinity'—the leaning tower inhabited by the likes of W.H. Auden and Stephen Spender—in favour of a world 'without classes and towers' (*E6* 274).[39] Multilateral education was a route to democratic 'common culture' so that the essay's close, with its advocacy of the 'common ground' gained through reading and writing, might refer to institutional class commonality as well as the power of autodidacticism or public libraries. Woolf was familiar with proponents of comprehensive education: she had read T.C. Worsley's *Barbarians and Philistines: Democracy and the Public Schools* (1940) and R.H. Tawney, who had called for 'secondary education for all' in 1922, and was President of the W.E.A. from 1928 to 1944.[40] 'The Leaning Tower' is 'haunted by political potential of the institution' and represents, as Periyan demonstrates so convincingly, a corrective to the notion that Woolf's educational philosophy was solely non-institutional in focus.[41]

In *Three Guineas* we find perhaps Woolf's most extensive thinking on women's education, in particular the economic basis of the self-perpetuating cycles of women's exclusion from and marginalization within the university. One of the letters the narrator (the daughter of an educated man) has to respond to before she can donate to the barrister's peace fund, is from the treasurer of a women's college rebuilding fund (based on a letter Woolf received from Joan Pernel Strachey on behalf of Newnham College in 1936). Given that the framing question of *Three Guineas* is how women can help to prevent war, this prompts consideration of the role education plays in promoting war and whether support should be given for women to enter the existing university system with its emphasis on competition, display, hierarchy, and patriotism.

The narrator's research confirms a pervasive belief in the value of education as 'among the greatest of all human values' and she documents, through the individual stories of Mary Kingsley and Sophia Jex-Blake, the sacrifices and struggles of women to secure an education, as well as the reasons women are denied education by fathers who have the

---

[37] Natasha Periyan, '"Altering the Structure of Society": an institutional focus on Virginia Woolf and working-class education in the 1930s', *Textual Practice* 30.7 (2017), 1–24, at 11.

[38] For further reading see Brian Simon, *The Politics of Educational Reform, 1920–1940* (London: Lawrence & Wishart, 1974).

[39] Periyan, 'Altering', 15.

[40] Periyan, 'Altering', 15, 3.

[41] Periyan, 'Altering', 18.

financial ability to provide it (*TG* 110). Once within the university, however, the narrator finds (through a stark discourse of sums and figures) not only that 'the colleges for the sisters of educated men are, compared with their brothers' colleges, unbelievably and shamefully poor', but that women 'have no say in that education' (*TG* 115, 116). Not only that, she discovers that 'the finest education in the world, does not teach people to hate force, but to use it' (*TG* 115). What would the ideal university look like, she wonders? The 'experimental', 'adventurous' college would be poor, a place where 'society was free; not parcelled out into the miserable distinctions of rich and poor, of clever and stupid; but where all the different degrees and kinds of mind, body and soul' (*TG* 118). It would refuse to teach the 'arts of dominating other people' or the 'arts of ruling, of killing, of acquiring land and capital' (*TG* 118). But reality and pragmatism intrude and the narrator admits that 'we must help to rebuild the college which, imperfect as it may be, is the only alternative to the education of the private house' (*TG* 123). The guinea given, the narrator exhorts women to remain outside, to eschew the love of spectacle and ceremony: the ribbons, gowns, and ermine that adorn academics just as they do soldiers. Women, 'who have been shut out from the universities so repeatedly, and are only now admitted so restrictedly', are 'members not of the intelligentsia but of the ignorantsia' and can use their marginal position to protect intellectual and cultural freedoms (*TG* 166–7).

Outside the Institution

While, as outlined, much recent scholarship has explored Woolf's neglected engagement with educational institutions, much of her thinking represents an alternative pedagogy based in outsiderness and refusal. Her emphasis is more often on the democratizing potential of reading (and writing) as a site of education and the valorization of the active, dialogic common reader. The more we learn about Woolf's own active and wide-ranging reading practices—her continual self-education—the less surprising is the emphasis she placed on eclectic, pleasurable but intellectually demanding and resistant reading. Melba Cuddy-Keane has employed the term 'democratic highbrow' to characterize this reader and to signal Woolf's uncoupling of highbrowism or intellectualism from class categories and associations. For Cuddy-Keane, this is an intellectualism occurring outside elite institutions, therefore rejecting a focus on particular syllabi or canons and particular ways of reading and 'testing' or accrediting that reading. Woolf works in the 'genre of the informal essay' and trains her readers, not in a particular style of reading or criticism, but in broader skills in wide-ranging, pluralist reading and in lateral thinking and independence of judgement. She thus recasts '"highbrowism" as radical social practice.'[42]

---

[42] Cuddy-Keane, *Intellectual*, 2.

Public libraries, as well as the books in them, become another key site of education and Woolf's support of the Women's Service Library (now Women's Library) in the late 1930s reveals the importance in relation to women and their histories.[43] In 'The Leaning Tower' she tracks the route to reading: 'This book was not bought; it was not hired. It was borrowed from a public library. England lent it to a common reader' (*E6* 276). Her utopian valorizing of the library space as one of liberation and equality places it at the centre of her alternative pedagogy: 'To admit authorities, however heavily furred and gowned, into our libraries and let them tell us how to read, what to read, what value to place on what we read, is to destroy the spirit of freedom which is the breath of those sanctuaries' (*E5* 573). It also indicates the topicality of her interest in the common reader given contemporary debates about literary and cultural education due to rising literacy rates, mass market publication, and the extension of adult education. Furthermore, the 'institutionalization of English studies within the universities augured an increasing gap between specialized theoretical discourse and the generalist reader', as Cuddy-Keane has outlined so carefully and compellingly.[44] Woolf worked against insistence on the legitimacy and rigour of literary study in the academy, whether I.A. Richards's focus on scientific rigour and close textual analysis or on the Scrutiny critics, F.R. and Q.D. Leavis's emphasis on uplift and guidance for working-class or general readers in how and what to read with a view to 'preserving cultural value'.[45] Woolf's model is anti-hierarchical and eschews specialization and institutional validation. In her essay 'Why?' (written for *Lysistrata*, the magazine of Somerville College, Oxford), she asks 'why learn English literature at universities when you can read it for yourselves in books' (*E6* 34). The academic study of literature is deadened and limited by the pedagogical structures of higher education, in particular the lecture form, which 'incites the most debased of human passions—vanity, ostentation, self-assertion, and the desire to convert?' (*E6* 33).

While Woolf may not have outlined or adhered to one specific philosophy of education, she demonstrates a complex and multi-layered engagement with the inequalities and limitations of the education system particularly in relation to gender and class. As well as critique, she offers a rethinking of the term 'education' itself—based around a broader understanding of learning and knowledge, the places in which they occur, and the reasons and means by which they are sought. Literature remains at the heart of this understanding: 'Literature is open to everybody. I refuse to allow you, Beadle though you are, to turn me off the grass. Lock up your libraries if you like; but there is no gate, no lock, no bolt that you can set upon the freedom of my mind' (*ARO* 57).

---

[43] See Anna Snaith, '"Stray Guineas": Virginia Woolf and the Fawcett Library', *Literature and History* 12.2 (2003), 16–35.

[44] Cuddy-Keane, *Intellectual*, 1.

[45] Cuddy-Keane, *Intellectual*, 70.

SELECTED BIBLIOGRAPHY

Bell, Quentin, *Virginia Woolf: A Biography* (London: Grafton Books, 1978).
Cuddy-Keane, Melba, *Virginia Woolf, the Intellectual and the Public Sphere* (Cambridge: Cambridge University Press, 2003).
Dalgarno, Emily, *Virginia Woolf and the Visible World* (Cambridge: Cambridge University Press, 2001).
Daugherty, Beth Rigel, 'Virginia Woolf Teaching/Virginia Woolf Learning: Morley College and the Common Reader', in Helen Wussow, ed., *New Essays on Virginia Woolf* (Dallas: Contemporary Research Press, 1995), 61–77.
Faithfull, Lilian M., *In the House of My Pilgrimage* (London: Chatto and Windus, 1924).
Harrison, Jane, *Alpha and Omega* (London: Sidgwick and Jackson, 1915).
Jones, Clara, *Virginia Woolf: Ambivalent Activist* (Edinburgh: Edinburgh University Press, 2015).
Kenyon Jones, Christine, and Anna Snaith, ' "Tilting at Universities": Virginia Woolf at King's', *Woolf Studies Annual* 16 (2010), 1–44.
King's College Magazine, Ladies' Department, number XI, Michaelmas term 1900.
Lambert, Andrew, *The Foundations of Naval History: John Knox Laughton, the Royal Navy and the Historical Profession* (London: Chatham, 1998).
Lee, Hermione, *Virginia Woolf: A Biography* (London: Vintage, 1996).
McWilliams Tullberg, Rita, *Women at Cambridge*, rev. ed. (Cambridge: Cambridge University Press, 1998).
Midgley, Nicholas, "Virginia Woolf and the University", *Woolf Studies Annual* 2 (1996), 147–59.
Mills, Jean, *Virginia Woolf, Jane Harrison and the Spirit of Modernist Classicism* (Columbus: Ohio State University Press, 2014).
Periyan, Natasha, ' "Altering the Structure of Society": an institutional focus on Virginia Woolf and working-class education in the 1930s', *Textual Practice* 30.7 (2017), 1–24.
Snaith, Anna, ' "Stray Guineas": Virginia Woolf and the Fawcett Library', *Literature and History* 12.2 (2003), 16–35.
Stengers, Isabelle, and Vinciane Despret, *Women Who Make A Fuss: The Unfaithful Daughters of Virginia Woolf*, trans. April Knutson (Minnesota: University of Minnesota Press, 2014).
Zink, Suzana, *Virginia Woolf's Rooms and the Spaces of Modernity* (Basingstoke: Palgrave, 2018).

CHAPTER 23

WOOLF AND SUFFRAGE

BARBARA GREEN

During World War I and after the 1918 partial franchise was won, numerous suffragists and suffragettes endeavoured to make sense of the 'Cause' by placing suffrage struggles in historical and personal context, necessarily grappling with the problem of feminism's temporality as part of that project.[1] Interwar and World War I novels that featured the suffragist/ette in order to wrestle with the problem of a feminist modernity include May Sinclair's *The Tree of Heaven* (1917), Cicely Hamilton's *William: an Englishman* (1919), Rebecca West's *The Judge* (1922), Edith Zangwill's *The Call* (1924), Vera Brittain's *Honourable Estate* (1936), and two of Virginia Woolf's novels that took up suffrage most directly, *Night and Day* (1919), and *The Years* (1937).[2] Like many of the feminist texts of the post-vote period, Woolf's two suffrage novels self-consciously explored the centrality of feminism to the meaning of a gendered modernity, discovering new ways of telling feminist time.

By 'feminist time' I mean to evoke not only early twentieth-century feminist conversations about the temporality of feminism, but also a whole set of mid- to late-twentieth century, and even contemporary, meditations, worries, and anxieties about how feminism contributed to the cultures of modernity. These range from the still unsettled question of the 'modernism' of suffrage writing and activism, to the relationship of feminist movements to one another in a temporal frame (what we generally call the 'waves' of feminism), to the dating of modernism's emergence (what would happen,

---

[1] I am grateful to Anne Fernald, Catherine Clay, and Elizabeth Evans for their comments and suggestions.
[2] May Sinclair, *The Tree of Heaven* (London: Cassell & Co., 1917); Cicely Hamilton, *William: an Englishman* (London: Skeffington and Son, 1919); Rebecca West, *The Judge* (London: Hutchinson, 1922); Edith Zangwill, *The Call* (London: G. Allen & Unwin, 1924); Vera Brittain, *Honourable Estate* (London: Victor Gollancz, 1936); Virginia Woolf, *Night and Day (1919)*, ed. Michael H. Whitworth (Cambridge: Cambridge University Press, 2018); Virginia Woolf, *The Years (1937)*, ed. Anna Snaith (Cambridge: Cambridge University Press, 2012). All in-text references to *Night and Day* and *The Years* are to these volumes.

for example, if we granted the women's vote the same centrality we do the Great War in histories of modernism's evolution?).³

Perhaps predictably, suffrage scenes play a more dominant role in those of Woolf's writings that preoccupy themselves with the problem of feminist time (as distinct from the larger issue of time itself that informs her various literary experiments, as described by Jesse Matz in Chapter 11 of this volume). *The Years*, for example, adopts time as a protagonist, as Anna Snaith has shown, in order to investigate women's changing roles in modernity including suffrage activism through the form of the family saga; *Night and Day* portrays the arrested development of modern femininity when it is burdened by the backward-looking project of constructing a family history and archive, and measures that project against the forward-looking activities of the suffragist.⁴ Of course, a kind of feminist time also explicitly organizes other texts by Woolf—*Three Guineas* (1938), for example, constructs a feminist archive of 'fact' out of its efforts to retrace women's institutional and private histories; *A Room of One's Own* (1929) encourages us to 'think back through our mothers' (*ARO* 57); and the draft 'essay-novel' *The Pargiters* aimed to extend feminism's story from the 1880s into the future—but without animating the figure of the suffragist/suffragette in order to think through a feminist modernism as do *The Years* and *Night and Day*.

Though there is a long tradition of vibrant writing about 'Woolf's feminism and feminism's Woolf', the more specific question of Woolf's relationship to the suffrage movement has been, relatively speaking, less studied.⁵ In recent years, however, scholars have connected Woolf's feminist writing to writings emerging from the Edwardian suffrage movement and pre-war feminist circles as well as to the writings of interwar feminist groups published between the wars. Molly Hite's *Woolf's Ambiguities: Tonal*

---

³ For work on suffrage and modernity, see, for example, Mary Chapman, *Making Noise, Making News: Suffrage Print Culture and U.S. Modernism* (Oxford: Oxford University Press, 2014); Carey Snyder, 'Beatrice Hastings: Debating Suffrage in the *New Age* and *Votes for Women*', in Faith Binckes and Carey Snyder, eds., *Women, Periodicals and Print Culture in Britain, 1890s–1920s: The Modernist Period* (Edinburgh: Edinburgh University Press, 2019); Claire Eustance, Joan Ryan, and Laura Ugolini, eds, *A Suffrage Reader: Charting Directions in British Suffrage History* (London: Leicester University Press, 2000); Barbara Green, *Spectacular Confessions: Autobiography, Performative Activism, and the Sites of Suffrage* (New York: St. Martin's Press, 1997) and *Feminist Periodicals & Daily Life: Women and Modernity in British Culture* (New York: Palgrave Macmillan, 2017); Janet Lyon, *Manifestoes: Provocations of the Modern* (Ithaca: Cornell University Press, 1999); Sowon Park, 'Political Activism and Women's Modernism', in Maren Tova Linett, ed., *The Cambridge Companion to Modernist Women Writers* (Cambridge: Cambridge University Press, 2010), 172–86; June Purvis and Sandra Stanley Holton, eds, *Votes for Women* (London and New York: Routledge Press, 2000); Laura Winkiel, *Modernism, Race and Manifestoes* (Cambridge: Cambridge University Press, 2011); Ewa Ziarek, 'Right to Vote or Right to Revolt? Arendt and the British Suffrage Militancy', *Differences* 19, no. 5 (2008), 1–27.

⁴ Anna Snaith, '*The Years* and Contradictory Time', in Jessica Berman, ed., *A Companion to Virginia Woolf* (Chichester: John Wiley & Sons, 2016), 137.

⁵ Laura Marcus, 'Woolf's Feminism and Feminism's Woolf', in Sue Roe and Susan Sellers, eds, *The Cambridge Companion to Virginia Woolf* (Cambridge: Cambridge University Press, 2006), 209–44. Also see Chapter 20 'Feminism' by Stephanie Brown and Chapter 31 'Feminist Theory' by Jean Mills in this volume.

Modernism, Narrative Strategy, and Female Precursors, for example, places Woolf in conversation with the polemical fictions of her literary precursor, suffragist Elizabeth Robins.[6] Clara Jones's *Virginia Woolf: Ambivalent Activist* pushes beyond an acknowledgement of Woolf's sceptical attitude toward suffrage feminism to more thoroughly investigate Woolf's relationship to various activist organizations during the modern period including her work for the People's Suffrage Federation (PSF) in the 1910s.[7] Woolf's early work with the constitutionalist PSF suggests to Jones a source for the investments in 'democratic social reform' in her early novel *Night and Day* as well as for the 'adultist agenda' found both in this novel and elsewhere in Woolf's writing.[8] (The term 'adultist' here refers to the standpoint of feminists, especially socialist-feminists, who campaigned for extending the vote to all women and unfranchised men, regardless of their status as property holders.) Mary Jean Corbett's rich study, *Behind the Times: Virginia Woolf in Late-Victorian Contexts*, considers Woolf's attitudes toward suffrage in the context of feminist generations.[9] Sowon Park's excellent 'Suffrage and Virginia Woolf: "The Mass Behind the Single Voice",' places Woolf's thinking about feminism much more centrally, and less ambivalently, in the field of suffrage activism and culture, 'shift[ing] the emphasis—from Woolf in suffrage to suffrage in Woolf'.[10] Each of these builds on Naomi Black's classic *Virginia Woolf as Feminist*, which associates Woolf with 'social feminism, based on women's differences from men'.[11] And in a broader look at suffrage modernism conducted through an exploration of the suffrage reprints made available by Persephone Press, Urmila Seshagiri, while not considering Woolf in particular, productively 'align[s] material politics of feminism with developments in modern literary form'.[12] Elizabeth Evans's recent work on the 'new public woman' suggests that this link between material politics and form might have a great deal to do with women's walking in London in *Night and Day* and *The Years* since these novels 'imagine changes in opportunities for women' 'through the employment of spatial tropes'.[13]

As the terms 'ambivalent' and 'ambiguities' appearing in the titles of two of the aforementioned works suggest, the question of Woolf's hesitations regarding suffrage continue to worry scholars invested in considerations of movement feminism as a context for Woolf's thoughts regarding gender. Indeed, the relative quiet in conversations regarding Woolf and suffrage may spring in part from Woolf's own expressed indecision

---

[6] Molly Hite, *Woolf's Ambiguities: Tonal Modernism, Narrative Strategies, Feminist Precursors* (Ithaca: Cornell University Press, 2017).

[7] Clara Jones, *Virginia Woolf: Ambivalent Activist* (Edinburgh: Edinburgh University Press, 2016).

[8] Jones, *Virginia Woolf: Ambivalent Activist*, 77.

[9] Mary Jean Corbett, *Behind the Times: Virginia Woolf in Late-Victorian Contexts* (Ithaca: Cornell University Press, 2020), 190–225.

[10] This is Sowon Park's phrasing; see her 'Suffrage and Virginia Woolf: "The Mass Behind the Single Voice",' *The Review of English Studies* 56, no. 223 (2005), 122.

[11] Naomi Black, *Virginia Woolf as Feminist* (Ithaca: Cornell University Press, 2004), 10.

[12] Urmila Seshagiri, 'Making it New: Persephone Books and the Modernist Project', *MFS Modern Fiction Studies* 59, no. 2 (2013), 261.

[13] Elizabeth Evans, *Threshold Modernism: New Public Women and the Literary Spaces of Imperial London* (Cambridge: Cambridge University Press, 2018), 111, 129.

regarding the impact of the vote on women's advancement or the wisdom of suffrage activism itself. In *A Room of One's Own*, for example, Woolf's narrator downplays the significance of the 1918 act that expanded the franchise to include property owners and women over thirty in favour of a legacy from a relative that gave her five hundred pounds a year ('Of the two—the vote and the money—the money, I own, seemed infinitely the more important') (*ARO* 29).[14] In *Three Guineas*, Woolf famously burns the word 'feminist' ('Look, how it burns!') as 'a dead word, a corrupt word' drained of meaning since women have earned the 'only right' that is significant, the 'right to earn a living' (*TG* 179). The difficulty we have in assessing the significance of the 'fact' of suffrage culture to Woolf's feminism may also stem from our sensitivity to Woolf's well-noted dissatisfaction with the 'polemical tendencies' expressed in some women's fiction.[15]

Reading Woolf's suffragists/ettes Mary Datchet in *Night and Day* and Rose and Eleanor Pargiter in *The Years* in relation to a suffrage activist who was featured in a 'movement' novel proper—by 'movement novel' I mean a novel that circulated in feminist networks and was promoted in the feminist press during the suffrage period—encourages a reconsideration of questions of feminist ambivalence. In addition, attending to the activist Vida Levering, who appears in Elizabeth Robins's *The Convert*, alongside Woolf's own feminist heroines also invites new questions regarding the temporality, and the modernity, of the suffragist/ette. Woolf's ambivalence about suffrage, demonstrated in the framing of suffragette Rose Pargiter's militancy as tied to trauma and in satiric representations of suffragist Mary Datchet's distracted office work, gives us a new way of thinking about the conversion narrative that undergirds much suffrage fiction of the early twentieth century, thus allowing us to better appreciate its own ambivalent temporality. My choice of the term 'ambivalence' to describe a range of hesitations and temporal delays is meant to nudge a term and its relations ('ambiguity', 'abstruseness') away from their singular association with properly 'modernist' texts or attitudes and toward both earlier and contemporary polemical or social realist writing. Ambivalence and ambiguity are said to be what makes Woolf's feminism exceptional. From another perspective, however, these qualities mark her as typical. Woolf's focus on failed conversion in *Night and Day* particularly in the novel's satiric office scenes, and on feminist trauma in *The Years*, points us to a greater appreciation of the complex temporalities of earlier movement fictions that also incorporated acknowledgement of feminist ambivalence, even if ultimately to overcome it.

Documentary impulses undergird the conversion narrative—one of the dominant forms of suffrage era writing—since a protagonist's growing attachment to the 'Cause' hinges on close encounters with suffrage culture, generally described in detail in movement fictions. With a title like *The Convert* it should be no surprise that Elizabeth Robins's 1907 suffrage novel works as a primer for the conversion narrative

---

[14] See also Alex Zwerdling, *Virginia Woolf and the Real World* (Berkeley: University of California Press, 1986); Jane Marcus, 'Art and Anger', *Feminist Studies* 4 (1978), 68–98.

[15] Hite, *Woolf's Ambiguities*, X. Corbett notes Woolf's rejection of a feminist 'tendency to reproduce ... existing structures of domination' (*Behind the Times*, 192).

as a sub-genre. Robins was an American actress, playwright, and novelist who spent much of her career in London, joined the Women's Social and Political Union (WSPU) in 1906, and became a founding member and President of the Women Writers Suffrage League (WWSL) in 1908. Her novel *The Convert* was based on her 1906 suffrage play, *Votes for Women*; both wove together a fictional romance plot with semi-documentary treatments of open-air meetings, closed-door sessions, and other elements of suffrage activism. At first glance, like many pre-war suffrage fictions, *The Convert* suggests a simple progressive history to suffrage's temporality, one that traces the feminist subject's development as she evolves from an alignment with private life to a commitment to public life.

Persuasive discourse in the form of reproduced speeches and political conversation is a key feature of the conversion narrative. *The Convert*, for example, turns upon an initiate's intimate encounters with an experienced suffragist/ette as well as large public scenes of witnessing where, by accident or design, the recruit stumbles upon or deliberately attends an open-air meeting to hear suffrage arguments, speeches that are reproduced in full in the pages of the novel. In suffrage set-pieces, the rational-critical discourse of suffrage oration takes centre stage and inflects the functioning of dialogue and exchange between women. Even in intimate domestic scenes, where Vida invites a suffragette to her home to discuss gender politics, conversation becomes purposeful: the suffragist persuades both through disinterested argument and the recitation of individual experiences of sex oppression so that persuasive prose and emotionally laden conversation work to rouse her auditor and also, presumably, the reader.[16] Conversion, as a trope and as a narrative mechanism, *moves* subjects (and readers) from one position to another, from detachment to affiliation, from scepticism to alignment with suffrage values, from ignorance (willed or no) to awareness and action.[17] In *The Convert*, Vida shifts her position from spectator to speaker as she joins the movement, ultimately offering the feminist discourse that nudges the reader to a new political position. This feature of suffrage fiction has posed problems for many modernists trained to be suspicious of texts that invite us to 'join a society, or, more desperately, to write a cheque' to borrow Woolf's own language regarding the Edwardian fictions of Wells, Bennett, and Galsworthy (*E*3 427). Indeed, in keeping with Woolf's tendency to withhold such guiding direction (what Hite calls her 'tonal ambiguity'), suffrage speech is muted in *Night and Day* and *The Years*. Feminist conversation in *Night and Day*, for example, is rarely persuasive and generally fails to make things happen. Similarly, feminist conversation in *The Years* is largely omitted: suffrage speeches are left out of representations of meetings, and references to suffrage activism are telegraphic rather than expansive.

Woolf's *Night and Day*, generally not as well known as her later more experimental fictions, is in some ways a conventional heterosexual romance, tracking the slow development of a relationship between Katharine Hilbery, an upper-class member of a

---

[16] Glenda Norquay, 'Introduction', in *Voices & Votes: A Literary Anthology of the Women's Suffrage Campaign* (Manchester and New York: Manchester University Press, 1995), 9.

[17] Conversion narratives may also carry a spiritual dimension (Norquay, *Voices & Votes*, 14).

literary family, and Ralph Denham, a working lawyer with a poetic sensibility, and has been read as 'highly derivative'.[18] Given the fact that the suffragist figure in this novel abandons activism before the conclusion, it might seem that we have little to learn about the complexity of feminist activism from this text. But, like many modernist novels of the early twentieth century, *Night and Day* poses questions regarding suffrage's relation to a feminist future, especially where the well-being of the unmarried woman who lives at home is concerned. The novel juxtaposes public and private, activism and intellectual life in the figures of unpaid suffrage office worker Mary Datchet and Katharine Hilbery who might be described as one of the 'daughters of educated men' Woolf would come to describe in *Three Guineas*. The problem of the woman whose 'profession' is to be a young woman who 'lived at home' (*ND* 39), as characterized by Katharine, or the parallel difficulty of being mired in the 'details of domestic life' even when one works in an office (*ND* 28), a problem represented in the character of Ralph's sister Joan, are, at least initially, seemingly resolved by suffrage worker Mary Datchet who enjoys a room of her own, an occupation, and the modern thrill of moving through public space as 'a private in the army of workers' (*ND* 42). Yet, in the novel's closing pages, Mary is aligned with the future, developing 'plans for the good of a world that none of them were ever to know' (*ND* 536), largely because she has turned away from suffrage to a broader 'new society' (*ND* 410) that boasts more revolutionary, if undefined, goals.[19]

Though Mary's disaffiliation from the suffrage movement has been read as either related to Woolf's impatience with the narrowness of suffrage concerns, or is identified as a sign of Woolf's adultist perspective, we are given little material with which to judge Mary's anti-conversion.[20] Instead of the detailed polemics and persuasive speech that generally fill movement novels, Woolf withholds activist argumentation. For example, Mary and Katharine recognize the link between women's exclusion from the franchise and from political debate, but their conversation trails off into silence as the 'desire to talk about herself or to initiate a friendship' leaves Katharine (*ND* 53, 55).[21] Katharine's refusals don't engage suffrage argumentation, but instead shut it down as when she lapses into silence during a visit to Mary's suffrage office, (she 'stared into the swirl of the tea, and remained silent' (*ND* 87)). A 'convert already' (*ND* 93) who is disinclined to participate, she denies the novel the conventional mechanisms of conversion that organize movement fictions. Similarly, the many documents that Mary handles in the movement headquarters are never represented, even in part; instead suffrage speech is represented as 'old arguments' and a growing 'pile of letters' (*ND* 77–8).

---

[18] Linden Peach, *Critical Issues: Virginia Woolf* (New York: St. Martin's Press, 2000), 40. Julia Briggs notes that Woolf herself viewed the novel as a 'step backwards' (*Virginia Woolf: An Inner Life* (New York & London: Harcourt, 2005), 34). See Evans, *Threshold Modernism*, for an alternate reading. Corbett reads *Night and Day* productively in relation to Woolf's understanding of feminist generations (*Behind the Times*, 194–201).

[19] See Jones, *Virginia Woolf: Ambivalent Activist*, (67–92); Black, *Virginia Woolf as Feminist*, 36–7.

[20] Zwerdling, *Virginia Woolf and the Real World*, 214; Jones, *Virginia Woolf: Ambivalent Activist*, 79.

[21] I'm grateful to Anne Fernald for pointing out the initial reference to the vote in Katharine and Mary's conversation.

While *Night and Day* traces something like conversion's reversal, recording Mary's disenchantment with the 'Cause' and Katharine's refusal to engage it at all despite her approval, *The Years* skips over the question of how one becomes attached to feminism altogether, or, as some have argued, merely offers a psychologized account that roots activism in trauma. Though suffrage history underwrites *The Years* in various ways—for example, Dame Ethel Smyth, a member of the Women's Social and Political Union, was a model for the militant Rose Pargiter (*Y* 458–9) and Smyth acted as a source for Woolf as she was developing the novel—feminist history is fragmented history in *The Years* so that what gets woven into the text are traces gathered from the suffrage archive. For example, galley proof text (available in the Cambridge edition) highlights only the fact of Rose's speech at a suffrage meeting without providing the feminist text as a movement novel might do (Woolf's final text omits even these omissions): 'And now, Rose thought, what about my speech? What am I going to say? [...] Then I shall say ... her lips moved; she had rehearsed her speech in her bath that morning. I shall say, more or less, this ... she said. / Then he will say ... Then I shall say.... She smiled. And that'll clinch the matter, she thought' (*Y* 630–1, first ellipses mine, all others in the original). In *The Years*, the suppression of suffrage speech enables a particular vision of suffrage history, one that compresses the movement's rhetorical expansiveness and favours instead abbreviated and fragmenting symbols and phrases that memorialize suffrage's own promotional flourishes—in the 1914 section, for example, '[a]n old straw hat with a purple ribbon round it' (*Y* 212) and '[a] lady, fashionably dressed with a purple feather dipping down on one side of her hat' (*Y* 218) cite the militant WSPU's colours of purple, white, and green. Both seem aftershocks to Martin and Sally's abbreviated discussion of Rose's militant activism at their luncheon: '"A damned unpleasant thing" he said, "being in prison"'; '"Sitting on a three-legged stool having meat crammed down her throat!"'; '"Crash came a brick!" she [Sally] laughed, flourishing her fork' (*Y* 209). The thrown brick, forcible feeding, the purple band, and the purple feather function as echoes that indicate how suffrage activism saturates the landscape, colouring (quite literally) marginal figures in the background. On one level, these incidental asides preserve a different register of suffrage's rhetoric, one that is tied to the advertising strategies and repetitive sloganeering of the militant WSPU ('Deeds Not Words', 'Who Wins the Eye Wins All', 'Votes for Women'). They also indicate how suffrage is everywhere and nowhere at once: as a visible element of modern commodity feminism, the suffrage colours are an omnipresent part of the landscape but the horrors of suffrage imprisonment and governmental torture through forcible feeding are partially hidden and resist full understanding. Details of forcible feeding and imprisonment are only hinted at in *The Years* and are relegated to an existence off-stage, serving as a backdrop to the experiences of others. For example, in the holograph manuscript *The Pargiters*, Bobby [Martin] thinks of Rose at Kitty's dinner: '"What other world does one want? He asked himself. And Rose is sitting on a three legged stool in a cell, he remembered [...] a tube down her throat. But my dear Rose, he said to himself, you've not the ghost of a chance against this. Think of throwing a stone at that man's plate glass? As he sits eating his kipper with a golden spoon!"' (*Y* 785). The contrast between Kitty's luxurious and highly ritualized dinner in *The Years* (the dining-room 'harmoniously shrouded; pictures with hooded bars of light under them shone out; and the dinner table glowed' (*Y* 226)) and Rose's hunger strike, imprisonment, and forcible feeding explicitly referenced in *The Pargiters* underscore the ways in which suffrage's trauma provide a framework for considering the gendered modernity that both *Night and Day* and *The Years* represent.

Similarly, that the meeting that anchors the 1910 chapter is devoted to suffrage and is also, most likely, a meeting of the militant WSPU is barely visible in the final published version of *The Years*. The presence of Rose, the militant suffragette, is one remaining hint, as is Kitty's remark to Eleanor afterward that '"[f]orce is always wrong"' (*Y* 162), a clear reference to debates in the feminist community regarding the WSPU's use of militant methods as noted by Snaith (*Y* 465). The bringing together of characters with different preoccupations and orientations for a single organizational meeting is another clue: Eleanor, the dedicated servant of social philanthropy; Martin, not obviously connected to women's issues elsewhere; Kitty, dressed for the opera and displaying her 'great ladies' manner' (*Y* 160); Rose, the militant suffragette; and Sally, the mocking observer, sitting quietly in the corner. These characters would generally not find themselves in the same space for political purposes. As Snaith notes, the year 1910 encouraged such collaborative efforts when a Suffrage Bill was promoted by a Conciliation Committee for Women's Suffrage and was backed by militants and non-militants alike (*Y* 465). These efforts, along with the deliberate suspension of militant activities in support of that Bill, encouraged and required inter-organizational co-operation, and necessarily brought militants like Rose together with other non-militant supporters of the Bill. Early versions of *The Years* made the references to suffrage and to militancy explicit: the holograph manuscript of *The Pargiters* held at the Berg library reads 'The question before the meeting, which was whether [...] to join the militant branch of the suffrage movement or not' (*Y* 778). Snaith notes an additional explicit reference to suffrage in the holograph manuscript of the *The Pargiters*: 'Elvira's account of the meeting leads to a discussion about the vote: "Yes, but if one had a vote, One would be an Englishwoman. I don't want to be an Englishwoman"' (*Y* 779).

One could argue, of course, that Woolf's decision to move away from such explicit reference was part of an attempt to decouple larger questions of activism or political commitment from particular organizations. Sally's summary of the event in the published version of the novel is singularly unhelpful, for example, since she recounts for Maggie only an impressionistic view, refusing to offer a report of its central preoccupations: '"A meeting", Maggie interrupted her. "What for? What about?" "There were pigeons cooing", Sara went on. "Take two coos, Taffy. Take two coos ... Tak ... And then a wing darkened the air, and in came Kitty clothed in starlight; and sat on a chair"' (*Y* 169). Eleanor's notes of the meeting are not recorded for us, and we are only told that, to Eleanor, Martin 'speaks very well' and that Martin, Mr Spicer, Kitty and Rose 'were all at loggerheads' (*Y* 159, 160). Woolf's strategy of draining much of the suffrage content from these representations of meetings while retaining references that act as a shorthand for suffrage ('[f]orce is always wrong') reveals women's activism as a backdrop that can be assumed rather than described in detail, saturating the urban landscape.

By decoupling suffrage from a progressive narrative of conversion, Woolf's two suffrage novels invite reconsiderations of feminism's temporality, and offer new questions, as I will argue, for our reading of movement fictions. Though *Night and Day* most likely takes place during the height of suffrage activism in 1909 or 1910, its 1919 publication gave it an odd temporality, positioning it as slightly out of step with its moment for some readers.[22] Katherine Mansfield's view that the novel seemed 'unaware of what has been happening' and was problematically unmarked by the conflict of the Great War, aligns to a certain extent with contemporary scholarship that views the novel as awkwardly placed temporally: for Elizabeth Outka the novel displays a divided 'Vicmod' sensibility; for Mary Jean Corbett, the novel does not fully acknowledge its many debts to New Woman novels of the late nineteenth century.[23] Though many scholars see the text as shaped by a conflict that manages to inform the novel without blemishing the novel's surface (for Outka the war is 'hiding in plain sight'),[24] it is clear that *Night and Day* stands out from a group of novels published during and shortly after the war that focused on the ways in which the Great War dwarfed the suffrage movement in its significance, such as Cicely Hamilton's *William—An Englishman*, created a frame through which suffrage could be examined, such as May Sinclair's *The Tree of Heaven*, or that positioned the suffrage struggle and the war as exerting comparable, and equal, claims on the British public such as Edith Zangwill's *The Call*. By contrast, Woolf's near erasure of the war places suffrage culture in the spotlight alone without its modern partner, thus enabling an interrogation of feminist discontent with 'single-issue' feminism that is separate from, rather than generated by, the 'larger' wartime crisis. Woolf's choice highlights Mary Datchet's emergent dissatisfaction with suffrage and Katharine's reluctance to align herself with a movement she sees as pointless, allowing us to isolate a complex response to modern feminism and judge it on its own terms.

Suffrage's modernity in *Night and Day* is necessarily measured against the demands of the past, a demand that Woolf's characters debate and consider, even while organizing their daily activities around the claims of history. Though *Night and Day* is not marked by the formal play with temporality that defines much of Woolf's later work, the novel is filled with time talk. Katharine's desire to 'free herself from the past', for example, coexists with a feeling that 'the past had completely displaced the present' (*ND* 38). Katharine imagines that she and her mother are existing in a 'deep pool of past time' and are 'bathed in the light of sixty years ago' (*ND* 114). Domestic life too seems backwardly oriented: the Hilbery home functions as museum and archive; the suffragist Mary Datchet's family home has 'narrow red bricks which were said to be five hundred years old' and 'other evidence of incontestable age' (*ND* 198); and Ralph Denham, despite his

---

[22] Jones, *Virginia Woolf: Ambivalent Activist*, 78.
[23] Katherine Mansfield, 'A Ship Comes Into the Harbour', *Athenaeum*, 21 November 1919, 1227; Elizabeth Outka, 'The Transitory Space of *Night and Day*', in Jessica Berman, ed., *A Companion to Virginia Woolf* (Chichester: Wiley-Blackwell, 2016), 56; Mary Jean Corbett, 'Virginia Woolf and "The Third Generation"', *Twentieth-Century Literature* 60, no. 1 (2014), 30–1.
[24] Outka, 'Transitory', 57.

protests against the Hilbery's reverence for their literary ancestor, wants to write a 'history of the English village from Saxon days to the present time', certainly not a forward-leaning project (*ND* 236). The characters in *Night and Day* are so attentive to questions of time that in one memorable scene, William times Katharine's silences, '"the time between one remark and the next"', with the result of '"ten minutes and twenty seconds"', suggesting that time is both something to measure and suffer through (*ND* 183).

The relentless demands of the past are most visible in the rhythms of the archival project that organizes the Hilbery family's efforts to preserve the legacy of Katharine's grandfather, a famous poet. Part museum, part archive, the Hilbery home is a space designed to display, memorialize, preserve, and document his life and is animated by the paintings, manuscripts, and objects that retain the past, so that, for Mrs Hilbery, "'Dear chairs and tables!"' are '"like old friends"' (*ND* 15) and domestic space itself is characterized as archive, museum, 'chapel', or 'grotto' (*ND* 7). For Mrs Hilbery, the project of writing her father's life entails immersing herself in private memories of the 'ancient disaster' of the dissolution of her parents' marriage as well as in the carefully preserved documents associated with her celebrated father's creative work (*ND* 102). Her relationship to the past is an anxious one, since she is haunted by the 'ghost of her parent's sorrow' (*ND* 102) and filled with a desire to rewrite the past, to 'set things straight which had been crooked these sixty years' (*ND* 102). History-writing, however, is a non-productive enterprise. Mrs Hilbery's writing project is a stalled one, her writer's block, inability to organize her thoughts, and failure to prioritize the mass of information before her, means that each writing day resembles the last without moving the project any closer to a conclusion: 'the book still remained unwritten. Papers accumulated without much furthering their task, and in dull moments Katharine had her doubts whether they would ever produce anything at all fit to lay before the public' (*ND* 34).

Given this ambivalence regarding an investment in the past, one might expect Mary Datchet's role as a secretary for an unnamed (but clearly non-militant) suffrage organization would signal the future-oriented perspective of feminism. Indeed, for Mary's suffrage co-worker Sally Seal, the movement of feminism is linear, progressive, future-oriented, even if admittedly slow: '"That's what I feel, you know, about these meetings. Each one of them is a step onwards in the great march—humanity, you know. We do want the people after us to have a better time of it"' (*ND* 176). Yet for suffragist Mary Datchet as for Katharine Hilbery, women's time is archival time. Office labour, like the Hilberys' literary project, is repetitious and non-productive. *Night and Day*'s investment in reading suffrage labour as office work rather than as street activism and the novel's juxtaposition of suffrage intellectual and secretarial labour against the backward-looking archival projects of history writing in the aesthetically-minded Hilbery family, suggest that femininity's move into the future must be understood in relation to its management of the detritus of the past. The shared activities of record collection, book-keeping, and document production tie the activities of the progressive and public-oriented Mary Datchet to the aesthetically and domestically-oriented routines of Katharine Hilbery.

Though dedicated, Mary insists that she and her co-workers are 'all sick to death of women and their votes' (*ND* 84). Office work is arranged through the repetition of 'old arguments' (*ND* 77) and the recirculation of old jokes 'with scarcely any variation of words' (*ND* 78). On her way to the office, Mary becomes aware that she is 'already in a groove, capable, that is, of thinking the same thoughts every morning at the same hour' (*ND* 76). Mary's dreams about work are more about office efficiency, since 'great organizers always pounce, to begin with, upon trifles' (*ND* 76), than about the pressing issues of feminism so that the bureaucratic rhythms of office life become a kind of content. Representations of office work were rare in suffrage novels, but featured prominently in the pages of the WSPU's paper *Votes for Women* where they functioned to document the personalities and spaces of suffrage. In *Night and Day*, by contrast, the office appears as a 'dream' to Katharine, an 'unreal' space of 'enchanted people in a bewitched tower' (*ND* 92).

Ultimately, Woolf's suffragist Mary Datchet functions as a distracted office worker, whose break with suffrage stems from office work's inability to hold her attention, rather than from an argument regarding goals or strategies. In a central scene of disaffiliation, Mary finds herself unable to focus on the work at hand, her attention drifting to issues of romantic love and loss. Despite the fact that '[a] pleasanter and saner woman than Mary Datchet was never seen within a committee-room', she becomes increasingly distracted so that 'she had great difficulty in reducing her mind to obedience; and her reading lacked conviction, as if, as was indeed the case, she had lost the power of visualizing what she read' (*ND* 172). Thoughts of her object of desire, Ralph Denham, captivate her so that throughout the meeting she 'had thus to do battle with the sceptical presence of Ralph Denham' who 'threatened to have it all his own way' (*ND* 172). Despite 'half a dozen methods' of reigning her attention back to the task at hand, Mary is possessed by the presence of a more pressing reality outside of the meeting room walls: her pencil is bewitched so that on its own it 'drew a little round figure on the blotting-paper', her focus is hijacked by numerous 'unsuitable suggestions', she fails to 'attach more weight to one project than to another' (*ND* 172, 173). Finally, '[a]s if emerging from a mist', 'without conscious effort' and 'by some trick of the brain', her attention returns to the present: '[c]ertain articles were to be written; certain editors approached' (*ND* 173).

Similarly, in *The Years*, Eleanor is struck by the repetition and futility folded into the modern organizational meeting: 'I've heard all this, I've done all this so often, she was thinking.... People's faces even seemed to repeat themselves' (*Y* 158). Like Mary, Eleanor finds herself distracted, pulled away from the demands of paperwork and necessary bureaucracy of activism, thinking instead of Mr Pickford's life in Westminster, of a 'green glade' and 'flowering tree' in Kew that she can visit imaginatively, of the fact that Kitty attends the meeting dressed for the opera, or of Martin's impatient response to Kitty's 'great ladies' manner' (*Y* 158–60). These distractions bifurcate subjectivity ('she seemed able to divide herself into two') and temporality, so that she finds 'that her pencil could take notes quite accurately while she herself thought of something else' (*Y* 158). Katharine's abstract algebraic symbols from *Night and Day* ('dots and dashes and twisted bars' (*ND* 317)), and Mary's 'little round figure on the blotting paper', as well as Woolf's own cypher from *The Pargiters*, are reprised here as Eleanor turns dutiful notes into a symbolic trace of her wandering mind: 'digging a little hole in the blotting paper' and 'drawing a spoke from the hole in the middle' (*Y* 158).[25] Office work thus bends to the interrupting temporality of the daydream, a temporality that opens feminism to the everyday and encompasses its messiness.

Ambivalence structures *Night and Day*'s turn away from suffrage activism and also truncates references to militant activism in *The Years*. In both works, that ambivalence is tied to a complex temporality, a feminist time, that allows for distraction and delay rather than offering a simple progressive temporality. Woolf's ambivalence teaches us to notice the prevalence of doubt and uncertainty in suffrage fictions themselves. Even the silence that replaces suffrage speech in Woolf's novels has a role to play in movement fictions such as *The Convert* where the reticence of the novel ties gaps, silences, and restraint to the feminist subject's traumatic past. The lessons of *The Convert* suggest that trauma will be enfolded, eventually, into present and future activism; this process is difficult and involves a negotiation between the claims of the public sphere and the demands of privacy. A layering of silence and speech, of sexual and representative politics, complicates and slows the forward-moving thrust of the suffrage novel's temporality. One of the more sensational aspects of the plot of *The Convert* and the play *Votes for Women* upon which it was based—so scandalous from the perspective of suffrage leaders that Robins was asked to change her heroine's name to further distance her from Christabel Pankhurst—was that the feminist heroine had a 'past', a phrase that marries temporality with sexual experience. In glimpses, through gossip and cautious confessions, we learn that Vida Levering as a younger woman had begun an affair, had become pregnant, and had an abortion after being abandoned by the would-be politician Geoffrey Stoner who could not afford to lose his inheritance by marrying. Suffrage scholars note that it is through this experience, framed as one of maternal longing and loss, that Vida forges an alliance with a mixed-class feminist collectivity—sexual politics creates bonds between women.[26] What is harder to notice, however, since the narrative handles its scandalous sub-text so carefully, are the ways in which this private history presents a drag on the forward-motion of conversion. Indeed, because this experience remains hidden and marks the female subject (and only the female subject) with a determining secret, Vida's past organizes the pace and shape of her activism as well as that of the novel.[27] Vida Levering's affair, pregnancy, and abortion are positioned as a trauma narrative—haunting the subject, determining present and future articulations of subjectivity, resistant to discourse as the unsayable heart of the narrative. When Vida's maid Wark turns to the past, noting that Vida returned from abroad as '"different"' and '"turned into somebody else"', and then links that memory

---

[25] See Anna Snaith, *The Cambridge Edition of the Works of Virginia Woolf: The Years* for a reproduction of the 'doodle' from *The Pargiters*, xl.

[26] See Hite, *Woolf's Ambiguities*, 94; Jane Eldridge Miller, *Rebel Women: Feminism, Modernism and the Edwardian Novel* (London: Virago Press, 1994), 133–5.

[27] Miller, *Rebel Women*, 135.

to other scenes of domestic sexual exploitation, Vida cautions her that '"we never speak of that"' thus instructing readers that the feminist rhetoric that undergirds and propels the conversion narrative co-exists alongside omissions and elisions.[28] Trauma theory's insight that testimony requires an audience able to receive and properly witness a narrative of trauma seems pertinent here, especially since, within the logic of the novel, a feminist community both within and outside of the novel can only be constructed through the confessional utterance that depends on its very existence.[29] Vida's personal trauma is also associated with a hidden history of patriarchal exploitation and harassment of women that organized the domestic household in which she grew up, an '"ugly thing"' that was '"going on under [her] father's roof"'.[30] Only by reckoning with the past, by acknowledging it and connecting with it in a veiled but public confession, can the heroine fully affiliate with the movement: '"the time has come when a woman may look about her and say, What general significance has my secret pain? Does it 'join on' to anything?"'.[31] However, this project of 'joining on' requires sustained effort and comes with emotional and social costs. When we are told that a 'beholder' in the presence of Vida holding a child would find himself 'uneasily' 'search[ing] the eyes for tears', we are reminded of the complex feelings—perhaps even ambivalence—that accompany a slow affiliation with the 'Cause'.[32] As conversion narrative *and* trauma narrative, *The Convert* is forward-looking *and* backward-looking, both invested in a model of progressive history and ambivalent about the costs of confronting a painful past.

In its framing of the feminist time of conversion as bound up with a consideration of a traumatic past, *The Convert* thus shares something of the uneasy sensibility of Woolf's 'ambivalent' and 'ambiguous' suffrage novels. Thus reading backward—bringing questions from Woolf's suffrage novels back into the feminist archive of movement fictions—illuminates aspects of their temporal movements that are more difficult to see when they are read in isolation from one another. For example, *The Years*, which, as Snaith reminds us, provides a layered temporality in its 'exploration of the past always happen[ing] in conjunction with an awareness of the present moment', also offers an important linking of trauma and militant activism.[33] Rose's commitment to militant activism has been read by some as pathologized or overdetermined by the childhood trauma of sexual harassment (or what Woolf herself called 'street love' in her essay-novel draft later published as *The Pargiters*). For Christine Froula, for example, Rose's feminist commitments are inextricably tied to the ways in which the awareness of sexual danger teaches repression and 'inculcates femininity as a loss of speech, voice, witness,

---

[28] Elizabeth Robins, *The Convert* (1907) (London: The Women's Press, 1980), 29, 30.
[29] Dori Laub and Shoshana Felman, *Testimony: Crises of Witnessing in Literature, Psychoanalysis and History* (New York: Routledge Press, 1991).
[30] Robins, *Convert*, 225.
[31] Robins, *Convert*, 303.
[32] Robins, *Convert*, 6.
[33] Snaith, '*The Years* and Contradictory Time', 139.

never acknowledged as such and never mourned'.[34] Thomas Davis goes further, writing that 'the novel makes it difficult to see anything heroic or progressive in Rose's trajectory from childhood guilt and shame to activism. What first appears to be a narrative of political awakening inverts into one of psychopathology'.[35] However, reading *The Years* through the lens of *The Convert* suggests that its manipulation of the trauma narrative shares qualities with this suffrage fiction since they both exploit silences and gaps in order to connect sexual politics and representative politics, rather than separate them. Rose is on her way to a suffrage event, after all, when she meets with her cousins Maggie and Sally and contemplates her desire to thread together the past and the present ('for some reason she wanted to talk about her past; to tell them something about herself that she had never told anybody—something hidden' (*Y* 150)). Though she fails—'What is the use, she thought, of trying to tell people about one's past? What is one's past?' (*Y* 151)—her effort to integrate family history, sexual trauma, and representative politics suggests a determination to make private history visible in the public sphere. As Vida puts it, to have personal pain 'join onto' something larger. Similarly, Rose's recognition that children '"can't tell anybody"' about their initiations into patriarchy's cruelty (*Y* 143) echoes Vida Levering's cautionary phrase '"we never speak of that"'. Silence, combined with trauma's inherent resistance to discourse, leads to the destabilizing features of the past that both inform and unsettle the present.[36] Past trauma 'haunts' *The Years*, to borrow Snaith's term, just as past trauma ghosts and informs Vida Levering's activism in *The Convert*, though, admittedly, the surface of Woolf's text more visibly bears the scars of that wounding.

Woolf's engagement with suffrage culture allows us to see ambivalence as a feminist gesture (or perhaps as the feminist gesture) rather than as an anomaly or as critique—something to be lived through or with rather than overcome. Moments of distraction or references to trauma in Woolf's suffrage texts encourage us to reconsider moments of hesitation in seemingly more enthusiastic or single-minded suffrage fictions that emerged during the suffrage campaign. What if Mary Datchet's rejection of suffrage office work, Eleanor's distraction in an activist meeting, along with Rose's relationship to activism as a response to trauma, or Vita's silence regarding her own private motivations for her activism, were not symptoms of feminism's limitations but instead provided routes to a richer and more deeply felt feminism (if not always for the character, then perhaps for us)? Rather than a turning away from feminism, I want to consider these scenes of ambivalence or hesitation (on a character's part as well as on the author's part) as a reconsideration and reframing of feminism, one that encourages new readings of

---

[34] Christine Froula, *Virginia Woolf and the Bloomsbury Avant-Garde: War, Civilization, Modernity* (New York: Columbia University Press, 2005), 237.

[35] Thomas S. Davis, *The Extinct Scene: Late Modernism and Everyday Life* (New York: Columbia University Press, 2016), 86.

[36] Snaith notes that the 'historical continuum' of *The Years* is 'disrupted' by 'moments of shock and rupture' such as the wounds carried by Rose's body ('*The Years* and Contradictory Time', 146).

pre-war suffrage novels, explorations of the moments of indecision and hesitation that appear in movement novels 'before' conversion as well as 'after'.

Selected Bibliography

Black, Naomi, *Virginia Woolf as Feminist* (Ithaca, NY: Cornell University Press, 2004).
Corbett, Mary Jean, *Behind the Times: Virginia Woolf in Late-Victorian Contexts* (Ithaca: Cornell University Press, 2020).
Hite, Molly, *Woolf's Ambiguities: Tonal Modernism, Narrative Strategy, Feminist Precursors* (Ithaca: Cornell University Press, 2017).
Jones, Clara, *Virginia Woolf: Ambivalent Activist* (Edinburgh: Edinburgh University Press, 2016).
Marcus, Laura, 'Woolf's Feminism and Feminism's Woolf', in Sue Roe and Susan Sellers, eds, *The Cambridge Companion to Virginia Woolf* (Cambridge: Cambridge University Press, 2006), 209–44.
Park, Sowon, 'Political Activism and Women's Modernism', in Maren Tova Linett, ed., *The Cambridge Companion to Modernist Women Writers* (Cambridge: Cambridge University Press, 2010), 172–86.
Park, Sowon, 'Suffrage and Virginia Woolf: "The Mass Behind the Single Voice"', *Review of English Studies* 56, no. 223 (2005), 119–34.
Robins, Elizabeth, *The Convert (1907)* (London: The Women's Press), 1980.
Snaith, Anna, '*The Years* and Contradictory Time', in Jessica Berman, ed., *A Companion to Virginia Woolf* (Chichester: John Wiley & Sons, 2016), 137–49.

CHAPTER 24

IMPRESSIONISM AND POST-IMPRESSIONISM

TAMAR KATZ

VIRGINIA Woolf spent her life immersed in visual art as well as literature. She grew up in a family that was not only embedded in literary circles but knew many of the Victorian era's major painters. Portraits of her parents by Burne-Jones and G.F. Watts hung on the walls, and she frequently visited artists' houses as well as museums and exhibitions.[1] As an adult, her intimate circle of family and friends included artists and art critics and Woolf herself wrote repeatedly about art in her letters, essays, and fiction. It is not surprising then that, searching for principles of composition for her own work, she drew on debates about contemporary art. Two important recent developments in European painting offered her language for thinking about fiction as well. These included the flowering of Impressionism in late nineteenth-century France and the rise of Post-Impressionism in the early twentieth century—the latter shepherded into England by her friends. For Woolf—and for other modernist writers who attempted experiments we now term Impressionist—literature explored a series of problems that it shared with visual art.

Two central concerns persist throughout Woolf's writing and reveal her engagement with the ideas of Impressionism and Post-Impressionism. The first is the importance of consciousness in shaping our access to the world. Like both painterly and literary Impressionists, Woolf suggests that we apprehend our environment differently than conventional narratives would have it. She proposes that the world itself takes a radically fluid form, determined by the sequence and intensity of our perceptions rather than by the regularity of calendrical time or the social norms that designate some events more important than others. But while Woolf proposes remoulding fiction to the self's impressions, like Post-Impressionist artists and critics she searches for forms to shape

---

[1] Maggie Humm, 'Virginia Woolf and Visual Culture', in Susan Sellers, ed., *The Cambridge Companion to Virginia Woolf*, 2nd ed. (Cambridge: Cambridge University Press, 2010), 214–30.

that flux, alternative fictional patterns that could frame the ephemerality of the mind's experience, especially for women. While art critics—especially Post-Impressionist ones—cast these two movements as opposed, and while Woolf turned her attention more fully to impressions and abstract structure at different stages of her work, her writing consistently fused innovative narrative form with an attention to consciousness.

Woolf was one of modernism's most important theorists as well as novelists and she often anchored her philosophy of the novel in the importance of impressions to the way we inhabit the world. In one of her best-known manifestos, 'Modern Fiction' (1925), she redefined life and art by arguing that both must centre on consciousness. Criticizing an earlier generation of novelists for depicting the external world rather than their characters' understanding, she asserts that the mind is not composed as conventional fiction would have it. Instead it receives a constant flow of fleeting sensory perceptions and passing ideas. 'Examine for a moment an ordinary mind on an ordinary day. The mind receives a myriad impressions—trivial, fantastic, evanescent, or engraved with the sharpness of steel. From all sides they come, an incessant shower of innumerable atoms' (E4 160). She claims that once we recognize the importance of these impressions, we will understand perception, experience, and art differently. Woolf's fiction offers some of modernism's most radical experiments in imagining that 'ordinary mind on an ordinary day'. She would also come to test Impressionism's limits at providing aesthetic form, as she turned in later work to different kinds of patterning to remake the novel.

In arguing for the centrality of impressions to the way we engage the world, Woolf draws on a set of earlier aesthetic experiments that focused on these same concerns. The most prominent was the work of French Impressionist painters who began to reconceive visual representation in the decades before Woolf was born. She would have been familiar with the movement and the related work of artists in England not only by visiting galleries, but also through discussions with her sister, the painter Vanessa Bell, and at Bell's artists' Friday Club beginning in 1905.[2] Impressionist painters provided an aesthetic model by transforming the visual arts, experimenting with new ways of representing the external world that emerged when the artist focused closely on the structures of perception. The movement arose in 1860s and 1870s Paris, in the work of painters like Claude Monet, Pierre-Auguste Renoir, Berthe Morisot, and Camille Pissarro. They rebelled against official standards maintained by the French national academy, forming their own artists' society and exhibiting their work independently in 1874. Turning to scenes of ordinary life and to landscapes for their subject, they exploited techniques like loose, highly visible brushstrokes (earlier associated with preliminary sketching) to capture a sense of movement and dramatize the momentary effects of light on the eye.[3] In doing so they deemphasized drawing and outline,

---

[2] Diane Filby Gillespie, *The Sisters' Arts: The Writing and Painting of Virginia Woolf and Vanessa Bell* (Syracuse: Syracuse University Press, 1988), 34–5.

[3] Mary Tompkins Lewis, 'Introduction', in Mary Tompkins Lewis, ed., *Critical Readings in Impressionism and Post-Impressionism: An Anthology* (Berkeley: University of California Press, 2007), 1–19.

which seemed to propose an objective, orderly world that could appear recognizably to all viewers. Instead Impressionists shaped their canvases through the play of colours, underscoring painting's appeal to the senses.[4] Press accounts labelled the new style of painting Impressionist, drawing on the title of Monet's painting *Impression, Soleil Levant* [*Impression, Sunrise*]. As Jules-Antoine Castagnary explained in *Le Siècle* at the time: '"They are impressionists in the sense that they render not the landscape, but the sensation produced by the landscape."'[5]

Painterly Impressionism was susceptible to two contradictory interpretations. For much of the twentieth century, art critics understood it primarily 'as an art of objective, visual truth', an extension of the positivist belief that 'only the tools of science—direct observation and empirical analysis—provided the means to credible knowledge' by reproducing the way light reaches the eye.[6] Indeed, as we will see, this is how Virginia Woolf's fellow Bloomsburyite and Post-Impressionist theorist Roger Fry understood the movement. While some critics who interpreted Impressionism in this manner praised the work for its truthfulness, others objected that it was insufficiently artful, merely imitating the world. However—and importantly for Woolf and writers of Impressionist fiction that preceded hers—Impressionism could also point to quite a different conclusion. The movement showed how fully sensations mediate our access to the world, which we can thus know *only* through our senses.[7] In making the artist's gestures visible, Impressionist brushstrokes emphasized that painting was a highly subjective act. They also dislodged the assumption that there was a commonly agreed-upon shape to the world that painters could represent according to traditional conventions.

In diary entries and essays written across her life, Woolf sometimes frames her own experience in Impressionist terms, as she considered the challenge of conveying sensation in language. As Ann Banfield has suggested, when Woolf represented her own perceptions and consciousness, she sometimes adapted a 'Monet-like analysis of appearances'.[8] In a diary entry from 1928, for instance, she describes the difficulty of representing rooks as they beat 'up against the wind' in language that captured the movement of the bird's wing and the texture of air, as if the latter 'were full of ridges & ripples & roughnesses ... But what a little I can get down with my pen of what is so vivid to my eyes, & not only to my eyes: also to some nervous fibre or fan like membrane in

---

[4] James H. Rubin, *Impressionism* (London: Phaidon Press, 1999), 32.

[5] Quoted in Stephen F. Eisenman, 'The Intransigent Artist or How the Impressionists Got their Name', in Mary Tompkins Lewis, ed., *Critical Readings in Impressionism and Post-Impressionism: An Anthology* (Berkeley: University of California Press, 2007), 149–61, at 150.

[6] Lewis, 1.

[7] For analysis of how Woolf used colour as a political intervention, see Jane Goldman, *The Feminist Aesthetics of Virginia Woolf: Modernism, Post-Impressionism, and the Politics of the Visual* (Cambridge: Cambridge University Press, 1998). On Impressionism's reliance on the senses, see Jesse Matz, *Lasting Impressions: The Legacies of Impressionism in Contemporary Culture* (New York: Columbia University Press, 2016), 50–4.

[8] Ann Banfield, *The Phantom Table: Woolf, Fry, Russell, and the Epistemology of Modernism* (Cambridge: Cambridge University Press, 2000), 270.

my spine' (*D3* 191). Around the same time, in essays such as 'Street Haunting' (1927) and 'The Sun and the Fish' (1928), she meditates on how the urban and the natural world appeal to the eye. And later, in an unpublished account of her early life, 'A Sketch of the Past' (1939), Woolf describes her earliest recollections in sheerly sensory terms— as 'colour-and-sound memories' (*MB* 66). From recalling 'red and purple flowers on a black ground' (her mother's dress) to 'hearing the waves breaking, one, two, one, two ... and then breaking, one, two, one, two, behind a yellow blind', she summons her first moments of awareness through visual and auditory impressions (*MB* 64). She goes on to suggest that an art adequate to these memories would resemble Impressionist painting in its attention to colour and refusal of firm outline. 'If I were a painter I should paint these first impressions in pale yellow, silver, and green.... I should make curved shapes, showing the light through, but not giving a clear outline' (*MB* 66).

Impressionism, however, did not emerge in painting alone. Starting in the second half of the nineteenth century and continuing into Woolf's own time, British writers too began reimagining the world filtered through impressions, in essays and later in novels.[9] The most influential early advocate for this view was a nineteenth-century critic Woolf long admired, Walter Pater. She often praises the beauty of Pater's style, which many of his contemporaries considered exemplary, finding there a pleasure anchored in the senses. In her 1920 essay 'English Prose', Woolf describes re-encountering this favourite writer, 'who from words made blue and gold and green; marble, brick, the wax petals of flowers; warmth too and scent; all things that the hand delighted to touch and the nostrils to smell, while the mind traced subtle winding paths and surprised recondite secrets. This, and much more than this, comes back to me with renewed delight' (*E3* 172–3).

Pater also insisted on the radical value of perception in terms that prefigure 'Modern Fiction'. He was particularly notorious for an early manifesto, the 1873 'Conclusion' to *The Renaissance: Studies in Art and Poetry*, in which he claims that sensations are all we have. He argues that as we reflect on what we know of the outside world, it dissolves into 'a group of impressions—colour, odour, texture—in the mind of the observer'.[10] For Pater, this insight reveals how far impressions ground art and ethics in subjective experience, rather than empirical evidence. In a spiritually and aesthetically valuable life, he writes, 'not the fruit of experience, but experience itself, is the end'.[11]

When Woolf redefines life in 'Modern Fiction', she draws on Pater in claiming that consciousness undergirds our experience. She also demands that novels change to represent this new view properly. She calls for writers to transcribe the experience of receiving impressions: 'Let us record the atoms as they fall upon the mind in the order

---

[9] For overviews of literary Impressionism, see Tamar Katz, *Impressionist Subjects: Gender, Interiority, and Modernist Fiction in England* (Urbana: University of Illinois Press, 2000); Jesse Matz, *Literary Impressionism and Modernist Aesthetics* (Cambridge: Cambridge University Press, 2000).

[10] Walter Pater, *The Renaissance: Studies in Art and Poetry*, ed. Donald L. Hill (Berkeley: University of California Press, 1980), 187.

[11] Pater, *The Renaissance*, 188.

in which they fall, let us trace the pattern, however disconnected and incoherent in appearance, which each sight or incident scores upon the consciousness' (*E4* 161). She insists too that modern fiction must encompass the changed scale of importance that becomes clear when we make impressions central: 'Let us not take it for granted that life exists more fully in what is commonly thought big than in what is commonly thought small' (*E4* 161).

In evaluating literature, Woolf often referred to a cluster of modernist authors, her immediate predecessors and her contemporaries, who were experimenting in just this fashion, placing sensory impressions at the core of consciousness and finding in them art's best method of communicating. Of these writers—including Joseph Conrad, Dorothy Richardson, and James Joyce—Conrad provided her with the most consistent touchstone for the best of modern fiction. In his turn-of-the-century novels *Heart of Darkness* and *Lord Jim*, he altered realist convention by emphasizing how subjects struggle to understand the external world through its impressions upon them, by expanding the gap between the moment a narrator—or reader—sees objects and motion, and the time later, if ever, when he can understand them.[12] Conrad had earlier claimed explicitly that literature relies on the senses, linking his aesthetic goal to the reader's impressionability. He described his project in 1897 as 'by the power of the written word to make you hear, to make you feel—it is, before all to make you *see*'.[13] Although Woolf cites Conrad only briefly in 'Modern Fiction,' she praises him repeatedly in reviews of his reissued novels. She especially values *Lord Jim* for Conrad's '"moment of vision"', and for the way his novel's characters 'are enveloped in the subtle, fine, perpetually shifting atmosphere of [the narrator] Marlow's mind' (*E2* 142).[14]

Woolf had a far more complex response to a closer contemporary, Dorothy Richardson. Richardson's extended novel *Pilgrimage*, composed of thirteen volume-length chapters, began to appear shortly after Woolf's own first novel, *The Voyage Out*, in 1915, and continued publication until after Richardson's death in 1957. *Pilgrimage* pioneered stream-of-consciousness technique by tracing the flowing perceptions and emotions of its protagonist, Miriam Henderson, as she encounters daily life. For Woolf, *Pilgrimage* exemplified one promising path for modern fiction, but her reviews of several volumes find Richardson's scope limited. One source of Woolf's ambivalence was her conflicted reaction to female literary contemporaries.[15] As she noted in her diary,

---

[12] Another Impressionist writer, Ford Madox Ford, theorized his own and Conrad's fiction, defining this new technique as 'render[ing] those queer effects of real life that are like so many views seen through bright glass'. See 'On Impressionism, I', *Poetry and Drama* 2 (1914), 167–75, at 174.

[13] Joseph Conrad, 'Preface', *The Nigger of the Narcissus* (Garden City: Doubleday, 1926), xi–xvi, at xiv.

[14] For a sample of Woolf's comments on Conrad, see the following essays, many of them reviews of Dent's reissue of his work: 'Lord Jim' (*E2* 140–3), 'Mr Conrad's "Youth"' (*E2* 158–9), 'Mr Conrad's Crisis' (*E2* 226–8), 'A Disillusioned Romantic' (*E2* 229–32), 'A Prince of Prose' (*E2* 288–93).

[15] See Molly Hite, *Woolf's Ambiguities: Tonal Modernism, Narrative Strategy, Feminist Precursors* (Ithaca, NY: Cornell University Press, 2017), chapter 4; Anne E. Fernald, 'Virginia Woolf and Experimental Fiction', in Robert DeMaria, Jr., Heesok Chang, and Samantha Zacher, eds, *A Companion to British Literature: Volume IV: Victorian and Twentieth-Century Literature 1837–2000* (Hoboken: John Wiley & Sons, 2014), 246–59.

at times she hesitated to review Richardson because she was aware of her as a potential competitor. 'The truth is that when I looked at it [*Pilgrimage*'s fifth volume, *Interim*], I felt myself looking for faults; hoping for them. And they would have bent my pen, I know. There must be an instinct of self-preservation at work. If she's good then I'm not' (*D1* 315). But Woolf's more extended comments on Richardson in her reviews of *The Tunnel* earlier in 1919 and of *Revolving Lights* in 1923 also reveal her concern with the potential difficulties of Impressionism when narrowed to the scope of a single mind. Richardson aims, she says, to 'descend to the depths and investigate the crannies of Miriam Henderson's consciousness' (*E3* 367). This 'is, we are bidden to believe, the source beneath the surface, the very oyster within the shell' (*E3* 10–11). However Woolf does not find that Richardson has reached sufficient depths, or significant ones. She criticizes *The Tunnel* for leaving the reader 'distressingly near the surface' (*E3* 11), and she praises *Revolving Lights* in notably mixed terms: 'we feel that the trophies that Miss Richardson brings to the surface, however we may dispute their size, are undoubtedly genuine' (*E3* 367). Here she echoes a comment in her diary that what 'ruins Joyce & Richardson' is 'the damned egotistical self', which can leave the novel 'narrowing & restricting' (*D2* 14).

Woolf's own experiments in Impressionist fiction evolved to resist the danger of fictional solipsism. For while she explored how consciousness apprehends and composes the world, as her writing developed, she increasingly expanded her focus beyond the single mind. We can see this progression in the shift between her early short fiction focused on impressions and the first novel of hers we might term fully Impressionist, *Jacob's Room* (1922) as the latter radically expands the perspectives it brings together. Woolf began composing fiction in an overtly Impressionist mode as she worked out the ideas she would eventually articulate most fully in 'Modern Fiction'. She wrote an early version of that essay, entitled 'Modern Novels' in 1919; around the same time, she wrote a series of short sketches and stories that would appear in 1921 as *Monday or Tuesday*. Of these, 'Blue and Green' comes closest to painterly Impressionism's fascination with the power of colour to change the outlines we assume objects possess. The sketch consists of two paragraph-long descriptions: in 'Green', light passing through a lamp's pendants creates a transformed landscape, so that we barely discern the lamp, but encounter a world remade by light. 'The light slides down the glass, and drops a pool of green.... But the hard glass drips on to the marble; the pools hover over the dessert [sic] sand; the camels lurch through them; the pools settle on the marble' (*CSF* 136). Longer stories in the collection explore the way objects are transformed by perception. 'The Mark on the Wall', for instance, subsumes the objects of perception in the play of consciousness upon them, as the narrator ponders the turns of her own thoughts when she notices a black spot. Meandering from meditations on what the mark might be (is it a nail, a hole, a small rose leaf?) to the associations it prompts (how many objects one loses in a lifetime!), the story provides a metacommentary on socially sanctioned knowledge and the way the mind catches hold of ideas as they pass.

Woolf affiliated her third novel, *Jacob's Room*, with these briefer works, imagining them all 'taking hands & dancing in unity' (*D2* 14). But where the short fiction attends to at most a few minds, the novel juxtaposes a drastically expanded range of consciousnesses. In doing so it experiments radically with narrative form, for Woolf refuses to structure *Jacob's Room* through realist plot conventions or the coherence of an omniscient narrative view.[16] Instead the novel was to have, as she put it, 'no scaffolding' (*D2* 13). She presents its protagonist, the young Jacob Flanders—who will die in World War I before the novel's end—through 'a polyphony of ... voices' of some 160 characters.[17] The novel's resistance to giving the reader any authoritative perspective by multiplying views that do not ultimately cohere suggests that the world consists of incommensurable minds. It also makes visible how far the objects of perception are invented rather than known. Each character sees a different Jacob; their thoughts reveal their own subjectivities and social predicaments more than they do his. Indeed, though we occasionally inhabit Jacob's view, the novel never fully articulates his consciousness. The result both marks him as a mere type—a conventional young man formed by the institutions of pre-war England—and suggests that other minds remain essentially unknowable to us.[18]

Jacob's Room is the high point of Woolf's Impressionist experiments. In her subsequent work, rather than rejecting frame and shape, she will investigate different sorts of fictional 'scaffoldings'. But her writing retains Impressionism's premise that we make meaning of the world by filtering it through our perceptions. Indeed, the social, psychological, and ethical insights of Woolf's fiction emerge from the collision among multiple views, conflicting assessments that the reader must weigh against each other. Thus her next novel, *Mrs Dalloway* (1925), invites the reader to evaluate Clarissa Dalloway's life through her own judgement of its worth and also that of others. It asks the reader to comprehend post-war London through the jostling perspectives of characters, major and minor, who see the same things (a paused motorcar, advertising skywriting, an unhappy couple in the park), but interpret them differently. Even Woolf's later novels that, as we will see, have been more consistently interpreted through Post-Impressionism, like *The Waves*, insist on the priority of sensations to experience and the need to juxtapose radically incompatible interpretations of the world.

In the novels that follow *Jacob's Room*, Woolf turns her attention explicitly to questions of literary form and pattern. These concerns reveal her increasing affiliation with a later artistic movement, Post-Impressionism. While she learned about Impressionism by reading English critics and discussing French painting, her contact with Post-Impressionism was more direct and intimate: Woolf's family and social circle included all the movement's major figures. She thus shared a personal as well as an

---

[16] Linda Martin reads the novel differently, arguing that the narrator's mind is the 'most consistently developed' in the novel. See Linda Martin, 'Elegy and the Unknowable Mind in *Jacob's Room*', *Studies in the Novel* 47, no. 2 (Summer 2015), 176–92.

[17] Francesca Kazan, 'Description and the Pictorial in *Jacob's Room*', *ELH* 55, no. 3 (Autumn 1988), 701–19, at 702.

[18] Kate Flint, 'Introduction', in Virginia Woolf, *Jacob's Room* (Oxford: Oxford World's Classics, 2008), xxi–xxviii, at xvii.

intellectual relationship with the movement, living through its public events as well as sharing its ideas.

Indeed Post-Impressionism seemed to arrive on the British art scene *as* an event. In November 1910, well before Woolf began writing fiction and testing the literary experiments that would lead up to *Jacob's Room*, her friend the art critic Roger Fry opened the innovative exhibit *Manet and the Post-Impressionists* at the Grafton Gallery in London.[19] The show was designed to introduce modern French painting—including work by Paul Cézanne, Paul Gauguin, and Vincent van Gogh—to a British audience. It produced immediate shock waves in the British art world and society. Critics reacted with disgust and scorn, attacking the paintings as barbaric—their colours intense and unnatural, their technique lacking refinement. The influential *Times*, Woolf noted, described the exhibit as 'the rejection of all that civilization has done' (*RF* 155). 'The public in 1910 was thrown into paroxysms of rage and laughter' (*RF* 153). As Desmond MacCarthy, the exhibition secretary, recalled, 'One great lady asked to have her name removed from the Committee. One gentleman ... laughed so loud at Cézanne's portrait of his wife that "he had to be taken out and walked up and down in the fresh air for five minutes"' (qtd. in *RF* 154). But however resistant the public, the conventional press, and the art establishment, the first Post-Impressionist exhibit helped initiate an avant-garde art scene in pre-war London and galvanized a new generation of artists in England. A second show followed in 1912, including work by young British painters, among them Woolf's sister. By the 1920s, when Woolf looked back, Post-Impressionism had been accepted by the mainstream art world and work from Fry's first exhibit hung in the National Gallery.[20]

Woolf's Bloomsbury circle encompassed Post-Impressionism's central advocates and practitioners. Both Fry and MacCarthy were close friends of Woolf and her husband Leonard; Leonard himself would serve as secretary for the second exhibit. Vanessa, whose paintings appeared in this second show, became one of England's most important Post-Impressionist artists. Vanessa's husband, the art critic Clive Bell, wrote the introduction to the second exhibition catalogue and became one of the main theorists of the movement; the Post-Impressionist painter Duncan Grant lived with Vanessa after she separated from Clive.

Post-Impressionist cultural events yielded frivolous pleasures too. In 1911, Virginia and Vanessa, along with other Bloomsburyites, attended a fancy-dress dance costumed as 'Gauguin girls'.[21] Vanessa later described this Post-Impressionist Ball for the Memoir Club, remembering that 'we got stuffs I had lately found at Burnetts' made for natives in Africa with which we draped ourselves, we wore brilliant flowers and beads, we

---

[19] Critics often cite this exhibit as Woolf's reference point for the tongue-in-cheek claim in 'Character in Fiction' (1924): 'On or about December 1910, human character changed' (*E3* 421).

[20] Jonathan R. Quick, 'Virginia Woolf, Roger Fry and Post-Impressionism', *The Massachusetts Review* 26, no. 4 (Winter 1985), 547–70, at 548.

[21] Hermione Lee, *Virginia Woolf* (New York: Vintage Press, 1999), 287.

browned our legs and arms and had very little on beneath the draperies'.[22] Although she recalls that respectable members of the party were 'horrified'—and her son Quentin writes that 'indignant ladies ... swept out in protest'—Vanessa recollects her friends' exhilaration.[23] 'Our own pleasure in our appearance was such that we decided to paint ourselves or such of ourselves as weren't painters'.[24] Bloomsbury here shared modernist art's troubling fascination with racial primitivism. Merging Gaugin's Tahitians with Africans, Vanessa relished dressing as the fantasy of a composite non-Westerner. In this, the party also echoed the group's more notorious Dreadnought Hoax of a year earlier, in which Woolf, her brother Adrian, and several friends dressed up as the Emperor of Abyssinia and his entourage, spoke an invented mock-African language, and fooled the British navy into welcoming them aboard the British battleship HMS Dreadnought as an official delegation.[25]

As an aesthetic movement, however, visual Post-Impressionism explored a cohesive set of artistic principles. It shared many of painterly Impressionism's concerns, most notably by using vibrant, non-naturalistic colour to move the viewer. MacCarthy's introduction to the first exhibit's catalogue concedes that its 'connection with Impressionism is extremely close'.[26] However, advocates of the new movement often defined it as a reaction to what they saw as Impressionist principles. Fry, Post-Impressionism's earliest and most consistent advocate, set the new painting against its predecessor. In a 1908 letter to the *Burlington Magazine* entitled 'The Last Phase of Impressionism', he criticized the earlier movement as an unfiltered naturalism, while looking for signs of a new art that might replace it.

> Impressionism accepts the totality of appearances and shows how to render that; but thus to say everything amounts to saying nothing—there is left no power to express the personal attitude and emotional conviction. The organs of expression—line, mass, colour—have become so fused together, so lost in the flux of appearance, that they cease to deliver an intelligible message.[27]

---

[22] Vanessa Bell, 'Memories of Roger Fry', in Lia Giachero, ed., *Sketches in Pen and Ink* (London: Pimlico Press, 1998), 117–47, at 133–4.

[23] V. Bell, 'Memories of Roger Fry', 134. Quentin Bell, *Virginia Woolf: A Biography* (New York: Harcourt, 1972), 170.

[24] V. Bell, 'Memories of Roger Fry', 134. Woolf too mentions this, in a letter to Molly MacCarthy, 'I have to dress up again as a South Sea Savage, to figure in a picture. It's an awful bore!' (*L1* 455).

[25] On the hoax and the press response see Lee, *Virginia Woolf*, 278–83; Urmila Seshagiri, 'Orienting Virginia Woolf: Race, Aesthetics, and Politics in *To the Lighthouse*', *Modern Fiction Studies* 50, no. 1 (Spring 2004), 58–84, at 63–5.

[26] Desmond MacCarthy, 'The Post-Impressionists', in J. B. Bullen, ed., *Post-Impressionists in England* (London: Routledge, 1988), 94–9, at 95.

[27] Roger Fry, 'The Last Phase of Impressionism', in Christopher Reed, ed., *A Roger Fry Reader* (Chicago: University of Chicago Press, 1996), 72–5, at 73.

While Fry acknowledges resemblances between the two modes of art, not least as pivotal moments of aesthetic transformation, he emphasizes the way Post-Impressionists turn away from a fidelity to the 'appearance' of the external world.

Fry proposes that Post-Impressionists, in contrast, 'stir the imagination [of the viewer] most deeply' by foregrounding painting's compositional structure, especially by reviving the outline that Impressionism obscured, fusing it with colour.[28] Writing of Cézanne and Gauguin, he stresses 'They have already attained to the contour, and assert its value with keen emphasis. They fill the contour with wilfully simplified and unmodulated masses.'[29] He will continue in numerous essays to locate the essential virtue of the new movement in the way its emphasis on line and pattern produces an abstract compositional unity made of mass, colour, and form. We can see examples of this focus, not only in the work of a painter like Cézanne, whom Fry idealized for the way 'all is reduced to the purest terms of structural design', but also in the work of Vanessa Bell.[30] Bell's paintings characteristically render domestic or social scenes through partial abstraction, emphasizing the balance of masses in a canvas as both compositional unity and commentary on the gendered worlds she represents. In work like *A Conversation* (1913–1916) or *Studland Beach* (1912), she 'distil[s]' female and familial 'social experience' and the complex dynamics of feminine communication and alienation into counterbalanced, semi-abstract masses.[31]

After writing *Jacob's Room*, Woolf increasingly searched for literary forms that she imagined lie beneath conventional character and plot, and she turned to comparably spatial metaphors for her narrative method.[32] In contrast to her earlier aspiration to create a novel with 'no scaffolding', she describes the composition of *Mrs Dalloway* in terms of deep structure. Writing in her diary about the novel's composition, she feels most confident about the book's 'design' (*D2* 272), and sees her new method as 'dig[ging] out beautiful caves behind my characters… The idea is that the caves shall connect, & each comes to daylight at the present moment' (*D2* 263). As Banfield has discussed, both Woolf and Fry share this ideal with Cambridge philosophers like Bertrand Russell and Alfred North Whitehead, whose theories of knowledge analyse the mind less through its reliance on sight than through a more essential logical structure.[33]

---

[28] Roger Fry, 'Post Impressionism', in Christopher Reed, ed., *A Roger Fry Reader* (Chicago: University of Chicago Press, 1996), 99–110, at 100.

[29] Fry, 'Last Phase', 73.

[30] Fry, 'Paul Cézanne', in J. B. Bullen, ed., *Vision and Design* (Mineola, NY: Dover Press, 1998), 179–85, at 185.

[31] Lisa Tickner, qtd. in Grace Brockington, 'Relationships: Formal, Creative and Political', in Grace Brockington, ed., *In Focus: Abstract Painting c. 1914 by Vanessa Bell* (London: Tate Research Publication, 2017), www.tate.org.uk/research/publications/in-focus/abstract-painting-vanessa-bell/relationships.

[32] Quick, 567.

[33] Banfield draws attention to the way Woolf figures insight through visual perception even as she offers the contrary figure of 'reality itself' (Banfield, *The Phantom Table*, 252) as something that cannot be visualized, '"all eyeless and featureless"' (*D3* 76; qtd in Banfield, *The Phantom Table*, 252).

Woolf will investigate how aesthetic principles can be faithful both to sensory impressions and to a deeper logic. In *To the Lighthouse* (1927), the novel she wished she had dedicated to Fry, Woolf makes these premises explicit by taking a painter, Lily Briscoe, as one of her protagonists. Lily visits the Ramsay family in Cornwall and struggles to capture on canvas the house and her beloved Mrs Ramsay herself—both before and after Mrs Ramsay's death. As she does so, she thinks about her art in Post-Impressionist terms, wrestling with the importance of colour, design, and unity. But these problems are far from merely formal in the novel. Woolf wrote *To the Lighthouse* to memorialize her parents and understand her own grief. Through Lily, she joins questions of technique to the problem of how art can pay tribute to human relationships in non-representational terms.

In *To the Lighthouse* Lily searches for a new principle of composition as she paints. She focuses on her design and on stark colour in part to rebut a tamed version of Impressionism, exemplified by a popular visiting artist whose faint hues and 'etherealized' shapes Lily and the novel seem to reject (*TL* 67). Approaching her canvas in the novel's first section, she thinks, 'The jacmanna was bright violet; the wall staring white. She would not have considered it honest to tamper with the bright violet and the staring white, since she saw them like that, fashionable though it was, since Mr Paunceforte's visit, to see everything pale, elegant, semi-transparent' (*TL* 26). We can recognize affinities here with Fry's belief that Impressionism lacked the 'emotional conviction' of the new movement he calls for.[34] But *To the Lighthouse* does not wholly reject the premises of this earlier movement. Lily considers Paunceforte's style less 'honest' than the approach she seeks, but she uses the language of Impressionism in doing so. She insists on fidelity to what she *sees*, invoking perception as one of the standards to which art must be true. Throughout the novel, Woolf joins the language of the senses she developed in writing about impressions with a discussion of shape and structure. She merges both in the simultaneously perceptual and abstractly creative notion of vision with which Lily ends the novel: 'It was done; it was finished. Yes, she thought ... I have had my vision' (*TL* 281).

Readers who seek Post-Impressionist theories will be alert to the way Lily thinks about her canvas in terms of the formal structures that unify a work of art: 'Then beneath the colour there was the shape' (*TL* 27). Here she echoes not only Fry's theories, but the more widely-circulated polemical claims of Clive Bell in his 1913 manifesto, *Art*. Bell insists that the essence of all good art is 'significant form', the combination of lines, colours, and forms that alone 'stir[s] our aesthetic emotions'.[35] Lily repeats similar terms throughout the novel, expanding their resonance from the visual composition of her painting to a broader aspiration to comprehend an underlying non-representational truth: 'But what she wished to get hold of was that very jar on the nerves, the thing itself before it has

---

[34] Fry, 'Last Phase', 73.
[35] Clive Bell, *Art* (New York: Perigee Books, 1981), 17.

been made anything' (*TL* 260–1). However Lily's painting is not simply about the composition of lines or a solely aesthetic emotion, but also about the human relationships and desires art can evoke. Like Vanessa Bell, she uses abstraction to recreate the essence of domestic bonds. Indeed, she considers intimacy between people to be the mystery at the heart of life. 'What art was there, known to love or cunning, by which one pressed through into those secret chambers [of another's heart]?', she wonders, thinking of Mrs Ramsay. 'What device for becoming, like waters poured into one jar, inextricably the same, one with the object one adored?' (*TL* 70).

When Lily paints, she tries to capture the essence of Mrs Ramsay, who appears to her in intimate relation to others—to her son James, and then to Lily herself. As she explains to Mr Bankes early in the novel, her painting 'reverence[s]' Mrs Ramsay while refusing to represent her realistically. When Mr Bankes asks, 'What did she wish to indicate by the triangular purple shape, "just there?"' (*TL* 72), Lily responds:

> It was Mrs Ramsay reading to James, she said. She knew his objection—that no one could tell it for a human shape. But she had made no attempt at likeness, she said. For what reason had she introduced them then? He asked. Why indeed?—except that if there, in that corner, it was bright, here, in this, she felt the need of darkness.... Mr Bankes was interested. Mother and child then—objects of universal veneration... might be reduced, he pondered, to a purple shadow without irreverence.
>
> But the picture was not of them, she said. Or, not in his sense. There were other senses, too, in which one might reverence them. By a shadow here and a light there, for instance. Her tribute took that form, if, as she vaguely supposed, a picture must be a tribute. A mother and child might be reduced to a shadow without irreverence. (*TL* 72–3)

Lily's purple triangle supports the painting's compositional demand: to balance a bright corner with a dark shape. But more importantly the abstraction summons Mrs Ramsay reading to her son without resorting to 'likeness', providing 'other senses... in which one might reverence' the intimacy between people.

In *To the Lighthouse*, form crucially provides a model for bridging daily life and art. When Lily considers her memories, for instance, she becomes aware that they function 'like a work of art' (*TL* 217). The resemblance allows her to recognize art in Mrs Ramsay's own compositional skills:

> Mrs Ramsay bringing them together; Mrs Ramsay saying 'Life stand still here'; Mrs Ramsay making of the moment something permanent (as in another sphere Lily herself tried to make of the moment something permanent)—this was of the nature of a revelation. In the midst of chaos there was shape; this eternal passing and flowing... was stuck [*sic*] into stability. Life stand still here, Mrs Ramsay said.... She owed this revelation to her. (*TL* 218)

The passage explicitly links Lily's own painting and Mrs Ramsay's ability to make the moment permanent. Both summon a Post-Impressionist anxiety about the fleeting and ephemeral that critics like Fry projected onto Impressionism, proposing that art can give form and permanence to this flux.

Lily's 'revelation' is central to the novel. Her work does not simply strive to create an aesthetically balanced composition, or to evoke Mrs Ramsay through abstraction, but also to embody the simultaneous existence of art within ordinary life and painting. Thus when a stray movement in the house throws a new 'triangular shadow over the step' in the final section, she seizes the opportunity. 'One wanted, she thought, dipping her brush deliberately, to be on a level with ordinary experience, to feel simply that's a chair, that's a table, and yet at the same time, it's a miracle, it's an ecstasy. The problem might be solved after all' (*TL* 272). Immediately after, her longing for Mrs Ramsay resolves. Her grief 'too became part of ordinary experience, was on a level with the chair, with the table' and Mrs Ramsay herself reappears, 'casting her shadow on the step. There she sat' (*TL* 272). Lily's illumination concludes her mourning and art at once.

To the Lighthouse articulates Post-Impressionist ideas about artistic structure and abstraction more explicitly and affirmatively than do Woolf's other novels. However, these same issues also recur through much of her writing from *Mrs Dalloway* through her most experimental novel, *The Waves* (1931). *Mrs Dalloway* not only explores characters' consciousnesses in Impressionist fashion but compresses the novel to the shape of a single day. This structure allows the narrative to comment on Clarissa's thoughts about mortality and human connection, as it sets the relentlessly linear progression of the day's clock time against alternative modes of temporality, recursive and circular, emerging in metaphorical motifs and narrative flashbacks.

The Waves offers the high point of Woolf's formal composition. Imagined as an 'abstract, mystical, eyeless book' (*D3* 203), it presents the monologues of six speakers at a series of discrete life stages, from childhood to death. *The Waves* frames these stages and their implicit linearity, by bracketing them with italicized interludes that describe the progression of light in an uninhabited house over the course of a day. Similarly the interludes' waves on the beach provide a cyclical form for the speakers, rising individually and crashing back into the undifferentiated ocean.

These speakers—less realist characters than voices marked by image clusters and varying social backgrounds—seek patterns much like those structuring the novel.[36] Louis, for instance returns several times to the image of a circular chain, using it to evoke a unity deeper than sensations or individuation. He notes that although the characters '"have tried to accentuate differences ... there is a chain whirling round, round, in a steel-blue circle beneath"' (*W* 108). The other outsider in *The Waves*, Rhoda, also looks for solace in forms that she imagines are deeper than the social world. '"But what is the thing that lies beneath the semblance of the thing? ... let me see the thing. There is a square; there is an oblong.... The structure is now visible; what is inchoate is here stated"' (*W* 128–9).

---

[36] Woolf puzzles in her diary that a reviewer for The Times 'shd praise my characters when I meant to have none' (*D4* 47).

While offering an experimental example of how fiction might share Post-Impressionism's concern with abstract pattern, *The Waves* also begins to suggest Woolf's growing dissatisfaction with abstraction as an overarching principle. The novel begins to question the limits of abstract form metaphorically. Louis's 'steel-blue circle' is coercive as well as foundational, and Rhoda's square and oblong offer an inadequate escape from the terrors of crowds and social expectations. Pattern gives shape, but it also confines.

In Woolf's final novels, which follow *The Waves*, she increasingly questions the promise of compositional, as well as social, unity. As a result, she moves away from the abstracted structures of Post-Impressionism, and even to an extent from the Impressionist vision of perception remaking the world into sheer colour. In *The Years* (1937), while the central character Eleanor Pargiter wonders whether life is shaped by 'a gigantic pattern, momentarily perceptible' (*Y* 333), the novel stretches compositional unity beyond cohesion. It spreads across multiple generations and spaces, rising to many moments of revelation but always falling away again into the disparate details of ordinary life. Woolf's final novel, *Between the Acts* (1941), written against the civilization-dissolving forces of World War II, consistently expresses scepticism about the power of art to compel unity. Instead it emphasizes disruption and fragmentation. The novel's central event, a village pageant, tries to bring a community together by compressing all of English history into one performance. But the pageant is notable instead for the gaps between its scenes and above all for the echoing gramophone which suggests that those who listen are just 'scraps, orts and fragments' (*BA* 135–6), as it repeats '*dispersed are we*' (*BA* 69, 141–2). These late novels focus on the violence and authoritarianism spreading across Europe. In that context, Woolf suggests, art is better suited to exploring the gaps in form, the spaces that prevent art and society from cohering, rather than drawing them together in unified composition.

It was also under the shadow of impending war that Woolf returned to thinking intensely about her friend Roger Fry. Fry died in 1934 and his family asked Woolf to write his biography. Composing this text during the late 1930s sometimes provided relief from the daily anticipation of Hitler's aggression. But it also often frustrated her, as she was constrained by the genre's demands, the bulk of correspondence and factual material she must integrate, and the need to write a work conventional enough to satisfy Fry's bereaved family. It was not, in short, to be the unfettered alternative narration of life's 'unknown and uncircumscribed spirit' that she insisted fiction could offer in 'Modern Fiction' (*E4* 160). However, Woolf hoped to break loose once she could begin to describe Fry as *she* knew him: 'I think I will go on doggedly till I meet him myself—1909—& then attempt something more fictitious' (*D5* 155). When Woolf does so she reveals an incessantly curious, infectiously enthusiastic art lover who fuses qualities associated with Impressionism and Post-Impressionism. Fry is most compelling to Woolf for his ability to see and experience the world anew. He insists that 'The critic...must trust his sensibility, not his learning; he must lay himself open to all kinds of impressions and experiences; to science, to music, to poetry, and must never be afraid to revise a view which experience has altered' (*RF* 116). 'To the end of his life [he] would never write a book or deliver a lecture without seeing the pictures themselves, whether a fresh sight confirmed his opinions or upset them' (*RF* 121). The power of looking was central to what Woolf valued in Fry, and indeed his 'curious power of observation' made possible the revelation of 'some hidden centre' (*RF* 150). For Woolf, then, Fry was less an advocate of one particular school of art, than an embodiment of a new aesthetic and ethical way to understand the world. Woolf's fiction and her manifestos on art sought to make that reinterpretation of the world concrete.

Selected Bibliography

Banfield, Ann, *The Phantom Table: Woolf, Fry, Russell, and the Epistemology of Modernism* (Cambridge: Cambridge University Press, 2000).
Bell, Clive, *Art* [1913] (New York: Perigee Books, 1981).
Fry, Roger, *Vision and Design* [1920], ed. J. B. Bullen (Mineola: Dover Books, 1998).
Fry, Roger, *A Roger Fry Reader*, ed. Christopher Reed (Chicago: University of Chicago Press, 1996).
Goldman, Jane, *The Feminist Aesthetics of Virginia Woolf: Modernism, Post-Impressionism, and the Politics of the Visual* (Cambridge: Cambridge University Press, 1998).
Gillespie, Diane Filby, *The Sisters' Arts: The Writing and Painting of Virginia Woolf and Vanessa Bell* (Syracuse: Syracuse University Press, 1988).
Katz, Tamar, *Impressionist Subjects: Gender, Interiority, and Modernist Fiction in England* (Urbana: University of Illinois Press, 2000).
Lee, Hermione, *Virginia Woolf* (New York: Vintage, 1999).
Lewis, Mary Tompkins, *Critical Readings in Impressionism and Post-Impressionism: An Anthology* (Berkeley: University of California Press, 2007).
Matz, Jesse, *Lasting Impressions: The Legacies of Impressionism in Contemporary Culture* (New York: Columbia University Press, 2016).
Matz, Jesse, *Literary Impressionism and Modernist Aesthetics* (Cambridge: Cambridge University Press, 2001).
Rubin, James H., *Impressionism* (London: Phaidon Press, 1999).

CHAPTER 25

OCEANS AND EMPIRE

MAXWELL UPHAUS

'*Nous sommes des poissons*': 'We are fish'. Thus in 1886 did Lord Salisbury, the British prime minister, summarize to a German envoy (in diplomatic French) the core principle underlying his country's foreign policy.[1] Salisbury's statement distilled a self-conception held by many Britons throughout Virginia Woolf's lifetime: a conviction that the sea was so fundamental to Britain's national prosperity and imperial power as to practically be its natural environment, and that in using the sea to create, control, and expand its empire, Britain was only doing what it was naturally suited to do. This naturalized connection between the British Empire and the ocean formed an ideological cornerstone of British imperialism.

Within the first few chapters of her first novel, *The Voyage Out* (1915), Woolf already shows herself to be keenly attuned to the ideological importance of ideas of the sea and Britishness like those voiced by Salisbury. In the novel's third chapter, two passengers join the titular voyage to a South American tourist colony: the imperialist politician Richard Dalloway and his wife Clarissa. Alone in their cabin, the Dalloways discuss how '[b]eing on this ship' heightens their sense of national identity and imperial mission, or in Clarissa's words, 'what it really means to be English': 'One thinks of all we've done, and our navies, and the people in India and Africa ...' (*VO* 51). (Richard's reflections in response to this explicitly invoke Salisbury.) Shortly afterwards, the novel directly portrays the naval power that the Dalloways see as a linchpin of Britain's imperial identity; as it does so, it both echoes Salisbury's 'We are fish' and casts this idea in a very different light. At the end of the fourth chapter, Woolf's characters spot a pair of British warships: 'two sinister grey vessels, low in the water, and bald as bone, one closely following the other with the look of eyeless beasts seeking their prey' (*VO* 72). This ominous description assimilates the warships to the oceanic environment they are patrolling. 'Bald as bone' recalls the 'fossilized fish' with which the novel's protagonist, Rachel Vinrace, toys in an

---

[1] E. T. S. Dugdale, trans., *German Diplomatic Documents, 1871–1914*, vol. 1 (London: Methuen, 1928), 249.

earlier scene (*VO* 14), while 'eyeless beasts' evokes the 'blind monsters ... at the bottom of the sea' about which another character discourses (*VO* 19), as well as the similar deep-sea fauna—'fish with lights in their heads, they lived so deep'—described at the beginning of the chapter in which the warships appear (*VO* 55). By drawing a line between the 'sinister grey vessels' and these forms of marine life, Woolf naturalizes the warships even as she prompts us to look askance at them. The novel presents these means of imperial power-projection as malevolent sea creatures—natural inhabitants of the ocean. In other words, Woolf transforms Salisbury's positive, legitimizing characterization of British sea power into a negative, threatening representation of it, while maintaining the underlying naturalization of that sea power. Woolf's British warships still seem like fish—just predatory ones. In these scenes from *The Voyage Out*, Woolf thus highlights the ocean's crucial place in the theory and practice of British imperialism, and she folds aspects of this maritime-imperial thinking, together with a critique of it, into her own novelistic practice.

Throughout her career, Woolf continues both to draw on and to subvert ideas of a natural connection between the British Empire and the ocean. Fleshing out the way in which Woolf engages with such ideas represents a promising new direction for Woolf studies. Woolf critics have recognized the ocean's centrality in her work for as long as there have been Woolf critics: as Winifred Holtby points out in her 1932 study, the first book on Woolf in English, 'The thought of the sea haunts her writing.'[2] Since the 1990s, scholars have similarly demonstrated the equally haunting presence of the empire in Woolf's writing, and the question of how she represents British imperialism remains a pressing one for Woolf scholarship. Only in the last fifteen years, however, have critics taken up in earnest the task of reinterpreting Woolf's oceans in the light of the integral link between the ocean and imperialism during her lifetime.[3] This burgeoning line of inquiry dovetails with the growing subfield of oceanic studies, which urges renewed attention to the ocean in literature as a location with historical and material as well as purely psychological or metaphorical significance—or as one oceanic-studies manifesto has it, 'The sea is not a metaphor.'[4] Whereas a longstanding view of Woolf's oceans construes them as exactly that—a 'radical metaphor'[5]—these new perspectives in Woolf

---

[2] Winifred Holtby, *Virginia Woolf* (London: Wishart, 1932), 14.

[3] See Laura Doyle, *Freedom's Empire: Race and the Rise of the Novel in Atlantic Modernity, 1640–1940* (Durham and London: Duke University Press, 2008), 413–43; Nels Pearson, 'Woolf's Spatial Aesthetics and Postcolonial Critique', in Jessica Berman, ed., *A Companion to Virginia Woolf* (Chichester: Wiley-Blackwell, 2016), 427–40; Nicole Rizzuto, 'Maritime Modernism: The Aqueous Form of Virginia Woolf's *The Waves*', *Modernist Cultures* 11, no. 2 (July 2016), 268–92; Laura Winkiel, 'A Queer Ecology of the Sea: Reading Virginia Woolf's *The Waves*', *Feminist Modernist Studies* 2, no. 2 (2019), 1–23.

[4] Hester Blum, 'The Prospect of Oceanic Studies', *PMLA* 125, no. 3 (May 2010), 670.

[5] Patrizia A. Muscogiuri, 'Woolfian Seamarks: Commodified Women and the Racial Other on the Shores of Empire', in Helen Wussow and Mary Ann Gillies, eds, *Virginia Woolf and the Common(wealth) Reader: Selected Papers from the Twenty-Third Annual Conference on Virginia Woolf* (Clemson: Clemson University Digital Press, 2014), 179. Elsewhere, Muscogiuri qualifies this metaphorical interpretation of Woolf's oceans by acknowledging the ocean's material, historical importance; see Patrizia Muscogiuri, 'Sea and Coast between Metaphor and History in Virginia Woolf's Writing', in Anna-Margaretha

scholarship stress the necessity of going beyond purely figurative interpretations of oceanic space in her work. Instead, they direct attention to how—in moments like the literalization of British imperial power in *The Voyage Out*'s warships scene—Woolf's portrayal of the ocean responds to its concrete importance for the imperial Britain she inhabited.

Reassessing Woolf's depictions of the sea as responses to the sea's mobilization by the British Empire can also add to, and reframe, Woolf scholarship's still-developing picture of her work's complex relationship to that empire. By reading Woolf's seas in the light of the imperial culture of her time, Woolf scholars can sharpen their understanding of how and why she reproduces many tenets of that culture. At the same time, such readings clarify how her work resists the imperialist culture in which it is implicated—specifically, how it resists that culture from within, through parody, appropriation, and subversion. Woolf's oceans have widely been seen as spaces outside the scope of patriarchal imperialism. Viewing them this way, however, misses the full force of Woolf's critique. Her oceans should instead be seen as sites where she takes on the British Empire in what men like Salisbury considered its natural element.

Woolf's treatment of the ocean, in short, epitomizes her subversive critique of empire while also highlighting that critique's limitations. Scholars have emphasized Woolf's depiction of the ocean as naturally antithetical to empire: an element that represents resistance to patriarchal imperialism or exemplifies patriarchal imperialism's contingency within non-human nature and deep time. As Salisbury's 'We are fish' and its echoes in *The Voyage Out* attest, though, the imperialist discourse of Woolf's era represented the ocean in a very different way: as a natural facilitator of empire, integral to imperial identity. If Woolf scholars take into consideration Woolf's familiarity with such conceptions, they can better discern how her portrayals of an antithetical relationship between oceans and empire carry a subversive edge. In pitting the ocean against the empire, that is, Woolf was not drawing on an opposition that could simply be taken for granted: rather, she was striking at the core of prevailing imperialist ideas by wresting from the empire the oceanic space that supposedly constituted it. Yet, by focusing on this subversion of imperialist oceanic conceptions, Woolf leaves largely unchallenged, and indeed frequently perpetuates, an imperialist view of the empire's human subjects: Clarissa Dalloway's 'people in India and Africa'. In its emphasis on undoing the empire's connection of itself with the ocean, Woolf's work thus demonstrates profound critical insight into imperial self-conceptions while remaining, in another sense, deeply myopic.

Over the last twenty-five years, a now-ample body of scholarship on Woolf and empire has firmly established Woolf's preoccupation with and opposition to imperialism: in one critic's words, 'that Woolf was in outlook a committed anti-imperialist

---

Horatschek, Yvonne Rosenberg, and Daniel Schäbler, eds, *Navigating Cultural Spaces: Maritime Places* (Amsterdam and New York: Rodopi, 2014), 257–72.

there now seems little doubt'.[6] Yet alongside this account of Woolf's anti-imperialism, a parallel line of criticism has shown how Woolf remained bound up in the imperialist culture of her time—especially in her inability or unwillingness to consider the perspective of colonial subjects, which (it has been argued) reproduces the othering and effacing of non-European peoples that was an integral part of imperialism.[7] In the light of such arguments, the question for Woolf scholarship has become, not whether Woolf remains in some sense complicit in imperialism, but how scholars should 'theorize the *weight* of her complicity'.[8] Does Woolf's overt opposition to empire outweigh her enduring enmeshment in it? Or does the deep imprint throughout her writing of imperial ideologies, institutions, and attitudes render her work's posture towards the empire 'intentionally ambivalent'?[9] One way forward for Woolf critics as they continue to debate these questions is to explore how Woolf contests or draws on imperialist conceptions of the sea—an element whose imperial significance Woolf criticism is just beginning to recognize.

According to most existing scholarship, Woolf's oceans would seem to offer further evidence for a straightforwardly anti-imperial interpretation of her work. Studies of the ocean in Woolf's writing have emphasized the ways in which Woolf positions oceans and empire as inherently antithetical. This idea of an inherent opposition between oceans and empire arises from two distinct perspectives: one focused on gender, the other on nature and the non-human world. From a feminist perspective, one common approach

---

[6] Helen Carr, 'Virginia Woolf, Empire and Race', in Susan Sellers, ed., *The Cambridge Companion to Virginia Woolf*, 2nd ed. (Cambridge: Cambridge University Press, 2010), 199. Important studies of the anti-imperialism of Woolf and her circle include Jane Marcus, 'Britannia Rules *The Waves*', in Karen R. Lawrence, ed., *Decolonizing Tradition: New Views of Twentieth-Century 'British' Literary Canons* (Urbana and Chicago: University of Illinois Press, 1992), 136–62; Kathy J. Phillips, *Virginia Woolf Against Empire* (Knoxville: University of Tennessee Press, 1994); Patrick Brantlinger, '"The Bloomsbury Fraction" Versus War and Empire', in Carola M. Kaplan and Anne B. Simpson, eds, *Seeing Double: Revisioning Edwardian and Modernist Literature* (Basingstoke: Palgrave Macmillan, 1996), 149–67; Anna Snaith, 'Leonard and Virginia Woolf: Writing Against Empire', *Journal of Commonwealth Literature* 50, no. 1 (2015), 19–32.

[7] See Urmila Seshagiri, *Race and the Modernist Imagination* (Ithaca and London: Cornell University Press, 2010), 140–91. See also Patrick McGee, 'The Politics of Modernist Form; Or, Who Rules *The Waves?*' *Modern Fiction Studies* 38, no. 3 (1992), 631–50; Jane Garrity, *Step-Daughters of England: British Women Modernists and the National Imaginary* (Manchester: Manchester University Press, 2003). For an argument that positing Woolf's 'inability or unwillingness to imagine herself into the lives' of non-European peoples is 'ultimately of limited use for thinking about ... Woolf's novels', see Valerie Reed Hickman, 'Clarissa and the Coolies' Wives: *Mrs Dalloway* Figuring Transnational Feminism', *Modern Fiction Studies* 60, no. 1 (2014), 52–77 (quotation at 54).

[8] Jeanette McVicker, 'Postcolonial Approaches', in Anna Snaith, ed., *Palgrave Advances in Virginia Woolf Studies* (Basingstoke: Palgrave Macmillan, 2007), 212. Emphasis in original.

[9] James F. Wurtz, '"I Have Had My Vision": Empire and the Aesthetic in Woolf's *To the Lighthouse*', *Woolf Studies Annual* 16 (2010), 98. Valuable studies of the formal imprint of imperial structures in Woolf's fiction include Jed Esty, *Unseasonable Youth: Modernism, Colonialism, and the Fiction of Development* (Oxford: Oxford University Press, 2012), 127–42; and Paul Stasi, *Modernism, Imperialism, and the Historical Sense* (Cambridge: Cambridge University Press, 2012), 108–35.

to Woolf's seas is to construe them as 'woman's space'.[10] This approach highlights how Woolf uses aquatic or oceanic imagery to represent women's lives and modes of perception, or to evoke what their lives and modes of perception could be like when free of patriarchal dominance. An array of Woolfian female protagonists—Rachel Vinrace in *The Voyage Out*, Cam Ramsay in *To the Lighthouse* (1927), Rhoda in *The Waves* (1931), even the landlocked Clarissa Dalloway in *Mrs Dalloway* (1925)—identify with the sea as a space of authenticity or liberation, while in works like 'The Mark on the Wall', (1917), Woolf envisions such freedom from 'the masculine point of view' (*CSF* 80) in explicitly aquatic terms: '[a] world without professors or specialists or house-keepers with the profiles of policemen, a world which one could slice with one's thought as a fish slices the water with his fin' (*CSF* 81).[11] Furthermore, given the connection Woolf herself establishes between patriarchy and imperialism, such interpretations of Woolf's oceans also view them, insofar as they are intrinsically opposed to patriarchy, as intrinsically opposed to empire. According to Kathryn Simpson, Woolf draws on a conception of the ocean as 'the binary opposite of "masculine" land and all it represents', including 'empire'.[12] As such, Woolf's oceans represent the opportunity for escape from patriarchal imperialism, or at least the desire for such escape. For instance, when Rachel Vinrace is molested aboard ship by Richard Dalloway, the imperialist advocate of 'enclos[ing] ... enormous chunks of the habitable globe' within British rule (*VO* 51), she turns in response to the 'sea-birds' swimming '[f]ar out between the waves' and finds comfort in this vision of what cannot be thus enclosed: '"You're peaceful", she said. She became peaceful too' (*VO* 80). The ocean's status as the antithesis of empire also carries over from escape to resistance: besides standing for the prospect of a 'peaceful' life apart from empire, the ocean can also embody the struggle against it. *The Waves*, for example, likens its titular oceanic phenomenon—'[t]he waves drumm[ing] on the shore'—to 'turbaned men with poisoned assegais who ... advance upon the feeding flocks, the white sheep' (*W* 58). By casting the naturally unruly waves as 'agents of anti-colonial resistance', this simile crystallizes what many critics have seen as the oppositional force of *The Waves*' oceanic imagery and 'saturated', aquatic style.[13] In this respect, *The Waves* provides some of the best evidence for the idea that Woolf's seas intrinsically oppose patriarchal imperialism.

While they illuminate many aspects of how Woolf deploys her oceans, however, the figurative approach taken by such feminist analyses leaves them open to oceanic

---

[10] Anca Vlasopolos, 'Staking Claims for No Territory: The Sea as Woman's Space', in Margaret R. Higonnet and Joan Templeton, eds, *Reconfigured Spheres: Feminist Explorations of Literary Space* (Amherst: University of Massachusetts Press, 1994), 72–88.

[11] On Woolf's use of such aqueous, piscine imagery to suggest specifically feminine forms of imagination and creativity, see Jane Marcus, *Virginia Woolf and the Languages of Patriarchy* (Bloomington and Indianapolis: Indiana University Press, 1987), 151–6.

[12] '"Queer Fish": Woolf's Writing of Desire Between Women in *The Voyage Out* and *Mrs Dalloway*', *Woolf Studies Annual* 9 (2003), 56.

[13] Rizzuto, 'Maritime Modernism', 288, 277. See also Jessica Berman, *Modernist Fiction, Cosmopolitanism, and the Politics of Community* (Cambridge: Cambridge University Press, 2001), 139–56; Muscogiuri, 'Woolfian Seamarks'.

studies' critique of metaphorical readings of the sea in literature. Furthermore, viewing the sea as a material reality rather than a metaphor underscores the fact that no human being could actually inhabit the subaquatic perspective desired, for example, in 'The Mark on the Wall'—that the ocean is, in its material nature, completely inhospitable to human existence.[14] Taking this fact into account, though, arguably only deepens the sea's anti-imperial significance. From a perspective attuned to the ocean's distinct characteristics as a material environment, Woolf's oceans can be seen to oppose patriarchal imperialism not by emblematizing human opposition to it but by exemplifying empire's contingency—like that of all human institutions and structures—within non-human nature and deep time. Woolf often uses the ocean or oceanic life to criticize anthropocentrism and emphasize the inconsequence of the tiny slice of space and time that humans inhabit. In a 1924 review of the new aquarium at the London zoo, for example, she reflects on how 'That crude human egotism which supposes that Nature has wrought her best for those who walk the earth is rebuked at the aquarium. Nature seems to have cared more to tint and adorn the fishes who live unseen at the depths of the sea' (*E3* 404). The ocean similarly decentres or circumscribes human existence throughout Woolf's fiction. *Jacob's Room* (1922) counters ideas of a human-centred universe with 'the old old fact—how there is a sea coldly, greenly, swaying outside' (*JR* 225), while the 'Time Passes' section of *To the Lighthouse* famously depicts humanity's transience in the face of oceanic nature, as 'winds and waves ... like the amorphous bulks of leviathans' (*TTL* 110) wear away at and threaten to engulf the human world represented by the Ramsays' summer home. In such an oceanic universe, the hegemonic claims of empire recede to insignificance or collapse altogether. Bernard, the primary voice in *The Waves*, suggests as much when, describing a visit to Rome, he juxtaposes the fragmented remnants of empire visible there with the ocean's ultimate horizon: 'Imagine ... the aqueducts and the broken Roman pavement and the tombstones in the Campagna, and beyond the Campagna, the sea, then again more land, then the sea' (*W* 150). *The Waves* here envisions what, as Nicole Rizzuto argues, it also asserts formally: the ocean's status as an element preceding, circumscribing, and outlasting everything human, including especially empire.[15]

Whether Woolf's oceans are understood as 'woman's space' or as the epitome of the non-human, in short, they frequently exist in an antithetical relationship with empire. Recently, Woolf critics have begun to look anew at this naturalized antithesis and reconsider the political work it performs. Nels Pearson has proposed, for example, that by associating the ocean with the 'identity-subsuming universality' of abstract global space and non-human time, and by contrasting this oceanic 'universality' with the secure

---

[14] One way in which feminist scholarship on Woolf's oceans has dealt with this fact is by arguing that the ocean represents not just escape from or opposition to patriarchy but also the subordination, deformation, and destruction patriarchy imposes. See Simpson, ' "Queer Fish" ', 57; and David Bradshaw, ' "The Purest Ecstasy": Virginia Woolf and the Sea', in Lara Feigel and Alexandra Harris, eds, *Modernism on Sea: Art and Culture at the British Seaside* (Oxford: Peter Lang, 2009), 101–15.

[15] 'Maritime Modernism', 277.

intelligibility of 'imperially ordered' terrestrial spaces, Woolf actually perpetuates, rather than challenges, an imperialist mindset: 'Woolf... thus stages her continued implication in the imperial binary that opposes historicized or cultured space to global fluidity.'[16] While it has much to recommend it, though, this line of analysis does not acknowledge the degree to which Britons during Woolf's lifetime imagined the ocean as itself an 'imperially ordered' space—the space, indeed, upon which the empire was founded. However paradoxical it may seem today, this idea of the British Empire's oceanic foundation was widely held in Woolf's time. Conversely, while the idea of an intrinsic opposition between the ocean and human polities has a very long history and was certainly also common among Woolf's contemporaries, it could not be so fully taken for granted between the 1880s and the 1940s. The imperial culture of Woolf's upbringing envisioned a natural *connection* of the ocean and empire, rather than a natural antithesis between them. In framing her work's opposition of the empire to the ocean, Woolf does not just envision alternatives to patriarchal imperialism; she does so by reclaiming the very element that patriarchal imperialism saw as intrinsically its own.

Take, for example, a passage from a late Victorian poem that Woolf came to know well:

> [T]hey left us a kingdom none can take—
> The realm of the circling sea—
> To be ruled by the rightful sons of Blake,
> And the Rodneys yet to be.[17]

These lines, from Henry Newbolt's poem 'Admirals All', frequently rang in Woolf's ears around the turn of the century. In a recollection of her father, Leslie Stephen, written shortly after his death in 1904, she recounts how he 'shouted Mr Henry Newbolt's "Admirals All" at the top of his voice as he went about the house or walked in Kensington Gardens, to the surprise of nursery-maids and park-keepers' (*E1* 129). Leslie Stephen was not alone in his enthusiasm: Newbolt's 1897 collection, which included the poem, sold 21,000 copies in a few months.[18] The poem expresses the turn-of-the-century British view that oceans and empire were fundamentally connected. Newbolt asserts that Britain's empire, first and foremost, *is* the ocean. The 'kingdom' bequeathed to the rule of modern Britons by their seafaring ancestors, the 'admirals all' of the poem's title, is not any overseas territory but 'the realm of the circling sea' itself. The sea, by implication, constitutes Britain's dominion: Britain rules the ocean before it rules anything else, and it only rules anything else because it rules the ocean. This poem with which Woolf

---

[16] 'Woolf's Spatial Aesthetics', 432, 437.

[17] Henry Newbolt, *Admirals All and Other Verses* (London: Elkin Mathews, Vigo Street, 1898), 7. Robert Blake (1598–1657) and George Brydges Rodney (1718–1792) were both famous Royal Navy admirals.

[18] Vanessa Furse Jackson, *The Poetry of Henry Newbolt: Patriotism Is Not Enough* (Greensboro: ELT Press, University of North Carolina, Greensboro, 1994), 67.

became so familiar thus encapsulates the sea's significance, both ideologically and materially, for British imperialism.

Newbolt's view of the sea as essential to Britain's 'realm' had an important element of truth. As an array of writers like Newbolt reiterated throughout Woolf's lifetime, Britain's national power and economic prosperity rested on the sea. By Woolf's day, Britain had become the greatest maritime nation on earth: in 1910, Britons owned a third of the world's merchant marine, and British ships carried forty per cent of all seaborne trade.[19] Britain's unrivalled merchant fleet also underpinned its industrial economy by ensuring the dependable trans-oceanic circulation of goods—raw materials in, manufactures out—on which that economy depended. The need to finance and insure its seaborne commerce had fuelled the growth of the country's financial services sector. In short, 'everything that by 1914 made [Britain] economically pre-eminent depended on maritime trade'.[20]

Britain's maritime mercantile supremacy was guaranteed by Newbolt's topic in 'Admirals All': the country's maritime military supremacy. Newbolt's poem recounts the exploits of British naval heroes from the late sixteenth to the early nineteenth centuries. It thereby outlines the growth of Britain's naval power over the same period, a process that culminated in the British fleet's complete victory over its chief rival, France, in the Napoleonic Wars. This triumph made Britain the world's undisputed pre-eminent sea power, thereby enabling the nation's all-important maritime commerce to flow unthreatened. For most of the nineteenth century, Britons took their naval predominance for granted, but by the 1880s would-be challengers were again starting to emerge, posing what seemed to be a renewed danger to Britain's maritime livelihood. Accordingly, Woolf's early years witnessed a surge of interest in the navy and an intensified commitment to maintaining British supremacy at sea. In 1889, Lord Salisbury oversaw the passage of the Naval Defence Act, which allocated £21,500,000 for an enormous naval building programme and mandated that the Royal Navy be kept at a size equal to that of the next two largest fleets in the world combined (the so-called 'Two-Power Standard'). By 1914, the Naval League, the main organization advocating for the preservation of British naval superiority, boasted a larger membership than any contemporary political party.[21] In this environment, the navy acquired enormous popular significance as the guarantor of Britain's maritime lifeblood and hence became a symbol, even an embodiment, of the nation itself.[22]

Beyond its perceived importance for the nation's very existence, Britain's sea power was also the single most important factor in the creation and preservation of its empire—a

---

[19] Glen O'Hara, *Britain and the Sea Since 1600* (Basingstoke: Palgrave Macmillan, 2010), 39.
[20] O'Hara, *Britain and the Sea*, 37.
[21] W. Mark Hamilton, *The Nation and the Navy: Methods and Organization of British Navalist Propaganda, 1889–1914* (New York and London: Garland Publishing, 1986), 23, 33.
[22] See Cynthia Fansler Behrman, *Victorian Myths of the Sea* (Athens, Ohio: Ohio University Press, 1977), 121. See also Jan Rüger, *The Great Naval Game: Britain and Germany in the Age of Empire* (Cambridge: Cambridge University Press, 2007).

fact stressed again and again during Woolf's formative years. A case in point from Woolf's own experience appears in *English Seamen in the Sixteenth Century*, originally published in 1895 by the imperialist historian James Anthony Froude. In keeping with her lifelong interest in the history and literature of sixteenth-century seafaring, Woolf reviewed a reissue of *English Seamen* in 1918, by which point the book had gone through several editions (it would subsequently go through several more).[23] The book opens with a vivid presentation of the empire as an oceanic entity. Britain has 'spread the English race over the globe' and 'made her Queen Empress of India', in Froude's eyes, 'entirely in consequence of her predominance as an ocean power': 'Take away her merchant fleets; take away the navy that guards them: her empire will come to an end; her colonies will fall off, like leaves from a withered tree; and Britain will become once more an insignificant island in the North Sea.'[24] Even more overtly than Newbolt, that is, Froude argues that the ocean constitutes Britain's empire. It enabled Britain to spread its people and its power worldwide and now provides the means of perpetuating that global imperial sway. This depends, however, on Britain's unflagging commitment to maritime 'predominance'. If that sea power disappears—if the navies and merchant fleets of other nations replace those of Britain on the ocean, cutting Britain's links with its offshoots overseas—then the empire disappears.

Froude goes a step beyond simply proclaiming the necessity of sea power to the empire's existence. His simile of tree and leaves also naturalizes the link it asserts between Britain, its empire, and the sea. This image casts the British Empire as a living thing, animated and sustained by the waters Britain rules in the same way that a tree is nourished and its leaves animated by the water circulating through it. As long as Britain remains committed to maritime supremacy, the ocean makes reigning over the empire as natural as the growth and efflorescence of a tree. By naturalizing the ocean's empire-building role in this way, Froude also tacitly assimilates the ocean as the empire's natural element, its essential and intrinsic foundation.

With the sea thus imaginatively annexed as an essential, natural basis of the empire, Britain's seaborne imperial dominance could be presented as equally natural: a matter of geographical destiny. According to the geographer Halford Mackinder, Britain's global maritime expansion was all but foreordained by its status as an island, which gave it 'universality' by virtue of the access it afforded to 'the ocean-highway, which is in its nature universal'.[25] By granting Britain an uninterrupted travel route all around the

---

[23] Alice Fox, *Virginia Woolf and the Literature of the English Renaissance* (Oxford: Clarendon Press, 1990), 32. For Woolf's review of Froude's book, see E2 329–30. On Woolf's admiration for the Tudor voyagers and their main contemporary record, Richard Hakluyt's *Trafficks and Discoveries*, see also Anne E. Fernald, *Virginia Woolf: Feminism and the Reader* (New York: Palgrave Macmillan, 2006). As Fox and Fernald emphasize, Woolf admired Elizabethan seafaring, especially as recounted by Hakluyt, despite, rather than because of, the imperial significance claimed for it by men like Froude.

[24] *English Seamen in the Sixteenth Century: Lectures Delivered at Oxford Easter Terms 1893–4* (London: Longmans, Green, 1901), 1–2.

[25] *Britain and the British Seas, 1902* (New York: Haskell House, 1969), 11.

world, the sea seemed to license the country's indefinite aggrandizement.[26] From this perspective, all Britain had done in acquiring its empire, and all it needed to do to hold on to that empire, was pursue the natural avenue for expansion offered by the sea. This point is made in another study of Tudor seafaring Woolf reviewed, Walter Raleigh's *The English Voyages of the Sixteenth Century*: 'As a people ... we follow the sea; it will be an ill day for us when the tides that wash the world run their ancient courses, and we may not follow.'[27] In Raleigh's conception, British imperialism simply follows the course the ocean sets for it. As long as Britain keeps 'follow[ing] the sea', its power will flow around the world as naturally as the ocean tides.

This naturalizing trajectory culminated in a portrayal of the British themselves as an essentially oceanic people, naturally suited to take to the seas and thereby create an empire. As well as being Britain's geographical destiny, maritime imperialism, in this view, reflected the country's innate national character. James Anthony Froude stated the case plainly: 'the sea is the natural home of Englishmen'.[28] In his capacity as editor of the *Cornhill Magazine*, Leslie Stephen published a wryer take on this idea, Robert Louis Stevenson's essay 'The English Admirals', which argues that the English self-conception of themselves as 'endowed with natural parts for the sea', however 'unwarrantable', was 'seated beyond the reach of argument': 'We should consider ourselves unworthy of our descent if we did not ... please ourselves with the pretension that the sea is English.'[29] Lord Salisbury, as we have seen, gave this line of thinking its pithiest expression. According to Salisbury, to Froude, and even to Stevenson, 'the realm of the circling sea' was not just the element on which Britain's power had come to be based; it was a domain for which its people were inherently suited. In using their command of this oceanic realm to create and rule an empire, Britons were merely making the most of their natural environment. Empire lived and moved and had its being in the ocean.

Woolf scholarship has not let British imperialism's conscription of the ocean pass altogether unnoticed. Indeed, criticism on Woolf and empire effectively began with an essay, Jane Marcus's 'Britannia Rules *The Waves*', which highlights Woolf's scathing treatment of the maritime-imperial ideology invoked in the essay's title. In Marcus's words, *The Waves* is a 'mockery of English maritime power'.[30] By more fully taking into consideration the ways in which British imperial discourse naturalized the empire's connection with the sea, Woolf scholars can better understand an aspect of this mockery that Marcus's essay leaves unexplored: Woolf's recurrent portrayal of oceans and empire as naturally *opposed*. That is, Woolf's portrayal comes into focus as profoundly subversive: a challenge to a core tenet of British imperial ideology. Woolf

---

[26] See Gillian Beer, 'The Island and the Aeroplane: The Case of Virginia Woolf', in Homi Bhabha, ed., *Nation and Narration* (London: Routledge, 1990), 272.

[27] *The English Voyages of the Sixteenth Century* (Glasgow: James MacLehose, 1906), 194. For Woolf's review of Raleigh, see E1 121–2.

[28] *Oceana or England and Her Colonies* (London: Longmans, Green, 1886), 14.

[29] 'The English Admirals', *Cornhill Magazine* 38, no. 223 (July 1878), 36.

[30] 'Britannia Rules *The Waves*', 142.

mocks the maritime-imperial ideas of men like Froude and Salisbury by exploding their naturalizations of maritime power—by asserting that the sea is *not* actually 'the natural home of Englishmen' and that it does not intrinsically animate, convey, and sustain the empire. Woolf's habit of setting oceans and empire at odds punctures these maritime-imperial tropes and severs the empire's naturalized connection with the sea. Moreover, by recurrently depicting the ocean as 'woman's space', Woolf reclaims 'the realm of the circling sea' on behalf of Britain's subordinated, disenfranchised women rather than its dominant, imperialistic men. When, in works like 'The Mark on the Wall', she likens the liberated female imagination to 'a fish slic[ing] the water with its fin', she essentially throws Salisbury's maritime-imperial dictum back in his face: no, you men are not fish; *we women* are fish. In this sense, Woolf's opposition of oceans to empire is one of the most potent ways in which her work subverts contemporary British imperialism.

Simultaneously, though, the nature of Woolf's engagement with maritime-imperial ideology also detracts from this subversive project. Woolf's focus on disrupting the empire's appropriation of the ocean helps perpetuate an imperialist mentality in other respects, especially insofar as it augments Woolf's blind spots regarding race and the representation of colonial subjects. In part, this is due to a fact about the ocean's place in the empire that may seem obvious but bears underlining: no imperial subjects actually lived there. However integral the sea was to the empire, it was not a space in which imperialism's effects on non-European peoples were directly apparent or directly felt—at least not during Woolf's lifetime. (The period of Britain's participation in the Atlantic slave trade was a different story.[31]) Focusing on the sea thus allows Woolf to contest one of the empire's conceptual cornerstones while keeping its human consequences at arm's length, if not altogether out of sight. Like Clarissa Dalloway's in *The Voyage Out*, that is, Woolf's oceanic vantage point on the empire affords, at most, only a distant, condescending view of 'the people in India and Africa'.

Woolf also uses racial difference as a means to the end of subverting maritime imperialism in a way that leaves imperialist ideas about racial difference intact. This dynamic can be seen in one of the most famous instances of Woolf's 'mockery of ... maritime power': her participation in the *Dreadnought* Hoax of February 1910. This escapade involved Woolf and five other Bloomsburyites posing as a delegation from Abyssinia—complete with blackface and, in Woolf's case, male garb—and conning their way into an official inspection tour of HMS *Dreadnought*, the leading representative of Britain's new generation of warships. The hoax embarrassed the navy and made an embodiment of British sea power into a laughing stock: officers of the *Dreadnought* going ashore

---

[31] Although a fuller development of this point is beyond the scope of this chapter, I do not mean to suggest that the legacy of the Atlantic slave trade was not still potent during Woolf's lifetime or that Woolf's work does not reckon with this legacy—simply that the ocean in Woolf's day was no longer itself a site of British imperial violence against non-European peoples in the way it had been during the centuries of British involvement in this trade. For studies that consider how Woolf's work engages with the history and legacy of Atlantic slavery, see Jane Marcus, *Hearts of Darkness: White Women Write Race* (New Brunswick and London: Rutgers University Press, 2004); Doyle, *Freedom's Empire*, and Winkiel, 'A Queer Ecology of the Sea'.

found themselves greeted with shouts of 'bunga bunga', the nonsense phrase with which the hoaxers supposedly responded to everything they were shown on the ship.[32] The hoaxers' use of racial pantomime, however, indicated that their primary interest was in undermining the mystique of maritime power rather than the racial stereotypes that, in practice, they ended up enacting.[33] Woolf was not one of the instigators of the hoax, but her mature experiments with using the sea as a setting or symbol for 'racialized challenges to British hegemony'[34] still typically reveal the grip of imperialist racial perspectives: for instance, *The Waves*' description, quoted above, of breakers on the beach as 'turbaned men with poisoned assegais' is tinged with primitivist imagery and assumptions.[35] Furthermore, such overt associations of the ocean with racialized anti-colonial resistance are the exception rather than the rule. The people on whose behalf Woolf reclaims the ocean from white British men are principally white British women; the 'we' in her version of 'we are fish' remain primarily white and British. In short, Woolf's subversion of imperial maritime ideology both greatly strengthens her anti-imperial critique and, by amplifying her tendency to subordinate or ignore the perspectives of colonial subjects, significantly constrains it.

Woolf's short story 'Scenes from the Life of a British Naval Officer' (1931) exemplifies both sides of the coin. The story is a relatively extended portrayal of maritime imperialism in action, taking its readers onto a warship of the kind that *The Voyage Out* only observes in passing. As it goes through the motions of naval routine in order to satirize them, moreover, the story functions as a literary equivalent of the *Dreadnought* Hoax. If *The Waves* mocks British maritime power, then 'Scenes from the Life'—likely written soon after *The Waves* was published—intensifies this project in a way that highlights both its efficacy and its limitations.

The story's opening locates us in an imperial sea route depicted as a space of energy, vitality, and even violence: 'The rushed waters of the Red Sea dashed past the porthole; occasionally a dolphin leapt high into the air, or a flying fish exploded an arch of fire in mid air' (*CSF* 226). Together with the Suez Canal, which issues into it, the Red Sea formed one of the British Empire's most important maritime arteries—the crucial 'passage to India' that Woolf's friend E.M. Forster had invoked a few years previously. This setting's imperial significance is subtly underscored by its very name, which colours the sea 'red': the classic British imperial hue. The story therefore primes readers to see its ocean setting as an inherently imperial space, pervaded by and conveying the lifeblood of empire. By placing her naval vessel in the midst of onrushing seawater and vibrant sea life, Woolf sets the stage for a view of the ship, and by extension the empire it represents, as similarly filled with life and energy. In addition, by describing the flying fish 'explod[ing] an arch of fire', Woolf gives the ocean's natural inhabitants some of the

---

[32] Peter Štanský, *On or About December 1910: Early Bloomsbury and Its Intimate World* (Cambridge, Massachusetts, and London: Harvard University Press, 1996), 29–30.
[33] See Seshagiri, *Race and the Modernist Imagination*, 146.
[34] Seshagiri, *Race and the Modernist Imagination*, 147.
[35] Pearson, 'Woolf's Spatial Aesthetics', 434.

attributes of the warship in a manner that suggests continuity between them. If actual sea life is fiery and explosive, at least in metaphor, then the warship—with its literally fiery engines and explosive ordnance—might not seem so foreign to the sea, and might, in fact, seem to belong there. In this way, Woolf's opening lays the groundwork for another naturalization of British maritime power: a portrayal of the sea as an intrinsic part of the empire, where the presence of Britons and their ships is as natural as that of fish.

The sketch proceeds, however, in a very different direction. Instead of substantiating a sense of correspondence between maritime imperialism and the ocean, Woolf destroys the basis for such a belief. The titular naval officer, Captain Brace, is immediately revealed to be the opposite of the oceanic world outside his porthole. While the sea and its creatures are almost violently animated, the captain is an automaton. The story follows him through the rigid rounds of his routine: he studies a map and his chronometers, begins charting a course, reviews the ship's company, dines, and climbs to the crow's nest to look through a telescope. Woolf portrays the chronometers the captain studies as 'white faced instruments whose dials ... were moving, sometimes with so slow an advance as to be imperceptible, sometimes with a sudden decisive spring' (*CSF* 226), and the sketch makes clear that he and his crew are more such 'white faced instruments' themselves: machines strictly and mindlessly performing their operations. Everything on the ship is done 'exactly', 'precisely', and as 'an automatic action', without volition (*CSF* 227). When the captain reviews his crew, '[f]ive hundred right hands flew exactly to their heads' and '[f]ive seconds later the Captain's right hand flew to his head'; when he dines, '[t]he red fluid in the wine glass slowly sank, rose, sank[,] rose and sank again' (*CSF* 227). Woolf combines this imagery of mindless activity with a further impression of solidity and rigidity. The captain's face has a 'carved look' (*CSF* 226), and the end of the sketch describes his telescope as 'a horn casing ... enclos[ing]' him: 'When he moved the telescope up and down it seemed as if his own long horn covered eye were moving' (*CSF* 228). From beginning to end, Woolf's representative British naval officer is orderly, regulated, rigid, and inanimate.

The story thus counteracts the idea of congruity between empire and ocean that it begins by evoking. The captain embodies British maritime imperialism, but he has no affinity at all with the oceanic domain that men like him claimed to rule by nature: he is rigid where it is fluid, lifeless where it is vital, systematic and machine-like where it dashes, leaps, and explodes. In this respect, 'Scenes from the Life' echoes Woolf's frequent association of masculinity or patriarchy with fixity, solidity, and structure, opposed to oceanic fluidity.[36] Captain Brace demonstrates an impulse to order, fix, and regulate that Woolf elsewhere casts as quintessentially masculine, as when he charts a course: 'He took a pair of compasses, and began to draw on a large sheet neatly divided into squares a design of such immense elaboration and exactness that each stroke seemed to create an immortal object that would endure precisely so for ever' (*CSF* 226–7). This masculine impulse, the story implies, is of a piece with the imperialism

---

[36] See Bradshaw, '"The Purest Ecstasy"', 109.

the captain also represents, and the captain's chart projects such patriarchal imperialism onto the ocean. The captain rules the ocean on his map, dividing and measuring its cartographic space, just as Britain claims to rule the waves in reality. Yet Woolf disrupts this inscription of empire onto the sea, revealing instead a total disjuncture between patriarchal imperialism and the ocean.

In this sense, 'Scenes from the Life' corroborates a feminist interpretation of Woolf's oceans as 'woman's space', antithetical to patriarchal empire. From a different point of view, the story provides another example of Woolf's tendency to use the sea to rebuke anthropocentrism: it compares the captain unfavourably to the vibrant marine life glimpsed at its beginning in the same way as, in Woolf's essay 'The Sun and The Fish', for instance, the '[b]lue and silver armies' of fish in the London zoo make '[t]he most majestic of human evolutions' seem 'feeble and fluctuating' (*E4* 523). However, the story silently juxtaposes such views of ocean and empire as antithetical with notions of the sea as the natural home of Englishmen—notions that Woolf initially proffers and then proceeds to subvert. This idea of a natural accord between the empire and the ocean forms the story's unspoken subtext, its point of departure. To an audience primed to see an intrinsic link between empire and the sea, Woolf gives a story in which no such link exists. The story is animated by this discrepancy between the 'received idea' that Britannia naturally ruled the waves—an idea '"instinct" in the English imaginary' of Woolf's time—and the reality Woolf depicts.[37] In other words, the story is profoundly subversive: it flies straight in the face of such received ideas about an innately oceanic imperial identity. This also means, though, that the story still assumes certain maritime-imperial tenets: in order for its depiction of complete discordance between the empire and the ocean to have maximum effect, its readers must have internalized the idea that oceans and empire are naturally connected. The story remains bound up with the maritime imperialism it repudiates.

The story's residual ties to imperialist ideology are more glaringly evident in the way that its subversive representation of a maritime-imperial agent hinges on a racist depiction of imperial subjects. Woolf describes Captain Brace's 'carved look' through an extended primitivist simile, which likens his face to a statue 'cut by a negro from a well seasoned log', 'dried in a tropical sun', 'sluiced by tropical rains', and 'erected before grovelling multitudes as their idol', where it stands silently 'for many centuries' (*CSF* 226). This description exemplifies the story's mockery of maritime empire. The simile establishes the captain's stolid rigidity and thereby does the initial work of opposing him to the ocean he supposedly rules. Furthermore, by portraying the captain as an 'idol', Woolf casts the reverence accorded the navy by 'multitudes' of her fellow Britons as only so much empty idolatry. She thus frames maritime imperialism as antiquated, irrational, and superstitious—something with no logical or natural basis. In this respect, Woolf delivers perhaps the ultimate insult to empire: she likens it to its own image of the very type of 'primitive' culture it rules and to which it sees itself as innately superior.

---

[37] Rizzuto, 'Maritime Modernism', 273.

Yet by portraying the captain in these terms, the story, like the *Dreadnought* Hoax, also engages in the same kind of othering and racial stereotyping as the imperial culture it critiques. The very simile whereby the story first goes about subverting the idea of an intrinsic connection between the ocean and empire also reiterates racist assumptions about African fetishism and primitiveness. The story thus strikes at an imperialist mentality in one form while reasserting it in another. Woolf later notes the captain's racism when describing his meal: 'When the hands [serving him] were not white, they were dismissed' (*CSF* 227). However, when it evokes the life-world of 'a negro' in order to suggest that its protagonist not only has nothing to do with the vibrant oceanic world around him but is stuck in the past and lacks a fully realized humanity, Woolf's story replicates the captain's dismissive gesture. Alongside its subversion of maritime empire, the story perpetuates racist attitudes consonant with imperialism—another instance of what Jane Marcus has called 'a racist buzz' audible throughout Woolf's writing.[38] The story's act of subversion, indeed, cannot be separated from the racism it perpetuates.

'Scenes from the Life' thus undermines one of British imperialism's central claims while also highlighting the limitations of Woolf's method of undermining that claim. By making a mockery of maritime imperialism's naturalizing presumptions, 'Scenes from the Life' wrests the ocean out of the grasp of empire. In so doing, the story prompts Woolf scholars not to take Woolf's ocean/empire oppositions for granted. Rather, it highlights how subversive this opposition was, and how Woolf uses it 'to reform the attitudes of her time.'[39] Simultaneously, though, the story shows how Woolf's method of reforming one set of contemporary imperialist attitudes could leave another set of such attitudes unchallenged, and even reaffirm them.

While illustrative, 'Scenes from the Life' only tells part of the story of how Woolf engages with maritime imperialism. We can see this by returning briefly to *The Voyage Out*'s warships scene. That passage subverts the naturalization of British sea power in a different way: by appropriating and recasting it. The strike against *The Voyage Out*'s warships is not that they are completely unlike the sea they supposedly rule, as in 'Scenes from the Life'; it is that they are too much like it. In their predatory prowling through the oceans, the 'eyeless beasts' with which Britain controls its seaborne empire are identical to fish, just as Lord Salisbury said they were—but rather than a natural warrant for what they are doing, in Woolf's hands this becomes a sign of how *un*natural that imperial project is. Rather than openly invalidating the idea Salisbury voiced, *The Voyage Out* both echoes it and critiques it—critiques it *by* echoing it. Like her relationship with the empire in general, then, Woolf's engagement with maritime imperialism is multi-dimensional. If in some cases she simply overturns this ideology, in other cases she incorporates its tenets and assumptions, builds on them, and turns them against each other. Woolf scholarship will need to keep these multiple dimensions in view as it

---

[38] Marcus, *Hearts of Darkness*, 22.
[39] Carr, 'Virginia Woolf, Empire and Race', 211.

continues to explore how Woolf's depiction of the ocean epitomizes her mingled opposition to and enmeshment in the empire.

Selected Bibliography

Behrman, Cynthia Fansler, *Victorian Myths of the Sea* (Athens, Ohio: Ohio University Press, 1977).
Blum, Hester, 'The Prospect of Oceanic Studies', *PMLA* 125, no. 3 (May 2010), 670–7.
Bradshaw, David, '"The Purest Ecstasy": Virginia Woolf and the Sea', in Lara Feigel and Alexandra Harris, eds, *Modernism on Sea: Art and Culture at the British Seaside* (Oxford: Peter Lang, 2009), 101–15.
Carr, Helen, 'Virginia Woolf, Empire and Race', in Susan Sellers, ed., *The Cambridge Companion to Virginia Woolf*, 2nd edition (Cambridge: Cambridge University Press, 2010), 197–213.
Doyle, Laura, *Freedom's Empire: Race and the Rise of the Novel in Atlantic Modernity, 1640–1940* (Durham and London: Duke University Press, 2008).
Marcus, Jane, 'Britannia Rules *The Waves*', in Karen R. Lawrence, ed., *Decolonizing Tradition: New Views of Twentieth-Century 'British' Literary Canons* (Urbana and Chicago: University of Illinois Press, 1992), 136–62.
Marcus, Jane, *Hearts of Darkness: White Women Write Race* (New Brunswick and London: Rutgers University Press, 2004).
Muscogiuri, Patrizia A., 'Woolfian Seamarks: Commodified Women and the Racial Other on the Shores of Empire', in Helen Wussow and Mary Ann Gillies, eds, *Virginia Woolf and the Common(wealth) Reader: Selected Papers from the Twenty-Third Annual Conference on Virginia Woolf* (Clemson, SC: Clemson University Digital Press, 2014), 173–82.
O'Hara, Glen, *Britain and the Sea Since 1600* (Houndmills, Hampshire: Palgrave Macmillan, 2010).
Pearson, Nels, 'Woolf's Spatial Aesthetics and Postcolonial Critique', in Jessica Berman, ed., *A Companion to Virginia Woolf* (Chichester, West Sussex: Wiley-Blackwell, 2016), 427–40.
Rizzuto, Nicole, 'Maritime Modernism: The Aqueous Form of Virginia Woolf's *The Waves*', *Modernist Cultures* 11, no. 2 (July 2016), 268–92.
Rüger, Jan, *The Great Naval Game: Britain and Germany in the Age of Empire* (Cambridge: Cambridge University Press, 2007).
Seshagiri, Urmila, *Race and the Modernist Imagination* (Ithaca and London: Cornell University Press, 2010).
Vlasopolos, Anca, 'Staking Claims for No Territory: The Sea as Woman's Space', in Margaret R. Higonnet and Joan Templeton, eds, *Reconfigured Spheres: Feminist Explorations of Literary Space* (Amherst: University of Massachusetts Press, 1994), 72–88.
Winkiel, Laura, 'A Queer Ecology of the Sea: Reading Virginia Woolf's *The Waves*', *Feminist Modernist Studies* 2, no. 2 (2019), 1–23.

CHAPTER 26

BIOPOWER

MADELYN DETLOFF

VIRGINIA Woolf was an astute theorist of power, although she was not generally considered a political theorist by her contemporaries, perhaps because her understanding of power was inextricable from her feminism, and feminism was at the time considered 'merely' a women's issue and therefore not a matter extending to the whole of the polis. Leonard Woolf's oft-quoted description of Woolf as 'the least political animal' is tempered, Anna Snaith argues, by his recognition of her political awareness:

> In his autobiography, Leonard Woolf wrote: 'Virginia was the least political animal that has lived since Aristotle invented the definition', but he also wrote that she was 'highly sensitive to the atmosphere which surrounded her, whether it was personal, social, or historical. She was therefore the last person who could ignore the political menaces under which we all lived.'[1]

Snaith examines Woolf's complex negotiation of public and private spheres, and scholars such as Melba Cuddy-Keane, Erin Carlston, and Christine Froula (among others) have written thoughtfully on Woolf's role as a public intellectual and political thinker.[2] Given the wealth of scholarship on Woolf's political thought (now recognized as inseparable from her feminism) by decades of Woolf scholars, this chapter will not attempt to summarize the wide scope of Woolf's political thinking, but rather will focus on one aspect of her political theorizing—her early illumination of the workings of biopower and its imbrication with the relatively new phenomenon (in Woolf's lifetime) of fascism. Not content merely to identify the problem, Woolf sought to cultivate what she thought of as an inoculation against ultra-nationalist violence. From a Foucauldian

---

[1] Anna Snaith, *Virginia Woolf: Public and Private Negotiations* (New York: Palgrave Macmillan, 2003), 5.

[2] Christine Froula, *Virginia Woolf and the Bloomsbury Avant-Garde: War, Civilization, Modernity* (New York: Columbia University Press, 2003); Erin Carlston, *Thinking Fascism: Sapphic Modernism and Fascist Masculinity* (Stanford, CA: Stanford University Press, 1998); Melba Cuddy-Keane, *Virginia Woolf, the Intellectual, and the Public Sphere* (New York: Cambridge University Press, 2003).

perspective, such violence is the apotheosis of biopower's employment of 'state racism'.[3] To be clear, Woolf herself was far from perfect in her own resistance to the otherizing lure of biopolitical logic, but her effort to 'think peace into existence' in the last years of her life demonstrates her commitment to divergent thinking as an ongoing practice with ethical and political consequences.

A brief overview of biopower and its connection to 'state racism' will help to set the stage for Woolf's intervention. Like most of the concepts that Foucault develops, biopower is a historical constellation that he arrived at inductively through an expansive analysis of the mechanisms, institutions, and rationalizations for the exercise of power in the 'West' (Western Europe and North America) from roughly the seventeenth through the twentieth centuries. Foucault's hypotheses are not as meticulous as historians or political scientists might desire, but as speculations on the history of thought they are useful for formulating questions about why certain forms of and rationalizations for power gained traction at particular times and places. Not incidentally, Woolf found the question 'why?' especially powerful for breaking open unexamined pieties and staid conventions.[4]

Biopower is the third type of power system that Foucault describes in 'Right of Death and Power over Right', the final section of his 1976 *La Volonté de Savoir* (*The Will to Knowledge*), originally translated into English as *The History of Sexuality Volume One*.[5] While Foucault's three formulations of power (sovereign, disciplinary, and bio-) appear to develop sequentially in his history, he is clear that they are not mutually exclusive. Sovereign power, associated with the right of a ruler 'to take life or let live' and therefore more prevalent in pre-Enlightenment monarchies than parliamentary republics, is still wielded by contemporary democratic republics that exercise the death penalty, for example.[6] Disciplinary power, arising for Foucault in the seventeenth century and 'centered on the body as a machine' that undergoes rigorous training for maximal self-control and efficiency, coexists with the slightly later appearance of biopower, which is concerned with the 'species body, the body imbued with the mechanics of life and serving as the basis of the biological process' and regulated through a 'biopolitics of the population'.[7] Disciplinary power is focused on the individual at the level of the body, while biopower is focused on the masses at the level of population. Foucault explains this bifurcation more clearly in his 1976 lecture, 'Society Must be Defended':

---

[3] Michel Foucault, ' "Society Must Be Defended", Lecture at The Collège de France, March 17, 1976', in Timothy Campbell and Adam Sitze, eds, *Biopolitics: A Reader* (Durham, NC: Duke University Press, 2013), 61–81, at 74.

[4] For example, see E6 30–5. For other discussions of Woolf and biopolitics/biopoetics, see Derek Ryan, *Virginia Woolf and the Materiality of Theory: Sex, Animal, Life* (Edinburgh: Edinburgh University Press, 2013) and Carrie Rohman, *Choreographies of the Living: Bioaesthetics in Literature, Art, and Performance* (New York: Oxford University Press, 2018).

[5] Michel Foucault, *The Will to Knowledge: The History of Sexuality: Volume One*, trans. Robert Hurley (New York: Penguin, 1998). (See copyright page for publication and translation history.)

[6] Foucault, *The Will to Knowledge*, 136. (Italics in original.)

[7] Foucault, *The Will to Knowledge*, 139. (Italics in original.)

discipline tries to rule a multiplicity of men to the extent that their multiplicity can and must be dissolved into individual bodies that can be kept under surveillance, trained, used, and, if need be, punished. And that the new technology [biopower] that is being established is addressed to a multiplicity of men, not to the extent that they are nothing more than their individual bodies, but to the extent that they form, on the contrary, a global mass that is affected by overall processes characteristic of birth, death, production, illness, and so on. So after a first seizure of power over the body in an individualizing mode [i.e. disciplinary power], we have a second seizure of power that is not individualizing but, if you like, massifying, that is directed not at man-as-body but at man-as-species.[8]

For Foucault, the coexistence of 'massifying' biopower and 'individualizing' disciplinary power explains why sexuality (a meaning-making system that grafts cultural intelligibility [or unintelligibility] to our pleasures) evolves as an especially 'dense transfer point for relations of power' during the nineteenth and twentieth centuries.[9] Sexuality is a conduit for disciplinary power insofar as it regulates individual behaviour, thought, desire, practice, and eventually sense of interiority, of self. Sexuality is a conduit for biopower insofar as population, birth rates, and mortality rates are influenced by reproduction, health and illness, and living arrangements (such as families), which all have some connection to sexual practice and social norms regarding sexual relations. For this reason, institutions dedicated to the health and welfare of populations, such as medicine, law, government, education, religion, urban planning, and physical culture have been preoccupied with sexuality.

Sexuality is not the only power-knowledge system that operates in this bipartite manner. Racism and ableism also draw on the individuating, normative force of disciplinary power as well as the massifying, otherizing force of biopower in similar fashions. Nor are these three phenomena—sexuality, scientific racism, and eugenic ableism—mutually exclusive. They are, rather, braided systems (something like the braided copper strands in an electrical cord) that serve together as conduits of power. The strands might be hypothetically separated for analysis, but they work together in ways that are difficult to untangle in everyday practice. Not coincidentally, these strands are similarly enmeshed and examined in Woolf's life and work.

Of particular concern to Woolf, who wrote during the apotheosis of fascism in the early twentieth century, was the otherizing force of what Foucault calls 'state racism' as an alibi for the deadly aspects of biopower (which alleges to foster life rather than threaten death, and thus needs a rationalization for its commitment to deadly force). Woolf is more attuned than Foucault to the links connecting state racism to what we might call 'state genderism', which she analyses in depth in her anti-fascist epistolary essay *Three Guineas* (1938). For Foucault, state racism is necessary to biopower because power that is wielded in service to the life of the people would contradict itself if it were

---

[8] Foucault, '"Society Must be Defended"', 64. (Clarifications in square brackets are mine.)
[9] Foucault, *The Will to Knowledge*, 103.

to engage in the sovereign power to take life, to kill. Therefore, populations need to be separated into the people to be protected and others—beings and groups who are imagined to be threats to the people and therefore killable. State racism thus serves as a rationale for killing others. By extension, state genderism and state ableism serve as rationales for devoting resources to those deemed men and those deemed able-bodied while withholding resources from those deemed not men and/or not able-bodied. As Judith Butler contends, [bio]power construes 'which lives are livable, and which are not' 'by regulating access to resources—material, affective, political, epistemological—that give some people greater odds of flourishing and others lesser (if any) odds'.[10] Biopower, with its braided strands of state racism, state genderism, and state ableism thus begins to look a lot like eugenics with its insistence on the 'health of the race' and the fitness of the individual. The 'health' of the people, the good of the population, the fitness of the race and the life of the (privileged) individual are all biopolitical aims, and they are all caught up in the relationship between reproduction and population. Thus, we can see how and why biopower and the rudiments of fascism co-evolved.

Woolf begins to develop a theory of state racism and genderism in *A Room of One's Own* (1929) through her narrator's meditations on why 'Professor von X' and his ilk are so angry about the supposed 'Mental, Moral, and Physical Inferiority of the Female Sex' (*ARO* 24). While Woolf's text is stylistically playful and wittily hyperbolic, if we follow its logic, *A Room of One's Own* presents a theory of massified othering that is consistent with Foucault's description of the workings of biopower. For Woolf, the sheer difficulty of living calls for 'gigantic courage and strength' (*ARO* 27). To exert at least the fantasy of control over the 'arduous' nature of life, man (more specifically, white man) develops the 'self-confidence' necessary to conquer and colonize by cultivating a belief in his 'innate superiority ... over other people' (*ARO* 27). It is no coincidence that's Woolf's chain of logic ends on the subject of power:

> Without self-confidence we are as babes in the cradle. And how can we generate this imponderable quality, which is yet so invaluable, most quickly? By thinking that other people are inferior to oneself. By feeling that one has some innate superiority—it may be wealth, or rank, a straight nose, or the portrait of a grandfather by Romney—for there is no end to the pathetic devices of the human imagination—over other people. Hence the enormous importance to a patriarch who has to conquer, who has to rule, of feeling that great numbers of people, half of the human race indeed, are by nature inferior to himself. It must indeed be one of the chief sources of his power. (*ARO* 27)

There is a feedback loop operating in Woolf's depiction of the patriarch's power. Self-confidence is necessary to overcome the relative helplessness of living beings (who are

---

[10] Judith Butler, *Undoing Gender* (New York: Routledge, 2004), 4; Madelyn Detloff, 'Woolf and Crip Theory', in Jessica Berman, ed., *A Companion to Virginia Woolf* (Malden, MA: John Wiley, 2016), 277–90, at 280–1.

likened to 'babes in a cradle'). Imagining the inferiority of others boosts self-confidence, which facilitates killing, conquering, ruling others, which reinforces the fantasy of superiority, which facilitates self-confidence ... and repeat. State racism enacted on others is simultaneously a form of bolstering the well-being of those imagined to be the people represented by the state. This is the logic of biopower.

For her part, Woolf extends her analysis to women, developing connections between Foucauldian state racism and Woolfian state genderism in her depiction of the relationship between women (as a massified group) and men (as a massified group):

> Women have served all these centuries as looking-glasses possessing the magic and delicious power of reflecting the figure of man at twice its natural size. Without that power probably the earth would still be swamp and jungle.... Whatever may be their use in civilized societies, mirrors are essential to all violent and heroic action. That is why Napoleon and Mussolini both insist so emphatically upon the inferiority of women, for if they were not inferior, they would cease to enlarge. (ARO 28)

The relationship between state racism and state genderism, however, cannot be articulated as a simple matter of analogy (racism is like sexism, or vice versa) because in any particular context one may be operating more perniciously than the other, and both may be operating simultaneously to otherize women of colour and non-binary people of colour. It important to note that Woolf herself was far better at discerning and describing state genderism than state racism, as Jane Marcus (among others) has argued in *Hearts of Darkness: White Women Write Race*. In her chapter on Woolf, 'A Very Fine Negress', Marcus analyses the exclusionary logic embedded in the passage from *A Room of One's Own* from which Marcus gets her chapter title:

> They [women] are not even now as concerned about the health of their fame as men are, and, speaking generally, will pass a tombstone or signpost without feeling an irresistible desire to cut their names on it, as Alf, Bert, or Chas. must do in obedience to their instinct, which murmurs if it sees a fine woman go by, or even a dog, Ce chien est á moi. And, of course, it may not be a dog, I thought, remembering Parliament Square, the Sièges Allée and other avenues; it may be a piece of land or a man with curly black hair. It is one of the great advantages of being a woman that one can pass even a very fine negress without wishing to make an Englishwoman of her. (ARO 38–9)

As Marcus notes, Woolf's logic in this passage—which begins by critiquing the possessiveness that motivates, for Woolf, not only patriarchal control over women, but white imperialist attempts to dominate lands inhabited by people considered racial inferiors—ventures into trouble through a failure to think intersectionally in the final sentence of the passage. Woolf fails to consider that an Englishwoman can be a woman of colour (i.e. that there are, and were during Woolf's time, Englishwomen of colour). Thus, while critiquing white patriarchy, Woolf nevertheless conflates Englishness and whiteness.[11] Woolf identifies this gambit in her critique of white English colonialism as it applies to white Englishmen colonizing men of colour, but does not extend her analysis to white Englishwomen, who may not have been the main drivers of English imperialism in Woolf's lifetime, but were nevertheless prone (as Woolf's rhetorical slip demonstrates) to conflate the dominant race with the nation. Thus Woolf's critique of state racism and her complicity with its premises are operating simultaneously in *A Room of One's Own*.

It is not productive to excuse or explain away Woolf's lapse. Several scholars, including Maren Tova Linett, Urmila Seshagiri, and Janet Lyon (in addition to Jane Marcus) have analysed and contextualized anti-Semitic, racist, and/or ableist incidences in Woolf's writing.[12] Similar studies have been done of other prominent modernist writers, so Woolf is far from alone.[13] There is much we can learn about the cultural dissemination of biopolitical logic in its braided entanglements of racism, ableism, and hetero-cis-normativity by acknowledging such instances and analysing the cultural work they contribute to the massifying discourse that accompanies and abets biopower. At the same time, it is possible to read Woolf reparatively—meaning to read for the tools she gives us to challenge and combat the lethal logic of biopower while acknowledging and holding her to account for her moments of toxicity or participation in the biopolitical logic of state racism and ableism.[14] On balance, Woolf has more illuminating moments than toxic ones (sometimes on the same issue). For example, she illustrates the eugenicist, ablest, masculinist strains of biopower in her depiction of Sir William Bradshaw, the 'nerve specialist' who insists on divine proportion and arguably provokes Septimus Smith's suicide by suggesting that his life (as someone with a psychiatric condition) is not acceptable, and thus not liveable.[15] Woolf traces even more fully the operations of biopower on the queer/crip character Sara in *The Years,* and she gives us a means to make connections between toxic masculinity, authoritarianism, the desire to possess and control people (including one's children), and national 'memory and tradition' in *Three Guineas*.[16]

---

[11] Jane Marcus, *Hearts of Darkness: White Women Write Race* (New Brunswick: Rutgers University Press, 2004), 30.

[12] Maren Tova Linett, *Modernism, Feminism, and Jewishness* (New York: Cambridge University Press, 2007) and *Bodies of Modernism: Physical Disability in Transatlantic Modernist Literature* (Ann Arbor: University of Michigan Press, 2017); Urmila Seshagiri, 'Orienting Virginia Woolf: Race, Aesthetics, and Politics in To the Lighthouse', *Modern Fiction Studies* 50, no. 1 (Spring 2004), 58–84; Janet Lyon, 'On the Asylum Road with Woolf and Mew', *Modernism/modernity* 18, no. 3 (January 2011), 551–74.

[13] For example, see McIntire on T. S. Eliot's overtly racist early poetry in Gabriele McIntire, *Modernism, Memory, and Desire: T. S. Eliot and Virginia Woolf* (New York: Cambridge University Press, 2008); Barbara Will, *Unlikely Collaboration: Gertrude Stein, Bernard Faÿ, and the Vichy Dilemma* (New York: Columbia University Press, 2011); Janet Malcolm, *Two Lives: Gertrude and Alice* (New Haven: Yale University Press, 2007); Andrew Parker, 'Ezra Pound and the "Economy" of Anti-Semitism', *Boundary 2* 11, no. 1/2 (Autumn/Winter 1982–1983), 103–28.

[14] For more on the intricacies of reading Woolf reparatively, see Madelyn Detloff, *The Value of Virginia Woolf* (New York: Cambridge University Press, 2016), 71–92.

[15] For more on this topic, see Detloff, *The Value of Virginia Woolf*, 58–70.

[16] On Sara, see Detloff, 'Woolf and Crip Theory', 285–6.

When read reparatively, Woolf's work offers a springboard to consider the braided threads of heteronormativity, compulsory able-bodiedness, and state racism as entwined conduits of biopower. The entwining of state racism and state genderism is particularly emphasized in *Three Guineas*, which identifies the enmeshed exclusionary mechanics of fascism and patriarchy, arguing that 'the public and private worlds are inseparably connected; that the tyrannies and servilities of the one are tyrannies and the servilities of the other' (*TG* 214–15). Woolf does not end her analysis by making this connection, but rather contemplates the response called for by that recognition of entwinement: 'But the human figure [of a tyrant or dictator] even in a photograph suggests other and more complex emotions. It suggests that we cannot dissociate ourselves from that figure, but are ourselves that figure. It suggests that we are not passive spectators doomed to unresisting obedience but by our thoughts and actions can ourselves change that figure' (*TG* 215).

Woolf's important insistence that we are not 'doomed to unresisting obedience' may overshadow her other implication in this passage—that 'complex emotions' can inspire change in 'our thought and actions' (*TG* 215). Woolf's attention to affect, moreover, contributes to a peculiar feature of *Three Guineas*—its repeated emphasis on the smell, or 'odour' of sexism in British professional life. Through her use of pointedly olfactory language in *Three Guineas*, Woolf, picks up on the affinity between the affect 'disgust' and what affect theorist Silvan Tompkins calls 'dissmell'—the rejection of something that smells unpleasant.[17] Unlike shame, which involves an unrelinquished attachment to an object, 'in dissmell the object is the object is entirely rejected'.[18] Woolf's evocation of dissmell, therefore implies that biopolitical exclusion operates viscerally, at the level of the body, even in situations that should, on paper, be considered non-exclusionary. Describing the 'atmosphere' that permeates the male-dominated world of 'Whitehall' (a metonym for British civil service and government) Woolf repeatedly references odours, and in one instance, 'flavour':

> We are trying, remember, to discover what flavour attaches itself to sex in a public office; we are sniffing most delicately not facts but savours. And therefore it would be well not to depend on our own private noses, but to call in evidence from outside. Let us turn to the public press and see if we can discover from the opinions aired there any hint that will guide us in our attempt to decide the delicate and difficult question as to the aroma, the atmosphere that surrounds the word 'Miss' in Whitehall. (*TG* 133)

Woolf's olfactory language is thus more than mere wit, although it may undoubtedly be read as a satirical critique of the nepotistic practice of men in power that 'queers the professions' by granting positions to male relatives or the male relatives of friends (*TG*

---

[17] Eve Kosofsky Sedgwick and Adam Frank, eds, *Shame and Its Sisters: A Silvan Tomkins Reader* (Durham, NC: Duke University Press, 1995).

[18] Sedgwick and Frank, *Shame and Its Sisters*, 224.

132). Her sensory language builds upon an earlier premise in *Three Guineas*—that affects such as 'horror and disgust', which, according to Woolf's fictional letter writer, unify herself and her male interlocutor in their response to photographs of corpses from the Spanish Civil War, play an important role in civic life (*TG* 96). Photos are effective rhetorical devices precisely because they are not addressed to logic, but rather to affect:

> Those photographs are not an argument; they are simply a crude statement of fact addressed to the eye. But the eye is connected with the brain; the brain with the nervous system. That system sends its messages in a flash through every past memory and present feeling. When we look at those photographs some fusion takes place within us; however different the education, the traditions behind us, our sensations are the same; and they are violent. You, Sir, call them 'horror and disgust'. We also call them horror and disgust. And the same words rise to our lips. War, you say, is an abomination; a barbarity; war must be stopped at whatever cost. And we echo your words. War is an abomination; a barbarity; war must be stopped. (*TG* 96)

While horror and disgust are apparently unifying responses for Woolf, dissmell is segregating and directed towards others or objects outside the self. Because it is not readily acknowledged as affect by those who express (or rather project) it, dissmell reeks of plausible deniability. The female letter writer in *Three Guineas* thus opens something of an investigation to discover the source of the 'odour' that makes the public realm of Whitehall so inhospitable to women:

> After considering the evidence contained in those three quotations, you will agree that there is good reason to think that the word 'Miss', however delicious its scent in the private house, has a certain odour attached to it in Whitehall which is disagreeable to the noses on the other side of the partition; and that it is likely that a name to which 'Miss' is attached will, because of this odour, circle in the lower spheres where the salaries are small rather than mount to the higher spheres where the salaries are substantial. As for 'Mrs', it is a contaminated word; an obscene word. The less said about that word the better. Such is the smell of it, so rank does it stink in the nostrils of Whitehall, that Whitehall excludes it entirely. (*TG* 134)

Although the words 'Miss' and 'Mrs' appear at first to be the source of the foul odours that 'stink in the nostrils of Whitehall', the narrator's investigation lays the blame on the masculinist culture of Whitehall, rather than on the women who bear the titles of 'Miss' or 'Mrs', for the 'atmosphere' that disadvantages women. 'There! There can be no doubt of the odour now. The cat is out of the bag; and it is a Tom' (*TG* 134). Woolf's colloquialism calls to mind the image of a tomcat marking his territory, thus characterizing the exclusionary attitudes of the men in power as atavistic, even animal-like. Later in *Three Guineas*, Woolf reinforces her suggestion that the male-dominated professions are affectively toxic due to 'their possessiveness, their pugnacity, their greed' by suggesting that women who practise 'mental chastity' (refusal to compromise one's intellectual integrity for money) 'can join the professions and yet remain uncontaminated by them'

(*TG* 163). Woolf finds this integrity, consisting of 'having a mind of your own and a will of your own', crucial to 'abolish the inhumanity, the beastliness, the horror, the folly of war' (*TG* 163).

The charged descriptors—'inhumanity', 'beastliness', 'horror'—explicit in Woolf's call for the 'daughters of educated men' to resist the seduction of war emphasize that 'thinking peace into existence' requires intervention at the level of the affective register. With this in mind, perhaps the term 'biopolitical logic', which I used earlier to describe the conceptual structure of biopower, is less accurate than the term 'biopolitical affective force', which would account for the anger of Professor von X, the horror and disgust of Woolf's fictional letter writers, and the dissmell in Whitehall (*ARO* 26; *TG* 96, 134). The potentially atavistic force of affect, moreover, might explain the brutality of biopower's effects, despite its avowed purpose of fostering life. As Foucault notes,

> wars were never as bloody as they have been since the nineteenth century, and all things being equal, never before did regimes visit such holocausts on their own populations ... Wars are no longer waged in the name of a sovereign who must be defended; they are waged on behalf of the existence of everyone; entire populations are mobilized for the purpose of wholesale slaughter in the name of life necessity: massacres have become vital.[19]

As Woolf reminds us in the face of this brutality, however, 'we are not passive spectators doomed to unresisting obedience but by our thoughts and actions can ourselves change that [authoritarian] figure' associated with what I will call here biopolitical rage (*TG* 215).

The 'thoughts and actions' Woolf advocated in *Three Guineas* and her 1940 essay in *The New Republic*, 'Thoughts on Peace in an Air Raid', involve the cultivation of 'intellectual liberty' and the imperative to 'compensate the man for the loss of his gun' by giving him 'access to the creative feelings' (*TG* 165; *E6* 244). Cultivating intellectual liberty, for Woolf, involves participating in the public sphere without the desire for publicity, something that is achieved through the relative inexpensiveness of reading and writing. At the level of reading, Woolf's letter writer explains why at least three daily and three weekly newspapers are necessary to cut through the partisanship of the allegedly objective news:

> each paper is financed by a board; ... each board has a policy ... each board employs writers to expound that policy, and if the writers do not agree with that policy, the writers, as you may remember after a moment's reflection, find themselves unemployed in the street. Therefore if you want to know any fact about politics you must read at least three different papers, compare at least three different versions of the same fact, and come in the end to your own conclusion. Hence the three daily papers on my table. (*TG* 174)

---

[19] Foucault, *The Will to Knowledge*, 136–7.

The financial precarity of [mostly male] journalists who risk losing their livelihood for straying from the party line extends to women writers. For this reason, Woolf arrives at the controversial position that protecting intellectual liberty depends on having enough money to render one free from depending on one's writing to make a living (*TG* 171). Having enough to live on, meaning a modest yearly income, frees the writer from various motives—power, vanity, publicity, and advertisement—that may get in the way of disinterested thinking and writing (*TG* 175). This somewhat utopian view of disinterestedness is influenced by Woolf's own modest inheritance of £2,500 from her Aunt Caroline in 1909. Biographer Hermione Lee provides some context for Woolf's wariness about editors and editorial boards as well as Woolf's desire to avoid the motivations of vanity or publicity, given that her early journalism was dampened by the censorship of editors as well as internal self-censorship. 'She couldn't be as rude as she wanted to be ... she couldn't speak frankly about sex or religion ... and the *Cornhill* wouldn't call "a prostitute a prostitute or a mistress a mistress," ' Lee explains. 'And she was terrified of showing sentimentality or egotism, and of being laughed at.'[20] From this standpoint, the inheritance her aunt provided her did free her from external (if not internal) censors, as her modest financial independence allowed her to write what she wished to write without capitulating to editors. Co-owning a small press, The Hogarth Press, with her husband furthered her capacity to write on her own terms. Her insistence on the necessity of financial independence for intellectual liberty thus may be coloured by her personal experience of how difficult intellectual independence could be for writers whose livelihoods depended on pleasing the public, impressing an editor, or adhering to oppressive social norms.

Despite Woolf's wariness about journalism, however, she did contribute over six hundred essays and stories to journalistic venues, including the *Times Literary Supplement*, *The New Republic*, *Vogue*, *Good Housekeeping*, and *The Atlantic*—for which she published sections of *Three Guineas* as the lead story, 'Women Must Weep—Or Unite Against the War' in May 1938.[21] In other words, Woolf wrote for the general public even after she received her aunt's inheritance, and this writing can be considered a form of public intellectual work consistent with her call to resist state racism and state genderism with 'thoughts and actions'.[22] Two years after 'Women Must Weep' was published, Woolf recorded the oft-quoted phrase 'thinking is my fighting' in her diary (*D5* 285). She did not mean this in an abstract or passive sense. Thinking and writing were for her the means to combat fascism, or what she and her contemporaries called Hitlerism. She arrives at this sentiment after a meandering account of the mundane events of a spring

---

[20] Hermione Lee, *Virginia Woolf* (New York: Random House, 1996), 214.

[21] For discussion of Woolf's unsigned *Times Literary Supplement* essays, see Anne E. Fernald, *Virginia Woolf, Feminism, and the Reader* (New York: Palgrave, 2006), 85–116. Alice Wood discusses Woolf's *Good Housekeeping* essays and includes a brief note on her *Vogue* essays in Alice Wood, 'Made to Measure: Virginia Woolf in *Good Housekeeping* Magazine', *Prose Studies* 32, no. 1 (April 2010), 12–24. Virginia Woolf, 'Women Must Weep—Or Unite Against the War', *New Republic* 161, no. 5 (May 1938), 585–94.

[22] On Woolf as a public intellectual, see Cuddy-Keane, *Virginia Woolf*.

day sprinkled with the intrusions and tensions of wartime living. I quote this entry at length, as the interruptions of war into everyday life are matched by the interruptions of references to writing. It is almost as if writing is positioned as a retort to war, even in this casual private writing:

> An appeal last night for home defence—against parachutists. L. says he'll join. An acid conversation. Our nerves are harassed—mine at least: L. evidently relieved by the chance of doing something. Gun & uniform to me slightly ridiculous. Behind that the strain: this morning we discussed suicide if Hitler lands. Jews beaten up. What point in waiting? Better shut the garage doors. This a sensible, rather matter of fact talk. Then he wrote letters, & I too: thanked Bernard Shaw for his love letter. Copied my lecture contentedly. A thunderous hot day. Dutch laid down arms last night. The great battle now raging. Ten days, we say, will settle it. I guess we hold: then dig in; about Nov. the USA comes in as arbitrator. On the other hand—Mabel just come. She says theyre building wooden bridges beside the others on the Thames. Pop-pop-pop, as we play bowls. Probably a raider over Eastbourne way. Now thunder rain sets in. L. & P[ercy] discussing Miss Emery's fruit. John wishes we'd come up. Mr Pritchard (the old one) dead at last. No, I dont want the garage to see the end of me. I've a wish for 10 years more, & to write my book wh. as usual darts into my brain. L. finished his yesterday. So we've cleared up our book accounts—tho' its doubtful if we shall publish this June. Why am I optimistic? Or rather not either way? because its all bombast, this war. One old lady pinning on her cap has more reality. So if one dies, it'll be a common sense, dull end—not comparable to a days walk, & then an evening reading over the fire. Hospital trains go by. A hot day to be wounded. Anyhow, it cant last, this intensity—so we think—more than 10 days. A fateful book this. Still some blank pages—& what shall I write on the next 10? This idea struck me: the army is the body: I am the brain. Thinking is my fighting. (*D5* 285)

In this diary entry, Woolf oscillates from matter-of-fact planning in the event of a Nazi invasion, commenting on mundane tasks and events, reporting gossip and speculation about course of the war, sounds of guns within hearing range of her house in Sussex, and existential commentary on the absurdity of war. Woolf ultimately presents herself here as fighter prepared to use her best weapon, 'thinking', to resist the Nazis.

Thinking was not solitary for Woolf, but rather communal and communicated in the form of writing—the action of 'thoughts and actions' that are necessary to challenge 'unresisting obedience' to state racism and genderism (*TG* 215). Thus, Woolf contemplates finishing her book (*Between the Acts* (1941)), copying her lecture (perhaps for the local Women's Institute), and filling the pages she has left in her notebook at the same time that she discusses with Leonard their contingency plans in the event that the Nazis do succeed in an invasion of England.

Echoing her May diary, Woolf formalizes her focus on the importance of thinking as resistance in her October 1940 essay, 'Thoughts on Peace in an Air Raid':

> The Germans were over this house last night and the night before that. Here they are again. It is a queer experience, lying in the dark and listening to the zoom of a

> hornet which may at any moment sting you to death. It is a sound that interrupts cool and consecutive thinking about peace. Yet it is a sound—far more than prayers and anthems—that should compel one to think about peace. Unless we can think peace into existence we—not this one body in this one bed but millions of bodies yet to be born—will lie in the same darkness and hear the same death rattle overhead. Let us think what we can do to create the only efficient air-raid shelter while the guns on the hill go pop pop pop and the searchlights finger the clouds and now and then, sometimes close at hand, sometimes far away a bomb drops. (E6 242)

'Thinking peace into existence', Woolf continues, means engaging in public discourse about the direction and values of the nation, even when one is not invited to engage in that discourse. Noting the exclusive masculinity of the British government, she writes:

> There is no woman in the Cabinet; nor in any responsible post. All the idea makers who are in a position to make ideas effective are men. That is a thought that damps thinking, and encourages irresponsibility. Why not bury the head in the pillow, plug the ears, and cease this futile activity of idea making?

She rejects the temptation of 'irresponsibility' with a kind of pep talk for women:

> Are we not stressing our disability [as women kept out of the seats of power] because our ability exposes us perhaps to abuse, perhaps to contempt? 'I will not cease from mental fight,' Blake wrote. Mental fight means thinking against the current, not with it. (E6 242–3)

In order for thinking against the current to have any uptake, it needs to reach beyond the solitary thinker to a wider community. This 'mental fight' is strenuous due to ingrained 'memory and tradition' that propels the 'current' of thought in the direction of state racism and genderism. In *Three Guineas*, Woolf links 'memory and tradition' directly to education—its mode of delivery as well as its content. Discussing 'facts from history and biography' about access to education for women, Woolf's letter writer notes that battles for access to education 'prove that education, the finest education in the world, does not teach people to hate force, but to use it ... and are not force and possessiveness very closely connected to war?' (*TG* 115). Moreover, memory and tradition are closely connected to masculine rituals of national and cultural belonging, which Woolf satirically describes as processions of educated men dressed in ridiculous ceremonial garb (*TG* 102–7).

For Woolf, 'memory and tradition' as they are conveyed by masculinist educational systems cultivate loyalty among insiders to an exclusive population—in this case, white British men who identify with the Englishness (*TG* 102).[23] It is not unsurprising that

---

[23] On Woolf's 'disloyalty' as an act of resistance to fascism in *Three Guineas*, see Carlston, *Thinking Fascism*, 136–86.

loyalty to the nation is one of the key features of fascism, and that loyalty is both affective and ceremonial, as Robert Paxton explains:

> At its fullest development, fascism redrew the frontiers between private and public, sharply diminishing what had once been untouchably private. It changed the practice of citizenship from the enjoyment of constitutional rights and duties to participation in mass ceremonies of affirmation and conformity. It reconfigured relations between the individual and the collectivity, so that an individual had no rights outside community interest. It expanded the powers of the executive—party and state—in a bid for total control. Finally, it unleashed aggressive emotions hitherto known in Europe only during war or social revolution.[24]

Paxton's mention of 'aggressive emotions' in particular resonates with Woolf's investigation of affect in *Three Guineas*, which I have outlined above. How then, are aggressive emotions lanced and detoxified? Woolf's answer is through a reprogramming of 'memory and tradition' so that the aggressive emotions are discouraged. In *Three Guineas*, she suggests revamping the educational system so that it is focused not on competition and domination, but on living: 'It should teach the arts of human intercourse; the art of understanding other people's lives and minds, and the little arts of talk, of dress, of cookery that are allied with them. The aim of the new college, the cheap college, should be not to segregate and specialize, but to combine' (*TG* 118–19). She goes further in 'Thoughts on Peace in an Air Raid' to suggest that women (a class of people at the time who are less enthralled by 'memory and tradition' because of their lack of access to the toxicity of traditional education) must 'help the young Englishmen to root out from themselves the love of medals and decorations. We must create more honorable activities for those who try to conquer in themselves their fighting instinct, their subconscious Hitlerism' (*E6* 244). While Woolf does not provide a useful catalogue of honourable activities that we can use to counter the lure of biopolitical affective force, she does suggest that affects associated with creativity are key to supplanting the toxic affects associated with war and internal 'Hitlerism'. 'The emotion of fear and of hate is therefore sterile, unfertile. Directly that fear passes, the mind reaches out and instinctively revives itself by trying to create' (*E6* 244). These creative instincts are for Woolf, connective, and therefore appropriate counters to the destructive instincts that are associated with exclusion and segregation. Woolf was not a fool. In *Three Guineas*, her fictional letter writer's many ambivalences and compromises between the world as she wished it to be and the world as it was, indicate that Woolf was aware that 'memory and tradition' were not easy currents to oppose. Her words in 'Thoughts on Peace in an Air Raid' indicate, however, that she knew the stakes of passively consenting to 'memory and tradition', which had become an alibi for the brutal effects of biopolitical exclusion in the form of state racism and genderism. Given these stakes, she was not willing to remain silent.

---

[24] Robert O. Paxton, *The Anatomy of Fascism*, Kindle Edition (New York: Knopf, 2005), Kindle Location 234–8.

Selected Bibliography

Carlston, Erin, *Thinking Fascism: Sapphic Modernism and Fascist Masculinity* (Stanford, CA: Stanford University Press, 1998).
Cuddy-Keane, Melba, *Virginia Woolf, the Intellectual, and the Public Sphere* (New York: Cambridge University Press, 2003).
Fernald, Anne E., *Virginia Woolf, Feminism, and the Reader* (New York: Palgrave, 2006).
Foucault, Michel, *The Will to Knowledge: The History of Sexuality: Volume One*, trans. Robert Hurley (New York: Penguin, 1998).
Foucault, Michel, '"Society Must Be Defended", Lecture at The Collège de France, March 17, 1976', in Timothy Campbell and Adam Sitze, eds, *Biopolitics: A Reader* (Durham: Duke University Press, 2013), 61–81.
Froula, Christine, *Virginia Woolf and the Bloomsbury Avant-Garde: War, Civilization, Modernity* (New York: Columbia University Press, 2003).
Linett, Maren Tova, *Bodies of Modernism: Physical Disability in Transatlantic Modernist Literature* (Ann Arbor: University of Michigan Press, 2017).
Lyon, Janet, 'On the Asylum Road with Woolf and Mew', *Modernism/modernity* 18, no. 3 (January 2011), 551–74.
Marcus, Jane, *Hearts of Darkness: White Women Write Race* (New Brunswick, NJ: Rutgers University Press, 2004).
Sedgwick, Eve Kosofsky, and Adam Frank, eds, *Shame and Its Sisters: A Silvan Tomkins Reader* (Durham, NC: Duke University Press, 1995).
Woolf, Virginia, 'Women Must Weep—Or Unite Against the War', *The New Republic* 161, no. 5 (May 1938), 585–94.

CHAPTER 27

THE NATURAL WORLD AND THE ANTHROPOCENE

CLIFF MAK

Woolf's lifelong engagement with natural history writing, aristocratic sports writing, and evolutionary ethics offers more than mere fodder for her literary figurative practice. Moreover, Woolf herself worried that the cross-species and ecocritical ethics thematized in her work—from the experimental focalization of a dog's interiority in *Flush* (1933) to the repletion of flower's-, snail's-, butterfly's-, and thrush's-eye views in 'Kew Gardens'—lacked any basis beyond mere metaphor and anthropocentric projection. At a number of points throughout her career, Woolf was forced to reckon with the possibility that literalizing too blithely such figuratively based ethics would risk essentializing individuals by reducing their personalities and actions to mere products of animal instinct, and, in the process, actually undercut her own work towards exploring modes of subjectivity and agency beyond the limits of traditional humanist representation. For Woolf critics, too, interested in exploring modernism's ambit beyond the Anthropocene, revisiting Woolf's relationship to the natural world affords an opportunity to contend with the pitfalls and difficulties of deriving an ethics from her work.

There has been no shortage of recent studies on Woolf's relationship to the natural world. Reflecting the rise to prominence of ecocriticism, posthumanism, and critical animal studies more largely across the humanities, scholars have produced a number of important investigations into the status of animality, non-humanity, nature, and nature-cultures in Woolf's works. Bonnie Kime Scott, most recently, for example, has provided a comprehensive survey of the field as it has taken shape, not only taking stock of the numerous subfields of literary Woolf studies that have emerged in the wake of the larger ecocritical studies but also noting how Woolf herself was an important figure for early ecocriticism and eco-feminism some time before the latter was taken up as a critical banner by literary Woolfians.[1]

---

[1] Bonnie Kime Scott, 'Ecocritical Woolf', in Jessica Berman, ed., *A Companion to Virginia Woolf* (Malden, MA and Oxford: Wiley-Blackwell, 2016), 319–21. See also Kristin Czarnecki and Carrie

Indeed, as Scott's survey suggests, such studies have been a long time coming. Perhaps no other major modernist writer (with the possible exception of Marianne Moore) has had not just a body of work but a biography so saturated with interest in and concern for the non-human natural world. In addition to the countless animals proliferating throughout her fiction and essays, for example, Woolf herself was raised in a family that prized the pursuit of entomology, natural history, and botany and, in addition, had strong opinions about the ethics and appeal of related aristocratic sports such as fly-fishing (for example, in 'A Sketch of the Past' (*MB* 71, 135)).[2]

In Woolf studies more broadly, one recent turn has been to read an ethics out of Woolf's aesthetics. Emily Hinnov puts the case succinctly: 'Woolf views aesthetics as a vehicle for social action that might bring about humanistic […] coherence and interconnectivity.'[3] And Jessica Berman more specifically argues that Woolf locates her ethics *in* aesthetic judgement and in the epistemology of immediate experience: ethics here being a folding-together of a Levinasian emphasis on radical alterity and a feminist emphasis on care and intimacy.[4] These readings have come as a corrective to earlier phases of criticism that either relegated, along the pat lines of modernist autonomy, Woolf to the realm of aesthetics—'the immured priestess in the temple of art'[5]—or completely politicized her, reducing her work to a set of ideological effects.[6] Against that tendency to focus solely on one aspect of Woolf, then, these more recent ethical recuperations seek to read Woolf comprehensively, giving credence to the weight Woolf herself placed on seeing the ethical and the aesthetic as parts of a whole.

The criteria of these ethical readings have been naturally assumed by animal-studies approaches to Woolf. Berman's emphasis on a Levinasian philosophy of the intimate, face-to-face encounter with radical alterity in *Orlando* (1928), for example, is echoed quite closely in studies of *Flush*. Alice Kuzniar, in her work on the affective powers of human–dog relationships, celebrates Woolf's account of the therapeutic potential of

---

Rohman, eds, *Virginia Woolf and the Natural World: Selected Papers from the Twentieth Annual International Conference on Virginia Woolf* (Clemson: Clemson University Digital Press, 2011).

[2] For an overview of Woolf's childhood relationship to entomology and taxonomy, see Christina Alt, *Virginia Woolf and the Study of Nature* (Cambridge: Cambridge University Press, 2010), 72–8.

[3] Emily M. Hinnov, 'The Nature of Time and Cosmic (Comm)unity in Virginia Woolf's The Waves', in Kristin Czarnecki and Carrie Rohman, eds, *Virginia Woolf and the Natural World: Selected Papers from the Twentieth Annual International Conference on Virginia Woolf* (Clemson: Clemson University Digital Press, 2011), 214–20, at 218.

[4] Jessica Berman, 'Ethical Folds: Ethics, Aesthetics, Woolf', in Maren Linett, ed., *Virginia Woolf: An MFS Reader* (Baltimore, MD: Johns Hopkins University Press, 2009), 257–79.

[5] The phrase is Alex Zwerdling's and ostensibly a paraphrase of Quentin Bell's characterization of his aunt. See Alex Zwerdling, *Virginia Woolf and the Real World* (Berkeley: University of California Press, 1986), 9. For a critique of Zwerdling's hyperbole and method, see James Gindin, 'Politics in Contemporary Woolf Criticism', *Modern Language Quarterly* 47, no. 4 (1986), 422–32.

[6] Such criticism—as in, for example, Jane Marcus's seminal essay on *The Waves*—reduces even Woolf's undeniably substantial aesthetics to a 'parody' or 'swan song' of the Romanticism that sustains white British colonialism, mocking 'the complicity of the hero and the poet in the creation of a collective national subject through an elegy for imperialism'. Jane Marcus, 'Britannia Rules *The Waves*', in Margaret Homans, ed., *Virginia Woolf: A Collection of Critical Essays* (Englewood Cliffs: Prentice Hall, 1993), 235.

canine intimacy.[7] Derek Ryan, more recently, makes a case for canine subjectivity in *Flush* by naming 'four key moments where Flush and Miss Barrett gaze at each other'; for Ryan, it is Flush's face and eyes that mark a legible site of subjectivity.[8]

The humanistic strength of these ethical readings, however, is also their limitation. While they effectively draw our attention to the work of modernist beauty as an interconnective interface between different human subjectivities and, even, open up a space for thinking about how humans might ethically interact with non-human alterity, they openly rely upon a metonymic understanding of relation that necessarily limits the sphere of ethical relation to beings with some sort of sufficient—namely, facially expressive—resemblance to humans. Thus both Kuzniar and Ryan—and animal-studies approaches to Woolf more generally, especially those that focus primarily on *Flush* (despite the fact that Woolf herself dismissed the novel as 'a little joke' in a December 1932 letter)—propound an ethics of overcoming radical alterity that already presumes and relies upon the pre-existence of a shared but still anthropocentric, discursive grammar behind (and built into) the face of the other (*L*5 140). That is, when it comes to pets and other companion species, the otherness we encounter turns out to be less radical than we at first wanted to believe.

What we take, after all, to be the legibility of canine subjectivity specifically—in their facial expressions, vocalizations, behaviour, sociality, linguistic interpellation—must be remembered, as companion-species theorist Donna Haraway insists, as the product of aeons of human–canine co-evolution, co-habitation, and domestication. (Jacques Derrida, too, speculates from a Lacanian perspective that there can be no desire or even unconscious for animals, except, perhaps, for domestic or tamed animals that have 'translated' into themselves the unconscious of humankind via some kind of 'contagious transference or mute interiorization'.)[9] What may seem each time we meet the gaze of a dog like a spontaneous and epiphanic reckoning with non-human otherness has, in fact, already been deeply conditioned, even predetermined, by history. The animal-studies approach to Woolf that privileges the epistemological novelty of canine faces over and against the fact that canine faces are, in an evolutionary sense, the *least* novel of non-human faces thus symptomatically reproduces and valorizes a modernist ideology that oscillates between the instantaneous and the archaic, between the opaque surface and the bad infinity of absolutely transparent interiority. At its extreme, the temporization of co-evolutionary history demonstrates how easily the moderns' penchant for impersonal mystification lends itself to the mechanics of sentimental, anthropomorphic projection.

---

[7] Alice A. Kuzniar, *Melancholia's Dog* (Chicago: University of Chicago Press, 2006), 120–3.

[8] Derek Ryan, *Virginia Woolf and the Materiality of Theory: Sex, Animal, Life* (Edinburgh: Edinburgh University Press, 2013), 143–50.

[9] Donna Haraway, *The Companion Species Manifesto: Dogs, People, and Significant Otherness* (Chicago: Prickly Paradigm Press, 2003), 26–32; Donna Haraway, *When Species Meet* (Minneapolis and London: University of Minnesota Press, 2008), 15–42; Jacques Derrida, *The Animal That Therefore I Am*, ed. Marie-Luise Mallet, trans. David Wills (New York: Fordham University Press, 2008), 121.

In other words, implicit within Scott's observation that many critical animal studies and ecocritical scholars have found in Woolf a prescient precursor is this chapter's stronger claim that modernist ideology has indelibly shaped key parts of contemporary 'inhumanist'-humanities approaches to the reality of the Anthropocene—and often in a reductive, essentialist manner. Thus, even before attending to recent calls to expand modernist studies' critical remit beyond the human, it is necessary to reassess the ways in which the aesthetic and ideological parameters of modernism itself often restrict the scope of investigation into non-human subjectivity. While the centrality of *Flush* indexes the lasting appeal of a certain strand of modernism for critical animal studies (the convergence of dogs' exemplarity as a co-evolutionary companion species and their exceptional familiarity among the rest of the animal kingdom privileges them as *the* non-human figure for a sentimental solution to the social alienations of modernity), it is the culmination of only one particular stage of development in Woolf's trademark epistemology of intersubjectivity (fundamentally an aestheticized physiognomy). During the later stages of her career, Woolf in fact extends her interest in intersubjectivity beyond human–canine relations to other human–animal configurations, in the process illuminating the ways in which it is not actually anything like 'agency' or 'autonomous interiority' that is naturalized by the epiphanic mode of modernist intersubjectivity but rather the deterministic and disingenuously instrumentalizing 'instinctual' skill of the human observer, or author, herself.

An aristocratic and seemingly arcane tradition firmly ensconced within the exclusive purview of men, fly-fishing is not commonly associated with Woolf. Indeed, previous studies of animals in Woolf's writing have tended to dismiss the ethical and artistic significance that fishing actually had for Woolf, opting to read her father Leslie Stephen's well-known but mild distaste for fishing and Woolf's bland response (as recorded by Woolf in 'A Sketch of the Past') as the starting point for a definitive aversion to fishing altogether—if they note it at all.[10] And as a sport with its own celebrated literary apparatus dating back to 1496 (with the publication of the *Treatise of Fishing with an Angle*), fly-fishing was often given to a rarefied technical pedantry understandably not to Woolf's tastes.[11] Fly-fishing, however, was nonetheless a practice that, in its particular relationship to its animal objects—both as a sport and as a discourse about sport— resonated with important aspects of Woolf's own writing practice. In 'A Sketch of the Past', Woolf follows her anecdote about her father's opinion of fishing with a passage

---

[10] 'It was a perfect lesson', Woolf writes. 'It was not a rebuke; not a forbidding; simply a statement of his own feeling, about which I could think and decide for myself. Though my passion for the thrill and the tug had been perhaps the most acute I then knew, his words slowly extinguished it; leaving no grudge, I ceased to wish to catch fish' (*MB* 135).

[11] The *Treatise of Fishing with an Angle* is attributed to Dame Juliana Berners, to whom is also sometimes attributed the *Book of St. Albans* (later editions of which would include the *Treatise of Fishing*), which was the first text to codify a number of collective nouns for animals that we still use today—for example, a school of fish. See also, for your amusement, James Lipton, *An Exaltation of Larks: The Ultimate Edition* (New York: Penguin, 1991).

linking fishing to a mode of penetrative vision, urban flânerie, and counterfactual speculation unmistakably continuous with her own narrative style:

> But from the memory of my own passion I am still able to construct an idea of the sporting passion. It is one of those invaluable seeds, from which, since it is impossible to have every experience fully, one can grow something that represents other people's experiences. Often one has to make do with seeds; the germs of what might have been, had one's life been different. I pigeonhole 'fishing' thus with other momentary glimpses; like those rapid glances, for example, that I cast into basements when I walk in London streets. (*MB* 135)

Woolf's recollection in 1939 of her childhood desire to experience 'the sporting passion' indicates the degree to which she had already, at a young age, alloyed fly-fishing to an eminently modernist epistemology of the 'momentary glimpse'. But the fond nostalgia of this anecdote, which turns a scene of domestic animal-centred pedagogy into one possible origin story for Woolf's modernist aesthetics, also belies the degree to which, in the decade before writing 'A Sketch of the Past' that saw such experimental works as *Flush*, *The Waves* (1931), and *Three Guineas* (1938), she had already begun consequentially interrogating the ethics and politics not only of fly-fishing but also, because of their shared valorization of invasive and deterministic epistemologies, her own modernist ideology.

In 1936, Woolf reviewed the book *My Sporting Life*, an aristocratic sport memoir written by none other than her own brother-in-law: the intrepid fly-fisher, lepidopterist, and popular MP John Waller ('Jack') Hills. As first Stella Duckworth's suitor and, later, husband, Hills was a familiar presence in the Stephen household as Woolf was growing up, and was the first to introduce Woolf to her lifelong love of lepidoptery. He is usually cited as one of the more progressive voices in Woolf's family biography, though he drifted away from Woolf's circles in the decades after Stella's death in 1897. Hills is, though, maybe most important for being what a number of critics have argued is the original model for Richard Dalloway, who first appears on the scene in *The Voyage Out* (1915), mocking Helen Ambrose's recreational activities:

> 'May I ask how you've spent your time? Reading—philosophy?' (He saw the black book.) 'Metaphysics and fishing!' he exclaimed. 'If I had to live again I believe I should devote myself to one or the other.' (*VO* 77)

Dalloway then goes on to read a sentence of Helen's book, which is apparently G.E. Moore's *Principia Ethica*, before trivializing the entire venture of moral philosophy as 'the kind of thing we used to talk about when we were boys' (*VO* 78).

Here, Dalloway's first appearance in Woolf's fiction helpfully encapsulates two major and opposing aspects of the way fish and fishing function more generally throughout Woolf. First, fish are surprisingly, perhaps, often associated with systematic thinking, or the texture of thought and cognition more broadly, especially of the sort that might have anything to say about ethics. Hence, for example, the famous extended metaphor for thought at the start of *A Room of One's Own* (1929), in which Woolf compares 'the sudden conglomeration of an idea' to a fish at the end of a line (*ARO* 4).[12] And second, what is clear in the scene is Woolf's marked distaste for what she perceives as the anti-intellectual chauvinism characteristic of fly-fishers, or fly-fishing writing in general. Thus, the metaphor in *A Room of One's Own* is completed when, submerged in thought, Woolf is interrupted and shooed off the turf lawn by an Oxbridge beadle, sending her 'little fish into hiding'. Cast in this scenario as the fly-fisher who intrusively catches a fish only to reject it as 'insignificant', so the beadle here echoes Richard Dalloway's dismissive boorishness: he forces Woolf's narrator into a position where she has no choice but to acquiesce automatically to gender convention out of '[i]nstinct rather than reason' (*ARO* 6–7).

And indeed, when critics, again, do discuss the significance of fishing in Woolf, they tend to emphasize its association with violence in her fiction; the brutal instrumentalization, objectification, and killing of fish usually taken as a symbol for a social regime that violently restricts the agency of women. The scenes of fishing in *To the Lighthouse* (1927) and *Between the Acts* (1941), for example, are taken, firstly, as a 'display of dominance over nature' that, secondly, foretell later social and sexual discord—the masculine displays of violent prowess themselves 'capturing' the women in the novel, whether it is the marital strife between Giles and Isa or the friction between implacable old imperial Bart and his sister Lucy.[13]

But these readings neglect, I argue, the attention Woolf pays to the particular modes of organizing knowledge, affect, and virtue that are historically attached to fly-fishing, and also especially to how the violence of fishing *and* these attendant phenomenologies together cannily reflect Woolf's own style. We see in the following passage, for instance, not just the ugly violence of fishing, red in tooth and claw, but also an organizational (technical, technological) fastidiousness that we will see is characteristic of the sport:

> Lucy, [Bartholomew's] sister, was three years younger than he was. The name Cindy, or Sindy, for it could be spelt either way, was short for Lucy. It was by this name that he had called her when they were children; when she had trotted after him as he fished, and had made the meadow flowers into tight little bunches, winding one long grass stalk round and round and round. Once, she remembered, he had made her take the fish off the hook herself. The blood had shocked her—'Oh!' she had cried—for the gills were full of blood. And he had growled: 'Cindy!' The ghost of that morning in the meadow was in her mind as she replaced the hammer where it belonged on one

---

[12] In 'On Not Knowing Greek', Woolf also valorizes the philosophical clarity—and brutality—of ancient Greek thought against the 'vagueness' and 'confusion' of the modern Christian age; Sophocles in particular '[glides] like a shoal of trout smoothly and quietly, apparently motionless, and then, with a flicker of fins, off and away' (*E4* 50).

[13] Christina Alt's study is representative of this kind of reading, Woolf's fish being regarded merely as 'symbolic of human fate' or just 'negatively symbolic' and thus in line with Leslie Stephen's prohibition. See Alt, *Virginia Woolf and the Study of Nature*, 165, 206.

> shelf; and the nails where they belonged on another; and shut the cupboard about which, for he still kept his fishing tackle there, he was still so very particular. (*BA* 15)

Here what is recognizable as Bart's lifelong bullying of his sister manifests as a sort of fastidiousness of style. Recalling Woolf's description of Hills himself as eminently 'scrupulous' in 'A Sketch of the Past', this passage draws our attention to how the fastidiousness and particularity of the fisherman function as both features of personality (or personal style) and as a kind of moral virtue in their own right—though one that blindly inflicts violence on others.[14] (No less than Wordsworth, tellingly, calls it a 'blameless sport'.[15]) Indeed, having introduced the basic prominence of fly-fishing in Woolf, I turn now to fly-fishing proper and examine how fishing's specific phenomenologies sublimate, under the ethical rubric of self-discipline, the violence visited upon one's concrete animal others.

The single most defining feature of fly-fishing is its phenomenology of time. As Hills and the longer tradition of fly-fishing writing before him stress, fly-fishing cultivates patience and an openness to failure that other aristocratic sports do not quite afford. In his 1921 *History of Fly Fishing for Trout*, Hills surveys an English history of the genre since the Middle Ages and notes that it is the formal convention to begin with a prologue justifying not only the virtue of sport in general but also the virtue of fishing above all other sport. For where all sport is laudable for helping to prevent the sin of idleness, fishing in particular surpasses the rest by virtue of its contemplative character. Where other sports such as hunting are about activity and are therefore 'too laborious', fishing by its very nature must be done in relative solitude and quiet. 'It enables a man to eschew all contrarious company and all places of debate where he might have any occasion of melancholy', writes Hills. 'Perhaps this is the reason why politicians in all ages have found relaxation in fishing.'[16]

As a correlative, the temporality of the actual act of waiting for fish is mirrored by the temporality of learning one's way around the technical apparatus. According to fishing writers, fishing surpasses other sports in the quantity and quality of technical information required to pursue the sport successfully. Fishing lore—especially that concerning the tackle, and the construction of an angling rod—is a special art handed down and refined over centuries, and Hills warns the 'casual reader', faced with the exceptional amount of fastidiously technical detail in any given fishing book, from thinking that 'the practical part of the book is worthless'.[17] It is, in fact, the opposite, and for Hills, the ability of pedantically profuse technical directions (especially in the pre-modern

---

[14] 'He was scrupulously clean; he washed all over ever so many times a day, and was scrupulously well dressed, as a Victorian city solicitor; also as a countryman. The word "scrupulous" suggests itself when I think of Jack Hills' (*MB* 103).

[15] William Wordsworth, 'Written Upon a Blank Leaf in "The Complete Angler"' (1819).

[16] John Waller Hills, *A History of Fly Fishing for Trout* (New York: Frederick A. Stokes, 1921), 16.

[17] Hills, *Fly Fishing*, 22.

treatises) to *snap* together and nigh-miraculously describe an 'uncommonly' effective fishing rod, for example, reveals that '[n]ot only are they excellent; they are modern'.[18]

Thus, in two ways, fly-fishing is structured around the sudden, almost epiphanic, synchronic synthesis of a longer or larger quantity either amassed or experienced diachronically through time. That quantity could be the wait that culminates dramatically in the agonistic big catch—as Hills quotes the sixteenth-century fisher-poet John Dennys: 'When you have hookt him, give him leave, keeping your Line stright, and hold him from rootes and he will tyre himselfe. This is the chiefe pleasure of Angling'—or it could be the sheer volume of technical and optical data that resolve into the physics of a simple rod and tackle.[19]

In each case, moreover, the actual mechanism by which quantitative technique or practice suddenly resolves into something qualitatively new is never fully elucidated. It remains vague, mystified under the sign of 'intuition'—what Hills can only call 'the imponderable element which places you in the right temper'.[20] Unable to see the trout deep beneath the surface of the stream and across the length of line and rod, the fisher's primary skill is learning how to sense, somehow, the fish's approach by intuition alone. Hills speaks in the second person of the fisher's 'day' of good fortune, when the multiplicity of unaccountable and uncontrollable factors align and the trout is 'yours':

> On your day—and such days come to all of us, to make up for the many when we are either maddened or drugged and stupefied by our incurable ineptitude—how delicately and how surely you throw. [...] You know exactly what to do, and you do it. Wherever the fish may be rising, your fly sails over him, hardly touching the water, wings up, floating like a cork, following every crinkle of the slow current. You gain an extraordinary sense of power. Your rod and line, right down to the fly, are part of yourself, moved by your nerves and answering to your brain.[21]

The perceptual and cognitive synthesis beautifully unites the fisher, his nerves, and his brain with his surroundings and even the trout itself, providing a brief, flashing moment of cross-species contact. Later on, in *My Sporting Life*, Hills, in a very revealing analogy that Woolf will latch onto in her review, describes fishing in terms of learning Latin and Greek in a classroom:

> That quick correlation of nerves and sense that knowledge that comes like a flash from nowhere that a fish has taken my fly, that steady stare over the broken water of an unknown river to make sure where the trout will be lying. And when I prove myself right, when a trout and another and then another rise confidently, I get the same exhilaration from solving the unknown as I got long ago in quite different circumstances. It is as though I stepped back through the years to some Eton or

---

[18] Hills, *Fly Fishing*, 22.
[19] Hills, *Fly Fishing*, 42.
[20] Hills, *My Sporting Life* (London: Philip Allan, 1936), 10.
[21] Hills, *Fly Fishing*, 135–6.

Oxford examination, and were staring at a piece of unseen Latin or Greek which I had to translate. Twisting it this way or that, trying to bore through it, seeing no meaning, nothing but words; suddenly it springs to life, there it is lying open to me, vital and real. So with a new river: I can read it, make sense of it, I know where trout are, and where they are not. Thus do the most opposite experiences give similar emotions.[22]

Or as Hills gracefully puts it a little later: 'You must know your river in all its moods and tenses.'[23] The opacity of the object and the spontaneous vision that burns all that opacity away; the extreme patience and technical detail required; the crucial but ineffable burst of instinct that locks everything together. We could hardly ask for a better description of Woolf's own prose.

This resemblance, in fact, is what Woolf focuses on in her review of Hills's book. The first half of the essay, succinctly entitled 'Fishing', is mostly a record of Woolf's half-tongue-in-cheek surprise at how effective Hills's prose is, hyperbolically comparing his writing to Flaubert's:

> Now, if the art of writing consists in laying an egg in the reader's mind from which springs the thing itself—whether man or fish—and if this art requires such ardour in its practitioners that they will readily, like Flaubert, give up all their bright spring mornings to its pursuit, how does it come about that Major Hills, who has spent thirty years in the House of Commons, can do the trick? (*E6* 493)

But Woolf is also relatively serious about the compelling mimesis of Hills's language. 'All books are made of words', she writes, 'but mostly of words that flutter and agitate thought. *This* book on the contrary, though made of words, has a strange effect on the body. It lifts it out of the chair, stands it on the banks of a river, and strikes it dumb' (Woolf's emphasis, *E6* 492). There is something hypnotic about Hills's immersive, so frequently second-person prose—something akin to the experience of fishing itself.

Woolf's wonder at what we might call Hills's aerodynamics of thought pivots through a number of different considerations, first linking the history of the English novel to its intimacy with the English countryside: for without the old fishermen of centuries past, Woolf asks, where would Scott, Dickens, and Eliot be? 'No wonder, since the poachers are gone, that fiction is failing' (*E6* 494).[24] But perhaps more pertinently compared

---

[22] Hills, *My Sporting Life*, 10.
[23] Hills, *My Sporting Life*, 36.
[24] Woolf is being slightly funny with her assertions again, but fishing, and especially fishing writing, was indeed fiercely nationalistic. The French, for example, may have written the first hunting manual (according to Hills, *La Chace dou Serf* from the thirteenth century), but it was up to the English to write the first *fishing* manual, an aristocratic tradition that would culminate with Lord Grey himself writing a wildly popular tome in 1899. So nationalistic was fishing writing that in 1883, in the midst of the Victorian Shakespeare craze, one Rev. Henry Nicholson Ellacombe, Vicar of Bitton, had to claim the Bard himself as one of their own, publishing the short treatise *Shakespeare as an Angler*. This bald proposition, of course, was brought into question a mere thirty-five years later in 1918 with Max Hühner's seminal intervention into the field, *Was Shakespeare an Angler?*

to poets—'if to bare reality is to be a poet'—Hills's writing does what effective poetry should do. As Woolf describes it, while the conscious reading mind is occupied with the embodied phenomenology of fishing—it 'must be all body'—the unconscious mind 'leaps to the top and strips off veils' (E6 493). And this transparency effected by Hills's prose is again much the same as the spontaneous transparency the fisher quietly waits for, standing alone in the river. Can we know, for example, what Hills himself dreams about?, asks Woolf. Can we tell from his prose what his highest aspirations are? What we glean from his book is that he dreams only of the catch. But reading Hills's dreams is for Woolf (echoing no less than Freud abortively pondering the dream-life of animals) the same as trying to penetrate the mind of a fish: 'the trout subtle, the salmon ingenuous; each with its nerves, with its brain, its mentality that we can dimly penetrate, movements we can mystically anticipate, for just as, suddenly, Greek and Latin sort themselves in a flash, so we understand the minds of fish?' (E6 495).[25] The phenomenology of cross-species contact now daringly comes to resemble a basic intersubjectivity: to know the gentleman fisher, it seems, is to know the fish.

Yet Woolf's aim in elucidating Hills's remarkably transparent and mimetic prose is not to celebrate it uncritically but to suggest that there is, in fact, an *ethics* of transparency, and that Hills's prose is in the business of actively appropriating the transparency of its object in bad faith. Woolf's point when speculating about the content of Hills's dreams is to ask what he elides when he raises the Big Catch to the mountaintop of his dreams—namely, his political ambitions. ('For dream he does. "I always, even now, dream that I shall astonish the world. An outstanding success..." The Premiership is it?' (E6 495).) It is hence with this elision in mind that Woolf actually begins her review with a curious invocation of Oriental wisdom: 'While there is a Chinese proverb which says that the fisherman is pure at heart "as a white sea-shell," there is a Japanese poem, four lines long, which says something so true but at the same time so crude about the hearts of politicians that it had better be left in its original obscurity' (E6 492).[26] Woolf is here suggesting that the performance of moral purity is ultimately a dissemblance of political crudeness—a crudeness that ultimately turns on what Woolf says is 'a confusion in the mind of the reader between fish and men'. That is, Hills's confusion, stemming from his lifelong immersion in both fly-fishing and politics, leaves him unable or unwilling to distinguish ethically between animals and men.

My Sporting Life ends with an apology for sport in general, arguing against claims that sport is animal cruelty by constructing an ad hoc economy of benevolence, in which social compassion and animal compassion are found to have incommensurate ethics and cannot therefore be compared. How can one, after all, compare the beating of a child, for example, with the killing of an animal? 'Which is right?' Hills asks, 'Are we, on both sides, ruled by those inscrutable and eternal contradictions lying deep in our spiritual and material nature?'[27] This inscrutable incommensurability 'deep' in our nature: Hills's

---

[25] Sigmund Freud, *The Interpretation of Dreams*, in *The Standard Edition of the Complete Psychological Works of Sigmund Freud*, ed. James Strachey, vol. 4 (London: Hogarth Press, 1900, 1953, 1958), 131–2.

[26] The editors of Woolf's collected essays have been unable to trace the source of either.

[27] Hills, *My Sporting Life*, 275.

ethical language takes on the topological rhetoric of fish and rivers with which we are now familiar. The ethical justification for sport, Hills seems to be saying, should be as clear to you, ultimately, as the movement of trout is to him—forgetting for a second that this movement is by no means at all clear. Like Woolf's own epiphanic aesthetics, which centres an epistemology of instinct and intuition that cannot help but risk undercutting a larger ethics of interconnective subjectivity via its reliance on an essentializing and deterministic metonymy, Hills here founds the authority of his ethical claims only on a mystifying recourse to the natural world.

Indeed, Hills consistently repeats this language elsewhere and ends up (unwittingly) calling the legitimacy of his own ethical position into question by chalking up a number of not-even-difficult questions to a kind of theological inscrutability—the same epistemological gap that the fly-fisher feels between himself and the trout beneath the water. Discussing a traditional fly-fishing dictate against fishing with bait (using bait can lead to overfishing), Hills dismisses the entire debate, claiming that it is ultimately not a matter of reason but, seemingly more importantly, of the fishers' essence: 'But the greater is one of those eternal contradictions which lie at the root of all powerful emotions. We are not ruled by reason. We follow a different law, and we recognize its sanction. It is not the less binding because we cannot set it out in words. It is a part of our make-up as an angler.'[28] Certainly, in each case here—whether concerning the ethics of sport in general, or the practical ecological considerations necessary to keep fishing sustainable—there are substantive reasons for choosing to proceed one way or another. But in each case, Hills defers to mystification, and despite his protest that child abuse and killing an animal are ethically incommensurate, he effectively flattens ethical judgement and athletic judgement, humans and animals, into a single, clumsy mess of 'intuitive' or 'instinctual' gut feelings. The fisherman's valorization of his own pure heart, turns out, is itself the root of the politician's crudeness. Transparency—seemingly such a simple matter when it comes to reading the minds of fish—ends up blind to its own violent implications.

It is only appropriate, then, that a novelist and thinker as ethically meticulous as Woolf would eventually recognize how the seemingly instantaneous clarity afforded by an aesthetics and characterology of instinct can all too easily naturalize subjective difference in a deterministic fashion that actually obfuscates the particularities required for good-faith ethical judgement, and it is revealing to see how the seeds of this recognition were present even in Woolf's earliest work. Looking back at Woolf's portrait of Richard Dalloway in *The Voyage Out*, her first novel, it is even clearer now the extent to which his character's ethos is informed by Hills's. Dalloway's blowhard emphasis on liberal world systems, for example, or what he calls the 'unity of aim, of dominion, of progress', relies ultimately on the elision of particulars and is made possible by the agency of what he calls 'political instinct' (*VO* 67, 69). Like Hills, whom Woolf whimsically remembers living as if he had 'a system plainly marked in front of him', Dalloway is given to easy synchronic organizations of data, which the faculty of 'instinct' makes

---

[28] Hills, *My Sporting Life*, 21.

more facile by allowing him to see the political world as an ethological world—with himself, of course, as the top dog (*MB* 47).

But it is not just Richard Dalloway and the other characters in *The Voyage Out* whose political and social ambitions rely on a naturalistic 'confusion in the mind of the reader between [beasts] and men'. (St. John Hirst, for example, patronizingly views all the other characters as cattle, hens, or rats.) The animalizing, physiognomic figure is one of the most frequent and reliable devices in Woolf's toolbox, occurring sometimes as frequently as once every other page in her novels—starting with *The Voyage Out* and extending throughout most of her other fiction and much of her essayistic prose.[29] Often it is her characters' favourite way of sneering at other characters and themselves. In *The Voyage Out*, Helen Ambrose mocks a woman for having 'the face of an impertinent but jolly little pig', for example, 'mottled red under a dusting of powder', and in her fictional debut, Clarissa Dalloway writes home, with a not inconsiderable amount of self-satisfaction, to demean Mr Pepper as 'an ill-conditioned fox-terrier', going on to remark that 'it's a pity, sometimes, one can't treat people like dogs!' (*VO* 179, 50). Later, in her own eponymous novel, just after musing that '[h]er only gift was knowing people almost by instinct', she considers with pity her own 'ridiculous little face, beaked like a bird's', an observation that it is the sole function of the one-off character Scrope Purvis to independently confirm (*MD* 8, 9). Mr Ramsay reminds Mrs Ramsay of 'the great sea lion at the Zoo tumbling backwards after swallowing his fish and walloping off so that the water in the tank washes from side to side' but thinks of his own eyes a few paragraphs later as having the 'leathern eyelid of a lizard' (*TTL* 36, 39). But physiognomy is importantly a device favoured by Woolf's own voice, too, not only for aesthetic and rhetorical purposes—in 'Kew Gardens', a shaky older man jerks his body 'in the manner of an impatient carriage horse tired of waiting outside a house'; in *The Voyage Out*, the narrator reproaches a group of men for their self-satisfaction by giving them 'the appearance of crocodiles so fully gorged by their last meal that the future of the world gives them no anxiety whatever'—but also for polemical ones as well—Woolf's critique of the Plumage Bill of 1921 nevertheless lays into a description of the 'stupid face' of an unfortunate woman as having 'something of the greedy petulance of the pug-dog's face at tea-time' (*CSF* 86; *VO* 205; *E3* 242). Any consideration of what Woolf might contribute to critical animal studies, posthumanism, or modernist studies' encounter with the Anthropocene

---

[29] Physiognomy, despite waning in popularity as a pseudo-scientific practice after its heyday in the nineteenth century, nevertheless enjoyed an important afterlife among modernist writers with an investment in naturalism. D.H. Lawrence, most prominently, espoused in his 1921 book *Fantasia of the Unconscious* a self-proclaimed 'pseudo-philosophy' in which elaborate physiognomies of facial features provided a shorthand through which to figure a character's interior life instantly and transparently, condensing a certain amount of empirical data into an isolated phenomenological unit. Or as Woolf herself admiringly writes—seemingly untroubled by the racialist foundation of such thinking—Lawrence's 'impatience, the need for getting beyond the object before us, seems to contract, to shrivel up, to curtail scenes to their barest, to flash character simply and starkly in front of us. We must not look for more than a second; we must hurry on.' See Lawrence, *Fantasia of the Unconscious* (New York: Seltzer, 1922), xiv; and Woolf, 'Notes on D. H. Lawrence', *E6* 466.

more largely is therefore incomplete without accounting for Woolf's late confrontation with the violent epistemology of her own modernist style.

In the introduction to the recent 'Modernist Inhumanisms' special issue of *Modernism/modernity*, Aaron Jaffe provocatively calls for the broad range of recently minted inhumanist rubrics and disciplines to recognize and explore their own stakes within the modernist archive more fully and in so doing, '[expand] modernist reference beyond the Anthropocene'. To do so, Jaffe writes, scholars should attend more closely to those tenets of modernist aesthetics that have long been canon but that have only recently been understood as potentially 'ex-anthropic'—namely, 'modernism's weird fixations on becoming minimal and becoming inhuman'.[30] Naturally, one of Jaffe's primary case studies is Woolf, whose signature call for more realistic representations of women's subjectivity simultaneously indexed the need to see 'something besides (or, outside) representative subjectivity—to possible modes of extrasubjectivity to be accessed at impersonal, even inhuman scales'.[31]

Here, Jaffe neatly lays out the question Woolf herself grapples with in her review of Hills's sporting memoir. For Woolf, along with most of her modernist cohort, one of the problematic objectives of the realist writer is to make the interior of another being instantly, epiphanically accessible—something Hills, too, surprisingly and troublingly accomplishes in the mimetic style of his prose. The problem for modernism, however—that is, where modernism canonically finds its impassable representational limit and aesthetic starting point—is that many of the techniques for making unique interiorities accessible or transparent paradoxically erase interiority altogether, or render it irrelevant.

This question, after all, is not only the question behind the humanistic ethical turn in Woolf criticism (which, as I have noted, often problematically locates faciality as the site of intersubjective ethics), it is also a central point of contention in many earlier feminist recuperations/repudiations of Woolf. The fragmentary and constantly mutating aesthetic practices associated with Woolf's modernist experimentation have been taken to be at odds with, for example, a feminist politics committed to a historical realism made efficacious primarily through the Lukacsian reconstruction of a 'complete human personality'.[32] This is even more of a problem when the object of such aesthetic representation is an especially demanding kind of asubjective and, to some, adamantly anti-identitarian experience.[33] By way of conclusion, then, what I want to suggest is that Woolf's writing has been a unique and vital focal point for so many opposing and accelerated polemics because at key points throughout her career, Woolf was working

---

[30] Aaron Jaffe, 'Introduction: Who's Afraid of the Inhuman Woolf?', *Modernism/modernity* 23, no. 3 (September 2016), 491–513, at 496, 497.

[31] Jaffe, 'Introduction', 493.

[32] Toril Moi, *Sexual/Textual Politics: Feminist Literary Theory* (London: Methuen, 1985), 4–5; Georg Lukács, *Studies in European Realism*, trans. Edith Bone (New York: Howard Fertig, 2002), 5.

[33] See also Toril Moi, 'I Am Not a Woman Writer: About Women, Literature, and Feminist Theory Today', *Feminist Theory* 9, no. 3 (December 2008), 267.

through precisely these problems of representation via the particular epistemological device of the *type*.

Specifically, any account of Woolf's relationship to the natural world has to consider how her interest in exploring asubjective experience led her to animal typology in particular as a suitable novelistic method. Typology, when it simply assigns an individual on the basis of external characteristics to a larger, homogenized group such as a species, risks the ugly essentialisms of physiognomy, for instance, but it also opens up, as part of a longer tradition of post-Darwinian social ethics, a way to represent an understanding of agency and intersubjectivity that treads the importantly complex space between sovereign self-determination and naturalistic determinism. For Woolf, these two poles marked the opposing tendencies of her modernist aesthetics and characterology, and it is precisely to the degree that her ethical practice simultaneously entertained both of them that she saw their potential real-world consequences reflected back to her in John Waller Hills's writing, and that modern *Flush* scholars have symptomatically reproduced them (in the way that, for example, a liberal cross-species interconnectivity with Flush disingenuously summons the deterministic conditioning of co-evolutionary history for the sake of a seemingly spontaneous and epiphanic reckoning with nonhuman alterity). Hence, while there is certainly, as Jaffe and many other Woolf scholars have pointed out, an important case to be made for how the impersonal and inhumanist rubrics of modernism create a space for thinking feminism beyond liberal monadic autonomy, it is also important to remember how Woolf herself became increasingly wary of the ways in which the deterministic aspects of any inhumanism that goes 'beyond the Anthropocene' only reinstantiates the epistemological grounds for the imperialist, antifeminist sovereign ego (whether, say, interrogating those grounds in Hills's fly-fishing self-justifications, flagging the same tendency in the character of Richard Dalloway, or even ironizing her own narratorial impulses in the form of Clarissa's self-regarding but blinkered 'gift' for instinct).

In 'The Climate of History', Dipesh Chakrabarty's seminal challenge to humanists to reckon with the idea of the Anthropocene, Chakrabarty, drawing from the work of scientists E.O. Wilson and Paul J. Crutzen (the latter, along with collaborator Eugene F. Stoermer, having coined the term 'Anthropocene' for 'the new geological epoch when humans exist as a geological force' in 2000), encourages humanists to begin thinking of humanity's historical function as a species—that is, no longer just the subject of history but one collective actor among many in a deep history of the ecological and geological world.[34] For Chakrabarty and Wilson, this is an urgent matter of our self-knowledge and historical consciousness in the face of catastrophic climate change. At the same time, Chakrabarty concedes that humanists as a discipline have a built-in resistance to 'the biological-sounding talk of species':

---

[34] Dipesh Chakrabarty, 'The Climate of History: Four Theses', *Critical Inquiry* 35, no. 2 (Winter 2009), 197–222; Paul Crutzen and Eugene Stoermer, 'Have We Entered the "Anthropocene"?', *IGBP [International Geosphere-Biosphere Programme] Newsletter* 41 (October 2000).

They feel concerned about their finely honed sense of contingency and freedom in human affairs having to cede ground to a more deterministic view of the world. Besides, there are always, as [Daniel Lord] Smail recognizes, dangerous historical examples of the political use of biology. The idea of species, it is feared, in addition, may introduce a powerful degree of essentialism in our understanding of humans.[35]

Is there, then, actually a way for the human disciplines to adopt the language of the natural world without collapsing into bare essentialism? It is in this context of the biological idea of the human 'species' that Woolf's signature call as a modernist to '[l]ook within' and convey 'life', that elusive 'essential thing', can most usefully be read ('Modern Fiction', *E4* 160). For despite using the rhetoric of essence, Woolf, in the spirit of Chakrabarty's challenge, is not ultimately leaning into any essentializing notion of 'human nature', but is rather searching for a language to describe that quality that enables beings to live and move freely through the modern world—on the one hand, unconstrained by a deterministic 'air of probability', and on the other, to still, in that freedom, maintain their integrity and legibility even as they are battered from all sides by 'myriad impressions', 'an incessant shower of innumerable atoms' (*E4* 160). (Here again, Woolf imagines the novelist as a fisher. Her version of Mr Bennett has a 'magnificent apparatus for catching life' but has unfortunately cast his line 'just an inch or two on the wrong side'. Like an elusive trout, '[l]ife escapes' (*E4* 159).) And it is along these lines that Woolf's place in the tradition of typological thinking becomes most apparent.

In *The Order of Things*, Foucault explains that, as taxonomical thinking gave way to biological thinking at the turn of the nineteenth century, classes of beings were liberated from synchronic tables of classification and reinserted into diachronic history. This new episteme culminated most visibly in the rise of Darwinian evolutionary theory: more fundamentally, though, the shift was to a preoccupation with how beings are able to move through time while remaining discrete, whole, and intact. Or, in other words, living and organic. The type, therefore, rather than the externally imposed taxon, became a container, a unit of vitality, for understanding the dynamic principles of inner necessity that kept, at any given moment in history, either individual bodies, beings, or classes of beings recognizably coherent and functional (and also open to evolution).[36]

Crucially, the type is not a frozen and essentialist taxonomy, but rather a heuristic for facilitating a being's successful biological and social existence. As historian of science Lorraine Daston reminds us, typological practice and its generalizations were not necessarily essentialist: that is, there is a difference between finding a coherent set of descriptors for any type, even when they suggest a principle of inner necessity, and concluding that such a unity necessarily indicates an a priori predetermined essence.[37] Darwin himself, for example, (as Chakrabarty does note via Smail) concludes in the first

---

[35] Chakrabarty, 'Climate of History', 214.

[36] Michel Foucault, *The Order of Things: An Archaeology of the Human Sciences* (New York: Vintage, 1994), 278.

[37] Lorraine Daston, 'Type Specimens and Scientific Memory', *Critical Inquiry* 31 (Autumn 2004), 168.

two chapters of *On the Origin of Species* that there is, in fact, no such thing as an actual 'species' in nature: for if animals of a kind are ever-evolving heterogeneously, how exactly can one delimit where one species ends and another begins?[38] And along these lines, twentieth-century scientists seeking to understand the precise relationship of determinism to autonomous development—whether animal ethologists such as Julian Huxley or sociologists like Erving Goffman (himself inspired by Huxley)—proposed various typological mechanisms (the concept of display, most notably) by which patterns of collective human or animal behaviour might consolidate themselves over time in a way neither fully intentional or spontaneous nor wholly predetermined by genotype, environment, or a kind of universal human essence (à la Durkheimian 'ultimate beliefs')—as if in the middle voice, neither active nor passive.[39]

Woolf's father Leslie Stephen anticipated these later twentieth-century analogies of biological and behavioural typology in his oft-overlooked *The Science of Ethics* (1882). Like Darwin and Goffman, Stephen insisted not on any essentializing function of typology but on the utility of type for expedient, vital social interaction—that is, ethics—and hence analogized the formation of personality types, like social displays, to self-organizing evolutionary principles found in animal life. Where Stephen went beyond his scientific counterparts, however, and where Stephen's speculative interests begin to resonate with Woolf's own, was in analogizing the structure of evolutionary and personality types to principles behind man-made aesthetic and mechanical forms as well. From the gracefully self-evident utility of physical tools like a bow to the exemplary refinement of Greek sculpture, or even the haphazard but undeniable aesthetic unity of a dish like roast pig, Stephen argued that all these classes of made objects are types in the sense that, although we might not be able to explain how a type was first discovered, it nevertheless recognizably presents as 'the solution of an amazingly complex problem', 'rolled in countless minds till it is rounded to perfection, like the pebble on the sea-beach'.[40] To make this equivalence, furthermore, was also to claim that aesthetic forms lack any absolute essence or deterministic function apart from their detectable mechanisms of necessity: external conditions present a 'problem' to which aesthetic forms are 'only' the solution, in the same way that a new animal species 'solves' an environmental 'problem'; likewise, any new solution modifies its environment and becomes in turn 'a set of data for a new problem'. In other words, what may *appear* at any

---

[38] Thus, the original grammar of Darwin's title takes on a sharper significance: the work is distinctly not just about the origin of *the* species as a plurality of empirically concrete groups but more fundamentally about the origin of the idea of species itself.

[39] See Julian Huxley, 'Introduction: A Discussion on Ritualization of Behavior in Animals and Man', *Philosophical Transactions of the Royal Society of London. Series B* 251, no. 772 (1966); Erving Goffman, *Gender Advertisements* (New York: Harper, 1969), 1. Huxley himself (the brother of Aldous Huxley and the grandson of T.H. Huxley) built off the work of geneticist C.H. Waddington and, further down the line, Darwin's own.

[40] Stephen is somewhat whimsically citing Charles Lamb's 'Dissertation upon Roast Pig' (1823), in which a clumsy ancient Chinese man, naturally, is said to have discovered the dish by accidentally burning his house down. See Leslie Stephen, *The Science of Ethics* (London: Smith, Elder, 1882), 74, 76, 77.

given time as the necessity of essence is immediately reassessed in its own turn as contingency: 'As the bow is felt out, the animal is always feeling itself out': and for Stephen, this meant that the artwork, too, must feel itself out—understanding itself neither as a singular work of genius (just as any given animal is never an unprecedented problem to be solved by evolutionary history) nor as a mere symptom of historical conditions (just as an animal is not simply the solution to an environmental problem) but as a continual process of both inhabiting a received world and making that world habitable for itself.[41]

The utility of typological thinking both for Woolf herself and for Woolf scholars becomes clear when we consider a later, more experimental work like *The Waves* as a reassessment of the epistemology of character. Not only, for example, do the persons in the novel explicitly contemplate the need to break out of both physiognomically deterministic constraints (Rhoda: 'The human face is hideous ... I am sick of prettiness') and epiphanic interiority (Bernard's 'world seen without a self'), but Woolf's structural decision to follow a group of six individuals from young childhood to maturity effectively casts those individuals as *animals* in the midst of transformation, learning to adapt, evolve, individuate, proliferate, and perhaps, even, achieve an equilibrium among equals in a way that figures ethical balance as ecological stability—that is, as animals feeling themselves out (*W* 115, 213). In this manner, type might be considered a more appropriate denomination than character for the organizing unit of agency and perception in much of Woolf, for whom a being moves less like a discrete actor through the mechanical stagecraft of life and more like 'a density of meaning, a conglomeration of loveliness' (recall 'the sudden conglomeration of an idea at the end of one's line'!) through life conceived of as a substance, a 'luminous halo, a semi-transparent envelope surrounding us from the beginning of consciousness to the end' (*JR* 108; *E4* 160).[42]

Indeed, the whole of Woolf's style is generally directed not quite at the 'essence' of experience (especially not any particular 'human essence') but at an intrinsic necessity that seems to make experience cohere (in a manner continuous across species lines). Woolf's fiction thus tends to be built gradually through a slow, descriptive, even quantitative elaboration to a sudden and qualitatively revelatory finish: from the syntactical structure of her prose (the familiar three beats followed by a flash of insight) to the macrostructure of her novels (and their famously bracing final sentences). So wrought, each of Woolf's individual works seems to attain an integral completeness that detaches both the work and the characters it contains from the reader's own temporality and judgement. On the ending of *To the Lighthouse*, for example, Eric Hayot writes,

---

[41] Stephen's concept of the animal as both solution and problem, moreover, cannily anticipates Bergsonian and, eventually, Deleuzian theory. See Stephen, *The Science of Ethics*, 79.

[42] Suggestively, the keyword 'instinct' appears nineteen times in *The Voyage Out*, while appearing only three times in *The Waves*. The novelistic perspective has moved from outside the animal to inside the animal. 'Instinct' is no longer a phenomenological category to be noted insofar as it indexes the opacity of cross-species difference in an economy of perceived intentionality vs. observed behavior.

> The charm of imaginary art, like that of imaginary artists, lies in its unimaginability; whatever it does, however it produces and organizes an aesthetic world internal to the novelistic or poetic space in which it appears, in the end justifies itself directly in proportion to the audience's inability to evaluate it on terms other than its own. [...] The conjunction of that metafictional ending and Lily's line guarantees, more than any mental picture of her painting, the authority and legitimacy of her judgment.[43]

Woolf thus achieves for her works that desired effect of modernist aesthetic autonomy, made durable and intensely graspable like one of Woolf's solid objects, while the characters rise towards a metafictional coincidence with Woolf herself, their latest ethical apprehensions necessarily unavailable to the reader's judgement but deemed, for the time being, provisionally sufficient.

Selected Bibliography

Chakrabarty, Dipesh, 'The Climate of History: Four Theses', *Critical Inquiry* 35, no. 2 (Winter 2009), 197–222.
Foucault, Michel, *The Order of Things: An Archaeology of the Human Sciences* (New York: Vintage, 1994).
Hills, John Waller, *A History of Fly Fishing for Trout* (New York: Frederick A. Stokes, 1921).
Hills, John Waller, *My Sporting Life* (London: Philip Allan, 1936).
Jaffe, Aaron, 'Introduction: Who's Afraid of the Inhuman Woolf?', *Modernism/modernity* 23, no. 3 (September 2016), 491–513.
Scott, Bonnie Kime, 'Ecocritical Woolf', in Jessica Berman, ed., *A Companion to Virginia Woolf* (Malden, MA and Oxford: Wiley-Blackwell, 2016), 319–30.
Stephen, Leslie, *The Science of Ethics* (London: Smith, Elder, & Co., 1882).

---

[43] Eric Hayot, *The Hypothetical Mandarin: Sympathy, Modernity, and Chinese Pain* (New York: Oxford University Press, 2009), 177.

CHAPTER 28

WAR AND PEACE

BERYL PONG

From the fact that many of the Bloomsbury Circle were conscientious objectors, to Leonard Woolf's work on the League of Nations, to Julian Bell's death in the Spanish Civil War: war touches almost all aspects of Woolf's biography and social life. Her preoccupations with the political violence of her time are in many ways exemplary of the modernist generation. As Marina MacKay has observed, modernism was 'stunned into disaffection by the trauma of the First World War' before becoming 'a writing compelled into and out of commitment by the Spanish Civil War', with texts like Arthur Koestler's *Spanish Testament* (1937), W.H. Auden's 'Spain' (1937), and George Orwell's *Homage to Catalonia* (1938) taking centre stage in their proclamations to political commitment. The latter conflict then became a signal event not only of a difficult present, but of an anxious future: 'some of the most important so-called late modernist "war writing" is essentially proleptic, concerned with the war to come rather than with wars ongoing.'[1]

Instead of tracing war through Woolf's life—territory already covered with great detail and insight by Hermione Lee's biography, *Virginia Woolf* (1996)—this chapter focuses on how war impacts her fiction with respect to the intersection between aesthetic style and politics. I suggest that prolepsis can run in tandem with, rather than necessarily after, sentiments like disaffection and commitment as a mode that spills across temporal boundaries of pre- or post-war. For much of Woolf's writings need to be understood in relation to a sense that wars to come were, precisely, also wars ongoing: that is, that the end of one war appears to run into another, such that her era is hurtling towards catastrophes expected or even already known. In this way, prolepsis represents a sense of fatalistic repetition. For Woolf, it also functions crucially as a creative strategy for galvanizing commitment to the future, as bearing witness is only useful in terms of its implications for catalysing resistance. Her thinking about war is thus inextricable from her thinking about peace, and her thinking about the future is inextricable

---

[1] Marina MacKay, 'Violence, Art, and War', in Peter Brooker, Andrzej Gasiorek, Deborah Longworth, and Andrew Thacker, eds, *Oxford Handbook of Modernisms* (Oxford: Oxford University Press, 2010), 461–76, at 473.

from her thinking about the present and the past. In paying attention to the various temporal modes that structure Woolf's writing, I argue that war and peace serve as an important bridge between two areas not often examined together in Woolf studies—her philosophical thinking about time and her political activism.

To think of Woolf as a canny, self-conscious, and foreboding presentist-futurist: this might seem like a counter-intuitive claim. Because criticism has been historically dominated by Woolf's interest in capturing life as 'a luminous halo, a semi-transparent envelope surrounding us from the beginning of consciousness to the end', her fidelity is arguably to the lived present, rather than the social future (E4 160). The deep investment in subjective or psychological time has led to charges of apoliticism and contentions that modernist temporality obscures the broader socio-political conditions underpinning it.[2] Even critics who read the privileging of psychology favourably tend to sidestep Woolf's politics and her pacifism. For example, Ann Banfield argues that Woolf attempts to translate the fleeting into the eternal by writing or aestheticizing the moment, but she does not discuss *The Years* (1937): a historical novel whose narrative hops through half a century of everyday moments rendered in the present to address a range of conditions concerning Irish Home Rule, suffrage, homosexuality, and class relations.[3]

Conversely, if not the present in and of itself, Woolf scholarship has often examined the writer's interest in the present as a repository for memory and the past. This has become a particularly productive area of inquiry for trauma studies. In Freud's well-known articulation of trauma in *Beyond the Pleasure Principle* (1920), he delineates several dimensions to the 'traumatic neurosis', including 'fright' and the 'repetition-compulsion', where the unconscious unwittingly repeats or re-enacts the traumatic event. Because the infliction of trauma constitutes its own lacuna, making the moment itself inassimilable and ungraspable, trauma cannot be known in the first instance and can only be felt as haunting; understanding and reconciliation are hence both belated and deferred. David Eberly and Suzette Henke's edited collection, *Virginia Woolf and Trauma: Embodied Texts* (2007) is an exemplary treatment in this regard. The book as a whole examines not just how trauma and the emergence of traumatic memory underpin much of Woolf's writing, but why, in light of her own past childhood abuse, 'a haunting, if sometimes repressed trauma narrative can be found embodied over a lifetime of literary production', making the writer's entire body of work an autobiographical chronicle of her own relationship with belatedness.[4]

---

[2] The more well-known arguments about modernist temporality's apoliticism are articulated by Wyndham Lewis in *Time and Western Man* (1927) and later, by Georg Lukács in *The Meaning of Contemporary Realism* (1963).

[3] Ann Banfield, 'Time Passes: Virginia Woolf, Post-Impressionism, and Cambridge Time', *Poetics Today* 24, no. 3 (Autumn 2003), 471–516.

[4] Suzette Henke and David Eberly, assisted by Jane Lilienfeld, *Virginia Woolf and Trauma: Embodied Texts* (New York: Pace University Press, 2007), 1.

The temporality of trauma has broader implications for understanding Woolf's approach to temporal experience overall, as Martin Hägglund's work shows. Taking an opposite tack to Banfield's, he claims that modernist time is often misread as a desire for the transcendental and the immortal, when it is actually invested in 'the radical temporality of life' and in temporal finitude.[5] He posits that Woolf is primordially concerned with the desire to exist and survive in mortal time, a concept he calls chronolibido. This characterizes the 'traumatic' aspect of Woolf's writing about temporality, because temporal experience itself involves a structure of deferral and delay similar to that of trauma. Where the apprehension of trauma is always too soon (unexpected and therefore incomprehensible) as well as too late (not available to consciousness until it imposes itself again as nightmare or memory), Woolf is attuned to the ways in which temporal apprehension, too, manifests as delay or deferral: characters are always in the process of comprehending the past, but their present experience can only be apprehended in retrospect. Hägglund therefore identifies in Woolf's writing nothing less than a 'structural link between the possibility of trauma and the constitution of time'.[6]

While focused on the writer in relation to phenomenologies and temporalities of being, Hägglund's work might be taken in a different direction to illuminate Woolf's political philosophy and peace work. Although his argument is anchored to her earlier modernist texts and precludes her work in the 1930s as well as the posthumously published *Between the Acts* (1941), by temporalizing and extending her relationship to chronolibido over a wider period, we can see how her thinking about time becomes increasingly overt in its politics. It is especially striking that Hägglund's argument pivots on the anticipation of death: since 'the notion of chronolibido seeks to elucidate that it is *because* of temporal finitude that one cares about life in the first place', one's investment in the present is not only inflected by the traumatic past, but by the always-present expectation of a traumatic future.[7] I suggest that this broader trauma of temporal understanding becomes enmeshed with the trauma of being threatened with one's own erasure within the changing historical situation, as the spectre of crises like the Spanish Civil War and World War II began shadowing the inter-war present. From the 1920s through to the 1930s, Woolf's preoccupation with the past and present coexist with the shaping of a war-time future in discomfiting ways, when death feels that much more political and that much more imminent, and when she sought to fight, in her present, against the dehumanizing effects of future war.

One cannot stress enough the inextricable role of history in this anxious futurity. As Woolf wrote in her diary of 13 September 1938: '1914 but without even the illusion of 1914. All slipping consciously into a pit' (*D*5 170). The conscious slide into mid-century historical cataclysm is marked by prolepsis, by the sense of return to an earlier period of wartime disenchantment. But because this is an imperfect return—a return without even

---

[5] Martin Hägglund, *Dying for Time: Proust, Woolf, Nabokov* (Cambridge, MA: Harvard University Press, 2012).

[6] Hägglund, *Dying for Time*, 61.

[7] Hägglund, *Dying for Time*, 8.

the illusion of the past—Woolf's feeling is not only that of repetition or prolepsis but of *lateness*: of catching up with events whose momentum exceeds one's capacity to apprehend or abate it, and of grappling with circumstances whose similarity to, but *unlikeness* from, the past makes the present and one's relationship to it profoundly vexed.

This is a historically-specific understanding of lateness that departs from the transtemporal and transcultural way in which the term has been theorized, especially with regards to style. From Johann von Goethe to Georg Simmel, from Theodor Adorno to Edward Said, late style has been understood in terms of aesthetics' relationship to mortality and death. Where the earlier critics argued that lateness is broadly characterized by a sense of completion and by the sublime consummation of an artist's earlier work, Adorno and Said have suggested that it is often defined by fragmentation and rupture, indicating 'intransigence, difficulty, unresolved contradiction' rather than summation or refinement.[8] Part of the critical debate over how to delimit late style comes from the way it is often deployed as an amalgam of two German terms and their meanings: as a style of posterity and timeless canonicity to which a select group of artists has been elected (*Spätstil* or 'late style'), and as change or development in individual style that comes with advancing age (*Altersstil* or 'old-age style').

In light of the latter meaning, it is to be expected that '[a]ny notion of "late" Woolf is, of course, complicated and retrospectively defined by her suicide in 1941', as Anna Snaith points out.[9] This is especially the case since Woolf's earlier writings are typically read in terms of *Spätstil* while her later works have been seen as inferior and languishing in *Altersstil*. Recent criticism of late Woolf has indeed hinged on the dynamic relationship between her age and aesthetic development—or, as some critics would have it, her anti-development—but age is understood in terms of both person and epoch. Since Jed Esty's argument in *A Shrinking Island: Modernism and National Culture in England* (2004), a familiar narrative of late Woolf and late modernism has focused on ideas of national insularity and re-entrenchment under the weight of imperial decline.[10] Similarly, John Whittier-Ferguson's *Mortality and Form in Late Modernist Literature* (2014) focuses on a constellation of ageing high modernists, arguing for the influence of imminent mortality on Woolf's late style as it is inflected by the coming of World War II and by aesthetic modernism's own expiation.[11] These critical works demonstrate why late modernism presents a distinctive problem for typical accountings of late style. While *Spätstil* is about historical transcendence, *Altersstil*, being about age, is concerned with the historical situatedness that can militate against the former. These tensions are brought to the fore in Woolf's works, which are by turns concerned with the age of her own person

---

[8] Edward Said, *On Late Style: Music and Literature Against the Grain* (London: Bloomsbury, 2006), 3.

[9] Anna Snaith, 'Late Virginia Woolf', *Oxford Handbooks Online*, www.oxfordhandbooks.com/view/10.1093/oxfordhb/9780199935338.001.0001/oxfordhb-9780199935338-e-28.

[10] Jed Esty, *A Shrinking Island: Modernism and National Culture in England* (Princeton: Princeton University Press, 2004).

[11] John Whittier-Ferguson, *Mortality and Form in Late Modernist Literature* (Cambridge, MA: Cambridge University Press, 2014).

and of her era, and by turns concerned with mass violence, both as a definitive element of the twentieth century and as a seemingly perennial historical condition.

Nevertheless, despite being faced with a sense that 'history ... is a nightmare from which [one is] trying to awake', to paraphrase Joyce's *Ulysses* (1922), Woolf saw the lateness of her historical era not as a fatalistic principle, but as the grounds for her own pacifist commitments. However much early Woolf might seem to transform the momentary into the eternal, the worldly into the transcendent, and however much late Woolf might seem to recede into the past and into expressions of sameness and expiation, her overall writing trajectory is, in a politically chronolibidinal fashion, fundamentally invested in the present in relation to catastrophes both past and future. She repeatedly marshals other temporalities in service of a present that demands critical thinking about the ethics of state violence. By the late modernist period, Woolf's late style, in several understandings of that term, would crystallize; but rather than simply expressing national insularity or creative exhaustion, her style reflected her increasingly geopolitical agenda, as her dedication to peace only got stronger as war seemed more and more to be an inevitable condition of modernity. In this way, disaffection, commitment, and prolepsis merge, because her drawing attention to historical belatedness becomes a clarion call for activist work in the present.

Since lateness is not exclusively specific to temporal categories or periods at all, but rather speaks to particular thematic preoccupations or aesthetic forms within a given historical moment, Woolf's development as a writer can be understood in relation to Said's reading of Adorno. His is a reading that emphasizes self-conscious historicity, where one's apprehension of the century's unstoppable wars is simultaneously belated and anticipatory: 'lateness is the idea of surviving beyond what is acceptable and normal'.[12] At a time when the newness of martial innovation and global war became disillusioningly iterative and even tired and cyclical, surviving and persisting in mortal time, with awareness of one's temporal finitude, was precisely what was needed to advocate for an urgent vision of peace.

The impact of war on Woolf's writing, in both content and form, needs to be traced back to *Jacob's Room* (1922), though initial reviews either made no mention of the war at all or only in passing. Perhaps due to the lack of direct references to the conflict within the text itself, it was not until 1932, with Winifred Holtby's *Virginia Woolf: A Critical Memoir* (the first full-length critical work on Woolf) that *Jacob's Room* was called a 'war book'.[13] A fragmented and abortive take on the *Bildungsroman*, the novel traces two and a half decades in the short life of Jacob Flanders, from 1890 to the outset of World War I, and it is comprised of episodic vignettes of the character's childhood in Scarborough, his university years at Trinity College in Cambridge, his friendship with

---

[12] Said, *On Late Style*, 8.

[13] Winifred Holtby, *Virginia Woolf: A Critical Memoir* (London: Bloomsbury, 2007). For more on the early reception history of *Jacob's Room*, see Karen L. Levenback, *Virginia Woolf and the Great War* (Syracuse: Syracuse University Press, 1999), 44.

Bonamy and relationships with various women, a trip to Greece, and finally, his death at war. Now largely recognized as an attempt to write about the Great War indirectly, from its shadows and effects, the text is typically read within the elegiac mode alongside *Mrs Dalloway* (1925) and *To the Lighthouse* (1927) as an attempt to lament and bereave the war dead. As Woolf mused in her diary in 1925, 'I have an idea that I will invent a new name for my books to supplant "novel". A new——by Virginia Woolf. But what? Elegy?' (*D3* 34).

Critics have been divided in their assessments regarding just how sincere the text's elegiac vision really is, with some reading the novel as a sentimental and straightforward act of literary mourning, and others calling it a 'satiric elegy' that criticizes the patriarchal intellectual and political structures to which Jacob belongs, and which send men like him to war.[14] The answer, of course, is that Woolf's novel is both an attempt at articulating war-time grief as well as a critique of England's educational, political, and social institutions.[15] The two projects, far from mutually exclusive, are intertwined; they inform much of her mature fiction, when Woolf's feminism increasingly dovetailed with her anger at violent injustices perpetrated by the same patriarchal structures upholding inequality abroad and at home. As Christine Froula argues, Woolf came of age at the turn of the century when political and social movements gave hope that Europe 'might really be on the brink of becoming' civilized, to use Leonard Woolf's words, only to find barbarities 'within the walls' of European civilization itself: in the form of nationalisms and imperialisms, of disparities within class and sex and gender systems, and in the waging of the 1914 '"Civil War" that rent what had been an increasingly international civilization'.[16]

In *Jacob's Room*, the elegiac mode is both undercut and given further resonance by two narrative features. The first is the hollowness and opacity of Woolf's characterization of Jacob, who remains known to the reader primarily as the object of others' affections, rather than as his own person. The text is self-conscious of this fact: 'It is no use trying to sum people up', the narrator states, 'One must follow hints, not exactly what is said, not yet entirely what is done' (*JR* 37). Or again: 'It seems that a profound, impartial, and absolutely just opinion of our fellow-creatures is utterly unknown […] Such is the manner of our seeing' (*JR* 96). The narrator, whom we know nothing about, except that she is female and a decade older than Jacob, repeatedly interjects that she has no access to interiority to justify her portrait of the titular character.[17] The overall effect is that of negative space or absent presence, with the novel giving shape and form to the

---

[14] Alex Zwerdling, *Virginia Woolf and the Real World* (Berkeley: University of California Press, 1986), 74.

[15] Linda Martin makes this argument concretely in 'Elegy and the Unknowable Mind in Jacob's Room', *Studies in the Novel* 47, no. 2 (Summer 2015), 176–92.

[16] Christine Froula, *Virginia Woolf and the Bloomsbury Avant-Garde: War, Civilization, Modernity* (New York: Columbia University Press, 2005), 17.

[17] 'Whether we know what was in his mind is another question. Granted ten years' seniority and a difference of sex, fear of him comes first; this is swallowed up by a desire to help' (*JR* 128).

lack that death both represents and entails. In this sense, *Jacob's Room* is more of an anti-elegy. Through Jacob's distance and inaccessibility to the reader, the novel mourns his death without sentimentalizing it. Ending with Jacob's mother and Bonamy standing in his room after his death, 'everything [left] just as it was', with a pair of his old shoes never to be worn again, the novel formalizes how war steals and deprives without acceding to narrative consolation (*JR* 246).

Bonamy's final lamenting cry—'Jacob! Jacob!'—is a refrain that brings us back full circle to the novel's beginning, when the character as a child is similarly called by his older brother: '"Ja—cob! Ja—cob!" Archer shouted' (*JR*, 4–5; echoed on 247). This bookending signals a second narrative feature of the novel's approach to elegy: that of return or prolepsis, given weight by a disjointed narrative time and tone that signals circularity or return, but also, foreknowledge of a future that it does not yet tell. For the fact of war, and Jacob's future death in it, seems to shadow the narrative at every turn. From the comings and goings of various admirals and captains throughout Jacob's life, to others' constant comparisons of him with past war heroes, to his very surname Flanders, suggestive of the French–Belgian area where many of the war's battles were fought: Jacob seems predetermined to die in war, his life taken from him from the very beginning.

There are other notable moments of prolepsis: when the narrator, for example, jarringly remarks, 'And now Jimmy feeds crows in Flanders, and Helen visits hospitals', thereby moving Flanders from metaphor to burial site, and polluting the narrative present with the violent future (*JR* 131). Vincent Sherry identifies another arresting moment of prolepsis, during Jacob's continental tour in late spring or early summer of 1914, when the narrator states in a single-sentence paragraph: 'And then, here is Versailles' (*JR* 176).[18] With the Treaty of Versailles lying outside of the novel's narrative time, but invoking for the reader intense and uncomfortable associations in 1922, the year of the text's publication, *Jacob's Room* menacingly brandishes a future beyond that of the Great War and Jacob's death. In doing so, it suggests the prolepsis of war not only as a literary structure, but as a historical principle. As Bloomsbury economist John Maynard Keynes wrote in 1919:

> In England the outward aspect of life does not yet teach us to feel or realize in the least that an age is over ... We are busy picking up the threads of our life where we dropped them. But perhaps it is only in England (and America) that it is possible to be so unconscious. In continental Europe the earth heaves and no one is aware of the rumblings. There it is not just a matter of extravagance or 'labor troubles'; but of life and death, of starvation and existence, and of the fearful convulsions of a dying civilization.[19]

---

[18] See Vincent Sherry, '*Jacob's Room*: Occasions of War, Representations of History', in Jessica Berman, ed., *A Companion to Virginia Woolf* (London: Wiley, 2016), 67–78.

[19] John Maynard Keynes, *The Economic Consequences of the Peace* (Harmondsworth: Penguin, 1995), 4.

In hindsight, Keynes's commentary in *Economic Consequences of the Peace* would take on a sense of the prophetic. Soon enough, history would prove how the burden and humiliation of the financial reparations imposed on Germany would lead to the nationalism, resentment, and desire for retaliation that spurred Nazism. But because he was writing this at the end of one war and before confirmation of the next, Keynes himself is expressing not only prolepsis but an anticipatory sense of belatedness or eventuality. He perceives another war on the horizon as a realization of that which has already been set in motion. *Jacob's Room* brings up this idea in both historical-epochal and aesthetic terms to demand the reader's critical vigilance in linking past and future.

This understanding of historical momentum also informs Woolf's next novel, *Mrs Dalloway*. Published six weeks before her diary musings about the elegy form, *Mrs Dalloway* takes place on one June day in 1923, but its inter-war setting is crucial to its position as a war elegy that makes the most of the genre's capacity to dramatize and mediate psychic, social, and other forms of violence. Certainly, in its rendering of shell-shocked soldier Septimus Smith, the novel makes explicit its project to mourn those irredeemably scarred by war. Physically back in London but unable to reintegrate psychically or emotionally, Septimus sees his dead friend Evans, whom he had witnessed blown to smithereens on the battlefield, around city parks and street corners; others' 'post-war' is still his war time. But there is added insult to injury created by the political-medical institutions to which Septimus is subjected. This shifts the novel from lament to critique. Sir William Bradshaw and Dr Holmes, and their policy of 'Conversion' to social norms, pathologize his condition as the 'deferred effects of shell shock' (*MD* 164), though his interrogation by Sir William reveals this to be only part of the story:

> 'You served with great distinction in the War?'
> The patient repeated the word 'war' interrogatively.
> [. . .]
> 'Yes, he served with the greatest distinction', Rezia assured the doctor; 'he was promoted'.
> [. . .]
> He had committed an appalling crime and had been condemned to death by human nature.
> 'I have—I have—', he began, 'committed a crime—'
> 'He has done nothing wrong whatever', Rezia assured the doctor.
> [. . .]
> 'I—I—', he stammered.
> But what was his crime? He could not remember it.
> 'Yes?' Sir William encouraged him. (But it was growing late.)
> Love, trees, there is no crime—what was his message? (*MD* 86, 88)

In Septimus's confession that he has committed a crime, he attempts to bypass war's vocabulary of distinction and heroism to get at something deeper: the pathology is not shell shock, but the commission of violence and murder that society demanded of its young. Wracked with survivor's guilt but unable to feel, he wonders if 'the world itself is without meaning' (*MD* 79). But since he considers that 'his brain [i]s perfect'—he can read the Inferno, for instance, and can add up his bill—he surmises that 'it must be the fault of the world' that 'he could not feel' (*MD* 79). Seeing his own nation's institutions to blame, he tries to 'tell the whole world' his 'message' about modern violence and the collective responsibility in promoting or resisting it (*MD* 63, 75). And when that fails, he acts out his 'astonishing revelation', bearing his message by falling out of the window in a sacrificial death (*MD* 63).

Mrs Dalloway's move from individual to collective elegy—from mourning Septimus to mourning his victimization by a war-making society—suggests that the future is imperilled, since one's blindness to forms of violence at home and abroad threatens to help history repeat itself. The bitterness and anger displayed by Doris Kilman, Clarissa's daughter's tutor, suggests a fictional manifestation of Keynes's prophecy that an impoverished and humiliated Germany would seek to avenge itself. Miss Kilman's family (then Kiehlman) had emigrated from Germany in the eighteenth century, but despite being an Englishwoman whose brother fought and died for England in the war, she finds herself poor, outside of the Dalloways' class, and a racialized other. She 'evokes a defeated and still belligerent post-war Germany, thrust like a pariah outside the Allies' international community, while the decadent Clarissa whom Miss Kilman would re-educate personifies an England tyrannical in victory and heedless of the political consequences of the international class oppression instituted at Versailles'.[20] What Clarissa fears, Woolf writes, is not Miss Kilman herself, but 'the idea of her', which 'had become one of those spectres with which one battles in the night ... dominators and tyrants' (*MD* 11). The novel transposes onto these women the geopolitical tensions and apprehensions of the inter-war period as they were gradually bubbling to the surface.

With an eye cast to wars both past and future, the novel is self-conscious about a post-war peace that is transmuting into an inter-war breathing space. It is no wonder, then, that *Mrs Dalloway* announces its Janus-faced relation to war time from the very beginning: 'For it was the middle of June. The War was over, except for some one like Mrs Foxcroft at the Embassy last night eating her heart out because that nice boy was killed and now the old Manor House must go to a cousin; or Lady Bexborough who opened a bazaar, they said, with the telegram in her hand, John, her favourite, killed; but it was over; thank Heaven—over' (*MD* 4).[21] When and for whom is war truly over? When does a conflict end if it leads to another?

In Paul Saint-Amour's reading of *Mrs Dalloway*'s skywriting scene, Londoners are fascinated not only by the advertising potential of the aeroplane, but by the spectre of

---

[20] Froula, *Virginia Woolf and the Bloomsbury Avant-Garde*, 104.
[21] Froula, *Virginia Woolf and the Bloomsbury Avant-Garde*, 4.

future aerial warfare that it encapsulates.[22] '[I]t always seems utterly impossible that one should be hurt' by the Zeppelins (*D1* 32), Woolf had remarked in her diary during World War I, but their auguring of civilian vulnerability would soon find renewed and more acute consummation: not only in the Second Sino–Japanese War and the Spanish Civil War, but even earlier, in the British use of aerial bombardment for policing colonial territories in Iraq, among other countries.[23] Future-oriented air-anxiety thus meshed uncomfortably with the act of mourning the past: what is elegized is not just the traumatic effects of a previous war, but the fact that future conflicts are already rearing their heads. Indeed, while the trauma of the future is theoretically impossible in Freudian terms, this is precisely Saint-Amour's hypothesis, which grounds Hägglund's sense of time's inherently ontological-epistemological trauma within a historical-cultural frame. For Saint-Amour, Woolf's attentiveness to future geopolitical conflict means that we need a way of accounting for 'the traumatizing power of anticipation' and for the possibility of a '*pre*-traumatic stress syndrome': for trauma as a temporal affect that transcends its own tenses.[24] Understanding war both as an event and as a condition of everyday life, *Mrs Dalloway* finds a distinctive idiom for Woolf's post-war, inter-war present.

Refrains of non-human agency and negative space from *Jacob's Room* ('listless is the air in an empty room') and *Mrs Dalloway* ('The doors would be taken off their hinges') find later and more heightened manifestation in the second section of *To the Lighthouse*, 'Time Passes' (*JR* 247; *MD* 3). Focused largely on the inanimate environment, the narrative describes scenes of the Ramsays' deserted house, interrupted only by devastating reminders of war-time events rendered shockingly in brackets: '[A shell exploded. Twenty or thirty young men were blown up in France, among them Andrew Ramsay, whose death, mercifully, was instantaneous.]' (*TL* 181). Andrew's death arrives in the midst of other family tragedies, including the sudden passing of Mrs Ramsay, who had been, till now, the novel's protagonist; they are dispatched with in a manner made all the more brutal due to the narrative's prior investment in their interior, psychic lives. Andrew's death is as impersonal and as instantaneous as the way in which it is narrated, and as significant as it is bathetic: merely one of twenty or thirty victims, in a conflict that would claim millions, his passing is traumatizing to those who knew him but peripheral to those who did not. Befitting the brackets themselves, his death is both an aside and a core event.

As James Haule has discussed, earlier drafts of this section were in fact much more explicit in referring to the war, and in critiquing what he describes as the 'male destructiveness and sexual brutality' driving it.[25] While World War I doubtless remains

---

[22] Paul Saint-Amour, *Tense Future: Modernism, Total War, Encyclopedic Form* (Oxford: Oxford University Press, 2015), 110–20.

[23] See Saint-Amour, *Tense Future*, 71–6, for a discussion on colonial air raids during and around 1922, modernism's *annus mirabilis*.

[24] Saint-Amour, *Tense Future*, 17; 7–8 (his emphasis).

[25] James M. Haule, '*To the Lighthouse* and the War', in Mark Hussey, ed., *Virginia Woolf and War: Fiction, Reality, and Myth* (Syracuse: Syracuse University Press, 1991), 164–80, at 166.

central to the section, and quite literally, on a structural level, to the novel as a whole, the published version of 'Time Passes' is notable for the way it layers the war onto the drama of human time and temporal experience overall. Where the first and third sections of *To the Lighthouse* indulge in interweaving complex streams of thought over the course of a single day, in 'Time Passes', a decade passes by in a few pages, largely in the form of external details like the settling of dust in a room. The war is both the period's key, temporally dislocating and catastrophic event as well as a part of a meditation on the ruthless nature of time itself.

The dialectic of violence and time, understood simultaneously as ageless and cyclical yet historically-specific and dislocating, would, by the 1930s, become a key topic of debate. With the rise of fascism, the fact of World War II moved from being a possible to a foregone outcome; what remained to be seen was its scale and magnitude. World War II would differ from World War I in a myriad of ways: from the understanding that violence would reach civilians and not just soldiers, to the long, drawn-out sense of foreknowledge and inevitability that preceded its actual declaration, and to the impression of global war itself as a form of prolepsis and return. Accordingly, there was a large-scale discussion of war and mass violence among 1930s' intelligentsia—including Sigmund Freud, Albert Einstein, Aldous Huxley, Bertrand Russell, and of course, Leonard Woolf—who struggled to theorize war in one or both of two ways: the first considered the broader, more primal question of whether war and barbarity are themselves intrinsic to the human condition, and the other focused on specific social and geopolitical contexts for promoting pacifism and literary activism at this historical juncture. There was a 'tendency to conjoin—or, of equal importance, to juxtapose—two kinds of inquiry', Sarah Cole explains: 'a pragmatic approach which focused on how the Western nations might prevent wars, primarily through the expansion and development of international organizations devoted to world peace, and the anthropological or psychological account of violence as a central feature of human kind'.[26]

The sense of the 1930s as simultaneously distinct and unique, but somehow perennial, cyclical, primordial, and bygone, would inform the late phase of Woolf's writings as they grappled simultaneously with the sense that the road to World War II was already paved, but that, despite and indeed because of this, pacifist engagement was all the more demanded of art. Throughout the decade, Woolf conceived of a generically hybrid text that would alternate fictional 'extracts' or chapters with a book of explanatory essays of social critique, a 'novel-essay' called *The Pargiters* (1937). Two works eventually resulted from a more definitive division along the hyphenated lines. The first is the polemical anti-fascist, pacifist, and feminist essay, *Three Guineas* (1938), which radically rails against the fascist tendencies and patriarchal oppressions of Woolf's own native culture. It is an exemplary reflection of the contemporary debates concerning war but with a feminist stance: asked to think about how to prevent the imminent conflict, the narrator

---

[26] Sarah Cole, *At the Violet Hour: Modernism and Violence in England and Ireland* (Oxford: Oxford University Press, 2012), 205.

of *Three Guineas* tackles the question of why men go to war in the first place, addressing war and militarism in general and the long-term effects of deep-rooted gender inequality from past generations that undergird them. And *Three Guineas* served pacifist agendas beyond its content: Woolf sold manuscripts of the text to raise money for the Refugees Society and signed copies to support the League of Nations.[27]

The second work to emerge from Woolf's thinking is the more subdued and, at first glance, seemingly apolitical historical novel, *The Years*. Begun in 1931, when a split in the Cabinet over the budget caused the government to resign, *The Years*' composition evolved alongside the rise of fascism in Germany as well as the growth of the British Union of Fascists at home. Woolf also worked on the proofs as the Spanish Civil War began, and her diaries at this time oscillate between these artistic and political concerns. Tracing half a century of British history from 1880 to an unspecified 'Present Day', the novel refers to events such as the deaths of Queen Victoria and Charles Stewart Parnell, women's suffrage, the Balkan conflicts, and World War I. These remain incidental to the text's portrait of three generations of the Pargiter family. Not only do the details of everyday life appear to take precedence over world-historical events, the narrative seems to undercut its own chronological structure: although chapter headings pinpoint the particular years in which events are set, Woolf's writing is characterized by repetition and recursiveness, with phrases, songs, actions, and objects reappearing at various points throughout the text and hence, throughout different periods of time. This suggests the suspension and curtailment of linear or progressivist versions of history. In Thomas Davis's reading, *The Years* 'treats conflicts and antagonisms in a notably non-dialectical manner': 'on the one hand, they are the generative, mobilizing force of history; on the other hand, such destruction and violence foreclosures any possibility of historical progress'.[28] In designing a narrative temporality that is both diachronic and synchronic, both chronological and circular, the novel depicts the historical present as at once retrogressive and inexorable, both momentous as well as understandable only in relation to other temporalities. The text's generic rewriting of the historical novel thus gives expression to the particular lateness of the mid- to late thirties as a period of imminent temporal rupture, but also, as the linear result of past events.

While critics have read *The Years*' turn to history as a return to Victorian conservatism, the novel suggests ways in which temporal dislocation and disjuncture could serve as a critical strategy through which to recuperate alternative understandings of the political present. Woolf herself thought deeply about contemporary historiography; she was familiar, for example, with the work of R. G. Collingwood, whose *Idea of History* included the 'presentist' notion that history is 'the knowledge of the past in the present [...] the present revival and reliving of past experiences'.[29] Given such intellectual and

---

[27] Virginia Woolf, *A Room of One's Own and Three Guineas*, ed. Anna Snaith (Oxford: Oxford University Press, 2015), xxvii.
[28] Thomas Davis, *The Extinct Scene: Late Modernism and Everyday Life* (New York: Columbia University Press, 2016), 82.
[29] R. G. Collingwood, *The Idea of History* (Oxford: Oxford University Press, 1993), 175.

historiographical interests, Snaith argues that Woolf's novel engages anticipatorily with the historical materialism of Walter Benjamin, for whom thinking about the past always begins with its stakes in and 'recourse to a consciousness of the present'.[30] Two early titles for *The Years*, when considered alongside one another, are indicative of Woolf's investment in how to understand historical time presently: 'Time Passes' and 'Here and Now'.[31]

The implicit interrelations, and mutual implications, between past, present, and future are nowhere more apparent than in the incessantly rewritten '1917' chapter of the novel, in which Woolf drew on her own past war-time diaries to depict the Pargiters sheltering from an air raid during World War I. Surely, the scene needs to be read as prolepsis, as both a memory of a past event and an imaginative rehearsal of things to come. But while depicting an air raid, the scene also acts as a creative air-raid siren of sorts, sounding the need to think critically, to 'fight with the mind', as Woolf exhorts in her later essay 'Thoughts on Peace in an Air Raid' (1940) (*E6* 242). In the scene, Eleanor recognizes Nicholas's homosexuality and Polish ethnicity with a 'sharp shiver of repugnance ... Then she realized it touched nothing of importance ... All the evening, off and on, she had been feeling about him; this, that, and the other; but now all the feelings came together and made one feeling, one whole-liking' (*Y* 269). The loss of physical civilian immunity during an air raid has given way to another, more inter-social kind of immunity that would buttress against the ethnic and sexual prejudices driving the war to come. While suggesting how one could and should bear history in mind when acting in the future, Woolf gives the briefest of spaces to this insight, making it barely perceptible. Political indirection characterizes another scene towards the end of the text, when North briefly and offhandedly observes Oswald Mosley's fascist insignia on a London street: 'somebody had chalked a circle on the wall with a jagged line in it' (*Y* 279). Such fleeting moments, Davis points out, accumulate throughout the novel, demanding of the reader a critical-interpretive practice even before—especially before—the arrival of historical catastrophe. It makes startlingly legible the potential banality of evil.

As Elizabeth Evans has shown, *The Years*' final form is motivated by a belief in anti-didacticism and in the avoidance of explicit critique, due to Woolf's opposition to proselytizing and propagandizing.[32] The opposition to didacticism, and to univocality and monologism as totalitarian aesthetics, continues through to *Between the Acts*. Centring on the staging of an annual village pageant of English history in the grounds of a remote country home, Woolf's last novel describes the various goings-on and interactions of the community, with the pageant itself operating as an anticlimax. The narrative finds a level of interpretive openness and looseness that seems to suggest triviality: 'Did the plot matter? [...] The plot was only there to beget emotion', one character

---

[30] Anna Snaith, '*The Years* and Contradictory Time', in Jessica Berman, ed., *A Companion to Virginia Woolf* (Chichester: Wiley-Blackwell, 2016), 137–50, at 140.

[31] Snaith, '*The Years* and Contradictory Time', 137.

[32] Elizabeth Evans, 'Air War, Propaganda, and Woolf's Anti-Tyranny Aesthetic', *Modern Fiction Studies* 59, no. 1 (Spring 2013), 53–82.

says (*BA* 66). Here, too, we find expressions of war as simultaneously primordial and dislocating, ever-present and ruptural, though on even larger timescales. On the one hand, the landscape is a palimpsest of past violence where, '[f]rom an aeroplane ... you could still see, plainly marked, the scars made by the Britons; by the Romans; by the Elizabethan manor house; and by the plough, when they ploughed the hill to grow wheat in the Napoleonic wars' (*BA* 3). Images of pre-history, supplied by Lucy Swithin's imaginative reading of a book called *Outline of History* interpolate the narrative.[33] On the other hand, such suggestions of deep history and chronology are threatened by the 1939 present: '[t]welve aeroplanes in perfect formation like a flight of wild duck' interrupt the pageant and sever Reverend Streatfield's words, reminding the audience and the reader of the threat of present-day bombers (*BA* 138). In Woolf's meditation on being between the acts of two world wars, the long past as well as the future are at stake.

Despite often being read as an epitomic text of late modernist nostalgia and insularity, *Between the Acts* is persistently concerned with how to think carefully about the global crisis during the text's conception. Notably, the final scene of the pageant brings the audience up to 'the present moment. It was now. Ourselves'; this was not done in the popular Parkerian pageantry in the 1930s, which prioritized historical re-enactment and epochal distance (*BA* 133).[34] Pageant playwright La Trobe wanted to 'expose them [the audience], as it were, to douche them, with present-time reality', Woolf writes (*BA* 129). The novel also rallies against any notion of enforced univocality, which it equates with the oppressive forces of totalitarianism contemporaneous with its writing. When the pageant dissolves into a dialogic chorus of unidentifiable voices that form a 'rambling capricious but somehow unified whole', as Woolf describes it in her diary entry, even the unexpected intrusion of bellowing cows in the countryside becomes a 'primeval voice' that 'filled the emptiness and continued the emotion' of the actors (*D5* 135; *BA* 101, 102). 'Dispersed are we; who have come together', goes the pageant's central refrain: 'Unity—Disperity' (*BA* 141, 144). Spoken near the end of the novel, this claim of togetherness and dispersion, of communality and divergence, insists on heterogeneity, plurality, and deviation as a more democratic ethos that is distinct from the uniformity of fascist regimes that punished outliers from the perceived 'normal'.

Prolepsis is folded into the writing of the novel itself, as Woolf had already included the presence of bomber planes flying over England in the March 1939 draft before World War II began in earnest. Furthermore, set on one June day in 1939, months before war's outbreak when fears of the conflict remained anticipatory rather than known, *Between the Acts* returns to the use of prolepsis in *Jacob's Room*. Where Versailles in the earlier novel suggested a peace that would itself lead to another war, with Woolf's last novel, the war becomes its own endgame while commenting on the constant ebb and flow of historical violence.

---

[33] The book is a fictional amalgamation of two actual works, H. G. Wells's *The Outline of History* (1920) and G. M. Trevelyan's *History of England* (1926).

[34] Esty, *A Shrinking Island*, 61.

From the 1920s to the early 1940s, then, we come full circle in Woolf's own use of prolepsis. But, as with the proleptic mode itself, this is a repetition with a difference. Future- rather than past-oriented, Woolf's use of prolepsis is always in service of a historical present that seems too late to be redeemed in terms of the mass violence of the twentieth century, but that nevertheless demands self-questioning and proactive critique as a way forward. 'What remedy was there for her at her age—thirty-nine, the age of the century—in books?' Isa thinks (*BA* 14).[35] In Woolf's fiction, the answer, it would appear, lies precisely in the literature itself, where writing and the creative imagination have the capacity and the burden to make historical consciousness—and historical conscience— legible for her contemporary moment. It also lies in connecting philosophical thinking about time and history with political activism, to fashion a narrative style that responds to the temporal politics of war with a pacifist politics of time.

Selected Bibliography

Banfield, Ann, 'Time Passes: Virginia Woolf, Post-Impressionism, and Cambridge Time', *Poetics Today* 24, no. 3 (Autumn 2003), 471–516.

Cole, Sarah, *At the Violet Hour: Modernism and Violence in England and Ireland* (Oxford: Oxford University Press, 2012).

Collingwood, R. G., *The Idea of History* (Oxford: Oxford University Press, 1993).

Davis, Thomas, *The Extinct Scene: Late Modernism and Everyday Life* (New York: Columbia University Press, 2016).

Esty, Jed, *A Shrinking Island: Modernism and National Culture in England* (Princeton: Princeton University Press, 2004).

Evans, Elizabeth, 'Air War, Propaganda, and Woolf's Anti-Tyranny Aesthetic', *Modern Fiction Studies* 59, no. 1 (Spring 2013), 53–82.

Froula, Christine, *Virginia Woolf and the Bloomsbury Avant-Garde: War, Civilization, Modernity* (New York: Columbia University Press, 2005).

Hägglund, Martin, *Dying for Time: Proust, Woolf, Nabokov* (Cambridge, MA: Harvard University Press, 2012).

Haule, James M., '*To the Lighthouse* and the War', in Mark Hussey, ed., *Virginia Woolf and War: Fiction, Reality, and Myth* (Syracuse: Syracuse University Press, 1991), 164–80.

Henke, Suzette, and David Eberly, assisted by Jane Lilienfeld, *Virginia Woolf and Trauma: Embodied Texts* (New York: Pace University Press, 2007).

MacKay, Marina, 'Violence, Art, and War', in Peter Brooker, Andrzej Gasiorek, Deborah Longworth, and Andrew Thacker, eds, *Oxford Handbook of Modernisms* (Oxford: Oxford University Press, 2010), 461–76.

Martin, Linda, 'Elegy and the Unknowable Mind in Jacob's Room', *Studies in the Novel* 47, no. 2 (Summer 2015), 176–92.

Saint-Amour, Paul, *Tense Future: Modernism, Total War, Encyclopedic Form* (Oxford: Oxford University Press, 2015).

---

[35] Esty, *A Shrinking Island*, 14.

Sherry, Vincent, '*Jacob's Room*: Occasions of War, Representations of History', in Jessica Berman ed., *A Companion to Virginia Woolf* (London: John Wiley & Sons, 2016), 67–78.

Snaith, Anna, '*The Years* and Contradictory Time', in Jessica Berman, ed., *A Companion to Virginia Woolf* (Chichester: Wiley-Blackwell, 2016), 137–50.

Whittier-Ferguson, John, *Mortality and Form in Late Modernist Literature* (Cambridge: Cambridge University Press, 2014).

CHAPTER 29

WORK

MARY WILSON

The opening lines of *Mrs Dalloway* (1925) may be the most famous of all Virginia Woolf's opening lines, and they are told from the perspective of a servant: Lucy, Mrs Dalloway's harried but devoted maid:

> Mrs Dalloway said she would buy the flowers herself.
> For Lucy had her work cut out for her. The doors would be taken off their hinges; Rumplemayer's men were coming. And then, thought Clarissa Dalloway, what a morning—fresh as if issued to children on a beach. (*MD* 3)

Lucy's voice is presented through an aside in Woolf's slippery free indirect discourse; the colloquialism of 'her work cut out for her' and the formal address of her employer in the first sentence hint at the point of view Woolf's narrator temporarily occupies. Quickly, though, the narrator moves on. Lucy is a starting place, a jumping-off point, left on the house side of that open threshold as Clarissa ventures off into public space and her own remembrances.

This idiom, 'work cut out', is unusual in Woolf's writing, appearing only four times: once each in *The Voyage Out* (1915), *The Years* (1937), *A Room of One's Own* (1929), and *Mrs Dalloway*. It denotes a significant, perhaps almost overwhelming task, a job that must be done and that requires concentration and effort. The phrase's association here with Lucy's preparations for Mrs Dalloway's party adds another layer of meaning as Clarissa walks out the door. Not only are Lucy's responsibilities daunting, they are also set out for her by her mistress, who—liberated from such responsibilities—is free to choose whether or not she goes out to buy her own flowers.

In another sense, until relatively recently, the work of domestic servants has largely been cut out of Woolf studies. But redirecting critical attention to domestic space and to the cross-class economic and emotional relationships housed there is important work cut out for us in understanding Woolf. Attending to the particulars of the opening moments of *Mrs Dalloway* reveals a still under-explored element of Woolf's writing: the ubiquity, and necessity, of domestic servants, to the stories Woolf tells, to the way in which she tells them, and to the circumstances that enabled her to write at all. Servants revitalize the neglected house at the heart of *To the Lighthouse* (1927) after the Ramsay family's many losses. Crosby, ' "still with us" ' (*Y* 149) for much of *The Years*, becomes a symbol of Victorian domestic stasis to be escaped in modern life. Mrs Moffatt sweeps up in *The Waves* (1931); the scullery maid tells ghost stories in *Between the Acts* (1941). Servants are part of the fabric of domesticity (even creating that fabric in the short story 'Nurse Lugton's Curtain'), but rarely are they given the opportunity to speak for themselves or permitted to have their own stories. Flush gets his full biography while the life of Lily Wilson, Elizabeth Barrett Browning's maid, is sectioned off in a (four-page) footnote. Like Lucy as *Mrs Dalloway* begins, these Woolfian servants are at once central and marginal.

Recently, critics have begun to insist on the value of turning our attention to domestic servants in Woolf's life and in her writing. Acknowledging their presence, in turn, suggests a need to re-examine Woolf's depictions of domesticity in terms of class, and her depictions of class in terms of domesticity. This project is more complex than it may initially appear. Bringing servants into the critical conversation means more than facing up to and trying to reconcile the mocking nastiness and middle-class prejudice that often characterizes Woolf's private comments on her servants with her commitment to women's need for independence and self-direction. It involves grappling with the unique qualities of cross-class relationships in shared domestic space, which distinguishes the particular context of domesticity and class from more wide-ranging investigations of class in Woolf.

As Victoria Rosner notes, 'No other major novelist of the period was so preoccupied with the critique of Victorian domesticity or so explicit about the relationship of literary modernism to the changing nature of private life.'[1] Woolf's writing about domesticity explicitly addresses the question of how modern women can confront the wide-ranging cultural, social, and personal impacts of patriarchal control of individuals and institutions. Woolf also recognizes that domestic service is part of this patriarchal legacy, calling it 'a fine rubbish heap left by our parents to be swept' (*D3* 220). Woolf's choice of metaphor is revealing: she finds the 'system' of domestic service to be a mess, but her passive construction leaves open who will do the sweeping. In 'Mr Bennett and Mrs Brown', Woolf argues that the tools of the Edwardian novelists will not work for Georgian writers who want to capture the changed human character of twentieth-century modernity. Her deep engagement with remaking her own domestic spaces, from the time she and her siblings first set up house in Bloomsbury, shows that she extended this narrative critique to ways of living. But Woolf could never get free from servants, never completely constructed a domesticity that did not depend on the labour of others—specifically other women. As Selina Todd explains:

---

[1] Victoria Rosner, *Modernism and the Architecture of Private Life* (New York: Columbia University Press, 2005), 15.

the keeping of servants enabled middle-class women to lead increasingly independent lives without challenging the sexual and class divisions of labor. Self-consciously emancipated women like Virginia Woolf and Vera Brittain raised the question of how women could combine love and work, domesticity and citizenship—but ultimately they felt unable to create 'a penurious but unhumiliating independence in Bloomsbury' without the domestic assistance of working-class women.[2]

Servants are a persistent reminder that the independence Woolf craved is predicated on the availability of other women to do the domestic work that the woman writer sets aside.

In these intimate and personal relationships worked out in servant-supported domestic space, in the private house that is not purely private, we can most clearly see how, as Woolf argues in *Three Guineas* (1938), that 'the public and the private worlds are inseparably connected ... the tyrannies and servilities of the one are the tyrannies and servilities of the other' (*TG* 214). Domestic space matters because patriarchy has made the history of women the history of the private house, a history that has been systematically denied importance and that Woolf makes central to her work. Jane Marcus sees the footnotes in *Three Guineas* as 'provid[ing] a reading list for an alternative history that includes the domestic with the national and international',[3] and in so doing creates a discourse that can recognize the domestic as foundational to the system of class and gender oppression that also operates on national and international levels. Woolf consistently gives her feminist attention to the private sphere as the locus of women's lives, and she lives and writes during a period of extraordinary upheaval in the day-to-day experience of living, including in the institution of domestic service. Even if her conclusions about service are contradictory, her emotions inconsistent, her attitudes unenlightened and her depictions, particularly in her private writings, sometimes downright cruel, Woolf demonstrates a lifelong intellectual and personal engagement with the problems and benefits of domestic service, for both the daughters of educated men and for the women who served them. Like Isa Oliver, Woolf too was 'pegged down ... by a myriad of hair-thin ties into domesticity' (*BA* 14). The inescapable intersection of domesticity and class is one of the most profoundly constructive contexts of Woolf's life. Woolf's experience of domesticity and class varies over the course of her lifetime, but her (sometimes unwilling) dependence on the care of servants, particularly women, remains constant. If not for the home-making labours of servants like Sophie Farrell, Nellie Boxall, Lottie Hope, Annie Thompsett, and Louie Everest, Woolf's novel-making could not have taken place. Their work was the necessary condition for hers.

The consequences of that dependence, in Woolf's life and in her writing, are profound. It is not just Lucy in *Mrs Dalloway* who has 'her work cut out for her'. When the

---

[2] Selina Todd, 'Domestic Service and Class Relations in Britain 1900–1950', *Past & Present* 203 (May 2009), 201.

[3] Jane Marcus, 'Introduction', in Virginia Woolf, *Three Guineas*, ed. Jane Marcus (New York: Harcourt, 2006), lix.

phrase appears again in *A Room of One's Own*, it refers to the task at hand for Woolf's modern woman novelist, Mary Carmichael. This echoing phrase both draws together Mary and Lucy as women at work even as it reminds us of their social separation: Mary must observe and write while she 'still wear[s] the shoddy old fetters of class on her feet' (*ARO* 67). Woolf writes while wearing those fetters as well, but throughout her work demonstrates her awareness of them. Even if servants' voices are scaled back as Woolf moves through drafts of her novels and stories, they are not cut out entirely. Servant characters appear in all of Woolf's novels, in her book-length essays, and in many short stories. A servant illustrates the 'change in human character' that necessitates a new kind of novel-writing in 'Mr Bennett and Mrs Brown', and talk about servants allows Mrs Brown herself to avoid a difficult conversation on the train in that essay. Servants' sometimes ghostly presences in the texts encourage us to look and to read more closely—particularly as a means to considering the relation between domestic service and writing itself, both as forms of work and in the form of the works Woolf produces. Like—and so unlike—her servants, Woolf also worked at home; their shared domestic space was also their workplace. Her servants' labours in her homes enabled her to write. Virginia Woolf's writing demonstrates a fundamental connection between these two kinds of work taking place in the home: the home-making efforts of servants and the novel-making labour of the writer.

Anna Snaith insists, 'There can be no doubt that [Woolf] thought carefully about her class position, its benefits and drawbacks, and how it affected what and whom she could write about.'[4] While noting that Woolf held many of the prejudices towards servants and other members of the 'lower orders' that were common in her circle, Kathryn Simpson points out, 'less typical was her self-consciousness about such attitudes and her scrutiny of her own snobbish and class-biased responses and feelings'.[5] Jean Mills argues that Woolf's 'diaries, her essays, and her fiction point to a woman grappling with the disparities of class and the consequences and frustrations of both trying to resist and yet being forced to be constrained by the demands of a class-bound patriarchal society', and explains further that 'issues of class, which Virginia Woolf saw as inseparable from gender, remain prevailing and effective discourses, both overtly and within the subtexts of her life and work'.[6] Woolf's engagements with leftist politics and women's education were tied up with ethical attentiveness to the position of working-class men and women. Her work at Hogarth Press shows her commitment to publishing working-class voices. Her private writings demonstrate a critically self-aware understanding that 'the stability of her class depended' on the 'contentment' of lower-class workers.[7]

---

[4] Anna Snaith, *Virginia Woolf: Public and Private Negotiations* (New York: St. Martin's Press, 2000), 116.

[5] Kathryn Simpson, 'Social Class in *To the Lighthouse*', in Allison Pease, ed., *The Cambridge Companion to* To the Lighthouse (Cambridge: Cambridge University Press, 2015), 110.

[6] Jean Mills, 'Virginia Woolf and the Politics of Class', in Jessica Berman, ed., *A Companion to Virginia Woolf* (Chichester: Wiley-Blackwell, 2016), 220–1.

[7] Alice Wood, 'Facing *Life as We Have Known It*: Virginia Woolf and the Women's Co-Operative Guild', *Literature and History* 23, no. 2 (Autumn 2014), 23–4.

Some of the most important and revealing recent work on Woolf and class has looked specifically at domestic space and domestic service, most significantly Alison Light's revelatory *Mrs Woolf and the Servants*. Light excavates the biographies of the women who served Woolf throughout her life and places them alongside Woolf's own life story. For Light, the story of Woolf's relationship with her servants is 'a story about mutual—and unequal—dependence but it [is] also about social differences, about class feelings and attitudes which were generated and sustained by women at home and indoors rather than by men in their workplaces'.[8] Ultimately, Light argues that 'the figure of the servant and of the working woman haunts Woolf's experiments in literary modernism and sets a limit to what she can achieve'.[9] However, Pamela L. Caughie suggests that we see Woolf's reluctance to ventriloquize working-class characters as an ethical position. In fact, Caughie claims, 'the assumption that in refusing to identify with servants, Woolf fails to give them their due' misses the point of Woolf's modernism, which attempts to 'enter into those social spaces, the manifold and shifting social spaces between the classes, and to respond to "the absolute alterity of the neighbour"'.[10]

Light's and Caughie's positions point to the difficulty of reconciling what seem like fundamental contradictions in Woolf's living with and thinking and writing about servants, and to the larger questions about feminist domesticity that those contradictions reveal. As Mary Childers argues, 'A willingness to hear the voice of the relatively privileged woman crack under the pressure of class position is essential to a feminism that acknowledges differences among and within women.'[11] Woolf's voice cracks frequently when she turns to domestic servants. Often her fictional servants are largely instrumental or idealized—such as, for instance, *Mrs Dalloway*'s Lucy, who remains a servant even in her fantasies: 'She was Lady Angela, attending Princess Mary, when in came Mrs Dalloway' (*MD* 34). Even as she works to extricate women from oppressive social structures, her own continued reliance on domestic service underscores Woolf's complicity in patriarchal systems of power. Examining the interrelations of domesticity and class may shed light on some persistent questions: Why are servants so vexing in Woolf's writing that she repeatedly edits out servant characters over the course of working on a novel or a story? How could Woolf, analysing so skilfully the circumstances that have stunted women's development as writers, recognize the need for money and a room of one's own but fail to include explicit analysis of how her own ability to write depended on using some of that money to pay someone else to keep that room clean? What is at stake for Woolf in the ways that she seems sometimes able to see servants clearly and at other times not at all? How does Woolf's understanding of her own gendered oppression in a patriarchal society intersect with her class consciousness? In thinking about her fiction, Woolf recognizes the juiciness, the clear narrative potential, in servant

---

[8] Alison Light, *Mrs Woolf and the Servants* (London: Bloomsbury Press, 2008), xiv.
[9] Light, *Mrs Woolf*, xviii.
[10] Pamela Caughie, 'Dogs and Servants', *Virginia Woolf Miscellany* 84 (Autumn 2013), 38.
[11] Mary Childers, 'Virginia Woolf on the Outside Looking Down: Reflections on the Class of Women', *Modern Fiction Studies* 38, no. 1 (Spring 1992), 62.

stories, as when she declares in her diary that, were she reading it, 'I think I should seize with greed upon the portrait of Nelly [Boxall], & make a story—perhaps make the whole story revolve round that—it would amuse me. Her character—our efforts to be rid of her—our reconciliations' (*D3* 274) but is never able to write that story out. Throughout her adult life, Woolf questioned the need, the usefulness, and the ethics of keeping domestic servants. Yet Woolf was never without servants in her employ, frustrated as both servant and mistress might be in their relationship of mutual dependence.

It appears there is something significantly different about class experienced in a domestic context than in the public sphere. The usual touchstone for Woolf's ideas about the working class—her introduction to *Life as We Have Known It*, a collection of writings by members of the Women's Co-operative Guild, also published separately as 'Memories of a Working Women's Guild'—has questionable relevance for an analysis of domesticity and class, because it presupposes separate domestic spaces for these women of different classes. Woolf claims that 'One could not be Mrs Giles because one's body had never stood at the wash-tub, one's hands had never wrung and scrubbed and chopped up whatever the meat may be that makes a miner's dinner' (*E4* 137). Critics such as Mary Childers, Laura Marcus, and Evelyn Tsz Yan Chen have read this statement as a failure of empathy and imagination; others, including Q.D. Leavis—often cutting in her analyses of Woolf's class-bound imagination—see it as an honest admission of the limits of her ability to speak across lines of class.[12] Strikingly, though, this and other examples of working-class life Woolf cites in her introduction do not include examples of domestic service work—the closest regular contact Woolf would have to working women, and the kind of work that it might seem easiest for her to imagine. Instead, Woolf seems to find servants particularly hard to think through, to the point that they become conspicuous by their absence. Woolf's description of the gulf between the experiences of the middle-class woman and the working-class woman provides a near-perfect example of servants and their labour being 'cut out': 'They did not stroll through the house and say, that cover must go to the wash, or those sheets need changing. They plunged their arms in hot water and scrubbed the clothes themselves' (*E4* 137–8). For Mary Childers, this passage is another example that 'usefully reveals what Woolf, or a woman in her position, may have particular trouble seeing.... Woolf's two sentences about laundry deftly omit the fact that when the women who stroll give orders, they give them to other women, often women of the same class represented in these essays.'[13] Childers's analysis suggests that cutting out the work of servants is crucial to the argument Woolf (problematically) makes in her essay, precisely because Woolf's repeated insistence that middle-class

---

[12] See Childers, 'Outside Looking Down'; Laura Marcus, 'Woolf's feminism and feminism's Woolf', in Sue Roe and Susan Sellers, eds, *The Cambridge Companion to Virginia Woolf* (Cambridge: Cambridge Univesity Press, 2010), 142–79; Evelyn Tsz Yan Chan, *Virginia Woolf and the Professions* (Cambridge: Cambridge University Press, 2014); Anna Snaith, *Virginia Woolf: Public and Private Negotiations*; Q. D. Leavis, 'Lady Novelists and the Lower Orders', *Scrutiny* 7, no. 2 (1935), 128.

[13] Childers, 'Outside Looking Down', 67.

women and working-class women have nothing in common would be undercut if she acknowledged that they are domestic cohabitants.

To acknowledge how, and to what end, the work of servants is cut out of 'Memories of a Working Women's Guild' is to see its engagement with class in a new and important light. Woolf claims that her sympathies with working-class women are blunted by the distance between her experience and theirs, but her problems with imagining domestic servants stem from their proximity. It is not that servants are too distant from her experience, but that they are too close. Victorian domestic life—the 'fine rubbish heap' of a system Woolf decries—operated through strict separations that created a sense of distance among family and servants sharing the same domestic space. These divisions were significantly less possible to maintain in the homes Woolf made as an adult. Woolf lives through—and actively engages in—a time of extraordinary upheaval in domestic life, from the Victorian houses of her childhood to the modernist domestic spaces she and her peers created. She nods to this change in her depiction of the two cooks in 'Mr Bennett and Mrs Brown':

> The Victorian cook lived like a leviathan in the lower depths, formidable, silent, obscure, inscrutable; the Georgian cook is a creature of sunshine and fresh air; in and out of the drawing room, now to borrow the *Daily Herald*, now to ask advice about a hat. Do you ask for more solemn instances of the power of the human race to change? (*E*1 320)

Though the description of the Georgian cook seems, on the surface, far more positive than the Victorian, it has an edge of concern too: she is no longer confined to her own separate space, and she may share her employers' tastes in reading and fashion. This newfound mobility and closeness are a problem for both Woolf the writer and Woolf the employer. Her attempts to resolve it in both arenas become another instance of 'work cut out', as Woolf reduces the presence of servants in her fiction and moves towards daily help in her life, rather than the live-in service that characterized her earlier experiences of domestic labour.

Virginia Stephen was born into a household at once blended and stratified. It comprised eighteen people: eleven family members, with seven servants to wait on them. The architecture of 22 Hyde Park Gate reinforced the social divisions among the classes of people under its roof. Maids slept in attic bedrooms above the study where Leslie Stephen worked. The long-time family cook, Sophie Farrell, laboured in the basement, like the 'Leviathan of the lower depths' Woolf would describe in 'Mr Bennett and Mrs Brown'. That lowest floor also provided space for the servants' sitting room, which Woolf remembered as 'at the back; very low and very dark' (*MB* 116). The family had their spaces—nursery, bedrooms, sitting rooms, drawing room—in the floors between. The house was substantially expanded in 1886 when Virginia was four years old, increasing its size by a third. Maintaining such a space and the people in it demanded near-constant effort. While the mistress of the house was responsible for directing her servants' labour—Alison Light notes that 'Julia [Stephen] began the day by descending to the kitchen to discuss the meals' with Sophie Farrell[14]—the servants were charged with making the house into a home. Together, Julia Stephen and her household staff enabled Leslie Stephen to dedicate himself to his work in the room of his own.

Between 1830 and 1880, one in six English women was in service.[15] The 1881 census reported a total of 1,230,406 women working as domestic servants, nearly half a million more than were in service thirty years earlier. The rise in the servant population paralleled the growth of the middle class in the nineteenth century. Servant-keeping was a clear indicator of class status: '[f]or any nineteenth-century family with social pretensions at least one domestic servant was essential'.[16] When, in *Night and Day* (1919), Joan Denham proposes 'fewer servants' as a means to reduce their lower-middle-class family's expenses, her brother Ralph quickly responds '"It's out of the question"' (*ND* 24). The non-aristocratic servant-keeping class encompassed a wide range, from those struggling to pay a single maid-of-all-work to those who, like the Stephens, were able to employ an array of women to care for their home and its inhabitants.

For Virginia and her social contemporaries, servants were both ubiquitous and invisible, their labours evident throughout the main house while their living quarters were sectioned off and hidden. Architectural design reinforced such estrangement. Servants often had their own separate set of stairs, sectioned off by a door covered with green baize cloth to soften noise; at Hyde Park Gate, a 'plush curtain hung over the top of a staircase in the dining room, muffling the servants' activities and keeping the cooking smells, no longer considered suitable for genteel noses, at bay'.[17] This physical separation had both practical and ideological dimensions. Books on household management by such domestic authorities as Mrs Beeton argued for strong control of servants by the mistress of the house, advice balanced by conduct books for servants that encouraged servants to remember their lesser place. Emily Augusta Patmore—the model for the Angel in the House in her husband's poem—suggested in *The Servants' Behaviour Book* that '[you] should remember that, as long as you are in service, you are always in the house of another, and have strangers round you'.[18] Given the necessarily intimate relationship of domestic servants to the bodies and emotions of their employers, Patmore's instruction suggests a need to reinforce an ideology of estrangement to counteract a lived experience of uncanny proximity and deep knowledge. The revelation of servant closeness can be deeply unsettling.

Intriguingly, Woolf finds herself in an unexpected place when she tries to 'describe the cage—22 Hyde Park Gate' in which she was 'shut up' with her 'tyrant father' in 'A Sketch of the Past': not in any of the family's spaces, but rather 'at the basement; in the

---

[14] Light, *Mrs Woolf*, 34.
[15] Theresa McBride, *The Domestic Revolution: The Modernisation of Household Service in England and France 1820–1920* (London: Croom Helm, 1976), 34.
[16] Pamela Horn, *The Rise and Fall of the Victorian Servant* (Wolfeboro Falls: Alan Sutton, 1991), 17.
[17] Light, *Mrs Woolf*, 32.
[18] Emily Augusta Patmore (Mrs Mary Motherly), *The Servant's Behaviour Book* (London: Bell and Daldy, 1859), 41.

servants' sitting room' (*MB* 116). This spatial memory leads to a vivid recollection of the moment when a housemaid unexpectedly opined about the basement conditions:

> It was a dark insanitary place for seven maids to live in. 'It's like hell,' one of them burst out to my mother as we sat at lessons in the dining room. My mother at once assumed the frozen dignity of a Victorian matron, and said (perhaps): 'Leave the room'; and she (unfortunate girl) vanished behind the red plush curtain which, hooped round a semi-circular wire, and anchored by a great gold knob, hid the door that led from the dining room to the pantry.
> It was in the dining room, at the long baize covered table, that we did our lessons. (*MB* 116–17)

Remembering her own sense of entrapment points Woolf to the physical suppression of the Stephens' maids, suggesting an incompletely explored identification that also surfaces in some other references to servants and servitude. Woolf also explicitly connects this moment to education. What, exactly, is the lesson that Virginia Stephen learns here?

Most overtly, Julia Stephen is teaching her children about how to deal with servants who violate what Victoria Rosner describes as 'the code of invisibility' that hides 'the tremendous discrepancy between life on one side of the curtain and the other'.[19] The 'baize covered table' invoked at the start of Woolf's new paragraph is protected by the same material often used to separate servants and employers; the reference reinforces the writer's turn away from the servant's experience and towards her own domestic education. Unlike Thoby and Adrian, who start their education at the dining table with Julia but continue through public school and Cambridge, Virginia's and Vanessa's education will be primarily (though not exclusively) domesticated. What's going on in this moment is another instance of work being cut out: the daily lived drudgery of menial work cut out, separated and sanitized, from the middle-class work of education. Looking back, the adult Woolf has some sympathy for the maid, but once the servant 'vanishes' to the other side of the curtain, she is gone for good—she never reappears in 'A Sketch'. Though her parentheses indicate that she feels for the girl's situation, Woolf does not, perhaps cannot, follow the servant imaginatively into the 'hell' of the basement.

Woolf notes elsewhere in 'A Sketch of the Past' that 'one only remembers what is exceptional', a fact that she links to the difficulty of writing about the majority of lived experience, which consists of 'non-being': 'A great part of every day is not lived consciously. One walks, eats, sees things, deals with what has to be done; the broken vacuum cleaner; ordering dinner; writing orders to Mabel; washing; cooking dinner; bookbinding' (*MB* 69–70). Servants are part of non-being, their work only obliquely acknowledged. Only certain standout moments, such as the one between Julia and the maid in the dining room, are memorable.

---

[19] Rosner, *Modernism*, 67.

Julia's lesson makes class difference, and not gender solidarity, fundamental to domestic space. In so doing, it elides the fact that both the daughters of educated men and domestic servants have a problematic class identity that is directly related to their positions in the private house. In *Three Guineas*, Woolf questions the applicability of the language of class to the daughters of educated men because of the specific issues of gender: 'if the term "bourgeois" fits her brother, it is grossly incorrect to use it of one who differs so profoundly in the two prime characteristics of the bourgeoisie—capital and environment' (*TG* 218, n2). Since the daughters of educated men have been systematically restricted to the space of the private house and denied access to those tools that determine class position and power, Woolf suggests that a characteristic of her class is to see and experience their own class at an oblique angle. But servants are in a similar position. Selina Todd highlights 'the silence on service that characterizes the major historical studies of class in twentieth-century Britain'.[20] Explaining why servants have tended to be ignored by historians despite their ubiquity in modern Europe, Theresa McBride notes that:

> The servant has not interested the social or labour historian concerned with class struggle since servants did not form a true social class. Although recognised by law as a distinctive social group, servants did not have a class identity, since for most domestics, household employment was not a permanent occupation.... Moreover, servants were isolated from the mainstream of working-class activities and aspirations.... Working alone or with only one or two other domestics in a middle- or upper-class household, the servant gained no sense of class solidarity and the great majority remained politically inactive.[21]

The nature of domestic service inhibits the development of a class consciousness, encouraging servants to identify with (or against) the family they serve and the relatively few other servants in the house, not with the broader array of other servants doing similar work in other houses. This isolation persisted despite the fact that domestic servants made up the vast majority of the population of working women in Woolf's lifetime; in Britain, service was 'the largest single female occupation ... until at least 1945'.[22]

In her own writings about domestic service, Julia Stephen rhetorically elides the distinction she so sharply drew in Woolf's anecdote. In her essay 'Domestic Arrangements of the Ordinary English Home', Stephen characterizes the system of domestic service as based on choices made by both masters and servants, and therefore not demeaning to either: 'when the work which we choose to call menial and which in our daily life we find convenient to relegate to others, is chosen by those whose choice is free, it is clear that domestic work carries with it no stigma'. Confronted with the argument that domestic servants are degraded by a working situation that makes them dependent on

---

[20] Todd, 'Domestic Service', 181.
[21] McBride, *Domestic Revolution*, 9.
[22] Light, *Mrs Woolf*, xv.

their employers, she responds that the domestic servant 'is dependent, as we all are, on those with whom she lives. As surely as we know anything we are convinced that dependence on each other is the most unvarying as it is the happiest law of life.'[23] For her daughter, though, the mutual dependence of self and servant is a consistent source of anxiety, not of happiness. In 'A Sketch', Woolf intuits an oblique connection between herself and the servant in their domestic location, which for both lower-class maid and middle-class girl feels like a site of imprisonment, but one they cannot fully share. Shared gender draws them together in their domestic situations; class differences keep them on opposite sides of the curtain.

Perhaps nowhere in Woolf's writing is this complicated experience of identification and disavowal more memorably presented than at the beginning of the third chapter of *Three Guineas*. Woolf's narrator illustrates her surprise at being asked for her opinion by the son of an educated man with a quick sketch of a servant:

> Consider, Sir, in the light of the facts given above, what this request of yours means. It means that in the year 1938 the sons of educated men are asking the daughters to help them to protect culture and intellectual liberty. And why, you may ask, is that surprising? Suppose that the Duke of Devonshire, in his star and garter, stepped down into the kitchen and said to the maid who was peeling potatoes with a smudge on her cheek: 'Stop your potato peeling, Mary, and help me to construe this rather difficult passage in Pindar,' would not Mary be surprised and run screaming to Louisa the cook, 'Lawks, Louie, Master must be mad!' That, or something like it, is the cry that rises to our lips when the sons of educated men ask us, their sisters, to protect intellectual liberty and culture. But let us try to translate the kitchenmaid's cry into the language of educated people. (*TG* 165)

Woolf uses the apparent absurdity of a kitchen maid construing Pindar to show the utter strangeness of the request being made of her. In crafting this example, though, Woolf opens up the connections that domesticity creates among women, whatever their class, whose opinions have been disregarded and whose sights are supposed to be set on homely and private acts of service and care, whether Mary's potato peeling or Julia Stephen's sickroom attendance. Mary's blurted exclamation of shock echoes of the voice of that outspoken servant in 'A Sketch of the Past', and here Woolf almost joins her voice to that cry even as she gives the servant the same name as her novelist in *A Room of One's Own*. But just as quickly Woolf shuts down this cross-class identification, declaring her intent to 'try to translate the kitchenmaid's cry into the language of educated people'. Woolf has had her domestic lessons; she is one of the educated people; servants, by definition, are not. Education and its lack become the key distinction between these women, and allows for the daughters of educated men to hold a higher class status than

---

[23] Julia Duckworth Stephen, 'Domestic Arrangements of the Ordinary English Home', in *Stories for Children, Essays for Adults*, ed. Diane Gillespie and Elizabeth Steele (Syracuse: Syracuse University Press, 1987), 254.

servants despite the closeness of their domestic positions—their mutual, gendered relegation to the private sphere, their exclusion from the structures of formal education, their lack of power in the larger patriarchal system. Mary peels potatoes in service of Woolf's rhetorical point, which requires the servant simultaneously to be very like, and fundamentally unlike, her mistress. Of course, this identification only goes one way. The servant's reaction mirrors the confused shock of the daughters of educated men—but those daughters do have ideas about how to protect intellectual liberty and culture. In this construction, it is not possible to conceive that Mary might have any ideas about Pindar.

In her diary Woolf again and again worries 'the question of Nelly; the perennial question'—the question of her servants and of service itself. She finds the fault in 'the system': 'How can an uneducated woman let herself in, alone, into our lives—what happens is that she becomes a mongrel, & has no roots any where' (D3 220). Woolf's language again indicates that deep intimacy of domestic life and her revulsion at their closeness. After all, Nellie Boxall or Woolf's other servants have not 'let themselves in'; rather, they have been hired to provide labour—to do, as Julia Stephen put it, 'work which we choose to call menial and which in our daily life we find convenient to relegate to others'. These examples show just how embedded 'the perennial question' is in Woolf's thinking about her own class position and the labour relationships that enable her domestic and working life, and how much depends upon the maintenance of a clear line that would disrupt too-close identification across these lines of class. Light notes how often Woolf identifies herself with servants as she complains about the women who work for her, perhaps prefiguring that connection between her child self and the maid laid out in 'A Sketch of the Past'. Like her mother, Woolf does not seem to see the work of domestic service as inherently demeaning or problematic for the servants necessarily, but—unlike Julia—she finds the presence of servants oppressive for the middle-class woman, quite possibly because of the far greater degree of physical proximity between the classes in modern domesticity.

Julia Stephen's domestic lesson endeavours to draw a sharp line between the spaces of the family and those of the servants—achievable in Hyde Park Gate, with its many floors and separate stairways, but not in the domestic spaces of Woolf's adult life. There was a curtain at Monk's House, but it was strung up to give some privacy to Leonard and Virginia who took their baths in the kitchen, not to section off the servants' space.[24] Rather than off in a distant attic, Nellie Boxall's bedroom was next door to Leonard's. Woolf's modern experience of domestic service put the intimacy that had always been at the heart of the system on direct and uncomfortable view.

As impossible as it seems for Woolf to think herself into the body of a working woman—as much as she fantasized about a servantless existence; as much as she enjoyed aspects of domestic labour, particularly cooking—Woolf was keenly aware that her ability to write rested on her servants' work. While Nellie Boxall was hospitalized

---

[24] Light, *Mrs Woolf*, 171.

in 1930, Woolf 'had a glimpse of what it might actually mean to be a housewife',[25] exclaiming in a letter to Quentin Bell 'I cannot write when I must be planning dinner. How any woman with a family ever put pen to paper I cannot fathom' (*L4* 176). Clarissa Dalloway's opening declaration that she will buy the flowers herself still rests on Lucy staying home to prepare the house for Rumplemayer's men.

Woolf's response, ultimately, is not to live without service, but rather to live without servants. Virginia's stormy, complicated relationship with Nellie ended with Nellie's dismissal from their service in March 1934. From then on, the Woolfs had no live-in help at Monk's House, and in 1940 their last live-in servant at Tavistock Square, Mabel Haskins, left as well. The same diary entry that refers to Nellie as 'uneducated' and a 'mongrel' and rails against the Victorian legacy of domestic service also includes Woolf's idea for a better system: 'I could put my theory into practice by getting a daily of a civilized kind, who had her baby in Kentish town; & treated me as an employer, not friend' (*D3* 220). Here Woolf is referring to Annie Thomsett, whom she described elsewhere in the diary as 'an ideal servant' (*D3* 255), and who did work for several years providing daily help to the Woolfs at Monk's House. Annie Thomsett was one of several such people whose daily work kept the Woolfs' households running. Alison Light notes, with some frustration, that in his autobiography Leonard Woolf 'paradoxically'[26] credits his long-time gardener, Percy Bartholomew, and their cook, Louie Everest, with enabling the Woolfs 'to live in comfort without servants'.[27] Leonard explains:

> the Victorian domestic system, in which we were both brought up, assumed that one's comfort depended upon having servants living in the house, and we still had a cook and house parlourmaid in the nineteen-twenties. But it is really much more comfortable not to have servants living in, provided that you have enough money to organize your physical life without them.[28]

The Woolfs can live in comfort without servants thanks to the work of two servants because their comfort depends on reducing their servants' physical proximity—work cut out, once again. The shared domestic space divided by a curtain in Hyde Park Gate now becomes separate domestic spaces: Percy and Louie live in cottages owned by the Woolfs. Cutting the servant out while maintaining their labour becomes the means of establishing control over modern domestic space, and preserving the lines of class that modern domestic service blurred. A similar kind of cutting out characterizes Woolf's fictional presentation of servants as well. Woolf often writes servants in such a way as to emphasize their difference and distance from her middle-class characters, but the haunting effect of her revisions and excisions often betrays that lingering and

---

[25] Light, *Mrs Woolf*, 194.
[26] Light, *Mrs Woolf*, 284.
[27] Leonard Woolf, *The Journey Not the Arrival Matters* (Orlando: Harvest, 1969), 101.
[28] L. Woolf, *The Journey*, 99–100.

uncomfortable sense of identification and proximity that comes through so clearly in 'A Sketch of the Past'.

Woolf's published fiction is full of servants, and—as critics look more into the composition and revision history of her novels—her early drafts even more so. Woolf's domestic servants—unlike discomfiting characters like Miss Kilman—usually do not disrupt or unsettle domestic space, as Julia Stephen's unnamed maid or Woolf's own cook, Nellie Boxall—memorably did. Instead, these characters—Lucy, Crosby, Mildred, Mrs Moffatt, Mrs Sands, and others—often operate in the narratives like the women who make up 'the grey tide of service' (*MD* 97) at Lady Bruton's luncheon in *Mrs Dalloway*:

> And so there began a soundless and exquisite passing to and fro through swing doors of aproned white-capped maids, handmaidens not of necessity, but adepts in a mystery or grand deception practised by hostesses in Mayfair from one-thirty to two, when, with a wave of the hand, the traffic ceases, and there rises instead this profound illusion in the first place about the food—how it is not paid for; and then that the table spreads itself voluntarily with glass and silver, little mats, saucers of red fruit; films of brown cream mask turbot; in casseroles severed chickens swim; coloured, undomestic, the fire burns; and with the wine and the coffee (not paid for) rise jocund visions before musing eyes, gently speculative eyes; eyes to whom life appears musical, mysterious; eyes now kindled to observe genially the beauty of the red carnations which Lady Bruton (whose movements were always angular) had laid beside her plate, so that Hugh Whitbread, feeling at peace with the entire universe and at the same time completely sure of his standing, said, resting his fork:
> 'Wouldn't they look charming against your lace?' (*MD* 93–4)

This passage exemplifies the tensions at the heart of Woolf's representations of domestic servants. Woolf recognizes and skewers the ideal of service as creating an illusion of self-sufficiency and liberation from commodification that in the end upholds the sexual system of patriarchal certainty. But by that end, as the narrative focus turns from the aproned white-capped maids to the admirable Hugh, the passage itself performs the same action it begins by criticizing as Hugh and his carnations eclipse the labouring bodies of the maids. While Woolf engages in critique here, she also betrays, as Mary Childers would say, 'what [she] ... may have particular trouble seeing'.[29] In this case, it may be more appropriate to point to what Woolf has trouble hearing: the doors swing open here soundlessly, not creaking on their hinges like the memory-sparking doors at the novel's beginning. The maids here start out by not being heard, and they end up not being seen. Such a representation of invisible, inaudible service is a direct legacy of Victorian domestic ideologies, and Woolf is not endorsing it here. But it is nonetheless expressive of a means of smoothing the rough edges of service for narrative ends, of making characters who could be potentially disturbing by their proximity into ones who essentially 'live out' of the texts in which they appear—thus, for example, the relegation

---

[29] Childers, 'Outside Looking Down', 67.

of the life of Lily Wilson to a footnote in *Flush* (1933); thus it is that the lurching, leering women who revitalize the Ramsay house in 'Time Passes' are dailies, themselves just passing through.

Late in *Three Guineas*, Woolf reveals the psychological motivations behind certain topics of discussion, when subconsciously held patriarchal attitudes begin to be felt in conversations between men and women:

> Intellectually, there is a strong desire either to be silent; or to change the conversation; to drag in, for example, some old family servant, called Crosby, perhaps, whose dog Rover has died ... and so evade the issue and lower the temperature.... Often, to be candid, while we are talking about Crosby, we are asking questions—hence a certain flatness in the dialogue—about you. (*TG* 203)

There is a risk, Woolf admits, of 'flatness in the dialogue', because the servant is serving primarily as a cover for the real and difficult topics at hand. But Woolf's example highlights how servants are supposed to work, both in literature and in life: to enable avoidance of difficulty, intimacy, and mess. To make things easier. Woolf here both interrogates that servant function and calls on it, pointing out its immediate utility and its long-term flaws in relationships among members of the educated class. But even this exposure of the servant-signifier as a signifier depends on the continued flatness in the character of the servant and not just the dialogue, to make Crosby, like the potato-peeling Mary, usable as a narrative tool.

Woolf's representations of servants are so often disappointing, whether because they are 'tinged with revulsion'[30] or haloed with nostalgia. They disappoint because it seems there should be a more open acknowledgement of the value of their labour and its necessity to artistic creation. But focusing too much on the very real limitations of Woolf's representations—limitations she herself clearly recognized—in turn limits our ability to engage with the work servants do in her texts, particularly as they demonstrate her negotiations with the discomfort produced by lower-class domestic proximity. The work cut out for us is first simply to notice the servants who appear, often just momentarily, throughout Woolf's novels, and to see the ways in which their presences reinforce the classed nature of domestic space. Jacob Flanders's room stands as a synecdoche for an interior that the women around Jacob—including the narrator—cannot access, but the maid who empties Jacob's chamber pot is 'aware' that 'he had grown to be a man' (*JR* 191) precisely because her labours bring her into his otherwise private space. Lily Briscoe's painting will be 'hung in the attics' (*TL* 281); the same space that housed the broken-hearted Swiss maid Marie in 'The Window'. In both instances, Woolf invokes servants to highlight their difference from the middle-class characters at the centre of the novels, but in so doing also highlights servants' closeness to those characters and their narratives. Servants are never at the centre of Woolf's domestic spaces, but they are also never long absent; the novels, like the houses, cannot run without them.

---

[30] Light, *Mrs Woolf*, 203.

Woolf, like Mary Carmichael, is well aware that she writes from her own classed perspective, with the fetters of class still on her feet. Woolf's acknowledgement of her own limitations invites our critical engagement with the representations she does produce. It matters deeply that we accept the work cut out for us in reading Woolf's servants by bringing them back into the critical conversation, reading Woolf's engagement with class in terms of domesticity.

SELECTED BIBLIOGRAPHY

Caughie, Pamela L., 'Dogs and Servants', *Virginia Woolf Miscellany* 84 (Autumn 2013), 37–9.
Childers, Mary, 'Virginia Woolf on the Outside Looking Down: Reflections on the Class of Women', *Modern Fiction Studies* 38.1 (Spring 1992), 61–79.
Horn, Pamela, *The Rise and Fall of the Victorian Servant* (Wolfeboro Falls: Alan Sutton, 1991).
Light, Alison, *Mrs Woolf and the Servants* (New York: Bloomsbury, 2008).
Marcus, Jane, 'Introduction', in Virginia Woolf, *Three Guineas*, ed. Jane Marcus (New York: Harcourt, 2006), xxv–lxxii.
McBride, Theresa, *The Domestic Revolution: The Modernisation of Household Service in England and France 1820-1920* (London: Croom Helm, 1976).
Mills, Jean, 'Virginia Woolf and the Politics of Class', in Jessica Berman, ed., *A Companion to Virginia Woolf* (Chichester: Wiley-Blackwell, 2016), 219–34.
Rosner, Victoria, *Modernism and the Architecture of Private Life* (New York: Columbia University Press, 2005).
Simpson, Kathryn, 'Social Class in *To the Lighthouse*', in Allison Pease, ed., *The Cambridge Companion to* To the Lighthouse (Cambridge: Cambridge University Press, 2015), 110–21.
Snaith, Anna, *Virginia Woolf: Public and Private Negotiations* (New York: St. Martin's Press, 2000).
Todd, Selina, 'Domestic Service and Class Relations in Britain 1900-1950', *Past & Present* 203 (May 2009), 181–204.
Wilson, Mary, *The Labors of Modernism: Domesticity, Servants, and Authorship in Modernist Fiction* (New York: Routledge, 2013).
Wood, Alice, 'Facing *Life as We Have Known It*: Virginia Woolf and the Women's Co-Operative Guild', *Literature and History* 23, no. 2 (Autumn 2014), 18–34.

CHAPTER 30

CONSUMER CULTURE

ELIZABETH M. SHEEHAN

Virginia Woolf's life coincided with the rise of key elements of consumer culture in Britain, including the ascendance of department stores, advertising, the ready-made clothing industry, and celebrity fashion designers. Her writing is intimately concerned with these historical phenomena; consumer culture is a frequent subject of her fiction and non-fiction, and it shapes her experimental techniques. In turn, it is as objects of consumption that Woolf and her works continue to circulate and be remade. Woolf's current fame fuels and is fuelled by the proliferation of commodities related to her and the Bloomsbury Group, from commercial and academic books to dolls, textiles, clothing, and holiday tours.[1] During the late 1980s—an era that is, like the 1920s, known for 'conspicuous consumption'—a wave of scholarship on modernism and early twentieth-century consumer culture gathered force, and it has generated decades of work addressing how Woolf and her texts relate to shopping, marketing, celebrity, and fashion.[2] Now, scholars look to Woolf's work for the way it theorizes, represents, and provides an object lesson in consumer culture.

Consumer culture is not simply a context in which to read Woolf's work, but also a framework for examining how Woolf's work is consumed, including what scholarly interpretations prevail at a given moment. Many of Woolf's texts anticipate such interpretive issues as they describe how various characters read the world, especially aspects of consumer culture. In *Mrs Dalloway* (1925), for instance, Peter Walsh senses during his stroll through London that there has been a profound transformation since his last

---

[1] On the market for Bloomsbury, see Regina Marler, *Bloomsbury Pie: The Making of the Bloomsbury Boom* (New York: Henry Holt, 1997). On popular images of Woolf, see Brenda Silver, *Virginia Woolf, Icon* (Chicago: University of Chicago Press, 2000).

[2] During the 1990s, moreover, Jennifer Wicke credits Bloomsbury with facilitating 'the famous turn to "deficit spending" that is now the hallmark of the bourgeois liberal state, and, in comparison to the brutalities of supply-side economics, is a veritable state of grace'; see her 'Coterie Consumption: Bloomsbury, Keynes, and Modernism as Marketing', in Kevin H. J. Dettmar and Stephen Watt, eds, *Marketing Modernisms: Self-Promotion, Canonization, Rereading* (Ann Arbor: University of Michigan, 1996), 109–32, at 130.

visit: 'those five years—1918 to 1923—had been, he suspected, somehow very important' (*MD* 64). Peter first registers that change via women's clothing ('even the poorest dressed better than five years ago') and their use of cosmetics, including the 'curls of Indian ink' decorating women's faces. That phrase suggests how colonial production becomes imperial consumption and it inscribes this process on London women's bodies.[3] Peter works as a colonial administrator in India, where resistance movements had begun to challenge British rule, yet he understands the transformation in London during those years predominantly as a matter of style and adornment rather than economics or politics ('there was design, art, everywhere'). Despite just having witnessed a group of young men honouring those killed in the war, Peter does not wonder whether changes in women's appearance might be connected to that loss and violence, let alone to women's enfranchisement in 1918 and their increased presence in the workforce (which were both facilitated by war). Peter, in short, does not consider what overlapping contexts might relate to changes in London fashion. His misapprehensions, however, are not ours. Rather, critical frameworks from postcolonial and feminist studies have attuned scholars to how his impressions about developments in consumer culture in London simultaneously register and occlude dynamics of empire and gender.

Peter's musings prompt further questions about consumer culture, its distinction from art and politics, and its relation to ideas and experiences of gender and class in the early twentieth century. The term *consumer culture* describes the ideas, behaviours, and relations generated with and through commodities (purchasable objects or services) and consumption (the act of buying or using commodities). Consumer culture also often designates the way that, under capitalism, seemingly all aesthetic and social phenomena involve consumption or commodities. Furthermore, consumer culture's entwinement with myriad aspects of social and political life helps to establish capitalism as seemingly natural or inevitable. For instance, Peter's perceptions register how consumer culture shaped the experience of London. With the success of department stores by the late nineteenth century and the increased production of relatively low-cost clothing and home goods, more middle- and lower-middle- class women took to the streets to shop or browse.

Some cultural historians describe the increased availability of a larger variety of relatively affordable goods, especially garments, as a process of 'democratization'.[4] Peter's sense that 'even the poorest dressed better' exemplifies the perception that the proliferation of commodities benefitted working- and lower-class people. Yet increased access to commodities did not necessarily signal a more democratic society. Early twentieth-century fashion, for example, reinscribed gender, ethnic, and class distinctions through its styles and patterns of production and consumption, including by employing growing numbers of working-class and immigrant women in the garment trade. Peter's roving

---

[3] On *Mrs Dalloway*'s critique of the imperial dimensions of consumer culture, see Alissa G. Karl, *Modernism and the Marketplace* (New York: Routledge, 2009), 62–80.

[4] See, for example, Peter Gurney, *The Making of Consumer Culture in Britain* (London: Bloomsbury, 2017), especially 133–8.

gaze also underscores how consumer culture made women of all classes newly visible in the public sphere—from streets to periodicals to political debates. Yet it also trivialized and commodified women's position in public life, confirming that women should be evaluated according to their appearance and their relationships to clothing and shopping. Accordingly, for over a century, various feminist accounts of early twentieth-century consumer culture depict it as a realm of possibilities, contradictions, and limitations, especially for gendered and racialized subjects.[5]

Woolf's writing and career register, respond to, and exemplify consumer culture in complex, sometimes contradictory ways. Her involvement with the Omega Workshop in Bloomsbury and British *Vogue* magazine demonstrates how the convergence of art and fashion shaped her personal relationships and work. In turn, her writing's distinctive formal elements and central political commitments were reactions to and products of consumer culture, including the feminization of consumption, the commodification of art, and bourgeois conceptions of history. *Orlando* (1928) in particular illuminates how consumer culture encourages certain theories of history and thus determines what it means to read in historical context.

Woolf grappled with the relationship between literature and consumer culture through her and Leonard's ownership and management of the Hogarth Press. While the Hogarth was not a large commercial press, scholars Peter D. McDonald and Helen Southworth emphasize that it never separated itself from the market or sought an exclusive readership.[6] In addition, Woolf wrote extensively for and about the 'common reader', whom she contrasted with the critic and the scholar, since the former 'reads for his own pleasure rather than to impart knowledge or correct the opinions of others' (*E4* 19). Woolf's conception of the common reader cut across distinctions between high and low or mass culture, which featured in discussions of consumer culture in the early twentieth century and which shaped scholarship on modernism in the 1980s and 1990s.[7]

---

[5] See, for example, Rachel Bowlby, *Just Looking: Consumer Culture in Dreiser, Gissing, and Zola* (New York: Metheun, 1985); Rita Felski, *The Gender of Modernity* (Cambridge, MA: Harvard University Press, 1995); and Rishona Zimring, 'The Make-up of Jean Rhy's Fiction', *Novel* 33, no. 2 (Spring 2000), 212–34.

[6] Peter McDonald, *British Literary Culture and Publishing Practice 1880–1914* (Cambridge: Cambridge University Press, 1997), 299 and Helen Southworth, 'Introduction', in Helen Southworth, ed., *Leonard and Virginia Woolf, the Hogarth Press, and the Networks of Modernism* (Edinburgh: Edinburgh University Press, 2010), 1–16. See also Alice Staveley, Chapter 16 in this volume.

[7] Andreas Huyssen's *After the Great Divide: Modernism, Mass Culture, Postmodernism* (Bloomington: Indiana University Press, 1987) and Lawrence Rainey's *Institutions of Modernism: Literary Elites and Public Culture* (New Haven: Yale University Press, 1998) demonstrate modernism's deployment of various logics and tropes of mass culture, such that modernism undoes the distinctions between art and commerce, high and low, that (they argue) it also asserts. Subsequent work has emphasized how the high versus low divide fails to describe modernism's relationship to consumer culture, including in Woolf's texts. See, for example, Jane Garrity, 'Virginia Woolf, Intellectual Harlotry, and 1920s British *Vogue*', in Pamela Caughie, ed., *Virginia Woolf in the Age of Mechanical Reproduction* (New York: Garland, 2000), 185–218; Elizabeth Outka, *Consuming Traditions: Modernity, Modernism, and the Commodified Authentic* (New York: Oxford, 2009); and Kathryn Simpson, *Gifts, Markets, and Economies of Desire in Virginia Woolf* (Basingstoke: Palgrave Macmillan, 2008).

Woolf at times described consumer culture as a threat to literature; in a 1939 essay, for example, she lamented that the business of reviewing made writers akin to tailors repairing clothing in a shop window as a critical crowd looked on, thereby inhibiting their creativity (*E6* 197). But distinctions between art and commerce and between high and low culture can conceal alternative formations and points of connection and continuity, such as Woolf's common reader.

Woolf's texts and life also engage and illuminate consumer culture's production and reconfiguration of the categories of public and private. By the early twentieth century, a wide range of relatively affordable decorative objects were sold for the home. Such items linked English domestic spaces to various parts of the British empire and the globe and undermined the idea that a feminized, private realm might shelter occupants from the public, masculine operations of the market and the public sphere. Woolf's essay 'Street Haunting: A London Adventure' and a number of those collected in *The London Scene* draw attention to the affective and social power of commodities, and to the acts of shopping, browsing, and observing trade. At the same time, many commodities for the home celebrated the domestic as a sanctified, non-commercial realm and upheld a vision of England detached from its colonial dimensions and populations. That enshrinement of the domestic could help to sell goods.

Such marketing tactics are related to what Elizabeth Outka argues is the early twentieth-century emergence of the 'commodified authentic': a commercial aesthetic that paradoxically celebrates what is traditional and seemingly uncommodified, such as the home.[8] (Imagine, for example, a display in a department store window that evokes life in a rural English cottage in order to sell mass-produced wooden furniture.) Outka connects both the commodified authentic and the department store window display to the form of Woolf's work. She argues that the depiction of pre-war life in Woolf's second novel, *Night and Day* (1919), resembles an elaborate display of nostalgic, 'authentic' goods in a shop window; the novel depicts the pre-war moment, while making clear that this fictionalized near past is separated from the reader as if by a transparent but uncrossable barrier—a barrier that, Outka says, is akin to glass windows in front of department store displays, which were themselves evidence of irreversible cultural change.[9]

While World War I fuelled a commodified nostalgia for past moments, it also ensured that consumption was understood vis-à-vis citizenship. As part of the British government's efforts to direct consumer spending, for example, a poster distributed by the National Savings Committee in 1916 announced, 'To dress extravagantly in war time is worse than bad form. It is unpatriotic.'[10] The poster assumes that women have a key role in supporting the nation but that they might easily fail their patriotic duties due to their desire to consume. An association between feminine fashion and political and intellectual inadequacy emerged with particular force during the mid-1920s, as the British government considered extending suffrage to all women between the ages of

---

[8] Outka, *Consuming Traditions*, 4–7.
[9] Outka, *Consuming Traditions*, 152.
[10] Parliamentary Recruitment Committee, 'Why Aren't You in Khaki?'

twenty-one to twenty-nine. (Women over thirty who met certain standards of property ownership gained the vote in 1918, as did all men over twenty-one.) Full suffrage for women over twenty-one was derided as granting the 'flapper vote', a phrase that linked young women to excessive consumption, since the flapper was known by bold dress and make-up as well as her frank expressions of desire.[11] As the debate over the 'flapper vote' shows, consumer culture was a matter of great political concern, even as women's participation in consumer culture could disqualify them from full political participation. Yet if a woman rejected fashion and shopping altogether, she would be open to charges of failing her feminine and domestic duties. Accordingly, many suffragettes used dress to signal that they could be simultaneously feminine and politically engaged. Parades of women marching in white dresses served, as Barbara Green argues, to transform 'the feminine body into a civic body'.[12]

In Elizabeth Dalloway, Woolf represents a young woman who would be enfranchised by the 'flapper vote'. Elizabeth's interest in politics and professions is rather idle, although her thoughts about her future suggest unprecedented opportunities. Alone on a bus speeding through London, Elizabeth considers the possibility of becoming 'a doctor, a farmer, possibly go into Parliament, if she found it necessary' (*MD* 122). Unlike the stereotypical flapper, however, Elizabeth is uninterested in consumer culture; Clarissa admits her daughter 'cared not a straw' for gloves or shoes, and Elizabeth appears indifferent to the goods and delicacies available at the Army and Navy Stores, which she visits with Mrs Kilman (*MD* 10). Nevertheless, the novel underscores that dress and beauty remain the lens through which others see Elizabeth—and through which she knows she is seen. As Elizabeth rides the bus, we get an account of how 'to each movement of the omnibus the beautiful body in the fawn-coloured coat responded freely like a rider, like the figure-head of a ship' (*MD* 121). The nautical metaphor implies that Elizabeth's position within the British empire is at stake in her negotiation with the protocols of dress. Despite the freedom offered by such modern conveniences as the bus and her disavowal of fashion, she may become yet another feminine figure glorifying masculine achievement.[13] Via Elizabeth, *Mrs Dalloway* stages the contradictory dynamics by which consumer culture promised and foreclosed changes to the social and political position of women, especially middle- and upper-class white British women.

Woolf's insistence on taking consumer culture seriously should be understood as part of her resistance to patriarchy. In *A Room of One's Own* (1929), she observes, 'it is the masculine values that prevail. Speaking crudely, football and sport are "important"; the worship of fashion, the buying of clothes "trivial"' (*ARO* 56). She notes 'these values inevitably transfer from life to fiction', thereby limiting how critics receive a book and what

---

[11] See Bellie Melman, *Women and the Popular Imagination in the Twenties: Flappers and Nymphs* (New York: St. Martins, 1988), 15–37.
[12] Barbara Green, *Spectacular Confessions: Autobiography, Performative Activism, and the Sites of Suffrage 1905–1938* (New York: Palgrave Macmillan, 1997), 1.
[13] For a related discussion of Elizabeth, see Rachel Bowlby, *Feminist Destinations and Other Essays on Virginia Woolf* (Edinburgh: Edinburgh University Press, 1997), 84.

authors write. All of Woolf's novels and many of her short stories and essays examine the phenomena of fashion or shopping in some way. As we see in *Mrs Dalloway*, fashion, dress, and shopping are key to capturing the gendered cultural and political dynamics of a given moment.

Fashion and fiction are both ways of expressing time via form and style. In a sense, any work of literature that gives textual shape to a particular moment could be compared to a garment. But Woolf's modernism is especially linked to *la mode* in that many of her texts use innovative techniques to thread together various characters' perceptions to represent part of the social fabric. Woolf's concern with timeliness and what is of the moment (*modo* in Latin) with respect to literary form and social life links her modernist project to *la mode* (i.e. fashion) as a way of capturing, inhabiting, or reimagining an instant in time.[14] In *Jacob's Room*, for instance, Woolf deploys a method of interweaving characters' thoughts, which she further developed in *Mrs Dalloway* and *To The Lighthouse* (1927). This technique does not always hinge on representations of dress, of course, but given garments' status as time-bound, shifting borders between the self and others, they often facilitate Woolf's exploration of different perspectives and their relationships with each other. In the scene in which Elizabeth rides the bus, for example, the 'fawn-coloured coat' provides a pivot for the narrative to shift briefly from Elizabeth's perspective to those of the people around her and then back. In short, fashion is a subject and method for Woolf.

Woolf pursues fashion and modernism's impulse to 'make it new'—a sartorial and literary tendency that, paradoxically, involves remaking or even maintaining the old.[15] Many of Woolf's works—like many modernist texts—are concerned with the multiplicity of time, from the ephemerality of fleeting moments to the way the past interrupts the present via memory; in that way, her texts match well with fashion's complex temporality, which involves rapid changes, the recycling of past styles, as well as the idea of timeless chic.[16] Once again, that dynamic describes both Woolf's content and form. From *The Voyage Out*'s (1915) interrupted bildungsroman—a genre built to narrate the development of a middle-class subject—to *Between the Act*'s (1941) pageant in which British history is conjured via a parade of costumes and commodities, many of Woolf's works contemplate how a given present continues or reconfigures the past. Mrs

---

[14] On this point, see Elizabeth M. Sheehan, *Modernism à la Mode: Fashion and the Ends of Literature* (Ithaca: Cornell University Press, 2018), 28–9. On fashion as a subject and method for Woolf, see also Lisa Cohen, '"Frock Consciousness": Virginia Woolf, the Open Secret, and the Language of Fashion', *Fashion Theory* 3, no. 2 (1999), 149–74; Jennifer Wicke, 'Frock Consciousness: Virginia Woolf's Dialectical Materialism', in Jessica Berman and Jane Goldman, eds, *Virginia Woolf Out of Bounds* (New York: Pace University Press, 2001), 221–35; and Randi Koppen, *Virginia Woolf, Fashion and Literary Modernity* (Edinburgh: Edinburgh University Press, 2009).

[15] On this phrase, see Hugh Kenner, *The Pound Era* (Berkeley: University of California Press, 1971), 447–8.

[16] On the temporality of fashion, see Caroline Evans, *Fashion at the Edge: Spectacle, Modernity, and Deathliness* (New Haven: Yale University Press, 2003) and Ilya Parkins, *Poiret, Dior, and Schiaparelli: Fashion, Femininity, and Modernity* (London: Berg, 2012).

Dalloway's silver mermaid dress—designed before the war, but still appropriate for a chic party in 1923—illuminates fashion's multiple, sometimes conflicting temporalities, for it makes clear that fashionability is not always about wearing the newest thing. Rather, in dress and in literature, fashion involves finding the right relationship between the present and a particular past. Woolf's attunement to fashion does not mean, however, that she celebrates it. Woolf depicts a society shaped by consumer culture, including fashion, often using methods of description that emerge with and from that culture, but also serve as a way of critiquing that culture. In doing so, she establishes the feminized, trivialized phenomenon of fashion as a powerful representational, affective, and epistemological tool.

Woolf's interest in the power of fashion and consumer culture reflects her position within the Bloomsbury Group, whose members experimented with innovative ideas and modes of consumption. These include Roger Fry, Vanessa Bell, and Duncan Grant's direction of the Omega Workshops from 1913 to 1919, an artists' collective producing avant-garde decorative arts and design; John Maynard Keynes's influential economic theories, which put spending and consumption at the heart of that discipline; and the publication and promotion of writing and art by Bloomsbury members, friends, and lovers in British *Vogue* during the editorship of Dorothy Todd (1922–1926). Bloomsbury's forms of intimacy flourished through commodities and practices of consumption, whether via the playful decoration of private spaces or the circulation of erotic and financial capital within the group.

Academic debates about the significance and impact of Bloomsbury rest partly on assumptions and assertions about how consumer culture enables or limits desired forms of social transformation, from the cultivation of egalitarian communities to the dismantling of the British imperial order. In an influential essay, cultural critic Raymond Williams argues that Bloomsbury introduced into the British bourgeoisie a 'new *style*', which included informal interpersonal relationships, anti-imperialist sentiments, and the ambiguous position of women, who were part of the group but excluded from the institutions, like Cambridge University, that fostered it.[17] While emphasizing that Bloomsbury critiqued dominant early twentieth-century values, Williams asserts that the late twentieth-century British bourgeoisie and Bloomsbury share a 'cult of appreciative-conspicuous-consumption'.[18] In Williams's view, Bloomsbury's styles of relation are inextricable from its styles of consumption, and both fuel the development of the bourgeoisie. Jennifer Wicke, in turn, affirms Williams's connection between Bloomsbury's social and economic practices when she proposes that the group engaged in 'coterie consumption', which involved consuming certain goods, promoting art created by members of the coterie, and pursuing unconventional ways of living.[19] She locates Woolf at the heart of Bloomsbury's experiments by situating her alongside Keynes as an influential theorist of the market.

---

[17] Williams, *Culture and Materialism* (London: Verso, 1980), 154.
[18] Williams, *Culture and Materialism*, 166.
[19] Wicke, '*Mrs Dalloway* Goes to Market', *Novel: A Forum on Fiction* 28, no. 1 (Autumn 1994), 6.

Subsequent accounts of Bloomsbury have placed different emphases on the group's reinforcement and divergence from prevailing configurations of sexuality, gender, class, and colonial power. Christopher Reed, for example, argues that Bloomsbury's creation and consumption of decorative art fostered their unconventional sensibilities and ways of living, and he explores the countercultural aims and implications of a group that supported same-sex relationships when sexual activity between men was illegal in Britain.[20] By contrast, Jane Garrity analyses Bloomsbury's appearances in British *Vogue* under the editorship of Dorothy Todd and concludes that the group participated in what Garrity describes as *Vogue*'s sexist, colonialist techniques of 'selling culture to the "civilized"'—namely, its wealthy readers.[21]

Woolf herself had her photograph and writing published in *Vogue*, and she explicitly defended that choice.[22] Writing to Vita Sackville-West, Woolf implied that any writing for periodicals was a type of intercourse: 'whats [sic] the objection to whoring after Todd? Better whore I think, than honestly and timidly and coolly and respectably copulate with the Times Lit. Supp' (L3 200). Responding to a writer who thought writing for *Vogue* would debase her style, Woolf contrasted Todd's permissiveness with the *Times Literary Supplement*'s choice to censor 'irreverent' material in an acquaintance's essay: 'Todd lets you write what you like and its your own fault if you conform to the stays and the petticoats' (L3 158). Even as Woolf refers disparagingly to 'stays and petticoats', she imagines *Vogue* as an outlet for frank expression, including references to the body.

Woolf's references to sex and intimate garments underscore that the commodification of feminine sexuality is central to consumer culture and that such commodification has multiple effects, from enforcing conformity to facilitating marginalized modes of expression and desire. Accordingly, consumer culture's capacity to facilitate alternatives to prevailing gender and sexual norms informs Woolf's reaction to *Vogue*, just as it is pivotal to many scholarly accounts of the Bloomsbury group. In fact, clothing, including 'stays and petticoats', connected Woolf's relationship to consumer culture with her position within the Bloomsbury group. Through the Omega Workshops, Woolf's relationship to fashion became entwined with her ties to Bloomsbury just before, during, and after World War I—a crucial period when Woolf began her career as a published novelist.[23] Woolf's diaries and letters record her purchase of several Omega garments as well

---

[20] Christopher Reed, *Bloomsbury Rooms: Modernism, Subculture, and Domesticity* (New Haven: Yale University Press, 2004).

[21] Jane Garrity, 'Selling Culture to the "Civilized": Bloomsbury, British *Vogue*, and the Marketing of National Identity', *Modernism/Modernity* 6, no. 2 (1999), 29. For a contrasting account of 1920s *Vogue*, stressing the magazine and Todd's queer sensibility, see Christopher Reed, 'Design for [Queer] Living: Sexual Identity, Performance, and Décor in British *Vogue*, 1922–1926', *GLQ* 12, no. 3 (2006), 377–404.

[22] See Garrity, 'Virginia Woolf, Intellectual Harlotry, and 1920s British *Vogue*'.

[23] On the Omega's impact on Woolf, see Elizabeth M. Sheehan, *Modernism à la Mode*, 51–7. For a history of the Omega, see Judith Collins, *The Omega Workshops* (London: Martin Secker, 1983); and on Omega garments, see Elizabeth M. Sheehan, 'Experiments in Art and Fashion: Vanessa Bell's Dress Design', in Alexandra Gerstein, ed., *Beyond Bloomsbury: Designs of the Omega Workshops 1913–19* (London: Courtauld Gallery and Fontanka Press, 2009), 50–9.

as her reactions to the workshop's designs, especially those by her sister. In a letter to Bell in 1916, Woolf requests that Bell design a coat for her, praises a 'blue summer dress' she has just gotten from the Omega, and jests, 'I think even as an advertisement I should pay the Omega, as I'm always being asked who made my things' (*L2* 92). While this comment is light-hearted, it is striking that, nearly a decade before her appearance in *Vogue*, and well before she became a symbol of Englishness, intellectualism, modernism, elitism, feminism, lesbian identity, or all the above, Woolf refers to herself as selling a bit of Bloomsbury. Her joke also registers the Omega's engagement with consumer culture, including the rise of lifestyle marketing, celebrity designers, and a market for affordable fashion. What then would Woolf be advertising by advertising for the Omega? And how might that relate to Woolf's sense of her own developing subjectivity as an artist as well as her works' responses to consumer culture?

The Omega represents a striking attempt to bring together modernist art, consumer culture, and Bloomsbury's cultural and political values. Fry founded the Omega with Grant and Bell in the hope that it could employ struggling artists and develop the British public's taste for art and design. As Woolf later observed in her biography of Fry, developing that appetite was part of Fry's vision for how to bring about a better society—true 'civilisation' (*RF* 213). The Omega also drew inspiration from fashion, especially the pre-war era's most influential couturier, Paul Poiret.[24] Poiret was one of the first designers to sell a way of living, complete with textiles and furniture in a recognizable house style. If consumer culture increasingly invited people to imagine they could access or create entire worlds via goods, then Poiret endeavoured to design that world for his clients. Poiret also established himself as a patron of art, and his aesthetic recalled aspects of what Fry had dubbed the 'Post-Impressionist' style, exemplified by Cezanne, Gaugin, Picasso, and Van Gogh.

The Omega's stylistic engagement with the overlapping worlds of French art and fashion is apparent in surviving photographs and descriptions of Omega garments: their bright or contrasting colours, bold prints influenced by Japanese and Turkish design, and loose silhouettes all show Poiret's influence. Woolf's letters suggest that she found some of the Omega designs too daring, but she also expressed great pleasure in the garments, particularly those she purchased.[25] Elizabeth Wilson observes that 'fashion speaks a tension between the crowd and the individual' for it is a materialization of society's values and dictates and a medium through which people forge a sense of self.[26] With respect to Woolf's work and modern British fiction more broadly, Celia Marshik argues that depictions of garments often dramatize 'the difficulty of becoming a person—a

---

[24] Fry cited Poiret's design workshop as a model and potential collaborator with the Omega in his 'Omega Workshops Fundraising Letter', in Christopher Reed, ed., *A Roger Fry Reader* (Chicago: University of Chicago Press, 1996), 197.

[25] Writing to Bell, Woolf claimed that an outfit designed by her sister 'wrenched her eyes from her sockets' (*L2* 111).

[26] Wilson, *Adorned in Dreams: Fashion and Modernity*, rev. ed. (New Brunswick: Rutgers University Press, 2003), 11.

singular self—in the early twentieth century, the precise historical moment when the proliferation of consumer goods suggests that the process of individuation should have been getting easier'.[27] Yet for Woolf, the Omega dress cut across a division between 'the crowd and the individual' by confirming her position within an intimate community—what Reed has described as the Bloomsbury subculture, a term that registers the group's simultaneous place within and opposition to prevailing norms. By buying clothing at the Omega, Woolf could keep the transaction among friends and financially support Bloomsbury's artistic and (increasingly) political endeavours.

The resulting combination of intimacy, clothing, and embodiment emerges in a flirtatious letter that Woolf sent to her friend Saxon Sydney-Turner in February of 1917, during his affair with Barbara Hiles, an artist employed as a dressmaker at the Omega along with Faith Henderson. Woolf laments the possibility that Hiles would leave the Omega, claiming, 'I want to feel that for ever and ever she will make my clothes—and in fact I had a vision of some adaptation of dress contrived by her and Faith to do away with underclothes and be attached by a solitary button' (*L2* 141). If, seven years later, Woolf used 'stays and petticoats' to symbolize the restraints of mainstream fashion culture, here she jokes that the Omega will make all such garments unnecessary. The reduction of undergarments and 'attachments' was in fact one of the greatest shifts in women's dress over the course of the twentieth century. This change has been read as an index of shifting norms regarding women's sexuality, and it strengthened the long-standing associations between women's desires to consume and their sexual appetites. Woolf's joke plays with such connotations.

However, the pleasures of Omega garments are inextricable from forms of violence. By 1917, the Omega was fundraising for Belgian refugees, serving as a meeting place for pacifist activists, and staging productions and creating illustrated books and art with overt anti-war messages.[28] Bell's work at the Omega, including dressmaking, helped to support her life in Sussex, where she and her children moved with Grant so he could avoid arrest as a conscientious objector by labouring on a farm. (Saxon-Turner and Hiles camped temporarily at their home.) Meanwhile, the most reliable patron of Omega dresses, the aristocrat and pacifist Ottoline Morrell, opened her country home to other conscientious objectors, many of whom were associated with Bloomsbury. In this context, the Bloomsbury coterie was at once a seemingly frivolous social formation and a means of survival for members who sought to stay out of jail and out of uniform.

At the brink of another world war just decades later, Woolf would observe in *Three Guineas* (1938): 'the connection between dress and war is not far to seek; your finest clothes are those that you wear as soldiers' (*TG* 105). *Three Guineas* does not suggest

---

[27] Marshik, *At the Mercy of Their Clothes: Modernism, the Middlebrow, and British Garment Culture* (New York: Columbia University Press, 2017), 3–4. Marshik discusses how this dynamic emerges via the mackintosh, the evening dress, fancy dress, and second-hand clothing and includes discussions of Miss Kilman's mackintosh, Mrs Dalloway's gown, and Ottoline Morrell's wardrobe.

[28] See Grace Brockington, *Above the Battlefield: Modernism and the Peace Movement in Britain, 1900–1918* (New Haven: Yale University Press, 2011).

that dressing differently or consuming certain goods are sufficient anti-war strategies. Rather, Woolf urges women to refuse prevailing values, from modes of consumption and dress to forms of professional accomplishment, since they uphold the current patriarchal, warmongering system. Nevertheless, Woolf's line highlights her ongoing interest in how dress and various aspects of consumer culture, including literary texts, facilitate or interrupt violence, intimacy, and desire. The final section of this chapter shows how these questions animate *Orlando*, which was inspired by Woolf's affair with the fashionable aristocrat Vita Sackville-West. *Orlando* begins in the Elizabethan era, centuries before the explosion of consumer culture, and does not seem especially concerned with war. Yet the novel bears witness to the way consumer culture and especially fashion set the terms by which history and the body are understood, and, in doing so, inscribes war as a defining phenomenon of human society. The novel asks whether consumer culture and war are inevitable contexts for writing and reading.

Orlando's opening line stages a relationship between dress and war. The first sentence reads: 'He—for there could be no doubt of his sex, though the fashion of the time did something to disguise it—was in the act of slicing the head of a Moor which swung from the rafters' (*O* 13). This head is a spoil of war collected by 'Orlando's father, or perhaps his grandfather', and is used to train the young Orlando for the battles he will presumably fight as an Elizabethan nobleman. The narrator's gesture to fashion, meanwhile, reveals that knowledge of Orlando's 'sex' is a matter of historical and sartorial perspective. Garments for elite Elizabethan men and women were quite distinct, but the narrator finds those gendered sartorial signs confusing, apparently because he or she is of another time.

The term 'sex' also draws attention to the novel's shifting historical ground, for it was published before contemporary definitions and distinctions between biological sex, gender, and sexual orientation took hold; in the 1920s, for example, some experts proposed that men sexually attracted to other men were effectively women born in men's bodies—and vice versa.[29] The narrator's assumptions about historical *continuity* also are revealing; while Orlando's clothing is confusing, the narrator's confidence that Orlando is male may be because his violent 'slicing' is clearly something only 'he' would do, no matter what the century.[30] These first lines, then, raise questions about what the relationship is between commodities, gender, sexuality, empire, race, and war-making over time. In particular: can the phenomenon of changing fashions deliver on what is here a faint promise to interrupt the cultural grammar that naturalizes masculine violence against a racially and ethnically marked enemy? Does the confusion produced

---

[29] Celia Marshik and Allison Pease explore this point with respect to *Orlando* in *Modernism, Sex, and Gender* (New York: Bloomsbury, 2018), 1.

[30] For a discussion of how this sentence addresses the relationship between gender and imperialism, see Jamie Hovey, '"Kissing a Negress in the Dark": Englishness as a Masquerade in Woolf's *Orlando*', *PMLA* 112, no. 3 (1997), 393–404; Urmila Seshagiri, *Race and the Modernist Imagination* (Ithaca, NY: Cornell University Press, 2010), 178–9; and Celia R. Caputi Daileader, 'Othello's Sister: Racial Hermaphroditism and Appropriation in Virginia Woolf's Orlando', *Studies in the Novel* 45, no. 1 (2013), 59–79.

by fashion foreshadow Orlando's divergence from norms of gender and war-making? Conversely, does the fact that Orlando's dress appears feminine centuries later suggest that sword play also might not always be so obviously masculine, so that someday we might be just as likely to find that 'she' is in 'the act of slicing' a head? If so, that would be in keeping with Woolf's concern in *Three Guineas* that women's advancement in male-dominated activities and professions will not itself help to prevent war.

The tension between the narrator's present and Orlando's past also attunes us to the particular logic of cultural history and periodicity that the narrator deploys. The narrator refers to 'the fashion of the time', and it is a commonplace idea that a particular sartorial style characterizes a given historical era, decade, year, or even season. But that way of marking time itself has a history, and one that is rooted in consumer culture. In the eighteenth century, as consumer culture, and especially fashion, immersed Britain in a stream of more quickly outdated goods and garments, people came to think of time as a swift, irreversible flow and of history as organized in particular periods.[31] This bourgeois version of history facilitated by consumer culture contrasts with older aristocratic models in which ancestral lands, buildings, and titles embody and contain the past, present, and future.

Modern and aristocratic ideas of time and history clash and converge in *Orlando*. Orlando is a nobleman-turned-woman who lives for centuries and whose memories traverse the time and space of what becomes the British empire. In that sense, she and her magnificent hereditary estate exemplify history as continuity, stasis, and return. Yet Orlando's possession is imperilled by her longevity, change of gender, and illicit affairs, since she ends up facing legal suits alleging that she is dead, a woman, or has sons with claims on her estate. (Sackville-West did not inherit her own family home because of her gender.) The novel also parodies the technique of describing historical periods via their signature commodities, including clothing; as Randi Koppen observes, the novel presents 'history as a sequence of fashions'.[32] Those fashions are literary as well as sartorial, since the novel imitates Elizabethan, Romantic, Restoration, and Victorian tropes and styles as it moves through the centuries. Finally, we can also understand Orlando's transition from a man to a woman in terms of the emergence of a consumer vision of history, given that consumer culture was (and is) framed as feminine and feminizing. In short, Orlando's gender transition and romps through history draw attention to multiple ways that consumer culture shaped concepts and experiences of identity and time. The novel flaunts the parallels between fashion and literature as ways of giving particular forms to time.

That returns us to the question of if and how consumer culture enables or constrains non-normative forms of intimacy and embodiment. For the novel appeared at a moment when fashion was giving form to lesbian identity as a legible, categorizable way of being. In the late 1920s, it became fashionable for upper- and upper-middle-class

---

[31] See Timothy Campbell, *Historical Style: Fashion and the New Mode of History, 1740–1830* (Philadelphia: University of Pennsylvania Press, 2016).

[32] Koppen, *Virginia Woolf, Fashion and Literary Modernity*, 57.

women to wear masculine garments. As Laura Doan shows, that style was not necessarily perceived in terms of same-sex desire or challenges to masculine authority; for example, the popular terms 'boyish' or 'à la garçonne' suggest that such masculine styles were in keeping with some sense of women's subordination.[33] At the same time, masculine clothes allowed women like Vita Sackville-West to display their sexuality as an open secret; those already in the know might perceive their dress as a sign of same-sex desire rather than a simple display of fashionability. We can thus read Orlando's tendency in 1928 to 'change her skirt for a pair of whipcord breeches and leather jacket' upon her return to her estate as a reminder of the ambiguity of fashion and of configurations of gender and desire (O 287). As Doan argues, however, men's clothes became more firmly associated with lesbian sexuality after the sensational obscenity trial brought against Radclyffe Hall's *The Well of Loneliness* in 1928 thanks to widely circulated photographs of Hall in masculine garments.[34] Doan's analysis emphasizes fashion's limits as a medium for challenging regimes of gender, sexuality, and class. Masculine garments did not necessarily subvert male authority before 1928, and the subsequent establishment of a visible code for 'the lesbian' dovetailed with emerging discourses that sought to define, delineate, and often pathologize non-normative sexuality.

Orlando has been read as a rejoinder to such narrow, taxonomizing understandings of gender and sexuality. Nevertheless, reading in context makes it clear that Orlando's gender transition, costume changes, and romps reflect, reproduce, and extend as well as defy concepts of gender and time generated by consumer culture. If fashion and fiction give form to time, *Orlando* makes clear those sartorial and literary forms embed and are embedded within constructions of gender and sexuality. That is in keeping with the recognition that Woolf and her works are themselves part of consumer culture with its multivalent dynamics and effects, including its perpetuation of violence. *Orlando* stages the question of whether its narrative recapitulates tropes of consumer culture in the last chapter during Orlando's visit to a department store in 1928. As she rises in the lift and goes to buy linens for her estate, key scenes of the novel recur to her: first 'lying with Sukey—or whatever her name was' in a boat in Wapping; then lying 'on the deck of the *Enamoured Lady*' after having 'first turned woman'; then skating with Sasha, whom Orlando suddenly thinks she sees in the form of a fellow shopper, 'a fat, furred woman, marvellously well preserved, seductive, diademed, Grand Duke's mistress' (O 274, 275). Just as the department store brings a new 'slice of the world' to Orlando at every floor, so too does it serve up the past as a series of seductive, exotic encounters (O 274). The department store presents the past as irrecoverable but also tantalizingly close and perceptible. While *Mrs Dalloway* and *Night and Day* register how consumer culture shaped modes of perceiving the present, here *Orlando* stages how consumer culture mediates perceptions of the past.

Orlando's visit connects the department store's model of history (in which commodities generate a sense of the past as a series of lost yet reimaginable moments)

---

[33] Laura Doan, *Fashioning Sapphism: The Origins of Modern English Lesbian Culture* (New York: Columbia University Press, 2001), 105–6.

[34] Doan, *Fashioning Sapphism*, 122–5.

to war's material conditions and its production of cultural and historical knowledge. Orlando has gone shopping to replace the sheet on the 'royal bed' in which a servant, Louise, has found a hole. Though 'many kings and queens had slept there—Elizabeth; James; Charles; George; Victoria; Edward', Louise blames the Prince Consort for damaging the linens. She curses him as a 'sale bosch'; as the narrator explains parenthetically 'there had been another war; this time against the Germans' (O 275). The narrative pokes fun at Louise's xenophobic logic, which seems even more absurd given George, Victoria, and Edward's German roots. Like the opening scene, however, this passage reminds us that war-making has been a prime function of the monarchy and that they both entail a vision of the steady march of British history and identity. Accordingly, war is a dominant mechanism for marking time and transformation. Yet if, for Orlando in 1928, war amounts to a hole in a royal sheet and the purchase of fresh linens, does that suggest that consumer culture's endless circulation of goods has come to compensate for or distract from geopolitical violence—at least for those with purchasing power? Furthermore, if Orlando now patches up after the monarchy in her ancestral estate-turned-museum, how fundamentally does that diverge from the young Orlando's military destiny?[35] An aristocratic model of history as continuity seems to have settled alongside the periodized, contrastive accounts of history produced by consumer culture, and both work in the service of war-making.

The long-standing British fashion house Burberry found Orlando's combination of gender ambiguity and transformation as well as historical white Englishness particularly fitting for its autumn/winter 2016 season, which showed a collection of 'androgynous' clothing inspired by Woolf's *Orlando*, copies of which were given to audience members. The show included men's and women's clothing featuring Elizabethan collars, slouchy silhouettes, and military frogging, and it broke with tradition by making the garments immediately available in Burberry stores.[36] The event shrewdly took advantage of the increased visibility of gender nonconformity in popular culture, while employing a direct-to-consumer strategy and simultaneously affirming Burberry's English heritage via Woolf. With distribution across the globe, Burberry's revenues depend upon the worldwide consumption of Englishness. The company recast *Orlando* and Woolf's more critical treatment of British imperialism and fashion in celebratory, marketable terms. But this move is in keeping with the ways that *Orlando* drew energy from early twentieth-century fashion, including its construction of history and its simultaneous reconfigurations and reinforcements of gender and colonial norms. Burberry's efforts recontextualize Woolf's work, providing the opportunity to consider what sensuous alternatives and critical edge *Orlando* might still offer us in the present, when art and fashion are even more tightly linked and alternatives to capitalism seem even more distant.

Orlando's attention to consumer culture helps us to see that its critique of prevailing concepts and systems of gender, sex, intimacy, history, and war emerges with and from

---

[35] On the way that enduring white Englishness subtends *Orlando*, see Seshagiri, *Race and the Modernist Imagination*, 176–91.

[36] 'Burberry inspires nostalgia, Christopher Kane elevates Crocs', *Reuters* 19 September, 2016, reut.rs/2dcrDSQ.

an often-pleasurable entanglement with those phenomena, which are themselves various, complex, and contradictory. In that sense, *Orlando*, like many of Woolf's works, dramatizes what it means to exist and create—as well as read—in context. Woolf's texts invite us to consider what pleasures and attachments as well as material conditions shape our own reading practices. For example, feminist critics who discuss Woolf's relationship with consumer culture effectively repeat her insistence on taking fashion and shopping seriously. That repetition underscores how deeply readers' political investments, affective attachments, and critical approaches depend upon their material circumstances, which, in this moment of late capitalism, extend clearly from Woolf's era of consumer culture. To read Woolf in the context of consumer culture is to confront the dimensions of our own historical moment and the reasons people continue to consume her work.

Selected Bibliography

Bowlby, Rachel, *Feminist Destinations and Other Essays on Virginia Woolf* (Edinburgh: Edinburgh University Press, 1997).

Cohen, Lisa, '"Frock Consciousness": Virginia Woolf, the Open Secret, and the Language of Fashion', *Fashion Theory* 3, no. 2 (1999), 149–74.

Evans, Caroline, *Fashion at the Edge: Spectacle, Modernity, and Deathliness* (New Haven, CT: Yale University Press, 2003).

Garrity, Jane, 'Virginia Woolf, Intellectual Harlotry, and 1920s British *Vogue*', in Pamela Caughie, ed., *Virginia Woolf in the Age of Mechanical Reproduction.* (New York: Garland, 2000), 185–218.

Green, Barbara, *Spectacular Confessions: Autobiography, Performative Activism, and the Sites of Suffrage 1905–1938* (New York: Palgrave Macmillan, 1997).

Karl, Alissa G., *Modernism and the Marketplace* (New York: Routledge, 2009).

Koppen, Randi, *Virginia Woolf, Fashion and Literary Modernity* (Edinburgh: Edinburgh University Press, 2009).

Marler, Regina, *Bloomsbury Pie: The Making of the Bloomsbury Boom* (New York: Henry Holt, 1997).

Marshik, Celia, *At the Mercy of Their Clothes: Modernism, the Middlebrow, and British Garment Culture* (New York: Columbia University Press, 2017).

Outka, Elizabeth, *Consuming Traditions: Modernity, Modernism, and the Commodified Authentic* (New York: Oxford, 2009).

Reed, Christopher, *Bloomsbury Rooms: Modernism, Subculture, and Domesticity.* (New Haven: Yale University Press, 2004).

Sheehan, Elizabeth M., *Modernism à la Mode: Fashion and the Ends of Literature* (Ithaca: Cornell University Press, 2018).

Silver, Brenda, *Virginia Woolf, Icon* (Chicago: University of Chicago Press, 2000).

Simpson, Kathryn, *Gifts, Markets, and Economies of Desire in Virginia Woolf* (Basingstoke: Palgrave Macmillan, 2008).

Wicke, Jennifer, '*Mrs Dalloway* Goes to Market', *Novel: A Forum on Fiction* 28, no. 1 (Autumn 1994), 5–23.

PART VI
AFTERLIVES

PART V

AFTERLIVES

CHAPTER 31

FEMINIST THEORY

JEAN MILLS

WHETHER as an icon, an invocation, or in the replication of her own work, Virginia Woolf has guided or been central to key conversations in feminist theory. In the discourses of women's sexual liberation, Black and Latinx feminisms, lesbian feminism, trans feminism, and feminist pacifism, Virginia Woolf's theoretical positions outlined in both her fiction and non-fiction work continue to shape feminist thought in relation to gender, sexuality, race, class, and the potential for peace. With a focus on Woolf's inquiries into feminist identity, the limits and possibilities of feminist community, and the uses of feminist anger, this chapter delineates the arc of her influence on feminist theory as it also investigates the relevance and efficacy of her ideas in a twenty-first-century digital landscape across which much of feminist theory is now mediated and produced.

The historical trajectory of Virginia Woolf's influence has been evident in feminist thinking generated in work by Simone de Beauvoir, Doris Lessing, Carolyn Heilbrun, Adrienne Rich, and Sara Ahmed, as representative examples, from the 1940s to today. In documenting women's cultural, sexual, social, and historical experiences in her classic, *The Second Sex* (1949), Beauvoir relied on Woolf's fictional portrayal of Shakespeare's sister in *A Room of One's Own* (1929) to point to the disparities between 'the meager and restricted life' of a woman and Shakespeare's 'life of learning and adventure'.[1] In addition to her use of Woolf's essay, Beauvoir deployed narrative examples from Woolf's fiction, as well—Jinny in *The Waves* (1931) for her discussion of adolescent girls whose 'dreams of the future hide its futility',[2] and Woolf's heroines in *Mrs Dalloway* (1925) and *To the Lighthouse* (1927), to investigate the condition of women in relation to religion and revelation. In her analysis of women's character and sense of identity in relation to spirituality within the context of patriarchal society, Beauvoir writes:

> There is a justification, a supreme compensation, which society is ever wont to bestow upon woman: that is, religion. There must be religion for woman as there must

---

[1] Simone de Beauvoir, *The Second Sex*, rev. ed. (1949; repr., New York: Bantam Books, 1964), 98.
[2] Beauvoir, *The Second Sex*, 344.

be one for the common people, and for exactly the same reasons. When a sex or a class is condemned to immanence, it is necessary to offer it the mirage of some form of transcendence.[3]

Revelations and spiritual ownership for women, as for many of Woolf's protagonists in her novels, according to Beauvoir, 'are those in which they discover their accord with a static and self-sufficient reality: those luminous moments of happiness [...] of supreme recompense', are joy experienced not 'in the free surge of liberty' as men often experience religion, but in 'a quiet sense of smiling plenitude'.[4] Man, Beauvoir writes, 'enjoys the great advantage of having a God endorse the codes he writes; and since man exercises a sovereign authority over woman, it is especially fortunate that this authority has been vested in him by the Supreme Being'.[5] While Beauvoir sees religion and a woman's turn towards religion as filling 'a profound need', she also argues that it is 'much less an instrument of constraint than an instrument of deception',[6] and she frames her discussion with allusions to Woolf's fiction. In *Mrs Dalloway*, Clarissa loathes not so much Miss Kilman, her daughter's tutor, herself, but Miss Kilman's unquestioning devotion to God, 'it being [Clarissa's] experience that the religious ecstasy made people callous (so did causes)' (*MD* 10). She views Miss Kilman's attentions towards her daughter, Elizabeth, with jealousy and suspicion, accusing her of deceptively trying to convert her young mind to her religious beliefs. Highly critical of the institution of religion, Woolf nonetheless often explored the nature of her characters' spirituality. Indeed, much of the spiritual joy experienced in *Mrs Dalloway* occurs between same-sex unions—the adolescent kiss between Clarissa and Sally Seton, for example, which she describes as 'the revelation, the religious feeling!' (*MD* 32) or the bond between the traumatized war veteran Septimus Smith and his friend Evans. Written in the language of the spiritual ecstatic, these scenes offer examples of radical trespass and violations of patriarchal hierarchies, which helped guide Beauvoir in constructing her feminist positions on women and religion in *The Second Sex*.

In terms of feminist identity, Virginia Woolf has also been central to the work of Doris Lessing and her inquiries into sexual liberation and to Carolyn Heilbrun's investigations into the implications of androgyny. Useful comparisons have been made between Lessing's character Anna Wulf in *The Golden Notebook* (1962) and Woolf's Lily Briscoe in *To the Lighthouse*, each independent creative women whose struggles to maintain independence and establish a sense of identity in a male-dominated world are key themes to their respective narratives. In *Toward a Recognition of Androgyny* (1964), Carolyn Heilbrun characterized androgyny as 'a condition under which the characteristics of the

---

[3] Beauvoir, *The Second Sex*, 585.
[4] Beauvoir, *The Second Sex*, 584.
[5] Beauvoir, *The Second Sex*, 585.
[6] Beauvoir, *The Second Sex*, 585.

sexes and the human impulses expressed by men and women are not rigidly assigned',[7] a position that built upon Woolf's exploration of the mind as potentially androgynous, possessive of 'no single state of being' in *A Room of One's Own* (*ARO* 73). Heilbrun also deployed Woolf's biography as a means to rethink the genres of biography, memoir, and life-writing as a feminist methodology in *Writing a Woman's Life* (1988). She drew upon Woolf's writing career to demonstrate the pressure women writers experience to conform to a literary and cultural climate dominated by men, and the ways in which women writers, such as Woolf, rejected gendered scripts of women's roles under patriarchy to develop and shape narratives more true to women's lived experiences.

More recently, Sara Ahmed, whose work builds on decades of women of colour feminist research, also found Woolf's fiction to be instructive in how one acquires a 'feminist consciousness'.[8] Like Beauvoir, Ahmed uses the narrative arc of Mrs Dalloway herself as one example of a feminist path—one often filled with false starts, disappointments, obstacles, and changes in purpose and momentum. She counts *Mrs Dalloway* as a 'feminist classic' and a key component of her feminist 'killjoy survival kit'.[9] Indeed, Ahmed's blog *The Feminist Killjoy* resonates with Woolf's Angel in the House, in *A Room of One's Own*, whom Woolf argued women had metaphorically to kill in order to carve out the space and time to write. Like Woolf, Ahmed questions gendered prescriptions and expectations assigned to the trajectories of women's lives. In *The Promise of Happiness*, she cautions that the processional path of women's narratives from girlhood to adulthood must include 'refusing to follow other people's goods, or [...] refusing to make others happy'.[10] Ahmed's plea insists that our negative feelings, be they rage, anger, or unhappiness, be deployed repeatedly by 'the feminist killjoy', to achieve feminist aims, maintain and sustain vigilance over women's rights, and lead a feminist life.

In one of her more comedic and fantastical novels, the mock-biography, *Orlando: A Biography*, Woolf upends many of the assumptions about gender performance and expectations, across four centuries of historical context. She connects the relationship between women's experiences in the home and the pressure to marry and bear children with the reach, both domestically and abroad, of state power. Woolf notes that England of the nineteenth century rises out of the damp, as the muffin and crumpet were invented and coffee replaced the drinking of port after dinner, but '[t]he sexes drew further and further apart' (*O* 209). Her biographer/narrator reports that, 'The life of the average woman was a succession of childbirths. She married at nineteen and had fifteen or eighteen children by the time she was thirty; for twins abounded. Thus the British Empire came into existence' (*O* 209). Orlando, who has by this point in the novel transitioned into a woman, feels, but balks at, the social pressure to conform, repeat, and find a husband. She envisions '"Life! A Lover!" not "Life! A Husband!"' (*O* 222),

---

[7] Carolyn Heilbrun, *Toward a Recognition of Androgyny* (New York: Alfred A. Knopf, 1964).
[8] Sara Ahmed, *Living a Feminist Life* (Durham, NC: Duke University Press, 2017), 47.
[9] Ahmed, *Living a Feminist Life*, 235.
[10] Sara Ahmed, *The Promise of Happiness* (Durham, NC: Duke University Press, 2010), 60.

challenging the predetermined progression of a woman's life, which Ahmed and others have argued feminists need to re-examine and disrupt.

The novel, which depicts a gender transformation, while not a trans novel, has nevertheless been a notable part of new developments in feminist and trans theory for the ways in which it illustrates ideas of gender fluidity and outlines anti-patriarchal positions in favour of multiple perspectives. Though not a trans-authored text, nor a text with a trans protagonist, the novel can and has been read through a transgender theoretical lens. Pamela Caughie's comparison between Woolf's fantastical parodic novel and the real-life memoir of transsexual Elnar Wegener offers a pointed analysis of literature's capabilities in an era of scientific experimentation to shape our understanding of feminist identities. She writes that, 'By focusing on the nexus of scientific experimentation with the real and aesthetic experimentation with representation as reciprocal cultural forms, I uphold the power of literature, not just the promise of science, to reshape notions of gender and identity in the modernist era.'[11] Enjoying a resurgence in attention, in 2019 the novel was also the focus of an edition of the fine art photography journal *Aperture*, entitled *Orlando*, and guest edited by Tilda Swinton, who played the lead in Sally Potter's film version of the novel in 1992. The edition included 'Inspired by Virginia Woolf', which featured trans artists and trans subjects in conversation with the novel. *Orlando* continues to generate and guide discourses on notions of selfhood.

In the ever-changing evolution of feminist thought, Virginia Woolf's exploration of feminist identity has raised questions about her own positionality and feminist politics in relation to class and race. Critics such as Jane Marcus have argued in favour of Woolf's working-class credentials reading her depictions of charwomen in her novels such as Mrs McNab in *To the Lighthouse* and Crosby in *The Years* (1937), as not speaking for the working class, but in concert with them, and as blistering critiques of the ruling classes that created them. In a generative analysis, Marcus writes:

> [T]he voices of the charwomen, the cooks and maids, the violet sellers and the caretaker's children in *The Years*, [...] act as chorus in all her novels. We hear it in the 'ee um fah um so/foo swee too eem oo' of the tube station ancient singer in *Mrs Dalloway* to the pidgin Greek of the janitor's children in *The Years*: 'Etho passo tanno hai,/Fai donk to tu do,/Mai to, kai to, lai to see/To dom to tuh do.' If women's language, then lesbian language, is being made out of 'words that are hardly syllabled yet', every Woolf text suggests that other oppressed voices of race and class, of difference and colonial subjectivity, are beginning to syllable themselves, like the Kreemo, Glaxo, Toffe or KEY spelled by the mysterious sky-writing airplane in *Mrs Dalloway*.[12]

---

[11] Pamela Caughie, 'The Temporality of Modernist Life Writing in the Era of Transsexualism: Virginia Woolf's *Orlando* and Elnar Wegener's *Man into Woman*', *Modern Fiction Studies* 59, no. 3 (Autumn 2013), 501–25, at 502.

[12] Jane Marcus, Introduction to *Virginia Woolf and the Languages of Patriarchy* (Bloomington: University of Indiana Press, 1987), 11.

Although highly critical of her own class, Woolf and her relationship to the servants she grew up with in the late Victorian age and the ones she reluctantly managed in her own intellectual middle-class British household have been the focus of studies, which have found Woolf's positions on class to be problematic and indicative of the ways in which one's politics can sometimes be at odds with one's personal biases and blind spots. Despite these limitations, Alison Light points to the fact that Woolf 'was highly unusual in examining many of her reactions and feelings, probing her sore spots, especially in her diaries'[13] about her interactions and experiences with Britain's servant class. As Adrienne Rich has claimed, when Woolf was writing about women's poverty and lack of funding and support in *A Room of One's Own*, she was 'aware of the women who are not with us here because they are washing the dishes and looking after the children'.[14] But nearly five decades after its publication, in the early 1970s when Rich was writing, she noted that very little had changed to help fund and support women's creative and intellectual lives. Rich added to Woolf's inquiry into women and fiction, 'thinking also of women whom she left out […] women who are washing other people's dishes and caring for other people's children, not to mention women who went on the streets last night in order to feed their children'.[15] Ultimately, Virginia Woolf's personal and public relationship to class has been both reclaimed and challenged by feminist scholarship, which has noted the ways she exposed the vagaries and cruelties of the British class system, while also being complicit in its advantages and privileges as a result of her class status.

In *A Room of One's Own*, Woolf promoted women's contributions to cultural and literary production, theorizing a tradition of women writers who 'think back through our mothers', an idea that feminist thinkers such as Alice Walker and Toni Morrison found useful, but also, as women of colour scholars, and authors, exclusionary and in need of updating. It became important to many women of colour feminists to distance themselves from Woolf and push beyond her limitations, especially on issues of race. Indeed, Woolf's omissions or audiences she refused to claim to speak for, sometimes justifiably, as she was often very clear about her own position as both an othered British subject and a white woman of privilege, but at other times, as a result of her own personal and historical racial and class biases, have created ellipses of their own, gaps in the text, to unpack and speak across. Alice Walker, for example, examined African American women's experiences and contributions, invoking and extending Woolf's argument that 'Anon, who wrote so many poems without signing them, was often a woman', including women of colour creatives under the difficult aegis of anonymity (*ARO* 38). Walker's pathbreaking work outlined her 'womanist theory' as 'A black feminist or feminist of color.

---

[13] Alison Light, *Mrs Woolf and the Servants: An Intimate History of Domestic Life in Bloomsbury* (New York: Bloomsbury Press, 2008), xviii.

[14] Adrienne Rich, 'When We Dead Awaken: Writing as Re-vision (1971)', in *Adrienne Rich: Culture, Politics, and the Art of Poetry, Essential Essays*, ed. Sandra M. Gilbert (New York: W.W. Norton & Company, 2018), 3–19, at 7.

[15] Rich, 'When We Dead Awaken', 7.

From the black folk expression of mother to female children and also a woman who loves other women, sexually and/or nonsexually. Appreciates and prefers women's culture. Committed to survival and wholeness of entire people, male and female.'[16] She was writing in response to a white, liberal feminist movement, which marginalized women of colour in its own bid for equality and freedom of expression. In 2007, characterizing the history of feminist thought, Gill Plain and Susan Sellers pointed out that within the women's movement there was 'a pretense to a homogeneity of experience covered by the word sisterhood that does not in fact exist', and that too often 'white women focus upon their oppression as women and ignore differences of race, sexual preference, class, and age'.[17] This myopic view of the circumference of feminist thinking has been questioned, challenged, rethought, and expanded upon by decades of Black, Latinx, lesbian, trans, and multicultural scholarship, which insists on feminism's plurality and continues to invigorate and extend feminist theoretical discourse. In addition to Alice Walker, African American critics and authors such as bell hooks, Angela Davis, Audre Lorde, Toni Morrison, and Tuzyline Allan have found Woolf's work useful in disclosing her limitations regarding race and the racialized self.

This work delivered incisive critiques of both Woolf and the feminist movement in their own contemporary moments, while also demonstrating Woolf's work as generative. By the late 1990s, African American women's writing had begun to enjoy wider audiences, but, as Robyn Warhol-Down and Diane Price Herndl noted in 2009, African women's writing was being eclipsed and 'left out of histories and commentaries on African literature'.[18] Many African women writers, such as Beba Cameroonian author Juliana Makuchi Nfah-Abbenyi, following Walker's example, according to Warhol-Down and Price Herndl, 'have hesitated to self-identify as "feminist" because of the Western roots of feminist theory and practice'.[19] Some prefer 'womanist' or other spellings of the word, as they use a feminist methodology to adapt to their own purposes. This rethinking of feminist identity resonates with Woolf's own negotiation of the term 'feminist', when, in *Three Guineas* (1938), she ironically asks if we perhaps shouldn't 'write that word in large black letters on a sheet of foolscap; then solemnly apply a match to the paper', because, with access to the professions achieved, there was no longer a need to fear that men and women wouldn't work together for justice, equality, and freedom for all (*TG* 179). The scene, however, is meant as a foil to her argument pointing to the ways in which other words such as 'tyrant' and 'dictator' remain current and alive, as well as the similarities between both the patriarchal state and the fascist state, a comparison that continues to make us uncomfortable today.

---

[16] Alice Walker, *In Search of Our Mothers' Gardens: Womanist Prose* (New York: Harcourt Brace Jovanovich, 1983).

[17] Gill Plain and Susan Sellers, eds, *A History of Feminist Literary Criticism* (Cambridge: Cambridge University Press, 2007), 269.

[18] Robyn Warhol-Down and Diane Price Herndl, eds, *Feminisms Redux: An Anthology of Literary Theory and Criticism* (New Brunswick: Rutgers University Press, 2009).

[19] Warhol-Down and Herndl, *Feminisms Redux*, 7.

The questions and positions Virginia Woolf theorized about women's privacy as well as the nature of feminist community and women's relationship to the public sphere anticipate and sometimes reflect parallel development of similar questions feminist theorists face today in negotiating a relationship to social media. Indeed, any apprehension of her positions in relation to twenty-first-century feminist theory must inevitably involve a reckoning between feminist theory and social media, as conversations on feminist community are created, shaped, and reconsidered within its framework.

The fact that the discourse is both relentlessly replenished online and insatiably disseminated in a variety of social media platforms raises questions about both the content of the feminist conversation as well as the nature and efficacy of the methodology. As Urmila Seshagiri wrote in 2017, 'Feminism is repetitive because patriarchy is undead.'[20] She was pointing to a curious disjunction between a subject area that recognizes that women, feminists, and feminist women fundamentally shaped modernism and modernity and a body of scholarship responding to that subject, which continues to neglect women's roles, experiences, and contributions. She was also writing within the political context of a rise in misogynistic rhetoric, an uptick in the commission of hate crimes, and policy initiatives aimed at rolling back women's rights across the globe. Noting protest signs, such as 'I can't believe I still have to protest this shit', displayed at the Women's March in Washington, DC in January 2017, Seshagiri was also remarking upon a deep-seated frustration at having to repeat rationales to theoretical debates for women's equity and equal treatment, many considered to have been won and translated into real policy decades earlier.

Since the political watershed of 2016 outlined a world leaning globally and with enthusiasm towards right-wing populist ideologies, resurgent nationalisms, and anti-feminist thought, feminist theory has increasingly been shaped and directed across a digital landscape of visual and verbal play in response. Indeed, the hashtag and the links and memes, GIFs, and images, which social media generate create their own kinds of feminist community, and, in my view, have become in and of themselves artefacts and indicators of a contemporary feminist zeitgeist. The spirit of the age, which Woolf satirized so incisively in *Orlando* as being much more varied and complex than the masculinist prescriptives of her father's late Victorian age, in our own times finds us awash in an open-ended, infinite, and intersectional web of multiple interpretations and voices, similar to those 'many thousand' selves Woolf described in the final passages of the novel, as Orlando travels through centuries to her own contemporary time, and 'now looked down into this pool or sea in which everything is reflected' (*O* 282, 295). The infinitude is both exhilarating and overwhelming, as Orlando, as a woman, must decide whether to submit to or resist its directives. Remarkably, Woolf's embrace and interrogation of illegibility and ambivalence (sometimes in and of themselves as forms of resistance) throughout her work makes her somewhat of a twenty-first-century literary

---

[20] Urmila Seshagiri, 'Mind the Gap! Modernism and Feminist Praxis', *Modernism/Modernity* Print Plus 2, no. 2 (August 2017).

poster child for a digital generation, which very much sees itself as 'a society for asking questions' (*CSF* 125) about which Woolf once fantasized for women in her 1921 short story 'A Society', which advocated for women's reproductive freedom, access to education and the professions, and the inclusion of women's voices and experiences in literary and cultural production.

Currently, as memes and hashtags are born and replicated, some, such as #MeToo, for example, dedicated to narratives of sexual assault and sexual harassment, gain traction and evolve to become phenomena, marking profound shifts in any given conversation. As in the case of #MeToo, a transition in theoretical discourse sparked several political movements and activism devoted to issues raised in the conversation. The phrase was first coined in 2006 by civil rights activist Tarana Burke on the social media platform Myspace, and later popularized on Twitter in October 2017 by American actress Alyssa Milano, in response to a widely publicized case of sexual assault and harassment by film producer Harvey Weinstein. Interestingly, even though it's possible to discover the first mention of #MeToo on social media as a proliferating digital artefact, #MeToo is unencumbered by the boundaries of provenance, authorship, or origins.

While the feminist community generated by the MeToo hashtag far exceeds the reach of a twentieth century understanding of 'the public', social media's democratization of the conversation speaks to Virginia Woolf's challenges to and explorations of cultural gatekeeping, hierarchies, and pretentiousness. These she identified as male-driven and male-dominated, and as basic principles connected to egotism that she personally loathed. She rejected 'the loudspeaker' voice of the academy, was conflicted by both a desire for and a lack of formal education, ('I thought how unpleasant it is to be locked out; and I thought how it is worse perhaps to be locked in' (*ARO* 19), and cautioned against using one's influence, as women gained rights, the vote, and access to the professions, to re-enact the same power plays men in positions of authority often inflict upon women in the workplace. She wrote two collections of essays dedicated to everyday reading practices, entitled *The Common Reader* (1925) and *The Second Common Reader* (1932), as well as two major essays based on talks (not lectures), *A Room of One's Own* and *Three Guineas*, whose conversational and collaborative rhetorical styles are intimately bound up with their arguments, which investigate the architecture and hierarchies of inclusion and exclusion integral to a patriarchal society and its treatment of women.

The internet's unbridled posturing, its freedom, and lack of curatorial concision are also marked by gender, race, and class, which paradoxically replicate and often reify many of the same biases women bristled at and resisted for years. While the online conversation in feminist theory has in many ways been invigorated by social media's reach and efficacy, in other ways, it has led to an extraordinary loss of privacy and personal control and a documented increase in unfiltered and shameless hostility and hatred towards women. On the one hand, forewarned is forearmed, and certainly 2016 with the help of social media served as an unveiling and public airing of racism, sexism, homophobia, transphobia, and personal invective on a scale that made locating one's enemies easy. On the other hand, the pool of widespread and unapologetic extremism is so vast that a sense of urgency, which begins around an issue of gross, disturbing, even unprecedented injustice and wrong-doing, too often quickly deteriorates into a lack of social engagement and a debilitating sense of being overwhelmed by information, misinformation, and disinformation.

Virginia Woolf's involvement in as well as her ambivalence about public political discourses has been noted by critics such as David Bradshaw and Clara Jones, among others, especially in relation to Woolf's responses to political changes during the 1930s. The decade of the 1930s, that earlier global turn towards fascism and nationalism, Anna Snaith notes, 'saw Woolf battling with her "repulsion from societies" and yet her abhorrence of political developments at home and abroad'.[21] While part of Snaith's aim in '"Stray Guineas": Virginia Woolf and the Fawcett Library' is to outline Woolf's anti-fascist positions and political support and involvement on behalf of women's suffrage, refugees, and intellectual freedom, her investigation into the ways in which Woolf negotiated her responses to political causes also reveals a frustration on Woolf's part—a frustration that resonates with today's struggle to construct feminist community amidst relentless requests (whether via email or social media) to sign, donate, join, and protest. Snaith writes, 'Her feeling of bombardment during the '30s also involved awareness of the commodification of her signature. Desire for anonymity made her question public endorsement per se, regardless of the cause'.[22] A desire for privacy, personal control, and a respite from the din of ceaseless public pressure concerned Woolf as she investigated its effects upon feminist thinking. She also recognized the ways in which capital, culture, and war combine to perpetuate patriarchy and its entrenched persecution of women, a system that Woolf sought to dismantle.

Three Guineas is relevant to anyone's contemporary moment due to its subject matter, the need to prevent and end war. Yet it also remains current due to its inquiries into methodology. The essay outlining Woolf's pacifism and patriarchy's connection to women's oppression in both the private and public spheres, is also, as Snaith points out, 'a deliberation on the complexities and implications of various kinds of political and charitable support'.[23] In other words, in addition to its analysis of the complexities of pacifism and its usefulness and interconnectedness to feminist theory and activism, *Three Guineas* resonates with the challenges we face today as we grapple with the advantages and disadvantages of the political post-card versus the phone call to a representative, the online donation to Change.org, for example, versus a birthday fundraising appeal for a personal cause on Facebook. But within the panoply of these various media and the questions it raises about method, *Three Guineas* is, as Snaith claims, 'an enactment of her preferred form of resistance: the text'.[24]

Virginia Woolf used both her fiction and non-fiction work to question the nature of this vast public conversation, as she tried to identify and navigate her own role in

---

[21] Anna Snaith, '"Stray Guineas": Virginia Woolf and the Fawcett Library', *Literature and History* 12, no. 2 (November 2003), 16–35, at 16.
[22] Snaith, 'Stray Guineas', 18.
[23] Snaith, 'Stray Guineas', 18–19.
[24] Snaith, 'Stray Guineas', 16.

relation to it. In the essay, she is very clear about her own positionality, as a white woman of a certain class, collectively 'the daughters of educated men', as she identifies herself in *Three Guineas* (*TG* 180). In another characteristic interactive, collaborative stylistic signature, she begins as if in the middle of a conversation, theorizing a relationship between feminist interconnectedness in the public sphere and the need to maintain a specific, localized methodology in advancing a feminist agenda:

> 'But,' she may say, '"the public"? How can that be reached without putting my own mind through the mincing machine and turning it into sausage?' '"The public," Madam,' we may assure her, 'is very like ourselves; it lives in rooms; it walks in streets, and is said moreover to be tired of sausage. Fling leaflets down basements; expose them on stalls; trundle them along streets on barrows to be sold for a penny or given away. Find out new ways of approaching "the public"; single it into separate people instead of massing it into one monster, gross in body, feeble in mind.' (*TG* 176)

In an essay whose premise is framed around a response to a male correspondent asking her to sign a manifesto for peace, donate money, and join a society, her narrator investigates 'some of the active ways in which you […] can put your opinions into practice' on behalf of a cause, while noting the challenges women face in particular in building coalitions in the public sphere (*TG* 176). She points out how men and women are similarly appalled at the horrors of war. She returns again and again to the 'photographs of dead bodies and ruined houses' in the war-torn landscape of the Spanish Civil War, verbal images of destruction, the responsibility for which she lays at the feet of men in power (*TG* 150). But our differences based on gender, she reminds us, are 'profound and fundamental', making a request of support and funds from a member of the patriarchy that oppresses, dismisses, and marginalizes women, difficult to satisfy (*TG* 181).

In outlining and identifying the structure of patriarchy, she is also making suggestions, devising feminist strategies and theories about ways to subvert it. She writes that even '[t]he very word "society" sets tolling in memory the dismal bells of a harsh music: shall not, shall not, shall not. You shall not learn; you shall not earn; you shall not own; you shall not', which complicates her relationship to the public request for funds (*TG* 182). Her challenge to what seems a simple and obvious solicitation on behalf of peace becomes an intricate and deeply thought-out meditation on the consequences of systemic oppression, until 'inevitably we ask ourselves, is there not something in the conglomeration of people into societies that releases what is most selfish and violent, least rational and humane in the individuals themselves? Inevitably we look upon society, so kind to you, so harsh to us, as an ill-fitting form that distorts the truth; deforms the mind; fetters the will' (*TG* 182).

We face similar challenges today as we struggle to engage with the internet as a tool both for constructing and maintaining a genealogy of feminist thought and for supporting feminist activism, only to realize that the echoes of the past continue to remind and sometimes to admonish us in the present. Not only do the size, scale, and scope of the internet work both for and against the advancement of feminist theory, but many of the issues and the movement's aims, with few exceptions, have largely remained the same. Co-creating a feminist tradition of theory and activism with the past, while also pointing to the brutal, barbaric, and often life-threatening realities of the treatment of women under patriarchy, Woolf ultimately aligns the nineteenth-century fight for women's rights by 'those queer dead women in their poke bonnets and shawls' with the twentieth-century fight against fascism.

Woolf's narrator in *Three Guineas*, albeit conditionally, agrees to sign the manifesto and to send money for the peace effort, but she refuses to join his society, recording a separate tradition of feminist community and activism and instructing future generations of women by theorizing potential pathways for organizing resistance. She writes, 'we believe that we can help you most effectively by refusing to join your society; by working for our common ends—justice and equality and liberty for all men and women—outside your society, not within' (*TG* 183). She famously creates the Society of Outsiders, which has no hierarchies, no oaths, no offices, no secretaries, no meetings, and no conferences, but values 'elasticity' and 'secrecy' instead and insists on achieving peace, intellectual liberty, and justice 'by the means that a different sex, a different tradition, a different education, and the different values which result from those differences have placed within our reach' (*TG* 189). Instead, she calls on women to build their coalitions and advocacy efforts outside of the establishment, to maintain and practice indifference and disinterest, to offer her brothers 'neither the white feather of cowardice nor the red feather of courage, but no feather at all', to refuse to take part in patriotic displays and refuse to bear arms. In other words, she has been asked by her male correspondent to sign a peace manifesto, which she does, but only as she rewrites and posits, instead, one of her own. Woolf's essays, but her entire body of work, in both the diaries and letters, her fiction, and journalism, as well, not only have created, but continue to create feminist communities of their own, as her arguments, investigations, images, and examples return to remind us of the need for sustained vigilance as well as new methods, new theories, and new ways of looking at the world.

As the methodologies of the internet work both for and against feminist aims, rage, too, is a multivalent sword. Feminist anger has acted both as an important tool for resistance and invigoration of a cause as well as a justification for committing acts of violence against women. In the wake of a widespread increase in right-wing ideologies, nationalism, fascism, racism, and anti-feminist thought, women's rage has returned to the forefront of feminist theoretical discourse. As one leading feminist journal *Signs: A Journal of Women in Culture and Society* states quite plainly in its most recent call for papers for a special issue devoted to the complexities of rage to be published in Summer 2021: 'Feminists are raging', and for good reason. In addition to running the online Feminist Public Intellectual Project, the journal will now be airing their site, Ask a Feminist, as a podcast with its first episode featuring recent titles fuelling the debate. Soraya Chemaly's *Rage Becomes Her: The Power of Women's Anger* (2018), for example, argues that 'a society that does not respect women's anger is one that does not respect women; not as human beings, thinkers, knowers, active participants, or citizens'[25] and Charlene A. Carruthers's *Unapologetic: A Black, Queer and Feminist Mandate for Radical Movements* (2018) provides a manifesto and manual for activism and effective organization from a Black, queer, and feminist perspective seeking to counter a 'mainstream narrative propped up by patriarchy and misogyny (straight-up hatred of women)'.[26]

Virginia Woolf's work, biography, and example have figured prominently in the feminist uses of anger and its efficacy as political currency. Anger, and the ways in which she navigated her anger both on the page and in her personal life, became a key focus for women reading her work both in English and in translation throughout the 1960s and 1970s. In 1971, Adrienne Rich wrote about re-reading *A Room of One's Own* and of recognizing, but also being struck by what she characterized as Woolf's suppression of her anger in the text:

> I was astonished at the sense of effort, of pains taken, of dogged tentativeness, in the tone of that essay. And I recognized that tone. I had heard it often enough, in myself and in other women. It is the tone of a woman almost in touch with her anger, who is determined not to appear angry, who is willing herself to be calm, detached, and even charming in a roomful of men where things have been said which are attacks on her very integrity.[27]

While Woolf was addressing women in her 'talk', Rich claimed that she felt acutely the implied male presence in the room, because the political climate had not changed to the point 'when women can stop being haunted, not only by "convention and propriety" but by internalized fears of being and saying themselves'.[28] This suppression of women's anger is further investigated by Jane Marcus, who sought to encourage women to 'spit out' their 'rage and savage indignation',[29] as Marcus wrote in an essay, which she anthologized ten years later in her collection of essays *Art and Anger: Reading Like a Woman* (1988), noting the typical prolepsis that often occurs in the development of women writers, as feminist literary criticism strives to catch up to feminist politics as goals were achieved within the movement. Marcus admits that some of the earlier essays in the collection seem 'too polite and well-mannered, now that Woolf *is* the subject of so much critical debate' and hardly worth 'the uproar it caused at the 1975 MLA'.[30] With one of the aims accomplished, to reshape the male-driven critical response to her work in the 1940s and 1950s as the 'lyrical British novelist' Mrs Woolf, feminists now were

---

[25] Soraya Chemaly, *Rage Becomes Her: The Power of Women's Anger* (New York: Simon & Schuster, 2018).

[26] Charlene A. Carruthers, *Unapologetic: A Black, Queer and Feminist Mandate for Radical Movements* (New York: Beacon Press, 2018).

[27] Rich, 'When We Dead Awaken', 6.

[28] Rich, 'When We Dead Awaken', 6.

[29] Jane Marcus, *Art and Anger: Reading Like a Woman* (Columbus: The Ohio State University Press, 1988).

[30] Marcus, *Art and Anger*, xiv.

'paying attention to Woolf's politics'.[31] Marcus noted an adjustment in the tenor of the debate, which focused very much on women's personal anger and the need for women to express their emotions. She wrote that her interest in Woolf's anger 'clearly grew out of my own anger and the anger of my generation of feminist critics, who were trying to change the subject without yet having developed a sophisticated methodology',[32] marking the importance of women's anger as a resource and rationale for devising approach, strategy, and action in response to oppression. She characterized the trajectory of change indicated in the form of address: 'Now that the subject has been changed, we can record the history of that process.'[33] The earlier criticism on Woolf 'address[es] the establishment with a clenched fist [...] cursing the literary hegemonic fathers. The later essays address a discursive community of feminist readers.' 'Now', she writes 'we look forward to the work of the "daughters of anger" '[34] in a bid to secure the future of feminism in a more forthright posture, implying confidence and a freedom of expression of anger.

Virginia Woolf was perhaps more ambivalent, or at least more realistic about the complexities and uses of rage and the size and scope of the burden of resistance upon the shoulders of future generations of feminists. In the 1921 'A Society', after the women's collective (representative of the feminist movement) has been truncated by the guns and battle cries of World War I, the women reconvene at the end of the story to assess the accomplishments of the group, but now, against the backdrop of the 'proper explosion of the fireworks' (CSF 136), for peace. Woolf also identified these 'proper' celebrations as complicit in the cycles of war and remembrance, issues that she saw as intersecting with the experiences of women and children, and as consequential relationships she questioned and hoped to break. In the final scene of the satire, Woolf's narrator, Cassandra, aptly named for the prophetess who spoke the truth, which no one believed or could understand, says, referring to one of the member's daughters, whom they hope to carry on the legacy of the collective, 'It's no good [...] Once she knows how to read there's only one thing you can teach her to believe in—and that is herself' (CSF 136). Castalia agrees, noting that, 'that would be a change'. The women gather the papers and minutes of their society, and 'though Ann was playing with her doll very happily, we solemnly made her a present of the lot and told her we had chosen her to be President of the Society of the future—upon which she burst into tears' (CSF 136).

Succeeding generations of feminist scholars have both questioned or built upon this earlier characterization of Woolf's rage as being 'suppressed'. Recently, conceptions of Woolf's anger and how we understand it in relation to her feminist theoretical positions and strategies for future activism have been challenged by investigations into affect theory. In 'After Anger: Negative Affect and Feminist Politics in Virginia Woolf's *Three Guineas*', Margot Kotler argues that Woolf's Society of Outsiders and her juxtaposing

---

[31] Marcus, *Art and Anger*, xiv.
[32] Marcus, *Art and Anger*, xxi.
[33] Marcus, *Art and Anger*, xxi.
[34] Marcus, *Art and Anger*, xxi.

of image and text outline her 'impersonal method', which 'provides a model for collective feminist politics that complicates the teleological narrative of feminism in which emotion operates as a site of truth'.[35] Kotler's aim is not to dismiss or ignore our emotions, but to rethink the 'personal is political' as 'the personal is factual'.[36] In an instructive essay that insists we read Woolf's feminist uses of anger more strategically, Kotler writes that Woolf:

> [...] demonstrates the danger of a feminist politics that uncritically exploits the personal and the emotional as a source of truth and makes them the first step of a political project that will end in its own obsolescence. Instead, Woolf maintains that feminists would be better served by both transforming personal emotions into collective negative feelings, as shown in her use of impersonal anger as a feminist methodology, and harnessing this *attributed* anger and unhappiness to launch collective critique, via unsympathetic and indifferent response, of the emotionally exploitative rhetoric and imagery of the fascist and patriarchal state.[37]

Understood in this way, rage becomes not personally exhausting as an emotion, but as a key tool and resource 'that supports a more sustainable feminist politics',[38] one that is more useful and effective moving forward, because, as Kotler claims in the essay, for Woolf, there really is no such thing as 'after anger'.[39] Woolf, in an earlier era, strove to carve out a way forward for future generations of women readers, writers, and thinkers through a commitment to art and language, and through the transformation of her anger into an effective political tool of feminist thought.

In the historical documentation of her influence on feminist identity and community and in the replenishment of her work across new digital methodologies, Virginia Woolf continues to be a major vitalizing force in feminist theory, as states and individuals continue to attempt to police and regulate women's lives. In seeking to dismantle patriarchy and theorize a world we have yet to create, Virginia Woolf exposed the cruelty of hierarchies, while also noting the repetitive nature of oppression that continues to sing the same old song as in the children's nursery rhyme 'Here We Go Round the Mulberry Bush', a refrain she used in *Three Guineas* to illustrate the same hypocrisies and injustices born on the backs of women's unpaid labour. Challenges to feminist essentialism, female chauvinism, heterosexist assumptions overlooking lesbian and trans texts, and ableist bias have invigorated feminist theoretical discourse and activism on behalf of feminist causes. Both the embraces of and challenges to Virginia Woolf's work, I would argue, have led to a more explicit acceptance of difference among women, and created a

---

[35] Margot Kotler, 'After Anger: Negative Affect and Feminist Politics in Virginia Woolf's *Three Guineas*', *Woolf Studies Annual* 24 (2018), 35–54, at 37.
[36] Kotler, 'After Anger', 41.
[37] Kotler, 'After Anger', 53.
[38] Kotler, 'After Anger', 53.
[39] Kotler, 'After Anger', 53.

myriad of feminist approaches, which continue to enrich and diversify an ongoing feminist narrative and critical debate.

Selected Bibliography

Ahmed, Sara, *Living a Feminist Life* (Durham, NC: Duke University Press, 2017).

Ahmed, Sara, *The Promise of Happiness* (Durham, NC: Duke University Press, 2010).

Carruthers, Charlene A., *Unapologetic: A Black, Queer and Feminist Mandate for Radical Movements* (New York: Beacon Press, 2018).

Caughie, Pamela, 'The Temporality of Modernist Life Writing in the Era of Transsexualism: Virginia Woolf's *Orlando* and Elnar Wegener's *Man into Woman*', in *Modern Fiction Studies* 59, no. 3 (2013): 501–25.

Chemaly, Soraya, *Rage Becomes Her: The Power of Women's Anger* (New York: Simon & Shuster, 2018).

De Beauvoir, Simone, *The Second Sex* [1949] (New York: Bantam Books, 1964).

Heilbrun, Carolyn, *Toward a Recognition of Androgyny* (New York: Knopf, 1964.

Jones, Clara, *Virginia Woolf: Ambivalent Activist* (Edinburgh: Edinburgh University Press, 2016).

Kotler, Margot. 'After Anger: Negative Affect and Feminist Politics in Virginia Woolf's *Three Guineas*', *Woolf Studies Annual* 24 (2018): 35–54.

Light, Alison, *Mrs Woolf and the Servants: An Intimate History of Domestic Life in Bloomsbury* (New York: Bloomsbury Press, 2008).

Lorde, Audre, 'The Uses of Anger: Women Responding to Racism', Keynote Address to Women's Studies Association Conference, Storrs, CT, 1981.

Marcus, Jane, *Art and Anger: Reading Like a Woman* (Columbus: The Ohio State University Press, 1988).

Marcus, Jane, *Virginia Woolf and the Languages of Patriarchy*. (Bloomington: University of Indiana Press, 1987).

Morrison, Toni, *The Source of Self-Regard: Selected Essays, Speeches, and Meditations* (New York: Knopf, 2019).

Nfah-Abbenyi, Juliana, *Gender in African Women's Writing: Identity, Sexuality and Difference* (Bloomington: Indiana University Press, 1997).

Plain, Gill, and Susan Sellers, eds, *A History of Feminist Literary Criticism* (Cambridge: Cambridge University Press, 2007.

Rich, Adrienne, 'When We Dead Awaken: Writing as Re-vision (1971)', in Sandra M. Gilbert, ed., *Adrienne Rich: Culture, Politics, and the Art of Poetry, Essential Essays* (New York: W.W. Norton & Co., 2018), 3–19.

Seshagiri, Urmila. 'Mind the Gap! Modernism and Feminist Praxis', in *Modernism/Modernity*, vol. 2, cycle 2 (7 August 2017), https://doi.org/10.26597/mod.0022.

Snaith, Anna, ' "Stray Guineas": Virginia Woolf and the Fawcett Library', *Literature and History* 12, no. 2 (November 2003): 16–35.

Walker, Alice, *In Search of Our Mothers' Gardens: Womanist Prose* (New York: Harcourt Brace Jovanovich, 1983).

Warhol-Down, Robyn, and Diane Price Herndl, eds, *Feminisms Redux* (Rutgers University Press, 2009).

CHAPTER 32

DISABILITY, ILLNESS, AND PAIN

ELIZABETH OUTKA

> this monster, the body, this miracle, its pain
> Woolf, 'On Being Ill'

THIS line from Virginia Woolf's essay 'On Being Ill' captures her contradictory treatments of ill and impaired bodies (*E4* 318). Lurking on one side of 'the body' lies the monstrous, while on the other, the body transforms into 'this miracle', evoking the possibility of new insights despite (or because of) 'its pain'. The very ambiguity of references—Is the miracle the pain or the body? Is the monster the body or the miracle?—reflects the mingled representations of bodies in Woolf's work. The slippage between monster and miracle, though, also suggests Woolf's incongruous attitudes towards bodies outside what Rosemarie Garland-Thomson terms 'the normate'.[1] On one hand, Woolf evinces in her writing a profound understanding of bodies experiencing some forms of physical and mental health issues, detailing the challenges and insights arising from such altered states. On the other hand, when representing bodies with more visible and more permanent structural or cognitive differences—traits Woolf at times all too clearly sees as monstrous—she often displays callous, deeply normate reactions, with disturbing alliances to the eugenics movement of her time.[2]

---

[1] The normate, Garland-Thomson argues, is a constructed figure defined 'by the array of deviant others whose marked bodies shore up the normate's boundaries'. *Extraordinary Bodies: Figuring Physical Disability in American Culture and Literature* (New York: Columbia University Press, 1997), 8.

[2] See Matt Franks's analysis in 'Serving on the Eugenic Homefront: Virginia Woolf, Race, and Disability', *Feminist Formations* 29, no. 1 (Spring 2017), 1–24.

Assessing Woolf's treatment of bodies demands an approach that encompasses these contradictions. To date, though, critical work on Woolf typically approaches illness and disability separately, drawing on two distinct theoretical models. Using what could roughly be characterized as a medical humanities model, critics from the 1970s on have investigated Woolf's representations of illness, with particular attention to the figure of the invalid and its gendered construction and to characters experiencing psychiatric differences.[3] The mental health struggle of Septimus Smith in Mrs Dalloway (1925) has received particularly detailed analysis, and 'On Being Ill'—and its relationship to Woolf's mother's work on nursing, Notes from Sick Rooms—has been the subject of renewed attention.[4] When assessing Woolf's treatment of bodies with structural or cognitive impairments, however, scholars have used a disability studies model. While definitions of disability do encompass both chronic illness and mental health issues, most critics assessing Woolf through disability theory focus on her (often strikingly negative) representations of bodies with typically more permanent physical and cognitive differences.[5] These scholars largely set aside questions of chronic or mental illness, though they observe the contradictions between Woolf's more nuanced treatment of such topics versus her treatment of bodies she defined as non-normate.

Disability studies and medical humanities approaches should be brought together to assess Woolf, despite the significant challenges to such a move: these two fields work within different, even incompatible, frames. The medical humanities typically view illness and disability as issues located within the body, and as issues that may—and even should—be cured or addressed through intervention. As critic Anna Mollow observes, however, the 'founding paradigm' of disability studies is the adoption of a social and not a medical model;[6] disability is not located in a body but in the 'architectural, attitudinal,

---

[3] Early work by Quentin Bell and Jean Love, carried on by Kimberly Coates, Cheryl Hindrichs, and others, assesses the interplay between Woolf's personal experiences with illness and her broader aesthetic projects: Quentin Bell, *Virginia Woolf: A Biography* (New York: Harcourt Brace Jovanovich, 1972); Jean Love, *Virginia Woolf: Sources of Madness and Art* (Oakland: University of California Press, 1978); Kimberly Coates, 'Phantoms, Fancy (And) Symptoms: Virginia Woolf and The Art of Being Ill', *Virginia Woolf Annual*, 18 (2012), 1–28. See, too, Cheryl Hindrichs's edited issue 'Virginia Woolf and Illness' for *Virginia Woolf Miscellany*, 90 (Autumn 2016), 1, 44–68 and Douglas Orr, *Virginia Woolf's Illnesses*, ed. Wayne Chapman (Clemson: Clemson University Digital Press, 2004).

[4] See, for example, Karen DeMeester, 'Trauma and Recovery in Virginia Woolf's *Mrs. Dalloway*', *MFS Modern Fiction Studies* 44, no. 3 (Autumn 1998), 649–73; and Suzette Henke and David Eberly, eds, *Virginia Woolf and Trauma: Embodied Texts* (New York: Pace University Press, 2007). Also, see Virginia Woolf and Julia Stephen, *On Being Ill with Notes from Sick Rooms* (Ashfield: Paris Press, 2012).

[5] Critics such as Janet Lyon, Maren Linett, Madelyn Detloff, and Matt Franks offer incisive critiques of how Woolf constructs non-normate bodies in her diaries and essays, and in characters such as Mrs. McNab in *To the Lighthouse*, Sara in *The Years*, and Rhoda's teacher in *The Waves*: Janet Lyon, 'On the Asylum Road with Woolf and Mew', *Modernism/modernity* 18, no. 3 (Sept. 2011), 551–74; Madelyn Detloff, '"The Law Is on the Side of the Normal": Virginia Woolf as Crip Theorist', in Ann Martin and Kathryn Holland, eds, *Interdisciplinary/Multidisciplinary Woolf* (Clemson: Clemson University Digital Press, 2013), 102–8; Maren Linett, *Bodies of Modernism: Physical Disability in Transatlantic Modernist Literature* (Ann Arbor: University of Michigan Press, 2017); Matt Franks, 'Serving on the Eugenic Homefront'.

[6] Anna Mollow, 'Disability Studies', in Imre Szeman, Sarah Blacker, and Justin Sully eds, *A Companion to Critical and Cultural Theory* (New York: John Wiley & Sons, 2017), 339–56, at 340.

political, and economic structures that enforce the marginalization of disabled people'.[7] Disability scholars and activists work to change not bodies but the cultural norms that constrict them. Each approach offers different narratives about the body, with different areas of concern and erasure. The medical humanities cover a wider range of illness states (from acute to chronic) and diagnose the body's pain and ways it might be addressed; this approach, though, risks reinforcing the idea of a correct 'normate' body, ignoring ways that the 'problems' of certain bodies are in fact socially constructed. Disability studies, in turn, recognizes that longer forms of illness, like 'mental illness ... chronic physical illnesses, and chronic pain—can produce disability'.[8] And yet, despite these inclusions, disability studies tends to focus less on chronic or mental illness, and more on bodily states such as sensory and structural impairments and cognitive differences outside of the psychiatric. The focus is understandable: the temporal frames may differ between chronic illness and a more permanent structural difference, and disabling illnesses may be less visible, and treatment—to rid a body of cancer, say—signifies differently than attempts to force a structurally different body into a normate form.[9] Adding to the complications, as Diane Herndl observes, is that 'most people in the disability community do not want to be considered ill, and most people who are ill don't want to be considered disabled'.[10]

These distinctions between illness and disability, and between medical humanities and disability studies, are critical to maintain, yet these differences may also obscure three things: conditions that overlap the two, the way illness and disability may be used against each other, and the way this very use may obscure the tangled differences in visibility inherent to each. In Woolf studies, critics have, for good reasons, generally used a medical humanities approach for illness, and a disability studies approach for physical and cognitive differences. Because, though, these analyses are generally applied separately, they often elide how Woolf uses certain forms of illness and disability to make other forms less visible. Chronic illness and mental health issues—categories that may straddle both illness and disability and unfold across varying time frames—also tend to fall out of sight when using only a disability studies approach for Woolf, reinforcing the

---

[7] Mollow, 'Disability Studies', 342.
[8] Mollow, 'Disability Studies', 341. For work on mental health and disability, see Andrea Nicki, 'The Abused Mind: Feminist Theory, Psychiatric Disability, and Trauma', *Hypatia* 16, no. 4 (Autumn 2001), 80–104; and Elizabeth Donaldson, 'Revisiting the Corpus of the Madwoman: Further Notes toward a Feminist Disability Studies Theory of Mental Illness', in Kim Q. Hall, ed., *Feminist Disability Studies* (Bloomington: Indiana University Press, 2011), 91–113. Susan Wendell examines disability and chronic illness in 'Unhealthy Disabled: Treating Chronic Illnesses as Disabilities', *Hypatia* 16, no. 4 (Autumn 2001), 17–33.
[9] Feminist scholars of disability studies note how the field's rejection of the medical model risks eliding issues surrounding pain and bodily suffering. See, for example, Liz Crow, 'Including All of Our Lives: Renewing the Social Model of Disability', in Jenny Morris, ed., *Encounters with Strangers: Feminism and Disability* (London: Women's Press, 1996), 206–26; and Mollow, 'Disability Studies', 350.
[10] Diane Herndl examines the two fields in 'Disease versus Disability': The Medical Humanities and Disability Studies', *PMLA* 120, no. 2 (2005), 593–8, at 593.

ways these conditions were often elided at the level of the culture—something Woolf herself is intent on observing.

Investigating Woolf's treatment of illness and disability alongside each other, without collapsing them together, requires on two levels what I term a composite gaze. As critics, we must approach her representations through overlapping sightlines, illustrated here through three clusters of examples that combine portraits of ill bodies, of structurally or cognitively different bodies, and of bodies experiencing mental health issues that might encompass both illness and disability. Each cluster, in turn, reflects a second gaze, that of a composite observer, one who embodies what the culture would consider a non-normate form yet who observes and defines other bodies as non-normate. Deploying a composite approach, rather than a bifurcated one, recognizes the overlapping qualities of bodies and grants ways to acknowledge the unclear borderlands between disability and illness while maintaining the critical distinctions between the two. I begin with passages from Woolf's early diary that model her contradictory treatments of bodies and the ways she creates hierarchies among bodily differences. From these more private, less aesthetically crafted accounts, I turn to her essays 'On Being Ill' and 'Street Haunting' that rewrite aspects of the earlier diary entries, reifying her hierarchies while introducing a problematic new aesthetic 'cure'. Finally, I investigate instances in *Mrs Dalloway* where the diary accounts are again re-envisioned, now in fully fictional form. Building on the previous two clusters, I offer a series of sightlines that allows for a multi-modal approach, framing representations of bodies through both medical humanities and disability studies lenses. Taken together, these clusters keep Woolf's contradictory treatments of different conditions—and her vacillations between what Maren Linett terms 'othering and selving'—clearly in view.[11] Making the *contradiction* central allows us to see distinctions between illness and disability without participating in Woolf's attempts to use one to hide the other.

Composite Perspectives I: The Diary

Two moments from Woolf's diary of 1915, written two days apart, concern confrontations with ill or impaired bodies. In the first, Woolf recounts visiting a sick friend, Janet Case:

> She is in bed, & will have to stay in bed for weeks. Her nerves are thoroughly wrong. She can't read, or do anything—I can guess what she feels like—& how miserable she must be very often—especially since she is growing old, & Emphie must be wearisome with her repetitions, & general enthusiastic vagueness … Still she is trained to be brave, & so unselfish by nature. (*D1* 11)

---

[11] Linett, *Bodies of Modernism*, 204.

Two days later, she tells of a startling encounter on a country walk that has received considerable attention from disability studies scholars:

> On the towpath we met & had to pass a long line of imbeciles. The first was a very tall young man, just queer enough to look twice at, but not more; the second shuffled, & looked aside; & then one realised that every one in that long line was a miserable ineffective shuffling idiotic creature, with no forehead, or no chin, & an imbecile grin, or a wild suspicious stare. It was perfectly horrible. They should certainly be killed. (*D1* 13)

These two passages easily can—indeed in many ways should—be evaluated through distinct theoretical lenses. For the first, critical work on Woolf and illness allows us to frame it as a familiar Victorian-tinged tableau: a sickroom with a passive female invalid and a female relative who nurses her, two roles Woolf sought firmly to reject. She finds both Case, and by extension the scene itself, to be 'growing old', and the nursing by the sister (Emphie) 'wearisome', with Case trained (or is it by nature?) in bravery and unselfishness in language that suggest passivity. Woolf reinforces, even as she rejects, these rigid modes of defining the ill female body, and certainly all this is familiar feminist ground. Such a moment does not obviously fall within a more recent disability studies framework—Case is ill, and seemingly temporarily so—but the second entry has been productively read through a disability model. Janet Lyon, for example, has brilliantly analysed how, for Woolf and for many critics, the subjects of Woolf's gaze become anonymous background material in ways that reify their culturally constructed 'disability'. Lyon instead details the laws surrounding the treatment of those with 'mental deficiencies', and the Foucauldian formulations of biopower on display as the state quarantined and institutionalized such individuals, a move Woolf appears to endorse.[12]

Without contradicting the force of Lyon's argument, reading the towpath moment alongside the sickroom moment grants a more comprehensive view of Woolf's uneven treatment of bodily conditions. Taken together, the entries reveal how Woolf treats illness, as well as issues surrounding mental health, with insight, often making visible—even as she at times reinforces—cultural constructions surrounding illness and gender. By contrast, Woolf often represents bodies with structural or intellectual differences as distinctly 'other', exemplifying, as she does in the second passage, how certain bodies are constructed as non-normate by separating them from her (equally constructed) normate position. Woolf's contradictory reactions are captured by the two uses of 'miserable'. Woolf can empathize with how 'miserable' Case is, and the misery is something Case would feel internally; by contrast, Woolf labels each towpath figure a 'miserable' creature, collapsing their individuality while defining how they look to her—miserable—not how they might feel. Taken together, the two entries suggest the subtle ways Woolf uses illness, here and elsewhere, as a foil or shield against structural or intellectual impairments. Even as she laments Case's isolation, limited company, and

---

[12] Lyon, 'On the Asylum Road'.

invisible suffering—and potentially eases those by her visit—she declares the towpath group should be hidden and even killed. She builds a hierarchy of bodily differences, borne out in her later work.

The two passages also suggest, however, that these divisions—both the ones reinforced by Woolf and the different critical frames for each passage—are not as neat as they might seem. Woolf positions herself as a separate observer in both scenes, but her body and her experiences overlap with the bodies she sees, part of a continuum she works to deny. One of the complicating factors here is that, obscured in both passages, are the conditions that straddle elements of both illness and disability: chronic illness and mental health issues. At the time of the diary entries, Woolf herself was in the midst of ongoing mental health challenges, often being forced into rest and isolation. When she had made a second suicide attempt in 1913, it was in fact Case who helped stand vigil by her bed;[13] she could indeed 'guess what [Case] feels like'. Just what Case is suffering from—do nerves suggest a psychological complaint?—is obscured, perhaps deliberately so. Woolf also knew, though, that when a case of 'nerves' moved from a temporary condition to a chronic mental health issue, the very real threat of institutionalization arose; she too could be declared a 'lunatic', part of this line she passes on the towpath. As a composite observer, Woolf does not, quite, *occupy* an ableist or normate position in relationship to the bodies she observes, however much she wanted to define herself that way, and however much her response in the second case reflects such an attitude. Despite her attempts to distance herself from both situations—subtly with Case and viciously with the towpath group—these are not encounters between neatly separate bodies, something that indeed seems to fuel Woolf's rejection. In the towpath entry, Lyon points out that Woolf's horror grows as the line passes,[14] but it is also true that as the group metaphorically and literally comes closer to her, she uses the structural, physical differences (the lack of chin or forehead) along with the suggestions of mental deficiency to facilitate her violent dismissal. Woolf aligns herself with Case and an illness framework, where mental health issues are 'nerves' and categorized as temporary, and separates herself from the towpath group by constructing them as permanently disabled, different, and unfit to live. Woolf uses illness as a way to, ironically, establish a kind of normate disability against which to define what she sees as a non-normate disability. As critics, we can reify the distinction Woolf makes here by only seeing Woolf's views on illness or only focusing on her more callous treatment of structural and cognitive differences, and not seeing the complicated ways these categories may define each other. Mental health issues, which are often framed as both illness and disability, also become obscured, as does Woolf's own composite position.

---

[13] See Henry Alley, 'A Rediscovered Eulogy: Virginia Woolf's "Miss Janet Case: Classical Scholar and Teacher"', *Twentieth Century Literature* 28, no. 3 (Autumn 1982), 290–301, at 292. For Woolf's mental health, see Hermione Lee, *Virginia Woolf* (New York: Knopf, 1997), 171–96.

[14] Lyon, 'On the Asylum Road', 558.

Composite Perspectives II: 'On Being Ill' and 'Street Haunting'

Over a decade later, Woolf formalized the contradictory elements of the diary entries in two published essays, 'On Being Ill' (1926) and 'Street Haunting' (1927/1930). The essays are not typically considered together, capturing as they do the two different frames I've outlined. Critics explore 'On Being Ill' largely from a medical humanities angle, investigating how the essay is shaped by Woolf's own experiences with illness and setting the essay into broader discussions of nursing, gender, and the invalid.[15] 'Street Haunting', which recounts a twilight city walk where the narrator encounters a range of differently abled bodies, has been fruitfully analysed through a disability studies lens, revealing Woolf's normate assumptions about these bodies.[16] These two critical frames remain essential: people with short-term illnesses are not disabled; people with structurally different bodies are not ill. Investigating the essays alongside each other, however, reveals how each rewrites the previous diary entries in ways that reify Woolf's hierarchies of bodies, and the stark ways she singles out structural and cognitive impairments. Woolf remains a composite observer, both in the way she herself embodies the experiences of illness and disability and in the way she occupies both normate and non-normate positions. Her composite position in turn highlights the way mental health issues occupy a no man's land, tangled between illness and disability, a rogue difference these works—and the culture more broadly—cannot quite find a way to categorize and represent.[17] Instead, the essays offer differing aesthetic 'cures' that privilege or erase some bodies over others.

In 'On Being Ill', Woolf explores the reasons illness is so often ignored in literature and argues for the surprising compensatory insights it may bring. The essay references different categories of illness, including acute diseases that fall clearly into an 'illness' definition and long-term conditions that shift into a disabling category, such as tuberculosis and—surprisingly—influenza, the complications of which had potentially killed Woolf's mother and, as she and her doctors believed, weakened Woolf's own heart.[18] Influenza, in fact, serves as a palimpsestic marker, at once a reference to a common, typically non-fatal acute disease, and a reference to the far more serious and disabling strain

---

[15] See, for example, Coates, 'Phantoms, Fancy (And) Symptoms'.
[16] Linett, *Bodies of Modernism*, 19–21; and Lyon, 'On the Asylum Road', 561–4.
[17] Ted Bogacz notes how, during and after the war, shell shock was referred to as a 'no man's land' because it blurred distinctions between physical and mental illness and between British demarcations of the sane and insane; see his excellent 'War Neurosis and Cultural Change in England, 1914–1922: The Work of the War Office Committee of Enquiry into "Shell-Shock"', *Journal of Contemporary History* 24, no. 2 (April 1989), 227–56, at 246.
[18] See Orr, *Virginia Woolf's Illnesses*, 7, 27, 93–8. Woolf's mother's influenza was not during the pandemic.

that the world had so brutally experienced in the influenza pandemic of 1918–1919.[19] Woolf also hints at mental health issues, though only once directly when she speaks of 'the oncome of melancholia' (*E4* 318). Scattered throughout the essay, however, are symptoms that might apply equally to both mental and physical conditions, from the hallucinatory or delirious visions that punctuate the narrative, to the sense of suffering, pain, and isolation illness may bring, to her sly references to Hamlet and King Lear.

Woolf had herself experienced these mingled health issues. In the essay, she reimagines illness in ways that push against the Victorian invalid—or nurse—roles exemplified in the Case visit. She eschews sympathy and nursing as performed by 'the laggards and failures' and instead extolls the radical new perspectives illness may bestow (*E4* 320). In many ways, Woolf evaluates illness through a disability studies-like lens, rejecting a medical model, with its focus on cures, and re-envisioning a bodily difference not as disability but as potentially advantageous, opening aesthetically generative vistas.[20] The essay works to make illness and its benefits visible, and as such pushes against the isolation and hidden qualities such states may impose. While mental health issues remain cloaked, Woolf nevertheless brings visibility to impairments—and then redefines that impairment as strength.

'Street Haunting' reminds us, though, that Woolf maintains a strict hierarchy of impairments: illness may be redefined as strength, but not structural or cognitive differences. The narrator recounts a city walk in the early evening, noting that street haunting allows one to become a neutral observer, a roving 'enormous eye' (*E4* 481). This allegedly impartial eye, however, has decidedly ableist vision. In the starkest example, the narrator relates her encounter with a woman with dwarfism trying on shoes in a store. The moment invites a disability studies reading, as Maren Linett and Janet Lyon have offered, with Woolf's attitude a textbook example of normate constructions of bodily differences.[21] Unlike the mingled identifications from the diary entries, here the narrator relentlessly constructs divisions, selecting an example where differences are visually clearly marked and insisting that the woman's stature is a deformity. She is escorted by two women 'of normal size' who seemed to 'disclaim[e] any lot in her deformity', the narrator tells us, and the smaller woman 'wore the peevish yet apologetic expression usual on the faces of the deformed' (*E4* 483). Having defined the woman as 'other', the narrator constructs herself as 'normal' and omniscient, assuming she knows what the woman is thinking as she tries on shoes. As Lyon observes, 'We don't really know what the woman is imagining ... because Woolf does not grant her speech.'[22] The

---

[19] For more on Woolf and influenza, see Elizabeth Outka, '"Wood for the Coffins Ran Out": Modernism and the Shadowed Afterlife of the Influenza Pandemic', *Modernism/modernity* 21, no. 4 (2014), 937–60; and Outka, *Viral Modernism: The Influenza Pandemic and Interwar Literature* (New York: Columbia University Press, 2020). Jane Fisher also explores the pandemic and Woolf in *Envisioning Disease, Gender, and War: Women's Narratives of the 1918 Influenza Pandemic* (New York: Palgrave, 2012).

[20] Claire Barber-Stetson's 'On Being Ill in the Twenty-First Century', in Hindrich's *Virginia Woolf Miscellany* issue, also notes its links to disability studies, 48–50.

[21] See Linett, *Bodies of Modernism*, 19–21; and Lyon, 'On the Asylum Road', 561–3.

[22] Lyon, 'On the Asylum Road', 562.

narrator's tone throughout is confident and condescending, offering a more urbane cruelty that accentuates the differences more starkly than even the brutal dismissal of the diary. Woolf's representation becomes what David Mitchell and Sharon Snyder would term a 'narrative prosthesis', a way for Woolf to use bodily difference to then re-establish a picture of 'normalcy'.[23]

The narrator's attitude towards the woman quickly encompasses other bodily differences. When the narrator returns to the street, she suddenly sees disability everywhere, as if the woman 'had called into being an atmosphere which ... seemed actually to create the humped, the twisted, the deformed' (E4 484). The street scene becomes a mocking rewrite of the towpath scene, with a 'little convey' of blind men, a 'feeble-minded boy', and other disparate figures (E4 484). As if bodily differences were themselves a coercive contagion (rather than subjected to coercion) the narrator claims that 'the dwarf had started a hobbling grotesque dance to which everybody in the street now conformed' (E4 484). She keeps herself rigidly separate from these bodies—at least at first—and perhaps for this reason, she seems less threatened than in the towpath scene. And while in 'On Being Ill', she grants visibility to impaired bodies and translates differences into strengths, here she grants visibility to impaired bodies—but only to uphold definitions of structural, cognitive, and sensory differences as deformities.

These stark divisions are both reinforced and upended, however, when we investigate parallel street confrontations in each essay in which the narrators explore the thorny question of sympathy, an issue that links to both caregiving and a recognition of a contiguous identity with another. In 'On Being Ill', the narrator notes the problems with giving sympathy to the ill—only 'laggards' offer it, the ill crave indifference, and it's impossible anyway, as each experience of illness is unique and cannot be imparted, and general suffering is so great that sympathy for illness is overwhelming: 'sympathy we cannot have. Wisest Fate says no. If her children, weighted as they already are with sorrow, were to take on them that burden too' all art and endeavours would cease, leaving only 'horror and despair' (E4 319). She then offers a mini street scene where she becomes the well observer who dismisses certain bodies:

> As it is, there is always some little distraction—an organ grinder at the corner of the hospital, a shop with book or trinket to decoy one past the prison or the workhouse, some absurdity of cat or dog to prevent one from turning the old beggar's hieroglyphic of misery into volumes of sordid suffering, and the vast effort of sympathy which those barracks of pain and discipline ... ask us to exert on their behalf, is uneasily shuffled off for another time. (E4 319–20)

As the passage unfolds, the narrator imposes greater distance from other bodies: she becomes a 'one', and bodies become buildings, moving from a hospital—an institution closer to Woolf's own situation—to institutions at more distance from her, like the

---

[23] See David Mitchell and Sharon Snyder, *Narrative Prosthesis: Disability and the Dependencies of Discourse* (Ann Arbor: University of Michigan Press, 2001).

workhouse and the prison. The 'misery' is somewhere between the two uses of the word in the diary: in part a recognition of the beggar's suffering, as she feels for Case, and in part a more callous dismissal akin to her labelling of the towpath group. Here, she sees the misery but implies it is a 'hieroglyphic', something unreadable (to her) and something the narrator may block through trivial distractions. She has some acquaintance with the 'barracks of pain and discipline' imposed by doctors—and the passage is within an essay where she is often inside the ill body—but she also pushes against seeing herself as one of these bodies. Notably, the essay leaves out any discussion of bodies with structural or cognitive differences.

Compare this moment to a parallel confrontation in 'Street Haunting'. After the narrator passes what she terms the 'maimed company of the halt and the blind', she continues to re-enforce boundaries, concluding 'They do not grudge us ... our prosperity' (E4 484). Then, though, another confrontation halts her thoughts: 'suddenly', she says 'we come upon a bearded Jew, wild, hunger-bitten, glaring out of his misery; or pass the humped body of an old woman flung abandoned on the step of a public building' (E4 484). These sights seem different for the narrator; these make 'the nerves of the spine ... stand erect', and 'a question is asked which is never answered' (E4 484–5). Lyon argues that this moment marks an imaginative blockage for Woolf 'beyond which Woolf's narrative sentience does not go'.[24] While I do not disagree, I want to offer another reason the narrative shifts at this moment: the differences for Woolf become more personal, veering towards conditions she could recognize as extending to her own body. The woman in the shoe store, the blind men, and the 'idiot boy' are, in her schema, relegated to a different sphere, but the next figures suggest different categories: poverty (which Woolf did not face) and ageing and mental health issues, which she did. The shift potentially occurs not because Woolf fails to imagine their lives but because they move uncomfortably close to 'misery' she knew. Like the towpath group, with their 'wild suspicious stares', the 'wild' bearded man 'glar[es]', suggesting a connection Woolf wants to ignore. The moment parallels the confrontation in 'On Being Ill', which has Woolf avoiding a mingled set of conditions she both knew and did not, yet here, the avoidance is temporarily breached by the man's gaze back at her.

This gaze disrupts the narrative and unsettles the narrator's attempts to separate herself from the bodies she sees. Mental health issues again seem to blur the categories—the bearded man can't be neatly defined as ill with a case of 'nerves' in a hidden sick room, or a body she can easily mark as radically different from her own; even her designation of him as Jewish, while in part prejudicially marking him as separate from her, connects him to Woolf's (nominally) Jewish husband. And the mental health issues this body evinces blur the location of the problem. As disability studies reminds us, the challenges that the woman with dwarfism, the 'idiot boy', and the individuals with sensory impairments face are due less to their bodily differences than to the way the culture has defined and limited those bodies. The poverty, isolation, and homelessness of

---

[24] Lyon, 'On the Asylum Road', 563.

the bearded man and older woman are likewise problems not intrinsic to a body but to conditions within which that body is forced to live. In illness, though, the challenge often lies within the body—though such bodies are, of course, also subject to socially imposed definitions. The bearded man, and the mental health issues he suggests, blur the categories both for Woolf and for critics. The man simultaneously threatens the neat divisions between the bodily differences Woolf constructs, reveals the problematic ways she defines certain impairments against others, and highlights her own composite position. At the literary critical level, the potential mental illness the man reflects disrupts divisions between illness and disability, crashing in, as it were, to analyses that seek to set aside mental health issues from assessments of Woolf and disability.

The two essays finally offer different aesthetic responses to all these bodily differences in ways that highlight the hierarchies Woolf identifies. In 'On Being Ill', Woolf details the compensatory advantages of illness. Importantly, she does not present these advantages as a cure—these are benefits that arise *from* the bodily differences and grant a greater vision unseen by those who are well. In 'Street Haunting', though, Woolf offers three telling aesthetic fantasies: the first erases all bodily differences, the second imagines a tentative structure that might recast difference as strength, and the third recuperates mental health differences by hiding structural and cognitive ones. Immediately after the street scene, she launches into the first fantasy, where a 'house' seems to stand in for the body. She imagines she can create 'all the chambers of a vast imaginary house' from the disparate elements that surround her, furnishing it 'at one's will', while being 'happily under no obligation to possess it', able to 'dismantle it in the twinkling of an eye' (*E4* 485). Art, she suggests, allows for such control. On one hand, there's an unsettling sense of erasure, a retreat into fantasy where anything discordant with her sense of beauty might be dismantled; it's uncomfortably close to the medicalized model that seeks to 'correct' difference. On the other hand, the fantasy potentially speaks to the power of re-definition, the power to redefine the body 'at one's will', unhampered by the limits of the culture.

This second reading is bolstered by the next fantasy, one that momentarily offers a reconsideration of the street scene. After noting the absurdity of her house fantasy—how at odds it is to her surroundings—she observes how mixed the self is, 'streaked, variegated, all of a mixture' (*E4* 486). It is only 'circumstances' and 'convenience' that demand one role for each person: 'The good citizen ... must be banker, golfer, husband, father; not a nomad wandering ... a mystic staring ... a debauchee in the slums ... a soldier heading a revolution, a pariah howling with scepticism and solitude' (*E4* 486). The list of forbidden roles contains what the narrator might consider a sanitized, tidier version of her non-normate street scene, and also at least a mild acknowledgement of how constructed and limiting are notions that 'a man must be whole' (*E4* 486).

Still, Woolf goes on to offer a third moment—a mix of fantasy and description—that notably erases parts of the street scene while reimagining others. Following her chaotic thoughts on the street, the narrator enters, 'none too soon' the 'second-hand bookshops'. In such spaces, the narrator says, 'we find anchorage in these thwarting currents of being; here we balance ourselves after the splendours and miseries of the streets' (*E4*

486). The scene is a comforting domestic one. The shopkeeper talks 'about hats', and there's a troubling replacement of the previous shoe scene, with the bookseller's 'foot on the fender' suggesting that part of the comfort for the narrator lies in the woman's normate body and prosaic conversation (E4 486). The reference to the hat, though—and the practical comfort it seems to impart to the narrator's turbulent thoughts—also recall the final scene between Septimus Smith and his wife in Mrs Dalloway, when Septimus's hallucinatory despair briefly gives way to a moment of connection as they design a hat. In the link to Septimus, Woolf hints of the narrator's own mental health issues, as she seeks a refuge from the 'thwarting currents' she herself contains. Woolf then imagines a possible redefinition and acceptance for the bodies on the street—though only, it would seem, those linked to illness, poverty, and mental health—by translating them into books. As Woolf writes, 'second-hand books are wild books, homeless books' having 'a charm which the domesticated volumes in the library lack' (E4 487). Here, friendships might be found 'with the unknown and the vanished', despite a 'grayish-white' appearance and an 'air of shabbiness and desertion' (E4 487). The narrator comforts herself, and seemingly translates the 'wild' misery of the bearded Jewish man, and the homelessness and desertion of the old woman, into books that may be accepted both in and through their differences (though only after translating them into objects). Despite this reimagining, though—which we can miss when focused only on Woolf's treatment of structural and cognitive differences—Woolf again privileges bodies suffering from mental health issues while (and even by) blocking out other non-normate bodies.

Composite Perspectives III: Sightlines in *Mrs Dalloway*

Mrs Dalloway offers a particularly potent nexus for discussing illness and disability—and the interactions of disability studies and medical humanities. Woolf wrote her novel in the aftermath of two unprecedented generators of illness and bodily impairments: World War I and the influenza pandemic of 1918–1919. Critics have exhaustively documented how the war impacted bodies. Structural and burn injuries were widespread and could lead to physical and cognitive impairments. Alongside these injuries, the war's relentless traumas produced short- and long-term mental health issues, most notably in what was identified as shell shock. Then, as the war was ending, another, more hidden vector of bodily impairment emerged in the influenza pandemic, which worldwide killed five to ten times as many as the war and left many with ongoing health issues. This strain of the virus produced short-term illness in dramatic forms, causing delirium, haemorrhaging, and often lethal damage to the lungs akin to poison gas. Full recovery could take months, and for many, morphed into chronic illness and disability. The virus could cause permanent cardiovascular and pulmonary problems, induce deafness, and damage joints and nerves. And there were widespread cases of the virus producing mental health issues from hallucinations to depression to psychosis. It was, in short, an illness that could then produce disability.[25]

While often evaluated through the lens of the war alone, *Mrs Dalloway* is structured around the central overlapping sources of disability and illness, the war and the pandemic: Clarissa Dalloway is recovering from influenza and its lingering damage, and Septimus Smith struggles with the aftermath of war.[26] Septimus, though, also serves—both in the novel and this essay—as a composite figure for both the war and the pandemic, and for the mingled elements of illness and disability. Septimus reflects various elements of what we might term an illness continuum: short-term illness, and chronic physical and mental illness. He also contemplates and imaginatively inhabits structurally and cognitively different bodies. These composite qualities demand a continued composite approach; borrowing from the shifting perspectives that structure Woolf's novel, I investigate four moments that both separately and together suggest overlapping sightlines and bodies. Approaching these moments from multiple perspectives avoids prioritizing one view and reveals how the war and the pandemic together deepened the contradictory and yet mingled aspects of illness and disability.

Mingled Sightlines: Take One

Midway through the novel, in a moment of despair, Septimus perceives in his surroundings only brutality and suffering; he watches the street and recalls a scene reminiscent of my earlier examples:

> vans roared past him; brutality blared out on placards; men were trapped in mines; women burnt alive; and once a maimed file of lunatics being exercised or displayed for the diversion of the populace (who laughed aloud), ambled and nodded and grinned past him ... each half apologetically, yet triumphantly, inflicting his hopeless woe. And would *he* go mad? (*MD* 81)

Seen through a disability studies lens, the moment captures several layers of ableist framing. The 'lunatics' are 'maimed' and are equated with live entombment and being burned alive. The passage also describes a brutal norming, in the way these individuals are on display for the 'diversion' of a public who laughs and uses them to construct a normate self. And yet, Woolf uses them in this way too, as an aesthetic device to prove a moral point, and the people themselves drop off the reader's gaze as individuals.[27] Approaching the passage from the standpoint of medical humanities, we see how

---

[25] See Outka, '"Wood for the Coffins"'; and John Barry, *The Great Influenza: The Story of the Deadliest Pandemic in History* (New York: Penguin, 2004).

[26] Outka, '"Wood for the Coffins"', 953–4 and *Viral Modernism*, 112–41.

[27] Lyon sees a sharp difference between Woolf's treatment of Septimus and this grouping: 'On the Asylum Road', 569.

depression infuses what Septimus sees and what he remembers. The ambiguity of 'his hopeless woe'—it could refer to Septimus or the 'each' or both—suggests the identification Septimus makes with the line he sees, and the blurring of the two, while the question of the last line articulates his own fears of joining them. As we saw with Woolf, Septimus occupies both the normate position (and seems anxious to stay there) and the non-normate one, but here, Woolf more clearly displays the overlaps between the positions, and the fears that govern the demarcations.

Mingled Sightlines: Take Two

Throughout the novel, Septimus displays an abiding fear that his own body, or those of others, will suddenly be injured, in what we might call an anticipatory fear of disability. The anxiety, though, is different than the fear of identification discussed earlier. Septimus's perception of his body and those around him appears shaped by flashbacks; Septimus wonders on the street why he could 'see through bodies', and he feels 'the flesh was melted off the world. His body was macerated until only the nerve fibres were left' (*MD* 61). Towards the end of the novel, in a brief moment of clarity as he helps his wife trim a hat, he tries to assure himself that his view of his wife's face will not suddenly shift:

> He shaded his eyes so that he might see only a little of her face at a time, first the chin, then the nose, then the forehead, in case it were deformed, or had some terrible mark on it. But no, there she was, perfectly natural, sewing.... there was nothing terrible about it, ... for what was frightening or disgusting in her as she sat there ...? (*MD* 127)

To view the moment though disability studies, here we see the construction of what is 'natural' by what is 'deformed' or marked or disgusting. Also present is a depiction of post-traumatic stress and a fear experienced by many soldiers after the war and by both victims and caregivers during the pandemic. Septimus's fears are not metaphoric or merely hallucinatory; they reflect very real, lived experiences, both of soldiers, who occupied a world where bodies could at any moment be burned or injured or changed or penetrated (in ways that could indeed allow bodies to be 'seen through'), and of flu victims, whose bodies were invaded with alarming speed with burning fevers, hallucinations, and attacks on the nervous system. The resulting bodies were then subject to definition as 'deformed' or disabled in problematic ways, but the fear of such injury goes beyond buying into a normate position. It encompasses both the very real injury of post-traumatic stress disorder, which shapes how Septimus is seeing his own body and the bodies of others, as well as the suffering and pain experienced by bodies in the aftermath of injury.

Mingled Sightlines: Take Three

Woolf makes clear, however, that much of Septimus's suffering stems from the biopower of the state, represented by the two doctor figures in the novel and their damaging treatment; scholars routinely note Woolf's unusually vicious portrait of these doctors.[28] Woolf offers Sir William Bradshaw as an embodiment of state power, a brutal enforcer of normate values, demanding all conform to his definitions, and ensuring that England 'secluded her lunatics, forbade childbirth, penalised despair' (*MD* 89). He diagnoses Septimus almost on sight, defining him entirely through his mental health issues, and dictates his treatment. At the moment of Septimus's suicide, Woolf makes clear that his decision comes not from his illness but from the way it is defined and treated by his doctors: suicide, he thinks 'was their idea of tragedy, not his.... He did not want to die. Life was good' (*MD* 133). It is only when one doctor arrives that he jumps.

Mingled Sightlines: Take Four

Septimus nevertheless has moments of insight and pleasure, moments when the very fact of what Bradshaw would term his mental illness allows him to see the world in new ways. As he hears a nursemaid reading the letters an airplane has traced in the sky, for example, he finds that his hallucinatory perception allows his senses to mix pleasurably:

> Septimus heard her say 'Kay Arr' close to his ear, deeply, softly, like a mellow organ, but with a roughness in her voice like a grasshopper's, which rasped his spine deliciously and sent running up into his brain waves of sound which, concussing, broke. A marvellous discovery indeed. (*MD* 20)

Potentially troubling hints lurk: he is misinterpreting his surroundings to some extent, there is an hallucinatory quality here, and the breaking of waves on his brain—with the word 'concussing'—suggests neurological damage. Nevertheless, he appears to experience the world at this moment with pleasure, the language rich with positive bass notes—deep, soft, mellow, delicious, marvellous, discovery. His synaesthesia grants him a perspective that seems absent from the minds that surround him. Such moments occur throughout the novel, always a direct contradiction to the narrow and regimented ways the doctors work to define him and his condition. As she does in 'On Being Ill', Woolf redefines Septimus's condition as potentially beneficial, one that allows a new way of seeing and interpreting the world.

These mingled sightlines, together with the earlier examples, illustrate the importance of a multi-modal approach for evaluating both illness and disability in Woolf's work. A medical humanities model may reveal how adept Woolf is at illustrating the problematic constructions defining ill bodies and those experiencing mental health

---

[28] See, for example, Detloff, '"The Law is on the Side of the Normal"', 103–4.

issues but also risks suggesting—as indeed Woolf does—that differently abled bodies are medically deviant and in need of curing. A disability studies model may reveal how problematic Woolf's representations of bodies with structural, sensory, and cognitive differences often are but tends to downplay her treatment of disabling forms of illness and mental health issues and her own role as a composite observer. When we divide the analysis, we also risk missing how Woolf uses different categories to define and to dismiss others, and indeed we risk ignoring certain categories ourselves in a kind of zero-sum critical game. A composite model that does not collapse the categories together highlights the multiple subject positions a single body may occupy and brings visibility to conditions like chronic illness and mental health that straddle both theoretical frames. Such an approach remains attentive to the different sites and causes of 'misery' bodies may experience, from the systemic disorders an illness may produce within a body, to the outside regulation and control of differently abled bodies. Coming full circle, Woolf captures both her own and the scholarly contradictions present in 'this monster, the body, this miracle, its pain'.

Selected Bibliography

Barry, John, *The Great Influenza: The Story of the Deadliest Pandemic in History* (New York: Penguin, 2004).

Coates, Kimberly, 'Phantoms, Fancy (And) Symptoms: Virginia Woolf and The Art of Being Ill', *Woolf Studies Annual* 18 (2012), 1–28.

Detloff, Madelyn, ' "The Law Is on the Side of the Normal": Virginia Woolf as Crip Theorist,' in Ann Martin and Kathryn Holland, eds, *Interdisciplinary/Multidisciplinary Woolf* (Clemson: Clemson University Digital Press, 2013), 102–8.

Franks, Matt, 'Serving on the Eugenic Homefront: Virginia Woolf, Race, and Disability', *Feminist Formations* 29, no. 1 (Spring 2017), 1–24.

Garland-Thompson, Rosemarie, *Extraordinary Bodies: Figuring Physical Disability in American Culture and Literature* (New York: Columbia University Press, 1997).

Herndl, Diane, 'Disease versus Disability: The Medical Humanities and Disability Studies,' *PMLA* 120, no. 2 (2005), 593–8.

Hindrichs, Cheryl, ed., 'Virginia Woolf and Illness', *Virginia Woolf Miscellany*, 90 (Autumn 2016), 1, 44–68.

Linett, Maren, *Bodies of Modernism: Physical Disability in Transatlantic Modernist Literature* (Ann Arbor: University of Michigan Press, 2017).

Lyon, Janet, 'On the Asylum Road with Woolf and Mew', *Modernism/modernity* 18, no. 3 (September 2011), 551–74.

Mitchell, David, and Sharon Snyder, *Narrative Prosthesis: Disability and the Dependencies of Discourse* (Ann Arbor: University of Michigan Press, 2001).

Mollow, Anna, 'Disability Studies,' in Imre Szeman, Sarah Blacker, and Justin Sully, eds, *A Companion to Critical and Cultural Theory* (New York: John Wiley & Sons, 2017), 339–56.

Outka, Elizabeth, ' "Wood for the Coffins Ran Out": Modernism and the Shadowed Afterlife of the Influenza Pandemic', *Modernism/modernity* 21 no. 4 (2014), 937–60.

Outka, Elizabeth, *Viral Modernism: The Influenza Pandemic and Interwar Literature* (New York: Columbia University Press, 2020).

Wendell, Susan, 'Unhealthy Disabled: Treating Chronic Illnesses as Disabilities', *Hypatia* 16, no. 4 (Autumn 2001), 17–33.

Woolf, Virginia, and Julia Stephen, *On Being Ill with Notes from Sick Rooms* (Ashfield: Paris Press, 2012).

CHAPTER 33

THE ACADEMY AND PUBLISHING

VARA NEVEROW

VIRGINIA Woolf's critical reception during her lifetime was strong, and she was sufficiently respected that she inspired the British novelist Winifred Holtby to write *Virginia Woolf: A Critical Memoir*, published in 1932. Just three years later, American writer and journalist Ruth Gruber published her dissertation, *Virginia Woolf: A Study*.[1] On the Continent, multiple scholarly works on Woolf were published in Germany and France between 1933 and 1937,[2] and this international engagement with Woolf's oeuvre continues today.[3] In addition to these book-length works, Woolf's fiction was widely critically assessed.[4] The number of scholarly reviews and academic analyses of Woolf's work increased steadily during the same period in France and Germany as well as Belgium and Italy. Victoria Ocampo, who edited the Argentinian journal *Sur*, was acquainted with Woolf and inspired by her, and Jorge Luis Borges translated Woolf's *A Room of One's Own* in 1936 and *Orlando* in 1937.

Scholarly articles published in the United States during the 1920s and 1930s show deep respect for Woolf's work. In the *English Journal* (1928), Helene B. Bullock praises the innovative and radical modernist strategies of authors such as Woolf and Dorothy

---

[1] The volume has been updated and republished a number of times, most recently in 2005, retitled as *Virginia Woolf: The Will to Create as a Woman* (New York: Carroll & Graf, 2005); the 2005 edition includes an Introduction and historical documents.

[2] See Thomas Jackson Rice, *Virginia Woolf: A Guide to Research* (New York and London: Garland Publishing, 1984), for a primary bibliography of Woolf's publications and an annotated secondary bibliography of scholarship and reception.

[3] See, for example, Mary Ann Caws and Nicola Luckhurst, eds, *The Reception of Virginia Woolf in Europe* (London: Continuum, 2002); Natalya Reinhold, *Woolf Across Cultures* (New York: Pace University Press, 2004); Jeanne Dubino, Paulina Pająk, Catherine W. Hollis, Celiese Lypka, and Vara Neverow, eds, *The Edinburgh Companion to Virginia Woolf: Global Contemporary Literature* (Edinburgh: Edinburgh University Press, 2021).

[4] See Robin Majumdar and Allen McLauren, eds, *Virginia Woolf: The Critical Heritage* (New York: Routledge, 1997).

Richardson and imagines the benefits of pairing such techniques with the teaching of composition. In 'Virginia Woolf and the She-Condition' (1931), Mary Electa Kelsey weaves her reading of Woolf's novels into an argument that emphasizes androgyny without ever mentioning the term. Kelsey observes that, 'Mrs Woolf herself inveighs specifically against the present state of sex-consciousness, thinking it "one of the tokens of the fully developed mind that it does not think specially or separately of sex".[5] John Hawley Roberts writes explicitly of the sexual intimations in *Mrs Dalloway*, noting that, when Clarissa 'fell in love with Sally Seton, [she] knew "something warm which broke up surfaces and rippled the cold contact of man and woman, or of women"'.[6] Roberts argues that, '[O]ur symbolic Clarissa is bisexual, just as Septimus, who loved both Rezia and the soldier Evans, is bisexual'.[7] This engagement with feminism, gender, sexual attraction, and sexual orientation in Woolf's work continues to be central to contemporary scholarship.

However, not every American scholar valued Woolf. Joseph Warren Beach (1937) lauds some of Woolf's techniques, but he thinks her work is too 'mystical'[8] and suggests she has no 'comprehension of the social forces underlying the world she describes';[9] further, he prefers the writing styles of Arnold Bennett and John Galsworthy. With more than a hint of venom, Lodwick Hartley, in 'Of Time and Mrs Woolf' (1939) writes that, 'For about two decades Virginia Woolf has been a test of taste. Among discriminating people failure to appreciate her has been tantamount to admitting, if not outright Philistinism, at least immature perceptibility.'[10] Hartley snubs Woolf by praising Jane Austen, 'a critic of life, not a poetess singing in an ivory tower the beautiful unaccountability of human existence'.[11] Hartley's snarky phrasing is all too familiar. Despite E.M. Forster's valiant attempt to debunk both this persistent supercilious 'ivory tower' slur and what he terms the 'legend of the Invalid Lady of Bloomsbury',[12] this phantom continues to manifest itself even in fictional works such as Michael Cunningham's 1998 Pulitzer Prize winning novel *The Hours*, and Stephen Daldry's 2001 film version featuring Nicole Kidman with a prosthetic nose playing a fragile, selfish, bitchy, tantrumical Woolf.[13]

---

[5] See Mary Electa Kelsey, 'Virginia Woolf and the She-Condition', *The Sewanee Review* 39, no. 4 (October–December 1931), 425–44, at 425.

[6] John Hawley Roberts, 'Toward Virginia Woolf', *Virginia Quarterly Review* 10, no. 4 (October 1934), 587–602, at 595. (www.vqronline.org/essay/toward-virginia-woolf).

[7] Roberts, 'Toward Virginia Woolf', 595.

[8] Joseph Warren Beach, 'Virginia Woolf', *The English Journal* 26, no. 8 (October 1937), 603–12, at 610.

[9] Beach, 'Virginia Woolf', 611.

[10] Lodwick Hartley, 'Of Time and Mrs Woolf', *The Sewanee Review* 47, no. 2 (April-June 1939), 235–41, at 235.

[11] Hartley, 'Of Time and Mrs Woolf', 241.

[12] E.M. Forster, *Virginia Woolf: The Rede Lecture*, rev. ed. (1942; repr., Cambridge: Cambridge University Press, 2016), 5.

[13] For the prosthetic nose, see Patricia Cohen, 'The Nose Was the Final Straw', *New York Times*, 15 February 2003, nytimes.com/2003/02/15/movies/the-nose-was-the-final-straw.html.

Woolf has been judged based on her inherited privileges as the daughter of an educated man in some scholarly settings. Other members of the Bloomsbury Group,[14] Woolf's circle of close friends, have similarly been blamed and derided for their purported elitism. During the era of the Bloomsbury Group, the 'Bloomsberries'[15] were subjected to the contempt of their peers from such literary figures as Wyndham Lewis and D.H. Lawrence and ridiculed as mediocre, precious, frivolous, and pretentious. Leslie A. Fiedler observes in 'Class War in British Literature' (1958) that this antagonism was persistent. Fiedler notes that, for the new generation of Angry Young Men, 'Bloomsbury' had become 'a handy label for a hated world'.[16] Brenda Helt and Madelyn Detloff in their introduction to *Queer Bloomsbury* (2016) remind us that the 'mainstream stereotypes of Bloomsbury' still portray the life-long friends as a 'group of elite and snobbish dilettantes'.[17] The misnomer 'the Bloomsbury "Set"' is a gaffe that appears regularly in journalistic news items, especially in the United Kingdom, where the term is typically used to position the members as indulgent and spoiled. The BBC Radio 4 series titled *Gloomsbury* is meant to parody the group in a gentle fashion, but such attention does not fully offset the hostility that is expressed elsewhere.[18] The Bloomsbury Group has for many decades been depicted in variants of the phrase 'They lived in squares, painted in circles, and loved in triangles', an expression derived from a bit of dialogue by the British novelist Margaret Irwin.[19]

As the primarily British term Bloomsbury 'Set' suggests, Woolf was much more frequently and harshly criticized in the United Kingdom than in the United States. Among Woolf's contemporaries, British scholars who viewed her and her work as supercilious

---

[14] Reliable scholarly resources on the Bloomsbury Group include J.K. Johnstone's *The Bloomsbury Group: A Study of E.M. Forster, Lytton Strachey, Virginia Woolf and their Circle* (New York: Noon Day Press, 1954) and S.P. Rosenbaum's six volumes which feature the set of *Victorian Bloomsbury* (London: Palgrave Macmillan, 1987); *Edwardian Bloomsbury* (London: Palgrave Macmillan, 1994); and *Georgian Bloomsbury* (London: Palgrave Macmillan, 2003) and the separate publications *The Bloomsbury Group Reader* (Oxford: Blackwell Publishers, 1993), *Aspects of Bloomsbury* (New York: St. Martin's Press, 1998), and *The Bloomsbury Group Memoir Club* (New York: Palgrave Macmillan, 2014). Also relevant to an understanding of Bloomsbury culture are Regina Marler's *Bloomsbury Pie: The Making of the Bloomsbury Boom* (New York: Henry Holt, 1997); Helt and Detloff's 2016 collection, cited later; and Derek Ryan and Stephen Ross, eds, *The Handbook to the Bloomsbury Group* (London: Bloomsbury Academic, 2018).

[15] Katherine Mansfield referred to them as the 'Blooms Berries'. See Gerri Kimber, 'To Hell with the Blooms Berries: Katherine Mansfield in *Mansfield* and the Work of C.K. Stead', in Elizabeth Wright and Paul Edwards, eds, *Bloomsbury: Inspirations and Influences* (Cambridge: Cambridge Scholars Publishing, 2014), 110–25, at 110.

[16] Leslie A. Fiedler, 'Class War in British Literature', *Esquire*, 1 April 1958, 79–81, at 80.

[17] Brenda Helt and Madelyn Detloff, *Queer Bloomsbury* (Edinburgh: Edinburgh University Press, 2016), 4.

[18] See, for example, Philip Hensher, 'Virginia Woolf Makes Me Want to Vomit', *Telegraph*, 24 January 2003, telegraph.co.uk/comment/personal-view/3586663/Virginia-Woolf-makes-me-want-to-vomit.html.

[19] See Stuart N. Clarke, 'Squares where all the couple are triangles', *Virginia Woolf Bulletin* 57 (January 2018), 42–44; and Vara Neverow, review of *Queer Bloomsbury* by Brenda Helt and Madelyn Detloff, *Virginia Woolf Miscellany* 91 (Spring 2017), 38–40, at 39.

and irritating as well as inferior included F.R. Leavis and his wife, Q.D. Leavis. F.R. Leavis founded the academic *Scrutiny* with L.C. Knights in 1932, and *Scrutiny* systematically took Woolf to task.[20] With regard to these 'Scrutineers',[21] Molly Abel Travis contends that F.R.Leavis 'devalued Woolf by comparing her unfavorably to those writers he valued ... us[ing] her fiction as a constant negative measure to point to the positive qualities of James, Conrad, and Lawrence'.[22] But it was Q.D. Leavis who 'attacked Woolf in terms of class and gender, labeling her effete, sterile and unnatural'.[23] In a scathing review, she not only reviled Woolf's feminist essays but viciously attacked the author herself, remarking that, 'there is no reason to suppose Mrs Woolf', a daughter of an educated man, 'would know which end of the cradle to stir'.[24]

As Thomas Jackson Rice observes, during the 1940s and 1950s, the intensity of the scholarly receptions of James Joyce and D.H. Lawrence verged on 'explosions' while '[t]he Woolf industry ... developed more gradually'.[25] American academic journals in the period continued to focus on Woolf's work after her death, but most British ones did not. As an example, in 1956, the newly launched American journal *MFS Modern Fiction Studies* devoted an entire issue to Virginia Woolf, featuring strong essays that engage variously with such topics as Woolf's writing style, her short story 'Moments of Being' (1929), and the works *Mrs Dalloway* (1925), *Orlando* (1928), and *Between the Acts* (1941). The issue also features a detailed bibliography of the scholarship from 1920 to 1956.[26] *MFS Modern Fiction Studies* has gone on to publish three more dedicated issues, and, in 2009, *Modern Fiction Studies: An MFS Reader*, edited by Maren Linett, commemorated the journal's fiftieth anniversary with a curated selection of the previously published articles on Woolf.

The British journal *Essays in Criticism* (created in 1951), which released in January 1964 an issue featuring four articles dedicated to *Scrutiny*, has published a scant number of articles dedicated to Woolf over the decades. These few include Kate Flint's 'Virginia Woolf and the General Strike' (1986), Hermione Lee's 'Biomythographers: Rewriting the Lives of Virginia Woolf' (1996), and Kirsty Martin's 'Virginia Woolf's Happiness' (2014). Another British journal, *Critical Quarterly*, created in 1959 as a replacement

---

[20] From 1932 to 1952, close to twenty different book reviews and essays in *Scrutiny* make mention of Woolf either as the focal point or in passing. Nearly every reference is hostile. Five of these pieces are by F.R. Leavis, and five are by Q.D. Leavis. To view the comments, go to: http://www.unz.com/print/Scrutiny/Search/?PubType=All&Text=virginia+woolf&Action=Search.

[21] See Raymond Williams, 'Our Debt to Dr. Leavis', *Critical Quarterly* 1, no. 3 (September 1959), 245–7.

[22] Molly Abel Travis, 'Eternal Fascism and its "Home Haunts" in the Leavises' Attacks on Virginia Woolf', in Merry Pawlowski, ed., *Virginia Woolf and Fascism: Resisting the Dictators' Seduction* (London: Palgrave Macmillan), 165–77, at 171.

[23] Travis, 'Eternal Fascism', 173.

[24] Q.D. Leavis, review of 'Caterpillars of the Commonwealth Unite!: *Three Guineas* by Virginia Woolf', *Scrutiny* 7 (September 1938), 203–14, at 210, http://www.unz.org/Pub/Scrutiny-1938sep-00203.

[25] Rice, note on preface to *Virginia Woolf: A Guide to Research*, xi.

[26] Maurice Beebe, 'Criticism of Virginia Woolf: A Selected Checklist with an Index to Studies of Separate Works', Virginia Woolf: A Special Number, *MFS Modern Fiction Studies* 2, no. 1 (February 1956), 36–45.

for *Scrutiny*,[27] featured Raymond Williams's 'Our Debt to Dr. Leavis' in the third issue, so it may not be surprising that this journal also has published few scholarly articles dedicated exclusively to Woolf over the years.[28]

In the British *Review of English Studies*, launched in 1925, a small number of reviews of scholarly monographs on Woolf appeared between 1954 and 1980. During its entire history, the *Review* has offered just five research articles dedicated to Woolf's work, starting with an article by Ronald McCall in 1987. Similarly, *English: Journal of the English Association* published reviews of Woolf's work and some early criticism in the 1940s, but twenty-three years followed before a scholarly review evaluated Dorothy Brewster's *Virginia Woolf* and two other works unrelated to Woolf. With just one exception (an article on Woolf's feminism by J.B. Batchelor published in 1968), it was more than thirty years before Tracy Hargreaves's 2001 '"I should explain he shares my bath": Art and Politics in *The Years*' was offered to readers. Since then, six articles on Woolf articles including Leena Kore Schröder's 2006 '"The lovely wreckage of the past": Virginia Woolf and the English Country House' have been published, suggesting that this journal has become more welcoming toward Woolf scholarship.

Leonard Woolf's unremitting efforts kept Woolf's oeuvre in print posthumously. Leonard finished the unrevised manuscript of *Between the Acts*, published the novel in 1941, and continued to release collections of unpublished essays and stories starting with *The Death of the Moth* in 1942 and *A Haunted House, and Other Short Stories* in 1944. He also compiled *A Writer's Diary* (1953), a highly (and controversially) curated selection of Virginia Woolf's personal journals designed with the intent to respect privacy and avoid risk.[29] The essays were eventually compiled into the four-volume set of *Collected Essays* (1967). The Hogarth Press continued to release Woolf's work in the 1970s, publishing *Mrs Dalloway's Party: A Short Story Sequence* (1973), the five essays of *The London Scene* (1975),[30] and Woolf's only play, *Freshwater: A Comedy* (1976).

When Aileen Pippett's *The Moth and the Star: A Biography of Virginia Woolf*, the first posthumous full-length work on Woolf's life and work, was published in 1955, it was reasonably well received,[31] and it increased awareness of Woolf's life and work. The volume

---

[27] Wendy Pollard, *Rosamond Lehmann and Her Critics: The Vagaries of Literary Reception* Hants, (England and Burlington, VT: Ashgate, 2004), 7.

[28] The publications include C.B. Cox, 'The Solitude of Virginia Woolf', *Critical Quarterly* 1, no. 4 (December 1959), 274–366; Morris Beja, 'Matches Struck in the Dark: Virginia Woolf's Moments of Vision', *Critical Quarterly* 6, no. 2 (June 1964), 137–52; Maud Ellman, 'The Woolf Woman', *Critical Quarterly* 35, no. 3 (September 1993), 86–100; and Andrew Shail, '"She looks just like one of we-all": British Cinema Culture and the Origins of Woolf's *Orlando*', *Critical Quarterly* 48, no. 2 (July 2006), 45–76.

[29] Even though many of Woolf's friends, acquaintances, and contemporaries had died, Leonard's choices in the volume emphasize her literary opinions over her social and political life.

[30] These essays were originally published serially in *Good Housekeeping* between 1931 and 1932.

[31] For reviews, see V.S. Pritchett, 'She Cast a Spell on Bloomsbury', *New York Times*, 25 September 1955, 7; and Virginia Kirkus, review of *The Moth and the Star: A Biography of Virginia Woolf*, *Kirkus Review*, 15 March 1956, 23, kirkusreviews.com/book-reviews/aileen-pippett/the-moth-and-the-star-a-biography-of-virginia-w/.

was not authorized by Leonard Woolf, and Anne Olivier Bell, who edited the complete set of Woolf's diaries, indicates that Leonard himself had at first refused to allow Pippett to include passages in *A Writer's Diary* but later 'relented to the extent of allowing publication in America only—where the book made a further contribution to the distorted image of Virginia Woolf'.[32] Bell also speculates that Leonard's own decision to publish *A Writer's Diary* may have 'create[d] or reinforce[d] the popular journalistic image of Virginia Woolf, the moody, arrogant, and malicious Queen of Bloomsbury'.[33] After fifteen years of fending off requests, Leonard Woolf persuaded Quentin Bell, Virginia's nephew, to undertake the task, but that work was not completed until 1972.

Woolf's status was not secure in the 1960s. The front matter of A.D. Moody's slim 1963 volume categorized Woolf as a second-rate writer whose 'genius places her with the minor rather than the major modern novelists'.[34] More sagacious in his assessment of Woolf's potential value, Carl Woodring presciently states in his 1966 volume that readers should appreciate Vanessa Bell's beautifully designed covers and '[n]ever buy a Woolf novel without its dust jacket'.[35] A major shift in Woolf's status in the 1960s can be linked to Jean Guiguet's *Virginia Woolf et son œuvre: L'art et la quête du reel*, published in France in 1962.[36] Guiguet was partially motivated to undertake the project because 'the majority of critics had not done full justice to the special qualities of Virginia Woolf'[37] even though he was frustrated by the lack of access to Woolf's private correspondence and diaries.

Herbert Marder's *Feminism and Art: A Study of Virginia Woolf* (1968) was also a turning point. Marder radically redefines and realigns Woolf's other works with her feminist manifestoes, *A Room of One's Own* and *Three Guineas*, although he makes clear that he does not like the latter work. Marder connected Woolf directly to the turbulent rise of second-wave feminism in America. As Mark Hussey unequivocally asserts in the United States 'Woolf studies [became] virtually synonymous with feminist criticism'[38] during a period when the United Kingdom did not fully recognise Woolf's value. However, Hussey points out that 'The situation [in the United Kingdom] is now entirely different. Textual scholarship and the editing of Woolf's writings have been almost

---

[32] Anne Olivier Bell, 'Editing Virginia Woolf's Diary' in James M. Haule and J.H. Stape, eds, *Virginia Woolf: Interpreting the Modernist Text* (London: Palgrave, 2002), 11–24, at 12.

[33] Bell, 'Editing Virginia Woolf's Diary', 11.

[34] A.D. Moody, *Virginia Woolf* (Edinburgh and London: Oliver and Boyd, 1963), no pagination.

[35] Carl Woodring, *Virginia Woolf: A Portrait* (New York: Columbia University, 1966), 8. Woodring's recommendation was wise. Recently, a first edition, first impression of *To the Lighthouse* with a dust jacket sold for £32,000.

[36] *Virginia Woolf and Her Works*, the English translation, was published by The Hogarth Press in the United Kingdom and Harcourt, Brace & World in the United States in 1965.

[37] Jean Guiguet, *Virginia Woolf and Her Works*, trans. Jean Stewart (London: The Hogarth Press, 1965), 13.

[38] Mark Hussey, 'Virginia Woolf in America', in Nancy E. Green and Christopher Reed, eds, *A Room of Their Own: The Bloomsbury Artists in American Collections* (Ithaca: Herbert F. Johnson Museum of Art, Cornell University, 2008), 48–57, at 49.

entirely a British affair, spearheaded by Julia Briggs's "feminist" edition of Woolf for Penguin, where English editors dominate'.[39]

Quentin Bell's two-volume biography of his aunt was greeted with praise by many scholars but was met with rage in the feminist literary community in America. Ellen Hawkes Rogat in 'The Virgin in the Bell Biography' (1974) systematically and methodically rejects Bell's depiction of Woolf as 'pale figure of a neurotic virgin cloistered from experience'[40] and argues that Bell's numerous 'references to [Woolf's] madness, defensive virginity, and frigidity' are an attempt to reduce Woolf's 'art to a symptom of her terrified retreat from the world'.[41] Furthermore, Rogat finds that Bell far too often lauds his parents, Clive Bell and Vanessa Bell, at the expense of his aunt. Ongoing and contentious confrontations between Bell and Jane Marcus, one of the most passionate American advocates for Woolf, continued well into the 1980s. Marcus entered the debate with a vengeance in 1977 with '"No More Horses": Virginia Woolf on Art and Propaganda'.[42] In 'Storming the Toolshed' (1982), Marcus sums up the heated political climate of the moment writing that Bell 'is not amused by feminist criticism of Virginia Woolf. He has invented a name for us. He calls us "lupines",[43] a term that, for Marcus, deliberately disparages American feminists. In his introduction to Issue 20 of the *Virginia Woolf Miscellany*, Peter Stansky triggered another squabble between Bell and Marcus[44] that continued in *Critical Inquiry* in the mid-1980s.[45]

In 1975, the floodgates opened and most of Woolf's private letters, diaries, and memoirs began to flow forth, providing academics with a vast amount of material that has informed and underpinned the analysis of Woolf's work ever since. Six volumes of Woolf's letters were released from 1975 to 1980. In 1976, *Moments of Being*, a collection of Woolf's autobiographical essays, was published, offering full texts of the key sources Bell had used in crafting some sections of his biography. Between 1977 and 1984, five volumes of Woolf's diaries were released. In 1983, Houghton Library at Harvard University added the six Monk's House photograph albums to their archival collection.[46] The letters of Vita Sackville-West and Virginia Woolf were published in 1984, and, beginning in 1986, Woolf's six volumes of collected essays—both published and previously unpublished—were released in chronological order, the last in 2000. Also published during this time

---

[39] Hussey, 'Virginia Woolf in America', 56, n12.
[40] Ellen Hawkes Rogat, 'The Virgin in the Bell Biography', *Twentieth Century Literature* 20, no. 2 (April 1974), 96–113, at 96.
[41] Rogat, 'The Virgin in the Bell Biography', 102.
[42] See Clara Jones, *Virginia Woolf: Ambivalent Activist* (Edinburgh: Edinburgh University Press, 2015), 8–13.
[43] Jane Marcus, 'Storming the Toolshed', *Signs* 7, no. 3 (Spring 1982), 622–40, at 632.
[44] See Peter Stansky, 'To the Readers: An Editorial Comment on Woolfians and Lupines', *Virginia Woolf Miscellany* 20, (Spring 1983), 1.
[45] Quentin Bell, 'A "Radiant" Friendship', *Critical Inquiry* 10, no. 4 (June 1984), 557–66; Jane Marcus, 'Quentin's Bogey', *Critical Inquiry* 11, no. 3 (March 1985), 486–97, at 489.
[46] Maggie Humm, *Snapshots of Bloomsbury* (New Brunswick: Rutgers University Press, 2006) features selected material from this collection. The Harvard collection is now digitalized and can be viewed online.

frame were transcribed holographs of Woolf's work, including *The Waves* in 1976 and, in 1982, both *Melymbrosia* (*The Voyage Out*) and *To the Lighthouse*. Brenda R. Silver's *Virginia Woolf's Reading Notebooks*, published in 1983, offers meticulous documentation of Woolf's notations.[47] This glorious profusion of primary sources and previously inaccessible work created a seismic shift in both the biographical and scholarly understanding of Woolf's life and work. But these treasure troves of primary sources were not the only factors in Woolf's incremental posthumous rise to her current status, that of *Virginia Woolf Icon*, declared in the righteous title of Silver's 1999 volume.

Marcus had a massive influence on Woolf in the academy in America. She was both a major contributor to feminist scholarship on Woolf and an active player in advancing the publication of feminist interpretations of Woolf. In addition to numerous articles in journals, her own collected essays are *Virginia Woolf and the Languages of Patriarchy* (1987), *Art and Anger* (1988), and *Hearts of Darkness: White Women Write Race* (2004). Her first edited collection, *New Feminist Essays on Virginia Woolf* (1981), features landmark perspectives on Woolf's feminism, and, appropriately, Marcus proclaims in the very first sentence of her own essay 'Thinking Back through Our Mothers', 'Writing, for Virginia Woolf, was a revolutionary act', thus establishing an enduring stance that Woolf was an activist—'a guerrilla fighter in a Victorian skirt'.[48] Marcus's second edited collection, *Virginia Woolf: A Feminist Slant*, published in 1983, provided similarly insightful work on Woolf's feminist approaches, and the majority of the contributors went on to shape the field of Woolf studies. Lydia Blanchard in her 1985 review-essay of Marcus's *New Feminist Essays on Virginia Woolf* and *Virginia Woolf: A Feminist Slant* and Patricia Clements and Isobel Grundy's *Virginia Woolf: New Critical Essays* describes the tense critical moment deftly: 'Polarized into establishment and anti-establishment camps, Woolf scholars appear to spend their time in combat. Some go forth wearing their lupine as a military decoration, "proudly" and with "wild Woolfian abandon" as Jane Marcus has suggested; others counterattack against what they perceive as the "lunatic fringes"'.[49] This phase of confrontational standoffs in Woolf studies seems now to have passed.

In the United States, the Centennial Conference celebrating Woolf's one-hundredth birthday was held at West Virginia University from March 18 to 20 in 1982. The selected papers from the conference—*Virginia Woolf: Centennial Essays*—were edited by Elaine K. Ginsberg and Laura M. Gottlieb and published in 1983. In Fall 1982, Woolf Centenary Lectures at the University of Texas were organized by Jane Marcus, and in 1983, Marcus published *Virginia Woolf and Bloomsbury*, a collection of essays derived from the lectures. A third event dedicated to Woolf's centenary was held in September 1982 at

---

[47] Access to Silver's volume is now available for free in an electronic scan with live links to sections at https://collections.dartmouth.edu/ebooks/silver-virginia-1983.html.

[48] Jane Marcus, 'Thinking Back through Our Mothers', in *New Feminist Essays on Virginia Woolf* (Lincoln: University of Nebraska Press, 1981), 1–30, at 1.

[49] Lydia Blanchard, 'Virginia Woolf and Her Critics: 'On the Discrimination of Feminisms', *Studies in the Novel* 17, no. 1 (Spring 1985), 95–103, at 95.

Fitzwilliam College, University of Cambridge, and was organized by Eric Warner, an American scholar at the university who had realized that there were no plans at all for Woolf's centenary in the United Kingdom.[50] He edited the collection of essays *Virginia Woolf: A Centenary Perspective* (1984) drawn from the event.

Despite all this positive attention, Woolf came under scrutiny from some American feminists who undervalued or even mocked her. For example, Elaine Showalter took her title *A Literature of Their Own* (1977) from a phrase by John Stuart Mill. She then used it to savage *A Room of One's Own*, pointedly lampooning Woolf's intellectual and creative integrity by contending, for example, that, when 'Refined to its essences, abstracted from its physicality and anger, denied any action, Woolf's vision of womanhood is as deadly as it is disembodied. The ultimate room of one's own is the grave.'[51]

Despite critical attention, Woolf was only rarely on the syllabus in colleges and universities in the United States prior to the 1970s. Barbara Christian writes:

> Today everyone reads [Woolf]. But this is 1994, 20 years after the Virginia Woolf fever of the 1970s. And you [Toni Morrison] went to graduate school in the 1950s.... Did you have one of those crazy teachers who insisted on exposing his students to odd writers?... Even in 1965, some 10 years later when I was a graduate student at Columbia, Virginia Woolf was still a suspect writer.[52]

Many graduate students had to spar with their advisers to justify their desire to explore Woolf's undervalued work.[53]

The young scholars who invested in Woolf during their graduate studies in the 1960s and early 1970s and completed their doctoral degrees—whether or not they wrote their dissertations on Woolf—became professors. Nonetheless, it took them nearly twenty years to bring Woolf fully into the curriculum.[54] As Lillian S. Robinson writes, '"*Beowulf* to Virginia Woolf" is a pleasant enough joke, but, though lots of surveys begin with the Anglo Saxon epic, not all that many conclude with *Mrs Dalloway*'.[55] Between 1980

---

[50] For an overview of the conference, see Eric Warner, ed., introduction to *Virginia Woolf: A Centenary Perspective* (New York: St. Martin's Press, 1984), 1–11.

[51] Elaine Showalter, *A Literature of Their Own*, rev. ed. (1977; repr., Princeton: Princeton University Press, 1998), 297.

[52] Barbara Christian, 'Layered Rhythms: Virginia Woolf and Toni Morrison', Toni Morrison Double Issue, *MFS Modern Fiction Studies* 39, no. 3/4 (Fall/Winter 1993), 483–500, at 488. See also J. J. Wilson, 'From Solitude to Society in Reading Virginia Woolf', in Mark Hussey and Vara Neverow, eds, *Virginia Woolf: Emerging Perspectives: Selected Papers from the Third Annual Conference on Virginia Woolf* (New York: Pace University Press, 1994), 13–18.

[53] Based on ProQuest Theses and Dissertation data, fifty dissertations on Woolf were completed between January 1950 and December 1969, primarily in the United States.

[54] Maren Linett, ed., preface to *Modern Fiction Studies: An MFS Reader* (Baltimore: Johns Hopkins, 2009), ix–xiii, at ix.

[55] Lillian S. Robinson, 'Treason Our Text: Feminist Challenges to the Literary Canon', *Tulsa Studies in Women's Literature* 2, no. 1 (Spring, 1983), 83–98, at 85. How accurate Robinson was. In 1982, the reading list for my doctoral comprehensive examination at New York University featured more than four hundred works beginning with Anglo Saxon texts from the 600s and ending with the year 1945. Of

and 1995, Woolf's oeuvre moved gradually but steadily toward the centre of the literary canon in the United States.[56] Since Woolf was valued not only for her modernist style but also for her feminist and Sapphist perspectives, her advocacy for pacifism, and her socialist inclinations, her relevance in the United States was, from the start, implicitly multi-disciplinary. As English studies gradually assimilated Woolf in the United States, so too did Women's Studies. Women's Studies programmes often integrated *A Room of One's Own* and *Three Guineas* into the curricula, while the lesbian academic community, closely associated with Women's Studies in most institutions, particularly embraced Woolf. A significant number of articles on Woolf's Sapphism began to be published in the 1980s and 1990s. Among the book-length works published were Suzanne Raitt's 1993 *Vita and Virginia: The Work and Friendship of V. Sackville-West and Virginia Woolf* and Eileen Barrett and Patricia Cramer's 1997 edited collection *Virginia Woolf: Lesbian Readings*, both of which further explored and informed Woolf's life and work. Louise DeSalvo's controversial *Virginia Woolf: The Impact of Childhood Sexual Abuse on Her Life and Work* (1989) also resonated for those in Women's Studies who had begun to tackle the systemic societal indifference to molestation, assault, and rape endured by women and girls. Peace studies programmes in the United States welcomed Woolf's pacifist perspectives, and volumes such as Hussey's 1992 collection of essays, *Virginia Woolf and War: Fiction, Reality, and Myth*, and Karen Levenback's 1999 monograph, *Virginia Woolf and the Great War*, helped inaugurate Woolf's role in the field.[57]

The techniques and rationales for teaching Woolf have enhanced her academic status. A search of the *MLA International Bibliography* indicates that from 1931 to 2019 at least sixty-seven essays focusing on the topics of 'teaching', 'pedagogy', and/or 'education' were published specifically on Woolf, including several essays that focus on Woolf's work being taught in the community college setting. Hussey's *Virginia Woolf: A to Z* in 1995,[58] an encyclopaedic resource of all things Woolfian has been an extraordinary resource for Woolf scholars and teachers over the years. The meticulously compiled volume offers a detailed alphabetical compendium of information ranging from the various members of Woolf's family, friends, acquaintances, contemporaries, and historical events to lucid summaries of critical reception and scholarship on each of Woolf's

---

those four hundred plus works, only six were by women, and Ralph Ellison was the only Black author on the list.

[56] The *MLA International Bibliography* lists eight hundred and nine articles in academic journals, five hundred and five book articles, two hundred and thirty-eight dissertations, and one hundred and eighteen books on Woolf published between 1980 and 1995. Substantial numbers of these works address feminism, sex, social class, politics, and pedagogy, but only a few of these engage with race or post/colonialism.

[57] Among more recent publications are Jane M. Wood's collection *The Theme of Peace and War in Virginia Woolf's War Writings: Essays on Her Political Philosophy* (Lewiston: Edwin Mellen Press, 2010) and Sarah Cole's *At the Violet Hour: Modernism and Violence in England and Ireland* (New York: Oxford University Press, 2012). Also of relevance for this area of inquiry are the various studies that focus on trauma in Woolf's work, including Suzanne Henke and David Eberly eds, *Virginia Woolf and Trauma: Embodied Texts* (New York: Pace University Press, 2007).

[58] The volume was out of print for some time, but Cecil Woolf Publishers reprinted it in 2011.

major and minor publications and her letters and diaries. Hussey also oversaw the creation of *Major Authors on CD-ROM: Virginia Woolf* (1996), one of the first forays into the digital world of Woolf but in a format sadly no longer compatible with most computers. Merry Pawlowski digitalized a complete set of photographs of Woolf's *Three Guineas* reading notebooks held in the University of Sussex Monks House archive (2001) accessible through a subscription-based website (woolf-center.southernct.edu[59]). Woolf Online (woolfonline.com), which is free to users, was conceived by Julia Briggs and allows readers to compare variants of *To the Lighthouse*. The website Modernist Archives Publishing Project [MAPP] (modernistarchives.com) features a trove of information about The Hogarth Press. The Modern Language Association published both *Approaches to Teaching Woolf's* To the Lighthouse (2001) and *Approaches to Teaching Woolf's* Mrs. Dalloway (2009), volumes that focus on pedagogical techniques.

Yet, even as early as the 1970s, while Woolf's work was beginning to be accepted in the academy in the United States, some of her controversial views began to provoke debates. Segments of Woolf's writings, both public and private, have continued to raise concerns because they reveal clear evidence of white privilege, class hierarchy, racism, and anti-Semitism as well as harsh perspectives on disability, factors that never directly impacted the majority of the 'daughters of educated men' for and of whom Woolf spoke in *Three Guineas*. These critiques also coincided with contemporary debates relating to race, class, post-colonialism, oppression, domination, and discrimination in academia.

Alice Walker in her eponymous short essay published in *In Search of Our Mothers' Gardens* (1973) counters Woolf's depiction of the obstacles that Judith Shakespeare (the white playwright's white imaginary sister in *A Room of One's Own*) would have endured and lists, in her very visible square brackets, the harsh actualities experienced by Phillis Wheatley, a real enslaved Black woman, an African American poet of the 1700s:

> Virginia Woolf wrote ... speaking of course not of our Phillis, that 'any woman born with a great gift in the sixteenth century [insert eighteenth century, insert Black woman, insert born or made a slave] would ... have gone crazed, shot herself, or ended her days in some lonely cottage outside the village, ... (A) highly gifted girl ... would have been so thwarted and hindered ... [add chains, guns, the lash, the ownership of one's body by someone else, submission to an alien religion] that she must have lost her health and sanity to a certainty.[60]

Walker, who in the same volume speaks of Woolf as a woman writer 'who has saved so many of us,'[61] does not engage directly with Woolf's notoriously problematic phrase

---

[59] The Modernist Archives Publishing Project is now in the process of acquiring permission from the Society of Authors to display the images from the *Three Guineas* reading notebooks on that website.

[60] Alice Walker, 'In Search of Our Mothers' Gardens: Womanist Prose', in *In Search of Our Mothers' Gardens: Womanist Prose* (New York: Harcourt Brace Jovanovich, 1973), 231–43, at 235. Brackets in original; ellipses and parentheses by Neverow.

[61] Alice Walker, 'Saving the Life that Is Your Own: The Importance of Models in the Artist's Life', in *In Search of Our Mothers' Gardens: Womanist Prose* (New York: Harcourt Brace Jovanovich, 1973), 3–14, at 14.

in *A Room of One's Own*: 'It is one of the great advantages of being a woman that one can pass even a very fine negress without wishing to make an Englishwoman of her' (*ARO* 39). But Walker does criticize Woolf for eradicating women of colour unless they are depicted as the Other, as curiosities and oddities. More recently, Sonita Sarker observes that: 'Woolf's feminism informs her ambivalent nationalism, [and] both are inflected by an Englishness which constitutes itself as the unracialized norm against which Others are marked'.[62] Gretchen Holbrook Gerzina situates 'Bloomsbury within a racialized popular, social and aesthetic context'[63] and engages with a variety of relevant issues including Woolf's participation in the *Dreadnought* Hoax, her references to race in *Orlando*, and the implications of Roger Fry's fascination with African art.

While Marcus contends that *The Waves* is 'concerned with race, class, colonialism, and the cultural politics of canonicity itself',[64] Urmila Seshagiri argues that Marcus 'oversimplifies' the novel when she 'compresses imperial, class, and gender issues into the same critical model'.[65] Seshagiri offers a much more nuanced and intricate analysis of 'The "question of the West & the East" that infiltrates many of Woolf's major works, transforming Englishness and modernity into sites defined by racial difference, imperialism, and Orientalism',[66] concluding that, 'To read *To the Lighthouse* merely as an opposition to imperialist or nationalist violence is to ignore the rich cultural texture of Woolf's writing: the several discourses operating in the novel's exploration of feminism and aesthetics rewrite Englishness as a confluence of racially differentiated perspectives'.[67]

Woolf's aversion to Otherness and raciality also intersects with her anti-Semitism, despite her marriage to a Jewish man. One of the earliest essays focusing specifically on Woolf and Jewishness is Catherine A. Civello's 'Ham, Bacon, and Shellfish: Virginia Woolf and Anti-Semitism' (1994). Leena Kore Schröder delves into the details of Woolf's diaries and finds that not only does Woolf 'regularly efface the individual Jew and reduce him or her to an identity that is generalized and conceptual rather than unique'[68] but also that, for Woolf, 'class and race opinions are almost always couched in such terms of physical revulsion'.[69] Maren Linett (2002), Youngjoo Kim (2012), Emma Sutton (2014), and Kathryn Simpson (2014) have all contributed to the ongoing conversation about

---

[62] Sonita Sarker, 'Locating a Native Englishness in Virginia Woolf's *The London Scene*' *NWSA Journal* 13, no. 2 (Summer 2001), 1–30, at 6.

[63] Gretchen Holbrook Gerzina, 'Bushmen and Blackface: Bloomsbury and "Race"', *South Carolina Review* 38, no. 2 (Spring 2006), 46–64, at 46.

[64] Jane Marcus, 'Britannia Rules *The Waves*', in Karen Lawrence, ed., *Decolonizing Tradition: New Views of Twentieth-Century 'British' Literary Canons* (Champagne-Urbana: University of Illinois Press, 1992), 136–62, at 142.

[65] Urmila Seshagiri, 'Orienting Virginia Woolf: Race, Aesthetics, and Politics in *To the Lighthouse*', *MFS Modern Fiction Studies* 50, no. 1 (Spring 2004), 58–84, at 61–2.

[66] Seshagiri, 'Orienting Virginia Woolf', 59.

[67] Seshagiri, 'Orienting Virginia Woolf', 79.

[68] Leena Kore Schröder, 'Tales of Abjection and Miscegenation: Virginia Woolf's and Leonard Woolf's "Jewish" Stories', *Twentieth Century Literature* 49, no. 3 (Autumn, 2003), 298–327, at 298.

[69] Schröder, 'Tales of Abjection and Miscegenation', 303.

Woolf's anti-Semitism. A special section in Issue 19 of *Woolf Studies Annual* (2013) is dedicated to the topic of Woolf and Jews.

With regard to British race and class issues, Woolf also differentiates herself from the Other. She is white and English; she is decidedly not a Jew; she is of the privileged classes; and, when she argues for women's autonomy, she generally speaks only of the benefits she seeks for the daughters of educated men. As Mary Childers writes, 'Early in [*Three Guineas*], which works to show that middle-class and upper-class women are poor and their labor uncompensated, the speaker blithely refers to the fact that one of the few things women and men of her class have in common is that maids serve them food and clean up after them.'[70] Similarly, Alison Light in *Mrs Woolf and the Servants* (2008) explores the class issues revealed in the complicated relationships between Woolf and the women who served her and her family during her life. Engagement with problematic aspects of Woolf's oeuvre and personal writings is essential to her critical reception in academia. Racism, anti-Semitism, classism, and a range of other awkward assertions that Woolf makes in her private writings and in her published work must, however, be balanced in such discussions by recognition of the many other valuable attributes in her oeuvre.

Woolf's sustained scholarly presence and relevance in the twenty-first century can be linked not only to the sustained publication of articles and books but also the founding of societies and journals dedicated to Woolf studies. The *Virginia Woolf Miscellany* (virginiawoolfmiscellany.wordpress.com/), which originated in 1973, has served as a platform for sharing perspectives on Woolf for more than forty-five years. The International Virginia Woolf Society (originally the Virginia Woolf Society) was formed in 1976 at the MLA Convention in New York City, a development that was coordinated in part by the editors of the *Miscellany*. The *Selected Papers*, originally published by Pace University Press, emerged from the annual conferences on Virginia Woolf launched in 1991 by Mark Hussey. The publication transitioned to Clemson University Press and, as of 2018, Clemson works in tandem with Liverpool University Press in publishing a collection of longer essays two years after each conference. The *Woolf Studies Annual*, founded by Hussey, released its first volume in 1995 and is hosted by Pace. Hussey is stepping back in 2021, and Benjamin Hagen will take over as the editor of the *WSA*. The *Virginia Woolf Bulletin* was started in 1999 as a key element in the founding of the Virginia Woolf Society of Great Britain. Other Woolf societies have been established in Europe including in France and, more recently, in Italy. There is also a Woolf society in Japan, and a Korean–Japanese Woolf conference. The thirtieth Annual Virginia Woolf Conference, hosted by Hagen, was scheduled for June 2020, but, due to COVID-19, will be held virtually in June 2021. (The annual conference is independent, is hosted by the academic institution where it is held, and has no formal association with any of the Woolf societies).

---

[70] Mary M. Childers, 'Virginia Woolf on the Outside Looking Down: Reflections on the Class of Women', *MFS Modern Fiction Studies* 38, no. 1 (Spring 1992), 61–79, at 73.

In 2020, also due to the pandemic, many Woolf communities started to explore the benefits of online meetings. The first such event—a 'Woolf drop-in' on Zoom—was organized by Elisa Kay Sparks and held on 13 June 2020, the day that the annual Woolf conference would have begun. The Italian Virginia Woolf Society hosted 'Dalloway Day' online on 17 June 2020 (the event, always held on the third Wednesday in June, was originally created by the Virginia Woolf Society of Great Britain). Inspired by Sparks, Shilo McGiff, Hagen, Drew Shannon and Amy Smith started a series of Woolf-focused 'Salons' on Zoom with the first web-based event on 23 June 2020. On 4 January 2021, the VWSGB hosted its initial virtual gathering.

The Hogarth Press celebrated its one-hundredth anniversary[71] with a cake designed by Cressida Bell, Quentin Bell's daughter, and a speech by Cecil Woolf, Leonard Woolf's nephew, during the twenty-seventh Annual Conference on Virginia Woolf in Reading, United Kingdom in June 2017. However, The Hogarth Press no longer holds the copyright for Woolf's work. In the United Kingdom, Woolf's work came out of copyright from 1992 to 1995 but then was subject to the 'revived copyright' from January 1996 to December 2011.[72] The Shakespeare Head Press Editions of Virginia Woolf were launched in 1992 as soon as the original copyright expired. Penguin and Oxford University Press also took advantage of this opportunity and released all of Woolf's novels and *A Room of One's Own* and *Three Guineas* with introductions and annotations.

Current American copyrights remain in effect for seventy years after the death of the author or the executor of the author. Since Leonard Woolf had renewed Virginia's copyrights in 1953, some of her work will continue to be under copyright with Harcourt in the United States. In 2004, Hussey and Daugherty petitioned Harcourt to reprint all of Woolf's novels that were still under copyright as well as *A Room of One's Own* and *Three Guineas* in the format of annotated scholarly editions similar to those published by Penguin in the United Kingdom in 1992. Woolf's *The Voyage Out* and *Night and Day* were excluded, but *Jacob's Room*, although out of copyright, was published along with the other Harcourt volumes, each of which features an introduction and extensive annotations. Hussey served as the general editor of the collection published between 2005 and 2008. The Cambridge Edition of the Works of Virginia Woolf is now the standard resource for researchers. Each volume is based on the first British publication of the copy-text of the work. In the field of academic publishing, Woolf scholarship is booming, especially in the United Kingdom, notably with Edinburgh University Press, Bloomsbury Publishing, Cambridge University Press, and Oxford University Press.

As Woolfian scholarship has become a lucrative option for publishing, Woolf's oeuvre has been woven into a broad and multifaceted swath of intellectual exploration that crosses disciplines, genres, genders, cultures, and nations. Woolf, as the founder of a Society of Outsiders, has invited her readers—whether common or academic, marginalized or privileged—to wrestle with the complex pleasures and challenges of

---

[71] It is now a part of the Crown Publishing Group/Penguin Random House.
[72] For this information, see the Harry Ransom Center, University of Texas at Austin, 'WATCH: Writers Artists and Their Copyright Holders', norman.hrc.utexas.edu/watch/uk.cfm.

modernist writing and the arts, to analyse politics, to confront and defy oppression, to resist Fascism, to endeavour to overthrow the innumerable obstacles created by hierarchy, to fight for women's autonomy, to accept and explore sexual fluidity and queerness, and to honour nature, its creatures, and the living world. As numerous facets of Woolf's critical reception continue to evolve, the emerging perspectives enrich and inform the academy, bringing new insights to bear both on the moment and on the paths of history in Woolf studies.

Selected Bibliography

Barrett, Eileen, and Patricia Cramer, eds, *Virginia Woolf: Lesbian Readings* (New York: New York University Press, 1997).
Bullock, Helene B., 'The Denial of Our Teaching', *The English Journal* 17, no. 9 (November 1928), 750–5.
Caws, Mary Ann, and Nicola Luckhurst, *The Reception of Virginia Woolf in Europe* (London: Continuum, 2002).
Christian, Barbara, 'Layered Rhythms: Virginia Woolf and Toni Morrison', Toni Morrison Double Issue, *MFS Modern Fiction Studies* 39, no. 3/4 (Fall/Winter 1993), 483–500.
Guiguet, Jean, *Virginia Woolf and Her Works*, trans. Jean Stewart (London: The Hogarth Press, 1965).
Helt, Brenda, and Madelyn Detloff, *Queer Bloomsbury* (Edinburgh: Edinburgh University Press, 2016).
Hussey, Mark, *Virginia Woolf A to Z: A Comprehensive Reference to Her Life, Works, and Critical Reception* (New York: Facts on File, 1995).
Majumbar, Robin, and Allen McLaurin, eds, *Virginia Woolf: Critical Heritage* (New York: Routledge, 1997).
Marcus, Jane, ed., *New Feminist Essays on Virginia Woolf* (Lincoln: University of Nebraska Press, 1981).
Marcus, Jane, *Virginia Woolf and the Languages of Patriarchy* (Bloomington: Indiana University Press, 1987).
Rice, Thomas Jackson, *Virginia Woolf: A Guide to Research* (London: Garland Publishing, 1984).
Seshagiri, Urmila, 'Orienting Virginia Woolf: Race, Aesthetics, and Politics in *To the Lighthouse*', *MFS Modern Fiction Studies* 50, no. 1 (Spring 2004), 58–84.
Silver, Brenda R., *Virginia Woolf Icon* (Chicago: University of Chicago Press, 1999).
Virginia Woolf Miscellany, Issue 1, Fall 1973-present. https://virginiawoolfmiscellany.wordpress.com/.
Wilson, J. J., 'From Solitude to Society Through Reading Virginia Woolf', in Mark Hussey and Vara Neverow, eds, *Emerging Perspectives: Selected Papers from the Third Annual Conference on Virginia Woolf* (New York: Pace University Press, 1994).

CHAPTER 34

MODERN WOOLFIAN FICTION

ROXANA ROBINSON

CHARTING the influence of Virginia Woolf is a bit like charting the influence of the Gulf Stream—a warm current that swirls its way across the planet, seeping into distant tides, washing onto unknown shores, and affecting everything it meets, even the climate. Virginia Woolf has influenced nearly every contemporary novelist writing in English, whether we know it or not. No matter how distant we might feel from her work, some trace of that vivifying current has found its way into our writing.

Woolf challenged all sorts of conventions: prose style, the patriarchy, interior monologue, plot, chronology, even the sentence itself. But for someone whose ideas were so radical, she was surprisingly cool and reserved: her voice was mild and composed. She didn't rant because she didn't need to. She wasn't an outsider, shouting up at the fortress walls. She was an insider, born into the upper echelons of the literary establishment. She wasn't intimidated by its giants; they were friends and kin. She didn't harangue, she merely made irrefutable observations. She merely reconsidered the novel itself. She created her own prose style: meditative, subjective, and lyrical. She discarded action in favour of awareness.

In much of this, Woolf was influenced—actually, enchanted—by Marcel Proust. While reading *Remembrance of Things Past*, she wrote about the heady sense of possibility it offered:

> But Proust so titillates my own desire for expression that I can hardly set out the sentence. Oh if I could write like that! I cry ... Scarcely anyone so stimulates the nerves of language in me: it becomes an obsession. (Letter to Roger Fry, 6 May 1922, *L2* 525)

Proust made narrative into a kind of hypnotic digression, lapsing into parenthetical asides until the sense of forward movement was lost, lulled by an endless spreading awareness that encompassed everything—sense and mind and heart. Proust's work gave Woolf that heady moment of excitement and permission that all novelists recognize—permission to do something entirely new, to move into unexplored terrain.

Woolf adopted Proust's immersive approach to consciousness and his inventive approach to the sentence. She stretched it to an impossible length or cropped it abruptly short, but she was never disrespectful of its language or its structure. Each sentence is clear, beautiful, and infused by the interior glow of poetry.

Poetry had always been a large part of Woolf's life. As a child she had memorized it, and had listened to people recite it at tea, or while walking on the lawn. She knew the Victorians and Edwardians, their galloping rhythms and dramatic action, the rhymes and cadences addressing each other, meeting and repeating throughout the work. As a child she heard them; as an adult she read *The Oxford Book of English Verse* at breakfast (Letter to Vanessa Bell, 24 Oct 1916, *L2* 124–5). Poetry was a deep part of her interior life and it informed her prose. Because her sentences are so exquisite, so close to poetry, they require reading at two levels: one for comprehension, one for delight.

Freed from the demands of plot, Woolf used interior monologue as a narrative engine, and her characters' thoughts provide much of the story's movement. Earlier writers had, of course, used interior monologues—Anthony Trollope's urbane observations, Charlotte Brontë's confessional asides—but these were carefully composed for the public. Woolf's meditations are private. They come from the deepest recesses of the mind; dim, silent spaces where thoughts shift and flow, broken, barely articulated, flickering in and out of sight, creating the vast and complicated reef of consciousness.

So, these are some of what forms Woolf's literary heritage—a cool, radical feminism; a dreamlike running commentary; intensity of the moment; sentences like jewellery. Woolf made a slow incantatory reflection into an integral part of fiction. As Proust had done for her, she offered future novelists that heady moment of permission: a view into new meadows.

The name of novelists influenced by Woolf is legion, but a small sampling would include Michael Cunningham, Rachel Cusk, Ian McEwan, Zadie Smith, Monica Ali, Tessa Hadley, and this writer.

Michael Cunningham's lovely 1998 novel, *The Hours*, freely borrows from Woolf's novel *Mrs Dalloway* (1925). Cunningham translates many of Woolf's characters and scenes into contemporary life, shifting genders and sexual orientation and introducing new narrative lines. His fluid, glinting prose style pays direct homage to hers.

Woolf's novel presents a day in the life of Clarissa Dalloway, a society matron who's about to give a party. In *A Room of One's Own* (1929), Woolf wrote about sexist bias against such subject matter. 'This is an important book, the critic assumes, because it deals with war. This is an insignificant book because it deals with the feelings of women in a drawing-room' (*ARO* 56). In *Mrs Dalloway*, Woolf implicitly asked the question, 'Can a novel about a society hostess be significant?'

Woolf's beautiful and capacious answer, of course, is yes. What Woolf wants to know, as she takes up her pen in the morning, is what it's like to be human. A woman's story will be just as important as a man's.

Mrs Dalloway consists mostly of Clarissa's musings, but it also includes the suicide of Septimus Smith, a young veteran suffering from shell shock. Smith hears voices and sees visions of his dead comrade. He longs to end the tumult, but that's not why he jumps to his death. He does so to escape the doctor who's about to seize control of his life. Woolf's complicated narrative includes war, empire, trauma, and power. Death. These are far more than the concerns of a hostess, but Woolf takes those seriously, too, because they are also part of what it is to be alive.

Michael Cunningham's novel refers to Woolf's in obvious ways: the characters, the lyrical style, the interior commentary, the party, the suicide. But Cunningham enters the earlier text's fabric in other, more profound ways. For the reader, suicide has an ominous significance in Woolf's book that the writer can't know, since it's not only a reference to the trauma of war, but also a dark foreshadowing of her own end. Cunningham addresses this by directly confronting Woolf's death—by chronicling it.

His book opens in the last hour of her life, as Woolf walks towards the River Ouse. With startling fluency Cunningham conjures up Woolf, the war, her bond with Leonard, and her madness. In six pages we arrive at the moment of her death.

It's shockingly bold of Cunningham, to dare to write in Woolf's voice, to invite the comparison between his writing and hers, to declare ownership of her thoughts during the last half-hour of her life.

I was deeply sceptical of the idea that another writer—especially a man!—could speak in her voice. Certainly the words would sound bogus, the voice forced.

But the book is shockingly good.

Cunningham's style—pellucid and elegant—mirrors Woolf's. Simple declarative sentences are interspersed with lucent observation.

> She hurries from the house, wearing a coat too heavy for the weather. It is 1941. Another war has begun. She has left a note for Leonard, and another for Vanessa. She walks purposefully toward the river, certain of what she'll do, but even now she is almost distracted by the sight of the downs, the church, and a scattering of sheep, incandescent, tinged with a faint hint of sulfur, grazing under a darkening sky. She pauses, watching the sheep and the sky, then walks on. The voices murmur behind her; bombers drone in the sky, though she looks for the planes and can't see them.[1]

By the third line, after 'Leonard' and 'Vanessa', we know who this woman is. 'Purposefully' and 'river' identify the day and the hour; 'murmuring voices' remind us of the reason. What gave me pause was 'the scattering of incandescent sheep, tinged with sulfur'. That descriptive language, precise and hallucinatory, seemed eerily like Woolf's. I wondered if Cunningham had found a portal to her mind.

Even more boldly, Cunningham then includes Woolf's own writing. Here is perhaps the last thing she ever wrote, a sacred text, the farewell note to Leonard.

> Dearest,
>
> I feel certain that I am going mad again: I feel we can't go through another of these terrible times. And I shan't recover this time. I begin to hear voices, and cant

---

[1] Michael Cunningham, *The Hours* (New York: Farrar, Straus, and Giroux, 1998), 3.

concentrate. So I am doing what seems the best thing to do. You have given me the greatest possible happiness.[2]

What's remarkable about the juxtaposition of the two voices is that it's apparently seamless. There seems to be no jointure between Cunningham and Woolf. When I read that passage I felt a kind of chill: the two voices seemed miraculously to be the same.

Cunningham, like Woolf, creates a web of consciousness that contains everything—memory, reality, fact, emotion, humour, and pathos—a fine jumble of gossamer threads, airy and strong, which makes up the private, meditative state that dominates both *Mrs Dalloway* and *The Hours*. This state of awareness is central to Woolf's writing: it's the state into which we often slip, the solitary part of life that paces, unseen, alongside the public one.

Mrs Ramsay muses on it in *To the Lighthouse* (1927):

> To be silent; to be alone. All the being and the doing, expansive, glittering, vocal, evaporated; and one shrunk, with a sense of solemnity, to being oneself, a wedge-shaped core of darkness, something invisible to others. Although she continued to knit, and sat upright, it was thus that she felt herself, and this self having shed its attachments was free for the strangest adventures. When life sank down for a moment, the range of experience seemed limitless. And to everybody there was always this sense of unlimited resources, she supposed; one after another, she, Lily, Augustus Carmichael, must feel our apparitions, the things you know us by, are simply childish. Beneath it is all dark, it is all spreading, it is unfathomably deep; but now and again we rise to the surface and that is what you see us by. (*TL* 85)

With the last sentence Woolf moves from interior realism into a dream-state of metaphor: 'Beneath it is all dark, it is all spreading'. What is this 'it'? Consciousness? The world? She doesn't identify it, but she doesn't need to: we understand her on an intuitive level, not a rational one. Something dark and spreading, unfathomably deep: this is the landscape of the dream. This is the way we use mysterious iterations of the natural world to represent our most private feelings.

Michael Cunningham dips into metaphor and dreamscape as easily as Woolf does. Here, his character of Woolf is asleep and dreaming:

> It seems, suddenly, that she is not in her bed but in a park, impossibly verdant, green beyond green—a Platonic vision of a park, at once homely and the seat of mystery, implying as parks do that while the old woman in the shawl dozes on the slatted bench something alive and ancient, something neither kind nor unkind, exulting only in continuance, knits together the green world of farms and meadows, forests and parks. Virginia moves through the park without quite walking; she floats through it, a feather of perception, unbodied... Virginia moves through the park as if impelled by a cushion of air; she is beginning to understand that another park lies

---

[2] Cunningham, *The Hours*, 6. See also *L6* 481.

beneath this one, a park of the underworld, more marvelous and terrible than this; it is the root from which these lawns and arbors grow. It is the true idea of the park, and it is nothing so simple as beautiful.[3]

This magical shifting between real and surreal, from fact to metaphor, allows our understanding to expand, encompassing something greater than ourselves. This takes place not in the realm of reason, but of poetry and intuition. This fluid, effortless shift is part of Woolf's legacy, and one that Cunningham uses to great effect.

Cunningham uses Woolf's characters and style as though they were his own. His work is so closely aligned with hers that reading it is a kind of hallucinatory experience, as though Cunningham has persuaded Woolf to reorder her book in a new version. It is both unsettling and marvellous.

Cunningham explores his own issues: gender and homosexuality, the AIDS epidemic, the effects of the next world war. Like Woolf, Cunningham writes about ordinary people and sees women's lives as important ones. Woolf offers a hint of homosexuality; Cunningham proposes a world in which gay can mean settled, normal, bourgeois.

I was mesmerized by Cunningham's imaginative tribute to Woolf. It was so daring! Jane Smiley once said that she wrote her novel *The Greenlanders* because she admired Scandinavian literature so much that she wanted to join its company. I admired the idea that a fiction writer could simply enter the literature of another time and country by choice, through an act of empathetic imagination.

Michael Cunningham may have been even more daring than Smiley, in entering a country guarded closely by those who feel such a deep ownership of Woolf. Hasn't she spoken to us in so many ways, in our most interior places? Hasn't she spoken about how men demean women, and doesn't he belong to that tribe of demeaners? Isn't she a woman, and doesn't that make her more ours than his?

Yes to all those questions, but I think Cunningham has earned the right to join the Woolfian community. Except for the fact that I put all my fiction in one room, in alphabetical order, I would put *The Hours* among the Woolfiana—the diaries, letters, essays, biographies, Bloomsbury books, and other works that cluster around Woolf's literary persona.

His book is in with all the other novels, including Woolf's. I can't even put Cunningham's book next to hers, because of the alphabet. Still, I can feel the invisible connection, the charged thread crisscrossing the shelves, running between Woolf and Cunningham; also between her and her admired friend E. M. Forster, Rosamund Lehmann, Elizabeth Bowen, Elizabeth Taylor, John Updike and the others, tracing the river of her influence through the literary oceans.

One of Woolf's skills is her ability to create a community and enter inside every person within it. Her voice is intimate and authoritative: in *To the Lighthouse*, she speaks

---

[3] Cunningham, *The Hours*, 30.

as six-year-old James Ramsay and as the elderly, widowed William Bankes. She seems to hover over the household, ready to alight on whom she will illuminate.

Zadie Smith, in *White Teeth*, shifts similarly between the minds of the characters. The two writers inhabit different communities: Woolf's world consists mostly of the educated upper middle class (even Septimus Smith, a modest clerk, seems very like the others, and is untrammelled by class issues). Smith revels in diversity and draws on a wide variety of ethnic origins, politics, race, religions, accents, and classes.

The opening of *White Teeth* echoes of the plot from *Mrs Dalloway*, with an attempted suicide by an English war veteran who is married to an Italian wife—though here it's the wife, not the husband, who has lapsed into madness, and the husband, Alfred Archibald Jones, survives his attempt.

But Smith's tone is very different from Woolf's; Smith's voice is light, knowing, and sardonic. Both writers offer close observations of London, but their cities are very different.

As Clarissa Dalloway stepped out of her house in Westminster,

> It was June. The King and the Queen were at the Palace. And everywhere, though it was still so early, there was a beating, a stirring of galloping ponies, tapping of cricket bats; Lords, Ascot, Ranelagh and all the rest of it, wrapped in the soft mesh of the grey-blue morning air, which, as the day wore on, would unwind them, and set down on their lawns and pitches the bouncing ponies, whose forefeet just struck the ground and up they sprung, the whirling young men, and laughing girls in their transparent muslins who, even now, after dancing all night, were taking their absurd woolly dogs for a run; and even now, discreet old dowagers were shooting out in their motor cars on errands of mystery ... and she, too, loving it as she did with an absurd and faithful passion, being part of it, since her people were courtiers once in the time of the Georges, she, too, was going that very night to kindle and illuminate; to give her party. (*MD* 4–5)

Woolf mocks the political establishment, but she loves the leafy bowers of Westminster and the unwitting charm of the aristocracy.

Smith mocks everything, with exuberant irreverence. The man who saves Archie's life is Mo Hussein-Ishmael. Like Clarissa, he lives in London, and like her, he feels a vital connection to it—though this is not because his people had been courtiers in the time of the Georges. Mo is Muslim and runs a halal butcher shop. He plays his own version of cricket by leaning out the window and swiping at pigeons with a cleaver. After laying waste to that morning's flock,

> Mo wiped the sweat off his forehead, snorted, and looked out over Cricklewood, surveying the discarded armchairs and strips of carpets, outdoor lounges for local drunks; the slot-machine emporiums, the greasy spoons, and the mini-cabs—all covered in shit. One day, so Mo believed, Cricklewood and its residents would have cause to thank him for his daily massacre; one day no man, woman, or child on the Broadway would ever again have to mix one part detergent to four parts vinegar

to clean up the crap that falls on the world. *The shit is not the shit,* he repeated solemnly, *the pigeon is the shit.* Mo was the only man in the community who truly understood.[4]

Smith offers the chaotic wreckage of the immigrant's London, one far outside the network of Oxbridge and those connections who could get you a minor secretaryship when you've failed in India and need a job back in England. Smith's London is not full of parks; no ponies gallop there, no debutantes walk their woolly dogs. Most of Smith's characters come from the Asian subcontinent and the Caribbean. They are not white; they are not affluent. They are impecunious outsiders, enterprising and intrepid, determined to wrest some kind of success from this incomprehensible British world. They are more active and vigorous than Woolf's characters; they must be.

Unlike Woolf's nearly plotless works of introspection, Smith's tale is a tangled skein of action and complication. Smith chooses not to move into the darker, more troubling depths of Woolf's narrative. Smith's characters struggle and flail on a choppy surface, while Woolf's drift deeper into the surge, falling through bands of light and darkness.

Ian McEwan shares Woolf's record of productivity and her glittering felicities of style, as well as a deep attentiveness to the moment. He records them with such precision and exactitude, it's as though each moment has been arrested for the purpose of his thorough investigation.

His novel *Saturday* opens with a quote from Saul Bellow on:

> what it means to be a man. In a city. In a century. In transition. In a mass. Transformed by science. Under organized power. Subject to tremendous controls. In a condition caused by mechanization. After the late failure of radical hopes. In a society ... which spent billions against foreign enemies but would not pay for order at home ... As megatons of water shape organisms on the ocean floor. As tides polish stones. As winds hollow cliffs.[5]

This murmured account reads like a gender-reversed description of the intention of *Mrs Dalloway*; just as Woolf does, it moves from the urban to the natural world.

Like Clarissa, the protagonist of *Saturday* has a domestic task. 'Mrs Dalloway said she would buy the flowers herself' (*MD* 3); Henry Perowne is going to make a family dinner. 'Perowne's plan is to cook a fish stew. A visit to the fishmonger is one of the simpler tasks ahead.'[6]

Both novels observe the classical unities of time, place, and action. They take place within a twenty-four-hour span, and explore the intimate complexities of family, as well as those of work, politics, and culture. Both raise questions of morality and humanity.

---

[4] Zadie Smith, *White Teeth* (London: Hamish Hamilton, 2000), 5.
[5] Ian McEwan, *Saturday* (London: Anchor Press, 2006), 1. Quoting Saul Bellow, *Herzog* (New York: Viking Press, 1964).
[6] McEwan, *Saturday*, 55.

Both are narrated with fastidious precision, mostly from the point of view of the protagonist:

> Some hours before dawn Henry Perowne, a neurosurgeon, wakes to find himself already in motion, pushing back the covers from a sitting position, and then rising to his feet. It's not clear to him when exactly he became conscious, nor does it seem relevant. He's never done such a thing before, but he isn't alarmed or even faintly surprised, for the movement is easy, and pleasurable in his limbs, and his back and legs feel unusually strong. He stands there, naked by the bed—he always sleeps naked—feeling his full height, aware of his wife's patient breathing and of the wintry bedroom air on his skin. That too is a pleasurable sensation. His bedside clock shows three forty. He has no idea what he's doing out of bed; he has no need to relieve himself, nor is he disturbed by a dream of some element of the day before, or even by the state of the world. It's as if, standing there in the darkness, he's materialized out of nothing, fully formed, unencumbered.[7]

Here are many echoes of Woolf: the close rendering of time and place, the specificity of detail, the mandarin prose, the deep attentiveness to consciousness itself. Like Clarissa, Henry Perowne is supernally aware of the life he is living.

Dr Henry Perowne, like Clarissa Dalloway, enjoys an agreeable affluence. He's educated, upper middle class, and successful; he loves his work, his spouse, and his children. He feels gratitude and humility for this; he feels fortunate that he can contribute to the world.

Perowne feels part of some larger plan, benign, unknowable, one that tends mysteriously towards good. '"There's grandeur in this view of life."'[8] This phrase from Darwin drifts into Perowne's mind on waking. Mrs Dalloway, resting before her party, thinks, 'What she liked was simply life. "That's what I do it for", she said, speaking aloud, to life' (*MD* 109).

When Perowne looks out over his square, his thoughts—proprietary, interested, appreciative—mirror hers:

> He likes the symmetry of black cast-iron posts and their even darker shadows, and the lattice of cobbled gutters. The overfull litter baskets suggest abundance rather than squalor; the vacant benches set around the circular gardens look benignly expectant of their daily traffic—cheerful lunchtime office crowds, the solemn, studious boys from the Indian hostel, lovers in quiet raptures or crisis, the crepuscular drug dealers

And, in an unmistakable nod to Mrs Dalloway's crazy singing woman:

> the ruined old lady with her wild, haunting calls. Go away! She'll shout for hours at a time, and squawk harshly, sounding like some marsh bird or zoo animal.[9]

---

[7] McEwan, *Saturday*, 1.
[8] McEwan, *Saturday*, 53.
[9] McEwan, *Saturday*, 3.

Henry Perowne, like Clarissa, takes pleasure in London's material presence; they both have a guileless trust in the civilization it represents. They both find comfort in their surroundings.

> Standing here ... gazing towards Charlotte Street, towards a foreshortened jumble of facades, scaffolding and pitched roof, Henry thinks the city is a success, a brilliant invention, a biological masterpiece—millions teeming around the accumulated and layered achievements of the centuries, as though around a coral reef, sleeping, working, entertaining themselves, harmonious for the most part, nearly everyone wanting it to work.[10]

Both Clarissa and Perowne witness aeronautical mysteries: Clarissa sees a stunt-pilot write an illegible word against the sky in letters of smoke. Perowne sees a plane hurtling towards Heathrow, one engine aflame against the night.[11] Woolf's vision is remote, whimsical, amused; McEwan's is private and dark, disturbing. These enigmatic visions seem like intimations of metaphysical mysteries of human endeavour, technology and commerce, and the bottomless blue of the empyrean itself.

One of the most appealing things about both writers' work is the presence of literature itself, rippling beneath the text. References to fairy tales, poetry, plays, novels, and novelists all appear, like small bright portals into other landscapes.

To the Lighthouse begins with Mrs Ramsay reading a fairy tale to her son James. Like a Chinese box, 'The Fisherman and his Wife' opens into another version of the Ramsays' own story: the fisherman's wife is impossibly selfish and demanding, and her imperious requests have catastrophic consequences. Mr Ramsay, famously selfish, famously demanding, strides up and down on the lawn. He recites poetry, and one of his texts is 'The Castaway' by William Cowper, in which a sailor is swept overboard and left to drown. This reiterates Mr Ramsay's worst fear: that he and his work will be forgotten. '"We perished", and then again, "each alone"'; he mourns, with voluptuous self-regard, '"But I beneath a rougher sea/Was whelm'd in deeper gulfs than he"' (*TL* 224, 225). Both Woolf's novel and Cowper's poem contain the slow drumming of the sea, the imagined one of the poem set against the real one, which murmurs in the background throughout Woolf's book. The two are connected like lines of harmony, rising and falling against each other to make the melody.

In Woolf's work, all the characters know poetry. Even Clarissa Dalloway—(who isn't clever, and barely reads anything except memoirs, in bed)—quotes from *Cymbeline*. Poetry was central to Woolf's prose—rhythm and rhyme and cadence were part of her literary consciousness; they thrummed throughout her prose.

In McEwan's *Saturday*, poetry is also rampant: both Perowne's father-in-law, old Grammaticus, and Perowne's daughter Daisy are poets. Strangely, though McEwan's voice is grounded in a kind of ultra-reality, here poetry takes on an urgent nearly magical

---

[10] McEwan, *Saturday*, 3.
[11] McEwan, *Saturday*, 14.

power. Because, though this is a story about medical science, one which contains the risk of great physical harm, it is poetry that saves lives. The Perowne house is invaded by marauding thugs who threaten mayhem. Daisy, who is most at risk, reads one of her own poems out loud to the strange assembly. The grave, beautiful language and the humanity of its message have a transformative effect, and that small shift in mood allows for a different ending to the story.

In *Atonement*, McEwan's 2001 novel, literature is the current in which the narrative moves. One of the main characters, Bryony, yearns to be a writer. She submits her work to Cyril Connolly, who sends her a response from Elizabeth Bowen. McEwan takes a risk similar to Cunningham's, mimicking the voice of a famous and accomplished writer. He succeeds with a virtuoso performance, imitating her polished, intelligent style.

Woolf's voice echoes within McEwan's work in many ways, through the generosity of spirit, the crystalline prose, the deep attentiveness to the moment. Reading McEwan's work makes me remember Woolf's with pleasure, reminding me of the way in which great writing can move through the generations, slipping into our sentences, whispering into our ears, sliding onto our keyboards.

Rachel Cusk, another English writer, writes fiction, memoir, and a sort of hybrid of the two, in which a narrator recounts a story that seems autobiographical but may not be. In any case, her narrators are masters of perception.

Her short story, 'Freedom', is set in a beauty salon, described with blazing precision.

> By now it was completely dark outside. Inside the salon, all the lights were on. There was music playing, and the droning sound of passing traffic could be faintly heard from the street. There was a great bank of glass shelves against one wall where hair products stood for sale in pristine rows, and when a lorry passed too close outside, it shuddered slightly and the jars and bottles rattled in their places. The room had become a chamber of reflecting surfaces while the world outside became opaque. Everywhere you looked, there was only the reflection of what was already there. Often I had walked past the salon in the dark and had glanced in at the windows. From the darkness of the street, it was almost like a theater, with the characters moving around in the bright light of the stage.[12]

I like the fact that Cusk writes unapologetically about a beauty salon. In 1929, Woolf commented sardonically in *A Room of One's Own* that women's subjects, such as fashion, and the buying of clothes, were considered insignificant compared to men's subjects, such as football and war. Woolf's observation of such literary sexism surely played a part in the sea change that followed; now Rachel Cusk can write a story for *The Paris Review* about a woman who wants to dye her hair. Cusk needn't apologize for the fact that women care about how they look, or that they spend time and money on it. She can write a serious story about such intimate and mundane moments in a woman's life.

---

[12] Rachel Cusk, 'Freedom', *Paris Review* 217 (Summer 2016), 23–4.

Cusk's unnamed narrator wants to conceal her grey hair; her hairdresser warns her of a lifelong commitment. Unlike Woolf's narrators, Cusk's is only an observer. We don't know her thoughts, as her hairdresser reveals a drastic life-shift, and a patron takes shattering action. The narrator sits passive and silent as her hair is washed and coloured, watching the story unfold in a series of unexpected vistas, like forest pools descending down a hillside to end in a wild cascade.

Cusk's work is more heavily ironic than Woolf's. Woolf uses equal strands of irony and compassion in her complicated weave, but Cusk makes irony the thicker thread. *In The Fold*, her 2005 novel, coolly eviscerates the romantic notion of upper-class English life. She reveals those stock literary characters, the charmingly eccentric gentry, benign guardians of the countryside, as rotten to the core. Cusk expands mercilessly on Woolf's wry social commentary, her violent message all the more startling because of the poised elegance of her prose.

The distinguished fiction writer Tessa Hadley has written several story collections and a novel, *The Past*. Like Woolf, she uses a sharply precise form of descriptive observation; like Woolf she chooses the domestic world as setting.

Here is the opening of *The Past*:

> Alice was the first to arrive, but she discovered as she stood at the front door that she had forgotten her key. The noise of their taxi receding, like an insect burrowing between the hills, was the only sound at first in the still afternoon, until their ears got used to other sounds; the jostling of water in the stream that ran at the bottom of the garden; a tickle of tiny movements in the hedgerows and grasses. At least it was an afternoon of balmy warmth, its sunlight diffused because the air was dense with seed floss, transparent-winged midges, pollen; light flickered on the grass, and under the silver birch leaf-shadows shifted, blotting their penny-shapes upon one another. Searching through her bag, Alice put on a show of amusement and scatty self-depreciation.[13]

Hadley's graceful, ruminative style, her descriptive skill, and her awareness of the natural world are all reminiscent of Woolf. So, too, is her attentiveness to the domestic setting: the novel is set in a grandparents' house, out in a bucolic countryside. The house itself, its structure and history, and its charm, is essential to the narrative:

> The house was a white cube two storeys high, wrapped round on all four sides by garden, with French windows and a veranda at the back and a lawn sloping to a stream; the walls were mottled with brown damp, there was no central heating and the roof leaked. On the mossy roof slates, thick as pavings, you could see the chisel marks where the quarrymen had dressed them two hundred years ago. Alice and Kasim stood peering through the French windows: the interior seemed to be a vision of another world, its stillness pregnant with meaning, like a room seen in a

---

[13] Tessa Hadley, *The Past* (London: Jonathan Cape, 2015), 3.

mirror. The rooms were still furnished with her grandparents' furniture; wallpaper glimmered silvery behind the spindly chairs, upright black-lacquered piano and bureau. Paintings were pits of darkness suspended from the picture rail. Alice had told her therapist that she dreamed about the house all the time. Every other house she'd lived in seemed, beside this one, only a stage set for a performance.[14]

The novel takes place during a week in the summer, when four siblings and their children gather in a rectory owned by their grandparents. The house is unchanged; the bedrooms still contain the same children's books, the limp-cushioned armchairs, the ponderous bureaus. The outdoor landscape is still full of open meadows and rushing brooks. But, of course, the siblings have changed, and the narrative charts the slow collision between their shared past and their separate presents.

The summer house, as a repository of family history, as setting for memories and personalities, a place in which to chronicle and celebrate and explore the whole messy, complicated organism of kin, has a precedent, of course. This is one against which all other literary vacation houses may be measured.

Never was a family so lovingly and ruthlessly chronicled as are the Ramsays, in *To the Lighthouse*. Shabby was the word for their rented place: 'The mat was fading, the wallpaper was flapping. You couldn't tell anymore that there were roses on it' (*TL* 39). But this isn't shameful; it's not due to poverty, though the Ramsays aren't rich, and can't afford to do it up. In fact, there's a great deal of cultural value accorded to a summer house full of ancient family furniture. This kind of shabbiness is actually evidence of bounty: the Ramsays have eight exuberant children, a vast shoal of friends and a generous tradition of hospitality. Both Mr and Mrs Ramsay attract admirers, and the house is full of lively conversation and good food. The shabbiness is due to liveliness and activity: the children will track in sand, they'll nail seaweed on the wall, they'll dissect crabs and collect stones. The house guests will carry easels through the sitting room. There is no point in getting good chairs.

And faded chintz and sandy carpets is the other side of decorum. The striking of the gong calls the family to a candlelit table and an elegant meal; but this is a cloth laid over the churning ferment of the emotional life. The children ripple with mocking laughter at their mother's rant; everyone remembers Mr Ramsay whizzing a soup plate out the window because of an earwig in it.

The vacation house is full of the shadowy presence of the stilled family past: the mildewed furniture can't be replaced without destruction of a part of childhood itself. These houses, remote and insular, are always fixed on the calendar at summer.

Woolf uses the ageing of the house, in 'Time Passes', to represent the devastating changes within the family (the deaths of Mrs Ramsay, Prue, and Andrew). Hadley uses the ageing as a prelude to her narrative, which is an examination of the family's history.

---

[14] Hadley, The Past, 4–5.

Hadley offers intimate, specific details—the walls mottled with damp, the fact that what quarriers do to roof slates is called 'dressing'. I like learning these details just as I liked learning the surgical procedures that Henry Perowne had performed: clipping the neck of a middle cerebral artery aneurysm, a craniotomy for a meningioma, and relief of a *tic douloureux*.[15] This information is delivered with such specificity and authority that we believe that we are in the midst of a real life.

In *Mrs Dalloway*, Richard Dalloway happens to amble along the street with Hugh Whitbread. Whitbread sees a Spanish necklace in a shop window, and steps into the jeweller's:

> 'I should like to see Mr Dubonnet', said Hugh in his curt worldly way. It appeared that this Dubonnet had the measurements of Mrs Whitbread's neck, or, more strangely still, knew her views upon Spanish jewellery and the extent of her possessions in that line ... Hugh was on his legs again. He was unspeakably pompous. Really, after dealing here for thirty-five years he was not going to be put off by a mere boy who did not know his business. For Dubonnet, it seemed, was out, and Hugh would not buy anything until Mr Dubonnet chose to be in; at which the youth flushed and bowed his correct little bow. It was all perfectly correct. And yet Richard couldn't have said that to save his life ... Hugh was becoming an intolerable ass. (*MD* 102–3)

The kind of necklace and the length of Hugh's patronage, the little bow of the snubbed salesman—these are like small nails with studded tops, tapped in a neat line along the edges of a chair to show its shape. Here is the world, say these writers; here are the facts that define it.

One of Hadley's recurrent themes is the driving current of illicit sexuality that runs beneath the bland terrain of middle-class life. It's present, too, in Woolf's work: the affairs of Minta Rayley that capsize her marriage; Mrs Dalloway's remembered kiss from Sally Seton. Peter Walsh remembers Clarissa's genteel shock at learning that a neighbour has married his housemaid. The family receives her, dressed like a parakeet, and talking non-stop, but when Clarissa learns she'd had his child before her marriage, she declares she can never see the woman again. Prudish, Peter Walsh thinks Clarissa. And, of course, the whole story of *Orlando* (1928) is a coded reference to a brief erotic fling between Woolf and Vita Sackville-West.

In Hadley's work, illicit sexual encounters operate as unacknowledged moments in bourgeois lives, hidden rocks beneath the smooth current. A married woman needn't tell about the afternoon in that empty house, or comment on the fact that a child looks like no one in the family. In the story 'An Abduction', a teenage girl is taken off for the night by some posh teenage boys. She gets a crush on the handsome one. They all shoplift at a local store, then move to a house absent of parents. That night the boy deflowers her; the next day she's returned. She never tells her family. The episode forms a gap in

---

[15] McEwan, *Saturday*, 5.

her life, a lacuna that she can't reveal. She's stalled, frozen by it. She never knows how to understand it, any more than Clarissa understands how to consider Sally's kiss, or the housemaid's shame. These sexual episodes have a kind of secret unexplained weight in peoples' lives, morally neutral but psychologically powerful.

Modernism offered writers new ways to approach the idea of time. Woolf does what she wants with it, stretching and shrinking it as though she's playing an accordion. She intersperses memories of the past with moments in the present and imaginings of the future. She changes time into something else altogether, as in 'Time Passes', in *To the Lighthouse*. That was written during the General Strike in London, in May 1926, when for nine days the world did seem to stop. Here Woolf treats time itself as action, its passage recorded only through the changes of the natural world—the stately circuits of the sun and moon; the nearly invisible rise of damp, the subtle loosening of wallpaper. In *Mrs Dalloway*, the passage of Clarissa's day is notated by the regular chiming of Big Ben, in one of Woolf's most exquisite sentences: 'The leaden circles dissolved in the air' (*MD* 4).

This liberation of chronology has affected all subsequent novelists; narratives now swing freely through past and present, future, and other imagined tenses, through a freewheeling universe where time does what we tell it.

I was asked to include myself in this essay, and I'll confess that Woolf is an enormous influence on my work. At times, I was worried that I'd be accused of some sort of aesthetic plagiarism, for I was filling my mind with her words and ideas, and writing my way out of that swarm.

While I'm writing a novel, I use another book as a kind of touchstone. In the mornings, before I begin to work, I pick up that book and read a few pages, sometimes just a few paragraphs. This is a book that offers a connection to my writing and some kind of literary sustenance. While I was writing my novel, *This is my Daughter*, in the mornings I read *The Journals of John Cheever*. Cheever's beautifully simple, unadorned prose, his humility, his compassion, his interest in the family, the domestic, the spiritual, all made his journals deeply helpful to me. It was like a companion on my path, or like the path itself.

I wrote the end of my novel *Sweetwater* while staying alone in a house in Maine. I wrote during the day; at night I read the new translation of *Anna Karenina*, by Pevear and Volokhonsky. It made me hopeful about the whole endeavour of writing fiction, the idea that you could set down your ideas about marriage, and the heart, and the landscape and your spiritual relationship to it, and make it important. So, in my mind, that book became part of my own.

While I was writing my next novel, *Cost*, I used one book to start off every morning's writing. I had a copy of *The Hours* in my study, and I'd flip it open to read a bit. I didn't usually want the beginning or the end, and though I admired the Mrs Brown sections, they were too removed from my own book—set in the 1950s, and way down in southern California. It was Virginia I wanted, in London or in Rodmell. I loved the passage about the burial of the thrush. '"Hello, changelings"', says Virginia, playful, magically unpredictable, when she sees Vanessa's children.[16] It was that sleight of hand, that magical ability to speak in someone else's voice that I was trying to find, moving across my own dim twilit landscape. How did Cunningham find those words? How did he transport himself inside her mind? That's what I wanted to do—find my way inside the mind of my character.

In *Cost*, I started out in the mind of a woman in her eighties who was losing her memory:

'Her memory was gone.'[17]

Because of the tradition of the use of third person, this statement could be made either by an omniscient observer or by Katherine herself, just as the sentence 'Mrs Dalloway said she would buy the flowers herself' could be spoken by an interior or exterior voice.

I wanted the interior one. I wanted the characters to speak in their own voices, securely cached inside the cocoon of privacy, that place in which Mrs Ramsay loses herself in meditation, where she allows herself the deep intimacy of her own thoughts. That acknowledgement of herself was something essential, something modern. The real interior self could not be observed by the nineteenth-century narrator. Woolf identified the private self, she named the wedge-shaped darkness. This has no public persona, it exists only in the mind:

> It came to Katharine like a soft shock, like a blow inside the head. She was in the yellow bedroom at her daughter's house in Maine, standing at the bureau, getting ready for lunch. She'd just finished doing her hair, smoothing it back to her modest bun, tucking in the small combs to hold it in place. The combs were hardly necessary now, her long fine hair—still mostly black—had turned wispy and weightless, and no longer needed restraint. But vanity, like beauty, is partly habit, and Katharine still put the combs carefully into her thinning hair, though now they slipped easily out, then vanished, beneath the furniture, against the patterns of the rugs.
>
> Hair done, combs briefly and precariously in place, Katharine looked around for her scarf. It was an old soft cotton one, a blue paisley square. She'd worn it once at a birthday party, and now, for a moment, in her daughter's guest room with its faded yellow walls, the sunlight slanting onto the worn wooden floors, the idea of the scarf and the party seemed confusingly to merge. She had a sudden sense of the party blooming around her—a blur of voices, laughter, a fireplace—a sense of pleasure at being with these people, whoever they were. Green demitasse cups, those tiny tinkling spoons, a tall brass lamp by the fireplace—or was that somewhere else?[18]

Katharine's daughter is Julia Lambert, a painter in her fifties. She's successful enough; she shows at a good gallery and gets good reviews. There are people who collect her work, but she doesn't enjoy the same prestige given to the men in her generation. They've

---

[16] Cunningham, *The Hours*, 116.
[17] Roxana Robinson, *Cost* (New York: Farrar, Straus, and Giroux, 2008), 3.
[18] Robinson, *Cost*, 3–4.

become stars, some are superstars. This might be merit; she suspects it's partly gender. Men's work brings higher prices, it's a fact.

She knows her situation is perilous: an artist can slide into nowhere in an instant, and it's more likely to happen to a woman. Julia has to keep reminding herself that it's the work that's important, not the way the world sees you.

While I was writing Julia I had Lily Briscoe in mind. Lily, who wants to create, and who struggles to ignore Charles Tansley's derisive refrain: ' "Women can't paint, women can't write" ' (*TL* 67).

Those words have power over Lily, over Julia, and over me. As I write them now, they still unsettle me. This is one reason why Virginia Woolf's writing is so important: she calls up the self that lies silent and unnameable, and she speaks the words that have kept us mute and motionless for centuries.

Julia, at her opening, sees a male contemporary who has become famous, as she has not:

> There were moments when Julia could not help it, she burned with the pure gemlike flame of envy. Because what was the point of all this, all this groping, year after year, for something hidden and mysterious, the struggle to find the secret harmonies within the music of the world, this struggle to play the great chords of the human soul, if the world were so utterly indifferent to your efforts?
> ... But there were also moments ... that Julia was simply grateful for the life she had, grateful that she was allowed to do this —make art.[19]

It's only by steadfastly resisting Charles Tansley's unspoken refrain, only by finding the interior refuge, that Lily and Julia are able to work:

> Lily stepped back to get her canvas—so—into perspective. It was an odd road to be walking, this of painting. Out and out one went, further and further, until at last one seemed to be on a narrow plank, perfectly alone, over the sea. And as she dipped into the blue paint, she dipped too into the past there. (*TL* 232)

Lily is suspended in her own luminous consciousness like a mote in a sunbeam—serene, absorbed, productive.

The writer, too, walks that narrow plank. We never know where we will next set our feet: the next step, into the void, is an act of faith. With luck, there will be something solid below.

With every book, and every piece of writing, I remember Woolf's statement about women's work. Men think women can't do it; women must put that thought from them. Men think women's work is not important; women must remember that it is.

So while I wrote that book, every morning I read from *The Hours*, hearing Woolf's voice, spoken by Cunningham. And I thought of Lily Briscoe, bracing herself against

---

[19] Robinson, *Cost*, 385–6.

Charles Tansley's taunts, making herself believe that she—and I—could take another step.

Selected Bibliography

Cunningham, Michael, *The Hours* (New York: Farrar, Straus, and Giroux, 1998).
Cusk, Rachel, 'Freedom', *Paris Review* 217 (Summer 2016), 23–4.
Hadley, Tessa, *The Past* (London: Jonathan Cape, 2015).
McEwan, Ian, *Saturday* (London: Anchor Press, 2006).
Robinson, Roxana, *Cost* (New York: Farrar, Straus, and Giroux, 2008).
Smith, Zadie, *White Teeth* (London: Hamish Hamilton, 2000).

CHAPTER 35

MAGIC REALISM AND EXPERIMENTAL FICTION

LAURA Mª LOJO-RODRÍGUEZ

INTRODUCTION: A PAN-AMERICAN COLLECTIVITY

IN 1934, Argentinian editor and writer Victoria Ocampo commissioned Jorge Luis Borges the translations of Virginia Woolf's *A Room of One's Own* (1929) and *Orlando* (1928), to be published in 1935 and 1937, respectively, under the auspices of the intellectual circle 'Sur' ('South').[1] Despite the controversial and equivocal circumstances of Borges's translations, these were to play a major role in the reception of Woolf's works in Spanish-speaking countries. It is a fact that *Orlando* would stand out as a major source of inspiration for generations of writers, attracted by Woolf's use of subversive narrative strategies to trespass physical and psychological boundaries, and by her innovative conception of time, history, and gender, which anticipated what later came to be known as 'magic realism'. This essay explores the ways in which Woolf's influence affects the construction of alternative ontological realms that both coexist with and transcend identifiable historical sites in the work of Jorge Luis Borges, Gabriel García Márquez, William Faulkner, Toni Morrison, Michèle Roberts, and Jeanette Winterson. Despite obvious differences, these writers unsettle received assumptions pertaining to history and its fictional accounts, and all propose alternative rewritings of it, while establishing an intertextual dialogue both with Woolf and among themselves articulated by *Orlando*'s

---

[1] This essay benefits from the collaboration of the research group *Discourse and Identity* (GRC2015/002; ED431C, 2019/001, GI-1924, Xunta de Galicia) and the research project *Intersections: Gender and Identity in the Short Fiction of Contemporary British Women Writers* (FEM2017-83084-P, AEI, FEDER), Ministry of Economy and Competitiveness, Government of Spain.

fantastic blend of 'satire and wildness' where the past becomes 'expressive, articulate' (*D3* 131, 125).

Understanding the complex process of reception of Woolf's work in Hispanic countries requires examination of the rich web of cultural interrelations between North and South America in the second half of the twentieth century, resulting in what Moya and Saldívar have called the 'trans-American imaginary' in terms of a 'chronotope, a contact zone, that is both historical and geographical'.[2] Such a transnational conception of American literature was already implicit in Victoria Ocampo's cultural agenda when she founded the journal *Sur* (*South*) in 1931, as well as its two related publishing houses, Sur and Sudamericana. In fact, Ocampo's efforts mirror Woolf's and her cultural agenda of the Hogarth Press publications, which not only published Anglophone writers beyond the United Kingdom, but also first introduced Russian writers and psychoanalysis in Britain. As Battershill and Southworth have argued, the Hogarth Press soon transcended the domestic, amateurish concerns of its inception to quickly develop 'into a full-scale international publishing business' by also establishing collaborative bonds with other European and American publishing houses.[3]

In her vision of a pan-American collectivity, Ocampo was indebted to Waldo Frank, whom she met in Buenos Aires in 1929. This meeting signalled for Ocampo 'an important event in my life. My interest in the United States, its writers, its cities, its way of life, was suddenly aroused'.[4] As I have elsewhere argued,[5] Frank's view of a pan-American collective identity was summarized in his short-lived editorial project *Seven Arts* (1916–1917), as the Frenchman Romain Rolland explains in the first issue of the journal, in an article significantly entitled 'America and the Arts', translated by Frank himself: 'Rejoice in the founding of a magazine in which the American Spirit may seek and achieve consciousness of its nature and of its role. My faith is great in the high destinies of America [...] On our old Continent, civilization is menaced. It becomes America's solemn duty to uphold the wavering torch.'[6] Like Frank, Rolland lays out a picture of a decadent European culture that can, however, be revitalized through American paths. In this, Frank aligns himself with Ortega, whose work he had reviewed in the *Nation & Athenaeum* of London and who, in turn, published translations of Frank's work in his *Revista de Occidente* [*Journal of the Western World*]. As Gayle Rogers has suggested, Ortega's 'wide-ranging and mutually influential dialogues with the American journalist and novelist Waldo Frank and the Argentine writer, publisher and feminist Victoria Ocampo evince a shared conviction that Europe might be resuscitated best in

---

[2] Paula Moya and Ramón Saldívar, 'Fictions of the Trans-American Imaginary', *Modern Fiction Studies* 49, no. 1 (Spring 2003), 1–18, at 2.

[3] Claire Battershill and Helen Southworth, 'Woolf, the Hogarth Press, and Global Print Culture', in Jessica Berman, ed., *A Companion to Virginia Woolf* (Oxford: Blackwell, 2016), 377–95, at 378.

[4] Victoria Ocampo, *Autobiografía VI. Sur y Cía* (Buenos Aires: Sur, 1984), 50–1.

[5] Laura Mª Lojo-Rodríguez, 'Woolf in Hispanic Countries: Buenos Aires and Madrid', in Jessica Berman, ed., *A Companion to Virginia Woolf* (Oxford: Blackwell, 2016), 467–80.

[6] Romain Rolland, 'America and the Arts', *Seven Arts* 1, no. 1 (November 1916), 47–51, at 47.

Madrid, New York, and Buenos Aires.[7] In short, Frank, Ortega, and Ocampo's common work as dissemination through the literary journals that they respectively ran aimed to counterbalance what they saw as a decadent European aesthetics via Hispanic routes of inspiring connections among cultural capitals in the inter-war period.

Two Women in Conversation: Virginia Woolf and Victoria Ocampo

In the winter of 1928, Victoria Ocampo (1890–1979), a well-to-do Argentinian with literary aspirations, travelled to Paris. Ocampo's journey had been prompted by a profound conviction that only the French capital could satisfy what she defined as her intellectual 'hunger', her thirst for knowledge, intellectual relations, and acquaintances, which the temporary visits to her Buenos Aires home of prominent European intellectuals such as José Ortega y Gasset and Hermann Keyserling could only partly satiate. Through Ortega, Keyserling, and Drieu de la Rochelle, Ocampo was introduced to a number of active characters in the cultural life of France, such as Paul Valéry, Benjamin Fondane, Maurice Ravel, and Anna de Noailles, the poet whom Victoria had so passionately read in her adolescence. Although grateful to Ortega and Keyserling for helping her out in various literary projects, Ocampo, herself a writer, was eager to find a role model who could bring about a productive change in literary terms, thus leaving behind what she saw as a panorama of patriarchal oppression and literary stagnation for women writers in her own country. That was partly produced because, as a woman, Ocampo found it difficult to find a voice and a place of her own in a literary panorama dominated by male standards and critical perspectives: 'My one ambition is to be able to write one day […] as a woman […] [who] cannot find relief of her feelings and thoughts in a male style; inasmuch as she cannot talk in a man's voice.'[8]

Thanks to a letter of introduction by Keyserling, Ocampo was received by Noailles, who soon engaged her in a 'loquacious, voluble chatter […] almost without giving you time to reply', as Ocampo recalls in her 1933 essay 'Anna de Noailles'.[9] Despite her charm and intelligence, Ocampo was soon put off by Noailles's anti-feminism and by her ruthless criticism of women writers, which Ocampo regarded as an excess of pride and vanity. In her diary, Virginia Woolf herself recalls the two women's meeting as rendered

---

[7] Gayle Rogers, 'The Circulation of Interwar Anglophone and Hispanic Modernisms', in M. Wollaeger, ed., *The Oxford Handbook of Global Modernisms* (Oxford: Oxford University Press, 2012), 461–76, at 468.

[8] 'Mi única ambición es llegar a escribir un día […] como una mujer […] [que] no puede aliviarse de sus sentimientos y pensamientos en un estilo masculino, del mismo modo que no puede hablar con voz de hombre.' Victoria Ocampo, *Testimonios I* (Madrid: Revista de Occidente, 1935), 12. All translations, unless otherwise indicated, are mine.

[9] Ocampo, *Writer, Feminist, Woman of the World* (University of New Mexico Press, 1999), 134–5.

by Ocampo: 'And so to Mme de Noailles, dying of extinguished vanity in a small flat. She lay in bed, bedizened, covered with dozens & dozens of veils & c: began plucking them off; was never still a moment; lighting lamps & putting them out; demanded worship; was not old, but had outlived her fame. Nothing wrong with her but the death of her great fame' (D5 263–4). Woolf used similar derogatory terms for Ocampo, a 'South American rasta', an 'opulent millionaire from Buenos Aires […] very ripe & rich; with pearls at her ears, as if a large moth had laid clusters of eggs; the colour of an apricot under glass; eyes I think brightened by some cosmetic' (D5 263). Woolf's rendering of Ocampo's vision of Noailles as well as her own impressions of the Argentinian suggesting exuberant excess and exoticism not only reveal Woolf's imperial prejudice, but also hint at a particular construction of herself by articulating difference, standing as a sober role model for other women writers.

Ocampo's first attempt to establish a connection with other women writers turned out to be a disappointing experience, yet on her visit to La Maison des Amis des Livres and Shakespeare and Company in Paris, respectively run by Adrienne Monnier and Sylvia Beach, Ocampo was deeply impressed by the generous dedication of these women to the intellectual community in Paris. Sylvia Beach gave Ocampo a copy of Virginia Woolf's *A Room of One's Own*, which not only triggered Ocampo's artistic imagination, but also opened the door to the process of reception of Virginia Woolf's *oeuvre* in the Spanish-speaking world.

SUR, JORGE LUIS BORGES, AND *ORLANDO*

Ocampo's encouraging experiences during this third trip to Europe culminated in the founding of the literary journal *Sur* [*South*] in 1931, and of the two related publishing houses—Sur and Sudamericana. In November 1934, Ocampo met Virginia Woolf in London, expecting to find answers to what she called her 'hunger, authentically European', and also hoping that Woolf would agree to the publication of some of her works in the Spanish translation in her publishing houses.[10] As their correspondence shows, Woolf advised Ocampo to begin with *A Room of One's Own*, to be followed by *Orlando* and *To the Lighthouse* (1927) (L5 358). Ocampo commissioned the translation of the first two to Jorge Luis Borges: *Un cuarto propio* was published in *Sur* between 1935 and 1936 and in book form in Editorial Sur in 1936, to be followed by *Orlando* in 1937.

When *Orlando* was launched in translation in July 1937, Ocampo delivered a lecture at Sociedad de Amigos del Arte (Art's Friends Society) entitled *Virginia Woolf, Orlando y Cía* (Virginia Woolf, Orlando, and Co), where she carefully analysed the novel's feminist slant and its attack on patriarchy. Just as Woolf warns her readers about the playful nature of *Orlando*, Ocampo chooses to deviate from traditional exegesis and critical

---

[10] Ocampo, *Testimonios I*, 11.

commentary of Woolf's novel, and addresses her audience as Woolf's 'common reader', whose definition echoes Woolf's and whom Ocampo defines as one who 'differs from the critic and the scholar in reading only for pleasure, without having to worry about transmitting his or her knowledge. The common reader does not have a method, only a passion: reading.' Following such a method, Ocampo produces this imaginative piece that intertwines personal reflection, recollections of the writer's correspondence and meetings, and her own personal understanding of Woolf's text:

> I am going to speak to you as the 'common reader' [English in original] of Virginia Woolf's work. I am going to speak to you of the image I keep of her. Do not expect to hear pure literary criticism; you'd be disappointed. For my encounter with the author of *Orlando* has given me once more—among other things—the certainty that nothing I have imagined about this woman, dreamt for her, defended in her name is false, exaggerated or in vain. And in thinking of Virginia Woolf, I cannot forget it for a moment.

Once more, Ocampo construes her criticism of Woolf's work as the memory of a personal encounter to be shared with her audience and readers. By doing so, Ocampo engages herself in a process of appropriation by establishing comparisons between Woolf's fictional scenarios and her native Argentina, where social prejudice often discouraged women from developing literary aspirations. In her lecture, Ocampo emphasized Woolf's feminist message in *Orlando*, which she relates to *A Room of One's Own*, clearly paraphrasing some passages from Woolf's essay in her talk: 'Things seem to have changed a great deal since then [Elizabethan England], and to hear of those prehistoric customs makes us smile. We must note, however, that if they have changed for men, they have hardly begun to change for women. All those women who have written have repeated, in one way or another, Jane Austen's gesture of hiding her manuscript under blotting paper when visitors or servants entered her room.'[11]

Jorge Luis Borges's reading and subsequent translations of Woolf's texts moved in a different direction from Ocampo's, though: he admitted that *A Room of One's Own*

---

[11] Ocampo, *Virginia Woolf, Orlando y Cía* (Buenos Aires: Sur, 1938), 46. 'Voy a hablarles a ustedes como "common reader" [sic] de la obra de Virginia Woolf. Voy a hablarles de la imagen que conservo de ella. No esperen ustedes oír crítica literaria pura; se decepcionarían. Pues el encuentro con la autora de Orlando me ha traído una vez más—entre otras cosas—la certidumbre de que nada de lo que yo había imaginado de la mujer, soñado para ella, defendido en su nombre, es falso, exagerado ni vano. Y al pensar en Virginia Woolf no puedo olvidarlo ni un momento.' Ocampo, *Virginia Woolf, Orlando y Cía*, 7; 'Las cosas parecen haber cambiado mucho desde entonces y nos hace sonreír el relato de costumbres de trogloditas. Conviene advertir que si han cambiado para los hombres, apenas empiezan a cambiar para las mujeres. Todas las que han escrito han hecho, de un modo u otro, el gesto de Jane Austen ocultando su manuscrito bajo un secante cuando los visitantes o los criados entraban en su cuarto.' Ocampo, *Virginia Woolf, Orlando y Cía*, 26; 'Las cosas parecen haber cambiado mucho desde entonces y nos hace sonreír el relato de costumbres de trogloditas. Conviene advertir que si han cambiado para los hombres, apenas empiezan a cambiar para las mujeres. Todas las que han escrito han hecho, de un modo u otro, el gesto de Jane Austen ocultando su manuscrito bajo un secante cuando los visitantes o los criados entraban en su cuarto.' Ocampo, *Virginia Woolf, Orlando y Cía*, 26.

interested him less than *Orlando*, since 'I am a feminist myself, I do not need a vindication to convince me.' However, *Orlando* deeply impressed Borges's imagination, probably because he regarded Woolf's novel as a perfect correlation for his own combination of fantastic realms and historical sites. Despite the controversy surrounding Borges's translations of Woolf's works—he teasingly suggested that *Un cuarto propio* had been his mother's translation, rather than his own—he was impressed by Woolf's literary achievement in *Orlando*, which he defined in 1936 as 'one of the most singular and exasperating [novels] of our times'. Of particular interest to Borges was Woolf's suggestive intersection of 'magic, bitterness and happiness' and the alternation of 'dream and reality' in a delicate balance that made of Woolf one of the most intelligent and imaginative writers in the literary panorama of his day.[12] Significantly, Borges's description of Woolf's technical achievements in *Orlando* already seemed to put forward a definition of what later came to be known as magic realism. Borges's emphasis on a fluid understanding of time, able to encompass different chronological dimensions, and the simultaneous combination of magic and historical sites somehow anticipates the seminal features of the genre that Alejo Carpentier famously put forward in his prologue to *The Kingdom of this World* (1949) and defined as the 'marvellous real' in a conflation inherent to and reaffirmed throughout American history and to be found 'at every stage in the lives of men who inscribed dates in the history of the continent'.[13]

Orlando would become one of Woolf's most popular novels in South America, opening up the path for a particularly fruitful tradition in South American letters, namely, magic realism. It could be argued that the juxtaposition of the marvellous real, past and present, or fact and fantasy were elements already present in Woolf's novel,[14] which Borges emphasized both in his translation and in his critical comments on Woolf's novel. In a way, *Orlando*'s indeterminacy in relation to literary genre, gender, and history places Woolf's novel in an interstitial position of liminality that has been signalled as one of the most characteristic traits of magic realism: 'Magic realism emerges as a form of genre indeterminacy, pointing toward ontological uncertainties with regard to the statues of both realities and fantasies. By a combination of basically realistic plot structures with supernatural elements, without resolving the conflict, Magic Realism emerges as genre-specific form of liminality.'[15]

---

[12] Gabriella A. Ferrari and Jorge Luis Borges, Diálogos (Barcelona: Seix-Barral, 1982), 306; Jorge Luis Borges, Textos cautivos: Ensayos y reseñas en El Hogar, eds, Enrique Sacerio-Garí and Emir Rodríguel Monegal (Barcelona: Tusquets, 1986), 122–3; Borges's fascination with *Orlando* is stated in one of his 'Biografías Sintéticas' ['Synthetic Biographies'] dedicated to Woolf, published in the journal *El Hogar* [The Home] on 30 October 1936. Woolf's biography was accompanied by Borges's translation of a fragment from Orlando's first chapter.

[13] Alejo Carpentier, 'On the Marvelous Real in America' [1949], in Louis Parkinson Zamora and Wendy Faris, eds, *Magical Realism: Theory, History, Community* (Durham, NC: Duke University Press, 1995), 75–88, at 87.

[14] Jill Channing, 'Magical Realism and Gender Variability in Orlando', *Virginia Woolf's Miscellany* 67 (Spring 2005), 11–13, at 11.

[15] Jochen Achilles and Ina Bergmann, eds, *Liminality and the Short Story: Boundary Crossings in American, Canadian, and British Writing* (London: Routledge, 2015), 18.

Orlando influenced authors such as Julio Cortázar and Gabriel García Márquez, who himself affirmed to have found in Woolf's novel 'a style and an art'. Borges's *Historia Universal de la Infamia* (*The Universal History of Infamy*) (1935) itself brings to mind Woolf's novel in its playful fictionalization of history as well as in its combination of fantasy, realism, and social satire.[16] Given Borges's personal interest in magic realms and fantasy, he approached the translation of *Orlando* primarily in those terms, which featured prominently in his understanding of Woolf's novel over social and feminist critique. As a result, some critics have recently pointed out how Borges's translations (both in *A Room of One's Own* and *Orlando*) consistently minimize Woolf's feminist message, approaching Orlando's gender shift as a magical event rather than as an instance of Woolf's social critique. A clear example, commented by Leone and Badenes and Coisson can be found in Orlando's first awareness of gender shift, which Woolf playfully mirrors in the syntax of the narrative through a similar shift of possessives and pronouns:[17]

> Orlando had become a woman—there is no denying it. But in any other respect, Orlando remained precisely as he had been. The change of sex, though it altered their future, did nothing whatever to alter their identity. Their faces remained, as their portraits prove, practically the same. His memory—but in future we must, for convention's sake, say 'her' for 'his', and 'she' for 'he'—her memory then, went back through all the events of her past life without encountering any obstacle. Some slight haziness there may have been, as if a few dark drops had fallen into the clear pool of memory; certain things had become a little dimmed; but that was all. The change seemed to have been accomplished painlessly and completely and in such as way that Orlando herself showed no surprise at it. Many people, taking this into account, and holding that such a change of sex is against nature, have been at great pains to prove (1) that Orlando has always been a woman, (2) that Orlando is at this moment a man. (*O* 128)

In his translation, Borges completely omits the free indirect discourse passage in between dashes that signals Orlando's gender shift, substitutes the possessive for the third-person plural ('their')—which emphasizes Orlando's double nature—for the third-person singular ('su' (his or her), and uses the adjective 'anormal' (abnormal) to refer to Orlando's transformation ('tales cambios de sexo son anormales'). In Woolf's text, this reads that 'such a change of sex is against nature' (*O* 128):

---

[16] Luis Harss, 'Gabriel García Márquez, o la cuerda floja', in *Los nuestros* (Buenos Aires: Editorial Sudamericana, 1966), 381–419, at 400; Susan Jill Levine, '*Cien años de* soledad y la tradición de la biografía imaginaria', *Revista Iberoamericana* XXXVI 72, (June 1970), 453–63, at 455.

[17] Leah Leone, 'La novela cautiva: Borges y la traducción de Orlando', *Variaciones Borges* 25 (2008), 223–36, at 224, 225. Borges's textual manipulations have been also signalled by and Guillermo Badenes and Josefina Coisson, 'Woolf, Borges y Orlando. La manipulación antes del manipulacionismo', *Mutatis Mutandis* 4, no. 1 (2011), 25–37, at 34.

> Orlando se había transformado en una mujer—inútil negarlo. Pero, en todo lo demás, Orlando era el mismo. El cambio de sexo modificaba su porvenir, no su identidad. Su cara, como lo pueden demostrar sus retratos, era la misma. Su memoria podía remontar sin obstáculos el curso de su vida pasada. Alguna leve vaguedad puede haber habido, como si algunas gotas oscuras enturbiaran el claro estanque de la memoria; algunos hechos estaban un poco desdibujados: eso era todo. El cambio se había operado minuciosamente y de manera tan perfecta, que la misma Orlando no se extrañó. Muchas personas, en vista de lo anterior, y de que tales cambios de sexo son anormales, se han esforzado en demostrar que (a) Orlando había sido siempre una mujer (b) que Orlando es ahora un hombre.[18]

As Mónica Ayuso explains, Borges's presence is 'more clearly felt in the rendering of gender in which he adopts a critical masculine presence which sabotages the texts'. Similarly, Patricia Willson finds textual evidence of Borges's dismantling of Woolf's syntax in the text and of inversion of salient thematic expressions, which affect the rhetorical structure of Woolf's novel in Borges's translation.[19] Borges's understanding of Woolf's novel, and especially of Orlando as a magical character rather than as the expression of Woolf's concerns regarding gender, may have been in tune with a predominant understanding of the novel as such in the conservative Argentina of the late 1930s. However, Borges's canonical position as a writer has also affected the status of his translations, which were seldom contested, to the point of even being argued that his translation somehow improves Woolf's original narrative: 'The translation of the Argentinian narrator is, in many cases, more concise and imaginative than the original itself.'[20]

Woolf's *Orlando* became a landmark of stylistic innovation achieved through the novel's parody of a traditional genre (biography) and by its radical reformulation of time and chronology. As has been often argued, Borges's translations go beyond a linguistic transposition of a text, thus often representing a critical comment on authors, their texts, and contexts, appropriating and transforming narratives 'without seemingly changing anything', and *Orlando* was no exception.[21] Borges's biographer, Emir Rodríguez Monegal, explains how his translation of *Orlando* was to become a seminal book in the South American literary tradition by its contemporary reassessment of 'fantastic narratives', the most ancient and unquestionable form of fabulation until the

---

[18] Woolf, *Orlando: Una biografía*, trans. Borges (Barcelona: Edhasa, 2009), 121–2.

[19] Monica Ayuso, 'The Unlike[ly] Other: Borges and Woolf', *Woolf Studies Annual* 10 (2004), 241–51, at 249; Patricia Willson, *La constelación del Sur: Traductores y traducciones en la literatura argentina del siglo XX* (Buenos Aires: Siglo XXI, 2004), 154; and Leah Leone, 'A Translation of His Own: Borges and A Room of One's Own', *Woolf Studies Annual* 15 (2009), 47–66, at 53.

[20] Levine, Susan Jill, '*Cien años de* soledad y la tradición de la biografía imaginaria', *Revista Iberoamericana* XXXVI (1970), 72, June–September: 453–63.

[21] 'La traducción del narrador argentino es, en muchos casos, más concisa e imaginativa que el mismo original.' Levine, '*Cien años de* soledad', 454; Sergio Gabriel Waisman, *Borges and Translation: The Irreverence of the Periphery* (Lewisburg, PA: Bucknell University Press, 2005); Efraín Kristal, *Invisible Work: Borges and Translation* (Nashville, TN: Vanderbilt University Press, 2002), xiii.

advent of realism in the eighteenth century. *Orlando* was to become a major source of inspiration for one of the greatest South American novels, García Márquez's *A Hundred Years of Solitude* (1967). Both Woolf and William Faulkner worked as major points of departure for García Márquez's unique reassessment of the literary tradition, as both challenged received assumptions pertaining to time, space and, ultimately, identity. Woolf inspired García Márquez in her particular conception of time as a large temporal span that connects different moments in a historical continuum. In turn, Faulkner's creation of an imaginary region and his unique combination of alienation and submerged historical layers resistant to dominant cultural modes triggered Márquez's invention of fictional Macondo.

ORLANDO AND GABRIEL GARCÍA MÁRQUEZ'S *A HUNDRED YEARS OF SOLITUDE*

Woolf's *Orlando* was published a year after Gabriel García Márquez was born in Aracataca, Colombia, and Borges's translation of the novel was to be published ten years later. García Márquez's first reference to Woolf dates from April 1950 in an essay entitled '¿Problemas de la novela?' ('Problems of the Novel?'), as part of his intense activity as a journalist at *El Heraldo* (*The Herald*), Barranquilla. In this article, García Márquez regrets the stagnation of the Colombian novel, and attributes this to a parochial attitude that ignores inspiring and innovative assessments of the genre, as understood by Joyce, Faulkner, or Virginia Woolf. Márquez cites *Orlando*, praises Woolf's 'manejo del tiempo' ('treatment of time') as one of the writer's greatest achievements, and laments that Woolf's influence is nowhere to be perceived in his homeland:[22]

> In Colombia, a novel undoubtedly and fortunately influenced by Joyce, Faulkner or Virginia Woolf remains yet unwritten. And I am saying 'fortunately', since I don't believe that we, Colombians, are an exception, for the time being, to the game of influence. In her prologue to *Orlando*, Virginia acknowledges her influences. Faulkner himself could not have denied Joyce's influence on himself. There's something—especially about the handling of time—between Huxley and, again, Woolf... If we,

---

[22] 'Todavía no se ha escrito en Colombia la novela que esté indudablemente y afortunadamente influida por los Joyce, por Faulkner o por Virginia Woolf. Y he dicho "afortunadamente", porque no creo que podríamos los colombianos ser, por el momento, una excepción al juego de las influencias. En su prólogo a "Orlando", Virginia confiesa sus influencias. Faulkner mismo no podría negar la que ha ejercido sobre él, el mismo Joyce. Algo hay—sobre todo en el manejo del tiempo—entre Huxley y otra vez Virginia Woolf... Si los colombianos hemos de decidirnos acertadamente, tendríamos que caer irremediablemente en esta corriente. Lo lamentable es que esto no haya acontecido aún, ni se vean los más ligeros síntomas de que pueda acontecer alguna vez.' Gabriel García Márquez, '¿Problemas de la novela?' [1950], in *Obra Periodística. Volume 1: Textos Costeños*, ed. Jacques Gilard (Barcelona: Bruguera, 1981), 267–9, at 269.

Colombians, had to rightly choose, we'd have to fall under that movement. It's regrettable that this has not happened yet, or that there are not the slightest symptoms that this could ever happen.[23]

García Márquez aimed to reverse the literary stagnation of his own tradition through his writing practice. As he openly admitted in conversation with Plinio Apuleyo Mendoza, 'I would have been a different writer if I hadn't read that sentence in *Mrs Dalloway*':

> But there could be no doubt that greatness was seated within; greatness was passing, hidden, down Bond Street, removed only by a hand's-breadth from ordinary people who might now, for the first and last time, be within speaking distance of the majesty of England, of the enduring symbol of the state which will be known to curious antiquaries, shifting the ruins of time, when London is a grass-grown path and all those hurrying along the pavement this Wednesday morning are but bones with a few wedding rings mixed up in their dust and the gold stoppings of innumerable decayed teeth. (*MD* 15)

García Márquez mentions *Mrs Dalloway* (1925)—and not *Orlando*—as the novel that triggered his literary imagination, and his own reformulations of time and space in his writing practice. Significantly, the quoted passage partakes of *Orlando*'s imaginative conception of time as a historical continuum, in which Clarissa's perceptions of the present moment fluidly overlap with a primaeval vision of the beginning of times, all transfixed by the realization of the inevitability of death. Woolf's radical transformations of realistic conceptions of natural time into a composite that intertwines in the character's mind different epochs, ages, and periods fascinated García Márquez: 'Woolf radically transformed my sense of time. She allowed me to glimpse in an instant Macondo's process of decomposition and its final destiny. I also wonder if this would be the remote origin of *The Autumn of the Patriarch* [1975], which is a book about the human enigma of power, of its solitude and its misery.'[24]

Only a year after the publication of *A Hundred Years of Solitude*, the Uruguayan critic Rodríguez Monegal, Borges's biographer, hinted at Woolf's influence in García Márquez's novel, emphasizing as a major affinity García Márquez's use of what he called 'the time of fable', characterized by a free conception of time void of the laws of causality

---

[23] Jorge Luis Borges translated William Faulkner's *The Wild Palms* [*Las palmeras salvajes*] in Ocampo's publishing house, Sudamericana, in 1940. In the previous year, Borges had written a review of this work published in *El Hogar* [*The Home*] praising the technical achievement of Faulkner's *Light in August*, *The Sound and the Fury* and *Sanctuary*, regarding Faulkner as 'the first novelist of our time'. Borges, *Textos cautivos*, 320.

[24] 'Yo sería un autor distinto del que soy si a los veinte años no hubiese leído esta frase de *La Señora Dalloway*... porque transformó por completo mi sentido del tiempo. Quizás me permitió vislumbrar en un instante todo el proceso de descomposición de Macondo, y su destino final. Me pregunto, además, si no sería el origen remoto de *El otoño del patriarca*, que es un libro sobre el enigma humano del poder, sobre su soledad y su miseria.' Gabriel García Márquez, *El olor de la guayaba: Conversaciones con Plinio Apuleyo Mendoza* (Barcelona: Bruguera, 1982), 67–8.

or existence, and by its 'magic' potential, which implies the quiet acceptance of the supernatural, the existence of parallel dimensions to reality, and the inspiring intersections between the marvellous and the quotidian.[25] By so doing, García Márquez's particular understanding of Woolf paved the way for magic realism with its radical modification of the realist mode, the combination of realism and the fantastic, and a particular cultural environment that destabilizes effects by signalling 'the hybrid nature of much postcolonial society', which Wendy Faris considers as a major trait of this tradition. García Márquez himself has often stressed how myth and fantasy are to be understood as integral components of what is known as 'reality':

> I came to understand that reality also comprises people's myths, beliefs and legends; these are not born from scratch, but are produced by people and are, therefore, their history, their quotidian life where their triumphs and failures intervene. I came to understand that reality is [...] also about the mythology and legends that are part of people's lives, and all this must be incorporated [to the novel].[26]

A Hundred Years of Solitude is also an 'imaginary biography of Latin America'. In fact, Márquez's construction of the chronotope he named Macondo—the most famous of Colombian landscapes which, paradoxically, is not to be found on any map—is a metaphor for human hatred and resentment that returns to haunt the living in an atmosphere of 'bad conscience and rancour', as Márquez explained to Harss in a famous interview a year prior to the publication of the novel. Both Woolf and Márquez rewrite several literary genres and, by doing so, they transcend their barriers and construct alternative spaces that emphasize the fictional and contradictory nature of history, and of its dependence on fiction. By redefining time, both writers offer a powerful parody of history, since 'through the unchanging and immortal Úrsula and the endlessly autumnal patriarch, García Márquez satirizes the history of a continent'.[27]

---

[25] Emir Monegal, 'Novedad y anacronismo de *Cien años de soledad*', 129, in *García Márquez: El escritor y la crítica*, ed. Peter Earle (Madrid: Taurus), 114–38.

[26] Wendy B. Faris, *Ordinary Enchantments: Magical Realism and the Remystification of Narrative* (Nashville, TN: Vanderbilt University Press, 2004), 1. 'Me di cuenta de que la realidad es también los mitos de la gente, es las creencias, es sus leyendas; que no nacen de la nada, son creadas por la gente, son su historia, son su vida cotidiana e intervienen en sus triunfos y sus fracasos. Me di cuenta de que la realidad no era sólo los policías que llegan matando gente, sino también toda la mitología, todas las leyendas, todo lo que forma parte de la vida de la gente, y todo eso hay que incorporarlo.' Gabriel García Márquez y Mario Vargas Llosa, *La novela en América Latina: Diálogo entre M. Vargas Llosa y G. García Márquez* (Lima: Universidad Nacional de Ingeniería, 1969), 52.

[27] Susan Jill Levine, 'A Second Glance at the Spoken Mirror: Gabriel García Márquez and Virginia Woolf', *Inti: Revista de literatura hispánica* 16 (1982), 53–60, at 55; Alexander Coleman, 'Bloomsbury in Aracataca: The Ghost of Virginia Woolf', *World Literature Today* 59, no. 4 (1985), 547. Alexander Coleman, 'Bloomsbury in Aracataca: The Ghost of Virginia Woolf', *World Literature Today* 59, no. 4 (1985), 547.

The Latin American 'Boom' and Toni Morrison

Woolf's *Orlando* triggered a series of literary conversations with various South American writers, who found in her work an inspiration to break away with what they saw as obsolete literary modes, thus resisting the pervasiveness of realism that was simply 'inadequate' to render a reality that escaped rationalizations and a common-sensical understanding of it. In this, both Borges and García Márquez parallel Woolf: their works in translation also travelled swiftly to the North American continent during the so-called 'Boom' of the 1960s.

Woolf's fiction and essays often question artificially erected barriers between fiction and non-fiction, literature and politics: both *Orlando* and *A Room of One's Own* (the Woolfian texts that first travelled to South America) partake of this premise in order to affirm positions in a world defined by injustice and inequality, literature being a means to overcome these. The coexistence of magic realms as sites of both otherness and ideological resistance with ordinary life often implies not only displacing and questioning dominant discourse, but also constructing alternative worlds that correct the dominant reality from which the dispossessed—on account of their class, ethnicity, language, or gender—may access, D'haen explains, the 'main body of Western literature'.[28]

As was the case of Gabriel García Márquez, the early Toni Morrison was influenced by both William Faulkner and Virginia Woolf, probably because she found in Woolf's fiction inspiring strategies to resist dominant discourses by imagining ideologically powerful spaces of otherness. As is well known, Morrison wrote a Master's thesis at Cornell University on Virginia Woolf and William Faulkner's treatment of madness and alienation, which John Duvall affirms to stand 'as a piece of intellectual autobiography that provides a glimpse into the development of the novelistic imagination.'[29] Morrison's second novel, *Sula* (1973), draws from Woolf's exploration of shell shock and madness through the character of Shadrack, yet Morrison displaces her characters from a metropolitan environment and places them in Medallion, a segregated town in Ohio, thus emphasizing periphery and alienation. Both Woolf and Morrison engage with otherness, and both claim for their right to reassess an inherited tradition in their own terms: 'The imagination that produces work which bears and invites re-readings, which motions to future readings as well as contemporary ones, implies a shareable world and

---

[28] D'haen, Theo, 'Magical Realism and Postmodernism', in Lois Parkinson Zamora and Wendy Faris, eds, *Magical Realism: Theory, History, Community* (Durham, NC: Duke University Press, 1995), 191–208, at 195.

[29] John Duvall, 'Doe Hunting and Masculinity: Song of Solomon and Go Down, Moses', *Arizona Quarterly* 47, no. 1 (Spring 1991), 95–115, at 96.

an endlessly flexible language. Readers and writers both struggle to interpret and perform within a common language shareable imaginative worlds.'[30]

As Barbara Christian explains, Morrison was 'confronted with some of the same issues of narrative technique which she [Woolf] had to content'.[31] Isolation and the problematization of the woman writer emerge in Morrison, as in Woolf, as new forms of writing in order to find engaging ways to express female subjectivity by focusing on the intersections between personal memory and history, thus creating a literary form for those who have been left out, as Morrison herself explains in a 1983 interview with Nellie McKay:

> It is generally true that contemporary black women writers consistently look back to their mothers and grandmothers for the substance and authority in their voices. I suspect this is an important and distinguishing element of black women's approach to their art. In contrast, many white women writers say they are inventing the authority for the voices pretty much from scratch in an effort to break the silence of Shakespeare's sisters. Black women writers—having the example of authoritative mothers, aunts, grandmothers, great-grandmothers—have something to contribute to the world. They have a distinctive and powerful artistic heritage. It is not white, and it is not male.[32]

The passage brings to mind some of Woolf's most famous statements in *A Room of One's Own* regarding a silenced tradition of women writers, while also connecting Morrison with other African American women writers. In that sense, Alice Walker significantly rephrased Woolf's claims in terms of ethnicity in order to voice the oppression and acknowledge the will of women such as Phillis Wheatley, a great example of artistry and survival, who having no room of her own, nor enough money to support herself since she 'owned not even herself' did write.[33] Whereas Morrison establishes a position of affinity with Woolf's narrative as a woman in terms of invisibility and displacement, she also distances from her on account of race. For Morrison, being part of the African American community privileges the power of the spoken word over the written one in a heritage that is orally transmitted from generations to generations of black women, which she recovers in her magic realist narratives. Just as García Márquez celebrated the story-telling inheritance from his grandfather and his superstitious grandmother in the androgynous narrative voice that controls *A Hundred Years of Solitude*, Morrison evokes in her novels submerged folk narratives, 'kinetic orality', and places these at the core of her novels, thus making women 'simultaneously the site of the historical and

---

[30] Toni Morrison, *Playing in the Dark: Whiteness and the Literary Imagination* (New York: Vintage, 1992), xii.
[31] Barbara Christian, 'Layered Rhythms: Virginia Woolf and Toni Morrison', *Modern Fiction Studies* 34, no. 3/4 (Autumn/Winter 1993), 483–500, at 493–4.
[32] Nellie McKay, *Critical Essays on Toni Morrison* (Boston, MA: Hall, 1988), 141.
[33] Alice Walker, 'In Search of Our Mothers' Gardens', in Alice Walker, *In Search of Our Mothers' Gardens: Womanist Prose* (London: Phoenix Press, 2005), 231–43, at 235.

the magical': 'We don't live in places where we can hear those stories anymore; parents don't sit around and tell their children those classical, mythological, archetypal stories that we heard years ago. But new information has to get out, and there are several ways to do it. One is the novel.'[34] By doing so, and as Lisa Williams has suggested, both Woolf and Morrison employ narrative strategies that 'disrupt linear notions of time and space as the dead arise from the past to find their rightful place in the present moment'.[35] In a sense, García Márquez's and Morrison's communal voice mirrors Woolf's late interest in the oral origins of the literary tradition, best embodied by 'Anon', the 'simple singer, lifting a song or a story from other peoples [sic] lips, and letting the audience join in the chorus' (*E6* 582).

In Morrison's narratives, space often becomes the site of transcendent mythical experiences, linking the local population to a strong cultural ancestry predating the colonial event. Such strategies enable unspeakable secrets and silenced stories to emerge, as in Woolf's *Orlando* and Morrison's *Beloved*, in a fantastic realm that defies spatial and chronological rationalizations through the creation of magical sites that, however, question received notions of a particular construction of the historical past, out of a desire 'to find out something about this country and that artistic articulation of its past that was not available in history, which is what art and fiction can do but sometimes history refuses to do'.[36]

WOMEN IN CONVERSATION: MICHÈLE ROBERTS AND JEANETTE WINTERSON

In an inspiring reassessment of autobiography and its formal conventions, Michèle Roberts explained how 'writing this memoir [*Paper Houses: A Memoir of the '70s and Beyond*, 2007] joins up all the scattered bits of me, makes them continuous, gives me a conscious self existing in history'.[37] By consciously blurring boundaries between history and autobiography, fact and fiction, and self and other, Roberts—like Woolf—refutes the epistemological certainty of history and validates personal experience, memory, and recollection as powerful narratives accounting for the past of the self. Roberts's fiction shows a concern with a need to rewrite history, myth, and religion from a feminist

---

[34] Gabrielle Foreman, 'Past-on Stories: History and the Magically Real, Morrison and Allende on Call', in Lois Parkinson Zamora and Wendy Faris, eds, *Magical Realism: Theory, History, Community* (Durham, NC: Duke University Press, 1995), 285–303, at 287; Toni Morrison, 'Rootedness: The Ancestor as Foundation' in Mari Evans, ed., *Black Women Writers* (New York: Anchor Books, 1984), 339–45, at 340.

[35] Lisa Williams, *The Artist as Outsider in the Novels of Toni Morrison and Virginia Woolf* (Westport, CT: Greenwood Press, 2000), 129.

[36] Toni Morrison, 'Faulkner and Women', in Doreen Fowler and Ann J. Abadie, eds, *Faulkner and Women: Faulkner and Yoknapatawpha* (Jackson: University Press of Mississippi, 1986), 295–302, at 296.

[37] Michèle Roberts, *Paper Houses: A Memoir of the '70s and Beyond* (London: Virago, 2007), 6.

perspective, and her narrative offers alternative constructions of Eve, Mary Magdalen, Mrs Noah, Saint Theresa of Ávila, George Sand, or the Brontë sisters in a particular female genealogy descending from Shakespeare's sister. But Roberts often does so by juxtaposing realist and magical realms, which enables the existence of a feminist space of exchange where women participate in empowering conversations across time and history.

In so doing, Roberts has overtly acknowledged her debt to Virginia Woolf, a major influence on her as a young woman reader, though she simultaneously articulates difference, especially in what relates to their differing conception of the role of the body in fiction, which, for Roberts, 'is not really visible' in Woolf's novels. Significantly, Roberts particularly praises Woolf's autobiographical writings in *Moments of Being*, which, in her view, connect the bodily life of the child with the desire to write while offering a space that blurs boundaries between fact and fiction or self and other. Despite admitting an ambivalent relationship of 'love and hate' in what relates to Woolf's literary legacy, Roberts has often drawn from Woolfian models in her depictions of the material conditions of women's lives and their artistic concerns through time and history, and also in putting forward imaginative spaces for mutual conversation and alternative outlets of dissidence that inspire women's work and interrogate hegemonic versions. Woolf's influence on Roberts has been discussed in relation to, for example, *Impossible Saints*, *Daughters of the House*, and *The Book of Mrs Noah*: the last triumphally closes with a celebration of Mrs Noah's female ancestry, including fairy-tale characters and women writers in conversation, which brings to mind Woolf's *A Room of One's Own*. Similarly, the short story 'Anger'—included in Roberts's first collection of short fiction *During Mother's Absence* (1993)—presents a terrifying vision of women trapped in silence and anonymity that reaches back to Woolf's Joan Martyn or to Shakespeare's sister, while also explicitly establishing an intertextual dialogue with Morrison's *Beloved* in the female protagonist's failed attempt to murder her daughter to spare her the pain of joining the 'lives of the obscure'.

Roberts's *Flesh and Blood* (1998) rests on a fluid conception of time as a continuum of different layers that overlap, and whose central section is a long prose poem significantly entitled 'Anon', which Clare Hanson has read as an invitation to move beyond time and history to an imaginary site of female resistance. Roberts's Edenic garden recalls the Woolfian 'moist and mossy floor' and the 'matted boughs' of the forest where the poet Anon sings. In addition, Susanne Gruss has seen in Roberts's second section of the novel, 'Cherubina', an intertextual connection with *Orlando* in what relates to notions pertaining to sexuality and gender.[38]

---

[38] Claire Hanson, 'During Mother's Absence: The Fiction of Michèle Roberts', in Abby Werlock, ed., *British Women Writing Fiction* (Tuscaloosa: University of Alabama Press, 2000), 229–47, at 243; Virginia Woolf, ' "Anon" and "The Reader": Virginia Woolf's Last Essays', ed. Brenda R. Silver, *Twentieth Century Literature* 25, no. 3/4, (Autumn 1979), 356–441, at 382; Susanne Gruss, *The Pleasure of the Feminist Text: Reading Michèle Roberts and Angela Carter* (Amsterdam: Rodopi, 2009), 135–6.

In this sense, Roberts's construction of the female *flâneur* in *Paper Houses*, observing the city through time, mirrors Woolf's *Orlando* in its concern to 'loop between sketches of thinking, dreaming and writing and sketches of the culture that made this activity possible', both being witness to and actor of these events.[39] Apart from assessing the formal and ideological conventions of biography and autobiography as literary genres, *Paper Houses* also addresses female sexuality and gender boundaries in its protagonist's conception of sexual identity and her questioning of compulsory heterosexuality. In addition, *Paper Houses* also poses forward a particular conception of history as a site to be revisited or as a myth to be carefully digested, which, however, helps to make sense of the present world. Thus, in 'Flâneuse'—a story included in Roberts's *Mud: Stories of Sex and Love* (2010)—its protagonist, Polly, a young writer having an affair with an editor, suddenly metamorphoses into an eighteenth-century lady after attending a musical performance in London, and is mistaken for a prostitute walking the London streets unchaperoned.

Significantly, Roberts—like Morrison—draws on Woolf's feminist revisions of history, time, and place via the phantasmagorical narrative excess of magic realism, aiming to transfigure historical accounts by undermining the naturalness of history, by laying bare the ideology that has sustained it as a narrative, and by emphasizing its fictional nature. By doing so, both Roberts and Morrison aim to liberate 'history's destructive aspect', while also posing forward 'an imaginative sense of future', a concern backbone of most magic realist narratives. In a sense, Jeanette Winterson's oeuvre partakes of similar premises; for Roberts, Winterson's fiction is 'set on an eternal postmodernist present, refusing traditional notions of time, space and history'.[40]

Jeanette Winterson's literary debt to Virginia Woolf in general, and to *Orlando* in particular, has been explored by numerous critics.[41] Winterson herself has often pointed out this connection in numerous essays and interviews, has made a documentary on Woolf's *Orlando* for the BBC2 series, *Art That Shook the World* (2002), and has written the introduction for Woolf's *Orlando* published by the Folio Society (2013). In her collection of essays *Art Objects: Essays on Ecstasy and Effrontery* (1995), Winterson included two essays on Woolf's *Orlando* and *The Waves* (1931) in the section entitled 'Transformations', thus acknowledging not only Woolf's capacity to transform tradition and convention, but also the various ways in which she herself, as a writer, had

---

[39] Roberts, *Paper Houses*, 6.

[40] David Mikics, 'Derek Walcott and Alejo Carpentier: Nature, History, and the Caribbean Writer', in Lois Parkinson Zamora and Wendy Faris, eds, *Magical Realism: Theory, History, Community* (Durham, NC: Duke University Press, 1995), 371–404, at 382; Roberts, *Food, Sex & God*, 95.

[41] Sonya Andermahr, *Jeanette Winterson: A Contemporary Critical Guide* (London: Continuum, 2007), 136; Fiona Doloughan, *Contemporary Narrative: Textual Production, Multimodality and Multiliteracies* (London: Continuum, 2011), 91; Merja Makinen, *The Novels of Jeanette Winterson* (London: Palgrave Macmillan, 2005); Susana Ónega Jaén, *Jeanette Winterson* (Manchester: Manchester University Press, 2006), 87; Agata Woźniak, 'A Reflection of My Own: Jeanette Winterson, Virginia Woolf and the Narcissism of Hommage', in E. H. Wright, ed., *Bloomsbury Influences: Papers from the Bloomsbury Adaptations Conference* (Cambridge: Cambridge Scholars Publishing, 2014), 68–86, at 70.

been transformed by Woolf's *oeuvre*, as she made clear in an interview: '[*Orlando*] felt liberating. It does still. I realised that you can call a novel a biography, that walls are there to be climbed over, and that the point of life is the quality of the questions, not the satisfaction of the answers. You can't solve life. You can't explain life. You can celebrate it and conjure with it, mourn it and hold it in your arms. But you can't contain it, and art doesn't. Exuberant impossible unlikely lucky life.'[42] Echoing Woolf's famous statement in *A Room of One's Own*—'we think back through our mothers if we are women'—Winterson acknowledges Woolf as a significant forerunner in her writing practice: 'A writer uninterested in her lineage is a writer who has no lineage. The slow gestations and transformations of language are my proper study and there can be no limit to that study. I cannot do new work without known work.'

Winterson not only praises *Orlando* for its transgressive proposal in terms of gender and sexuality, but also for Woolf's move away from realist modes by posing 'an immediate challenge to conventional genre-boxing' along with an invitation to trigger the readers' disbelief in accordance to Woolf's description of *Orlando* in her diary: 'truthful; but fantastic' (*D3* 157).[43] As Borges and García Márquez had been before her, Winterson was fascinated by Woolf's treatment of time, which she handled as if it were 'an element, not a dimension', and by the novel's freedom from all constraints: 'historical, fantastical, metaphysical, sociological'.[44] For Winterson, *Orlando* successfully draws away from 'the mimicry of Realism' through spells, artifice, and wild connections across time and space—'through the inner and outer worlds of imagination and experience'.[45]

Most significantly, Winterson's particular conversation with Woolf entails an emphasis on the ideological possibilities of alternative magical sites that overlap with ordinary worlds, in line with Toni Morrison's and Michèle Roberts's readings of Woolf's work. One might wonder, however, why Roberts's and Winterson's narratives—unlike Morrison's—are seldom examined through the lens of magic realism, despite their obvious affinities. It is certainly assumed that magic realism originally stemmed from a post-colonial, peripheral background of 'otherness' with respect to mainstream culture, but at present the term has moved beyond Latin American literature of American literature produced by Latinos, and must be understood as a 'worldwide phenomenon', rather related to the growth of a postmodern literary sensibility.[46] Discussing William Faulkner's possible consideration as a magic realist writer, Theo D'haen has pointed out the reluctance of American scholarship to apply this particular term to American literature, showing a preference for the term 'postmodernism'. Such a preference not only underscores the political repercussions and implications of contemporary texts such as

---

[42] Jeanette Winterson, 'The Books That Changed My Life', *Telegraph*, 4 July 2017, www.telegraph.co.uk/culture/books/11209010/Jeanette-Winterson-the-books-that-changed-my-life.html.

[43] Winterson, *Art Objects: Essays on Ecstasy and Effrontery* (London: Vintage, 1995), 172, 67, 71.

[44] Jeanette Winterson, 'Shape shifter: The joyous transgressions of Virginia Woolf's *Orlando*', *The New Statesman*, 18 February 2013, www.newstatesman.com/culture/culture/2013/02/shape-shifter-joyous-transgressions-virginia-woolf%E2%80%99s-orlando.

[45] Winterson, *Art Objects*, 72, 73.

[46] Faris, *Ordinary Enchantments: Magical Realism and the Remystification of Narrative*, 3.

Faulkner's, but also unveils the 'privileged centre ideology that they claim to combat'. By describing magic realism as the 'cutting edge of postmodernism', D'haen actually advocates for its strong, materialist concerns: 'By stubbornly restricting the term to a geographically limited segment of literature, these critics [inside and outside the United States] fail to see that the really significant resistance within the international postmodern movement is being put up by magic realism.'[47]

Woolf's *Orlando* could itself be regarded as a prototype of a magic realist text in its suggestive and innovative understanding of time, its destabilization of narrative conventions, its blurring of fictional boundaries, and in its conception of gender and sexuality.[48] Most importantly, Woolf opens up a space that both entails dissident voices with the mainstream of culture and the possibility of articulating an empowering discourse for women.

Conclusions

In an essay entitled 'A Work of My Own'—whose title brings to mind Woolf's *A Room of One's Own*—Jeanette Winterson affirms that 'the writer has to choose a word, every word, that is solid enough for its meaning and powered enough for its flight. The word will have to cross time, the word will have to survive assault.'[49] Winterson seems here to underline the power of the written word to signify itself, independent from its context, ready to be reassessed in the reader's mind, which seems to be prophetic of *Orlando*'s reception in America through the novel's translation, personal readings, and artistic appropriation by a number of influential writers.

The influence of *Orlando* spread through South American countries as swiftly as the colourful butterflies that Woolf imagined to inhabit the Argentine *pampa*, as she wrote in a letter to Victoria Ocampo: 'And you [Ocampo] are about to voyage to the land of great butterflies and vast fields: which I still make up from your flying words' (*L5* 365). In turn, Ocampo had been fascinated by a woman writer whose 'novels seem herbaceous borders of the gardens in her country, a mixture of flowers, spots of colours which seem to sprout in happy disorder and where, however, everything is inspired foresight, confident selection, art and discipline'.[50]

Such a masterful combination of fantasy and technical control encouraged Jorge Luis Borges, at Ocampo's suggestion, to translate *Orlando* into Spanish, which, whether

---

[47] D'haen, 'Magical Realism and Postmodernism', 200, 201.
[48] Channing, 'Magical Realism and Gender Variability in *Orlando*', 11.
[49] Winterson, *Art Objects*, 167.
[50] 'Esa es la mujer cuyas novelas se parecen a los 'herbaceous borders' [sic] de los jardines de su país, mezcla de flores, en manchas de color, que parecen brotar en feliz desorden y donde sin embargo todo es previsión inspirada, selección segura, arte y disciplina.' Victoria Ocampo, *Testimonios III* (Buenos Aires: Sudamericana, 1946), 97.

intentionally or not, opened up the path for what is known as magic realism. Borges's personal reading of Woolf's *Orlando* certainly underscored Woolf's feminist message and privileged in his critical reflections on the novel the character's miraculous transformation and its voyage through time as a primordial example of magic ordinariness. Similarly, Gabriel García Márquez acknowledged Woolf as a major contemporary writer, whose particular conception of time and psychological insight triggered his imagination in becoming himself a writer. Like García Márquez, Toni Morrison found inspiration in the fruitful intertwining of real and fantastic realms to voice the anger and frustration of the dispossessed, and Jeanette Winterson modelled herself as a writer by reading Woolf.

Across time and cultures, and in varied ways, all these writers appropriated, reassessed, and were inspired by Virginia Woolf. In so doing, they embody Woolf's 'continuing presences' through their particular understanding of her work since, as Woolf famously declared in 'Craftsmanship', words are inherently overloaded with meaning, and are therefore endlessly reinterpreted and invested with personal significance: 'Now, this power of suggestion is one of the most mysterious properties of words. Everyone who has ever written a sentence must be conscious or half-conscious of it. Words, English words, are full of echoes, of memories, of associations—naturally. They have been out and about, on people's lips, in their houses, in the streets, in the fields, for so many centuries. And that is one of the chief difficulties in writing them today—that they are so stored with meanings, with memories, that they have contracted so many famous marriages' (*E6* 95). These being 'out and about' of English words—of Woolf's 'flying words'—seems, indeed, to reflect the fate of *Orlando* and its process of reception: rich in invested meanings, full of appropriations, open to reassessments and new readings, all of which was radically to alter modes of viewing and understanding the world and literary practices and their relation to the writer's imagination, which, as Woolf expressed in her essay 'Reading' (1919), is both a physical and emotional effort, revealing a 'landscape not printed, bound or sewn up, but somehow the product of trees and fields and the hot summer sky, like the air which swam, on fine mornings, round the outline of things' (*E3* 142).

Selected Bibliography

Channing, Jill, 'Magical Realism and Gender Variability in *Orlando*', *Virginia Woolf's Miscellany* 67 (Spring 2005), 11–13.
D'haen, Theo, 'Magical Realism and Postmodernism', in Lois Parkinson Zamora and Wendy Faris, eds, *Magical Realism: Theory, History, Community* (Durham, NC: Duke University Press, 1995), 191–208.
García Márquez, Gabriel, '¿Problemas de la novela?' [1950], in *Obra Periodística. Volume 1: Textos Costeños*, ed. Jacques Gilard (Barcelona: Bruguera, 1981), 267–9.
García Márquez, Gabriel, *El olor de la guayaba: Conversaciones con Plinio Apuleyo Mendoza* (Barcelona: Bruguera, 1982).

García-Sánchez, Soraya, 'A Conversation with Michèle Roberts, about Novels, History and Autobiography', *Journal of International Women's Studies* 12, no. 1 (January 2011), 183–91.

Hanson, Clare, 'During Mother's Absence: The Fiction of Michèle Roberts', in Abby Werlock, ed., *British Women Writing Fiction* (Tuscaloosa: University of Alabama Press, 2000), 229–47.

Leone, Leah, 'A Translation of His Own: Borges and A Room of One's Own', *Woolf Studies Annual* 15 (2009), 47–66.

Levine, Susan Jill, 'A Second Glance at the Spoken Mirror: Gabriel García Márquez and Virginia Woolf', *Inti: Revista de literatura hispánica* 16 (1982), 53–60.

Lojo-Rodríguez, Laura Mª, 'Woolf in Hispanic Countries: Buenos Aires and Madrid', in Jessica Berman, ed., *A Companion to Virginia Woolf* (Oxford: Blackwell, 2016), 467–80.

Morrison, Toni, 'Rootedness: The Ancestor as Foundation', in Mari Evans, ed., *Black Women Writers* (New York: Anchor Books, 1984), 339–45.

Morrison, Toni, *Playing in the Dark: Whiteness and the Literary Imagination* (New York: Vintage, 1992).

Roberts, Michèle, *Food, Sex & God: On Inspiration and Writing* (London: Virago, 1998).

Rogers, Gayle, 'The Circulation of Interwar Anglophone and Hispanic Modernisms', in M. Wollaeger ed., *The Oxford Handbook of Global Modernisms* (Oxford: Oxford University Press, 2012), 461–76.

Walker, Alice, 'In Search of Our Mothers' Gardens', in Alice Walker, *In Search of Our Mothers' Gardens: Womanist Prose* (London: Phoenix Press, 2005), 231–43.

Winterson, Jeanette, *Art Objects: Essays on Ecstasy and Effrontery* (London: Vintage, 1995).

CHAPTER 36

VIRGINIA WOOLF IN THE CANON OF WOMEN'S LITERATURE

Narrative Futures of The Feminist Novel

TONYA KROUSE

At the conclusion of *A Room of One's Own* (1929), Virginia Woolf reminds readers of the limitations that women have historically faced in their creative pursuits. Nevertheless, she advocates optimism for the future, arguing that the women writers of today and tomorrow give life to the woman writer of the past, whose potential was thwarted: 'She lives in you and in me, and in many other women who are not here tonight, for they are washing up the dishes and putting children to bed. But she lives; for great poets do not die; they are continuing presences; they need only the opportunity to walk among us in the flesh' (*ARO* 85–6). Woolf understands that women's economic independence facilitates this opportunity, and she argues 'that if we live another century or so', her imagined Shakespeare's sister will be born (*ARO* 86). Woolf confirms her investment in a historical literary tradition, and she seeks to establish women's place in it. She argues that women's economic and personal autonomy produces the necessary conditions for women's creative excellence, from which a canon of women's literature can emerge.

Although Woolf does not characterize her novels as feminist undertakings, she does give readers cause to understand her authorial agenda as feminist. Woolf's fiction identifies gender as a typical justification for structural inequality, and it suggests that patriarchy relies on the systematic oppression of women for its power. Furthermore, Woolf's novels meet one of the necessary conditions for the feminist novel that Roxane Gay outlines in her provocative 'Theses on the Feminist Novel'. A feminist novel, writes Gay, 'is a novel where the concerns of women and womanhood are the alpha and the omega of the narrative but it also deals explicitly with the stories, with the lives of women'.[1] If feminism is a cultural and political movement that advances the cause of equality between the sexes, Woolf advances feminist objectives not only in her polemical works but also in her fiction. Nearly a century beyond Woolf's *A Room of One's Own*, we can re-evaluate how Woolf's feminism informs her choices for representing women characters in her novels. Doing so deepens our knowledge of the roles available to women not only in the fiction of Woolf and the women writers who follow her but also in the world.

Woolf returns repeatedly in her novels to three archetypal roles for women characters: the Angel, the Artist, and the Girl. These archetypes messily overlap and filter through each other, marking 'woman' as a complex creative site. Thus, this chapter finds inspiration in what Toril Moi describes in her influential *Sexual/Textual Politics: Feminist Literary Theory* as Anglo-American 'images of women' criticism. Moi assesses this type of woman-centered analysis as both refreshing in its 'insistence on the *political* nature of any critical discourse' and problematic for its resistance against more theoretically nuanced and self-aware feminist approaches.[2] Moi's comments more than thirty years ago anticipate a reaction against this type of interpretive framework in favour of more abstract poststructuralist feminist approaches. This reaction persists into the twenty-first century and can stall attempts to understand the literary historical bonds between the authors of feminist fiction today and their precursors.

In the introduction to the 1999 *What is a Woman? And Other Essays*, Moi complicates her earlier interrogation of 'images of women' approaches. She explains, 'My new work is an attempt to work my way out from under poststructuralism ... and to see what happens when one goes elsewhere'.[3] This chapter similarly seeks to find a way out from under poststructuralism, which might allow readers to refocus on a canon of women's literature and the ways in which women are represented in that literature. By examining how more recent women authors deploy Woolf's archetypes of female identity, readers can witness Woolf's lingering influence. As one critic aptly argues, 'Conclusively, "feminist" to Virginia Woolf did not denote freedom; women had to free themselves from invisible forces like the "Angel in the House" and survive even by "telling lies." Therefore it is left to the future generation of women writers to assert themselves and to speak and write nothing but the truth'.[4] To understand Woolf's impact on feminist fiction, we must learn not only to 'think back through our mothers' (*ARO* 57) but also to think ahead through Woolf's daughters, the diverse women writers of today and tomorrow.

---

[1] Roxane Gay, 'Theses on the Feminist Novel', *Dissent* 61 no. 4 (2014), 45.
[2] Toril Moi, *Sexual/Textual Politics: Feminist Literary Theory* (London: Methuen, 1985), 49.
[3] Toril Moi, *What Is a Woman? And Other Essays* (Oxford: Oxford UP, 1999), xii.
[4] B. Sudipta, 'Feminism and Virginia Woolf', *Literary Half-Yearly* 35, no. 2 (July 1994), 43.

Narrative Futures: Woolfian Archetypes, the Feminist Novel, and the Canon of Woolf's Daughters

The 'Angel in the house' perhaps constitutes Woolf's most powerful and pervasive fictional image for womanhood. Symbolizing an ideal of submissive femininity that compromises women's full participation in political, social, and cultural life, the Angel gets her power from her complicity with oppressive patriarchal and heteronormative structures. For this reason, Woolf concludes that the woman writer must kill the Angel in order to create.

Many scholars have taken Woolf's concluding call to action as her last words on the Angel. For example, in their groundbreaking work of feminist literary criticism *The Madwoman in the Attic: The Woman Writer in the Nineteenth Century*, Sandra Gilbert and Susan Gubar understand the ideal of the Angel as compelling 'the surrender of [woman's] self—of her personal comfort, her personal desires, or both—that is the beautiful Angel-woman's key act, while it is precisely this sacrifice which dooms her both to death and to heaven'.[5] Gilbert and Gubar are not alone in consigning the Angel to the grave: critics including Elaine Showalter in *A Literature of Their Own*,[6] Jane Marcus in *Art and Anger*,[7] and many who follow them suggest that Woolf's feminism and Woolf's feminist characters rise from the Angel's ashes. And yet, the Angel persists both in Woolf's fiction and in the feminist fiction that follows Woolf.

Woolf's fictional Angels operate neither as monsters to be slain nor paragons of creativity to be revered but as complex identities through which readers discover aesthetic, political, sexual, and social structures that stretch into the present and look forward to the future. Most significantly, Woolf depicts her fictional Angels as always already dead or dying. *Mrs Dalloway*'s (1925) Clarissa Dalloway, *To the Lighthouse*'s (1927) Mrs Ramsay, and *The Years*' (1937) Mrs Pargiter do not exist as fully alive women who can either be killed or embraced. Woolf's fictional Angels embody a dying or dead ideal of femininity, an ideal that haunts women and with which they must reckon to find their own voices.

Clarissa Dalloway perfectly embodies Woolf's Angel archetype. Unfortunately, Woolf's rich characterization of Clarissa sometimes encourages readers to misinterpret her as a site of creativity and possible redemption rather than as a doomed figure. In fact, the narrative of *Mrs Dalloway* does not bear out such an optimistic interpretation, nor do the narratives of Woolf's other Angels. Clarissa feels 'herself suddenly shriveled,

---

[5] Sandra M. Gilbert and Susan Gubar, *The Madwoman in the Attic: The Woman Writer and the Nineteenth-Century Literary Imagination* (New Haven: Yale UP, 1979), 25.
[6] Elaine Showalter, *A Literature of Their Own: British Women Novelists from Bronte to Lessing* (Princeton: Princeton University Press, 1977).
[7] Jane Marcus, *Art and Anger: Reading Like a Woman* (Columbus: The Ohio State University P, 1988).

aged, breastless'; she construes herself through what she lacks, 'something central which permeated; something warm which broke up surfaces and rippled the cold contact of man and woman, or of women together' (*MD* 28). Clarissa, a ghostlike presence, goes through the motions, but for Woolf, going through the motions does not affirm life nor does it result in art.

Woolf offers similarly bleak characterizations of Mrs Ramsay and Mrs Pargiter, who, unlike Clarissa, do not survive to their novel's ends. Gilbert and Gubar rightly note that Mrs Pargiter's 'death, like Mrs Ramsay's, heralds changes on which the rest of the novel meditates. Unlike Mrs. Ramsay, however, Mrs Pargiter is neither beautiful nor powerful.'[8] By the time Woolf writes *The Years*, her interest in and patience with the 'the Angel in the house' has nearly disappeared. The Angel might serve as a catalyst for the women who come after her, but in herself she no longer holds interest. Indeed, as Woolf's career progresses, she seems progressively less invested in the Angel archetype, and by the time she writes *Between the Acts* (1941), she doesn't bother to write the Angel in the house at all: Mrs Oliver is dead before the action of the novel begins.

In feminist fiction after Woolf, however, the Angel lives on. Unlike Woolf, who portrays the Angel as a holdover from a repressive Victorian past, literary novels including Margaret Drabble's *The Garrick Year* and *The Waterfall*, Doris Lessing's *The Memoirs of a Survivor* and *The Good Terrorist*, Buchi Emecheta's *Second Class Citizen*, and Helen Oyeyemi's *Boy, Snow, Bird*, as well as many young adult novels including J.K. Rowling's *Harry Potter* series and Suzanne Collins's *The Hunger Games* trilogy, repeatedly resurrect the Angel in new guises. In some cases, contemporary authors revive the Angel as Woolf's villain that must be slain or as a role model that real women attempt, but always fail, to emulate. In others, authors revive the Angel and transform her into a saviour with the power to right society's wrongs and to assist the next generation of women in leading creative, fulfilling lives. While critics such as Barbara Hill Rigney in *Madness and Sexual Politics in the Feminist Novel: Studies in Bronte, Woolf, Lessing, and Atwood* and Roxanne J. Fand in *The Dialogic Self: Reconstructing Subjectivity in Woolf, Lessing, and Atwood* have to varying degrees discussed contemporary revisions of Woolf's Angel, they have not fully accounted for the lingering power of this archetype, nor have they discussed the larger implications of what contemporary novelists use the Angel to achieve. An analysis of the differing portrayals of the Angel in Margaret Atwood's *The Handmaid's Tale* and Zadie Smith's *On Beauty* can illuminate the Angel's ongoing significance.

In Atwood's *The Handmaid's Tale*, the Angel is embodied by the Commander's Wife, Serena Joy, the primary antagonist to the novel's narrator and protagonist, Offred. Atwood paints Serena Joy, and not the Commander, as Offred's most dangerous enemy, combining in her the characteristics of popular culture Angel icons from the 1970s and 1980s, Tammy Faye Bakker and Phyllis Schlafly. Offred remembers first watching Serena

---

[8] Sandra M. Gilbert and Susan Gubar, *No Man's Land: The Place of the Woman Writer in the Twentieth Century. Volume III: Letters from the Front* (New Haven: Yale UP, 1994), vol. 3, 50.

Joy while her 'mother slept in on Sunday mornings', and later reading a profile about her once she had begun to make speeches objecting to the women's movement: 'She was good at it. Her speeches were about the sanctity of the home, about how women should stay home. Serena Joy didn't do this herself, she made speeches instead, but she presented this as a failure of hers, as a sacrifice she was making for the good of all'.[9] This passage shows the ways in which Serena Joy embraces power that depends on complicity with patriarchal oppression of women, much like Woolf's Clarissa and Mrs Ramsay do.

As with Woolf's Angels, Serena Joy's complicity gives her a measure of power, but it also limits her freedom: 'She doesn't make speeches anymore. She has become speechless. She stays in her home, but it doesn't seem to agree with her. How furious she must be, now that she's been taken at her word'.[10] From Offred's perspective, Serena Joy's fury at her own subjugation drives her desire to subjugate Offred, making Serena Joy a direct agent of the very patriarchal power that oppresses her; only by fighting the Angel, even as she befriends the Commander, can Offred preserve a sense of her self-identity. Offred's opposition to Serena does not eradicate the Angel: it reanimates her as a villain onto which Offred can project all her own frustrations. Significantly, by construing the Angel, Serena Joy, as the villain, the narrative forecloses the potential for women in Gilead to unite in a feminist rebellion against their oppressors. Atwood brings Woolf's Angel back to life, and in so doing, she enacts a narrative regression of the feminist progress that Woolf's body of work predicts.

In contrast, Smith's *On Beauty* revives the Angel in her character, Mrs Kipps, to rethink the Angel's demonization in feminist discourse. Like Mrs Ramsay, Mrs Kipps stands in the shadow of her academic husband. She rarely leaves the house; her life revolves around her husband and children. As Mrs Kipps's husband Monty explains, 'She doesn't enjoy social conflagration. It's fair to say she is more warmed by the home hearth'.[11] Nevertheless, Smith's Angel does not merely duplicate those we see in Woolf's novels. A black Caribbean immigrant of around sixty years old, Mrs Kipps may espouse the values of Woolf's Angels, but she looks nothing like them, and her sociohistorical context is dramatically opposed to theirs. Of all the characters in *On Beauty*, Mrs Kipps alone has the power to create harmony and synthesis for those who enter her orbit, and her ability to do so depends on rigid divisions between masculine and feminine, outside and inside, public and private, mind and body. Her racial and colonial identity, however, gives her the potential also to operate as an ally to the novel's contemporary black working mother, Kiki Belsey. Through Kiki, Smith encourages readers to encounter the Angel with fresh eyes and brings the Angel down to earth.

In the end, Mrs Kipps dies suddenly, having hidden her aggressive cancer from everyone. Here readers perceive two similarities between the Angel in *On Beauty* and the Angel in *To the Lighthouse*: like Mrs. Ramsay, the narrative kills Carlene Kipps without fanfare, almost as a parenthetical aside; also like Mrs Ramsay, Carlene Kipps

---

[9] Margaret Atwood, *The Handmaid's Tale* (New York: Anchor Books, 1998), 45.
[10] Atwood, *Handmaid's Tale*, 45.
[11] Zadie Smith, *On Beauty: A Novel* (London: Penguin Press, 2005), 115.

lives on through a painting. Beyond these two points, however, the similarities cease. Unlike Mrs Ramsay who is lost to the living characters in *To The Lighthouse*, the spirit of Mrs Kipps presides over the two discoveries that propel the novel toward its conclusion—Kiki's discovery of the painting of the goddess Erzulie and Zora's discovery of her father's infidelity. These discoveries also propel mother and daughter, Zora and Kiki, toward reunion with each other and toward reconciliation and renewal: 'Zora now reached the top of the stairs leading down to the basement. Howard begged her for a little more time. There was no more time. Mother and daughter were already calling for each other, one running upstairs and one running down, each with her rich, strange news'.[12] In this moment, Carlene transforms from Angel to goddess, and by bringing Zora and Kiki together, she transfers the resolve and certainty of her own role to the formerly confused and uncertain contemporary women. The Angel might die, but in her afterlife as goddess instigates feminist redemption.

As Atwood's and Smith's two very different adaptations show, feminist novelists continue to find in Woolf's Angel a dynamic source of inspiration for their own narratives. Whether the Angel operates as a villain or saviour, a stereotype to be rejected or an unattainable ideal, she stands as a critical counterpoint to real contemporary women who struggle to understand and express themselves. The Angel may not need to be slain, these authors suggest, but instead revived so that women can use her to learn about themselves. Nevertheless, she certainly is not as attractive an option for female identity from the standpoint of late twentieth- and early twenty-first-century feminist novelists as Woolf's next archetype: the Artist.

The Artists that stand out most notably in Woolf's novels are *To the Lighthouse*'s Lily Briscoe and *Between the Acts*' Miss LaTrobe. As Kristin Bluemel summarizes, 'Second wave feminist critics embraced *To the Lighthouse* and *Between the Acts* as works that uphold for feminist consumption and emulation images of individual, eccentric, psychologically exiled female artists triumphing, in their middle years, against the odds of an antagonistic history'.[13] However, just as Woolf returns to the archetype of the Angel throughout her oeuvre in order to confront and consign to history the ideals of womanhood that she inherits from the Victorian period, she returns to the archetype of the Artist to depict a role that promises liberation but fails to deliver it. If the Angel's identity depends on embodying a patriarchally endorsed feminine ideal, the Artist's depends on rejecting it. In this, the Artist denotes a necessary step toward empowerment and equality, but Woolf suggests that women must surpass this archetype if they want full personhood.

In *To the Lighthouse*, Lily Briscoe appears, upon first reading, to offer a feminist solution to the problem of female creativity that the Angel Mrs Ramsay poses. Unlike Mrs Ramsay, Lily attempts to forge a feminist aesthetic, and she resists the voices of the Charles Tansleys of the world that say, 'Women can't write, women can't paint' (*TTL* 71).

---

[12] Smith, *On Beauty*, 433.
[13] Kristin Bluemel, 'Feminist Fiction', in Robert L. Caserio (ed.), *The Cambridge Companion to the Twentieth-Century English Novel* (Cambridge: Cambridge UP, 2009), 123.

For this reason, many critics look to Lily's narrative as a model for coherent womanhood that the Angel does not provide. According to Raphael Ingelbein: 'Although Woolf contemplates chaos, dispersal and the loss of unity in *To the Lighthouse*, she eventually works to restore order through Lily's vision—the last words of the novel, 'my vision', reassert both coherence and subjectivity'.[14] The coherence that Lily represents, however, also mystifies the very real conflicts and structures of oppression that characterize relations between the sexes in the novel, and in their mystification, these conflicts and structures dominate Lily's choices as an artist and exhaust her powers of creativity. Lily's completion of her painting at the novel's end does not satisfy. Completing her painting affords Lily independence from the feminine ideal that Mrs Ramsay represents, but it does not afford her feminist closure, which would grant her the ability, as Gay says feminism should, 'to move through the world with the same ease as men'.[15]

In the posthumously published *Between the Acts*, Woolf returns to the Artist in the figure of Miss LaTrobe, an outcast who constantly sees herself failing as an artist, the next play that she might write nagging at her before the current production has finished (*BTA* 46). The novel's conclusion offers her no consolation or redemption; she judges her attempt a failure and disappears with the downpour that marks her play's unscripted end. By the time Woolf writes *Between the Acts*, the Artist archetype limits women's creative potential just as surely as the Angel archetype does.

Nevertheless, the *kunstlerroman*, or novel that focuses on tracing the development of a central Artist figure, remains a standard form for Woolf's successors. To characterize women primarily as Artists—and not primarily as daughters, sisters, wives, or mothers—allows women authors to challenge conservative, patriarchal beliefs that locate women's identity in their relationships to men. As Gayle Greene argues in *Changing the Story: Feminist Fiction and the Tradition*, 'prototypical *Kunstlerroman* and *Bildungsroman* of contemporary women's fiction' present 'questing protagonists' who 'seek "something new": and "something new," a term which recurs in Lessing's works, means more than individual freedom or fulfillment—it means something radically oppositional to 'the nightmare repetition' of the past'.[16] Yet, reviewing Woolf's influence on later feminist fiction makes apparent that although embodying the Artist role may allow women to resist becoming an Angel, it does not free women from the constraints of feminine gender expectations.

For women authors after Woolf, the Artist blocks a path toward self-actualization and embodied creativity for women. While readers frequently regard these fictional Artists as role models for female empowerment, the woman authors who write them often see these characters as blocked, angry, and isolated. Two paradigmatic examples of novels that illustrate this point are Doris Lessing's *The Golden Notebook* and Claire Messud's *The*

---

[14] Raphael Ingelbein, 'Intertextuality, Critical Politics and the Modernist Canon: The Case of Virginia Woolf', *Paragraph: A Journal of Modern Critical Theory* 22, no.3 (November 1999), 284

[15] Gay, 'Feminist Novel', 45.

[16] Gayle Greene, *Changing the Story: Feminist Fiction and the Tradition* (Bloomington: Indiana UP, 1991), 7.

Woman Upstairs. Written about fifty years apart, both novels feature Artist protagonists whose creative lives are compromised by their gender and life circumstances, and both challenge the idea that they will be freed by inhabiting the role of the Artist. Lessing and Messud are not alone in setting this challenge: readers see similar critiques of the Artist archetype in many feminist novels, including A.S. Byatt's *Possession: A Romance*, Margaret Drabble's *The Witch of Exmoor*, Buchi Emecheta's *The Bride Price*, Erica Jong's *Fear of Flying*, Jeanette Winterson's *The PowerBook*, Margaret Atwood's *Cat's Eye* and *The Blind Assassin*, Meg Wolitzer's *The Wife*, Chimamanda Ngozi Adichie's *Americanah*, and Zadie Smith's *Swing Time*. In these more recent works, the Artist typically has her independent income and room of her own, but she remains overdetermined by cultural expectations for normative femininity. The Artist may not make her home inside the house of patriarchy, but she lives trapped by her need to resist it.

In *The Golden Notebook*, Lessing depicts her protagonist, Anna Wulf, as a woman in crisis at a historical moment that is characterized by world war, the threat of nuclear annihilation, and immense political upheaval. She believes that her historical position distances her from the writers who came before her: 'There is something new in the world. And I don't want to hear, when I've had encounter with some Mogul in the film industry, who wields the kind of power over men's minds that no emperor ever did, and I come back feeling trampled on all over, that Lesbia felt like that after an encounter with her wine-merchant'.[17] These observations comprise the source of Anna's writer's block, and they underwrite her alienation.

Unlike Woolf's Artists who retain some faith in the potential to find unity or self-expression in art, Lessing's Wulf has lost all faith: 'I have decided never to write another novel.... I suffer torments of dissatisfaction and incompletion because of my inability to enter those areas of life my way of living, education, sex, politics, class bar me from'.[18] Although Anna continues to write her notebooks and does, by the novel's end, go on to write a second novel, the redemptive possibilities of art, which ground the completion of Lily Briscoe's painting and even Miss LaTrobe's pageant production, have been exhausted. She writes a book that isn't very good and goes on living. The Artist achieves no meaning: she engages in endless repetition.

In *The Woman Upstairs*, Messud's Nora, like Anna Wulf, and like Woolf's Artists before her, is lonely, dissatisfied, and invisible. While the outside world views her as a competent third-grade teacher, a dutiful daughter, and a loyal friend, she nurtures artistic ambitions that she shrinks to fit inside her 'studio', the second bedroom of her modest apartment. Her art takes the form of elaborate, miniature, true-to-life dioramas of other women artists' living and working spaces. When she meets Sirena, an installation artist who creates worlds out of everyday domestic objects, and agrees to share a larger studio space with her, her ambitions expand to fill that space, even though Sirena and the world continue to regard her as 'the woman upstairs'.

---

[17] Doris Lessing, *The Golden Notebook*. 1962. (New York: HarperPerennial Modern Classics, 2008), 452.

[18] Doris Lessing, *The Golden Notebook*, 59

At the beginning of the novel, Nora thinks of the woman upstairs as a quiet, non-threatening identity: 'We're not the madwomen in the attic—they get lots of play, one way or another. We're the quiet woman at the end of the third-floor hallway, whose trash is always tidy, who smiles brightly in the stairwell with a cheerful greeting, and who, from behind closed doors, never makes a sound.'[19] By the novel's end, Nora's articulation of 'the woman upstairs' transforms to reveal fury, bitterness, and disappointment: 'My anger is prodigious. My anger is a colossus. I'm angry enough to understand why Emily Dickinson shut out the world altogether, why Alice Neel betrayed her children, even though she loved them mightily. I'm angry enough to see why you walk into the water with rocks in your pockets, even though that's not the kind of angry I am.'[20] Messud positions the enraged Nora Eldridge on a continuum with other women artists including Woolf. The woman artist's creativity collapses beneath the weight of patriarchal oppression. The challenge Messud sets for her readers in *The Woman Upstairs*– not unlike the challenge Lessing sets in *The Golden Notebook*—is to envision what a woman might achieve creatively if we stop seeing her as 'the woman upstairs' and start seeing her as a living, breathing human being.

In the end, Lessing and Messud both object to reducing women to the Artist role and to confining artists to their identities as women, not only in their fiction but also in their public comments about their own accomplishments. Famously, Lessing's 1971 introduction to *The Golden Notebook* disavows feminist interpretations, which deploy Lessing's novel as 'as a useful weapon in the sex war.'[21] As a result, feminist scholars of Lessing's fiction have spent fifty years trying to account for Lessing's antagonism. Sometimes they have done so by analysing Lessing's writing comparatively with that of other women writers, most frequently Woolf's. For example, many essays in the field-shaping collection *Woolf and Lessing: Breaking the Mold*, Aaron Rosenfeld's 'She Was Where? Lessing, Woolf, and Their Radical Epistemologies of Place', and my own ' "Anon," "Free Women," and the Pleasures of Impersonality' take this approach. Alternatively, scholars have accounted for Lessing's claims independently. For example, Marjorie J. Lightfoot's "Breakthrough in the Golden Notebook," Roberta Rubenstein's *Novelistic Vision of Doris Lessing: Breaking the Forms*, and Magali Cornier Michael's *Feminism and the Postmodern Impulse: Post-WWII Fiction* do this. In all cases, Lessing's comments about *The Golden Notebook*, as well as her unsympathetic portrayal of her artist-protagonist, seem to demand an alibi before scholars can embark on feminist interpretations.

Similarly, Messud provoked controversy when an interviewer suggested that women authors should create characters that readers want to befriend. 'What kind of question is that?' Messud responded, asking whether readers would want to befriend a long list of characters ranging from Oedipus to 'any of the characters in anything Pynchon has ever written'. Messud then defended her unsympathetic characterization of Nora

---

[19] Claire Messud, *The Woman Upstairs* (New York: Knopf, 2013), 6.
[20] Claire Messud, *The Woman Upstairs* (New York: Knopf, 2013), 253.
[21] Doris Lessing, *The Golden Notebook*, xii.

Eldridge: 'Her rage corresponds to the immensity of what she has lost'.[22] The debate that resulted from this interview reminds readers of how critics have addressed Lessing's contentious claims about her intent in writing *The Golden Notebook*. For this reason, evaluating *The Golden Notebook* and *The Woman Upstairs* to understand their engagement with Woolf's Artist archetype makes sense. Both Lessing and Messud powerfully illustrate, in their novels and their public comments, the limitations of the Artist as a model for female empowerment.

In the end, Woolf's only archetype that offers women hope of creating and living freely is the Girl, the woman of the future who will benefit from the labours of the Angel and the Artist before her and who will not face the constant struggle either to embody or to resist patriarchy's norms. Woolf and the feminist authors who follow her use the Girl to experiment with possibilities for feminist narrative. As Rachel Blau DuPlessis describes in 'Feminist Narrative in Virginia Woolf', 'Trying to make fiction talk about women and their concerns, especially when a woman is the speaking subject, may necessarily lead to a critical transformation of narrative structures, to reversals, reassessments, reweightings of all sorts'.[23] Through the Girl, this project begins.

Woolf fleshes out this archetype most dynamically in the figure of Cam in *To the Lighthouse*, although she also gestures toward her in the forms of Elizabeth Dalloway, the boy and woman Orlando, and even Isa in *Between the Acts*. Cam's characterization reveals a path toward agency and creativity unbound from her gender, a vision of the individual in fluid relationship with the world that she inhabits. The boyish girl Cam runs and darts; she seems not to notice the world around her—only her own ultimate goal, which neither characters nor readers can intuit: 'For Cam grazed the easel by an inch; she would not stop for Mr. Bankes and Lily Briscoe; though Mr. Bankes, who would have liked a daughter of his own, held out his hand; she would not stop for her father, whom she grazed also by an inch; nor for her mother, who called 'Cam! I want you a moment!' as she dashed past. She was off like a bird, bullet, or arrow, impelled by what desire, shot by whom, at what directed, who could say?' (*TTL* 54). As a girl, Cam possesses boundless energy and does not acknowledge the desires or demands of others, particularly those desires or demands that would compel her to embrace or reject cultural imperatives for feminine behaviour.

By the time readers meet Cam at the novel's end, she has grown from this girl into a young woman whose energy, it appears, now turns totally inward. She loses herself in her own thoughts and in the physical sensations produced by dragging her hand through the water as she makes the journey away from dry land and toward the lighthouse. Unlike both Mrs. Ramsay and Lily Briscoe, Cam floats on a tide of emotion and sensory experience that instigate vast leaps in her imagination. Unlike Mr. Ramsay, who continually

---

[22] Annasue McCleave Wilson, 'An Unseemly Emotion: PW Talks with Claire Messud'. *Publisher's Weekly* (blog), 29 April 2013. Accessed 23 May 2018. https://www.publishersweekly.com/pw/by-topic/authors/interviews/article/56848-an-unseemly-emotion-pw-talks-with-claire-messud.html.

[23] Rachel Blau DuPlessis 'Feminist Narrative in Virginia Woolf'. *Novel: A Forum on Fiction* 21, no. 2–3 (January 1988): 323–330. *MLA International Bibliography*, EBSCOhost (accessed October 14, 2017), 325.

seeks community and connection—which the narrative indicates has hindered his work—Cam does not. She revels in her autonomy: 'But as, just before sleep, things simplify themselves so that only one of all the myriad details has power to assert itself, so, she felt, looking drowsily at the island, all those paths and terraces and bedrooms were fading and disappearing, and nothing was left but a pale blue censer swinging rhythmically this way and that across her mind. It was a hanging garden; it was a valley, full of birds, and flowers, and antelopes.... She was falling asleep' (*TTL* 204). In this passage, Cam's imagination takes over and produces a truth made possible by lapsing out of her subjective consciousness and her relationship to others. She absents herself from the triangle of herself, her father, and James; she refuses to play the role of Angel or Artist, and she refuses to serve as a conduit between her father and brother. Rather, Cam imagines a fecund world, a foreign world: she refuses to play any assigned role.

Perhaps unsurprisingly, the creative potential of the Girl captures the imagination of more recent women writers. Novels such as Doris Lessing's *The Memoirs of a Survivor*, Margaret Atwood's *Cat's Eye* and *The Robber Bride*, Kathy Acker's *Blood and Guts in High School*, Anne Enright's *The Gathering*, Toni Morrison's *Beloved*, Meg Wolitzer's *The Interestings*, and Zadie Smith's *White Teeth* and *NW* use this archetype to create a positive framework for female identity and creativity that can live on into the future. Two of the most generative examples for understanding the Girl's life in the feminist novel after Woolf are Fatima, in Fatima Mernissi's autobiographical *Dreams of Trespass: Tales of a Harem Girlhood*, and Stella, in Jenni Fagan's post-apocalyptic *The Sunlight Pilgrims*. Fatima and Stella illustrate the transformative potential of the Girl as a model for female subjectivity, accommodating women from a range of intersectional identities, cultural backgrounds, and gender histories. Unlike the Angel and the Artist, the Girl operates as a fertile space within which women can tell their own stories and write their own futures.

Mernissi's *Dreams of Trespass: Tales of a Harem Girlhood* centres on the Girl Fatima, who watches the women in the harem who surround her and who learns from them both the necessity of creative expression and the frustrations of being denied basic human freedoms. Mernissi's novelistic account of her girlhood emphasizes not just the obstacles to happiness that her mother and the other women face as a result of patriarchy but also the Girl Fatima's desire to take pleasure in the woman-centred world of the harem and to create and to advocate out of joy and not just anger. For example, considering the women of the harem's performances of feminists' lives, Fatima considers: 'Deep down, though, the problem with feminists' lives was that they did not have enough singing and dancing in them.... The feminists' lives seemed to be all about fighting and unhappy marriages, never about happy moments, beautiful nights, or whatever it was that gave them the strength to carry on.... I decided then and there that if I ever led a battle for women's liberation, I definitely would not forget about sensuality.'[24] The Girl Fatima's

---

[24] Fatima, Mernissi, *Dreams of Trespass: Tales of a Harem Girlhood* (New York: Basic Books, 1994), 132–3.

perception that for feminism to achieve success—as political action, as art, as social change—it must encompass the full range of human emotions and experiences, without limitation, connects strongly to Woolf's assertions in *A Room of One's Own* about the necessary preconditions for female creativity, as well as to Woolf's experiments near the end of her life with attempting to articulate women's experiences in *The Pargiters* (1937), which would become *Three Guineas* (1938) and *The Years*, and in *A Sketch of the Past* (1939) and other short pieces written for The Memoir Club, which are collected in *Moments of Being* (1985).

Mernissi, like Woolf before her, connects women's personal stories, influenced as they are by family, culture, social class, religion, and education, with the larger enterprise of feminist politics. Beyond that, Mernissi uses the Girl to imagine new approaches for narrating women's lives and evaluating the intersecting emotions, experiences, and events that hold significance for women. By weaving a tale of a young Girl coming into womanhood, a Girl who is both Fatima the author and an invented character named Fatima, Mernissi successfully co-opts Woolf's archetypal Girl to interrogate the relationships between imperialism and patriarchy, global politics and family dynamics, and historical, geographical, and environmental context and the formation of self-identity.

Fagan's project in *The Sunlight Pilgrims* differs dramatically from Mernissi's. Unlike Mernissi, Fagan locates her Girl not in the real world but in a near-future dystopia framed by environmental apocalypse. Further, Fagan does not share Mernissi's emphasis on ethnicity, religion, and family as indexes of identity. Nevertheless, these are superficial differences. Fagan's novel is as indebted as Mernissi's to Woolf's Girl archetype. As with Woolf's portrayal of Cam Ramsay and Mernissi's portrayal of Fatima, Fagan's portrayal of Stella insists that girlhood—and the transition to fully embodied, fully autonomous womanhood—neither complies with nor does battle with patriarchy. Instead, the archetype of the Girl advances an ideal of self-actualization through free and authentic expression, through telling the truth about one's own experience.

Stella, a trans girl who dreams of gender confirmation surgery, feels and expresses certainty about her present identity and her future. Her certainty is rooted in sexual, social, and intellectual desire. Echoing Gertrude Stein, she thinks: 'A girl is a girl, is a girl, is a girl. That's all she has. Also, her obsession with Lewis is becoming creepy, she might do anything at this point—if he would kiss her again. Anything. She'd even beg. She'd take a kiss anywhere. Even on the elbow. He doesn't know what to make of her, though, does he? She could ask him out on a date. She is not afflicted with her mother's zealous self-reliance and totalitarian independence from state and fellow man—she isn't scared to say she wants something'.[25] This passage elucidates the difference between the Girl and the Artist: the Girl sees no glory in cutting herself off from human connection in order to secure her independence; the girl sees happiness as a positive value, as or more valuable than self-reliance or even art. This is not to say that the Girl does not have

---

[25] Jenni Fagan, *The Sunlight Pilgrims* (New York: Hogarth, 2016), 27.

insecurities, anxieties, or frustrations of her own. For example, Stella has many, most of which connect to her trans identity: 'There was *Boys Don't Cry* and she has a few models to look up to now, but other than that she feels like she is forever searching to find girls like her who are still wanted and attractive and normal'.[26] Even still, Stella's insecurities, anxieties, and frustrations do not define her as they define the Artist or the Angel in the house. She searches for models, but the Girl creates herself.

THE FUTURE OF THE FEMINIST NOVEL: FORGING BONDS BETWEEN WOMEN

The Girl archetype offers Woolf and female novelists after her a site through which to imagine female subjectivity as autonomous, productive, and, at least to some extent, free. The Girl does not have the power to destroy patriarchy or unilaterally to escape its punishing effects. Like the Angel and the Artist before her, the Girl lives within patriarchy. Unlike them, however, she possesses the ingenuity to invent a space for her own growth, and she can picture new possibilities for not only female-male relationships but also relationships between women. These newly imagined affiliations, particularly between girls and women, predict the future of the feminist novel after Woolf.

Unlike Angels who understand themselves only as helpmeets to men, and unlike Artists who understand themselves as alienated and isolated by their creative ambitions, Girls understand themselves through their connections to other women. In this way, these fictional Girls provide a framework through which women authors can understand their embeddedness in a canon of women's literature and within a community of women novelists—past, present, and future. As Woolf writes, 'All these relationships between women... are too simple. So much has been left out, unattempted' (*ARO* 62). Woolf seeks to represent these complex relationships, with greater and lesser success, not only in her discussion of Chloe and Olivia in *A Room of One's Own* but also in the relationships that she depicts between Elizabeth Dalloway and Miss Kilman in *Mrs Dalloway*, the Girl Orlando and the prostitutes from the brothel in *Orlando: A Biography*, and Peggy and Eleanor in *The Years*.

Women writers after Woolf also make this attempt, most notably in novels featuring the Girl. They forge strong ties between female characters that allow girls and women both to retain their independence from one another and to rely on each other for support, constructive criticism, and inspiration. Women authors' depiction of friendship between women might, according to Judith Taylor, forge 'a new feminist orientation to friendship' that 'would work against a kind of compulsory gender

---

[26] Fagan, *Sunlight Pilgrims*, 41.

conforming interdependence'.[27] Rather than idealizing friendship between women, or presenting women as competitors for men upon whom they must depend, this model would promote independence as a feature of women's relationships: 'The expectation should be that friends are very different people with some important points of connection, with varied histories and families and views, or goals, and they need not merge these, but learn from and enjoy one another's. Focusing on gender and sexual conformity and more on desire and freedom can be beneficial and, at the very least, it's more honest'.[28] Indeed, this is the project of feminist fiction today, and of the women authors who write it.

A canon of women's literature, as Woolf intuited, relies not only on women writers attaining an independent income and room of their own but also on them using their creative talents to connect imperfectly with other women. Further, it requires a space within which women authors can value those areas of life that are conventionally regarded as private, emotional, or domestic. As Zadie Smith said to Christopher Bollen in an interview about her novel *NW*, 'You have this sense that women's matters are not serious. I remember one year a Booker judge saying, "Oh, these books are too domestic," and the judge held up my book as an example of a book that wasn't domestic, thinking that was a compliment. But I don't consider that a compliment—to have a women's field, if that's what it is, denigrated'.[29] When Woolf envisions relationships between women in fiction that exist independently from their relationships with men, in which women dare to like each other and to connect in complicated ways, she implies a similar belief.

Often, critical accounts of feminist fiction assign it to one of two categories: fiction that rails against women's subjugation within patriarchy, and fiction that celebrates the new opportunities that feminism makes possible. As Roberta Rubenstein argues in 'The Feminist Novel in the Wake of Virginia Woolf', 'Since the mid-twentieth century, feminist novels have expressed two divergent though often overlapping perspectives: critiques of the confining circumstances of women's lives in patriarchy before feminism; and celebrations of the increasing potentialities for the growth, self-discovery, and full humanity that feminism has made possible'.[30] Similarly, in 'Re-Envisioning Feminist Fiction', Emma Parker writes, 'While feminist fiction of the 1970s and 1980s traces the struggle for women's liberation, in the 1990s writers increasingly interrogate the meaning of freedom'.[31] These accounts introduce an unnecessary and unfortunate division in women's literary history and in the history of the feminist novel. When we acknowledge Woolf's archetypes for female subjectivity, and when we trace

---

[27] Judith Taylor, 'Beyond "Obligatory Camaraderie": Girls' Friendship in Zadie Smith's *NW* and Jillian and Mariko Tamaki's *Skim*', *Feminist Studies* 42, no. 2 (2016), 453.

[28] Taylor, 'Beyond "Obligatory Camaraderie"', 468.

[29] Christopher Bollen, 'Zadie Smith' *Interview Magazine* (blog), 24 August 2012. Accessed October 14, 2017. https://www.interviewmagazine.com/culture/zadie-smith.

[30] Roberta Rubenstein, 'The Feminist Novel in the Wake of Virginia Woolf', in Brian W. Shaffer (ed.), *A Companion to the British and Irish Novel, 1945–2000* (Oxford: Blackwell, 2005), 62.

[31] Emma Parker, 'Re-Envisioning Feminist Fiction', in David James (ed.), *The Cambridge Companion to British Fiction since 1945* (Cambridge: Cambridge UP, 2015), 81.

their pervasive influence on the novels that women following her write, we discover more continuity than division.

Following Woolf, writers of feminist novels, including those discussed here and many more, engage with the Angel, that symbol of a woman thoroughly embedded in patriarchal norms for female identity, and the Artist, that symbol of a woman who breaks free from patriarchy to write her own story and reject normative femininity. They also, following Woolf, create a new identity in the form of the Girl, who neither accepts nor rejects those norms that patriarchy encodes. Woolf inspires these writers to create narratives of affiliation, particularly between women, that are complicated, contentious, loving, and true. Gay concludes 'Theses on the Feminist Novel' with one final axiom: 'A feminist novel, at its best, allows for hope and the possibility of a better world, even if that hope is shrouded in darkness'.[32] This is the future for feminist fiction for which Woolf lays the groundwork.

Bibliography

Acker, Kathy. *Blood and Guts in High School* (New York: Grove Press, 1978).
Adichie, Chimamanda Ngozi. *Americanah* (New York: Anchor Books, 2013).
Atwood, Margaret. *The Blind Assassin* (New York: Anchor Books, 2000).
Atwood, Margaret. *Cat's Eye*. 1988. (New York: Anchor Books, 1998).
Atwood, Margaret. *The Handmaid's Tale*. 1986. (New York: Anchor Books, 1998).
Atwood, Margaret. *The Robber Bride*. 1993. (New York: Anchor Books, 1998).
Bollen, Christopher. 'Zadie Smith' *Interview Magazine* (blog), 24 August 2012. Accessed October 14, 2017. https://www.interviewmagazine.com/culture/zadie-smith.
Bluemel, Kristin. 'Feminist Fiction', in Robert L. Caserio, ed., *The Cambridge Companion to the Twentieth-Century English Novel* (Cambridge: Cambridge UP, 2009), 114–130. Cambridge Companions to Literature (CCtL).
Byatt, A.S. *Possession: A Romance* (New York: Vintage International, 1990).
Collins, Suzanne. *The Hunger Games* (New York: Scholastic Press, 2008).
Drabble, Margaret. *The Garrick Year* (Boston: Houghton Mifflin Harcourt, 2013).
Drabble, Margaret. *The Waterfall* (New York: Penguin Putnam, 1971).
Drabble, Margaret. *The Witch of Exmoor* (New York: Harvest, 1996).
DuPlessis, Rachel Blau. 'Feminist Narrative in Virginia Woolf'. *Novel: A Forum on Fiction* 21, no. 2-3 (January 1988): 323-330. *MLA International Bibliography*, EBSCOhost (accessed October 14, 2017).
Emecheta, Buchi. *The Bride Price* (New York: George Braziller, 1976).
Emecheta, Buchi. *Second Class Citizen* (New York: George Braziller, 1974).
Enright, Anne. *The Gathering* (New York: Grove/Atlantic, 2007).
Fagan, Jenni. *The Sunlight Pilgrims* (New York: Hogarth, 2016).
Fand, Roxanne. *The Dialogic Self: Reconstructing Subjectivity in Woolf, Lessing, and Atwood* (Selinsgrove: Susquehanna University Press, 1999).
Gay, Roxane. 'Theses on the Feminist Novel.'" *Dissent*, 61 no. 4 (2014): 45-48.

---

[32] Gay, 'Feminist Novel', 47.

Gilbert, Sandra M. and Susan Gubar. *The Madwoman in the Attic: The Woman Writer and the Nineteenth-Century Literary Imagination* (New Haven: Yale UP, 1979).

Gilbert, Sandra M. and Susan Gubar. *No Man's Land: The Place of the Woman Writer in the Twentieth Century. Volume III: Letters from the Front* (New Haven: Yale UP, 1994).

Greene, Gayle. *Changing the Story: Feminist Fiction and the Tradition* (Bloomington: Indiana UP, 1991).

Ingelbein, Raphael. 'Intertextuality, Critical Politics and the Modernist Canon: The Case of Virginia Woolf'. *Paragraph: A Journal of Modern Critical Theory* 22, no. 3 (November 1999): 278–292. *MLA International Bibliography*, EBSCOhost (accessed 14 October 2017).

Jong, Erica. *Fear of Flying* (New York: Penguin, 1973).

Krouse, Tonya. ' "Anon", "Free Women", and the Pleasures of Impersonality' in Debrah Raschke, Phyllis Sternberg Perrakis, and Sandra Singer, eds. *Doris Lessing: Interrogating the Times* (Columbus: The Ohio State University Press, 2010), 32–57.

Lessing, Doris. *The Golden Notebook*. 1962. (New York: HarperPerennial Modern Classics, 2008).

Lessing, Doris. *The Good Terrorist*. 1985. (New York: Vintage International, 2008).

Lessing, Doris. *The Memoirs of a Survivor*. 1974. (New York: Vintage, 1988).

Lightfoot, Marjorie J. "Breakthrough in The Golden Notebook." *Studies in the Novel* 7 (1975): 277–84.

Marcus, Jane. *Art and Anger: Reading Like a Woman* (Columbus: The Ohio State University Press, 1988).

Mernissi, Fatima. *Dreams of Trespass: Tales of a Harem Girlhood* (New York: Basic Books, 1994).

Messud, Claire. *The Woman Upstairs* (New York: Knopf, 2013).

Michael, Magali Cornier. *Feminism and the Postmodern Impulse: Post-World War II Fiction* (Albany: State University of New York Press, 1996).

Moi, Toril. *Sexual/Textual Politics: Feminist Literary Theory* (London: Methuen, 1985).

Moi, Toril. *What Is a Woman? And Other Essays* (Oxford: Oxford UP, 1999).

Morrison, Toni. *Beloved*. 1987. (New York: Vintage, 2004).

Oyeyemi, Helen. *Boy, Snow, Bird* (New York: Riverhead Books, 2014).

Parker, Emma. 'Re-Envisioning Feminist Fiction', in David James, ed., *The Cambridge Companion to British Fiction since 1945* (Cambridge: Cambridge UP, 2015), 79–94. Cambridge Companions to Literature (CCtL).

Rigney, Barbara Hill. *Madness and Sexual Politics in the Feminist Novel: Studies in Bronte, Woolf, Lessing, and Atwood* (Madison: University of Wisconsin Press, 1978).

Rosenfeld, Aaron. 'She Was Where?: Lessing, Woolf and Their Radical Epistemologies of Place', *Doris Lessing Studies* 26, no. 2 (2007): 8–14.

Rowling, J.K. *Harry Potter and the Sorcerer's Stone* (New York: Scholastic, 1997).

Rubenstein, Roberta. 'The Feminist Novel in the Wake of Virginia Woolf', in Brian W. Shaffer, ed., *A Companion to the British and Irish Novel, 1945–2000* (Oxford: Blackwell, 2005), 45–64. Blackwell Companions to Literature and Culture (Blackwell Companions to Literature and Culture): 28.

Rubenstein, Roberta. *The Novelistic Vision of Doris Lessing: Breaking the Forms of Consciousness* (Urbana: University of Illinois Press, 1979).

Showalter, Elaine. *A Literature of Their Own: British Women Novelists from Bronte to Lessing* (Princeton: Princeton University Press, 1977).

Smith, Zadie. *On Beauty: A Novel* (London: Penguin Press, 2005).

Smith, Zadie. *NW* (New York: Penguin, 2012).

Smith, Zadie. *Swing Time* (New York: Penguin, 2016).
Smith, Zadie. *White Teeth* (New York: Vintage, 2001).
Sudipta, B. 'Feminism and Virginia Woolf'. *Literary Half-Yearly* 35, no. 2 (July 1994): 36–44.
Taylor, Judith. 'Beyond "Obligatory Camaraderie": Girls' Friendship in Zadie Smith's NW and Jillian and Mariko Tamaki's *Skim*'. *Feminist Studies* 42, no. 2 (2016): 445–468. *MLA International Bibliography, EBSCOhost* (accessed 14 October 2017).
Saxton, Ruth, Jean Tobin. *Woolf and Lessing: Breaking the Mold* (New York: St. Martin's Press, 1994).
Wilson, Annasue McCleave. 'An Unseemly Emotion: PW Talks with Claire Messud'. *Publisher's Weekly* (blog), 29 April 2013. Accessed 23 May 2018. https://www.publishersweekly.com/pw/by-topic/authors/interviews/article/56848-an-unseemly-emotion-pw-talks-with-claire-messud.html.
Winterson, Jeanette. *The Power Book* (New York: Vintage, 2000).
Wolitzer, Meg. *The Interestings* (New York: Riverhead, 2014).
Wolitzer, Meg. *The Wife* (New York: Scribner, 2003).

CHAPTER 37

CREATIVE NON-FICTION AND POETRY

STACEY D'ERASMO

VIRGINIA Woolf's two book-length essays, *A Room of One's Own* (1929) and *Three Guineas* (1938), have had a long and pervasive influence on poetry and what we now call creative non-fiction.[1] Both works use clear, expository prose to argue for women's rights and the liberation of female consciousness; along the way, Woolf fully dissects patriarchal consciousness, anatomizing it down its last narcissistic cell. Her tone is measured, bemused, ironic. The central image of *A Room of One's Own*—the eponymous room of the title and the necessary £500 a year—along with the creation of Shakespeare's sister, have become fundamental feminist tropes. *Three Guineas* expanded on the themes of *A Room of One's Own*, raising the question of how women might create new systems of education, pacifism, and citizenship. This text, which concerns ambivalence, has drawn passionately ambivalent responses. Susan Sontag begins her own long essay 'Regarding the Pain of Others' by responding to *Three Guineas*, questioning its assumptions and the grammar of its class privilege. For any feminist writer, or any writer considering the tenets of feminism, Woolf's non-fiction work on these topics is a touchstone. While there is some amount of formal play in these essays—the epistolary conceit of *Three Guineas*, the running interior monologue of *A Room of One's Own*—they are more direct than inventive, meant to persuade and convince through logic, example, and evidence.

However, Woolf's influence on non-fiction writing is as powerfully wielded, and possibly more so, via her style in her fiction, her less instrumental non-fiction, and her diaries. Moreover, that style embodies an ethics that has become constitutive of the *ars poetica* of many contemporary non-fiction writers. Sontag may have taken on *Three Guineas* intellectually, and with mixed feelings, in 'Regarding the Pain of Others', but she followed Woolf's stylistic method, and the worldview it embodies, without hesitation

---

[1] Portions of this essay have been adapted from Stacey D'Erasmo, 'Influence: A Practice in Three Wanders', *New England Review* 31, no. 4 (2010–2011), 31–42. Reprinted with permission.

in her short piece 'The Way We Live Now', a piece that can only be called 'fiction' if one squints very hard. Published in *The New Yorker* in 1986, 'The Way We Live Now' begins:

> At first he was just losing weight, he felt only a little ill, Max said to Ellen, and he didn't call for an appointment with his doctor, according to Greg, because he was managing to keep on working at more or less the same rhythm, but he did stop smoking, Tanya pointed out, which suggests he was frightened, but also that he wanted, even more than he knew, to be healthy, or healthier[2]

Written as a response to the then accelerating AIDS crisis, the piece flows from voice to voice of a group of people around an unnamed central figure (modelled on photographer Robert Mapplethorpe) who is becoming very ill. Like Woolf pieces such as 'Kew Gardens' or her novel *The Waves*, the centre—in this case, a mortally ill man—is an occasion more than a narrative engine, the rock thrown into the pond. The subject is the pond as it ripples, not the rock. As a narrative design, it is markedly decentralized. Sontag took issue with Woolf's stance in non-fiction work such as *Three Guineas*, but she seems to have found great mobility and depth in Woolf's centripetal style. The force of 'The Way We Live Now' is in no small part due to this stylistic choice; we feel that the people around the man are co-creators of him, just as he has been a co-creator of all of them. The disease is a virus, and so is the narrative; it is contagious, collective, and it moves very fast as the long sentences hurtle down the page.

With this piece, Sontag might be regarded as one among many of Woolf's aesthetic heirs, who have made innovative uses of Woolf's fictional techniques in constructing creative non-fiction and poetry. As Woolf's place in the canon became increasingly assured over the latter half of the twentieth century and novels such as *Mrs Dalloway* (1925) and *To the Lighthouse* (1927) became mainstays on syllabi, the decentralized style of her fiction became familiar to entire generations of readers and writers. Several major non-fiction writers have made use of that decentralized style in their work. Digression, associative logic, a diffident or disappearing central subject, collective narration, the use of flickering perceptions, and an emphasis on the liminal are some of the elements of that style that have become powerful tools for non-fiction writers working long after Woolf's death. Moreover, as I will argue, that style is also an ethics and a politics in and of itself.

The roots of that style lay close to home for Woolf, in several senses, as I wrote in the *New England Review*.[3] In 1913, Roger Fry founded the design company called the Omega Workshop, located at 33 Fitzroy Square in London. His ideals were more or less socialist, crossed with a vision of artists as the new elite. In a just world, he wrote, society 'might choose its poets and painters and philosophers and deep investigators and make of such men and women a new kind of kings'.[4] To this end, he wished to employ

---

[2] Susan Sontag, 'The Way We Live Now', *The New Yorker*, 24 November 1986.
[3] D'Erasmo, 'Influence: A Practice in Three Wanders'.
[4] Roger Fry, *Vision and Design* (New York: Brentano's, 1924), 78.

artists to bring cutting-edge artistic movements into home design, into furniture, textile design, pottery, stained glass, and so on. The designers of Omega were members of the Bloomsbury Group—Vanessa Bell, Duncan Grant, Edward Wolfe, and Fry himself. Despite Fry's visionary intentions, the work produced by Omega was expensive, in limited quantities, and the company collapsed altogether in 1919.

But Fry's basic idea—an idea that derives from the earlier Arts and Crafts Movement—that the boundaries between the decorative and the fine arts should be erased is, indeed, quite radical. In one stroke, it frees art from gallery walls and the curators who decide what goes on them while simultaneously elevating the home to an artistic zone. It took art away from the academicians who governed it and delivered it to the people. The Omega designs for rugs and linens funnelled the new Modernist shapes and motifs into the infinite repetition favoured by domestic design. In doing so, they favoured the repeated image over any central image. They fundamentally altered the composition itself by removing the frame and multiplying the image. The centre was no longer relevant or even visible as a discrete entity.

Meanwhile, Fry's close friend Woolf was struggling to find her way toward a new kind of writing. Her first two novels, *The Voyage Out* (1915) and *Night and Day* (1919), were more or less conventional forays with a feminist edge. But by 1919 she was restless. In the 1925 essay 'Modern Fiction', she wrote:

> Examine for a moment an ordinary mind on an ordinary day. The mind receives a myriad impressions—trivial, fantastic, evanescent, or engraved with the sharpness of steel. From all sides they come, an incessant shower of innumerable atoms; and as they fall, as they shape themselves into the life of Monday or Tuesday (*E4* 160).

That last phrase, of course, is the title of the title story in the collection *Monday or Tuesday* (1921), the first book Woolf published with the Hogarth Press—established by her husband, Leonard—in a print run of a thousand copies, with woodcuts by her sister, Vanessa Bell. The press liberated Woolf to be, as she put it, 'the only woman in England free to write what I like' (*D3* 43). *Jacob's Room* (1922), the novel that followed *Monday or Tuesday*, was also published by Hogarth, as were all her books.

From this point forward, the fully brilliant Woolf came into being. Liberated from conventional publishing, she was liberated as well from the conventional notions of the time concerning character, consciousness, and narrative. In the essay 'Character in Fiction', she throws down the gauntlet to her immediate predecessors such as Arnold Bennett, H.G. Wells, and Hugh Walpole when she argues, essentially, for insight and metaphor over reams of realistic description of houses, clothing, and landscape. 'Those tools are not our tools', she exhorts the aspiring writers of her time, 'and that business is not our business. For us those conventions are ruin, those tools are death' (*E3* 430).

Her tools were different, closer to her compatriots in Omega than to literary predecessors such as Walpole and Bennett. The evidence for this web of influence is subtle, but palpable. Both Woolf and Fry were strongly influenced by the Impressionists and Post-Impressionists, who loosened the central object from its moorings, setting it adrift and dissolving it in perception. At the same time, Woolf's ties to Fry were so close that she wrote and published his biography in 1940. She was famously ambivalent—or even actively resistant—to writing that biography. Nevertheless, she casts Fry as a modernist hero, a sensitive, multiply talented, extraordinarily intelligent man, a revolutionary of the new aesthetic the members of the Bloomsbury Group both produced in their work and embodied in their lives. Over and over, she remarks upon his vigorous curiosity, his openness to transformation, and, not least, the many ways in which his aesthetics and his life were inextricable from each other. Of his later life, she writes that he had found 'a balance between the emotions and the intellect, between Vision and Design' (*RF* 245). Whatever mixed feelings she had about the man, and the biography, clearly she valued this balance in him, and saw its pursuit as central to his life story. The only other biographies she wrote were *Flush* (1933), from the point of view of Elizabeth Barrett Browning's cocker spaniel, and *Orlando* (1928), the fabulistic fictional biography inspired by the life of her lover Vita Sackville-West. Her biography of Fry was the penultimate book she published before her suicide in 1941. Like Fry, Woolf sought that balance of Vision and Design; it seems telling that she used that particular title of one of Fry's books to figure the emotion and the intellect. 'Design' is a very different word than, say, 'structure' or 'architecture' or 'plot' or even 'art'. It is visual, more commonly used in relation to clothing, buildings, and graphics than it is to, say, novels.

What one sees in Woolf's work as she made her breakthrough around 1919 could be called a revolution in design: an extraordinary intricacy and suppleness in the use of visual patterning in her fiction and, further, a radical use of what one might call the ethics of that patterning to structure her fiction overall. *Monday or Tuesday* contains the short piece 'Kew Gardens', in which the narrative point of view flows seamlessly among the insects, the people, the city at large, the past, the present, the real and imagined, the living and the dead, with no boundaries or hesitation whatsoever. Scale shifts constantly, vertiginously, gorgeously. But it also makes continual use of repeated visual patterns, a method that Woolf expanded considerably in the novel that followed it, *Jacob's Room*.

Consider this short passage from *Jacob's Room*, where young Jacob is sailing with a friend around the Cornwall coast:

> The Scilly Isles were turning bluish; and suddenly blue, purple, and green flushed the sea; left it grey; struck a stripe which vanished; but when Jacob had got his shirt over his head the whole floor of the waves was blue and white, rippling and crisp, though now and again a broad purple mark appeared, like a bruise; or there floated an entire emerald tinged with yellow. He plunged. He gulped in water, spat it out, struck with his right arm, struck with his left, was towed by a rope, gasped, splashed, and was hauled on board. (*JR* 61–2)

Here, the colours are, in fact, the plot. We begin at 'bluish', which then multiplies into 'blue, purple, and green' that flush the sea then empty it of colour ('left it grey'), then strike a stripe; the verbs, and the agency, belong to the colours, which drive the action. The blue is the first note rung again in the second sentence, followed again by the purple, and then, as before, by the green, but the green now shifts to 'emerald', ringing a change on the pattern and changing the visual rhythm as well as the sonic one. The emerald tows in its wake a little yellow (which is, of course, a constituent of green). Meanwhile, Jacob takes off his shirt, swims, and is 'hauled' in, like a fish, but the colours through which he swims constitute an active narrative medium of their own, a zone of perpetual transformation, a body ('like a bruise') that is not a human body, but that is abundantly physical, responsive, and generative. As every child knows, blue is a component of purple; blue and yellow are components of green; as the initial blue, which is actually a reflection of the Scilly Isles, blends with other colours, the multiple iterations of colour that result 'flush' the sea, like bringing blood to the surface of skin, but blood of a different colour and kind than human blood and the 'skin' is the surface of the water. Jacob, by contrast, is an isolated, impermeable noun. When he gulps the water, it does not change him, or the water. Nothing is generated by his interaction with the water. The change and interactions, arranged in and as a repetitive visual pattern, belong to the colours.

This kind of patterning suffuses *Jacob's Room*, scene after scene. All lyrical enough, one might even say, decorative enough, very nice, very Post-Impressionist, and so on. But this does not get at the brilliance of *Jacob's Room*. The brilliance of *Jacob's Room* is that Woolf uses this aesthetic of patterning and repetition to tell the entire story of Jacob's life, birth to death, on its edges, often without him being, literally, present at all—we see him, we infer him, like the colours in the aforementioned scene, even when he isn't being named. Jacob is a refrain, a textual recurrence, a collection of repeated impressions: around him cluster, over and over, the sea, books, beauty (his own and the world's), a series of messy, well-appointed rooms. It is as if he is a colour made of the reflections of all the colours of the world around him. We never know him, not really. His character, such as it is, is pointedly, limpidly diffuse. He repeats in an open, syncopated rhythm until he disappears, leaving an empty room behind him after his death in the war: 'the rooms are shapely, the ceilings high; over the doorways a rose or a ram's skull is carved in the wood' (*JR* 93–4). Jacob, like Sontag's mortally ill man in 'The Way We Live Now', is more the point around which the world of the novel revolves than the character driving it; he's like Woolf's famous mark on the wall from her short piece of the same name, or like Wallace Stevens's jar on a hill in Tennessee. There are several passages that describe a room of Jacob's that he isn't even in, invoking him through his objects, his shoes ('His slippers were incredibly shabby, like boats burnt to the water's rim' is just one such description), his walls, his doorways, his furniture (*JR* 49).

Moreover, this aesthetic of patterning, repetition, of spirals of self that curve upward and upward toward death is not decorative, not a particularly elegant way of compressing information. It implies an ethics, an envisioning of fiction as a way of life, which is to say: Woolf demonstrates over and over that every life—no matter how deeply felt individually, no matter how unique we feel ourselves to be (and are)—is exquisitely, hopelessly enclosed in an overall pattern of life and death, of colour and light and movement, over which no single consciousness, not even the Queen's, is master. Ironically, for a woman who was herself such a great writer, she doesn't appear to believe in Greatness. Instead, throughout Woolf's work, we see that we are woven into a fabric much larger than ourselves—often figured as a city, or a day, or a garden, or a single house—and the writer reveals the shining warp and woof of that fabric, the web of interconnections not necessarily ever fully known by the characters themselves. For example, in *Mrs Dalloway*, Lady Bruton, beginning to doze after lunch, imagines everyone she loves being 'attached to her by a thin thread ... which would stretch and stretch, get thinner and thinner ... as if one's friends were attached to one's body ... by a thin thread ... [like] a single spider's thread' (*MD* 101). Each of us is a mark on the wall, a thread in a vast pattern not woven by any single creature. This is not a decorative technique. This is not a clever way to write description. This is an ethics, a vision of what it is to be alive in the world. It essentially takes the long, generous view of human desire, the view suffused with the knowledge that it passes—all desires, all our most wilful acts, our most heroic stances and worst blunders alike, pass into the glorious, collective hum and blur of the human. On the last page of *Jacob's Room*, after Jacob's death in World War I, his old friend Bonamy looks out the window to see vans, buses, and horses; engines, brakes, and voices are all sounding in the London street below. When Bonamy says, 'Jacob! Jacob!' his voice raised in grief might be simply one among many at that moment, on that day, in that city, in that world (*JR* 247).

Similarly, in the very last sentences of 'Kew Gardens', the point of view pulls farther and farther back, beginning with the everyday noises in that public space:

> Voices. Yes, voices. Wordless voices, breaking the silence suddenly with such depth of contentment, such passion of desire, or, in the voices of children, such freshness of surprise; breaking the silence? But there was no silence; all the time the motor omnibuses were turning their wheels and changing their gear; like a vast nest of Chinese boxes all of wrought steel turning ceaselessly one within another the city murmured; on the top of which the voices cried aloud and the petals of myriads of flowers flashed their colours into the air. (*CSF* 95)

Synaesthesia organizes this passage. The separation between the voices and the colours is lifted and they flow into one another. As with the colours in the earlier passage cited from *Jacob's Room*, the sounds here are the actors in the scene, not the people making the sounds. They flow vigorously from voices to gears to steel turning to the overall 'murmur' of the city itself and back to voices with their own logic and choreography. By the time we get to the flowers '[flashing] their colours into the air', the colours seem somehow to be sonic as well, another sort of thing that is released into, and transmitted by, the air. The patterning is Woolf's *ars poetica* and, indeed, her genius. In *A Room of One's Own*, Woolf argued eloquently against the system of values that asserted that important books deal with wars, while trivial ones deal with 'the feelings of women in a drawing-room' (*ARO* 56). As Woolf and the other members of the Bloomsbury Group attempted to take down these barriers of value between wars and drawing rooms—Lytton Strachey, of course, was the first English translator of Freud, who, one might say, placed a high value on interior space—aesthetic barriers between the 'decorative' and the 'artistic' began tumbling as well. The homey, decorative, domestic use of patterning—on wallpaper, on sheets, on dresses—became a new way not only of looking at but also of understanding and conceptualizing, the world. Via this aesthetic of vision and design, we see that we are all part of a larger, very beautiful pattern that repeats over and over. As seen on a skirt or a sheet of wallpaper, a flower or a bus or a person might all have the same visual weight, or the flower might be greater than the person or the bus. The principles of visual design do not conform to human biases about value or obey patriarchal structures of power. No great man, or even woman, weaves the pattern of existence. That thin thread winds them all round.

This conception of Woolf's—the spiralling narrative design that structures and drives her fiction—seems to be shared by creative non-fiction writers working today such as Rebecca Solnit, Maggie Nelson, Maureen McClane, and others. If *A Room of One's Own* prescribed agency both economically and spatially for women artists, the decentralized method of Woolf's fiction offered some ideas about what the woman artist might see from the windows of that room, not unlike what Bonamy saw from the windows of Jacob's room: a vast pattern of life over which no single consciousness or narrative reigns. Hisham Matar observed in *The New Yorker* that the Woolfian sentence is:

> a freely progressing, long, fractured series of observations and insights, unburdened and unhurried by the need to tell the 'story,' yet moving with the unrelenting progression of a scalpel. It steals away, like 'a light stealing under water,' revealing not merely information but the cadence and temper of inner lives, and how they resonate against the images and sensations of the physical world.[5]

The motion of that freely progressing sentence is also visible in the freely progressing structure of non-fiction by Solnit, Nelson, and many others.

Of course, this Woolfian influence on non-fiction is not limited to women writers. W.G. Sebald, in an interview with Michael Silverblatt on the literary chat show *Bookworm*, discussed how reading her essay 'The Death of the Moth' taught him that 'a subject which at first glance seems quite far removed from the undeclared concern of a book can encapsulate that concern'.[6] Sebald was freed to pursue his own radical wanderings by reading Woolf, among others; his digressive, *sui generis* work was not only made possible for him as a writer by Woolf but we as readers, particularly readers in English, are also able to read him because we have long read Woolf. If a reader has read the freely progressing Woolfian sentence, that reader can read the freely progressing Sebaldian book, which works in something of the same way.

The novelist and essayist Teju Cole, whose style is notably digressive and associative, has remarked on Woolf's influence in several pieces, particularly on the 'intensity of her attention to life, and the epiphanic moments that intermittently illuminated the gloom' of her last years.[7] His novel *Open City* ranges at will geographically over New York

---

[5] Hisham Matar, 'The Unsaid: The Silence of Virginia Woolf', *The New Yorker*, 10 November 2014.

[6] W. G. Sebald on the literary chat show *Bookworm*, hosted by Michael Silverblatt and produced by KCRW, available at www.kcrw.com/culture/shows/bookworm/w-g-sebald and as a podcast.

[7] Teju Cole, 'Blind Spot', in *Known and Strange Things* (New York: Random House, 2016) 379.

City as the narrator wanders it, and intellectually over myriad topics, memories, and observations. Cole appears to find a sympatico cosmopolitan sensibility in Woolf, because of her 'sense of embracing human variety ... that emotional range ... makes her much more valuable to me than Henry James'.[8] He allows that while she was as class-bound as James, she is 'freer'.[9] Again and again, that word—'free'—comes up when writers talk about Woolf's influence on them. She made them feel free, at least on the page.

Woolf's wish that all women would be freed economically and politically did not come true in her lifetime (she herself only got the vote in 1918, when she was thirty-six years old), nor in ours. However, in 1919 she liberated the English sentence and, in doing so, also liberated readers of any and all genders to read more freely than they ever had before.

Also liberated were certain contemporary non-fiction writers who have a distinctly Woolfian echo, or way of moving, in their prose. The turn of the twenty-first century saw the rise of what might be called the New Bricoleurs, a group that includes Rebecca Solnit, Maggie Nelson, Leslie Jamison, Lia Purpura, Durga Chew-Bose, Sarah Manguso, Rachel Cohen, Maureen McClane, and Akiko Busch. These writers share a method of narrative design—which is to say, an apparently un-designed design that favours bricolage over a unitary structure that drives toward a single, argumentative point. These writers move from the personal to the historical, from high to low culture, from statistic to speculation, and in some cases from non-fiction to fiction, as if by ungoverned and ungovernable interior forces or chance encounters. Indeed, Rachel Cohen's 2005 book *A Chance Meeting: Intertwined Lives of American Writers and Artists* uses actual meetings—some momentary, some lifelong friendships—between various American writers and artists and writes into these meetings with the force and intimacy of fiction, freely imagining the thoughts and feelings of the subjects.

Many of these writers specifically reference Woolf as an influence. Maggie Nelson included *To the Lighthouse* on a list of her ten favourite books of all time[10] and her mother's PhD dissertation was on Woolf.[11] Claudia Rankine, whose book *Citizen*, a work, simultaneously, of fiction, non-fiction, prose, poetry, visual imagery, and criticism, frequently invoked Woolf and responded to imagery from Woolf's texts in her own. Rankine might well not include herself in the aforementioned list of writers. In interviews she has said that, prior to writing *Citizen*, 'I was writing poems that nobody understood ... and they had to do with my own thoughts about this and that, and they were involved with, like, Virginia Woolf'.[12]

---

[8] Teju Cole, 'Teju Cole Reminds Us of Life Beyond Politics, and the Beauty of Art', interview by Adam Fitzgerald, *Lithub*, 8 November 2016, https://lithub.com/teju-cole-reminds-us-of-life-beyond-politics-and-the-beauty-of-art.
[9] Teju Cole, *Lithub* interview, 8 November 2016.
[10] Maggie Nelson, 'My 10 Favorite Books: Maggie Nelson', *The New York Times*, 7 October 2016.
[11] Hilton Als, 'Immediate Family: Maggie Nelson's life in words', *The New Yorker*, 18 April 2016.
[12] Claudia Rankine, as transcribed in 'Claudia Rankine: "I Think We Need to Be Frightened", Highlights from Her Talk at BAM's Eat, Drink, and Be Literary' by Emily Temple, *Lithub*, 11 May 2017.

In fact, Rankine's 2001 book of poetry *Plot*, muses on Woolf in several long sequences. The eight-part poem sequence 'Eight Sketches' is subtitled 'After Lily Briscoe's Purple Triangle'. Because *Plot* concerns, among many other things, the ambivalence of a painter named Liv about her pregnancy, 'Eight Sketches' refigures Briscoe's famous abstraction (the purple triangle) of Mrs Ramsay reading to James as a meditation on motherhood and the body of the mother. The purple triangle becomes 'pelvic-shaped',[13] a 'purpling bruise',[14] and a 'bruised purple surface'.[15] In another long sequence, 'Painting after the death of Virginia Woolf entitled Beached Debris', Liv creates an image of Woolf drowned in the river Ouse. At one point she 'applies a cold cloth to clot Woolf's drips',[16] as if bandaging an actual body. At another point in the sequence, she (mis)quotes *The Years*: ' "What would the world be with an I in it?" (Virginia Woolf)'.[17] In the Afterword to the poem, she seems to close the conversation with Woolf and Lily Briscoe by a moment in which a person called Mom or M. reflects that 'She was trying to come up with something: Ouse to Other)'[18] and 'M. needing Woolf for a model was stopped dead in madder hue.'[19] One has the sense that Liv no longer needed or could identify with Woolf as a model once she became a mother, and that Woolf's suicide was a termination point for a female artist beyond which she intended to live—'Ouse to Other'. Rankine has indicated that after James Byrd was killed, her subject matter and political consciousness changed radically.[20] Her freely moving method, however, did not change, except, perhaps, to intensify. *Plot* moves very freely within language, but *Citizen* widens substantially to include visual images ranging from paintings to screen grabs; scripts; essayistic reflections on Serena Williams, Judith Butler, and a YouTube character among many others; satire; and accounts of myriad racist microaggressions. In *Plot*, Rankine shed the image of suicidal female artist, buried her in a painting, and went on in *Citizen* to take artistic freedom to greater heights and depths than she had ever taken it before.

Akiko Busch, in her essay 'Rereading Mrs Dalloway', references Clarissa Dalloway's 'flickering sense of presence' as an image of 'transitory identity', an image in which she finds particular resonance in her discussion of the potential power of social invisibility as experienced by, say, middle-aged women like Clarissa.[21] Clarissa, she writes, 'found that being unseen was not a matter of being ignored or dismissed, but of being intuitively present and fully integrated into the world around her'.[22] Busch links Dalloway

---

[13] Claudia Rankine, *Plot* (New York: Grove Press, 2001), 40.
[14] Rankine, *Plot*, 41.
[15] Rankine, *Plot*, 43.
[16] Rankine, *Plot*, 60.
[17] Rankine, *Plot*, 62. Woolf quote adapted from *The Years*, 218.
[18] Rankine, *Plot*, 101.
[19] Rankine, *Plot*, 101.
[20] Rankine, *Lithub*, 11 May 2017.
[21] Akiko Busch, 'Rereading *Mrs Dalloway*' in *How to Disappear* (New York: Penguin, 2019), 142–3.
[22] Busch, *How to Disappear*, 146.

to dancers, Alfred Hitchcock's *The Lady Vanishes*,[23] Whitney Otto's novel *Now You See Her*,[24] psychological studies on social status and altruism,[25] Mystique from the *X-Men* movie series, a collaboration between the model Versuchka and photographer Holger Trulzsch, and various other cultural points as she considers the possibility that 'Opacity itself can work as a connective tissue.'[26]

Jamison has said that when she read Woolf's essay 'On Being Ill':

> it felt like encountering a long-lost relative: the banner I'd never known I'd always been fighting under: *Bodies matter—we can't escape them—they're full of stories—how do we tell them?* Her argument might have the urgency of a battle cry but it's also vulnerable; it's posing questions; it's got mess and nerve—it's leaking some strange fluid from beneath its garments, hard to tell in the twilight, maybe pus or tears or blood. Even her syntax feels bodily—full of curves and joints and twists, shifting and stretching the skin of her sentences.[27]

After reading this essay, Jamison was freed to compose her book *The Empathy Exams* and centre it on the poetics of physicality, and vice versa, a topic she had felt ashamed of (and been advised against) pursuing previously.[28] Durga Chew-Bose's 2017 essay collection *Too Much and Not the Mood* takes its title from a 1931 diary entry of Woolf's.

Essayist Lia Purpura has written that Woolf's concept of 'moments of being' constitutes an ethics that Purpura calls an 'ecology of presence'. Purpura writes:

> her drive to observe her own perception, to take an ice-core sample of an instant, or of a day, or of a memory, is at heart a *restorative gesture* in the face of her era's intensified speed, instability, and violence. Woolf's particular flavor of modernism is rooted in the drive to gather, hold, and deepen moments, to make the shimmering moment of perception the base upon which 'reality' rests. Her sensibility honors the fleeting, fragile instances of a person's life. These small, often untethered moments saved for use (like string in wartime), teased forth, and accepted as a partial picture (for it's a 'sketch' of the past she wrote, and not a 'portrait')—these form the basis of a sensibility muscular enough to meet, as she says, 'the myriad impressions of an ordinary day, trivial, fantastic, evanescent or engraved with the sharpness of steel' (E4 160).
>
> This drive to *preserve* a fleeting, fragmentary genuineness, a shimmery state, fat with existence, to recognize and assert it, to keep it from the ruinous effects of the war, commerce, the strictures of upper-class British society, and more—this drive I'll call an *ecology of presence*.[29]

---

[23] Busch, *How to Disappear*, 140.
[24] Busch, *How to Disappear*, 141.
[25] Busch, *How to Disappear*, 144–5.
[26] Busch, *How to Disappear*, 150.
[27] Leslie Jamison, qtd in Joe Fassler, '"We Sweat, Crave, and Itch All Day": Why Writing About Bodies Is Vital', *The Atlantic*, 1 April 2014.
[28] Jamison, *The Atlantic*, 1 April 2014.
[29] Lia Purpura, 'Woolf and The Ecology of Presence', *TriQuarterly*, 27 August 2014.

We can see from the work of these innovative writers that there are, in a sense, at least two facets of Woolf's vision and design, her ethical aesthetics and aesthetic ethics, that have had a strong influence on the writers who came after her. One is the more or less straightforward argument of *A Room of One's Own*: women, and we might extend this to all human beings, need economic agency and full access to education and political participation in order to be accountable and empowered citizens. *Three Guineas* continues this line of thought in arguing that those who are not fully empowered citizens cannot simply be folded into current political movements, no matter how necessary those movements might be, or how much the disempowered may agree with their aims.

The other facet is what we see in Woolf's narrative design: an aesthetic that is also an ethics that values the transitory, the embodied, the unbounded, the decentralized, the subjective, the wayward, and the unstable nature of perception itself. At times in Woolf's work, and that of her literary progeny, these two facets appear to be one; at others, they diverge. Like Woolf, these latter-day writers do not live in a world where all bodies and minds are universally free. As with Woolf, and Rankine, these writers deal in various ways with the tension between the degrees of their personal and intellectual freedom and the freedom denied to others. In a time of political turmoil, that 'unburdened and unhurried'[30] Woolfian sentence Matar describes might seem an unaffordable luxury. Who can wander when it's time to march? Serpentine sentences don't fit on protest signs. More ominously, aren't some people rendered more evanescent than others? Where do liminality and marginality converge to the detriment of some of the citizens of this world? And what is the writer's role in that world, which is, after all, lived off the page and on contested ground? As of this writing, it costs £16.50 to enter Kew Gardens. Which people can afford that, and why? Alternately, to a writer such as Purpura, the Woolfian way of moving through and in language might seem itself an act of restoration and survival, a powerful method of resistance to 'war, commerce',[31] and the barriers of class.

This tension is highly visible in the trajectory of the work of Rebecca Solnit. In her essay 'Woolf's Darkness: Embracing the Inexplicable', she states directly that:

> Virginia Woolf is present in five of my books in this century, *Wanderlust*, my history of walking; *A Field Guide to Getting Lost*, a book about the uses of wandering and the unknown; *Inside Out*, which focused on house and home fantasies; *The Faraway Nearby*, a book about storytelling, empathy, illness, and unexpected connections; and *Hope in the Dark*, a small book exploring popular power and how change unfolds.[32]

At least three of those five books involve extensive, literal wandering—walking, driving, flying—and all of them wander at will through self and culture, near and far, the present moment, and myriad points in history. For Solnit, Woolf's work granted that

---

[30] Matar, *The New Yorker*, 10 November 2014.
[31] Lia Purpura, *TriQuarterly*, 27 August 2014.
[32] Rebecca Solnit, *Men Explain Things to Me* (Chicago: Haymarket Books, 2014), 89.

permission. She writes, 'All of Woolf's work as I know it constitutes a sort of Ovidian metamorphosis where the freedom sought is the freedom to continue becoming, exploring, wandering, going beyond.'[33]

Solnit is not Woolfian at the level of the sentence. Her work is not painterly in that way; she doesn't make extensive use of images; her sentences are of moderate length and complexity. However, the organization of the five books she mentions resonate deeply with the structure of the Woolfian sentence, and of Woolf's prose, especially her fiction, in general. In the space of a few pages, Solnit might move from a library where she's working in Iceland, to the history of terns, to the white nights of the far north, to the profound value of night and darkness, to mazes, labyrinths, and the human inner ear.[34] The liberation she found in Woolf seems to have allowed her to move not only literally, but also intellectually, taking unpredictable routes over the page. For example, what is the central subject of *The Faraway Nearby*? It is not determinable. It is, simultaneously, about fairy tales, Alzheimer's disease, family dynamics, breast cancer, *Frankenstein*, apricots, and Iceland. None of these topics is privileged over any other. Instead, Solnit moves fluidly from *topos* to *topos* without necessarily resolving any of the particular narratives that are in play; without, as it were, arriving at any final destination. She wanders the earth. Her mind wanders the universe, enacting that freedom to continue becoming at will.

As Solnit herself suggests, she did not, perhaps could not, as a writer, remain in that open-ended Woolfian mode intellectually. Beginning around 2014, Solnit's work became increasingly focused on the American politics of the moment, particularly regarding gender issues. Certainly, those concerns threaded through her earlier work. Her 2008 essay 'Men Explain Things to Me'—in which, among other things, a man attempted to demonstrate his superiority to her by citing a book that, unbeknownst to him, she had written—launched the phrase 'mansplaining' into the culture. However, as significant portions of the United States moved to the right, and with the election of Donald Trump, Solnit did not seem to feel as free to wander in any sense. Her 2017 essay collection, *The Mother of All Questions*, focused exclusively on women's concerns, loosely organized around tropes of silence and breaking silence. Even here, she invokes Woolf, but with a difference. She begins the volume by recounting an incident wherein, at the end of a talk she gave on Woolf, during the question and answer period, 'the subject that seemed to most interest a number of people was whether Woolf should have had children'.[35] This difference in the presentation of Woolf—from powerful liberator to misperceived and pathologized woman whom Solnit patiently attempts to rescue from misogynistic diagnoses—might be said to mark a shift in Solnit's sensibility. From unbounded wanderer, she has become a defender, particularly of the rights of women, and a guardian of all those rendered vulnerable by systems of oppression. Moreover, her later work does not tend to move from association to association in the manner of the

---

[33] Solnit, *Men Explain Things to Me*, 103–4.
[34] Rebecca Solnit, *The Faraway Nearby* (New York: Penguin, 2013), 181–8.
[35] Rebecca Solnit, 'The Mother of All Questions', *Harper's*, 3 August 2015.

five volumes she cited. Generally, it delivers sobering, incisive, complete arguments with specific and identifiable points. It is advocacy of high literary quality, driven by a sense of political urgency. Solnit appears to have moved from liberated voyager to liberator herself, seeking, via clear and cogent civic argument, to break the chains that bind large portions of humanity.

A much earlier post-Woolfian, the poet and essayist Annie Dillard, turned this tension inside out in her 1976 piece 'The Death of a Moth'. Dillard's 1975 book *Pilgrim at Tinker Creek*, a blend of personal narrative, scientific fact, the exploration of the natural world, theology, and history, seems to partake of Woolf's ethics of decentralization, a sequence of moments of being noted by one particular pilgrim during one particular year in her life. In her short essay 'The Death of a Moth', she took the image Woolf used in 'The Death of the Moth' and refashioned it from the subtly political to the spiritually personal. As W.G. Sebald noted in that same *Bookworm* interview, 'The Death of the Moth' doesn't seem to have anything to do with anything other than a moth dying, but the sense of analogy to far more worldly concerns is clear. He said:

> And it's written somewhere, chronologically speaking, between the battlefields of the Somme and the concentration camps erected by my compatriots. There is no reference made to the battlefields of the Somme in this passage, but one knows as a reader of Virginia Woolf that she was greatly perturbed by the First World War, by its aftermath, by the damage it did to people's souls—the souls of those who got away and, naturally, of those who perished.[36]

By contrast, Dillard's 'The Death of a Moth' also concerns a moth's demise, but in this case it is a female moth whose head is on fire, and Dillard observes her immolation as she is trying to summon her own dampened passion to write. Dillard writes:

> She burned for two hours without changing, without bending or leaning—only glowing within like a building fire glimpsed through silhouetted walls, like a hollow saint, like a flame-faced virgin gone to God, while I read by her light, kindled, while Rimbaud in Paris burnt out his brains in a thousand poems, while night pooled wetly at my feet.[37]

Dillard does not generally cite Woolf as an influence (she most often cites Thoreau), but she clearly calls on Woolf's famous essay during a time when she was, she writes, seeking the inspiration to write that she had had as a teenager reading Rimbaud. The image of the burning moth, an image she takes explicitly from Woolf, 'kindles' her. The essay ends on a sense of her renewal in her faith in writing, and in herself as a writer. Woolf's obliquely political image is transformed in Dillard's homage into a spiritual image, an image of a saint, burning herself up in her belief. Like Solnit, like Jamison, like Purpura, Dillard is

---

[36] W. G. Sebald, *Bookworm* interview, see note 6.
[37] Annie Dillard, 'The Death of a Moth', *Harper's*, 5 March 1976.

freed as a writer by Woolf, in this instance by a single image, or perhaps it would be more accurate to say that she is freed by remaking a famous image of Woolf's into an image closer to her own aesthetic and ethical bent. She introjects Woolf's method—using the death of a moth to embody much greater and more consequential sacrifices—and reinvigorates her own practice in so doing.

The tension between a style of decentralization and subject matter of great urgency is not necessarily resolvable, nor is it required to be. Woolf's tremendous innovations are not required to suit every literary or political project. However, it may be the case that this tension is least onerous when the ethics of dissolving the putative subject are most aligned with the themes of the text. For example, by making Jacob, the bright young image of the British Empire pre-World War I, into a mark on the wall, however beloved a mark he was, Woolf redistributes the value of one sort of life over others. Jacob is not the point, and his loss is not the point. The world is the point. Or perhaps it would be more accurate to say that there is no single point of highest value. Everyone around Jacob and the sounds in the street are as important as he is.

Non-fiction writers, as I have shown, have taken from the style of Woolf's fiction what they have needed to free their own work. Sontag took her polyvocality, Rankine the abstract consciousness of Lily Briscoe and Woolf's freedom with language, Sebald her sleight of hand with the placement of subject, Purpura her emphasis on fleeting and embodied moments of perception, Jamison her physicality within language, Cole her flaneur's way of moving through the world, Busch her porousness of identity, Solnit her freedom of juxtaposition as well as her feminism, Dillard her use of very small things to suggest far larger, even spiritual, matters. Few, however, appear to have wished to undermine or hollow out their ostensible subject matter by means of design. They have not wished to redistribute value by dissolving the very thing they appear to be discussing.

However, in her 2015 book-length essay *The Argonauts*, Maggie Nelson does just this with—ironically enough when the literary ancestor is Woolf—gender. Organized as a series of associative fragments that range from the deeply personal to Wittgenstein,[38] D.W. Winnicott,[39] *The Shining*,[40] the poet James Schuyler,[41] visual artist Catherine Opie, and myriad other topics, *The Argonauts* unfolds and refolds around a period in Nelson's life during which her fluidly gendered partner, Harry Dodge, had a mastectomy and began taking testosterone while she herself was pregnant and ultimately gave birth. Nelson uses the mythic image of the Argonauts, who entirely rebuilt the boat on which they were sailing across the ocean in the middle of the journey, not only as the title but also as the aesthetic of both text and theme of her book. Nelson and Dodge both literally and figuratively wander among, around, through, under, over, and near gender as they rebuild their lives. Nelson does not assert gender, or even champion the rights of the fluidly gendered, via a digressive or associative style. She dissolves it. What we think we

---

[38] Maggie Nelson, *The Argonauts* (Minneapolis: Graywolf Press, 2015), 3.
[39] Nelson, *Argonauts*, 33.
[40] Nelson, *Argonauts*, 56.
[41] Nelson, *Argonauts*, 103.

know or feel about gender (also love, family, and language, among other things) is her Jacob, her mark on the wall, her lighthouse to which arrival is incidental at best. Gender identity is not the point, but the departure point; not the subject, but an occasion for multiple iterations of subjectivity. Here, diffusing any sense of urgency when it comes to delineating gender is, in fact, what the book wants to do. Gender, suggests Nelson, is the opposite of urgent, not an answer but a perpetual question. It is wayward, liminal, collaborative, contingent, mobile, and in a continual, open-ended process of transformation. The boat, always under construction, is always at sea. So is the book. Dissolution and digression are not just the method, but also the topic. An imperial approach to gender is precisely what Nelson seeks to subvert, and does.

As a writer, Woolf could give the reader an experience of freedom through the act of reading. She additionally gave the writers who came after her not only a style but also a way of perceiving reality itself that has proven to be astonishingly generative, particularly to those writers working in poetry and creative non-fiction. By exploding the idea of the central subject and, instead, seeing all subjects and subjectivities as matters of equal weight, Woolf freed non-fiction from all received hierarchies of value. The writers who have continued to make use of that freedom ask, in various ways and to various ends, What if everything and everyone mattered? What if no story had dominion over any other? What would the world look like to us then, and what would we make of all that we see?

Selected Bibliography

Als, Hilton, 'Immediate Family: Maggie Nelson's life in words', *The New Yorker*, 18 April 2016.
Busch, Akiko, *How to Disappear* (New York: Penguin, 2019).
Cole, Teju, *Known and Strange Things* (New York: Random House, 2016).
Dillard, Annie, 'The Death of a Moth', *Harper's*, 5 March 1976.
Jamison, Leslie, qtd in Joe Fassler, '"We Sweat, Crave, and Itch All Day": Why Writing About Bodies Is Vital', *The Atlantic*, 1 April 2014.
Matar, Hisham, 'The Unsaid: The Silence of Virginia Woolf', *The New Yorker*, 10 November 2014.
Nelson, Maggie, *The Argonauts* (Minneapolis: Graywolf Press, 2015).
Purpura, Lia, 'Woolf and The Ecology of Presence', *TriQuarterly*, 27 August 2014.
Rankine, Claudia, *Plot* (New York: Grove Press, 2001).
Sebald, W. G. on the literary chat show *Bookworm*, hosted by Michael Silverblatt and produced by KCRW, available at www.kcrw.com/culture/shows/bookworm/w-g-sebald.
Solnit, Rebecca, *Men Explain Things to Me* (Chicago: Haymarket, 2014).
Solnit, Rebecca, *The Mother of All Questions* (Chicago: Haymarket, 2017).
Sontag, Susan, 'The Way We Live Now', *The New Yorker*, 24 November 1986.

CHAPTER 38

VIRGINIA WOOLF, FILMMAKER

JACQUELINE SHIN

REGARDLESS of how Woolf may have imagined the future's interest in her life and works, she likely could never have imagined the extent to which she would become a cultural icon after her death—instantly recognizable, commodified, celebrated, fought over, and even feared. As Holly Williams summarizes, Woolf is:

> famous far beyond her work: people know [her] as an icon of 'the writer'—often with a side order of 'tortured genius' and 'difficult woman'. She's inspired countless books, films, plays, even ballets, and achieved notoriety as everything from lesbian icon to symbol of high art, from trailblazing feminist to ghastly snob. For many years, she was the best-selling postcard at the National Portrait Gallery: perhaps because it is so easy to see whatever we want in her image.[1]

This ubiquitous image Williams refers to of a youthful Virginia Stephen is notable for the sitter's preoccupied expression, which suggests an inwardness that the camera can capture but not access or reproduce. Taken in 1902, the black and white portrait now graces t-shirts and coffee mugs, book bags and smart phone covers bought and sold across the globe.

Woolf is part of a pantheon of iconic British authors with famous faces and huge fan bases, including William Shakespeare, Jane Austen, Charles Dickens, and James Joyce. Michael Cunningham, whose novel *The Hours* responds to and adapts both *Mrs Dalloway* and Woolf's life, insisted that no one but Woolf has 'inspired this level of devotion and fascination and adulation'; there 'aren't many figures in the twentieth century, or ever, really, who have inspired this particular kind of ardent, hair-splitting devotion'.[2]

---

[1] Holly Williams, 'From The Roaring Queen to Downton Abbey: the afterlives of Virginia Woolf', *New Statesman*, 28 February 2016.

[2] Michael Cunningham, qtd in Monica Latham, *A Poetics of Postmodernism and Neomodernism: Rewriting* Mrs Dalloway (London: Palgrave Macmillan, 2015), 1.

Surely, devotees of Austen ('Janeites') or worshipers of Shakespeare (practitioners of 'bardolatry') would challenge such extravagant claims. In fact, it is not the intensity of adoration for Woolf that sets her legacy apart; it is its doubleness—what Brenda Silver identifies, in *Virginia Woolf Icon*, as the 'double movement of iconization and iconoclasm' that her name and face conjure.[3] More than most authors, the love that Woolf has inspired is counterbalanced by an equally potent fear, one with deep roots in misogyny. Woolf's legacy has been (perhaps unsurprisingly) a uniquely contentious one.

According to Silver, the author's posthumous rise to iconic status, specifically within Anglo-America, is intimately tied up with second-wave feminism, with its 'shifting attitudes towards gender, sexuality, and cultural class'.[4] A transgressive figure, crossing the borders 'between high culture and popular culture, art and politics, masculinity and femininity, head and body, intellect and sexuality, heterosexuality and homosexuality, word and picture, beauty and horror', Woolf has been hailed by some as a revolutionary and cast by others as a monster, part sphinx, part medusa.[5] Different versions of a 'monstrous Woolf', childless and castrating, are evident in Edward Albee's *Who's Afraid of Virginia Woolf?* (1962), Alan Bennet's *Me, I'm Afraid of Virginia Woolf* (1978), and Hanif Kureishi's *Sammy and Rosie Get Laid* (1987).[6] There is also a gendered component to the depictions of a 'mad, sad Woolf', whose history of mental illness and tragic death by suicide cast a shadow over her body of works, quashing out the 'shimmering, inventive, life-affirming elements'.[7] As Williams ruefully observes, different versions of a charmless, 'miserable Woolf' 'brought back to life only to focus on her death', can be found in the film *The Hours* (1998), Katie Mitchell's play *Waves* (2006), and Wayne McGregor's ballet triptych *Woolf Works* (2015).[8]

Whether motivated by an impulse towards iconization or iconoclasm, creative responses to Woolf have tended to overlook her incredible multiplicity—a multiplicity that Maria DiBattista, in *Imagining Virginia Woolf*, deems 'the highest achievement' of Woolf's art.[9] In what follows, I limit my focus to a small number of contemporary (male) filmmakers who seem intent on acknowledging the richness of Woolf's *works* rather than engaging with the details of her life, riffing off her ideas to expand and focalize their own. Whereas in 1999, Silver could convincingly claim that Woolf's 'being a woman

---

[3] Brenda Silver, *Virginia Woolf Icon* (Chicago: Chicago University Press, 2000), 5.
[4] Silver, *Virginia Woolf Icon*, 4–5.
[5] Silver, *Virginia Woolf Icon*, 10–11.
[6] Silver, *Virginia Woolf Icon*, 82–3.
[7] Holly Williams, 'Virginia Woolf Should Live On, But Not Because of Her Death', *The Guardian*, 27 May 2015. As Patricia Cohen notes in 'The Nose Was the Final Straw', *New York Times*, 15 February 2003, 'For years the standard take on Woolf was as the invalid lady of Bloomsbury, a frail, snobbish madwoman.' Woolf's role as madwoman fits into the history of linking 'femaleness and madness' traced by Sandra M. Gilbert and Susan Gubar in their seminal work *The Madwoman in the Attic: The Woman Writer and the Nineteenth-Century Literary Imagination* (New Haven: Yale University Press, 1984), 62.
[8] Williams, 'Virginia Woolf should live on'. For all that these works present limited versions of Woolf herself, we should also acknowledge the richness and inventiveness of their responses to Woolf's writing.
[9] Maria DiBattista, *Imagining Virginia Woolf: An Experiment in Critical Biography* (Princeton: Princeton University Press, 2009), 10.

may ultimately be the most significant factor in her conflicting iconic representations', such a statement does not hold true in the twenty-first century, at least not in the medium of film.[10] For Mark Cousins, François Ozon, David Lowery, and Alex Garland, Virginia Woolf does not signify a (mad)woman, feminist, bisexual, lesbian, or elitist snob. Instead, she is embraced as one of them: that is, as an experimental 'filmmaker' and fiercely intelligent thinker.

Film is a medium that Woolf was fascinated by and theorized about, yet one in which her legacy has floundered. By bringing together an eclectic assortment of films, including *What Is This Film Called Love?* (2012), *Under the Sand* (2000), *A Ghost Story* (2017), and *Annihilation* (2018), I gesture towards an alternative legacy for Woolf, one in which she and her works are essentially vaporized and reconfigured. No longer are her biography or her body (including her nose) or even particular works at the forefront of her legacy.[11] Instead, Woolf is dispersed, part of a multitude, spread out into a web of intertextuality. For Cousins, Ozon, Lowery, Garland, and others, Woolf's gender and politics no longer seem to matter, and in my conclusion, I take up the significance of this 'neutering' of Woolf. What does it mean for a domesticated, safe—one might even say sanitized—version of Woolf to survive into the future?

Modernist fiction is notoriously difficult to adapt into film. First, *any* 'translation' of fiction into film encounters thorny challenges. In her 1926 essay 'The Cinema', Woolf famously attacks cinema as a rapacious predator gluttonously feeding upon all 'the famous novels of the world', with results 'disastrous to both'. As she sees it, the 'alliance' between fiction and film is an 'unnatural' one (*E4* 350). As novel readers, our intimate familiarity with the inside of characters' minds (such as Anna Karenina's) is outraged by the presentation of clumsy outward signs: bodies, costumes, gesticulations, actions, and props are meant to stand in for complex interiority. Writing just before the advent of synchronized sound in cinema, Woolf zeroes in on film's inability to convey the subtleties of thought and feeling. Although she does not discuss narration explicitly, she is pinpointing what happens when the narrative voice is lost in translation. Without a narrator there is nobody and nothing to step into the void when a character is silent or when their words are at odds with what is going on in the quickness of their mind or body. Impeded by the photographic nature of the medium, which is devised to 'record and reveal physical reality', adaptations of novels, according to Woolf, are doomed to fail.[12]

Woolf imagines a future in which film evolves into a more abstract medium, when some 'secret language' of visual signs such as a squiggle can almost instantaneously convey the 'likeness' of a thought. In the meantime, Woolf wants film to play to its strengths, insisting that what is 'accessible to words, and to words alone, the cinema must avoid' (*E4* 351). So much of modernist fiction, including the works of Woolf, Joyce,

---

[10] Silver, *Virginia Woolf Icon*, 10.
[11] See Cohen, 'The Nose Was the Final Straw'.
[12] Siegfried Kracauer, *Theory of Film: The Redemption of Physical Reality* (Princeton: Princeton University Press, 1960), 2.

Joseph Conrad, and Marcel Proust, is accessible to words alone, rendering the already difficult task of adapting novels into film even more challenging. Woolf's works in particular are unimaginable without her narrative consciousness, which picks up on visual and verbal patterns to thread voices and lives together only to pull them apart again, registering sensations trembling through the air with the accuracy of a seismometer. Woolf's narrators have an unprecedented freedom of movement that only language can convey. She is an intensely visual writer but also fundamentally a literary and discursive one. Who would be foolhardy enough, given all this, and knowing Woolf's own disdain for adaptations, to adapt her novels into film?

A few brave filmmakers have made the attempt, although, as Earl G. Ingersoll notes in *Screening Woolf: Virginia Woolf on/and/in Film*, the list is a very short one.[13] It includes a BBC adaptation of *To the Lighthouse* by Hugh Stoddart and Colin Gregg (1983); Eileen Atkins's performative reading of *A Room of One's Own* (1990); Sally Potter's take on *Orlando* (1992); and Marleen Gorris's adaptation of *Mrs Dalloway* (1997). For the most part, these works endeavour to remain faithful to the original source text. In Potter's notes on adapting *Orlando*—the most critically acclaimed and noteworthy of these adaptations—she insisted that her task was to 'find a way of remaining true to the spirit of the book and to Virginia Woolf's intentions, whilst being ruthless with changing the book in any way necessary to make it work cinematically'.[14] Woolf's 'direct addresses to her reader' are translated into Tilda Swinton's expressive and amusing 'looks to the camera'; Potter brings the novel up to her present moment, celebrating some of the wins of feminism that Woolf in 1928 could only look forward to. She claims that 'it would have been a disservice to Virginia Woolf to remain slavish to the letter of the book'; we might say that her film is successful to the extent that it departs from Woolf's novel, whereas the other adaptations are more 'slavishly' tied to their originals.[15]

The most well-known and commercially successful cinematic response to a novel by Woolf, *The Hours*, is, as Ingersoll describes it, 'a variety of "bio-pic", in which "Woolf" is a "fictional" character, caught in a web not of her own making'.[16] Stephen Daldry (director) and David Hare (screenplay) adapt Cunningham's novel, which 'adapts' *Mrs Dalloway*, weaving the novel together with two other narratives—one of which is Woolf's life—that mirror and intersect with the novel in significant ways. Both versions of *The Hours* are not so much adaptations as forms of homage. Cunningham claimed that rather than rewriting *Mrs Dalloway* he saw what he was doing as 'more akin to music, to jazz, where a musician will play improvisations on an existing piece of great music from the past— not to reinvent it, not to lay any kind of direct claim to it, but to both honour it and try to make other art out of an existing work of art'.[17] *The Hours* represents a departure from

---

[13] Earl G. Ingersoll, *Screening Woolf: Virginia Woolf on/and/in Film* (Madison: Fairleigh Dickinson University Press, 2017), 21.
[14] Sally Potter, 'Notes on the Adaptation of the Book *Orlando*', University of Alabama in Hunstville, https://www.uah.edu/woolf/Orlando_Potter.htm, last updated 14 September 2010.
[15] Potter, 'Notes on the Adaptation of the Book *Orlando*'.
[16] Ingersoll, *Screening Woolf*, 21.
[17] Michael Cunningham, qtd in Ingersoll, *Screening Woolf*, 113.

adaptation as an attempt at reproduction—a movement towards alternative 'modes of engagement' with source texts that the filmmakers I discuss continue and push further.[18]

In *Screening Woolf*, Ingersoll traces the theoretical shift away from fidelity in adaptations towards a looser relationship with source texts. Christopher Orr, in the 1980s, built on Roland Barthes's discussion of intertextuality and his insistence that the 'source text', rather than being privileged, is one text amongst many that make 'the filmic text intelligible'.[19] Robert Stam was 'especially drawn to [Gérard] Genette's construct of hypertextuality within which, for example, film adaptation represents a "hypertext" and its anterior fictional text represents a "hypotext"'.[20] These theories underpin the work of Cousins, Ozon, Lowery, and Garland. Like Cunningham, they do not rewrite or adapt Woolf so much as they take cues from her works, attempting to see and think through the lens of her writing. Evidently, Woolf's works are terrible for adaptation but marvellous for filmmaking. As experimenters testing the limits of their medium, just as Woolf did with fiction, these twenty-first-century filmmakers turn to her to the extent that her aesthetic resonates with theirs, particularly in their explorations of identity, loss, and survival. Hermione Lee recognizes that 'Virginia Woolf's story is reformulated by each generation'; she takes on different shapes 'depending on who is reading her, and when, and in what context'.[21] Woolf has now become a filmmaker, one without a camera, but with a filmmaker's sensibility.

What Is This Film Called Love? (2012) is, in the words of its Northern Irish filmmaker Mark Cousins, 'about three days I spent in Mexico City, wandering around with my camera, trying to film what [Woolf] might have filmed'.[22] Cousins does not take on any 'big subject' or tackle social change (as in his previous works), but instead attempts to capture 'what it's like to be alive on an ordinary day' rather than an 'exceptional day'—as Woolf would put it, the life of Monday or Tuesday. His use of an amateur flip camera dictates the improvisational poetics of the film, allowing him to get 'really close to someone', to the 'rough and tumble of everyday life', as he put it. Cousins walks around the streets of Mexico City holding a photograph of the celebrated Soviet filmmaker Sergei Eisenstein (who himself visited the city and made a film about it in the 1930s). Addressing him directly, Cousins says that his film will be 'about me, walking around talking to you, seeing what happens'. He tells 'Sergei' what he sees, while a wry female narrator (voiced by Scottish painter Alison Watt) tells us what Cousins sees and does and thinks and dreams. Cousins sees *with* Eisenstein, showing and sharing the city to and with him; we see the city as Woolf might. The film is grounded in her observing presence.

---

[18] Hutcheon, *A Theory of Adaptation*, 22.
[19] Robert Stam, qtd in Ingersoll, *Screening Woolf*, 20.
[20] Ingersoll, *Screening Woolf*, 20.
[21] Hermione Lee, *Virginia Woolf* (New York: Vintage Books, 1999), 758.
[22] Cousins, Mark, 'My Influences: Mark Cousins', Frieze (website), 30 March 2018, frieze.com/article/my-influences-mark-cousins.

In the first few minutes of *What is this Film*, we hear the narrator stating, 'So the story began. It wasn't much of a story, to be honest, as you're about to see, it doesn't have much of heroics or romance or even events. It was about a guy who was always doing something, doing nothing.' We see images of an airplane wing, a plastic cup on the tray of an airplane seat, a hotel room, flashes from dreams. Throughout the movie we are shown everyday objects that reflect life in the city: a broken sunflower on the street, people walking, a cat entering and exiting the frame, kiosks displaying magazines. Cousins's first-person addresses to 'Sergei' are offset by the third-person narration, the two voices alternating between intimacy and detachment. He peevishly insists, for instance, that he will turn his back on a procession honouring the late Pope John Paul; she drily tells us that he does not turn his back, then relays what he sees. Together these voices make meaning out of the images flitting across the screen, helping to demarcate the three days and our movement through the city.

Cousins's 'Virginia Woolf' is the author of 'Street Haunting: A London Adventure' (1927), a narrative essay that is referred to and quoted in the film.[23] Both Cousins and Woolf are keen observers of the city, ramblers who find delight in the mundane, who are in love with the imaginative possibilities presented by strangers, who follow the meanderings of the streets and the associations of the mind. In 'Street Haunting', the attention of Woolf's narrative persona is caught by one anomalous sight and thought after another as she sets out on the silly yet still plausible pretext of buying a lead pencil. The pencil gives her 'an object, a purpose, an excuse for walking half across London between tea and dinner' (*E4* 480). Woolf notes how, as we leave our homes, the carapaces of our identities and experiences vanish, leaving only 'a central oyster of perceptiveness, an enormous eye' (*E4* 481). This eye is 'not a miner, not a diver, not a seeker after buried treasure'; instead, it 'floats us smoothly down a stream' (*E4* 482). As in *What Is This Film*, Woolf's essay balances the recording of visual pleasure with commentary. When the eye becomes sated, her mind delves deeper, imagining what it might be like to be other people: the 'dwarf' she sees buying shoes, the woman who might wear the pearls that she observes in a jeweller's window.

Cousins, rather than searching for a pencil, decides to investigate what Eisenstein might have meant when he wrote about Mexico City (or his response to it) as being ecstatic. This 'quest', like Woolf's, turns 'doing nothing into doing something', allowing him to dwell with a sense of purpose on otherwise random sights. He reflects on the 'hint of worship' in low-angle shots as he frames a statue; on the ecstasy of political protest as he films a crowd gathering; on the beauty of a plant that illustrates Eisenstein's notion of 'non-indifferent nature'—how it seems 'like it's trembling, like you can see its blood, its nervous system, like your friend'. He wonders about other lives, both human and non-human. Observing an elderly man getting on a bus, he says to 'Sergei', 'look at this, a

---

[23] Jessica Kiang, 'Mark Cousins On "What Is This Film Called Love," PJ Harvey, "Prometheus" & "The Sadness Of Time Passing"', Indiewire, 14 July 2012, https://www.indiewire.com/2012/07/mark-cousins-on-what-is-this-film-called-love-pj-harvey-prometheus-the-sadness-of-time-passing-108445.

man gets on a bus'. We see the doors of the bus close and it inches forward, then stops. The man gets out. 'Is this the shortest journey in the world?' he asks playfully. 'Were his feet that sore?' Jumping from one 'wee' sight and thought to another, briefly forgetting himself each time, Cousins comes to realize what ecstasy means: being 'out of myself'. 'A moment ago', he tells 'Sergei', 'I also realized something so fucking obvious: my way of getting out of myself is walking.'

To get out of oneself, to imagine living other lives, having other bodies and selves, is fundamental to Woolf's aesthetic as a novelist. She articulates and performs this imaginative practice in 'An Unwritten Novel' (1920) and 'Mr Bennett and Mrs Brown' (1924) as well as in 'Street Haunting'. This putting on the bodies and minds of others is a form of what DiBattista deems the 'non-egotistical sublime'. This term aligns Woolf 'with the tradition of Romantic selfhood to which she, in fact, belongs', mediating between John Keats's notion of 'negative capability' and William Wordsworth's 'egotistical sublime'.[24] Essentially, it involves imaginatively becoming someone else while still being an embodied 'I', without losing oneself in the process. Woolf is adamant that our selves are multiple; we are 'neither here nor there, but something so varied and wandering that it is only when we give rein to its wishes and let it take its way unimpeded that we are indeed ourselves' (*E4* 486). The narrator of Cousins's film underscores the importance of this exercise in becoming by quoting three lines from 'Street Haunting', invisibly splicing together sentences from three different sections of the essay: 'One captures a word in passing and from a chance phrase fabricates a lifetime. One can put on, briefly, the bodies and minds of others. To escape is the greatest of pleasures, street haunting in winter the greatest of adventures.' Woolf's vision is aligned with a fundamental aspect of cinema that is showcased in *What Is This Film*: the waywardness of the camera. Whatever catches its attention and settles within its frame becomes a subject worthy of looking at and becoming absorbed by. Wherever the camera goes, there our attention follows. This promiscuity is everywhere apparent in Cousins's film—it is as if the camera would, if it could, follow each 'one of [the] 21 million people in the city'.

Cousins builds on the 'varying and wandering' nature of the camera and our selves to perform two essentially Woolfian acts of cinematic magic. As he leaves the city after his three days of street haunting, the narrator calmly states: 'And then to cap it all there's something else you should know about this story. As the guy sat on the plane an event occurred. It's not clear when or how'. The voices of the narrator and of Cousins start to overlap and meld as neon lights flash. Her voice continues: 'And then he was me. He left manhood and became a woman, the woman who has been telling you this tale. Did you wonder how I knew what he did and thought? I knew because I *am* him.' In this *Orlando* moment, imaginative becoming morphs into *actual* becoming. Similarly, the very end of the film holds a long static shot outdoors, leafy and green. A deer with antlers rests on the ground against a wall. Cousins (in the voice of Watt) reminds us, 'So this has been the small story of a guy who's on an airplane and walked a lot and became a girl. Old

---

[24] DiBattista, *Imagining Virginia Woolf*, 26.

FIGURE 38.1 Mark Cousins, *What is This Film Called Love?*

Virginia says that we can put on the bodies of others and old Sergei says that ecstasy is getting out of yourself.' The viewer is addressed in subtitles:

> Here I am lying in the shade / looking at you / breathing / My story has been about the joy of walking and changing / Could it be your story too? / If you look at me lying here and see yourself in me / it could be your story too / Just like *The Wizard of Oz* could be your story / Or an earthquake you hear on the radio / could be your story/ Now it's nice just lying here / My walking's done for the day / I'm old and young / I'm having my dinner

The credits roll against this static shot. In getting out of himself, putting on the bodies of others, Cousins has *become* this deer, just as he became the female narrator. He pushes Woolf's vision further: from leaving one's self to travel into 'the heart of the forest where live those wild beasts, our fellow men', to encompass animal life (*E4* 491). The film invites us to 'become' someone or some*thing* else in our turn (Figure 38.1).

'Old Virginia' (comfortable, familiar) is fundamental to the fabric of this movie, just as is 'old Sergei'. She and her works become part of an intertextual web that also includes *The Wizard of Oz*, Robert Frost's 'Apple-Picking', Alfred Hitchcock's *Vertigo*, works by Austen, Chris Marker, and others. Woolf's works and vision, though, do much to focalize Cousins's film, helping to convey the sense of adventure, of 'delight and wonder' that can exist in an ordinary day exploring a city (*E4* 490). As Cousins affirms in another context, 'I always think of Woolf as a filmmaker.'[25] The same might be true for

---

[25] Mark Cousins, 'Mark Cousins: the films that influenced I Am Belfast', British Film Institute, 20 June 2016, https://bfi.org.uk/news-opinion/news-bfi/features/mark-cousins-films-influenced-i-am-belfast. In

Ozon, Lowery, and Garland as they turn to her works to help centre their meditations on ghosts and afterlives.

Like the medium of cinema in general, there is an elegiac quality to much of Woof's fiction, as if loss suffuses every particle of reality. Woolf accepted ghosts and hauntings as part of everyday life. In her diaries she records her various encounters with them: the ghosts of loved ones, of her past and future selves, of the unborn selves whose voices she would channel in her fiction, who 'keep up their hauntings by day and by night' (*W* 232).[26] There is no sense of the uncanny or fear in her accounts, only a kind of sadness and the comfort of familiarity.[27] French filmmaker François Ozon, in *Under the Sand*, and American filmmaker David Lowery, in *A Ghost Story*, turn to Woolf as a fellow experimenter whose aesthetic (along with those of others) guides and structures their own. For Ozon, Woolf helps uncover the absence within everyday life and relationships; for Lowery, her work presents a positive take on ghosts that he transforms into something much darker and more melancholy. All three artists are interested in the impossibility of separating the 'before' of a loss from 'after'.

Ozon's *Under the Sand* centres on a woman who seems unable to accept the loss of her husband, Jean (Bruno Cremer), after he disappears while she is asleep on the beach. After some time, her references to her husband as if he were still alive and a part of her life alarm her friends, who want her to move on. Yet for Marie Drillon (Charlotte Rampling) he is still there even though he is physically absent. She talks to him as she is getting dressed to go on a date with another man; she buys him a tie when out shopping. As Roger Ebert puts it, Marie's life 'doesn't go on without [Jean].... This is not so strange. I know many people who talk about the departed in the present tense.'[28] Whereas 'many people believe that their loved ones are with them in spirit', though, Marie 'refers to her husband Jean as if he is actually still present as a force in her life'. We, too, see him and hear him. His physical reality is just as substantial or as spectral as hers; if he is a ghost, so is she—a ghost inhabiting her past life, trying to make sense of what she has lost, and when.

At one point in the film, Marie, who is a literature professor, reads to her class a passage from Woolf's *The Waves* (1931), signalling that this novel is one of Ozon's intertexts. The excerpt is from one of Bernard's monologues, where he describes what Woolf would call a 'moment of being':

> I, standing with my razor in my hand, became suddenly aware of the merely habitual nature of my action (this is the drop forming) and congratulated my hands,

his interview with Jessica Kiang, Cousins also says, 'I have to say I think Virginia Woolf was the first great documentary filmmaker even though she never made a documentary film.'

[26] See, for example, entries for 9 March 1920, 26 July 1922, 17 October 1924, 26 December 1929, 17 March 1932, 21 April 1932, 19 January 1935, 8 February 1935, 28 August 1938, and letter from January 1932.

[27] Cf. her description of Henry James's ghosts from 'Henry James's Ghost Stories': 'They have their origin within us. They are present whenever the significant overflows our powers of expressing it; whenever the ordinary appears ringed by the strange' (*E3*, 324).

[28] Roger Ebert, *Under the Sand* Review, Rogerebert.com, 10 August 2001.

ironically, for keeping at it. Shave, shave, shave, I said. Go on shaving. The drop fell. All through the day's work, at intervals, my mind went to an empty place, saying, 'What is lost? What is over?' And 'Over and done with,' I muttered, 'over and done with,' solacing myself with words. People noticed the vacuity of my face and the aimlessness of my conversation. The last words of my sentence tailed away. And as I buttoned on my coat to go home I said more dramatically, 'I have lost my youth.'

Ozon takes his cue from this everyday epiphany, from Bernard's sudden awareness of loss and emptiness. *Under the Sand* is very much about late mid-life, when the comfort of being settled can easily skate into boredom or disaster. Marie realizes that there was a great deal that she did not know about her husband before his disappearance. The questions, 'What is lost? What is over?' echo throughout the film, just as Jacob's name echoes throughout the pages of *Jacob's Room* (1922), searching, mournful, hopeful, rendering the solidity of reality more and more insubstantial. The structure of Ozon's film also draws on *The Waves* as well as *Jacob's Room*; these works are organized around a central absence. Jean, like Percival, like Jacob, is already absent, even when he is alive.

In *Under the Sand*, Marie's loss seems at first like an unusual case of grief in that she is not sure whether her husband is dead (by accident or suicide) or whether he just chose to leave her, bored of her and their life together, as her mother-in-law cruelly suggests. She cannot mourn because the nature of the loss is so uncertain. Yet, as Woolf often explores in her fiction, and as the film suggests, we are all in a sense ghosts to one other whether we have left this life or not. At the end of the film Marie sits on the beach and digs her hand under the sand while sobbing. She sees a man who from a distance resembles her husband; she runs towards him and then seems to swerve past him as the camera pulls back and the movie ends. We are left not knowing whether Jean is alive or dead. We only know that the lines between certainty and uncertainty, life and death, presence and absence are blurred. Ozon, through Woolf, suggests that there is no time when Marie's husband was not in some way absent to her. The 'art of losing' is both devastating and utterly commonplace.

Lowery's *A Ghost Story* also explores loss and the tension between absence and presence. Lowery has acknowledged Woolf's vital influence on his film, referring to her as a 'kindred spirit'. At the Sundance Film Festival, he said that 'Woolf is everywhere in *A Ghost Story*' and that her writing 'corresponds perfectly' to his 'difficult-to-grasp perspectives on ghosts and specters and their relationship to life and time'.[29] In an interview he stated that his film 'takes cues' from Woolf's work, specifically her short impressionistic story 'A Haunted House', but also, according to him, *Mrs Dalloway*, *To the Lighthouse*, and *Orlando* (with other hypotexts including *Beetlejuice*, *Poltergeist*, the films of Tsai Ming-liang, *Boyhood*, *The Tree of Life*, and *Ghost*).[30] Lowery affirms that 'Virginia Woolf's literature really transformed [his] own ideas about how to formally

---

[29] Manuel Betancourt, '*A Ghost Story* is Haunted by Virginia Woolf', *Electric Lit*, 3 August 2017.
[30] Matthew Jacobs, 'Movies And Books That Inspired *A Ghost Story*', *The Huffington Post*, 10 July 2017.

represent the passage of time and how time affects us.' I would suggest that Lowery underplays his *differences* from Woolf—*A Ghost Story* draws on her works but takes a much darker and more nihilistic perspective on loss and survival.

The film's epigraph is the first line from 'A Haunted House' (1921): 'Whatever hour you woke there was a door shutting' (*CSF* 122). Casey Affleck (as 'C') and Rooney Mara (as 'R') are a couple whose story unfolds against a cosmic backdrop. They have disagreed about moving out of their house, but C agrees to the change; he suddenly dies in a car accident and returns to the house as a ghost—a figure wearing a plain sheet with two eye holes cut out. He watches R grieve and move on and leave while he stays behind and waits. And waits. He stays on as others inhabit the house and as it becomes dilapidated; he watches it being demolished, stands in a giant pit as foundations for a high-rise building are being laid, and moves into the future where he is surrounded by men and women in suits conducting business meetings. He goes out onto a ledge of the high-rise, surveying a futuristic skyline, jumps, and plummets to the earth, rising to see a family of settlers arrive on the land long before the house was built. He watches himself and C walk around the house for the first time as they decide to rent it; he watches himself return to the house as a ghost as time forms a loop.

Like *Under the Sand* and much of Woolf's fiction, *A Ghost Story* depicts the fluidity of time and the way that loss infuses everything, both in the present and retrospectively. Yet in taking on the point of view of a ghost for much of the film, Lowery turns what might be consoling—the presence of a ghost watching over his lover—into something that is not, focusing more on the ghost's loss and how his new relationship to time expands his grief and loneliness. As Manuel Betancourt puts it, 'Lowery steers away from the [ghost story's] more supernatural elements, and instead focuses on the tragedy of being a person who remains.'[31] Some time after the accident, the ghost of C is in the living room facing their bedroom door, the camera positioned behind him. R walks out of the room and out the front door. Without seeming to cut, the door of the bedroom immediately opens again, and R walks out and leaves by the front door wearing a different outfit. We get another nearly imperceptible cut as a differently dressed R walks out of their room and out the front door yet again. Like Woolf, Lowery is adept at showing time's passage.

Later, C sits disconsolately on the bed, waiting, watching. The woman he loves is moving on while he holds on, tethered to the house; they inhabit the same space, yet exist on different planes. R eventually returns to the house with a man; she hugs him at the door, and they kiss. We hear ominous music, lights flash, and electricity sounds. Shots of the flickering lamps alternate with a close-up of a bookcase; suddenly, a stack of books flies onto the floor, one tumbling open. R kneels to examine the open book, which has 'A Haunted House' just visible on the inside flap. As she reads, the camera pans in extreme close-up shots on the pages of Woolf's story, continuing to urgently cut and pan.

---

[31] Betancourt, '*A Ghost Story* is Haunted'.

Finally, the camera zooms in on the entire page of the book that it had been obsessively zooming in on and panning across (Figure 38.2):

> Death was the glass; death was between us; coming to the woman first, hundreds of years ago, leaving the house, sealing all the windows; the rooms were darkened. He left it, left her, went North, went East, saw the stars turned in the Southern sky; sought the house, found it dropped beneath the Downs. 'Safe, safe, safe,' the pulse of the house beat gladly. 'The Treasure yours.' (*CSF* 123)

The scene cuts to black.

Woolf's story, about two ghosts who are separated when one dies and who are reunited in death at the house that they inhabited, is a happy one. The narrator, part of the couple that lives in the house hundreds of years later, notices that the ghosts are looking for their treasure and wonders where it could be, without feeling a hint of alarm or concern. The ghosts are a happier version of the human-like 'airs' that move around the summer house in the 'Time Passes' section of *To the Lighthouse*, questioning, wondering, giving 'off an aimless gust of lamentation' (*TL* 173) before we learn of the deaths of Mrs Ramsay and two of her children. The story presents a gentle fantasy of love and reunion that Lowery contrasts with his darker tale. Directing R to 'A Haunted House'

FIGURE 38.2 David Lowery, *A Ghost Story*

FIGURE 38.3 Alex Garland, *Annihilation*

seems to be a way for the ghost to communicate his desire and grief. 'Death was between them', and will remain so; and perhaps something always separated them in life as well, as various flashbacks suggest. The ghost in this story is the one haunted by loss, the one whose love lasts longest, 'when existence or when hope is gone'.[32]

When the ghost sees himself first entering the house *as* a ghost, we realize that the camera's perspective all along has been that of this 'Ghost Stage 2' and that the first ghost was there at the beginning of the movie, watching, hitting the keys of the piano, dropping books, even when C was alive. 'Before' and 'after' form a circle as the first ghost collapses and disappears and as the second continues the cycle, with no point in which absence was not present, in which loss was not part of the film's reality. As in *Under the Sand*, loss suffuses everything, yet for Lowery the span of loss is stretched to its limits, becoming more melancholy than elegiac. One of the centrepieces of *A Ghost Story* is an extended monologue given by a man who is at a party at the house long after R has left. He talks about what endures—about the ultimate pointlessness of any human endeavour: 'So, you can write a book, but the pages will burn. You can sing a song and pass it down. You can write a play and hope that folks will remember it, keep performing it'. But ultimately, it 'doesn't matter'. All will end. This zooming out to the end of the universe makes loss a part of the fabric of the cosmos. It is a far more nihilistic vision of the afterlife of individuals, works of art, and humanity than Woolf's—or Garland's in *Annihilation* (Figure 38.3).

Garland, like Woolf herself, is a hybrid artist. For Woolf, borders are where change often happens and where limits—such as those between the arts—are tested. It is where new things are made, where old things are broken down and reconfigured. Some artists work primarily in this space of conversation, 'making raids into the lands of

---

[32] Austen, *Persuasion*, 189.

others', whereas others burrow 'deeper and deeper into the stuff of their own art' (*E6* 45). Garland's film, *Annihilation*, is an adaptation of Jeff VanderMeer's 2014 novel, yet is a work in its own right, and I will discuss it as such. The connections between Woolf and this film are looser than with the others discussed here, yet aspects of its plot and structure reflect on this tenuousness, offering an allegory for the kind of intertextuality or hypertextuality that Garland's work is performing. Garland playfully nods to Woolf, drawing on her works and ideas to shape his film's exploration of identity and survival. He takes the hybrid nature of film as the jumping off point for his creation of new and unexpected combinations.

The film, like the novel, concerns an expedition undertaken by a small group of female scientists into a mysterious region called 'Area X'. Lena (Natalie Portman) is a biologist and professor, researching 'the genetically programmed life cycle of a cell'. She is the only one to survive the expedition and, at the start of the film, is being questioned about it while closely observed; the narrative jumps back and forth between her interrogation, the expedition itself, and an earlier timeline when her husband Kane (Oscar Isaac) decides to go on a similar expedition and returns with his body shutting down. Kane is monitored at the headquarters of the Southern Reach—the 'clandestine government agency that dealt with all matters connected to Area X'.[33] Here, Lena meets psychologist Dr Ventress (Jennifer Jason Leigh), who takes her to the boundary, a giant moving wall like a pink-purple-turquoise soap bubble. She tells Lena that Area X was discovered three years previously, when a national park reported that a lighthouse was surrounded by this 'Shimmer'. 'Since then', Ventress explains, 'we've approached by land, by sea, sent in drones, animals, and teams of people. But nothing comes back. And the boundary is getting bigger, it's expanding.' Soon it will swallow the area they are standing in, and 'then we're talking cities, states, and so on'. Kane is the only one who has returned. Lena joins the next expedition to find out what is inside; Ventress holds out a lure and a promise to her: 'You can save him.'

Unlike the novel, Garland's film is divided into three sections: Area X, The Shimmer, and The Lighthouse. Thus, Garland's nod to Woolf and her novel, which builds towards a final voyage to a lighthouse in its third and final section. As Josephine Livingstone aptly notes, Woolf's building 'represents an always-out-of-reach object for human desire—that thing that propels us through life and toward each other. You are never in the lighthouse, only moving towards it' (except that in *Annihilation* members of the group do reach it). The group, which also includes a geomorphologist, paramedic, and physicist, are determined to reach the lighthouse, the original source of the mystery. We see them walking warily towards the Shimmer with their rifles drawn and ready; they have no memory of crossing over, and wake up days later.

As the members of the expedition explore the 'unnervingly lush landscape', they come across strange hybrids that should not be physically possible.[34] Some are quite

---

[33] Jeff VanderMeer, *Annihilation* (New York: Farrar, Straus and Giroux, 2014), 12.
[34] Ed Power, '*Annihilation*: who are the Southern Reach and what on earth is The Shimmer?', *The Telegraph*, 12 March 2018.

innocuous and even beautiful. The women walk past a fence covered in beautiful flowers of different varieties, some of which are growing from the same branch. 'It's like they're stuck in a continuous mutation', Lena marvels. Later, they spy two antelopes, doubles, that have flowering branches for antlers, and encounter graceful human-like figures made of leaves and flowers. The physicist, Josie (Tessa Thompson), realizes that the leaves of these figures must contain human genomes, the kind that define the physical structure of the body. Other hybrids are different degrees of horrifying. After killing a giant alligator, the members of the group look into its mouth and see that it has the teeth of a shark. In another scene, the amiable geomorphologist, Sheppard (Tuva Novotny) is dragged off in the darkness of night by a bear and screams out, 'Help me! Help me!' while the others run behind, unable to do anything. Lena later finds Sheppard's body in the woods, her throat ravaged. When the bear returns to their camp it has Sheppard's voice, distorted, crying, 'Help me!' and we can see that its face is partially a skull with a human skull grafted onto one side.

While examining the leaf-like figures, Josie grasps that the Shimmer 'is a prism that refracts everything'—not just light rays and radio waves, but 'Animal DNA. Plant DNA. All DNA.' Genes are broken down, scrambled, and remixed to form new combinations, beautiful, monstrous, or both. Livingston reads this splicing of genes psychoanalytically, as an illustration of how '[w]hen one being causes suffering in another, the suffering fragments and embeds within the being that caused it'. The presence of Woolf's novel 'leavens' the film with 'psychological sophistication', she claims, with the 'Shimmer's prismatic refractions [...] an allegory, at least in part, for the perceptive warping of human subjectivity'. I would add that the 'brilliant splicing' that Livingstone points out in the title of her essay—between Woolf and David Cronenberg, known as one of the originators of the body horror genre[35]—signals an alternative allegory: a more playful meta-allegory for what Garland is doing with texts, artists, and genres in *Annihilation*.

Garland's film is a 'brilliant splicing' of its many intertexts and hypotexts: Ed Power lists H.P. Lovecraft, Jorge Luis Borges, and David Lynch's *Twin Peaks*; Livingstone includes Andrei Tarkovsky's *Stalker*, Steven Spielberg's *Jurassic Park*, and Cronenberg's *The Fly*.[36] We might add Conrad's *Heart of Darkness*, Francis Ford Coppola's *Apocalypse Now*, John Carpenter's *The Thing*, as well as Spielberg's *Raiders of the Lost Ark*, Fritz Lang's *Metropolis*, and Woolf's *Mrs Dalloway*. These and other texts are broken down and recombined, giving them a strange and twisted kind of afterlife. This prismatic recombination is a different way of imagining and conceiving of intertextuality: it breaks references down to fragments (a title, a concept, a structure, a phrase, a scene, an image) that are just barely recognizable before splicing them with something else. *Annihilation* does the most of any of the films I discuss to vaporize and reconfigure Woolf.

In *Mrs Dalloway* Woolf notably imagines a gentler but similar form of dismantling and splicing in Clarissa's vision of the afterlife:

---

[35] Josephine Livingston, '*Annihilation* Is a Brilliant Splicing of Woolf With Cronenberg', *The New Republic*, 27 February 2018.
[36] Power, '*Annihilation*'.

> somehow in the streets of London, on the ebb and flow of things, here, there, she survived, Peter survived, lived in each other, she being part, she was positive, of the trees at home; of the house there, ugly, rambling all to bits and pieces as it was; part of people she had never met; being laid out like a mist between the people she knew best, who lifted her on their branches as she had seen the trees lift the mist, but it spread ever so far, her life, herself. (*MD* 8)

Garland borrows and twists this concept of survival. Each intertext in the film spreads 'ever so far', like a mist, part of other things, other texts. In the lighthouse, Lena finds Dr Ventress, who had gone on ahead of the group. Her face shadowed, the psychologist intones how the lighthouse is 'inside' her now, and explains her understanding of the alien being that now inhabits it/them: 'It's not like us. It's unlike us. I don't know what it wants. Or if it wants. But it will grow until it encompasses everything. Our bodies and our minds will be fragmented into their smallest parts until not one part remains. Annihilation.' She screams and particles of light stream upwards from her mouth, swirling around her as she is pulled apart, the scene echoing one from *Raiders of the Lost Ark*. Some of Lena's cells then get mixed with the source of the Shimmer, dividing repeatedly and splicing with the alien genes, creating a strange golden double that mirrors her every move. Lena is just barely able to kill it before it kills her, after which the Shimmer disappears. Back in the observation room her interrogator asks her what this alien being wanted. He insists that it was there for a reason, mutating the environment and destroying everything. Lena responds: 'It wasn't destroying. It was changing everything. It was making something new.' Out of this (modernist) mutation and reconfiguration a strange, sometimes terrible, beauty is born. Working on the sunny and not-so-sunny margins between different media, hybrid artists like Garland create new afterlives for artists like Woolf. *Annihilation* playfully fractures and splices what has come before, bringing about horror as well as wonder.

Rather than being cordoned off in a separate feminist space, viewed as intimidating, daunting, and hyper-politicized (by those who might be disturbed by her power), Woolf has been embraced within the popular medium of film in the twenty-first century. She has joined a company of men as a 'filmmaker' whose works help focalize their exploration of 'universal' themes such as identity, loss, time, and survival. She has also become just one cultural reference in a postmodern sea of cultural references—one influence among many in a spreading web of intertextuality or hypertextuality. This afterlife has much to recommend it. It gives Woolf her due as a thinker and experimenter whom other artists take seriously in engaging with her oeuvre. Her works are turned to with respect and even affection and love. This afterlife requires that Woolf be a recognizable icon, yet democratizes her so that anyone can reference her, without fear. Woolf herself and all the details of her life do not factor much, if at all, into this afterlife; she is no bogeywoman, no figure of derision or pity.

On the other hand, 'old Virginia' as a writer and 'filmmaker' has become safe and even sanitized, neutered, and domesticated. Cousins, Ozon, Lowery, and Garland have nothing to say about her challenges to patriarchy and fascism, to violence, war, oppression, or normative sexuality, her demand that women have a room of their own in which to think and write, in which they can kill the angel of the house who censors what they say. Has too much been let go to drop the 'tortured' and 'female' from 'artist'? What would it mean to keep Woolf's feminism and historical context intact? Every reader of Woolf must answer these questions for themselves. I would only suggest that future filmmakers can certainly turn to Woolf's works while addressing her gender and politics, and that the company of artists she is welcomed into need not be comprised of all men. Moreover, the fact that filmmakers have been and still are turning to her works suggests that her legacy is very much alive, there to be turned to, pushed against, and experimented with. Perhaps this is the kind of afterlife that Woolf would have approved of: surviving 'on the ebb and flow of things', 'spread ever so far' in the works of others, forming unexpected and fresh reconfigurations.

Selected Bibliography

Austen, Jane, *Persuasion* (Oxford: Oxford University Press, 2004).

Betancourt, Manuel, '*A Ghost Story* is Haunted by Virginia Woolf', *Electric Lit*, 3 August 2017, https://electricliterature.com/a-ghost-story-is-haunted-by-virginia-woolf.

Cousins, Mark, interview/Q&A by James King, ICA London, 13 February 2013, https://soundcloud.com/icalondon/what-is-this-film-called-love.

Cousins, Mark, interview at Belfast Film Festival, vimeo.com/64100631.

Cousins, Mark, 'Mark Cousins: the films that influenced *I Am Belfast*', British Film Institute, 20 June 2016, https://bfi.org.uk/news-opinion/news-bfi/features/mark-cousins-films-influenced-i-am-belfast.

Cousins, Mark, 'My Influences: Mark Cousins', *Frieze*, 30 March 2018, https://frieze.com/article/my-influences-mark-cousins.

DiBattista, Maria, *Imagining Virginia Woolf: An Experiment in Critical Biography* (Princeton: Princeton University Press, 2009).

Ebert, Roger, *Under the Sand* Review, Rogerebert.com, 10 August 2001, rogerebert.com/reviews/under-the-sand-2001.

Hutcheon, Linda, with Siobhan O'Flynn, *A Theory of Adaptation* (New York: Routledge, 2006).

Ingersoll, Earl G., *Screening Woolf: Virginia Woolf on/and/in Film* (Madison, NJ: Fairleigh Dickinson University Press, 2017).

CHAPTER 39

WOOLFIAN AFTERLIVES

LAURA SMITH

VIRGINIA Woolf has had a catalysing role on artists working in non-verbal media, including the arts, music, dance, and design. An analysis of Woolf's impact beyond the medium of her writing allows for a trans-historic and international study of her legacy, charting her influence from, for example, landscape painting in Cornwall to Japanese Butoh; and from North American opera to the Ballet Russes. Tracing many of the vital and fluid connections between Woolf, her contemporaries, and those whose work she has inspired, demonstrates how her legacy manifests visually. Her resonance operates on many different levels, inspiring a range of reactions from allusion to affinity, and pastiche to homage. Across generations, from her own family and friends to more distant allies—unknown to her—but making work via her impulse today, Woolf has influenced artists, dancers, designers, and musicians.[1] Herein the work of her sister, the painter Vanessa Bell will be considered alongside that of pioneering contemporary feminist artist Judy Chicago; while the musical compositions of Woolf's close friend Ethel Smyth will be charted in tandem with modern-day, US-based, folk-rock duo The Indigo Girls; as the balletic moves of Bloomsburyite Lydia Lopokova are discussed along with British choreographer Wayne McGregor's recent exploits.

The enduring reverence for Woolf among scholarly and literary communities, often posits her as a solo woman genius, working in relative isolation within and against a patriarchal society that excluded all but the luckiest of creative women. However, such

---

[1] A broad range of scholarship connects Woolf to the practitioners she inspired. For an examination of her impact on the visual arts, see Maggie Humm, ed., *Virginia Woolf and the Arts* (Edinburgh: Edinburgh University Press, 2010); Frances Spalding, *Virginia Woolf: Art, Life and Vision* (London: National Portrait Gallery Publications, 2014); and Jane Goldman, *The Feminist Aesthetics of Virginia Woolf: Modernism, Post-Impressionism, and the Politics of the Visual* (Cambridge: Cambridge University Press, 2009). For dance, see Susan Jones, *Literature, Modernism & Dance* (Oxford: Oxford University Press, 2014); and Rishona Zimring, *Social Dance and the Modernist Imagination in Interwar Britain* (Farnham: Ashgate, 2013). And for musical explorations, see Emma Sutton, *Virginia Woolf and Classical Music: Politics, Aesthetics, Form* (Edinburgh: Edinburgh University Press, 2013).

an account neglects to mention the expansive community of creative practitioners into which Woolf was born; as well as those peers that she strove to promote and endorse; and those that she stimulated in successive generations. And these relationships, of influence and inspiration, were—and are—vital to Woolf's own conception of creativity and community: 'For masterpieces are not single and solitary births; they are the outcome of many years of thinking in common, of thinking by the body of the people, so that the experience of the mass is behind the single voice' (*ARO* 49). The following passages will thus situate Woolf's extraordinary accomplishments alongside the achievements of other practitioners, demonstrating that her legacy is not that of a solitary voice singing out of a silent vacuum but part of a polyphonous choir whose shared voices are louder and stronger as a result of one another. My purpose here is to open these conversations out to the far-reaching and surprising range of creatives who have taken inspiration from Woolf, not to chart a particular direction of influence, but to reveal just how wide and impactful her legacy is.

Woolf's most unswerving ally was her older sister, the painter Vanessa Bell (1879–1961). Throughout their lives, Woolf and Bell shared a mutually influential relationship founded on emotional support, creative appreciation, and aesthetic affinity. As children, the sisters worked alongside each other in what Woolf, in 'A Sketch of the Past' called a 'close conspiracy ... of instantaneous sympathy' (*MB* 143). In this memoir, as in most of her depictions of her childhood, Woolf places her sister and their family life at the centre of her own creativity and happiness. Significantly when doing so she consistently imagines her medium as visual rather than verbal: 'If I were a painter ... if I were painting myself' (*MB* 66–73). As such she creates a resolute link between her sister and her own visual imagination, unequivocally reflecting the impact that Bell had on her writing. And while Bell was frequently a subject for Woolf, she also wrote her own memoir 'Notes on Virginia's Childhood' in which she affirms their alliance and enduring ambitions:

> I cannot remember a time when Virginia did not mean to be a writer and I a painter.... Our happiest afternoons were spent in a small room handed over to us opening out of the drawing-room.... In this room we used to sit, I painting, and she reading aloud. She read most of the Victorian novelists in this way and I can still hear her voice if I read George Eliot or Thackeray.[2]

Just as Bell's love of fiction endured, so too did Woolf's affection for the visual arts. As is evident in her 1934 essay on Walter Sickert, in which she states: 'Words are an impure medium.... Better far to have been born into the silent kingdom of paint' (*E6* 39). Bell was a gifted and committed painter whose fervour for creativity echoed Woolf's own. Her Charleston home, which she shared with fellow painter Duncan Grant, would, for

---

[2] Vanessa Bell, 'Notes on Virginia's Childhood', in *Sketches in Pen and Ink, A Bloomsbury Notebook*, ed. Lia Giachero (London: Pimlico, 1998), 63–4.

her, become a lifelong application of this 'kingdom of paint'—though it was anything but silent. Almost every surface, from doors to headboards to wardrobes to walls, retain Bell's (and Grant's) Post-Impressionist, decorative aesthetic of colours, shapes, and curves that are almost synaesthetic in their clamour.

Evident in the dual creative output of both Woolf and Bell is a search for light, freedom, and pattern: a serious retort to the gloomy interior of the Stephen family home in Hyde Park Gate and the oppressive Victorian middle-class ideals of femininity extolled there. Such overbearing familial standards resulted in oscillating emotions of fascination and revolt in the sisters, a discord that they later exploited as creative practitioners. Following the death of their mother, Julia Stephen in 1895 and their father, Sir Leslie Stephen, in 1904, Virginia, Vanessa, and their brothers moved out of their Hyde Park Gate home to Gordon Square in Bloomsbury. In these 'rooms of their own', all the things that were previously unthinkable or unsayable were suddenly possible and for both sisters, despite the looming threat of war, those years were full of discovery and newfound freedoms. Bell's paintings from this period embody such energy and curiosity. *Studland Beach* (1912) is a large seascape that depicts several women and children seen only from behind as they huddle to look out to sea or cluster around a changing hut. The work reveals Bell's early influence from Henri Matisse—as well as what her husband, the critic Clive Bell, and her lover, the painter Roger Fry, were calling 'significant form', a style of painting that emphasized colour, shape, and line rather than subject matter. That said, the work also shares striking similarities with many Woolfian tropes: Bell's confident reduction of detail to only the most essential components mirrors the way that Woolf often takes shortcuts with our understanding or circumnavigates dogmatic description; the way that the painting employs empty space, which is somehow taut with emotion; Bell's use of light and dark as a structuring device; and her focus on the ocean as representative of freedom or liberty, are all reminiscent of, or perhaps inspired by, Woolf's prose (Figure 39.1).

Bell's portraits also operate through similar affinities; *Helen Dudley* (c. 1915) presents her friend, through minimal detail, as self-assured and quietly commanding; *Mrs St. John Hutchinson* (1915) is a less flattering portrayal of her husband Clive's mistress, shown, again with paired down detail, as suspicious and sombre; while *Iris Tree* (1915) is a sparse depiction of the eighteen-year-old poet and actress painted as slightly awkward but remaining calm and poised. These are paintings of real women whose varying features—both physical and emotional—Bell captures with a knowing solidarity and a scarcity of ornament. Once again, this way of describing and presenting her subjects finds many parallels in her sister's writing, as Woolf herself stated upon seeing Bell's cover designs for her 1919 short story 'Kew Gardens': 'God made our brains upon the same lines, only leaving out 2 or 3 pieces in mine' (*L2* 289).

In addition to Bell, the only other artist who Woolf commissioned to illustrate her own published texts was Dora Carrington (1893–1932). The Hogarth Press, which Woolf founded with her husband Leonard in 1917 and through which the majority of both of their texts were published (providing them freedom outside of commercial concerns or editorial pressures), not only gave the couple the ability to publish the texts that they

FIGURE 39.1 Vanessa Bell, *Studland Beach* © Estate of Vanessa Bell. All rights reserved, DACS 2020. Photo © Tate

were interested in, but also to commission art by the artists they admired. Carrington became a regular contributor.

One of a generation of younger artists and writers who were well known to Woolf (including Nina Hamnett, Dolores Courtney, Barbara Hiles, and Dorothy Brett), Carrington was given the nickname 'crophead' by Woolf who seemed to approach her with a mixture of admiration and curiosity: 'She is odd from her mixture of impulse and self consciousness. I wonder sometimes what she's at: so eager to please, conciliatory, restless, and active.... But she is such a bustling eager creature, so red & solid, and at the same time inquisitive, that one can't help liking her' (*D1* 153). Carrington's notable body of work, which took the form of painting, printmaking, and the decorative arts, combines elements of Post-Impressionism, primitivism, and surrealism. Most of her paintings are landscapes and portraits, but beneath her perceptive representations of her subjects, a sort of strange psychology is in operation: one that, again, seems to operate on a similar level to the often penetrating intimacy of Woolf. Just as Woolf frequently wrote her family, friends, and homes into her fiction, Carrington's interest in personal subjects—landscapes of her home and portraits of personal acquaintances—subtly reveal her enduring interest in showing us the emotion of a place or person.

FIGURE 39.2 Dora Carrington, Farm at Watendlath, Tate. Photo © Tate

At first glance her *Farm at Watendlath* (1921) could be seen as a straightforward painting of the farm in the Lake District where Carrington spent her honeymoon with Ralph Partridge, but there is something suggestive about the curves and voluptuousness of the hills and mountains in the background. So much so that it appears that the two figures—a woman and a girl—that look back at these curves (their backs to us) show women at different stages of their lives directly contemplating their own sexuality. At a time when Carrington's hitherto ambiguous sexuality had seemingly been established as heterosexual (having just married a man) still, her desires remained divided between two men (her new husband, and Lytton Strachey with whom she shared a lifelong, mutual—though non-sexual—love) and she seems to have channelled many of these emotions into this work (Figure 39.2).

Carrington also endowed later landscapes with allusions to women's bodies and their sexualities. Her *Spanish Landscape with Mountains* (c. 1924), painted during her travels across France and Spain has been described, by those who knew the geography of the area, to be quite imaginative, a departure from the actual landscape toward a depiction that resembles breasts and skin. Or, as Frances Partridge, the second wife of Ralph, suggests: 'like knees under bedclothes'.[3]

So, while Carrington might not have consciously described herself as a feminist—and neither would Woolf for that matter, the two of them—as well as Bell—were undeniably feminist in their resolve to live according to their own nature—particularly in their attitudes to sexuality and relationships, as well as their approach to making work: 'Literature is open to everybody. I refuse to allow you, Beadle though you are, to turn me off the grass. Lock up your libraries if you like; but there is no gate, no lock, no bolt that you can set upon the freedom of my mind' (ARO 57).

In this way, Woolf, Carrington, and Bell followed particular endeavours that sought to reassess the social and material conditions that prevented so many women from having access to means of personal expression and the attentions of recorded history. To discuss what is perhaps the most striking and relevant of these endeavours, we must return to Bell. In 1932, Vanessa Bell and Duncan Grant were commissioned by Sir Kenneth Clark to design a one hundred and forty-eight-piece dinner service.[4] However, two years later, Bell and Grant presented Clark with a set of fifty hand-painted Wedgwood blank ceramic plates, each decorated with a portrait of a famous woman from history. The subjects are depicted in loose brushwork, surrounded by capricious line and circle motifs, in blue, brown, and yellow glazes. It was not quite what Clark had in mind: 'it turned out differently to what we had expected', he wrote, noting that the plates showed 'Bloomsbury asserting its status as matriarchy'.[5]

A playful and challenging chronicle of women through history, *The Famous Women Dinner Service* encompasses women from the realms of ancient history to the (then) present moment including actresses and queens, pin-ups and literary figures, muses and saints, and, of course, Bell and Woolf. This trans-historical sorority exhibits an extraordinary scope of reference that resonates with the broader quest that Bell shared with Woolf, to create proper ways to celebrate women's histories. Woolf had written essays about many of the women commemorated in the set, including Jane Austen, Emily Brontë, Emily Barrett Browning, Dorothy Osborne, Sappho, Madame de Staël, Sarah Churchill, Ellen Terry, and Christina Rossetti. Bell and Grant's emphasis on honouring this community of women applauds the notion of the 'group'—and the strength of bonds between women—over the individual, a visual affirmation of Woolf's notion that as creative women we 'think back through our mothers' (ARO 57).

Such a work can be cited as a significant forerunner to some of the most important feminist art projects of the 1960s and 1970s, particularly Judy Chicago's *The Dinner*

---

[3] Frances Partridge, qtd in Jane Hill, *The Art of Dora Carrington* (London: A&C Black Publishers, 1994), 136.

[4] Bell's notebook records the original order in full: '36 large plates, 12 smaller plates, 36 side plates, 12 soup cups & saucers, 1 salad bowl & stand, 2 junket dishes, 6 oval dishes at different sizes, 2 sauce boats & stands, 4 pepper pots, 4 salt pots, 4 mustard pots, 2 sauce tureens & stands & handles, and 3 Liverpool jugs'. In Hana Leaper, 'The Famous Women Dinner Service: A Critical Introduction and Catalogue', *British Art Studies* 7 (2017), www.britishartstudies.ac.uk/issues/issue-index/issue-7/famous-women.

[5] Leaper, 'The Famous Women Dinner Service'.

Party (1974–1979). Chicago (b. 1939) is a feminist artist most well known for her large-scale installations, which examine the role of women in history and culture. *The Dinner Party* consists of three banqueting tables arranged in a triangle. Each of the three tables holds place settings (hand-painted china plate, ceramic cutlery, and goblet on an embroidered placemat) for thirteen mythical and historical famous women, making thirty-nine women in total. These women include goddesses, ancient queens, modern artists, writers, activists, politicians, and—of course—Virginia Woolf (though sadly Bell is absent). They are 'seated' according to their historical era: pre-history to classical Rome, Christianity to the Reformation, and the American Revolution to the Women's Revolution. The entire triangle then stands on 'The Heritage Floor', made up of over two thousand white, triangular-shaped tiles inscribed with the names of nine hundred and ninety-nine additional famous women in gold script.

Woolf's hand-painted china plate—in pinks and greens—resembles a blossoming flower or stylized vulva, which Chicago states is intended to symbolize Woolf's resolute affirmation of unrestricted expression. It also contains seed forms in its centre, similar to many of the powerful fertility images of the goddesses' plates on the pre-history table. The centre of Woolf's plate though seems to burst out from its petals, an allusion to Chicago's sense of 'Woolf as a woman who urged other women to break free from the confines of pre-existing, predominantly masculine literature and instead to write in a style reflective of themselves'.[6] The plate sits on an embroidered place-mat in which a wave pattern embroidered around the letter 'V' frames her name, and from beneath the plate glows a stitched and painted light beam reminiscent of an old fashioned lighthouse, illustrating for Chicago the way that Woolf 'illuminated a path toward a new, woman-formed literary language'.[7]

Another feminist artist from this period who cites Woolf as a direct influence is Rebecca Horn (b. 1944). Best known for her installations, films, and the body-modifying sculptures she began making in 1968, Horn is interested in manipulating the contact between a person and their environment. Works such as *Pencil Mask* or *Finger Gloves* (both 1972) are reminiscent of the ways in which Woolf ties her depictions of landscapes, objects, and colours to her main characters' consciousnesses in order to explain their psychological natures—their inner landscapes—as in this passage from *Jacob's Room* (1922) in which a sorry-for-himself Jacob becomes almost camouflaged with the street at the sight of his love with another man: 'The light from the arc lamp drenched him from head to toe. He stood for a minute motionless beneath it. Shadows chequered the street. Other figures, single and together, poured out, wavered across, and obliterated Florinda and the man. The light drenched Jacob from head to toe' (*JR* 128). Perhaps the most obvious of Horn's allusions to Woolf is a work entitled *Orlando* (1988). An installation consisting of a pair of androgynous-looking black shoes placed on the floor, scattered with pieces of coal—symbolic of the transformation of one substance into another. On

---

[6] Judy Chicago, *The Dinner Party* (New York: Bantam, 1981), 151.
[7] Chicago, *The Dinner Party*, 151.

the wall above the shoes and coal, two copper rods point toward one another, connected by two snaking cables to an electrical current. The ends of the rods are a few centimetres apart, a space that every twenty-five seconds is closed by a crack of electricity sparking between them in alternating directions. Through titling this work *Orlando*, Horn is speaking directly to Woolf's own treatment of her protagonist and their shifting gender. The back and forth of Horn's electricity is an enactment of Orlando's oscillating sex and the freedom that can be found in obscuring the mechanisms that we employ for the performance of gender, clothes, and shoes:

> it is clothes that wear us and not we them; we may make them take to mould of arm or breast, but they mould our hearts, our brains, our tongues to their liking.... The man has his hand free to seize his sword, the woman must use hers to keep the satins from slipping from her shoulders. The man looks the world full in the face, as if it were made for his uses and fashioned to his liking. The woman takes a sidelong glance at it, full of subtlety, even of suspicion. Had they both worn the same clothes, it is possible that their outlook might have been the same. (*O* 173)

The absence of a body in Horn's *Orlando*, and the presence of the empty shoes, playfully suggests that the wearer of the shoes may have been magically metamorphosed from a gendered body into a new electric identity in which more than one gender is present and possible. This is reminiscent of Woolf's affirmation that 'In every human being a vacillation from one sex to the other takes place, and often it is only the clothes that keep the male or female likeness, while underneath the sex is the very opposite of what it is above' (*O* 173–4) (Figure 39.3).

In addition to Horn, many contemporary and emerging artists today also cite Woolf as a catalyst, influence, or inspiration. Glasgow-based, Sara Barker (b. 1980) makes sculptural paintings, or painted sculptures, which challenge the parameters of what a painting or a sculpture might be. Her skeletal brass and steel structures trace wonky rectangular shapes over painted aluminium, wood, and Perspex sheets or trays, coloured in Bloomsbury-esque forms or patterns with layers of oil paint, car paint, gouache, and watercolours. Numerous contradictions exist within Barker's works; both sculptures and paintings, they are also simultaneously landscapes and interiors, they employ figurative as well as abstract languages, and they also challenge any stereotypical notions of what a male or female artist might be expected to make. As Barker comments:

> Often I draw on female writers like ... Virginia Woolf ... who write about their own creative space. I always felt that space was a metaphor for creative freedom and was something I wanted to make work about. Often, dealing with glass and big metal works and welded structures, it's something you feel confronted by. Who made this work? Was it a man or a woman?[8]

---

[8] Sara Barker quoted in Catherine Deveney, 'Rising Stars of 2015: Artist Sara Barker', *The Guardian*, 28 December 2014.

FIGURE 39.3 Rebecca Horn, *Orlando*, © 2020 Artists Rights Society (ARS), New York / VG Bild-Kunst, Bonn. Photo © Tate

Painter Laura Owens (b. 1970) is also challenging certain conventions—this time, of painting. In her large-scale canvases she works against hierarchies of imagery, allowing the most peripheral or diminutive details—or features that would ordinarily be downgraded to the decorative—to hold a central position. The quality and strength of the attention that she pours onto the smallest of elements creates an energy around them akin to Woolf's descriptions of a still life:

> This table, these chairs, this metal vase with its three red flowers, are about to undergo an extraordinary transformation. Already the room ... wears the wavering, unreal appearance of a place where one waits expecting something to happen. Things quiver as if not yet in being. The blankness of the white table-cloth glares (*W* 93)

Woolf is a key influence for Owens—both in her treatment of the still life, but also significantly through her founding of the Hogarth Press in 1917. The laborious process of typesetting by hand led Woolf to appreciate a sentence as an object that could be physically constructed. This was revelatory for Owens, who also prints and binds her own books: 'Making books, hand binding, doing all the slow work and thinking with the other side of my brain about signatures, orientation, gluing and which page is going where etc, but also allowing myself to put "anything" into a book, is helping me see my paintings differently.'[9]

For Owens then, the ongoing practice of bookmaking is a productive extension of her painting and a direct response to Woolf as a creative stimulus. Owens's books feed her paintings with ideas and imagery, as well as granting her the freedom to embrace the details of the everyday or the minutiae of the commonplace.

Contemporary artist Aleana Egan's (b. 1979) sculptures and installations also highlight familiar details from our daily lives with a Woolf-like energy and precision. Her recent exhibition at London's Drawing Room included references to literary texts such as Jean Rhys's *Good Morning, Midnight* (1939) and Woolf's *The Waves* (1931), in which Woolf asks: 'What is the thing that lies beneath the semblance of the thing?', a question that has become central to Egan's artistic explorations (W 128). Her postminimalist sculptures are eclectic in their materials and content but quiet and elegant in their construction; in *It is noon and one of them wanders off* (2012), several coloured steel and plaster shapes lie atop two sheets of unrolled roofing felt, seemingly discarded like bits and pieces left scattered on empty twin beds. *Room after room* (2012), resembles an enlarged but delicate 'm' shape as a line of welded steel traces three gently undulating bumps. Egan's works are often complemented by found objects too: a discarded shirt without its buttons; a 1936 leaflet from the Royal Irish Academy; a mezzotint of Maria Gunning, one of the famous eighteenth-century Irish sisters who emigrated to London to marry noblemen. Together these found fragments and their sculpted counterparts generate the realization in a viewer that feelings and emotions can be stimulated by (often) incomplete and subjective histories, memories, and environments. Egan's works are at times elegant, anxious, and fragile, and sometimes robust and awkward. With a stillness reminiscent of the 'Time Passes' section of *To the Lighthouse* (1927), these sculptures operate along different levels of individual and collective memory and experience, making that which is potentially private feel public, and vice-versa:

> So loveliness reigned and stillness, and together made the shape of loveliness itself, a form from which life had parted; solitary like a pool at evening, far distant, seen from a train window, vanishing so quickly that the pool, pale in the evening, is scarcely robbed of its solitude, though once seen. Loveliness and stillness clasped hands in the bedroom, and among the shrouded jugs and sheeted chairs even the prying of the wind, and the soft nose of the clammy sea airs, rubbing, snuffling, iterating, and reiterating their questions—'Will you fade? Will you perish?'—scarcely disturbed

---

[9] Laura Owens, qtd in a press release for her exhibition at Galerie Gisela Capitain, Cologne, 18 May 2011, https://www.galeriecapitain.de/exhibition/309/312.

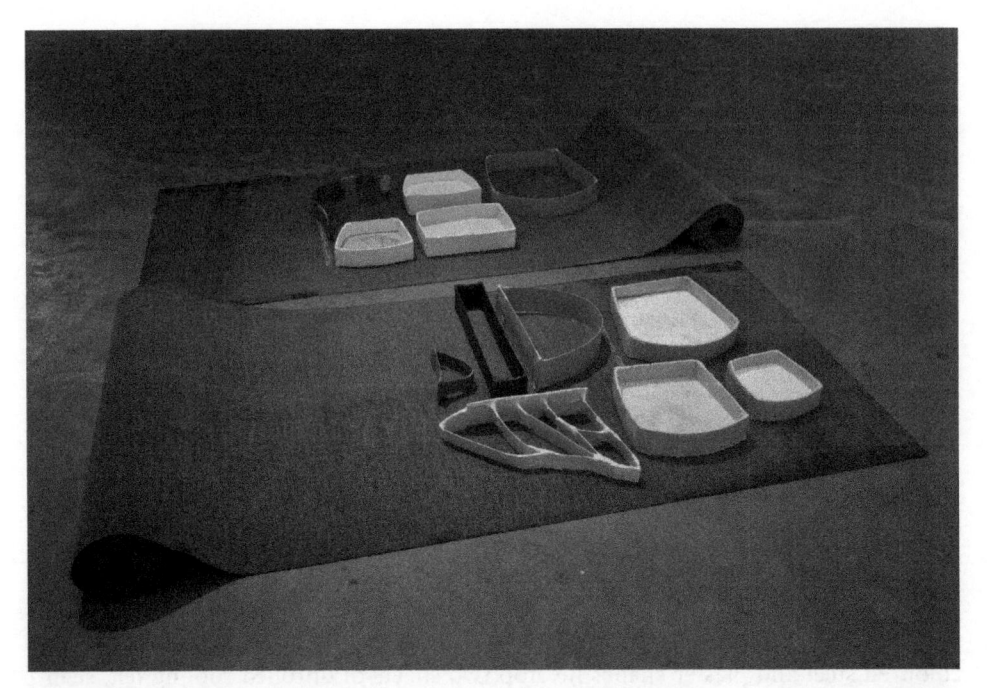

FIGURE 39.4 Aleana Egan. *It is noon and one of them wanders off* (2012) Image courtesy of the artist and Kerlin Gallery, Dublin

the peace, the indifference, the air of pure integrity, as if the question they asked scarcely needed that they should answer: we remain. (*TL* 176) (Figures 39.4 and 39.5)

So many other visual artists have referenced, summoned, quoted, mentioned, been inspired or influenced by, and/or paid tribute to Woolf and her extraordinary catalogue of writings—so much so that there are too many to discuss in detail here, though all deserve a place in the constellation of creatives in which she is situated.[10] Furthermore, outside of the visual arts, Woolf's influence also abounds. Her legacy is widespread across film, theatre, dance, music, and design. In a letter to her friend Violet Dickinson in 1902, Woolf famously said: 'I would give all my profound Greek to dance really well ... but I think Providence inscrutably degreed some other destiny for me' (*L1* 63). Indeed, perhaps the most well-known and recent of the creative endeavours inspired by Woolf's output is Wayne McGregor's ambitious ballet *Woolf Works* performed at The Royal Opera House, London (2015–2017).

---

[10] Barbara Hiles (1891–1984), Dorothy Brett (1883–1977), Nina Hamnet (1890–1956), Ethel Sands (1873–1962), Nan Hudson (1869–1957), and Ray Strachey (1887–1940), all of whom were known and—to varying degrees admired—by Woolf, also cite and draw on her output. As do contemporary collage artists; Linder (b. 1954) and Penny Slinger (b. 1947), painters Lucy Stein (b. 1979) and Caragh Thuring (b. 1972) and filmmakers and photographers Moyra Davey (b. 1958) and Eve Fowler (b. 1964).

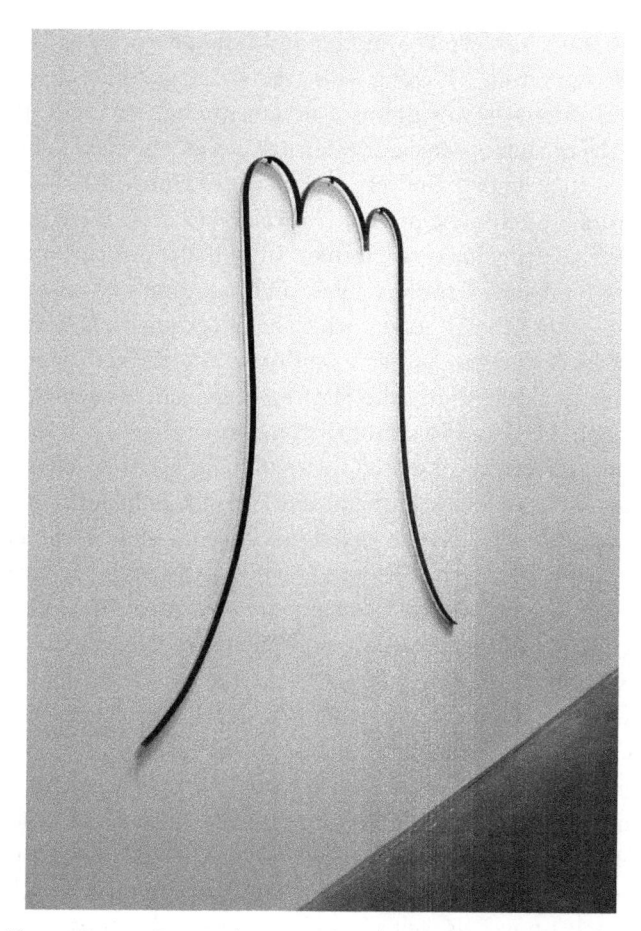

FIGURE 39.5 Aleana Eagan. *Room after room* (2012) Image courtesy of the artist and Kerlin Gallery, Dublin

McGregor was appointed resident choreographer at the Royal Ballet, London in 2006. He is the first Royal Ballet director to express a serious interest in literature since Kenneth MacMillan stepped down in 1977. That said, *Woolf Works* isn't a narrative ballet, instead, McGregor, along with theatre director and writer Uzma Hameed, crafted three acts that draw on three of Woolf's novels, and are also layered with images from Woolf's own life. This format allowed McGregor to experiment with form and abstraction—as is his great skill—while allowing Hameed to mine some of the rich imagery in Woolf. The ballet opens with Woolf's own voice, reading from her essay *On Craftmanship* in a unique archive recording made by the BBC in 1937, in which she asks: 'How can we combine the old words in new orders so that they survive, so that they create beauty, so that they tell the truth?' It is almost as though McGregor and Hameed are setting themselves this formidable challenge—one that they rise to with intelligence and nuance.

The first of the three sections 'I now, I then' is inspired by *Mrs Dalloway* (1925). Set to a commissioned score by Max Richter—which in fact complements the whole ballet—this opening segment shifts between the interior and exterior worlds of Clarissa Dalloway and Septimus Warren Smith. Opening with grainy vintage film of bygone London by Ravi Deepres, and a slowly revolving spare architectural set by Ciguë, the ballet shows Clarissa's day, as she organizes her society soirée that evening. Clocks chime throughout Richter's score—as they do in the novel—as a means of pulling Clarissa out of her nostalgic rememberings and into the present. The role of Clarissa is shared by Alessandra Ferri and Beatriz Stix-Brunell. Ferri, a former Royal Ballet principal plays the present-day Clarissa, her fluid limbs, modest lines, and hauntingly precise movements are celebrated by McGregor's choreography, which has an exquisite, flickering quality. Stix-Brunell plays Clarissa's younger self with a gentle restraint, beneath which seems to burn aching desire. Francesca Hayward, who plays Sally, quivers as an enchanting memory. She dances with both Ferri and Stix-Brunell's versions of Clarissa, as the two remember and enact a single kiss they once shared with Sally. Gary Avis is deliberately blank, almost invisible, as Clarissa's dullard husband, and Federico Bonelli smartly provides both the charm and naivety of Clarissa's rejected suitor, Peter. Meanwhile, Edward Watson carries the raw misery of the shell-shocked Septimus through his tearing and angst-ridden moves. The novel's feeling of collaged time is underpinned by Lucy Carter's layered lighting, Richter's lamenting score, and Ciguë's restrained set.

The second section 'Becomings' is based on *Orlando*. Depicting the urgency and gender-play of the novel, Richter's score shifts from Elizabethan strings to marching electronica, while Carter's bold lighting fills the stage and the auditorium with laser beams cutting through plumes of dry ice and smoke. Natalia Osipova (as Orlando)'s famously expressive talent is utilized in fast fidgety movements and a series of hyperextensions while Eric Underwood (also as Orlando) moves with a majestic authority; together their androgynous moves serve to make the sexes seem indistinguishable. The swagger and dynamism of Woolf's novel, as well as its playfulness and pathos, are all there in the frantic and relentless velocity of this section, which is perhaps the most abstract part of the whole ballet (Figure 39.6).

'Tuesday', the final section of *Woolf Works*, is inspired by *The Waves*. The section opens with a reading of Woolf's suicide note to Leonard, spoken by the actress Gillian Anderson against a black-and-white projection of slowly breaking waves. The reading leads us into a slight soundtrack of fleeting children's voices and sounds of the sea as McGregor's choreography solemnly alludes to the fleeting passages of life and light. Ferri returns to the stage in this section to play—it seems—Woolf herself as the watery imagery of *The Waves* melts into a depiction of Woolf's last moments. Brief moments from her life story are retold as wave after wave of dancers flood the stage, pooling and swirling, framing and partnering Ferri who dances with liquid grace and self-resolution. Her performance is pensive and heartfelt, an apt way to close a show that is both an exercise in narrative metamorphosis and a platform for the intersecting emotional dimensions so characteristic of Woolf's writing.

Contemporary dancer and choreographer Setsuko Yamada (b. 1950) also finds significant influence and inspiration in Woolf's works. Originally trained in the practice of Butoh, from 1977 Yamada has honed her signature style of flowing movements culled

FIGURE 39.6 Wayne McGregor, *Woolf Works*. Premiere: The Royal Ballet, 2015. Image: Tristram Kenton

from Japanese breathing techniques, tai chi, and the martial arts. Yamada's solo dance *Wearing Rose Pink*, originally performed at the Patravadi Theatre, Bangkok (2009) was inspired by both *To the Lighthouse* and *The Waves* as well as Andrew Wyeth's well-known painting *Christina's World* (1948). Yamada's dance is a subtle, tense exploration of inner consciousness and the multiplicity of voices and perspectives across several characters, which operates in both of these novels by Woolf. Yamada is able to convey through movement what Woolf conveys through words, combining memories, aspirations, and desires in the choreography of a 'dance on the poignancy and elegance of life'.[11]

A dancer also worthy of mentioning in direct relation to Woolf is the celebrated Russian ballerina Lydia Lopokova, or Baroness Keynes (born Lidia Vasilyevna Lopukhova, 1892–1981). Lydia trained at the Imperial Ballet School and in 1910 joined the Ballet Russes on their European tour. In 1921, she danced the Lilac Fairy and the Princess Aurora in Diaghilev's lavish production of *The Sleeping Beauty*. Although the production was not a success, her performance attracted the attention of John Maynard Keynes and the two soon became lovers and married in 1925. Keynes was closely linked to the Bloomsbury Group and was close friends with Vanessa Bell, Duncan Grant, Virginia Woolf, and Lytton Strachey, all of whom, upon first meeting Lydia, found her difficult to accept despite her friendships with many other significant cultural figures, including T.S. Eliot, H.G. Wells, and Picasso, who drew her many times.

---

[11] Review of *Wearing Rose Pink*, At Bangkok (website), 20 November 2009, https://at-bangkok.com/detail_news.php?new_id=691.

Bloomsbury's disinterest in Lopokova perhaps exposes something about the group's own cultural preferences. Lopokova's work was dramatic and expressive, whereas much of their output was—on the surface at least—intellectual and domestic. However, Woolf was evidently curious about Lydia, basing the character of Rezia, the friendly milliner in *Mrs Dalloway*, in part on her. Lopokova dressed unconventionally and had a particular passion for hats, a detail that Woolf explicitly transferred to her fictional character. That said, she also paints a more antagonistic picture; for all of Rezia's kindliness, her single flaw is that she is incapable of understanding Septimus Smith's post-traumatic stress. In depicting this inadequacy in Rezia, Woolf creates a parallel with her own considerations of Lopokova as a partner for Keynes, as she writes: 'You can't argue solidly when Lydia's there' (*L*3 115). Lopokova was hurt by Bloomsbury's rebuffs but eventually the long and happy union that she and Keynes enjoyed (until he died in 1946) convinced them that the marriage had not been a mistake, and even Woolf became more fascinated by the ballerina: 'how does her mind work? Like a lark soaring, a sort of glorified instinct inspired her?' (*D*3 18).

Another individual with whom Woolf became increasingly fascinated was the composer and suffragette Dame Ethel Mary Smyth, (1858–1944). Smyth was born in Sidcup, Kent, the fourth of a family of eight children, whose father John Hall Smyth was a major general in the Royal Artillery and much opposed to music as a career option. Undeterred and determined to become a composer, Smyth undertook private tutelage before attending the Leipzig Conservatory, where she began to make both her name and her prolific output of compositions for piano, chamber music, orchestral works, choral works, operas, and suffrage march songs as well as several semi-autobiographical pieces of published writing. In recognition of her work, Smyth was made a Dame Commander of the Order of the British Empire in 1922, the first female composer to be awarded a damehood. She also received honorary doctorates in music from the Universities of Durham and Oxford. Smyth joined the Women's Social and Political Union (WSPU) in 1910. In 1911, her composition *The March of the Women* became the anthem of the women's suffrage movement and in 1912, when the WSPU's leader, Emmeline Pankhurst, called on members to break windows in the houses of any politicians who opposed votes for women, Smyth was amongst the 109 members who answered her plea in the affirmative and were subsequently arrested, spending two months in Holloway Prison. Rumour then goes that when Smyth's friend Thomas Beecham visited her in prison, he found the suffragettes marching and singing in the yard while Smyth conducted them from a window using a toothbrush.[12]

Woolf met Smyth in 1930 when she, recovering from the flu, allowed Smyth (who had just read and was inspired by *A Room of One's Own*) to interview her in bed. The interview lasted hours and became what Woolf later described as the 'basis of an undying friendship' (*D*3 291). From that point on, the pair maintained frequent correspondence,

---

[12] See Geoffrey Norris 'Ethel Smyth: From Prison to the Proms', *The Telegraph*, 31 July 2008, or Judith Abbs, 'Ethel Smyth Belongs on the List of Great Women Composers', *The Guardian*, 12 March 2015.

which offers significant insights into the differences between their respective disciplines as well as the ways in which they influenced one another. In many ways, the bond that formed between Smyth and Woolf was unsurprising as they shared much in common, from their respective endeavours to achieve professional success in male-dominated industries, to their polemics on the under-representation of women in their disciplines, and their interest in biography, autobiography, and the telling of women's lives. Their friendship brings together one of the most productive autobiographers amongst composers, and a writer whose many texts now form the foundations for modern biographical thinking.

In her letters, Woolf provides several images of Smyth, including her first impression—from an encounter years before they actually met:

> I suppose I told you how I saw you years before I knew you?—coming bustling down the gangway at the Wigmore Hall, in tweeds and spats, a little cock's feather in your felt, and a general look of angry energy, so that I said, 'That's Ethel Smyth!'—and felt, being then a mere chit, she belongs to the great achieved public world, where I'm a nonentity. (*D6* 439)

And elsewhere, she gave this impression of Smyth during a rehearsal of her opera *The Prison* (1930):

> On Monday I went to hear her rehearse. A vast Portland Place house with the cold wedding cake Adams plaster: shabby red carpets; flat surfaces washed with dull greens. The rehearsal was in a long room with a bow window looking on, in fact in, to other houses ... a barren brick outlook ... Ethel stood at the piano in the window, in her battered felt, her jersey and short skirt, conducting with a pencil. There was a drop at the end of her nose ... Ethel's pince nez rode nearer and nearer the tip of her nose. She sang now and then; and once, taking the bass, made a cat squalling sound—but everything she does with such forthrightness, directness, that there is nothing ridiculous ... As she strides and turns and wheels about to use perched mute on chairs she thinks this is about the most important event now taking place in London. And perhaps it is. (*D4* 9)

The correspondence between Woolf and Smyth reveals a symbiotic relationship in which each encouraged one another to write more and more on their own lives and their own creativity. In her 'Professions for Women' speech of 1931, Woolf referred to Smyth's texts as masterpieces and the following year urged her: 'If you've one duty, this side of the grave, it is to go on memorializing ... please please please write more' (*L5* 112). And in 1934 she wrote to Smyth again: 'please I beg of you devote yourself to memoir writing for posterity ... This I consider your most sacred duty' (*L5* 326).

Woof's conception of biography was as a fluid and unfixed genre, in which multiple times and consciousnesses overlap. Musician, photographer, and writer Patti Smith (b. 1946) shares this understanding, asking—in her own autobiography—what is 'real time' and whether it does, indeed, move with linearity:

> Is it time uninterrupted? Only the present comprehended? Are our thoughts nothing but passing trains, no stops, devoid of dimension, whizzing by massive posters with repeating images? Catching a fragment from a window seat, yet another fragment from the next identical frame? If I write in the present yet digress, is that still real time? Real time, I reasoned, cannot be divided into sections like numbers on the face of a clock. If I write about the past as I simultaneously dwell in the present, am I still in real time? Perhaps there is no past or future, only the perpetual present that contains this trinity of memory.[13]

Smith is a long time and self-professed fan of Woolf. At the opening of her 2008 retrospective exhibition at Fondation Cartier, Paris, Smith celebrated Woolf's *The Waves* by performing a mesmerizing dramatic performance in which a single sentence from Woolf's original text became the prompt for a sort of free improvisation homage. Uncoincidentally, the start of the exhibition fell on the sixty-seventh anniversary of Woolf's death. Of which, Smith said, 'I do not think of this as sad. I just think that it's the day that Virginia Woolf decided to say goodbye. So, we are not celebrating the day, we are simply acknowledging that this is the day. If I had a title to call tonight, I would call it "Wave". We are waving to Virginia.'[14]

Smith's exhibition included a set of photographs taken at Monk's House in 2003. These photographs are intimate portraits though devoid of human beings, they embody the 'Time Passes' section of *To the Lighthouse* wonderfully, wherein Woolf writes: 'What people had shed and left—a pair of shoes, a shooting cap, some faded skirts and coats in wardrobes—those alone kept the human shape and in the emptiness indicated how once they were filled and animated' (*TL* 175–6).

Also in 2003, Smith travelled to Charleston, Vanessa Bell's Sussex home, to perform two acoustic shows—entitled *Returning a Wave*—of her own music and writing produced across her forty-year career. During one of the performances Smith was moved to tears while singing her *Pissing in a River* 1976, the lyrics of which refer to voices, beckoning us to come back, over and over.

For Smith, Woolf has become a close friend and a fiercely creative influence: 'I went through a transformation last night', Smith is reported to have said following the show, 'I mean, it was really eerie in places. Some of the passages had the same kind of language. It was one of those times where I actually learnt something new about myself.'[15]

Numerous other musicians and composers have been influenced, inspired and motivated by Woolf's writing. Contemporary singer/songwriter Patrick Wolf's (b. 1983) song 'To the Lighthouse' appeared on his *Lycanthropy* album of 2003. The song's melody is based on a descending tetrachord, a repeating four-note pattern that is

---

[13] Patti Smith, *M Train* (London: Bloomsbury, 2016), 84.

[14] Patti Smith, qtd. in Open Culture, 'Watch Patti Smith Read from Virginia Woolf, and Hear the Only Surviving Recording of Woolf's Voice', 30 January 2013, http://www.openculture.com/2013/01/watch_patti_smith_read_from_virginia_woolf_and_hear_the_only_surviving_recording_of_woolfs_voice.html, accessed 25 August 2017. Of note is that fact that Smith also named her fourth studio album of 1979 *Wave*.

[15] Patti Smith quoted in Sean O'Hagan, 'American Icon', *The Observer*, 15 June 2003.

often used to signify a lament. It recounts images of war and emotions of anxiety, lost dreams, and fear, with lyrics such that exhort the addressee to build a castle, rather than collecting stones for a descent into the river.

From the Diary of Virginia Woolf 1974 is an eight-part song cycle written by Dominick Argento (b. 1927) for the English mezzo-soprano Janet Baker. The work won the Pulitzer Prize for Music in 1975. Argento often uses literary sources as the stimulus for his compositions; his original idea for the piece was to use excerpts from *The Waves* but, after having read Woolf's diaries, he made the decision to work with these texts instead, in order to illuminate Woolf's inner world in a more immediate way.

British band The Smiths (formed in Manchester in 1982) named their 1985 non-album single 'Shakespeare's Sister' (which later appeared on the 1987 compilation albums *Louder Than Bombs* and *The World Won't Listen*). Directly referring to *A Room of One's Own* wherein Woolf imagines Shakespeare's unrecognized sister of equal genius:

> Now my belief is that this poet who never wrote a word and was buried at the crossroads still lives. She lives in you and in me, and in many other women who are not here tonight, for they are washing up the dishes and putting the children to bed. But she lives; for great poets do not die; they are continuing presences; they need only the opportunity to walk among us in the flesh. (*ARO* 85–6)

The Smiths' front man, Morrissey, is said to have embraced Woolf's essay as a teenager and its call to write, to create, despite personal or societal difficulties.

And in the United States, feminist folk-rock duo Indigo Girls (formed in Atlanta in 1985) produced their own ode to Woolf: 'Virginia Woolf', in 1992. Emily Saliers of the Indigo Girls cites the profound connection she felt with Woolf upon reading her diaries. The song's lyrics describe this experience as: 'a kind of a telephone line through time, and the voice at the other end comes like a long-lost friend'. Woolf's impact on and significance to Saliers is profound ('like a letter to my soul') and, as for so many creative practitioners, exists outside of time and continues to find potency so many years on, as the song concludes, directly addressing Woolf: the singer herself becomes proof of Woolf's endurance.

With its striking imagery, rhythms, colour, and flow, Woolf's writing has always suggested a strong affinity with other media. Her enduring emphasis on redefining biography and finding new forms for women's (often) un-narrated lives and stories, as well as her endeavour toward a multiplicity of narrators in place of one unified authorial voice, has spawned countless re-readings and appropriations of her work and ideas in paint, sculpture, installation, music, song, and dance, reasserting her claim that: 'masterpieces are not single and solitary births' (*ARO* 49).

Perhaps it is this generosity of spirit, creativity, and correspondence, and the honesty with which she approached her own autobiographical writing, not to mention her patronage, that has led to her influence as one of the most cited, referenced, queried, challenged, celebrated, and honoured writers of the last century. And one whose work has initiated so many divergent and multitudinous creative endeavours.

Woolf asks us to read, write, and create in a way that challenges conventions. To carve out different temporal and spatial arrangements for our own creativity that fit with our own subjective understandings of the world and our place within it. In so doing, she asks us to embrace difference and discord and to see these qualities as exciting, positive, and the foundations of cultural production, as she calmly avows in *Three Guineas*: 'though we see the same world, we see it through different eyes. Any help we can give you must be different from that you can give yourselves, and perhaps the value of that help may lie in the fact of that difference' (*TG* 102).

Selected Bibliography

Bell, Vanessa, *Sketches in Pen and Ink: A Bloomsbury Notebook*, ed. Lia Giachero (London: Pimlico, 1998).
Chicago, Judy, *The Dinner Party* (New York: Bantam, 1981).
Goldman, Jane, *The Feminist Aesthetics of Virginia Woolf: Modernism, Post-Impressionism, and the Politics of the Visual* (Cambridge: Cambridge University Press, 2009).
Hill, Jane, *The Art of Dora Carrington* (London: A&C Black Publishers, 1994).
Humm, Maggie, *The Edinburgh Companion to Virginia Woolf and the Arts* (Edinburgh: Edinburgh University Press, 2010).
Jones, Susan, *Literature, Modernism & Dance* (Oxford: Oxford University Press, 2014).
Smith, Patti, *M Train* (London: Bloomsbury, 2016).
Spalding, Frances, *Virginia Woolf: Art, Life and Vision* (London: National Portrait Gallery, 2014).
St. John, Christopher, *Ethel Smyth: A Biography* (London: Longmans, Green, and Co., 1959).
Sutton, Emma, *Virginia Woolf and Classical Music: Politics, Aesthetics, Form* (Edinburgh: Edinburgh University Press, 2013).
Zimring, Rishona, *Social Dance and the Modernist Imagination in Interwar Britain* (Farnham: Ashgate, 2013).

Index

A

1917 Club 237–39, 259
Abbot, H. Porter 161
abstraction 176, 388–90, 598, 633
academy 250, 299, 360, 378, 496, 521–35
Acker, Kathy 583
activism 316–17, 320, 324, 362–76, 441, 450, 454, 476, 486, 496–502 *see also* suffrage
adaptation 169, 200, 481, 578, 607–9, 618
Addison, Joseph
Adichie, Chimamanda Ngozi 90, 208, 353
Adorno, Theodor 443–44
Aeschylus 100
aesthetics 19, 32, 63–64, 70–72, 90, 92, 109, 113, 122, 183, 253, 294, 311–12, 322n42, 423, 443, 532, 593
　commercial 475
　epiphanic 432
　ethical 600
　European 555
　experience 63, 282, 322
　feminist 67
　judgement 321–22, 423
　modernist 426, 434–35
　of reflexivity 71
　totalitarian 452
affect 106, 187–92, 194–95, 277, 280–82, 285, 287–90, 414–16, 420, 427 *see also* emotion
　temporal 449
　theory 185, 501
afterlives 3, 306, 613, 620, 622–40
agency 152, 228, 279, 336, 422, 425, 427, 432, 435, 438, 449, 582, 593, 596, 600, 618
Ahmed, Sara 189–90, 194, 287, 326, 328–31, 335–39, 341, 489, 491–92
Albee, Edward 606
Ali, Monica 537
Allan, Tuzyline 494

alienation 8, 90, 95–96, 107, 238, 386, 425, 561, 564, 580
allusion 108, 128, 197–211, 236, 250, 279n5, 288, 290, 354, 490, 622, 626, 628
alterity 69, 84, 88, 96, 112, 115, 182, 186–89, 194–95, 423–24, 435, 460 *see also* otherness
Altes, Kiesbeth Korthals 181
Anand, Mulk Raj 22, 231n21, 233–34
Anderson, Gillian 634
androgyny 106, 208–9, 490–91, 503, 522
Anthropocene 425, 434
anti-imperialism 103, 106, 112, 127, 394–97, 482, 532
Aquinas, Thomas 92
archive 63, 65, 67–68, 115, 119, 122, 124, 202, 211, 248, 253–55, 348, 350, 363, 368, 370–71, 374, 434, 531, 633
Argento, Dominick 639
Aristotle 91, 101, 180, 183–85, 197, 263n2
Armstrong, Nancy 137
Arnold, Edward 243
Arnold, Matthew 57, 93
Atkins, Eileen 608
Attridge, Derek 182, 186–89
Atwood, Margaret 576–78, 580, 583
Auden, W. H., 23, 121, 358, 440
Austen, Jane 77, 80, 90–91, 139, 159–60, 203, 277, 285, 289, 522, 557, 605–06, 612
autobiography 50, 58, 109–10, 212–224, 236, 238, 242, 249, 254, 285n10, 295–96, 408, 468, 566, 568, 637 *see also* memoir
autonomy 23, 156, 181, 250, 316, 333, 423, 439, 533, 535, 573, 583
　aesthetic 439
avant-garde 44, 78, 85, 94, 238, 249, 384
Avis, Gary 634
Ayuso, Mónica 560

B

Badenes, Guillermo 559
Bailey, John 68
Baker, Janet 639
Bakhtin, Mikhail 159, 174, 201, 262n2
Banfield, Ann 113n34, 139n22, 379, 386, 441–42
Baring, Maurice 241
Barker, Sara 629
Barkway, Stephen 252
Barrett, Eileen 530
Barrett Browning, Elizabeth 1, 118, 123, 219, 457, 593, 627
Barthes, Roland 101, 609
Bartholomew, Percy 468
Batchelor, J. B., 525
Battershill, Claire 248, 252, 254–55, 554
Battle of Britain 127–28
Bayly, Thomas Haynes 210
Beach, Joseph Warren 135, 522
Beach, Sylvia 556
Beale, Dorothea 356–57
Beaumont, Caitriona 316
Beauvoir, Simone de 489–91
Beecham, Thomas 636
Beer, Gillian 113–14, 210
Beerbohm, Max 277, 280–83, 289–90
Bell, Anne Olivier 17, 103, 229, 526
Bell, Clive 22, 28, 36, 49, 63, 212, 231–32, 317, 318n27, 347, 384, 387
Bell, Cressida 534
Bell, Quentin 9, 10, 45–46, 48, 311, 347, 468, 505n3, 526–27, 534
Bell, Vanessa 7, 11, 15, 23–25, 44–45, 154, 221, 224, 229, 233, 238, 253, 257, 378, 386, 388, 478, 526–27, 537, 592, 622-2, 627, 635, 638
Bellow, Saul 542
Benjamin, Walter 112n26, 254, 292n4, 294, 299, 452
Ben Jelloun, Tahar 327, 330, 335, 337, 339, 342
  The Sacred Night 338
  The Sand Child 330–31, 335–39, 341
Bennet, Alan 606
Bennett, Arnold 83, 85–86, 97, 151–52, 158, 522, 592
Bergson, Henri 97, 168–70, 217, 219, 438n41
Berman, Jessica 69, 90n3, 91, 111–12, 113n37, 144, 186–87, 292n1, 329, 334, 339, 423

Bernard, Henry 238
Bernhardt, Sarah 266–67, 275
Besier, Rudolf 219
Betancourt, Manuel 615
Bibesco, Elizabeth 123
Bildungsroman 1, 13, 76, 212, 444, 477, 579
biopower 408–421
Birmingham Group 233
Birrell, Francis 243
Biryukov, Paul 295
Bishop, Edward 253, 255n36, 272n21
Black, Naomi 122, 364
Blair, Sara 228–29, 233, 238, 239n41
Blanchard, Lydia 528
Bloomsbury 2, 7, 9, 22–23, 37, 45, 58, 144n27, 224, 227–35, 238–39, 241–45, 457–58, 474, 522, 624
Bloomsbury Group 2, 27, 31–32, 37, 47, 58, 118, 142, 183–85, 212, 214, 230–34, 237–38, 240, 242, 249, 252, 302, 317–18, 321, 347, 384–85, 440, 446, 472, 478–81, 522–23, 526, 532, 540, 592–93, 595, 627, 629, 635–36
Bloomsbury Memoir Club 15, 44, 212, 220–21, 224, 384, 584
Bluemel, Kristin 578
Bluestockings 248
Blyth, Ian 108
Bollen, Christopher 586
Bonelli, Federico 634
book history 250, 251n14, 255n33
Booth, Charles 17
Booth, Wayne 181
Borges, Jorge Luis 521, 553, 556–62, 564, 569–71, 619
Bos, Jacques 153
Bosanquet, Theodora 118
Bostridge, Mark 54
Boswell, James 214
Bowen, Elizabeth 28, 540, 545
Bowlby, Rachel 89n2
Boxall, Nellie 458, 461, 467, 469
Bradbury, Malcolm 227–28
Bradford, Gamaliel 217
Bradshaw, David 235, 497
Brailsford, H. N., 238
Brenan, Gerald 32, 69

Bressey, Caroline 238
Brett, Dorothy 240, 625
Brewster, Dorothy 235, 525
Briggs, Julia 83, 89n1, 155–56, 253, 367n18, 527, 531
British Museum 84–85, 198, 235, 237, 242–43, 287–88
Brittain, Vera 458
Brontë, Charlotte 42, 90, 121, 285, 289, 537, 567, 576
   Jane Eyre 289
Brontë, Emily 103, 285, 567, 627
Browne, William 99
Browne, Thomas 206
Browning, Elizabeth Barrett 1, 118, 123, 208, 219, 457, 593, 627
Bullock, Helene B., 521
Burke, Edmund 77
Burke, Tarana 496
Burne-Jones, Edward 17, 377
Busch, Akiko 597–58, 603
Bussy, Jane 301–2
Butler, Judith 64, 411, 598
Byatt, A. S., 580

C

Cameron, Julia Margaret 53, 154, 229
capitalism 3, 342, 473, 485–86
Carlston, Erin 408
Carlyle, Thomas 51, 208, 241, 277
Carpenter, John 619
Carpentier, Alejo 558
Carrington, Dora 22, 34, 231–32, 240, 624–27
Carroll, Lewis 45
Carruthers, Charlene A., 500
Carter, Lucy 634
Case, Janet 29, 198, 239–40, 317, 320n38, 347, 355, 507–9, 511
Castagnary, Jules-Antoine 379
Caughie, Pamela 123, 327, 460, 492
Cavarero, Adriana 114
Cecil, Nelly 29, 215, 266, 317
Cézanne, Paul 232, 384, 386, 480
Chakrabarty, Dipesh 435–36
Chapman, Guy 243
character: as caricature 150–55, 161–62
   complexities of 97
   and form 149–163
   as type 83, 150, 154, 156–57, 383, 435–38
   and visual portraiture 154
Chaucer, Geoffrey 85, 90–91, 97, 136, 205, 208
   The Canterbury Tales 205
Cheever, John 549
Chekhov, Anton 100
Chemaly, Soraya 499
Chen, Evelyn Tsz Yan 461
Chew-Bose, Durga 597–99
Chicago, Judy 622, 627–28
Childers, Mary 460–61, 469, 533
Christian, Barbara 529, 565
Churchill, Sarah 627
cinema 64, 70, 155, 250, 607–8, 611, 613 *see also* film
Civello, Catherine A., 532
Clark, Kenneth 627
Clarke, Stuart N., 279, 302
class 2–3, 13, 17, 34, 45, 47–48, 51, 55, 113, 118, 119, 123, 140, 249, 259, 286, 314, 318n26, 321, 324, 352, 357, 359, 373, 441, 445, 448, 456–68, 470–71, 473, 479, 484, 489–90, 492–94, 496, 498, 523–24, 531–33, 564, 576, 580, 584, 597, 600, 606
   middle 15, 48, 51, 55–58, 119, 122, 123, 137, 229, 235, 316, 320, 322, 476–77, 493, 541, 543, 548, 624
   privilege 355, 590
   upper 366, 476, 483, 546, 599
   working 44, 252, 315, 320, 322–23, 345, 352–53, 356, 358, 360
Clay, Catherine 316
Clements, Patricia 528
Clough, Anne Jemima 356
Cohen, Rachel 597, 606n7
Cohn, Dorrit 145, 175
Coisson, Josefina 559
Cole, Sarah 450
Cole, Teju 596–97
Colefax, Sibyl 241
Coleridge, Samuel 203–04, 274, 353
Coleridge, Sara 275
Collingwood, R. G. 451
Collins, Suzanne 451
colonialism 34, 108, 240n42, 413, 423n6, 531–32
   see also empire; imperialism

commodities 252, 472–73, 475, 477–78, 482–84
Connolly, Cyril 241, 545
Conrad, Joseph 90, 165, 227n2, 262, 265,
    270–71, 381, 524, 608, 619
  Heart of Darkness 381, 619
  Lord Jim 270, 381
  The Secret Agent 165
consciousness 15, 19, 21, 97, 101, 113n34, 144,
    146–48, 168, 172, 175–76, 187–88, 191,
    195, 256–57, 262, 270, 284, 336, 377–83,
    435, 438, 441–42, 452, 454, 491, 522, 537,
    539, 543–44, 551, 554, 583, 590, 592, 594,
    596, 598, 603, 608, 635
  self-, 64, 67–68, 72, 222, 283–84, 459
Cons, Emma 350
consumer culture 1, 472–86
Coppola, Francis Ford 619
Corbett, Mary Jean 370, 319n29
Cortázar, Julio 559
cosmopolitanism 228
Costelloe, Karin 239
Courtney, Dolores 625
Cousins, Mark 607, 609–13, 620
Cowper, William 544
Cramer, Patricia 530
Craye, Julia 350
creative non-fiction 590–604
Crenshaw, Kimberlé 315
critical animal studies 422, 425, 433
Cromwell, Jason 328, 337
Cronenberg, David 619
Crutzen, Paul J., 435
Cuddy-Keane, Melba 180, 182n8, 192, 271n19,
    321–22n42, 352, 359–360, 408
Cunningham, Michael 250, 522, 537–40, 545,
    550–51, 605, 608–9
Currah, Paisley 330
Cusk, Rachel 537, 545–46

D

Daldry, Stephen 522, 608
Dante, Alighieri 198, 210
Darwin, Charles 11, 94, 435–47, 543
Daston, Lorraine 436
Daugherty, Beth Rigel 89n2, 351–52, 534
Davies, Emily 56, 355
Davies, Margaret Llewellen 57

da Vinci, Leonardo 282
Davis, Angela 494
Davis, Thomas S., 375
death 11, 15, 19, 24, 33–35, 45, 47–49, 54–55, 58,
    72, 78, 203, 206, 209, 214, 219, 222, 229,
    275, 280, 295, 316–17, 334, 336–38, 372,
    381, 398, 409–10, 419, 426, 440, 442–43,
    445–49, 524, 534, 538, 556, 562, 575–76,
    592, 603, 614, 616–17, 624
  in *Between the Acts*
  in *Jacob's Room* 13, 85, 158, 167, 594–95
  in *Mrs. Dalloway* 21, 187–88
  in *To the Lighthouse* 20–21, 95, 98–99, 387
  in *The Waves* 389
  Woolf's, 2, 23, 31, 117, 591, 598, 605–6, 638
  see also mortality
De Certeau, Michel 66
Deepres, Ravi 634
Defoe, Daniel 77, 90, 103, 272
Deleuze, Gilles 91, 186
de Medici, Catherine 265
Dennys, John 429
De Quincey, Thomas 109–11, 224
Derrida, Jacques 186, 242
DeSalvo, Louise 530
desire 22, 27, 30, 32, 36, 39, 51, 80, 95, 98, 110, 115,
    120, 122, 124–25, 128, 183–84, 188, 191,
    200, 205, 221, 253, 276n29, 280, 282, 285,
    299, 306, 315, 322, 326–29, 332–33, 337–
    39, 344, 351, 360, 367, 370–72, 375, 396,
    409–13, 416–17, 424, 426, 442, 445n17,
    447, 470, 475, 479, 482, 484, 497, 529, 536,
    567, 577, 582–84, 586, 595, 617–18, 634
  queer 191, 342
  same-sex 106–7, 313, 484
detachment 37, 102, 115, 161, 170, 282, 322–24,
    329, 366, 610
Detloff, Madelyn 184, 193, 204, 523
D'haen, Theo 564, 569–70
diary 13, 23–24, 32–34, 36–37, 39–40, 45, 56,
    63, 65, 70–74, 85, 89, 93, 96–96, 108,
    119, 128, 144n27, 153, 155, 160–61, 209,
    216, 218–19, 221, 228–29, 231, 234, 238,
    266, 292, 305, 319, 351, 379, 381–82, 386,
    389, 417–18, 442, 445, 447, 449, 453, 461,
    467–68, 507, 509–13, 525–26, 555, 569,
    599, 639 *see also* private writings

DiBattista, Maria 606, 611
Dickens, Charles 136, 159, 161, 234, 354, 430, 605
Dickinson, Emily 581
Dickinson, Violet 2, 29–30, 37, 41–42, 215, 220, 263, 317, 632
Dillard, Annie 602–3
disability 336, 419, 504–19, 531
disability studies 505–8, 510, 511, 513, 515–17, 519
dispossession 14, 335
Disraeli, Benjamin 214, 303
Doan, Laura 313n12, 484
domesticity 13, 17, 19–21, 329, 457–58., 460, 466–67, 471
Donne, John 136, 203, 209
Doolittle, Hilda 227n2, 231
Dostoevsky, Fyodor 90, 96, 153, 265, 270
Drabble, Margaret 576, 580
Dreadnought Hoax 385, 402–3, 406, 532
Duckworth, Gerald 17, 222–23, 244
Duckworth, Stella 19–20, 48, 55, 426
Dujardin, Édouard 138–39
Dunbar, William 227
DuPlessis, Rachel Blau 582
Durkheim, Émile 437
Duvall, John 564

E

Eagleton, Terry 153
early novels 76–88, 318
Easdale, Joan Adeney 252
Eberly, David 441
Ebert, Roger 613
ecocriticism 422
Eddington, Arthur 113
education 2, 29n4, 52–53, 56–57, 109n15, 121, 125–26, 169n8, 176, 229, 285, 290, 312, 314, 316–17, 344–61, 415, 419–20, 445, 464, 466–67, 498–99, 530, 580, 584, 590, 600
   alternative pedagogy 346, 359–60
   essays on 345–46, 354–56
   fiction on 346, 353–54
   self-, 346–47, 357, 359
   women's, 313, 320n38, 459
   Woolf as student 347–50

   Woolf as teacher 350–52 *see also* Woolf, Virginia: life
Egan, Aleana 631–32
egotism 40–41, 69, 86, 134, 138, 203, 397, 417, 496
Einstein, Albert 450
Eisenstein, Sergei 609–10
elegy 2, 20, 97–98, 203, 210, 383, 423, 445–48
Eliot, George 45, 90, 160, 193, 234, 277–78, 285, 623
Eliot, T. S., 232, 278, 635
   'Tradition and the Individual Talent', 199
   The Waste Land 199, 259
Ellis, Havelock 217
El Saadawi, Nawal 327, 330–33, 336, 339, 342
   Woman at Point Zero 330–31
embodiment 137, 209, 218, 327–28, 330, 335, 337, 399, 402, 481, 483, 518
Emecheta, Buchi 576, 580
emotion 33, 41, 96, 109, 126, 146, 185, 223–24, 268, 271, 277, 280, 282, 284, 287–90, 295–96, 388, 420, 452–53, 502, 539, 582, 589, 593, 624–25 *see also* affect
empire 1, 3, 45, 47, 111, 113, 119, 127, 165, 178, 184, 228, 315, 319, 349, 392–407, 473, 475–76, 482–83, 491, 538, 603, 636 *see also* colonialism; imperialism
England 2, 8, 10, 23, 50, 56, 108, 119, 125–29, 142, 193, 205, 227–28, 230, 244, 246, 250, 255, 302–3, 312, 329, 348, 351, 360, 377–78, 383–85, 418, 443, 445–46, 448, 453, 475, 491, 510, 518, 542, 557, 562, 592
Englishness 8, 126–27, 303, 412, 419, 480, 485, 532
Enke, Finn 334
Enright, Anne 583
Esposito, Roberto 74
essays 18, 24, 50, 59, 64–66, 72, 82–90, 92, 96, 99–101, 103–5, 113–15, 119, 121–22, 151–52, 166, 201–2, 209, 212–13, 244, 252, 262–64, 266, 268, 271–72, 274–292, 302, 318–20, 324, 345–46, 349, 351, 377, 379, 380, 386, 417, 423, 450, 459, 461, 477, 496, 499–501, 505n5, 507, 510, 514, 524–25, 527–30, 530, 532–33, 535, 540, 564–65, 567, 574, 581, 590, 627
Esty, Jed 127, 208

ethics 64, 69, 71–72, 84, 90–92, 96, 111, 180–96, 219, 292, 380, 422–24, 426–27, 431–32, 434–35, 437, 444, 461, 590–95, 599–603
see also narrative ethics
Evans, Elizabeth 364, 452
Everest, Louie 458, 468

F

Fagan, Jenni 583–84
Faithfull, Lilian 348, 350
Fand, Roxanne J., 576
Faris, Wendy 563
Farrell, Sophie 51, 458, 462, 463
fascism 112–13, 117, 119–20, 122–23, 125–26, 128–29, 134, 326, 346, 408, 410–11, 414, 417, 419n23, 420, 450–51, 497, 499, 535, 620
fashion 45, 53, 98, 241, 268, 327, 462, 472–86, 545
Faulkner, William 139, 165, 553, 561, 562n23, 564, 569–70
The Sound and the Fury 135, 139, 165
Fawcett, Henry 50, 53
Fawcett, Millicent 50
Fawcett, Philippa 53
femininity 52–53, 339, 363, 371, 374, 575, 580, 587, 606, 624 *see also* womanhood
feminism 1–2, 14, 47, 67, 103, 106, 108, 115, 117, 120, 122, 124, 183, 251n14, 279, 311–25, 339, 345, 357, 362–365, 368, 370–73, 375, 408, 417, 422, 435, 445, 460, 480, 489, 494–95, 501–2, 522, 525, 526, 528, 530, 532, 537, 575, 581, 584, 586, 590, 603, 606, 608, 621
and aesthetics 67
ambivalent 501
and Bloomsbury Group 317–19
and critique 102, 181, 257n38, 324, 336, 559
difference 315
eco-, 422
first-wave 312
global 14
intersectional 315
lesbian 489
New Woman debates 313
New Woman novel 313
second-wave 578, 606

women of colour critique of 493–94
see also feminist novel; feminist theory; gender; lesbian; suffrage; women's literature; women's rights
feminist novel 573–89
feminist theory 109n15, 260, 489–503
Fernald, Anne 199, 279, 285n10, 320n38, 321
Ferri, Alessandra 634
Fewster, Anna 254
fiction: experimental 553–72
highbrow 249
middlebrow 252
modernist 103, 117, 145, 185–86, 607
short 2, 24, 101, 154, 256, 382, 567
suffrage 365–66, 375
women's, 106, 290, 573–89
Woolfian 536–52
Fiedler, Leslie A., 523
film 70, 81, 250n13, 492, 496, 522, 580, 606–15, 617–21, 632, 634 *see also* cinema
filmmaker 605–21
Finch, Anne (Lady Winchilsea) 203, 289
Fisher, H. A. L., 353
Fisher, Jo 55
Fitzgerald, Edward 98
Fitzjames, James 263
Flaubert, Gustave 139, 430
Flint, Kate 524
Fondane, Benjamin 555
Ford, Ford Madox 231, 381n12
foreignness 8, 293, 299, 300–1
form: aesthetic 9, 71, 172, 176, 378
epistolary 67–70, 125, 295n14, 300
literary 136, 153, 162, 170, 172, 175, 364, 383, 477, 565
narrative 174–78, 181–82, 215, 257, 277, 378, 383
novel 105
soliloquy 111–12
formalism 71
Forster, E. M., 22, 29, 31–32, 78, 100, 176, 184, 212, 233–34, 238, 243, 317, 347, 407, 522, 540
Aspects of the Novel 32, 176
Foucault, Michel 64, 66, 71, 73–74, 409–11, 416, 436
Frank, Waldo 554

free indirect discourse 85–86, 134, 138–43, 158–59, 187, 262, 267, 456, 559
Freeman, E. A., 351
Freeman, Elizabeth 328
Freud, Sigmund 23, 82, 217, 222–23, 239, 244, 431, 441, 450, 595
Freund, Gisèle 22
Friday Club 229, 233, 378
Friedman, Susan Stanford 18
friends 13, 24, 27–43, 44, 50, 52, 54, 69–70, 85, 95–96, 109, 121, 144, 159, 161, 215, 230–33, 237, 243, 249, 295, 320, 333, 345, 347, 371, 377, 384–85, 414, 478, 481, 523, 525, 530, 536, 547, 556, 586, 595, 613, 622, 625, 635
Froebel, Friedrich 345
Frost, Robert 227n2, 612
Froude, James Anthony 400–2
Froula, Christina 77, 84, 374, 408, 445
Fry, Roger 22, 63, 68, 144, 184, 212, 219–23, 231–33, 243, 268, 274, 317, 379, 384–87, 398–91, 478, 480, 532, 536, 591–93, 624
Furbank, P. N., 238

G

Galsworthy, John 239, 522
Garland, Alex 607, 609, 613, 617–20
Garland-Thomson, Rosemarie 504
Garnett, David 219, 233, 243
Garnett, Edward 243
Garrity, Jane 479
Gaskell, Elizabeth 98, 201
Gauguin, Paul 232, 384, 386
Gay, John 246
Gay, Roxane 573
gender 38, 54, 90, 106, 109, 112n27, 113, 123, 135–36, 153, 194, 207, 217, 258, 277–78, 285, 288, 290–91, 298, 303, 314, 324, 327–30, 334–36, 339–41, 345, 354, 360, 364, 366, 395, 427, 445, 451, 458–59, 465–66, 473, 479, 482–85, 489, 491–92, 496, 498, 508, 510, 522, 524, 532, 540, 542, 551, 553, 558–60, 564, 568–70, 573, 579–80, 582–86, 601, 603–4, 606–7, 621, 629, 634
  roles 2, 50
  studies 108, 334
  see also transgender

generic hybridity 102, 105, 110–11, 114
Genette, Gérard 609
genre 1–2, 9, 67–68, 76, 89, 97, 105, 107n7–8, 108–9, 114, 133–36, 138, 142, 147, 151, 153, 175, 212, 214, 217, 247, 254, 266, 277, 279, 288, 290, 320, 330, 345, 359, 366, 390, 428, 447, 477, 491, 534, 558, 560–61, 563, 568–69, 619, 637
Gerould, Katherine Fullerton 135
Gertler, Mark 231–32, 239–40, 242
Gerzina, Gretchen Holbrook 532
Giddens, Anthony 228
Gilbert, Sandra 575–76, 606n7
Gillespie, Diane 161, 252–53
Ginsberg, Elaine K., 528
Goethe, Johann von 443
Goffman, Erving 437
Goldman, Mark 252
Goldstone, Harmon 347
Gordon, Elizabeth Wilson 252
Gorky, Maxim 23, 294
Gorris, Marleen 608
Gottlieb, Laura M., 528
Graham, John 161
Grant, Duncan 28, 58, 212, 229–30, 232, 317, 384, 478, 480–81, 592, 623–24, 627, 635
Gray, Thomas 203, 210
Great War 13, 20, 82, 84, 363, 370, 445–46, 530
  see also World War I
Green, Barbara 476
Greene, Gayle 579
Greene, Graham 118
Greene, Nick 208
Gregg, Colin 608
Gruber, Ruth 521
Grundy, Isobel 528
Gruss, Susanne 567
Gualtieri, Elena 89n2
Gubar, Susan 575–76, 606n7
Guiguet, Jean 526
Gunning, Maria 631

H

Hackett, Robin 331
Hadley, Tessa 537, 546–48
Hagen, Benjamin 90, 533–34
Hägglund, Martin 442, 449

Hall, Radclyffe 32, 107, 335, 484
  The Well of Loneliness 32, 107, 335, 484
Hameed, Uzma 633
Hamilton, Cicely 318, 362, 370
Hamilton, Molly 238
Hammill, Faye 249
Hamnett, Nina 625
Hampson, John 233
Hankins, Leslie 253
Hanson, Clare 193, 340, 567
Haraway, Donna 424
Hardy, Thomas 17, 272, 357
Hare, David 608
Hargreaves, Tracy 525
Harris, Alexandra 228
Harrison, Jane Ellen 29, 107n8, 320n38, 350, 355
Harss, Luis 563
Hartley, Lodwick 522
Harvey, Benjamin 253
Harvey, David 228
Haskins, Mabel 468
Haule, James 449
Hawkins, Ethel Wallace 135, 136n13
Hayot, Eric 438
Hazlitt, William 207, 277–78, 280, 284, 286, 288–90
Heard, Gerald 113
Heilbrun, Carolyn 489–91
Helt, Brenda 523
Hemingway, Ernest 262, 270–72
Henderson, Faith 481
Henke, Suzette 441
Hepworth, Barbara 239
Herndl, Diane Price 494, 506
Hiles, Barbara 481, 625
Hill, Octavia 51–52, 55–56, 351
Hills, John Waller 48, 426, 428–32, 434–35
Hinnov, Emily 423
Historiography 105, 108, 177, 208, 339, 351, 451
history: English 2, 127, 177, 327, 351, 390, 428, 452
  family 1, 12, 38, 363, 375, 547
  literary 78, 159, 162, 200, 205, 208–9, 277–79, 289, 586
  women's 47, 586
Hitchcock, Alfred 599, 612
Hite, Molly 189, 192, 363, 366

Hobson, J. A., 238
Hogarth Press 23–24, 28, 35–37, 89, 214, 227–28, 231–34, 237–38, 240–44, 246–61, 272, 292–96, 319, 322, 417, 459, 474, 525, 531, 534, 554, 592, 624, 630 *see also* Hogarth House; publishing
Hogarth, William 246
Hollander, Rachel 186
Hollis, Catherine 253
Holtby, Winifred 279, 393, 444, 521
hooks, bell 494
Hope, Lottie 458
Horn, Rebecca 628
Hours, The (Cunningham) 250, 522, 537, 539–40, 549, 551, 605, 608
Hours, The (Daldry) 522, 606, 608
Howells, William Dean 265–65
Howsam, Leslie 257
Hudson, Nan 241
Hulme, T. E., 91, 136
Humphrey, Robert 133n2, 136n11, 145n30
Hunt, Holman 241
Hunt, Leigh 239, 241
Hussain, Iqbalunnisa 327, 330–31, 333–35, 339, 342
  Purdah and Polygamy 330, 333–34, 336, 342
Hussey, Mark 158, 188, 210, 249, 252, 526, 530–31, 533–34
Hutchinson, Mary 231, 241–42
Huxley, Aldous 57, 238, 450, 561
Huxley, Julian 437
Huxley, Thomas Henry 11
Hynes, Samuel 121

I

identity 9, 23, 35, 89, 91, 101, 127, 162, 188, 194, 212–13, 216–18, 222, 224, 248, 250, 275, 283, 313, 319, 324–25, 327–30, 337, 392, 394, 397, 405, 465, 479–80, 483, 485, 489–90, 492, 494, 502, 512, 532, 553–54, 559, 561, 568, 574, 577–79, 581, 583–85, 587, 598, 603–4, 609, 618, 620, 629
illness 20, 50, 54–55, 78, 410, 504–19, 600, 606
immediacy 64, 67, 74, 222, 223, 275
imperialism 112, 119, 127–28, 195, 354, 359, 392–99, 401–2, 404–6, 423, 445, 485, 532, 584
  see also colonialism; empire
impersonality 106, 581
Impressionism 377–91

Indigo Girls 622, 639
individualism 112, 134, 137, 321
Ingelbein, Raphael 579
Ingersoll, Earl G., 608–9
inspiration 3, 27–28, 31, 33, 35, 41–42, 109, 197, 205, 207, 228, 237, 244, 254, 480, 523, 553, 561, 564, 574, 578, 585, 602, 623, 629, 634
interiority 107, 111, 137–38, 256, 410, 422, 424–25, 434, 438, 445, 607
interior monologue 114, 133, 138–39, 142, 145, 155, 175, 537, 590 *see also* stream of consciousness
internationalism 128, 314
intersubjectivity 68, 425, 431, 435
intertextuality 108, 199, 211, 579, 588, 607, 609, 618–20
intimacy 8, 22, 27–28, 30, 32–33, 36–37, 64, 68–69, 90, 96, 99, 140, 143, 147, 182, 185, 187–89, 193–95, 242, 280, 293, 296–97, 324, 335, 388, 423–24, 430, 467, 470, 478, 481–83, 485, 550, 597, 610, 625
Irwin, Margaret 523
Isherwood, Christopher 121

J
Jaffe, Aaron 434–35
Jailant, Lise 252
James, C. L. R., 233, 237
James, Henry 17, 233, 241, 265, 544, 597
James, William 134, 145–46, 147, 241
Jameson, Storm 243
Jamison, Leslie 597, 599, 602–3
Jex-Blake, Sophia 358
Joad, Marjorie Thomson 29, 238, 244, 259
John, Augustus 231
Johnson, Samuel 65, 109, 263, 275, 278, 354
Jones, Clara 24n42, 320, 351, 364, 497
Jonson, Ben 203, 208–9
Joyce, James 92, 97, 133, 135–36, 138–39, 154, 199–200, 207, 381–82, 444, 524, 561, 605, 607
  Ulysses 97, 133, 135–36, 139, 199, 207, 444

K
Kant, Immanuel 63
Keats, John 94, 98, 101, 207, 239, 262–63, 297–98, 353, 611

Kelsey, Mary Electa 522
Keynes, John Maynard 22, 28, 211, 212, 215, 230, 233, 237, 317, 347, 446–48, 478, 635–36
Keyserling, Hermann 555
Kidman, Nicole 250, 522
Kim, Youngjoo 532
Kingsley, Mary 358
Kittler, Friedrich 64
Knights, L. C., 524
Knutsen, Ane Thon 254
Koestler, Arthur 440
Kolocotroni, Vassiliki 154, 293n11
Kopley, Emily 254
Koppen, Randi 158, 483
Koteliansky, S. S., 240, 293–96, 306
Kotler, Margot 501–2
Kureishi, Hanif 606
Kuzniar, Alice 423–24

L
labour 11, 24–25, 51, 82, 90, 98, 200, 238, 250, 259, 288, 314, 371, 457–59, 461–63, 465, 467–70, 502, 582 *see also* work
Lacan, Jacques 424
Lahr, Charles 237
Lakoff, George 73
Lamb, Charles 201, 437n40
Lamb, Henry 239
Lanchester, Elsa 238
Lang, Fritz 619
Lanone, Catherine 234
Larson, Jil 183
late modernism 120, 443
late works 117–29
Laughton, John Knox 349, 351
Lawrence, D. H., 135, 231, 237, 239, 240–41, 433n29, 523–24
Leavis, F. R., 103n2, 360, 524
Leavis, Q. D., 103n2, 360–61, 524
Le Bon, Gustave 144
Lee, Hermione 10, 28, 33, 36, 38, 40, 49–50, 57, 73, 154, 214, 230, 240n42, 249, 250n13, 266–67, 347, 417, 440, 524, 609
Lee, Sidney 213–14
Lees, Derwent 229

legacy 1, 3, 57, 112, 203, 249, 350, 365, 371, 402, 457, 468–69, 501, 540, 567, 606–7, 621–23, 632
Lehmann, John 28, 233
Lehmann, Rosamund 540
Leone, Leah 559
lesbian 107–8, 185, 313–14, 326–27, 480, 483–84, 489, 492, 494, 502, 530, 605, 607 see also queerness; sapphist
Lessing, Doris 489–90, 576, 579–83
letters 1–2, 7, 14, 17, 29–30, 34, 36–37, 40, 42, 47, 53, 55, 63–70, 84, 89, 98, 103, 105, 119, 122, 212–13, 219–21, 233, 258, 260, 266–67, 270, 275, 292, 294–95, 344, 351, 358, 367, 377, 418, 479–80, 494, 499, 518, 527, 531, 540, 544, 558, 637 see also private writings
Levenback, Karen 530
Levering, Vida 365, 373, 375
Levinas, Emmanuel 112, 182, 186–87, 191, 195, 423
Levine, Caroline 71
Lewis, Day 121
Lewis, Wyndham 136, 227n2, 231, 244, 523
Leys, Norman 231–32
Light, Alison 51, 460, 462, 468, 493, 533
Lightfoot, Marjorie J., 581
Linett, Maren Tova 413, 505n5, 511, 524, 532
little magazine 244
Livingstone, Josephine 618–19
Lockhart, John 262–63, 274
Lodge, David 199
London: literary 2, 35, 227–45
Lopokova, Lydia 622, 635–36
Lorde, Audre 494
loss 20, 27, 160, 221, 258, 336, 340, 372–74, 416, 452, 473, 496, 579, 603, 609, 613–15, 617, 620
Lovecraft, H. P., 619
lovers 27–43, 106, 238, 295, 305, 340–41, 478, 543, 635
Lowe, Gill 17, 270, 293, 306
Lowell, James Russell 17
Lowery, David 607, 609, 613–17, 620
Lubbock, Percy 135, 265, 268, 278
Luckhurst, Nicola 72
Ludwig, Emil 217

Lukács, Georg 137n16
Lynch, David 619
Lynd, Robert 273
Lynd, Sylvia 118
Lyon, Janet 413, 505n5, 508–9, 511, 513
Lyric 106, 112, 209–10, 296n20, 298, 303
Lyttelton, Kathleen 30, 263, 264

M

Macaulay, Rose 238
MacCarthy, Desmond 212, 230, 241, 268, 384–85
MacCarthy, Molly 15, 230
Macdonald, Ramsay 237
Macé, Marielle 337, 517
MacKay, Marina 440
Mackinder, Halford 400
MacMillan, Kenneth 633
MacNeice, Louis 121
magic realism 553–72
Malory, Thomas 209
Manguso, Sarah 597
manifesto 18, 102, 104, 136, 230, 272, 344, 363, 378, 380, 387, 391, 428, 499–500, 526
Mann, Thomas 171
Mansfield, Katherine 2, 22–23, 29, 33–36, 78, 80, 136, 216–17, 227, 231, 236–37, 239–40, 257, 302, 319, 370
Mapplethorpe, Robert 591
Marcus, Jane 80, 107n7, 109n15, 111, 121, 144, 287, 406, 412–13, 423n6, 458, 492, 500, 527–28, 532
Marcus, Laura 15, 106, 150
Marder, Herbert 39, 526
Marker, Chris 512
Marler, Regina 230
Marlowe, Christopher 84–85, 208
Márquez, Gabriel García 553, 559, 561–66, 569, 571
Marsden, Dora 244
Marshik, Celia 189–90, 480, 481n27
Martin, Kirsty 524
Martin, Linda 383n16
Masefield, John 84–85
Matar, Hisham 596, 600
materiality 113, 151, 254–55, 257–58, 294, 296
Matisse, Henri 624

mature works 89–116
Matz, Jesse 83, 363
Maurice, F. D., 351
Maurois, André 214, 217, 302–3, 305
Maxse, Kitty 29, 317
Mayor, F. M., 319
McBride, Theresa 465
McCall, Ronald 525
McClane, Maureen 596–97
McDonald, Peter D., 474
McEwan, Ian 534, 542, 544–45
McGiff, Shilo 534
McGregor, Wayne 606, 622, 632–35
McKay, Claude 238
McKay, Nellie 565
McLaurin, Allen 142
McNeillie, Andrew 15n23, 22, 104, 229, 264n8, 269n18, 271n20, 279
McNichol, Stella 160
McTaggart, Ursula 247
medical humanities 505–7, 510, 515–16, 518
Meisel, Perry 281–82
Memoir Club, The 15, 44, 212, 220–21, 224, 384, 584
memory 11–12, 14, 21, 44, 52, 82, 147, 160–62, 167–68, 201, 213, 221–23, 246, 326, 328, 332, 346, 373, 413, 415, 419–20, 426, 441–42, 452, 464, 469, 477, 498, 539, 550, 557, 559, 565–66, 599, 618, 631, 634, 638
Mendoza, Plinio Apuleyo 562
mental health 19, 504–11, 513–16, 518–19
Meredith, George 17, 241
Mernissi, Fatima 583–84
Messud, Claire 579–82
metaphor 13, 21, 67, 70, 73, 98, 134, 136, 146, 150, 153, 157, 159, 197–211, 264, 271–72, 274, 280, 288, 291–92, 294, 296n17, 300, 304, 386, 389–90, 393, 397, 404, 422, 427, 446, 457, 476, 491, 517, 539–40, 592, 629
  analogy 73, 80, 134, 145–48, 251, 264, 266, 412, 429, 437, 602
  metonymy 154, 258, 432
  organic 200, 205–6, 209
  sexual 204
  simile 73, 145, 255, 396, 400, 405, 406
  synecdoche 150, 154, 294, 470

Michael, Magali Cornier 581
Micir, Melanie 175n25, 327
Midgley, Nicholas 353
Milano, Alyssa 496
military 40, 54, 127, 340, 354, 399, 485, 528
Mill, John Stuart 11, 51, 529
Mills, Jean 252, 294n13, 321n42, 459
Milman, Sylvia 229
Milne, Herbert J. M., 240
Milton, John 202–4, 208–9, 355–56
Ming-liang, Tsai 614
Minow-Pinkney, Makiko 152, 188
Mirrlees, Hope 231, 254
Mitchell, David 512
Mitchell, Katie 606
Mockerie, Parmenas Githendu 232
modernism 58, 77, 80, 82, 86–87, 103, 106, 120, 136n10, 137, 149, 199, 227–28, 246, 249–52, 255, 257, 259, 323, 362–64, 378, 422, 425, 434–35, 440, 443, 457, 460, 472, 474, 477, 480, 495, 549, 599
  critique of 137
modernist studies 149, 250–51, 295n14, 425, 433
modernity 70, 79, 82, 112n26, 164, 174, 228, 241n45, 247, 255, 313, 362–63, 365, 369–70, 425, 444, 457, 495, 503, 532
Moi, Toril 574
Mollow, Anna 505
Monegal, Emir Rodríguez 560, 562
Monet, Claude 378–79
Monnier, Adrienne 556
Monson, Tamlyn 112
Montaigne, Michel de 72, 90, 99, 100, 277, 280, 283–86, 289–90
Moody, A. D., 526
Moore, G. E., 91, 180, 183–86, 228
Moore, Lisa Jean 330
Moore, Marianne 423
Moore, Olive 237
Morisot, Berthe 378
Morley, Edith 350–52
Morrell, Ottoline 7, 231, 240–41, 481
Morris, William 255
Morrison, Toni 493–94, 503, 529, 553, 564–69, 571, 583
Morrissey, Steven Patrick 639

mortality 13, 21, 389, 410, 443, 455 *see also* death
Moya, Paula 554
Muir, Edwin 118
Murry, John Middleton 135n7, 231, 239, 240, 244
music 2, 27, 39, 41, 43, 100, 111, 127, 210, 227, 275, 295–96, 298–99, 302–03, 333, 353, 390, 443, 469, 498, 545, 551, 568, 608, 615, 622, 632, 636–39
Musil, Robert 145
myth 54, 303, 530, 563, 566, 568

N

narrative ethics 180–96
narrative theory 250
Nash, John 229
Nash, Katherine Saunders 192
Nash, Paul 231
nationalism 111–13, 119, 125, 128, 497, 499, 532
natural world 205, 207, 209, 211, 380, 422–39, 539, 542, 549, 602
Neel, Alice 581
Nelson, Maggie 596–97, 603–4
Neo-pagans 230
Nevinson, C. R. W., 229
Newbolt, Henry 398–400
Newton, Adam Zachary 181
Nfah-Abbenyi, Juliana Makuchi 494
Nicholls, Norah 253
Nicholson, Ben 239
Nicholson-Weir, Rebecca 186
Nicolson, Harold 38, 65n13, 107n9, 214–15, 217, 272
Nightingale, Florence 51, 53–54, 56, 213
Noailles, Anna de 555–56
non-fiction 278–79, 285, 288, 314–15, 351, 472, 489, 497, 564, 590–604 *see also* creative non-fiction
notebooks 63–66, 70, 75, 119, 279n5, 286, 528, 531, 580 *see also* Woolf, Virginia: private writings
novel
  experimental 176, 389
  feminist 573–89
  of manners 77
  modernist 104–5, 133
  movement 365, 368

Novotny, Tuva 619
Nussbaum, Martha 180–82

O

objects 25, 45, 50, 170, 191, 210, 298, 314, 339, 371, 381–83, 388, 415, 425, 437, 439, 472–73, 475, 515, 568, 580, 594, 610, 628, 631
Ocampo, Victoria 22, 521, 553–57, 562n23, 570
oceans 389, 392–407, 540, 542, 603, 624
Ogden, Charles Kay 238
Omega Workshops 231–32, 243, 474, 478–79, 591
Opie, Catherine 603
Orage, A. R., 240
Orr, Christopher 609
Ortega y Gasset, José 554–55
Orwell, George 231n21, 234, 440
Osborne, Dorothy 67, 69, 627
Oser, Lee 91, 185–86, 195
Osipova, Natalia 634
otherness 89, 90, 93, 95, 182, 194, 424, 532, 564, 569 *see also* alterity
Otto, Whitney 599
Outka, Elizabeth 370, 475
Owens, Laura 630–31
Oxbridge 201, 230, 233, 286, 427, 542
Oyeyemi, Helen 576
Ozon, François 607, 609, 613–14, 620

P

pacifism 102–103, 107n8, 126, 313, 315, 338, 345, 441, 450, 489, 497, 590
pain 69, 90, 93, 289, 332, 339, 374–75, 504–20, 567, 590
painting 46, 94, 173, 268n17, 346, 377–80, 383–91, 439, 470, 551, 578–80, 598, 622–26, 629–31, 635
Pankhurst, Christabel 318, 373
Pankhurst, Emmeline 636
Park, Sowon S., 321, 364
Parker, David 181
Parker, Emma 586
Parnell, Charles Stewart 451
parody 33, 70, 112, 160, 175, 394, 423, 523, 560, 563
Partridge, Frances 627
Partridge, Ralph 259, 626

Pater, Clara 29, 347, 349
Pater, Walter 267, 281–82, 380
Patmore, Coventry 53–54, 207
Patmore, Emily Augusta 463
patriarchy 2–3, 66, 80, 88, 95, 107, 109, 115, 119–20, 122–24, 127–28, 184, 228, 323, 326–27, 330–34, 336, 339, 342, 375, 396, 397n14, 404, 412, 414, 458, 476, 491, 495, 497–500, 528, 536, 556, 573, 580, 582–87, 620
   critique of 323, 327, 342
Pawlowski, Merry 531
Paxton, Robert 420
peace 11, 24, 73–74, 80, 93, 112, 122, 124–26, 144, 173, 210, 220, 277, 358, 396, 409, 416, 418–20, 440–55, 469, 489, 498–99, 501, 530, 532
Pearson, Nels 397
perception 113, 118, 134, 139, 142–45, 148, 181–82, 184, 186, 190, 212–13, 219, 249, 262, 283, 313, 336, 377–83, 386–87, 390, 396, 438, 473, 477, 484, 517–18, 539, 545, 562, 584, 591, 599–600, 603
   collective 145, 148
Periyan, Natasha 357–58
personal essay 22, 285 *see also* creative non-fiction; essays; non-fiction
Pevear, Richard 549
Phare, E. E., 260
phenomenology 97, 178, 428, 431
philosophy 11, 66, 72, 98, 112–14, 181–82, 217, 224, 232–33, 358, 360, 378, 423, 426, 433, 442, 530
photography 64, 492
Picasso, Pablo 480, 635
Piozzi, Hester Lynch Thrale 275
Pippett, Aileen 525–26
Pissarro, Camille 378
place 7–26
Plain, Gill 494
Plato 90–91, 97–98, 349, 539
pleasure 27–28, 31–32, 38, 41, 45, 49, 52–53, 57, 91, 93, 98, 109, 159, 184, 191, 193, 195, 199, 202, 207, 210, 249n10, 252, 280–81, 283, 289, 331–32, 336, 340, 380, 384–85, 410, 429, 441, 474, 480–81, 486, 518, 534, 544–45, 550, 557, 581, 583, 610–11

Plotinus 217, 219
poetry 2, 78–79, 90, 97–100, 102–7, 109–12, 114–15, 117, 127, 201, 203–8, 242–43, 254, 261, 267, 289, 296, 322, 380, 390, 413, 431, 537, 540, 544–45, 590–604
Poiret, Paul 480
politics 11, 29, 66–67, 70, 73, 105, 107, 109, 112–14, 117–22, 124, 126, 128, 137, 153, 177, 184, 186, 234, 252, 254, 277, 279, 292, 311, 312n5, 318–19, 322–23, 325, 358, 364, 366, 375, 409, 416, 426, 431, 434, 440–42, 454, 473, 476, 492–93, 500–03, 525, 530, 532, 535, 541–42, 564, 574, 576, 580, 584, 591, 601, 606–7, 621–22
   feminist 67, 187, 318, 434, 492, 500–503, 584
   international 66
   pacifist 454
   sexual 375, 576
Pope, Alexander 208, 246, 336, 340, 353, 610
Post-Impressionism 19, 25, 377–91, 625
Potter, Sally 608
Pound, Ezra 136, 227, 231, 237, 244
Power, Ed 619
Price, Leah 260
primitivism 331, 385, 625
print culture 247, 249, 254
privacy 50, 64, 67–68, 244, 373, 467, 495, 525, 550
private writings 63–75 *see also* diary; letters
Proust, Marcel 135, 145, 147, 171, 272, 303, 536–37, 608
   In Search of Lost Time 171
Pryce-Jones, David 241
publishing 23, 227–28, 244, 247–55, 283, 318, 459, 521–35, 554, 556, 592 *see also* Hogarth Press
Purpura, Lia 597, 599–600, 602–3
Pynchon, Thomas 581

Q

Queen Victoria 2, 16, 33, 47, 49, 214–16, 219, 244, 314, 451
queerness 175n25, 191, 326, 330–33, 342, 535
queer theory 3, 108, 326–43
Quigley, Megan 83

R

race 3, 13, 93, 123, 324, 400, 402, 411–13, 462, 482, 489, 492–94, 496, 528, 530–33, 541, 565
racism 406, 409–14, 417–18, 420, 496, 499, 531, 533
  scientific 410
  state 409–14, 417–18, 420
Rainey, Lawrence 252
Raitt, Suzanne 79, 108, 530
Raleigh, Walter 401
Rankine, Claudia 597–98, 600, 603
Ravel, Maurice 555
Raverat, Gwen 229
Raverat, Jacques 29, 231
Ray, Man 118
Read, Herbert 118
Rebel Art Centre 231
Reed, Christopher 479, 481
Reid, Panthea 96
relationality 69, 145, 147, 159, 180, 182, 184
Renoir, Pierre-Auguste 378
reviewer-critic 260, 262–76, 290, 389
Reynier, Christine 89n2
Rhys, Jean 631
Rich, Adrienne 489, 493, 500
Rice, Thomas Jackson 524
Richards, David A. J., 184
Richards, I. A., 360
Richardson, Dorothy 133, 135–37, 381–82, 522
  Pilgrimage 135–36, 381–82
  Revolving Lights 382
  The Tunnel 382
Richmond, Bruce Lyttleton 229, 264
Richter, Max 633–34
Ricoeur, Paul 171–72, 174–76, 178
Rigney, Barbara Hill 576
Rimbaud, Arthur 602
Rizzuto, Nicole 397
Roberts, John Hawley 522
Roberts, Michèle 553, 566–69
Robins, Elizabeth 365–66, 373
Robinson, Lillian S., 529
Rochelle, Drieu de la 555
Rogat, Ellen Hawkes 527
Rogers, Gayle 554
Rogers, Lillian 71

Rolland, Romain 554
Romain, Gemma 238
Romains, Jules 142
Romanticism 169, 303n33, 423n6
Rosenbaum, S. P., 215, 230
Rosenfeld, Aaron 581
Rosner, Victoria 230, 457, 464
Ross, Stephen 230
Rossetti, Christina 204, 627
Rossetti, D. G., 241
Rousseau, Jean-Jacques 221, 223
Rowling, J. K., 576
Rubenstein, Roberta 296n19, 581, 586
Ruskin, John 52, 55, 228
Russell, Bertrand 386, 450
Ruti, Mari 183
Ryan, Derek 230, 424
Rylands, Dadie 244

S

Sackville-West, Vita 1, 7, 29, 33, 36–39, 41–43, 102, 107–10, 116, 162, 205, 214, 216, 218, 244, 247, 313, 327–28, 479, 482–84, 527, 530, 548, 593
Said, Edward 443
Saint-Amour, Paul 448
Saint-Saëns, Camille 302
Saldívar, Ramón 554
Saliers, Emily 639
Sand, George 567
Sandberg, Eric 150, 154
Sands, Ethel 241, 632n10
Sappho 297, 627
Sargent, John Singer 241
Sarker, Sonita 532
Sarraute, Nathalie 145
Sasken, Sassia 228
satire 17, 45, 108, 117, 151–52, 160, 162, 213, 246, 318, 501, 554, 559, 598
Schröder, Leena Kore 525, 532
Schuyler, James 603
Scott, Cyril 238
Scott, Bonnie Kime 200n10, 422
Sebald, W. G., 596, 602–3
Sedgwick, Eve Kosofsky 330
Sellers, Susan 494
Seneca 72

servants 16, 44–47, 51, 148, 456–71, 493,
    533, 557
Seshagiri, Urmila 251n14, 364, 413, 495, 532
sex 15, 19, 23, 29, 38, 53, 85, 88, 106–7, 113, 126,
    162, 176, 216–17, 221, 238, 258, 289, 312,
    327–28, 330, 331, 334–37, 366, 409, 411,
    414, 417, 424, 445, 479, 482, 484–85,
    489–90, 499, 522, 530, 559, 568, 572,
    580–81, 629
sexism 32, 39, 259, 335, 341, 412, 414, 496, 545
sexuality 32, 71, 107, 183, 217, 254, 313–14, 318,
    325, 327–29, 339, 341, 409–10, 479,
    481–82, 484, 489, 548, 567–69, 606,
    621, 626–27
  homosexuality 217, 441, 452, 540, 606
  queer 183
  women's, 313–14, 481
Shakespeare, William 66, 90, 94, 98–99, 105,
    186, 202–03, 206, 208–10, 236, 290, 342,
    430n24, 489, 567, 573, 590, 605–06, 639
  Cymbeline 98, 199, 544
  Hamlet 206, 511
  King Lear 210, 511
  Macbeth 210
  The Winter's Tale 342
Shannon, Drew 254, 534
Sheepshanks, Mary 317, 351
Shelley, Percy Bysshe 98, 198, 214, 240, 303, 353
Sherry, Vincent 446
Shklovsky, Victor 295
Showalter, Elaine 529, 575
Sickert, Walter 241, 623
Silver, Brenda R., 65n14, 118, 209, 528
Silverblatt, Michael 596
Sim, Lorraine 188
Simmel, Georg 443
Simpson, Kathryn 317n24, 396, 459, 532
Sinclair, May 135, 138–39, 141, 362, 370
Sitwell, Edith 242, 247
Sitwell, Osbert 242
Sitwell, Sacheverell 242
Smiley, Jane 540
Smith, Amy 534
Smith, Logan Pearsall 241
Smith, Patti 637–38
Smith, Reginald 264, 266
Smith, Zadie 537, 541–42, 576–77, 580, 583, 586

Smiths, The 639
Smyth, Ethel 2, 27, 29, 32, 39, 40, 43, 68–70,
    121, 219, 221, 223, 368, 622, 636–37
Smyth, John Hall 636
Snaith, Anna 34, 107n7, 123, 244, 252, 274n27,
    320n38, 363, 369, 374–75, 408, 443, 452,
    459, 497
Snyder, Sharon 512
social circle 27, 229, 383
social critique 64, 107, 450, 559
Solnit, Rebecca 596–97, 600–3
Sontag, Susan 590–91, 594, 603
Sorensen, Jennifer 254
Southworth, Helen 251–52, 474, 554
Spanish Civil War 120, 124, 415, 440, 442, 449,
    451, 498
Sparks, Elisa Kay 534
Spencer, Stanley 231
Spender, Stephen 121, 358
Spielberg, Stephen 619
Sprott, W. J. H., 274
Squier, Susan 234
Squires, J. C., 241
Staël-Holstein, Anne Louise Germaine de 627
Stam, Robert 609
Stansky, Peter 403, 527
Staveley, Alice 253
Stead, W. T., 314
Stein, Gertrude 23, 147, 238, 247, 584
Stephen, Adrian 11, 15, 17, 22, 229–30, 239, 347,
    351, 464
Stephen, Fitzjames 263
Stephen, Julia Prinsep 10–12, 15–17, 19–20, 25,
    45–46, 48, 50–59, 222, 224, 229, 317, 348,
    425, 437, 462–67, 469, 505, 520, 624
Stephen, Leslie 10–12, 15–17, 19, 22, 44–51, 53,
    58–59, 80, 95, 213, 222, 224, 236, 237,
    264, 278, 317, 347, 349, 398, 401, 425,
    427, 437, 439, 462–63, 523, 624
Stephen, Thoby 11, 15, 17, 20, 25, 45, 49–50, 229,
    231, 347, 464
Stevens, Wallace 594
Stevenson, Iain 249
Stevenson, Robert Louis 210, 401
Stimpson, Catherine R., 69
Stix-Brunell, Beatriz 634
Stoddart, Hugh 608

Stoermer, Eugene F., 435
Stopes, Marie 312, 315
Strachey, Alix 231, 319
Strachey, Joan Pernel 358
Strachey, Julia 319
Strachey, Lytton 22, 28–29, 31, 33–34, 44, 54, 107, 212–15, 230, 239, 317, 347, 355, 523, 595, 626, 635
Strachey, Pernel 355
stream of consciousness 1–2, 81, 133–48, 234, 381, 465
Stryker, Susan 330
Sturt, Mary 169–70
style 18, 32–33, 37, 41, 68, 71, 76, 79, 102, 104, 108, 110, 135–36, 139, 149–50, 153, 159, 234, 248, 262, 272, 277, 280–82, 284–85, 303, 305, 312, 318, 342, 351, 356, 359, 379–80, 387, 426–28, 434, 440, 443–44, 454, 473, 477–80, 483–84, 524, 530, 536–38, 540, 542, 545–45, 559, 590–91, 596, 603–4, 624, 634
    as ethics 590–91
    late 443–44
    and politics 440, 454, 591
subjectivity 64n22, 68, 70, 150, 165, 172, 175, 178, 183, 186, 196, 313, 373, 422, 424–25, 431–32, 434–35, 480, 492, 565, 576, 579, 583, 585–87, 604, 619
suffrage 3, 47, 50–52, 56–58, 79, 121, 125, 264n10, 311, 312n5, 314–15, 317, 320–21, 324–25, 362–76, 441, 451, 475–76, 486, 497, 636 see also feminism
suicide 21, 24, 118, 289, 413, 509, 518, 537–38, 541, 593, 598, 634
Sullivan, John Willian Navin 240
Sullivan, Melissa 252
Sutton, Emma 532
Swinburne, Algernon 241
Swinton, Tilda 492, 608
Swithin, Lucy 124, 143–44, 208, 453
Sydney-Turner, Saxon 28, 215, 481
sympathy 33, 69, 96, 187–88, 263, 284, 464, 511–12, 623

T

Tambimuttu, M. J., 234
Tarkovsky, Andrei 619
Tawney, R. H., 358

Taylor, Elizabeth 540
Taylor, Judith 585
technology 73–74, 254, 260, 410, 544
Tennyson, Alfred 98, 204, 208, 210, 237
Terry, Ellen 267, 275, 627
Thackeray, Minny 11
Thackeray, William Makepeace 11, 45, 52, 80, 201, 229, 346, 356, 623
Theophrastus 153–54
Thompsett, Anne 458, 468
Thomson, James 28, 208, 259, 504
time 164–79
    chronotope 173–75, 178, 554, 563
    duration 168–70, 205
    feminist 362–63, 373–74
    objective 165–66, 173, 177
    phenomenology of 428
    prolepsis 328, 440, 442–44, 446–47, 450, 452–54, 500
    queer 328
    subjective 164–67, 170, 173–74
Todd, Dorothy 478–79
Todd, Selina 457, 465
Toker, Leona 187
Tolstoi, Sophie 295
Tolstoy, Leo 90, 97, 159, 265, 270, 293–96, 307
Tomlinson, Barbara 287
Tompkins, Silvan 414
totalitarianism 122, 453 see also fascism
tradition 44–63, 67–68, 76, 78–82, 86, 98, 105–7, 126, 144, 148, 154, 162, 183, 199–203, 207–9, 220, 247, 267, 271, 277, 279–80, 285–88, 290, 314, 321, 334, 352, 354, 356, 363, 379, 395, 407, 413, 415, 419–20, 422, 425, 428, 430, 432, 435–36, 474–75, 485–86, 493, 499, 547, 550, 556, 558, 560–66, 568, 573, 579, 611
transgender 327–28, 330, 492
translation 240, 248, 252, 291–310, 355, 409, 500, 549, 553–54, 556–61, 564, 570, 607
trans theory 334, 492
Transue, Pamela J., 312
trauma 2, 19, 94, 160, 166, 170, 172, 223, 365, 368–69, 373–75, 440–42, 449, 490, 506, 515, 517, 530, 538, 636
Travis, Molly Abel 524
Trevelyan, Bob 241

Trevelyan, Hilda 241
Trollope, Anthony 537
Trotter, David 313
Trotter, Wilfred 144
Trulzsch, Holger 599
Turgenev, Ivan 270
Turner, J. M. W., 241
Tusan, Michelle 258
typology 435, 437

U
Underwood, Eric 634
Updike, John 540

V
Valéry, Paul 555
VanderMeer, Jeff, 618
van Gogh, Vincent 618
Vaughan, Emma 317
Vaughan, Madge 29
Vicinus, Martha 55–56
Victorian society 19, 51, 213
violence 2, 13, 20, 99, 122, 124, 144, 156, 170, 174, 181–82, 288–89, 329, 331–32, 341, 390, 402–3, 408–9, 427–28, 440, 444, 447–48, 450–51, 453–54, 473, 482, 484–85, 530, 532, 599, 620
  nationalist 408, 532
  sexual 2, 331
visual art 19, 25, 68, 111, 151, 154, 157, 161, 256, 277–78, 280–82, 284–85, 288, 372, 377–80, 385–87, 391, 495, 511, 593–94, 596–98, 603, 607–8, 622–23, 627, 632
Volokhonsky, Larissa 549

W
Wadsworth, Edward 229
Walker, Alice 531–32, 565, 593–94
Walpole, Hugh 592
war 1, 2, 10–11, 13, 17, 19–21, 24–25, 54, 73–74, 82, 84–85, 92, 95, 111–12, 115, 117–20, 124–28, 142–44, 160, 165, 174, 214, 221–22, 227, 234, 238, 240, 248, 253, 261, 292, 297, 303, 312–13, 315–16, 324–25, 338, 353–56, 358, 362–63, 366, 370, 375–76, 383–84, 390, 408, 415–20, 440–55, 473, 475, 478–83, 485, 490, 497–98, 501, 510–11, 515–17, 523, 530, 537–38, 540–41, 545, 555, 580–81, 588, 594–95, 599–600, 602–3, 620, 624, 639
  writing 440
Ward, Mary Augusta 52–53, 56–58
Warhol-Down, Robyn 494
Warner, Eric 529
Warr, George 347–49
Waterlow, Sydney 28, 240
Watson, Edward 634
Watt, Alison 609, 611
Watts, G. F., 17, 229, 377
Weaver, Harriet 244
Wegener, Elnar 492
Weinstein, Harvey 496
Wells, H. G., 238, 366, 592, 635
West, Rebecca 23, 157, 362
Wheatley, Phillis 531, 565
Whitehead, Alfred North 386
Whittier-Ferguson, John 443
Wicke, Jennifer 472n2, 478
Wilde, Oscar 262, 314n15
Williams, Holly 605–6
Williams, Raymond 478, 525
Willis, J. H., 244, 248
Wilson, Elizabeth 480
Wilson, E. O., 435
Wilson, Jean Moorcroft 237
Wilson, Lily 457, 470
Wilson, Nicola 253, 259
Wilson, Patricia 560
Winnicott, D. W., 603
Winterson, Jeanette 327, 339–43, 553, 566, 568–72, 580
  The Daylight Gate 339–41
  The Gap of Time 339–40
  The Passion 339–40
  Sexing the Cherry 339
  Written on the Body 339
Wittgenstein, Ludwig 603
Wittig, Monique 327
Wolf, Patrick 638
Wolfe, Edward 592
Wolfe, Jesse 185, 89
Wolitzer, Meg 580, 583
womanhood 48–49, 52, 136, 336, 529, 573, 575, 584
  Victorian 52
  see also femininity

women's literature 573–589
Women's Studies 530
women's rights 18, 51, 314–16, 420, 491, 495–96, 499, 590, 601
Women's Co-operative Guild 57, 67, 102, 112, 126, 129, 317, 322, 459, 461, 471
Woodring, Carl 526
Woolf, Cecil 534
Woolf, Leonard 23, 49, 57, 126, 184, 221, 227, 231, 233, 236–39, 242–43, 247, 249, 252, 259, 268, 273–74, 279, 294–96, 307, 316–17, 408, 440, 445, 450, 468, 525–26, 534
Woolf, Virginia, life 7–26
  Bloomsbury Group 2, 27, 31–32, 37, 47, 58, 118, 142, 183–85, 212, 214, 230–34, 237–38, 240, 242, 249, 252, 302, 317–18, 321, 347, 384–85, 440, 446, 472, 478–81, 522–23, 526, 532, 540, 592–93, 595, 627, 629, 635–36
  childhood/early life 7–23, 44–47, 51, 81, 213, 223–24, 426, 441, 462, 623
  death 2, 23–24, 31, 33, 117, 524, 538, 591, 598, 605–06, 638
  education 2, 29, 290, 347–51
  family 7–26, 44, 47, 229, 317, 377, 383, 423
  friends and lovers 27–43
  Hogarth Press 23–24, 28, 35–37, 89, 214, 227–28, 231–34, 237–38, 240–44, 246–61, 272, 292–96, 319, 322, 417, 459, 474, 525, 531, 534, 554, 592, 624, 630
  marriage 23, 28, 49, 234, 246–49, 316, 532
    see also Woolf, Leonard
  residence, places of
    Brunswick Square 22, 230–31, 233
    Fitzroy Square 22, 229, 231–32, 245, 591
    Gordon Square 22, 29, 49, 58, 229, 237–38, 317, 624
    Hogarth House 23, 227, 232, 234, 242–43, 246, 248
    Hyde Park Gate 10–11, 14–19, 22, 25, 44, 46–49, 51, 222, 224, 229, 231, 233, 462–63, 467–68, 624
    Mecklenburgh Square 23–24, 231
    Monk's House 7, 23–25, 46–47, 467–68, 527, 531, 638
    Talland House 10–15, 46, 222
    Tavistock Square 23–24, 57, 227, 233, 236, 238, 242–43, 248, 250, 468
Woolf, Virginia, works
  essays:
    '22 Hyde Park Gate', 224
    'Am I a Snob?', 37, 277, 321
    'An Andalusian Inn', 291
    'Anon', 209, 211, 213, 274, 276, 291, 300–301, 303
    A Room of One's Own 2, 19, 23, 38, 40, 50, 81, 102–07, 109, 110n19, 111–12, 114–15, 117, 121, 194, 199–202, 204–205, 208–209, 218, 230, 237, 245–46, 253, 260, 277, 280, 285–91, 311, 318–19, 326, 330–31, 335, 345, 350, 355, 367, 411–13, 427, 450, 456, 459–60, 466, 476, 489, 491, 493, 496, 500, 521, 526, 529–32, 534, 537, 545–46, 553, 556–57, 559–60, 564–67, 569–70, 572–74, 584–85, 589–90, 594–96, 600, 608, 621, 636, 639
    'The Art of Biography ', 162, 213, 215–16, 219–20
    'Body and Brain', 215
    'Byron and Mr Briggs', 268–69
    'Character in Fiction', 82, 86–87, 92, 149–52, 154, 166, 384, 592
    'The Cinema', 607
    'Coleridge as Critic', 274
    Collected Essays 279, 525
    The Common Reader 65, 89–92, 102, 279, 283–84, 496
    'Craftsmanship', 306, 571
    'The Death of the Moth', 277, 280, 596, 602
    The Death of the Moth 525
    'The Docks of London', 323
    'Dorothy Wordworth', 277
    'The Duchess of Newcastle', 280
    'Ellen Terry', 275
    'English Prose', 380
    'An Essay in Criticism', 268, 271
    'The Feminine Note in Fiction', 323
    'Fishing', 430
    'Friendships Gallery', 30
    'George Eliot', 277
    'Great Men's Houses', 239, 277
    'Haworth, November 1904, 18n29, 278
    'How it Strikes a Contemporary', 82, 264, 268

'How Should One Read a Book?', 110, 198, 262, 267–69
'The Humane Art', 68
'Jane Austen', 277
'JMK', 215
'Journeys in Spain', 278
'The Leaning Tower', 24, 121–22, 177, 358, 360
'Letter to a Young Poet', 68, 121
'Life and the Novelist', 268
'Lives of the Obscure', 277, 280, 567
'Literary Geography', 18n29
The London Scene 320n34, 475, 525
'The Man at the Gate', 274
'Mary Wollstonecraft', 277
'Memoirs of a Novelist', 212, 256
'The Memoirs of Sarah Bernhardt', 266
'Memories of a Working Women's Guild', 461–62
'Men and Women', 218
'The Modern Essay', 280, 283
'Modern Essays', 82
'Modern Fiction', 18–19, 42, 90, 92, 99, 136, 150, 186, 268, 277, 378, 380–82, 390, 436, 592
'Modern Letters', 68
'Modern Novels', 76, 82, 382
Moments of Being 527, 567, 584
'Moments of Being: Slater's Pins Have no Points', 350
'Montaigne', 283
'Morley Sketch', 351
'Mr Bennett and Mrs Brown', 44, 87, 137, 151–52, 166, 237, 266, 277, 283, 457, 459, 462, 611
'Mrs Thrale', 274
'The Narrow Bridge of Art', 97
'The New Biography', 214–15, 219
'Old Bloomsbury', 31, 229
'On Being Ill', 277, 504–05, 507, 510, 511–14, 518, 599
'On Not Knowing French', 301–304
'On Not Knowing Greek', 90–91, 296, 354, 427n12
'On Re-Reading Novels', 268
'Outlines', 280
The Pargiters 117, 121–22, 125, 176, 192, 357, 363, 368–69, 373–74, 450, 584

'The Perfect Language', 292
'Phases of Fiction', 103, 159, 272–73
'Poetry, Fiction, and the Future', 102, 104–06, 109, 110, 112n26, 114
'The Reader', 209
'Reading at Random', 272
'Reminiscences', 224
The Second Common Reader 103, 109–10, 496
'A Sketch of the Past', 46, 51, 95, 161, 212, 223–24, 277, 380, 423, 425–26, 428, 463–64, 466–67, 469, 584, 623
'The Stranger in London', 292
'Street Haunting', 277, 280, 306n41, 380, 475, 507, 510–11, 513–14, 610–11
'The Sun and the Fish', 380, 405
'Thoughts on Peace During an Air-Raid', 24, 74, 124, 277, 416, 418–20, 452
'A Walk by Night', 278
'A Week in the White House with Theodore Roosevelt,' 266–67
'What is a Novel?', 105
'Why?', 360
'Why Art To-Day Follows Politics', 120, 122
'Women and Fiction', 105, 114
'Women Must Weep—Or Unite Against the War', 417
lectures: 'Professions for Women', 49, 112, 117, 207, 637
letters: *Collected Letters* 30
non-fiction: *Roger Fry* 1, 24, 32, 118, 221, 223
novels:
　Between the Acts 2, 7–9, 24, 35, 41, 113n37, 114n40, 117–20, 122, 124, 126–28, 134, 142–44, 159, 177–78, 185, 200, 208–11, 219, 22, 291, 326, 342, 390, 418, 427, 442, 452–53, 457, 524–25, 576, 578–79, 582
　Flush 1, 21, 118, 123, 183, 212, 219, 245, 254, 422–26, 435, 457, 470, 593–94
　Jacob's Room 13–14, 76–77, 83–89, 100, 103, 135, 151–52, 155–58, 160, 167, 172, 174, 186, 196, 212, 216, 220, 230, 234–35, 237–38, 241, 254, 353–54, 356, 382–84, 386, 397, 444–47, 449, 453, 470, 477, 534, 592–96, 614, 628

Woolf, Virginia, works (*cont.*)
- *To the Lighthouse* 2, 9, 11, 19–20, 25, 46, 63, 89, 93–98, 135, 140–41, 143, 145, 150, 159, 165–66, 172–75, 181, 185, 193, 212, 221, 261–62, 286, 326, 386–89, 396–97, 427, 438, 445, 449–50, 457, 477, 489–90, 492, 505n5, 526, 528, 531–32, 535, 539–40, 544, 547, 549, 556, 575, 577–79, 582, 589, 591, 597, 608, 614, 616, 631, 635, 638
- *Mrs Dalloway* 9, 21, 32, 65, 71, 87, 89, 92–93, 96, 98–100, 135, 139–40, 143, 145, 147, 151, 155, 157, 159, 160, 163, 167–73, 185, 187–88, 190, 193, 199, 227, 231, 234–37, 250, 262, 283, 186, 326, 331–32, 342, 383, 386, 389, 395, 445, 447–49, 456–58, 460, 469, 472–73, 476–77, 484, 489–92, 505, 507, 515–16, 522, 524–25, 529, 537, 539, 541–43, 548–50, 562, 575, 585, 591, 595, 598, 605, 608, 614, 619, 633, 636
- *Orlando* 1, 21, 31, 33, 38, 102–11, 114–15, 151, 155–56, 158–64, 172, 175, 177, 183, 200, 205–09, 211–12, 214, 216–20, 241, 245, 313, 323, 326–31, 334–36, 339–42, 423, 474, 482–86, 491–92, 495, 521, 524, 532, 548, 553, 556–62, 566–71, 582, 585, 593, 608, 611, 614, 628–30, 634
- *Night and Day* 2, 23, 30, 34, 76–81, 84, 159, 180, 197, 228n6, 234–35, 241, 244, 255, 315, 362–73, 463, 475, 484, 534, 592
- *The Voyage Out* 1, 7, 23, 33, 76–78, 87, 98, 135, 154, 158–60, 198, 212, 234–35, 240, 244, 255, 291, 297–98, 315, 318, 349, 351, 353, 381, 392–94, 396, 402–03, 406, 426, 432–33, 438, 456, 477, 528, 534, 592
- *The Waves* 13–14, 31, 41–42, 76, 97, 102–107, 110–15, 117–18, 139, 142–44, 158–59, 172, 175–77, 180, 183, 185, 193, 198, 212, 218–19, 222, 245, 251, 258, 270, 326, 337, 380, 383, 389–90, 393, 395–97, 401, 403, 405, 423n6, 426, 438, 457, 489, 505, 528, 532, 568, 591, 593, 613–14, 631, 634–35, 638–39
- *The Years* 55, 111, 117–22, 124–28, 148, 159, 177, 180, 183, 185, 192–93, 219, 245, 298, 300, 326, 346, 349, 353–54, 356–58, 362–66, 368–69, 372–75, 390, 413, 429, 441, 451–52, 455–57, 492, 505, 525, 530, 575–76, 584–85, 589, 598

other: *The Hyde Park Gate News* 17–19, 45, 47, 154

plays: *Freshwater: A Comedy* 525

private writing:
- *A Passionate Apprentice* 70
- *A Writer's Diary* 525–26
- *Virginia Woolf's Reading Notebooks* 528

short fiction:
- 'Blue and Green', 382
- 'Friendships Gallery', 30
- 'A Haunted House', 614–16
- *A Haunted House, and Other Short Stories* 525
- 'The Hours', 96
- 'The Introduction', 92
- 'The Journal of Mistress Joan Martyn', 212
- 'Kew Gardens', 2, 24–25, 35, 155, 236, 422, 433, 591, 593, 595, 600, 624
- 'The Man Who Loved His Kind', 93
- 'The Mark on the Wall', 2, 7, 81, 155, 249, 255–59, 382, 396–97, 402
- 'Memoirs of a Novelist', 212, 256
- 'Moments of Being', 524
- *Monday or Tuesday* 154, 382, 592–93
- 'Mrs Dalloway in Bond Street', 92, 98
- *Mrs Dalloway's Party: A Short Story Sequence* 525
- 'The New Dress', 93
- 'Nurse Lugton's Curtain', 457
- 'Scenes from the Life of a British Naval Officer', 403
- 'A Simple Melody', 95
- 'A Society', 237, 501
- 'An Unwritten Novel', 151, 154–57, 158, 160, 166, 611

Woolmer, J. Howard 248
Wordsworth, Dorothy 277
Wordsworth, William 72, 353, 428, 611
World War I, 112n26, 126n31, 142, 240, 313, 315, 353, 356, 362, 383, 440, 444, 449, 451–53, 475, 479, 501, 515, 595, 602–03 *see also* Great War
World War II 118–19, 122, 142, 234, 248n8, 390, 442–43, 450, 481, 540
work 456–71 *see also* labour
Worsley, T. C., 358

Wright, Elizabeth 357
Wright, Joseph 357

Y
Yamada, Setsuko 634–35
Yonge, Charlotte M., 45
Young, John 252–53

Z
Zangwill, Edith 362, 370
Zemgulys, Andrea P., 241
Zhang, Dora 83
Zink, Susana 356
Žižek, Slavoj 194
Zwerdling, Alex 47, 312n5, 423n5